www.wadsworth.com

wadsworth.com is the World Wide Web site for Wadsworth and is your direct source to dozens of online resources.

At *wadsworth.com* you can find out about supplements, demonstration software, and student resources. You can also send email to many of our authors and preview new publications and exciting new technologies.

wadsworth.com
Changing the way the world learns®

A Child's
Odyssey

Child and Adolescent Development

THIRD EDITION

Paul S. Kaplan

**Suffolk County Community College and
The State University of New York at Stony Brook**

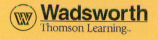 **Wadsworth**
Thomson Learning™

Australia • Canada • Mexico • Singapore • Spain • United Kingdom • United States

Executive Editor: Vicki Knight
Assistant Editor: Annie Berterretche
Editorial Assistant: Amy Wood/Erin Conlon
Marketing Manager: Marc Linsenman
Marketing Assistant: Jenna Burrill
Project Editor: John Walker/Tanya Nigh
Print Buyer: Karen Hunt
Permissions Editor: Susan Walker

Production Service: rosa+wesley
Text Designer: Gladys Rosa-Mendoza, rosa+wesley
Photo Researcher: Peggy Cooper
Copy Editor: Laura Lawson
Cover Designer: John Walker
Cover Image: Kristian Pierre *The Night Owl*/Superstock
Cover Printer: Phoenix Color Corporation
Compositor: Brian Wenberg, rosa+wesley
Printer: RR Donnelley, Willard

Printed in the United States of America
1 2 3 4 5 6 7 03 02 01 00 99

For permission to use material from this text, contact us by **Web:** http://www.thomsonrights.com
Fax: 1-800-730-2215
Phone: 1-800-730-2214

Library of Congress Cataloging-in-Publication Data

Kaplan, Paul S.
  A child's odyssey: child and adolescent development /
Paul S. Kaplan. — 3rd ed.
    p.   cm.
  Includes bibliographical references and index.
  ISBN 0-534-35503-X
  1. Child development. 2. Adolescence. I. Title.

RJ131.K36   1999
305.231—dc21   99-047373

For more information, contact
Wadsworth/Thomson Learning
10 Davis Drive
Belmont, CA 94002-3098
USA
http://www.wadsworth.com

International Headquarters
Thomson Learning
International Division
290 Harbor Drive, 2nd Floor
Stamford, CT 06902-7477
USA

UK/Europe/Middle East/South Africa
Thomson Learning
Berkshire House
168-173 High Holborn
London WC1V 7AA
United Kingdom

Asia
Thomson Learning
60 Albert Street, #15-01
Albert Complex
Singapore 189969

Canada
Nelson Thomson Learning
1120 Birchmount Road
Toronto, Ontario M1K 5G4
Canada

Contents in Brief

Part One   Prospects for Personhood   1

Chapter One   The Study of Child and Adolescent Development   2

Chapter Two   Perspectives on Child and Adolescent Development   36

Chapter Three   Mechanisms of Change: Genetic and Environmental Interaction   76

Chapter Four   Prenatal Development and Birth   114

Part Two   Infancy and Toddlerhood   155

Chapter Five   Physical Development in Infancy and Toddlerhood   156

Chapter Six   Cognitive and Linguistic Development in Infancy and Toddlerhood   196

Chapter Seven   Social and Personality Development in Infancy and Toddlerhood   232

Part Three   Early Childhood   275

Chapter Eight   Physical and Cognitive Development in Early Childhood   276

Chapter Nine   Social and Personality Development in Early Childhood   322

Part Four   Middle Childhood   367

Chapter Ten   Physical and Cognitive Development in Middle Childhood   368

Chapter Eleven   Social and Personality Development in Middle Childhood   418

Part Five   Adolescence   461

Chapter Twelve   Physical and Cognitive Development in Adolescence   462

Chapter Thirteen   Social and Personality Development in Adolescence   508

To my children:

Stacey, Amy, Jodi, and Laurie

Four of a kind
Each unique

About the Author

Paul S. Kaplan graduated from City College of New York and earned his Doctorate from New York University. He completed additional graduate work at the State University of New York at Stony Brook. He is a professor of psychology at Suffolk County Community College and also teaches at the State University of New York at Stony Brook. Dr. Kaplan was recently awarded the New York State Chancellor's Award for excellence in teaching. He has written a number of books in the areas of child development, human development, and the child with exceptional needs. He often speaks to professional and community groups and is active in the community. Dr. Kaplan is married with four daughters, to whom this book is dedicated, and one grandchild, Zachary.

Contents

Preface   xvii

Part One   Prospects for Personhood   1

CHAPTER ONE
The Study of Child and Adolescent Development   2

Child Development:
A Look at The Mystery   3
What Is Development?   4
The Nature of Development   5
Categories of Change   5

Recurring Themes in Child and
Adolescent Development   6
Theme/Issue 1: What Makes Change Occur?
  Heredity and Environment   6
Action/Reaction   Scott: On and Off the Timetable   7
Theme/Issue 2: Children Develop within
  Multiple Contexts   8
    Focus on the Family   8
    School and Community   9
    The Media   10
Action/Reaction   "It's My Right to Watch
  What I Want"   10
    Culture   10
    Subcultures in the United States   11

The Child in the 21st Century
Immigration, Custom, and Misunderstandings   13
Cultural Cautions   15
Theme/Issue 3: Children Are Affected
  by the Historical Time in Which They Live   16
Theme/Issue 4: How Important Is the Child's
  Early Experience?   16

The Child in the 21st Century
Talking About Our Generation   17

Theme/Issue 5: The Issue of Stability and Change   20
Issue/Theme 6: Social Influences Are Reciprocal   21
Theme/Issue 7: Continuity and Discontinuity
  in Development   21
Theme/Issue 8: Intervention Can Affect
  the Course of Development   22

Discovery: Research in
Child Development   22
The Importance of Research Methods   22
Choices in Research Methods   22
    Naturalistic Observation   23
    Case Studies   23
    The Survey Method   24
    Correlations   24
    The Experimental Method   25
    Quasi-Experimental Designs   27
Research Designs   28

Ethical Considerations in Research   30
Informed Consent   30
Deception   31

Child Development: What's in It for Me?   32
Personal Benefits   32
Careers in Working with Children   32
Research, Teaching, and Clinical Work   33
Influencing Public Policy   33

Summary   34
Review   35

CHAPTER TWO

Perspectives on Child and Adolescent Development   36

Could You Predict Their Reactions?	37
Theoretical Perspectives on Child Development	38
Why Bother with Theory?	38
Good Theory-Bad Theory	39
Usefulness	39
Testability	39
Predictability	39
Inclusiveness	39
Other Criteria	39
Categorizing Theories	39
Orientation to Life	39
Do Children Develop in Stages?	40
The Scope of the Theory	40
The Nature-Nurture Debate	40
Piaget's Theory of Cognitive Development	41
What Is Knowledge?	41
Factors in Development	42
Organization and Adaptation	42
Organization: Cognitive Structures, Schemata and Operations	42
Adaptation	43
The Stages of Cognitive Development	43
The Sensorimotor Stage	43
The Preoperational Stage	44
The Concrete Operational Stage	44
The Formal Operational Stage	44
Stance on Central Issues	45
Application and Value	45
Criticisms and Cautions	45
The Information-Processing Approach	46
Basic Assumptions and Principles of Information Processing	47
Stance on Basic Issues	49
Application and Value	49
Criticisms and Cautions	49
Freud's Psychoanalytic Theory	50
Levels of Consciousness	50
The Constructs of the Mind	50
Defense Mechanisms	51
The Psychosexual Stages	51
Action/Reaction *"Give Him Back!"*	52
Stages in Freud's Developmental Theory	52
The Oral Stage	52
The Anal Stage	52
The Phallic Stage	52
The Latency Stage	53
The Genital Stage	53
Stance on Basic Issues	53
Application and Value	53
Criticisms and Cautions	53
Erikson's Psychosocial Theory	54
The Psychosocial Stages	55
Stage 1: Trust versus Mistrust	55
Stage 2: Autonomy versus Shame or Doubt	55
Stage 3: Initiative versus Guilt	55
Stage 4: Industry versus Inferiority	55
Stage 5: Identity versus Role Confusion	56
Erikson's Later Stages	56
Socialization, Culture, and History	56
Stance on Basic Issues	56
Application and Value	57
Criticisms and Cautions	57
The Behavioral Approach	57
Classical Conditioning	58
Operant Conditioning	58
Stance on Basic Issues	59
Action/Reaction *"The Temper Tantrum"*	59
Application and Value	60
Criticisms and Cautions	60
Social Learning Theory	60
The Process of Imitation	61
Self-Efficacy	62
Reciprocal Determinism	63
Stance on Basic Issues	63
Application and Value	63
Criticisms and Cautions	63
Vygotsky's Sociocultural Theory	64
Stance on Basic Issues	66
Application and Value	66
Criticisms and Cautions	66
Bronfenbrenner's Ecological Theory	67
Stance on Basic Issues	69
Value and Strengths	69
Criticisms and Cautions	69
Developmental Theory: Yesterday, Today, and Tomorrow	70
How to Use Theories	70
The Child in the 21st Century *Chaos Theory*	71
Summary	73
Review	74

CHAPTER THREE
Mechanisms of Change: Genetic and Environmental Interaction 76

Questions Without Easy Answers 77
Genetic Transmission 78
The Sex Chromosomes 80
Action/Reaction *Determining the Gender of Your Child* 81
Transmitting Dominant and Recessive Traits 82
Polygenic Inheritance 82
Action/Reaction *A Secret to Keep?* 83
Sex-Linked Traits 84
Determining Genetic Contribution 85
Twin Studies 85
Adoption Studies 88
Physical Characteristics 88
Temperament 89
Behavioral Traits and Psychopathology 92
Action/Reaction *"Aggressive" Genes?* 93
Shared and Nonshared Environments: How Can Siblings Be So Different? 93
Rate of Development 94
Intelligence 95
The Child in the 21st Century *The Bell Curve: IQ Differences Among Groups?* 96
Modifying Intelligence 96
Genetic Influence on Disease 99
Cystic Fibrosis 99
Tay-Sachs Disease: Hope Through Research 100
Sickle-Cell Anemia 100
Phenylketonuria: A Success Story 101
Chromosomal Abnormalities 101
Down Syndrome 101
Sex-Linked Chromosomal Disorders 103
Predispositions to Disorders 103
Schizophrenia 103
Alcoholism and Genetics 104
The Child in the 21st Century *The New Genetics: Premises, Promises, and Problems* 105
Models of Genetic Influence 108
The Range of Reaction Model 108
Genotype/Environment Effects Model 108
The New Reality 110
Summary 111
Review 112

CHAPTER FOUR
Prenatal Development and Birth 114

The First Odyssey 115
Prenatal Development 116
The Beginning 116
The Germinal Stage 116
The Embryonic Stage 119
The Fetal Stage 119
Developmental Myths 120
The Developing Organism and the Environment 120
Medication 122
Drugs: Legal and Illegal 122
Nicotine 122
Alcohol 123
Commonly Used Illegal Drugs 124
Over-the-Counter Drugs 126
Pollution and Radiation 126
Disease and Pregnancy 127
Venereal Disease 127
The Mother's Medical Condition 129
The Rh Factor 129
Current Issues 129
Maternal Age 130
Action/Reaction *Too Old to Start?* 130
Maternal Nutrition 131
Stress during Pregnancy 132
The Father's Role 133
Technology and Reproductive Alternatives 134
Action/Reaction *Does the Child Need to Know?* 136
Technology, Pregnancy, and Birth 137
The Child in the 21st Century *Reproductive Surrogacy* 138
Birth 139
The Three Stages of the Birth Process 139
Cesarean Birth 140
The Effects of Obstetrical Medication 141
Birth Centers 142
The Lamaze Method 143
Action/Reaction *Under Pressure* 143
The Leboyer Method 144

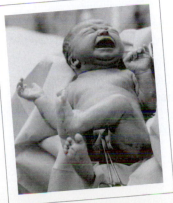

Prematurity: Born At Risk   144

   Action/Reaction *What If Something Happens?*   145

   The Child in the 21st Century:
   The Mystery of Prematurity:
   Not Just Poverty   147

Infant Mortality   148

After the Birth   148

Looking Ahead   150

Summary   151

Review   152

Part Two   Infancy and Toddlerhood   155

C H A P T E R F I V E

Physical Development in Infancy and Toddlerhood   156

"I Need an Instruction Book!"   157

The Newborn at a Glance   158

How the Infant Experiences the World   158

   Vision   159

     Form and Preference   159

     A Preference for Faces?   159

     Can Infants Recognize Different Faces?   159

     Color Vision   161

     Spatial and Depth Perception   161

     Visual Tracking   162

   Hearing   162

   Smell   163

   Taste   163

   Pressure and Pain   164

Infant States   164

   Infant Crying   166

Learning   167

Reflexes   168

Brain Development   169

   The Brain and Experience   170

Infant Health   171

   Sudden Infant Death Syndrome   171

   The Child in the 21st Century
   Disease Conquered… and Reappearing   172

Growth and Motor Development   176

   Principles of Growth and Development   178

   Cultural Differences and Motor Development   179

   The Effects of Practice and Stimulation   179

   Dynamic Systems Theory   180

Focus on the Toddler   182

   Action/Reaction *"Toddler Action Alert"*   185

Parenting Choices   186

   Infant Nutrition   186

   Gender Differences: How Parents View Sons
   and Daughters   188

     Gender Differences at Birth   188

   Action/Reaction *"I Don't Want Ken and Barbie!"*   188

   Toilet Training   190

Atypical Development: Early Intervention   191

Summary   193

Review   194

C H A P T E R S I X

Cognitive and Linguistic Development in Infancy and Toddlerhood   196

An Intelligent Infant   197

Piaget's Theory of Sensorimotor Development   198

   Trends and Premises in Infant Cognitive
   Development   198

   The Substages of Sensorimotor Development   198

     Reflexes (0–1 month): Substage 1   198

Primary Circular Reactions
(1–4 months): Substage 2   198
Secondary Circular Reactions
(4–8 months): Substage 3   199
Coordination of Secondary Reactions
(8–12 Months): Substage 4   199
Tertiary Circular Reactions
(12–18 Months): Substage 5   200
Invention of New Means through Mental
Combination (18–24 months): Substage 6   200
Object Permanence   200
Object Permanence and Infant Behavior   203
Piaget's Theory under Scrutiny   203
Putting It All Together   205

Information-Processing Skills   206
Memory   206
Memories from Infancy and Toddlerhood   207

Predicting Later Intelligence   208

Parents and Cognitive Development   210
Action/Reaction *How Much Is Too Much?*   211
Programs to Help At-Risk Infants and
Toddlers Develop   211
The Question of Acceleration:
The "American Question"   212

The Child in the 21st Century
Teaching Parents to Parent   213

The Development of Language   215
The Nature of Communication   215
The Nature of Language   215
How Children Develop Language   216
Prelanguage Communication   216
The First Word   218
Action/Reaction *"Why Isn't My Child Talking?"*   218
Toddler's Language   219

How Do Children Learn Language?   221
Reinforcement and Imitation   221
Is Language Acquisition Innate?   222
Weaknesses of the Nativist Position   224
Cognitive Theory and Language
Development   225
Social Interaction and Language
Development   225
Culture and Early Language Usage   227
Social Class Differences in Language
Development   228

Encouraging Linguistic Ability   228

Summary   230

Review   231

CHAPTER SEVEN
Social and Personality Development in Infancy and Toddlerhood   232

Setting the Stage   233

Emotional Development   234
What Emotions Do Infants Show?   234
Secondary Emotions   235
Culture and Emotion   236
Can Infants Read the Emotional States of Others?   237
Using Information from Others: Social
Referencing   238
The Smile   239
Empathy   240

Attachment   241
The Nature of Attachment   241
Attachment Behavior   242
The Consequences of Poor Attachment   242
The Quality of Attachment   244
Infant Attachment and Later Behavior   245
Causes of Secure and Anxious Attachment   246
Maternal Sensitivity: A Look at the
Key Construct   247
Looking at the Caregiver-Child Relationship   248

The Child in the 21st Century
*Children of Depressed and Stressed
Mothers: Changing the Way We Look at
Attachment Problems*   249
Synchrony between Parent and Child   250
Infant Temperament and Attachment   251

The Child in the 21st Century
*Early Attachment and Adult
Romantic Relationships*   252
Some Basic Concerns with
Attachment Theory   253
Fear of Strangers   254
Separation Anxiety   254

The Father-Child Relationship   255
Where Is Father?   256
Action/Reaction *Angry, Frustrated, But in Love*   257
How Do Fathers Interact with Infants?   257
Do Infants Become Attached to Their Fathers?   258
Fathers as Caregivers   258

Maternal Employment   259
Do Employed Women Interact Differently
with Their Children Than Full-time
Homemakers?   260
Effects of Maternal Employment on Children   261

Day Care 262

    Action/Reaction *Split Shift* 263

    Day Care and Attachment 263

    Early Day Care and Social and Cognitive
Development 264

    Day Care after Age 1 266

Action/Reaction *"I Work, but . . . ."* 267

    Evaluating Day Care 267

Many Roads to Travel 268

    The Child in the 21st Century
The School of the 21st Century? 269

Summary 271

Review 272

Part Three   Early Childhood   275

CHAPTER EIGHT

Physical and Cognitive Development in Early Childhood 276

The Time-Life Remover 277

Physical Development in the Preschool Years 278

    Growth and Development 278

    Motor Abilities 278

    Fine-Motor Control 280

    Handedness 280

    Children's Art 281

    Safety 283

Nutrition: Why Preschoolers Eat What They Eat 284

    Action/Reaction *"He Eats Only Junk Food"* 286

Children's Health: A World View 286

Brain Development 288

Cognitive Development: The Preoperational Stage 290

    Language Development in Early Childhood 291

    How Preschoolers Reason 293

    Seriation and Classification 293

    Transitive Inferences 295

    Conservation 296

    Characteristics of a Preschooler's Thinking 297

    Appearance and Reality 297

    Irreversibility 297

    Transformations 298

    Egocentrism 298

    Animism and Artificialism 298

    Magical Thinking 299

Recent Challenges to Piaget's Views 299

    Harmonizing the Views 303

Information-Processing Abilities 303

    Attention 303

    Memory Skills 304

    The Importance of Prior Knowledge 305

    Scripts 306

    The Child in the 21st Century
Children Testifying in Court 307

The Preschooler's Environment: Home, Television, and Preschool 309

    The Home 309

    Television 310

    Barney and Friends 310

    Sesame Street 311

    Mr. Rogers' Neighborhood 312

    Action/Reaction *How Much TV Is Too Much TV?* 312

    Preschool Education 313

    Action/Reaction *The Nursery School Gambit* 314

    Do Nursery Schools Foster Development? 315

    Project Head Start 315

    The Future of Head Start and
Early Childhood Programs 316

    Kindergarten 317

    Questions for the Future 318

A Final Thought 318

Summary 319

Review 320

CHAPTER NINE
Social and Personality Development in Early Childhood　322

The Land of Make-Believe　323
A Sense of Initiative　324

The Self-Concept in the Preschool Years　325
Emotional Expression in Early Childhood　326
Childhood Fears　326

Play　327
The Development of Play　328
Action/Reaction *Saving the World from Invaders*　329
Pretend Play　330
Rough-and-Tumble Play　330
Gender Differences in Play　331
The Benefits of Play　332

Parents and Preschoolers　333
Parenting Styles　333
Discipline Style　334
Subculture and Discipline　336
Child Rearing in African American Homes　337
Child Rearing in Latino Homes　338
Child Rearing in Asian American Homes　339
Child Rearing among Native Americans　339

Sibling Relationships: Is It Always "Sibil War"?　341
Sibling Arguments　342
Action/Reaction *Should They Intervene?*　343
The Only Child　344

Peers: A New Relationship　345
Prosocial Behavior　345
Conflict　346

Gender Role Acquisition　347
Gender Differences　347
Three Considerations　348
Gender Identity, Gender Stability, and Gender Consistency　348
Sex Typing and Gender Roles　349
Biological Contributions　350
Hormones　350
Differences in Maturation　350
Genetic Differences　350
Behavior Theories　351
Different Treatment for Sons and Daughters　351
Action/Reaction *"But He's a Boy!"*　351
Role Models and Imitation　352
Psychoanalytic Theory: Identifying with Parents　353
Gender Schema Theory　353
Gender Role Theories Reconsidered　354

Atypical Development: Child Abuse　354
Sexual Abuse　355
Emotional Abuse　356
Why Are Children Abused?　357
Abusing Parents　357
Do Abused Children Grow Up to Abuse Their Own Children?　357
The Abused Child　358
The Situation　358
Acceptance of Violence　358

The Child in the 21st Century
To Spank or Not to Spank　359
Witnessing Domestic Violence　361
Preventing Child Abuse　362

Summary　363
Review　364

Part Four Middle Childhood 367

C H A P T E R   T E N

Physical and Cognitive Development in Middle Childhood 368

Books, Baseball, and Potato Chips 369

Physical Development in Middle Childhood 370

Height and Weight 370

Nutrition in Middle Childhood: "I'll Choose It Myself!" 370

Childhood Obesity 371

Action/Reaction *"Why Can't You Accept Me as I Am?"* 372

Physical Fitness and Health 373

Health Education 373

Organized Sports: Pro and Con 374

Dentition 376

Motor Skill Development 376

Readiness for School 377

The Stage of Concrete Operations 377

The Decline of Egocentrism 378

Reversibility, the Ability to Decenter, and Transformations 378

Conservation 379

Conservation of Number 379

Conservation of Weight 379

Conservation of Volume 379

Seriation and Classification 379

How the School-Age Child Thinks 381

Limitations of Concrete Operational Thought 381

Information-Processing Skills 382

Attention 382

Recall, Recognition, and Memory Strategies 382

Metamemory 382

Language Development in Middle Childhood 383

Children's Humor 385

The Elementary School Experience 389

Reading 389

Reading and Television 390

Math Skills 390

Computer Literacy: The New Basic 391

Rating the Schools 392

Success in School 394

The School Experience 394

The Home 396

Action/Reaction *To Change Teachers or Not to Change: That Is the Question* 398

Attitudes, Motivation, and Work Habits 399

Intelligence 399

The Stanford-Binet and Wechsler Tests 400

How Intelligence Tests Can Be Misused 401

Boys, Girls, and the School Experience 403

Bilingual Children in School 404

The Child in the 21st Century *Bilingual Programs: Do They Work?* 405

Ebonics 407

Atypical Development: Children With Exceptional Needs 408

Learning Disabilities 409

Attention Deficit/Hyperactivity Disorder 410

Mental Retardation 412

Gifted and Talented Children 413

The Total Child in School 414

Summary 415

Review 416

C H A P T E R   E L E V E N

Social and Personality Development in Middle Childhood 418

Through a Child's Eyes 419

Looking at Middle Childhood 420

Measuring Up 420

Action/Reaction *The All-American Boy's Brother* 420

The Latency Stage 421

"How I See Myself": The Self-Concept and Self-Esteem 421

Self-Esteem: Valuing Oneself 422

Building Self-Esteem 424

Child Rearing During Middle Childhood 424
  Child-Rearing Strategies Reconsidered 425
  Do Parents Agree on How to Raise Their
    Children? 425

The Changing Family 426
  The Experience of Divorce 426
    Immediate Reactions to Divorce 426
    Long-term Effects of Divorce 427
    Action/Reaction *That Seven-Letter*
    Word: Divorce 429
    Divorce and the Age of the Child 429
    Does Divorce Affect Boys and Girls
      Differently? 430
    Prescriptions for Divorcing Parents 430
    The Child in a Single-Parent Family 430
  Stepfamilies 432
    Action/Reaction *What's a Mother to Do?* 434
  Latchkey or Self-Care Children 434
  Homeless Families 435
  Gay and Lesbian Households 438

Best Friends 439
  Acceptance and Rejection 440
  Friendship Patterns and Gender 440
  Gender Stereotypes in Middle Childhood 441

Moral Development 441
  Piaget's Theory of Morality 441
  Kohlberg's Theory of Moral Reasoning 442
    Level I: Preconventional Morality 442
    Level II: Conventional Morality 443
    Level III: Postconventional Morality 443
    Is Moral Reasoning Related to Moral
      Behavior? 444
    Moral Reasoning and Gender 444
    Evaluating Kohlberg's Theory 445
  The Psychoanalytic Conception of Morality 446
  The Learning Theory Approach to Morality:
    Studying the Behavior Itself 446

Prosocial and Antisocial Behavior 447
  Helping Others 447
  The Child in the 21st Century
  Raising a Moral Child 448
  Aggression and Antisocial Behavior 450
  Creating the Aggressive Child 451
  Exposure to Crime and Violence 452
  Television and Antisocial Behavior 453

Atypical Development: Children and Stress 454
Middle Childhood In Perspective 456
Summary 457
Review 458

Part Five Adolescence 461

CHAPTER TWELVE
Physical and Cognitive Development in Adolescence 462

Will the Real Teenager Please Stand Up! 463
Puberty and Adolescence 464
  Development of the Female Adolescent 465
    Menstruation 466
  Development of the Male Adolescent 467
  The Secular Trend: Taller, Earlier, and Heavier 467
  What Causes Puberty? 467

The Timing of Puberty 469
  Early and Late Maturation 469

The Health of Teenagers Today 471
  Suicide 471

Physical Activity, and Nutrition 473
  Physical Activity 473
  "I'm Really Fat": Teenagers and Body Image 474
  Action/Reaction *Mirror, Mirror on the Wall* 476

Atypical Development: Eating Disorders 477
  Anorexia Nervosa 477
  Bulimia 478
  Obesity 479

**Sleep: Why Many Teenagers Are
Always Tired** 480

Cognitive Advances in Adolescence 482
  The Stage of Formal Operations 482
    Combinational Logic 482
    Separating the Real and the Possible 483
    Using Abstractions 483
    Hypothetical-Deductive Reasoning 483
    Thinking about Thinking 484
  Evaluating Piaget's Ideas 484
  Cognitive Functioning Beyond
    Formal Operations 484

Adolescent Thought Processes and Risk Taking 485
The Imaginary Audience 486
The Personal Fable 486
Risk Taking 486

Morals and Values In Adolescence 488
Cognitive Development and Moral Reasoning 488
Values and Attitudes 489
Religious Beliefs 490

Sexual Expression 491
The Revolution in Sexual Attitudes 491
Dating 492
Dating Violence and Acquaintance Rape 493
Sexual Behavior 494
Contraceptive Use 495
Action/Reaction *What Did You Find?* 496
Sexually Transmitted Diseases 496

The Child in the 21st Century
Sex Education: Just the Facts? 497
Teenage Pregnancy 499
Consequences of Teenage Pregnancies 500
Sexual Orientation: Homosexual Behavior 502

Adapting to Change 504
Summary 505
Review 506

CHAPTER THIRTEEN
Social and Personality
Development in Adolescence 508

Rites of Passage 509
The Self-Concept and Self-Esteem in Adolescence 510
In Search of an Identity 513
The Four Identity Statuses 514
Identity Diffusion 514
Identity Foreclosure 515
Identity Moratorium 515
Identity Achievement 516
Do Males and Females Take Different Paths to Identity Formation? 517
Concerns about Identity Status 517

The Child in the 21st Century
Identity, Minority Status, and the Bicultural Experience 518

Achieving Emotional and Behavioral Autonomy 519
Achieving Emotional Autonomy: Renegotiating Relationships with Parents 519
Behavioral Autonomy: The Issue of Conformity and Independent Action 521
Conflict between Parents and Adolescents 523
Action/Reaction *How Much? How Soon?* 525
Communication with Parents and Peers 526
Different Views: Same Family 527
Successful Parenting in Adolescence 527
Cultural Differences 528

The Secondary School Today 529
The Junior High/Middle School Experience 529
The High School 531
High Schools: A Different View 533
Gender and Achievement in High School 534
Minorities in High School 536
Dropping Out of School 538

Career Choice 538
Women and Careers 539
Socioeconomic Status 541
Teenagers and Work 542

Atypical Development: Drug Abuse and Violence 544
Drug Use 544
Alcohol 544
Nicotine 544
Marijuana 546
Cocaine and Crack 546
Can Drug Abuse Be Predicted? 546
Action/Reaction *When Daniel Comes Home from College . . . Drunk* 548
Drug Education 548
Violence and Delinquency 549
Family Processes and Relationships 549
Individual/Peer Factors 550
School and Community Factors 550
Protective Factors 551
Can Violence Be Curbed? 551

Exploding the Myths 552
Summary 553
Review 554

Glossary 557
References 563
Name Index 623
Subject Index 638

A Child's Odyssey

THIRD EDITION

Preface

It is amazing how much the development of a child from birth to adulthood is similar to a journey. As one plans a journey, so parents plan for their children. Just as children make more of their own decisions with age, so do travelers make more decisions on their own as they gain experience. Just as the person on a journey is faced with challenges and tasks, so is the developing child faced with many age-related challenges and tasks. Just as there is a sense of adventure and mystery in an odyssey, so is the child's developmental odyssey filled with a sense of wonder, mystery, and adventure. Just as there is more than one way to get from one place to another, research shows that there are many ways to develop a healthy sense of self, good interpersonal relationships, a strong body, and competent intellectual abilities. Just as traveling companions influence the quality of an individual's experience on a journey, so do the child's parents, siblings, extended family, friends, and teachers influence the child's odyssey.

This third edition of *A Child's Odyssey* is substantially changed from the second edition. However, it still offers the balance of scientific research, the sense of empathy with the individual, and the even-handed approach to controversial issues that made it special. The third edition has been thoroughly updated with many new features and new areas of content added.

One of the strengths of the previous editions was their extensive variety of pedagogical devices. In this text, some of the original devices have been retained and several new ones added. Each chapter begins with motivational true-false questions. Within each chapter, a special feature entitled "The Child in the 21st Century" focuses on the challenges and issues facing children at the beginning of the new century. Another feature, called "Action/Reaction," invites the reader to consider a scenario in which concepts learned in the text may be used to analyze an issue or a challenge faced by a particular child or family.

A new feature entitled "Guideposts" alerts the reader to the most important points in the text. The new "Review" feature allows readers to demonstrate their understanding of the key concepts and terms covered in the chapter. A feature entitled "For Your Consideration" presents a number of thought-provoking questions that encourage readers to think critically about issues. The "Trends" feature points out changes occurring in children's health and educational achievement as noted by two major government initiatives in these areas. A "Datagraphic" feature offers pictorial views of demographic changes. All key terms are highlighted by bold print, and the definition is provided on the same page. A glossary is also found at the end of the book. A point-by-point chapter summary appears at the conclusion of each chapter. In addition, many new figures and tables have been added. All these pedagogical features are designed to help the reader focus on the most important points and to apply the material to actual situations and issues.

This third edition contains much new material. Two general changes can be easily noted from a casual look at the text. First, there is much more material concerning cultural perspectives in the body of the text. Second, since many child development specialists take a more contextual view, emphasizing the importance of understanding the child developing in multiple contexts, references to this are found throughout the text. A new section entitled "Atypical Development" emphasizes such areas as eating disorders, stress, early intervention for infants and toddlers with disabilities, and children with learning disabilities, attention-deficit/hyperactivity disorder and mental retardation.

Although all sections of the text have been updated, many new areas have been added. Careful attention has been given to the length of the text, and through rewriting and judicious editing, the addition of material has not substantially increased the page count. In Chapter 1, an introduction to the concept of multiple contexts, including culture and subculture, is given. In addition, attention is given to quasi-experimental designs and time-lag and sequential designs. The theories chapter has been reorganized to present Vygotsky's sociocultural theory and Bronfenbrenner's ecological theory as well as a section on new trends in child development. Our understanding of genetics is changing rapidly, and Chapter 3 contains new material on the Genome Project, on twin and adoption studies, and on models of genetic/environmental interaction. In Chapter 4, "Prenatal Development and Birth," new material on technology and reproductive alternatives, on the father's role, and on the effects of cocaine is included.

The chapters on infancy and toddlerhood reflect our growing appreciation of the abilities of infants and toddlers. New material on neonate and infant sensory abilities, infant health, sudden infant death syndrome, dynamic systems theory of motor development, the needs of toddlers, modern views of Piaget's sensorimotor stage, culture and emotions, advances in attachment theory, the father-child relationship, and new research on day care has been added along with new material on culture and early language usage.

Chapters 8 and 9 cover early childhood, and offer more on nutrition, children's health, handedness, brain development, language development including private speech, self-concept, magical thinking, preschool education, the only child, subculture and discipline, child-rearing strategies in different cultures, child abuse, and exposure to violence. Chapters 10 and 11 look at middle childhood and introduce new material on health education, participation in organized sports, the elementary school experience, gender differences in the school experience, homelessness, aggression, and prosocial behavior.

The chapters covering adolescence include much new research on nutrition and physical activity in adolescence, postformal operational reasoning, religious beliefs, the development of the self-concept and self-esteem in adolescence, new perspectives on the parent-adolescent relationship, behavioral and emotional autonomy, and new perspectives on risk-taking, teenagers and employment, drug use, violence, values, acquaintance rape, sex education, and homosexuality. There is also expanded coverage of the junior and senior high school experience, on the experience of males and females, and adolescents from different minority groups.

Ancillaries

Ancillaries for this edition include the following:

Study Guide: The Study Guide contains study questions and a review for each chapter, important terms and concepts, practice tests in both multiple-choice and true-false formats, and activities to accompany each chapter.

Instructor's Manual: The Instructor's Manual contains chapter learning objectives, lecture notes, discussion questions, case studies, suggestions for teaching, suggested activities for students, and transparency masters.

Test Bank: The Test Bank contains approximately 1,200 multiple-choice questions and 150 essay questions, with correct answers and page references to the main text. The test bank is available electronically in both Macintosh and Windows formats as well as in hard-copy form.

Film and Video Library: Instructors may choose from a variety of programs from *Films for the Humanities and Sciences* and from the *Annenberg/CPB Discovering Psychology* series.

Web Site: The Web Site provides several useful Internet links and additional study questions to accompany each chapter. Students and instructors can access the web resources through http://psychology.wadsworth.com

Acknowledgments

Listing only the author's name on the cover of a book is somewhat misleading, for the text you see before you is truly a team effort. Developmental editors, production editors, reviewers, artists, and many other professionals who often go unappreciated are involved. I have had the great fortune to deal with excellent editors; Peter Marshall at West Publishing Company and Stacey Purviance at Wadsworth. In addition, I would like to thank the many other people at Wadsworth who have helped make this third edition of *A Child's Odyssey* a reality.

I also want to express appreciation for the time and effort invested by the authors of the various ancillary books, including Elizabeth Rider (Elizabethtown College), Stephen Buggie (University of New Mexico–Gallup Campus), and Michael L. Jaffe (Kean University). In spite of tight schedules, they all did excellent work.

The quality of a textbook depends greatly on the quality of the prepublication reviews by psychology professors around the country. The professional reviewers listed below deserve special acknowledgment for their constructive criticisms that led to many improvements in this book. I am very grateful to all of them.

Martha Arterberry
  Gettysburg College
Jill Chafetz
  Rhode Island College
Nancy Coghill
  University of Southwest Louisiana
Jack Demick
  Suffolk University
Susanne Denham
  George Mason University
K. Laurie Dickson
  Northern Arizona University
Michelle Dunlap
  Connecticut College

Shari Ellis
  Virginia Commonwealth University
Rick Fabes
  University of Arizona
Vivian Harper
  San Joaquin Delta College
Kimberly Klein Dechman
  Mary Washington College
Charles LaBounty
  Hamline University
Deborah Leong
  Metropolitan State College of Denver
David Lockwood
  Humber College

Graham Mathews
  Georgia College
Phil Mohan
  University of Idaho
Ligaya Paguio
  University of Georgia
Elizabeth Robertson
  University of North Carolina-Greensboro
Judith Ward
  Central Connecticut State University
Richard Willis
  Catonsville Community College

I would also like to thank Vicki Knight, who has served as my editor. I am also grateful to Laura Lawson for copy editing; to Gladys Rosa-Mendoza who performed superbly as the production editor; to Gladys Rosa-Mendoza of rosa+wesley who created the new design; to Brian Wenberg who did valiant work on the page layouts; to Peggy Cooper who provided outstanding photo research. Others who have made significant contributions to this project include Joanne Terhaar (marketing), Annie Berterretche (editorial assistant), John Walker and Tanya Nigh (project editors), Stephen Rapley (creative director), and Leslie Krongold (media editor).

I would further like to thank David Quinn, Joyce Garbrielle, and Delores Perillo of Suffolk County Community College's library for their help in obtaining many resources that were required in the writing of this text.

Finally, writing a book is a bit like running a marathon. It takes perseverance and time. I wish to thank my wife, Leslie, as well as my daughters, Stacey, Amy, Jodi, and Laurie, for their patience, encouragement, and understanding that made the writing of this book easier and more pleasant.

Prospects *for* Personhood

1 The Study of Child and Adolescent Development

2 Perspectives on Child and Adolescent Development

3 Mechanisms of Change: Genetic and Environmental Interaction

4 Prenatal Development and Birth

The *Study of* Child

CHAPTER OUTLINE

Child Development: A Look at The Mystery

Recurring Themes and Issues in Child and Adolescent Development

Discovery: Child Development

Ethical Considerations in Research

Child Development: What's in It for Me?

ARE THESE STATEMENTS
True *or* False?

1. Preschool children consider everyone they play with in nursery school a friend.
2. If we know that a child is negotiating a particular stage of development, psychologists can predict exactly when the child will enter the next stage.
3. Despite the increase in maternal employment, a majority of mothers with children under 18 years are still full-time homemakers.
4. Parents raising their children in poverty are just as likely to rate their children's health as "excellent" as middle class parents.
5. American children spend more time watching television than in any other activity except sleep.
6. Children who experience a very poor early environment can benefit greatly from a significant improvement in their environment later in childhood.
7. Surveys are especially useful when the researcher wants to gather information from a great many people.
8. Most Americans today believe that the younger generation will make the United States a better place to live.
9. Young children believe that if they can't see a car approaching, a car cannot be there.
10. Most psychological experiments cause no physical or psychological harm to the people who participate in them.

ANSWERS: 1. *True.* 2. *False.* 3. *False.* 4. *False.* 5. *True.* 6. *True.* 7. *True.* 8. *False.* 9. *True.* 10. *True.*

and Adolescent Development

Child Development: A Look at The Mystery

A mother took her young daughter to a toy store to buy a birthday present for one of her preschool classmates. The child's eyes brightened as she spied a toy she wanted. She led her mother over to the toy and pleaded with her to buy it.

"But I don't have the money," her mother explained.

"You have 'moneys,'" the child replied. Her mother smiled and picked up the toy to buy it.

At the checkout counter, the mother placed the $20 on the counter, receiving three $1 bills, two quarters, a dime, a nickel, and three pennies change. She was surprised when the child informed her that she now had more "moneys" than she had before. As far as the child was concerned, her mother had made a profit on the exchange!

We are often surprised when children see the world differently than adults. After all, we know that five $1 bills equals a $5 bill and that 100 pennies equals $1, but we are puzzled when young children balk at giving us 100 pennies in exchange for a dollar bill or two nickels for one small dime.

"But you have moneys." This young child may believe that when her mother buys her the toy with a $20 bill and receives three singles, two quarters, a dime, a nickel, and three pennies change, that her mother actually made money on the deal since she has more "moneys" now than when she started.

Childhood is a time of mystery and charm. We have been led to believe that once we are adults the world of the child is permanently closed to us. In one way it is. None of us will ever again experience the first day of school or the joy on our seventh birthday when we received the toy we "always wanted." Still, our status as adults gives us an opportunity to understand that world better and appreciate the changes in behavior that occur as children develop.

What Is Development?

The term **development** describes the sequence of physical, cognitive, social, and personality changes that occur to human beings as they age. *Child development* is the scientific study of these changes throughout the childhood years.

The process of development is common to all of us, and many aspects of development unfold in a predictable way. Children sit before they walk, and they walk before they run. This predictability permits the scientific study of development. But within this predictability is individuality. The "average child" is a myth. Each child experiences different events, and each experiences the same events differently. Some develop quickly and dramatically; others require more time. Each child is at the same time similar to others and yet unique.

What is child development?

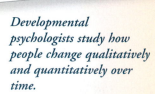

Developmental psychologists study how people change qualitatively and quantitatively over time.

development

The sequence of physical, cognitive, social and personality changes that occur to human beings as they age.

Many young children define a friend as someone they are playing with at the time. Everyone in the nursery school class is a friend. As children develop, their concept of friendship changes.

The Nature of Development

To better understand the nature of development, we must look at the way a child progressively deals with a problem or a concept. For example, a child's understanding and practice of friendship changes as the child grows (Rubin, Bukowski, & Parker, 1998; Selman, 1981). Through infancy and toddlerhood, friendship is defined by physical proximity or by a desire to play with the other child's toys. Three- and 4-year-olds see friendship in terms of playmates. A friend is someone who plays with you. In the early school years, helping and sharing are important and a definite give-and-take is seen in children's friendships. However, they are motivated by self-interest, not mutuality. Later in elementary school a different perspective develops, and friends are now seen as people with whom children can share good times and problems. They share feelings as well as material needs. However, there is jealousy and possessiveness here. The final stage, where friendship involves mutuality and trust, is seldom attained before adolescence.

Here we see the development of children's concept of friendship. The changes are predictable in terms of the order in which they will appear. What is not predictable is the exact age at which the child will exhibit a particular stage of understanding. Some children of the same age will be more advanced than others. Knowing how a child sees his or her friends, we can now predict the next progression in that child's understanding of friendship, but pinpointing the exact age at which a change to a newer conception of friendship will occur is difficult.

Preschool children consider everyone they play with in nursery school a friend.

If we know that a child is negotiating a particular stage of development, psychologists can predict exactly when the child will enter the next stage.

Categories of Change

Developmental changes can be placed into two distinct categories: quantitative change and qualitative change (Appelbaum & McCall, 1983). **Quantitative changes** involve changes in amount, frequency, or degree. Such changes are usually quantified easily, for example, in terms of inches or pounds. Any changes that involve an increase or decrease in some characteristic are considered quantitative.

Qualitative changes involve changes in process, function, structure, or organization. A child's understanding of friendship is an example of qualitative change. This understanding cannot be understood strictly in terms of more or less; it is best described in terms of "difference." Try this experiment. Cut out sixteen pictures from various magazines. Make certain that four pictures show food, four show pieces of furniture, four show toys, and four show items of clothing. Ask children of various ages first to look at all the pictures and then to try to recall as many

quantitative changes
Changes that can be considered solely in terms of increases or decreases, such as changes in height or weight.

qualitative changes
Changes in process, function, structure or organization

pictures as they can after a minute or two of study. As you would expect, the older children will remember more of the items than the younger children will. This is basically a quantitative change in ability to recall information. However, if you observed the children studying the pictures, you probably noticed a qualitative change in the strategies they used to help them remember the items (Kail & Hagen, 1982; Schneider & Bjorklund, 1998). Younger children do not make use of the categories, while older children do.

Recurring Themes in Child and Adolescent Development

As we explore child and adolescent development, certain themes and issues will arise repeatedly. You will come to recognize these themes and issues in many different contexts throughout this text.

THEME/ISSUE 1:
What Makes Change Occur? Heredity and Environment

When we watch a baby begin to walk, we are seeing a being impelled toward progress. Time after time, the baby will try, fall, perhaps cry, get up, and try again. In more subtle ways, the process goes on in a multitude of areas throughout one's life.

What causes these changes? The two mechanisms of genetics and environment or learning are often advanced to account for change. You may have heard someone say that some change was due to genetics and another change to environmental factors, but such thinking is antiquated. Some areas of development, such as physical growth, are indeed determined mostly, though not entirely, by one's genetic endowment; other areas, such as being able to program a computer, are affected mostly by learning. However, both genetic and environmental determinants are important in understanding behavior.

Psychologists use the term **maturation** to describe the unfolding of an individual's unique genetic plan. Maturation largely explains such things as the time a child's teeth erupt, a child's developing the ability to grasp objects and to walk, and the time at which a female first menstruates. The maturational process depends most strongly on the individual's genetic master plan. This master plan, which functions as a timetable of sorts, largely (but not entirely) determines when certain events will occur. The genetic master plan may limit progress as well. For example, before a baby can walk, he or she must have the necessary strength and balance—prerequisites that are determined largely by maturation. The child is ready to walk only when these prerequisites are met. However, the environment must also be taken into consideration, because adequate nutrition and experience are also important (Cratty, 1986). Infants need opportunities to practice their skills. Most of the time, it is not too difficult to provide these basic experiences.

Evidence indicates that an overwhelmingly poor environment has a disastrous effect on the rate of maturation. Children raised under very poor conditions are often far behind in many areas of development but with extra care and attention, the negative effects of a poor environment can be overcome to some degree (Clarke & Clarke, 1976). There is also evidence that environmental enrichment can optimize the development of these skills (Zelazo, Zelazo, Cohen, & Zelazo, 1993). The maturation process proceeds in much the same way for people in all cultures. Unlike the learning process, whose course is largely determined by external events, maturation is determined largely by internal signals.

maturation
A term used to describe changes that are due to the unfolding of an individual's genetic plan. These changes are relatively immune to environmental influence.

Any relatively permanent changes in behavior caused by interaction with the environment are the result of **learning.** When a child recites the alphabet, imitates a brother's fear of spiders, sings along with Daddy, or recognizes Mommy, learning has occurred. A child's understanding of gender roles, morality, language, and problem solving is dependent on learning. Yet we cannot see learning; we can only infer it from behavioral change. The child who solves a mathematics problem that he or she could not solve the week before is said to have learned.

In contrast to maturation, learning is extremely dependent on the environment. Children learn what they see and experience. A child whose parents habitually fight, scream at their children, and encourage their children to take an aggressive stance toward other people will learn to be aggressive. A child whose parents settle disputes calmly and encourage their children to do the same is likely to learn to settle disputes in a peaceful manner. Yet the relationship is not an exact one. Peaceful and calm people sometimes emerge from traumatic environments, whereas a tranquil, supportive environment does not guarantee a well-adjusted child. Parents are not the only influence on their children. As the child's social world expands, peers, teachers, television, and a host of other environmental factors influence what the child learns.

To fully understand the nature of development, we must appreciate both genetic and environmental factors and how they interact. Let us say that it is helpful to have good eye-hand coordination and quick reflexes to hit a baseball well. Let us further hypothesize that genetic factors underlie these abilities. An individual who has better eye-hand coordination and better reflexes may have an initial advantage. However, what if this individual is not given any practice in hitting? The person would then never reach his or her potential. At the same time, through constant practice, an individual with average eye-hand coordination and reflexes may become a very good player. The situation is even more complicated, though, for it only makes sense to talk about genetic contribution within a particular context. The genetic contribution to the ability to swing a bat well is probably more

learning
Relatively permanent changes in behavior due to interaction with the environment.

important at the major league level, where the ball is thrown at 90 miles an hour with considerable skill, and less important at the neighborhood level, where practice is probably sufficient to hit the ball reasonably well.

The same analysis may be used for understanding a number of other characteristics, such as intelligence. As will be discussed in Chapter 3, to understand intelligence, both the genetic endowment of the individual and the environment must be taken into account. For example, two children with similar genetic potential who are raised in very different environments will have different intelligence scores. If one child is raised in an enriched and stimulating environment and the second in an unstimulating environment, the intelligence levels of these children will differ. On the other hand, what if we were to take five people from similar environments and backgrounds and expose each of them to an enriched and concentrated educational program? Some of the people would still do better than others, partially because of differences in genetic endowment. The environment may encourage or discourage the development of a genetic potential in a certain area, and different aspects of our genetic potential may be developed depending on the environment in which we find ourselves. We must look at both genetic and environmental factors if we are to understand behavior and development.

THEME/ISSUE 2:
Children Develop within Multiple Contexts

Development does not occur in a vacuum. Each individual's life is embedded in a series of multilevel contexts (Kreppner & Lerner, 1989). The most immediate context is the family, but other contexts such as the school, peer group, neighborhood, religious institution, and the political system under which the child is living are important. The different facets of the environment affect each other. Political changes, such as the availability of government- and private-sponsored day care services, may affect interactions in the family, and changes in the family structure, such as more mothers seeking employment, affect the economic and political system. The functioning of an individual, then, is the product of interactions between the person and the many facets of the environment that continually emerge and change over time (Fisher & Lerner, 1994). The contextualization of development is one of the most important changes in child psychology.

Focus on the Family The family is the most important context for development. The family today in the United States (and many other developed countries) is quite a different institution from what it was 50 years ago. The traditional family consisting of a mother who is a homemaker and a father who is employed full-time is far less common. In fact, only about 12% of American children live in such families, largely because of the rise in the percentage of mothers who are employed and the growth of single-parent families (Hernandez, 1997). In 1940, only 10% of all mothers were employed, while today the figure stands at more than 60% (Hernandez, 1997). Many of these employed mothers have young children and require substitute child care (Scarr, 1998). The child in the early 21st century is more likely to spend some part of his or her early childhood in a day care center or other substitute care arrangement. Supervision becomes a key concern as the number of self-care, or latchkey children (children who do not have a parent or older person waiting for them when they come home from school) has increased.

About 20% of all children now live in single-parent families, which have increased with the rise in divorce and of unmarried mothers. Most divorced parents remarry, and many children will negotiate a series of marital transitions from intact family to single-parent family to stepfamily relationships.

Guideposts

How do genetic and environmental factors interact?

Although there are some abilities that are probably influenced by genetics, such as eye-hand coordination and speed of response, which make hitting a baseball easier, the genetic contribution is more important at the major league level than at the little league level. Practice is important at both levels.

Despite the increase in maternal employment, a majority of mothers with children under 18 years are still full-time homemakers.

Guideposts

How have families changed in the last 50 years?

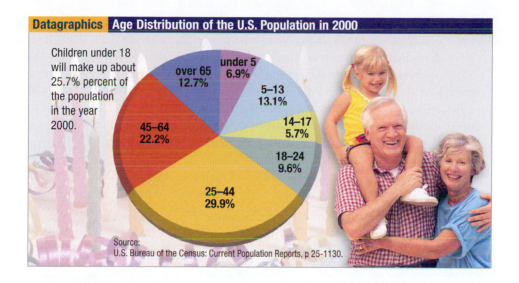

Datagraphics Age Distribution of the U.S. Population in 2000

Children under 18 will make up about 25.7% percent of the population in the year 2000.

over 65 12.7%
under 5 6.9%
5–13 13.1%
14–17 5.7%
18–24 9.6%
25–44 29.9%
45–64 22.2%

Source:
U.S. Bureau of the Census: Current Population Reports, p 25-1130.

School and Community   A child's day is organized around attendance at school, and this is beginning much earlier in life. Many young children attend a preschool, and most children now attend kindergarten, about half attending it for a full day. Unfavorable comparisons between American children and their peers in other countries on various measures of academic achievement have produced changes in curricula and calls for educational reforms (Kaplan, 1990). As a result, kindergartners today are more likely to be exposed to academic work.

The child is also a product of the neighborhood. A child raised in a poverty-stricken area will have an experience that is quite different compared with a child raised in a suburban or rural area. A child who is raised in an area in which drug sales and violence are common will differ greatly from a child's experience in an area in which it is unusual to even lock one's doors.

Where one lives and, to some extent, the school one attends is dependent on socioeconomic status. People living in poverty tend to live in areas where children are exposed to more violence (McLoyd & Wilson, 1991). Poverty affects every area of life. Without adequate financial resources, medical care for low-income families is often substandard and bills cannot be paid. Vaccination rates are also lower (Wood, 1995). Compared with middle-income parents, many fewer parents living in poverty circumstances consider their children as being in excellent health (Adams & Benson, 1990). Poverty is related to many problems, such as homelessness, prematurity, inadequate nutrition, and lack of intellectual stimulation in the home.

T F
4

Parents raising their children in poverty are just as likely to rate their children's health as "excellent" as middle-class parents.

The contextualization of development means that psychologists look at the entire context in which children develop. How will the experiences of these children differ?

About 22% of all American children live in poverty (McLoyd, 1998). This figure has not varied much since 1981, but it is an increase from the 15% level in 1970. Children are much more likely to live in poverty than are adults (Hernandez, 1997; Larson, 1992). African American, Latino, Native American and some subgroups of Asian Americans are more likely than whites to live in poverty (Wolf, 1995). The gap between rich and poor is wider in the United States than in most other industrialized countries (Bradsher, 1995) and has grown since 1980.

Poverty has increased for many reasons. First, the number of single-parent families has risen, and poverty among female-headed single-parent families is much greater than poverty among married couples (Burns & Scott, 1994). Most are the product of divorce, but the number of single parents who are unmarried has increased dramatically as well, until very recently (Glazer, 1993). Since 1991, the teen birth rate has significantly declined, although the rate is still relatively high (Coles, 1999). Other reasons for the increase in the number of children living in poverty are the loss of blue-collar, well-paying jobs and the inability of federal poverty programs to keep up with the need (Huston, McLoyd, & Coll, 1994).

The Media   The influence of the media must also be recognized. Children spend more time watching television than engaging in any other activity except sleeping (Dorr & Rabin, 1995). People are greatly influenced by what they see on the television or in the movies as well as what they listen to on the radio. Many people are concerned about the effect watching violent television programs or listening to violent song lyrics may have on children. Television sets now often come with a v-chip, which allows parents to screen out programs containing violence, profanity, or nudity (Healey, 1995).

ACTION / REACTION

"It's My Right to Watch What I Want"

The Moores don't know what they are going to do with their 13-year-old Kellen. Kellen is a good student and has good friends, but he insists that he has the right to watch any television program he wants. The Moore's cable television gets about 40 stations, and they believe that some of the programs are not suitable for a boy his age.

Kellen argues that he understood his parents' concerns when he was younger, but now it is time for them to "trust him." He feels he is old enough to choose what he wants to see on television.

If you were Kellen's parents, how would you answer his argument?

ACTION / REACTION

Culture   A child raised in the Japanese culture encounters a different set of values and attitudes and has a different life experience than a child developing in Ecuador. Often what seems strange or unusual to one individual may seem very common and natural to another. Trading for profit is not very common among young children in Great Britain or the United States, but it is very common in Zimbabwe, Africa (Jahoda, 1983).

Various cultures deal with developmental challenges in different ways and misunderstandings can arise when two cultures interact (see *Immigration, Customs and Misunderstandings* on page 13). Medical and agricultural volunteers learned this lesson while doing volunteer work in New Guinea among the Dani tribe. Each morning the volunteers would buy food from the Dani farmers. The Dani would

American children spend more time watching television than any other activity except sleep.

For Your Consideration

What would be the advantages and disadvantages of not having a television in a child's home?

hold up their fingers on one hand to indicate how much currency they would accept for their vegetables. One volunteer noticed that they would often walk away disappointed, and none of the advisers could understand why since they always paid the price indicated. The Dani would not talk about their disappointment. Finally, one of the Dani who worked in the hospital solved the mystery for the volunteers.

When you hold up two fingers you are indicating that you want two of whatever you are signaling. However, in the Dani culture, what you want is indicated by the number of fingers that are *not* raised (E. Riccardo, 1999, personal communication). When a Dani farmer held up two fingers, he was signaling his desire for three, while they were only being given two. In Dani culture, it is considered inappropriate to complain.

One's general outlook on life and priorities are prescribed by one's culture. For example, these volunteers were able to fly in some candy canes and gave them out to those who were present during an assembly. The Dani are very poor, and this was a rare treat. The volunteers became concerned when they finished giving out their supply and saw many people coming over the hills to join the assembly. Would there be a confrontation between those who had and those who didn't? Sharing is a value much admired in the Dani culture, and those who had been given the treats shared with the newcomers without any protest.

Subcultures in the United States   It is easy to accept cultural differences, especially among those that are very different, such as the Dani. However, within complex societies, a number of groups exist each of which differ from the majority culture in attitudes, child-rearing strategies, beliefs, values, and communication patterns. If these minority groups differ significantly from the dominant culture and think of themselves as different, they are considered **subcultures** (Henslin, 1999; Light, Keller, & Calhoun, 1994). The principal minority groups within the United States are African Americans, Latinos, Asian Americans, and Native Americans. The percentage of Americans belonging to these groups is expected to increase substantially in the 21st century (see Table 1.1). Subcultures need not be ethnic or racial groups, for we may speak of a subculture of teenagers or older people living in retirement communities.

Children raised in other cultures have different experiences and are deeply affected by the cultural context.

Table 1.1   Resident Population of the United States: Today and Tomorrow

(Percentage of the U.S. Population)

	White	African-American	Native American	Latino	Asian
1997	72.9	12.1	.7	10.7	3.6
2000	71.8	12.2	.7	11.4	3.9
2010	68.0	12.6	.8	13.8	4.8
2020	64.3	12.9	.8	16.3	5.7
2030	60.5	13.1	.8	18.9	6.6
2040	56.7	13.3	.9	21.7	7.5
2050	52.8	13.6	.9	24.5	8.2

The U.S. Bureau of the Census uses a low, medium, and high set of projected figures. These figures are taken from the middle series.
SOURCE: U.S. Department of Commerce (1998)

subcultures

Groups with a system of values, attitudes, modes of behavior, and life styles which are distinct from, but related to, the dominant culture of a society.

Each subculture exists within a larger, dominant culture, not completely apart from it. Understanding the values, child-rearing strategies and attitudes of a particular group is vital to understanding the context in which children are developing. For instance, African American children often take on family responsibilities quite early and are raised within extended kinship networks that offer support and comfort. Many Latino children are raised in an atmosphere that stresses cooperation and family pride rather than competition. Some Asian American children are used to a child-rearing regimen emphasizing family obligations, and many Native American children are raised with a value system that emphasizes group activities and sharing.

Cultures and subcultures differ from each other in many ways and, as shown in Figure 1.1, culture influences development in four specific areas (Pachter & Harwood, 1996). The physical and social setting of the home includes the way the home is set up as well as the social customs of the society—for example, the way girls and boys are treated within the society and family. In many Latino cultures, families are defined as including extended families, and children are taught the importance of the personal qualities of loyalty and family solidarity. Culture also influences customs regarding child care. Some cultures expect children to be more independent than others. Culture also influences caretaker psychology; the attitudes and values on which these customs are built. When Puerto Rican and Anglo-American mothers were asked about the most positive desirable child behavior traits, Puerto Rican mothers stressed qualities reflecting respect and social abilities, whereas Anglo mothers generated descriptions that were more individualistic, such as self-confidence and independence (Harwood, 1992).

Culture also influences the larger social and political conditions under which people live, which in turn may have far reaching effects on people's lives. Some political systems provide more family support, such as day care, than others. Child-rearing strategies may also be affected by the varying economic and social conditions that exist. For example, spoiling children is often a significant concern to many African American parents, and this belief may lead to stricter disciplinary procedures. Many African American parents perceive they are raising their children in a hostile physical and social environment, and they need to prepare the child to have the ability to live in a dangerous atmosphere and in a society in which rejection may occur (Pachter & Harwood, 1996).

Guideposts

In what specific ways does culture affect development?

Figure 1.1 The developmental niche

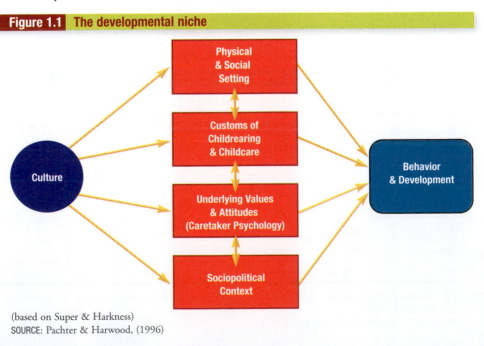

(based on Super & Harkness)
SOURCE: Pachter & Harwood, (1996)

The Child in the 21st Century

Immigration, Custom, and Misunderstandings

Give me your tired, your poor, your huddled masses, yearning to breathe free.

This is a line of Emma Lazarus's great poem that is inscribed on the base of the Statue of Liberty. The United States has always been a destination of immigrants, who have come for political freedom and economic opportunities. The number of immigrants entering the United States has waxed and waned over the years but has ranged from 800,000 to a little more than 1 million in the past 10 years (U.S. Department of Commerce, 1998). In the United States, today, 15% of all children are either immigrants or are living with at least one parent who is an immigrant (Hernandez, 1997). The greatest number come from Mexico, the Caribbean, and Central and South America, but many also immigrate from Asia, especially China, India, the Philippines, and Vietnam.

Imagine what it would be like if you immigrated to another country. You would probably have a poor knowledge of the language, the system of government would be strange to you, and the customs would be different. You may have been part of the majority group and culture in the country from which you came. You are now part of a minority group. Whenever a minority group comes into contact with the majority culture, some change occurs. It may take a few generations, but change is inevitable. This is called *acculturation*. Acculturation occurs when contact between cultures affects the cultural patterns of one or both groups (Hernandez, 1989). Your children would be the products of two cultures: the one you brought with you from your country of origin and the one in which they are raised. Immigrant parents face challenges in many areas of child rearing. Children's relationships with their parents may be more formal in some societies than in American society. Parents may be stricter or less strict than is common here. First-generation immigrants often have to decide just how to mix their original culture with American culture.

Physicians, teachers, and governmental officials must often communicate and work with immigrants, and this interaction is not always easy. With the extensive immigration to the United States and other Western countries, children are more likely to come in contact with other children who have newly arrived. Naturally, immigrants must come to appreciate and adjust to the realities of their new country, and the vast majority do so with enthusiasm. Cultural differences often remain, however, and understanding these cultural differences may be a key to better interpersonal relationships and reducing prejudice. At the same time, professionals must be aware of these customs if they are to serve these immigrant populations.

Consider the following situation. A Vietnamese mother comes into the doctor's office accompanied by her 1-year-old daughter. The physician rises and through an interpreter asks the mother what ails her child. The woman and the doctor both sit down. The doctor takes a relaxed position, sitting with his legs crossed, and smiles at the woman. To put the woman at ease, the doctor compliments her on her beautiful child, then continues asking about the child's symptoms.

It sounds simple and efficient, but the doctor has made so many mistakes and insulted the client so badly that his effectiveness may well be compromised. The doctor innocently believed he was acting correctly when he asked about symptoms, complimented the child, and sat in a relaxed position. But all three actions can cause problems.

First, among Southeast Asians it is considered impolite to ask direct questions immediately. People first make small talk, asking about the entire family and the like, before getting down to business. Second, complimenting a child on her beauty or health may be a problem if the parents come from a rural village in their home country. They may fear that a lurking evil spirit will hear the praise and take the child away. In some villages, children are not named until 2 years of age because giving the child a beautiful name may draw the jealous attention of the evil spirit. Third, if the patient is Laotian, crossing one's legs and allowing a toe to point toward the patient is considered an insult.

This point raises another problem. We tend to characterize all people who come from Southeast Asia as one group, but this is incorrect. Language, customs, and traditions differ widely among the Vietnamese, Cambodians, Laotians, and Thais. In one incident, a doctor, Marianne Felice, asked a Vietnamese interpreter to talk to a Laotian youth. The Vietnamese interpreter "indignantly" announced that he was Vietnamese and "stormed away." Later, Dr. Felice was told that if she had asked the Vietnamese interpreter to translate for a Cambodian patient, it would have been worse, because these two countries have been at war for centuries. Appreciating the differences between these groups is crucial to understanding the behavior of the people who come from the diverse cultures. For example, in Thailand a person who is angry at another does not show anger directly. Instead, the person may turn toward another object or person and scold it or him or her. A doctor must then understand that the words directed toward a dog or even a child in his presence may actually be directed at him. Although people from Southeast Asia are likely to forgive Westerners for their bad manners and chalk it up to ignorance, they may still be offended.

Anyone studying child development must also deal with cultural differences. For instance, most American children play pat-a-cake with their parents, but this game is not played in Southeast Asian families. Linguistic differences remain a problem too; for example, asking questions about the color of something can cause problems. In Vietnamese, the word for *blue* and *green* is the same, so if you ask what color the sky or a leaf is, the same word will be used to describe both.

Diet and folk medicine raise other problems. Especially in Vietnamese culture, good health is considered to be a perfect equilibrium between hot and cold elements; too much of one or the other is said to cause illness. Diarrhea is attributed to an excess of the cold element, while pustules are related to an excess of the hot element. Drugs and herbs are classified into hot and cold categories, too. Ginger is hot; ginseng is cold. Western medicines are hot; water is cold. Giving water to a patient who is already "cold" is considered poor medicine, and diets are carefully balanced according to this theory of hot and cold.

All of this discussion shows that we must take culture and background into account when dealing with people. If we understand the cultural background of the people we are dealing with or studying, we can develop an appreciation for and a sensitivity to their perceptions of the world, and we can avoid mistakes that contribute to disharmony among people.

What do you think?

You are at a presentation where the lecturer is discussing the importance of understanding the cultures of various immigrants. A member of the audience says that he appreciates the information but believes that immigrants have the responsibility to adapt to the culture and political-economic system of their adopted country. He further argues that maintaining certain cultural views from the culture of origin might even hinder this adaptation. This starts a heated discussion. Would you agree or disagree with his views?

You can explore the questions above using InfoTrac College Edition. Hint: enter search terms *acculturation* and *immigration*.

A few short years ago, the concept of American society as the melting pot was popular; that is, minority groups melted into American society as they took on the values of the dominant culture. Today, because the melting pot seems not to explain our society anymore (if it ever did), many psychologists and educators increasingly look at American society as well as many other Western societies in terms of cultural pluralism in which a number of cultural groups exist side by side. This new perspective has the advantage of encouraging the appreciation of how an individual's culture affects behavior and development.

To what extent should a person's cultural, religious, and racial group membership be taken into consideration when trying to understand behavior and development? Is an 8-year-old Latino child's experience in the United States that much different from an 8-year old white or African American child? The answer is both yes and no. Certainly, some of the developmental concerns are similar, as they are both in the third grade and dealing with similar developmental problems. However, their experiences may be different in other contexts. The Latino child may live in a different neighborhood, speak a different language, and be raised using different strategies. Although there are many similarities, the person's experience may be greatly affected by the cultural environment.

In addition, each group has a different history both in the United States and in the country of origin. The historic lack of opportunity available for some minority groups may influence their attitudes towards authority, education, and local and national politics (Ogbu, 1992).

Cultural Cautions The importance of understanding the diverse groups that comprise most Western societies today is reflected in many sections of this text. Although this new appreciation of culture is significant, the emphasis on culture has many pitfalls attached to it.

First, there is a tendency to define people in terms of their culture and forget the individual. For instance, if certain minority group cultures emphasize sharing, people may then stereotype any individual belonging to this group as an individual who shares because the culture values this behavior. However, variations among people in the culture are common and not every person in the group may show this behavior.

Second, people often view minorities as unified, monolithic wholes rather than as fragmented entities (Ryan, 1994). At times, the differences between subgroups in the minority culture are under-appreciated. For example, Latinos do not all belong to the same group. People from Cuba, Mexico, and Puerto Rico differ greatly. Latinos may share some elements of culture and attitudes, but they are certainly not identical. In addition, as you would expect, members of minority groups frequently differ among themselves in attitudes towards current issues.

Third, there is a tendency to stereotype all members of minority groups as poor. Although members of certain minority groups such as African Americans, Latinos, and Native Americans are more likely to be poor than whites, many are not poor. The African American and Latino middle class is growing in number, and many live in the suburbs, not the central city (O'Hare & Frey, 1992).

Fourth, it is important not to hold onto an idealized picture of one culture and denigrate another culture in the process. One culture should not be portrayed as pristine and pure, fighting against some bad dominating culture. If we say that American culture values individuality more than some other cultures, this does not make either American culture nor any other culture better or worse. Differences have to be understood and appreciated. While our new appreciation of the importance of culture is to be applauded, we ought not to steep cultures in myths and half truths and adopt simplistic notions about the goodness or badness of a particular culture.

Last, although cultural differences are important, it is also vital to appreciate similarities among various groups in hopes, values, and attitudes. An appreciation of culture does not have to be divisive, but too often we emphasize what divides us instead of what we share in common. Although cultural differences are illuminating, it would be wrong to leave the impression that members of one minority group differ in every, or even most, respects from members of other minority groups or the majority group.

The purpose of an explanation of culture is not to stereotype families but to become aware of a set of attitudes, values, and beliefs that may be considered when interacting with people of a particular group (Salend & Taylor, 1993). It is also important to appreciate the situation in which they now find themselves and to understand their history.

For Your Consideration ❓
How could an appreciation of culture sometimes lead to the danger of stereotyping and over-generalizing? Is there any way to counter this danger?

While appreciating cultural differences, it is important to understand the similarities in experience as well. In what ways will these children's challenges and experiences be similar?

For Your Consideration ?

In what ways do you agree or disagree with the idea that children (and adolescents) are the same today as they were 50 years ago?

Guideposts

How would the cohort effect explain some of the differences between how children and their parents see the world?

One reason children of the 1920's, 1960's, and 1990s differed in their behavior is because they grew up in different historical times with different options and experiences in the educational realm. Differences among age groups based upon such historical influences are called cohort effects.

cohort effect
The effect of belonging to a particular generation and of being raised in a certain historical time.

THEME/ISSUE 3:
Children Are Affected by the Historical Time in Which They Live

Besides the various contexts in which children find themselves, children are also affected by the historical time in which they live. Children born 40 years ago grew up in a world where most mothers were not employed, the cold war and the threat of nuclear catastrophe was great, and the female doctor or lawyer was statistically unusual. Computers were few and, by our current standards, primitive. Children born today will grow up with sophisticated computers and other technological devices. Even in their earliest years, they will be exposed to computers. They will not remember the cold war. They will grow up in a world where most women are employed and the female doctor or lawyer is not unusual.

The effect of growing up in a particular time period is known as the **cohort effect.** Look at the differences between generations. Many more children today grow up in single-parent families. The present generation has received more education than any previous generation. Events that occur at a particular point in time—such as economic depressions, epidemics, and revolutions—affect people's lives greatly. People in the same generation share common experiences. The differing experiences of the generations must be taken into consideration when evaluating their behavior and attitudes (see *Talking About Our Generation* on page 17).

THEME/ISSUE 4:
How Important Is the Child's Early Experience?

"The child is the father of the man," states an old proverb, and there is some truth to it. Early experience is important. Children who do not receive enough emotional care may show abnormal behavior patterns that limit later social and emotional functioning (Bornstein, 1995; Rutter, 1979). Indeed, the psychological makeup of terrorists has been linked to terrorists' experiences in childhood involving hopelessness and rage and a lack of nonviolent role models; the only effective role models terrorists had belonged to terrorist groups. In addition, about half the terrorists studied described a life-threatening childhood illness that few in their culture survive. This led them to deny the risk of death in adulthood (Goleman, 1986).

Aggression as well as altruism can be traced to childhood influences. New research also relates early nutrition as important both in later obesity and heart disease. For example, plasma cholesterol is a major factor in heart disease. In countries where the incidence of heart disease is high, children have average to high levels of plasma cholesterol, whereas in countries where the heart disease rate is lower,

The Child in the 21st Century

Talking About Our Generation

A few years ago, my wife's aunt gave us a black and white television set that she was no longer using that we placed in the den. One day I walked in to find my 8-year-old daughter fiddling with the controls. I asked her what was wrong.

"Daddy, I can't get the color," she answered.

"That's because there isn't any," I explained.

We sat down to watch something. After a few minutes, she got up and said, "How can you watch that?" and went downstairs to watch the program on the color television set.

People usually appreciate the differences between themselves and their children in terms of developmental differences and role changes. This book will outline many developmental differences among children, adolescents, and adults in the way they think, act, and perceive the world. We also realize that as we develop we take on different roles. Children entering first grade are now students with particular responsibilities and behaviors expected of them. Adults may act somewhat differently because we are parents and have a set of responsibilities and behaviors attached to that role. Many parents are surprised to hear themselves admonish their children to "be careful" or to "show more respect" just as their parents did before them.

Another possibility, often overlooked, is the cohort effect, the influence of growing up in a particular generation. We usually think of different historical times in terms of the Middle Ages and note how different children's lives were in those times. Children were exposed to a great deal more of adult life and they were often brutalized and had no rights. But times are changing much more quickly than in the past. Technological advances mean that the childhood experiences of children today differ greatly from what their parents and grandparents experienced when they were young. Most of today's teenagers have never wound a watch, dialed a telephone, or used a manual typewriter, but many have no difficulty formatting floppy disks, downloading music off the Internet, or setting the videocassette recorder (VCR) to watch their favorite program (Woodyard, 1998). People are bounded by their cohorts and deeply affected by the historical time in which they are raised.

A poll taken of parents in 1890 found that just 16% of parents thought independence was one of the most important goals of child rearing, while 64% thought obedience was one of the most important objectives of child rearing. In 1924, about one in four thought it was important to raise a child to be independent but one third gave it top priority in 1945 and by the late 1970s three of four put independence at the top of their list. Evidence indicates that it remains a most important goal of child rearing. Teaching obedience as one of the three most important goals has plummeted from 64% in 1890, to 45% in 1924 to only 17% in 1978. Today, parents are raising children to think for themselves. When parents are asked to rate how important various outcomes of child rearing are on a scale of 1 (less important) and 5 (most important), independent thinking averaged 4.4, far higher than

raising children to work hard (3.2), help others (3.2), obey (2.8), or be well liked (1.4). Now imagine how this change in emphasis might affect how children are raised and how these children think. Children raised to think for themselves rather than just obey authority figures might look at the world quite differently.

People have also changed significantly in the way they discipline their children. In 1962, spanking was the preferred method of disciplining children, while in 1992 *time out*, a procedure in which the child is removed from a reinforcing situation to one that is less reinforcing, was much more popular (see Table A on page 18) (Bruskin/Goldring Research, 1993).

The experiences of each generation also differ greatly because of the historical events that occur. People born between 1946 and 1964 are called the baby boomers. The older baby boomers are in their early fifties, but the younger baby boomers are still raising young children. The baby boom generation was brought up generally in stable intact families in which few mothers worked, and they had solid relationships with their community. Baby boomers rebelled against the system, and the civil rights, women's, and antiwar movements were shaped by them and at the same time affected them deeply. They believed they could change the world. The one word that defines this generation is *individualism* (Russell, 1995). It was a generation raised to think for themselves and be independent, and they raised their own children to believe in independence.

The next generation, called Generation X, includes people born between 1965 and 1977 and experienced

Table A	Methods of Discipline Favored by Parents 1962 and 1992	
Type of Discipline	1962	1992
Timeout	20%	38%
Lecture them (in a nice way)	23%	24%
Spanking	59%	19%
Take away television privileges	38%	15%
Scold them (not in nice way)	17%	15%
Ground them	5%	14%
Take away allowance	4%	2%

NOTE: Parents could cite more than one method.

SOURCE: Data from Bruskin/Goldring Research (1993)

a very different world than their parents. Early adults in Generation X are more likely to have experienced the divorce of their parents than previous generations, and 40% of all young adults spent some part of their childhood in a single-parent family (Zill & Robinson, 1995). They are more likely than previous generations to have stepparents and stepsiblings and more likely to have taken care of themselves at an early age. They are more insecure about intimacy and marriage. They are marrying later than their parents did. As adults and young parents today, they will take it for granted that both parents will work as they raise their children, but they have more day care alternatives than their parents had. Generation Xers are also more open in their desire to balance job, family life, and leisure than baby boomers (Ritchie, 1995).

The next generation, the children of older baby boomers, born in the very late 1970s and 1980s are called Generation Y. These teenagers are growing up in an expanding economy and are interested in being entrepreneurs. They tend to be optimistic, embrace environmentalism, and are skilled in technology. Their knowledge of computers, including E-mail, the Internet, and Web pages, leads to an "I can do it myself" attitude (Woodyard, 1998).

And what of children who will be born in the year 2000 or are very young children now? Their world also differs. Many baby boomers grew up with television as a family affair as they sat with their families and watched a program. Generation Xers tended to watch by themselves, but their children will probably have more televisions and many more channels to watch. Interactive television is technologically possible and in the near future may become commonplace. People watching television may be able to change their view of a show or a sporting event at the touch of a button. This generation of children is being raised with technology from birth. A few weeks ago I found myself in a software store. A little 3-year-old walked up to a computer, climbed into the chair, and without asking any questions turned the computer on, clicked on her favorite program, and began playing a game. She could not talk too well, but she knew how to use a computer.

This present generation of children will not really know of the cold war or the East-West confrontation. For them, the world will be a smaller place, and they will wonder how other generations got along without immediate access to the information superhighway.

This is also a generation that is more likely to be raised in a pluralistic environment. As you can see from Table 1.1 on page 11, the percentage of people from minority groups that comprise the population in the United States will increase into the next century. Today's child is much more likely to interact with people from other ethnic and racial groups.

It is difficult to predict the exact ways that this generation of children will differ from its parents and grandparents, but it is reasonable to assume that each generation will continue to differ significantly in attitudes and experiences as we enter the 21st century.

What do you think?

How will your children's world differ from your present reality? How will these changes affect them?

You can explore the questions above using InfoTrac College Edition. Hint: enter search terms, *cohort effect, Baby Boomers, Generation X,* and *Generation Y.*

children have low levels of the substance (DeBruyne & Rolfes, 1989). It seems that all we have to do is look at factors in childhood to explain adult behavior. But consider these two cases:

> *Boy, senior year secondary school, has obtained certificate from physician stating that nervous breakdown makes it necessary for him to leave school for six months. Boy not a good all-around student; has no friends—teachers find him a problem—spoke late—father ashamed of son's lack of athletic ability—poor*

adjustment in school. Boy has odd mannerisms, makes up own religion, chants hymns to himself—parents regard him as "different."

Girl, age sixteen, orphaned, willed to custody of grandmother, who was separated from alcoholic husband, now deceased. Mother rejected the homely child, who has been proven to lie and steal sweets. Swallowed penny to attract attention at five. Father was fond of child. Child lived in fantasy as the mistress of father's household for years. Four young uncles and aunts in household cannot be managed by the grandmother, who is widowed. Young uncle drinks, has left home without telling the grandmother his destination. Aunt, emotional over love affairs, locks self in room. Grandmother resolves to be more strict with granddaughter since she fears she has failed with own children. Dresses granddaughter oddly. Refused to let her have playmates, put her in braces to keep back straight. Did not send her to grade school (Goertzel & Goertzel, 1962, p. xiii).

These descriptions of the early environments of two children would make it difficult for you to give a positive prognosis for their later adjustments or accomplishments in life. But the first case describes Albert Einstein; the second describes the early life of Eleanor Roosevelt, wife of President Franklin D. Roosevelt and a powerful figure in her own right. So it is apparently not so easy to make sweeping generalizations and predictions based on early childhood data. (More will be said about children who, despite experiencing poor environments, still grow up to be fine adults in Chapter 11.)

Early experiences are important, but later experiences can compensate at least partially for poor early experiences. Children raised under very poor conditions often progress very slowly in many areas of development, but with extra care and attention the effects of their environment can to some degree be compensated for (Clarke & Clarke, 1976). Psychologists often focus on early experience because most children who have a poor start continue to be victims of a poor environment throughout childhood and adolescence, resulting in poor interpersonal relationships in adulthood. If children enter school already behind in certain important skills and

The cases of Albert Einstein and Eleanor Roosevelt demonstrate how difficult it can be to make predictions for people based on early childhood experiences.

Children who experience a very poor early environment can benefit greatly from a significant improvement in their environment later in childhood.

For Your Consideration ?

*Suppose you could choose one of
two life paths before you were
born. Path 1 would give you an
excellent first five years of life
followed by a poor second five
years (ages 6 to 10). Path 2
would have you experiencing
a very poor first five years of life
followed by an excellent second
five years. Which path would
you choose and why?*

nothing is done to help them catch up and achieve, they may fall further behind and never fulfill their potential. This can affect vocational opportunities, the nature of their social world, and their interests in adulthood. In other words, often early childhood experience seems so important because there is no change in the environment in later childhood. Where a positive change does occur, better outcomes are the rule. Of course, prevention is easier and superior to remediation, and it is best to create a positive early environment for children instead of trying to reverse the problems caused by poor early experience.

THEME/ISSUE 5:
The Issue of Stability and Change

If an individual was sociable and friendly as a 6-year-old, could we make any prediction about the individual at age 12 or 14? If a child was aggressive or shy at 6 years, could you predict the child's behavior in adolescence and adulthood?

These questions reflect the issue of stability and change. If we could say that a particular behavior at age 6 is linked to a behavior later on, it would provide the knowledge necessary to try to alter the pattern. Indeed, some constancy has been noted. Children who showed temper tantrums at 8 to 10 years of age were later judged to be more undercontrolled, irritable, and moody than their even-tempered peers (Caspi, Elder, & Bem, 1987).

Yet, there is also much evidence of change. Often, the relationship between early and later behavior is positive, though very moderate or even low (Clarke & Clarke, 1986; Rutter, 1987).

Many studies seeking stability in intellectual performance and personality find very low relationships and change more common. For example, when children were followed through childhood, there was certainly a group of children whose problems at early ages continue throughout childhood and adolescence, but the general relationship between behavioral ratings at ages 7, 11, and 16 was low, with many troubled children at one age moving into the "normal" category later on. In fact, a majority of children in the extreme group (labeled deviant) had moved out of that category (Fogelman, 1983).

We can find both continuity and change in development. The finding that change occurs compels us to be careful when making general statements about the future of children at different ages. Changes in environment can change the developmental pattern. In addition, it is a mistake to view the developing child as essentially a passive object on which people operate. The child experiences the environment as an individual, and individual differences in reactions to environmental factors must be taken into account. For instance, one child will react to a stressful situation, such as divorce or family turmoil, differently from another.

Because specific behaviors change with time, stability is sometimes difficult to see, but the underlying personality structure may still be similar. If we examine the intensity of a child's reactions to a stimulus we find an interesting progression. An intense child may cry loudly at the sound of thunder at 6 months, laugh hard when a parent plays roughly at 1 year, rush to greet his father and get hiccups when very excited at 5 years, and tear up an entire page of homework if one mistake is made or slam the door of his room when teased by his younger brother at 10 years (Thomas, Chess, & Birch, 1970). We would hardly expect a 10-year-old to show the same behavior as a 1-year-old, even though the same structure—in this case, intensity—underlies all these behaviors and is relatively stable.

Guideposts

Why is it difficult to see stability
in children's behavior and
personality?

THEME/ISSUE 6:
Social Influences Are Reciprocal

It is far too easy to look at these themes and come to the conclusion that outside influences, parents, teachers, friends, and even psychologists act on a passive organism, as the hold of a potter does on clay. This is not the case, for it ignores the effect the child has on these people. Do you remember a child in school who was always being discourteous to others, whose health habits were poor, who did not seem to have the social skills necessary to interact with others, and who was aggressive? This child was probably rejected. We could look at how the other students in the class treated the child. But more correctly, we should also look at how this child's behaviors affected others. In other words, we must look at both how the child affected and was affected by others (Bugental & Goodnow, 1998).

This perspective emphasizing how both parties in an interaction affect each other is called **reciprocal interaction.** We both affect and are affected by the people around us. Spend some time observing the interactions between a parent and an infant. Perhaps the parent hugs the baby, who responds with a smile. The parent then says something to the baby, who reacts with a vocalization. The baby's vocalization brings a string of verbal praise from the parent. For years, psychologists have looked at the caregiver-child relationships in terms of what the mother or father did to the child, but the effect of the child on the parents was rarely considered. Today, child psychologists look at how each affects the other.

In the preceding example, the actions of both parties served as responses and stimuli, which promoted new actions. The baby's smile stimulated the parent to speak to the child, and this in turn stimulated the baby to vocalize. The interaction proceeded rapidly, with both parties affecting the behavior of the other. The system is bidirectional, with information flowing from one party to the other and back again (Bell, 1968, 1979).

This approach is very useful in understanding and perhaps predicting problems. For example, a child may be slow in developing reading skills leading his parents to react with impatience and criticism. These parental behaviors may cause the child to avoid reading or put in only the minimum effort possible. The child's reduction in effort leads to further parental criticism. A knowledgeable teacher may alert parents to the possibility that this scenario could occur and suggest other ways for the parents to react to the child's progress. Any analysis of behavior, then, must consider the effect each party has on the other.

THEME/ISSUE 7:
Continuity and Discontinuity in Development

Do children develop in leaps and bounds or in a more gradual manner? Consider the child who begins to speak. The child has been making other noises, including crying, cooing, and babbling. Would you consider the child's speech as just another gradual and expected improvement in vocalization coming directly from earlier abilities, or a completely different step forward in development, distinct from the vocalizations of the past?

Child psychologists have long debated the question of continuity and discontinuity in development. Those who support *discontinuity* argue that development can be seen in terms of stages, each one qualitatively different from those that came before, much like a ladder with many rungs. Children proceed from stage to stage of development just as they would climb the rungs of a ladder. Psychologists who argue in favor of *continuity* of development see development in terms of smooth, small steps, explained by looking at past achievements. They see no stages but rather gradual development. This debate is ongoing, and some of the theorists

Guideposts

What is reciprocal interaction?

Guideposts

How do the views of psychologists who believe children develop in a discontinuous manner differ from those who believe that children develop in a continuous manner?

reciprocal interaction
The process by which an individual constantly affects and is affected by the environment.

presented in Chapter 2 will argue for a stagelike discontinuity, while others will argue that development is best seen in terms of continuity.

THEME/ISSUE 8:
Intervention Can Affect the Course of Development

Since environmental factors influence development, we can intervene at certain points of development to enhance it or change its direction (Ramey & Ramey, 1998). Special programs are designed to stimulate premature infants to enable them to function better in life (Hack, Klein, & Taylor, 1995). Preschool programs are designed so that children can improve their skills and succeed later in their school years. Often, such intervention aims at either preventing a problem from arising or reducing the severity of the problem and helping the child deal with the difficulty. Although this text emphasizes typical development, particular developmental difficulties will be discussed along with programs that are aimed at prevention and treatment.

Discovery: Research in Child Development

Discovering how and why a change occurs—and describing the nature of that change—is exciting. Researchers actively seek such information through well-defined methods of data gathering and experimentation. These methods allow us not only to understand some of the mysteries of childhood but also to answer many practical questions. They do so in a way that allows other researchers to reproduce or **replicate** their studies. To do so, the researcher must clearly define the subjects in the study, the manner in which the study will be carried out, and the statistical analyses used.

The Importance of Research Methods

Many students ask why a knowledge of research methods is important. They say, "It's the information that matters. Why worry about how the researcher got it?" But this attitude misses the point. The way a researcher obtains the information—the research methods—largely determines the legitimacy of the study's conclusions. A poorly designed study will produce invalid results. Knowing about research methods allows people to better evaluate information. We live in an information-rich environment. Daily we read of new findings concerning parenting practices or nutritional advice in the newspapers. Not all the studies that lead to these reports are carefully designed or unbiased. A knowledge of research methods can help people determine which information deserves attention and which should be ignored.

Choices in Research Methods

Researchers have a number of methods from which to choose, and each method has its advantages and disadvantages.

replication
The duplication or repetition of an experiment or a piece of research. The description of a study must be so detailed that other researchers may reproduce the study.

Naturalistic Observation   No matter which method is chosen, observation may enter the picture. Sometimes, a researcher will simply observe people in their natural environment. This method is called **naturalistic observation.** For example, Bonnie Klimes-Dougan and Janet Kistner (1990) wanted to know whether abused preschoolers would react differently from nonabused children when faced with some distressed peers. The researchers watched abused and nonabused preschoolers on a playground react to naturally occurring crying, screaming, or such verbalizations as "ouch," "stop," or "help." They found that abused preschoolers showed more aggression toward, as well as withdrawal from, distressed peers than did nonabused preschoolers. Abused children were more likely to initiate actions that caused others distress. These results are especially interesting because these inappropriate responses persisted despite prolonged exposure to and interaction with nonabusive peers and caregivers at a day care center. Certainly new approaches to countering these early experiences are required.

As valuable as naturalistic observation is, it presents problems. First, observers may disagree as to what they have seen. To counter this possibility, subjects may be videotaped. Second, observers themselves may influence a subject. Would you act the same way if someone was watching you? The very presence of an adult sitting in a classroom or watching parents play with their children may cause subjects to act differently. Research shows that some subjects try to present themselves in their best light, while others may show the opposite reaction (Repp, Nieminen, Olinger, & Brusca, 1988). For this reason, observations must be conducted with an eye to blending into the background as much as possible. Third, although naturalistic observation yields interesting information, it cannot tell us anything about cause and effect.

Guideposts

How can observation be used to study children's development?

For Your Consideration

People being observed often act differently. How would you design an observational study to reduce this problem?

Case Studies   What if you wanted to know how a fourth grader spends an average school day? Perhaps you could follow the child around, noting all activities for the day. You might interview parents, teachers, and friends and generally try to obtain as much relevant information as possible. A researcher following the progress of a subject over an extended period of time is conducting a **case study.** The researcher painstakingly records the person's behavior, seeking to identify patterns. In some cases, psychological testing is performed.

Case studies often yield interesting insights into the functioning of a particular child. Case studies can be especially useful when investigating an unusual situation, one in which relatively few people find themselves (Lehman, 1991). For example, one case study investigated an 11-year-old boy who was verbally gifted, had a learning disability in mathematics, and had a serious health impairment. The child was receiving homebound instruction and had little contact with the school. The investigators looked at the child's learning characteristics and educational experiences, trying to discover something about the unique experiences of this child (Moon & Dillon, 1995).

Case studies can be useful, especially in generating experimental questions that can then be looked at using other means (Wells, 1987). They also present a unique look at the individual, which is sometimes necessary, since other methods

naturalistic observation

A method of research in which the researcher observes people in their natural habitat.

case study

A method of research in which a person's progress is followed for an extended period of time.

For Your Consideration ?

It isn't always easy to produce good survey questions. Choose a topic, such as attitudes about spanking children, and construct five questions that you would ask your friends to determine, in an unbiased fashion, their attitudes.

In what situations would a psychologist use a survey?

survey

A method of study in which data are collected through written questionnaires or oral interviews from a number of people.

of research rely on the group. Although a valuable technique, the case study approach is of limited use. One can never be quite certain that the child being studied is similar to other children who are the same age or who have a particular condition. Therefore, it is necessary to do many case studies to demonstrate a common behavioral pattern, and by their very nature such observations are time-consuming and expensive. Second, the words that the observer uses in describing the subject of the case study can cause difficulties. The descriptions of the behavior may contain phrases that reflect judgment on the part of the observer. Another researcher might use words with other connotations or may describe a particular scene differently.

The Survey Method   What if you wanted to find out how children feel about eating their vegetables or the nature of adults' attitudes toward the younger generation? If data from a large group are required, a survey is often used. In a survey or interview, researchers ask a large number of people questions about their own behavior or that of others, and the answers are tabulated and reported.

In a startling recent survey, adults were interviewed concerning their evaluations of teenagers and younger children. Only 37% believed that today's youngsters will make the United States a better place to live, and two-thirds of the adults surveyed came up with negative adjectives such as "rude," "wild," or "irresponsible" when asked to describe teenagers. Nearly half described younger children as spoiled, and a third used the term "lazy" (Public Agenda, 1997). These results reflect a significant change from similar earlier surveys. Previous surveys found adults critical of teenagers but much more charitable toward younger children.

Adults are focusing their attention on such areas as ethical behavior, integrity, respect, civility and compassion to a greater extent than in the recent past. More than 60% believed that teenagers fail to learn fundamental moral values, and 90% of all adults felt the problems were widespread—that is, found among all socioeconomic groups. Many blame both the school and the home. Of course, it is not clear from this report whether adult opinions are reflecting real behavioral changes in children and adolescents, or simply reflecting what adults see in the media.

The survey technique has limitations. For instance, we must ask about the nature of the respondents. If we want to generalize from this sample, we would have to be certain that it accurately reflected the nature of the American public. Second, some people just refuse to participate, and it is difficult to determine whether these nonparticipants differ from those who willingly do so. In some personal surveys on sex, sometimes as many as half may refuse to participate. Third, you cannot be certain that respondents are telling you truthfully how they feel or act. Finally, it is difficult to construct a fair and unbiased questionnaire. The researcher must be quite careful about how the questions are worded. For example, imagine being asked a number of questions concerning how you discipline or punish your child. If the question is, How often do you spank your child? you might answer one way, but if the question is, How often do you beat your child? you might answer quite differently.

Surveys can be very useful because they allow the researcher to gather a great deal of data in a fairly short amount of time. Still, questionnaires must be constructed with care, the sample carefully chosen, and the interpretations cautiously made.

Correlations   Often researchers involved in collecting and analyzing data wish to discover the relationships between two elements in the environment. For example, there is a relationship between scores on intelligence tests and school achievement. Higher intelligence scores are related to higher achievement levels in school. Researchers use the term **correlation** to describe such a relationship.

There is a relationship between acting out in school and poor achievement, but this does not establish a cause and effect relationship. It is possible that other factors, such as lack of attention, poor motivation, reading difficulties or personal problems are factors that underlie both.

For Your Consideration

A positive correlation exists between having high self-esteem and academic achievement, self-confidence and being able to bounce back from stress. Why would it be incorrect to conclude that high self-esteem causes these outcomes?

A correlation can be positive, negative, or zero. A positive correlation indicates that relatively large scores on one factor are associated with large scores on another and relatively small scores on one factor are associated with small scores on another. As intelligence increases, so does academic achievement. A perfect positive correlation is written +1.00. A negative (or inverse) correlation indicates that as one factor increases, the other decreases. A perfect negative correlation is written −1.00. For example, we may find a negative correlation between misbehaving in class and grades on a child's report card: the greater the number of incidents of misbehavior in class, the lower the grades. A zero correlation indicates that there is no relationship between the two factors; for example, there is no relationship between the color of a child's hair and the child's intelligence.

Most correlations are far from perfect. The correlation between scores on an intelligence test and achievement in school as measured by grades hovers between .50 and .60, which is high but not anywhere near perfect (Kubiszyn & Borich, 1987). Other factors besides intelligence, such as motivation and perseverance, are involved in school success.

Guideposts

What is meant if two behaviors are positively correlated?

Correlations do not establish cause-and-effect relationships. Certainly students who misbehave tend to receive poor grades, but it may not be correct to state that misbehavior causes poor grades. There are other possibilities. Students who misbehave do not pay attention in class, study hard, do their homework, or do well on exams. It may be these factors, rather than misbehavior, that caused the poor grades. Only more research can determine whether this is the case. The important facts to remember about a correlation are that it tells us that a relationship exists, the direction of the relationship (whether it is positive or negative), and the magnitude of that relationship.

The Experimental Method   The research methods discussed thus far are very useful in describing a particular behavior or situation. However, they do not normally allow us to make cause-and-effect statements. If, for example, we want to state that under a particular circumstance some action, such as praise, causes some specific outcome, such as a more positive attitude toward chores, we must perform an **experimental study.** The watchword of the experimental approach is control. We must choose two (or more) groups that are equivalent and do something to one group that we do not do to the other(s). In this instance, we must control for every factor possible to make certain that the only difference between the two groups is the amount of praise that children are given.

correlation

A term denoting a relationship between two variables.

experimental study

A research strategy using controls that allows the researcher to discover cause-and-effect relationships.

The factors of an experiment that are manipulated by the experimenter to determine their effects on subjects' behavior are called **independent variables,** while the responses measured in the study for example, their thoughts, feelings, behavior, or physiological reactions are called the **dependent variables** (Leary, 1995). In our proposed study of the effects of praise on children's attitude toward chores, there is one independent variable (whether the child receives praise) and one dependent variable (a measure of attitude toward chores).

Experimental research typically entails selecting a sample of subjects, randomly assigning these subjects to experimental and control groups, exposing only the experimental group to a treatment that serves as the independent variable while the other group (called the control group) is not exposed to such a treatment, and finally measuring the dependent variable and comparing the groups.

An experiment begins with a question of some interest to the researcher. The question must be worded in such a way that it can be answered experimentally. For example, What do we mean by praise? or What kind of statements can be considered praise? We must also define a way of measuring the dependent variable. All past relevant research must be searched to learn what is already known about the question. This ensures that our research rests on solid ground. It also would allow us to make hypotheses (educated predictions) about what will happen in our experiment.

Now we are ready to choose our sample. We must decide what characteristics we wish our sample to have. Do we want to use children of just one age group? Does it matter whether the children live in a house or an apartment? Does it matter whether they have siblings or if they are only children? Each decision is important, for if we find that praise causes an improvement in attitude toward chores, we must limit our conclusion according to the characteristics of our sample. If we used 8-year-olds, we cannot say that the same thing would necessarily be true of teenagers.

Since we want both the experimental group and the control group to be similar, we would try to assign children randomly to either group. That way each child chosen for the study has the same opportunity to be placed in either the experimental or control group. Sometimes, when random assignment is not possible, subjects in the experimental and control group are matched on critical characteristics, such as age or socioeconomic status.

We now instruct the parents of children in the experimental group to praise their children when doing chores. You might think that we would simply tell the parents of the children in the control group not to praise their children when they are performing their chores. However, if we created an experimental group in which the children were praised, and a control group in which children were not praised, and a significant difference in attitude toward chores was later found, we could not be certain if the difference was due to the praise or to the attention they received. When children receive praise, they are also receiving attention. In order to equalize the attention both groups receive, we would ask the parents of the children in the control group to engage their children in routine conversation when they were doing the chores. If we then found significant differences between the experimental and control group, we would then know it was due to praise and not just attention. Some researchers might even create two control groups, one group of children that receives attention in the form of neutral conversation and another group that receives neither attention nor praise.

Experimentation is the lifeblood of any science and such research studies often have practical applications. For example, Chris Boyatzis and colleagues (1995) questioned the effect of watching a popular children's television show, *The Mighty Morphin Power Rangers,* has on aggressive behavior. The Power Rangers are

independent variable

The factor in a study that will be manipulated by the researcher.

dependent variable

The factor in a study that will be measured by the researcher.

a group of racially diverse superheroes who battle monsters trying to take control of the Earth. The National Coalition on Television Violence, which has analyzed violence on television since 1980, claims that it is the most violent children's program ever studied, averaging more than 200 violent acts per hour.

An ethnically diverse sample of boys and girls ranging in age from 5 to 11 years was randomly assigned either to an experimental group that watched an episode of the program or a control group which did not. On the first day of the study, the researchers observed the children in regular play, and the number of aggressive acts was recorded. The next day the experimental group watched the television show and then were allowed to play in their regular fashion while the children's play was observed and the number of aggressive acts recorded.

The results showed that children who watched the Power Rangers program committed seven times the number of aggressive acts as the control group children. Boys were much more likely to be affected than girls, perhaps because so many more Power Rangers are males. An interesting observation is that a number of the violent acts were almost exact replicas of what was seen on the program, such as flying karate kicks. This study demonstrated that viewing this program leads to more aggressive actions.

Experimental studies are often difficult to perform because a researcher must exercise such great control over the environment. However, the effort is often worth the extra trouble, since only experimental studies can demonstrate cause-and-effect relationships.

Quasi-Experimental Designs   Psychologists cannot always use the degree of control that they would like to make causal inferences. Sometimes, randomizing is not possible. For example, what if a developmental psychologist was interested in determining what the result of exposure to violence in a civil war would be on the children in some nation. The psychologist could not randomly assign children into those areas ravaged by conflict and relatively safer areas. In these cases, psychologists use **quasi-experimental designs,** which are studies that are used when sufficient control over the variables is lacking (Ray, 1997). Quasi-experimental designs do not involve random assignment of subjects to conditions, but rather compare groups that already exist or measure changes that exist within a single group of people before and after some event transpired or treatment was administered (Leary, 1995).

In this latter case, a control group may simply not be available. For instance, after conducting anonymous questionnaires a school finds that it has a definite drug problem and begins an extensive drug education program. At a later time, the effects are measured, and the researchers find that a reduction in drug use has occurred. The design of this study, called a single-group pretest-posttest design, might lead us to conclude that the program was effective, but we do not know whether some reduction would have occurred anyway. The design could be improved if we could consult the results of earlier surveys that might give us some idea of the fluctuation of drug use over time and if other posttests were included continuing throughout the year.

Studies that use quasi-experimental designs can provide fairly strong circumstantial evidence about cause-and-effect relationships, but they certainly remain open to interpretation (Leary, 1995). Sometimes, they can be designed so as to reduce the number of possible alternative explanations. For example, perhaps we would compare the rates of drug use to those of students in another school that has reasonably similar students but does not offer the drug prevention program. This nonequivalent control group at least allows some comparison, but because randomization did not occur, it would prevent us from making very strong statements about cause and effect.

For Your Consideration ?

Design an experiment to determine if training new fathers in child care techniques would improve the father-child interaction.

Guideposts

What elements comprise a good experimental study?

quasi-experimental design

A research design used when sufficient control over the variables under study is lacking. Because of the lack of control, definitive statements about cause and effect cannot be made.

A cross-sectional study shows that young children (below the age of 9) unfortunately tend to believe that if they can't see the car it isn't there.

Guideposts

What is the difference between cross-sectional and longitudinal studies?

cross sectional study

A research design in which people at different ages are studied to obtain information about changes in some variable.

longitudinal study

A research design in which subjects are followed over an extended period of time to note developmental changes in some variable.

At one time, quasi-experimental designs were not very respected, but recently this bias has lessened. Certainly, the well-designed, randomized, controlled experimental study is preferable, but many psychologists realize that not all topics can be studied using well-controlled experimental designs (Leary, 1995). When such randomization is not possible for practical or ethical reasons, quasi-experimental studies can address these questions even though their limitations should be kept in mind.

Research Designs

Developmental research is often concerned with measuring change over time. We may be interested in discovering how children of various ages perceive their parents or how they approach various problems. If you were an investigator interested in the first topic, you could find groups of 8-, 10-, and 12-year-olds, measure their perceptions of their parents, and compare their perceptions. This is an example of a **cross-sectional** design. On the other hand, you could use a group of 8-year-olds and measure how they perceive their parents today, then wait until they are 10 and measure their perception of their parents again, then wait another two years and do it a third time. This is an example of **longitudinal** design. Both methods are popular, and each has advantages and disadvantages.

Cross-sectional studies are easier to perform. Groups of different-aged subjects are tested at the same time, and the results are compared. In one study, 5-, 8-, and 11-year-old children were tested on their ability to perceive traffic sounds (Pfeffer & Barnecutt, 1996). This ability is important because prior research demonstrated that most accidents occur at bends, crossroads, and other locations where visibility is restricted.

Recordings were made of a car in a number of conditions. In the "toward" condition, the car approached and reached the microphone; in the "away at speed" condition, the car drove away from the microphone at 30 miles per hour; in the "away from start" position, the car started at the microphone and drove away from that point, gradually gaining speed; and in the "passing" condition, the car approached and passed the microphone. Each child was tested individually on a total of twelve sounds, three of each condition. Before the test the experimenters made certain the children understood the concepts of away and towards. Children were individually tested to determine their ability to judge the movement and location of the vehicle.

The results were both interesting and disturbing (see Table 1.2). Children in the 5-year age group were only able to respond correctly on one-third of the sounds; the 8-year-olds averaged about half correct, and the 11-year-olds responded correctly about 60% of the time. Five-year-olds had the most difficulty identifying the sound of an approaching vehicle, which has implications for their safety. Earlier studies found that children below the age of 9 years rely on limited cues, mostly the visible presence of a vehicle, and often believe that if they don't see a vehicle it can't be there. Only at 9 years of age do they begin to understand that places where vision is obscured are unsafe. Young children do not seem to pay attention to auditory cues, perceive them correctly, or interpret them correctly.

Table 1.2 Mean Correct Responses by Age and Condition

(from a total possible score of 3 for each condition and 12 for all conditions combined)

Age (years)	Toward	Away at speed	Away from start	Passing
5	.55	1.05	1.20	1.35
8	1.55	1.45	1.35	1.55
11	2.00	1.90	1.85	2.05

SOURCE: Pfeffer & Barnecutt, (1995)

Children also had confidence in their judgments even though they were frequently wrong. It may be possible to educate children to use their auditory skills better, to understand that just because they don't see a vehicle doesn't necessarily mean it isn't there and to identify dangerous places.

Cross-sectional studies are useful, but they have their faults. It is difficult to understand the growth and decline of any attribute over an extended period of time, because the same people are not being followed (Nunnally, 1982). In addition, when comparing subjects who differ significantly in age, the effect of growing up in a different generation, the cohort effect, must be taken into account.

Longitudinal studies are not as easy to execute as cross-sectional studies. Subjects must be followed over some period of time and retested at stated intervals. Longitudinal studies allow scientists to identify changes within subjects over age. Such questions as Do obese children become obese adults? and Do aggressive children remain aggressive into adulthood? can best be studied using longitudinal research designs.

In one longitudinal study, fathers' parenting behaviors were assessed when their children were 13 months old and again at 5 years of age. Fathers' total involvement increased. During infancy, mothers were the primary caregivers and both parents were equally involved in play activities. When the children were 5 years old, fathers were more involved in the caregiving, and again the degree of social interaction with the child was about the same (Bailey, 1994). Still, mothers performed the greater share of the caregiving at both ages. Paternal participation was related to maternal employment. If Mother was employed, Father participated more in the caregiving. Perhaps mothers simply had less time and fathers felt more responsible.

Longitudinal studies also have weaknesses. They are more time-consuming, and maintaining contact with subjects over the long term is difficult. Some subjects move away; others simply do not return their questionnaires at various testing periods, leaving the researcher with incomplete data. It is difficult to determine whether those who drop out differ from those who remain throughout the study. In addition, the effect of practice and retesting must be investigated (Blanck, Rosenthal, & Snodgrass, 1982). Let's say you want to measure the changes in intelligence over the years. If you use the same or a very similar test, the children might become wise to the test and show an improvement simply as a result of practice. On the other hand, using different measures may create problems, because one measure may not be directly comparable to another. As with the cross-sectional approach, the cohort effect should be taken into account. Longitudinal studies performed 30 years ago are interesting, but they may be confounded by specific generational problems, and such studies have to be updated.

To reduce or eliminate the problems with cross-sectional and longitudinal studies, developmental psychologists may use **sequential designs.** These require the use of at least two cross-sections or two longitudinal analyses (Stevens-Long & Commons, 1992). The researcher studies at least two different cohorts at two or

T
F
9

Young children believe that if they can't see a car approaching, a car cannot be there.

sequential design

The use of at least two cross-sections or two longitudinal analyses in the same study.

more different times of measurement. For example, what if we wanted to measure health practices, including eating and exercise patterns? We could begin the study in the year 2000 with a sample of 5-year-olds and measure these behaviors every two years. This is a longitudinal study. To find out whether there are any cohort effects, we might then start another such study in 2010 of a different group of 5-year-olds and follow them every two years as well. Two longitudinal studies, then, cover the same age ranges but at different times. Another way of conducting a sequential study would be to use a cross-sectional approach comparing children who were 5, 10, and 15 years of age on these variables and then following them every two years (Schaie, 1994).

At times, a researcher may want to know whether 5-year-olds today are different from 5-year-olds twenty years ago on some variable, or whether parents have changed the way they deal with their children. In a **time lag study,** two or more data collections occur at different times and data that already exists before the study was even planned are used for comparison. You may examine the same variable in 5-year-olds today and compare them with similar studies done in 1970. For example, you may find data on children's opinions of environmental issues in 1970 and then use a similar survey to obtain data about today's children. If they are similar, you might then argue that age may have something to do with particular attitudes. However, if they differ greatly you may be witnessing a change in culture. Of course, two different groups of people were involved in this study, which makes interpretation somewhat difficult (Hayslip & Panek, 1993).

Ethical Considerations in Research

Ethical problems arise whenever research is performed. In most universities today, committees review the ethics of each research proposal involving animals or human beings, and many professional organizations as well as the federal government have published ethical standards for research (Cooke, 1982). Most psychological experiments cause no physical or mental pain. Studies that contain anything considered even remotely dangerous are rare. Although there are many ethical questions in psychological research, two of the main concerns have to do with the issues of informed consent and deception.

Informed Consent

Ideally, subjects should be told specifically what is expected of them and be encouraged to decide for themselves whether or not they wish to participate in a study. Federal guidelines specify many important features of informed consent (Cooke, 1982; Miller, 1998). The subjects should be told the purpose of the research, the procedures involved, the risks and benefits, and be presented with a statement noting that they are free to withdraw from the study along with an invitation to ask questions about their participation. Some studies involve small children who naturally cannot give their permission. In such a case, the study is explained to the parents, who then consent to the child's participation. It is assumed that the parents are both capable and responsible for making decisions that are in their child's best interests. If the child is above 7 or so, the child's consent should definitely be obtained (Cooke, 1982). However, the researcher should try to get the permission of children even younger than 7. Often, however, young children have difficulty understanding the research process, and their limited cognitive abilities do not

10

Most psychological experiments cause no physical or psychological harm to the people who participate in them.

time lag study

A study that compares data presently gathered to data gathered at an earlier time, before the study was contemplated.

allow them to understand fully their rights, especially their right to withdraw from the study (Thompson, 1990).

Recently, a new question about consent has been raised. In recent years, Congress has canceled proposed studies funded by the federal government on sensitive topics, such as the sexual behavior of teenagers, because many legislators felt the questions were too graphic or offensive. In the past, parents were often, but not always informed that a questionnaire would be given to their children. Only if the parents objected by phone or mail would their children be prevented from participating. Now, under this rule, parents will have to sign a written consent to have their children participate on anonymous surveys on such topics as sexual behavior, religious attitudes, or illegal or antisocial activities (Lane, 1995).

Some social scientists claim that such a law would lead to tremendously increased costs and would also lead to questions about the accuracy of their studies, since parents would have to take a positive action—signing a consent, rather than simply a passive one, not objecting. In one school where a survey on drinking and drug use was being conducted only 17 of 100 parents returned the form (Lane, 1995). Many parents, even those who do not object, may just not sign the consent form because of lack of time or interest. Perhaps a compromise would be best. A federal regulation requiring parental notification and allowing withdrawal by telephone, but not requiring active agreement might satisfy the concerns of both sides.

Deception

The most serious ethical problem confronting researchers today is deception. Some researchers argue that they cannot always inform subjects about the true objectives of their study. If they do, the subjects may alter their behavior to match the desires of the researcher. What if the researcher wants to determine whether the gender of the author of a composition would affect students' evaluations of the work? The researcher may tell the subjects that the study is concerned with the content of the story itself and not even mention the name of the author, which appears at the top of the page and clearly reflects the writer's gender. Is this deception warranted? Today, sexism and racism are not fashionable, and if psychologists are to study these areas, subtle deceptions may be necessary. Other psychologists disagree, arguing that deception is morally wrong and harmful to the profession (Baumrind, 1985).

This difference of opinion among researchers will continue. Those researchers who use deception take on extra responsibilities. After the study, subjects must be informed as to the study's true nature. It is necessary to look into the possible impact on the subject's self-esteem, feelings toward authority figures, and alienation from society, especially for subjects who already perceive themselves to be rejected or alienated from society (Fisher & Tryon, 1988). In addition, during the study, subjects may acquire knowledge that may trouble them, and researchers must provide help for subjects trying to work through what they have learned about themselves (Holmes, 1976a, 1976b).

Children of different ages are vulnerable to different types of problems (Thompson, 1990). For example, challenges to a child's self-concept are likely to become more stressful with age. If a study purports to find a child's intelligence, the discovery of the score will affect a child of school age more than it will a younger child.

For Your Consideration

Under what circumstances, if any, would you agree that a researcher is justified in using deception to obtain research results?

Guideposts

What are the two most common ethical concerns of researchers conducting studies in child development?

On the other hand, a very young child is more likely than an older child to be stressed if separated from an adult. In addition, special risks are taken when we do research on children with disabilities or on children who show behavioral problems. We must continue to be aware and sensitive to the way children experience the research process. We also need to minimize the stresses for children who participate as part of the field's commitment to establish and maintain standards for the decent treatment of children who are subjects of experiments.

Child Development: What's in It for Me?

Whenever one approaches a new subject, it is natural to ask about its relevance. "What's in it for me?" is a common question and deserves an answer.

Personal Benefits

Most people marry and raise children. A better understanding of children can lead to a greater appreciation of the problems and potential of children and enable parents to experience more fully the joys of parenting. For example, an understanding of cognitive (intellectual) development may help parents appreciate why their child enjoys a particular game. Very young children enjoy playing peek-a-boo because they are just learning that people still exist even though they can't see them. The child generates an expectation that the parent is still there, which is subsequently validated. When the child sees that the expectation is correct, the child reacts with glee. This reaction means much more to the parent who understands how a child is perceiving the game.

An appreciation of where the child is in the developmental cycle can enable parents to help their children. Knowing what skills are necessary for reading would help a parent understand the best time to begin a particular activity related to learning to read. At the same time, warning signs can be spotted and remedial action taken. In one case, a 9-month-old had stopped babbling. The parents suspected that their child might be experiencing a hearing problem, took the child for a checkup, and discovered that they were correct.

Careers in Working with Children

People who work with children, including teachers, mental health personnel, nurses, nutritionists, child care workers, nursery school personnel, parent educators, and playground supervisors, need a knowledge of child development. The practical possibilities are endless. For example, teachers could avoid much frustration by understanding that the way they present questions to their students greatly affects how the students answer the questions. Nurses may need to communicate with children in stressful situations, such as undergoing surgery or experiencing a separation due to divorce or the death of a parent, and an understanding of how to explain such occurrences would be helpful. Nutritionists who understand the thinking processes of children are better able to develop strategies to encourage children to eat balanced diets.

Understanding how children think, their concerns, and their abilities can help professionals deal more effectively with children.

Research, Teaching, and Clinical Work

Child development is a growing field. Many child development specialists teach in colleges and universities and perform research. As you read this text, you may begin to form research questions that you may someday be in a position to answer. In addition, parenting courses have become very popular, and child psychologists are often called on to design and offer such programs.

Influencing Public Policy

Research can answer practical public policy questions. Child development specialists are often called on by government agencies to create and evaluate programs aimed at improving the lives of children. For example, child abuse is a national problem, and researchers are seeking new ways to prevent child abuse and treat its victims. Mental health is a major national problem, and research into the causes and prevention of emotional problems is an ongoing concern. Questions about the effects of television and television advertising on children have been researched, and child development specialists are suggesting ways that television can be improved for young children (Huston, Watkins, & Kunkel, 1989). Research into the effects of day care on children (see Chapter 7) has made important contributions toward improving the day care experience for young children (Lamb, 1998). By influencing public policy toward children on local, state, and national levels, the nation can carefully nurture its most valuable resource—its children.

In this introductory chapter, we examined some of the central themes and issues that surround child and adolescent development and looked at ways psychologists perform research to find the answers to particular questions. However, the research questions are often suggested by a theoretical approach, and a knowledge of different approaches is indispensable to understanding child development. It is to these important theoretical approaches that we turn next.

Summary

1. Child development involves the study of the sequence of physical, cognitive, social, and personality changes that occur to children as they age. Quantitative changes involve changes in amount, frequency or degree, while qualitative changes involve a change in process, function, structure or organization.

2. Although some behaviors or aspects of development are probably due more to genetic influence and others to environmental influence, both genetic and environmental influences interact to cause the changes that child development specialists seek to investigate.

3. Changes that are relatively immune to environmental influences and are caused by the unfolding of the individual's unique genetic plan are considered maturational in nature. Learning is defined as a relatively permanent change in behavior which can be attributed to interactions with the environment.

4. A child is enmeshed in many contexts including the immediate and extended family, the community, school and even the political system under which the child lives. The child's culture influences the physical and social aspects of the home, child-rearing customs, caretaker psychology, and the political and social systems under which children develop.

5. The effect of belonging to a particular generation is known as the cohort effect. The experiences of children today differ significantly from those of children a few decades ago.

6. Early childhood experiences can have a profound influence on later development and behavior. However, the effects of a poor early environment can be remedied, at least to some extent, by improving the environment.

7. Psychologists are interested in the question of stability and change. Although there is some evidence for stability throughout childhood and adolescence for some characteristics, there is much evidence for change.

8. When investigating any relationships, developmental psychologists emphasize reciprocal interaction; that is, they look at how children both affect and are affected by their environment.

9. Psychologists dispute whether children develop in a discontinuous manner—that is, in an orderly, sequential set of stages qualitatively different from one another—or in a more continuous manner, with new behaviors directly arising from older behaviors.

10. There are many methods of conducting research. In naturalistic observation, the researcher carefully observes and records what occurs in the natural environment. The case study method involves carefully observing a subject for a substantial period of time and collecting a great deal of information about an individual. Researchers using the survey method question a number of people, then tabulate and analyze their data. Researchers may also attempt to discover correlations or relationships between variables. These relationships show the extent to which one factor is related to another. Researchers using the experimental method control the environment, allowing only the desired variables to vary. Such experiments may demonstrate cause and effect. When the situation does not allow for randomization or the use of control groups psychologists use quasi-experimental designs.

11. In cross-sectional studies, children from various age groups are tested at a particular time. In a longitudinal study, a single group of children is tested at particular intervals. Sequential designs require the use of at least two cross-sections or two longitudinal analyses. A time lag study compares data that is presently gathered to data gathered at an earlier time.

12. Most psychological experiments cause no physical or psychological harm to their subjects. Today, universities have committees that examine the ethics of each experiment. Two of the most common ethical problems involve consent and deception.

13. The study of child development yields great personal benefits, helps people deal better with their children, opens up new vocational possibilities, and suggests ways society may be able to improve the lives of children.

Review

The sequence of physical, cognitive, social, and personality changes that occur as people age is called (1)_____ . Child development specialists divide change into two categories. (2)_____ change involves a change in amount, while (3)_____ change involves a change in process or function. Changes are usually due to the interaction of (4)_____ and (5)_____ factors. Psychologists use the term (6)_____ to describe the unfolding of the genetic plan.

The most important context for development is the (7)_____ . Two important changes in the family is the growth of (8)_____ families and the fact that about 60% of all women with children are employed. Another context is the community and where one lives is influenced by socioeconomic status. The percentage of children in poverty has recently (9)_____ (increased/decreased). African American and Latino children are (10)_____ (more/less) likely to live in poverty than white children. Another context is one's culture and when minority groups differ significantly from the majority group and consider themselves different they are often called (11)_____ . The four principal minority groups in the United States are (12)_____ , (13)_____ , (14)_____ , and (15)_____ . The minority group's culture changes as it comes in contact with the majority group in a process called (16)_____ . Children are also affected by the historical time in which they are raised, called the (17)_____ effect. Psychologists also know that the child affects the parents just as the parents affect the child, which is known as (18)_____ .

Psychologists often argue over how children develop. Some believe that children develop in a stagelike progression called (19)_____ development, whereas others believe they develop in very small improvements that come from earlier abilities.

Child psychologists use many methods to investigate children's development. Sometimes, they observe children in their homes or schools, called (20)_____ . At other times, psychologists may conduct a (21)_____ in which they follow one subject for a period of time, learning as much as they can about the subject. To gain information from many subjects in a relatively short period of time, a psychologist can conduct a/an (22)_____ . At other times, psychologists may wish to find a relationship between two variables known as a/an (23)_____ . If a psychologist wants to discover cause and effect relationship, a/an (24)_____ study must be performed. The factor that is manipulated by the experimenter is called the (25)_____ variable, while the factor being measured is called the (26)_____ variable.

Psychologists sometimes compare children of different ages at the same time called (27)_____ studies or follow a group of youngsters over a period of time called (28)_____ studies. Sometimes psychologists use a (29)_____ design in which the researcher follows at least two groups of different ages for a period of time. Researchers may want to compare children today to children of the same age growing up a generation or so ago. Psychologists can use a/an (30)_____ study in which children are tested and then the responses are compared to children's responses reported years ago. Ethical issues arise in the context of conducting research. The two most common problems involve (31)_____ and (32)_____ .

InfoTrac

For additional readings, explore InfoTrac College Edition, our online library. Go to http://www.infotrac-college.com/wadsworth. Hint: enter the search terms *Early Readers, Conflict of Generations,* and *Child Development Research.*

What's on the web

Society for Research in Child Development
http://www.srcd.org/publica.htm

Developmental Psychology Links
http://www-osf.wesleyan.edu/psyc/devel.htm

The Wadsworth Psychology Study Center Web Site
Go to the Wadsworth Psychology Study Center at http://psychology.wadsworth.com/ for quiz questions, research updates, hot topics, interactive exercises, and suggested readings in the InfoTrac College Edition related to this chapter.

Answers 1. development; **2.** Quantitative; **3.** qualitative; **4.** heredity; **5.** environmental; **6.** maturation; **7.** family; **8.** single parent; **9.** increased; **10.** more; **11.** subcultures; **12.** African American; **13.** Latino; **14.** Asian American; **15.** Native American; **16.** acculturation; **17.** cohort; **18.** reciprocal interaction; **19.** discontinuous; **20.** naturalistic observation; **21.** case study; **22.** survey; **23.** correlation **24.** experimental; **25.** independent; **26.** dependent; **27.** cross-sectional; **28.** longitudinal; **29.** sequential; **30.** time-lagged; **31.** deception; **32.** informed consent

Perspectives *on* Child

CHAPTER OUTLINE

Could You Predict Their Reactions?

Theoretical Perspectives on Child Development

Piaget's Theory of Cognitive Development

The Information-Processing Approach

Freud's Psychoanalytic Theory

Erikson's Psychosocial Theory

The Behavioral Approach

Social Learning Theory

Vygotsky's Sociocultural Theory

Bronfenbrenner's Ecological Theory

Developmental Theory: Yesterday, Today, and Tomorrow

How to Use Theories

ARE THESE STATEMENTS True *or* False?

1. Theories can both describe present behavior and predict future behavior.
2. The stage of cognitive development a child is negotiating is accurately determined by considering the child's chronological age.
3. All useful theories in child development posit a discrete number of stages.
4. There are no qualitative advances in children's intellectual development after age 6.
5. Studies show that there is a limit to the amount of information human beings can process at one time.
6. Freud believed that young children experienced the same sexual urges as adults.
7. It is dangerous for a small and vulnerable toddler to develop a sense of autonomy.
8. Reinforcers must be tangible to be effective with children.
9. The relationship between children and their parents may be affected by such long-range factors as their parents' work environment and parents' network of friends.
10. Developmental psychologists consider it appropriate to use one theory to understand cognitive development and another theory to understand social development.

ANSWERS: 1. *True.* 2. *False.* 3. *False.* 4. *False.* 5. *True.* 6. *False.* 7. *False.* 8. *False.* 9. *True.* 10. *True.*

and Adolescent Development

Millions of people watched the Space Shuttle Challenger *explode a minute and a half into its flight. Many children were watching the takeoff and people were especially concerned about its effect on children.*

Could You Predict Their Reactions?

On the morning of January 28, 1986, millions of people around the country watched on television the long-awaited Challenger space shuttle launch. More children than usual were watching because the shuttle carried a teacher, Christa McAuliffe, who was to give a science lesson in space. In less than a minute and a half into the mission, the space shuttle exploded. Shock and grief spread throughout the country, together with some concern about how the children who had witnessed this tragedy would respond.

Suppose you had been a teacher or a parent watching the Challenger blast off with preschool, school-age (6 to 12 years), or teenage children. Could you have predicted how each age group would have responded to the incident?

Many psychologists could have, and in fact did, because they know how children at various developmental levels reason and deal with information. The day after the tragedy, Nanci Monaco and Eugene Gaier (1987) conducted a study that, in part, demonstrated just how well psychologists' theories can be used to understand how children at particular age levels will react to an event. Teachers asked students of various ages for their comments and questions and found that these could have been predicted by Jean Piaget's theory of cognitive (intellectual) development. In other words, a teacher or parent familiar with Piaget's theory could easily both understand and predict how children of various developmental levels would reason about the tragedy.

Theoretical Perspectives on Child Development

Many students react to the word *theory* with a groan. A student once told me, "We want the facts, not a bunch of theorizing." It's unfortunate that theory has such a bad reputation, for it is a useful aspect of psychology.

Why Bother with Theory?

Without a theoretical perspective, data cannot be interpreted. Theory gives facts their meaning. Armed with a knowledge of Piaget's theory, developmental psychologists can accurately predict and explain how children will react to various experiences.

Imagine that you have access to a computerized database of research findings in child development. You ask for data on intellectual development, and the computer spews out thousands of pages of data from study after study. How do you know which studies are germane to your questions? How do you pull the information together to make it intelligible? To give cohesiveness to this voluminous data, you adopt a theory.

A theory can also help us relate one fact to another. Asked to determine who has behaved worse—Larry, who broke four dishes while helping to clear off the table, or Howard, who broke two dishes while trying to sneak an extra cookie—most 5-year-olds will respond, "Larry." Because young children do not take intent into consideration when judging an action, they see Larry's actions as worse because he broke more dishes (Piaget, 1932). Children who are 8 or 9 years old begin to factor intent into the equation and say Howard's actions were worse. To understand this developmental progression fully, we need a theory that relates the behavior and thought processes at one age to the behavior and thought processes at another age.

Theory can be of practical help as well. Imagine a mother near the end of her patience. Her 5-year-old twins—one with a cup of juice and the other with a glass of juice—are both complaining that the other has more juice. The mother has demonstrated that the cup and the glass contain the same amount of juice, but the twins continue to fight over who has more juice. The mother wants to know whether this constant bickering over who received more will ever end. By relating earlier behavior to later actions and one behavior to another, theory can help the mother understand why the twins continue to fight and at what point in their development the conflict will end.

Theories also allow us to predict what will happen next. For instance, if a person is negotiating the teenage years, Erik Erikson's psychosocial theory would emphasize the importance of an adolescent's developing a personal identity, with all the complexities that entails.

Finally, theory is useful in formulating the right questions for studying and understanding child behavior. Proponents of the various theoretical perspectives ask different questions about the same behavior. Each theorist seeks to understand why children act the way they do, but each approaches the subject differently.

The field of child development does not offer one unified theory. Even within a particular area such as social or cognitive development, a number of theories vie for acceptance.

Good Theory–Bad Theory

How can we tell a good theory from a bad one? Some qualities, such as usefulness, testability, predictability, and inclusiveness make a particular theory more useful than another.

Usefulness   Theories are neither right nor wrong; they are just useful. The best theory is the one that is the most useful in understanding and making predictions about the phenomenon in which one is interested. Some theories explain some areas better than others, and some theories are aimed at particular areas of interest.

Testability   Ideally, a theory is testable. Researchers should be able to perform experiments that test the theory's hypotheses. This seems simple enough, but this requirement can create quite a problem, since certain theories are harder to test than others. Freud's psychoanalytic theory, for example, is difficult to test experimentally because its main ideas are difficult to define in a way that allows them to be tested empirically (Cairns, 1998).

Predictability   Good theories can be used both to describe and understand present events and to predict future behavior. Think for a moment about the twins complaining over who had more juice. One of the mother's first questions was "When will they ever stop fighting?" A good theory would predict the point in the twins' development at which the children would be able to understand that both the cup and the glass could hold the same amount of juice. In the *Challenger* tragedy, the researchers could have predicted that young children would perceive the tragedy one way and older children in a different way.

Inclusiveness   A theory should be as inclusive as possible. No single theory explains all the concerns of child development, but a theory formulated to help us understand cognitive or social development should answer as many related questions as possible.

Other Criteria   A number of other criteria may be used. For instance, a good theory is economical; that is, it introduces as few new terms and concepts as possible and is clear and concise. Also, good theories tend to spark a great deal of valuable research and give people in the field a new slant on a particular issue.

Categorizing Theories

Just as there is no single theory of development that explains all facets of child development, there is no single way to categorize theories. Theories can be categorized in terms of their orientation to life, their stand on the issue of stages, the scope of the theory, and their view of the nature-nurture controversy.

Orientation to Life   Some theorists take the *organismic* view that human beings are active organisms constantly in the state of becoming, of developing. These psychologists, believe development is impelled by forces within the individual and that scientists should study the processes of development as they occur within the whole organism.

T F
1

Theories can both describe present behavior and predict future behavior.

Guideposts

What are the elements of a "good theory"?

Guideposts

How do organismic, mechanistic, and contextual theories differ from each other?

2

The stage of cognitive development a child is negotiating is accurately determined by considering the child's chronological age.

Guideposts

What are the components of a stage theory?

T F
3

All useful theories in child development posit a discrete number of stages.

In contrast, *mechanistic* theory views human beings as basically machines composed of parts that can be studied individually and independently. External forces cause reactions in the organism that impel development from one degree of skill and ability to another.

The *contextual* viewpoint argues that human development can only be appreciated when one looks at the individual's behavior within the wider social context. They argue that too often the individual is studied almost in a vacuum, as isolated from the social fabric, and this is artificial and inherently wrong. Contextualists broadly consider all the social, historical, and cultural contexts as well as the immediate social environment involving family, peers, and siblings.

Do Children Develop in Stages? Some psychological theories emphasize the concept of stages while others do not. Stage theories present development in terms of age-related periods in which people are faced with particular problems and have specific abilities. People in a particular stage should act or reason similarly. These theories see development as occurring in a steplike, discontinuous sequence. Progression from stage to stage occurs in an invariant order, and each child progresses through the same stages (see Table 2.1). Children cannot skip a stage but may enter or leave a particular stage at different times, so it is incorrect simply to equate ages with stages. The ages given throughout this text are nothing more than averages and guides and should not be thought of as absolutes.

Other psychologists believe that development is a more continuous process and do not agree with the concept of stages. These psychologists see development in terms of smooth, small steps, explained by looking at past achievements. They see no stages but rather gradual development.

The Scope of the Theory Some theories are useful in understanding cognitive development, others are stronger in their approach to personality development, and still others emphasize social development. The problem here is that each of the areas—personality, physical, cognitive, and social development—affect each other. Some theories also emphasize overt behavior while others investigate the processes of thought.

Some theorists argue that the child is motivated by forces within the individual. Other theorists emphasize the importance of forces outside the child, while still other authorities argue that psychologists can only understand the child's behavior by looking at it in the larger social context. Theorists representing each approach would ask different questions and emphasize different aspects of development.

The Nature-Nurture Debate Although every psychologist today agrees that both heredity and environmental factors interact, some theories emphasize one more than the other. Some theories take a more biological or maturational viewpoint while others, although not totally denying the importance of biology, do not emphasize it.

The first theoretical approaches we will investigate, Piaget's cognitive theory and the information-processing approach, focus on cognitive development. We will then look at the theoretical approaches of Freud and Erikson, which emphasize personality development. Theoretical approaches that highlight the importance of learning form the third portion of this chapter, while ecological theory and sociocultural theory, approaches that present development in a broader social context, will be presented last.

Table 2.1	Classic Stage Theories
Stage theories share some common features.	
1. Stages are sequential.	The child proceeds from stage 1 to stage 2, to stage 3, and so on.
2. No stages are skipped.	Children cannot proceed from stage 1 to stage 3. They must go through stage 2 during their developmental odyssey.
3. No regression can occur.	Development occurs in the forward direction. The child does not return to stage 2 after being in stage 3.
4. Each stage shows a qualitative change in abilities.	The defining aspect of each stage is a particular behavioral pattern, be it cognitive or social, which is qualitatively different from the behaviors shown in the previous stage. The particular stage a child is negotiating is determined by what the child is doing.
5. There are individual differences in the age at which children enter and leave any particular stage.	*Age* and *stage* are not synonymous terms. Some children spend more time in a particular stage than other children.

Piaget's Theory of Cognitive Development

People go to space to find stars and foods for people.
People shouldn't go in the sky.
The rocket died.
Somebody shouldda moved the clouds.

These are a few of the comments made by 5-year-olds the day following the *Challenger* tragedy. Even a casual look at the comments is enough to convince anyone that children do not think like adults. In fact, one of Piaget's central ideas is that children are not little adults. Perhaps you shrug your shoulders at this rather simple statement, but for years people did not understand that a child's way of thinking and dealing with problems is qualitatively different from an adult's. People interpreted the differences between the thinking of children and that of adults as mistakes or as signs of stubbornness against growing up. Piaget devoted his adult life to studying the cognitive (intellectual) development of children. His work is monumental, and his discoveries have a number of important implications.

Jean Piaget conducted research by presenting children of varying ages with problems to solve, noting how they approached the problem and the nature of their reasoning.

What Is Knowledge?

For most people, knowledge is a set of facts or concepts that an individual has been taught. This rather static view of knowledge allows only for adding more facts to one's storehouse. To Piaget, though, knowledge is equated with action. "To know something means to act on that thing, with the action being either physical, mental or both" (Thomas, 1979, p. 29). The 8-year-old's knowledge of a crystal is based on the interaction between the child and the object, and this interaction changes as the child matures and becomes more experienced (Piaget, 1970). Knowledge, then, is a process rather than some stable state. Piaget was interested in discovering the different ways children interact with their world to create knowledge. As children mature, their ways of knowing the world change.

Factors in Development

According to Piaget, development involves the continuous alteration and reorganization of the ways in which people deal with their environment (Piaget, 1970). Development is defined by four principal factors: maturation, experience, social transmission, and the process of equilibration. We discussed maturation—the gradual unfolding of one's genetic plan for life—in Chapter 1. Experience involves the active interaction of the child with his or her environment. Social transmission refers to the information and customs that are transmitted from parents and other people in the environment to the child. We can consider this the educational function in the broad sense. Finally, the process of **equilibration** defines development. Children seek a balance between what they know and what they are experiencing. When faced with information that calls for a new and different analysis or activity, children enter a state of disequilibrium. When this occurs, they change their way of dealing with the event or experience, and a new, more stable state of equilibrium is established. In this way, children progress from a very limited ability to deal with new experiences to a more mature, sophisticated level of cognitive functioning. For example, let us say that a child believes that heavy things are big and light things are small. The child is introduced to a Styrofoam beam, which looks like wood but is, of course, much lighter. The child is forced into disequilibrium and is motivated internally to find out more and establish a new equilibrium. This the child does by changing his or her ideas.

To Piaget, children are not simply passive receivers of stimuli. Children actively interact with their environment, and their active experiences impel them to new heights in cognitive functioning and action. Therefore, the child's cognitive development is based not only on information directly and formally transmitted from parents and teachers to the child but also on the child's personal experiences.

Organization and Adaptation

Two of the most important concepts in Piagetian theory are organization and adaptation. First, people must organize their knowledge in a way that makes the knowledge useful. Second, to survive, every organism must adapt or adjust to its environment. As the forces in the environment change, so must the individual's ability to deal with them change.

Organization: Cognitive Structures, Schemata and Operations Children perceive and deal with the world in more sophisticated ways as they mature. Piaget used the term **schema** to describe an organized system of actions and thoughts that are useful for dealing with the environment and may be generalized to many situations (Piaget, 1952). For example, an infant may place a block in her mouth and suck on it. This is the sucking schema. She may do the same with many items. The infant is also master of other schemata (the plural of *schema*), including looking, listening, grasping, hitting, and pushing. Schemata are tools for learning about the world, and new schemata are developed as the child matures.

Infants' schemata are basic and involve types of overt behavior, such as sucking and picking things up. Later on, schemata become more symbolic and mental. The 8-year-old given a block can mentally operate on the block. He can imagine placing two blocks together and taking them apart even if he does not always do so physically. These symbolic schemata that characterize older children are referred to as **operations;** they are internalized actions that are part of the child's cognitive structure. Such actions include plans or rules for solving problems (Piaget, 1974).

equilibration
In Piagetian theory, the process by which children seek a balance between what they know and what they are experiencing.

schema
A method of dealing with the environment that can be generalized to many situations.

operation
An internalized action that is part of the child's cognitive structure.

For example, Piaget wrote extensively about the operation of reversibility—that is, being able to return to one's point of origin. If 3 plus 5 equals 8, then subtracting 5 from 8 will leave 3. You can add something to 3 and then take it away and think your way from one condition to another and then return to the starting point. Schemata and operations form what Piaget calls the *cognitive structure* of the child.

As children develop, their cognitive structures become more and more similar to those of adults. For instance, consider what happens when a magnet is given to children in different stages of development. The infant merely puts the magnet in his or her mouth or perhaps bangs it against the floor. The 3-year-old might realize that some objects stick to or want to stay with the magnet. The 9-year-old child realizes that certain objects with certain characteristics are attracted to the magnet and tests out which ones and at which distances. The adolescent forms an abstract theory of magnetism that involves the size and shape of the magnet and distance from the object (Miller, 1993).

Adaptation   The second major concept in Piagetian theory is adaptation, which involves two complementary processes: assimilation and accommodation. **Assimilation** refers to the taking-in process, whether of sensation, nourishment, or experience. It is the process by which new information is filtered or modified to fit already existing structures (Piaget & Inhelder, 1969). When we assimilate something, we alter the form of an incoming stimulus to adapt to our already existing actions or structures (Piaget, 1983). For example, if a child sees an odd-shaped piece of paper and uses it as a paper airplane, the child has assimilated the paper into his or her structure and knowledge of an airplane. A baby may bang a rattle against the side of the crib, but when given another toy, perhaps a plastic block, the baby will assimilate it by banging it against the crib as well.

Accommodation involves modifying existing schemata to meet the requirements of a new experience (Piaget & Inhelder, 1969). When we accommodate, we create new schemata or modify old ones. For example, a child may be very good at using a one-handed pickup schema—that is, lifting an item with one hand—but when faced with a heavier item, the child has to accommodate—that is, use a two-handed pickup schema.

Assimilation and accommodation work together. Suppose you are riding in a car with a young child and the child points to a large, new Cadillac and says, "Car." "That's right," you remark as you continue driving. The child then spots an old, rusty Volkswagen Beetle and again says, "Car." You are suitably impressed. After all, even though the Cadillac and the Volkswagen are noticeably different, the child understands that they are both cars—an example of assimilation. As you drive on, the child points to a large truck and says, "Car." You correct her, saying, "No, that is a truck." After a while, the child points out a few more trucks. She has accommodated. Now she has separated her conception of car from that of truck. In this way, using assimilation and accommodation, the child begins to understand her world.

The Stages of Cognitive Development

Piaget (1954) argued that children's cognitive development can be viewed as occurring in a sequence of four stages. Each of these stages represents a qualitative advance in a child's ability to solve problems and understand the world.

The Sensorimotor Stage   Between birth and about 2 years of age, infants progress through the sensorimotor stage (see Chapter 6). They investigate their world using

Guideposts
How are actions and thoughts organized?

Guideposts
How do assimilation and accommodation operate?

assimilation
   The process by which information is altered to fit into one's already existing cognitive structures.

accommodation
   The process by which one's existing structures are altered to fit new information.

sensorimotor stage
   The first stage in Piaget's theory of cognitive development, in which the child discovers the world using the senses and motor activity.

During the second year, young children can use one thing to represent another.

the senses and motor activity. They develop **object permanence**—the understanding that objects and people do not disappear merely because they are out of sight. For instance, when a parent leaves the room, an infant is likely to cry. Young infants may believe that the parent has disappeared. Reappearance of the mother or father brings joy and relief. Children in the later part of the second year, at the end of this stage, also show the beginnings of representational thought, that is the ability to use one thing to stand for another. For example, a child may use a cardboard box to stand for a hat. This ability continues to develop in the next stage.

The Preoperational Stage From about age 2 through age 7, children negotiate the lengthy preoperational stage (see Chapter 8). Children's ability to use representation improves greatly and the child's developing use of symbolism shows itself in their expanding linguistic abilities. Language allows children to go beyond direct experience, opening up a new and challenging world.

This stage has a number of limitations, though. Children cannot understand conservation—that is, that quantities remain the same despite change in their appearance. Preschoolers often do not understand, for example, that a short wide glass and a tall, narrow glass can hold the same amount of liquid.

Early in this stage, children attribute the characteristics of living organisms to inanimate objects. The child who described the *Challenger* tragedy with the words "The rocket died" shows this type of thinking.

The preoperational child is also egocentric, believing that each person sees the situation just the way the child does. If a parent is tired or not feeling well, a child may bring the parent a favorite toy. He doesn't understand that Daddy or Mommy would rather have some peace and quiet and perhaps something to read. Children in this stage believe that everything in the world was created to meet their needs; for example, the sun was created to make the child warm and give the child light. Children in this stage are also artificial, which means that they interpret all phenomena, including natural phenomena, as made by human beings. The child who noted that "Somebody shouldda moved the clouds" as an explanation for the shuttle explosion exemplifies this manner of thinking.

The Concrete Operational Stage From age 7 to about age 12, children progress through the stage of concrete operations (see Chapter 10). In this stage, many of the preoperational deficiencies are slowly overcome, and children develop the ability to conserve. The child in the stage of concrete operations has difficulty with abstract terms such as freedom or liberty. Things are understood concretely and literally. A saying such as "You can lead a horse to water, but you can't make him drink" is often met with a questionable frown, and political cartoons mean nothing to the child in this stage. In short, children in this stage understand the world on a concrete, tangible level. There is much less egocentrism, and these children can see things from other people's points of view. One child in the concrete operational stage noted, "It was sad that Mrs. McAullife's children lost their mother." There is also a sense of fairness shown here, as some said that it's not fair that she died so young.

The Formal Operational Stage During adolescence, children enter the stage of formal operations (see Chapter 12). They develop the ability to test hypotheses in a mature, scientific manner and can understand and communicate their positions on complex ethical issues that demand an ability to use abstractions. These children can consider hypotheses, deal with future orientations, and consider many aspects of a problem. When asked about the *Challenger* incident, many believed that space exploration must continue, since so much energy and time had already been committed to the endeavor, and they systematically looked and evaluated positions regarding the future of manned space missions. Others looked at the possible lessons learned from the tragedy.

Stance on Central Issues

Piaget's theory is clearly organismic. Children are active participants in their own development as they explore the world. Motivation for development comes from within the organism. Piaget also clearly believed in stages as he posited distinct stages of development. Piaget argued for the interaction between innate and experiential forces. The physical maturation of the child allows new opportunities to develop. Piaget's theory emphasizes cognitive development and extensively describes the intellectual development of the child.

Application and Value

Piaget's ideas comprise the most influential theory in all child development (Beilin, 1992). His explorations into the way children develop their concepts of time, space, and mathematics, for example, show that children see the world differently from the way adults do. To serve the needs of youngsters better, parents and teachers must understand children's thought processes. Piaget's theory also recognizes previously unsuspected intelligence in infants and young children, and encourages us to determine what abilities infants possess at birth, what abilities children possess at later points in development, and what developmental processes allow children to make these transitions (Siegler, 1991). Piaget's emphasis on the active, searching mind of the child implies that children should be encouraged to discover and to experience, that they are not mere passive receivers of stimulation. Children initiate action and react to stimuli in the environment and are shaped by and actively shape their own environment (Kagan, 1992). Piaget's theories have also been fruitful in encouraging an incredible diversity of research that has greatly furthered our understanding of child development.

Criticisms and Cautions

Critics of Piaget's theory argue that Piaget underestimated the influence of learning on intellectual development. In addition, there is evidence both for and against the idea that children progress through a series of stages in cognitive development (Flavell, Miller, & Miller, 1993). Furthermore, although there is little doubt that if you test Piagetian stage-related concepts such as conservation exactly the way Piaget did, you get the same results, different results are sometimes obtained if the test situation is altered. For example, when investigating conservation of substance using a number of different substances including metal cubes, wire coils, and plastic wires, children could understand the conservation of some substances but not others (Uzgiris, 1968). If the same cognitive structures underlie children's thinking, it should not matter which substance is used. The nature of the task and of the past learning experiences of the child may be more important than Piaget realized (Flavell, 1992).

Guideposts

What are Piaget's four stages of development?

There are no qualitative advances in children's intellectual development after age 6.

concrete operations

The third stage in Piaget's theory of cognitive development, in which the child develops the ability to conserve and becomes less egocentric.

formal operations

The fourth and last stage in Piaget's theory of cognitive development, in which the adolescent develops the ability to deal with abstractions and engage in scientific logic.

While many theorists are impressed by Piaget's descriptions, they emphasize different processes to explain phenomena described by Piaget. For example, how do children proceed from one stage to another? Piaget argued that equilibration was the mechanism, but many disagree. For example, Robbie Case (1988, 1998) argues that it is not equilibration that is the major mechanism for change in development but rather changes in the child's short-term memory storage space or working memory capacity. This increases at a regular rate and in an orderly fashion and gives children the opportunity to form new and more complex cognitive structures.

Summary	Piaget's Developmental Theory of Cognitive Psychology

Basic Premises

1. Children do not think or solve problems in the same manner as adults.
2. This theory emphasizes the importance of the child's active interaction with the environment.
3. It sees maturation and experience as more important than formal learning in the child's cognitive development.
4. It views cognitive development as occurring in four stages. Each stage shows a qualitative leap forward in the child's ability to solve problems and reason logically.
5. It offers the most complete description of cognitive development from infancy through childhood available.

Value and Strength

1. The theory emphasizes the importance of active experience in a child's development. It leads to a view of young children as little scientists sifting through information and actively coping with the world.
2. Its descriptions of the way in which children think and approach problems are very helpful in understanding children's behavior.
3. Many of the sequences for understanding specific concepts are very challenging.

Criticisms and Weaknesses

1. It may underestimate the influence of learning on cognitive development and the nature of task on the child's performance.
2. Piaget's style of research has been criticized. Piaget presented children with a problem and sought to discover how they reasoned and tried to solve the problem. His studies were not controlled.

The Information-Processing Approach

Information-processing theory emphasizes the way children take in information, process it, and then act on the information. Such factors as attention, perception, memory, the mediating process by which an individual does something to the information, and a response system are important. Each of these cognitive processes is investigated in a detailed manner.

Information-processing specialists often use the computer as an analogy to the workings of the human mind, but this does not mean that they see human beings as computers or robots. The computer analogy helps us understand how children solve problems and use information (Gardner, 1998). What we type into the computer (the input) is roughly analogous to information we gather from the environment through our senses. Some operations are performed on the information according to the program, and the information is encoded and stored in some

information-processing theory
An approach to understanding cognition that delves deeply into the way information is taken in, processed, and then acted on.

way that is retrievable. Some processes must occur in our minds that enable us to attend to a particular stimulus, organize it, and remember it so it can be used in the future. The information that is retrieved and used if the proper command is given could be considered output. In the human being, the output could be some motor activity, such as moving the arm to catch a baseball, or it could be verbal, such as coming up with the answer to a math problem. Finally, an individual receives feedback—information noting whether the movement or answer was effective. Just as the title of a computer program gives some clue as to what the general results of the program will be, human beings

may have an upper executive plan, which coordinates activities and guides purposeful behavior.

Information-processing theorists are interested in following the information through the system to learn how it is encoded, processed, and retrieved (Sternberg, 1985). Thus, they look at cognition on a very detailed level, investigating the processes of perception, attention, representation, memory, and retrieval. For example, what if you ask a child to read a paragraph containing instructions for solving a puzzle and then ask him to use the information to do so? Information processors would ask some very specific questions about the child's behavior. For example, how fast did the child process the information? Which details were processed, and which were ignored? How did the child relate the information to prior activities that were similar and meaningful? What methods did the child use to transfer the information from what he read to solve the problem? If we can answer these questions (and others), we can understand the process by which the child has taken in the information about the task, related it to information already known making the new information meaningful, and, finally, decided how and when to use it. An information-processing specialist investigating the way children understood the *Challenger* explosion would analyze what elements of the situation children of various ages paid attention to and what they ignored, how children related what happened to what they already understood, the nature of the questions asked of the children, and the strategies children used to answer these questions.

Basic Assumptions and Principles of Information Processing

A number of assumptions and principles of information processing can help us understand the theory (Bjorklund, 1995). First and simplest is that people process the information; that is, they do something to the information they receive to make it useful. For example, if you did not know how to read, these letters, words and sentences would be unintelligible. You must process them—that is, do something to them in your mind to make sense out of the printed word.

A little less obvious is the notion of limited capacity. We cannot process any and all information; we can deal with only a finite amount at a time. We have only so much mental space in which to operate. For example, most of us have enough capacity to walk and talk at the same time. But if someone asks you to figure out the percentage of people in your class who passed a test, there is a noticeable change in your rate of walking or talking. To solve the problem, you must use some of the

The information processing approach uses the computer as an analogy for the workings of the human mind, but this does not mean that psychologists using this approach see human beings as computers or robots.

Guideposts

How do information-processing theorists use the analogy of a computer to explain human thinking and problem solving?

Studies show that there is a limit to the amount of information human beings can process at one time.

capacity that you used before for walking and talking. Some things are so well learned that they become automatic and require little attention, whereas others require a great deal of attention. For example, a young child learning to read must use a great deal of this processing capacity to sound out words, making it difficult to get much meaning from the words and making reading a chore. As one becomes more experienced, the decoding part of reading requires less attention, allowing for more processing of meaning. However, even now, if faced with a very difficult, long word, you will slow down and focus a great deal of your capacity on it.

Another assumption is that information moves through a system (see Figure 2.1). Information first enters sensory memory, in which it remains intact for a very short amount of time. From here, it passes to short-term memory, where capacity is smaller and the storage lasts 30 seconds or so. Short-term memory is also referred to as working memory which describes its function as the place where we mentally live, think and apply strategies to solve problems. By rehearsing, memories are kept in working memory and the process of transferring information to long-term memory begins.

Figure 2.1 Model of Memory

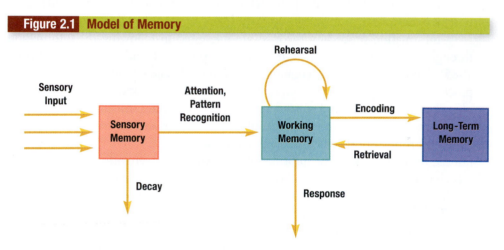

SOURCE: Leahey & Harris, (1997)

Psychologists believe that long-term store is laid down in networks where various concepts are related to one another in a meaningful manner. Strong associations are made between closely related concepts, weaker ones between loosely related concepts, and no associations at all between others. If we are thinking about Columbus, such things as discovering America and being Italian might be strongly related. A bit less strongly related is that Columbus sailed for Spain, and unrelated to Columbus might be that the capital of New York is Albany (Kaplan, 1990). Long-term memory is a dictionary organized by meaning.

A child's knowledge base plays a very important role in how the child processes information. New memories are not laid down in a vacuum but are related to older ones. The richer the network of memories in a particular area, the easier it is for the child to relate a new incident to an older one. We often have a framework on which to hang our memories. For instance, before learning about Columbus, we may have seen a film about explorers or heard or read about what they do. This makes learning about Columbus easier.

Last, people use strategies to solve problems and process information in a meaningful manner. Children use different strategies as they develop. When given some pictures to study, a young child may simply look at them, the older child will rehearse, while still older children may use different strategies, such as classifying the pictures, to remember them.

The information-processing viewpoint is not always seen in a developmental framework, but it can be. Developmental changes in the ability to process information, control one's attention, and use memory strategies develop in a manner allowing one to take a developmental perspective.

Stance on Basic Issues

Information processing uses the computer model, which replaces the human being as machine model. Its look at separate subprocesses would certainly be mechanistic. On the other hand, information processing posits an executive function that has overall control of behavior, an organismic element (Miller, 1993).

Information-processing theory does not offer the type of stagelike development Piaget advanced, but it does view qualitatively different strategies as appearing over time (Miller, 1993). Information-processing theory does not take any stand on the influence of environment and biology, although this may change in the near future. Finally, this is a theory that emphasizes the importance of cognition.

Application and Value

The information-processing approach allows us to delve more deeply into the same kinds of phenomena that interested Piaget. The Piagetian and information-processing viewpoints can complement each other, giving parents and teachers new ways to analyze a child's cognitive growth.

Criticisms and Cautions

The information-processing perspective is so new that it is difficult to analyze it critically at this point. It is hardly a unified field. A number of models have been advanced to account for the numerous subprocesses, such as encoding, memory, and retrieval, involved in processing information. No one yet knows how far the computer analogy can be taken. More important, we also do not know whether the mind will yield to the step-by-step analysis of subprocesses vital to the success of the information-processing approach. Furthermore, the approach devotes little attention to individual differences in most cases, which remains an important aspect of child development (Cairns, 1998). Although the viewpoint is interesting, much work remains before we can truly judge its value for understanding how children develop and process information.

For Your Consideration ?

A child has difficulty placing 10 sticks in size order. What questions would the Piagetian and information-processing views ask about the child's behavior?

Summary	Information-Processing Theory

Basic Premises

1. It emphasizes the importance of the manner in which children take in information, process it, and then act on it.
2. Such processes as attention, perception, memory, and processing strategies are studied.

Value and Strengths

1. It yields a detailed look at the processes involved in taking in and processing information.
2. It may serve as a diagnostic aid in discovering where people have difficulties in solving problems.

Criticism and Weaknesses

1. It is not a unified approach. A number of models have been advanced.
2. It still awaits adequate testing.

conscious

Freudian term for thoughts or memories of which a person is immediately aware.

preconscious

Freudian term for thoughts or memories that, although not immediately conscious, can easily become so.

unconscious

Freudian term for memories that lie beyond normal awareness.

Guideposts

Why is the unconscious an important concept in Freudian theory?

id

The portion of the mind in Freudian theory that serves as the depository for wishes and desires.

pleasure principle

The principle by which the id operates which involves the achievement of satisfaction as quickly as possible through the reduction of discomfort and tension.

ego

The part of the mind in Freudian theory that mediates between the real world and the desires of the id.

reality principle

The process by which the ego satisfies the organism's needs in a socially appropriate manner.

superego

The part of the mind in Freudian theory that includes a set of principles, violation of which leads to feelings of guilt.

Freud's Psychoanalytic Theory

Many people have an opinion about Freud's theory. Usually, they are either fascinated by it or reject it out of hand. But if you ask people what Freud said, many do not understand it well at all. Psychoanalytic theory comprises the following major elements.

Levels of Consciousness

Sigmund Freud (1900/1957, 1923/1962, 1933/1961) posited three levels of awareness. The **conscious** involves one's immediate awareness and makes up only a small portion of the total mind. The **preconscious** comprises memories that can easily become conscious. Finally, some memories are stored in the **unconscious**—the portion of the mind that is beyond normal awareness. Motives may arise from here. The unconscious shows itself in many ways, for instance, through dreams and slips of the tongue.

Freud (1933/1961) believed that behavior could be caused and maintained by early experiences that had apparently been forgotten. These experiences, which are stored in the unconscious, are beyond normal awareness but can still have a profound effect on behavior. For instance, a person may experience sexual difficulties in a marriage because of a traumatic sexual experience in childhood the individual no longer remembers.

Freud insisted that we may not be aware of our true motives or wishes because they are unacceptable to us or because society forbids us to gratify them. If a child who is angry at his mother kicks a younger sibling, a situation referred to as *displacement*, the child may refuse to admit to feelings of hostility toward his mother. The child is not lying but is probably unaware of those feelings.

The Constructs of the Mind

Freud explained the workings of the mind using three constructs (Freud, 1923/1962): the id, the ego, and the superego. The **id** is the source of all wishes and desires. It is unconscious and exists at birth. The id wants what it wants when it wants it and cannot tolerate delay. It operates through the **pleasure principle,** which entails achieving satisfaction as quickly as possible through the reduction of discomfort and tension. The infant is, in this sense, complete id.

Within the first year, the **ego** comes into being. Some needs, such as hunger, can be satisfied only by interacting with the real world. The ego, which is partly conscious, operates through the **reality principle.** It is responsible for dealing with reality and satisfying the needs and desires of the id in a socially appropriate manner. Whereas the id knows only its subjective reality (I want), the ego must also understand the world outside the mind and the self. As the child grows and matures, the ego becomes stronger, being able to delay gratification and balance the desires of the id with the restraints of the third construct, the superego.

The **superego** is analogous to one's conscience. It contains a set of principles gathered from interacting with others in society and serves as an internal gyroscope. The superego compares your behavior to your **ego ideal**—that is, what you think you should be like. The superego is perfectionistic, seeking to inhibit the id's antisocial desires and causing an individual to experience guilt when transgressing or even considering a misdeed. The ego must mediate between the prohibitions of the superego and the desires of the id. Tension may arise from the pull of the id, the nature of society's prohibitions, and the weight of superego restraint. Life is a compromise, and proper adjustment is a matter of maintaining a delicate balance.

Table 2.2 Defense Mechanisms

Defense mechanisms are used to reduce or eliminate unpleasant feelings such as anxiety or emotional conflict. This table shows some of the more prominent mechanisms.

Defense mechanisms	Description	Example
Rationalization	Making up plausible but inaccurate excuses to explain some behavior.	A student who is getting poor grades in school explains it away by telling you "It's not your grades that are important" or "Schools teach nothing useful anyway."
Denial	A person refuses to believe something has occurred or is occurring.	A person refuses to believe that someone has died or that he or she has a problem with using alcohol or drugs.
Compensation	Making up for a real or imaginary deficiency by putting effort into a similar area (direct compensation) or into a different area (indirect compensation).	An unathletic person who feels physically inferior may buy bodybuilding equipment and work out until he is a first-class weight lifter (direct compensation) or put his efforts into schoolwork to become the best student he can (indirect compensation).
Reaction Formation	An individual experiences feelings that are unacceptable to him or her and so acts in a manner that is contrary to those feelings.	A junior high school girl who likes a boy may act very rude or even hit him to "prove" to her friends that she doesn't really like him.
Projection	Feelings that are unacceptable to oneself are attributed to someone else.	A child who feels angry at her mother for not driving her to a friend's house asks her, "Why are you angry with me?" instead of telling her she is angry at her.
Regression	Returning to a time in life that was more comfortable.	A 3-year-old boy who is talking and toilet trained begins to talk baby talk and wet his pants after a baby brother is brought home from the hospital.
Repression	Memories are barred from consciousness so they no longer bother a person.	A person who accidentally struck another with his bat during a baseball game cannot remember the incident.
Displacement	The transfer of feelings from one person or object to another.	A child is angry at her father but yells at her brother.
Rechannelization (Sublimation)	Unacceptable impulses are rechanneled into socially appropriate pursuits.	An aggressive person learns to express himself through sports or music.

Defense Mechanisms

The ego has a difficult job. Sometimes it is overwhelmed, and the tension that results is experienced as anxiety. If the anxiety becomes too great, the ego may defend itself by using a large number of protective maneuvers called **defense mechanisms.** A defense mechanism is an automatic and unconscious strategy that serves to relieve or reduce feelings of anxiety or emotional conflict (Laughlin, 1970). Some of the more common defense mechanisms are presented in Table 2.2 above.

The Psychosexual Stages

One of the most challenging Freudian concepts is that of infantile and childhood sexuality, the idea that infants and children experience sexual feelings. Freud did not believe that young children experienced adult sexual feelings. His idea of sexuality resembles what we might consider sensuality and pleasure. Freud saw life as the unfolding of the sexual instinct that he called *eros*. The energy emanating from it is known as the **libido.** The libido attaches itself to different portions of the body as the child grows and matures. This is the basis for Freud's psychosexual stages. Freud stressed the importance of early experience in the formation of behavior and focused attention on parent-child interactions.

ego ideal
The individual's positive and desirable standards of conduct.

defense mechanism
An automatic and unconscious strategy that reduces or eliminates feelings of anxiety or emotional conflict.

libido
In Freudian theory, the energy emanating from the sex instinct.

Freud believed that young children experienced the same sexual urges as adults.

oral stage

The first psychosexual stage, in which sexuality is centered on the oral cavity.

anal stage

The second psychosexual stage, in which sexuality is centered on the anal cavity.

phallic stage

The third psychosexual stage, in which sexuality is centered on the genital areas.

"Give Him Back!"

When Taliya was pregnant with her second child, she explained what was happening to her 3-year-old, Tanya. After she gave birth, her husband brought Tanya to the hospital. She rushed to her mother's bed, saw her baby brother, and screamed, "No, no, Mommy—bad Mommy." Taliya started to cry but the worst was not over.

Tanya wants nothing to do with the baby. Although she has never tried to hurt her brother, she resents him. She seems jealous of the gifts he gets and the attention that he is given. She wants her brother to be "given back." Tanya was talking well and was even toilet trained; now she is talking in baby talk and wetting her pants. Taliya and her husband, Wallace, are worried and want to know what to do.

1. *Why is Tanya now using baby talk and wetting her pants?*
2. *If you were Tanya's parents, how would you handle the situation?*

ACTION / REACTION

Stages in Freud's Developmental Theory   The infant is negotiating the **oral stage.** At birth, infants gain pleasure through sucking and then later biting, which are both oral activities. If a child is either frustrated or overly stimulated, the infant may become fixated and partially remain in the stage of psychosexual development, and development is partially arrested (Eidelberg, 1968). The child's personality will show some characteristic of this fixation. Fixation at this stage, if it involves sucking, may lead to gullibility, dependence and inactivity, and a belief that others will provide the comforts of life for the child. Freud also noted an increase in such oral activities as eating and drinking in orally fixated individuals. Fixation at the biting stage may result in a sarcastic or biting personality that is always in conflict with others.

The Anal Stage   At about 18 months of age, the libido becomes attached to the anal cavity, and this coincides with attempts to toilet-train the child. A power struggle over bowel and bladder control may give rise to anal-retentive character. In such a case, the child shows such traits as miserliness, obstinacy, and extreme orderliness and neatness. If, on the other hand, the child relents and releases feces, especially at inappropriate times, anal-expulsive traits such as cruelty and messiness result.

The Phallic Stage   At about the age of 4, the libido becomes attached to the genital organs: the penis in males and the clitoris in females. The child now experiences sexual feelings toward the opposite-sex parent but fears that these desires will earn the displeasure of the same-sex parent and lead to punishment. The child wishes to be rid of the same-sex parent and have the opposite-sex parent all to him- or herself. This is called the **Oedipus complex** in boys and the **Electra complex** in girls. Children resolve this conflict by learning to identify with the same-sex parent. Problems in the phallic stage can lead to a variety of personality disturbances. For example, if the resolution of the Oedipus conflict is not positive, a boy may resent his father and generalize this resentment to authority figures later in life (Nye, 1975). A number of sexual problems also date from difficulties in the phallic stage.

Although this is not exactly what Freud had in mind, during the toddler years, toilet training takes center stage. According to Freud, the early interaction between child and parent is very important in determining the course of development.

The Latency Stage   From about age 6 until puberty, the child's sexuality lies dormant. Since a boy has identified with his father, he tends to imitate him at every turn. Boys have also repressed their feelings toward their mothers, but because they are so young, their repression generalizes to all females. Thus, 8-year-old boys are likely to stay apart from 8-year-old girls. The sexes segregate, and boys play with other boys and girls with other girls during this stage. In a similar way, girls identify with their mothers. However, the resolution of the Electra complex in females is less severe, and at this stage girls show somewhat less of an aversion to boys than boys do to girls.

The Genital Stage   The emergence of puberty, with its hormonal changes and sexual arousal, throws the child out of the latency stage into the genital stage. The young adolescent boy turns his attention to a girlfriend, while the young adolescent female seeks a boyfriend. This is the beginning of mature adult sexuality.

Stance on Basic Issues

Although it can be debated, Freud's theory would fit loosely into the organismic camp but certainly also contains some mechanistic elements. The child is an active organism, coping with drives and needs (Miller, 1993). On the other hand, the child is basically reacting to biological needs and is passively shaped by the early interaction with parents—an essentially mechanistic idea.

Freud's theory posits a group of stages, each of which is qualitatively different from the other. His theory emphasizes the primacy of biological needs, desires, and maturation, although he obviously realized the importance of the parent-child relationship. Freud's theory concentrates on emotional and personality development rather than dealing with social or cognitive development.

Application and Value

Freud's emphasis on the importance of the early interaction between parent and child has been largely accepted by psychologists (Cairns, 1998). Freud felt that injuries during the early stages left indelible marks on children, but today we have a more flexible view that allows for subsequent experience to ease the negative effects of poor early experiences. In addition, Freud's theory presented the development of the child in a stage setting that has become very popular. Some of Freud's ideas concerning the unconscious have been of great interest as well (Emde, 1992), and Freud's description of defense mechanisms has allowed psychologists to obtain new understandings of what were in the past incomprehensible behaviors. Finally, Freud's theory has served as a focal point for criticism and as a basis for the development of other theories.

Criticisms and Cautions

Psychoanalytic theory was formulated on the basis of Freud's clinical experiences and evolved from extensive observations of single individuals over a long period of time (Cairns, 1998). Freud's patients were troubled, and psychoanalytic theory may have more to say about abnormal development than typical development. It may be a mistake to base our ideas concerning normal development and child rearing on clinical experiences with emotionally troubled people. In addition, Freud's formulations are difficult to test empirically, and Freud, himself, showed a disdain

Guideposts

How does a child's personality develop from Freud's psychosexual stages?

For Your Consideration

Freud's theory is quite controversial. Consider the following Freudian concepts: sex instinct, Oedipus complex, anal personality, unconscious motivation, id-ego-superego. Which of these concepts do you believe are useful in understanding children's development, and which do you reject?

Oedipus complex
The conflict during the phallic stage in which a boy experiences sexual feelings toward his mother and wishes to do away with his father.

Electra complex
In Freudian theory, the female equivalent to the Oedipus complex, in which the female experiences sexual feelings toward her father and wishes to do away with her mother.

latency stage
The psychosexual phase in which sexuality is dormant.

genital stage
The final psychosexual stage, occurring during adolescence, in which adult heterosexual behavior develops.

Summary	Freud's Psychoanalytic Theory

Basic Premises

1. Behavior is motivated by unconscious thoughts, memories, and feeling.
2. Life is the unfolding of the sex instinct.
3. The child's early experience is crucial to his or her later personality. The manner in which the parents satisfy the child's basic needs is important to later mental health.
4. Children develop through a sequence of stages called psychosexual stages.
5. People protect themselves from anxiety and other negative emotions through unconscious and automatic reactions called defense mechanisms.

Value and Strengths

1. It encourages developmental specialists to look beyond the obvious visible behavior and seek insights into the unconscious.
2. It emphasizes the importance of the child's early experience and relationships, which in turn focuses our attention on the caregiver-infant relationship. The idea that later problems may be due to disturbed early relationships is challenging.
3. The concept of stages in Freudian theory has become a popular way of viewing the development of children.
4. Its emphasis on sexuality, while debatable, still alerts us to the existence of sexuality at all ages.
5. This theory serves as a focal point for other theorists.

Criticism and Weaknesses

1. Since theory is based on clinical experiences with troubled people, it may have more to say about unhealthy than healthy development.
2. Hypotheses are very difficult to test.
3. It fails to appreciate the importance of culture.

for systematic experimental work (Cairns, 1998; Miller, 1993). Some of his concepts, such as instinct and psychic energy, are vaguely or even poorly defined, and none is defined in a manner that would make testing easy. Finally, Freud's emphasis on sexuality may have grown out of the society in which he lived. Sexuality was frowned on in Vienna at that time, and the idea that sexuality is sinful and unhealthy may have been the cause of many of the problems Freud treated. His ideas may not be as universal as he thought.

Erikson's Psychosocial Theory

Although accepting some of Freud's concepts, a number of Freud's followers have rejected others. Freud's emphasis on sexuality has troubled many, as has his lack of consideration for the effect cultural differences may have on a child's development. Of all Freud's followers, Erik Erikson has had the greatest influence on the study of child development. Erikson (1963, 1968) argued that human beings develop according to a preset plan called the **epigenetic principle.** This principle consists of two main elements. First, personality develops according to predetermined steps that are maturationally set. Second, society is structured so as to invite and encourage the challenges that arise during these particular stages. Maturation brings about new skills that open new possibilities for the person, but it also increases society's demands on the individual's functioning. Societies have developed ways to meet the person's need at each step in the maturation process, such as parental care and schools (Miller, 1993).

epigenetic principle

The preset developmental plan in Erikson's theory consisting of two elements: that personality develops according to maturationally determined steps and that each society is structured to encourage challenges that arise during these stages.

The Psychosocial Stages

According to Erikson, each individual proceeds through eight stages of development from cradle to grave. Each stage presents the individual with a crisis. If a particular crisis is handled well, a positive outcome ensues. If it is not handled well, the resulting outcome is negative. Few people emerge from a particular stage with an entirely positive or negative outcome. In fact, Erikson argues that a healthy balance must be struck between the two poles. However, the outcome should tend toward the positive side of the scale. Although people can reexperience these crises during a life change, by and large, the crises take place at particular times in life. The resolution of one stage lays the foundation for negotiating the challenges of the next stage (Baltes, Lindenberger, & Staudinger, 1998).

According to Erikson, two-year-olds need to develop a sense of autonomy, a feeling of confidence that they are people on their own within a safe and secure environment.

Stage 1: Trust versus Mistrust The positive outcome of the stage of infancy is a sense of trust. If children are cared for in a warm, caring manner, they are apt to trust the environment and develop a feeling that they live among friends. If the parents are anxious, angry, or incapable of meeting a child's needs, the child may develop a sense of mistrust. Trust is the cornerstone of the child's attitude toward life. For example, children with a sense of trust are inclined to believe that others will come through for them and that people are generally good, while people with a low sense of trust focus on the negative aspects of other people's behavior (Hamachek, 1988).

Stage 2: Autonomy versus Shame or Doubt Two- and three-year-olds are no longer completely dependent on adults. Young children practice their new physical skills and develop a positive sense of autonomy. They learn that they are someone on their own. If children of this age either are not allowed to do the things they can do or are pushed into doing something for which they are not ready, they may develop a sense of shame or doubt about their own abilities and fail to develop self-confidence. People with a sense of autonomy have a basic attitude of "I think I can do it" and "I have something of value to offer" (Hamachek, 1988).

It is dangerous for a small and vulnerable toddler to develop a sense of autonomy.

Stage 3: Initiative versus Guilt By the time children reach about 4 years of age, they can formulate a plan of action and carry it through. The positive outcome of this stage is a sense of initiative, a sense that one's desires and actions are basically sound. If parents encourage children of this age to form their own ideas, the children will develop a sense of initiative. If a child is punished for expressing his or her own desires and plans, the child develops a sense of guilt, which leads to fear and a lack of assertiveness. Children with a sense of initiative accept new challenges, are self-starters, and have a strong sense of personal adequacy, while those with a sense of guilt show the opposite patterns (Hamachek, 1988).

Stage 4: Industry versus Inferiority During the middle years of childhood, children must learn the academic skills of reading, writing, and mathematics as well as a variety of social skills. If a child succeeds in acquiring these new skills and the child's accomplishments are valued by others, the child develops a sense of industry and has a positive view of his or her achievements. But children who are constantly compared with others and come up a distinct second may develop a sense of inferiority. If a child's cultural, religious, or racial group is considered inferior, a sense of personal inferiority may also develop. Children with a sense of industry enjoy learning about new things and experimenting with new ideas, persevere, and take criticism well (Hamachek, 1988).

Stage 5: Identity versus Role Confusion   During adolescence children must investigate various alternatives concerning their vocational and personal future and develop a sense of who they are and where they belong. The adolescent who develops a solid sense of identity formulates a satisfying plan and gains a sense of security. Adolescents who do not develop this sense of identity may develop role confusion and a sense of aimlessness and being adrift. Those with a sense of identity are less susceptible to peer pressure, have a higher level of self-acceptance, are optimistic, and believe they are in control of their own destinies, while those with a sense of confusion can be described in the opposite manner (Hamachek, 1988).

Erikson's Later Stages   Erikson's final three stages cover the period of adulthood. Erikson sees the positive outcome of early adulthood as the attainment of intimacy, while a person who is fearful or chooses not to enter into close interpersonal relationships may develop a sense of isolation. In middle age, people must find a way to remain productive and to help others. This positive outcome Erikson called generativity, the negative outcome and danger is a feeling of stagnation. Finally, in old age people must develop a positive sense of pride about their accomplishments in life, which Erikson called ego integrity. If, on the other hand, all they see is missed opportunities, they may become depressed and bitter, developing a sense of despair.

Socialization, Culture, and History

Erikson broadened Freud's conception of growth and development by stressing the importance of socialization, culture, and history. The resolution of each crisis depends on a person's interaction with his or her culture. The search for identity is different for an American than for a South Sea Islander. In our society, industry, the positive outcome of middle childhood, is somewhat dependent on formal school achievement. This is not true in many other cultures. Although children in every culture proceed through the same stages, each culture has its own way of directing and improving the child's behavior at each age (Miller, 1993).

Erikson (1975) also noted the importance of the historical period in which people live. Each generation is raised under different social, political, and technological circumstances. Erikson believed that certain historical changes, such as industrialization or the Great Depression of the 1930s, resulted in institutions changing to meet people's needs.

Stance on Basic Issues

Erikson's theory contains both organismic and contextual elements. The individual actively seeks to fulfill the challenges of development, an organismic view. Erikson's theory also emphasizes the importance of culture, the historical time in which a person lives and the socialization of children into their culture, which are contextual elements.

Erikson also described development in terms of stages and expanded them to include the entire life cycle. His theory is largely an explanation of personality development. Erikson argued that maturation both determined the sequence of the stages and also set limits. It is the family, society, and the environment, that determines how they are resolved.

Guideposts

In what ways does Erikson's theory differ from Freud's?

Basic Premises

1. It explains development in terms of the epigenetic principle. Personality develops according to predetermined steps that are maturationally set. Society is structured to encourage the challenges that arise at these times in a person's life.
2. It describes development in terms of eight stages from cradle to grave. Each has positive and negative outcomes.
3. It emphasizes the importance of culture and the historical period in which the individual is living.

Value and Strengths

1. It sees development as continuing over the life span.
2. The importance it places on culture and historical period adds to our appreciation of factors that affect children's development.
3. It provides a good general overview of crises that occur at each stage of a child's life. Some of these crises, such as identity versus role confusion, have become important in understanding specific periods in a child's life.

Criticism and Weaknesses

1. It is difficult to test experimentally.
2. The theory is rather general.

Application and Value

Erikson's theory, which is clear and easy to understand, serves as an excellent introduction to the general concerns of people at different ages. His emphasis on the importance of culture, socialization, and the historical moment extends our view of the factors that influence children. Erikson sees psychosocial development as continuing throughout life rather than stopping at adolescence. Finally, Erikson's conception of identity has become a cornerstone for understanding adolescence.

Criticisms and Cautions

Criticisms of Erikson's theory follow the criticisms of Freud's theory. Erikson's theory is difficult to test experimentally. Some support for Erikson's concept of identity exists, but little research has been done on the other stages. In addition, Erikson's theory is rather general and global, and some authorities doubt the existence of all of his stages (Thomas, 1979). Despite these criticisms, Erikson's theory offers a convenient way of viewing development throughout the life span.

The Behavioral Approach

Freud, Erikson, and many other psychologists look at an individual's mental states and events that occur within the individual to explain behavior. But not all psychologists believe it is necessary to do so. Some psychologists called **behaviorists** argue that the environment determines behavior and that if the environment is altered adequately, behavior change will follow. How does this occur? Behaviorists explain behavior in terms of the processes of learning, including classical and operant conditioning.

behaviorist

A psychologist who explains behavior in terms of the processes of learning, such as classical and operant conditioning, and emphasizes the importance of the environment in determining behavior.

Reinforcers must be tangible to be effective with children.

Classical Conditioning

Classical conditioning involves the pairing of a neutral stimulus with a stimulus that elicits a particular response until the stimulus that was originally neutral elicits the response. For example, suppose every time Kindra is taken to the doctor she experiences some sort of pain—often an injection. After a while, just seeing the doctor will be enough to cause her to cry. The sight of the doctor was probably neutral at first, but when paired with discomfort or pain, it eventually elicited crying. Now whenever Kindra sees the doctor, she may cry.

An **unconditioned stimulus** is the stimulus that elicits the response prior to the conditioning. In this case, the shot is the unconditioned stimulus, because it caused the crying response before the conditioning took place. The **unconditioned response** is the response to the unconditioned stimulus. The child's crying after receiving a shot is the unconditioned response. The **conditioned stimulus** is the previously neutral stimulus that elicits a response when it is associated with an unconditioned stimulus. In this case, the doctor is a conditioned stimulus. Only when the doctor's presence was paired with the shot did it cause Kindra to cry. Finally, the **conditioned response** is the learned response that becomes attached to the conditioned stimulus. In this case, it is the child's behavior of crying when she sees the doctor.

Kindra may also exhibit this response with a number of other people who look similar to the doctor. This is called **stimulus generalization.** Experience will teach Kindra to differentiate between the doctor and people of similar appearance. This occurs through the process of **discrimination.** She may then cry when she sees the doctor, but not when she sees other people. Will Kindra's fear ever end, or will she always cry in the doctor's office? Perhaps after many pain-free visits to the doctor, Kindra will no longer cry in response to the situation. This process is called **extinction.** Classical conditioning is especially useful for understanding emotional response, such as a child's response to the voice of a warm, supportive parent or a critical teacher.

Operant Conditioning

In **operant conditioning,** the child's behavior is followed by some event that increases or decreases the frequency of the behavior that preceded it. If the event increases the likelihood that the behavior will recur, the action is said to be reinforced. If it decreases the chances of its occurring, it is said to be punished. In operant conditioning, then, behavior is governed by its consequences. Suppose a 2-year-old brings you the newspaper. You respond with a smile, a hug, or a thank you. You may then find that this toddler brings you not only the newspaper but also your keys, wallet, handkerchief, and anything else the child can find on the table. The youngster has been reinforced for being helpful. A **reinforcer** is not always tangible; attention and praise can be and often are effective reinforcers.

Parents are the most important sources of reinforcement during the child's early years. As children grow and their social world expands, reinforcers are delivered by peers, teachers, and siblings. In fact, parents and siblings may reinforce children for different behaviors.

The setting is also very important. Children learn that if they behave in a certain way under some circumstances they will be rewarded, while that same behavior under other circumstances will not be. If Pat is reinforced for being aggressive by getting what he wants, he will show this behavior in many contexts, a phenomenon called *generalization*. He begins by taking toys away from a younger brother and generalizes this behavior to peers in school. However, he soon learns when this will work and when it will be counterproductive. In other words, Pat must learn to discriminate. Using profanity with friends may be acceptable, but it is inappropriate in front of Grandma. Being aggressive and hostile may be successful in getting his way in early childhood with some peers, but it is ineffective in late adolescence when trying to talk his way out of a speeding ticket.

The behavioral perspective emphasizes the past history of the organism, the setting, and the reinforcers available. No mention is made of what occurs within the mind, of thought processes, or of memory.

According to the principles of learning theory, when a behavior is reinforced, it is more likely to reoccur.

Stance on Basic Issues

Behaviorism is often used as an example of the mechanistic approach. The child is seen as basically clay in the hands of various potters who through reinforcement and punishment, mold the child. Behaviorists disagree entirely with the concept of stages; they don't need them to explain behavior. New behaviors emerge out of older ones in a very gradual manner.

It is often stated that behaviorists believe that the human being is born with a blank slate, and the environment just writes on it. This is really not true of modern behavioral thought. Many modern behaviorists admit that genetic factors place limits and potentials in many areas. Some people learn faster than others.

Guideposts

What does learning theory contribute to understanding children's behavior and development?

For Your Consideration ?

John Watson, a well-known behaviorist, once said that if he were given a group of infants and the ability to create any environment he chose, he could make the children into anything he wanted. Evaluate this statement: Are children as malleable as Watson suggests?

ACTION / REACTION

The Temper Tantrum

Almost every parent has to handle a child's temper tantrum at one time or another. But what do you do when it's an everyday occurrence?

Carrie is 4 years old and a bright, playful child, but when she doesn't get her way, she screams and throws things. She becomes inconsolable. Carrie engages in this behavior with both her parents, but most often with her mother. The mother's response is to give in, try to reason with her, or turn her attention to something else. Carrie's father usually gives in to her before the tantrum begins. When he doesn't, he spanks her. The girl then runs to her mother and screams even more. Since the mother doesn't believe in spanking, she tries to quiet Carrie by playing with her. She has told her husband that the child will become afraid of him when she gets older.

Carrie's mother is at the end of her rope. She can't take the screaming. Carrie's father wants Carrie's mother to ignore it or spank the child, which the mother does not believe to be the best policy. Carrie's mother doesn't know why the tantrums began or why they are getting worse—only that she has to do something.

1. *If you were Carrie's parents, how would you handle Carrie's tantrums?*
2. *If you were Carrie's mother, how would you deal with your husband's behavior toward the child?*

ACTION / REACTION

Summary	Behavioral Approach

Basic Premises

1. Human behavior may be explained by the processes of learning, including classical and operant conditioning.
2. The behavioral approach has been successful in modifying the behavior of people in many situations.
3. The behavioral approach does not deny consciousness and mental processes such thinking, but rather deals with behavior and development in a different manner.
4. Development is seen as continuous with no stages posited to explain progress.

Value and Strengths

1. Learning theories are clear, precise, and laboratory tested.
2. The emphasis on the environment is important.

Criticism and Weaknesses

1. Some consider it too mechanical. Its avoidance of mental processes such as consciousness and thinking may yield only a partial picture of behavior.
2. It sees little qualitative difference between humans and animals.

Application and Value

The behavioral view is valuable in pinpointing the importance of the environment. Even those who criticize behaviorism usually acknowledge that the environment has a tremendous effect on behavior (Rogers, 1980). The question is whether it has total control or whether internal, cognitive factors, such as thinking and information-processing abilities, must also be taken into account to understand the organism better. Another contribution of behaviorism is its emphasis on experimental methodology that produces high-quality work.

Criticisms and Cautions

The most common criticism of the behavioral view of child development is that it is too mechanical. This approach makes human beings seem too predictable, and the avoidance of such concepts as consciousness, thinking, and subjective experience is a problem. It is doubtful that all human development can be understood on the basis of the principles of learning.

Social Learning Theory

People also learn by observing and imitating others; they do not have to be reinforced or punished to change their behavior. If we see a person touch a hot stove and get burned, we do not have to repeat the action ourselves. **Social learning theory** investigates the process of imitation and observation learning (Bandura, 1986).

Observation learning can be seen in many behaviors. For instance, children learn to be aggressive or altruistic through observing respected people engaging in these behaviors. People also learn partly through observation how males and females are expected to act within a particular culture (Bandura, 1986).

Sometimes children imitate exactly the gestures and words they see and hear, as when a 2-year-old girl pointed as if lecturing and called out to her sister, "Darn

social learning theory

The theoretical view emphasizing the process by which people learn through observing others and imitating their behaviors.

Boys and girls who had watched an adult modeling violence were more likely to show violent behavior in that same situation than children who had not witnessed the model's violent behavior.

it, you better do that"—an exact imitation of her mother. However, imitation is not always so exact, and at times we learn general principles when watching others. Some children watched a model expound on ways to use a cardboard box creatively as a house or a hat. When asked to suggest uses for a tin can, these children showed more creativity but did not use the model's ideas. What they learned was that creativity was acceptable (Navarick, 1979).

The Process of Imitation

Imitation can be seen as a four-step process. A person must first pay attention to the model. Whether a person pays attention or not depends on the characteristics of the model, the value of the model's behavior, and the characteristics of the observer. Models who are regular associates or peers, who are personally engaging and prestigious, or who are seen as especially credible gain attention. Models who have high status or are successful, competent, and powerful are also effective. The characteristics of the learner, including arousal status, interest, and present and past performance, also influence attention. Second, the information must be retained in memory.

In the third step, the person must use the information in an attempt to reproduce the action. This is influenced by the developmental level of the child as well as by the child's history. A child who wants to hit a baseball like his or her favorite ballplayer may not physically be able to. Finally, some reinforcer must be available. According to Bandura, reinforcement provides children with information about what might happen in the future if they perform the particular behavior. It can also motivate children. Children may remember the consequences of the behavior and later use the information to attain their own ends. They do not have to experience the reinforcement personally.

Three processes function as motivation: direct reinforcement, vicarious reinforcement (seeing others reinforced), and self-reinforcement. If students study and get better grades, they are more likely to study again. In fact, students who anticipate that if they study they will be reinforced are more likely to study. But direct reinforcement is not necessary. Vicarious reinforcement can also affect the probability of performance. If the model is reinforced for doing something, it could

Guideposts

What is the process by which children learn through observation learning?

encourage such behavior in the observer. Observing others being punished conveys information about which behaviors are and are not tolerated. The third motivator is self-reinforcement, in which an individual reinforces him- or herself for performing a particular act.

Self-Efficacy

Social learning theorists divide behavior into two different processes: learning and performance. Children learn through a number of processes, including observing others. However, whether a person will exhibit the behavior (performance) depends partly on **self-efficacy,** which is one's beliefs about what one can and cannot do in a particular situation (Bandura, Barbaranelli, Caprara, & Pasterilli, 1996).

Judgments of self-efficacy, whether accurate or not, affect one's choice of activities (Bandura, 1986, 1992, 1997). People who believe a task is within their capabilities will attempt it, whereas they will avoid activities that they believe exceed their capabilities (Bandura, 1982).

Self-efficacy affects just how much effort a person will expend and the person's persistence (Bandura, 1997). People with a high degree of self-efficacy will place more effort into a particular task than those who have a low degree of self-efficacy. Self-efficacy is dependent on the task. A child may have a high degree of self-efficacy in solving mathematics problems, a low degree of self-efficacy concerning giving a speech in front of a class, and a moderate degree of self-efficacy concerning his ability to perform well on the athletic field.

Self-efficacy judgments arise from past experiences, observations of others, verbal persuasion and one's physiological state (Bandura, 1982; 1997). Past experiences in similar situations are one key, as a history of success in a particular situation increases self-efficacy, while repeated failures lower it. People also are affected by watching others succeed or fail and may reason that if others can do it, they can too. Sometimes, children can be persuaded that they can do something, although raising unrealistic expectations for success can undermine a child's self-efficacy. People also rely on information from their physiological state when judging their capabilities. A child may interpret sweating and the increase in her heart rate as signs of nervousness and uncertainty. High arousal when engaging in a complex task is associated with poorer performance. People are inclined to expect success when they are not experiencing great tension and agitation.

A child's judgment of self-efficacy may be a key to understanding some behavioral choices. For example, research demonstrates that how much children study may depend more on their sense of self-efficacy than on actual ability (Zimmerman, Bandura, & Martinez-Pons, 1992; Collins, 1982). Self-efficacy is considered a central concept of social learning theory.

One factor that may influence this child's performance is self-efficacy or one's beliefs about what one can and cannot do in a particular situation.

self-efficacy

A person's belief about whether he or she can successfully perform a behavior related to a personal goal.

Reciprocal Determinism

Social learning theorists also believe that to understand how people acquire such complex behaviors as helping and sharing, we must appreciate the relationship among the behavior, the environment, and personal and cognitive factors. Each factor can influence the other two and, in turn, be influenced by the other two, a concept called **reciprocal determinism.**

Stance on Basic Issues

Social learning has elements of all three orientations. It views people as actively influencing and being influenced by their environment. However, the theory is mechanistic as it does not stress qualitative changes as the organism develops and emphasizes outside influences more than internal motivation. It also has contextual elements as it highlights social contexts.

Social learning theory does not use stages and, in fact, argues against their use (Bandura, 1977). The theory emphasizes the importance of domain specific knowledge and skills, and a greater appreciation of the social environment. It is a theory with a wide scope, emphasizing how people learn social behaviors.

Application and Value

Social learning theory reminds us of the importance of observation learning and imitation in determining behavior. It is useful in understanding the genesis of many behaviors—from giving to charity to being aggressive, from choosing clothing to understanding speech patterns. The concept of self-efficacy is also useful and deserves special attention.

Criticisms and Cautions

Social learning theory is not without limitations. In the realm of child development, it completely lacks a developmental framework (Cairns, 1998; 1979). The process of imitation is described in terms that give little consideration to maturation or to the differences between the imitative behavior of a toddler and that of an adolescent (Thomas, 1979). As a result, although social learning theory explains some behaviors very well, it has difficulty with age-related developmental changes.

For Your Consideration ?

If a celebrity (an actor/actress or famous athlete) was convicted of possession of a controlled substance, should the celebrity receive a harsher, but strictly legal, sentence for the crime because he or she is a model? Why or why not?

Summary	Social Learning Theory

Basic Premises

1. Human behavior is partially explained through the process of imitation and observation learning.
2. The process of imitation may be explained using a four step process involving attention, encoding and memory, behavioral reproduction, and, finally, reinforcement.
3. Cognitive factors such as self-efficacy are important.

Value and Strengths

1. It is useful in understanding certain behaviors such as altruism and aggression.
2. It encourages us to look at the models in the person's environment.

Criticism and Weaknesses

1. It lacks a developmental framework. The process of imitation is viewed as the same no matter who is observing.
2. It does not explain age-related changes.

reciprocal determinism
A concept in social learning theory referring to the idea that a complex reciprocal interaction exists among individual factors, behavior and environmental stimuli, and that each of these components influences the others.

Vygotsky's Sociocultural Theory

In Chapter 1, the importance of the contextualization of child development was discussed. The emphasis on culture and context forms the basis for Lev Vygotsky's theory that is now becoming more influential in child psychology (Baltes et al., 1998).

Vygotsky (1962, 1978) argued that the basic unit of study is not the individual child's behavior but the child in a particular context performing some behavior. Behavior and development cannot be understood without an appreciation of the nature of the cultural, historical and social context which define and influence the child. Vygotsky's theory is known as *sociocultural theory* because children acquire ways of thinking and behavior that allow them to live in a particular culture.

Vygotsky emphasized the importance of culture. Within the dominant culture, subcultures also exist. Cultures provide tools that allow people to solve problems. Some cultural tools are physical such as the use of implements to plant crops; others are psychological tools, such as language. People develop tools to master their physical environment and create psychological tools to master their own behavior and influence that of others (Crain, 1992). The psychological tools that aid thinking and behavior, such as speech, writing, and numerical systems, are called *signs*.

Culture determines the types of skills that adults must teach their children. In our culture, reading is an important skill that adults teach to children. Cultures differ in the tools they use, and the tools available to the individual depend on the culture and the historical point in time. For example, a culture emphasizing memorization would require different skills than one emphasizing concepts and scientific reasoning.

Vygotsky was very interested in how cultures transmit these ways of thinking and behaving from one generation to another, and he argued forcefully that this occurs through social interaction between the child and parents, other adults, and more expert peers. One's culture is mirrored in these social interactions that form the basis of the individual's mental processes (Wertsch & Tulviste, 1992).

The teaching function is vital to understanding Vygotsky's approach. Children may develop some concepts on their own but will not develop many important ones without instruction. Children learn these concepts and skills through dialogues with adults and more advanced children who encourage these skills.

To understand how children learn through social interactions, consider the following scenario. Say two children are given some task to perform, and neither can do it alone. A competent adult guides each child, trying to help each understand and master the task. With such help, the first child is able to succeed but not the second. Are both children functioning on the same level? Some would say "yes," since neither was able to perform the task independently, but Vygotsky argued that they are quite different. The first child's potential in this task at this moment is much greater than the second child's. A static view of intelligence would rate them both equally, but one child can do so much more with adequate help than the other. Vygotsky (1978) called the difference between a child's actual development when working alone and the level of potential development determined by problem solving with the guidance of a competent partner the **zone of proximal development.** The adult may teach through prompts, clues, modeling, explanation, asking leading questions, discussions, and many other techniques (Miller, 1993). Vygotsky claimed that teaching should be based not on what the child can do by him- or herself but on the child's potential. The child is an active participant as he or she moves through the zone of proximal development. In fact,

Guideposts

How would Vygotsky's concept of the zone of proximal development guide instructional decisions?

zone of proximal development

Vygotsky's term for the difference between the child's actual developmental level as determined by independent problem solving and the higher level of potential development determined by problem solving under adult guidance or in cooperation with more capable peers.

some children may actively request help. Notice that in Vygotsky's system, social interaction energizes development.

What is learned first through social interaction eventually becomes internalized. All cognitive processes begin with social interactions that later are internalized, and Vygotsky argues that mental functioning can only be understood by looking at the social processes and cultural foundations from which they arise. This is a very controversial position. It is at odds with most Western psychologists, who argue that mental functioning arises from within the child, and such processes as thinking, memory and attention apply exclusively to the individual (Wertsch & Tulviste, 1992).

Vygotsky takes the opposite position—that cognitive processes such as thinking begin as social interactions. Social activity then shapes the mind. Children first interact with others, then with themselves, and only later internalize the patterns. The parent may model a particular type of thinking and engage in question and answer. Next the child has a conversation with him- or herself. For example, after being shown where to find something, the child may ask himself, "Now where can I find the answer?" Eventually, what was first overt and social becomes internalized and the child can perform the behavior without any help. The social origins of mental processes is one reason for Vygotsky's current appeal.

The development of thought also shows this. Vygotsky believed that at about 2 years of age, children learn to name objects and that words are basically symbols. At about age 3, speech splits into communication aimed at others and egocentric speech meant only for oneself (Miller, 1993). Egocentric speech involves a child in a dialogue with himself and the child uses this to guide his own behavior (Crain, 1992). For example, when cutting out the outline of a figure a child may say to himself, "Now cut along the lines." Just as children use language to guide others' behavior, they also use it to guide their own behavior.

Some supporting evidence for the importance of social interaction comes from a study in which young children were given the task of sorting small models of common household furniture and appliances into rooms of a dollhouse-like structure (Freund, 1990). For example, the child would be expected to place the stove in the kitchen and the bathtub in the bathroom. All children were first allowed to complete the task themselves. Then one group, the "interaction group," was presented with the task to complete with their mothers, while the second group, the "feedback group," completed the same task independently and was praised for their hard work, and the experimenter corrected any incorrect groupings. Mothers of children in the interaction group were not instructed to teach them anything, but to help their children group items as an adult would in any way they felt appropriate. Afterward, both groups were asked to sort the furniture again.

The results showed that the social interaction group performed significantly better than the feedback group on the retest. As Vygotsky's theory would predict, social interaction between adult and child during a problem-solving task led to improved independent performance. Children who interacted with their mothers created more correct adult groupings than children who practiced the task and were shown the correct solution. It should be noted that this task was just beyond the child's abilities and within the zone of proximal development, and social interactions might not help very much with tasks that were far beyond the child's abilities.

Lev Vygotsky called attention to a child's zone of proximal development: The gap between what a child can do alone and what the child can do with guidance. Education within the zone of proximal development can advance a child's reasoning abilities.

Guideposts

How does Vygotsky's view of the social nature of thought differ from most Western theorists?

For Your Consideration ?

What is the fundamental difference between how Piaget and Vygotsky view the origins of development?

Stance on Basic Issues

Vygotsky's theory is obviously contextual; he goes so far as to argue that the only way to investigate the child is to view the child in a particular context. As is the case with most contextual psychologists, he does not offer any stages, but nothing in the theory would oppose their use. Vygotsky argued for the interaction of biology and cultural forces, and the theory is a very broad one emphasizing higher mental processes.

Application and Value

Vygotsky's theory stresses the importance of the cultural and historical bases of development and the process of instruction. His concept of the zone of proximal development has educational applications. Vygotsky's focus on the importance of language as a tool and the social foundation of cognitive development are challenging as well.

Criticisms and Cautions

The theory has been criticized by many. First, Vygotsky challenged the idea that development comes from within the child by basically claiming that it mainly, but not exclusively, comes from outside the individual. Some argue that he replaced a narrow view of development with one that does not give proper significance to processes that occur within the individual. He may have overemphasized the influence of culture and underestimated processes that occur within the individual.

Vygotsky's work shows us the necessity of looking at the context and not isolating the individual, but it leaves little room to consider the role of the individual within the culture. Social and cultural processes determine individual processes. But how would one account for individual creativity and the fact that people often do criticize their own cultures?

Another problem involves the measurement of the zone of proximal development (Miller, 1993). The concept is brilliant, but measuring it precisely is difficult. In addition, if teachers continually give students difficult tasks that require

Summary	Vygotsky's Sociocultural Theory

Basic Premises

1. Children develop in a social context.
2. Parents, adults, and more expert children actively teach children concepts and skills through social interaction.
3. There is a difference between what children can do themselves and what they can do with the guidance of an adult called the zone of proximal development.
4. Behavior is first directed by others then is internalized.

Value and Strengths

1. Significant attention is given to social and cultural context.
2. It integrates everyday learning and development.
3. It stresses the importance of the teaching function.
4. It places an interesting emphasis on social interaction causing a behavior that is then internalized.

Criticism and Weaknesses

1. Zone of proximal development is difficult to measure.
2. Possible overemphasis is placed on thought arising from outside the organism through social interaction.
3. Social, cultural, and historical contexts are difficult to study.

adult assistance, this might cause an undesirable dependence on the adult and a loss of motivation (Crain, 1992).

Still another difficulty is found in researching some of the cultural and historical notions of the theory. Observing people in context is a nice idea, but wider contexts are often difficult to explore and research.

Despite these problems, Vygotsky's theory offers a different view to those that emphasize development as arising from within the individual. It reminds us of the importance of the social context and social forces as well as asking us to remember the importance of instruction in the development of a child.

Bronfenbrenner's Ecological Theory

The nature of the context in which people develop was well outlined by Urie Bronfenbrenner (1986, 1979; Bronfenbrenner & Morris, 1998). Bronfenbrenner suggests that people live their lives enmeshed in many different environments at the same time (see Figure 2.2). He uses the analogy of a set of Russian dolls with each inside the other. People both affect and are affected by these multiple layers of environment. Ecological theory systematically links these environments to each other and notes how they operate and affect each other. Four different environmental systems operate.

The **microsystem** consists of the immediate interactions of the person and the environment. This face-to-face interaction may occur in the home or school (Bronfenbrenner & Crouter, 1983). It is what the individual is presently experiencing. The microsystem includes where a child lives, the people in the home, and the activities they do together. At first the child's microsystem is limited to just the home and the family, but as the child develops, additional settings become important and more people enter the microsystem.

The **mesosystem** involves the interrelationships among two or more settings in which the person actively participates. For example, the mesosystem includes

---

SOURCE: Adapted from Kopp & Krakow, (1982)

Figure 2.2 The Ecological System

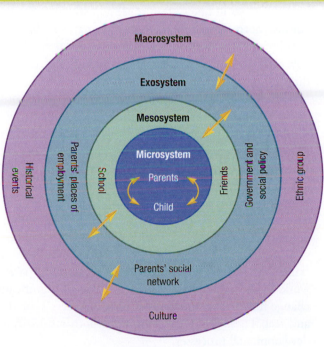

Microsystem refers to relations between the child and the immediate environment; *mesosystem* refers to the interrelationships of settings in the child's immediate environment; *exosystem* refers to social settings that affect the child but do not directly impinge on him or her; and *macrosystem* refers to the attitudes, mores, beliefs, and ideologies of the culture.

microsystem
The immediate interactions between the individual and the environment.

mesosystem
The interrelationships among two or more settings in which the person actively participates.

The relationship between children and their parents may be affected by such long-range factors as their parents' work environment and parents' network of friends.

exosystem

Settings in which the individual is not actively involved, at least at the present time, but yet affect the individual.

macrosystem

The ideology or belief system inherent in social institutions including ethnic, cultural, and religious influences, as well as the economic and political systems that exist.

the relationship between parents and the school, parents and day care center, parents and peer group. The entry of a child into a new setting causes changes in the other major settings. For example, the child's attendance in school may affect the pattern of activities and interactions occurring within the family (Bronfenbrenner & Crouter, 1983). It affects the family's routines and the time parents spend with the child.

The **exosystem** involves settings in which the child is not actively involved, at least at the present time, but yet affect the family and child, such as the parents' place of work, a class attended by older siblings (or younger ones), the parents' network of friends, or the activity of the local school board. The exosystem may directly affect the child. For example, if a school board increases class size, this may impact the children's education by affecting the teacher-child interaction. The exosystem may affect the child indirectly by making changes that impact positively or negatively on the parents' or other important people's lives. For example, the insecurity that a parent may experience at work may impact negatively on the parent-child interaction.

The **macrosystem** is composed of the ideology or belief system inherent in social institutions including ethnic, cultural, and religious influences, as well as the economic and political systems that exist (Seligman, 1991). For example, people in the United States live under a particular economic and political system that differs from that of people living in other countries. These differing social customs, ideologies, and economic systems affect the social institutions in the country and therefore the child. The availability of day care may be based on the political situation or the ideology of the system. Changes in social structure may also indirectly affect the child. For instance, the growth of single-parent families, the increased family mobility in the United States, and changes in the status of women have an effect on all systems. Within each society, a number of different micro-, meso- and exosystems operate depending on social class, ethnicity, and religious groupings.

Changes in one system cause adjustments in other systems. For example, the cultural norm of maternal employment affects the workplace, the economy, community affairs, as well as the child's microsystem. Flexible hours, the need for more day care, and more sharing of household and child-rearing responsibilities may directly impact the child's microsystem.

Ecological theory emphasizes the importance of looking beyond the current environment and appreciating the relationships between systems. A child's ability to learn to read in elementary school may depend not only on the way the child is taught in first grade but also on the relationship between the home and the school (Bronfenbrenner, 1979). It also will depend on the decisions made by others as far as school organization and staffing are concerned. Changes in political, social, and economic factors also both directly and indirectly affect the child. Since the direction of influence is reciprocal, we cannot reliably predict the future of either the environment or the person without understanding both.

Ecological theory also looks at the transitions that occur. Such ecological transitions include going to school, becoming a parent, or entering the world of work. These bring changes in roles that are significant. Roles have the power to change how people are treated, how they act, what they do, even how they think and feel. These ecological transitions both result from development and instigate developmental processes.

Stance on Basic Issues

Bronfenbrenner's stance on basic issues is similar to Vygotsky's. It is definitely contextual, is neutral on the use of stages, and accepts the interaction between the social and the biological while emphasizing the social aspects of life.

Value and Strengths

There is a growing appreciation of the various contexts that affect development (Parke, Ornstein, Reiser, & Zahn-Waxler, 1994). The fact that these systems affect each other and directly and indirectly affect children and adults expands our view of factors affecting development. The answers to seemingly simple questions such as "Does the day care experience help or harm the child?" depend on many contextual factors, such as the quality of the home and day care facility and attitudes toward day care and work. These are affected by a host of other factors. The concept of transitions and changes in role that occur encourages us to ask questions about preparation for these transitions. The acceptance of the concept of reciprocal interaction, that the person affects and is affected by the environment, means that the individual is not solely at the mercy of environmental factors; the individual has the power to affect the environment as well. Finally, ecological theory is broad enough to include social policy, cultural aspects of the environment and other macro- and exosystems.

Criticisms and Cautions

Although the theoretical view offered by ecological theory is popular, the difficulty may lie in its complexity. Most psychologists would agree that looking at the entire context of development is desirable; the question is whether it is practical. A theory that examines the individual as embedded and affected by so many social, political, and economic forces may simply be too complex to use as a basis for research. Although the conceptual view of ecological theory is valuable, it remains to be seen whether it can be practically used as a basis for research and interpretation.

For Your Consideration

One of the intriguing concepts in ecological theory is that contexts far from the child's immediate world may influence the child's development. How might the working environments of parents affect their children's lives?

Guideposts

How does Bronfenbrenner's theory expand the way child development specialists look at environmental influences?

Summary	Bronfenbrenner's Ecological Theory

Basic Premises

1. The person cannot be isolated from the context of development.
2. Human development is enmeshed in multiple environments at the same time.
3. Ecological theory links these environments to each other, noting how each operates and affects the others.
4. Transitions bring about changes in roles that change how people think and act and how they are treated.

Value and Strengths

1. It encourages a broader view of human development.
2. It shows how societal values and priorities that operate through public policy may affect the child.
3. It emphasizes the importance of specific transitions such as beginning school or becoming a parent.

Criticism and Weaknesses

1. This theory is very complex, requiring an in-depth look at the many contexts of development.
2. Some question whether the theory can be practically used as a basis for understanding development.

Developmental Theory: Yesterday, Today, and Tomorrow

A number of important advances have been made in theoretical approaches to child development that deserve some attention. First, most psychologists clearly accept the idea of reciprocal interaction, and we now understand the need to conceive of the organism as active in creating its own environment (Kagan, 1992). Rather than concentrating separately on the child or the parent, we concentrate on how each affects the other.

Second, a new appreciation of the complexity of the environment is accepted. Theoretical approaches, such as ecological theory, suggest that the environment is not a simple conception. Changes in one environmental factor may influence changes in other factors, influencing the individual's development and behavior (see *Chaos Theory* on page 71). Third, built into many relatively new theoretical approaches is an appreciation of the historical time in which the individual is living (Elder, Modell, & Parke, 1993). This appreciation emphasizes the changing nature of society and the fact that events and historical cycles are important to the understanding of development (Parke et al., 1994).

Fourth, a new appreciation of the importance of cultural variation is found. We are now more aware of cultural and subcultural membership and the need to do more research using samples of individuals whose experiences may not match those people from the majority group. In addition, we need to discover to what extent our theories hold in other cultures. This cultural sensitivity is found in Erikson's theory and also is prominent in ecological theory.

Fifth, the various areas of development interact with each other. Although it may be easier for conceptual purposes to look at the cognitive, physical, social, and biological aspects as separate realms, we know that these are integrated. The child's health may affect the child's cognitive abilities, and the child's cognitive level may affect the child's health practices (Parke et al., 1994). This linkage, although accepted, awaits further theoretical explanation.

How to Use Theories

Many child development specialists are aware that there are many ways to look at a particular behavior. This is a strength, not a weakness, since each approach has something different to offer. They are eclectic, that is, they adopt the most useful theory to explore an area rather than work from only one perspective. Such eclecticism is healthy if it allows us to appreciate the many ways a particular behavior can be studied (Rychlak, 1985).

Throughout this book, a number of different perspectives will be used. Each perspective may look at a particular aspect of development from a different point of view, but each has as its purpose a better understanding of the developing child.

Developmental psychologists consider it appropriate to use one theory to understand cognitive development and another theory to understand social development.

The Child in the 21st Century

Chaos Theory

We have soothed ourselves into imagining sudden changes as something that happens outside the normal order of things—an accident, like a car crash, are beyond our control, like a fatal illness. We do not conceive of sudden, radical, irrational change as built into the very fabric of existence, yet it is.

Chaos theory teaches us that straight linearity, which we have come to take for granted in everything from physics to fiction, simply does not exist. Linearity is an artificial way of viewing the world. Real life isn't a series of interconnected events occurring one after another like beads strung on a necklace. Life is actually a series of encounters in which one event may change those that follow in a wholly unpredictable, even devastating way.—Dr. Ian Malcolm, fictional mathematician, explains chaos theory in Michael Crichton's Jurassic Park. *(Crichton, 1989, p. 171)*

Few people had ever heard of chaos theory before reading the book or seeing the movie *Jurassic Park*. Yet, chaos theory has had an impact on physics, mathematics, and biology, and now psychologists are beginning to take notice.

As an introduction to chaos theory, think of a child being raised in a carefully controlled environment. A psychologist checks every parental action to make certain it is in keeping with our best theories of how to optimize the child's development. Nutritionists carefully monitor the child's diet, and doctors make sure the child gets enough sleep. Specialists design the child's social interactions and determine the programs the child watches on television. The entire environment is controlled, and nothing is left to chance.

Does this sound like nonsense to you? Of course it does. This is not the usual way people live. It is not the way children are raised. In reality, chance occurrences affect everyone; children and adults. Theodor Geisel (Dr. Seuss) had just had his book *And to Think That I Saw It on Mulberry Street* rejected by more than 20 publishers when he ran into an old friend on Madison Avenue in Manhattan who just happened to be an editor of children's books for a major publisher. He was interested in seeing Geisel's work and gave him a contract 20 minutes later. The book was a huge success, beginning a spectacular career, and the book has since had more than 20 printings (Wallace, Wallechinsky, Wallace, & Wallace, 1981). No one is claiming that Dr. Seuss would never have found a publisher, but the chance meeting which could not be predicted certainly changed Geisel's life and affected in some way the lives of many children. One of the theorists presented in this chapter, Albert Bandura (1982), discusses the notion that people's lives can be influenced by unusual and chance events. In the same way, people's environments are very complicated, and real life does not allow for the type of control that would make prediction simple and neat.

Rather than considering these chance events as "error," chaos theory welcomes them and considers them a source of study (Duke, 1994). Chaos theory attempts to understand and explain events that seem spontaneous and unpredictable. Phenomena studied by chaos theory display three general characteristics. First, the behavior appears to be disordered and random, such as the branching of a lightening bolt or the path of a falling leaf. Second, these behaviors can change radically in response to very brief and seemingly insignificant events, as a child blowing on that falling leaf will change the pattern of its fall. Third, phenomena that appear chaotic may actually follow detectable patterns if one looks closely or knows how to look at them ("Chaos Comes to Psychology," 1993). Some people misunderstand chaos theory, arguing that behavior and development are unpredictable. This is not true. Chaos theory proposes that, although a lack of predictability is to be expected when looking at specific patterns, definite patterns (which often include chance occurrences) are seen at a more global level of analysis (Duke, 1994). Chaos theory is actually a middle ground between a belief in total regularity and one in total randomness.

To explain this, one needs to understand the concept of an attractor, which is a point or a pattern around which some phenomenon is drawn. Attractors allow a degree of predictability. For instance, if you place a hot coffee cup down in a room it may be somewhat difficult to predict its exact temperature five minutes from now, but you can predict that eventually the coffee will become room temperature. The attractor concept allows us to understand how behavior can be seen as both stable and variable at the same time. The behavior of developing organisms is neither completely stereotyped nor random (Thelen, 1986). The behavior fluctuates, but only within limits, and within these boundaries we can see attractors. Traits such as morality, religiosity, competitiveness, or aggression around which many behaviors seem to revolve may be considered attractors.

Looking at the nature of a long-term loving relationship may make the concept of attractors somewhat clearer. Anyone who has been in a long-term relationship knows that there are times in which, despite the constant love, more harmony or discord exists. If someone conducting research chooses a point at which the relationship shows more discord and then generalizes this to be the nature of the relationship, the researcher will be in error. If you look at these patterns of harmony and discord over the long term you will see both as part of the relationship. The fluctuations are real and show a range of variation in the behavior around the relationship.

The pattern of behaviors around an attractor are recognizable but rarely identical. If you were asked to draw a number of circles, you would find that although all your drawings are easily recognizable as circles, they differ somewhat in size and form. A memory of an event, for instance, may be seen as an attractor but the memory may vary somewhat with each telling of the event.

Why does this occur? Chaos theory uses a concept called sensitive dependence on initial conditions to explain this lack of exact reoccurrence (Barton, 1994; Mandel, 1995). If two sets of conditions differ by even a very small degree at the outset, the specific solutions will diverge dramatically in the long run (Barton, 1994). Consider the problem of a person going on a 20-mile hike with a compass

that is off by only one degree. If the person discovers this problem after only five minutes or so, an easy correction can be made and the person will find that he is not far from where he should be. However, what if the group finds that a mistake has occurred after walking for many hours? Now that 1 degree mistake means much more, and they are far from their goal and probably lost. Small differences in the initial conditions, many of which may not be known, can result in significant differences in the long term.

This is sometimes called the *butterfly effect*, originally credited to Edward Lorenz, a meteorologist and an important figure in the development of chaos theory. If a butterfly flaps its wings in China, could it affect the weather in Oklahoma (Mandel, 1995)? Theoretically, such a trivial event at a critical time may have an important effect on the way an emergent weather system develops. Minor local events may then serve to reduce predictability by altering the course of future events.

This same phenomenon may be important to understanding development. Psychologists, naturally, look at major life events, especially traumatic ones, as causes of behavior. Chaos theory would have us look at small events that may occur at crucial times. A small discussion with a parent, a hug at the right time, a game of chess with a child may have as much or even a greater impact on a child's development than the major events that are often the focus of our research studies. Such minor events in the long run may be very important. Perhaps small changes in parenting practices or teaching strategies, especially when children are young, may not show immediate results but may be very significant over the long run (Duke, 1994).

How influential chaos theory will be is still a question. Many social scientists do not have the sophisticated mathematical knowledge necessary to fully appreciate the theory, which was originally meant for physicists and mathematicians (Mandel, 1995). The extent to which a theory borrowed from physics and mathematics can be applied to child development and behavior is also a question (Barton, 1994).

In the book *Jurassic Park*, chaos theory predicted that the scientists and gamekeepers in that park filled with dinosaurs could not control everything, and the resultant adventures and tragedy of that situation follow. However, chaos theory has its positive side as it leaves us with a deep sense of humility. It brings the mystery and adventure back into life. It emphasizes life's complexity, how small changes may reap large rewards over time, and how patterns of behavior may be similar yet not identical. At the same time it does not mean that predictability is impossible for over the long run events and behavior show patterns that can be identified. We may someday be able to understand how small changes at critical times fit into our lives, and this may give us a better understanding of an entire course of behavior and development.

What do you think?

To what extent do you believe that chance forces that are spontaneous and relatively unpredictable affect a child's development? What are some of these chance occurrences? How have they affected your life?

You can explore the questions above using InfoTrac College Edition. Hint: enter search terms *Chaos Theory, Children* and *Death*.

Summary

1. Theories give facts their meaning and help us interpret data. Theories allow us to relate one fact to another and predict behavior.

2. A good theory is determined by its usefulness, testability, ability to predict behavior, and inclusiveness.

3. Organismic theories perceive beings as internally motivated to develop, seeing them as actively involved in their own development and as organized wholes. Mechanistic views see organisms as machines who can be understood by examining how their discrete elements work. Development is impelled by external factors. Contextual theories look at how the organism develops within a particular context and historical time. Theories also differ in their attitude toward the use of stages, the balance between nature and nurture, and the type of behaviors with which they are most concerned.

4. Jean Piaget investigated children's cognitive, or intellectual development. He noted that children do not think like adults and described four stages through which children pass between birth and adolescence. Piaget's theory is noteworthy because of his discovery of the sequences of development leading to a mature understanding of such concepts as object permanence and causality. Piaget also viewed the child as actively involved with the environment and stressed the importance of discovery. His theory has been criticized because it may underestimate the importance of formal learning.

5. Information-processing theory focuses on the way people take in information, process it, and finally act on it. Such factors as attention, perception, memory, and response systems are investigated. It is a noteworthy approach because it yields specific information on how a child solves a particular problem. However, it is not as well-developed as other theoretical approaches, and only additional experimentation will determine how useful it will be.

6. Psychoanalytic theory emphasizes the importance of the early parent-child relationship. Freud argued that children progress through five psychosexual stages that involve the unfolding of the sexual instinct. Freud's concepts of stage development, infantile and child sexuality, unconscious motivation, and defense mechanisms are noteworthy. Psychoanalytic theory has been criticized because it is difficult to test, considers sexuality the prime motivation, and emphasizes deviancy.

7. Erik Erikson argued that people proceed through eight stages from the cradle to the grave. Each stage presents people with different tasks. If a task is successfully negotiated, there is a positive outcome; if not, there is a negative outcome. Erikson's theory is noteworthy because it provides a good framework for viewing development, emphasizes the importance of culture and history, and sees development as continuing throughout the life span. It has been criticized because it is overly broad and general, and difficult to explore experimentally.

8. Learning theorists or behaviorists do not emphasize the concept of stages but stress the importance of classical conditioning and operant conditioning. Behaviorism has been criticized for being too mechanical and not adequately taking consciousness and thought processes into consideration.

9. Social learning theorists emphasize the importance of observation learning to the understanding of behavior. Social learning theory has been criticized as lacking a developmental framework.

10. Vygotsky's sociocultural theory emphasizes the cultural context in which children live. Cultures transmit ways of dealing with the world through social interactions between older people and youth. Children internalize what they learn from social interactions. Vygotsky's work has become increasingly popular as psychologists begin to appreciate the importance of culture and context in child development. His emphasis on the teaching function is also of interest. His theory slights developmental processes that arise from within the child and does not adequately deal with the role of the individual within the culture.

11. Ecological theory takes a broad view of the environment. People are affected by multiple layers of context. The microsystem consists of the immediate interactions between the person and the environment. The mesosystem involves the interrelationships among two or more settings in which the person actively participates. The exosystem involves settings in which the person is not actively involved now but that affect the family and child, such as the parents' place of work. The macrosystem is composed of the ideology or belief system inherent in social institutions. Changes in each system have an impact on the other systems and eventually on the person's microsystem. This theory reminds us of the importance of the total environmental context, but some wonder whether it is really possible to investigate all the layers of context.

12. The field of child development lacks a unified theory that covers every aspect of development. A researcher will choose the theory that seems most useful in understanding the developmental phenomena of interest.

Review

Theories that view development as motivated chiefly by forces arising from within the individual and view human beings as constantly in the process of developing or becoming are referred to as (1)_____ theories. Other theories, called (2)_____ theories, see the human being as basically a machine composed of parts that can be studied independently and influenced by external forces. Some theories, called (3)_____ theories, argue that child development can only be understood by taking the entire environment into account, including the social, historical and political environment. Some theories view children as developing in a steplike, discontinuous process through various (4)_____ while others do not.

Jean Piaget is credited with a valuable theory of (5)_____ development. There are four elements to development: (6)_____ , (7)_____ , (8)_____ and (9)_____ . Children organize their actions and thoughts in terms of (10)_____ . When these actions and thoughts are organized in terms that are more symbolic and mental, they are called (11)_____ . Piaget also argued that children adapt to their environment through two processes. In the process of (12)_____ , information is changed to fit into one's already existing cognitive structure, In the process of (13)_____ , children change their cognitive structure in order to account for new information. Piaget described development in terms of four stages. In the first stage or (14)_____ stage, young children deal with the world through their senses and motor activity. They develop (15)_____ , the concept that things don't disappear just because they are out of sight. During the second stage, called the (16)_____ , children are egocentric and do not understand that a cup and a glass may hold the same amount because they don't look the same. In the third stage or (17)_____ stage, children are no longer as egocentric but still have difficulty coping with abstractions. The ability to understand abstract ideas arises during the last stage or (18)_____ stage.

Another theoretical view that is useful in exploring the cognitive development of children is called the (19)_____ approach, which emphasizes the importance of how people take in information, represent it in memory, and later retrieve it for use.

Freud's psychoanalytic theory argues that there are three levels of consciousness, the (20)_____ , (21)_____ , and the (22)_____ . To explain the workings of the mind, Freud postulated three constructs. The (23)_____ is the source of our drives, the (24)_____ mediates between what we want and what society allows, while the (25)_____ is the conscience. If anxiety becomes too great, people may adopt an unconscious and automatic strategy for dealing with it called a (26)_____ . In Freud's first stage, called (27)_____ , children gain satisfaction through sucking and later biting. Fixation during the second stage, called the (28)_____ stage, may result in a very fastidious or sloppy individual. During the (29)_____ stage, the child negotiates the Oedipus complex. Sexuality is dormant during the (30)_____ stage, and, finally, in the last stage or (31)_____ stage, adolescents turn their urges to a boyfriend or girlfriend.

Erik Erikson's psychosocial theory is based on the (32)_____ principle that children develop according to preset maturational steps and that societies are structured to invite and encourage challenges that occur during these stages. Erikson argued that people go through eight stages between birth and old age. For example, the first psychosocial crisis is (33)_____ versus (34)_____ during which it is important for the infant to develop a positive attitude toward life.

Some psychologists called (35)_____ argue that children's development and behavior is based on what they learn. It is the (36)_____ that determines behavior. One process of learning called (37)_____ involves the process whereby an individual associates one stimulus with a stimulus that causes a particular response until the original stimulus causes the response. Another process, called (38)_____ , is based on the premise that behavior is determined by its consequences.

(39)_____ theory looks at the models the child is exposed to and how the child learns through observation. A child's judgment of whether he or she can do something is called (40)_____ . The concept of (41)_____ argues that people's individual characteristics, behavior and environmental factors interact.

Vygotsky's theory, called (42)_____ theory, emphasizes the manner in which children acquire ways of thinking and behavior that allow them to live in a particular culture. Cultures transmit ways of thinking through (43)_____ . Vygotsky was most interested in the teaching function. He argued that psychologists should be more interested in children's potential and used the concept of (44)_____ to describe the difference between a child's actual development when working alone and level of potential development determined by problem solving with the guidance of a competent partner.

Another contextual theory is Bronfenbrenner's (45)_____ theory. It sees the individual as nested among many layers of environment. For example, the (46)_____ consists of the immediate interactions between the child and the environment, while the (47)_____ involves the interrelationships between two or more settings in which the child is involved. The (48)_____ consists of the settings in which the child is not yet involved but affect the child, such as the parents' place of work, and the (49)_____ consists of the ideology and political and economic system under which people live. Many child development specialists are (50)_____ ; that is, they use different theories under different circumstances.

InfoTrac

For additional readings, explore InfoTrac College Edition, our online library.
Go to http://www.infotrac-college.com/wadsworth.
Hint: enter the search terms *Freud on Civilization*, *Chaos Theory*, and *Pyschosocial Theory*.

What's on the web

Jean Piaget Society
http://www.piaget.org

Classic Theories of Child Devlopment
http://idealist.com/children/cdw.html

Sigmund Freud's Psychoanalytic Theory
http://www.utm.edu/research/iep/f/freud.htm

Vygotsky's Theory
http://csunix1.lvc.edu/~b_rehm/Vygotskyindex.html

The Wadsworth Psychology Study Center Web Site
Go to the Wadsworth Psychology Study Center at http://psychology.wadsworth.com/ for quiz questions, research updates, hot topics, interactive exercises, and suggested readings in the InfoTrac College Edition related to this chapter.

Answers 1. organismic; 2. mechanistic; 3. contextual; 4. stages; 5. cognitive; 6. maturation; 7. experience; 8. social transmission; 9. equilibration; 10. schemata; 11. operations; 12. assimilation; 13. accommodation; 14. sensorimotor; 15. object permanence; 16. preoperational; 17. concrete operational; 18. formal operational; 19. information-processing; 20. conscious; 21. preconscious; 22. unconscious; 23. id; 24. ego; 25. superego; 26. defense mechanism; 27. oral; 28. anal; 29. phallic; 30. latency; 31. genital; 32. epigenetic; 33. trust; 34. mistrust; 35. behaviorists; 36. environment; 37. classical conditioning; 38. operant conditioning; 39. Social learning; 40. self-efficacy; 41. reciprocal determinism; 42. sociocultural; 43. social interaction; 44. zone of proximal development; 45. ecological; 46. microsystem; 47. mesosystem; 48. exosystem; 49. macrosystem; 50. eclectic

Mechanisms *of* Change:

CHAPTER OUTLINE

Questions Without Easy Answers

Genetic Transmission

Determining Genetic Contribution

Physical Characteristics

Temperament

Behavioral Traits and Psychopathology

Shared and Unshared Environments:
How Can Siblings Be So Different?

Rate of Development

Intelligence

Genetic Influence on Disease

Models of Genetic Influence

The New Reality

ARE THESE STATEMENTS
True *or* False?

1. If genetic factors underlie a trait, it cannot be altered by environmental means.
2. Identical twins share the same genes, whereas fraternal twins are no more genetically similar than any other pair of siblings.
3. If neither the mother nor father show a particular trait, it cannot be transmitted to their offspring.
4. Color blindness is found mostly in males.
5. Psychologists believe that some behavioral differences observed among infants may be due to genetic factors.
6. Identical twins reared apart are more similar in intelligence than fraternal twins reared together.
7. Enrichment programs have failed to raise children's intelligence levels even over a short period of time.
8. Most children with Down syndrome are not diagnosed until they enter kindergarten or first grade.
9. Schizophrenia, like cystic fibrosis or Tay-Sachs disease, is transmitted directly from parent to child.
10. Reliable research demonstrates that genetic factors underlie alcoholism.

ANSWERS: 1. *False.* 2. *True.* 3. *False.* 4. *True.* 5. *True.* 6. *True.* 7. *True.* 8. *False.* 9. *False.* 10. *True.*

Genetic *and* Environmental Interaction

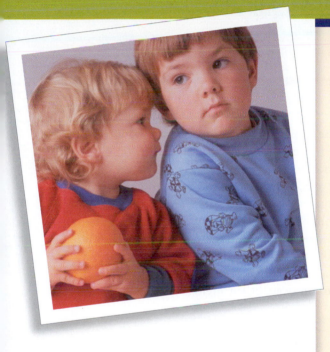

Questions Without Easy Answers

"How can my children be so different from one another?" one parent asked. *"My children have the same mother and father and share the same home, yet they don't seem to have much in common."* How can these large differences in the personality and behavior of siblings be explained?

You and your spouse decide to adopt a child. After a waiting period, you are told that an infant will be available for adoption very soon. Although you understand that you will not be told the parents' identities, would you have any questions about what the parents were like or their genetic background? Do you think you are entitled to some information about the parents?

Interest in the genetic influence on development, personality, and physical and mental health is greater than ever before. New research showing that particular genes place people at risk for diseases or predispose people to act in a certain manner constantly appears in newspapers and magazines. Yet, many people do not understand the true nature of genetic influence. For example, some people believe that having a gene for a particular trait means that the person is certain to show that trait. This is a gross overstatement.

In most cases, having a particular gene may predispose an individual—that is, make it more likely for that person—to show a trait, but the environment determines whether the individual actually shows it. If genetic endowment contributes to alcoholism or aggressiveness, someone who inherits these genes would have a greater chance of developing alcoholism or showing aggressiveness, but environmental factors would play a crucial role.

Other people incorrectly believe that if genetic factors underlie a trait, the trait cannot be altered. Genetic influence does not imply that the behavior cannot be changed. Although genetic endowment plays a role in determining intelligence, it is possible to raise a child's intelligence level by changing the child's environment. Nothing is as damaging as the belief that genetic influence means that some behavior or characteristic is carved in stone.

This chapter investigates the manner in which genetic and environmental factors influence development and behavior. As we shall see, the two interact in a complex manner to produce the developmental change and behavior we see in everyday life.

Genetic Transmission

The basic unit of heredity is the **gene,** which is composed of deoxyribonucleic acid (DNA). Human beings are believed to have between 50,000 and 100,000 genes (Cummings, 1995). Genes are carried on rod-shaped structures of various sizes called **chromosomes.** Each animal species has its own number of chromosomes. The normal human being has a complement of 46 chromosomes, or 23 pairs (see Figure 3.1). The same 46 chromosomes are found in every cell of the body except the **gametes,** or sex cells. Of the 23 pairs of chromosomes, 22 pairs are numbered according to their size, with chromosome 1 being the largest and chromosome 22, the smallest (Collins & Fink, 1995a). The 23rd chromosome pair is the sex chromosome and determines gender. In a process called **meiosis,** the sex cells divide

Figure 3.1	Chromosomes and Genes

Genes are carried on chromosomes. Each normal human being has 23 pairs of chromosomes.

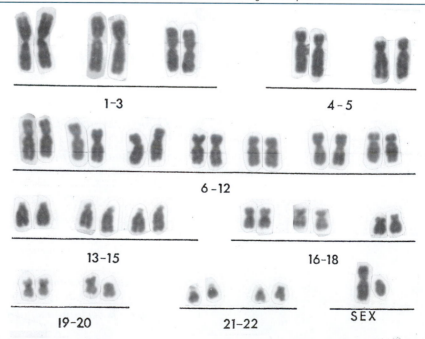

1–3   4–5
6–12
13–15   16–18
19–20   21–22   SEX

gene
The basic unit of heredity.

gametes
The scientific term for the sex cells.

chromosomes
Rod-shaped structures that carry the genes.

meiosis
The process by which sex cells divide to form two cells, each containing 23 chromosomes.

crossing over
The process occurring during meiosis in which genetic material on one chromosome is exchanged with material from the other.

monozygotic (identical) twins
Twins who develop from one fertilized egg and have an identical genetic structure.

dizygotic (fraternal) twins
Twins resulting from fertilization of two eggs by two different sperm and whose genetic composition is no more similar than any other pair of siblings.

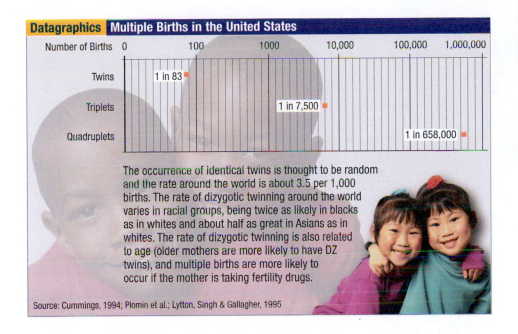

Number of Births: 0 — 100 — 1000 — 10,000 — 100,000 — 1,000,000

Twins — 1 in 83
Triplets — 1 in 7,500
Quadruplets — 1 in 658,000

The occurrence of identical twins is thought to be random and the rate around the world is about 3.5 per 1,000 births. The rate of dizygotic twinning around the world varies in racial groups, being twice as likely in blacks as in whites and about half as great in Asians as in whites. The rate of dizygotic twinning is also related to age (older mothers are more likely to have DZ twins), and multiple births are more likely to occur if the mother is taking fertility drugs.

Source: Cummings, 1994; Plomin et al.; Lytton, Singh & Gallagher, 1995

to form two cells containing 23 chromosomes each. This allows human beings to maintain the same complement of 46 chromosomes from generation to generation. The splitting of cells is random, and which one of the pair of like chromosomes ends up in which of the split cells is a matter of chance. There are over 8 million different possibilities in this process alone.

During the process of meiosis, some of the genetic material on one chromosome may be exchanged with material from another (Cummings, 1995). This exchange is called **crossing over.** When crossing over is taken into consideration, the chances that any two individuals are genetically identical are practically zero.

Although human beings share a common species inheritance—we each have two eyes, two ears, and one stomach—each person is also genetically unique. The only exception is identical twins, or **monozygotic twins,** who result from a single egg and sperm and who share the same genetic composition. Fraternal twins, or **dizygotic twins,** result from two different eggs being fertilized by two different sperm and are no more similar than any other pair of siblings. About 75% of all twin pairs are fraternal twins (Eder, 1995).

Identical twins share precisely the same genetic makeup. Fraternal twins are no more genetically alike than any other pair of siblings.

Guideposts

How does nature assure genetic uniqueness?

Identical twins share the same genes, whereas fraternal twins are no more genetically similar than any other pair of siblings.

For Your Consideration

If you had monozygotic twins, would you dress them identically? Would you treat them the same? Why or why not?

If this couple chooses to have another child, what are the odds that the child will be another girl?

The Sex Chromosomes

Twenty-two of the 23 pairs of chromosomes look identical. However, the 23rd pair is different. There are two types: the X chromosome and the Y chromosome. The genetic composition of a male is XY, while females have two X chromosomes. When meiosis occurs, a male contributes an X chromosome and a Y chromosome, while the female contributes two X chromosomes. If, during conception, the sperm carrying the X chromosome penetrates the egg's membrane, the offspring will be female. If the sperm carrying the Y chromosome penetrates, the child will be male. Figure 3.2 shows that the chances are 50-50 that the offspring will be a male. The situation is actually somewhat more complicated because environmental factors such as the conditions within the vagina can also influence the "odds" of conceiving a male or a female child.

From a strictly genetic point of view, the chances are the same for each conception. Even if you have seven boys, the chances are still 50-50 that the next child will be a girl. Many people fail to understand this basic point, and it is true for all inherited characteristics as well. Some people incorrectly believe that if their first child has a particular genetic problem, the chances of having a normal child are increased or decreased. Reproduction does not work that way. Every conception starts from square one again, and the same odds exist for every pregnancy.

Recently, techniques to increase the probability that a couple may conceive a boy or a girl as they choose, called **sex selection,** have been the focus of much media attention. Some techniques are quite sophisticated and require separating the X-carrying sperm followed by artificial insemination. Private companies provide this service and sometimes advertise that the method is 75 to 80% effective in choosing the gender of a child (Cummings, 1995). The use of sex selection is very controversial and the subject of much discussion.

Many societies have a tradition of preferring male children, especially for their first child, and most people who say they would use sex selection would do so to have a firstborn male (Steinbacher & Gilroy, 1996). Between 18% and 45% of all respondents say they are willing to use sex selection technology, and the overwhelming majority of both males and females who say they would use the techniques would do so to have a firstborn son. Evidence shows that the percentage of college students who say they would be willing to use the technology has increased (Gilroy & Steinbacher, 1983, 1991).

If sophisticated techniques were made available, the gender ratio might be placed in imbalance, resulting in an excess of males. In societies such as China, where there is a strong preference for sons and governmental policies encouraging families to have only one child, the extensive use of these techniques could cause

sex chromosomes

The 23rd pair of chromosomes, which determines the gender of the organism.

sex selection

Techniques that allow couples to choose the gender of their child.

Figure 3.2 **Determination of Sex**

The child's mother can contribute only an X chromosome, while the child's father can contribute an X or Y. Statistically, 50% of the conceptions will produce males, and 50% will produce females. However, other factors, such as conditions in the vagina, influence whether an X- or Y-carrying sperm will reach and penetrate the egg.

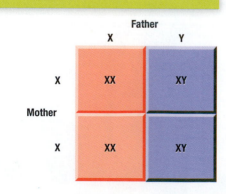

major demographic changes. Questions arise as to whether parents should have the right to use sophisticated laboratory techniques without regard to the possible social consequences or whether the government has the right to control the use of these techniques (Cummings, 1995). These are difficult questions to answer. The results of a survey of the attitudes of **genetic counselors** toward sex selection can be found in Table 3.1.

Table 3.1	Genetic Counselors and Sex Selection

Responses to outright requests for sex selection (n = 2,903 geneticists): % would perform prenatal diagnosis for sex selection and provide requested information (in parentheses: additional % who would refer)

Area/country	1. Single woman wants girl	2. Couple with four girls wants boy	3. Poor couple with five boys wants girl	4. Non-Western couple wants boy	5. Couple in 40s wants girl
English-speaking nations					
Australia	21 (7)	21 (29)	29 (36)	29 (29)	36 (21)
Canada	17 (33)	17 (34)	21 (32)	21 (39)	38 (29)
United Kingdom	8 (25)	12 (27)	14 (24)	17 (34)	22 (27)
United States	35 (36)	34 (38)	38 (37)	38 (38)	57 (28)
Western Europe					
France	4 (3)	8 (1)	9 (1)	10 (13)	24 (4)
Sweden	11 (11)	11 (11)	25 (8)	22 (11)	22 (11)
Asia					
China	34 (6)	24 (3)	28 (2)	35 (14)	29 (4)
Japan	10 (2)	18 (2)	22 (2)	19 (11)	19 (3)
Latin America					
Mexico	39 (3)	38 (3)	28 (2)	28 (2)	53 (3)
Total	27 (20)	29 (20)	31 (20)	35 (24)	44 (15)
Total excluding U.S.	23 (9)	26 (9)	27 (10)	33 (15)	39 (9)

1. A single woman wishes to become a mother. She wants a girl because a girl will be easier to raise. She may decide to terminate a male fetus.
2. A couple with four daughters desires a son. The woman is pregnant. They say that they will abort a female fetus.
3. A poor family has five sons. The sixth pregnancy is unwanted, but they say they will make financial sacrifices if the fetus is a girl. Otherwise, they will have an abortion.
4. A woman from a non-Western culture that prefers sons has so far given birth to two daughters. Her husband wants a small family but also wants a son. He says that if she has another daughter, he will divorce and send her and her daughters back to their own country and abandon them.
5. A professional couple in their early 40s has two teenaged sons. The pregnancy is unexpected. They were going to have an abortion but have decided to wait until they find out the fetus's sex. If it is a girl, they will carry it to term.

SOURCE: Wertz & Fletcher (1998)

ACTION / REACTION

Determining the Gender of Your Child

You have been married for 8 years and have three children, all girls. You and your spouse would like a fourth child, and both you and your spouse would prefer a boy since you already have three girls. You have both been reading about ways of increasing the odds that a male is conceived. You are thinking of trying a method of sex selection but are not certain.

1. *Assuming that the method is completely safe, would you use a method to increase your chances of conceiving a child of a particular gender?*
2. *If this was your first child, would you consider using it?*

ACTION / REACTION

genetic counselors
Specially educated professionals who help couples understand the genetic risks involved in producing offspring.

Transmitting Dominant and Recessive Traits

How do parents transmit traits to their offspring? With some select characteristics that are inherited because of one gene pair, the possibilities that an offspring will inherit a particular trait can be easily determined. A trait that is expressed when only one gene is present is considered **dominant.** Traits that become visible only when two genes (one from mother and one from father) are present are called **recessive.**

A number of genetic disorders follow this pattern, as do some characteristics in human beings. For instance, dark hair is dominant over blond hair, freckles over no freckles, and dimples over no dimples. These characteristics are all due to one gene pair. Figure 3.3 shows the transmission of a dominant trait, in this case six fingers.

Guideposts

How are dominant characteristics transmitted?

Figure 3.3   Transmission of a Dominant Trait: Six Fingers

A. When One Parent Has One Gene for Six Fingers
When one parent has one gene for six fingers, there is a 50% chance that the child will have six fingers.

B. When Both Parents Have One Gene for Six Fingers
When both parents have one gene for six fingers, there is a 25% chance that a child will have two genes for six fingers and thus have six fingers. There is a 50% chance that a child will have one gene for six fingers and, since this is a dominant trait, will have six fingers. There is only a 25% chance that a child will not have a gene for six fingers and so will have five fingers.

A

	Father	
	6 fingers	5 fingers
5 fingers	6 fingers 5 fingers	5 fingers 5 fingers
Mother		
5 fingers	6 fingers 5 fingers	5 fingers 5 fingers

B

	Father	
	6 fingers	5 fingers
6 fingers	6 fingers 6 fingers	5 fingers 6 fingers
Mother		
5 fingers	6 fingers 5 fingers	5 fingers 5 fingers

T
F
3

If neither mother nor father show a particular trait, it cannot be transmitted to their offspring.

Guideposts

How are recessive characteristics transmitted?

dominant traits
Traits that require the presence of only one gene.

recessive traits
Traits that require the presence of two genes.

carrier
A person who possesses a particular gene or group of genes for a trait, who does not show the trait but can pass it on to his or her offspring.

If neither you nor your spouse shows a particular trait, it can still be passed on to offspring if the trait is recessive. If both parents have one gene for a recessive trait such as the disease cystic fibrosis, a disease that causes respiratory problems, it is possible for a child to inherit the trait. Cystic fibrosis is caused by an abnormal pair of genes on chromosome 7, and it manifests itself only when both parents transmit the abnormal gene to their child (Stern, 1997). Since cystic fibrosis is caused by two abnormal genes, the only way a child can be afflicted with it is for both parents to have the abnormal gene. Neither the mother nor the father need show any symptoms of the disorder, because the disorder is recessive and requires two genes for it to show itself. A person who has one normal gene and one abnormal gene for a recessive trait is called a **carrier,** because the individual will not show the disorder but can pass the abnormal gene to his or her offspring. Figure 3.4 shows the odds of having a child with cystic fibrosis if two carriers marry.

Polygenic Inheritance

If the relationship between genetics and particular characteristics or behaviors were always so simple, predicting traits would be easy. But genetic transmission is not always so direct. Comparatively few human traits are transmitted in the manner just described. In addition, most of the characteristics discussed so far are caused exclusively by a person's genes. The effects of the environment on the expression of one's genetic endowment have scarcely been mentioned. In the real world, the relationship between genetic endowment and the behaviors or characteristics an individual shows is more complicated (Scarr & Kidd, 1983). Simple models of

Figure 3.4 Transmission of a Recessive Trait: Cystic Fibrosis When Each Parent Carries One Gene

When both the mother and the father carry the gene for cystic fibrosis, the chances are 25% that an offspring will have the disease (cystic fibrosis–cystic fibrosis), 50% that the child will be a carrier (cystic fibrosis–normal), and 25% that the child will not have the disorder or be a carrier.

NOTE: Some other genetic diseases such as Tay-Sachs disease and phenylketonuria are transmitted in the same way as cystic fibrosis.

	Father	
Mother	Normal gene	Cystic fibrosis
Normal gene	Normal gene / Normal gene	Cystic fibrosis / Normal gene
Cystic fibrosis	Normal gene / Cystic fibrosis	Cystic fibrosis / Cystic fibrosis

prediction soon break down as we consider characteristics determined by many gene pairs and that are affected by the environment.

When a characteristic is influenced by more than one pair of genes, the mechanism of inheritance is **polygenic** or **multigenic.** The term **multifactorial** describes a trait that is influenced both by genes and by the environment. However, the terms **polygenic, multigenic,** and **multifactorial** are often used interchangeably. Skin color is a polygenic trait; four gene pairs may be involved with no evidence of dominance (Cummings, 1995). The environment also influences the trait. If you have light skin and spend time in the sun, you might get tan. Your genetic makeup has not changed, but your outward appearance has.

To better describe the relationship between genes and environmental factors, scientists use the term **genotype** to refer to the specific composition of an individual's genes, and **phenotype** to refer to the observable characteristics of an individual. The phenotype and genotype may be the same or different. A person may have one hair color but choose to dye it, thereby changing the phenotype—that is, the color that is shown—but the genotype still remains. New hair that grows will show the original color.

Guideposts
What is multifactorial inheritance?

Guideposts
Does a person's genotype and phenotype have to be the same?

ACTION / REACTION

A Secret to Keep?

Kathy and Tom met in their second year of college and became engaged two years later. They agree on most things and are sensitive to each other's feelings. A few nights ago, they watched a television special on cystic fibrosis. The sufferings of a child afflicted with the disorder were depicted graphically, as were the parents' problems in dealing with the child's illness and the parents' own emotions.

Tom stated categorically that he couldn't take that situation and that "no life was better than that existence." Kathy felt a pang. Her sister had died from the disease five years before she and Tom met. Kathy had told Tom that her sister died of pneumonia. Kathy doesn't know whether she should tell Tom. She knows something about the disease, and since it doesn't run in Tom's family, their children won't have cystic fibrosis. (Kathy doesn't realize that Tom could be a carrier.) Why tell Tom something that could upset their marriage plans, when she reasons that it couldn't have any effect on their children? On the other hand, Kathy recognizes that not being completely honest with Tom is a poor way to start a marriage.

1. *If you were Kathy, would you tell Tom? Why or why not?*
2. *If you were Kathy's parents, would you insist that your child tell Tom?*
3. *If you were Tom, would you want to know? How would you react to the news?*
4. *Do people have a moral obligation to inform anyone about their genetic background?*

ACTION / REACTION

polygenic or multigenic traits
Characteristics that are influenced by more than one pair of genes.

multifactorial traits
Traits that are influenced both by genes and by the environment.

genotype
The genetic configuration of the individual.

phenotype
The observable characteristics of the individual.

Sex-Linked Traits

Sex-linked traits are those that are transmitted on the 23rd chromosome pair (sex chromosomes). The X chromosome is three times as large as the Y and contains many more genes than the Y. Many of the genes found on the X chromosome do not exist at all on the Y. This has profound consequences for males.

Consider what might happen if a female had one defective gene for a recessive trait and one gene for normal functioning that is dominant on the 23rd chromosome. Let us also assume that these genes are found only on the X, not on the Y. The female would not show the effects of the recessive gene, because she possesses a gene for normal functioning to counter it. But what would happen if she had children? She could pass on both her normal gene and the abnormal gene, but unlike our previous cases, the child's gender becomes crucial. As you can see in Figure 3.5, frame 4, if the mother passes on her abnormal gene on her X chromosome and the father passes his Y that does not contain any gene for this trait, the result is a male who will inherit the disorder. The defective gene on the X has no corresponding normal gene to counter it, so the defective gene on the X is in a position to show itself. Sex-linked traits involve female carriers, but it is the male who inherits the trait.

A considerable amount of interest in sex-linked traits exists today. Among the proven sex-linked traits are hemophilia (a severe blood disorder involving a deficiency in the blood's ability to clot) and color blindness. Because a female has two X chromosomes, her chances of being a hemophiliac are negligible. She is also far less likely to be color-blind. For example, red-green color blindness occurs in about 8% of all males but in less than 0.5% of females (Restak, 1988).

Could some of the other differences between males and females be genetically determined? Perhaps the fact that women normally outlive men can be explained partially by genetic endowment (Kermis, 1984). Psychologists differ sharply on such questions. Except for some genetic diseases and physical traits, the interaction of genes with the environment is crucial to understanding the end product. Still, the possibility of explaining some gender differences using the mechanism of sex-linked genetic transmission is tempting.

Color blindness is found mostly in males.

Why is it that males are more likely to show sex-linked traits than females?

Figure 3.5 **Sex-Linked Inheritance**

If the mother and father both contribute a normal X, as in frame 1, the child will be a female who will show no signs of the disorder and will not pass the disorder on to her offspring. If the mother contributes an abnormal gene on the X chromosome and the father contributes a normal gene for the same trait from the X, the child will be a female who will not show any signs of the disorder but will be a carrier like her mother (frame 2). If the mother contributes a normal gene and the father contributes his Y, as shown in frame 3, the offspring will be a male who will not show any signs of the disorder or be able to pass the disorder on. If the mother transmits the abnormal X chromosome and the father a Y, the resulting male offspring will show signs of the disorder and may pass it on to the next generation (frame 4). The abnormal gene on the X has no corresponding normal gene to counter it, so the abnormal gene on the X is in a position to show itself.

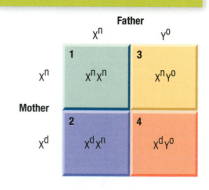

	Father	
	X^n	Y^0
Mother X^n	**1** $X^n X^n$	**3** $X^n Y^0$
X^d	**2** $X^d X^n$	**4** $X^d Y^0$

n = normal; d = gene for a disorder (for example, hemophilia or color blindness).

sex-linked traits
Traits that are inherited through genes found on the sex chromosomes.

Determining Genetic Contribution

How can scientists tell whether genetic factors are involved in a particular trait, be it extroversion, intelligence or alcoholism, and estimate the extent of that involve-ment? It isn't as easy as it seems. Consider the following. In a given family, the father, mother, and two children are quite overweight. Going back a few genera-tions, you find that almost everyone in the family is overweight. Can you conclude that obesity is genetic? Although you might suspect genetic involvement, you can-not conclude that it is so from this information. It is possible that the children may have learned how to eat from their parents. Perhaps the parents were totally absorbed with eating and modeled eating everything on their plate and taking sec-ond and third helpings. The children may have learned that behavior.

Trying to separate the possible environmental (learning) factors from the genetic involvement is difficult and requires the use of specific research methods. The term **heritability** is used to describe what proportion of the differences between people in a given population on a particular characteristic is caused by genetic factors (Cipriani, 1996). The term **environmentality** describes the proportion of the variation between people in a given population on a particular characteristic that may result from environmental factors. Two such methods useful for determining heritability are twin studies and adoption studies.

Twin Studies

Twin methods are based on the fact that monozygotic (identical) twins share 100% of their genes in common, and fraternal twins (dizygotic), as with all other siblings, share on the average only 50% of their genes in common (Kimble, 1993). A sim-ple method for evaluating the heritability of a trait is to find the extent to which if one twin has the trait, the other twin will have it also. This agreement between traits exhibited is called the **concordance rate.** If identical twins show the trait much more often than dizygotic twins, then some genetic influence can be assumed. If a trait is completely genetic, the concordance rate among identical twins is 1.00 and among fraternal twins is .50 (Cummings, 1995). When evaluat-ing the results of twin studies, it is the degree of difference between concordance

heritability
The proportion of the measured differences between people in a given population on a particular characteristic that is due to genetic factors.

environmentality
The proportion of the variation between people in a given population on a particular characteristic that is caused by environ-mental factors.

concordance rate
The degree of similarity between twins on any particular trait.

Research shows that there is a genetic component to weight, but that does not mean that these children are destined to be overweight, normally weighted, or even underweight. Environmental factors are also important.

in identical and fraternal twins that is important. The greater the difference, the greater the heritability (Cummings, 1994). For example, identical twins correlate about .90 for height and fraternal twins .45 (Pike & Plomin, 1996) (see Table 3.2 for other traits). A mathematical formula allows for a quantitative estimate of heritability from such data.

Sometimes, it is possible to research twins reared apart and together, which offers additional data (McGue, Bacon, & Lykken, 1993). When identical and fraternal twins in adulthood raised, together and apart, were studied, the identical twins had almost the identical body mass, a measure of weight corrected for height, whether reared apart or together. Fraternal twins varied much more than the identical twins even if they were reared together (Stunkard, 1990).

Table 3.2	Concordance Values in Monozygotic (MZ) and Dizygotic (DZ) Twins	
	Concordance values	
Trait	**MZ**	**DZ**
Blood type	100	66
Eye color	99	28
Mental retardation	97	37
Hair color	89	22
Down syndrome	89	7
Handedness (left or right)	79	77
Epilepsy	72	15
Diabetes	65	18
Tuberculosis	56	22
Cleft lip	42	5

SOURCE: JAMA (1986, 256: 51–54)

Recently, monozygotic and dizygotic twins, ages 11 and 17 years, were asked to rate the quality of their relationship with both their mother and their father (see Table 3.3). Monozygotic twins were consistently more similar than dizygotic twins on their ratings of parent-child relationships, especially father-child ratings. Notice also the greater magnitude of difference in the correlations between monozygotic and dizygotic twins at 17 years of age, showing that genetic influences have a stronger impact on parental relationships with older twins (Elkins, McGue, & Iacono, 1997).

Twin studies have their detractors. Early twin studies sometimes depended solely on appearances and did not test for whether these twins were identical or fraternal. New tests eliminate this problem, but interpreting older twin studies is still problematic. Second, twin studies assume that the environment of both twins is similar. It is possible that parents treat identical twins more similarly than fraternal twins. If this were so to any great extent, it might explain the greater concordance rates between identical twins, which would then be the result of a more similar environment than that experienced by fraternal twins (Reiss, 1993). Some studies do show that the treatment of monozygotic twins is more similar than the treatment of dizygotic twins, but this alone does not account for the findings from twin studies. Some even argue that identical twins know they are more similar and therefore may act in a particular manner. Last, studying twins and generalizing to the whole population has been questioned. Twins differ in many ways—for example, they are more likely to be premature, be born lighter, and perform worse on verbal tasks and language learning—although most of these differences disappear in the school years (Plomin, DeFries, & McClearn, 1990).

Table 3.3	Monozygotic (MZ) and Dizygotic (DZ) Intraclass Twin Correlations for Twin Reports of Parent-Son Relationships (PEQ) Factors			
	11-year-old twins		17-year-old twins	
	MZ	DZ	MZ	DZ
Relationship factor	(n = 172 pairs)	(n = 67 pairs)	(n = 92 pairs)	(n = 43 pairs)
PEQ primary factors				
Conflict with mother	.50	.33	.47[b]	.17
Conflict with father	.44	.36	.62[b]	.01
Involvement with mother	.47	.41	.47	.30
Involvement with father	.46	.28	.64[a, b]	.39
Son's regard for mother	.33	.34	.41[b]	.07
Son's regard for father	.32	.32	.58[a, b]	.24
Mother's regard for son	.38	.17	.38	.35
Father's regard for son	.34	.35	.53[b]	.14
Structure: mother	.30	.26	.44	.24
Structure: father	.27	.46	.43	.35
PEQ higher order factors				
Support: mother	.49	.33	.47	.24
Support: father	.45	.31	.64[a, b]	.15

NOTE: PEQ= Parental Environmental Questionnaire
(a) indicates that age differences in monozygotic correlations was significant. (b) indicates significant differences in monozygotic and dizygotic correlations for 17-year-olds. No significant age differences were found in dizygotic correlations or for differences in monozygotic and dizygotic correlations for 11-year-olds.
SOURCE: Elkins et al. (1997)

Adoption Studies

Studies of adopted children and their parents are also used to determine genetic influence. Consider a child of parents with a particular body mass adopted by parents with a significantly different body mass. Will the child be more similar to the adoptive or the biological parents? When adopted children's body mass was compared to the body mass of their biological and adoptive parents, a clear relationship between adoptee weight class of thin, medium, overweight, and obese and the body mass index of the biological parents was found (Stunkard et al., 1986). There was no relationship between adoptee weight class and the body mass of adoptive parents.

Adoption studies have been roundly criticized because the placement of adopted children is certainly not random. It is possible that children may be adopted by people with similar backgrounds to the biological parents. Second, parents may treat an adopted child differently from a biological child. This could lead to greater differences between adopted siblings than between biological siblings for solely environmental reasons (Reiss, 1993). Third, it is frequently difficult to find information about the biological fathers of adopted children (Nigg & Goldsmith, 1994). Fourth, the timing of adoption is a major question. The longer the child stays with the biological parents, the greater the influence of that environment. Last, it should be remembered that the womb itself is an environment (Lombroso, Pauls, & Leckman, 1994).

Twin and adoption studies are used to estimate the extent of any genetic contribution. However, these studies certainly show the importance of the environment. For instance, the Texas Adoption Project found that the intelligence scores of adopted children were more similar to their biological than adoptive parents. However, the relationships were all quite low, and most of the variability was not the result of genetic influences but of socioeconomic factors, such as neighborhood, friends, and schools (Cummings, 1995).

In addition, heritability depends on the population being measured and its environments. Many psychologists have asked that professionals conducting such studies sample subjects from a wider range of environments and measure the environments more accurately (Rowe & Waldman, 1993). Finally, these analyses of heritability consider groups and populations, not individuals.

Guideposts

How do twin and adoption studies help scientists determine whether a genetic base underlies a particular trait?

Physical Characteristics

The most striking genetic influence involves physical appearance. Hair and skin color, the shape of the nose, body build, and a thousand other physical characteristics are directly influenced by genes. Evidence that body weight is affected by genetics is clear (Ristow, Moller-Wieland, Pfeiffer, Krone, & Kahn, 1998). One's adult weight is not entirely predestined, but some people may be more likely to become obese, and programs to prevent obesity should be targeted at children who are at risk for obesity.

Most physical features are trivial, biologically speaking. A person's height or color of skin makes very little difference from the point of view of biological functioning. However, these and many other physical characteristics may or may not be valued by the society in which a person lives. For example, skin color is biologically trivial but may be socially important. Any discussion of a physical characteristic, then, must be investigated from both a biological viewpoint (does it lead to some advantage or disadvantage in functioning?) and a social perspective (how is that trait evaluated by the family and society?).

Temperament

Have you ever observed the behavior of two infants of about the same age? Did they behave in the same manner? The answer, as any parent of two or more children will tell you, is no. Children show behavioral differences from birth. Some are more easily distracted than others; some are considerably more active.

Each child is born with a **temperament,** an "individual style of responding to the environment" (Thomas, Chess, & Birch, 1970, p. 102). Alexander Thomas and his colleagues found nine behavior patterns that comprise a child's temperament (see Table 3.4).

The majority of children fit into one of three general types. Children with "easy" temperaments are generally happy, flexible, and regular. These children get along well with almost everyone and present few problems to parents or, later, teachers. "Difficult" children, on the other hand, are intense, demanding, and inflexible, and cry a great deal. Children in the third category—"slow to warm up"—do not respond well to changes in their environment, but their reactions are not intense. They exhibit a low activity level and have a tendency to withdraw from new stimuli.

Some psychologists do not use these categories and propose a different constellation of behavior patterns that define temperament. For example, Buss and Plomin (1984) suggest that temperament entails three characteristics: emotionality, activity, and sociability. *Emotionality* refers to the strength of arousal shown by infants in response to events. Emotional infants show strong fears, anger responses, or distress to even minimal negative stimuli and are less easily comforted. *Activity* is the extent to which the child requires movement and expends energy. *Sociability* is the child's desire for the rewards of being with other people, such as attention. Sometimes a fourth factor, *impulsivity,* measuring, among other characteristics persistence and sensation seeking, is also used. Substantial genetic involvement

temperament

A group of characteristics reflecting an individual's way of responding to the environment. These are thought to be genetic.

Table 3.4   Measuring Children's Temperaments

Alexander Thomas, Stella Chess, and Herbert Birch found that the majority of children could be classified as "easy," "slow to warm up," or "difficult" according to how they rate in key categories shown in color on a nine-point personality index.

Type of Child		Easy	Slow to warm up	Difficult
Activity Level	The proportion of active periods to inactive ones	Varies	Low to moderate	Varies
Rhythmicity	Regularity of hunger, excretion, sleep, and wakefulness	Very regular	Varies	Irregular
Distractibility	The degree to which extraneous stimuli alter behavior	Varies	Varies	Varies
Approach-withdrawal	The response to a new object or person	Positive approach	Initial withdrawal	Withdrawal
Adaptability	The ease with which a child adapts to changes in his or her environment	Very adaptable	Slowly adaptable	Slowly adaptable
Attention span and persistence	The amount of time devoted to an activity and the effect of distraction on the activity	High or low	High or low	High or low
Intensity of reaction	The energy of response, regardless of its quality or direction	Low or mild	Mild	Intense
Threshold of responsiveness	The intensity of stimulation required to evoke a discernible response	High or low	High or low	High or low
Quality of mood	The amount of friendly, pleasant, joyful behavior vs. unpleasant, unfriendly behavior	Positive	Slightly negative	Negative

SOURCE: Thomas et al. (1970)

---

is found on these dimensions (see Table 3.5) (Goldsmith, Buss, & Lemery, 1997; Schmitz, Saudino, Plomin, Fulker, & DeFries, 1996). There is no agreement on what factors actually comprise temperament, and different scientists have suggested different characteristics.

The extent to which temperament changes or remains stable is still at issue. There is evidence for relative stability. Ratings of infant temperament taken as early as 2 weeks are related to ratings at 2 months, and ratings at 2 months are related to 12-month ratings (Worobey & Blajda, 1989). Mothers' reports of approach (for example, reactions to new experiences), rhythmicity, persistence, irritability, cooperation-manageability, and inflexibility showed substantial continuity between birth and 8 years (Pedlow, Sanson, Prior, & Oberklaid, 1993).

Children considered undercontrolled at 3 years (a characteristic affected by temperament) scored high on measures of impulsivity, danger seeking, aggression, and interpersonal alienation at 18 years; whereas inhibited children scored lower on many such measures (Caspi & Silva, 1995). Styles of temperament observed at age 3 years continue to show themselves in the behaviors of adults at 21 (Newman, Caspi, Moffitt, & Silva, 1997). These relationships, though, are far from perfect.

Even if one argues for stability, we should not expect children to show their temperament in the same way as they mature. For example, at 2 months, a child who is easily distractible will stop crying for food if rocked, and at 2 years will stop a tantrum if another activity is suggested. The underlying characteristic of distractibility is present, but with age, different behaviors will be shown.

Others argue that there is evidence both for moderate stability and for change (Kagan, 1997; Plomin et al., 1993; Saudino & Plomin, 1996). When children's temperaments were measured at 2 months, 9 months, 6 years, and 15 years, substantial stability in activity level and a sociability factor were found. However, substantial change was found in a factor akin to emotionality (Torgersen, 1989). Perhaps some aspects of temperament change, whereas others may show stability. It is also possible that some aspects of temperament may become more stable with age (Lemery, Goldsmith, Klinnert, & Mrazek, 1999). In addition, one trait may

Table 3.5 — Correlations between Monozygotic (MZ) and Dizygotic (DZ) Twins on Four Dimensions of Temperament

Weighted Intraclass Correlations From Studies With the Emotionality, Activity, Sociability, Impulsivity (EASI) Temperament Survey, the EAS Questionnaire, and the Colorado Childhood Temperament Inventory (CCTI)

	Pair	
	MZ ($n = 567$)	DZ ($n = 633$)
Scale	ICR	ICR
Emotionality	.57	.11
Activity	.64	−.08
Sociability	.59	.10
Impulsivity	.66	.15

NOTE: MZ = monozygotic; DZ = dyzygotic; ICR = intraclass correlation.
Correlations are from the following studies: Plomin (1974; 1976), EASI administered to 60 MZ and 77 DZ pairs, *M* age = 4 years 6 months; Buss and Plomin (1975), EASI administered to 81 MZ and 57 DZ pairs, *M* age = 4 years 7 months; Harris and Rose (1977), EASI administered to 30 MZ and 23 DZ pairs, *M* age = 9 years 6 months; Neale and Stevenson (1989), EASI administered to 219 MZ and 322 DZ pairs, *M* age = 3 years 6 months; Plomin (unpublished; see Plomin & Foch, 1980), EASI administered to 51 MZ and 33 DZ pairs, *M* age = 7 years 7 months; Plomin and Rowe (1977), CCTI administered to 36 MZ and 31 DZ pairs, *M* age = 3 years 7 months; Plomin et al. (1993), CCTI administered to 90 MZ and 90 DZ pairs, *M* age = 1 year 8 months.
SOURCE: Goldsmith et al. (1997)

remain stable for a time, while another changes and vice versa (van den Boom, 1994). If temperament is substantially genetic in origin, genes may turn on and off, and different sets of genes may play a role at different stages of development (Buss & Plomin, 1984).

Children who exhibit different patterns of temperament show different physiological reactions (Huffman et al., 1998). For instance, children who show withdrawal in novel social situations, are easily frightened, and show anxiety when challenged are often labeled behaviorally inhibited. Children who show the opposite behaviors and approach new situations with confidence are labeled behaviorally uninhibited. Genetic involvement is strong in these behavioral patterns (Robinson, Kagan, Reznick, & Corley, 1992). Inhibited and uninhibited children differ on a number of physiological indicators, including heart rate and pupil dilation, suggesting greater reactivity on the part of the peripheral nervous system for children showing the inhibited behavior pattern. Inhibited children may be more at risk for developing some anxiety disorders later on, but more research needs to be conducted in this area (Kagan, 1998). Yet, other factors are also important. Parental response and such parental personality characteristics as extroversion, shyness, and avoidance may also affect the child's responses (Rubin, Hastings, Stewart, Henderson, & Chen, 1997).

Could there be genetic differences in temperament among various cultural and geographically related groups? Four-month-old infants from Boston, Dublin, and Beijing were tested on differences in ease and intensity of behavioral arousal to visual, auditory, and olfactory stimuli. The Chinese infants were significantly less active, less irritable, and less vocal than the infants in the other two samples. These differences in reactivity are part of many measures of temperament and may be partly genetic in origin (Kagan, 1984). The fact that some biological differences among groups exist has been accepted for many years. For instance, the proportion of Rh-negative (a chemical found in the blood, discussed in Chapter 4) individuals in China is less than 1% but greater than 15% in Europe (Cavalli-Sforza, 1991), and differences in response to medications have been noted (Lin, Poland, & Lesser, 1986). Although there is some environmental input in reactivity, Kagan (1984) notes that "it is reasonable to at least entertain the hypothesis of genetically influenced behavioral differences in infants belonging to populations that have been reproductively isolated for a long time" (p. 345).

Even though temperament appears to have a genetic basis, behavioral orientations may be affected by parenting practices and attitudes. In a study of infant temperament in three African societies, specific differences in temperament were attributed to each culture's child-rearing practices and parenting orientations (deVries & Sameroff, 1994). For example, mothers of infants in the Digo culture are not very concerned with time and are more likely to respond to a child's immediate needs. There is little emphasis on how long a child should sleep or the time a child should be fed. Perhaps as a result of this caregiving pattern, Digo infants were rated less regular than infants in the other two African cultures. A child's temperament, then, may also be influenced by environmental factors, including child-rearing practices.

A child's temperament may affect the parent-child relationship. If a child is irritable and difficult to soothe, parents may withdraw or adopt a negative style of parenting. This negative style may continue as the child matures (Neiderhiser, Reiss, Hetherington, & Plomin, 1999). Some evidence exists that demonstrates the effect of temperament on early parenting behaviors. Mothers of nonirritable infants show a high level of visual and physical involvement from the first month, combined with a gradual increase in effective stimulation. They rapidly respond to positive signs from their infants. Irritable infants are confronted with less visual

For Your Consideration ?

In your opinion, is temperament stable, or does it change as the child develops? Ask a parent whose child is in elementary school whether such behaviors as activity level, distractibility, responsiveness to other people, adaptability, mood, and intensity of responsiveness have stayed the same or changed as their children matured.

and physical involvement from birth, a very low level of effective stimulation, and a rapidly decreasing responsiveness.

What does temperament mean to parents and children? Temperament may affect how parents see themselves and their roles as parents. Parents who have a child who is rated difficult are more likely to believe that the child's behavior is not under their control, while mothers of easy infants are more likely to believe in their ability to control their child's behavior (Daniels, Plomin, & Greenhalgh, 1984; Sirignano & Lachman, 1985). Some, but not all studies, also find that mothers of difficult children are less responsive, and mothers of easy babies exhibit more positive maternal behaviors (Bates, 1987).

Children are fortunate if their inborn temperament meshes with the parents' abilities and styles. The "difficult" child thrives in a structured, understanding environment but not in an inconsistent, intolerant home. The "slow to warm up" child does best if the parents understand the child's needs for time to adjust to new situations. If the parents do not, they may only intensify the child's natural tendency to withdraw. Alexander Thomas, a pioneer in temperament research, urges parents to work with their child's temperament rather than try to change it. Children who are slow to warm up should be allowed to proceed at their own pace. Gentle encouragement is best. Difficult children should be handled in a very consistent and objective way. Easy children may also face problems related to temperament because sometimes they are unable to resolve conflict between their own desires and the demands of others.

It is generally agreed that temperament reflects behavioral tendencies, has biological underpinnings, is easiest to observe directly in infancy, and becomes more complex as the child matures (Bates, 1989; Goldsmith et al., 1987). Psychologists disagree about just how much of an infant's behavior emanates from temperament, the nature of the specific components that temperament comprises, and whether the term *difficult child* should be used at all because of its negative connotation. Despite these differences, the concept of temperament is useful in understanding the factors that underlie a child's tendency to react to stimuli in characteristic ways early in life.

According to some psychologists, inhibition is a characteristic affected by temperament, which remains stable.

Why is the concept of infant temperament important to understanding children's behavior?

Behavioral Traits and Psychopathology

If your parents are friendly and affectionate, will you be the same? Is extroversion (being outgoing) or introversion (being withdrawn) partially due to genetic endowment? Strong evidence exists that a genetic component underlies this personality dimension (Pike & Plomin, 1996). Between 20% and 45% of the variability in being extroverted, emotionally stable, agreeable, and conscientious results from genetic factors (Loehlin, 1992; Rose, 1995). Traits such as mental agility, religiosity, traditionalism, conduct problems, cheerfulness, danger seeking, self-control, hostility, and pessimism are strongly related in identical twins reared apart and much less related in fraternal twins reared apart (Cipriani, 1996; Rosenhan & Seligman, 1995). The heritability is only moderate on many of these traits, showing not only genetic influence but considerable environmental influence as well. Coping strategy, which may be related to temperament, also contains a genetic component (Mellins, Gatz, & Baker, 1996).

"Aggressive" Genes?

"You're just like your father!" Ina yelled at Les. "Go on, hit me! Show me what kind of man you are!" All the neighbors know Ina and Les—the couple is constantly fighting. The entire neighborhood can hear them, and their arguments often erupt into violence, with Les hitting Ina.

When interviewed, Ina noted that Les's father had behaved violently toward his own wife, so "it must be in his genes." "His father had a terrible temper," she stated, "just like Les does."

Les agrees. He states that although he loves Ina, he can't seem to control his temper, just as his father couldn't. Les had been a very aggressive child and was subject to temper tantrums. When a psychologist suggested that he could change, Les looked astonished, shook his head, and said, "Once it's in your genes, you can't get rid of it." Both Ina and Les also told the psychologist that their son was showing the same behavior pattern. They offered this as further proof of their genetics argument.

1. *If you were the psychologist, how would you deal with Les and Ina's attitude?*

2. *If you were Ina, what would you do?*

For Your Consideration ?

Your friend says that being criminally aggressive is a genetic trait and asks for your opinion. How would you respond?

Research evidence also implicates genetic factors in autism, attention deficit/hyperactivity disorder, aggressiveness, and anorexia nervosa, and they play a moderate role in depression, especially bipolar disorder (Deater-Deckard & Plomin, 1999; Farmer, 1996; Goodman & Stevenson, 1989; Rapkin, 1997; Thapar & McGuffin, 1994).

Just how would genes affect behavior? There are no known genes for behavior. Genes exert an influence on behavior through biological mechanisms, including enzymes, hormones, and neurotransmitters. Genes influence the individual's physiology, which in turn affects behavior.

Guideposts

How do genes influence behavior?

Shared and Nonshared Environments: How Can Siblings Be So Different?

At the beginning of this chapter, a parent asked how her two children could be so different. We all know families in which the siblings seem so different in personality, social skills, and physical abilities despite being raised in the same home by the same parents. If the siblings share, on the average, half their genes in common and the same environment, why should they be so different?

Environmental influences can be divided into two categories. First, there are those **shared** by siblings, including child-rearing strategies, socioeconomic variables, and parents' personalities (Pike & Plomin, 1996). Second, there are **nonshared** influences, the individual's unique experiences, such as being treated differently from one's siblings, different school experiences, and peer relationships. Some authorities claim that even shared features of the environment are experienced differently by siblings. After all, they are born at different times, their parents may be more or less at ease with their roles, and the family may be in different financial positions as the children develop. It is also possible that many factors usually considered shared may affect children in the same family differently. For example, divorce is obviously a shared experience by children in the same family, but it may affect siblings differently (Pike & Plomin, 1996).

shared environmental factors

Environmental factors, such as socioeconomic status or parental child-rearing styles, that are shared by siblings.

nonshared environmental factors

Environmental factors that are unique to the individual.

One question people always ask is how siblings who share the same biological parents, home, and community environment can be so different. The answer is simple. Siblings share on the average only half their genes in common. Most importantly, studies show that the child's unique experiences, called unshared environmental influences, are crucial.

For Your Consideration ?

Your neighbor cannot believe that her boys, who are only 11 months apart, are so dissimilar in their physical abilities, achievements, interests, and social skills since they have the same parents and share the same environment. How could you explain why the siblings are so different?

Guideposts

What are the implications of the concept of readiness for child rearing and education?

readiness

The point in development at which a child has the necessary skills to master a new challenge.

Nonshared environmental influence is more important in the areas of personality, cognitive ability, and psychopathology than shared environmental factors (Dunn & Plomin, 1990; Plomin et al., 1993; Saudino & Plomin, 1996). Nonshared environmental influences often work to make siblings in the same family more different from one another than similar (Dunn & Plomin, 1990). For example, many studies show that agreeableness, conscientiousness, and emotional stability are influenced by one's genes (Saudino et al., 1995; Loehlin, 1992). Genetic variance accounted for between 22% and 46%, shared environmental influences contribute between 0% and 11%, and nonshared environmental influences account for between 44% and 55% (Loehlin, 1992).

From a genetic viewpoint, siblings (except for identical twins) share, on the average, only half their genes in common. Half their genes, then, are not the same, and this type of nonshared inheritance can account for some behavioral differences as well (Plomin & Daniels, 1987). Siblings may be more similar to each other genetically than cousins or nonrelated people, but their genotypes also differ greatly from each other. When we look at both shared and nonshared environmental factors and genetic dissimilarity, and we realize the many ways in which they can interact, we can more readily understand why great differences in sibling behavior should be expected. In other words, the richness of genetic and environmental interaction should make us expect people in the same family to act differently, even if genetic factors underlie a particular trait. People often overestimate sibling similarity in the environmental and genetic aspects of life and underestimate the importance of the nonshared qualities of both.

Rate of Development

It is no secret that children develop at their own pace, and their rate of maturation reflects their unique genetic master plan. Such activities as standing, crawling, walking, and talking are largely, but not exclusively, dependent on the child's genetic endowment. Statistics may show that the "average" child walks or talks at a particular age, but wide variations exist within the range of typical development. When children fall far behind these norms, the situation should be investigated.

It is important to recognize that within the broad "normal" range, some children develop faster than others. Serious consequences may result from pushing a child to do something before the child is ready. **Readiness** implies that there is a point in development when a child has the skills necessary to master a particular task. When parents and teachers do not understand this, problems can result. For instance, if a child who does not understand the concept of numbers is forced by parents or teachers to try to add two numbers, the child is destined to fail. The child becomes frustrated because an understanding of numbers is essential to success in learning how to add. Bitter and unnecessary failure results. Repetition of such experiences may lead to a lack of self-confidence. The same argument may hold for any physical or mental challenge.

Intelligence

In the history of psychology, no issue has been more bitterly debated than the influence of genetics on intelligence (see *The Bell Curve: IQ Differences Among Groups?* on page 96). Two questions are usually asked: How much of the variable we call intelligence can be attributed to hereditary factors? and How modifiable is intelligence?

The first question involves discovering the heritability of intelligence. The existence of a genetic component in intelligence is well accepted (Petrill et al., 1997), but someone who offers a numerical percentage figure is likely to be criticized. Some authorities claim that it is impossible to estimate true heritability figures for human traits because we cannot control the environment (Feldman & Lewontin, 1975). After all, people with similar levels of intelligence tend to establish similar environments. Highly intelligent people create more stimulating environments than less intelligent people.

In the Louisville Twin Study, identical twins, fraternal twins, and nontwin siblings were compared (Wilson, 1977, 1983). The intelligence scores of the siblings were similar to those of their fraternal twins, which would be expected, since the two groups share about 50% of the genes in common, and again identical twins were more similar than any of the other pairs (see Table 3.6 for some representative values for monozygotic and dizygotic twins at different ages). In a study of identical twins reared apart, the average correlation of identical twins reared in different environments was .76, which is a higher value than for either fraternal twins or nontwin siblings reared in the same household and closer to the value found for identical twins in the same homes (Bouchard, 1984). When identical and fraternal twins separated in infancy and reared apart were followed, researchers found an astounding 70% of the variance in intelligence was associated with genetics (Bouchard, Lykken, McGue, Segal, & Tellegen, 1990).

These results have been criticized, with many scientists believing that this figure is too high (Adler, 1991). Most studies yield values closer to 50% (Cowan, Powell, & Cowan, 1998; Plomin & DeFries, 1980), which would ascribe approximately half the differences between populations in intelligence to genetic factors and the other half to the environment.

To what extent are the differences between children in intelligence due to genetic factors? The fact that a substantial genetic factor underlies intelligence does not mean that intelligence cannot be modified.

Identical twins reared apart are more similar in intelligence than fraternal twins reared together.

Guideposts

What are the conclusions of research studies on the heritability of intelligence?

Table 3.6	Within-Pair Correlations for the Intelligence of Monozygotic and Dizygotic Twin Pairs	
	Correlations	
Age	**Monozygotic**	**Dizygotic**
3 months	.66	.67
9 months	.67	.51
18 months	.82*	.65
30 months	.85*	.65
36 months	.88*	.79
4 years	.83*	.71
6 years	.86*	.59
8 years	.83*	.66
15 years	.88*	.54

* = statistically significant.
SOURCE: Wilson (1983)

The Bell Curve: IQ Differences Among Groups?

Rarely has a book generated as much fury and passion as The Bell Curve *by Richard Herrnstein and Charles Murray. It was the subject for cover stories in various magazines and was even brought up during a presidential press conference (Finn, 1995). As soon as it was published, reviews and letters to the editors decried the book, often calling it racist. What is it about the book that brings out such passions? To summarize the book's ideas, we will look at each of the book's four parts, presenting the authors' ideas and then noting some of the more thoughtful criticisms.*

Part I

American society has become more and more stratified according to intelligence level. Those with the highest intelligence attend certain universities, serve in certain positions in society, and reap the rewards. They form a cognitive elite and interact with each other, often marrying each other. Intelligence scores become even more important as jobs become more dependent on intellectual skills. The authors argue that general intelligence underlies performance in every job and is a function of both genetics and the environment. As environmental influences become more equal, genes become more important. The authors emphasize the importance of genetics in the variability of intelligence, claiming that the heritability figure lies between .40 and .80 (Herrnstein & Murray, 1994).

Criticisms

The idea that intellectual skills are becoming more important in our society and that America is becoming stratified by intelligence is intriguing, even if overstated. However, the relationship between skill level and intelligence is high but by no means perfect (Heckman, 1995). Factors other than ability, such as attitude and motivation, may also affect performance in school and on the job. Ability level and education are not the same, and people with less ability but with the motivation to study and attend school can succeed and reap the economic rewards of education (Heckman, 1995).

Some psychologists argue that there are many different intelligences, not just a general intelligence, an idea that will be discussed in Chapter 10 (Gardner, 1994). A person may be linguistically intelligent but not mathematically intelligent. Others have criticized for technical reasons the authors' use of a particular intelligence test in their assessment (Heckman, 1995). Finally, most psychologists certainly accept the idea that some genetic factors affect intelligence (Snyderman & Rothman, 1987), but the extent of the contribution is very much in doubt and depends on the environment and the skill that is being measured. Most scientists believe that the environment has not been adequately measured in many studies (Dolan & Molenaar, 1995).

Part II

The book's primary thesis is that intellectual ability can be adequately measured by intelligence tests, and that high intelligence is related to many desirable behaviors while low intelligence is related to many undesirable behaviors (Finn, 1995). Most people, of course, score somewhere in the middle. People with low intelligence scores, according to the authors, are more likely to drop out of school, be unemployed, give birth to

The data from adoption studies also indicate that the intelligence levels of adopted children are more closely related to the children's biological parents than to their adoptive parents, although the correlations are low (Horn, 1983; Jencks, 1972; Loehlin, Horn, & Willerman, 1989).

Modifying Intelligence

The second question regarding intelligence—that of modifiability—is more important. Some psychologists are afraid that studies that show a genetic basis for intelligence will be misinterpreted as meaning that the environment is unimportant (Cowan et al., 1998). This is certainly not the case, and any heritability figure out-of-wedlock children, use parenting strategies that are poorer, and commit crime, and are less likely to engage in political activity. Low intelligence is a better predictor of these conditions than socioeconomic status. The authors' statistical evidence is based on studies of whites, thereby circumventing any claim that racial variables confound their results. They emphasize that they are talking about groups, not individuals. They recognize that knowing the intelligence level of an individual does not allow you to predict much about the individual.

Criticisms

Much of the evidence presented in this section is based on correlations and does not demonstrate cause and effect. Is it poverty that leads to many of these social problems? Is it lack of intelligence? Is it some interaction between the two, with perhaps other variables being involved? Although the authors argue that it is lack of intelligence, many psychologists disagree. Environmental factors are often poorly described in many studies, making it difficult to determine what factors contribute to an outcome.

Part III

In the third and most controversial part of the book, the authors argue that differences in measured intelligence occur among various racial groups. They argue that differences in intelligence

among Asian Americans, African Americans, and whites are found at every socioeconomic level and are not due to any cultural bias among these tests. Although they believe that genetic factors play an important part in intelligence, they do not absolutely state that differences between racial groups are due to genetics (Azar, 1994), nor do they deny the possibility.

Criticism

It is hard to believe that these points are still being debated. Although the authors state that intelligence tests do not discriminate on the basis of group membership, this is still a very controversial position, with some psychologists arguing that these tests do not take cultural differences into consideration (Kaplan, 1996). Cultural and environmental factors are not identical, and therefore any discussion of causation is bound to be problematic. The fact that differences may exist does not indicate anything about what causes the differences. Further-more, heritability estimates are computed within the white population, and their usefulness in comparing intelligence scores between races is dubious at best (Kaplan, 1996).

A larger problem is the misunderstanding of the term *heritability*. If the heritability of IQ is placed at .6, this means that 60% of the differences in IQ scores among individuals in a large group (not a race) is due to genetic differences.

Most people incorrectly believe that 60% of an individual's IQ is determined by genes (Wright, 1995). In fact, the authors state that just because a trait is genetically transmitted in individuals does not mean that group differences in that trait are also genetic in origin. Heritability differs for different environments. These estimates apply only to the environment under study and say nothing about its modifiability.

Part IV

The authors argue that efforts to raise intelligence through social programs have basically failed. Resources have been taken from the intellectually able of all groups and directed toward those at the lower end, thereby reducing the educational experiences of gifted children.

The authors argue that we are facing a situation in which a caste system will arise as the differences between the cognitive elite and affluent grow and the underclass of people of all groups with low intellectual ability is created. The authors have little hope that environmental improvements will be sufficient. The cognitive elite's fear of the underclass will create what the authors call the "custodial state" in which social programs may be expanded to reduce violence, child abuse, and disorganization. The government will take over more of the parenting responsibilities from those who are inadequate for the job.

should be interpreted cautiously. Problems in defining what we really mean by intelligence, and difficulties in research design, combine to provide ammunition for both sides (Horn, 1985; Walker & Emory, 1985). Even the same set of data can be interpreted differently, especially if one researcher concentrates on one area of the study while another person favors data from a different portion (McCall, 1981). Psychologists accept the fact that an important environmental element underlies intelligence, because none of the correlations in the data noted previously are perfect (Snyderman & Rothman, 1987). No matter which estimate of heritability one uses, both environmental and genetic factors are involved in intelligence (Petrill et al., 1998; Scarr & Kidd, 1983).

Stricter policing and more segregation by class will result.

The authors argue that inequality of endowments is a reality that we all must accept. Trying to pretend that intelligence is unimportant or is easily modifiable leads to programs that do not work. They argue that any programs to improve the lot of people should be pegged at the correct level. For example, they note that if many women who have babies out of wedlock have below-average intelligence scores, then educational strategies that rely on abstract or future-oriented strategies will be of little use. If many adults who are chronically unemployed and without job skills have low intelligence scores, then job training should take this into account.

The authors state that the goal should be to create a society in which every person can find a valued place in the community. Since social problems are concentrated on the relatively few who have low intelligence scores, most people do succeed. To help these at-risk people, the authors believe that society should make it easier to make a living, begin a business, and fill out a tax form. Government bureaucracy and rules have become so complicated that many people cannot deal with them. Simplification is a solution. The authors argue for swifter justice and encourage birth control, but they are against government intrusion into the decision of whether to have a child. However, the authors argue that

people who have children outside marriage should not receive support from the government.

Criticism

Few people would deny the importance of focusing educational and training programs on the ability level of the people being served or the need to simplify rules to allow everyone to find a place in society. However, these ideas are rather simplistic. The book's critics fear that people may believe that intelligence is determined by genetic differences and that it is not malleable (Wright, 1995). Evidence exists that intervention can work and that cognitive skills can be improved, especially through intensive educational experiences (Kaplan, 1996; Nisbett, 1994). Just because genetic factors may underlie a trait does not mean that environmental change will be ineffective (Cowan et al., 1998). Believing that people's cognitive abilities are set in stone allows politicians to withdraw their support from programs to improve the cognitive functioning of children, incorrectly assuming that they can't work because intelligence is "genetic" (Cowan et al., 1998; Gates, 1994).

Conclusion: The Wrong Stuff

It is somewhat unfortunate that Herrnstein and Murray chose to needlessly complicate their ideas with a rather tired and dubious analysis of race and intelligence. It seems that these

same issues are raised in somewhat different forms every 20 years, so we can expect these arguments to rear again in the future. Advanced schooling and cognitive ability will certainly continue to be important, and questions about people with less schooling and/or ability deserve discussion. Questions about what we must do to provide opportunities for all people at all levels of ability to live reasonable lives and to be valued warrant attention, but without presenting intellectual differences in racial context (Heckman, 1995). It is unfortunate that they did not take this tack.

The Bell Curve could have served as a source of debate on issues of individuality, stratification, and the cost-benefit ratio of governmental programs. Unfortunately, the one question everyone will remember relates to race and intelligence, a question that should have been put to rest many years ago.

What do you think?

How important is IQ in our modern technological world? Herrnstein and Murray argue that divisions based upon IQ level exist in society and will become even more prominent in the future. If they are correct, what are the implications for society? Do you agree or disagree with their ideas in this area.

You can explore the questions above using InfoTrac College Edition. Hint: enter search terms *Intelligence and Society* and *IQ Levels.*

A number of studies testify to the modifiability of intelligence, but one by Skeels (1966) stands out. In the 1930s, Skeels was working in a bleak orphanage, where the children received little attention and were subjected to a rigid schedule. The children had no toys, and the environment was depressing. Skeels took a special interest in two girls who rocked back and forth and spent most of their time in bed. These two girls were later transferred to a mental institution, where they came under the influence of an older, retarded woman who showered them with attention. Their behavior changed, and they became much more responsive. Skeels decided to find out more about this phenomenon. A number of children were removed from the sterile setting of the orphanage and allowed to live with older children, who also had mental retardation, in a better environment. Their intelligence scores improved an average of 29 points, and one child's intelligence score actually rose by more than 50 points. The group that stayed in the depressing environment of the orphanage was found to have even lower intelligence scores than when the study had begun.

The conclusion that a change in environment accounts for the improvement in intelligence has been accepted by most psychologists today, although the methodology has been severely criticized (Longstreth, 1981). The genetic influence on intelligence does not limit its malleability (Scarr-Salapatek, 1975). Rather, the genetic factor affects the elasticity of intelligence. Few would argue that any enrichment program could turn a child of below-average intelligence into a genius, but a radical change for the better in the child's environment would probably have a significant effect on the child's intelligence score. Several programs have attempted to raise the intelligence scores of young children through a variety of educational programs aimed at both children and their parents. Many have been successful in the short term (see Chapter 8).

Enrichment programs have failed to raise children's intelligence levels even over a short period of time.

Genetic Influence on Disease

More than 3,000 diseases are linked in some way to genetics (Lynch, 1996). Many of these disorders are rare, and some show great variability in the severity of their symptoms. About 3% of all newborns have some genetic birth defect, and about 1 newborn in 200 has a chromosomal abnormality (Plomin et al., 1990).

Cystic Fibrosis

Cystic fibrosis is a recessive genetic disease of the glands that produce mucus, saliva, and sweat. It affects many organs, including the lungs, liver, and pancreas. A person with cystic fibrosis has a low resistance to respiratory diseases and a tendency to become dehydrated because of excessive salt in the sweat. About 1,000 children are born with the disease in the United States each year (National Institute of Health, NIH 1997). New antibiotics have increased the life expectancy of people with this disorder. Twenty years ago, the life expectancy of people with cystic fibrosis was 18 years, but today it is 28 years, with many living into their 30s and 40s (Wolfson, 1996). At this point, there is no cure for cystic fibrosis.

Recent research into this disorder shows great promise. Scientists have actually cured cystic fibrosis cells in the laboratory by inserting a healthy version of the gene that causes the disease (Angier, 1990a). A genetically engineered virus was used to place good copies of the gene into cells taken from the respiratory tract and pancreas of cystic fibrosis patients. As a result, the abnormal cells became healthier and functioned more normally. This is called *gene therapy* (Churchill, 1997). Several genetic diseases may be conquered by gene therapy, which has already been used successfully on a very rare genetic disorder in which children do not have the ability to fight off any disease (Angier, 1990b). New techniques hold a great deal of promise (Stephenson, 1999). However, progress in developing effective gene therapies against other conditions has been slow (Knowles & Boucher, 1996; Wheeler, 1995). Curing a few cells in the laboratory, although a significant achievement, is a long way from curing an actual individual. Although gene therapy certainly holds much promise, it will take much time before its promise will be fulfilled (Alton, 1996).

cystic fibrosis
A severe genetic disease marked by respiratory problems.

Tay-Sachs Disease: Hope Through Research

Some genetic diseases are more likely to be found in one group of people than another. For example, Tay-Sachs disease is most common among Jews whose ancestors came from Central and Eastern Europe, although members of any other group can inherit the disease (Richards, 1998). Many other diseases show a greater incidence in certain ethnic groups. Italians are more likely to suffer from thalassemia (a blood disease), and sickle-cell anemia is found more commonly among African Americans and Latinos. Tay-Sachs disease is a recessive disorder and is transmitted in the same manner as cystic fibrosis. Infants born with the disease seem healthy at birth, but after 6 months, their progress slows. The disease involves an inborn error in metabolism. The infant's body stores an excessive amount of a material called glycolipid in the cells of the nervous system, causing the cells to swell, rupture, and finally die. As more and more nerve cells die, the baby loses motor abilities and finally becomes mentally retarded. The disease is incurable. By the age of 2 or 3, the child dies.

A simple test can tell whether one is a carrier of Tay-Sachs. A blood test can determine the amount of a certain enzyme that breaks down the fatty substances in the nerve cells. People who are carriers will have only half as much of the enzyme as noncarriers, although this is enough for the carrier, and carriers never show any signs of the disease (March of Dimes, 1986c). The presence of the genetic disease in the fetus can also be determined. Current research is attempting to find a way to supply the brain with substitutes that will break down these fatty substances. Researchers are also looking into methods of transplanting genes from normal cells into defective cells to manufacture the chemical (March of Dimes, 1986c).

Sickle-Cell Anemia

Sickle-cell diseases are the most common serious genetic disorder in African Americans, occurring in one of every 400 to 500 births of African Americans in the United States (Noll et al., 1996). There are several types of the disease and more and less severe variants of each type. Sickle-cell anemia is an inherited defect in the structure of red blood cells. The sufferer, especially during periods of physical exertion or low oxygen, experiences considerable pain (Steinberg, 1999). Although most people with sickle cell anemia live normal lives, people with severe cases may suffer heart and kidney problems (Stefanatou & Bowler, 1997).

Sickle-cell anemia is a recessive disorder that results in abnormally shaped red blood cells.

tay-sachs disease
A fatal genetic disease most commonly found in Jews who can trace their lineage to Eastern Europe.

sickle-cell anemia
An inherited defect in the structure of red blood cells found mostly in African Americans and Latinos.

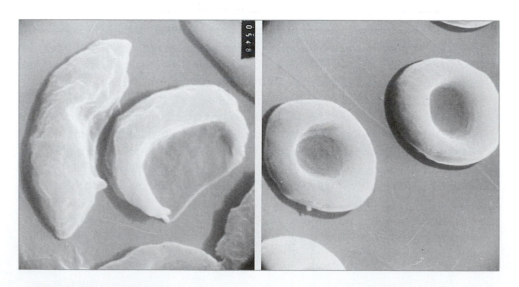

Periods of crisis requiring hospitalization are not unusual. Resistance to disease is decreased, and the health of the child with sickle-cell anemia is usually poor.

Approximately 1 in 10 African Americans is a carrier, and whether one is a carrier can be determined by a simple blood test. We can calculate that on the average, 1 marriage out of every 100 between African Americans has the potential for producing a child who will suffer from sickle-cell anemia. At present, antibiotics and improved medical treatment can help alleviate the symptoms, but some who suffer from severe cases of the disorder die in childhood (March of Dimes, 1986b). Doctors today are using the medication called hydroxyurea to turn on the expression of a gene for fetal hemoglobin that is normally turned off in adults to reduce the frequency of sickle-cell crises (Cohen, 1998; Stephenson, 1997). With improved treatment, many children with sickle-cell anemia will live more normal lives.

Phenylketonuria: A Success Story

Phenylketonuria (PKU) is a rare recessive disorder that occurs in approximately 1 in 12,000 births (Motulsky, 1997). It involves the inability to digest a particular amino acid called phenylalanine. If left untreated, brain damage leading to retardation results. Phenylalanine is found in all protein-rich foods, including fish, meats, poultry, eggs, and milk. It is also found in some soft drinks, many of which are now labeled. Most infants are screened, usually on the day they are scheduled to be discharged from the hospital, to determine whether they have PKU (Plomin et al., 1990).

Phenylketonuria is treated with a special diet low in phenylalanine. During middle childhood, the diet is relaxed or even abandoned. However, if the diet is abandoned too early, the child's intellectual abilities are negatively affected (Holtzman, Kronmal, Van Doorninck, Azen, & Koch, 1986). Some people should remain on the diet for life, which is not easy because the amino acid is found in so many foods (DeAngelis, 1993). A woman who has PKU should consult a physician before she becomes pregnant. If she becomes pregnant while not on the diet, the baby is likely to be born with mental retardation because of the mother's abnormal body chemistry.

Chromosomal Abnormalities

Some inherited disorders are due to chromosomal abnormalities, conditions in which a person has too few, too many, or incomplete chromosomes. Four of the most important are Down syndrome, Klinefelter's syndrome, Turner's syndrome, and the fragile X syndrome.

Down Syndrome   The most common chromosomal disorder is Down syndrome, which occurs in approximately 1 in every 1,000 births (Plomin et al., 1990). In the most common type, called trisomy, an extra chromosome is found on the 21st pair of chromosomes. The frequency of this disorder increases with the age of the mother (see Figure 3.6 on page 102). In about 5% of the cases, the disorder is linked to the sperm (Antonarakis, 1991). In the United States, about 5,000 children a year are born with Down syndrome (Dullea, 1989).

Children with Down syndrome are identified either at birth or shortly after by their physical appearance. Unusual physical features include folded eyes, short digits, flat face, protruding tongue, and harsh voice. Mental retardation is associated with the disorder, but the degree of retardation varies greatly. Today, many children with Down syndrome are given special treatment, including special

Guideposts

What are the symptoms and method of transmission for cystic fibrosis, Tay-Sachs disease, sickle-cell anemia, and phenylketonuria?

phenylketonuria (PKU)
A recessive genetic disorder marked by the inability to digest a particular amino acid and leading to mental retardation if not treated.

Down syndrome
A disorder caused by the presence of an extra chromosome, leading to a distinct physical appearance and often times mental retardation of varying degree.

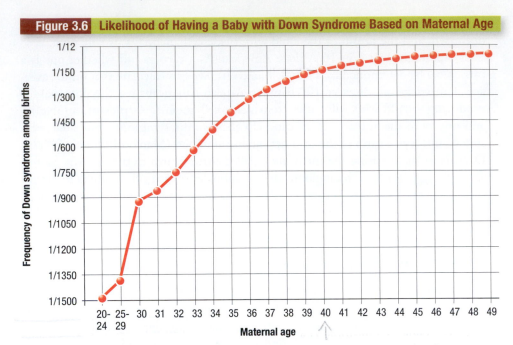

Figure 3.6 Likelihood of Having a Baby with Down Syndrome Based on Maternal Age

NOTE: This chart lists only the *approximate* frequency of babies with Down syndrome based on the mother's age. The figures are based on the *average* of the findings of four separate population surveys. SOURCE: Stray-Gundersen, (1986)

T F

8

Most children with Down syndrome are not diagnosed until they enter kindergarten or first grade.

preschool programs, which have improved their cognitive functioning, and many score in the mildly retarded range on intelligence tests (Kaplan, 1996). Years ago, most children with this disorder were institutionalized immediately after birth, but this is no longer the case. Many children with Down syndrome are now raised at home, which is usually beneficial.

Children with Down syndrome show the same developmental milestones as other children but at a much delayed pace. This includes smiling and laughing, eye contact during play, self-recognition, some attachment behaviors, and symbolic play (Roach, Barratt, Miller, & Leavitt, 1998). Not too long ago, the life expectancy for children with Down syndrome was 10 years or less. Congenital heart problems are common, and resistance to disease is low. However, medical advances have substantially increased the life span of these children. Although the mortality rate among young children with Down Syndrome is much higher than for other children, most who survive infancy live well into adulthood (Baird & Sadovnick, 1987). After the age of about 40, people with Down syndrome appear to be more susceptible to diseases that are related to old age. Many have brain lesions that look like the lesions of Alzheimer's disease, and many show symptoms of senility (Kolata, 1989). This may be because the genes associated with congenital heart defects, brain changes associated with a familial variety of Alzheimer's disease, and some other disorders are also found on the 21st chromosome. Much research today is being conducted into the relationship between various genes on the 21st chromosome.

Not only have the health and life expectancy of Down syndrome children improved, but their entire life has changed. This is the first generation who, with the help of early intervention programs, has ventured forth into the normal world of children. Some attend public schools (Schnaiberg, 1996). Although most are in special classes, some attend regular classes. They interact with nonretarded children and are tuned into the culture of childhood and adolescence. Some people with Down syndrome have been successful in the world of work with the help of job coaches and can live semi-independently, often in group homes (Kaplan, 1996).

Guideposts

What is Down syndrome? How have the lives of children with this disorder changed?

Sex-Linked Chromosomal Disorders   Three of the more common chromosomal disorders are caused by problems that occur on the sex chromosomes. In Klinefelter's syndrome, the male receives at least one more X chromosome than he should, thus creating an XXY genotype. This is found in approximately 1 in 600 male births. Children afflicted with this disorder have small sex organs and are sterile. Many, though not all, have mental retardation.

Turner's syndrome is caused by lack of an X chromosome. The genotype is expressed as XO. These females are sterile, short, and do not mature naturally. They often require estrogen treatments to attain adult stature. Though they often have specific learning problems, they are not usually mentally retarded (Kalat, 1980). They perform poorly on spatial, attention, and short-term memory tasks and show more difficulty accurately discriminating facial expressions. This last deficit may be the basis of some of their frequent problems in social relationships (McCauley, Kay, Ito, & Treder, 1987). Turner's syndrome appears in about 1 out of every 2,000 female births (Sutton, 1980).

The fragile X syndrome is a recessive sex-linked disorder in which the X chromosome is fragile and breaks easily. It is associated with mental retardation, hyperactivity, and short attention span, as well as a number of physical abnormalities (Hagerman, 1996). It occurs in just under 1 in 2,000 male births.

Down syndrome is the most common chromosomal disorder. It affects about 5000 children a year in the United States.

Predispositions to Disorders

Not all genetically based disorders are transmitted directly. Sometimes a predisposition to a disorder, rather than the disorder itself, is passed from parents to children. People with different genotypes may be differentially sensitive to various environments (Plomin & Rutter, 1998). This is true with the serious emotional disorder known as schizophrenia as well as with alcoholism.

Schizophrenia   Schizophrenia is a severe mental disorder characterized by hallucinations, delusions, emotional disturbances, apathy, and withdrawal. About 50% of the residents of mental hospitals at any one time suffer from the disorder. Schizophrenia is a major international health problem.

A number of twin and adoption studies have suggested that a genetic basis for schizophrenia exists (Nigg & Goldsmith, 1994). However, the evidence also indicates a strong environmental component. What appears to be transmitted is not the disease itself but rather a tendency or predisposition to acquire the disorder. All environmental factors being equal, an individual with a family history of schizophrenia is at greater risk for the disease than one with no family history of schizophrenia.

Prenatal, birth, and psychosocial factors also play a role. For example, some prenatal insults that cause brain abnormalities, such as lack of oxygen to the brain and birth trauma, some cognitive deficits, and chaotic family situations with communication problems may be implicated (Mirsky & Duncan, 1986). Genetic factors may make an individual more vulnerable to schizophrenia, but other factors can be important as well.

Guideposts

What does it mean if an individual inherits a predisposition to a disease?

T F
9

Schizophrenia, like cystic fibrosis or Tay-Sachs disease, is transmitted directly from parent to child.

schizophrenia
A severe mental disorder marked by hallucinations, delusions, and emotional disturbances.

Alcoholism and Genetics Twin and adoption studies consistently find a genetic basis for alcoholism (U.S. Department of Health and Human Services [USDHHS], 1993). When rates of alcohol abuse were studied in adoptees and their biological parents, adopted sons whose biological fathers were alcoholic were three times more likely to become alcoholic than adopted sons of nonalcoholic fathers (Bohman, 1986). If the mother was an alcoholic, the sons were twice as likely to become alcoholic. Studies also show a higher concordance rate for alcoholism among identical twins than fraternal twins (McGue, 1993; Sexias & Youcha, 1985). Most studies conclude that there is a genetic predisposition to alcoholism (Schukit, Tsuang, Anthenelli, Tipp, & Nurnberger, 1996), and some evidence links it to chromosome 11, which contains genes that metabolize alcohol (Rose, 1995). However, considerable evidence also exists that environmental factors are important as well. Most children of alcoholics do *not* become alcoholics, often because they have made the conscious choice not to drink. The cognitive factors that lead these people to refrain from alcohol use require more research. In addition, even people with no direct relative being alcoholic can become alcoholic. What is inherited is a predisposition to alcoholism.

Studies show that alcoholics and nonalcoholics have enzyme differences in the ability to break down alcohol. Alcoholics metabolize alcohol differently than nonalcoholics and build up tolerance more easily (Schukit, 1987). In one study, the sons of alcoholic fathers were compared with sons of nonalcoholic fathers. At the time of the study, none of the children were alcoholics. Even with the same level of alcohol in their systems, the sons of alcoholic fathers reported that they were less intoxicated than the sons of nonalcoholic fathers did (Schuckit, 1986). Some metabolic differences may be responsible for this difference. In addition, several neurological and chemical differences have been found between the two groups (Cloninger, 1987; USDHHS, 1993). It seems that people with a predisposition to alcoholism show a low intensity of reaction to alcohol as documented by subjective feelings of intoxication, measures of brain electrical activity, and the level of hormones known to be altered by alcohol (Schuckit, 1994).

Predispositions are inherited in a rather complex manner. Scientists are now trying to discover chemical or neurological markers that would allow us to discern which people are more at risk than others. Those at-risk individuals could then seek information and counseling that would help them understand their situation and deal with it. Our new knowledge of genetics presents us with many new opportunities but also new dangers, as discussed in *The New Genetics: Premises, Promises and Problems* on page 105.

Anyone can become an alcoholic, but research shows that a genetic predisposition to alcoholism exists.

The Child in the 21st Century

The New Genetics: Premises, Promises, and Problems

Magazines splash stories on the "new genetics" with a combination of incredible excitement over the possibilities for improving people's health and the possibilities for abuse. The discoveries in genetics have come fast and furious. It was only about 45 years ago that science finally confirmed that human beings carry 46 chromosomes, and today we are performing gene therapy.

Much of the recent progress is due to the most ambitious research project ever attempted, called the Human Genome Project (HGP) which began in 1990. Its 15-year goal is to map and sequence all 50,000 to 100,000 human genes. *Mapping genes* involves finding where the genes for particular characteristics are located on the chromosome, while *sequencing genes* refers to deciphering the language that tells the gene what to do and when.

Genes are made of deoxyribonucleic acid (DNA) and consist of four bases or nucleotides, adenine (A), thymine (T), guanine (G), and cytosine (C), which pair with themselves to construct the rungs of the double-helix DNA ladder. Most genes consist of between 10,000 and 150,000 code letters.

The progress in deciphering genes has been astounding and often faster than predicted, due to technological innovations that have aided researchers in their efforts (Guyer & Collins, 1993; Stephenson, 1998). This new knowledge has improved our understanding of many genetic diseases. Scientists have discovered the chromosome on which the defective gene is carried for a number of genetic diseases, including Huntington's

Disease (a fatal dominant genetic disorder whose onset is late middle age), Duchenne's muscular dystrophy, and familial Alzheimer's disease. The genetic basis for certain types of cancer, including colon and breast cancer, have been isolated (Lerman et al., 1999). New ways of determining carrier status as well as who is most at risk for a particular condition have been developed. This knowledge may eventually lead to methods which may alter the functioning of genes, preventing or even curing diseases. In 1994, scientists discovered a gene that keeps cancer from spreading; placing this gene in people who lack it or whose gene is not functioning properly could prevent the spread of a tumor (Weiner, 1996). A gene that seems essential for keeping the body's weight stable was copied in 1994. Although it is a long way from this feat to curing obesity genetically, since other genes and environmental factors are involved, it may be possible to control weight in this manner some day (Weiner, 1996). Genetic information will make it possible to diagnose people who have a disease well before any symptoms appear, and identify people at risk for developing a disease in the future (Churchill, 1997).

Our ability to screen for many genetic diseases has already yielded benefits. A Montreal team screened high school students for carrier status for Tay-Sachs disease and thalassemia (a blood disease) and, combined with counseling, reduced the frequency of these genetic diseases in Montreal. Careful study found that these students experienced no apparent psychological harm, and confidentiality was assured (McCabe, 1996; Mitchell, Capua, Clow, & Scriver, 1996). A screening program for thalassemia in

Hong Kong also reported success (Lau et al., 1996). The National Institutes of Health (NIH) recently recommended that screening for cystic fibrosis be offered as an option to all couples planning to have children and that insurance companies should cover the cost of the procedure ("Opposition to Human Cloning," 1997). The panel stressed the importance of education, counseling, and informed consent in all cases in which genetic testing is offered.

In many university clinics and hospitals, genetic counselors help people determine their risks of having a child with a genetic disorder. Counseling should be an integral part of any genetic test (Churchill, 1997). Most people who seek genetic counseling are faced with some kind of decision (Richards, 1998). A family with one child who has suffered from a genetic difficulty may have to decide whether to have other children. Others may have to decide whether they should even begin a family. Still others may be forced to decide whether to terminate a pregnancy based on laboratory tests showing that the fetus has some serious genetic defect—certainly a controversial question. Previous generations did not have the information needed to make such decisions, but success with some genetic disorders has provided an incentive for more screening to take place in the future (Richards, 1998).

The child in the 21st century will find that some genetic testing routine and the improvements it brings may allow the cure or reduction in the symptoms for many diseases. But many important issues remain in the use of such genetic technology and knowledge. As more diseases and predispositions to conditions and characteristics are discovered, will employers and insurance companies misuse such knowledge? For example, an employer may require a genetic examination and refuse to hire people with predispositions for particular personality traits, such as aggressiveness or withdrawal (Parens, 1996). Many people do not understand the concept of predisposition and may misinterpret a positive finding of an increased risk to incorrectly believe that the person is certain to develop the condition. In fact, people who have been found to have a known gene defect have been denied health insurance, employment opportunities, educational placements, and acceptance into the armed forces. In some cases, adoption agencies have refused to place children with prospective parents who had a genetic predisposition (Lynch, 1996). Several states have passed legislation and some members of Congress have introduced bills prohibiting such practices, but privacy remains a concern.

If a definite therapeutic option is available, there is little debate about the value of screening, since therapy coupled with counseling is appropriate. But what

about diseases for which there is no prevention available (Caskey, 1997)? For example, what if science develops the ability to screen for the genetic predisposition to schizophrenia or Alzheimer's disease? Since no preventive treatment for people at risk is available, the question arises as to why such screening should be done at all (Annas, 1995). Indeed, some screening is available for some late-onset diseases, and it is not often recommended because nothing can be done or no treatment is required for many years (Motulsky, 1997). However, the results may influence how people feel about themselves. After testing as carriers for cystic fibrosis, carriers had a poorer perception of their health than did noncarriers, even though they were told that carrier status did not and would not affect their health (Axworthy, Brocks, Bobrow, & Marteau, 1996).

In the longer term, there is the question of designer genes. Currently, science is focusing on disease, but what if researchers discover the genes that underlie height or some other physical characteristic, and the technology

involved in gene therapy is improved? Parents who learn that their child will be healthy but short may desire to alter the genes of the child so that the child is taller. If researchers isolate genes that underlie personality, perhaps even aggression, should parents be allowed to alter the child's genotype? Consider how this would affect the diversity of the human genotype. This leads to the question of which aspects of the genotype parents should be permitted to alter and which should be forbidden. This may sound like science fiction, but remember that just a few years ago the idea of screening for genetic abnormalities was considered futuristic.

Others are concerned about the impact this information may have on our traditional ideas about free will and personal responsibility. After presenting twin and adoption studies concerning obesity, I often hear students claim that they were destined to be fat and they had no control. This is certainly not true, but such an attitude could lead to resignation. Could an individual with a predisposition to aggression claim that his genes made him do the crime (Weiner, 1996)? These are important questions. On the other hand, such genetic information that may result in our reconsideration of complete free will may lead to a decrease in discrimination. Evidence showing a genetic basis for homosexuality has often been welcomed by the gay community because it is viewed as exploding the myth of sexual choice (Nelkin & Lindee, 1995). Gays may be discriminated against less if people believe that a genetic basis underlies sexual preference (Bailey, 1995). The idea that some genetic information may call into question the doctrine of complete free will does not mean that the information is incorrect. The idea of absolute free will is not necessary to encourage personal

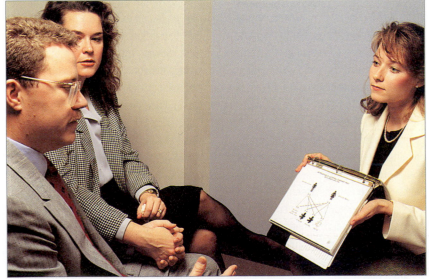

Genetic counselors help parents determine the risks of having a child with a genetic disorder.

responsibility (Parens, 1996). In fact, the change in attitude may even promote it. People with a predisposition to obesity or alcoholism may realize that they need to change their eating and drinking habits and that it is not only in their best interests but also in their power to prevent these conditions from arising.

Perhaps the most difficult question is the possibility that genetic information may be subverted into "demonstrating" that certain minority groups are somehow less competent or inferior to others and be used as a rationale for discrimination. In the past, mistaken genetic doctrines have been used to justify discrimination and even genocide. This must always be guarded against.

Yet, people who look only at the possible misuse of genetic research often make the error of assuming that because there is a possibility for abuse, therefore it definitely will be abused (Parens, 1996). A reasonable amount of money allocated for the Human Genome Project is being used to study the moral and ethical problems arising out of genetic advances. Many of the ethical problems have been studied, debated, and possible solutions suggested. There is a real danger that people and lawmakers may react emotionally to genetic research, limiting it unnecessarily due to their fear of the unknown.

Nothing shows this more than the reaction to an innocent-looking sheep named Dolly—the first mammal to be cloned from a single adult cell (Stephenson, 1997). When Ian Wilmut and his colleagues announced their success in cloning, they ignited a tremendous emotional reaction (Wilmut et al., 1997). The fear that someone would clone a human being led to shouts of outrage and the swift passage of laws against such an event. The director of the United Nation's World Health Organization

declared cloning of human beings to be ethically unacceptable ("Opposition to Human Cloning," 1997). The president of the United States announced a ban on the use of federal funds for any cloning of human beings and urged a private moratorium on any such project. It is ironic that in the rush to ban cloning of human beings, the fact that researchers, including Dr. Wilmut, agree that cloning humans would be wrong is often lost.

The problem is not the ban on cloning humans—almost everyone is in favor of this—but that many proposed laws are so broad that they would effectively ban basic and applied research on cloning techniques that could pave the way for exciting new treatments (Annas, 1998). For example, scientists may be able to clone a new organ from the cells of a person whose heart or liver is failing, thereby eliminating the problem of rejection (Weiner, 1996). Already, scientists in some countries have claimed that the broad laws interfere with their research. Norway's parliament passed a law against cloning human beings and highly developed organisms, and some scientists argue that it is so restrictive and hastily passed that it may interfere with their research into other areas ("Opposition to Human Cloning," 1997). A similar law was rejected in the United States (Annas, 1998).

There is no doubt that genetic advancements have the potential for benefit and misuse (Plomin & Rutter, 1998). Doctors may not understand the potential for problems. The results of a survey on the use and interpretation of a test for a mutation in a gene that causes colon cancer found that few patients received genetic counseling or even provided written consent before being tested (Giardiello et al., 1997). In the wrong hands, such information could affect a patient's insurability, employment, and

family relationships (Veatch, 1997). The need for rules concerning confidentiality and limiting the use of genetic testing in the workplace and by insurance companies is obvious. Genetic screening and testing provide information that differs substantially from family histories or the results of a cholesterol test. The genetic code of an individual is similar to a personal diary that, rather than offer the reader information about the past or the present, offers probabilistic information about the future (Annas, 1995). As with any diary, it should be private. Personal genetic information requires special privacy protection.

In the 21st century, the number of genetic tests available and the ability to influence one's genotype and that of the next generation may increase substantially. The possibility for important medical breakthroughs as well as the abuse of such research is real. Our society will face difficult challenges in determining just how this new information will be used.

What do you think?

Let's speculate that scientists have discovered the gene responsible for the predisposition to obesity and the genes that determine height. It becomes technically possible for doctors to allow parents to choose the characteristics of their children. A particular set of parents want only tall children and those without a predisposition to obesity. They are willing to pay for the service. Should parents be able to "design" their own children?

You can explore the questions above using InfoTrac College Edition. Hint: enter search terms *Genetic Screening* and *Genetic Screening Laws.*

Models of Genetic Influence

Perhaps you are impressed with the sheer array of characteristics, abilities, and disorders that are affected by one's genetic endowment. Psychologists, though, are not as interested in the degree of genetic involvement as in *how* genetics and environmental factors interact. It is easy to say that we must appreciate the constant genetic interactions between environmental and genetic factors to understand personality and development. But what is the nature of this interaction, and how does this interaction occur?

The Range of Reaction Model

Most human behaviors are the result of a highly complex reciprocal interaction between genetic and environmental factors. How our genes are expressed depends on the environment in which we exist, and how we respond to elements of our environment depends partially on our genetic endowment.

This is explained by the range of reaction model (Gottesman, 1966; Gottesman & Shields, 1972). Each genotype can produce a range of different phenotypes (its range of reaction) depending on the environment. One's genotype allows an individualized range of possible responses to the environment, and the environment determines the path. People differ in their responses to similar environments because their genetic makeup differs. Two children exposed to the same environment, perhaps one that is enriched or extremely unstimulating, will have different responses. Each child would be helped by the stimulating environment and hurt by the unstimulating environment, but due to their genetic differences, each would be affected to different degrees. The child's genotype for intellectual ability allows for a number of phenotypical paths, and it is the environment that determines which path the child follows.

Although this model seems reasonable, some psychologists view this model as too rigid. We cannot know the individual's genotype, and each new environment may have different influences on developmental outcomes that cannot be stated in advance of actual research investigation (Gottlieb, 1991). Therefore, the limits cannot be known.

Guideposts

How does the range of reaction model explain genetic/environmental interaction?

Genotype/Environment Effects Model

Perhaps the most interesting and controversial model describing how genes and environmental factors interact is the genotype/environment effects model (Scarr & McCartney, 1983). This model suggests three different genotype and environment effects.

The first is a *passive/environment* effect in which parents provide a rearing environment that is in itself affected by the parents' genes. Verbal ability is in some measure hereditary, and parents pass on genes for this ability as well as create an environment in which this ability can be developed. The environment created by the parents is, in part, shaped by their genetic endowment.

The second type of genotype/environment effect is called *evocative* because it represents the various responses that people with different genotypes evoke from the environment. For example, smiling, active babies receive more social stimulation than passive infants. Quick, attentive preschoolers receive more pleasant, mutually satisfying interactions than uncooperative, distractible children. A genetic basis for these behaviors exists. Some of the similarities in child-rearing strategies may be due to the genetic similarities of these children in that their behavior produces these parental reactions (Revelle, 1995). Some kinds of behavior evoke particular reactions from the environment.

The third kind of genotype/environment is called *active* and represents the child's selective attention to and learning from aspects of the environment that are influenced by the genotype. People seek out environments they find comfortable and stimulating. They actively select elements from the environment to pay attention to and learn about, sometimes called *niche picking* or *niche building*. These selections are related to the individual's motivation, personality, and intellectual ability, all partially affected by one's genotype. This is the most powerful connection between people and environment. For example, someone who enjoys athletics pays attention to all kinds of athletic stimuli, selecting athletic activities and participating in them thus becoming a better athlete.

As children grow, the relative importance of the three kinds of effects changes. Although infants are active in structuring their experiences by selective attention, they do not have much freedom or many opportunities. Their environments are created by parents and, according to this theory, reflect both genotype and environment. The effects of these passive genotype environments decline as the individual receives more opportunities to interact with the environment, replacing passive effects with more active ones. The importance of evocative effects remains throughout life.

According to this theory, a child with a particular genotype will receive certain kinds of parenting and be exposed to particular parent-created environments, evoke certain responses from others, and select particular aspects from the environment. Nothing is rigidly determined. The environment affects the child at every level of development.

This model nicely explains the fact that fraternal twins, adopted children, and siblings seem to become more different as they grow older (McGue et al., 1993). The early home environment is similar but because of genetic differences their active/environment interactions differ. They become more and more different as they become more independent. Identical twins, even when separated, remain more similar as they seek out similar experiences because they have the same genes. Scarr and McCartney argue that genes influence development by influencing the experiences children have. Genes become the quarterback of the nature-nurture team. Genes direct the course of human experience but experiential opportunities are required for development to occur. A restrictive environment does not allow children to develop their potential and abilities (Scarr, 1993).

This model offers a different way of explaining the dynamics behind a behavior. If we look at a child who is very warm and friendly and whose parents are the same, we might argue that the parents both model and reinforce such behaviors in their children. On the other hand, we can argue that a genetic basis underlies this and other traits. The parents are creating an environment consistent with their genes; the child is evoking positive reinforcement from the parents because he or she is acting in a particular way partially because of genetic endowment; and, lastly, the child seeks out these interactions, partially owing to genetic endowment.

You may be uncomfortable with this explanation. It seems as if as long as children are not raised in a terrible environment they will maximize their cognitive and social abilities. We may be in danger of forgetting environmental factors or, at

An active, smiling infant receives more social stimulation and positive feedback than a passive infant.

Guideposts

What are passive, evocative, and active effects?

least, relegating them to a secondary position, one they do not deserve. In fact, one of the objections to the idea that genotypes drive phenotypes is the problem of relegating such environmental elements as child-rearing practices or intellectual stimulation to a lower level of interest (Baumrind, 1993). Parents may believe that if a genetic basis underlies behavior, they have no power to change things. Other critics are concerned that an overemphasis on genetic factors will discourage intervention efforts (Jackson, 1993). With the exception of some rare genetic diseases, heritability estimates never even approach a figure that would allow one to argue that the environment is unimportant. Often genetic factors do not even explain 50% of the variability. It is also a myth, as noted previously, that if some aspect of development is influenced by genes, it cannot be changed (Cowan et al., 1998).

The New Reality

Our new understanding of genetic/environmental interaction has implications for the two situations described at the beginning of this chapter. Our understanding of shared and nonshared environments and genetics and how they interact means that we should expect siblings to be different. In the second case, some information about possible genetic diseases might be helpful for adoptive parents, and many professionals advocate that genetic family histories be made available to adoptive families (Bernhardt & Rauch, 1993). While accepting the fact of predispositions, parents must also appreciate the substantial effects that the environment has on children. Parents can enhance the environment and allow children to maximize their abilities (Creedy, 1994).

There is no doubt that the manner in which modern scientists view the interaction of genetics and the environment is more complicated than it has been in the past. Some people yearn for the "good old days," when general statements about what was inherited and what wasn't could be made. Things were certainly easier then, even if they were almost always incorrect. The more modern view of the nature-nurture controversy is certainly more complicated and precludes making grandiose statements about heredity causing one thing and the environment causing another. It is clear that we cannot speak of nature without nurture or of nurture without nature (Creedy, 1994). Our present knowledge, however, gives us the opportunity to marvel once again at the complicated process by which a tiny, one-cell fertilized egg develops into a person who then, guided by both genetic endowment and environmental factors, can fulfill his or her human promise.

Summary

1. The basic unit of heredity is the gene, which is composed of DNA and carried on chromosomes. Human beings have 23 pairs of chromosomes. In the sex cells, however, the chromosome pair splits, so that each sex cell contains 23 chromosomes. This split is random, assuring genetic individuality. The 23 chromosomes found in both the egg and the sperm cells combine during fertilization to maintain the same 46 chromosomes found in normal human beings.

2. The first 22 pairs of chromosomes appear to be alike, but the 23rd pair, the sex chromosomes, is different. A female has two X chromosomes, while the male has an X and a Y. The male determines the gender of the offspring, since he can contribute an X or a Y, while the female contributes only an X.

3. A trait that is expressed even if only one gene for it is present is called dominant. A trait that requires two genes to express itself is called recessive.

4. When a particular characteristic is influenced by many genes, we consider the mechanism of transmission to be polygenic, multigenic, or multifactorial. The term *multifactorial* is sometimes used to denote characteristics influenced by a number of genes as well as by the environment. The term *genotype* describes the genetic composition of the individual, while the term *phenotype* refers to the person's observable characteristics. An individual's phenotype and genotype may be different.

5. Since the X chromosome is three times larger than the Y, a number of genes found on the X are not present on the Y. When there is some defect on the X, a male may not be able to counter its effects, since males possess only one X and the gene may not be found at all on the Y. Traits inherited in this manner are called sex-linked traits. Females normally do not show them, because they have two X chromosomes, and only one normal gene is necessary to mask the effects of the defective gene. Hemophilia and color blindness are transmitted in this way to males.

6. The term *heritability* refers to that proportion of the measured variation between people in a given population on a particular characteristic that is the result of genetic factors. Scientists use twin and adoption studies to determine the extent to which a particular trait has a genetic basis. The agreement of twins on any particular characteristic is known as the concordance rate.

7. Our genetic endowment affects our physical characteristics. Since people react to one another on the basis of some of them, these characteristics can become socially important even if they are biologically trivial.

8. Human beings are born with a temperament, an individual way of responding to the environment. Temperament shows considerable stability in infancy, and after infancy evidence for both stability and change exists. Different physiological responses may underlie temperament. Children's temperament may influence how others react to them.

9. A genetic basis may account for many personality traits and some types of cognitive and emotional difficulties. There are no known genes for behavior, but genetic factors may influence behavior through physiological and neurological means.

10. Siblings differ from each other for genetic and environmental reasons. They share only on the average of half their genes in common. They also have many unique, individual experiences (nonshared environmental influences).

11. A child's rate of maturation is also affected by genetic factors. There appears to be a genetic basis for intelligence, although there is much dispute over the heritability figure. However, no matter what figure is used, an individual's environment greatly affects how these genes will be expressed. Educational programs can raise the intelligence scores of children.

12. A number of genetic disorders have been discovered, including cystic fibrosis, Tay-Sachs disease, sickle-cell anemia, and phenylketonuria.

13. If an extra chromosome somehow attaches itself to the 21st pair, the infant is born with Down syndrome. Such infants show mental retardation of varying degrees and have a number of distinctive physical attributes.

14. There is a significant genetic component in some major mental disorders, including schizophrenia, as well as in alcoholism. However, what is transmitted is not the disorder itself but rather a tendency or a predisposition to develop the disorder given a particular environment.

15. Some models seek to answer the question of how genes and environment interact to form a phenotype. The range of reaction model argues that for each genotype there are a number of possible outcomes, and it is the environment that determines which is shown. The genotype/environmental effects theory explains the interaction between genetic and environmental factors by using three types of interactions: passive, in which parents provide an environment for the child partly based on their genotypes; evocative, in which the child's behaviors that are partially based upon the genotype influence how others react to the child; and active, in which the individual, partially based on the genotype, chooses which aspects of the environment to attend to and which activities to engage in.

Review

The basic unit of heredity is the (1)_____ , which is made up of deoxyribonucleic acid. Genes are carried on (2)_____ . Each normal human being has a total of (3)_____ chromosomes. Every cell, except for the (4)_____ , has this total. During the process of (5)_____ , the sex cells divide to form two cells; during the process of (6)_____ , some of the genetic material from one chromosome may be exchanged for genetic material on the other chromosome. These processes ensure genetic individuality. (7)_____ twins develop from a single egg and a single sperm and share the same genetic composition, whereas (8)_____ twins develop from two different eggs that are fertilized by two different sperm.

If the male contributes an X chromosome, the offspring will be (9)_____ . If the male contributes a Y chromosome, the offspring will be (10)_____ . If only one gene is necessary to show a particular trait, the trait is said to be (11)_____ . If two genes, one from the mother and one from the father, are needed to show a particular trait, the trait is said to be (12)_____ . Sometimes, many genes contribute to a particular characteristic, a mode of transmission called (13)_____ ; and if many genes combine with environmental factors to produce a characteristic, the mode of transmission is called (14)_____ . The genetic makeup of an individual is called the (15)_____ , while the observable characteristics of an individual is called the (16)_____ . Traits that are transmitted through genes on the 21st chromosome are called (17)_____ traits.

Determining whether a particular characteristic has a genetic base is not easy. Scientists use the term (18)_____ to describe the proportion of the differences between people in a given population on a particular characteristic caused by genetic factors. Scientists also use the term (19)_____ to describe the proportion of variation between people in a given population on a particular characteristic due to environmental factors. Scientists often use either (20)_____ studies or (21)_____ studies to determine whether genetic influence underlies a particular behavior.

Children are born with an individual style of responding to the environment called, (22)_____ . Some psychologists divide these styles into easy, slow to warm up, and (23)_____ . Others use a different system measuring emotionality, activity level, (24)_____ and sometimes impulsivity. A genetic basis for many personality dimensions exists. Genes influence behavior through (25)_____ functioning.

People often ask how siblings can be so different? Siblings share, on the average, (26)_____ % of their genes in common, so they are genetically different. In addition, although they share the same home and neighborhood, called (27)_____ environmental factors, they have many different experiences unique to each, called (28)_____ environment.

How fast a child develops certain skills, such as standing and walking, is referred to as a child's (29)_____ and is affected by genetics. Psychologists use the concept of (30)_____ to describe the fact that the child has the skills necessary to master a new task. Intelligence is also affected by genetic factors, but to explain intelligence level, one must look at how genetic and (31)_____ factors interact. Many diseases are genetically transmitted. (32)_____ is a genetic disease affecting the child's mucus glands that causes respiratory problems. Another genetically transmitted disease is a blood disease called (33)_____ that affects mostly African Americans and Latinos. (34)_____ is a disease caused by the inability to digest a protein called phenylalanine. Other disorders are caused by chromosomal problems. Children with (35)_____ have a specific physical appearance and mental retardation caused by an extra chromosome on the 21st chromosome. Many disorders, such as schizophrenia and alcoholism, have a genetic basis, and people inherit a (36)_____ to the disease not the disease itself.

Psychologists today are more interested in how the environment and genetic factors interact than in how much of a trait can be explained by genetic factors. The (37)_____ model states that for each genotype there are many different possible phenotypes depending on the environment. The genotype/environment interaction model claims that there are three types of genetic/environment effects. (38)_____ effects involve the way a child's environment is structured, which partially depends on the parents' genetic endowment. (39)_____ effects involve actions on the part of the child that are partially determined by genetics, which may affect how others react to him or her. Finally, (40)_____ effects involve the individual's choices, which are influenced by genetic endowment.

InfoTrac

For additional readings, explore InfoTrac College Edition, our online library. Go to http://www.infotrac-college.com/wadsworth. Hint: enter the search terms *Common Genetic* or *Environmental Influences,* and *Genetic Transmission.*

What's on the web

Questionnaire used to Measure Temperament
http://www.temperament.com

Genetic Disorders
http://www.funkandwagnalls.com/encyclopedia/low/articles/g/g009000374f.html

American Society for Reproductive Medicine
http://www.asrm.org/mainpati.html

The Wadsworth Psychology Study Center Web Site
Go to the Wadsworth Psychology Study Center at http://psychology.wadsworth.com/ for quiz questions, research updates, hot topics, interactive exercises, and suggested readings in the InfoTrac College Edition related to this chapter.

CHAPTER FOUR

Prenatal Development

CHAPTER OUTLINE

The First Odyssey

Prenatal Development

Current Issues

Technology, Pregnancy, and Birth

Birth

Prematurity: Born at Risk

Looking Ahead

ARE THESE STATEMENTS
True *or* False?

1. Almost one-quarter of all American infants are born with some recognizable birth defect.
2. A fetus may suck its thumb in the womb.
3. Smokers are much more likely to give birth to premature infants than nonsmokers.
4. Infants exposed to cocaine while in the womb are less irritable, more placid, and smile more but at inappropriate times than infants who have not been exposed to cocaine prenatally.
5. Today, a medication exists that, when administered to pregnant women who test positive for the virus that causes AIDS, reduces the chances of the transmission of AIDS to the infant.
6. Mothers who have their first child in their 30s show more patience than younger mothers.
7. Chronic malnutrition in pregnant women can lead to a condition in which the child has fewer brain cells.
8. Exposure to chemicals in the workplace and some pesticides may affect the sperm cells, leading to fetal deformities.
9. Parents of children who have been conceived through in vitro fertilization (outside the womb in an artificial manner) are overprotective of these children but interact less with them than parents of children who have been conceived in the typical manner.
10. If a woman gives birth to a child by cesarean section, all her subsequent children must be born in the same way.

Answers: 1. False. 2. True. 3. True. 4. False. 5. True. 6. True. 7. True. 8. True. 9. False. 10. False.

and Birth

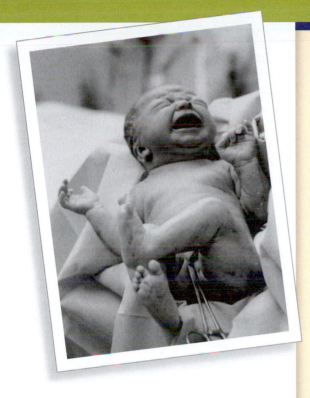

The First Odyssey

Look through the window of a hospital nursery and watch the infants for a few minutes. Some are sleeping, some fussing, and some crying. These infants all seem equally ready to begin their human odyssey. But this is not really so. Some of these infants are already starting at a disadvantage because of adverse experiences in the womb or during the birth process. Every child deserves a fair chance to develop healthfully, but all too often this is not the case because exposure to some agent during pregnancy may compromise development.

A number of environmental, physical, and viral agents can cause difficulties during pregnancy. Although the threats are real enough, the great majority of infants develop normally and emerge from the birth canal ready for life. About 7% of all the live births in the United States have low birth weight, and 3 to 7% have some recognizable birth defect (Wyrobek, 1993). Knowledge of the possible dangers allows prospective parents to alter their behavior to give their child the best start possible.

Almost one-quarter of all American infants are born with some recognizable birth defect.

115

Prenatal Development

People often do not appreciate the importance of what transpires during the prenatal period and act as though it had no relationship to life outside the womb (Hofer, 1988). This view is changing as scientific research is communicated to the public and people begin to appreciate the importance of the prenatal period.

The Beginning

During ovulation, one egg is allowed to pass into the fallopian tube, where it is exposed to any sperm that are present. Although many sperm may surround the egg cell, only one will penetrate the cell's outer wall. At this moment of conception, the mother's egg cell is fertilized by the father's sperm. When this occurs, there is a rearrangement and an exchange of genetic material, and the genetic endowment of the new being is set for life. This fertilized egg, or zygote, continues to travel down the tube into the uterus, or womb.

Within hours of conception, the fertilized ovum (zygote) divides, beginning a continuous process of cell differentiation.

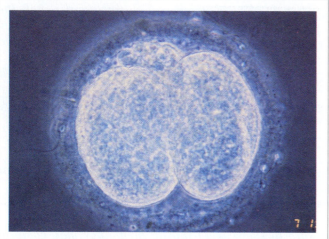

In some cases, two eggs may pass into the fallopian tube and be fertilized by two different sperm. The result is dizygotic, or fraternal, twins—two separately developing organisms that are no more genetically similar than any other pair of siblings. Identical twins develop from a single egg and a single sperm. A cell division takes place very early in development, and twins born from a single egg and single sperm have the identical genetic makeup.

From the moment of conception, the developing organism is affected by its genotype and its environment. During the nine months in the womb, its weight will increase one billion times over (Annis, 1978), and an infant will emerge with all biological systems ready for life outside the womb. Table 4.1 summarizes prenatal development.

The Germinal Stage

It takes anywhere from a week to ten days or so for the fertilized egg to embed itself in the lining of the uterus. During this period, called the **germinal stage,** the fertilized egg divides again and again and begins the process of specialization that results in the formation of its organs. On the second day, about 30 hours after fertilization, the cell divides into two new cells (Singer & Hilgard, 1978). At 60 hours, the two cells divide to become four cells. This division continues until, at the end of the first week, more than 100 cells are present. On the fifth day after conception, the cells rearrange to form a cavity. The hollow ball of cells is now called a **blastocyst** (Balinsky, 1970). The majority of cells are found in the outer layer, called a *trophoblast*, while the rest are found in the inner layer, called the *inner cell mass* (Moore & Persaud, 1993). The outer layer will become structures that enable the embryo to survive, including the yolk sac, the allantois, the amnion, and the chorion. The yolk sac produces blood cells until the developing organism can do so on its own, at which point it disappears. The allantois forms the umbilical cord and the blood vessels in the placenta. The amnion eventually envelops the organism, holding the amniotic fluid, which protects the organism. The chorion becomes the lining of the placenta. The inner cell mass becomes the embryo.

zygote

A fertilized egg.

germinal stage

The earliest stage of prenatal development, lasting from conception to about 2 weeks.

blastocyst

The stage of prenatal development in which the organism consists of layers of cells around a central cavity forming a hollow sphere.

Table 4.1

Table 4.1   Summary of Prenatal Development

Prenatal development is orderly and predictable.

Time Elapsed	Embryonic or fetal characteristics
4 weeks (1 month)	0.25–0.5 inch long. Head is one-third of embryo. Brain has lobes, and rudimentary nervous system appears as hollow tube. Heart begins to beat. Blood vessels form, and blood flows through them. Simple kidneys, liver, and digestive tract appear. Rudiments of eyes, ears and nose appear. Small tail.
8 weeks (2 months)	1.5 inches long. ⅓ of an ounce in weight. Human face with eyes, ears, nose, lips, tongue. Arms have pawlike hands. Almost all internal organs begin to develop. Brain coordinates functioning of other organs. Heart beats steadily and blood circulates. Complete cartilage skeleton, beginning to be replaced by bone. Tail beginning to be absorbed. Now called a fetus. Sex organs begin to differentiate.
12 weeks (3 months)	3 inches long. 1 ounce in weight. Begins to be active. Number of nerve-muscle connections almost triples. Sucking reflex begins to appear. Can swallow and may even breathe. Eyelids fused shut (will stay shut until the sixth month), but eyes are sensitive to light. Internal organs begin to function.
16 weeks (4 months)	6–7 inches long. 5–6 ounces in weight. Body now growing faster than head. Skin on hands and feet forms individual patterns. Eyebrows and head hair begin to show. Fine, downylike hair (lanugo) covers body. Movements may now be felt.
20 weeks (5 months)	10–12 inches long. 8–16 ounces in weight. Skeleton hardens. Nails form on fingers and toes. Skin covered with cheesy wax. Heartbeat now loud enough to be heard with stethoscope. Muscles are stronger. Definite strong kicking and turning. Can be startled by noises.
24 weeks (6 months)	12–14 inches long. 1.5–2 pounds in weight. Can open and close eyelids. Grows eyelashes. Much more active, exercising muscles. May suck thumb. May be able to breathe if born prematurely.
28 weeks (7 months)	16 inches long. 2.5–3 pounds in weight. Begins to develop fatty tissue. Internal organs (especially respiratory and digestive) still developing. Has fair chance of survival if born now.
32 weeks (8 months)	16.5 inches long. 4 pounds in weight. Fatty layer complete.
38 weeks (9 months)	Birth. 19–20 inches long. 6–8 pounds in weight (average). 95 percent of full-term babies born alive in the United States will survive.

SOURCE: Adapted from Cox (1984)

The survival of the fertilized egg depends on the egg's ability to burrow into the lining of the mother's uterus and obtain nourishment from the mother's system. This process is called **implantation,** which begins at the end of the first week and is completed by the end of the second week (Moore & Persaud, 1993). Digestive enzymes are secreted that allow the blastocyst to embed itself in the maternal tissues. It now develops the ability to feed off its host. It also prevents menstruation by releasing a hormone that maintains the conditions necessary for support.

At about seven or eight days, the inner cell mass has differentiated into two distinct layers: the *ectoderm* and the *endoderm*. The ectoderm will develop into the organism's external coverings, including the skin, hair, sense organs, and nervous system. The endoderm becomes the digestive system, the respiratory system, and the glands. At about the sixteenth day, another layer, the *mesoderm*, appears between the ectoderm and endoderm and develops into the muscles, connective tissues, and the circulatory and excretory systems.

implantation

The process by which the fertilized egg burrows into the lining of the mother's uterus and obtains nourishment from the mother's system.

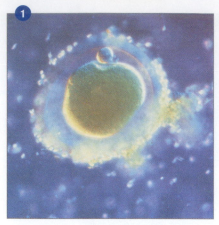

The fertilized ovum has divided for the first time. The chromosomes from the father and mother have united, and the genetic composition of the new life is fixed. Cell division starts at once, and the developing cluster of cells moves slowly down the fallopian tube toward the uterus.

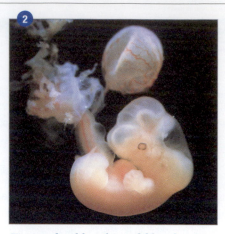

Five weeks old and two-fifths of an inch long. The major divisions of the brain can be seen as well as an eye, the hands, the arms, and a long tail. The upper part of the body develops more rapidly than the lower one— development takes place from the top down.

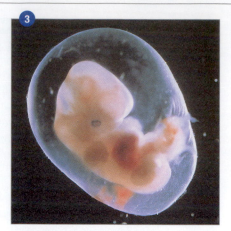

Six weeks old and three-fifths of an inch long. The embryo rests securely in its shock-absorbing amniotic sac. The heart beats rapidly. The brain is growing and the eyes are taking shape. The dark red swelling at the level of the stomach is the liver. The external ears are developing from skin folds.

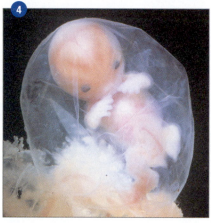

At eight weeks, 4 cm (1.6 inches), the developing individual is no longer an embryo, but a fetus. Everything that will be found in the fully developed human being has now been established. The fetal stage is a period of growth and perfection of detail. The heart has been beating for a month, and the muscles have just begun their first exercises.

The fetus in the third month. There is never any exchange of blood between mother and fetus. All exchanges of nutrients and oxygen occur by diffusion.

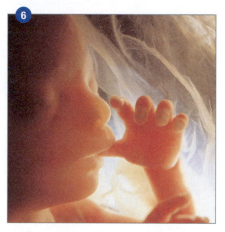

At four and one-half months, about 18 cm (just over 7 inches). When the thumb comes close to the mouth, the head may turn, and lips and tongue begin their sucking motions—a reflex for survival.

As development continues, the amnion swells and covers the developing organism. The trophoblast develops projections, or *villi*, that penetrate the uterine wall, allowing the developing organism to receive nutrients more efficiently. The villi on one side organize into the placenta, which is connected to the developing organism by the umbilical cord. The placenta delivers nutrients, removes wastes, and helps combat infection. The germ cell at the end of the first two weeks of life measures about 1/175 inch (Annis, 1978).

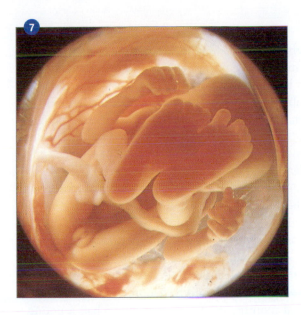

With specially manufactured equipment—a super-wide-angle lens with an ultrashort focal length—the whole fetus is photographed within the amniotic sac. This little girl is just over five months old and roughly 25 cm (10 inches) long.

The Embryonic Stage

The embryonic stage begins at about two weeks and ends at about eight weeks after conception. At two weeks, the tiny mass has just begun to depend on its mother for everything. It is hardly recognizable as a human being. Six weeks later, 95% of the body parts will be present (Annis, 1978). During the embryonic period, changes occur at a breathtaking pace. Each system's development follows a particular sequence. At day 31, the shoulders, arms, and hands develop; on day 33, the fingers develop; and on day 34 through day 36, the thumb is completed. The organs form and begin to function in a primitive manner. The first organ to function is the heart, which circulates the blood to the placenta and throughout the developing body by the end of the third week (Moore & Persaud, 1993). The circulatory system of the embryo is completely separated from the mother's, and no exchange of blood occurs. All exchanges of nutrients and oxygen occur by diffusion. By the end of the first month, the ears, nose, and mouth begin to form, and arms and legs make their appearance as buds. Fingers and toes become defined. Internal organs are now rapidly developing. During this time of extremely rapid growth, the organism is most vulnerable to environmental insult. The embryo is capable of some primitive behavioral reactions and is really very active, although too small for the mother to feel any of these movements. Reflex action occurs as early as the middle of the seventh week (Kisilevsky & Low, 1998). If the mouth is stimulated, the embryo flexes its neck to the opposite side.

The Fetal Stage

During the last seven months of development—the fetal stage—the fetus grows and develops at a tremendous rate. At the beginning of the third month, the average fetus is one and a half inches long and weighs less than one-third of an ounce. By the end of the third month, it is 3 inches long and weighs 1 ounce. During the sixth or seventh week after conception, if the developing child's genotype is XY, hormonal action will cause the development of male genitalia; otherwise, at 10 to 12 weeks the gonads develop into ovaries (Ruble & Martin, 1998). During the third month, the major organs are completed and bones begin to appear and muscles develop. The fetus now moves, kicks its legs, swallows and digests the amniotic fluid, and removes waste products through urination.

embryonic stage
The stage of prenatal development, from about 2 to about 8 weeks, when bone cells begin to replace cartilage.

fetal stage
The stage of prenatal development beginning at about 8 weeks and continuing until birth.

A fetus may suck its thumb in the womb.

During the fourth month, the fetus continues to grow at a fantastic pace. By the end of the month, it is 6 inches long and weighs 5 to 6 ounces. As it grows, it develops internally. By the fifth month, the fetus sleeps and wakes at regular intervals, and some reflexes, such as hiccuping and swallowing, have developed. The fetus cries and may suck a thumb. Beginning at about 16 weeks, fetal movements are likely to be felt by the mother, though some mothers experience movement earlier (Kisilevsky & Low, 1998). This is known as *quickening*. During the sixth month, the fetus attains a weight of about 2 pounds and a length of 14 inches. The facial features are clearly in evidence, and the fetus can make a fist.

During the last three prenatal months, the fetus gains a layer of fat that will help keep the infant warm after birth. Fetuses move less often during this time, but with more vigor (DePietro et al., 1996). By the end of the twenty-eighth week, the fetus measures about 15 inches and weighs about 2.5 to 3 pounds. Traditionally, seven months is considered the age of viability, since the fetus has a reasonable chance of survival if born at this time. This is misleading, however, for there is considerable individual variation in weight, health, and developmental readiness.

During the last two prenatal months, the fetus gains about half a pound a week. Its heretofore red, wrinkled appearance disappears somewhat as it puts on weight. The development of the lungs is especially important during these last months. By the end of the normal period of prenatal development, approximately 266 days, the infant is born. The entire process of fetal development proceeds without any need for conscious maternal intervention. It is directed by genetic forces that we are only just beginning to understand. However, the fetus is also affected by the environment.

Developmental Myths

People once believed that everything a woman did during pregnancy could have an effect on the developing embryo or fetus. Unusual occurrences in a pregnant woman's daily life were thought to influence the child's personality and physical well-being. Some believed, for instance, that if a rabbit crossed the mother's path the child would be born with a harelip (Annis, 1978). If the mother ate or squashed strawberries, the child would have a strawberry-shaped birthmark. The belief in total environmental control was replaced by the idea that nothing the mother did really mattered. The placenta was viewed as a barrier that did not allow any dangerous elements into the infant's environment and rendered various poisons harmless.

In the 1960s this view was shattered when a medication called thalidomide taken by pregnant women between the fourth and sixth week of pregnancy for morning sickness was linked to the birth of thousands of infants in Europe with missing or deformed arms and sometimes legs (Cook, Petersen, & Moore, 1990). Far from being a total barrier, the placenta allows a number of substances to pass into the system of the fetus. Although we no longer believe the superstitions about rabbits and strawberries, we know that the infant's environment greatly affects the health of the fetus.

The Developing Organism and the Environment

The embryo and fetus can be affected by many viruses, chemicals, and medications. Any agent that causes a birth defect is called a **teratogen.** The effects of these agents depend on the type of agent, the dosage, and the genetic characteristics of the fetus. The time at which the fetus is exposed is also important because some

Guideposts

What are the most important events to occur during the three prenatal stages?

teratogen

Any agent that causes birth defects.

teratogens are more likely to produce birth defects if they are ingested at a certain time during the pregnancy. This is called the **critical period,** the period during which a developing organism is most susceptible to a particular teratogen (Moore & Persaud, 1993). The time at which the organ is most rapidly developing is the period of greatest vulnerability. Figure 4.1 shows the critical periods for the major organs. Some organs such as the brain, teeth, and skeletal system have critical periods extending into childhood.

Before describing some of the more common teratogens, we should note three problems in the interpretation of research on teratogens. First, some research is based on animal research, and although the animal model is useful (Vorhees & Mollnow, 1987), any cross-species comparisons should be made with care.

Second, much of the data relating teratogens to human birth defects are correlational because we cannot experimentally expose pregnant women to particular teratogens and conduct controlled experiments. So when a correlation between ingestion of a particular agent and birth defects occurs, it is difficult to isolate the confounding variables such as diet, exercise, anxiety, and the mother's ingestion of other agents.

Finally, much of the evidence on the effects of specific teratogens deals with gross or very visible deformities or behavioral abnormalities. It is not always easy

Guideposts

Why is the concept of critical period so important to understanding the effects of a teratogen on the developing organism?

critical period
The period during which a particular event has its greatest impact.

Figure 4.1 Critical Periods in Prenatal Development

The darkest color shows the time during which that particular organ is at greatest risk.

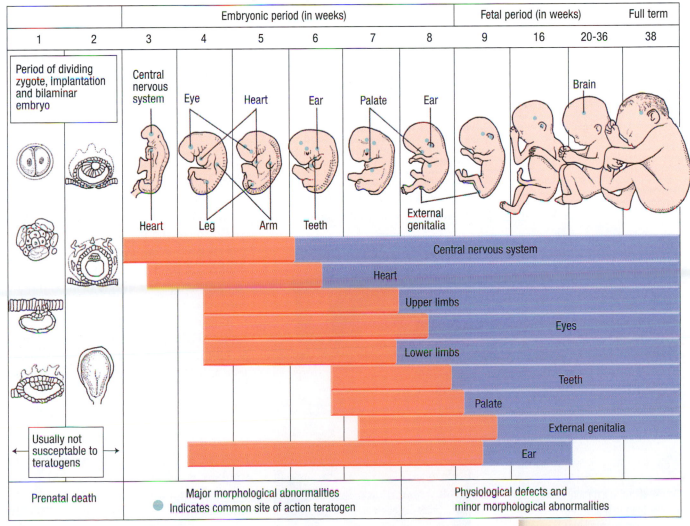

SOURCE: Moore & Pervaud (1993)

---

to discover the more subtle difficulties that may show themselves either later in a child's development or only at specific times, perhaps when the child is stressed.

Medication A number of medications have been linked to birth defects, and the research findings on still others are contradictory. Tetracycline, a commonly prescribed antibiotic, has been linked to permanent discoloration of the teeth and defective bone growth (March of Dimes, 1983). Most of the best-known teratogenic drugs cause a defect that is noticeable at birth.

One drug that does not fit this pattern is the synthetic estrogen called *diethylstilbestrol* (known as DES). From the 1940s through 1971, DES was widely administered to pregnant women who had a history of diabetes or who were apt to have miscarriages (New York State Department of Health, 1979). At first, there seemed to be little cause for concern. The children born to these women were healthy as infants, but in 1971 a link was found between prenatal administration of DES and a small number of cases of cervical cancer usually found only in women over 50 years. The chances of a daughter born to a mother who took DES developing the cancerous condition are about 1 or 2 in every 1,000 (Orenberg, 1981). However, many DES daughters suffer from genital tract abnormalities. All women whose mothers took the drug should be watched carefully by their doctors. DES sons are also affected by the drug. They sometimes experience genital tract abnormalities and benign cysts that require attention from a urologist. The DES story demonstrates that the effects of drugs taken during the prenatal stage may not show up for some time.

Drugs: Legal and Illegal Most drugs taken during pregnancy are not prescribed by doctors. They are available either legally, as in the case of nicotine and alcohol, or illegally, as with narcotics. The National Institute on Drug Abuse estimates that between 375,000 and 739,000 drug-exposed children are born each year (Sautter, 1992). Sometimes the damage is obvious, whereas at other times it may not be noticed for a number of years.

Nicotine Many pregnant women in the United States smoke (Lancashare, 1995). Nicotine causes a rise in heart rate, blood pressure, and respiration and constricts the flow of blood. The amount of oxygen the fetus receives is reduced. Newborns of mothers who smoke cigarettes are exposed to massive amounts of nicotine that

pass through the placenta, and some doctors believe they should be considered smokers or ex-smokers (Levy, 1997).

Although the effects of nicotine are dose related, smokers are twice as likely as nonsmokers to have low-birthweight babies (Hellerstedt, Himes, Story, Alton, & Edwards, 1997; Rasmussen & Adams, 1997). It is estimated that maternal smoking is responsible for between 20% and 30% of all cases of low birthweight and 10% of infant deaths in the United States (Dolan-Mullen, Ramirez, & Groff, 1994). Even if not premature, the infants of smokers weigh an average of 200 grams (about 0.5 pound) less than infants of nonsmokers (Vorhees & Mollnow, 1987). In addition, the infants of mothers who

Studies show that smoking during pregnancy presents a danger to the developing fetus.

Smokers are much more likely to give birth to premature infants than nonsmokers.

smoke are shorter; have smaller head, chest, arm, and thigh circumferences; and have lower neurological scores than the infants of nonsmokers (Metcoff, Coistiloe, Crosby, Sandstread, & Milne, 1989). Maternal smoking is also linked to miscarriages and increased risk of sudden infant death syndrome (see Chapter 5).

Injurious long-term effects from maternal smoking include increased risk of academic difficulties, especially in reading; hyperactivity and poor attention span; and deficits in long-term physical growth, intellectual performance, and behavioral development. Since women who smoke during pregnancy are very likely to continue after as well, it is difficult to determine to what extent these are related to smoking when pregnant, after pregnancy, or both (Naeye & Peters, 1984; Rasmussen & Adams, 1997). Some evidence even exists that maternal smoking during pregnancy may sensitize the fetus's brain to the effects of nicotine and other chemicals in tobacco, making it more likely that the child will smoke when an adolescent. Various chemicals may alter the release of neurotransmitters in the brain and change the threshold of these systems (Kandel, Wu, & Davies, 1995).

Women who stop smoking during pregnancy give birth to heavier infants (Floyd, Rimer, Giovino, Mullen, & Sullivan, 1993; Lieberman, Gremy, Lang, & Cohen, 1995), and evidence indicates that women who stop smoking prior to the fourth month of pregnancy reduce their risk of having low-birthweight infants (Butler, Goldstein, & Ross, 1972). Although giving up smoking is difficult, it is clear that the health risks are great, and pregnant and nursing women should try to quit.

Exposure to smoke in the environment, called *passive smoking*, is also related to lower birth weight (Martinez, Wright, Taussig, & the Group Health Medical Associates, 1994). Nonsmoking pregnant women exposed to cigarette smoke give birth to infants who weigh less than the infants of pregnant women who are not exposed to cigarette smoke in the environment (Eskenazi, Prehn, & Christianson, 1995). Recent studies find that mothers who continue to smoke while they care for their infants transmit nicotine and other chemicals through their breast milk, and this method of transmission may lead to even greater levels of such chemicals in the infant's system than direct inhalation from the environment (Mascola, Van Vunakis, Tager, Speizer, & Hanrahan, 1998). Both direct inhalation of smoke and transmission through breast milk are forms of passive smoking and can be injurious to the infant.

Alcohol The overwhelming majority of women drink at least once during pregnancy, and between 20 and 35% drink regularly (Rosenthal, 1990). A government study found that 3.5% of the mothers surveyed in 1995 admitted they had seven or more drinks or engaged in a drinking binge of five or more drinks at one sitting within the previous month, an increase from 1991 (*Newsday*, 1997).

Some children of alcoholic mothers show a distinct physical appearance and pattern of development. They are shorter and lighter than other children, and their growth and development are slow. They show a number of cranial and facial abnormalities, heart defects, poor motor development and coordination, and they tend to have mental retardation (Sampson, Bookstein, Barr, & Streissguth, 1995). Their mortality rate is also higher than average (Jones, Smith, Streissguth, & Myrianthopoulus, 1974). These characteristics describe **fetal alcohol syndrome.** Since most women are not alcoholics, people generally consider the negative

Guideposts

How does maternal smoking during the prenatal period affect the developing organism?

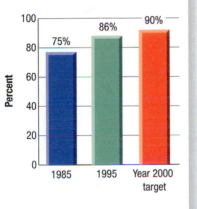

Trends in Development

Abstinence from tobacco use during pregnancy
Good progress has been made toward meeting this goal

Percent

75% (1985) 86% (1995) 90% (Year 2000 target)

Source: (USDHHS, 1998)

For Your Consideration

How would you reply to the comment "My mother smoked and drank a bit when she was pregnant with me, and I'm OK"?

fetal alcohol syndrome

A number of characteristics—including retardation, facial abnormalities, growth defects, and poor coordination—caused by maternal alcohol consumption during pregnancy.

Fetal alcohol syndrome

Progress has not been made on this objective, and the incidence has been moving away from the year 2000 objective. It is not clear whether this increase is due to improved reporting or to an actual rise in the incidence of fetal alcohol syndrome

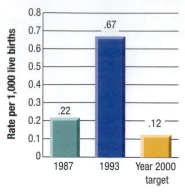

Source: (USDHHS, 1998)

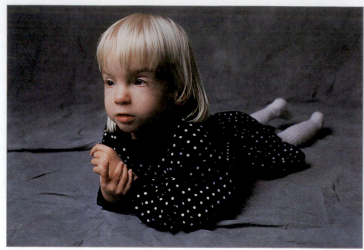

The girl's widely spaced eyes, flattened nose, and underdeveloped upper lip are three of the common physical symptoms of fetal alcohol syndrome.

Guideposts

What are fetal alcohol syndrome and fetal alcohol effect?

For Your Consideration

Why do some mothers continue to drink and smoke even after being told of the risk to the fetus?

fetal alcohol effect

An umbrella term used to describe damage to a child caused by the mother's imbibing alcohol during pregnancy that is somewhat less pronounced than fetal alcohol syndrome.

consequences of drinking something that happens to other people. Even the infants of confirmed alcoholics show the full syndrome in only about 35% of the cases for a variety of reasons, including the time during the pregnancy of the drinking (infants may be more or less vulnerable at different times) (Rosenthal, 1990). The term **fetal alcohol effect** is used to describe the less severe spectrum of damage done by alcohol (Casiro, 1994). Most common among these problems are severe learning and cognitive disabilities. The fetus is sensitive to alcohol, and the effects of alcohol seem to be dose related, with lower doses resulting in some, but not all, of the characteristics of fetal alcohol syndrome.

Even moderate drinking can affect the fetus. As little as one drink per day increases the risk of miscarriage during the middle months of pregnancy (Harlap & Shiono, 1980) and can lead to decreased fetal growth (Mills, Braubard, Harley, Rhoads, & Berendes, 1984). Prenatal alcohol exposure to 1.5 ounces of alcohol per day is related to a decrease in psychomotor skills (Larroque et al., 1995) and a reduction of about five points on intelligence tests at age 4 (O'Connor, Sigman, & Casari, 1993). Animal studies show that moderate alcohol consumption is sufficient to negatively affect attention and neuromotor functioning, even though the infants are of normal birth weight (Schneider, Roughton, & Lubach, 1997). Even women who do not drink regularly often can cause serious damage to their infants if they engage in binge drinking. A single binge can raise the alcohol level in an infant's system to the point of causing serious damage to the infant (Mendelson & Mello, 1987).

Commonly Used Illegal Drugs No drug has received the amount of attention in the media that cocaine has. Cocaine taken during pregnancy constricts the blood vessels in the placenta, decreasing blood flow to the fetus and increasing uterine contractions. It increases the chances of spontaneous abortion (Ness et al., 1999). Cocaine crosses the placenta, entering the fetus's system (Phillips, Sharma, Premachandra, Vaughn, & Reyes-Lee, 1996). It decreases the cellular oxygen and nutrient supply, alters neurotransmitters, and affects the parts of the brain responsible for learning, memory, behavior, and cognitive functions (Needelman, Zuckerman, Anderson, Mirochnik, & Cohen, 1993; Volpe, 1992). The use of cocaine during pregnancy is related to infant mortality, low birth weight, prematurity, and a number of medical problems including neurological damage and malformed circulatory and digestive systems (Neuspiel & Hamel, 1991; Scherling, 1994). Infants exposed to cocaine in the womb are more irritable and tremulous than the average newborn and are often unable to respond to the human voice or face (Berger, Sorensen, Gendler, & Fitzsimmons, 1990). They show more stress-related behavior (Eisen et al., 1991) and deficits in their ability to recover from a stressful episode (Bendersky & Lewis, 1998). They are emotionally labile and respond poorly to attempts to comfort them (Chasnoff, 1985, 1987). They show poorer reflexes, such as sucking, and smile less (Phillips et al., 1996). Both smiling and sucking intensity are behaviors that may affect maternal-infant bonding, and infants who smile less, have feeding problems, or are irritable and less consolable are more prone to abuse and neglect (Phillips et al., 1996).

Many such infants are jittery and show an abnormally high-pitched cry. They are overwhelmed by sensations, and some stiffen while being touched. Some cry when they hear music or voices or are brought into bright lights; others simply tune out and go to sleep. They show developmental delays in walking and talking, and some throw tantrums. Later, these children show language delays, emotional difficulties, impulsivity, low frustration tolerance, and attention problems (Scherling, 1994).

These initial difficulties are compounded as these troubled infants often do not receive the care they require. Sometimes, the babies are abandoned in the hospital to be raised by a foster family or a grandparent who may or may not be capable of dealing with infants who show so many behavioral and physical difficulties. If the infant is taken away after birth by welfare agencies, the child's lot may be a string of foster homes. If the child remains with the mother or both parents, the child is often subjected to an environment of poverty and inadequate parenting, which increases the risk of poor intellectual development. The parents often continue to use cocaine, which exposes the infants to extreme poverty, as the parent or parents use all the family resources to buy the drug (Wrightman, 1991). The lifestyle of these parents is chaotic, and the rate of neglect and physical abuse is high (Besharov, 1989). The mothers are often rigid and show a lack of pleasure in relating to their infants, are not responsive to their infants, and have very little emotional involvement with them (Burns, Chethik, Burns, & Clark, 1991). These infants experience both congenital problems due to prenatal exposure and subsequent damage due to poor parenting and the deficient environment in which they are raised during their early years.

This list of consequences is quite impressive, but some argue that the media has sensationalized the problem, often presenting the worst-case scenario. The effects of cocaine are dose related, with heavier exposure leading to greater difficulties (Alessandri, Bendersky, & Lewis, 1998). If we were to believe the popular media, we would incorrectly think that all cocaine-exposed children were severely affected, that little can be done for them, and that all medical, behavioral, and learning problems shown by these children are caused directly by their exposure to cocaine (Griffith, 1992). In reality, great individual differences exist in the behavior of children exposed to cocaine in utero. Many of the problems, especially oversensitivity to stimuli and problems in self-regulation, are caused by both the exposure to cocaine and other drugs in utero, as well as the deficient environment in which so many of these infants are raised.

The most damaging belief is that nothing can be done for these children. This view is simply not true, and society should not give up on these children (Mayes, Granger, Bornstein, & Zuckerman, 1992). Growing evidence exists that early treatment to eliminate drug use in pregnant mothers, along with prenatal care

Infants exposed to cocaine while in the womb are less irritable, more placid, and smile more but at inappropriate times than infants who have not been exposed to cocaine prenatally.

Guideposts

How does the home environment combine with prenatal exposure to cocaine to cause difficulties in young infants?

and follow-up examinations, can improve the long-term behavioral competence of these cocaine-exposed infants (Chasnoff, Burns, Schnoll, & Burns, 1992). When pregnant women who abused cocaine and other drugs received prenatal care, nutritional counseling, and drug treatment, the majority of infants were carried to full term, with premature infants born less than a month early. These children showed many classical signs of drug exposure, but they were helped when their parents were taught effective child-rearing strategies. Since these infants showed a deficiency in the quiet-alert state, a state during which infants are best able to process information, caregivers were taught to use comforting techniques such as swaddling, using pacifiers, and vertical rocking. The parents were taught how to maintain an appropriate environment as well as how to recognize when the child was approaching overstimulation. The majority of these children showed little difference at 3, 6, 12, 18, and 24 months from a group of nonexposed infants (Griffith, 1992). Only one-third showed delays in language development and problems in attention and self-regulation. Early intervention both to stop the drug taking and improve the environment can improve life for these children (Zuckerman & Frank, 1992). It is evident that cocaine-exposed infants and their families require immediate and intensive help if these infants are to have any chance of developing in a healthy manner.

The effects of marijuana smoking on the fetus are inconsistent, with some studies showing adverse effects (USDHHS, 1990). The use of marijuana has been linked to poor fetal growth and subtle neurological problems (Lester & Dreher, 1989; Zuckerman et al., 1989). Some studies have found behavioral differences for infants of mothers who are regular marijuana users, including lack of response to a light stimulus, tremors, and increased startling (Vorhees & Mollnow, 1987).

Babies of heroin addicts are born addicted to heroin and must go through withdrawal. They often show disturbances in activity level, attention span, and sleep patterns. Because these infants are frequently premature and very small, this is sometimes a life-or-death situation (USDHHS, 1990).

Over-the-Counter Drugs   Some over-the-counter drugs can also be dangerous, and concern is growing over the possible damage to the fetus from aspirin, antihistamines, diuretics, and antacids (Snow, 1998). If taken in the later months of pregnancy, aspirin may prolong labor and cause maternal heavy bleeding both before and after birth (Mendelson & Mello, 1985; March of Dimes, 1983). Heavy doses of aspirin are related to an increased rate of infant mortality and low birth weight (Snow, 1998). Researchers do not have enough evidence to form definite conclusions about the safety of many pain relief medications, and pregnant women should check with a doctor before taking these medications. Some, but not all, evidence indicates that heavy doses of caffeine may adversely affect the infant (Brooten & Jordan, 1983; Hronsky & Emory, 1987). Until the issue is conclusively decided, it is safer to eliminate caffeine from the diet or at least limit its intake severely.

Pollution and Radiation   Pollution and radiation can also adversely affect the developing fetus and are therefore causes for concern. For example, PCB, a contaminant sometimes found in water and fish, can cause immature motor responses, behavioral abnormalities, and deficits in information-processing abilities, such as visual discrimination (Jacobson, Jacobson, Fein, Schwartz, & Dowler, 1984; Jacobson, Jacobson, Padgett, Brumitt, & Billings 1992).

Radiation has been linked to fetal deaths as well as to a number of structural defects in infants. There is no safe level of radiation because radiation accumulates in the body, making repeated X-rays dangerous. Although there are times when an X-ray is medically required, pregnant women should avoid radiation as much as possible.

Disease and Pregnancy

Today's society has been spared the terrible epidemics of the past. We are no longer concerned about smallpox, diphtheria, and polio. Other diseases, however, can affect the developing organism. **Rubella** (commonly called German measles) is generally a very mild disease, yet the effects of the rubella virus on a developing embryo can cause serious disorders, such as congenital cataracts and other eye disorders, ear damage, congenital heart disease, and central nervous system damage as well as fetal death. In the epidemic of 1964-1965, about 50,000 babies were affected. Many died, while many others suffered injuries of varying degrees (Rugh & Shettles, 1971). With the advent of a vaccine for rubella, epidemics should become a thing of the past. Unfortunately, not every child is being protected, and isolated cases of rubella-induced defects still occur.

Venereal Disease In recent years, increased attention has been paid to the effects that AIDS (acquired immune deficiency syndrome), herpes, syphilis, gonorrhea, and chlamydia have on the fetus. Evidence is great that such diseases, which are usually transmitted during sexual intercourse, pose significant dangers to the developing fetus.

Women who have herpes can transmit it to the baby during the birth process. If the herpes virus reaches the baby's organs or brain, the prognosis is not good, and the mortality rate is high (Corey & Whitely, 1985). Antiviral treatment reduces the mortality rate, but impairment is still common (Stagno & Whitely, 1985). To prevent the spread of the disease, doctors often check for lesions in the birth canal and may recommend a **cesarean section** (discussed later in the chapter).

Syphilis in the expectant mother can cause a number of defects in the infant, including bone and facial deformities and nerve deafness, as well as fetal death. A number of those children who survive birth will develop syphilis. If the mother-to-be receives prompt treatment, the fetus may not be infected.

Fetuses exposed to gonorrhea are often premature and blind. The standard practice of placing a protective solution in an infant's eyes at birth is to protect the baby against blindness in case the mother has gonorrhea. In many hospitals, erythromycin or tetracycline is used. Erythromycin combats chlamydia, an infection that can also cause blindness in newborns (Simkin, Whalley, & Keppler, 1984). Chlamydia is more common than gonorrhea, and the infants of mothers with the disease may develop conjunctivitis and pneumonia and other lung disorders (Schachter, 1989). Chlamydia can also cause miscarriage, low birth weight, and infant death (March of Dimes, 1989). Unfortunately, women with chlamydia may not know they are infected because they are often asymptomatic, but newer tests allow for better screening. Once the disease is diagnosed, it is relatively easy to cure.

Today, the gravest concern centers on AIDS, which is a fatal disease affecting the immunological system and leads to an inability to fight off disease (Rosenberg & Fauci, 1994). It is caused by a virus called the human immunodeficiency virus (HIV). In 1996, 1,600 infants were born in the United States infected with the AIDS virus (Bettelheim, 1998), and worldwide about 500,000 infants are infected with the AIDS virus each year (Vuthipongse et al., 1998). AIDS is a worldwide concern.

rubella
A disease responsible for many cases of birth defects.

cesarean section
The birth procedure by which the fetus is surgically delivered through the abdominal wall and uterus.

Guideposts

How is the AIDS virus transmitted to infants?

Virtually all new cases of pediatric AIDS in the United States are caused by transmission of the virus prenatally or at birth (Anderson, Sedmak, & Lairmore, 1994; Rogers, Schochetman, & Roff, 1994). AIDS may also be transmitted through breast milk of HIV-positive mothers (Kuhn & Stein, 1997; Landau-Stanton & Clements, 1993).

The rate of HIV transmission between mother and child and the factors that determine such transmission remain somewhat uncertain (Futterman & Hein, 1994). Studies in the United States and other Western countries describe rates of transmission of between 15 and 40% (Dickover et al., 1996; Oxtoby, 1994). A number of factors have been suggested as predicting the likelihood of such transmission, including advanced HIV disease represented by altered immune system status and a high level of the virus in the system (Anderson et al., 1994; Mofenson & Wolinsky, 1994). Other studies suggest that a high risk of transmission exists with women who become HIV-positive during pregnancy itself (Oxtoby, 1994).

Infants infected with the virus are more likely than adults to develop symptoms of AIDS (Koup & Wilson, 1994; Sande, 1986). For unknown reasons, they show a more rapid progression from latent infection to symptoms to death (Koup & Wilson, 1994). The pregnant woman is also more susceptible to various viral, bacterial, and fungal infections and is more likely to die from these infections (Minkoff & Duerr, 1994). Although AIDS is certainly found in every ethnic and socioeconomic level, low-income, urban women and children are disproportionately involved (Capell et al., 1992; Hutchings, 1988). Of all children who acquired the virus through transmission from mother to child, 59% are among African American children and 26% are Latino children (Oxtoby, 1994). The reason is thought to be that many of these minority group women live in poor inner-city communities where the prevalence of HIV infection among drug users is high.

The prognosis for these infants is very poor, and the probability of long-term survival is presently low (Peckham & Gibb, 1995). Two distinct patterns have emerged. Some infants have profound immune deficiency and opportunistic infections during the first months of life; most of these children die before the age of 5. AIDS is the seventh leading cause of death in the United States for children between the ages of 1 and 4 years. A larger group gradually develops the immune deficiency during a period of several years up to age 10 and shows a pattern of disease development and mortality similar to that found in adults (Mayaux et al., 1996). These children with HIV are living into middle childhood and sometimes beyond.

Guideposts

What is the prognosis for infants with the AIDS virus?

For Your Consideration ?

Should testing for the presence of HIV in a pregnant mother be made mandatory? Why or why not?

Today, a medication exists that, when administered to pregnant women who test positive for the virus that causes AIDS, reduces the chances of the transmission of AIDS to the infant.

The question of testing all pregnant women for HIV is controversial. Some people argue that such information is vital and testing should be mandatory, which means without the woman's permission or even knowledge (Twomey & Fletcher, 1994). Opponents of mandatory testing argue that women at highest risk are most likely to receive poor, late, or no prenatal care, which would limit the benefits of the program. The program may also violate a person's civil rights. Today, testing for HIV in pregnant women is highly recommended and conducted in a voluntary but routine manner (Cotton, Currier, & Wofsy, 1994). One reason for the emphasis on early testing is the finding that giving AZT (zidovudine) to HIV-positive women during pregnancy prevents the transmission of AIDS in many cases (Dickover et al., 1996; Wade et al., 1998). With this possible preventive treatment available, such screening is highly desirable (Twomey & Fletcher, 1994). In fact, in the United States, the number of infants born HIV-positive has been reduced more than 40% as a result of such treatment (Painter, 1996). Unfortunately, this trend has not occurred globally, and each day many infants are born infected with the AIDS virus because of the cost of the treatment, which many underdeveloped nations simply cannot afford.

The Mother's Medical Condition

While noting some of the diseases that may affect the fetus, one should not forget the medical condition of the mother. Hypertension is related to poor fetal growth, increased perinatal death, and many neurological and developmental problems. Diabetes is also related to many birth defects. These disorders are dangerous to the mother as well. In both cases, as with so many other maternal medical conditions, competent medical advice and prompt treatment may improve the chances of delivering a healthy child and safeguarding the mother's health.

With many more women planning their first pregnancy when they are over 30 years old and with so many teens giving birth, a relatively new concept called *preconception care* has been advanced to reduce a woman's reproductive risks before conception. These preconception programs include risk assessment, which involves identifying health risks such as inadequate nutrition, health promotion, and interventions to reduce risk (Jack & Culpepper, 1990).

The Rh Factor   Perhaps the most famous maternal factor affecting the fetus is the **Rh factor**, which consists of a particular red blood cell antibody found in most human beings. Approximately 85% of all whites, 93% of African Americans, and nearly 100% of all Asians, Native Americans, and Eskimos have the factor; that is, they are Rh-positive (Stevenson, 1973).

In about 13% of Caucasian unions, the woman is Rh-negative and the man is Rh-positive. In such a situation, the baby may be Rh-positive and a problem may arise. Because the mother's blood is Rh-negative, her body reacts to the Rh-positive antigen in the fetus as it would to an invading germ or virus: by creating antibodies. However, since the blood of the fetus does not mix with that of the mother during her pregnancy, the mother is not likely to manufacture antibodies that might injure the fetus. Few fetal blood cells cross the placenta. During the birth, however, especially if it is long and difficult, some cells do cross the placenta, and the mother will manufacture the antibodies.

Since the first child of these parents is not likely to be exposed to many of these antibodies, the infant's chances of survival are good. Once these antibodies are manufactured, however, they tend to remain in the mother's body. The mother also becomes more sensitive to this factor in subsequent pregnancies. During the next pregnancy, the fetus will be exposed to the mother's antibodies, which will cross the placenta and destroy the red blood cells of the fetus (Ortho Diagnostic Systems, 1981). In each successive pregnancy, the risk to the fetus becomes greater and greater, until the chances that a child will be born healthy are quite low.

Since 1968, a preventive vaccine for Rh problems has been available. Within 72 hours after each birth, miscarriage, or abortion, a shot of the vaccine RhoGAM is administered to block the production of these antibodies. Before this vaccine was available, about 10,000 babies died every year, and 20,000 more were born with severe birth defects from Rh disease (Apgar & Beck, 1974).

Current Issues

As people learn more about the prenatal period, new issues are raised and old issues are perceived differently. Five such issues are especially current: (1) the relationship between the age of the mother and the health of the fetus, (2) the effect of maternal nutrition during pregnancy, (3) the effect of stress on the fetus, (4) the father's role during pregnancy, and (5) the effect of new technology on mother and child.

Guideposts
Explain what is meant by an Rh "problem."

Rh factor
An antibody often, but not always, found in human beings.

Many couples are deciding to wait to have their first child. Although the risks are somewhat greater, with good prenatal care, most women can give birth to healthy children.

6

Mothers who have their first child in their 30s show more patience than younger mothers.

Guideposts

What characteristics describe the parenting style of first-time mothers over age 30?

For Your Consideration ❓

In your opinion, what is the best age to start a family? What is the best spacing between children? Explain your answer.

Maternal Age The number of women having their first child at age 30 or older has increased substantially. Many contemporary couples have postponed having children for economic and career reasons. Since the middle 1970s, the birthrate for women above the age of 30 has grown steadily, increasing over 25%, although recently the birthrate for women over the age of 30 has stabilized (Lancashare, 1995).

First-time older mothers do very well. They are more likely than younger mothers to have good family support systems and economic stability and to plan the pregnancy. Certain age-related characteristics, such as patience and judgment, which are important in parenting, are more likely to be present, and some studies find that the age of the mother at birth shows a slight but consistent and positive association with the child's intelligence (Fonteyn & Isada, 1988). Older fathers (those having their first child above age 35) also do well. They spend more time in leisure activities with their children, have higher expectations for their children's behavior, and are more nurturing toward their children compared to fathers in their 20s (Heath, 1994).

The years between 20 and 30 are the safest for childbearing. As a woman ages, the incidence of high blood pressure and delivery complications increases (Fonteyn & Isada, 1988). Although the physical risks are somewhat greater, the availability of modern diagnostic procedures and better prenatal care reduces the risk somewhat. If there is no evidence of chronic disease, the outlook for the intelligent woman becoming a parent in her 30s is quite good (Berkowitz, Skovron, Lapinski, & Berkowitz, 1990).

The number of births at the other extreme is much more troublesome. The pregnant teenager belongs to the high-risk group for birth complications, birth defects, and prematurity (Croen & Shaw, 1995; Seitz & Apfel, 1994). This high rate of complications may be explained by the relationship between adolescent pregnancy and such factors as low socioeconomic status, poor education, and poor health care. Teenage mothers are likely to have repeat pregnancies and are less likely to experience high-quality prenatal care. Teenage pregnancy is part of a larger social

ACTION / REACTION

Too Old to Start?

When Dee and Will were married, they assumed that they would wait to have children for a few years and then would have a family of two children. A few years turned into 5 and then 10, and now they find themselves in their middle 30s and do not yet have any children. They delayed having children for career reasons and enjoyed being able to go on vacations without worries about child care. Now, however, they believe time is running out.

Some of Dee's friends are telling them that the transition to parenting will be much more difficult because they are used to such a different lifestyle and that neither of them will have much patience for the children because they are older. Dee also is concerned because she read that the chances of having a child with Down syndrome as well as complications from pregnancy increase with age. They would like to begin their family very soon but have some real concerns.

1. *How realistic are their concerns?*

2. *In your opinion, are their any special parenting challenges to starting a family later in life?*

ACTION / REACTION

and economic problem that must be approached educationally and medically. We will discuss this topic further in Chapter 12.

Maternal Nutrition The mother's nutritional history before pregnancy may also affect the infant's health (Sizer & Whitney, 1988). The mother may have suffered from nutritional problems that affect her own physical development and health, reducing her ability to bear a healthy child. The pregnant woman's nutritional needs are far greater during this period (see Figure 4.2). Malnourishment around conception may cause the placenta to fail to develop adequately, causing many different abnormalities. If this small infant is female, she runs an elevated risk of having a poor pregnancy outcome when she is an adult as well. A woman's pregnancy then can adversely affect not only her children but her grandchildren as well (Whitney, Cataldo, & Rolfes, 1994).

Trends in Development

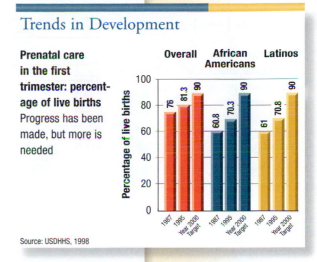

Prenatal care in the first trimester: percentage of live births
Progress has been made, but more is needed

Source: USDHHS, 1998

Figure 4.2   **Comparison of Nutrient RDA of Nonpregnant, Pregnant, and Lactating Women**

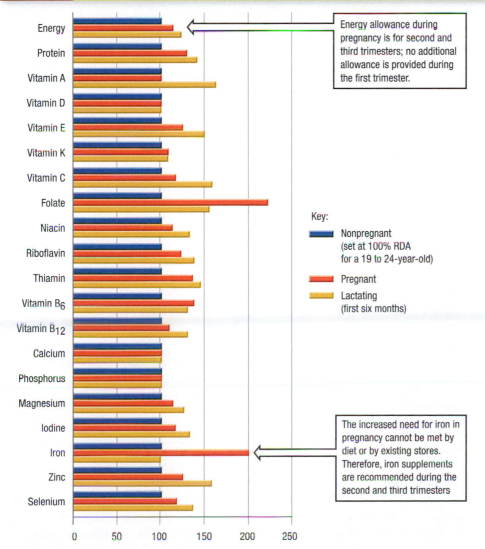

Energy allowance during pregnancy is for second and third trimesters; no additional allowance is provided during the first trimester.

Key:

■ Nonpregnant (set at 100% RDA for a 19 to 24-year-old)

■ Pregnant

■ Lactating (first six months)

The increased need for iron in pregnancy cannot be met by diet or by existing stores. Therefore, iron supplements are recommended during the second and third trimesters

SOURCE: Whitney & Rolfes (1996)

The RDA for pregnant and lactating women are not specific to age, as they are for nonpregnant women. This figure uses women aged 19 to 24 years as the nonpregnant standard. For several of the nutrients, the RDA do not differ during the childbearing years of 15 to 50. For a few, however, they do, and it is important to note that:

- For protein and vitamin K, the RDA increase slightly with age, so increased needs during pregnancy are more dramatic for women in the younger age groups.

- For vitamin D, calcium, and phosphorus, the RDA decrease at 25 years, so increased needs during pregnancy are more dramatic for women over 25.

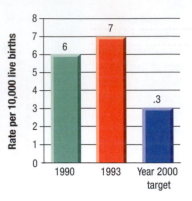

Spina bifida and other neural tube defects: rate per 10,000 live births
The rate has fluctuated between 6 and 7. No progress in this area is reported.

Source: USDHHS, 1998

Rate per 10,000 live births

1990 — 6
1993 — 7
Year 2000 target — .3

Chronic malnutrition in pregnant women can lead to a condition in which the child has fewer brain cells.

Guideposts

Explain the special importance of nutrition during pregnancy.

The past two decades have seen renewed interest in maternal nutrition during pregnancy. The finding that chronic malnutrition during the prenatal stage leads to an irreversible condition in which the infant has as much as 20% fewer brain cells than the normal baby (Winick, 1976) has done much to spur the interest in maternal nutrition. Malnutrition is related to fetal deformities and impaired physical and intellectual development. Mental retardation, low birth weight, cerebral palsy, and increased susceptibility to disease have been traced to malnourishment during pregnancy (Annis, 1978). Infants who were malnourished during the prenatal stage also show abnormal behavioral patterns, such as withdrawal and irritability (Birch, 1971). The significant correlation between nutritional status and prematurity is especially troublesome because extremely underweight infants are at risk for a variety of developmental problems (Ricciuti, 1980) and fetal deaths (DeBruyne & Rolfes, 1989).

Important research linking particular vitamins to fetal development and the possibility that supplements may prevent particular deformities has made nutrition before and during pregnancy an increasingly important issue. For example, giving folate (folic acid) supplements before and around the time of conception reduces the occurrence of neural tube defects, the most prominent being spina bifida in which the spine does not close properly (Johnston & Staples, 1998; Kurtzweil, 1996). When a group of women with low levels of zinc were given dietary supplements that included zinc, their infants had significantly greater birth weight and head circumference than a group of women given multivitamin tablets that did not contain zinc (Goldenberg et al., 1995).

Stress during Pregnancy   Some studies relate continuous stress to the birth of infants who are irritable, squirming, and generally more difficult to care for (Sontag, 1941, 1944; Stechler & Halton, 1982). These babies do not feed as well, and they cry more than infants whose mothers have not been under constant stress (Copans, 1974). In Finland, there is an old belief that stress during pregnancy affects the infant's temperament. Pregnant women in Helsinki, Finland, were asked about their stress during their regular visits to maternal outpatient clinics, and their ratings of stress were compared to measures of infant temperament when the infants were between 6 and 8 months. The results showed that mothers' subjective analyses of their own stress during the first trimester correlated well with such infant behaviors as slow adaptability, negative mood, easy distractibility, and high intensity. There were no relationships, however, between stress in the second or third trimester and infant temperament (Huttunen, 1989).

The mechanism by which stress leads to such problems is not entirely understood. Stress increases the production of hormones, particularly adrenaline, that may cause such reactions. Stress may also lead to anxiety that may increase metabolic rate and result in lower gestational weight gain. Anxiety may cause changes in hormonal balance that could contribute to early labor (Chomitz et al., 1995). Stress may also lead to poorer health habits, such as unhealthy eating habits, lack of sleep, or difficulty abstaining from cigarettes or alcohol, therefore causing prenatal difficulties.

So many factors confound the situation that the effect of stress on pregnancy remains a difficult question to answer. For instance, the stress may continue after the baby's birth, making it difficult to separate prenatal factors from postnatal factors when deciding what may have caused a problem. The research is suggestive but remains open to challenge.

Guideposts

How could maternal stress in pregnant women affect their developing infants?

The Father's Role

After noting the many maternal behaviors that affect the fetus, students often complain that the child's father seems to get away with everything during the prenatal stage. Yet, research demonstrates the importance of the father's behavior in affecting the pregnancy and the subsequent health of the fetus. Paternal drug taking prior to pregnancy as well as exposure to radiation may affect the father's genes and sperm and in turn directly affect the child.

Paternal exposure to particular chemicals prior to pregnancy is implicated in such outcomes as spontaneous abortion, low birth weight, and birth defects (Olshan & Faustman, 1993). Some agents can lead to reduced sperm quantity, less motility, and abnormal sperm structure (Wyrobek, 1993). An increase in spontaneous abortion is found in men working in occupational settings in which they are exposed to vinyl chloride, metals such as mercury, or chemicals used in the manufacture of rubber, plastics, and solvents (Aleser, Brix, Fine, Kallenbach, & Wolfe, 1989; Cordier, Deplan, Mandereau, & Hermon, et al. 1991; Taskinen, Antitila, Lindbohm, Sallmen, & Hemminki, 1989). Exposure to solvents and some pesticides have been linked to birth defects, and exposure to chemical toxins has been linked to cancer in the offspring (Wyrobek, 1993).

Fathers' use of alcohol and nicotine may also be implicated, as one large study found paternal cigarette smoking associated with increases in cleft lip and cleft palate and various other birth defects (Savitz, Schwingle, & Keels, 1991). In another study, fathers who had two or more drinks daily or at least five drinks on one occasion in the month before conception fathered infants who showed an average decrease of 181 grams in birth weight. The study controlled for such variables as maternal drinking, paternal smoking and other drug usage, and other factors (Little & Sing, 1987).

How could these chemicals affect the outcomes of pregnancy? First, these chemicals may directly affect sperm, causing a birth defect (Cicero, 1994). Second, evidence indicates that some chemicals and drugs, including cocaine, may be found in seminal fluid and transfer is possible (Olshan & Faustman, 1993).

The research on paternal exposure and adverse infant development, though, is plagued by incomplete reports and by the very small number of people studied (Wyrobek, 1993). Often, in occupational and environmental studies, the amount of exposure is not well researched (Shore, 1995). In many cases, the Environmental Protection Agency admits that the listing of a chemical or drug as having adverse affects on sperm is based on very few studies of each chemical, and the results may be expected to change as more information is provided (Wyrobek, 1993; Wyrobek, Watchmaker, & Gordon, 1994). In addition, the research is often inconclusive, and a definitive statement is difficult to make. Despite the inadequacies in research, the literature to date suggests potential associations between paternal exposure to drugs and chemicals and adverse pregnancy outcomes.

Aside from this, the father's behavior influences the expectant mother's actions. If women heed the warnings about drinking, smoking, and drug taking, they will increase their chances of giving birth to a healthy child, but if the father is indulging, the mother may find it more difficult to refrain from such behavior. In addition, the mother's need for emotional support places a responsibility on the father's shoulders. The father can help reduce the stress and anxiety experienced by the mother by being willing to understand the expectant mother's special needs for support and assistance. Such willingness can help the mother through this unique time in the couple's life.

T F 8

Exposure to chemicals in the workplace and some pesticides may affect the sperm cells, leading to fetal deformities.

Guideposts

How can the father's behavior affect the health of the developing child?

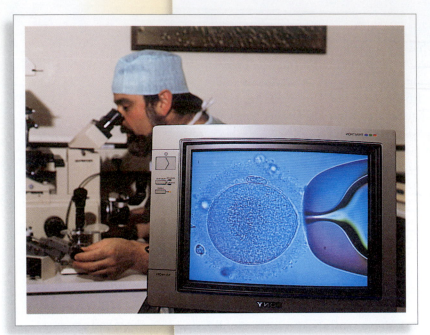

During in vitro fertilization, an egg taken from the mother is fertilized by sperm taken from the husband in a laboratory and then the fertilized egg is implanted into the mother's uterus.

Technology and Reproductive Alternatives

Many couples, for one reason or another, cannot have children. About 1 in every 13 couples is infertile, which is defined as the inability to conceive after a year or more of intercourse without contraception (Higgins, 1990). Many other couples have difficulty conceiving that doesn't last a full year.

More couples are entering high-tech treatment than ever before, and hope means everything to them. If you were told that a treatment had only a 10% chance of success, you wouldn't hold out much hope. Concentrating on the 10% probability, the infertile couple accepts hormones, surgery, and drug therapies that sometimes have annoying and painful side effects. Perhaps the most radical treatment is in vitro fertilization (IVF) in which the egg is taken from the woman's ovary through a process known as *laparoscopy*, which requires an incision. Next, the egg is fertilized with the husband's sperm and allowed to develop for two days before being implanted in the womb. More than 10% of couples seeking infertility treatment advance to IVF (Halpern, 1989). About 1% of the firstborn children in Western countries are conceived by IVF (van Balen, 1996), some 40,000 in the United States alone (Belkin, 1997). IVF requires commitment and some suffering, and it is also expensive. Injections of hormones are required, and much time is lost from work as people often have to spend weeks near a fertility clinic. The chances that one cycle of in vitro fertilization will result in a baby is low, so several attempts may be required (Meldrum & Gardner, 1998). In addition, there is a high rate of prematurity and an increased risk of prematurity in IVF pregnancies and therefore some concern about the health of these infants (Rosenthal, 1992; Templeton & Morris, 1998).

At one time, a number of possible questions and concerns were raised about the parenting of these children. Would these parents who waited so long to have children be overprotective or show an exaggerated concern for them? Would they expect too much too soon from these children? Would these parents who had been child-free for so long find the transition to parenting more difficult?

Sufficient pregnancies and births have taken place through IVF to assess its effects on children and parenting. When infertile couples who had their child via IVF were compared with fertile couples, the IVF mothers experienced more pleasure in their child and reported stronger feelings toward their child. There were no significant differences between the groups on expectations for achievement. The IVF mothers also reported behaviors that indicated more parental competence than the fertile mothers, but no differences on perception of burden were found. IVF mothers also characterized their children as more social and less obstinate. There was no higher degree of parental concern, protectiveness, or worry about the child. No significant differences were found among the fathers (van Balen & Trimbos-Kemper, 1993). These findings were also true for couples who had been infertile but finally had a child without needing IVF. Perhaps the experience of being infertile is associated with a greater awareness of the importance of parenthood (van Balen & Trimbos-Kemper, 1995).

There has been a boom in multiple births due to the growing number of couples in fertility treatment. "I had panic attacks when I heard it was triplets, but I would rather have my hands full than empty," said one mother who gave birth to two boys and a girl after 11 years of infertility treatments.

When parents who had children through in vitro fertilization and donor insemination (a process whereby sperm are inserted into the vagina without sexual intercourse, using medical procedures) were compared with adoptive and naturally conceived families, interesting differences in parenting style were found (Golombok, Cook, Bish, & Murray, 1995). Those who had used the new technologies showed more warmth to the child, were more emotionally involved, had more interaction, and experienced less stress (see Figure 4.3). Genetic ties appear much less important for family functioning than the strong desire to be parents. Parents who have conceived their children through in vitro fertilization and donor insemination appear to be very competent parents who are more involved with and value their experiences with their children but who are not overprotective.

IVF and other techniques presently available may go beyond helping couples who are infertile, though. What if a woman found out that she is carrying a gene that makes it quite likely that she will develop a very serious disease? She wants to

T F 9

Parents of children who have been conceived through in vitro fertilization (outside the womb in an artificial manner) are overprotective of these children but interact less with them than parents of children who have been conceived in the typical manner.

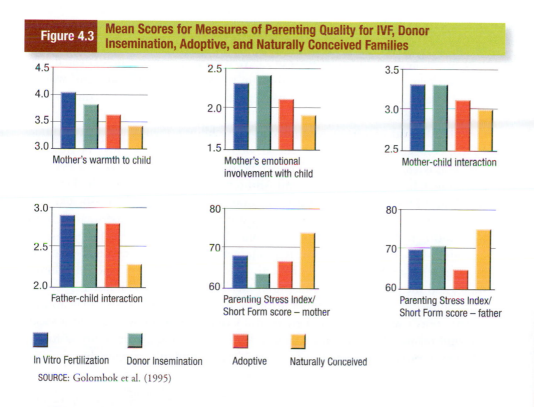

Figure 4.3 Mean Scores for Measures of Parenting Quality for IVF, Donor Insemination, Adoptive, and Naturally Conceived Families

In Vitro Fertilization   Donor Insemination   Adoptive   Naturally Conceived

SOURCE: Golombok et al. (1995)

Does the Child Need to Know?

Parents read special books to adopted children telling them about adoption. There are no secrets. Children are informed early of their status. But Ingrid and Stephen face a more difficult choice. Their daughter was conceived using a donor egg that was fertilized using in vitro fertilization and implanted into Ingrid's womb. They face the question of whether to tell their daughter and, if so, how to do it. The decision would be easier if it was just a case of in vitro fertilization, but because another woman's egg was used, the child carries those genes. They must decide whether their daughter has the right to know. Ingrid believes she does, but Stephen is not so certain.

1. *If you were in this situation, would you tell the child?*
2. *If your answer is yes, at what age and how would you tell the child?*
3. *If the child was conceived using in vitro fertilization but with the couple's own sperm and egg, should they inform the child of this?*

have children and does not wish to pass the gene on to her children. Under such a scenario, would you choose or would you encourage your wife to choose in vitro fertilization in which the egg is fertilized outside the womb, have genetic tests conducted on these embryos, and have those without the gene reimplanted in the womb? With more genes for various diseases and medical conditions being discovered each year, the question is germane. Such a test is available for cystic fibrosis. In one case, eight embryos of a British woman with a gene for cystic fibrosis were screened for the gene, two were reimplanted, and one survived to term (Wright, 1994). This process, called *preimplantation diagnosis technique*, permits examination of embryos for genetic defects before they are transferred to the uterus (Xu, Shi, Veeck, Hughes, & Rosewaks, 1999).

Given the present techniques, embryos can be conceived in vitro and preserved through cryopreservation. In one case, a custody battle occurred over seven frozen embryos conceived by in vitro fertilization. The parents, who were divorced, were fighting over legal custody (Angell, 1990). In another development, women in their 50s and even a few in their 60s have become pregnant and delivered. The oldest woman to deliver an infant is thought to be a 63-year-old California woman who delivered a daughter using a donor egg and her 60-year-old husband's sperm (Hellmich, 1997; Hellmich & Peterson, 1997). Menopause may no longer necessarily be the end of a woman's ability to bear children (Sauer, Paulson, & Lobo, 1990). Is it reasonable to help a woman become pregnant who may be 80 when her child is 18? On the other hand, men become fathers late in life—for example, the actors Charlie Chaplin at 73 and Anthony Quinn at 78 with little discussion (Phillips, 1994)—although expensive technology was not required. Isolated cases will certainly arise in which older women want to deliver and raise infants, but it is doubtful that this will become a trend. In response to these problems, the Canadian Royal Commission on Reproductive Technologies advocated that IVF be considered a proven treatment for only one type of infertility; blocked fallopian tubes, and the procedure not be used for any other purpose (Phillips, 1994).

Some advocates for people with disabilities are concerned that routine genetic tests coupled with the new reproductive technology will lead to a subtle pressure on people to terminate pregnancies whenever some disability is found. The new reproductive alternatives give new hope for infertile couples, but they also

For Your Consideration ?

A woman aged 58 wants to become pregnant and needs IVF to do so. Her insurance company refuses to pay for this. She claims this is age discrimination. In your opinion, who is correct? Why?

Guideposts

What are some of the social and familial implications of in vitro fertilization and other fertility techniques?

raise many social and medical issues (see *Reproductive Surrogacy* on page 138). These issues will have to be explored and the extent to which this technology is used monitored closely.

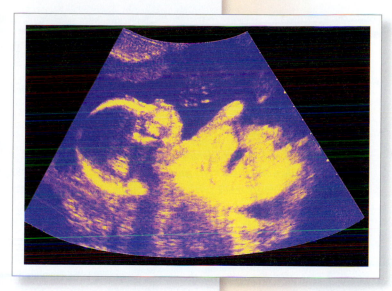

Technology, Pregnancy, and Birth

Today, a pregnant woman's experience of pregnancy and birth differs somewhat from that of her mother. Many pregnant women have **sonograms** (also called **ultrasound**) in which sound waves are used to produce a picture of the fetus. Sonograms can be used to determine the gestational age of the child, to learn whether a woman is carrying twins, and to diagnose a number of rare but important fetal defects. It can also help discover cardiac problems in the fetus (Buskens, Steyerberg, Hess, Wladimiroff, & Grobbee, 1997).

Some women undergo **amniocentesis,** which involves extracting a small amount of amniotic fluid from the womb. The fluid contains fetal cells that have been discarded as the fetus grows. The cells are cultured and examined for genetic and chromosomal abnormalities. In another procedure, called **chorionic villus sampling,** cells are obtained from the chorion during the eighth to twelfth weeks of pregnancy and checked for genetic problems. In some cases when a structural problem is found—perhaps through the use of ultrasound—it can be treated. For example, a 23-week-old fetus was surgically removed from his mother's womb, and an operation was performed to correct a blocked urinary tract. The fetus was then returned to the womb (Blackeslee, 1986). In another case, a small valve was implanted in the skull of a fetus that suffered from water on the brain to drain away the fluid, allowing the fetus to develop normally (Volpe, 1984).

Both amniocentesis and chorionic villus sampling are not used for every pregnant woman, since they require an intrusion into the area near the developing fetus. They are indicated when the mother is older or if there is some possibility of prenatal problems. Work is ongoing to develop techniques based on blood tests that will eliminate the need for invasive techniques such as amniocentesis and chorionic villus sampling (Phillips, 1994).

One such screening test is a blood test called the *maternal serum alphafetoprotein (MSAFP) test* which identifies pregnancies that are at higher-than-average risks for certain serious birth defects and other problems. Alphafetoprotein (AFP) is a substance that all fetuses produce; some of it gets into the amniotic fluid, and a little actually enters the mother's bloodstream. The test, which is given between the sixteenth and eighteenth weeks of pregnancy, measures the amount of AFP in the pregnant woman's blood. If the amount of AFP is either high or low, other tests are usually performed (Clark & De Vore, 1989; March of Dimes, 1989).

Another noninvasive procedure entails the use of fetal monitors. These devices tell the doctor how the fetus is reacting to maternal contractions during labor and presents an early indication of any potential fetal distress.

Each of these procedures has limitations and dangers. Some claim that fetal monitoring leads to unnecessary cesarean sections because a doctor may know

Sonograms, which are pictures of the fetus using sound waves, are helpful in diagnosing a number of problems as well as determining the exact gestational age of the child.

Guideposts

How are sonograms, amniocentesis, and alphafetoprotein tests used to diagnose problems in the developing organism?

sonogram

An image of the developing organism taken through the use of sound waves.

amniocentesis

A procedure in which fluid is taken from a pregnant woman's uterus to check fetal cells for genetic and chromosomal abnormalities.

chorionic villus sampling

A diagnostic procedure in which cells are obtained from the chorion during the 8th to 12th weeks of pregnancy and checked for genetic abnormalities.

The Child in the 21st Century

Reproductive Surrogacy

A 1991 trial held in New Jersey startled the nation. Elizabeth and William Stern contracted with Mary Beth Whitehead to act as a surrogate mother. Ms. Whitehead was impregnated with Mr. Stern's sperm through artificial insemination. Later, the surrogate mother did not wish to give up the child and wanted custody.

The New Jersey court handled the case as a custody case, therefore declaring the contract unenforceable. The court awarded custody to the biological father and permitted Elizabeth Stern to adopt the child. However, this was overturned by the New Jersey Supreme Court, which awarded custody to William Stern but did not allow Elizabeth Stern to adopt the child, granting Mary Beth Whitehead visitation rights (Ragone, 1994).

The term *surrogate mother* is really inadequate because it glosses over many important potential distinctions. For example, it is now possible to collect ova from almost any woman, fertilize the ova in the laboratory with sperm essentially from any man (in vitro fertilization), and implant a fertilized ovum into almost any woman with a uterus either immediately or after a time during which the fertilized egg is frozen. None of the parties to this technological feat need know each other; on the other hand, the parties involved may be intimately related.

In the past ten years or so, many celebrated cases of surrogate mothers have introduced new questions that have never had to be answered before. Many cases involve a couple unable to have children and another woman who allows herself to be artificially inseminated with the sperm from the first woman's husband. The second woman is called the *surrogate mother*. If the fertilized egg this woman nourishes is not her own but came from a different woman, would the woman still be called a surrogate mother?

Eugene Sandberg (1989) suggests that three different terms for mothers be used: the *genetic mother* is the producer or the donor of the egg, the *gestational*

Elizabeth and William Stern contracted with Mary Beth Whitehead, right, to act as a surrogate mother. Ms. Whitehead was impregnated with Mr. Stern's sperm through artificial insemination. Later, the surrogate mother did not wish to give up the child and wanted custody.

something is not quite right and decide to do a cesarean section even though the woman might be able to deliver vaginally. Amniocentesis and chorionic villus sampling are not risk-free procedures, and some complications do occur in a small minority of cases (Rhoads et al., 1989).

The MSAFP test has no risk attached, since it is a blood test, but the report of a high or low level of AFP can cause great anxiety to the family even though most times subsequent tests do not show that anything is wrong. Fetal surgery is risky, too, and we do not yet know which fetuses will benefit and which will not. Despite problems, it is clear that technology will continue to offer options that were only dreamed of a few years ago, and they will greatly affect how a woman and her developing child are treated at this important time in their lives.

mother is the developer of the fetus, and the *nurturing mother* is the custodian of the child. Today, the surrogate mother is usually a woman who carries her own fertilized egg for another couple, but this may not be so in the future. Most women who cannot have children can provide their own eggs but cannot carry the infant adequately. The egg of such a woman can be artificially inseminated and implanted in another womb. This has already been done. A 48-year-old woman delivered triplets for her daughter in South Africa after fertilization of the daughter's egg outside the womb and embryo transfer. A lesser number of women will simply need a genetic surrogate—that is, a donor ovum—but will be able to carry the child themselves. In vitro fertilization and surrogacy may become more common in the future.

The objections that are frequently raised concerning surrogacy involve the legal contracts and monetary issues as well as the potential exploitation of poor women to carry children for the wealthy.

As of the middle of 1992, England, Germany, and France have made such monetary contracts for surrogate parenting illegal, and 18 states have passed laws sharply limiting surrogacy arrangements ("Making Money," 1992; Phillips, 1994). Unpaid surrogate parenting remains legal. Today, eight established commercial surrogate mother programs operate in the United States, and a number of private individuals arrange surrogate contracts on a freelance basis (Ragone, 1994). Even the use of donor eggs remains controversial. Medical doctors do not allow anyone to be paid for donating organs, and payments by adoptive parents to birth mothers in private adoptions are limited by law to medical costs and living expenses. Yet, women "donating" eggs are often paid between $1,500 and $3,000 (and sometimes much more) because of the inconvenience and pain that is required, and some are asking whether recipients are being paid for the inconvenience or for the egg (Belkin, 1997).

By the year 2000, some forms of surrogacy will probably become acceptable. However, many issues remain unresolved. For instance, should a contract between a woman who agrees to carry a fertilized egg to term be enforceable in a court of law? Should people who do so be paid for their part? These and other questions are now being hotly debated. This new technology gives us many opportunities previously thought only science fiction. However, they open up many legal and ethical questions that need to be answered.

What do you think?

What are the arguments for and against the principle that contracts for surrogacy should be legal and enforceable in a court of law?

You can explore the questions above using InfoTrac College Edition. Hint: enter search terms *Surrogate Mothers* and *Surrogate Contracts*

Birth

Before birth, the average infant spends about 266 days, counting from conception, or about 280 days, counting after the beginning of the last menstrual period, developing in the womb. A century ago, most women gave birth at home, but today the overwhelming majority of births take place in hospitals.

The Three Stages of the Birth Process

The birth process is divided into three stages. During the **dilation stage,** the uterus contracts and the cervix flattens and dilates to allow the fetus to pass through the cervix (see Figure 4.4 on page 140). The general term **labor** describes this process. This stage can last from about 2 to 16 hours, or even longer. It tends to be longer with the first child. When the contractions start, they usually come at approximately 15- to 20-minute intervals and are generally mild. As they continue, they become stronger and more regular. Near the end of this first stage, the nature of the contractions changes. The contractions become more difficult, last longer, and are more frequent. This period, lasting about an hour, is called **transition** and is the most difficult time of labor for many women (Tucker & Bing, 1975). By the

dilation

The first stage of labor, in which the uterus contracts and the cervix flattens and dilates to allow the fetus to pass.

labor

A term used to describe the general process of expelling the fetus from the mother's womb.

transition

A period late in labor in which the contractions become more difficult.

Figure 4.4 **Stages of Labor**

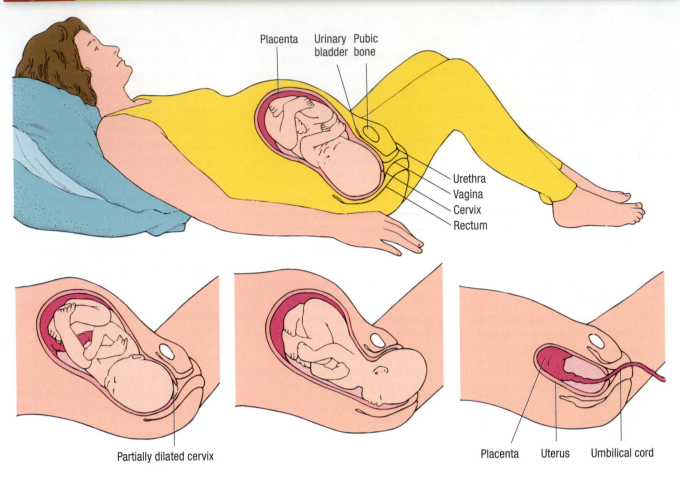

Placenta Urinary Pubic
bladder bone

Urethra
Vagina
Cervix
Rectum

Partially dilated cervix

Placenta Uterus Umbilical cord

(a) Postiiton of the fetus near birth. (b) Dilation stage: Uterine contractions push the fetal head lower in the uterus and cause the relaxin-softened cervix to dilate. (c) Expulsion stage: The fetus is expelled through the cervix and vagina. (d) Placental stage: The placenta is delivered.

SOURCE: Chiras (1993)

end of this stage, the cervix is open about 10 centimeters, and contractions are occurring every minute or so.

The second stage of birth involves the actual delivery of the baby. This **expulsion** stage is quite variable, lasting anywhere from 2 to 60 minutes. The baby's head appears, an event referred to as **crowning.** The rest of the body soon follows.

The third stage of the birth process involves the **delivery of the placenta,** or afterbirth. During this stage, mild contractions continue for some time. They help reduce the blood flow to the uterus and reduce the uterus to normal size.

Cesarean Birth

If it has been determined that there might be a problem in the birth process, the doctor may advise that the baby be removed surgically through the wall of the abdomen and the uterus. This is major surgery that typically involves a longer hospital stay. Cesarean sections, as this type of birth is called, increased substantially until the late 1980s, after which a reduction occurred (see Figure 4.5).

A number of explanations for the dramatic increase in cesarean sections have been advanced. The safety of the operation has improved markedly for both the

expulsion
The second stage of birth, involving actual delivery of the fetus.

crowning
The point in labor at which the baby's head appears.

delivery of the placenta
The third and last stage of birth, in which the placenta is delivered.

Figure 4.5 **Cesarean Operations Performed**

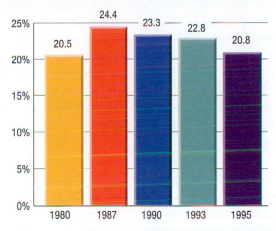

Before 1965, cesarean sections were performed in about 2 to 5% of all births.

SOURCE: U.S. Department of Health and Human Services (1998)

mother and the fetus. The practice of performing repeat cesarean sections, the increased threat of malpractice suits if anything goes wrong during a difficult vaginal delivery, and an increase in the number of problems that now indicate the need for the procedure are also reasons for the increase. Fetal monitors can alert a doctor to a possible problem early in labor, and the doctor may then opt to practice a conservative, defensive style of medicine rather than risk a possibly difficult vaginal delivery.

This increase in cesarean sections has become a controversial issue in recent years. One way to reduce the number of cesareans is to end the standard practice of automatically requiring a woman who has had one cesarean to deliver her other infants by the same method. Many women who have had cesarean sections are able to deliver subsequent babies vaginally, and the number of women doing so has increased substantially (Goldman, Pineault, Potvin, Blais, & Bilodueau, 1993; Quilligan, 1995). This is not always desirable, though, and must be decided on a case-by-case basis (Sachs, Kobelin, Castro, & Frigoletto, 1999).

A question often asked is whether there are any long-term consequences of cesarean birth. The research, although not very extensive, is quite encouraging. Simply stated, there are no negative long-term psychological consequences. Researchers find no differences on measures of maturity, temperament, or special problems (Entwisle & Alexander, 1987). However, parents of children born through cesarean section believed that their children had more academic ability and expected them to attain higher grades in reading and mathematics, although their standardized academic test scores did not differ from vaginally delivered children. The cesarean children did receive higher school grades, probably because their parents expected them to and supported superior achievement.

The Effects of Obstetrical Medication

In the United States, obstetrical medication is almost routinely administered to women in labor. There is little question concerning the effects of such medication on infants in the first few days of life. Medicated infants are more sluggish than unmedicated infants (Brackbill, 1979, 1982). In the second day of life, heavily medicated infants sucked at a lower rate, sucked for shorter periods of time, and

Guideposts

Why have cesarean sections increased in the United States?

If a woman gives birth to a child by cesarean section, all her subsequent children must be born in the same manner.

consumed less formula than infants whose mothers received no anesthesia or local anesthesia (Sanders-Phillips, Strauss, & Gutberlet, 1988). Infants of mothers who received a combination of an epidural and a narcotic to reduce pain during the delivery were less responsive, showed poorer reflexes, and were less easily consoled than babies whose mothers had received only an epidural or no medication at all (Emory, Schlackman, & Fiano, 1996). Today, many women giving birth in the United States are receiving epidural pain relief (Beilin, Leibowitz, Bernstein, & Abramovitz, 1999).

Some studies find the effects of the medication on infant behavior are quickly reduced during the first week after birth, but some differences between the medicated and unmedicated infants still exist (Murray, Dolby, Nation, & Thomas, 1981). By 1 month there were few differences between the groups, although mothers of unmedicated babies handled their babies more affectionately, and mothers of medicated babies spent more time stimulating their infants to suck. There were no differences in infant behavior, but the mothers of medicated babies perceived their infants as less adaptable, more intense, and more bothersome. Of course, more difficult deliveries may account for some of these findings.

Perhaps the major effects of medication, at least at one month, are found in the problems mothers have in interacting with infants who were heavily medicated during the first few days. These problems may carry over and be more important in the long term than the effects of the medications themselves (Murray et al., 1981). The early interactions may set up expectations and problems that may continue to influence the mother's responses (Emory et al., 1996).

The real controversy concerns the possiblity that long-term effects exist. Some argue that there are long-term behavioral and developmental differences (Lester, Heidelise, & Brazelton, 1982). Others disagree, with one study finding no significant differences in strength, sensitivity to touch, activity level, sleep or irritability between young children whose mothers received medication for pain during labor and those whose mothers did not (Kraemer et al., 1985).

The effects of obstetrical medication depend on the type of drug, the time of administration, the dosage, and a number of other individual factors not well understood. The use of medication during labor is a difficult issue. On the one hand, there is the mother's need for pain relief, while on the other there is some complicated and sometimes contradictory evidence on its effect on the child. Doctors, today are more aware of these considerations as well as the need to use the minimum amount of pain-relieving medication possible. However, only the mother truly can appreciate her own state and, together with input from medical personnel, make the decision as to what treatment she requires.

Birth Centers

Although most deliveries take place in a hospital, more births are taking place in birth centers attended by midwives. These centers may be useful for women who are at lower-than-average risk for problems in pregnancy (Rooks et al., 1989). There is even a suggestion to locate birth centers inside hospitals so that if emergency treatment is necessary, it is within easy reach of the patient (Lieberman & Ryan, 1989). Midwife-attended deliveries have increased, but the overwhelming majority of deliveries still take place in the hospital under a doctor's supervision (Lancashare, 1995).

The Lamaze Method

One popular birthing method was developed by Fernand Lamaze (1970), who advocated not only the father's presence but also his active participation in the birth process. Relaxation techniques, breathing methods for the various stages of labor, and a number of other procedures help reduce the discomfort of labor and birth, and consequently the need for painkillers. Finally, the method emphasizes the importance of experiencing the birth and sharing an emotional experience.

Lamaze procedures accomplish their goals. They reduce the amount of medication required, and women giving birth using Lamaze techniques report less discomfort and a more positive attitude toward the process (Charles et al., 1978; Cogan, 1980). This does not mean that the women feel no discomfort, although they do report experiencing less pain than women who do not undergo Lamaze training (Melzack, 1984).

The question of the effect that the father's experience may have on the father-infant relationship is still in doubt. At this time there is insufficient evidence to conclude that bonding is enhanced by the father's attendance at the birth (Palkovitz, 1985). Studies that find positive results for father attendance slightly outnumber studies that find no differences, but these positive studies tend to be less rigorously performed. However, evidence does confirm that the father's attendance at birth and early contact with the infant enhances the marital relationship and the father's feelings of being included, which can have a positive effect on the family.

In this prepared childbirth class, both mothers and fathers are getting ready for the experience of the birth of their child, as well as learning how to reduce the discomfort and pain of labor.

Guideposts

What does Lamaze birthing entail?

ACTION / REACTION

Under Pressure

When Lauren discovered she was pregnant, everything seemed perfect. Her husband Simon was happy, and both sets of prospective grandparents were thrilled. After reading some articles about childbirth, Lauren mentioned to Simon that she wanted to use the Lamaze method of childbirth and to give birth using the services of a midwife in a birth center, but Simon was not happy about that. Neither was Lauren's mother, who shook her head and said, "After you feel the first labor pain and get to the hospital, just have them put you out." Simon's mother was just as direct: "They've been delivering babies in the hospital the regular way for generations with no problems. Why try something new?"

Since Simon doesn't want to be in the labor or delivery room, Lauren has asked her best friend, Nilda, to be her coach. Simon sees this as an attack on his manhood, and everyone is pressuring Lauren to change her mind. Lauren is terribly upset and can't sleep.

1. *If you were Lauren, what would you do? What would you say to Simon and to the couple's mothers?*
2. *If you were Lauren's friend, how would you advise her?*
3. *If you were Lauren's doctor and saw how much pressure Lauren was getting from others, would you step in and make suggestions?*

The Leboyer Method

A different tack is taken by Frederick Leboyer (1975), whose method emphasizes the experience of the infant in what has come to be known as the Leboyer method of childbirth. Leboyer argues that birth is a traumatic experience for the infant. He believes that the baby feels everything and truly experiences the birth process and that what is easiest for the doctor may not be best for the baby. Among other things, Leboyer advocates using dimmed lighting and whispers in the delivery room, placing the infant on the mother's abdomen after birth, waiting minutes before cutting the umbilical cord, providing a bath in which the father plays a leading role, and having both parents massage the infant. He also notes the importance of preparation for childbirth.

Leboyer uses his clinical experiences and theoretical clarity as arguments in favor of his procedures. One study found that babies born by the Leboyer method were physically and behaviorally more advanced than would have been expected (Trotter 1975), but this study has been criticized because it lacked adequate controls. Better-controlled studies have found no differences between Leboyer babies and babies born in the more traditional manner on measures of behavior, cognitive development, or motor skills (Maziade, Boudreault, Cote, & Thivierge, 1986). The Leboyer method requires further testing and is not widely used in the United States because of the extra time needed by doctors (Snow, 1998). In the last analysis, the details of Leboyer's method may be less important than the humanistic attitudes and approach to birth that Leboyer advocates (Young, 1982).

Prematurity: Born At Risk

The greatest threat to an infant's survival is prematurity. A premature infant can be defined in terms of birth weight or the length of the gestation period. Currently, a baby weighing less than 2,500 grams (about 5.5 pounds) or one who has been born less than 37 weeks after conception is considered premature. A birth weight below 1,500 grams (about 3 pounds, 5 ounces) is designated very low birth weight, and an infant born at below 1,000 grams is designated as having extremely low birth weight. Each year, about 50,000 infants in the United States are born weighing below 1,500 grams (Singer et al., 1999). The rate of prematurity has been slowly rising and remains a significant problem.

Generally, premature infants are categorized into two groups. In the first group are infants born below the weight expected for their gestational age. Some of these babies are born at their normal term; others are born earlier. These infants are called **small-for-date babies.** The other group involves what are called **preterm infants,** those whose birth weights are appropriate for their gestational age but who are born at or before 37 weeks after conception (Kopp & Parmelee, 1979).

Years ago, the outlook for premature infants was very poor, but this has changed substantially. The mortality rate among infants with very low birth weight, and even for those with extremely low birth weight, has declined (Goldenberg & Rouse, 1998; Singer et al., 1998).

Premature infants are at risk for a number of physical and intellectual deficits during childhood (Horbar & Lucey, 1995; Middle, Alderdice, & Petty, 1996). Many low-birth-weight infants exhibit moderate to severe disabilities and many more milder forms (Doussard-Roosevelt, Proges, Scanlon, Alemi, & Scanlon, 1997). The smaller the infant, the more likely the child will have some disability, and children with the lowest birth weights often show major disabilities when observed at 1 or 2 years of age (Ehrenhaft, Wagner, & Herdman, 1989). Even with optimal environments, many will require special educational services, and about 20% show significant problems in the cognitive, physical, sensory, neurological, and/or language areas (Halsey, Collins, & Anderson, 1996; Horbar & Lucey, 1995).

The situation is complicated by the fact that not every premature infant suffers these setbacks. Many premature babies grow up to be superior children and to function well as adults. A variety of outcomes is possible, depending on the size and gestational age of the infant and on subsequent care and upbringing. In general, though, the lower the birth weight and the shorter the gestation period, the more potentially serious the consequences.

Premature infants are at risk not only because many diseased or genetically abnormal infants are born early, but also because the premature infant is likely to be born into a disadvantaged environment. Although prematurity is found in every socioeconomic group, it is far more common in women who live in poverty or in those who are young (McLoyd, 1998). White women between 20 and 30 years of age have about a 3% low-birth-weight rate, whereas economically disadvantaged teenagers have a 9% rate (Kopp & Kaler, 1989). Racial and ethnic group membership is also related to prematurity (see *The Mystery of Prematurity: Not Just Poverty* on page 147).

Advances in medical science have helped us save many lives of premature infants.

Guideposts

Why is prematurity considered the most important birth problem today?

ACTION / REACTION

What If Something Happens?

Often the actual reason a child is born prematurely remains a mystery. So it was with Ron and Hazel's baby. Jayne, born 6.5 months, was given only a small chance of surviving. After a few days in the hospital, Hazel went home. She returned to the hospital each day to feed Jayne and spend time with her, but Ron refused to see the baby at all. He told Hazel that if the baby died, it would be worse for him if he had become attached to her. Hazel felt the same way, but she told Ron it was their responsibility to care for Jayne. What if she, too, refused to see the baby? Ron said he would understand, and if she didn't want to see Jayne until her chances of surviving improved, he could respect that. Hazel was very angry at her husband's attitude and behavior.

Now Jayne is home and apparently will be all right. Ron now shows a great deal of love, but Hazel is distant with Ron because she is still angry with him. "He gave me no help when the baby was in the hospital," she complains. Her estimation of Ron has been reduced. Ron says that he understands Hazel's feelings but that continuing her cool behavior is pointless.

1. *If you were Hazel, how would you have handled Ron's behavior at the hospital?*
2. *If you were Ron, how would you deal with Hazel at home?*
3. *If you were Ron and felt the same way he did, how would you have dealt with the infant?*
4. *If you were the pediatrician, would you have intervened?*

ACTION / REACTION

Although we do not know the reasons for most premature births, a number of factors have been implicated, including the maternal health and nutrition prior to pregnancy; maternal age, weight, and weight gain during pregnancy; maternal smoking and use of other drugs; uterine problems; and lack of prenatal care (Kopp & Parmelee, 1979; Nathanielsz, 1995). Cigarette smoking is the largest single

prematurity
Infants weighing less than 5.5 pounds or born at or before 37 weeks after conception.

small-for-date infants
Infants born below the weight expected for their gestational age.

preterm infants
Infants born at or before the 37th week of gestation.

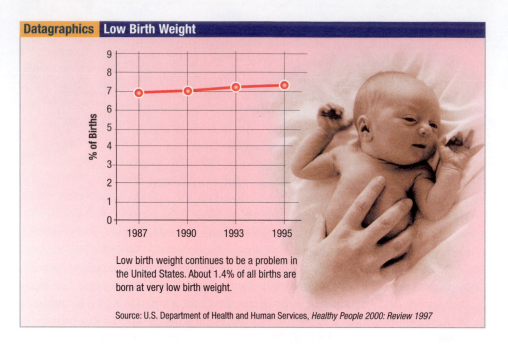

Datagraphics | **Low Birth Weight**

Low birth weight continues to be a problem in the United States. About 1.4% of all births are born at very low birth weight.

Source: U.S. Department of Health and Human Services, *Healthy People 2000: Review 1997*

modifiable risk factor and accounts for perhaps as much as 20% of low-birth-weight cases (Shiono & Behrman, 1995). These factors correlate with social class (Hughes & Simpson, 1995), because women living in poverty are less likely to eat a nutritious diet during pregnancy and are much less likely to receive high-quality prenatal care. Their health prior to the pregnancy is also likely to be worse, and they are more likely to be exposed to disease. It is no wonder that children born to these mothers are at a double risk, being they are more vulnerable at birth and more likely to be exposed to poor living conditions afterward (Roberts, 1997).

Tremendous improvements in the care of premature infants have been made. Today, effective tube-feeding techniques are available, and sophisticated machinery monitors the infant's vital signs. It is important that these children be stimulated. The effects of a deadening, nonstimulating hospital environment must be countered by giving the infants extra rocking and tactile stimulation as well as presenting them with things to look at and hear. Years ago, the policy was to avoid touching premature infants, but today we know that this is counterproductive. Gentle massaging and a program of appropriate stimulation is very helpful in fostering growth, weight gain, and development in general (Field, 1986). When preterm infants who received or did not receive special tactile stimulation were compared, those who enjoyed additional stimulation were discharged significantly earlier and were found to go from tube to other forms of feeding more quickly and to develop a better sucking response. At 15 months, they were superior in cognitive development as well (de Roiste & Bushness, 1996).

Various enrichment programs, some focusing on the child and others on the family, have been successful. In the Infant Health and Development Program, premature infants were randomly assigned either to an experimental group that received a training program based on child development principles, family support, and medical follow-up or to a control group that received only pediatric care for three years. The children who received the enrichment had significantly higher intelligence scores than children in the control group and showed fewer behavioral problems (Hack, Klein, & Taylor, 1995). Such programs are highly effective in improving the neurological, motor, and psychological development of premature infants. Premature infants require additional care, and family support programs are very successful in easing the pressure and helping children develop their cognitive abilities (Richmond, 1990).

The Mystery of Prematurity: Not Just Poverty

If prematurity is the greatest cause of infant mortality, prevention of low birth weight becomes a vital concern. Many studies have linked socioeconomic variables and drug taking to premature births, and these findings are widely accepted. Poverty status, with its greater exposure to disease, crowded conditions, and often poor nutrition, is related to low birth weight outcomes. People who take drugs or smoke are certainly more likely to have premature infants. Although many of these findings are based on correlations not allowing a cause-and-effect statement, the evidence is strong that these factors are somehow involved.

The first problem, that of improving prenatal care, has seen some success. The percentage of women in all socioeconomic groups receiving prenatal care has increased greatly, although some disparities still exist (USDHHS, 1995). Psychological factors also deserve attention. For example, having an attitude that chance plays a major role in determining one's health status is related to low birth weight. Women with this attitude may not believe their behavior can influence the infant's birth status, so they may not make healthy choices, including seeking out competent medical care (Shiono, Rauh, Park, Lederman, & Zuskar, 1997).

The second problem, that of reducing drug use, clearly requires more effort. Women are still smoking cigarettes and consuming alcohol at alarming rates, and cocaine and other drug abuse remains a significant problem. Reducing the incidence of cigarette smoking will reduce prematurity rates (Weissberg & Greenberg, 1998). In some areas of the country, the suggestion has been made that women whose babies test positive for cocaine be considered guilty of child abuse. This approach would certainly demonstrate how serious our society considers such behavior. After all, an individual who knows that it is dangerous to take such drugs and still puts her infant at considerable risk is knowingly injuring her child. Whenever this question is discussed in class, students of all backgrounds line up strongly in favor of this approach. It is popular among some professionals and politicians as well.

Yet, this is a questionable approach. Most crack users are from poor, minority group backgrounds, and the question of whether this is discriminatory can be raised. Should we consider people who drink or smoke cigarettes as doing the same thing and prosecute them (Marwick, 1998)? Without such authority, public welfare agencies still have the right to do what is in the best interests of the child. In addition, pregnant substance abusers may not seek out prenatal care if they are afraid of being arrested and prosecuted (Marwick, 1998). It is questionable whether such an approach is really needed.

Recently, though, many researchers are taking a closer look at some of the more puzzling aspects of prematurity. Scientists have known for many years that the prematurity rate varies considerably among various minority groups. The prematurity rate for African Americans is about 13%, twice that of whites (Lancashare, 1995; Paneth, 1995). This has often been explained by the fact that many more African Americans than whites live in poverty, and poverty is related to prematurity. The situation is much more complicated, though. The prematurity rate for Native Americans and Latinos is only very slightly higher than whites even though a relatively high proportion of women from these minority groups also live in poverty (Chomitz et al., 1995). The rate for Asian Americans, although somewhat higher than for whites, is still about half that for African Americans.

A recent finding may hold one key to answering the question of what additional factors besides poverty may be related to low birth weight. If Latinos are divided into two groups, a group that immigrated to the United States and has lived in the United States for less than five years and a group that has lived in the country for more than ten years, significant differences in prematurity rates become apparent (Zambrana, Scrimshaw, Collins, & Dunkel-Schetter, 1997). Latinos who have been living in the United States longer show a much higher prematurity rate than those who are recent immigrants. When compared on a number of variables, the group of Mexican Americans that had been living longer in the United States reported more prenatal stress, less support from the baby's father, less positive attitudes toward their pregnancies, and more drug and alcohol use, although there were no significant differences between groups on prenatal care. Just what leads to these undesirable changes is not yet known.

Growing evidence indicates that psychosocial factors as well as health-related behaviors during pregnancy are linked to prematurity. And often these variables correlate with one another. For example, prenatal stress is associated with substance abuse and very low social support. It may be that communal support, which is so important in reducing stress, may be a protective factor. Indeed, a study of African American women found that those living in predominantly African American neighborhoods had fewer low-birth-weight infants than African Americans of the same poverty status living in other areas, although the rate was still higher than for whites and most other groups (Roberts, 1997). Perhaps these women received more support from extended families living near them and neighbors. These social networks may offer important emotional support.

It is becoming increasingly clear that low birth weight is a more complicated problem than it first appears. Certainly, better access to prenatal care and more attention to drug use would help, but psychosocial factors are also related to poor birth outcomes, often in ways that are not well understood. The question of why some groups of women give birth to premature infants is not answered simply by looking at poverty status. Other communal, cultural, and support factors may be involved. At present, we do not truly understand the nature of these factors and how they operate, but at least we are now looking at new avenues of research to answer the question of why some groups of women living in poverty have much higher rates of premature births than others.

What do you think?

Controversy persists about whether pregnant women who engage in behaviors that are likely to cause injury to their infants should be held criminally accountable for their actions. For example, should women who drink alcohol, take cocaine, or smoke cigarettes be legally responsible for the harm they may do their infants? Would you be in favor of or opposed to legislation in this area?

You can explore the following questions using InfoTrac College Edition. Hint: enter search terms *Prenatal Care, Prenatal Care Social Aspects,* and *Prematurity.*

Infant Mortality

Congenital birth defects, prematurity, and low birth weight are the leading causes of infant mortality. In the area of infant mortality in the United States, there is both good news and bad news. The rate of infant mortality in the United States has declined consistently since 1933 and continues to drop (see Figure 4.6) (MacDormand & Rosenberg, 1993). However, the United States ranks twenty-second in the world in infant mortality, and its decrease in mortality rate is not equal to that of other industrialized countries (Shiono & Behrman, 1993).

The lack of prenatal care, drug taking, and a number of other factors are involved in the infant mortality rate. Today, more than three-quarters of all pregnant women receive prenatal care during the critical first trimester, the highest level ever reported. The percentage of those who did not receive any medical attention until the third trimester or not at all has fallen to 5% (Lancashare, 1995). Fewer Latinos (except Cuban), Native American, and African Americans receive care in the first trimester (National Center for Health Statistics, 1993). To improve the situation, access to health care before, during, and after pregnancy is required, as are changes in lifestyle such as reducing exposure to drugs.

After the Birth

By the end of the typical period of prenatal development, the average American male infant weighs approximately 7.5 pounds and measures approximately 20 inches. The average female weighs slightly less—about 7 pounds—but is more ready for life. She is about four weeks more mature as measured by skeletal age (Annis, 1978) and is more neurologically advanced. Hospitals have instituted specific procedures to measure the physical functioning and the capacity for independent survival of newborn infants. For example, infants can be evaluated using a rating system called the **Apgar Scoring System** (Apgar, 1953),

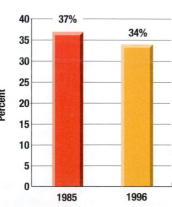

Trends in Development

Children's Health Index:
Has the United States reduced the percentage of infants born with one or more health risks?

There has been some improvement, as the percentage of infants born with one or more health risks has declined somewhat.

Source: National Education Goals Panel, 1998

Figure 4.6   Infant Mortality Rate by Race, 1980–1996

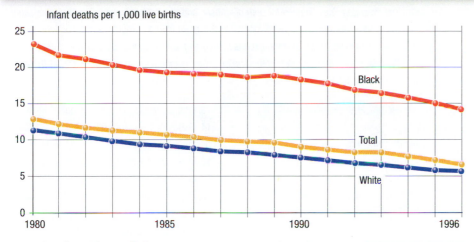

NOTE: Data for 1996 are preliminary.
SOURCE: Centers for Disease Control and Prevention, National Center for Health Statistics, National Vital Statistics System.

which measures five physical characteristics: heart rate, respiration, muscle tone, color, and reflex response (see Table 4.2). The neonate (newborn) is given a score of 0, 1, or 2 for each item according to a special criterion. For instance, if the newborn has a heart rate of 100 to 140 beats a minute, the infant receives a score of 2; for 100 beats a minute or below, the infant receives a score of 1: if there is no discernible heartbeat, a 0 is given (Apgar, Holaday, James, Weisbrot, & Berien, 1958). The highest possible total score is 10. Some studies suggest that there are differences among infants who have received scores of 7, 8, or 9 and those with a perfect 10. Infants who receive a score of less than 7 need additional watching and care. The Apgar score can alert those responsible for the infant's care to a possible problem.

A more complex assessment for infants is the **Brazelton Neonatal Behavior Scale,** which provides information concerning reflexes and a variety of infant behaviors (Brazelton, 1990). Among the behavioral items are measures of responsiveness to visual stimuli, reactions to a bell and a pinprick, and the quality and duration of the infant's alertness and motor activity (see Table 4.3) (Lester, Heidelise & Brazelton, 1982). The scale is a diagnostic tool but has also been used to research cross-cultural differences among infants.

Guideposts
How can the physical functioning and the abilities of the newborn be measured?

Table 4.2   The Apgar Scoring System

The Apgar Scoring System is a relatively simple scale used to rate newborns on survivability. Each child is rated on each of the five behaviors listed below. Each behavior can have a score of 0, 1, or 2. (Highest possible total score is 10.) If the total score is greater that 7, no immediate threat to survival exists. Any score lower than 7 is cause for great concern. If the score is lower than 4, the infant is presently in critical condition.

Area	Score 0	Score 1	Score 2
Heart rate	Absent	Slow (<100)	Rapid (>100)
Respiration	Absent	Irregular	Good, infant crying
Muscle tone	Flaccid	Weak	Strong, well flexed
Color	Blue, pale	Body pink, extremities blue	All pink
Reflex response			
Nasal tickle	No response	Grimace	Cough, sneeze
Heel prick	No response	Mild response	Foot withdrawal, cry

SOURCE: Based on Apgar (1953)

Apgar Scoring System
A relatively simple system that gives a gross measure of infant survivability.

Brazelton Neonatal Behavior Scale
An involved system for evaluating an infant's reflexes and sensory and behavioral abilities.

Table 4.3 The Brazelton Behavioral Assessment Scale

The Brazelton Scale is used for both diagnostic and research purposes. The examiner rates the child on each of these behaviors while the infant is in a particular state. For example, the child's response to an auditory response (such as the examiner's voice) is noted only when the infant is in the quiet alert state. The examiner is interested in discovering what the infant can do, not what he or she does.

1. Response decrement to repeated visual stimuli
2. Response decrement to rattle
3. Response decrement to bell
4. Response decrement to pinprick
5. Orienting response to inanimate visual stimuli
6. Orienting response to inanimate auditory stimuli
7. Orienting response to animate visual stimuli—examiner's face
8. Orienting response to animate auditory stimuli—examiner's voice
9. Orienting response to animate visual and auditory stimuli
10. Quality and duration of alert periods
11. General muscle tone—in resting and in response to being handled, passive and active
12. Motor activity
13. Traction responses as he is pulled to sit
14. Cuddliness—responses to being cuddled by examiner
15. Defensive movements—reactions to a cloth over his face
16. Consolability with intervention by examiner
17. Rapidity of buildup to crying scale
18. Rapidity of buildup to crying state
19. Irritability during the examination
20. General assessment and his capacity to control himself
21. tremulousness
22. Amount of startling
23. Lability of skin color—measuring autonomic lability
24. Lability of states during entire examination
25. Self-quieting activity—attempts to console self and control state
26. Hand-to-mouth activity

SOURCE: Lester & Brazelton (1982)

Looking Ahead

The study of prenatal development and birth is hopeful yet very frustrating. So much is known about preventing birth defects, yet every day we observe pregnant women drinking, smoking, eating improperly, and not availing themselves of proper prenatal care. Teenagers are giving birth at alarming rates, but often their knowledge of the effects of particular drugs such as cocaine on prenatal development is lacking (Hall & Rouse, 1996), and little effort is expended to teach these young parents about their infants' special needs. We have some of the answers to our problems, but improving programs to serve the needs of families during this important time of their lives is expensive. We pay for these failures in the years to come, since problems that develop at this stage often lead to psychological, social, and medical problems later in life that force their attention on us.

What does this information mean to prospective parents? Increasing knowledge allows them to make important decisions during pregnancy about what to avoid. Although there are no guarantees that their baby will be born healthy, they now have the information necessary to improve their chances of having a healthy infant. They can control their smoking and drinking and follow healthy routines in other areas, such as nutrition. Alternative birthing centers are also available if they wish. For these parents, the new medical knowledge and advances mean that their infant has a better chance of being born free of defects and developing healthfully in the years to come.

Summary

1. Fertilization occurs when a sperm cell penetrates an egg cell. The germinal stage lasts from conception until about 2 weeks. During this stage, the fertilized egg travels down the fallopian tube and embeds itself in the womb. The embryonic stage lasts from 2 to 8 weeks. During this time, the heart starts to beat, and 95% of the body systems are present. During the fetal stage, from 2 months until birth, the developing organism continues to develop internally and put on weight.

2. The time at which an event has its greatest impact is called the critical period. A teratogen is any agent that can cause a birth defect. For example, thalidomide, which was once prescribed to relieve the symptoms of morning sickness, caused many deformities. Diethylstilbestrol (DES) was prescribed for women who had histories of miscarriages. Although the infants were born healthy, some female offspring developed cervical cancer years later.

4. Cigarette smoking has been linked to low birth weight, learning difficulties, poor attention span, and behavioral difficulties. Children of alcoholic mothers may suffer from fetal alcohol syndrome, a condition consisting of physical defects and mental retardation. Even moderate drinking during pregnancy can cause some fetal abnormality, known as fetal alcohol effect.

5. The use of various narcotics during pregnancy is linked to many birth defects. The effects of cocaine are serious, and the environment these children live in is often poor, which adds to the problems. Studies show that these children's development can be improved significantly if they receive extra help.

6. Various diseases, such as rubella, AIDS, herpes, syphilis, gonorrhea, and chlamydia can cause fetal abnormalities or death.

7. The Rh factor is a particular red blood cell antibody. When the mother is Rh-negative and the father is Rh-positive, the offspring can be Rh-positive, and problems may arise. Antibodies from the mother can pass through the placenta and kill red blood cells in the fetus. Today, women with such problems receive a shot of the vaccine RhoGAM, which blocks the creation of the antibodies.

8. For financial, professional, and personal reasons, more women are having their first child when they are over 30. Although the risk is greater for both mother and baby, good prenatal care can reduce the risk somewhat. Older mothers and fathers are more stable and very capable parents. Many pregnant teenagers do not get proper prenatal care, are exposed to many teratogens, and may be malnourished; thus, the mothers and their infants are at high risk.

9. Serious malnutrition can lead to fewer fetal brain cells. Specific vitamin and mineral deficiencies can lead to fetal deformities. Malnutrition may serve to weaken the fetus. Specific nutritional supplements, such as folate and zinc, prevent some birth defects.

10. Paternal drug use or exposure prior to pregnancy may affect the father's sperm. If the father continues to drink and smoke, the pregnant woman may find it more difficult to refrain from such behavior herself.

11. Couples who have difficulty conceiving may seek treatment from fertility clinics. A number of procedures are available, including in vitro fertilization in which an egg is fertilized by sperm in a laboratory and then implanted in the womb. Parents of children conceived through alternative methods spend more time with their children but do not seem overprotective.

12. Maternal stress has been linked to babies who are irritable as well as to obstetrical problems.

13. New technologies now give the doctor and patient more information and choices with regard to fetal examinations. Sonography uses ultrasonic soundwaves to create a picture of the fetus in the womb. Amniocentesis and chorionic villus sampling are used to discover genetic problems. A screening test for alphafetoprotein can alert the physician to a possible problem. Fetal monitoring during labor gives doctors early warnings that something is wrong.

14. During the first stage of birth, the uterus contracts and the cervix dilates. The infant is delivered in the second stage, and the placenta during the third.

15. Cesarean births have increased significantly during the past 30 years because of improvements in safety, new technological aids allowing doctors to know sooner whether something is wrong, and the tendency for doctors to practice conservative medicine.

16. Infants born to mothers who have received obstetrical medication are more sluggish and not as alert. The long-term effects of obstetrical medication on the child are controversial at the present time.

17. The Lamaze method of prepared childbirth emphasizes the importance of both parents' participation in the birth process. Relaxation is used to reduce the discomfort of labor and birth, and usually less medication is required. The Leboyer method highlights the importance of the infant's experience during the birth process.

Review

18. A premature infant is one who weighs less than 5.5 pounds or who has spent fewer than 37 weeks in the womb. Infants born below the weight expected for their gestational age are small-for-date babies. Preterm infants are those whose birth weights are appropriate for their gestational age but who are born at or before 37 weeks. The cause of most cases of prematurity is unknown. Prematurity is related to infant mortality and intellectual, neurological, and developmental disabilities. Early intervention can help these infants develop more normally. The premature infant has special needs, and parents must learn to cope with these greater demands. Studies show that extra stimulation reduces the possibility that the infant will develop a disability.

19. The average American male infant weighs about 7.5 pounds and measures about 20 inches. Females weigh slightly less than males but are more mature as measured by skeletal age and more neurologically advanced. After birth, the child may be rated on the Apgar Scoring System, which provides caregivers with an idea of the infant's physical condition and chances for survival. A more involved assessment instrument called the Brazelton Neonatal Behavior Scale is both a diagnostic and research tool.

At the moment of (1)_____ , the father's sperm penetrates the mother's egg. The fertilized egg, called a (2)_____ , continues its journey down the fallopian tube. During this first prenatal stage, called the (3)_____ stage, the fertilized ovum divides again and again. During the process of (4)_____ , the fertilized egg burrows into the lining of the uterus. During the second prenatal stage, called the (5)_____ stage, changes occur at a fantastic pace so that at about 8 weeks almost all bodily systems are formed. The first organ to function is the (6)_____ , which starts functioning by the end of the third week. During the third prenatal stage, called the (7)_____ stage, growth continues at a tremendous rate.

During its time in the womb, the developing organism can be adversely affected by many agents called (8)_____ . The effects of most teratogens can be seen at birth, but the effects of (9)_____ were found many years later when some daughters whose mothers had taken the medication developed cancer. Mothers who smoke are likely to give birth to babies who weigh (10)_____ . Women who drink alcohol regularly or binge may give birth to babies who show a distinctive physical appearance and who have mental retardation, a condition called (11)_____ . Other infants exposed to alcohol may have some of the symptoms or show problems later in childhood, a condition called (12)_____ . Mothers who use (13)_____ during their pregnancies are more likely to deliver prematurely, and their infants often suffer many problems, including neurological damage and organ damage. A number of diseases can cause damage. The virus that causes (14)_____ may be transmitted either at birth, during the prenatal stage, or even during breast-feeding, causing infants to become fatally ill. If the mother is Rh-(15)_____ and the father is Rh-(16)_____ , the infant may be Rh-positive and may be damaged. This can be prevented if the mother receives a preventive vaccine after each birth or miscarriage.

A number of important issues can be raised. First, consider the mother's age. Many more women above the age of 30 are having their first child, mostly because of (17)_____ decisions. Another issue is maternal nutrition. Giving (18)_____ to pregnant women prevents neural tube defects, and giving (19)_____ supplements increases birth weight.

Some studies relate pregnant women's experience of a great deal of (20)_____ to poor infant adaptability and negative mood.

Through the process of (21)_____ , an egg is surgically removed and fertilized outside the body. During the pregnancy, the mother may receive a (22)_____ , which uses sound waves to produce a picture of the developing child. Some women have some amniotic fluid drawn and the fetal cells checked for abnormalities, a test called (23)_____ . A blood test for (24)_____ can be used to alert the doctor that something may be wrong. When the mother enters labor, her contractions may be followed using a (25)_____ , which informs the doctor of any possible problems.

There are three stages to birth. During the (26)_____ , the uterus contracts and the cervix dilates. The second stage, called (27)_____ , involves the delivery of the child. The third stage of labor is called (28)_____ . If there is a possible problem, the obstetrician may elect to deliver the baby through the abdominal wall and uterus by (29)_____ . Some parents elect to use the (30)_____ method of birth whereby both parents are present and have received training. Infants who weigh less than 2,500 grams or are born before 37 weeks of gestation are considered (31)_____ . Babies born below the weight typical for their gestational period are called (32)_____ infants, while others whose birth weights are appropriate for their gestation but are born before 37 weeks are called (33)_____ infants. The United States ranks (34)_____ among the world's nations in infant mortality rate. After the baby is born, the (35)_____ Scale may be administered, which measures five physical characteristics. Later, the (36)_____ Scale may be administered, which measures many reflexes and a variety of behaviors.

InfoTrac

For additional readings, explore InfoTrac College Edition, our online library.
Go to http://www.infotrac-college.com/wadsworth.
Hint: enter the search terms *Birth Weight, Low; Reproductive Surrogacy.*

What's on the web

Pampers' Infant and Toddler Development
http://www.totalbabycare.com/

Prematurity
http://www.comfortconnection.org/premature.htm

Planned Parenthood
http://www.plannedparenthood.org/

The Visible Embryo
http://visembryo.ucsf.edu

The Wadsworth Psychology Study Center Web Site
Go to the Wadsworth Psychology Study Center at http://psychology.wadsworth.com/ for quiz questions, research updates, hot topics, interactive exercises, and suggested readings in the InfoTrac College Edition related to this chapter.

Answers 1. conception; 2. zygote; 3. germinal; 4. implantation; 5. embryonic; 6. heart; 7. fetal; 8. teratogens; 9. diethylstilbestrol (DES); 10. less; 11. fetal alcohol syndrome; 12. fetal alcohol effect; 13. cocaine; 14. AIDS; 15. negative; 16. positive; 17. employment (career); 18. folate; 19. zinc; 20. stress; 21. IVF (in vitro fertilization); 22. sonogram (ultrasound); 23. amniocentesis; 24. alphafetoprotein; 25. fetal monitor; 26. dilation stage; 27. expulsion; 28. delivery of the placenta; 29. cesarean section; 30. Lamaze; 31. premature; 32. small-for-date; 33. preterm; 34. twenty-second; 35. Apgar; 36. Brazelton Neonatal Behavior Scale

Infancy
and Toddlerhood

5 Physical Development in Infancy and Toddlerhood

6 Cognitive Development in Infancy and Toddlerhood

7 Social and Personality Development in Infancy and Toddlerhood

CHAPTER FIVE

Physical Development

CHAPTER OUTLINE

"I Need an Instruction Book!"

The Newborn at a Glance

How the Infant Experiences
the World

Infant States

Learning

Reflexes

Brain Development

Infant Health

Growth and Motor Development

Focus on the Toddler

Parenting Choices

Atypical Development:
Early Intervention

ARE THESE STATEMENTS
True *or* False?

1 The newborn is born blind but within the first month develops vision that is similar to the vision of the average adult.
2 Neonates show an excellent sense of taste.
3 By about 2 weeks of age, neonates establish an adult day-night sleep pattern.
4 If parents are very responsive to their infant's cries during early infancy, the child cries less later in infancy.
5 Neonates can imitate simple facial gestures they see in their environment.
6 Most of the infant's reflexes become stronger during the first year.
7 Children actually grow more during the second year of life than during the first.
8 As a rule, girls walk, talk and toilet train earlier than boys.
9 Fathers are more likely to treat their sons and daughters differently than mothers.
10 The earlier parents start to toilet train their child, the shorter the amount of time it takes to do so.

ANSWERS: 1. *False.* 2. *True.* 3. *False.* 4. *True.* 5. *True.* 6. *False.* 7. *False.* 8. *True.* 9. *True.* 10. *False.*

in Infancy *and* Toddlerhood

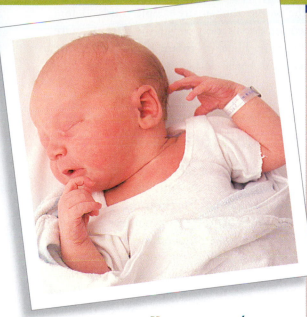

Human neonates have soft, dry, wrinkled skin. They usually weigh between 6 and 9 pounds and are about 20 inches in length. The neonate's head accounts for one-quarter of its entire length.

"I Need an Instruction Book!"

"Babies should come with instruction books and their vocalizations with subtitles," a young mother of a 6-month-old admitted to me. "They cry, but can't tell you why. They stare, but you can't tell what they can really see. They seem to hear, but you can't tell what they are listening to. They become cranky, but it is difficult to figure out what is wrong."

It isn't easy to care for infants or understand their behavior. Thankfully, psychologists have made tremendous strides in understanding the sensory abilities and behavior patterns of infants and toddlers. Much of what we have learned is surprising, and as we tear away the curtain of mystery, we become more impressed at the incredible abilities that even very young infants show.

The Newborn at a Glance

The newborn infant does not resemble the pictures on baby food jars, in soap advertisements, or in the movies. The newborn is covered with fine hair called **lanugo,** which is discarded within a few days. The baby's sensitive skin is protected in the womb by a thick secretion called **vernix caseosa,** which dries and disappears. The head is elongated and measures about one-fourth of the baby's total length. The thin skin appears pale and contains blotches caused by the trip through the birth canal. The head and nose may be out of shape because their soft, pliable nature allows an extra bit of give during birth. They will soon return to normal, but it will be about a year and a half before the bones of the skull will cover the soft spots, or **fontanels.** The legs are tucked in under the baby in a fetal position and will remain that way for quite a while. The newborn wheezes and sneezes and appears anything but ready for an independent existence.

But appearances are deceiving. The newborn has many impressive abilities and is much readier for life outside the womb than many people think. Before looking at these abilities, a few terms require explanation. When the term **neonate** is used, it refers to the baby's first month of life. The term **infant** refers to the entire first year of life. The **toddler** period begins at 1 year and continues until age 3.

How the Infant Experiences the World

Scientists can't ask infants what they can see or hear, so they have developed specific methods of measuring infant capabilities. One of the principle methods for measuring an infant's sensory abilities is through **habituation,** the process by which an individual spends less and less time attending to a familiar stimulus (Catania, 1998). An infant is presented with one stimulus, and the baby's behavior is closely observed. At first the infant shows some interest, but after a time the baby pays less attention to it, perhaps finally ignoring the stimulus altogether. Now the infant is presented with another stimulus, and the behavior is observed. If an increase in attention occurs, the infant has noticed the difference between the two stimuli. Neonates as young as 7 hours old show habituation. Neonates shown a figure first gazed at it but soon showed less and less attention. When the figure was rotated the infant stared about three times longer at the new figure (Slater, Johnson, Kellman, & Spelke, 1988).

Another technique identifies infant preferences for one stimulus over another. Two stimuli are projected, one to the left and one to the right. If the infant gazes at the one to the left significantly more, infants of that age can be assumed to have a preference for that stimulus. To be certain that the infant's preference is for the stimulus rather than the fact that it is on the right or left, the researcher switches the positions of the stimuli.

A third method is to measure the electrical activity of the brain when a particular stimulus is presented to an infant. These **event-related potentials,** as they are called, are transient changes in the brain's electrical activity that reflect the activity of a group of neurons responding to a stimulus. When 6-month-old infants were presented with their mother's face and faces of other people, infants showed different neural activity in response to their mother's face. Not only were the infants able to recognize their mother (they can do so at an earlier age), but different brain activity was found when the infants were presented with women looking similar to or very different from their mothers (de Haan & Nelson, 1997).

Guideposts

What methods do psychologists use to investigate the sensory abilities of infants?

Vision

Neonates can see at birth, but they are very nearsighted. Neonates have a visual acuity of between 20/200 and 20/400 at birth, which means they can see at 20 feet what an older child with normal vision could see at 200 or 400 feet (Haith, 1990).

The baby also has difficulty focusing (Kellman & Banks, 1998). When you look at a chair 5 feet away and then switch to a blackboard 20 feet away, the curvature of the lens of the eye changes to keep the visual image in focus. Newborns do show some visual accommodation, about a third of the adult level (Bremner, 1988). The best focal distance for the newborn is about 19 centimeters, or 7.5 inches (Haynes, White, & Held, 1965). Neonates cannot focus well on distant or approaching objects. As poor as their visual acuity is, though, it serves them well. When a mother holds her newborn, the baby's face is usually a bit less than 6 inches away, so the baby is able to see her during feeding. Visual abilities improve quickly (Bronson, 1994). By 2 months, the ability to focus approaches adult proportion (Aslin & Dumais, 1980), and within a year the infant's visual acuity approaches that of an adult (Haith, 1990). Young infants are motivated to search out visual stimuli and even when surrounded by darkness move their eyes searching for stimuli (Wentworth & Haith, 1998).

Form and Preference Newborns have visual preferences. They prefer curved lines to straight lines (Fantz & Miranda, 1975), a patterned surface over a plain one (Fantz, 1963), and high-contrast edges and angles (Cohen, DeLoache, & Strauss, 1979). The neonate's scanning is not random. It is directed by rules that cause the baby to concentrate on the outline of a figure rather than explore the figure's details (Haith, 1980). By 8 weeks or so, infants develop more adult patterns of scanning and will investigate the interior as well as the contours of a figure (Bronson, 1994; Maurer & Salapatek, 1976).

A Preference for Faces? How can visual patterns and preferences help the newborn survive? Because the newborn depends on others for the basic necessities of life, a visual preference for human faces would be adaptive. Some studies find that neonates (only 30 minutes old) visually track a face further than a scrambled face or a blank face pattern (Johnson, Dziurawiec, Ellis, & Morton, 1991) (see Figure 5.1 on page 160), but studies using other methods of testing, such as preferential looking, do not find a preference until about 2 or 3 months. For example, Fantz (1961) found that infants of 2 or 3 months spent more time fixating on faces than such patterns as a bull's eye, newsprint, or red, white or yellow discs. (see Figure 5.2 on page 160). By 2 to 4 months of age, infants prefer drawings of faces to any other drawings (Dannemiller & Stephens, 1988).

Can Infants Recognize Different Faces? Infants may recognize particular faces at an early age. Some researchers claim that neonates spend more time looking at their

The newborn is born blind but within the first month develops vision that is similar to the vision of the average adult.

The neonate's limited powers of accommodation and poor visual acuity make the mother's face look fuzzy (photo A) rather than clear (photo B): even when viewed close up.

Guideposts

What survival advantage would infants have if they were preprogrammed to pay most attention to faces?

Figure 5.1   **Mean Head and Eye Turning for the Face, Scrambled and Blank Stimuli**

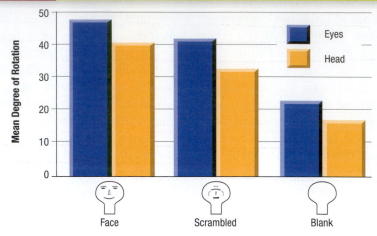

SOURCE: Johnson, Dziurawiec, Ellis & Morton (1991)

Figure 5.2   **Visual Preferences in Infancy**

The importance of pattern rather than color or brightness was illustrated by the response of infants to a face; a piece of printed matter; a bull's-eye; and plain red, white, and yellow disks. Even the youngest infants preferred patterns. Purple bars show the results for infants from 2 to 3 months old; green bars, for infants older than 3 months.

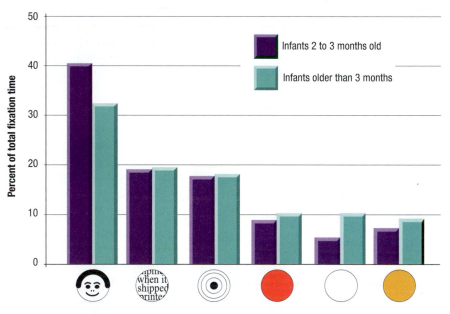

SOURCE: Fantz (1961)

mother's face than at a stranger's (Bushnell, Sai, & Mullin, 1989); others find that at 2 months infants can discriminate between their mother's face and those of female strangers. Certainly, this recognition is consistently found at 3 months (Kurzweil, 1988). The disparity in research results may be due to the different ways of testing the young infants (Pascalis, de Schonen, Morton, Deruelle, & Fabre-Grenet, 1995). Infants may also prefer certain types of faces (Rubenstein, Kalakanis, & Langlois, 1999). Two-month-old and 12-month-old infants gaze longer at attractive faces than at unattractive faces (Langlois, 1987, 1990).

Color Vision   Neonates can see some color, but their color vision is extremely limited, and different methods of testing neonates often result in very different results (Kellman & Banks, 1998). Neonates as young as 1 day old can tell the difference between a white stimulus and some shades of yellow-green (Adams, 1995). Four-day-old infants are able to discriminate red from green, and infants as young as 3 days prefer colored over noncolored stimuli (Adams, 1987, 1989). The size of the stimulus is important because in experimental situations neonates show some color discrimination to an 8-inch rectangle but not to a smaller one (Adams, 1995). Within some areas of the spectrum, neonates do not respond to color at all. By 2 months, color discrimination greatly improves (Kellman & Banks, 1998). It is impossible to say whether neonates see color the same way older people do. However, infants as young as 4 months do show the same color preferences as adults, gazing more at blue and red than at yellow (Banks & Salapatek, 1983).

Spatial and Depth Perception   Do babies live in a two-dimensional or three-dimensional world? To test an infant's depth perception, Gibson and Walk (1960) designed an ingenious experiment. A stand was constructed about four feet above the floor, and an infant was placed on the stand, which contained two glass surfaces. The first was a checkerboard pattern, the other a clear sheet of glass. On the floor beneath the clear glass was another checkerboard pattern, giving the impression of a cliff. This experiment, using what is called the **visual cliff,** showed that children 6 months or older would not crawl from the "safe" side over the cliff even if their mothers beckoned (see Figure 5.3).

But what about younger children? Testing very young infants on this apparatus is difficult because of their inability to crawl (Spelke & Newport, 1998). However, when infants as young as 2 months are placed on the deep side of the cliff, the heart rate of these infants slows, indicating interest, not fear (Campos, Langer, & Krowitz, 1970).

Babies develop depth perception at an early age; in this experiment, a six-month-old infant would not crawl across what looks like a cliff even though its mother beckoned.

Figure 5.3   The Visual Cliff Apparatus

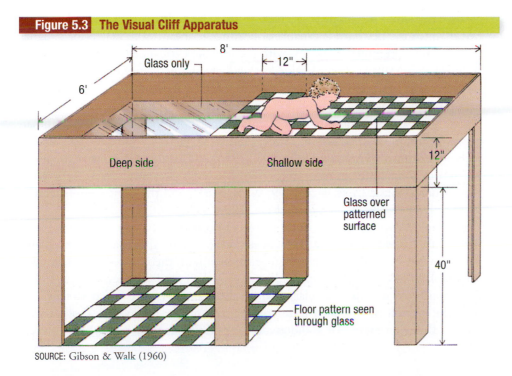

- 8'
- Glass only
- 12"
- 6'
- Deep side
- Shallow side
- 12"
- Glass over patterned surface
- 40"
- Floor pattern seen through glass

SOURCE: Gibson & Walk (1960)

visual cliff

A device used to measure depth perception in infants.

Guideposts

How do psychologists use the visual cliff to investigate depth perception?

Guideposts

What visual abilities do young infants show?

Although young children develop depth perception very early, it is only at 6 months or later that they develop a fear of the cliff. This contrasts with animals such as dogs, goats, and cats, which show a much earlier avoidance of the cliff.

Visual Tracking   Neonates can track slowly moving objects. When 1- to 4-day-old neonates were presented with a stationary light and a moving light that traced the outline of a rectangle, neonates reduced their sucking behavior more when presented with the moving light than when they were shown the stationary light (Haith, 1966). Three-day-old neonates look in the direction of a moving target, although the skill is not well developed (Kremenitzer, Vaughn, Kurtzberg, & Dowling, 1979). By 2 months, they can even anticipate where a visual stimulus will be. If a computer generates pictures that regularly appear alternately on the right and left sides, infants anticipate the appearance of the next picture shifting their eyes to where they think the next picture will come (Canfield & Haith, 1991; Wentworth & Haith, 1992).

Hearing

Some authorities claim that infants can hear in the womb. Newborns only 3 days old will change their sucking behavior to listen to their own mother's voice rather than to another female's voice (DeCasper & Fifer, 1980). The newborn does not have extensive experience with the mother's voice, so this effect may occur because the baby has heard its mother's voice while developing in the womb. Neonates whose average age was about 2 days demonstrated a preference for a specific passage that their mother read out loud during the last 6 weeks before birth when compared with one they were not exposed to during the prenatal stage (DeCasper & Spence, 1986).

Auditory capabilities are better developed in neonates than their visual abilities. Newborns react to pitch, loudness, and even rhythm, and they coordinate their body movements to other people's speech rhythms (Condon & Sander, 1974; Sansavini, Bertoncini, & Giovanelli, 1997). Neonates only 8 minutes old turn toward a sound (Werthheimer, 1961), but identification of sound location improves greatly after about 4.5 months (Mercer, 1998). The auditory threshold (the intensity at which the newborn is capable of hearing) is about 10 to 20 decibels higher than in adults (Bremner, 1988). As with the neonate's visual abilities, the newborn's auditory abilities have survival value as they help the neonate form a relationship with the caregiver. Human infants are exposed to many sounds—those made by pets, those made by inanimate objects, and those made by human beings—but they imitate those that most attract their attention and those are made by other human beings (Aslin, Jusczyk, & Pisoni, 1998). Human neonates respond to most sounds within the human voice range (Aslin et al., 1998) and are more responsive to sounds within the normal human voice range than outside it (Kearsley, 1973). Infants are also partial to music (Masataka, 1999; Walk, 1981), and rhythmic sounds tend to soothe a baby (Rock, Trainer, & Addison, 1999; Salk, 1960).

Many events in the real world provide information to more than one sense; they are multimodal in nature. The appearance of the mother is also often accompanied by her voice. As people walk toward the infant, their voices become louder. Infants show evidence of understanding this in their 1st year (Lewkowicz, 1996). Five-month-old infants were placed where they could see two video screens, one with the motion picture of a train coming toward the infant and another with the train moving away. An audiotape corresponding to either event was played.

Five-month-old-infants matched the auditory and visual information correctly, as measured by their visual fixation (Pickens, 1994). Six-month-old infants show the ability to pair touch and vision. An infant who touches and manipulates an object without seeing it and then has the opportunity to distinguish between this object and another can visually do so and some authorities believe this ability may exist at an earlier age (Rose, Gottfried, & Bridger, 1981; Rose, Feldman, Futterweit, & Jankowski, 1998).

Smell

The newborn can also use the sense of smell. Infants as young as seven days old turn preferentially to their mother's breast pad even if offered another woman's breast pad (MacFarlane, 1975), but this ability is not present in 2-day-old neonates. Two-week-old breast-fed children could recognize the smell of their mother when presented with gauze pads that had been worn in the mother's underarm area. However, these children could not recognize their father's odors, and non-breast-fed children could not recognize either the mother's or the father's odors (Cernoch & Porter, 1985).

Even bottle-fed neonates can identify the odor of lactating females. When presented with a pad that had been worn on the breast by a nursing mother and a pad that had been worn by a nonnursing mother, 2-week-old bottle-fed females turned preferentially toward a pad that had been worn on the breast by nursing mothers (Makin & Porter, 1989). This demonstrates that nursing mothers may produce a general odor that attracts infants as well as very specific odors that allow infants familiar with their mother's odor to distinguish their mother's odor from the scent of other mothers.

Taste

Neonates have an excellent sense of taste. When fed solutions that tasted bitter, sweet, sour, or salty, neonates only 2 hours old showed different facial responses to each taste except salty (see Figure 5.4) (Rosenstein & Oster, 1988). Some researchers believe that the newborn is more sensitive to taste stimuli in early infancy than at any other time (Reese & Lipsitt, 1973). While that is difficult to prove, we can conclude that the sense of taste is very well developed in the neonate.

Guideposts
What are the auditory abilities present in the neonate?

For Your Consideration
One approach to understanding the abilities that young infants show is to relate each sensory ability to an improvement in the chances for survival. How could the child's abilities to see, hear, smell, taste and experience touch and pain relate to survival?

T F 2
Neonates show an excellent sense of taste.

Guideposts
Describe the neonate's senses of smell, taste, and touch?

Figure 5.4	Sequence of Facial Expressions Elicited by the Sweet Solution

Initial Negative Facial Actions Followed by Relaxation and Sucking.
A sweet solution will elicit facial expressions in infants. Initial negative facial expressions are followed by relaxation and sucking.

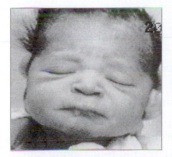
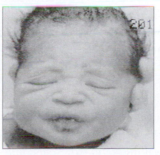

SOURCE: Rosenstein & Oster (1988)

Pressure and Pain

Neonates are responsive to tactile stimulation. A gentle touch can soothe a baby, and later in infancy touching leads to positive emotions in the infant and visual attention during parent-child interactions (Stack & Muir, 1992). They can also experience pain (Anand & Hickey, 1987; Azar, 1996). The neonate reacts to the needle taking blood from its heel with an angry cry (Hadjistavropoulis, Craig, Grunau, & Johnston, 1994). The human neonate's neural pathways and the brain centers necessary for pain perception are well developed.

Infant States

By about 2 weeks of age, neonates establish an adult day-night sleep pattern.

The neonate's favorite activity is sleeping, and neonates spend between 16 and 17 hours a day sleeping (Parmelee, Wenne, & Schulz, 1964). The newborn has no day-night sleep cycle, as any parent can attest (Harris, 1995). The neonate is as likely to sleep during the day as at night. The 24-hour sleep/wake cycle is usually established by between 12 and 16 weeks after birth, but individual differences exist, and children continue to awaken during the evening even after the pattern is established (Harris, 1995). As infants develop, they begin to sleep through the night, although nightly wakenings are common (Scher et al., 1995). However, the time it takes to put a child to bed actually increases around the second birthday perhaps due to separation protest, and the number of night awakenings increases as well between 16 and 24 months. The amount of time spent sleeping, feeding, and crying decreases during the 1st year (Michelsson, Rinne, & Paajanen, 1990).

The nature of the sleep periods shows some interesting differences among neonates, older children, and adults. When both children and adults are awakened from sleep in which they show rapid eye movements (REM), they report vivid dreams. The typical adult spends about 20% of sleep time in REM. Normally, the adult begins in non-REM sleep and after about 50 to 70 minutes switches to REM. About 50% of an infants' sleep—an astounding one-third of the infant's day—is spent in REM (Roffwarg, Muzio, & Dement, 1966). Premature infants show even more REM sleep, and REM periods are found in fetuses as early as at 18 to 20 weeks (Harris, 1995; Minard, Coleman, Williams, & Ingledyne, 1968). In addition, infants typically begin their sleep patterns in REM. By the age of 3 months, the amount of REM sleep is reduced to about 40%, and infants are no longer beginning their nights in that state (Harris, 1995; Minard et al., 1968).

The functions of sleep and REM are probably quite complex in the newborn. Sleep may serve to stimulate the central nervous system (CNS), to promote protein synthesis, to facilitate memory, and to maintain physiological functioning (Groome, Swiber, Atterbury, Bentz, & Holland, 1997). Perhaps newborns use the extra REM to provide a self-stimulatory experience, because they sleep so much of the day. The fact that REM sleep decreases as waking time increases provides some evidence in that direction. REM sleep may also foster brain organization and development, which is particularly rapid at this stage of life (Berg & Berg, 1979).

Besides waking and sleeping, newborns experience a number of transitional sleep states that fit into neither category (Figure 5.5). As the infant grows, these transitional states decrease, and the infant's state can more easily be measured and classified. These states reflect central nervous system functioning, and each state shows particular neurological brain wave patterns (Groome et al., 1997). Infants show seven sleeping and waking states (three sleeping states and four waking states) (Wolff, 1969).

Figure 5.5 Infant States

Infants spend more time sleeping than in any other activity.

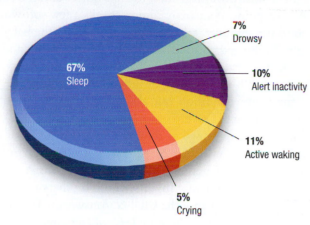

SOURCE: Berg, Adkinson, & Strock (1973)

1. *Regular sleep.* During this state the infant lies quiet, subdued, with eyes closed and unmoving. The child looks pale, and breathing is regular.
2. *Irregular sleep.* In this state, the infant does not appear as still, shows sudden jerks, startles, and a number of facial expressions, including smiling, sneering, and frowning. The eyes, though closed, sometimes show bursts of movement, and breathing is irregular.
3. *Periodic sleep.* This is an intermediate stage between regular and irregular sleep. The infant shows some periods of rapid breathing and has jerky movements followed by periods of perfect calm.
4. *Drowsiness.* In this state, the infant shows bursts of "writhing" activity. The eyes open and close and have a dull appearance.
5. *Alert inactivity.* The infant is now relaxed and has a bright, shining appearance but is inactive. The child searches the environment, and breathing is irregular.
6. *Waking activity.* The infant in this state shows a number of spurts in activity involving the entire body. Respiration is irregular. The intensity and duration of the baby's movements vary with the individual.
7. *Crying.* In this familiar state, the infant cries, and this is often accompanied by significant motor activity. The face may turn red.

Knowledge of infant states is important because the response of an infant to a stimulus is a function of the state in which the infant is tested (Ingersoll & Thomas, 1998; Parmelee & Sigman, 1983). Some reflexes are stronger and more reliable in one state than the other. The infant's sensory thresholds are also mediated by the baby's state. The concept of state has practical implications for parents as well (Brazelton, 1981). In the alert inactive state, infants may turn away from strong auditory stimuli toward more gentle voices (Parmelee & Sigman, 1983). During the transition states, the infant can go either way. If the stimuli awaiting the infant are pleasant, the infant is drawn out into an alert stage and is more responsive. The amount of alertness an infant shows may affect the neonate's opportunities for early stimulation. Parents have more opportunity to interact longer with an infant who shows more alert awake periods (Colombo & Horowitz, 1987). Infants learn about their environments most in periods of quiet alertness and attentiveness. An infant's state also influences adult behavior; when children cry, parents soothe them rather than play with them (Bornstein, 1995).

Guideposts

Why is the concept of infant state important to understanding the responses of an infant?

Infant Crying

A crying infant is totally distressed. At times, the lips quiver and the baby seems to be inconsolable. At that point, if a parent comes, speaks a few soft words, lifts the child from the crib to the shoulder, and pats the baby's back, the baby's world can become whole again. Prolonged episodes of crying are frustrating and exhausting for parents, who often question pediatricians about children's crying (Green, Gustafson, & McGhie, 1998). The cry of an infant has survival value. It not only informs others of the baby's condition but also encourages the parents or other caregivers to care for the infant. The cry of an infant can have a physical effect on parents. Mothers' heart rates increased as they watched videotapes of infants particularly, their own, crying (Weisenfeld & Klorman, 1978). The infant emits a number of different cries, and parents' sensitivity and responsiveness to infants' cries have a powerful effect on infants. Infants whose mothers respond promptly to cries exhibit less crying in later months (Bell & Ainsworth, 1972). Babies who are held may become more secure and require less contact later.

Young parents are often concerned that they will not understand what the infant is communicating through the cry, but most adults can easily tell the differences between infant cries (Thompson, 1998). In fact, as infants age, people pay attention to different acoustical features of the cry (Leger, Thompson, Merritt, & Benz, 1996). The raspy noise is a primary factor for understanding the intensity of the cry for a 1-month old but not for an older infant. There are qualitative differences in the types of cries infants show (Wolff, 1969). The hunger cry is heard when the infant is hungry as well as when there is any environmental disturbance. It starts out arrhythmically and low in intensity but gradually becomes louder and more rhythmic. The mad or anger cry follows the same general pattern as the hunger cry, except it is more forceful because more air is pushed past the vocal cords. The pain cry is different. The first cry is much longer, as is the first rest period. It lasts as long as seven seconds, during which time the infant lies still holding his or her breath. This is followed by the gasping intake of air and cries of shorter or varying duration. The pain cry begins suddenly, and no moaning precedes it. The initial segments of the pain cry are particularly potent stimuli for both adult males and adult females (Zeskind, Sale, Maio, & Weiseman, 1985).

Parents respond differently to these cries, and parenting style is more important than the form of crying in eliciting parental reactions. Parents do not respond to the hunger cry in any fixed way. Some always give the bottle or breast when they hear the cry; others check the diaper first. Experienced parents do not come as quickly as do inexperienced parents when they hear this cry. Parental response to the mad cry is less varied than the response to the hunger cry. Parents will go immediately to the crib to check on the baby, but they are not overly concerned. Both parents and nurses recognize the pain cry and rush to attend to the infant. Concern shows both on their faces and in the way they approach their caregiving responsibilities. Mothers with some experience are better than nonmothers at guessing the exact cause of the cries and spend more time in activities that might soothe the infant's distress (Gustafson & Harris, 1990).

Responding appropriately to infants when they are distressed and competently caring for the infants' physical and emotional needs are two of the key ingredients that foster what Erik Erikson called a sense of **trust,** which is the positive outcome of the psychosocial crisis of infancy. Infants with a sense of trust know that they can rely on their caregivers and that their environment is supportive and reassuring.

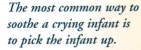

T F
4

If parents are very responsive to their infant's cries during early infancy, the child cries less later in infancy.

The most common way to soothe a crying infant is to pick the infant up.

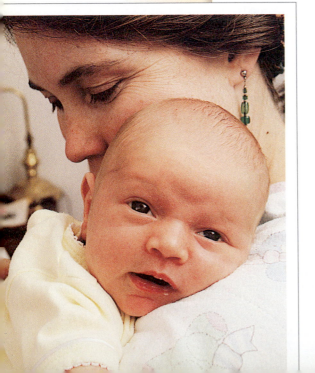

These children develop a positive relationship with others. The negative outcome, a sense of **mistrust,** arises when the infants' needs are met with rejection or hostility, and this leads to a perception of the world as a hostile, nonaccepting place. Much more will be said about the emotional needs of infants in Chapter 7.

Learning

For newborns to survive, they must learn about their new world. Researchers report some success using classical conditioning with infants (Rovee-Collins, 1987). The **sucking reflex** can be conditioned by sounding a tone that acts as the conditioned stimulus and following it by inserting a nipple that acts as the unconditioned stimulus (Lipsitt & Kaye, 1964). After pairing the tone and insertion of the nipple, the infants sucked to the tone (conditioned response).

Operant conditioning is easier to demonstrate in neonates. Infants who sucked on a nipple were rewarded by being allowed to hear music (Butterfield & Siperstein, 1972). The longer they sucked, the more music they heard. Two-day-old infants sucked longer and longer to hear the music but would not do so if sucking led to the music's being turned off. Infants can be conditioned to turn their heads in a particular direction if rewarded with milk each time they turn in the desired direction (Sameroff & Cavanagh, 1979).

Many studies indicate that neonates are capable of imitative behavior. Newborn infants, ages 0.7 to 71 hours, imitated an adult's facial gestures of opening the mouth and sticking out the tongue (Meltzoff & Moore, 1983), and infants less than 3 days old can imitate head turning (Meltzoff & Moore, 1989). Infants 12 to 21 days old imitate facial and manual gestures (Meltzoff, 1977). Infants opened their mouths and stuck out their tongues when the same behaviors were modeled by an adult (see Figure 5.6). There is also some evidence that neonates can match their own facial expression (happy face or sad face) to a model demonstrating these facial expressions (Field, Woodson, Greenberg, & Cohen, 1982; Reissland, 1988). Exactly when and what infants imitate is still debated, but the fact that they do is well accepted (Anisfield, 1991).

Figure 5.6   Imitation in Infants

These photographs, published in 1977, show 2- to 3-week-old infants imitating an adult's facial gestures. Andrew Meltzoff argues that very young infants can imitate.

SOURCE: Meltzoff (1977)

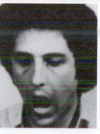
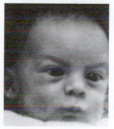
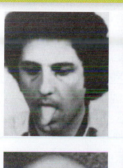

Reflexes

Psychologists today have a new respect for the neonate's sensory and perceptual abilities. Infants also enter the world preprogrammed with a number of specific responses to their environment in the form of reflexes that enable them to deal efficiently with stimuli in their environment (see Table 5.1). A **reflex** is a simple automatic reaction to a particular stimulus.

Reflexes connected with feeding are well established in the newborn. Place something in an infant's mouth, and the baby will respond with the sucking reflex. The infant also shows that **rooting reflex.** If you stroke the neonate's cheek, the baby turns in the direction of the touch. The swallowing reflex is also well developed in the newborn. A number of digestive reflexes—including hiccuping, burping, and regurgitation—are present as well. They allow the child to regulate the intake of food and eliminate gases.

The functions of other reflexes are either unknown or can only be guessed at. If you slide your finger along the palm of a neonate, the infant's fist will close. This **palmar grasp** reflex is strongest at birth, weaker by 2 months, and usually

Table 5.1 Some Neonatal Reflexes

Reflex	Eliciting Stimulus	Response	Developmental Duration
Babinski	Gentle stroke along sole of foot from heel to toe	Toes fan out; big toe flexes	Disappears by end of first year
Babkin	Pressure applied to both palms while baby is lying on its back	Eyes close and mouth opens; head returns to center position.	Disappears in 3-4 months
Blink	Flash of light or puff of air delivered to eyes	Both eyelids close.	Permanent
Diving reflex	Sudden splash of cold water in the face	Heart rate decelerates; blood shunted to brain and heart.	Becomes progressively weaker with age
Knee jerk	Tap on patellar tendon	Knee kicks.	Permanent
Moro reflex	Sudden loss of support	Arms extended, then brought toward each other; lower extremities are extended.	Disappears in about 6 months
Palmar grasp	Rod or finger pressed against infant's palm	The object is grasped.	Disappears in 3-4 months
Rooting reflex	Object lightly brushes infant's cheek	Baby turns toward object and attempts to suck.	Disappears in 3-4 months
Sucking reflex	Finger or nipple inserted 2 inches into mouth	Rhythmic sucking	Disappears in 3-4 months
Walking reflex	Baby held upright, soles of feet placed on hard surface; baby tipped slightly forward	Infant steps forward as if walking.	Disappears in 3-4 months

*The disappearance of the walking reflex has been questioned. Esther Thelen (Thelen, 1986; Thelen & Fisher, 1982) noted a similarity between the stepping reflex and infants' kicks when lying on their back. As infants mature, they show more kicking, and Thelen argues that these kicks are a forerunner of stepping. The walking reflex disappears because the increased mass of the their legs alters the way they can move. The infant's strength is sufficient when the body weight is supported as in the supine position (lying on the back) and its movement is aided by gravity. However, the strength is inadequate to lift the legs or support the weight when the infant is upright. The underlying mechanism, then, has not disappeared, but physical factors such as muscle strength make it impossible for the infant to show it.
SOURCE: Dworetzky (1984)

reflex

A relatively simple automatic reaction to a particular stimulus.

rooting reflex

The reflex in which a stroke on a cheek causes an infant to turn in the direction of the stimulus.

palmar grasp

The reflex in which placing something in the palm of an infant's hand causes a tight grasp.

moro reflex

A reflex elicited by a sudden loud noise or momentary change in position, causing the back to arch, an extension of the arms and legs, and finally their contraction into a hugging position.

disappears by about 3 months (Illingworth, 1974). In the evolutionary perspective, the grasping reflex might have some survival value. Most primates must hold onto their mothers for protection, and this reflex would facilitate that attachment. The reflex may have once had the same purpose for human infants. Persistence of this response well past the 3- to 4-month period may indicate brain damage.

If someone tickled you on the sole of your foot, your toes would curl in, but when the infant's sole is stroked, the toes fan out. This reflex, known as the **Babinski reflex,** normally disappears by the end of the first year. One of the most interesting reflexes is the walking (stepping) reflex. If infants are held upright and slanted a little forward and the soles of their feet make contact with some hard surface, they will show stepping motions.

Of all the reflexes, perhaps the strangest is the Moro reflex. This reflex may be elicited in a number of ways. A sudden loud noise or a momentary change in position may cause infants to extend their arms and legs while arching the back, then contract them into a hugging position. The infant also cries. What survival value might this reflex have? One psychologist described a film of a mother chimpanzee feeding while her baby plays at her side. The mother hears danger and "claps." The baby chimp exhibits the Moro reflex, ending with the baby's hugging himself to the mother's chest, and the mother and baby leave the scene of danger (Brazelton, 1981). It is quite an efficient system. Only 20% of normal infants in one study showed the Moro reflex at 5 months of age (Rushworth, 1971), and its presence past 6 months or so is a sign of possible neurological dysfunction.

Many other reflexes exist in the newborn. Most of them decrease and terminate with time and are replaced by voluntary behaviors. One popular theory argues that this occurs because the infant's cortex is not fully wired in, so nature allows the infant to run on these programmed reflexes. With time, the cortex, which is responsible for more voluntary activities, takes control and actively inhibits these early reflexes. Slowly, voluntary behavior replaces many automatic responses.

Brain Development

The change from automatic, preprogrammed, sensory, perceptual, and motor behavior to more voluntary activity is partly due to the development of the infant's central nervous system. The newborn's brain, which weighs about 25% of that of mature adult's, develops rapidly (Johnson, 1998). By 6 months it is 50% of the adult brain's weight, and at 2 years of age, it weighs 75% of what an adult's brain may weigh (Brierly, 1976). Brain growth allows the infant to develop new skills and capabilities.

Most areas of the brain are not well developed at birth. The brain stem and spinal cord are most advanced because they are involved in critical psychological functions and behavioral responses. Most areas of the upper region of the brain, the *cortex*, are relatively undeveloped. The sensory and motor areas are functional, but at a primitive level. The neurons that carry instructions from the cortex to the motor nerves lack the insulating cover called a *myelin sheath*, which is necessary for efficiently conducting impulses (Harris, 1995). This is one reason that the infant is slower in processing material. The process of myelinization is faster for the

Guideposts

What is the nature of the earliest neonatal responses to stimuli?

The grasping reflex is quite strong in infants.

Most of the infant's reflexes become stronger during the first year.

Babinski reflex

The reflex in which stroking the soles of a baby's feet results in the baby's toes fanning out.

sensory tract than for the motor area. This has survival value because the infant requires the information from the senses to negotiate the environment safely.

Between 3 and 6 months, a very important change occurs. The upper portion of the brain, the cortex, develops. This switch from control by the lower, more automatic section of the brain to control by the upper, more voluntary centers affects behavior, allowing more voluntary behaviors to replace programmed behavior. Many neonatal reflexes disappear within the first half-year of life, and many authorities argue that the upper centers of the brain are inhibiting these reflexes (Kalat, 1981).

Brain growth and development is related to behavior. Earlier, we noted two different findings about infants' preference for faces. Some research using visual tracking find preference within a day after birth, while others using preferential looking do not find it until about 2 months. It may be that two different neurological processes are involved. Visually guided behavior in the newborn is largely mediated by subcortical structures, and its influence over behavior declines, perhaps due to inhibition, during the second month of life. Visual preferences (how long the infant looks at a stimulus) depend on cortical maturity as well as exposure to faces over the first month of life and begins to influence infant preferences beginning at about 2 months (Johnson, 1998).

The brain can be divided into two hemispheres, the left and the right. The right side of the brain controls the left side of the body, and the left side of the brain controls the right side of the body. Some functions are localized on the left side or the right, and current evidence shows that these asymmetries in brain structure and lateralization exist at or prior to birth (Balaban, Anderson, & Wisniewski, 1998). A left-hemisphere bias for speech perception and a right hemisphere bias for perception of music is found in neonates (Young & Gagnon, 1990). Other asymmetries are also found early in life. Discriminating the visual shape of patterns is superior in the left hemisphere, and discrimination of location superior in the right hemisphere (Deruelle & de Schonen, 1991, 1995).

The Brain and Experience

The brain does not develop in a vacuum. The brains of rats raised in an enriched environment differ from those raised in an impoverished environment (Rosenzweig et al., 1972). The brains of the rats from the enriched environment have more dendrites, which serve as receivers when neurons send messages to each other. Experience makes an imprint on the brain, and lack of basic experience may hinder the brain's development. Although brain development is partly programmed by genes, experience is important. Visual experience speeds up myelinization of nerves in the visual cortex (Morrell & Norton, 1980).

The importance of experience was shown in a classic study in which one eye of a kitten was sewn shut for the first 4 to 6 weeks of life (Wiesel & Hubel, 1965). After cutting the sutures and allowing the kitten the full use of its eyes, the cells that would normally process visual information for that eye were unable to do so. There is a critical period of 4 to 6 weeks in which the cortical cells develop an ability to process information from the eye. After that period, suturing the eye had little or no effect on the kitten.

To better understand how experience can influence the brain, Greenough, Black, and Wallace (1987) argue that two different types of information and two different types of brain mechanisms should be taken into consideration. **Experience-expectant information** refers to environmental information that is common to all members of the species, such as being exposed to visual and

experience-expectant information

Environmental information acquired through experiences that are common to all members of the species, such as receiving visual information.

auditory information. In many sensory areas, the connections between nerve cells are overproduced, and which connections remain depends on the sensory experience of the individual. This would explain the research (some of it described previously) showing that there is a critical period for the development of many sensory functions.

The second type of information is called **experience-dependent information** and is unique to the individual. It involves learning about one's own environment and requires new connections between neurons to be formed in response to events in the environment. In fact, there is a dramatic growth of dendrites that receive transmissions from other cells, as well as the formation of synapses (the gap between these cells) early in life (Johnson, 1998). The development of the brain can help us understand cognitive development. Some authorities argue that there are spurts in the formation of the connections between neurons at particular ages, including 2 to 4 months, 7 to 8 months, 12 to 13 months, and 18 to 24 months in human infants. Perhaps one additional period in the first four months exists. These spurts are related to leaps in the infant's cognitive abilities (Fischer, 1987).

This modern understanding links the brain's development with various sensory, motor, and cognitive abilities. It also demonstrates that the relationship between experience and brain growth is reciprocal: Brain growth affects the child's abilities, and the child's experience affects the growth and development of the brain.

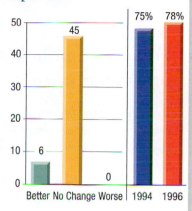

Trends in Development

Immunizations
Have states and the District of Columbia increased the percentages of 2-year-olds who have been fully immunized against preventable childhood diseases?

These figures represent the total percentage who are completely immunized at this time.

Source: National Education Goals Panel (1998)

Infant Health

Years ago, the death of a young child was common. But today, it is rare in developed countries. Most infants are spared the ravages of diseases that once plagued them, largely because excellent vaccines are available, although unfortunately not every child is vaccinated (see *Diseases Conquered and Reappearing* on pages 172–175).

The most common cause of infant death in developed countries during the first month of life is congenital or birth-related problems. After that, sudden infant death syndrome is responsible for this tragedy.

Sudden Infant Death Syndrome

It is every parent's nightmare. A seemingly healthy infant is put to sleep at night. In the morning, a parent discovers that the infant has died. No medical reason for it is ever found, and it is classified as **sudden infant death syndrome (SIDS).**

SIDS is defined as the sudden death of an infant under 1 year of age that remains unexplained after a thorough investigation (Kinney et al., 1995). It is responsible for over 6,000 deaths each year in the United States (Andolsek, 1997). Victims are most likely to be between 2 and 4 months of age. Some 90% are younger than 6 months; 97% are younger than 1 year.

No family, regardless of income and social status, is immune to SIDS. While infants who show low birth weight and whose mothers receive poor prenatal care are at greater risk, three-quarters of all SIDS infants are born into economically

experience-dependent information

Information acquired through experiences that are unique to the individual.

sudden infant death syndrome (SIDS)

The diagnosis given to young infants whose cause of death cannot be determined.

The Child in the 21st Century

Disease Conquered… and Reappearing

I can remember my grandmother telling me about the death of her 3-year-old daughter from measles in New York City in the early 1900s. As she told the story, I could see the sadness and the resignation. Deaths from childhood diseases were common.

How different the situation is today! The incidence of infectious childhood diseases has declined by 97% (see Table A). Credit largely goes to creation of effective vaccines, but cleaner water, public sanitation, and antiseptic hospitals also deserve some mention (Jost, 1993).

Many childhood diseases can be prevented by immunization: polio, measles, pertussis (Whooping cough), mumps, rubella (German measles), tetanus, and diphtheria. Relatively new vaccines for chicken pox, hepatitis B, bacterial meningitis, and haemophilus influenza type b (Hib), are now available ("Recommended Childhood Immunization Schedule," 1999b). With the exception of tetanus, all these diseases are contagious (Robinson et al., 1995). The Public Health Services advisory committee on immunization recommends that by 15 months children have a basic series of

Table A	Death from Infectious Deseases: The Effect of Vaccination	
	Prevaccine Maximum	**1997**
Measles	894,134 (1941)	135
Diphtheria	206,969 (1921)	5
Mumps	152,209 (1968)	612
Rubella	57,686 (1969)	161
Polio	21,269 (1952)	0

SOURCE: U.S. Public Health Service, 1997; *The Economist*, 1998

vaccinations on a particular schedule, a sample of which is shown in Figure A. The progress made in reducing the prevalence of these diseases must stand as one of the greatest achievements of 20th-century science.

Children in the United States cannot enter school without proof of inoculation, and so by age 6, almost all children are fully inoculated (Pollock, 1994). Vaccination levels for American infants and toddlers are at record-high levels, which is very good news ("Impact of Vaccines," 1999). However, these high averages hide the fact that many young children still have not received their full set of vaccinations on time (Bornstein, 1995; "Editorial Note," 1998). A significant difference exists between rates among poor and nonpoor children, with significantly more poor children not receiving their inoculations (USDHHS, 1995). In some inner-city areas, only

10% of the children are fully immunized (Williams, 1994). In urban areas, minority children are four to nine times as likely to get measles as white children (Williams, 1994). The problem is particularly great among homeless children. The disparity is alarming, and since poor children tend to live in clusters, the chances of an outbreak are greater.

The reasons for this lack of immunization are hotly debated. Some point to the cost of immunization (Children's Defense Fund, 1993). Although poor children receive vaccinations free, immunizations are too expensive for some low- and middle-income parents. In 1982, the cost of a complete set of childhood vaccines was $23.29, while in 1992 it stood at $243.90 (Pollock, 1994). It is easy, then, to blame the pharmaceutical companies for profiteering.

A more detailed investigation, though, shows that the situation is just

advantaged families whose mothers received good prenatal care (Blakeslee, 1989; "Infant Mortality," 1992). A risk factor that has been emphasized lately is cigarette smoking. Infants whose mothers smoke cigarettes are about 3.5 times more likely to die of SIDS (Klonoff-Cohen & Edelstein, 1995; Seachrist, 1995). It may be that nicotine-exposed children fail to produce stress hormones when faced with oxygen deprivation (Seachrist, 1995).

Research has found that some infants who die of SIDS may not be as healthy as they first seem. Between 40% and 50% of SIDS victims suffer from some respiratory infection right before their death. Some have a history of stress both before and after birth. The Apgar scores of these infants are significantly lower than those of babies who did not die from SIDS (Guntheroth, 1982). Abnormal heart rates and respiration problems are also found. These babies, then, appear to be

Figure A   Recommended Childhood Immunization Schedule, United States, 1999

Approved by the Advisory Committee on Immunization Practices (ACIP), the American Academy of Pediatrics (AAP), and the American Academy of Family Physicians (AAFP). Shaded bars indicate range of acceptable ages for vaccination. These recommended ages should not be thought of as absolute. Vaccine schedules are changed as new vaccines, combinations of current vaccines, and indications are licensed. (■)[1] All children and adolescents (through 18 years of age) who have not been immunized against hepatitis B may begin the series during visit. (■)[2] Those who have not previously received the second dose should schedule by the 11- to 12-year old visit. (■)[3] Those who have not had a documented case of chicken pox or have not been immunized should receive the vaccine. [4] Two poliovirus vaccines

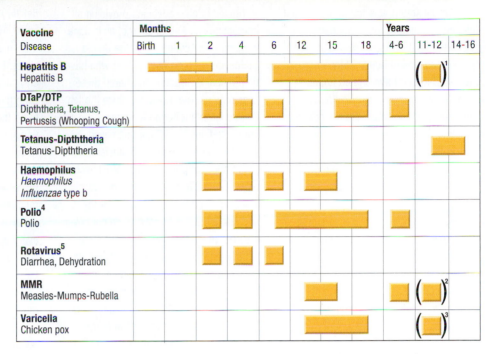

currently are licensed in the United States: inactivated poliovirus vaccine (IPV) and oral poliovirus vaccine (OPV). The ACIP, AAP, and AAFP now recommend that the two doses of poliovirus vaccine should be IPV. Use of IPV for all doses is also acceptable and is recommended for immunocompromised persons and their household contacts. [5] Clinicians temporarily should suspend administration of rotavirus vaccine to unimmunized and partially immunized children, pending collection and evaluation of additional information. Parents/patients should talk with their pediatrician about this recommendation.

NOTE: This information should not be used as a substitute for the medical care and advice of your pediatrician. There may be variations in treatment that your pediatrician may recommend based on individual facts and circumstances.

SOURCE: American Academy of Pediatrics (AAP), *Pediatrics* (1999)

not this simple. First, if producing vaccines was so profitable, why has the number of companies making vaccines fallen from 12 to 5 between 1984 and 1994 (Pollack, 1994)? Fewer companies want to make vaccines. One reason is the fear of liability and lawsuits for a child who has an allergic reaction, even to an approved vaccine (Pollack, 1994). In addition, the cost of bringing vaccines to market is much higher today, approaching $200 million. Most of the research on new vaccines is privately conducted. New vaccines, such as those for hepatitis B and bacterial meningitis, were very expensive to develop and market.

The pricing policies of pharmaceutical companies should, of course, still be scrutinized. However, blaming the cost of vaccines, especially when poor children receive vaccinations free, just doesn't match the facts. The major problems are a lack of access to health care, missed opportunities for administering vaccine,

members of an at-risk population, although they are essentially normal. The diagnosis of SIDS is even more complicated since some cases of infant deaths due to homicide or neglect (a conservative estimate is 2%) are incorrectly attributed to SIDS (Horgan, 1995; "Infant Mortality," 1992).

Because many victims of SIDS suffer from mild respiratory infections, research interest has centered on finding a relationship between SIDS and respiration. Many infants stop breathing for brief periods during sleep (a condition known as *apnea*), and some argue that SIDS is a form of prolonged sleep apnea. However, the SIDS infant does not have any more of these apneic spells than do babies who do not die of SIDS. Perhaps the SIDS victim does not recover from these periods. But why? The SIDS victim may be weaker and possibly does not develop the ability to react to threats to survival. In the first month and a lack of public awareness of the benefits of immunization.

Simply stated, it is too difficult to get children inoculated. Too many barriers exist. Many public health clinics are not open at convenient hours. They are understaffed and have limited hours. Procedural requirements also are a concern. Some require the child to undergo a complete physical examination, have a referral from a private physician, or enroll in a comprehensive well-baby program before immunizations are given (Jost, 1993).

Public complacency is also a problem, and some blame must be placed on the parents. Most parents have never heard of the diseases their children need to be inoculated against. They do not know anyone who has ever contracted one and so do not see the urgency of protecting their children. Occasionally, we are reminded that many of these illnesses are not eradicated but rather just controlled. In 1989, major outbreaks of measles hit American cities, with thousands of cases reported and more than 100 deaths recorded over 3 years (Jost, 1993). For some parents, language problems and cultural traditions that do not stress prevention make it difficult for them to take advantage of inoculation programs for their children (Curry & Rosensteel, 1995).

How can the percentage of infants and toddlers being inoculated be increased? Some advocate providing all immunizations free of charge, as is done in many other countries. In the United States, children on Medicaid or who have no medical insurance are offered these vaccinations free. However, since the federal government began funding immunizations in 1955, it has never required parents to prove financial need to get shots at public clinics. Most vaccinations, though, take place in private physicians' offices that charge for them, and some insurance policies do not cover the cost of vaccinations. There is a substantial debate on just how to distribute vaccines, where shots should be given, and who should receive them free of charge (Satcher, 1995; Thompson, 1995). Critics point out that giving them free to everyone would cover middle- and upper-class families who can pay for them and cause insurance companies to drop coverage. It would also be costly; that money, some authorities claim, would better be spent making the public health facilities more effective. After all, we are not exactly starting from scratch with very few children vaccinated. Making inoculations free to everyone would not do anything to correct the problems of service delivery and public apathy.

No matter how the inoculation problem is examined, making the health care delivery system easier to use is a necessity. Longer clinic hours and the use of mobile vans to make vaccinations more accessible are needed. Computerization on a local basis would surely help. For example, some parents lose or do not bring their child's record of vaccinations, which presents a problem if they use different clinics. Computerization would permit timely reminders and keep track of the vaccinations of each child. It is also recommended that physicians routinely check a child's immunization status at every opportunity, including hospitalizations and emergency room visits (Centers for Disease Control [CDC], 1993). Computerization would make all this much easier.

Efforts must also be made to rock people out of their apathy. Some advocate requiring proper inoculations for children entering day care. Such requirements successfully raised the inoculation rates for school-age children, so this idea is probably worth a try.

On the educational front, alerting parents and teachers of the importance of inoculations is necessary. Vaccination days are a possibility and community advertising, in the language of the people, is needed. Some special campaigns improve vaccination rates

Guideposts

What is sudden infant death syndrome, and what are some of the suggestions for preventing it?

or so, the infant's defensive reactions to respiratory distress are reflexive. However, a learned reaction soon takes its place. Perhaps the victim of SIDS fails to learn to defend against such dangers because of some subtle neurological problem (Lipsitt, 1982). Some researchers look at the developing brain for the clue, claiming that brain regions that control respiration develop abnormally (Travis, 1995). As previously noted, as new brain connections are being formed, myelin sheathing is taking place and old connections are dissolved. Perhaps something goes wrong with these critical switches. Other researchers are looking at subtle defects in different parts of the brain, including the brain stem, which is responsible for breathing and heart rate during sleep (Blakeslee, 1989).

At times, we can predict which infants will be at risk for the disorder, but again, not all SIDS victims fit any specific pattern. Among those who are most at risk are infants who have suffered an oxygen deficiency, have a high apnea rate, or have almost died once from the disorder. These infants may be monitored in their own home using an apnea monitor, a device that rings an alarm if the infant stops somewhat—for example, volunteers going door to door reminding parents of opportunities to vaccinate their children. Some nontraditional advertising, such as reminders on baby food jars and diaper boxes, are interesting additions to public health programs (Robinson et al., 1995). Computer-generated telephone reminders also help ("Evaluation," 1993).

State tracking can be especially helpful ("Painful Jabs," 1995). For example, Georgia health officials carefully audit records of public clinics, providing feedback to clinic personnel about children needing additional inoculations. A child's immunization status is checked whenever the child enters any health clinic and the needed shots are administered if the medical condition of the child allows. This program has raised the rate of immunizations for young children (Shalala, 1993).

The miracle of immunization has produced a worldwide reduction in childhood diseases. In 1977, the last case of smallpox occurred, and two years later the World Health Organization announced that for the first time a major disease, smallpox, had been completely eradicated from the globe. Vaccination rates are increasing markedly in underdeveloped nations ("How Poor Are the Poor?" 1994). By the year 2000, United Nations (UN) agencies have set a goal of eradicating polio and reaching an overall inoculation rate of 90% (UNICEF, 1991). The United Nations' active program is credited with saving two million lives a year (UNICEF, 1993). Even in some precarious political situations, vaccinations have gone forward. During the civil war in El Salvador, UN agencies persuaded both warring parties to declare a cease-fire during national vaccination days!

The problems faced by health care workers in underdeveloped countries differ somewhat from what is faced in more developed nations. Some diseases, such as polio, that have been all but eliminated in the United States and Europe continue to cause concerns, especially in more isolated regions (Cooper, 1995). Special problems also exist. For example, the limited health delivery systems in some underdeveloped countries cannot cope with multiple visits for vaccinations. The United Nations is now funding the development of a supervaccine that will allow all the vaccines to be given in one shot ("The U.N.'s Global Immunization Triumph," 1993). Although it is doubtful that this can be accomplished, a more convenient vaccination schedule could help. The need for refrigeration is also a major problem in these countries. A major scientific breakthrough may be at hand that would involve drying vaccines in such a way that they could be carried around in a briefcase rather than needing a refrigerator ("Extra Dry," 1995). Another problem is cost in underdeveloped nations ("The U.N.'s Global Immunization Triumph," 1993). Generally, if a vaccine costs more than $1, many countries simply won't use it, which is why many countries do not use the hepatitis b vaccine. Finally, new vaccines are needed around the world. Some are specific to geographic areas, such as the need for a vaccine for dengue fever and malaria, while the entire world waits for a vaccine for AIDS.

Progress from this point on, both in the world generally and in the United States, will be more difficult to achieve. As more children receive their inoculations, only the more difficult cases or most remote geographic areas remain to be served. The challenge for public health officials is to deliver the inoculations in a convenient, economically reasonable, effective manner, convincing parents of the need to have their children inoculated. While there is no denying the progress, many challenges also lie ahead. The real enemy, though, is complacency, which robs people of the will to continue the age-old battle against infectious diseases that, for the first time in history, human beings are in a position to finally win.

What do you think?

If you were charged with the responsibility of substantially improving the percentage of infants and toddlers who are vaccinated, what actions would you take?

You can explore the questions above using InfoTrac College Edition. Hint: enter search term *Childhood Immunizations.*

breathing for a specific period of time, allowing parents to respond to the problem. Use of a monitor does not guarantee the infant's survival. Some infants on monitors have died when they could not be revived. In addition, the monitor may cause parents much distress. Parents might feel that they cannot go out or use a noisy appliance because they will not be able to hear the monitor ring (Guntheroth, 1982). It must be noted, too, that the apnea hypothesis is still very controversial (Horgan, 1995).

While the cause of sudden infant death syndrome remains elusive, some suggestions for reducing the chance that an infant will die of SIDS have been advanced. One recommendation is that healthy infants be placed on their backs when put down for sleep (American Academy of Pediatrics Task Force on Infant Positioning, 1996). In countries in which the frequency of placing infants on their backs has increased, the incidence of SIDS has declined, sometimes by as much as

50%. A coalition of the federal government and private agencies are trying to get the message across via the "Back to Sleep" campaign directed at both the general public and health care providers. In the United States, where this recommendation is now being publicized, the incidence of SIDS has declined dramatically (Andolsek, 1997), but there is much room for improvement especially among low income families who live in the inner city (Brenner et al., 1998) and young mothers (Lesko et al., 1998). Most babies should sleep on their backs, but some babies have health conditions that might require a different sleeping position (AAP, 1999). It is best to consult the pediatrician about these matters. Other recommendations include keeping infants away from cigarette smoke (Adler, 1995); not placing anything with a soft fluffy surface, such as pillows or thick comforters in the crib; and not dressing the infant too warmly when putting the child to bed ("AAP Statement," 1997; Cadoff, 1995).

Many of these recommendations are based on studies in other cultures. Studies of various societies show that SIDS does not occur uniformly across groups. Asians, whether immigrants or not, have a lower rate of SIDS (Brooke, 1996). Perhaps this is because many of the suggestions, such as placing baby on the back, avoiding smoking, and avoiding overwrapping the infant, are culturally prescribed.

Sudden infant death syndrome is a family tragedy. Parents experience self-doubt, guilt, and pain. There is a high rate of marital problems and divorce following the experience. When a child is born very prematurely or suffers some lingering disease, parents have time to prepare for the possibility of an impending death, but SIDS does not afford parents that opportunity. The shock is great, the questions are many, and the answers are few.

Parents of SIDS victims can be helped to cope with their grief. Emotional support is available from groups of parents who have suffered similar tragedies. Parents of SIDS victims are given an opportunity to discuss their feelings and help one another. Religion may also play a role in adjusting to the sudden loss of a child (McIntosh, Silver, & Wortman, 1993). Religious institutions offer a supportive social network, and religious beliefs may provide a basis for finding meaning during the time of crisis. Professionals may also aid the family by offering parents the facts as we know them today. Sometimes just the knowledge that an autopsy shows no cause of death alleviates some of the guilt.

There is still much that scientists do not know about SIDS. Today there is hope that, with research, we may learn more about its causes and eventually be able to prevent this silent killer from striking.

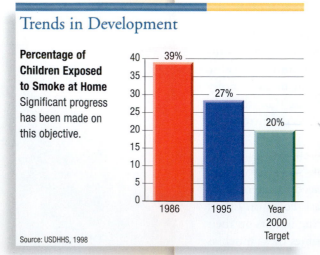

Trends in Development

Percentage of Children Exposed to Smoke at Home
Significant progress has been made on this objective.

Source: USDHHS, 1998

Growth and Motor Development

Infants grow rapidly. They rarely wear their clothes out; they grow out of them first. Growth in the first year is remarkable. After losing some weight during the first week or two, most infants double their birth weight by 4 months and triple it by 1 year. Within 6 months the infant has grown more than 5 inches, and in the next 3 months, 3 more inches will be added to the baby's length. Length usually increases by 50% during the first year. After infancy, the growth rate slows perceptibly. If it continued at this rate, a 10-year-old would be about 10 stories tall and weigh more than 220 tons (Brown, 1995)! In the second year, the child grows approximately 4 inches and gains less than 10 pounds (Lowrey, 1978; Whitney, Cataldo, & Rolfes, 1994).

Most scientists believe that growth is basically a slow but regular process, but some challenging research suggests a pattern of brief spurts and stops in which a child could grow as much as 0.5 inch in a day and then enter a considerable period of no growth (Lampl, Cameron, Veldhuis, & Johnson, 1992, 1995). This type of growth is called **saltatory growth,** after the Latin word *saltare,* which means "to jump or leap." Growth is determined by the secretion of growth hormones. During these periods children are more irritable, sleepy, and hungry. These findings are still controversial at the present time, with some experts arguing that growth takes place in a more gradual manner (Heinrichs, Munson, Counts, Cutler, & Baron, 1995).

Growth is, in many respects, a self-correcting process. If a baby's father is tall but the mother is short, the child's growth may be limited in the womb, but the child may catch up during the first six months and return to a normal growth rate (Tanner, 1970). Each child has a preordained path to travel in physical development (Waddington, 1957). Illnesses, stress, and nutritional inadequacy can deflect the path for a time, but a self-righting tendency called **canalization** takes place. The child's natural growth trajectory can be permanently deflected from its course if environmental deficiencies continue for a long period of time or are very severe.

Physicians check the child's growth and weight during well-baby checkups, using norms carefully prepared by the National Center for Health Statistics (see Figures 5.7 and 5.8). Heights and weights that fall between the 25th and 75th percentiles are usually considered normal. For instance, a 1-year-old male infant may weigh anywhere between 9.49 and 10.91 kilograms and still be within the normal range. Those that fall outside these figures should be examined by a pediatrician, but no problem may be indicated.

T
F
7
Children actually grow more during the second year of life than during the first.

Figure 5.7   Growth During Infancy and Toddlerhood (centimeters)

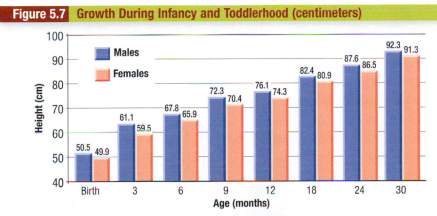

NOTE: Stature is given in centimeters. To convert to inches, multiply by .39.

Figure 5.8   Weight Gain During Infancy and Toddlerhood (kilograms)

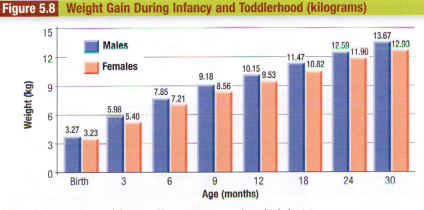

NOTE: All data are given in kilograms. To convert to pounds multiply by 2.2.
SOURCE: Hamill et al. (1977)

saltatory growth
Growth marked by brief spurts and stops.

canalization
The self-righting process in which the child catches up in growth despite a moderate amount of stress or illness.

Principles of Growth and Development

Infants do not develop in a haphazard manner. Their development follows consistent patterns and is governed by principles that are now well understood. For instance, the head and brain of the infant are better developed at birth than are the feet or hands. The **cephalocaudal principle** explains that development begins at the head and proceeds downward (**cephalocaudal** means from head to tail). Control of the arms develops ahead of control of the feet. A second rule of development notes that organs nearest to the middle of the organism develops before those farthest away. The **proximodistal principle** explains why the internal organs develop faster than the extremities. It also correctly predicts that control of the arms occurs before control of the hands, which predates finger control.

Muscular development follows a path from control of **mass to specific** muscles. First, the individual develops control over the larger muscles responsible for major movements. Then, slowly, control is extended to the fine muscles. This is why younger children use broad, sweeping strokes of the forearm or hand when coloring with a crayon. It is only later that the child gains the dexterity to use finger muscles in a coordinated manner.

Development is also directional. It moves from a state of largely involuntary, incomplete control toward one of voluntary control; from undifferentiation toward subtle differentiation. Under normal circumstances, the movement is forward, with new abilities arising from older ones.

Development occurs within a predictable sequence. Today we can predict what advancements in motor control will occur next, but not necessarily when they will happen. Mary Shirley (1933) made exhaustive observations of a group of children beginning on the day of their birth. These infants all progressed through the same sequence leading to walking. Shirley was interested only in when the baby first performed any of the acts on the chart (see Figure 5.9), such as sitting with support or standing with help, not in how well the baby performed the act. Each of these abilities is perfected with practice.

Guideposts

What are three principles that help psychologists understand physical development?

Figure 5.9 **The Sequence of Motor Development Leading to Walking**

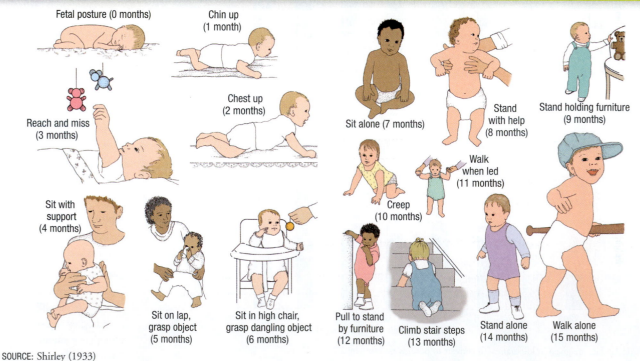

Fetal posture (0 months)

Chin up (1 month)

Reach and miss (3 months)

Chest up (2 months)

Sit alone (7 months)

Stand with help (8 months)

Stand holding furniture (9 months)

Sit with support (4 months)

Sit on lap, grasp object (5 months)

Sit in high chair, grasp dangling object (6 months)

Creep (10 months)

Walk when led (11 months)

Pull to stand by furniture (12 months)

Climb stair steps (13 months)

Stand alone (14 months)

Walk alone (15 months)

SOURCE: Shirley (1933)

Although the sequence of motor development is standard, the ages noted are merely guidelines. If the child's motor development is very late, it should be brought to the attention of a pediatrician, but there are no "average" babies. Each infant will negotiate each stage at his or her own rate. Some will stay longer at one stage than others. The age at which a child develops these abilities is a function of the child's maturation rate as long as the child is well-fed and healthy and has an opportunity to practice these skills.

Cultural Differences and Motor Development

Although individual differences in the rate of motor development are well accepted, the question of cultural differences is more difficult to resolve. Some research concludes that African infants are more advanced motorically at birth than European infants, while other research casts doubt on the conclusions (Geber & Dean, 1957; Keefer, Dixon, Tronick, & Brazelton, 1978). The question of just how African and European infants differ at birth, then, is still controversial. However, most researchers agree that African infants reach motor milestones, such as sitting and walking, before European or American infants do (Super, 1981).

The most obvious explanation for these differences lies in variations in the rate of maturation, which is largely influenced by genetics. While this may be partially true, another explanation is possible. In many African societies, infants are reinforced for their motor behavior, even at very early ages. Parents play games with them using these emerging motor skills. In some tribes, mothers begin walking training very early, and African children are placed in a sitting position and supported much more often than are American babies. Differences in child-rearing procedures may partly explain the motor advancement. African infants are precocious in motor skills on which they receive the most practice (Super, 1981).

This raises two questions. First, what is the effect of lack of practice on the development of motor skills? Second, can motor skills be accelerated through a special training program?

The Effects of Practice and Stimulation

No one doubts that some opportunity to practice motor skills is necessary for development of those skills, but there are many roads to mastering them. Hopi children who were reared in the restrictive environment of the cradleboard still walked at about the same age as infants not reared on the cradleboard (Dennis & Dennis, 1940). These children received excellent stimulation and were allowed off the cradleboard as they matured. Some evidence for flexibility is also found in a study of children raised in a substandard orphanage in Lebanon who were well behind in their motor development at age 1 year because of environmental restriction. When they received more opportunity to practice these skills, they were much improved by age 4 to 6 years (Dennis & Najarian, 1957). The greater opportunities these children experienced after the first year were sufficient to counter their poor early environments. If corrected, some of the effects of a deprived environment can be reduced, and children can catch up: if the environment doesn't improve, these children will not develop normal motor abilities. It should be remembered that Shirley's mean ages at which children achieve motor milestones are met only under favorable environmental conditions (Dennis, 1960). In other words, maturation alone is not sufficient to explain motor development. The environment must be stimulating and provide opportunities for practice as well.

cephalocaudal principle
The growth principle stating that growth proceeds from the head downward to the trunk and feet.

proximodistal principle
The growth principle stating that development occurs from the inside out—that the internal organs develop faster than the extremities.

mass to specific principle
A principle of muscular development stating that control of the mass, or large muscles, precedes control of the fine muscles.

There is, though, one necessary caution in the interpretation of the research on motor development. Generally, when studying motor development, the maturational aspects have been considered primary and the environment given a distinctly secondary place. The documented cases of catch-up have also unfortunately been used to place environment as an afterthought. However, studies of isolated and deprived infants do not show a complete catch-up (Razel, 1989). The idea that a small amount of practice later on is as good as a great deal of practice earlier is simply not true. These infants suffered severe and long-lasting difficulties. Therefore, although later training may help, the idea that the infant does not suffer from early deprivation or that such deprivation can be completely compensated for is inaccurate. The environment must provide meaningful opportunities for practice.

In most homes, children receive at least minimal stimulation and some opportunity to explore their environment. Parents are more interested in the possibility of hastening motor development. To that purpose, a number of programs aimed at improving motor development have been advanced, and some research has shown them to be effective. Infants given training that capitalized on the stepping reflex enabled them to walk at an earlier age than expected (Zelazo, Zelazo, & Kolb, 1972). Six-week-old infants who were given two 3-minute daily sessions of exercise in stepping or sitting or both for six weeks showed these abilities well before infants in two control groups who did not receive the exercise program. The effects of the practice were specific, affecting only the skills trained. The improvement did not generalize to other skills (Zelazo et al., 1993). The group that received training in both stepping and sitting naturally showed improvements in both.

Some infant exercise programs are valuable (White, 1993), and help children develop physical skills, but parents must take care not to put too much pressure on their children, seeking large gains and making such programs "work" rather than pleasure. Parents should be wary of stimulation programs that promise large gains in motor or cognitive development. Our effort would better be spent on optimizing the environment, allowing each child to take advantage of opportunities to explore and learn when the child is ready, and helping the child practice these skills.

Dynamic Systems Theory

Just a short time ago, this analysis would have been completely accepted. As the brain and body matures owing mostly but not entirely to genetic factors, new abilities come into play. Some practice is required, and those areas most practiced are best developed, but experience is considered a distinctly secondary factor. This seemed reasonable, and for many years few psychologists were interested in motor development.

Lately, this has changed, and a new view of motor development has emerged called **dynamic systems theory** (Thelen & Adolph, 1992; Thelen & Smith, 1998). The new approach focuses on understanding the process by which children learn new skills rather than simply listing these skills, and it seems that maturation does not tell the whole story even in excellent environments. Other biomechanical factors as well as perceptual skills are important. *Biomechanics* is the application of the principles of mechanics to the study of biological systems (Ernicke & Schneider, 1993). The structure of the legs and the muscles influences movement. The body is also affected by external forces such as gravity and other physical forces such as inertia. For example, infants show the walking reflex. If you hold an infant so that his feet meet a hard surface, the infant shows walking movements. This

dynamic systems theory
A theory of motor development emphasizing the interaction between the organism and the environment.

reflex "disappears" at about 3 months. Later, the infant develops the ability to walk. A leader in this new approach to motor development, Esther Thelen, found that kicking and stepping appear to be the same movement. Why would the brain inhibit the behavior while the infant stands but not when the infant is on his back?

Thelen argues that infants don't show the walking reflex because it requires a great deal of strength to lift a leg while upright but not while supine (Thelen & Fisher, 1982). At the time when the stepping reflex seems to disappear, infants have a rapid weight gain, most of which is fat, not muscle. Their limbs become somewhat heavier but not much stronger. The combination of increasingly heavy legs and a more demanding posture results in an inability to perform a behavior that once was performed with ease. Thelen argues that more than simple brain maturation is involved. Movement patterns emerge through interaction between the organism and the environment, and to understand motor skills, many aspects of the environment must be evaluated (Zernicke & Schneider, 1993).

This view invites us to consider a particular motor skill as the product of many elements that converge at a particular time. Some behaviors may be present very early in life but not shown because other systems are not ready. Only when all components reach a particular state and the environment is appropriate will the behavior be performed. With this understanding, it is sometimes possible to bring out these hidden skills using unusual means. When infants as young as 1 month were held supported under the armpits so that their legs rested on a small motorized treadmill, they performed coordinated alternating stepping movements that looked very much like adult walking (Thelen & Ulrich, 1991). Without the help of the treadmill, such patterns are not seen until at least 12 months, when babies begin to walk on their own. The treadmill movement is probably not voluntary, but it does indicate the sensitivity of motor skills to external conditions. The behavior will be shown when all factors are in readiness.

Perception and feedback from one's senses are also important to the development of motor skills. A child who wishes to grasp a toy is faced with a problem of how to accomplish this. The problem is solved as the infant first explores and tries out many movements, then narrows down the successful ones, selecting these and practicing them, becoming more proficient. The processes of exploration and selection are paramount. The first step is to discover patterns of behavior that help the baby get closer to the goal, such as a tentative crawl or a few steps. Then the infant tunes them and, with repetition, becomes proficient.

Often skills that are available are combined to solve these problems. Motor development involves increasingly complex combinations of previously acquired skills that are combined to produce a more advanced skill (Thelen, 1986). For example, when children are crawling they are really putting together kicking and rocking on all fours. When infants who have just developed sufficient muscle strength to support their abdomen and are learning to crawl on their hands and knees are observed, they try many crawling movements (Freedland & Bertenthal, 1994). Sometimes they even move backward, try moving one limb at a time or only use their arms. After a week or two of this trial and error, infants all arrive at the same method, and begin to crawl.

The brain does not contain a crawling "program," telling the infant just how to do it. Maturation may increase strength, but exploration and selection do the rest. These processes are demonstrated when a 6-month-old infant is placed in an infant jumper or bouncer.

According to dynamic systems theory, new motor skills emerge as infants reorganize their existing capabilities in order to achieve their objective.

How does dynamic systems theory break new ground in understanding motor development?

The infant is in a harness with a spring and the soles of the feet just touch the floor. Some movements will make the experience interesting, but the child must discover which. The infant must learn how much force to apply and when to do so (Goldfield, Kay, & Warren, 1993). The infant is trying to get the maximum bounce for the effort. The infant begins with only a few tentative bounces, varying in strength and timing. As the weeks pass, the infant increases the number of bounces and settles on a consistent amount and force. Using both visual information and feedback from muscles, the infant learns to use the most efficient strategy.

Obviously, perception is also involved. Perceptual abilities tell the infant where a rattle is and where the sound that interested him was coming from. It tells the infant in the baby bouncer where she is, and such feedback allows the infant to correct and change behavior. It shows children how close they have come to the goal. Young infants can combine information from more than one sense and coordinate movements with perception as they age. For example, consider the infant learning to walk. Not only is coordination of leg muscles required, but also the ability to shift body weight from one foot to another. Walking also requires infants to evaluate visual information, such as the nature of the floor, and adjust their posture as they walk (Bertenthal & Bai, 1989). When they locomote on their own, they make the necessary postural adjustments in response to the visual information.

This new view of motor development emphasizes its reciprocal nature. Tasks motivate infants to try new behaviors, and these new behaviors enable the infants to solve new tasks. Exploration and selection are the key processes by which infants develop these abilities. This does not mean that brain development is unimportant, just that it is not the only factor. No single factor causes walking. Rather, walking becomes a smoothly integrated action only when all its components, upright posture, leg alternation, weight shifting, and evaluation of sensory information are developed, and the child has sufficient opportunity to explore, select, and practice these movements.

Focus on the Toddler

"Infants are easy," said Daphne, running after her 2-year-old, who was heading for parts unknown. "You play with them, feed them, change them, and put them in their cribs—where they stay." Daphne, as well as most mothers of toddlers, can tell you that dealing with 2-year-olds is different. The skills of a 2-year-old in walking, muscle control, and communication make parenting a challenge. At 1 year of age, the child enters the toddler stage. The defining skill that differentiates an infant from a toddler is the ability to walk (Bornstein, 1995). Toddlers are active, engaging beings with a mind of their own. There is an exciting quality to their newfound capabilities, and they go from one activity to another with breathtaking speed. A new world is open to them. They prefer the wide open spaces and dislike confinement. There is wonder in everything they do. As Lieberman (1993) notes, "Who else could show us so convincingly that a wet, muddy leaf lying on the ground is actually a hidden marvel, or that splashing in the bath can bring ultimate joy? Toddlers have the gift of living in the moment and finding wonder in the ordinary. They share those gifts by helping the adults they love to reconnect with the simple pleasures of life" (p. 1).

Unfortunately, accidents are common at this age, and the health and safety of young children are prime parental responsibilities. Toddlers often become interested in things that parents miss on a casual inspection of an area. This is why it is important that the caregiver carefully evaluate the child's environment (see Table 5.2).

autonomy

The positive outcome of the second stage of Erikson's psychosocial stage: an understanding that the child is someone on his or her own.

shame or doubt

The negative outcome of Erikson's second psychosocial stage, in which the child has a sense of shame or doubt about being a separate individual.

According to Erikson, as children negotiate toddlerhood they should gain a sense of **autonomy,** an understanding that they are people on their own and have some control over their own behavior. However, if parents do not allow their children to do what they are able to do and are greatly overprotective, or if they push their children into doing something for which they are not ready, the children may develop a sense of **shame or doubt** concerning their ability to deal with the world around them. This negative outcome causes children to develop feelings of incompetence, insecurity, and unworthiness (Snow, 1998). The child's basic desire for self-assertion sometimes comes into conflict with parents' demands and restrictions (Snow, 1998). Parents support their children's attempts at autonomy by letting

Table 5.2 Important Accident Prevention Measures for Families to Observe during the Toddler Period

Potential Accident Situations	Prevention Measures for Health Teaching
Motor vehicles	Maintain child in car seat, not just seat belt; do not be distracted from safe driving by child in a car.
	Do not allow child to play outside unsupervised. Do not allow to operate electronic garage doors.
	Supervise toddler too young to be left alone on a tricycle.
	Teach safety with pedaling toys (look before crossing driveways; do not cross streets).
Falls	Keep house windows closed, or keep secure screens in place.
	Place gates at top and bottom of stairs. Supervise at playgrounds.
	Do not allow child to walk with sharp object in hand or mouth.
	Raise crib rails and check to make sure they are locked before walking away from crib.
Aspiration	Examine toys for small parts that could be aspirated; remove those that appear dangerous.
	Do not feed toddler popcorn, peanuts, etc.; urge children not to eat while running. Do not leave toddler alone with a balloon.
Drowning	Do not leave toddler alone in bathtub or near water (including buckets of cleaning water).
Animal bites	Do not allow toddler to approach strange dogs.
	Supervise child's play with family pets.
Poisoning	Never present medications as candy.
	Buy medications with childproof safety caps; put away immediately after use.
	Never take medications in front of child.
	Place all medications and poisons in locked cabinets or overhead shelves where child cannot reach.
	Never leave medication in parents' purse or pocket, where child can reach.
	Always store food or substances in their original containers.
	Use non-lead-based paint throughout the house.
	Hang plants or set them on high surfaces beyond toddler's grasp.
	Post telephone number of nearest poison control center by the telephone.
	In all first aid boxes, maintain supply of syrup of ipecac, an emetic, with proper instructions for administering if poisoning should occur.
Burns	Buy flame-retardant clothing.
	Turn handles of pots toward back of stove to prevent toddler from reaching up and pulling them down.
	Use cool-mist vaporizer or remain in room when vaporizer is operating so that child is not tempted to play with it.
	Keep screen in front of fireplace or heater.
	Monitor toddlers carefully when they are near lit candles.
	Do not leave toddlers unsupervised near hot-water faucets.
	Do not allow toddlers to blow out matches (teach that fire is not fun); store matches out of reach.
	Keep electric wires and cords out of toddler's reach; cover electrical outlets with safety plugs.
General	Know whereabouts of toddlers at all times. Toddlers can climb onto chairs, stools, etc., that they could not manage before; can turn door knobs and go places they could not go before.
	Be aware that the frequency of accidents increases when the family is under stress and therefore less attentive to children. Special precautions must be taken at these times.
	Some children are more active, curious, and impulsive and therefore more vulnerable to accidents than others.

SOURCE: Pillitteri (1992)

Toddlers have a great deal of energy and, because they do not always know what is dangerous, must be constantly monitored.

their toddlers make choices in ways that do not harm themselves or others, by helping them play and assert themselves safely and independently, and by rewarding and sharing in their children's accomplishments (Edwards, 1995). Erikson was well aware of the delicate balance necessary between encouragement and protection, and between freedom of self-expression and its suppression.

Toddlers are no longer completely dependent on other people. This independence is seen in their increasing annoyance when their activities are interrupted or when they are offered unwanted help. Toddlers want to do things in their own way. They have the physical abilities but not necessarily the understanding of what might happen if they do something. For example, that lovely vase within reach of the toddler may well be a thing of the past. It is not that the toddler wants to break it; it is that he or she may not know that it breaks. Even if you tell the child, it may not get through, and the child may not connect what you are saying with his or her behavior (Oppenheim, Boegehold, & Brenner, 1984). The toddler is also quite impatient and does not want to wait. After all, there are so many things to do and to explore.

Most of all, toddlers are explorers who have to balance their need to be independent and competent with the need for protection, love, and care (Lieberman, 1993). The motivation to explore forms the foundation on which learning occurs. Young children show a persistence and a drive to master skills. When learning to walk, the child may fall, get up, fall again, get up, and the pattern will continue (Hauser-Cram, 1996).

Toddlers can communicate verbally in an elementary manner, but they often become frustrated. They can't seem to put things effectively into words and often only gesture, repeating the same behavior over again until the parent shows understanding (Lieberman, 1993). Two-year-olds use their verbal skills to show their independence, saying "no," "me do it," and "mine" often. Although they may understand some commands, they may still be unable, or in some cases unwilling, to carry them out. The increased motor behavior, desire for independence, and tendency to be negative explains why parents often call this age the "terrible twos."

During toddlerhood control issues take center stage. Resistance and angry behavior peaks during the second year and then show a decline after and throughout the school years (Kopp, 1992). Mothers and fathers react more positively to 12-month-olds than to 18-month-old children, and self-reported enjoyment of child rearing declines from 18 to 24 months (Fagot & Kavanaugh, 1993). Mild conflicts are common; in fact, conflicts between 2-year-olds and their mothers are twice as common as those for 4- or 5-year-olds (Lieberman, 1993). Temper tantrums, a feature of this period, peak at between 18 and 21 months but clearly drop by 3 years.

On the other hand, toddlers do comply with requests quite often, and many parents don't seem to have a great deal of difficulty dealing with their 2-year-olds, despite the increase in motor activity (Kaler & Kopp, 1990). Actually, the "terrible twos" label may help somewhat, since parents faced with stubborn negative behavior may ascribe it to the child's age and not to the child him- or herself, telling themselves that the stage will pass (Lieberman, 1993).

Often parents believe that their toddlers are so difficult because they compare them with older children and sometimes long for the days when their schedules as infants allowed for longer naps. Simply stated, many people have inappropriate expectations for toddlers and do not understand the way toddlers learn. Toddlers learn with their whole bodies (Gonzalez-Mena, 1986). They learn through action, learning far more through active manipulation than through listening. Toddlers are explorers who are absorbed in their world. They do not have a short attention span for their age. When toddlers become interested in something, they can attend to it for a long time. As toddlers approach 3, they develop simple skills in the area of eye-hand coordination, and some of what seems like random exploration is reduced. The progression from movement that appears to occur just for the sake of movement to more controlled motor activity that seems increasingly oriented toward ends or consequences occurs during the toddlerhood stage (Bullock & Lutkenhaus, 1988).

Even if the "terrible twos" is an overstatement, some families have a very difficult time dealing with the typical behaviors shown by 2-year-olds and experience a great many management problems (Belsky, Woodworth, & Crnic, 1996). Families who have the most problems often use "negative control" strategies, which include statements and behaviors that convey anger and irritation. These control strategies include spanking, withholding basic needs such as food and love, or screaming at the child (Bigner, 1994). Children in these poorly functioning families show more negativity and power struggles escalate constantly. For example, toddlers whose mothers are affectionate, stimulate their children verbally, are responsive, and less frequently use punishment and restrictiveness, while using more positive methods of control, are more compliant (Olson, Bates, & Bayles, 1984). Children whose parents use many commands, physical control, or coerce their children into complying with instructions cooperate less with adults (Londerville & Main, 1981). Generally, parents who engage in more positive strategies, including reinforcing their toddlers for good behavior, giving children choices, and childproofing the environment, experience less conflict with their toddlers (Snow, 1998).

It takes special knowledge and skill to understand toddlers, to protect them from what they cannot do or what could injure them, yet not to hover over them, preventing them from learning. Parents must decide in which areas of the home toys are going to be allowed, where large-motor activities that are safe will be encouraged, and how they want to deal with the question of how many items the child can take out to play with at one time.

Toddlers can be very stubborn, and decisions about discipline must be made for the first time. Toddlers will test limits, and power struggles are common.

Guideposts
Why are the toddler years considered by parents to be so physically exhausting and demanding?

One way to deal with toddlers is to use choices to avoid these struggles (Gonzalez-Mena, 1986). For example, telling a child "I don't want you walking around while you eat, but you can eat in either the blue chair or the red chair" can resolve a problem. In addition, words may not be sufficient if danger is present, and preventing dangerous behavior by holding an arm before it hits someone or knocks the pot of boiling water off the stove may be necessary. Preventing problems is best, and this often involves understanding that some behaviors, such as wandering about, saying no, or crying, especially when tired, are to be expected.

Toddlers may hear many comments: protective ones such as "Don't step in the road," admonishments to wash their hands, and warnings to be careful or they will break something (Edwards, 1995). Children's compliance increases from the toddler through the preschool to the school years (Whiting & Edwards, 1988). Even children under 2 years comply when they understand a command and do not when they don't (Kaler & Kopp, 1990).

Parenting Choices

Most of the choices that affect young children are made by their parents. These include feeding, the extent to which children will be treated differently because of their gender, and toilet training.

Infant Nutrition

New parents have a million things to do, but if parents take the advice of many authorities, meal planing isn't one of them (Stehlin, 1995). The American Academy of Pediatrics (1992) recommends that infants receive breast milk for the first 6 to 12 months for good reason. Breast-feeding has important advantages for both mother and baby (Lawrence, 1991). Mother's milk is the natural food for human infants and meets all the nutrition requirements for infants, with the possible exception of vitamin D (Whitney et al., 1994). Vitamin D deficiency is rarely seen in breast-fed infants, though, since that vitamin is synthesized with the help of a normal amount of exposure to sunlight (Stehlin, 1995).

Research shows that breast feeding is superior to bottle feeding infants.

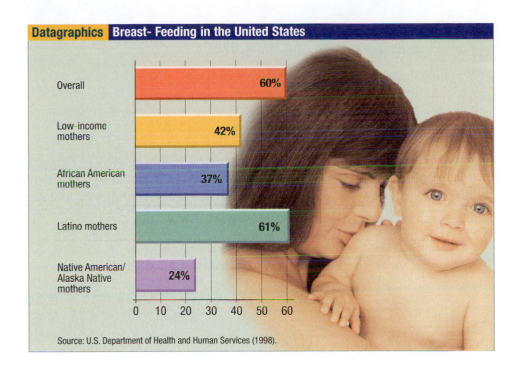

Datagraphics **Breast- Feeding in the United States**

Overall — 60%
Low-income mothers — 42%
African American mothers — 37%
Latino mothers — 61%
Native American/ Alaska Native mothers — 24%

0 10 20 30 40 50 60

Source: U.S. Department of Health and Human Services (1998).

Mother's milk contains a number of helpful substances not found in prepared formulas. Some antibodies protect the infant against intestinal disorders, and immunities are passed on in breast milk (Brown, 1995). Mother's milk also contains chemicals that promote the absorption of iron. Breast milk's protein content is well suited to a baby's metabolism, and the fat content is more easily absorbed and digested (Stehlin, 1995). Some preliminary evidence relates breast-feeding to the promotion of neurological development (Lucas, Morley, Cole, Lister, & Leeson-Payne, 1992). Breast-fed infants develop fewer allergic reactions, such as asthma, recurrent wheezing, and skin rash (Rolfes, DeBruyne, & Whitney, 1998). Some evidence indicates protection against some chronic diseases, such as diabetes, and better health, including a reduction in ear infections (Heinig & Dewey, 1996).

There are significant psychological benefits to the breast-fed infant. The close contact between mother and child encourages the growth and development of the mother-infant bond and satisfies the infant's need for warmth and physical contact.

Of course, infants can also be successfully raised on formula (Schmitt, 1979). The composition of infant formula is similar to breast milk but is not a perfect match, and the exact chemical makeup of breast milk is still unknown (Stehlin, 1995). However, whereas the infant's nutritional and psychological needs are normally satisfied naturally during breast-feeding, bottle feeding may require more thought and concern. The caregiver must be certain to hold the baby close to give the child the physical contact that is so important to infants. Most mothers can breast-feed (Brown, 1995), but it may be necessary to bottle-feed if the mother is taking certain medications. Mothers who are breast-feeding should watch their diet, as caffeine, alcohol, and environmental contaminants may be transferred to breast milk (Brown, 1995).

Many women do not breast-feed very long; in fact most stop by four months. Those mothers who receive early and repeated breast-feeding information are more likely to choose to breast-feed and do so longer (Saunders & Carroll, 1988). Education may be one important key to increasing the percentage of women who breast-feed their infants.

Guideposts
What are the benefits of breast-feeding?

For Your Consideration ?

Why don't more mothers breast-feed their infants?

Gender Differences:
How Parents View Sons and Daughters

The first announcement made to parents is the baby's gender. In fact, the first question people ask when told a new baby has arrived concerns gender (Intons-Peterson & Reddel, 1984). How important is gender to the way infants are treated? Do any inborn physical differences exist at birth?

Gender Differences at Birth   At birth, the average male is about 2% longer and about 5% heavier than the average female (Doyle & Paludi, 1991). Females are more mature at birth and continue to develop at a faster rate. Girls are four weeks more advanced in skeletal development at birth (Tanner, 1970), and they reach motor milestones faster than males. The average female child sits up, walks, toilet trains, and talks earlier than the average male child (Kalat, 1980). Another difference is that the average female infant performs more rhythmic behaviors, such as sucking and smiling, than the average male infant (Feldman, Brody, & Miller, 1980). Males exceed females in large musculature movements, such as kicking. They also show greater muscular strength and can lift their heads higher at birth (Korner, 1973). At the end of the first year, males show higher activity levels, but because this behavior is found through observation, the question of bias is raised.

These early physical and developmental differences may affect parental behavior, magnifying the effects of the differences. The more developmentally advanced females may be more responsive. By being capable of sitting, walking, or talking at an early age, they may be more reinforcing to the parents. Advanced development could then lead to more attention and different types of interaction with the caregivers.

The differences in how parents treat their sons and daughters, however, are more often based on the different expectations for each gender rather than on any real differences. For example, even when male and female infants are the same size, weight, and physical condition, parents see daughters as weaker and more sickly and males as sturdier and more athletic (Rubin, Provenzano, & Luria, 1974). When parents who had not even held their newborns, but merely had seen them

As a rule, girls walk, talk, and toilet train earlier than boys.

What physical differences exist between male and female neonates?

ACTION / REACTION

"I Don't Want Ken and Barbie!"

Jen and Peter have two children, Paula, 3 years, and Steven, 5 years old. Jen believes that each child should be raised as an individual and gender should not be an issue. She buys Paula "boy-type toys" and Steven "girl-type toys," believing that this is the best way to raise a child who will not be afraid to be him- or herself. She believes that children should be introduced to a variety of toys regardless of "gender appropriateness."

Her husband, Peter, feels differently. He sees nothing wrong with buying dolls for Paula and baseball equipment for Steven. He admits that he doesn't feel comfortable when Steven plays with dolls and believes that Jen shouldn't buy these things unless Steven specifically asks for them. He doesn't mind Paula playing with trucks and other such "boy-type toys" as much but sometimes feels that Jen is pushing this. Peter believes Jen won't accept the fact that boys and girls may be different and that she wants to mold them in her own way. Jen believes that Peter, although well meaning, is affected by stereotypes and that it would be better if they encouraged the children to explore things without regard to "gender appropriateness."

1. *As neighbors and friends, they ask you what you think. How would you deal with this issue?*
2. *If your 4-year-old boy asked you for a frilly doll, would it bother you?*

ACTION / REACTION

---

behind the nursery glass, were asked to describe their children, both fathers and mothers described their sons as more alert and stronger and the daughters as more delicate (Rubin et al., 1974).

Some evidence indicates that this labeling process continues throughout infancy and toddlerhood. When videotapes of 17-month-old children were shown to adults and the gender given, men described children labeled as male in such stereotyped terms as "independent," "aggressive," and "active" (Meyer & Sobieszek, 1972). These same actions were interpreted as delicate, passive, and dependent when they were told the child was a female. In another study, 13-month-old infants were observed in a play group. Although no gender differences were found in assertive acts or attempts to communicate with adults, the adults attended more to boys' assertive behaviors and less to those of girls. Adults attended more to girls when the girls used less intense forms of communication. Eleven months later, gender differences were observed as boys were more assertive, but girls talked to adults more (Fagot, Hagan, Leinbach, & Kronsberg, 1985).

As boys and girls develop, other differences become noticeable. Males are reinforced for attempts to develop gross-motor skills involved in large-scale physical play more than females are (Smith & Lloyd, 1978). Boys are allowed to play alone more than girls (Fagot, 1978). Even the physical environment provided for boys and girls in infancy and toddlerhood differs. Boys are provided with more sports equipment, tools, and large and small vehicle toys. Girls are given more dolls and children's furniture. Girls are dressed in pink and multicolored clothes more often, and boys are dressed in more blue, red, and white (Pomerleau, Bolduck, Malcuit, Cossette, 1990).

Some research studies find differential patterns of reinforcement, for example, girls receive more praise and more criticism (Fagot, 1978). Both parents are more likely to stop the play activities of boys. Parents give more positive feedback to boys when they play with blocks and more negative reaction when they play with dolls. Parents react more negatively when girls manipulate objects than when this is done by boys. Parents criticize girls more often when they attempt to participate in large-motor activities such as running, jumping, and climbing. More positive responses are given for their daughters' requests for help.

Parents often choose different toys for their sons and daughters. When mothers and fathers were videotaped playing with their 1- to 2-year-old children, no differential reinforcement of boys and girls for masculine or neutral play was found (Eisenberg, Wolchik, Hernandez, & Pasternak, 1985), but the child's gender affected parents' choice of toys during the interactions. Parents of boys chose more masculine toys, and parents of girls chose more neutral toys. Parental toy choice, but not parental reinforcement, was related to children's play choices. Parents did not actively discourage or encourage their young children to play with toys the children chose themselves. Merely by selecting play items, though, parents encouraged their children toward some toys and away from others.

The fact that parents and children select same sex-typed toys when they have a choice was amply demonstrated when parent-child pairs ranging in age from 18 to 23 months were observed during play (Caldera, Huston, & O'Brien, 1989). Each parent-child pair was asked to play with six different sets of toys. Toys were categorized as masculine (trains and wooden blocks), feminine (dolls and a kitchen set), and gender-neutral (puzzles and shape sorters). Each set of toys was placed in its own covered box, and parents and children engaged in play with these toys for four minutes after which they were told to put the toys away and go to the next box of toys.

Does the parents' early treatment of their sons and daughters lead to gender differences later in life?

For Your Consideration

Research shows few gender differences at birth, but parents perceive their infant males and females are quite different. How can you explain this difference between perception and reality?

T F
9

Fathers are more likely to treat their sons and daughters differently than mothers.

Guideposts

In what ways do mothers and fathers treat their infant sons and daughters differently?

Toddlers who are trained later train faster. Seldom is a child ready before the age of two at the earliest.

Even when no alternatives were available and parents' involvement was controlled, toddlers showed less involvement with toys stereotyped for the other gender than with those stereotyped for their own gender, and they more often rejected cross-gender toys than same-sex or neutral toys. Parents modeled more play with sex-stereotyped toys as well. Parents did not actively discourage play with cross-sex toys, though. Some parents did, however, have trouble complying with instructions when playing with cross-gender toys. One father playing with his daughter opened up a box with trucks and remarked, "Oh, they must have boys in this study," closed the box, and returned to playing with dolls. Mothers and fathers both showed these tendencies.

The nature of the toys influenced parent-child interaction. When playing with masculine toys, especially trucks, few questions were asked and more distance existed between child and parent. A great many animated sounds were made rather than verbal statements. Feminine toys elicited closer proximity, and more verbal interaction in the form of questions and comments. The neutral toys elicited the most positive verbal and informative verbal exchanges. These findings may have something to do with the nature of the neutral toys. Parents may associate puzzles and shape sorters with cognitive development. Generally, fathers tend to be more concerned than mothers with gender-appropriate behavior and are more likely to give negative feedback to boys who play with dolls and other soft toys.

Three main conclusions stand out quite clearly from the research in gender differences in early life. First, the initial differences between the genders are quite limited at birth. Second, the treatment of males and females tends to be more similar than different, although the differences may in the end turn out to be important. Parents give both sons and daughters affection and do not generally tolerate aggression from either. However, there is evidence that different patterns of behavior, even in the early years, are reinforced. Males receive greater reinforcement for engaging in physical play, while girls are positively reinforced for asking for help and for helping others. Both are reinforced for playing with gender-appropriate toys. Third, although parents often do not vocalize their gender-stereotyped opinions, they may show them in some of their behaviors toward their children and certainly in their toy preferences. Fathers are stricter than mothers in reinforcing these stereotyped gender-appropriate behaviors, especially in their sons. Parents are frequently unaware of how they may affect the development of their children and may need consciousness-raising if they are to follow their stated aim of allowing children to develop their own abilities.

Toilet Training

Of all the choices in dealing with very young children, toilet training seems to get the most attention. One of the most common questions is how early to start. Sometime in the course of the second year, toddlers begin to recognize the bodily sensations that allow them to take control of elimination. Besides the obvious maturational capability to control the muscles, individual and environmental factors are involved in toilet training. Some children do not like being soiled. Others may be aware that friends are not wearing diapers and may train easily and quickly. Still others may require more time and have many accidents. Once a child is maturationally ready, toilet training should not take long. Children can be introduced to the potty, taught about the procedures involved, and given encouragement and social reinforcement. The pressure on the child should be minimized, and parents should understand that some children will be ready for toilet training before others.

Some parents toilet train before the child understands what is expected and can become a willing partner. The ability to do so is rarely shown before between 15 and 18 months and may not occur until 24 to 30 months or even later (Lieberman, 1993). Some toddlers initiate the process themselves by calling their parents attention to the fact that they are eliminating. Beginning the process too early can lead to frustration and negativism, but it also makes the process slower. In one study, one twin from each of two twin pairs began toilet training as early as 2 months of age, while their siblings were allowed to wait (McGraw, 1940). The early training did not help; the later-trained children trained much more quickly and soon caught up to the others. Training started later is faster (Sears, Maccoby, & Levin, 1957). It is best to train a child when the child is ready.

Some parents place a great deal of importance on early toilet training. The expectation that a 1- or 2-year-old is going to be completely dry day and night not only is unreasonable but also may be harmful, for it leads to criticism from parents when the child has an accident. The age at which a child will be ready varies from child to child. Children's bowel control precedes bladder control, and the ability to control elimination in the day precedes the ability to do so at night (Oppel, Harper, & Rider, 1968). Girls are also somewhat ahead of boys in this area.

The earlier parents start to toilet train their child, the shorter the amount of time it takes to do so.

Under law, infants and toddlers with developmental delays are eligible for special early intervention services.

Atypical Development: Early Intervention

This chapter examined the sensory, perceptual, motor, and physical development of the child from birth through toddlerhood. The pattern of increased abilities and skills is impressive. It is clear that the infant is born ready for life, with many abilities that improve rapidly throughout this period. But what of young children who are not developing well? What can be done to help them?

States are required to provide services for infants and toddlers with developmental difficulties under a 1986 law, PL 99-457 (Hebberler, Smith, & Black, 1991). These services are called **early intervention programs** and are based on the idea that if problems can be diagnosed early and treatment received, the child's development may be enhanced and the effects of any disability reduced. In 1996, about 172,000 infants and toddlers received early intervention services (Office of Special Education, 1997). To receive such help, a child need not have a particular diagnosis; rather, eligibility is based on developmental and behavioral criteria (Bagnato, Neisworth, & Munson, 1993).

Children who are served may be experiencing a delay in development in a number of areas, including physical development, sensory development, cognitive development, or self-help skills. In addition, infants and toddlers who are at risk for developmental problems due to medical conditions, such as low birth weight, are also eligible. Some programs also target children raised in adverse social and environmental circumstances, such as children raised in abusive environments or by teenage parents in poverty, but services to this group are not required by federal statute (Kaplan, 1996). The potential services for infants and toddlers are shown

Guideposts

Why are early intervention programs necessary?

early intervention programs

Systematic efforts to assist young children between the ages of birth and 3 years and their families. Programs attempt to enhance development, minimize potential developmental delays, remediate existing problems, and improve overall family functioning.

in Table 5.3. Some services are aimed specifically at the child, such as physical therapy, while others focus on the family, attempting to help the family promote the child's development and deal with the child's additional needs.

Children who receive these services are superior to children who do not participate on various measures of development, including intelligence, motor skills, and language acquisition (Shonkoff & Hauser-Cram, 1987). Programs that are more intense, begin earlier, and focus on both the child and the family are most effective (Duwa, Wells, & Lalinde, 1993; Kaplan, 1996; Reynolds, 1995). These programs represent a significant step forward in society's attempt to enhance children's development and to help families provide for their children's special needs as early as possible so that every child may have a chance to grow and learn.

Table 5.3	Definition of Potential Services for Infants and Toddlers and Their Families	
Part H Services (Required by Law)	**Optional Part H Services**	**Other Services (Not Required)**
Audiology	Developmental child care	Housing
Assistive technology	Medical child care	Educational opportunities and vocational training
Family training, counseling, and home visits	Medical foster care	
	Therapeutic foster care/ shelter care	Family planning
Family assessment		Family therapy
Health services (only in order to benefit from other intervention)	Other health services	Culturally relevant special services
	Family support (respite, home-maker, parent-to-parent)	Family unification services
Intake—screening	Play/psychosocial therapy for children with emotional problems	Environmental adaptations for special needs (i.e., wheelchair ramp)
Medical services (only for diagnosis or evaluation)		
Multidiscplinary evaluation		Legal services
Nursing services		Comprehensive drug treatment
Nutrition services		Medications
Psychological services		Dental services
Service coordination		After-school care
Service planning (IFSP, IEP)		Training and professional support for early childhood, early intervention, and social support staff
Special instruction		
Social work service		
Therapy services (occupational, physical, and speech/language)		Outreach programs that make extended effort to locate child and families
Transportation services		
Vision services		

SOURCE: Service Delivery and Design Study: Options for Delivery of Early Intervention Services: New Approaches to Decision Making in Florida's Cost/Implementation Study for Public Law 99-457, Part H, Infants and Toddlers: Phase II Findings, © 1992, by M. A. Graham and L. Stone. Reprinted by permission.

Summary

1. Researching infant abilities is difficult. Scientists sometimes use habituation in which infants reduce the time they spend looking at a familiar object. When shown a different object, their attention may recover, showing that they notice the difference. Another research method aims at discovering infants' preferences for a particular stimulus by giving the infant a choice. A third method is to use event-related potentials in which the electrical activity of the brain is studied as the infant is presented with a particular stimulus.

2. Neonates are born with characteristics and abilities that make survival possible. Newborns can see, hear, smell, and taste. They can also experience pain. Their sensory abilities develop quickly.

3. Neonates spend most of the day sleeping and spend a great deal more time than adults in REM sleep. Infants' sleeping-waking state is related to behavior.

4. A number of cries have been identified in the infant, including the hunger, pain, and mad cries. Parents can correctly identify these cries.

5. Erik Erikson argued that the psychosocial crisis during infancy is trust versus mistrust. If the child's needs are met, the child develops a sense of trust. If not, a sense of mistrust may develop.

6. Classical and operant conditioning have been demonstrated in the infant. Infants can also imitate.

7. The neonate is born with a number of reflexes, such as the sucking, rooting (turning the head toward a source of stimulation when a cheek is stroked), grasping, and stepping reflexes. The functions of other reflexes, such as the Babinski reflex (fanning of the toes when soles of the feet are stroked) and the Moro reflex (extending arms and legs while arching the back, then contracting them in a hugging manner), are not known.

8. The brain grows rapidly in the months following birth, and such factors as nutrition and experience are important in optimizing brain growth.

9. Infant health has improved markedly with the advent of new vaccines, but not every infant and toddler is receiving the full complement of vaccinations.

10. The diagnosis of sudden infant death syndrome (SIDS) describes the death of an infant from unknown causes. Today, authorities advocate that healthy infants be put to bed on their backs, which seems to reduce the incidence of SIDS.

11. Growth and weight gains are sizable in infancy and slow down during toddlerhood. Some authorities believe that growth involves a steady process, while others argue that infants grow in spurts. Genetic considerations and nutrition both affect development. Acute illnesses and stress may deflect children from a normal growth trajectory, but a self-righting process enables children to return to normal when the illness or stress is past. Development occurs in a consistent pattern from the head downward (cephalocaudal) and from the inside out (proximodistal), and muscular development progresses from mass to specific.

12. Motor development also follows a specific pattern. The rate can be affected by culture, genetic endowment, and the environment. New research emphasizes the importance of biomechanical factors and perception, and looks at the processes of exploration and selection as leading to the development of important motor skills.

13. Walking separates infancy from toddlerhood. During toddlerhood, the psychosocial crisis is autonomy versus doubt. Infants must develop a sense that they are people on their own. Toddlers learn through doing, and they show a desire for independence. Toddlers have some limited verbal skills and may become frustrated when they cannot communicate. The toddler's physical abilities often outweigh the child's judgment, making home safety a first priority.

14. Significant nutritional and health advantages result from breast-feeding. Breast milk meets all the infant's nutritional requirements, except vitamin D, which is synthesized with the help of a little sunlight. Mothers pass on immunities through breast milk, and some evidence shows it promotes neurological development. Approved infant formulas are not identical to breast milk.

15. Gender differences in infancy are moderate and unstable. Girls are more mature at birth and develop at a faster rate than boys. Females show more oral and facial movements. Males show more large-musculature movements, such as kicking, and greater muscular strength.

16. Parents treat their infant sons and daughters differently. Activities requiring gross-motor control are more likely to be reinforced in male infants. In toddlerhood, girls are given more praise and criticism than are boys. Fathers are more rigid with regard to gender-stereotyped behavior than are mothers.

17. Toilet training is often a concern. Children who are toilet trained later take less time to train.

18. Infants and toddlers who show delayed development or who are at risk for developmental problems can receive help under PL 99–457. Such early intervention involves both direct services to the child and family support.

Review

At birth the newborn is covered with fine hair called (1)_____ and a thick fluid that protects the infant's sensitive skin called (2)_____ . In the 1st month of life, the newborn is called a (3)_____ , while the period of (4)_____ covers the entire first year. A child is considered a (5)_____ between ages 1 and 3 years. Psychologists investigate the sensory abilities of infants through a number of methods. Psychologists may present a stimulus a number of times, and slowly the child may lose interest in the stimulus, a phenomenon called (6)_____ . If the child regains interest after being shown another stimulus, the child has noticed the difference. In a (7)_____ test, psychologists may show the infant two stimuli and measure the amount of time the infant spends paying attention to the stimuli. Sometimes psychologists measure transient changes in neural activity when an infant is shown a stimulus, a technique called (8)_____ .

Neonates can see at birth but are quite (9)_____. Fantz noted that young infants pay more attention to (10_____ than to other stimuli. To test depth perception, Gibson and Walk used an apparatus called the (11)_____ and found that infants over 6 months would not crawl to the other side even if mother beckoned. Infants can hear even before birth and listen most intently to the sounds coming from (12)_____ . Neonates also show excellent senses of (13)_____ , (14)_____ , and (15)_____ . Young infants spend more time (16)_____ than in any other state. During their sleep infants show many more periods of (17)_____ than adults, but this declines as they age. Infants show a number of additional transitional (18)_____ . There are many different types of infant cries, and infants whose caregivers respond quickly and appropriately when they are very young cry (19)_____ (less, more) at 1 year.

In one study a tone was paired with nipple and after many trials the infant sucked to the tone, showing that neonates can learn through (20)_____ . If the infant is rewarded with music for sucking, the infant sucks for longer amounts of time, showing that neonates can learn through (21)_____ . Through the process of (22)_____ young infants can see a gesture and perform it. Neonates show a number of simple, automatic inborn patterns of behavioral response to stimuli called (23)_____ . For example, if you place a nipple in the neonate's mouth, the infant will show the (24)_____ reflex. If you stroke the side of the neonate's cheek, the infant turns toward that side, a behavior called the (25)_____ reflex. If you stroke the sole of the feet, the infant's toes curl out, showing the (26)_____ reflex. If you stroke the palm, the neonate shows the (27)_____ reflex in which the infant makes a fist. The (28)_____ reflex involves extension of the feet and legs outward while arching the back then contracting them into a hugging position and crying.

Brain development is rapid in infancy. One reason infants process information more slowly because most neurons still lack the covering that allows them to conduct impulses more efficiently, called the (29)_____ . Two kinds of information and two types of brain mechanisms can be used to explain brain development. (30)_____ information is common to the typical experiences of all members of the species which allows the formation of pathways through very dense nerve cells in the sensory cortex. (31)_____ information involves experiences that are unique to the individual and involves the dramatic growth of new (32)_____ as well as synapses.

The health of most children in developed countries is good, but many do not receive their (33)_____ by the age of 2. (34)_____ syndrome takes thousands of lives each year and is indicated when the cause of death is unknown.

Growth and weight gain in infants is quite impressive. Some experts believe that infants grow in regular intervals, but others argue for a (35)_____ growth pattern in which infants grow in spurts and stops. If the infant is temporarily ill, the child may not grow for a period and then catch up. This self-righting tendency is called (36)_____ . Infants develop in particular patterns. For example, the (37)_____ principle states that development occurs from the head downward, while the (38)_____ principle states that development occurs from the inside out. Muscular development is defined by the (39)_____ to (40)_____ principle, which states that the large muscles develop before the smaller muscles. Traditionally, the prime cause for motor development was (41)_____ with some need for (42)_____ . Lately, (43)_____ argues that other biomechanical and physical features are also important, and psychologists must understand the interaction between the organism and the environment. The key processes by which children develop new skills are (44)_____ and (45)_____ .

According to Erikson, the psychosocial crisis of infancy is (46)_____ versus (47)_____ , while the psychosocial crisis of toddlerhood is (48)_____ versus (49)_____ .

Parents have many choices to make. The American Academy of Pediatrics recommends that as far as feeding is concerned (50)_____ is best. Although physical and behavioral differences between boys and girls at birth are limited, parental (51)_____ of differences are much greater. When parents are compared concerning their treatment of sons and daughters, (52)_____ are more concerned about the gender appropriateness of toys. If an infant or toddler is not developing successfully, services are available under Public Law (53)_____ , which mandates help for young children who require it.

InfoTrac

For additional readings, explore InfoTrac College Edition, our online library.
Go to http://www.infotrac-college.com/wadsworth.
Hint: enter the search terms *Newborn Development, Infant Brain Development.*

What's on the web

Child's physical and emotional health
http://kidshealth.org/parent/index.html

Allowing Children Choices
http://digitalstarlight.com/tnpc/parentalk/toddlers/todd16.html

Toys suited to children's abilities at any age
http://www.etoys.com/toy/g/category/00/23/78/

The Wadsworth Psychology Study Center Web Site
Go to the Wadsworth Psychology Study Center at http://psychology.wadsworth.com for quiz questions, research updates, hot topics, interactive exercises, and suggested readings in the InfoTrac College Edition related to this chapter.

Answers 1. lanugo; 2. vernix caseosa; 3. neonate; 4. infancy; 5. toddler; 6. habituation 7. preference; 8. event-related potentials; 9. nearsighted; 10. faces; 11. visual cliff; 12. human beings; 13. smell; 14. taste; 15. pain, touch; 16. sleeping; 17. REM; 18. states; 19. less; 20. classical conditioning; 21. operant conditioning; 22. imitation (observation learning); 23. reflexes; 24. sucking; 25. rooting; 26. Babinski; 27. palmar grasp; 28. Moro; 29. myelin sheath; 30. Experience-expectant; 31. Experience-dependent; 32. dendrites; 33. vaccinations; 34. Sudden infant death; 35. saltatory; 36. canalization; 37. cephalocaudal; 38. proximodistal; 39. mass; 40. specific; 41. maturation; 42. experience; 43. dynamic systems theory; 44. exploration; 45. selection; 46. trust; 47. mistrust; 48. autonomy; 49. doubt; 50. breast-feeding; 51. perceptions; 52. fathers; 53. 99–457

CHAPTER SIX

Cognitive *and* Linguistic

CHAPTER OUTLINE

An Intelligent Infant

Piaget's Theory of Sensorimotor Development

Information-Processing Skills

Predicting Later Intelligence

Parents and Cognitive Development

The Development of Language

How Do Children Learn Language?

Encouraging Linguistic Ability

ARE THESE STATEMENTS
True *or* **F**alse?

1. A 6-month-old infant will not search for an object that is completely covered by a blanket.
2. Five-month-old infants show the ability to recognize faces and objects but only for a few minutes, after which they forget them.
3. Most adults can remember events that occured between 6 months and 1 year of age if they are reminded of them.
4. Infants' processing speed and memory abilities predict later cognitive abilities in early childhood.
5. Parents of the most advanced infants and toddlers tend to choose all the child's activities for them, programming the day so that the child is always busy learning something new.
6. Parents can often correctly interpret the meaning of their infant's babbling.
7. Toddlers who use sentences such as "Mommy go store" that leave out all the smaller, helping words such as *is* and *to* are very likely to have very poor linguistic skills later in childhood.
8. It is actually easier to learn a new language later in life than during early childhood.
9. Parents all over the world use simplified speech with exaggerated intonation when speaking to their infants and toddlers.
10. Middle-class children use more complex sentences and fewer commands than children of working-class families.

ANSWERS: 1. *True.* 2. *True.* 3. *False.* 4. *True.*
5. *False.* 6. *False.* 7. *False.* 8. *False.* 9. *True.* 10. *True.*

Development in Infancy and Toddlerhood

Is this child showing intelligent behavior? If intelligence is defined in terms of adaptive behavior, the infant certainly is.

An Intelligent Infant

A 6-year-old reads the word "tiny" from a comic book.

A 4-year-old tells his mother that the television show she is watching is "totally awesome."

A 3-year-old puts a simple puzzle together.

A 2-year-old tells her father that she wants a polar bear for a pet.

An 8-month-old repeatedly bangs a rattle against the side of the crib.

If you were asked which of these behaviors shows intelligence, you would probably say the first four. After all, three of them show verbal abilities, and one of them (putting together a puzzle) demonstrates problem-solving skills. Few people, however, would consider the baby's banging the toy against the crib intelligent behavior. But isn't it? If intelligence is considered adaptive behavior, this 8-month-old is learning about causality—that banging the rattle will lead to a predictable noise.

Piaget's Theory of Sensorimotor Development

During the first two years of life, children develop a basic understanding of the world around them. They learn to recognize objects and people, to search for objects that are not in their field of vision, to understand cause and effect, and to appreciate the concept of space. The average adult takes this knowledge for granted, but a child's understanding of these concepts takes many months to develop. The manner in which infants develop an understanding of their world was described in detail by Jean Piaget.

Trends and Premises in Infant Cognitive Development

Two important trends underlie Piaget's view of cognitive development in infancy. First, there is a trend from dependence solely on the objective content of the infant's environment toward internal representation. At first, the infant must experience everything. Later, children can create mental images of the world and understand and use language. Second, infants develop an appreciation that they are separate from other objects in the world and that the existence of those objects does not depend on the infant's perception of them.

Piaget's theory is based on two important premises. First, children are active participants in their own development. Second, development takes place in stages, and each stage acts as a foundation for a succeeding stage. No stage or substage can be skipped, and each must be negotiated in turn.

The Substages of Sensorimotor Development

The first stage of development is called the **sensorimotor stage** because infants learn about their environment through their senses (hearing, vision, touching) and their motor activity (reaching, grasping, kicking) (Piaget, 1962, 1967). Much of an adult's knowledge of the environment is not direct but rather symbolic, being based on words and language and requiring the ability to represent or create a mental picture of what is going on around the person. When your friend tells you not to sit on the chair that has spilled coffee on it, you don't have to see the coffee or get your pants soggy. You understand the idea behind the statement and can create a mental picture of what has happened. All this is far beyond the infant's abilities. The infant learns about objects through manipulation. Piaget described the development of such elementary concepts in terms of six substages (see Table 6.1).

Reflexes (0–1 month): Substage 1 In substage 1, the infant is basically an organism reacting to changes in stimuli. The behavior of infants is rigid and reflexive. Infants are almost entirely dependent on inborn patterns of behavior. Neonates do learn, though. For instance, an infant may suck harder on a bottle containing milk than on a toy placed in the mouth (Ault, 1977; Siegler, 1991).

Primary Circular Reactions (1–4 months): Substage 2 The most prominent feature of substage 2 is the emergence of actions that are repeated again and again. These are called **primary circular reactions.** They are primary because they are focused on the

---

For Your Consideration ?

Why is it difficult to see "intelligent" behavior in infants?

Guideposts

What are the two trends and two premises involved in Piaget's theory of infant cognitive development?

sensorimotor stage
The first stage in Piaget's theory of cognitive development in which the child discovers the world using the senses and motor activity.

primary circular reactions
Actions that are repeated again and again by infants.

Primary circular reactions are simple repetitive acts that center on the infant's own body, such as thumb sucking, hand clasping or foot grabbing.

Table 6.1	The Development of Representational Thought			
Substage 1	0–1 month	Reflexive Stage	Infant is dependent on reflexes, rigid patterns of behavior; can learn.
Substage 2	1–4 months	Primary Circular Reactions	Actions centered on the body are repeated.
Substage 3	4–8 months	Secondary Circular Reactions	Infant repeats actions that have made some impact on the environment.
Substage 4	8–12 months	Coordination of Secondary Circular Reactions	Infant can coordinate two or more strategies to reach a goal.
Substage 5	12–18 months	Tertiary Circular Reactions	Actions are repeated, but each action is no longer an exact copy of the one that preceded it. Novelty is sought.
Substage 6	18–24 months	Invention of New Means Through Mental Combination	The beginning of representation. Can think about objects mentally. Semiotic function arises in which symbols, such as using a picture of a car to stand for a car, and signs, such as words (arbitrary representations) can be used. Shows deferred imitation, can see something, remember it, and imitate the action at a later time.

The infant shaking a rattle is showing secondary circular reactions.

infant's body rather than on any outside object. They are circular because they are repeated. The infant tries to re-create some interesting event. For example, the infant may have had a thumb slip into his or her mouth by accident. This is pleasurable, so after the thumb slips out, the infant attempts to find his or her mouth again (Bjorklund, 1995).

Secondary Circular Reactions (4–8 months): Substage 3   New behaviors called **secondary circular reactions** are now seen. Infants now focus their interest not on their bodies but on the consequences of some action on their external environment. This is why they are secondary rather than primary reactions. The infant does something that creates some environmental reaction; for instance, an infant shakes a rattle and is surprised to find that the rattle produces a sound. The child may pause, then shake the rattle again, hear the sound, and continue the activity (Flavell et al., 1993).

Coordination of Secondary Reactions (8–12 Months): Substage 4   In substage 4, the child coordinates two or more strategies to reach a goal. This shows intention. Means and ends are now separated. The child shows perseverance in spite of being blocked. For instance, if you place your hand in front of a toy, the child will brush your hand away. The child is using the brushing away behavior in order to use a reaching or grasping behavior (Piaget, 1952).

secondary circular reactions

Repetitive actions that are intended to create some environmental reaction.

Tertiary Circular Reactions (12–18 Months): Substage 5 Tertiary circular reactions emerge during substage 5. Although actions are still repeated and thus circular, they are no longer carbon copies of each other. Children now seek out novelty (Ault, 1977). They are little scientists, experimenting with the world to learn its characteristics and mysteries. The substage 5 child picks up objects from the crib and throws them out, listening and watching intently to learn what they sound like and how they look on the floor (Willemsen, 1979). When you put the objects back in the crib, the child may throw them out again. Everything must be done physically. If a child wants to know whether a tricycle will fit under the table, he or she must physically do it; the child cannot tell just by looking at it (Bjorklund, 1995).

Invention of New Means through Mental Combination (18–24 months): Substage 6 Substage 6 marks the beginning of **representation** (Flavell et al., 1993). Toddlers can think about objects without having to directly and physically act on them. To some extent, trial and error can be performed in the mind (Bjorklund, 1995). The substage 5 child physically uses trial and error experimentation, but the substage 6 child can try out alternatives mentally by imagining them (Flavell et al., 1993). The child can now think of an object independent of its physical existence. Previously, spoons were something to suck on, eat with, or bang. Now a spoon may stand for or represent another unrelated object, such as a person or a guitar. Children can also use some language, which also reflects their ability to represent. The infant has moved from the realm of coordinated actions to that of symbolic representation.

Mental representation is made possible by what Piaget called the **semiotic function,** more generally called the **symbolic function,** or the ability to use an object to stand for something else (Piaget, 1952, 1983). The word, gesture, or object that stands for something else is called a *signifier* and what it stands for, the *significate*. Some signifiers show a direct similarity to the object they represent—for example, the child uses a toy car to stand for a real one—while others, such as words, are nothing more than arbitrary labels that everyone understands (Miller, 1993). The ability to use symbols allows greater flexibility and creativity since the child can imagine that a napkin is a hat and play with it. Piaget believes that the ability to use representative thought makes language possible, but language is only one mode of expressing thought. Others, such as gestures, are also possible.

The character of play and imitation also changes during this last substage of the sensorimotor stage. Children are now capable of **deferred imitation;** that is, they can observe some act and later imitate it. Before going to bed, an 18-month-old may make pedaling motions with the feet, just as the child saw older siblings do while riding their bicycles hours before. This deferred imitation also generalizes to other situations so the child uses the observed behaviors in novel situations (Barnat, Klein, & Meltzoff, 1996). During the second year, toddlers show a significant increase in symbolic and pretend play, such as drinking from miniature teacups or talking into toy telephones (Belsky & Most, 1982; McCune, 1995).

Object Permanence

"Out of sight, out of mind" the saying goes. But for the very young infant, objects that are out of sight quite literally cease to exist. Infants must tortuously develop an understanding that objects exist outside their perception of them—an understanding known as **object permanence.** Researchers study the development of object permanence by hiding objects in a variety of ways and observing children's

Guideposts

What are the major behavioral changes at each substage of sensorimotor development?

tertiary circular reactions
Repetitive actions with some variations each time.

representation
The ability to go beyond physical actions and to use symbols to portray events and feelings mentally.

semiotic function (symbolic function)
the ability to use one thing to stand for another.

deferred imitation
The ability to observe an act and imitate it at a later time.

object permanence
The understanding that an object exists even when it is out of one's visual field.

search patterns. Infants develop their ability to understand object permanence in a series of substages (Piaget, 1954) (see Table 6.2).

In substage 1 (0–1 month), infants look at whatever is in their visual field but will not search for an item or individual that disappears. For instance, the infant looks at mother but doesn't search for her when she leaves the room (Ault, 1977). Instead, the infant looks at something else.

During substage 2 (1–4 months), the infant looking at some item will continue to look in the direction of the item after it disappears. A 2-month-old follows her mother, but when she leaves the visual field, the infant may continue to gaze at the point where mother was, not anticipating her reappearance at another place (Bjorklund, 1995). Piaget (1954) did not see this as true object permanence, because the search is basically passive.

During substage 3 (4–8 months), a more active search pattern emerges. Now if an object is partially covered by a handkerchief, the infant tries to lift the cloth to discover the rest of the object (Diamond, 1982). Children who drop something from a high chair look to the ground for it. It is as if they can now anticipate the movement of an item. The child at this stage does not show complete object permanence, however, for the search for the hidden object consists only of a continuation of eye movement—some expectation that something in motion may continue its trajectory. The child will not search for an object that is completely hidden from view.

In substage 4 (8–12 months), the child will now search for an item that is completely covered by a handkerchief. It is here that the child makes an error that has fascinated psychologists for years, called the *AB search error*. If the child is allowed to find the item in one place, and the item is then hidden elsewhere while the child watches, the child will still search in the first location (see Figure 6.1) (Wellman, Cross, & Bartsch, 1987). Once the infant finds the object at the new location, if the toy is again hidden at the original location, the infant will now make an error by reaching back to the location that was most recently correct (Diamond, Cruttenden, & Neiderman, 1994).

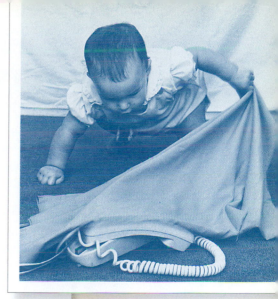

As infants develop, their search patterns become more sophisticated.

A 6-month-old infant will not search for an object that is completely covered by a blanket.

Guideposts

What are the major conceptual changes leading to object permanence?

Table 6.2		The Development of Object Permanence
Substage 1	0–1 month	Will not search for an object that leaves the visual field.
Substage 2	1–4 months	Will continue to look in the direction of where the object disappeared.
Substage 3	4–8 months	Will search for partially covered objects but not for objects that are fully covered. Can anticipate movement of an object.
Substage 4	8–12 months	Will search for a completely hidden object. Shows the AB search error. If a child is allowed to find an object hidden under cover A and the child witnesses the object hidden under cover B the child still searches in the first location.
Substage 5	12–18 months	The child no longer shows AB search error and can follow object through displacements. Object search is still based on visual information, and the child cannot form logical inferences that use mental representation.
Substage 6	18–24 months	Child does not need to have visual information as to location of object. Can imagine where object is located.

Figure 6.1 **The Stage 4 Search Task**

The experimenter hides the object in the first location (1), whereupon the infant searches successfully (2). But when the experimenter hides the object at the second location (3), the infant searches again at the original location (4).

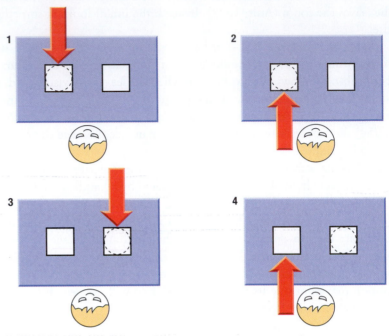

SOURCE: Bremner (1988)

According to Piaget, the child does not really have object permanence and has simply identified the object with a particular location (Diamond, 1982). Other psychologists disagree. Some suggest that the error results from memory limitations and the child's inability to inhibit what was earlier a successful response (Diamond et al., 1994). Others argue that the child's attention wanders back to position A, the original hiding place, and link this with specific brain mechanisms (Ahmed & Ruffman, 1998). Still other psychologists claim that the child actually knows where the object really is but perhaps cannot integrate knowledge and action (Baillargeon & Graber, 1988).

In substage 5 (12–18 months), children can follow the object through its displacements. They no longer search for an item under the first pillow if it is moved to a second one while they are watching (Piaget, 1954). The substage 5 child's understanding of object permanence is far from perfect, however. Piaget designed a simple test to demonstrate the child's limitations. His daughter had been playing with a potato and placing it in a box that had no cover. Piaget (1954) notes:

I then take the potato and put it in the box while Jacqueline watches. Then I place the box under the rug and turn it upside down thus leaving the object hidden by the rug without letting the child see my maneuver, and I bring out the empty box. I say to Jacqueline, who has not stopped looking at the rug and who has realized that I was doing something under it: "Give papa the potato." She searches for the object in the box, looks at me, again looks at the box minutely, looks at the rug, etc. but it does not occur to her to raise the rug in order to find the potato underneath. (p. 266)

Note that in this stage the movement from one hiding place to the other must be performed under the child's gaze. The child's search for a hidden object is still based on visual information. No logical inferences are formed, and there is no mental representation of the object.

During the last substage (18–24 months), children become free from the concrete information brought in through their senses. They can now construct a mental representation of the world and locate objects after a series of invisible displacements. They can imagine where an item might be (Diamond, 1982).

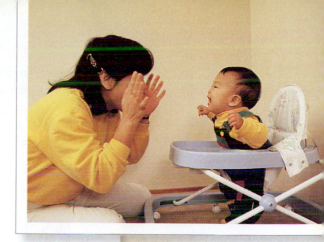

Playing peekaboo is an exciting activity for infants who are acquiring object permanence.

Object Permanence and Infant Behavior

Piaget's description of the infant's cognitive development explains some common infant behavior. For instance, a child in substage 5 of the sensorimotor period who is dropping toys out of the playpen despite pleas to stop is not doing this out of any malicious intent. The child is practicing tertiary circular reactions. Or take the example of the old game of peekaboo, in which you cover your face with your hands, then take your hands away. As a child gains more knowledge of object permanence, the child will pull down your hands, exposing your face. The child is validating the expectation that you are still there. Or perhaps a 4-month-old begins to cry hysterically after playing alone for a while. You notice that the baby has dropped a toy out of sight. Since young infants do not actively search for hidden objects, you may find that merely picking the toy up and placing it in the baby's field of vision is enough to stop the baby's crying.

Piaget's Theory under Scrutiny

Piaget's description of infant and toddler cognitive development is quite impressive, and studies conducted all over the world generally support Piaget's view of the sequence in which children develop these skills (Haith & Benson, 1998; Harris, 1989). Yet, important issues remain. Recent findings depart from Piaget's theory in two ways (Goubet & Clifton, 1998). First, young infants may know more about object permanence than Piaget thought. Second, Piaget emphasizes the importance of action as the main tool used by infants to gain knowledge, while recent research finds that infants know a great deal about objects well before they can reach for or manipulate objects. In addition, a fundamental error in logic may have crept into these studies. Just because infants do not successfully complete a particular task does not necessarily mean they can't do it. The child may have the ability to perform some task but may not be motivated to do so, or perhaps the infant simply cannot perform the physical movements necessary to search for and obtain an item in an object permanence experiment.

Whenever an infant cannot perform a particular task, Piaget interprets the inability in terms of competency; the child does not have the cognitive sophistication necessary. But some psychologists disagree, arguing that if the physical composition of the task were modified, perhaps the results would be different. For example, the type of cover used when hiding an object seems to make a difference. When plastic keys were hidden in a well and the keys were covered either by a 12-by-12 inch washcloth or a 7-by-7 inch piece of manila paper covered with blue felt, infants differed in their success with the task (Rader, Spiro, & Firestone, 1979). Some succeeded in uncovering the keys when the paper cover was used but not when the cloth cover was hiding them. The awkwardness of the covers used in an object permanence test may affect the test's outcome.

Piaget's object permanence tasks require youngsters to coordinate both knowledge and action (Mandler, 1998). The infant may understand object permanence but be unable to coordinate that knowledge with the action of crawling over and finding the object. When knowledge is separated from coordinated behavior, by using a child's attention and surprise as signs of understanding object permanence, some infants show an understanding of object permanence at a considerably earlier age than Piaget believed possible (Baillargeon et al., 1985; Mandler, 1998). Baillargeon and Graber (1988) showed 8-month-old infants an object that stood on one of two different placemats. Screens were pushed in front of the placemats, hiding the object from view. Next, a hand entered the apparatus through an opening in the right wall and "tiptoed" back and forth between the right wall and the right screen. After doing this for 15 seconds, the hand reached behind the right screen and came out with the object and shook it gently.

Sometimes at the beginning of the experiment, the object was located on the right placemat. When later in the trial the hand located the object behind the right placemat, this would not be surprising. The experimenters called this the "possible event." At other times, the object was initially located on the left placemat, so if the hand found the object behind the right placemat later, this would indeed be surprising. This was called the "impossible event" (see Figure 6.2).

The experimenters reasoned that if the infants remembered the object's location during the 15 seconds in which the hand tiptoed back and forth, they should be surprised at the impossible event (seeing the object retrieved from behind the right screen when they had last seen it occupying the left placemat). Since surprise

Figure 6.2 **Testing 8-Month-Olds' Location Memory in a Nonsearch AB Task**

In the possible event, the object is hidden behind the right screen and, after a delay, is taken from behind the right screen. In the impossible event, the object is hidden behind the left screen but later is taken away from behind the right screen. Will 8-month-olds pay more attention to the impossible event, therefore showing surprise and a knowledge of where the item should have been retrieved?

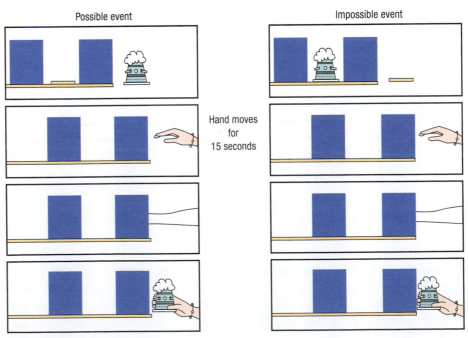

SOURCE: Baillargeon & Graber (1988)

usually shows itself by attention, infants should look longer at the impossible than the possible event. Indeed, infants did look much longer when the hand retrieved the object from behind the wrong screen (an impossible event) rather than from behind the correct screen where the object was actually hidden. This suggests that infants remembered the object's location during the entire 15 second delay, and their surprise was due to their knowing where the item should be. The researchers argue that there is a gap between what the infant knows about object permanence and the infant's ability to coordinate this knowledge with action.

Infants, then, may possess the notion of object permanence long before they can perform the coordinated movements necessary to show their knowledge on the standard Piagetian task (Johnson & Aslin, 1995). Some psychologists argue that infants as young as 2 to 4 months have some knowledge of object permanence (Johnson & Nanez, 1995; Slater et al., 1994). Most object permanence searches require the coordination of two distinct actions into a means-end sequence—for example, reaching for and removing a cover (the means) to grasp and play with a hidden toy (the end). The integration of separate schema into an intention-means-end sequence does not occur prior to substage 4 (about 8 months) according to Piaget, so Piaget may have been testing for object permanence using behaviors he believed infants were not yet capable of producing (Flavell et al., 1993). Piaget's supporters claim that studies that simplify Piaget's tasks are really not testing the same skill and offer alternative explanations for their findings (Rivera, Wakeley, & Langer, 1999). In addition, they argue that Piaget did understand that the nature of the tasks were important, but he considered his primary task to describe the general development of cognitive skills (Lourenco & Machado, 1996).

Similar problems arise when Piaget's concept of representation is studied (Mandler, 1998). Piaget argues that it is not until 18 months (substage 6) that representation is present, but studies of infants learning American Sign Language show that children as young as 6 to 7 months show clear symbolic signs (Meier & Newport, 1990). Piaget also argued that deferred imitation began in substage 6, but again, this belief is in doubt. When 9-month-old infants watched an adult model perform a series of actions, such as pushing a button on a box to produce a sound, and were not permitted to do so right after the demonstration but were presented with the materials a day later, they performed the action themselves at this later time (Meltzoff, 1988). Piaget considered the substages invariant, but it is now clear that these claims do not hold up well (Flavell et al., 1993).

Putting It All Together

Piaget's description of infant cognitive growth is an excellent starting point. At the same time, the evidence showing that other factors may affect performance should make us wary of making generalizations about what an infant or toddler can or cannot do. Infants follow Piaget's progression if tested in the standard Piagetian way. However, infants are very sensitive to the demands of the task. An analysis of what skills are necessary for success may provide information about why a child fails at a task. When a child must retrieve a hidden object, eye-hand coordination skills, motor skills, three-dimensional perception, and memory abilities are required. Piaget did not detail these skills. That task remained for others. Children who fail a particular task may lack any one (or more) of these skills or abilities. By looking more closely at the task, we begin to separate what the child knows from the specific methods Piaget used to test these abilities. It may well be that infants are more capable than Piaget believed they were.

Guideposts

What are the major criticisms of Piaget's concepts of infant cognitive development?

Information-Processing Skills

In earliest infancy, information-processing skills are tied directly to sensory and perceptual development. For instance, the development of the senses, such as the ability to focus, would affect the child's ability to process visual information. Even with perceptual limitations, infants do process information, although more slowly and certainly with more difficulty. One question, though, is whether infants have the ability to remember what they experience, and if they do, what is it that they remember?

Memory

Research on early memory focuses on recognition and recall. **Recognition** involves the ability to choose the correct response from a group of answers and is similar to the multiple-choice questions on a test. **Recall** involves producing the correct response on the basis of very limited cues and is similar to the task you face when taking an essay test. Recognition is excellent even in young infants. When three-month-old infants were presented with pictures of their mother, they were able to tell the difference between their mother's face and that of a stranger (Barrera & Maurer, 1981). Some researchers are impressed not only with infants' recognition ability but also with their retentive abilities. Five- and six-month-old infants who were familiarized with a face for only two minutes were able to recognize it after a delay of two weeks (Fagen, 1973). Neonates can retain memory for specific sounds over a 24-hour period (Swain, Zelazo, & Clifton, 1993). Recognition memory improves with age, with older infants showing superior retention on tests of recognition (Rose, 1981).

Infants are very sensitive to the conditions of the memory task. Three-month-old infants can be conditioned to kick in order to move a mobile and respond at a high rate if they are tested after a 24-hour delay on the same mobile. However, they do not respond if they are tested with a different mobile. They remember the details of their training mobile and discriminate between the situations (Bhatt & Rovee-Collier, 1994, 1996). Infants are even sensitive to reminders. Infants between 2 and 6 months old were conditioned to kick their foot to activate a mobile suspended over their crib. They were then made to wait for varying periods of time before being allowed to operate the mobile (Hayne & Rovee-Collier, 1995). Older children tolerated longer delays, but even after these time periods, if infants were offered a reminder by having the experimenter move the mobile around, infants showed retention for longer intervals (Hayne, 1990). However, if the mobile was just placed over the child, or the child saw only the stand or ribbon (which had been attached to the foot and the stand), no memory improvement took place. Reminders are only effective when infants encounter stimuli that are virtually identical to those present when the original learning occurred. These research studies also indicate that infants are capable of secondary circular reactions months earlier than Piaget suggested (Schneider & Bjorklund, 1998).

Studies of recall are not as plentiful as research on recognition. Piaget (1968) argued that children do not show true recall before one and a half to two years of age, but today many psychologists believe that recall probably begins somewhere in the first year (Mandler, 1990). Eight-month-old-infants were first trained to touch a lighted face by being reinforced by a number of pleasant sights and sounds (Brody, 1981). After the infants had learned to touch the light for a reward they were presented with a delay. After the face was lighted, the light was turned off, and a screen covered the face for 250 milliseconds. The screen was then lifted, and

Guideposts

How do infants show their ability to recall and recognize?

recognition

A way of testing retention in which the subject is required to choose the correct answer from a group of choices.

recall

A way of testing retention in which the subject must produce the correct responses given very limited cues.

the infants were reinforced for touching the face that had been illuminated before the lowering of the screen. After the infants had learned this response, the researcher varied the amount of time in which the screen covered the face by 3, 6, and 9 seconds. The 8-month-old and 12-month-old infants could remember the location of the stimulus during the 250-millisecond delay, but only the 12-month-old infants could tolerate the longer delays.

The period between 8 and 12 months of age is one of rapid change in the infants' cognitive abilities. Neurological changes that improve memory occur (Kagan, 1979a, 1979b). The infant develops an ability to spontaneously retrieve older information and apply it to current circumstances.

Memories from Infancy and Toddlerhood

If infants and toddlers can learn and remember, why is it that older children and adults can remember almost nothing from this period? Most adults rarely recall events that transpired before 3 or 4 years (Rovee-Collier & Boller, 1995), although some people can recall an occasional important incident that occurred from the age of 2 years (Peterson & Rideout, 1994). There are many possible explanations for this phenomenon called **infant amnesia.**

Most of an infant's day is spent in activities that are hardly memorable, so the lack of memories would be expected. In addition, retrieval occurs only when infants encounter stimuli that are virtually identical to those present during the original encoding situation. Any changes in perception, attention, or selection of which stimulus to look at makes it less likely the individual would remember anything, especially after very long intervals. This need for specific cues to retrieve these memories makes it difficult, if not impossible, for useful memories to be retrieved in present-day contexts. Furthermore, infant memories may be progressively updated and modified to reflect new circumstances and needs to such an extent that these early memories may no longer exist in their original form (Rovee-Collier & Boller, 1995). When memories are no longer useful—that is, they no longer guide current behavior—they may be permanently lost. What the young infant needs to know may not be useful later during childhood when verbal and motor skills are better, so these older, less useful memories are no longer adaptive and therefore forgotten.

Many psychologists, though, link childhood amnesia to linguistic difficulties. Infants do not understand language, and any memories are encoded perceptually by involving sights, sounds, and tactile sensations. Later, our memories are often linguistically linked. We do not know what happens to memories that were originally encoded without language, especially after an individual develops language. A retrieval failure might occur when linguistically capable individuals try to find memories that are primarily perceptually based (Hayne & Rovee-Collier, 1995). The importance of linguistic ability was shown in a study of the long-term verbal recall for a medical emergency (mostly broken bones or stitches). When the emergency occurred when children were 2 years or older and had some verbal skills, they could recall the experience a full two years later (Peterson & Rideout, 1998). If it occurred at a younger age, or if the 2-year-old did not have the ability to talk about the injury at the time it happened, the memory was either nonexistent or very limited. The ability to verbally narrate the experience was a key to memory. It is about the age of 2 when children begin to make limited references to the past, whereas before the age of 18 months they make few if any references (Veneziano & Sinclair, 1995).

This infant will probably not remember anything of his/her experience. The question of why we remember almost nothing before the age of about 2 has been answered in many ways.

Most adults can remember events that occured between 6 months and 1 year of age if they are reminded of them.

For Your Consideration

What are your first memories? Is there anything that makes these incidents special?

infant amnesia
The inability of adults to recall events that occur during infancy and toddlerhood.

Finally, certain brain structures, particularly in the limbic system, that are critical to the formation of memories are not fully formed until the fourth and fifth year of life, explaining the poor early memory and the improvement in memory during early childhood (Kandel, Schwartz, & Jessell, 1995).

Predicting Later Intelligence

By this time, you are probably willing to accept the fact that infants show intelligent behavior and are impressed by the rapid development of their cognitive abilities. But do these early infant abilities predict later cognitive abilities?

There is no single definition of intelligence, although most involve the ability to think, solve problems, learn, remember, and adapt to the environment (Snow, 1998). The difficulties surrounding the concept of intelligence will be explored in Chapter 10, when intelligence tests that are used with older children are discussed.

It is fair to ask why anyone would want to measure the intelligence of infants. First, this could lead to early detection of intellectual difficulties, allowing timely intervention. Second, it may help psychologists better understand the changes in intellectual functioning that occur between infancy and adulthood (Snow, 1998).

Intelligence tests meant for infants differ from those constructed for older children who are verbal. Infant intelligence tests measure mostly sensorimotor skills, and these are not the same skills that standardized intelligence tests measure later in childhood. One such test is the Uzgiris-Hunt Ordinal Scales of Psychological Development, which are based on Piaget's description of cognitive development during infancy, and measure such tasks as object permanence and understanding causality (Uzgiris & Hunt, 1975, 1987). For example, the observer presents the infant with a certain task, such as following a slowly moving object through a 180-degree arc, and notes the infant's reaction.

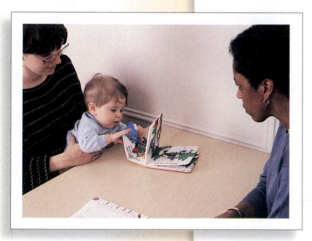

The Bayley Scales of Infant Development is the most commonly used measurement of infant intelligence.

The most commonly used evaluation instrument for measuring the intellectual abilities of infants and toddlers is the Bayley Scales of Infant Development (Bayley, 1969; Psychological Corporation, 1993). The Bayley Scales evaluate perceptual abilities, the response to various stimuli, memory, the beginnings of verbal communication, problem solving, motor abilities, persistence, and emotional and social behavior. Although these scales produce a valid description of the child's present development, the scores do not have predictive power with normal infants until about 18 months (Francis, Self, & Horowitz, 1987). Perhaps this is because the Bayley Scales largely measure sensorimotor abilities, whereas intelligence in older children depends largely on verbal abilities and learning.

If this is true, psychologists would need to measure basic information-processing abilities that underlie future intelligence if they wish to predict IQ. Indeed, some information-processing skills do predict later cognitive ability (DiLalla et al., 1990; Dougherty & Haith, 1997). Infants who habituate more quickly develop better cognitive skills, including later measures of Piagetian abilities and speaking vocabularies (Ruddy & Bornstein, 1982; Schneider & Bjorklund, 1998). Another skill, visual recognition memory at 6 months, predicts scores on tests of cognitive skills from 2 to 6 years in preterm infants (Rose & Wallace, 1985). Two particular information-processing skills, memory and processing speed, seem to underlie all

Guideposts

How can psychologists predict later intelligence from infant abilities?

Infants' processing speed and memory abilities predict later cognitive abilities in early childhood.

these abilities and predict intelligence later in life (Rose & Feldman, 1996, 1997).

Other authorities are impressed with social variables that may predict later intelligence. The child's socioeconomic status in the first 12 to 18 months appears to be a good predictor of later intellectual development (McCall, Hogarty, & Hurlbutt, 1972). Socioeconomic status is usually analyzed in terms of income, parental education, and occupational rating. Low-socioeconomic homes differ greatly from middle- and higher-socioeconomic homes, especially in the area of verbal behavior (Lawrence & Shipley, 1996). Perhaps lack of formal education or the stresses of poverty may prevent these parents from providing the verbal stimulation or the environment necessary for their children to develop adequate cognitive skills.

Yet, there is something unsatisfactory about the entire concept of socioeconomic status. It is far too broad and too general a consideration, and it ignores the wide variations that exist in intelligence within socioeconomic levels. General statements about the low-socioeconomic-status parent ignore these differences and stigmatize an entire group of people. A more specific approach stressing behaviors and specific environmental variables rather than social class may be more helpful in uncovering clues to intellectual development. Indeed, much convincing research demonstrates an important relationship between children's home environment and their health and cognitive development (Bradley et al., 1994; Molfese, DiLalla, & Lovelace, 1996).

One instrument frequently used to measure the quality and quantity of the emotional and cognitive elements of the home environment is called the Home Observation for Measurement of the Environment, or HOME scale (Elardo, Bradley, & Caldwell, 1977). Table 6.3 shows some selected items from the parental responsivity subscales of each of the HOME inventories.

A substantial relationship exists between the home environment in the first year and intelligence at age 3 (Bradley & Caldwell, 1980); between HOME scores at 2, 3, and 4 years and later intelligence (Bradley, 1989), and between HOME scores and achievement test scores and classroom behavior during middle childhood (Bradley, Caldwell, & Rock, 1988). Research indicates that such factors as the responsivity of the caregiver, parental involvement with the child, the variety of stimulation available, the organization of the environment, the caregiver's restrictiveness, and the play materials available at an early age predict later cognitive development.

Can you predict the child's later intelligence from his or her socioeconomic status? Although studies find some predictive ability, there are many problems with using socioeconomic status to predict later intelligence.

Guideposts

What elements of the home are most important in optimizing young children's cognitive abilities?

Table 6.3	Selected Items from Parental Responsivity Subscales of the HOME Inventory

Infant/Toddler Version

Parent responds to child's vocalization with a verbal response.
Parent caresses or kisses child at least once during visit.

Early Childhood Version

Parent holds child close 10 to 15 minutes per day.
Parent spontaneously praises child's qualities or behavior twice during visit.

Middle Childhood Version

Parent sometimes yields to child's fears and rituals (for example, allows night light, accompanies child to new experiences).
Parent responds to child's questions during interview.

SOURCE: Bradley (1989)

Guideposts

What are the qualities of the most competent parents, according to Burton White?

One point should be kept in mind, though. A healthy environment in infancy is usually carried over through childhood. An unhealthy environment in infancy rarely improves greatly in childhood. Some of the relationship between the environment during infancy and later intellectual ability is a reflection of the cumulative effects of the environment throughout childhood and does not solely demonstrate the importance of the earliest environment. Also, some areas of the home environment probably will be more important at different times than other areas.

Parents and Cognitive Development

Most factors that influence cognitive development are determined by the child's parents. Burton White (1971) studied the differences between mothers of competent infants and mothers of less competent infants and found three major differences. The mothers of competent children were designers—that is, they constructed an environment in which children were surrounded with interesting objects to see and explore. They were able to understand the meaning that an activity or experience might have for a child and build on it. Second, parents of competent children interacted frequently with their children in interplays of 20- to 30-second duration. The children were not smothered with attention, but the parents were always available and ready to help their children experience events. They often labeled the environment for the child and helped share the child's excitement. Third, the parents of these children were not overly permissive or overly punishing. They had firm limits, but they were not very concerned about such minor things as mess and bother.

Parents can create an environment conducive for learning by providing opportunities for exploration, labeling the environment, providing encouragement for communication, and reading to the child. The interactions need not be long and should take into account the child's attention span. Such activities should be low-key and fun. A problem arises when a child's parents believe they are conducting an academic activity and put pressure on their children to achieve too early (Zinsser, 1981). Parental disappointment, anxieties, and expectations can be communicated to young children quite early and may hinder the very development that parents seek to improve. Infants and toddlers have limited attention spans and may go from activity to activity quickly.

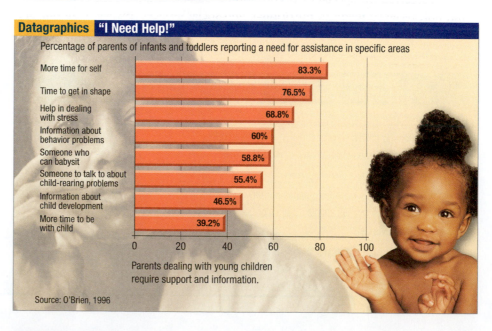

Datagraphics "I Need Help!"

Percentage of parents of infants and toddlers reporting a need for assistance in specific areas

More time for self	83.3%
Time to get in shape	76.5%
Help in dealing with stress	68.8%
Information about behavior problems	60%
Someone who can babysit	58.8%
Someone to talk to about child-rearing problems	55.4%
Information about child development	46.5%
More time to be with child	39.2%

Parents dealing with young children require support and information.

Source: O'Brien, 1996

How Much Is Too Much?

In the past decade, the importance of cognitive stimulation in infancy has been increasingly noted by authorities in the field. One night Lauren and Peter, who are expecting their first child very soon, were invited to Lester and Judy's home for the evening. Lester and Judy have a baby boy, William; naturally, the conversation turned to child behavior and child rearing.

Lester and Judy believe that early intelligence predicts later academic success. "Children need a head start from their parents," they argue. They are determined to work with William as he matures and to help him maximize his cognitive abilities. They both give William plenty of attention, have three mobiles over the crib, and have written the name of each item in the house on strips of paper that are pasted on each piece of furniture. They surround the child with plenty of pictures and are very involved in two exercise and cognitive growth programs. They tell their friends that to do anything less is to reduce William's chances of becoming a top student.

Lauren and Peter were impressed by the way their friends had structured the baby's environment, but they wonder whether the environment is too structured, too stimulating, and too confusing for their infant. They must decide just what course to chart for their own new baby.

If you were Lauren or Peter, what course would you choose?

ACTION / REACTION

Programs to Help At-Risk Infants and Toddlers Develop

If early parent-child relations and the environment of infants and toddlers are important, then helping parents and children during these early years might have lasting benefits. A number of programs seek to improve parenting skills (see *Teaching Parents to Parent* on page 213), and some directly target infants and toddlers at risk, providing them with early educational experiences. Still other programs combine parent education with special experiences for the young child. The Abecedarian Project, for example, tested whether mental retardation influenced by inadequate home environments could be prevented through intensive early programs together with medical and nutritional support (Ramey & Ramey, 1992). The program began between 6 and 12 weeks after birth. Both the treatment group, which received the special early education program, and the control group, which did not, received medical, nutritional, and social services. By age 3, all but one of the children in the control group who had mothers with intelligence scores below 70 scored in the range of mild mental retardation (less than 70) or borderline range (70 to 85). Every child in the early intervention group who received the intensive help 5 days a week, 50 weeks per year, scored in the average range at age 3. At 6, the intelligence scores of the early intervention group children ranged from 7.9 to 20.1 points higher than the control group children (Martin, Ramey, & Ramey, 1990). A follow-up of the program found that the intellectual gains persisted through 7 years of school (Campbell & Ramey, 1994).

Another project, Project CARE, sought to change parental attitudes and the home environment. In addition to the day care experience, a family support component was added (Wasik, Ramey, Bryant, & Sparling, 1990). Families whose children were judged to be at risk for delayed development due to social and educational factors participated in the study over an 18-month period. One group received both an educational day care–based program and family education, the second group got just family education, and the third did not receive either service although nutrition, medical care, and social services were available to every family in the study.

The day care program included activities aimed at enriching the child's intellectual and emotional abilities, especially language usage. Family education was designed to foster cognitive and social development through a series of weekly home visits in which the trained visitors discussed goals of parenting and problem solving strategies in rearing children. They discussed identifying problems, generating different ways of dealing with them, and making decisions. Home visitors also demonstrated techniques and discussed day care activities with the parents.

The results showed improved development and intelligence scores for the education plus family group, but the home base program alone was not sufficient to raise IQ scores, probably because it was not intensive enough to change parental attitudes (Ramey & Ramey, 1992). Apparently, a combination of professionally directed preschool experience and family education can be successful, but an intensive program is required to bring about sufficient change in the home environment of these at-risk children. A long-term evaluation of children who participated in both programs found that these children gained directly from these programs and indirectly because they positively influenced the family environment (Burchinal, Campbell, Bryant, Wasik, & Raney, 1997).

The Question of Acceleration: The "American Question"

The suggestions made for helping children develop their abilities emphasize doing so at the children's pace. There is no hint of accelerating infants cognitively to make them learn faster. This desire to accelerate is perhaps part of our culture. American educators and parents are often interested in the question of how fast or how early a child can accomplish some academic task. We are impressed with the child who is reading at the age of 4 or solving algebraic equations at 8. Reflecting this fascination with speed, researchers have raised the question of whether infants can be accelerated through the period of sensorimotor experience.

It is tempting to see the cognitive abilities of young children as basically nothing more than the immaturity of an inefficiently functioning organism. However, an alternative view suggests that the immaturity in many areas of developmental concern have specific purposes (Bjorklund & Green, 1992). For example, limited motor capabilities prevent young children from wandering from the mother, enhancing survivability. Limitations in information processing, sensory abilities, and perception reduce the amount of information the child has, thereby allowing the child to construct a more simplified and understandable view of the world. The way infants process material and their limited abilities, then, may be adaptive. If this is true, infants' cognitive abilities are not just immature cognitive processes but rather have definite functional uses. It would then be folly to rush children through them.

Piaget was reluctant to make any recommendations to teachers or parents concerning how to maximize a child's potential, let alone how to accelerate the child (Vernon, 1976). In the spirit of Piaget's theory, parents may help their children by designing an environment that is appropriate for the children at their particular point in development and elaborating on that environment, giving children plenty of opportunity to discover things on their own. For instance, when presenting children with objects of different textures, it is beneficial to have a variety of such objects in the environment and to allow the children to explore them at their own pace. This does not mean that the parents remain passive. Indeed, parents should be available, answer questions, interact with the child, and so on, but the emphasis is on discovery, not formal teaching and programming.

The Child in the 21st Century

Teaching Parents to Parent

Parents make important decisions every day. What should be done when a baby cries? What toys should a toddler have? How should the temper tantrums of a toddler be handled? These and hundreds more questions and challenges arise during the normal course of a day. Research demonstrates that the structure of the home and the early parent-child interaction are important for optimizing development. Child psychologists have the answers to some of the questions that parents most often ask, and can offer suggestions and techniques that can maximize the young child's development as well as reduce tension in the home.

Unfortunately, in the absence of any education about parenting practices, parents tend to continue to act on incorrect assumptions, such as a belief that young infants can't do anything, or hold expectations that are unreasonable for toddlers, such as expecting an unrealistically long attention span. Many parents do not understand what their young children are capable of doing. In one study, 61% of a sample of mothers did not expect newborns to see, and other studies reported estimates for the emergence of basic perceptual capacities involved in vision and hearing at weeks or even months beyond the correct time (Crouchman, 1985). After infancy, people tend to show the opposite pattern and overestimate what their children are capable of doing on memory tests and attainment of Piagetian skills (Miller, 1988). There is no doubt that parents

need more accurate information about their children's abilities. Although all parents could use a dose of information about child rearing, psychologists find that some groups are more at risk—for example, infants who are born premature or to very young parents or parents who are under a great deal of stress (Owen & Mulvihill, 1994).

Parent education programs can help parents by providing information, helping them learn new skills, changing parental attitudes, and providing important support for their child-rearing activities, thereby building confidence in the parents. An assumption underlying such programs is that the more skilled, knowledgeable, and supported parents are the better able they are to foster their child's development. Much research shows this to be true (Brems, Baldwin, & Baxter, 1993; Thomas, 1996). These programs help parents become more sensitive and responsive to their young children.

Parent education programs differ widely. Some involve simply giving information. Others require the active involvement of parents in the program. Still others offer services to both parents and the children. Those that require active participation are more successful than those that do not, and those that offer services to both parents and children tend to be the most successful. When teenage mothers (16 years old and younger) were given weekly classes covering such areas as ways to stimulate their infants, nutrition and family planning, and were offered a number of supportive services, significant improvements were found both in the mothers and in the infants (Badger, Burns, & Vietze, 1981). The infants showed higher

scores on the Bayley tests than a control group, and the mothers were more physically and emotionally responsive to their infants. One three-year program, called New Parents as Teachers (NPAT), tried to assess the value of high-quality parent education on the skills new parents need to optimize their children's development during the first three years of life (Pfannenstiel & Seltzer, 1989). The program consisted of providing parents with information on child growth and development, periodic developmental and health screenings, monthly home visits by parent educators, and group meetings at neighborhood resource centers. When compared with a control group, children whose parents were in the program scored significantly better on measures of intelligence, auditory comprehension, and language ability. Parents who participated were significantly more knowledgeable. One interesting finding was that the higher the quality of the parental participation and the more active the parent was in the program, the better their children performed. The high-quality parent involvement with the parent educator was the main reason for this program's effectiveness.

Some of the most recent programs take a more ecological perspective in keeping with Urie Bronfenbrenner's work (see pages 67–69). These programs view child-rearing behaviors as part of the overall social and economic situation, and offer a much broader range of services (McLoyd, 1998). They provide support services, help in gaining educational, health and social services, mental health services, job training, day care services, along with parenting education. The change in outlook is based on studies showing that parenting behaviors are affected by stress and the situation in which the family finds itself. For example, studies of fathers who lost their jobs during the Great Depression of the 1930s and whose economic situation had deteriorated and was often desperate, found that fathers became irritable, tense, and angry and that they were more likely to be arbitrary and punitive in their discipline. These parenting practices led to negativity and a host of poor behaviors in their children (Elder, Liker, & Cross, 1984). In the same way, parenting skills are adversely affected when families are under a great deal of daily stress (McLoyd, 1998). Mothers from diverse socioeconomic backgrounds who report high psychological distress exhibit fewer positive behaviors such as hugs, praise, and support and show more negative behaviors such as criticism, threats and slaps (Conger, McCarty, Yang, Lahey, & Kropp, 1984). Emotional problems such as depression lead to undesirable parenting consequences such as punitiveness, inconsistency, and unresponsiveness. When families receive social and emotional support, their parenting behaviors improve significantly as they become more sensitive, accessible, and responsive to their children (Crockenberg, 1987).

Some programs that combine services to children and to parents are called *two-generation programs.* Parenting education and social support are provided along with an array of services including day care, job and literacy training, and transportation so parents can participate (Smith, 1995). For example, the Comprehensive Child Development Program offers prenatal care, parenting education, health care, adult education, job training, and other supports, such as treatment for mental health problems and substance abuse. Literacy education, counseling, and job placement are also offered. Services are provided for the first 3 years along with home visits that focus on parenting skills (St. Pierre, Layzer, & Barnes, 1995). All members of the family receive services. Parenting attitudes and behaviors improved. Parents had more confidence and interacted in a more positive and stimulating manner with their children (Walker et al., 1995). They were less authoritarian, had higher expectations for the children's success, and spent more time with their children (St. Pierre et al., 1995).

Parents can benefit greatly from such programs if they are geared to the needs of the family. As both parents being employed is the norm, single parenthood is common, and many parents must deal with the stresses of poverty, different programs may be needed to serve particular groups. Of equal importance is the likelihood that parent education programs will be aimed at both mothers and fathers.

What does this mean for the child born in the 21st century? When parenting skills are improved, the infant becomes more responsive, and cognitive development is optimized. But these programs must also deal with the underlying stressors in the family and perhaps the poverty and powerlessness that many parents feel. There are possible implications for the field of developmental psychology as well. Just as early childhood day care is now considered a specialty, there will be a call for more people to be parenting educators. These educators not only will be involved in teaching parents and making home visits but also will have to develop skills that will allow them to encourage fearful parents to participate in such programs.

What do you think?

How would you answer a person who argues that people were parenting reasonably well years ago, and who sees no reason the government or even private agencies should get involved in training parents today?

You can explore the questions above using InfoTrac College Edition. Hint: enter search terms *Parenting* and *Parenting Styles.*

For Your Consideration ?

Following Piaget's ideas, how would parents encourage their children's cognitive development?

The purpose of improving interaction between parents and children and of designing a stimulating atmosphere for infants is to provide the best environment for children to develop their cognitive potential. The goal should be to provide a child-centered environment that will help the child develop according to his or her own abilities.

A number of programs emphasize adult-directed activities that promise to teach infants to read early, identify artists, and so on. Most of these programs are not based on sound research. Adults dictate how and when learning takes place. In White's (1993) research on development, children during the first 18 months who were considered superior in development chose most of their activities, except, of course, for maintenance activities such as feeding and bathing. The best course is to design stimulating environments for children and to interact with children so they gain the appropriate skills. Rushing a child through these growth stages accomplishes little. Accelerated development is not necessarily any better.

The Development of Language

Cognitive development and linguistic progress are intimately connected. Piaget linked them through the semiotic process, while information-processing specialists are fascinated by studies linking changes in attention, memory, and problem solving to language learning. As we will see, cognitive and linguistic growth are linked in a complicated manner, and each affects the other.

The Nature of Communication

Language and communication are not the same. Language is only one part of communication. **Communication** is the process of sharing information, including facts, desires, and feelings. It entails a sender, a receiver, and a message. **Language** involves arbitrary symbols with agreed-on meanings (Shatz, 1983). Most of the time it is verbal, but it need not be. American Sign Language (ASL), for instance, is a nonverbal language used by people with severe hearing impairments in the United States. It is a recognized language with a grammar of its own, even though it is not verbal.

The Nature of Language

Just what do children learn when they acquire language? Language has a number of subsystems, including phonology, morphology, syntax, and semantics, as well as rules for social language use, sometimes called pragmatics (see Figure 6.3).

Figure 6.3	Subsystems of Language

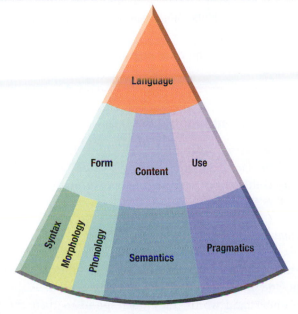

SOURCE: Owens (1992)

5

Parents of the most advanced infants and toddlers tend to choose all the child's activities for them, programming the day so that the child is always busy learning something new.

communication
The process of sharing information.

language
The use of symbols to represent meaning in some medium.

Not all communication is verbal. Pointing is an early but effective means of communication. By the end of the first year, children are calling attention to interesting objects and activities by pointing at them.

Guideposts

Describe the five subsystems of language.

phonology

The study of the sounds of language, the rules for combining the sounds to make words, and the stress and intonation patterns of the language.

morpheme

The smallest unit of meaning in a language.

morphology

The study of the patterns of word formation in a particular language.

syntax

The rules for combining words to make sentences.

semantics

The study of the meaning of words.

pragmatics

The study of how people use language in various contexts.

grammar

A general term that refers to the total linguistic knowledge of phonology, morphology, syntax, and semantics.

Phonology includes the sounds of a language, the rules for combining the sounds to make words, and the stress and intonation patterns of the language (Bloom, 1998). For example, the sound "cl," but not the sound "kx," occurs in English. Children must learn how these sounds combine to become words.

Morphology is the study of the patterns of word formation in a particular language. A **morpheme** is the smallest unit of meaning in a language. Some morphemes, such as *dog* and *little*, can stand by themselves, while others, such as *-ed* and *-ing*, must be added to another word. The rules of **morphology** make certain that some sequences, such as *walked*, will occur and that others, such as *walkness*, will not. Every language also has its own rules for combining words to make sentences, called **syntax.** For instance, "John hit Mary" conveys a meaning quite different from "Mary hit John."

Children must acquire a vocabulary and understand the meanings behind words. This area is called **semantics** (Carroll, 1994). Children must also be able to use language appropriately to express their ideas efficiently. This is called **pragmatics.** For example, children must learn the proper way to ask for something, how to greet others, how to apologize, as well as how to use language in a variety of social situations (Becker, 1988). Each language has its own rules, and each culture has its own idea of how language should be used. The general term **grammar** is used to refer to the total of the rules or principles that describe the structure of a particular language.

How Children Develop Language

Few events bring parents as much joy as their child's first word. It is easy to forget that much has taken place before the child says "dada" or "car." Under normal circumstances, every child in every culture proceeds through similar steps in reaching linguistic competence.

Prelanguage Communication   Communication between infants and their caregivers does not require language (Yale, et al., 1999). Smiles, cries, gestures, and eye contact all form a basis for later communication. The nonlanguage interaction between parent and infant approximates a conversation. Although very young infants cannot understand words, they do respond to their caregiver's language

(Fernald & Simon, 1984), and some linguistic abilities are present almost from birth. One-day-old infants respond to speech sounds by moving their bodies in rhythm to them (Condon & Sander, 1974). One-month-old infants are able to discriminate between certain vowels, such as "i-u" from "u-a" and "pa" from "pi" (Trehub, 1973). Neonates show some ability to discriminate vocalizations in their mothers' native language from those in another language (Mehler et al., 1988).

The infant's ability to respond to language and other nonverbal cues leads to a kind of turn taking called *protoconversations* (Bateson, 1975). A parent speaks, and the baby responds by smiling or, later, **cooing.** The parent then says something else, and the pattern continues. The interactions are spontaneous. Let's say a mother is playing with her baby. When the infant lets go of a toy, the mother says, "No, I don't want that any more. I want the ball." These interactions are the beginning of conversation mode and are the basis for later communication. Such conversations are not as random as they seem. Mothers use a rising pitch when their infants are not paying attention and the mothers want them to make eye contact (Stern, Spieker, & MacKain, 1982). In addition, yes-no questions are spoken with a rising pitch, whereas questions having to do with what and where as well as various commands are accompanied by a falling pitch.

The infant is also the master of another ability, cooing. Cooing involves production of single-syllable sounds, such as "oo." Vowel sounds are often led by a consonant, resulting in a sound like "moo." Infants enjoy listening to themselves vocalize, but these early noncrying vocalizations are not meant to be formal communication.

The next step in language development is **babbling,** which involves both vowel and consonant sounds strung together and often repeated. Babbling may begin as early as 3 months and gradually increases until about 9 to 12 months of age, after which it decreases as the child begins to use words (deVilliers & deVilliers, 1978). Most infants are babbling by the age of 6 months (Silverman, 1995). No one has been able to decipher the meaning of any of the babbles of infants. Although babbling begins as a relatively uncoordinated activity, social stimulation affects the amount of babbling children produce (Hedge, 1995).

Many of the important prerequisites for understanding language are shown at this point. Infants begin to pay attention to more frequently used words. Four-and-a-half-month-old infants show a preference for listening to their own names over other names that are matched or not matched for sound stress patterns (Mandel, Juscyk, & Pisoni, 1995). For example, if the child's name is Joshua, the child shows a preference for the name over Agatha (same stress) or Maria (different stress). Children have the ability to recognize and respond to frequently occurring sound patterns, which is a prerequisite for later relating sounds to meanings.

By 7.5 months, infants show some capacity for detecting the sound patterns of words in fluent speech (Jusczyk & Aslin, 1995) and begin to appreciate the nature of their own language. For example, in English most words have a stress on the first syllable. Nine-month-old American infants listen significantly longer to words with a strong/weak stress than with a weak/strong stress (Jusczyk, Cutler, & Redanz, 1993). This preference is not found in 6-month-olds. Pauses between phrases and sentences, and changes in pitch give infants cues to organize speech in memory, preparing the way for later linguistic mastery (Fisher & Tokura, 1996). Infants are also sensitive to repetitions. When 8-month-old infants listened to a computerized voice speak unbroken strings of nonsense syllables for only two minutes, the infants were able to recognize three-syllable sequences that were repeated as they paid more attention to them (Saffran, Aslin, & Newport, 1996). Being able to pick out words from rapidly spoken sentences or to pay attention to the stress

Parents can often correctly interpret the meaning of their infant's babbling.

cooing
Verbal production of single-syllable sounds, such as "oo."

babbling
Verbal production of vowel and consonant sounds strung together and often repeated.

patterns of words, and being able to pick out recurrent sounds shows the beginning of an understanding of the nature of words, a prerequisite for the later understanding of language.

The First Word Children's earliest recognizable language is in the form of single words. Children usually utter their first word any time between 10 and 15 months, but there is considerable individual variation. The development of the first 10 or so words is relatively slow, taking place from the later part of the first year gradually through the next few months (Durkin, 1995). Children's first words are related to those that they have heard frequently used by their parents (Hart, 1991). After they begin using language, the relationship between the frequency of parental use of particular words and children's utterances is much less (Barrett, Harris, & Chasin, 1991). The most common words, at least in one study, were *mom, dad, baby, kitty, duck, sock, good, see,* and *stop* (Hart, 1991).

Early word acquisition is a function of the general symbolic ability, and infants will learn words and other symbolic forms with equal ease at the onset of word acquisition (Namy & Waxman, 1998). Over 85% of all infants 11 to 24 months use symbolic gestures as well as words to label requests and express an intention (Acredolo & Goodwyn, 1985, 1988). For example, after seeing her mother repeatedly perform spider-crawling movements when singing "itsy-bitsy-spider," one infant began to perform a similar spider-crawling gesture not only during the song but also to refer to spiders in both pictures and the home. As Piaget would predict, gestures and words are used as mental representations of the object. Children produce their first symbolic gestures at about the same time or even a bit earlier than they produce words (Goodwyn & Acredolo, 1993).

The use of gestures, though, declines as the child develops more sophisticated verbal abilities. Sixteen-month-olds use both words and symbolic gestures to name objects, but by 20 months, their use of gestures lessens and learning new words takes on prominence over learning new symbolic gestures (Iverson, Capirci, & Caselli, 1994). Perhaps a common symbolic process underlies both word acquisition and the development of other symbolic forms of communication, such as gestures. This hypothesis is consistent with developmental studies of deaf infants learning a gestural language such as ASL, who learn it with a facility that is equal to children learning spoken languages (Petitto, 1988). The hearing infant switches to a verbal language as it is the most prominent form of communication in its environment, but it is clear that, at least at the outset of word acquisition, the infant's

---

ACTION / REACTION

"Why Isn't My Child Talking?"

Maya and Jack are very attentive parents of an 11-month-old son, Alexander, who is not babbling very much. He began babbling at about 4 or 5 months but doesn't do much vocalizing. Maya tried not giving him toys until he verbalized, and Jack is labeling everything in sight, but still the child does not seem to be verbalizing very much.

A neighbor's child seems to be much more advanced. At 10 months this child said his first word and seems to be progressing faster and easier than their child. Although Alexander seems healthy, his parents are concerned with his lack of progress in speech and language. They feel that with their prompting and supportive environment the child should be showing better developmental progress.

1. *If they asked you for your honest opinion, what would you tell them?*
2. *What precautionary acts can they take if they are so concerned?*

ACTION / REACTION

symbolic capacities are flexible enough to accommodate both words and gestures, and they can learn both quite easily.

Nelson (1973) studied early word acquisition in a number of children and was able to divide the children into two categories. **Expressive children** used words that were involved primarily in social interactions, such as "bye-bye" and "stop." The early language of **referential children** involved the naming of objects with such words as *dog* and *penny.* These differing styles followed the linguistic style used by the children's caregivers. The parents of referential children named objects very frequently, while those of expressive children directed their children's activities and emphasized social interactions. The early language of both groups differed. Referential children used many more different words. Expressive children began to use language in a social context, while referential children used it in a cognitive context, such as labeling items when looking at a book (Nelson, 1981). At 20 months, referential children were more likely than expressive children to point out objects to their mothers (Goldfried, 1990).

These findings demonstrate two important points. First, children's language is influenced by the language parents use; second, children may take different paths and still arrive at linguistic competence. Both expressive or referential children are linguistically competent, although they follow different styles and paths.

Words at first are used in isolation and then gradually are generalized to similar situations. A **holophrase** is a single word that stands for a complete thought (Carroll, 1994). For instance, a child says, "Up," and means "Pick me up," or the child says, "Wet," and wants to be changed. Parents must go beyond the word and use the context to interpret the child's ideas.

Toddler's Language

50 words   18 mos.

By around 18 to 20 months, most infants have a productive vocabulary of around 50 words. Words such as *no, mine,* and *hot* are common, although word usage is inconsistent; that is, a word may be used at one time in the day and not at another. Right before the child knows about 50 words, in the second half of the child's second year, a rapid acceleration in vocabulary occurs (Woodward, Markman, & Fitzsimmons, 1994). It could be called a naming explosion, because about three-quarters of these new words are nouns. By 24 months, the child is using 320 words and by 30 months, 570 words (Mervis & Bertrand, 1994).

320 word by Age 2

This vocabulary explosion is difficult to explain. It may be caused by some improvement in memory or some change in processing capacity (Woodward et al., 1994). Perhaps it is caused by some major cognitive advance, such as the child beginning to understand that everything can and ought to be placed in a category (Gopnick & Meltzoff, 1987). There may be a number of different factors that converge to cause this phenomenon, many of which are not well understood (Gershkoff-Stowe, Thal, Smith, & Namy, 1997). Between 20 and 22 months children show a spurt in comprehension as well (Reznick & Goldfield, 1992).

Children seem to employ a fast mapping strategy that enables them to connect a word and an object after only one or two exposures (Mervis & Bertrand, 1994). Between 2 and 5 years, children seem to pick up words at an astounding pace (Rice, Buhr, & Nemeth, 1990). This is true both in production and comprehension. Between about 1.5 and 6 years, children learn to comprehend over 14,000 words (Rice, Burns, & Nemeth, 1990). Young children learn words in a variety of contexts and situations (Akhtar, Carpenter, & Tomasello, 1996). They can even learn them from a television program, where the words are spoken quickly (Rice & Woodsmall, 1988). Children can hold a verb or a noun in their

expressive children

Children who use words involved in social interactions, such as *stop* and *bye-bye.*

referential children

Children whose early language is used to name objects, such as *dog* or *bed.*

holophrase

One word used to stand for an entire thought.

minds while something is being done or said and await the label at a later time (Tomasello & Barton, 1994). Some children, however, learn their words at a more gradual pace and maintain a balance of nouns and other kinds of words, especially verbs (Goldfield & Reznick, 1989). This may mean that there is no single "correct" strategy, and there may be more roads to linguistic competence than first thought.

It is easy to understand how children link a noun such as a chair with the label, but what about learning verbs? Parents also label action sequences, but in a number of ways. Parents label what they are doing, request the child's participation or comment on their own or the child's pending action. The last of these is most important and seems to lead to the most rapid learning of verbs (Tomasello & Kruger, 1992). Two-year-old children were taught the novel verb for an action, *plunk*, when a doll on wheels was placed at the top of a ramp and a button pushed beside the doll allowing the doll to roll down the ramp and through the hole. None of the children knew the verb *plunk* before the study. Some were introduced to the verb as the doll was in action ("Look, I'm plunking the man"), others when the action was finished ("Look, Jason, I plunked the man"), and others in an impending action condition ("Look, Jason, I'll plunk the man"). Children learned the verb best in the impending action context as measured by both comprehension and production.

During the toddler stage, the child's vocabulary increases greatly, two- to three-word sentences are spoken, and the first pronouns, such as *I*, appear. Some simple adjectives and adverbs are present, and the child often demands repetition from others. The child begins to announce intentions before acting and asks questions (Weiss & Lillywhite, 1976).

The two-word stage is well organized. The child's use of words is governed by rules that make the meaning of the communication easier to understand (Armon-Lotem, 1995). The meaning depends on specific word orders (Owens, 1994). For example, when expressing ownership, toddlers use a word to stand for the possessor and another for the item, as in "mommy ball" or "baby doll." When the toddler wants something that has happened to happen again, the child will use a recurrence word, such as *more* or *nuther*, and then the object, such as "nuther cookie" (Owens, 1994). Young children use an agent-action form such as "Adam hit" or an attribution form such as "big ball" (Durkin, 1995). Later, they expand on these. Toddler language contains a number of these rules. When about half the child's utterances contain two words, the child begins to use three words, and these sentences are still governed by specific rules.

The child's early speech leaves out small words such as *a*, *to*, or *from* and concentrates on the more important words. This is called **telegraphic speech,** because it is similar to the language found in telegrams, in which the sender includes only the words absolutely necessary for communication. Examples are "Mommy go store" and "Baby take toy." These important phrases are commonly stressed by other speakers in the environment, which makes them easier to imitate and learn (Brown, 1973).

Language development continues throughout childhood. We will look at this topic again in Chapters 8 and 10.

Guideposts

What are the main achievements in the linguistic area between birth and 3 years?

7

Toddlers who use sentences such as "Mommy go store" that leave out all the smaller, helping words such as *is* and *to* are very likely to have very poor linguistic skills later in childhood.

telegraphic speech

Sentences in which only the basic words necessary to communicate meaning are used, with helping words such as *a* or *to* left out.

How Do Children Learn Language?

Psychologists have been struggling over the question of how a child develops from a being who understands and produces no language to one who can use language with great ease. Four major factors contribute to our regrettably incomplete understanding of this process: the principles of learning, innate factors, cognitive factors, and social factors.

Reinforcement and Imitation

At first glance, it appears that children learn language through imitation. This seems true, especially for early vocabulary. Words are symbols that stand for things or ideas. The vocabulary of each language differs. The only way children can learn words is by hearing them and then copying them. Children learn the word *apple* when they have need for the word. They learn new words by hearing or overhearing words that are relevant to what they have in mind (Bloom, Margulis, Tinker, & Fujita, 1996). That is, children learn words that pertain to what they are attending to or thinking about.

The first scientific attempt to explain language acquisition is credited to B. F. Skinner (1957), who believed that language was learned in a similar way as everything else—through reinforcement and modeling. Language learning could be explained by environmental factors. Operant conditioning—including the processes of reinforcement, generalization, and discrimination—is responsible for language development. Children are reinforced for labeling the environment and asking for things. Through the processes of generalization and discrimination, children come to reduce their errors and use the appropriate forms. Children also imitate parental speech. Skinner looked at the acquisition of grammar as a matter of generalizing and making inferences. For example, a child may learn the meaning for the phrase "my teddy bear" and then infer that "my" can be used as in "my apple" or "my television." Generally, caregivers who reinforce their children for using complex language have children who indeed use such language. When mothers show approval of their children's verbal behavior, the children's mean length of utterance (MLU) increases. Parents may reward more mature forms of expression by praising or by giving children what they are requesting, thereby reinforcing particular ways of communicating.

Reinforcement and imitation also have an effect in some areas of pragmatics. For example, children who are reinforced for saying "please" and "thank you" or who have parents who use such politeness are more likely to use these expressions of courtesy.

Although imitation and reinforcement are helpful in understanding some areas of vocabulary acquisition and general language usage, they are inadequate to explain language acquisition itself. The overall amount of imitation decreases with age, especially after age 2 (Owens, 1988). In other words, the usefulness of imitation as a language-learning strategy decreases as language becomes more complex. Imitation, then, is most important at the single-word level.

It is also very difficult to explain how children create original sentences using reinforcement and imitation. All children create original sentences they have not heard before. Strong evidence against imitation is the finding that children invent new words and new forms they have not heard around them (Marcus et al, 1992).

In addition, how can a child of limited cognitive abilities master the complicated rules of grammar that even adults cannot explain—and do all this without formal training (Bloom, 1975; Durkin, 1995)? To use language correctly, children

Guideposts

How do behaviorists explain language learning?

"I drinked the waters."
Once children begin to
master the rules of
grammar, they often
overgeneralize them.

must acquire rules such as those for changing tense and creating word order. Some of the rules are quite complicated. Try describing the rule by which you would use the phrase "a thing" or "the thing." Most of us use the rule perfectly, but we would be hard-pressed to formulate it. Also, if only the processes of learning are involved, why do children make the same mistakes as they develop their language abilities. For example, once children begin to acquire some of the basic rules of English, they sometimes overuse them, saying *seed* and *goed* for the past tense of *see* and *go*. There is often an early period when the child correctly uses these irregular verbs before this over-regularization, as psychologists call it, appears (Johnson, 1995). With experience, most children gradually learn the exceptions with little or no formal training. Furthermore, why do they produce such childish speech patterns as telegraphic speech that they do not hear around them? Finally, consider the following seven-word sentence: "The boy is going to the store." There are 5,040 different ways to arrange the seven words, but only a very few will make sense. Any preschooler could easily tell you which make sense and which do not. How do they learn this? These problems, among others, have led some authorities to argue that some innate biological mechanism must be responsible for language acquisition.

Is Language Acquisition Innate?

Noam Chomsky (1959, 1965, 1972, 1987), the leading advocate for the biological or **nativist explanation,** argued that human beings are preprogrammed to learn language. Children require only exposure to the language prevailing in their own culture. Human beings are born with an innate, biological ability to learn language, called a **language acquisition device.** Children can acquire the grammar of the particular culture's language because their brain is innately patterned to understand the structure of languages. Children can understand the basic rules of language and form hypotheses about them, which they then test out.

Indeed, the difficulties of explaining grammatical constructions is daunting. Chomsky argues that since children learn the grammatical rules despite the fact that the rules are so abstract and children receive poor input means that they must have some basic understanding or capacity to understand language. Chomsky's position excited many psychologists. It explained the interesting similarities we find in language development around the world. Children in all cultures proceed through similar steps when learning language (Slobin, 1972) and make the same mistakes. These similarities could be explained if the acquisition of language rests on some shared neurological foundation.

In the nativist view, language acquisition is a maturational activity coinciding with brain development. Some authorities claim that there is a critical period between birth and adolescence for developing language (Lenneberg, 1967) and that if not developed during that time, the individual's language will be permanently disordered. There is evidence for and against this idea. What would happen if children were not exposed to any language? In a few cases of severe environmental deprivation and isolation, little or no language development occurred. When these isolated children are later exposed to language, they learn some early language but it is far from complete (Harris, 1995). The most interesting case is that of Genie, a girl who was kept socially isolated from 18 months until adolescence, without any exposure to language (Curtis, 1977). After intensive speech and

nativist explanation
An explanation of language development based on biological or innate factors.

language acquisition device
An assumed biological device used in the acquisition of language.

language therapy she reached a 2-year-old stage or so of language but did not really move past that. Her language usage consisted of two or three words loosely linked by meaning without any grammatical construction (Harris, 1995). If the nativist theory is correct, why did she learn any language? If the behavioral theory is correct, why was her language so poor? This remains a mystery. Perhaps the mechanisms for learning simple language and more complex forms are different.

It is certainly more difficult to learn language later in life. The importance of early language exposure is shown in a study in which Korean and Chinese immigrants to the United States took a grammar test that required them to choose which of a group of statements was grammatically correct. Some of the immigrants had settled in the United States as young children while others had done so in adulthood. All had been in the United States for about ten years. Those who learned English earlier showed much greater knowledge of English grammar (see Figure 6.4) (Johnson & Newport, 1991). Perhaps once past this critical period, language learning is certainly possible but more difficult.

Although Chomsky's theory is controversial, everyone accepts the fact that human beings are born with an impressive vocal apparatus that allows them to develop speech, and specific areas of the brain are devoted to language. The cerebral cortex in human beings is divided into two hemispheres: the right and the left. Most people are right-handed, and almost all have their language functions centralized in the left hemisphere. Half the left-handed people also have their language areas localized in the left hemisphere (Gleason, 1985). This specialization is present at an early age and other neurological changes related to language learning also occur early in life (Harris, 1995).

When specific areas of the brain are injured, certain language-related problems occur. For example, the area responsible for producing speech is called **Broca's area.** Damage here causes difficulties in producing language, but the person is still able to comprehend language. Damage to another area, called **Wernicke's area,** causes a person to have poor comprehension and speech filled with nonsense words, even though the speech is fluent (Harris, 1995). The brain also has areas associated with written language (Gleason, 1985).

In addition, a number of factors already noted indicate that some biological basis for language acquisition may exist. Human infants can make impressive

Guideposts

How does Noam Chomsky explain the development of language?

It is actually easier to learn a new language later in life than during early childhood.

Figure 6.4 The Relationship Between Age of Arrival in the United States and Total Score Correct on the Test of English Grammar

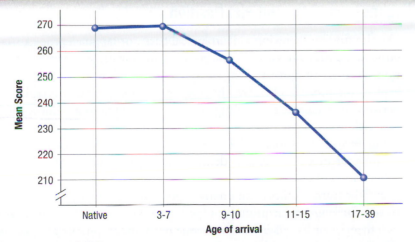

SOURCE: Johnson & Newport (1991)

Broca's area
An area in the brain responsible for producing speech.

Wernicke's area
An area in the brain responsible for comprehension of language.

phonetic distinctions and are attentive to speech quite early in life (Marean, Werner, & Kuhl, 1992). Some strategies for processing language may be innate (Slobin, 1973; McNeill, 1970). Infants show different brain wave electrical patterns to familiar and unfamiliar words (Harris, 1995).

One recent, but still controversial, area of research that may support the nativist position involves the question of how parents react to their children's ungrammatical statements. Parents correct their children's syntactical errors of word order, tense, or improper grammar about a third of the time. For example, if a child says, "That are a monkey," the parent would say, "That *is* a monkey." Parents also respond with expansions or recasts, in which adults reproduce major parts of the child's utterance but add something. For example, if a child said, "Lady dress on," the parent might say, "The lady has a dress on." Sometimes, parents respond with a question that clarifies the child's statement as well. While some authorities doubt whether the relatively small percentage of corrections and expansions really influence children's acquisition of language (Gordon, 1990), others argue that they may be important (Bohannon, MacWhinney, & Snow, 1990; Bohannon & Stanowicz, 1988).

Both the function and consequences of such corrective feedback, sometimes called *negative evidence* because it hypothetically shows children that something in their speech pattern is incorrect, is important to the Skinner-Chomsky debate. The nativist position is that since children are rarely informed about the grammatical correctness of their statements and learn language on the basis of relatively poor and limited linguistic input, the explanation of how language acquisition occurs must lie in the child's innate ability to learn language. On the other hand, if parental corrections and expansions are important in shaping children's language, it would provide evidence for the more environmental explanations (Bohannon, Padgett, Nelson, & Mark, 1996).

A recent study found no relationship between recasts and children's subsequent grammar or self-corrections (Morgan, Bonamo, & Travis, 1995, 1996). Recasts did not serve as corrections and did not reduce grammatical mistakes, but recasts did encourage children to use a variety of ways to express themselves. The results of this study may be seen as evidence for the nativist position. This study has been questioned on technical grounds, with some authorities arguing that the jury is still out (Bohannon et al., 1996), while its conclusions also have been defended (Morgan, 1996).

Weaknesses of the Nativist Position

Despite findings showing a neurological basis for language, the existence of a language acquisition device has not yet been demonstrated (Moerk, 1989). In addition, even if we agree that a neurological basis for language exists, it does not explain the processes involved in language learning. And although the similarities between how children learn language around the world are impressive, recent evidence shows that there are some differences that reflect the nature of the language being learned (Akiyama, 1984, 1985). So although some biological foundation for learning language is probable, the nativist position does not fully explain language acquisition either.

The learning theory and nativist positions thus both fail as a complete explanation for language acquisition. One expert, George Miller, put it well: "We had two theories of language learning—one of them, empiricist associationism (learning theory), is impossible; the other, nativism, is miraculous. The void between the impossible and miraculous remained to be filled" (in Bruner, 1978, p. 33). Two other approaches to language acquisition emphasizing the importance of cognitive and social factors are now popular and have begun to fill this void.

Cognitive Theory and Language Development

Language learning requires a number of cognitive processes such as attention, information processing, and retention. The development of skills in these areas affects a child's language abilities. For instance, paying attention to stimuli that are loud or attached to some vital activity (such as feeding), remembering them, making discriminations and judgments about them (such as whether they are the same or different), and classifying according to these judgments are all cognitive processes related to language learning (Peters, 1986). In fact, cognitive psychologists often question just how much of human language capacity is really innate, since we can program computers to learn particular rules of grammar (Shanks, 1993).

Cognitive psychologists argue that cognitive factors either precede or place a limit on language learning (Durkin, 1995). Children notice things in their environment and learn words best when parents focus on what children are paying attention to rather than forcing children to redirect their attention to something else (Dunham, Dunham, & Curwin, 1993; Bloom, 1998). To create sentences, children also need the cognitive ability to remember words. In addition, children must understand something about an object or an idea before using words in a meaningful manner. Linguistic growth necessarily parallels cognitive growth. The child first uses simple words to label things, then proceeds to define classes in terms of their more abstract qualities, such as color.

Piaget (1962; Piaget & Inhelder, 1969) argued that language emerges from nonlinguistic sensorimotor intelligence and represents the ability to create and understand symbols. It is difficult to understand how a child could express a thought such as "all gone" or understand the concept of disappearance unless he or she understood some measure of object permanence (Rice, 1989). Words that show disappearance emerge with the development of object permanence and the naming explosion discussed earlier may be related to developments in the ability to classify objects in spatial or temporal order (Gopnik, 1984; Gopnick & Meltzoff, 1987). Toddlers all around the world use locational terms, such as *out*, *down*, and *on* (Bowerman, De Leon, & Choi, 1995), which they could not do without some spatial understanding. Studies have generally not supported the idea that sensorimotor intelligence is a prerequisite for *all* aspects of language learning, but children's performance on some Piagetian tasks does predict specific linguistic achievements (Tomasello & Ferrar, 1984).

Even in the area of vocabulary, the cognitive aspects are now being appreciated. Children first talk about what they know—favorite things, people, and activities (Rice, 1989). Their first words aren't abstract and don't concern objects that aren't meaningful to them, such as *fax machine*. Rather, they name their bottles and other things that have meaning to them. Although cognitive advancements are not a total explanation for language development, cognitive processes cannot be ignored.

Social Interaction and Language Development

Children do not acquire language in a vacuum. They are affected by the linguistic environment that surrounds them, including the home and the day care center they may attend. Although there are many similarities in the way children develop

Guideposts

How do cognitive factors relate to language learning?

their linguistic skills around the world, some individual differences are also found (Elsen, 1995). These differences are not merely in pace of learning but in the path children take to learn language. Some individual differences in language development can be explained by the variations in linguistic environments that surround children. For instance, 1-year-old infants in day care are greatly affected by the quality of the care. The better the care measured by class size, number of adults, teacher education, as well as observations of teacher-child interactions, the better the children's ability to communicate (Burchinal, Roberts, Nabors, & Bryant, 1996).

The social interchanges between parent and infant or toddler are intense and begin early. When people talk to infants, they modify their speech. Parents talk to their older infants in shorter well-formed sentences that are simple and repetitious (Bowerman, 1981). Such speech contains many questions and commands and few hesitations, focuses on the present tense and is high pitched and spoken with an exaggerated intonation (Garnica, 1977; Masataka, 1998). The use of simplistic, redundant sentences is normally referred to as **motherese** or, more recently, **parentese** and is found almost universally (Fernald & Morikawa, 1993). Deaf mothers sign to their 6-month-old infants and their own friends differently. They sign slower, often repeat the same sign, and exaggerate the movements associated with each sign much more when signing to their infants. Young children show greater attention and responsiveness to infant-directed signing than adult-directed signing (Masataka, 1996). Even hearing infants pay greater attention, showing more positive facial expressions and vocalizations to gestures in Japanese Sign Language that are signed in motherese than those signed in regular Japanese Sign Language (Musataka, 1998). Infants who can hear pay more attention to spoken motherese than to other forms of speech (Fernald, 1985). They also show more positive emotions when motherese is used, and it facilitates the infant's detection and discrimination of linguistic features (Masataka, 1996). Even young children use motherese when talking to younger children, but they are not as proficient in its use (Tomasello & Mannle, 1985).

The child's reaction to parental speech determines the speaker's choice of words (Bohannon & Marquis, 1977). If a 2-year-old does not seem to understand, the adult immediately reduces the number of words in the next sentence. Children are not merely passive receivers of information—their comprehension or noncomprehension serves to control their linguistic environment.

Verbal exchanges between adults and young children do not constitute formal language lessons. The idea that parents somehow sit down and teach their children how to talk is not supported by the facts. However, there is no doubt that parental speech patterns affect the child's linguistic development. A strong relationship exists between parental language and children's vocabulary, especially in early language development (Barrett et al., 1991; Hart, 1991). Language acquisition involves learning a social skill that is useful in the interpersonal context and is purely functional. The purpose of speech and language is to communicate one's thoughts, ideas, and desires to others.

Language is also used to direct the actions of others. The child learns that communication involves signaling meaning, sharing experiences, and taking turns. One eminent psychologist, Jerome Bruner (1978b), sees language development in terms of problem solving. Children must solve the problem of how to communicate their wishes and thoughts to others. They learn language by interacting with others and by actively using language. The opportunity to engage actively in communication is necessary. Children acquire grammar and vocabulary because they are useful in accomplishing their aim of getting across to others what they want and what they are thinking. Notice that in this conception of language

Parents all over the world use simplified speech with exaggerated intonation when speaking to their infants and toddlers.

Guideposts

How does the early child-caretaker social interaction influence language learning?

motherese

The use of simple repetitive sentences with young children.

development, parents tune their linguistic input to the child's ability level. This theory is sometimes called the **fine-tuning theory.** Fine-tuned speech is not just motherese; that is, it is not just simpler sentences but communication that is matched to the child's developmental level and adapts as the child develops (Sokolov, 1993). It explains the finding that children encounter language in a very structured and progressively more difficult and complex manner. Language is learned as an extension of nonlinguistic communication. In fact, Bruner's (1983) theory is a kind of compromise between Skinner's and Chomsky's. Bruner believes that language develops from the interaction between the language and social environment created by the caregivers and whatever innate language potential children have (Levine & Mueller, 1988).

Culture and Early Language Usage

Cultural variation may help explain differences in language usage and development. For example, similarities and differences exist in the ways in which Japanese and American mothers use language. When observed playing with their children, both Japanese and American mothers accommodated their speech to their children's special needs by simplifying their speech, repeating themselves frequently, and using interesting sounds to engage their infant's attention. At the same time, Japanese and Americans differed in the way they interacted with their infants. These differences were shaped by their cultural beliefs.

American mothers focused more on target objects and provided labels consistently. Japanese mothers were less likely to label toys but used language more often in rituals of social exchange, such as giving, taking, and verbal politeness (Fernald & Morikawa, 1993). Americans mothers will say, "That's a car, see the car? You like it? It's got nice wheels." In contrast, Japanese mothers often omitted the name of the object—for example, "Here! It's a vroom-vroom. I give it to you. Now give this to me. Give me. Yes. Thank you." Japanese mothers were more likely to engage their infants in empathy routines, encouraging the infant to show positive feelings toward a toy: "It's a doggy here; give it a love love love love," while encouraging the infant to pat the dog gently. Japanese mothers also used more baby talk and used this form of expression longer.

When asked, Japanese mothers typically explained their goal was to talk gently to the child using sounds they felt were easy to imitate. American mothers were more likely to report their goals were to attract the infant's attention and to teach the infant words. American mothers were more interested in fostering linguistic competence, while Japanese mothers used language as a method of establishing emotional bonds (Fernald & Morikawa, 1993). Differences followed. American children had larger noun vocabularies than did Japanese infants at 19 months. These linguistic differences are now beginning to be investigated as a clue to the many paths children can take to become language proficient.

Japanese mothers are less likely to label toys, but use language more often in rituals of social exchange such as giving and taking, and verbal politeness.

fine-tuning theory
A theory noting that parents tune their language to a child's linguistic ability.

Middle-class children use more complex sentences and fewer commands than children of working-class families.

Guideposts

How do the language skills of children from poverty backgrounds and middle-class backgrounds differ?

Reading to young children promotes linguistic competence, but there are many ways to read to children. A developmentally appropriate active strategy is best.

Social Class Differences in Language Development

In the United States, the language environment of poor and more advantaged children differs (Walker, Greenwood, Hart, & Carta, 1994). Economically impoverished families play fewer language games that are conducive to early language learning and ask their children less often for language (Hart & Risley, 1992; Walker et al., 1994). Middle-class children use more expansive language and do better in language activities in school. Children of working-class parents use simpler sentences and more commands (Olim, Hess, & Shipman, 1967). Children reared in poverty environments have fewer early language experiences associated with optimal language development and this leads to differences between middle- and lower-income children in later reading and academic achievement. In fact, early language ability predicts success in school (Walker et al., 1994). Middle-class parents are more sensitive to the ages of their children, adjusting their length of utterance so that the children can understand them (Lawrence & Shipley, 1996). Middle-class parents also provide a richer vocabulary and more topic-continuing utterances, while working-class parents use more commands (Lawrence & Shipley, 1996).

Keep in mind, though, that language is functional and these children are not deficient in their own native environment. What is somewhat lacking are the specific language abilities required in school. When we consider how well a child can communicate in his or her own environment, no deficiency is found (Hart & Riley, 1992; Menyuk, 1977; Walker et al., 1994).

Encouraging Linguistic Ability

Most suggestions for improving children's linguistic competence are based on the premise that children learn language both by listening and by participating. Even at the earliest age, parents can talk to infants. Infants are sensitive to language and learn much about verbalizations and turn taking from early conversations. There are many opportunities to talk to a baby—for example, during feeding or changing (Honig, 1988). Parents can also help by labeling the environment and encouraging communication. When the child appears to be communicating in a prelinguistic mode, it is beneficial to say, "You want a cracker?" while holding the cracker up and emphasizing the word. As the child develops, parents should show a desire and a willingness to listen and communicate with their children. Children need an opportunity to talk, and as they develop, parents can ask who, what, where, why, and how questions and encourage them to use more than just a yes or a no answer. Parents may also find it helpful to expand on their children's statements. For example, if the child says, "Throw ball," a parent might say, "Throw the ball to Daddy." Such expansions may have a positive effect in broadening the child's language usage in some areas (Hovell, Schumaker, & Sherman, 1978). Since parents are models, using good speech and full sentences are also important.

Reading to a child is also beneficial, but there are many ways to do this. When the child is old enough to give some response, parents may ask questions that are age-appropriate and allow the child to participate in the story. When reading a story, a young child may be asked to point to the cow or the dog. In time, when children can talk, they can label things themselves and answer such questions as what color it is. Even later, the story may lead to a discussion about farm life and the like.

Reading can become a participatory activity with great benefits to children. Parents of toddlers were divided into two groups (Whitehurst et al., 1988). Parents in the experimental group were instructed to (1) use open-ended questions that required the children to use more than a yes/no response, (2) encourage the children to tell more, (3) ask the children function/attribute questions ("What is the farmer doing?"), and (4) offer expansions (repeating statements with some additions, such as when a child said, "Dog," the parent might say, "Big dog"). Parents were also told to respond positively to the children's attempts to answer the questions and to reduce the number of questions that the children could answer by pointing. These techniques required the children to talk about the pictured materials. The control group parents were instructed to read in their normal manner. After 1 month, children in the experimental group scored significantly higher on measures of expressive language ability and showed a higher mean length of utterance, a greater use of phrases, and a lower frequency of single words. Nine months later, the differences were somewhat less but still present.

Cognitive and linguistic growth in infancy and toddlerhood is indeed impressive. When you look at a 1-month-old-infant who cannot speak or understand language and whose cognitive abilities are very limited and then stare at the active, engaging 2-year-old, it is amazing how far the child has come in such a short time. It is only recently that scientists have begun to understand the ways in which young children develop the skills necessary to understand the world around them and to communicate effectively with others, and it is clear that there is still much to learn in these areas.

For Your Consideration ?

How does reading to young children improve their language skills?

Summary

1. According to Jean Piaget, in the first two years, children negotiate the sensorimotor stage during which they use their senses and motor skills to learn about the world.

2. The development of object permanence—the understanding that an object or person exists even when it is out of sight—is an important achievement in infancy.

3. Some psychologists argue that infants are more capable than Piaget believed. Infants are very sensitive to the physical requirements of the task, and other factors such as motivation and the need to coordinate action with thought may limit performance on a particular task.

4. Infants have the ability to recognize faces very early, and infants between 8 and 12 months of age have some recall abilities. Infants' retention under certain circumstances is impressive.

5. We do not remember events during infancy for many reasons including the fact that early memories are encoded without language, and these memories may be changed by subsequent experience.

6. Scores on infant intelligence tests do not predict later intellectual ability very well, but some information-processing abilities, such as speed of processing and memory, do.

7. There is a relationship between later cognitive development and the responsiveness of the caregiver, parental involvement with the child, the variety of stimulation the child receives, the organization of the environment, and the play materials available. Allowing children to explore their own world, labeling the environment, encouraging communication, reading to the child, briefly interacting with the child by sharing some experience, and tailoring activities to the child's development level promote cognitive growth.

8. The best way to optimize the child's intellectual ability is to improve the home environment. Programs aimed at improving the home environment and parent-child interaction have been successful. Active participation and providing emotional and social support are important factors determining the success of these programs.

9. Communication is the process of sharing information. It may be verbal or nonverbal. Language is a set of agreed-on, arbitrary symbols used in communication. The subsystems of language include phonology, morphology, syntax, semantics, and pragmatics.

10. Infants communicate with the people around them by smiling, crying, and gesturing. They are sensitive to speech sounds from the moment they are born. Babbling, which involves verbalization of vowel and consonant sounds often repeated, begins as early as 3 months. Children utter their first word anytime between 10 and 15 months of age. A holophrase is one word that stands for an entire thought. The child's early sentences are called telegraphic, because they contain only those words absolutely necessary for communicating meaning to other people.

11. Behaviorists, such as B. F. Skinner, use the processes of reinforcement and imitation to explain language acquisition. Noam Chomsky argues that a human being is biologically programmed to learn language and merely requires exposure to a language to master it.

12. Cognitive psychologists argue that such factors as attention and memory are involved in language acquisition. In addition, to use a word correctly, a child must know something about an object.

13. Adult speech to young children is well constructed and consists of short, simple sentences with many repetitions. Social interaction is important in language acquisition because children learn language through interaction with their caregivers, who fine-tune their language to the child's developmental level.

14. The linguistic environment that surrounds a child is important in the acquisition of language. Middle-class parents tend to use expansive language, while working-class parents tend to use more restricted speech patterns. Parents can do much to help their children develop linguistic competence.

Review

Piaget's first stage of cognitive development is called (1)_____ . During this stage, the young child learns about the world through the (2)_____ and through (3)_____ . Actions that are focused on the body and occur repeatedly are called (4)_____ reactions. Infants are showing (5)_____ reactions if their repetitive actions are focused on some outside consequence rather than on their own bodies. Children later show (6)_____ reactions as their actions are repetitive but are no longer carbon copies of each other and they seek novelty. Between 18 and 24 months, the child can now use (7)_____ , the ability to portray events and feelings symbolically in the mind. The child also shows (8)_____ in that he or she can witness something and show the behavior at a later time. During the first 2 years, the child also develops (9)_____ , an understanding that things don't disappear just because they are out of sight.

Research on infant memory often measures retention using the process of (10)_____ in which the child is required to pick out the correct answer from a group of possibilities, or (11)_____ in which, on the basis of very limited cues, the child must show the correct response. The most commonly used scales to measure infant intelligence are the (12)_____ , but they are not successful in predicting later intelligence in normal children. There is much evidence that (13)_____ skills such as processing speed may predict later intelligence. Psychologists use the (14)_____ Scale to determine aspects of parenting and the physical setup of the home that influences cognitive development. Piaget called the issue of accelerating children the (15)_____ question and he argued against such practices.

(16)_____ is the process of sharing information, while (17)_____ involves arbitrary symbols with agreed-on meanings. Language contains five systems. The study of the sounds of a language is called (18)_____ , the way words are constructed is called (19)_____ , the rules for creating sentences is called (20)_____ , and the study of word meanings is called (21)_____ . Finally, the study of the social use of language is called (22)_____ .

Most infants by 6 months are (23)_____ ; that is, they are using strings of vowel and consonants. Some children called (24)_____ children learn language involved in social interactions, while other children, called (25)_____ , use language more to name and label

objects. Children in the single-word stage use a (26)_____ , one word to stand for an entire thought. By about 18 to 20 months, children's vocabulary increases very quickly and they can learn a word after just one exposure in a process called (27)_____ . At about 2 years, the child begins to use (28)_____ speech, sentences that leave out the helping words such as *a* and *to*.

(29)_____ , such as B. F. Skinner, explain language learning in terms of reinforcement and imitation. The chief advocate of the nativist viewpoint, (30)_____ , disagrees. He argues that language is a property of mind and that each person is born with a (31)_____ that allows an individual to learn language from the fragmented input that the child hears. Language learning is also affected by such (32)_____ skills as memory and attention. The (33)_____ environment, including the interactions between child and caretaker, is also important. Parents use short, repetitive, simple utterances called (34)_____ with their young children. Jerome Bruner argues that parents carefully control the linguistic environment of their child and change it as the child matures. This theory is called the (35)_____ theory.

InfoTrac

For additional readings, explore InfoTrac College Edition, our online library.
Go to http://www.infotrac-college.com/wadsworth.
Hint: enter the search terms *Children Learning Language; Language Acquisition, Research; Language Awareness.*

What's on the web

Jean Piaget Society
http://www.piaget.org

Major Milestones in Infant Language Development
http://www.kidsears.com/milestones/milestone_intro.htm

The Wadsworth Psychology Study Center Web Site
Go to the Wadsworth Psychology Study Center at http://psychology.wadsworth.com/ for quiz questions, research updates, hot topics, interactive exercises, and suggested readings in the InfoTrac College Edition related to this chapter.

Answers 1. sensorimotor; 2. senses; 3. motor activities; 4. primary circular; 5. secondary circular; 6. tertiary circular; 7. representation; 8. deferred imitation; 9. object permanence; 10. recognition; 11. recall; 12. Bayley Scales; 13. information processing; 14. HOME; 15. American; 16. Communication; 17. language; 18. phonology; 19. morphology; 20. syntax; 21. semantics; 22. pragmatics; 23. babbling; 24. expressive; 25. referential; 26. holophrase; 27. fast mapping; 28. telegraphic; 29. Behaviorists; 30. Noam Chomsky; 31. language acquisition device; 32. cognitive; 33. social; 34. motherese; 35. fine-tuning

Social *and* Personality Development

CHAPTER OUTLINE

Setting the Stage

Emotional Development

Attachment

The Father-Child Relationship

Maternal Employment

Day Care

Many Roads to Travel

ARE THESE STATEMENTS
True *or* False?

1. Infants do not show identifiable emotions until the age of 4 months.
2. Most children can recognize themselves in the mirror or in pictures by 12 months.
3. Newborns will cry when they hear other neonates crying.
4. The quality of an infant's attachment predicts later social and emotional health during the early childhood years.
5. Infants who do not show a fear of strangers are at risk for later personality difficulties.
6. When mothers are employed, fathers participate more in the child care and housekeeping.
7. Infants can become attached to their fathers as well as to their mothers.
8. Mothers who are employed full-time tend to stress independence training for their children more than mothers who are not employed.
9. Most children in day care attend relatively large day care centers.
10. The majority of children in infant day care show secure attachments to their mothers.

ANSWERS: 1. *False.* 2. *False.* 3. *True.* 4. *True.*
5. *False.* 6. *True.* 7. *True.* 8. *True.* 9. *False.* 10. *True.*

in Infancy *and* Toddlerhood

Setting the Stage

Like so many American families, Lisa and Tim Walters needed every penny to keep their heads above water. With two children (Beth, age 2, and Jon, 8 months), a modest home, and two cars, they were just breaking even each month. They decided that Lisa would stay home and be a full-time homemaker until the youngest child entered elementary school. Then Lisa would return to work. Both agreed that this was the best strategy for them. It combined their belief that the early relationship between mother and child was important with the reality of needing two incomes as the children grew.

But Tim was laid off from his job. Unable to afford a long layoff, he took a lower-paying position and returned to school for retraining. Trapped by car payments and a hefty mortgage, Lisa and Tim fell into debt. They finally decided that Lisa should go back to work immediately.

The 2-year-old will have to enter a day care program, while the baby will be cared for by either a neighbor or Lisa's mother. They are very concerned about how these experiences will affect the children.

Many American families are asking the same questions. Over the past 30 years, the proportion of employed mothers has increased dramatically, and today over 60% of all women with preschoolers are employed (U.S. Department of Commerce, 1998). Fifty-nine percent of all mothers with infants are also employed.

Many people equate the employed mother with the single parent—and indeed most single parents are employed—but more than half of all mothers in two-parent families are also employed. So the Walters' dilemma is not unusual, and the questions the Walters ask are of concern to many parents today.

Emotional Development

Emotional development in infancy is not an easy area to research. Since infants cannot verbalize how they feel, psychologists investigate emotional development on the basis of facial gestures, physiological responses, or the sounds infants make in response to some stimulus.

What Emotions Do Infants Show?

Many parents argue that their very young infants show identifiable and definite emotions almost from birth. They are correct, according to **differential emotions theory**, which states that young infants possess a limited number of emotions (Malatesta, Culver, Tesman, & Shephard, 1989). These specific emotions are innate and include interest, disgust, physical distress, and a precursor of surprise, called a startle. The social smile emerges sometime between three and six weeks (Izard & Malatesta, 1987). Each of these emotions can be elicited at will. Novelty and human faces trigger interest, and bad-tasting foods result in disgust. The social smile is elicited at three weeks by a high-pitched human voice and at six weeks by the human face. Anger, surprise, and joy emerge in the next four months; sadness about the same time; and fear between five and seven months (Izard & Malatesta, 1987). These emotions are referred to as **primary emotions** because they appear early in life, can be easily recognized from facial expressions, and are found in infants all around the world. In fact, adults agree on the emotional expressions infants show (Emde, Izard, Huebner, Sorce, & Klinnert, 1985). Both trained and untrained college students have no difficulty identifying infant emotional responses to a variety of events, ranging from happiness during playful interactions to the pain from inoculations, to the expressions of surprise and sadness (Izard, Huebner, Risser, McGinnis, & Dougherty, 1980). These emotions result from biological programming (Izard, 1994).

Early infant emotions are related to specific infant behaviors. When newborns only two hours old were fed solutions that tasted bitter, sweet, sour, or salty, they showed different facial responses to each, except salt (see page 163). The reaction to a sweet substance sometimes involved an initial negative response that passed quickly and was considered a reaction to the syringe used to place the solution into the infant's mouth. It was followed by total facial relaxation. When the sour solution was given to the infants, they compressed their cheeks against their gums, tightly squeezed their eyes, lowered their brows, and pursed their lips. The reaction to bitter included a mouth gaping accompanied by elevation of the tongue in the back of the mouth and other actions that blocked swallowing. The researchers note that some of the facial actions in response to the nonsweet stimuli are components of adult expressions of disgust, but they are not willing at

Infants do not show identifiable emotions until the age of 4 months.

What emotions do neonates show?

differential emotions theory

The theory that neonates show a limited number of emotions that are biologically determined.

primary emotions

Emotions that appear early in infancy, are innately determined, can be recognized through facial expressions, and reflect a subjective experience.

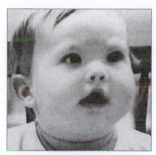
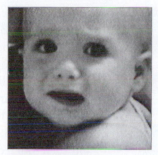

Interest: brows raised; mouth my be rounded; lips may be pursed.

Fear: mouth retracted; brows level and drawn up and in; eyelids lifted

Disgust: tongue protruding; upper lips raised; nose wrinkled.

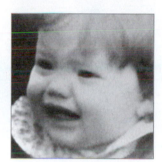

Joy: bright eyes lifted; mouth forms a smile

Sadness: corners of mouth turned down; inner portion of brows raised.

Anger: mouth squared at corners; brows drawn together and pointing down; eyes fixed straight ahead.

this time to draw any conclusions about the subjective nature of these infant responses (Rosenstein & Oster, 1988). Other psychologists are willing to consider the responses in terms of emotional expression.

Learning also plays a part in emotional expression. Hearing the mother's voice may bring forth a smile in the infant; later in infancy, seeing the doctor's office may lead to crying. Cognitive development is still another factor in emotional expression. Consider the emotional expressions of four- to eight-month-old infants who watched while someone wearing a scary mask approached them. The babies cried when the mask was worn by a stranger, but they laughed when their mothers wore the mask (Sroufe & Wunsch, 1972). This reaction demonstrates that infants at this age can use cognitive appraisal to "decide" which emotion to show.

Secondary Emotions

Other emotions such as shame, envy, guilt, contempt, and pride appear during the second year of life and are called **secondary emotions** (Izard & Malatesta, 1987). These secondary emotions require more sophisticated cognitive abilities than primary emotions (Lewis, Alessandri, & Sullivan, 1992). For example, to feel envy the child must be aware of the difference between oneself and others, which typically develops between 15 and 24 months (Lewis, Stanger, & Sullivan, 1989).

The emergence of the distinction between the self and other is usually tested by placing some rouge on the nose of a child, allowing the child to see his or her reflection in a mirror and observing reactions that would show self-awareness, such as touching the nose. Between 15 and 18 months, many infants begin to recognize themselves in a mirror, videotape, or picture; and by the end of the second year,

secondary emotions
Emotions that begin to appear in the second year of life and require sophisticated cognitive abilities, for example envy and pride.

Most children can recognize themselves in the mirror or in pictures by 12 months.

In the second half of the second year, children begin to recognize themselves in the mirror or in pictures.

Guideposts

What are the differences between primary and secondary emotions?

almost all children do this easily (Asendorpf, Warkentin, & Baudonniere, 1996).

Some secondary emotions such as guilt, shame, and pride require not only a sense of self but an ability to evaluate one's actions against a standard. Beth understands that the bridge she just built with toy blocks is good because she evaluates it against some standard and therefore feels pride. This type of evaluation begins to emerge somewhere around 18 to 24 months, slightly after self-consciousness, and becomes more sophisticated with time (Lewis et al., 1992). This is nicely shown in a study in which children were given tasks to perform, each of which had an easy and a difficult version. In the easy puzzle-solving chore, children had to complete a four-piece puzzle; in the difficult condition, a 25-piece puzzle missing some pieces. Children often showed pride when they successfully complete the difficult task, but not when they successfully completed the easy task. Likewise, children often showed shame when they failed the easy task, but not when they failed the difficult task (see Figure 7.1) (Lewis et al., 1992). By three years, children are capable not only of engaging in such self-evaluating behavior but also of taking task difficulty into account. Both self-consciousness and a capacity for self-evaluation are necessary for children to regulate their own behavior and experience emotional reactions to doing something wrong (Asendorpf et al., 1996). Self-evaluative statements increase greatly between 19 and 29 months and are found in almost every child by 30 months (Stipek, Gralinski, & Kopp, 1990).

Figure 7.1 Incidence of Pride and Shame as a Function of Task Difficulty

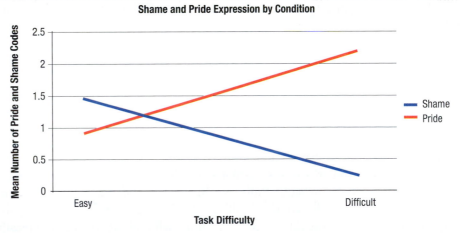

SOURCE: Lewis et al. (1992)

Culture and Emotion

Cultures have their own rules determining what emotions should and should not be shown in particular situations. Cultures often demand that people control their emotions and sometimes mask their negative feelings. Children begin to do this in the last half of the second year. A 20-month-old child falls but cries only if Mom is present (why pass up an opportunity for a good hug?). Three-year-olds can hide their emotions quite well. Preschoolers were told not to peek at a toy when the experimenter left a room and observed through a one-way mirror. Only 4 did not look; 29 sneaked a peak. When asked, the overwhelming majority lied, stating that they hadn't looked when they really did. Later, when shown videotapes of these children denying they had looked, psychologists could *not* tell who was lying and who was not by their facial and body movements (Lewis, Stanger, & Sullivan, 1989). It seems, therefore, that 3-year-olds can mask their emotional expression and use verbal deception (Polak & Harris, 1999).

This may seem unfortunate as the innocence of children seems to be so brief, but keep in mind that we teach children to hide their real feelings at times (but hopefully not to lie about what they did) for good reasons. The child who receives a shirt instead of that hoped-for toy from Grandpa is told to show gratitude and to say "Thank you" rather than show disappointment. The child also witnesses such displays. Mother may say that she doesn't want to see anyone because she is tired, yet she smiles and says, "Nice to see you," when the neighbor knocks on the door.

Guideposts

How does culture affect emotional expression?

Can Infants Read the Emotional States of Others?

Even young infants are aware of their parents' facial expressions. Infants as young as 2 or 3 months—and possibly even newborns—can discriminate a variety of facial expressions (Nelson, 1987). Two-month-old infants can discriminate a happy face from a neutral face, and three-month-olds discriminate happy, sad, and surprised faces (Nelson & Horowitz, 1983). Three-month-old infants recognize the difference between smiling and frowning expressions (Barrera & Maurer, 1981). Some studies have even shown that young infants not only can discriminate facial expressions but also can imitate a happy, sad, or surprised expression (Field et al., 1983). Infants between 4 and 9 months were shown color slides of happy, angry and neutral faces simulated by female models (see Figure 7.2 on page 238). Infants were able to discriminate and recognize the happy, angry, and neutral faces in all the female models (Serrano, Iglesias, & Loeches, 1995). Although there is little doubt about an infant's ability to differentiate among expressions, some researchers claim that in the first few months, infants may not be able to understand the true nature of emotional expression. It is only after the age of 6 months or on that infants reliably react to different expressions, behaving more negatively to a frowning, crying, or sad face than to a happy or neutral face (Kruetzer & Charlesworth, 1973). In the second half of the first year, infants not only can discriminate emotions but also are affected by them, therefore realizing that emotions have meaning (Bornstein, 1995; Repacholi, 1998).

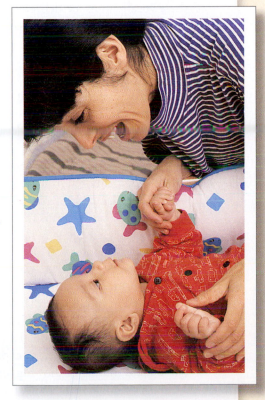

Even two- or three-month-old infants can discriminate a variety of facial expressions, but don't understand the true nature of emotional expression until six months when they first reliably react to different expressions.

Figure 7.2 **Modeling Emotions**

These models are simulating happy, angry and neutral facial expressions. Infants are able to discriminate among these different facial expressions.

Happy   Angry   Neutral

Using Information from Others: Social Referencing

Infants are surrounded by people making gestures, showing facial expressions, and displaying emotion in their voice and speaking. By 5 months, infants can discriminate vocalizations that indicate happy and sad emotions (Walker-Andrews & Gronlick, 1983). Five-month-old infants show more positive attention and smiling when they hear vocalizations that are approving rather than prohibiting, even if these vocalizations are delivered in an unfamiliar language (Fernald, 1993)! Infants cannot understand words but are affected by the physical form of the communication, including their tone and loudness. Infants can use not only the facial expressions of others but the tone of the communication to guide their own behavior.

The phenomenon in which a person uses information received from others to appraise events and regulate behavior is called **social referencing** (Hornik & Gunnar, 1988). Most studies of social referencing place an infant in an ambiguous situation while an adult displays a particular expression. The psychologist then observes how the expression affects the infant's behavior (Rosen, Adamson, & Bakeman, 1992). This is a common practice in everyday life. Parents may try to interest their children in something new by acting as if it were pleasurable through words, expressions, and vocalizations or show impatience at a particular behavior through these same means (Flavell & Miller, 1998).

Social referencing is reliably found at about a year. Recall the visual cliff described in Chapter 5. This, as you remember, is a table with a checkerboard pattern on one side and clear glass on the other side. Below the clear side is another checkerboard that makes the clear side look like a cliff. The height of the table can be adjusted in such a way that the infant will neither avoid the cliff because of fear nor find the cliff absolutely safe. The situation is ambiguous, and the infant is uncertain about what to do. The mother stands opposite the infant and is told to smile, show joy or interest, or express fear or anger. If an infant looks at the mother while she is smiling or showing joy or interest, most infants will cross the deep side.

social referencing

The phenomenon in which a person uses information received from others to appraise events and regulate behavior.

If the mother shows fear or anger, very few infants will cross. If the visual cliff is adjusted so that it is obviously safe, very few infants reference their mothers at all, and those who do and see their mothers showing fear hesitate but cross anyway (Sorce, Emde, Campos, & Klinnert, 1985).

Social referencing is most likely to take place when the situation is ambiguous. Under such circumstances, infants actively search for information (Rosen et al., 1992; Walden & Ogan, 1988). Although the expressions that most influence infants' behavior are negative, such as fear and sadness, positive emotions also affect the behavior of the infant. When 10-month-old infants' reactions to strangers were recorded, the reactions of the mother to the stranger influenced the child's behavior (Feinman & Lewis, 1983; Rosen et al., 1992). If the mother spoke to the stranger in a positive manner, expressing positive emotion, the infant was friendlier to the stranger than if the mother was neutral. Although mother is most often used in these studies, infants will social reference to their fathers and even to their day care center's staff (Camras & Sachs, 1991).

The visual cliff and the appearance of a stranger are reasonably strong fear-inducing situations. When milder stimuli are used, such as a new but strange toy, and mother is asked to show a happy or fearful emotion, the research evidence is mixed. Some studies show facial signals have an effect on the children's behavior and other studies do not (Klinnert, Emde, Butterfield, & Campos, 1986; Mumme, 1993). This is due to contextual differences. When the situation is deeply disturbing or fear inducing, infants use parents' facial expressions; in milder situations they may or may not.

In everyday situations infants are exposed to vocal expressions of emotion as well as facial gestures. In one study, infants were presented with a novel toy. Some mothers showed different facial expressions (fear, happiness, or a neutral expression), while other mothers presented their children with vocalizations reflecting happiness, fright, or neutrality. Infants reduced their exploration only when they heard their mother's frightened voice (Mumme, Fernald, & Herrera, 1996). A facial expression may be too weak to regulate an infant's behavior in approaching or not approaching a toy. In a very unusual, highly uncertain, and potentially dangerous situation, the mother's expression may be sufficient to influence the child's behavior (Hirshberg & Svejda, 1992). In less anxiety-arousing situations, vocal signals may also be required.

Social referencing can lead to some fairly sophisticated behavior patterns in young toddlers. When 14-month-old children saw an adult either look at or place a hand into one box and say "wow" while showing a happy expression, and either look at or place a hand into a second box and say "ech" while showing a disgusted facial expression, infants searched much more for the "happy" object than the object of disgust (Repacholi, 1998). The infants understood that the emotional display related to something inside the box, not the box itself, and used the adult's gaze and action to understand this while using the adult's emotions to guide the action.

There is no doubt that by the end of the first year the infant can distinguish and interpret emotions and is sometimes affected by the emotions of others. Research into infant emotions continues at a rapid rate, and some emotional responses have been researched thoroughly.

The Smile

Newborns show expressions that look like smiles, but these expressions occur either during sleep or when the infant is drowsy, and they are probably involuntary reactions (Lamb, 1988). By 3 to 6 weeks, however, infants show voluntary

Guideposts

How are children guided by the facial expressions and voice qualities of others?

smiling in the waking state. This smile is shown not only to social stimuli, such as voices, but also to nonsocial stimuli, such as bells or a bull's-eye. Gradually, smiles become more limited to social stimuli. Infants also smile when they have mastered an action reflecting pleasure or satisfaction.

After four or five months, the frequency of smiling becomes dependent on the infant's culture and family environment. Infant smiling that is reinforced with attention will increase in frequency (Etzel & Gewirtz, 1967). The social nature of the smile continues to develop in infancy. Older infants smile more when they are smiling at someone who is attentive than when the other person is not looking at them (Jones & Raag, 1989).

Every infant in every culture smiles. In fact, smiles are interpreted as positive expressions all around the world, and the development of the smile is basically the same in every society. Blind infants smile in response to social stimuli at about the same time as sighted children, even though they have not seen a smile (Kaplan, 1996).

The smile, then, begins as an inborn response, but it soon evolves from an undifferentiated response to internal stimuli to a response that is attached to social stimuli. Its frequency can be increased through reinforcement. If infants are rewarded for smiling by being picked up, talked to, and handled, the frequency of their smiling increases. The smile contributes to the establishment and maintenance of the infant-caregiver relationship, as most parents take pleasure in interpreting their child's smile as a positive response to their own activity, and their actions are thus reinforced by the child (Eveloff, 1971; Rochat, Querido, & Striano, 1999).

Empathy

When we hear someone crying, it usually has some emotional impact on us. This is true for infants as well. When newborns were exposed to tape-recorded cries of other neonates, the infants responded by crying (Simner, 1971). They were more sensitive to the cries of a 5-day-old neonate than to either a cry engineered through a computer or the cry of a 5.5-month-old infant. When one group of newborns listened to their own cries and another group heard the cries of another newborn, only the group of newborns exposed to the cries of another newborn decreased their sucking on a pacifier and showed facial expressions of distress (Dondi, Simion, & Caltran, 1999). Could such empathy be innate?

It is a possibility. When neonates who were either crying or calm listened to their own cries or those of other neonates, they demonstrated a remarkable degree of empathy (Martin & Clark, 1982). Infants who were originally calm cried when they heard the sounds of another neonate crying. Crying infants continued to cry when exposed to the cries of other infants but stopped when they heard recordings of their own cry. Calm infants, hearing their own cries, did not begin to cry. When newborns were presented with tapes of a crying chimpanzee, an 11-month-old child, and another newborn, those exposed to the cry of another newborn cried, but the newborns didn't cry when exposed to the cry of an 11-month-old or the chimpanzee. The researchers conclude that neonates as young as 18 hours can distinguish among their own cries, the cry of another infant, or an older child and that of a chimpanzee, and they will respond differently to these cries. Neonates seem to have an empathy that is astounding for their age.

Such reactions are an early and rudimentary form of empathy, but the further development of empathy requires cognitive advancements (see Chapter 9) (Hoffman, 1979). Before about 1 year, infants are empathically aroused without

For Your Consideration ?

Using the concept of reciprocal interaction, how can an infant's smile affect how he or she is treated?

Guideposts

How do neonates display empathy?

Newborns will cry when they hear other neonates crying.

the cognitive abilities that will later be important in experiencing empathy. They do not see themselves as distinct from others.

As children become aware of themselves as distinct from others, they know when another person is in distress and may themselves become very distressed. They may feel compassion, with a desire to help (Azar, 1997; Hoffman, 1984). However, they assume that the other person is feeling the same way as they are. For example, an 18-month-old will get his mother to comfort his friend who is crying, although the other child's mother is available. Since the first child is used to being comforted by his own mother, he assumes that his friend would also be comforted by the first child's mother and doesn't try to get the other child's mother to comfort him. Empathy continues to develop as the ability to take another person's point of view increases throughout childhood.

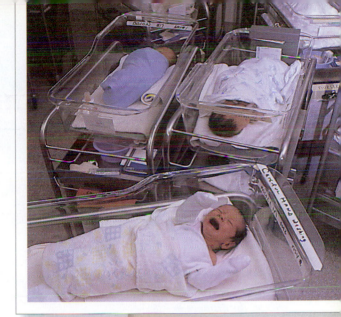

When one infant cries, others tend to do so as well. Some authorities argue that young infants experience empathy for others.

Attachment

Many of the questions Lisa and Tim have revolve around their ability to meet the needs of their young children. What do children require in order to feel that the world is a positive place and that they have value? What experiences in infancy will enable their children to feel confident enough to explore the world around them, develop satisfying peer relationships, and cope with adversity?

Many psychologists emphasize the importance of the early parent-child relationship. Erikson (1963) argued that developing a sense of *trust* was crucial to the child's development as it formed the basis for resolving all the other psychosocial crises of life. Young children develop a sense of trust when their physical and emotional needs are satisfied in a consistent and warm manner. If not, the child may develop a sense of *mistrust*, which may adversely affect future interpersonal relationships, as this early parent-child relationship serves as a model for later interpersonal relationships. To better understand the nature of this relationship, an appreciation of attachment theory is necessary (Karen, 1990).

Guideposts

What are the psychosocial crises of infancy and toddlerhood?

The Nature of Attachment

An **attachment** is an emotional tie that one person forms with another, binds them together in space, and endures over time (Ainsworth, 1974). Infants become attached to the primary caregiver, in most instances the mother, but they also become attached to their fathers, their grandparents, and day care workers.

Attachment is necessary for the survival and the healthy development of the infant (Ainsworth, 1974; Bowlby, 1973). According to a famous attachment researcher, John Bowlby (1969), attachment is a product of evolution and ensures survival since it leads to the protection of the child by the caregiver and the enhancement of the child's development. The infant is not born with a natural affinity to the mother. This affinity is learned (Waters & Deane, 1982). Attachment takes time to form, and it develops along with the child's cognitive abilities. So, although attachment has biological roots, learning and cognition also play a part.

attachment
An emotional tie binding people together over space and time.

If the child's world is threatened, the infant reduces the distance to the caregiver, which gives the child security.

Guideposts

What is the difference between attachment and attachment behavior?

Attachment Behavior

Although infants begin to recognize the difference between strangers and familiar people in the first four months (see Legerstee, Anderson, & Schaffer, 1998), it is only at about six months that proximity-maintaining behaviors, such as seeking out the caregiver when afraid or following the mother around, occur (Ainsworth, 1967). The concept of attachment differs from **attachment behavior,** which involves actions that result in a child's reducing the distance to another person who is viewed as better able to cope with the world (Bowlby, 1982). In other words, under certain circumstances, such as stress or anxiety, children are motivated to seek out the individual to whom they are attached. Such behaviors are shown only when a child's world is threatened in some manner (Colin, 1996). In safe circumstances, the level of attachment behavior is low, and the attachment figure is used as a secure base for exploration and play. The attachment system functions to balance proximity-seeking and exploratory behaviors. Under low-stress conditions, the presence of the caregiver supports exploration of the environment. As the situation becomes more stressful, infants typically show more proximity-seeking behaviors.

The Consequences of Poor Attachment

Knowledge of the importance of attachment and attachment behavior has grown steadily over the years. While working in a child guidance clinic, Bowlby noticed how often the early histories of adolescents in trouble included severe disruptions in their relationships with their mothers. He came to believe that these disruptions had a negative influence on the children's development. Bowlby was also influenced by the work of Konrad Lorenz (1937), who found that geese will follow and attach themselves to the first object they see. When the goslings opened their eyes and saw Lorenz, he became the object of attachment. They followed him everywhere. The geese were capable of forming such a relationship only in the first day and a half. This unlearned, rather rigid, irreversible behavior pattern is called **imprinting.**

Other theorists and research studies show that a breakdown in the early caregiver-child relationship can result in serious consequences (Rutter, 1979). Indeed, Freud (1935) argued that difficulties in this early relationship were the foundation for emotional disturbance. Children who do not receive adequate care become anxious and are unable to relate to others. The tragic consequences of the lack of any caregiver-child attachment was shown by Spitz (1945, 1965), who compared children raised in an orphanage, where they received impersonal care from the staff, with children raised by their mothers in what amounted to a prison nursery. The children raised in the prison nursery thrived, while those raised in the orphanage without much attention suffered greatly. Emotional disturbances, failure to gain weight, and mental retardation were common. The orphanage-raised children also suffered many more physical illnesses. Spitz coined the term **hospitalism** to describe these symptoms.

attachment behavior
   Actions by a child that result in the child's gaining proximity to caregivers.

imprinting
   An irreversible, rigid behavior pattern of attachment.

hospitalism
   A condition found in children from substandard institutions. It is marked by emotional disturbances, failure to gain weight, and retardation.

Children who have been deprived of a good early relationship with a caregiver can benefit greatly if the environment is improved. Dennis (1973) followed children raised in an orphanage in Lebanon. The children received little attention, and their life was one of uninterrupted boredom. When tested after the first year, they were extremely retarded, but after being adopted, they recovered quickly. Those adopted before the age of 2 recovered well. At about 6 years of age, those who were not adopted were transferred to other institutions—one for males, the other for females. The institution serving the females was just as bad as the one from which they had come. When tested during middle childhood, the girls were quite retarded. The institution for males, however, was run differently and provided a more stimulating environment filled with toys, educational equipment, and films. The boys had an average IQ of 80, far above the intelligence scores for the girls.

No matter whether the infant monkey was fed by the wire or by the cloth substitute mother, the infant ran to the cloth mother when frightened.

Dennis's observations led to two conclusions. First, these children suffered from a lack of stimulation; that is, their environments were so unstimulating that it prevented them from developing normally. The infant needs a rich diet of stimulation to develop in a healthy manner. Dennis's study shows the unfortunate consequences of understimulation in institutional environments (Bradley, 1995). Second, the consequences of these unfavorable environments, although quite serious, could be remedied to some degree by placing them in a better, more stimulating environment. The earlier this occurred, the better.

Years ago, many psychologists believed that attachment was chiefly based on feeding—that is, the satisfaction of the child's need for food—but a series of famous experiments by Harry Harlow brought this idea into grave doubt (Harlow, 1959, 1971; Harlow & Suomi, 1971). Harlow raised rhesus monkeys with either a terrycloth mother or a wire mother. The baby monkeys spent as much time as they could with the cloth surrogate, even when the wire mother did the feeding. Harlow noted that primates had a need for **contact comfort,** but there was more to it than the need for warmth and comfort. When frightened, the infant monkeys clung to and were comforted by the presence of the cloth mother, even when the wire mother had fed them. At times, these baby monkeys gained enough "courage" to investigate the feared stimulus, using the mother as a safe base of operations. But even though the monkeys raised with the cloth mother were more normal than those raised with the wire mother, they still exhibited abnormalities. They could not play normally, showed rocking movements, bit themselves, were withdrawn, and could not function sexually. If infant monkeys were well cared for but deprived of physical closeness, they showed fear and withdrawal and were unable to establish social relations with peers.

In other studies, Harlow demonstrated that the injurious consequences of a lack of mothering could be, to some degree, reduced if the maternal deprivation is addressed early enough (Harlow & Harlow, 1962). Although we must naturally be careful about transferring conclusions between monkeys and human beings, Harlow's studies suggest that touching and contact may be a prime need for infants and a key ingredient in promoting attachment.

Guideposts

What implications do the studies conducted by Spitz, Dennis, and Harlow have for institutions and caregivers?

contact comfort

The need for physical touching and fondling.

The Quality of Attachment

Up to this point, research clearly showed the importance of the caregiver-child attachment, that it was not based on feeding, and that the results of poor early relationships could be partially repaired. Most children, though, do develop some attachment to a caregiver, and it was Mary Ainsworth, a researcher who originally worked with Bowlby, who discovered how the quality of that attachment would influence the child's development. Ainsworth's (1967; Ainsworth et al., 1978) observations both in Uganda, Africa, and Baltimore, Maryland, pointed to the importance of the quality of attachment between parent and child. The infants' confident use of mothers as the secure base from which to explore was the primary evidence of secure attachment, and a show of anxiety or anger was interpreted as anxious attachment. Ainsworth noticed that if mother was present and the child's anxiety level was low, children would roam all around the room and explore things. If mother left the room, the infant became upset in Uganda but less so in Baltimore. Ugandan children are kept close and mother absence is unusual, whereas children in Baltimore were more used to the comings and goings of mother.

Such naturalistic observations are very time-consuming and difficult to control, so Ainsworth and her colleagues developed a structured way of measuring attachment behaviors using what is called the **strange situation** (see Table 7.1), a procedure in which young children experience a series of brief separations from and reunions with their caregivers, and their reactions are observed (Ainsworth & Wittig, 1969; Waters & Deane, 1982). The strange situation is one way to determine the quality of attachment.

Using the strange situation, infants were originally classified into three major categories depending on the pattern of behavior observed (Ainsworth, Blehar, Waters, & Wall, 1978). Later, a fourth category or major pattern of behavior was found, but not every researcher uses it (Main & Solomon, 1990; Waters, 1997).

Guideposts

How is the quality of attachment measured?

strange situation

An experimental procedure used to measure attachment behaviors.

secure attachment

A type of attachment behavior in which the infant in the strange situation uses the mother as a secure base of operations.

anxious/avoidant attachment

A type of attachment behavior shown in the "strange situation," in which the child avoids reestablishing contact with the mother as she reenters the room after a brief separation.

Table 7.1	The Strange Situation	
Episode	**People Present**	**Procedure**
1	B, C, E	E shows C where to put B and where to sit, then leaves. If necessary, C gets B to start playing with toys.
2	B, C	C does not initiate interaction but may respond.
3	B, C, S	S enters, sits quietly for a minute, talks with C for a minute, and engages B in interaction or play for a minute.
4	B, S	C exits. S lets B play. If B needs comfort, S tries to provide it. If B cries hard, episode can be terminated early.
5	B, C	C calls to B from outside the door, enters, greets B, and pauses. If B needs comfort, C may provide it. When B is ready to play with toys, C sits in her chair. If B is very upset and needs extra time with C, episode can be prolonged.
6	B	C exits. B is left alone. If B cries hard, episode can be terminated early.
7	B, S	S enters, greets B, and pauses. If B is OK, S sits. If B needs comfort, S tries to provide it. If B cries hard, episode can be ended early.
8	B, C	C calls to B from outside the door, enters, pauses, picks B up, comforts B if necessary, and lets B return to play when ready.

NOTE: B = baby; C = caregiver; E = experimenter; S = stranger.
SOURCE: Colin (1996)

Infants are classified as **securely attached** if, when reunited with their mothers, they greet them positively, actively attempt to reestablish proximity during the reunions, and show few if any negative behaviors toward them. Secure infants use their mothers as a base of operations to explore the environment when the mother is present (Ainsworth, 1979). When mother leaves they may protest or cry, but when she returns she is greeted with pleasure, and the child wants to be picked up and held close. They are easily consoled (Main & Cassidy, 1988).

Infants classified as **anxious/avoidant** ignore their mother's entrance into the room during the reunion episodes and may actively avoid reestablishing contact (Main & Cassidy, 1988). They explore the new environment without using their mother as a base of operations and don't care whether she is there. When their mother leaves, they are not affected, and on return they avoid the mother. They do not try to gain contact when distressed and do not like to be held.

Infants classified as **anxious/resistant** (also called anxious/ambivalent) show a great deal of anxiety on entering the room even before the session begins. They are clingy from the beginning and afraid to explore the room on their own. They become terribly anxious and agitated on separation, often crying profusely. They show an angry resistance toward the mother on reunion (Joffe & Vaughn, 1982). They are ambivalent, both seeking and resisting close contact (Ainsworth, 1979). These infants seek contact with their mother but simultaneously arch away from her in an angry fashion and refuse to be soothed.

The fourth group, **anxious/disorganized-disoriented,** show many different behaviors. Sometimes, the infant may first approach the caregiver and then show avoidance or suddenly cry out after having been quieted. The infant may also show contradictory behaviors at the same time, such as approaching the parent while taking great care not to look at the caregiver. Some even show fear of their caregiver. They appear confused, apprehensive, and sometimes depressed (Hertsgaard, 1995). Many abused and neglected children act in this manner. These infants show high levels of hormones indicative of stress (Grossman, 1993).

Generally, in most samples drawn from ordinary middle- or working-class families in the United States, about 60% to 65% of infants are classified as securely attached, between 20% and 25% as avoidant, and about 10% as resistant. The percentage of infants who are considered disoriented-disorganized varies greatly with the sample used; about 5% to 8% in a typical nonclinical sample (Waters, 1997), although some estimates are a bit higher. In some clinical samples involving maltreated children or children whose caregivers suffer from some serious mental disorders, the percentages can skyrocket to more than 50% (Colin, 1996; Lyons-Ruth, Easterbrooks, & Cibelli, 1990).

Infant Attachment and Later Behavior

The difference in the way children react in the strange situation is interesting in itself. Its importance is increased by the many studies finding a relationship between type of attachment and later behavior and development. At 2 years of age, infants who were classified as securely attached are more enthusiastic, more persistent, and less easily frustrated than the infants from the other two groups (Matas, Arend, & Sroufe, 1978). Securely attached infants are more socially and cognitively competent as toddlers (Waters, 1978). Securely attached infants also are better problem solvers during toddlerhood (Frankel & Bates, 1990). Securely attached children are more cooperative and comply more readily with mothers' instructions (Londerville & Main, 1981). Securely attached children at 18 months show a higher quality of play and more advanced verbal ability than anxiously

anxious/resistant attachment

A type of attachment behavior shown during the "strange situation," in which the child both seeks close contact and yet resists it during the mother's reentrance after a brief separation.

anxious/disorganized-disoriented attachment

A type of attachment behavior shown during the "strange situation" in which the child shows a variety of behaviors, such as fear of the caregiver or contradictory behaviors such as approaching while not looking at the caregiver, during the mother's reentrance after a brief separation.

Guideposts

How do researchers classify infants into the categories of secure, anxious/resistant, anxious/avoidant and anxious/disorganized-disoriented attachment on the basis of their behavior in the strange situation?

attached preschoolers. They are also more popular in middle childhood and show fewer negative and more positive emotions (Sroufe, Carlson, & Shulman, 1993). Anxiously attached youngsters are less effective in their interpersonal relations, less successful in their efforts to master challenging tasks, and show a higher incidence of behavioral problems (van den Boom, 1994).

The quality of the attachment to the caregiver has implications for all close personal relationships and is related to increased competence in interpersonal relationships (Belsky & Cassidy, 1994; Fagot, 1996; Park & Waters, 1989). When children were followed from infancy through middle childhood, children who were identified as aggressive were likely to be considered disorganized in their attachment at 18 months, while avoidant attachment in infancy was related to withdrawal (Lyons-Ruth et al., 1997). Securely attached children continue to have better interpersonal relations (Elicker, Englund & Sroufe, 1992). The inescapable conclusion is that anxious attachment in infancy is associated with a higher risk of problem behavior in the social and emotional domains later in childhood (van IJzendoor, Jeffer, & Duyvesteyn, 1995).

Causes of Secure and Anxious Attachment

What causes some children to be securely attached while others are anxiously attached? The core construct explaining why children differ in attachment security is maternal or more generally **caregiver sensitivity,** which involves being aware of infant cues, interpreting them correctly, and responding promptly and appropriately (De Wolff & van IJzendoorn, 1997; van den Boom, 1997). One-year-old infants of mothers rated as highly sensitive are significantly more likely to be securely attached than those of mothers rated as less sensitive (Isabella, Belsky, & Von Eye, 1989). Mothers of secure infants are more involved with their infants, more responsive to the infant's signals, more appropriate in their responses, and show more positive and less negative behaviors toward their infants than mothers of anxiously attached infants (Isabella, 1993). On the other hand, persistent lack of sensitivity and inconsistency are related to anxious attachment (van IJzendoorn et al., 1995).

Infants who show avoidant patterns of behavior in the strange situation have mothers who are angry, resentful, and irritable; are consistently in opposition to baby's wishes; are always scolding them; and physically interfere with what the infant is doing, often using verbal commands (Ainsworth et al., 1978). They are significantly more rejecting of their child's desires and behaviors than mothers of children placed in other categories. Owing to this maternal behavior, avoidant infants come to expect that interactions with caregiver will be aversive or disappointing, leading to a defensive strategy in which the child directs attention away from the mother and avoids her. They may have the desire for proximity but the experience of rejection. Avoidant mothers are sometimes highly active in infant-mother interactions, even to the point of overstimulation, but are not sensitive to their infant's reactions (Leyendecker, Lamb, Fracasso, Scholmerich, & Larson, 1997).

Mothers of children classified as resistant are best characterized by the term *inconsistent*. They are less involved than parents of securely or avoidant children. Although sometimes sensitive, they are more often insensitive. Their timing is poor, often interacting with their infants when the babies are uninterested or otherwise engaged. They are underinvolved, unavailable, and unpredictable, which accounts for the angry, ambivalent behaviors shown by infants.

The stability of these patterns is still controversial at the present time (Howes & Hamilton, 1992b; Belsky, Campbell, Cohn, & Moore, 1996). When attachment relationships were measured from infancy through nine years, 76% of the children showed no change, but almost a quarter changed attachment categories (Howes, Hamilton, & Philipsen, 1998). The quality of a relationship with a parent can change if there is a major improvement or even a decline in the quality of the child's environment leading to changes in parent-child interactions. A child may show a pattern of anxious attachment while the parents are going through a divorce and then later, if the parents solve their problems and become more sensitive to the child's needs, show a more secure pattern (Waters, 1997).

If sensitivity is a key, then it should be possible to increase the probability of secure attachment through parent training that promotes sensitivity (Wendland-Carro, Piccinini, & Millar, 1999). This has been successfully accomplished with parents of anxious/avoidant children. Parents were taught how to better read infant cues and to respond appropriately, and a change in attachment classification was sometimes accomplished (van den Boom, 1994). Some programs directly teach mothers to be more sensitive while others attempt to improve social support to parents. These often show some improvement in maternal sensitivity, but that improvement does not always translate into a change in classification category (van IJzendoorn et al., 1995). Perhaps this is because sensitivity may be only one of many components relating to attachment.

Maternal sensitivity is an important factor in determining attachment quality. Parental anger, resentment, and irritable behavior is related to a child's avoidant pattern of behavior.

Maternal Sensitivity: A Look at the Key Construct

The relationship between maternal sensitivity and attachment has been consistently found in study after study (Pederson et al., 1998) and across many cultures (Vereijken, Riksen-Walraven, & Kondo-Ikemura, 1997). The relationship between maternal sensitivity and attachment classification is only moderately strong, though, and other factors must be involved. For example, mutuality (positive exchanges between parent and infant), attentiveness to child, and the mother's ability to stimulate the child may also be important. Sensitivity cannot be considered the exclusive, and perhaps not even the most important, factor in the development of attachment.

Other psychologists argue that the focus on maternal behaviors is too simplistic, and maternal sensitivity should be seen as a characteristic of the relationship, not just of the mother (van den Boom, 1997). It might be seen in both the child's skill in signaling needs and parental readiness to respond. Still others want to expand this notion of sensitivity to include characteristics of the mother, child, and the situation. Taking this more contextual or ecological approach, the strains and stresses of life such as marital conflict, characteristics of the mother such as maternal depression, and characteristics of the child such as a difficult temperament may adversely affect attachment (Cummings & Davis, 1996; Davis & Cummings, 1994; De Wolff & van IJzendoorn, 1997).

Others question whether sensitivity shown in one situation may be more important for fostering secure attachment than in another (Thompson, 1997). Perhaps sensitivity shown when a child is fearful or distressed is more important than sensitivity shown in more typical situations. Age may also be a factor. Quick and appropriate responsiveness to infant crying may be more important early in the first year, while assistance during challenging or threatening experiences may be more important in the second year (Thompson, 1997). Last, children may differ in their susceptibility to the influence of maternal sensitivity due to environmental factors that buffer the impact of caregiver insensitivity (Belsky, 1997;

Cowan, 1997). Taken as a whole, these critics argue that although sensitivity is certainly a very important concern, the concept is in need of expansion and other aspects of the caregiver-child relationship should also be investigated.

Looking at the Caregiver-Child Relationship

Many factors may influence the caregiver-child relationship. The caregiver's emotional problems may affect parent-infant relationships, leading to anxious attachments (see *Children of Depressed and Stressed Mothers: Changing the Way We Look at Attachment Problems* on pages 249–250). Mothers who suffer from mental disturbance are not as responsive, resulting in children who are more likely to form insecure attachments. Mothers of anxiously attached children are prone to feelings of insecurity, which may result in maternal behaviors that affect the quality of mother-child interaction. These mothers are less social and less empathetic (Izard, Haynes, Chisholm, & Baak, 1991).

Another variable affecting attachment may be the caregiver's attachment status—that is, how the child's parents remember their early relationship with their own parents (van IJzendoorn, 1995). Using a structured interview called the Adult Attachment Interview (AAI), the early attachment experiences of adults and their current thoughts about them are uncovered (Colin, 1996; Main & Goldwyn, 1985; Sagi et al., 1994). Four categories—autonomous, dismissing, preoccupied, and unresolved—are used.

Adults characterized as *autonomous* find it easy to recall and discuss attachment related experiences. They integrate both positive and negative experiences, tolerate flaws, and do not idealize their parents (Benoit & Parker, 1994). They provide balanced and noncontradictory descriptions of their parents as loving or, if rejecting, understand why and show they have forgiven them.

Individuals classified as *dismissing* report few attachment memories of any value, do not value their memories, and show little concern for their early life. Sometimes, the memories contradict each other, saying that parents were perfect, an idealized view, yet describing rejection. Others simply cannot remember anything at all.

Those who are *preoccupied* are still enmeshed in their relationship with their parents, are extremely dependent on them, and still struggle to please them. They can tell many stories about childhood but cannot provide a coherent and organized description of early relationships.

Subjects with an *unresolved* experience describe abuse, loss, or some traumatic experiences and change quickly between positive and negative feelings, often giving irrational answers. They seem confused or disoriented when loss of a loved one or experiences of sexual or physical abuse are discussed.

Mothers' adult attachment scores predict subsequent mother-infant attachment for their own infants (Fonagy, Steele, & Steele, 1991; Ward & Carlson, 1995). For example, when the Adult Attachment Interview was administered before the child's birth, it successfully predicted later attachment status (secure and anxious attachment between mother and child) (Benoit & Parker, 1994). Mothers who were autonomous generally formed secure relationships with their own children, those with dismissing models most often had infants who were classified as avoidant, mothers with preoccupied attachments usually had infants who were ambivalent, and mothers with unresolved models generally showed disorganized/disoriented attachments (Steele, Steele, & Fonagy, 1996). Perhaps the parents' model of their early relationship influences their ability to perceive, interpret, and respond to their infants' signals (maternal sensitivity), which could influence attachment

Guideposts

How does the caregiver's own attachment status affect infant-caregiver attachment?

PART 2 Infancy and Toddlerhood

The Child in the 21ST Century

Children of Depressed and Stressed Mothers: Changing the Way We Look at Attachment Problems

Early research on attachment conducted by Bowlby and Spitz demonstrated the difficulties that follow when infants do not become attached to their caregivers, and later research shows quality of attachment has consequences for later behavior. Recently, researchers have turned their attention to investigating particular situations that may adversely influence the mother-child relationship and have been taking a more ecological and contextual view.

One of the areas of greatest interest is how maternal depression might affect the infant-caregiver relationship. Mothers who are depressed show more negative expressions, less positive interaction, and are less sensitive during interactions with their infants (Lyons-Ruth, Connell, Grunebaum, & Botein, 1990; NICHD, 1999). Maternal depression is associated with anxious attachment, including disorganized/disoriented attachment (Shaw & Vondra, 1993; Teti, Gelfand, Messinger, & Isabella, 1995). It may also lead to later aggressiveness and withdrawal (Shaw, Keenan, & Vandia, 1994). Depressive symptoms are linked to poor mother-toddler interactions and to problem behaviors in toddlers (Leadbeater & Bishop, 1994). For example, infants whose mothers were depressed for three months after birth show developmental and growth delays at 1 year (Field, 1992). The evidence is overwhelming that these children are at a risk for difficulties in attachment and social and emotional problems later on (Zeahan, Borris, & Scherringa, 1997).

How might maternal depression affect the child? Infants of depressed mothers may imitate their mother's state (Cohn & Tronick, 1989). Infants of depressed mothers display more sad and angry expressions and fewer interest expressions than infants of nondepressed mothers (Pickens & Field, 1993). In addition, the substandard parenting may directly affect the child's development. Children of depressed mothers are exposed to long periods of sadness, helplessness, hopelessness, irritability, and confusion, which may affect their development (Cichetti & Toth, 1998). Depressed mothers may not have the energy to care for their children (Cohn, Campbell, Matias, & Hopkins, 1990). They may go through the motions, not being very responsive, and children learn that their behavior has no effect on maternal behaviors (Leadbeater, Bishop & Raver, 1996). Furthermore, depressed mothers are less sensitively attuned to their infants and less reinforcing (Murray, Fiori-Cowley, Hooper, & Cooper, 1996).

classification (Grossman & Grossman, 1990; Main, Kaplan, & Cassidy, 1985). Some psychologists claim that this model of early relationships may even influence interpersonal relationships in adolescence and early adulthood (see *Early Attachment and Adult Romantic Relationships* on page 252).

The most important principle of attachment theory is that individual differences in infant-caregiver attachment are based on the type of relationship that the infant has with the caregiver (Bridges, Connell, & Belsky, 1988). Some caregivers are more competent than others, and psychologists have identified the characteristics of competent caregiving. For example, parents who are attentive, meet the infant's needs, provide a relatively anxiety-free atmosphere, are skilled in the physical care of the infant, permit increasing freedom with development, show empathy for the infant, and are sensitive to infant cues are competent caregivers. These competent parents express positive emotions; provide a safe atmosphere in which the infant can explore; frequently interact with infants; touch, hold, and smile at their infants a great deal; and provide a stimulating atmosphere for their infants (Jacobson, 1978).

Attitudes and expectations also affect the parent-child relationship. Parents who have positive expectations about parenting adapt well to their new roles, while those who are overly anxious do not (Maccoby & Martin, 1983). Parents who know what to expect of a child at a particular age are less likely to lose their

They are slower to respond and less likely to use motherese (Bates, 1988).

Similar findings exist for mothers who have just experienced severe personal and social adversity, and these experiences predict poorer outcomes (Murray et al., 1996). Studies of disadvantaged mothers show that many are under pressure, which may cause depression and a marked increase in interactions that are hostile, intrusive, or show withdrawal (Cohn, Matias, Tronick, Connell, & Lyons-Ruth, 1986). The effects of social adversity may be additive. Maternal depressive symptoms, lack of social support, and stress combine to lead to problem behaviors (Leadbeater & Bishop, 1994). Those living in poverty, then, are more likely to show these symptoms.

How might this work? Poverty may diminish the mother's capacity for supportive, consistent, and involved parenting and render the parents more vulnerable to the effects of negative life events. The major mediator in the link between economic hardship and parenting behavior is psychological distress derived from an excessive number of negative life events, undesirable chronic conditions, and disruptions in marriages and family life. Economic hardship adversely affects children's socioemotional functioning in part through its impact on the parents' behavior toward the child (McLoyd, 1990). Parents influence their young children through sharing face-to-face interactions, teaching, and managing their children's social environment. Disruptions in each and any of these areas is associated with later problems behavior (Dodge, 1990).

This research shows the new interest in identifying those circumstances under which children prosper or suffer and discovering the ways in which children are influenced by particular conditions. This modern emphasis on investigating specific conditions under which children thrive or do poorly is found when psychologists research other areas of interest as well. Psychologists are slowly turning away from such large questions as what are the effects of day care or maternal employment on children. In the future, questions concerning which children are most at risk and under what circumstances children are negatively or positively influenced by a set of circumstances will be explored. Psychologists are just now becoming aware of the many aspects of the environment that can influence the parent-child relationship. By identifying these elements, we can design more appropriate interventions that lead to better parenting and the prevention of later difficulties (Cichetti & Toth, 1998).

What do you think?

What are the advantages of turning away from answering larger but important questions, such as "What is the effect of maternal employment on children?" and focusing on the specific aspects of the situation that enhance or negatively influence children's development? Are there any disadvantages to such a change in focus?

You can explore the questions above using InfoTrac College Edition. Hint: enter search term *Maternal Depression*.

patience. For example, the parent who thinks that a newborn will sleep through the night or that a baby will be quiet during his or her favorite television program is likely to be disappointed.

The social support received from both family and friends is related to maternal sensitivity, which, as we've seen, is an important aspect of competence (Crockenberg & McCluskey, 1986). This is most true for parents of irritable infants and shows that mothers require the support of other people, especially when dealing with difficult infants or infants with special needs.

Synchrony between Parent and Child

Any understanding of the parent-child relationship must look at the second-by-second interactions between the two. This is often summarized under the heading **synchrony**—referring to the extent to which an interaction is reciprocal and mutually rewarding (Isabella et al., 1989). Watch a mother feeding her baby some mushy cereal, and the meaning of synchrony becomes obvious. The infant's head turns, the baby looks here and there, spits out a little, blows a bubble, and kicks both feet. At just the right second, as the baby looks up, the mother has the spoon ready.

synchrony

The coordination between infant and caregiver in which each can respond to the subtle verbal and nonverbal cues of the other.

The timing is amazing. The infant also was an active participant, looking at mother at just the right moment, knowing what was coming. The timing was based on an accurate reading of cues for both. People who do not have regular contact with a particular infant often find it difficult to do things with the child. For instance, they may not be able to read the child's signals and may find themselves shoveling cereal into a closed mouth.

Mother and child must cooperate, and each must adapt to the other's behaviors. The development of the warm relationship hinges on the development of this synchrony, this understanding of what will happen next. The beginning of this mutual understanding, as well as the basic attachment sequence discussed earlier, starts at birth. In fact, synchrony has been related to attachment quality. Mother-infant pairs developing secure attachments are characterized by many well-timed, reciprocal, and mutually rewarding behaviors. Those developing anxious relationships are characterized by interactions in which mothers are minimally involved, not responsive to infant signals, or in which mothers are intrusive (Isabella & Belsky, 1991).

Infant Temperament and Attachment

Certain characteristics of the child can help or hinder the formation of a viable caregiver-child relationship and influence the nature of their interactions. For example, the responsive, capable infant is more likely to elicit more favorable responses than an infant who is unresponsive (Brazelton, Koslowski, & Main, 1974). Infants who are less sociable interact less with their mothers, and this may produce anxious attachment relations (Lewis & Feiring, 1989).

The most important infant characteristic affecting attachment is the child's temperament (see pages 89–92) (Seifer, Schiller, Sameroff, Kesnick, & Riordan, 1996; Rosen & Burke, 1999). Individual differences in how infants react may influence the way parents respond to the infant (Izard et al., 1991). Maternal behavior is much more positive when dealing with non-irritable behavior in infants than when dealing with infants who are constantly irritable (van den Boom & Hoeksma, 1994). Mothers of children with a difficult temperament, defined in terms of negative emotionality, irritability, and fussy/crying behavior, often are less responsive to their child, which may lead to anxious attachment. Infants who are anxiously attached cry more, demand more attention, and show more negative emotions (Goldsmith & Alansky, 1987). Children with a less difficult temperament are more likely to show more secure attachment (Seifer et al., 1996).

A leading proponent of the importance of temperament, Jerome Kagan (1982), uses the term *behavioral inhibition* to describe the tendency of some infants and young children to withdraw and show negative emotions in response to new people, places, objects and events (Garcia-Cool, Kagan, & Reznick, 1984). Such infants require a great deal of time to adjust to new situations and need to be very close to their mothers. They show elevated levels of a hormone, cortisol, implicated in stress reactions (Kagan, Reznick,& Snidman, 1987). A relationship exists among early irritability, anxious attachment, and behavioral inhibition (Calkins & Fox, 1992). The resistant attachment reflects high inhibition; the avoidant low inhibition. Kagan (1984) argues that quality of attachment reflects temperamental responses to the strange situation and is an important factor helping determine attachment behavior.

There is some disagreement about just how important temperament is to the establishment of a secure attachment. Some studies support its importance, while the results of other studies are more equivocal (Calkins & Fox, 1992; Nachmias, Gunnar, Mangelsorf, Parritz, & Buss, 1996; Vaughn et al., 1992).

Guideposts

How does a child's temperament influence attachment?

Early Attachment and Adult Romantic Relationships

Could the nature of a child's early interactions with caregivers influence the nature of their relationships with others in adulthood? According to Bowlby (1973), infants and young children construct inner working models of themselves and their social interaction partners. These working models include expectations for the behavior of others in relationships, how one acts, and ways of regulating one's emotions and coping with negative emotions. These working models act as guides, allowing people to predict the actions of others and plan for these actions (Collins & Read, 1990). These early relationships could act as a prototype for later relationships even outside the family (Bartholomew & Horowitz, 1991). This possibility generated some fascinating research on adult attachment, based on the idea that patterns similar to those developed in infancy will generalize to other relationships later in life (Hazan & Shaver, 1990). There is some evidence to support this idea (Feeney & Noller, 1990; Fraley & Shaver, 1997).

Adults were asked to choose which of three descriptions best described their feelings toward relationships. These descriptions were translations of the secure, avoidant, and ambivalent classifications found in the infancy research (see Table A). Subjects were also asked about their most important romantic relationship as well as their memories of their early parent-child relationship

(Hazan & Shaver, 1987). A reasonably similar percentage of adults chose the categories of secure, ambivalent, and avoidant as found in infant studies. Indeed, subjects' descriptions of their early relationships with parents reflected these categories. Those who chose the secure status described their relationship with their parents as affectionate, caring, happy, and acceptant. Differences between the two categories of anxious subjects were less significant, but both differed substantially from those choosing the secure status, being much less positive. Subjects choosing the avoidant category perceived their mothers as cold and rejecting, while ambivalent subjects saw their fathers as unfair and unsupportive and reported a lack of independence.

Subjects in each of the attachment categories characterized their love relationships differently. Those in the secure category described their love experience as happy, friendly, and trusting and were able to accept and support their partner. Those choosing the avoidant classification showed a fear of intimacy and a

desire for independence. Anxious/ ambivalent subjects experienced love as an obsession, a desire for complete union, a roller coaster of emotional highs and lows, and showed tremendous jealousy.

Other studies show a similar picture. Those in the ambivalent category noted how easy it was to fall in love but how hard it was to find true love. They are dependent, require complete commitment, and worry about being abandoned (Carver, 1997). Those in the avoidant classification are mistrustful and want distance, finding it difficult to engage in self-disclosure (Cooper, Shaver & Collins, 1998; Feeney & Noller, 1990). Most studies show few if any sex differences. It seems that, as predicted, early social experiences produce relatively enduring differences in relationship styles, and the same three attachment styles shown in the infant literature are found in adult romantic love (Cooper et al., 1998; Feeney & Noller, 1990).

Studies linking the earliest childhood relationships to later relationship styles

Table A	Adult Attachment Types and Their Frequencies

Question: Which of the following best describes your feelings?

Answers and percentages:

Secure (56%): I find it relatively easy to get close to others and am comfortable depending on them and having them depend on me. I don't often worry about being abandoned or about someone getting too close to me.

Avoidant (25%): I am somewhat uncomfortable being close to others; I find it difficult to trust them completely, difficult to allow myself to depend on them. I am nervous when anyone gets too close, and often, love partners want me to be more intimate than I feel comfortable being.

Anxious/Ambivalent (19%): I find that others are reluctant to get as close as I would like. I often worry that my partner doesn't really love me or won't stay with me. I want to merge completely with another person, and this desire sometimes scares people away.

SOURCE: Hazen & Shaver (1987)

are interesting but should be interpreted very cautiously. First, the correlations obtained between childhood experiences and later relationship experiences are positive but not strong, and, in fact, continuity between the two declines as people age. Mental models do not have to remain stable. They are constructed, revised, and continuously integrated as the person has new experiences. In fact, one study found that 25% of the subjects reported a change in their romantic attachment styles during adulthood, mostly in the direction of becoming more secure. These changes were associated with being in a relationship that disconfirms the initially negative model of the self and other (Hazan & Hutt, 1990). For example, an avoidant individual may learn that his partner can be depended

on. Two major researchers in this field argue that it is difficult to defend the idea that a style adopted in infancy remains unchanged throughout childhood and adolescence (Hazan & Shaver, 1987). Change can and does occur.

Finally, evidence indicates that anxiously attached people can have meaningful relationships, and not all securely attached people have relationships that are satisfying and last (Kirkpatrick & Davis, 1994). Early models of relationships have an influence on people, and therefore we might expect some correlation between the nature of one's early interpersonal relationships and later ones. At the same time, the evidence for change demonstrates the dynamic nature of human behavior. Later experiences can change the way an

individual understands the nature of relationships and participates in them. The relationship between early attachment classification and adult behavior is interesting, but other factors are also obviously important.

What do you think?

Why would there be any relationship between early attachment category and later relationship style? What types of experiences might change the mental models of relationships that people carry with them?

You can explore the questions above using InfoTrac College Edition. Hint: enter search terms *Attachment* and *Early Relationships*

Some Basic Concerns with Attachment Theory

Attachment theory, as it presently exists, provides us with a map for understanding the early caregiver-child relationship and its consequences. Problems and questions remain, though, and criticisms of this approach deserve attention. Two major questions, already discussed, are the primacy of maternal sensitivity and the influence that children's characteristics and situational variables have on attachment (Rosen & Burke, 1999). Although most attachment theorists will admit that children's characteristics may influence attachment, perhaps by influencing parents' behaviors, they do not view them as being on par with maternal variables. Others suggest contextual variables may be more important than often realized (Rosen & Rothbaum, 1993).

Another problem is that the model of attachment in use is based on behaviors that occur during momentary separations, and a broader understanding of attachment may be needed to account for behaviors during natural, nonstressful situations (Field, 1993). The strange situation may tap individual differences in the children's coping with momentary stress, but it may provide less understanding of attachment than the way mother and child relate to each other when they are together under less stressful situations.

The question of the meaning of specific behaviors in the strange situation exists when conducting cross-cultural research as well. Let's say that we find that Japanese children react more strongly to separation, perhaps because in Japanese culture children are rarely separated from their mothers at an early age (Miyake, Chen, & Campos, 1985). How should this be interpreted? It is questionable whether one should interpret research in other cultures without a better knowledge of what behaviors may mean.

Kagan (1984) also questions the modern values that arise from the strange situation. Today we value autonomy in children, perhaps because so many

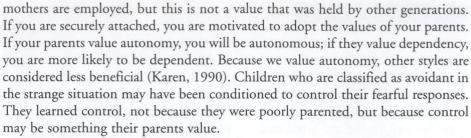
mothers are employed, but this is not a value that was held by other generations. If you are securely attached, you are motivated to adopt the values of your parents. If your parents value autonomy, you will be autonomous; if they value dependency, you are more likely to be dependent. Because we value autonomy, other styles are considered less beneficial (Karen, 1990). Children who are classified as avoidant in the strange situation may have been conditioned to control their fearful responses. They learned control, not because they were poorly parented, but because control may be something their parents value.

Attachment theory is certainly useful and explains many of the needs and behaviors of young children. It is now a cornerstone of our understanding of infants' social and emotional development. It is a growing, dynamic theory and hopefully will address these questions and criticisms in the future.

Although some infants and toddlers show a fear of strangers, new research shows that others do not.

Fear of Strangers

Some time in the second half of the first year, parents are surprised by the way their infants react to kindly strangers. In the past, the baby showed curiosity, but now the child may show fear, manifested by crying and agitation. Until about 4 months of age, infants smile even at strangers, but after that they do so less and less (Bronson, 1968). Most children go through a period in which they react with fear to strangers and even to relatives they do not see regularly. The stage usually comes between about 7 and 10 months and may last through a good portion of the second year (Lewis & Rosenblum, 1975).

Some studies question whether this fear of strangers is inevitable. When an adult female was allowed to interact with infants and their mothers for ten minutes before making any attempt to pick up the babies, and the mothers acted in a friendly manner toward the other woman, the infants were neither fearful nor upset and responded positively to the stranger (Rheingold & Eckerman, 1973). Infant response to strangers depends on the stranger and the context (Durkin, 1995). Infants show less or no fear of other children, perhaps because of the similarity in size (Lewis & Brooks-Gunn, 1972). Female strangers produce less fear than male strangers (Skarin, 1977). If the mother is present and the stranger appears in a familiar place, such as the child's home, less anxiety is generated than when the setting is unfamiliar. In addition, when infants are allowed to investigate the situation on their own, they do not always show stranger anxiety. It is wrong, then, to conclude that stranger anxiety is inevitable or that the appearance or lack of stranger anxiety indicates any problem (Goleman, 1989). Rather, we can say that stranger anxiety is reduced by a number of factors and depends on the situation.

T F
5

Infants who do not show a fear of strangers are at risk for later personality difficulties.

Separation Anxiety

Separation anxiety begins at about 8 or 9 months and peaks at between 12 and 16 months (Metcalf, 1979). It can be found throughout the preschool period in some children, although its intensity lessens with age. Some separations are predictable, as in the case of the mother who every weekday morning takes her child to the day care center. When the child can anticipate predictable separations and knows that mother will return, is familiar with the environment, and is well acquainted with

fear of strangers
A common phenomenon beginning in the second half of the first year, consisting of a fear response to new people.

the substitute caregivers, the child after a while will not show much, if any, separation anxiety when the mother leaves (Maccoby, 1980). Unpredictable separations, such as when a child must enter the hospital, are different. The child is now presented with a novel situation in an unfamiliar environment and with strange people.

How a child reacts to any separation depends on the child's age, how familiar the situation is, and previous experiences. In addition, if the child has familiar toys or a companion (such as a sibling) or is left with a substitute caregiver for whom he or she feels an attachment, separation anxiety will be reduced.

Even the possibility that the mother will leave can be enough to cause some problems, especially in the unpredictable situation. For example, when the mother begins to pack for a trip, the child, in anticipating the loss, may start to cry and cling to her. Any increase in the risk of a separation can trigger some anxiety (Bowlby, 1982).

Separation anxiety may also be a function of temperament. The brain wave patterns of ten-month-old infants who cried both before and after separation from their mothers were different from the brain wave patterns of infants who did not cry (Davidson & Fox, 1989). These differences may demonstrate that reactions to separation are at least partly based on variations in temperament.

Infants often show separation anxiety. They show less anxiety when they are left with familiar people.

The Father-Child Relationship

Up to this point, it must seem as if children have only one parent—the mother. What about the father? We know a great deal about mother-child attachment, but what about the father-child relationship?

Where Is Father?

Fathers are not as involved with their infants and toddlers as they are with their older children (Gottfried, Gottfried, & Bathurst, 1995). Most women have had more experience handling and caring for infants and toddlers than men have. This lack of experience, combined with the cultural prescriptions favoring mothers, causes fathers to be wary of interacting with their babies. In the United States, mothers greatly exceed fathers in the amount of time spent with their children. Even when the mother is employed outside the home, she is much more likely than the father to take time off to care for the children, and she is usually the person primarily responsible for arranging child care.

This may be slowly changing as one clear trend is the greater participation of fathers both with housework and child care when mother is employed (Gottfried et al., 1995). Men's average contributions to housework and child rearing have about doubled since 1970, whereas women's contributions have decreased by a third. The level of paternal care has shifted even since the mid-1980s, and men contribute nearly one-third to this activity in dual-earner couples (Parke, 1995). When mothers are employed, fathers spend significantly more time with their children on weekdays; changes in weekend time are not significant (Gottfried et al., 1995). This is especially true for time spent with sons.

When mothers are employed, fathers participate more in the child care and housekeeping.

separation anxiety
Fear of being separated from caregivers, beginning at 8 or 9 months and peaking at between 12 and 16 months.

Guideposts

How does the mother's employment status affect the relative contributions of fathers and mothers to child-rearing activities and housekeeping?

For Your Consideration ❓

Why has there been some increase in fathers caring for young children?

For Your Consideration ❓

Why are fathers less active in the care of their infants and toddlers than mothers (even when mother is employed full-time)?

When both parents work, there is some evidence that fathers help out somewhat more, although 50–50 splits are rare.

Despite the increase, men still participate much less in child care generally, and only minimally with their infants and toddlers (Hoffman, 1989; McBride & Mills, 1993). When couples with infants were asked to rate the average involvement of fathers on a 5-point scale (0 meant no participation, 5 performing all of the task), the mean score for all tasks was 1.7 for both child care (feeding, changing diapers, soothing baby when fussy, and getting up at night to care for the child) and housework. Interestingly, mothers' and fathers' ratings often did not match; fathers thought they were doing more than mothers perceived (Deutsch, Lussier, & Servis, 1993).

Although fathers are doing somewhat more, we should not go overboard, then, believing that there is true equality in family life. Every study finds that even when both parents are employed, the disparity in time spent is very obvious (Coltrane, 1996). In her research for the book *The Second Shift*, which describes dual-earner families, Arlie Hochschild (1989) found that fathers do not do much housework or child care, despite protestations in the newspapers to the contrary. Hochschild argues that women in dual-earner families work an extra month each year of 24-hour days. Women work approximately 15 hours a week longer than men. Only 20% of the men in her study shared housework equally. Even when couples share the work around the house in an equitable fashion, women do two-thirds of the daily jobs, such as cooking and cleaning up, and most of the daily chores with the children. Much of what men do involves home and car repairs. Men are likely to take their children on fun outings, while women spend more time on maintenance activities such as bathing and feeding. Most studies find that there is little change in the division of labor. Men tend to help out by shopping but don't do much ironing or washing dirty diapers.

It is important for fathers to become more involved. Father involvement is related to children's higher intelligence scores and academic achievement, greater social maturity, and better adjustment (Gottfried, Bathurst, & Gottfried, 1994; Gottfried, Gottfried, & Bathurst, 1988; McBride & Daragh, 1995).

Why don't employed women insist on a more equitable distribution of the work? Although some certainly do, many women believe that child care is principally the woman's responsibility, that their demands will adversely affect the marriage, or that their husbands are not competent to do the work (Pleck, 1985). A number of factors influence just how involved father will be. The father's

understanding of his role and the models he had as a boy may influence his parental behaviors. Also, the mother's attitudes may be important. Not all mothers want more help, perhaps because of their traditional notions or their belief that men are unaccustomed or careless about child care (Parke & Buriel, 1998). A number of other factors are also important—for example, marital satisfaction, employment and social support, sex role orientation, and maternal attitude regarding the importance of father involvement (De Luccie, 1996). A positive marital relationship provides emotional support for sensitive parenting, and fathers seem to need mothers' emotional support and encouragement to be more involved in parenting (De Luccie, 1996; McBride, 1995; McBride & Mills, 1993).

ACTION / REACTION

Angry, Frustrated, But in Love

When Grace was born, Sheila and Jan were ecstatic. Sheila took the first year off work to care for the baby full-time, after which she returned to her full-time job. During the day, Sheila's mother takes care of Grace in her own home. After work, Sheila picks up Grace and returns home. Jan gets home about a half hour later. Jan has always been a good husband and gives Sheila emotional support.

Since she has returned to work, Sheila notices that Jan helps out somewhat more. He does the food shopping, plays with the baby, sometimes does some dusting, and will take Grace for a trip to the park. However, Sheila still finds herself doing 90% of the feeding, diapering, and house cleaning. She feels frustrated and angry, but her friends tell her that she is lucky, since Jan does help out. If she asks Jan to do a specific chore, he does it. However, sometimes it takes him so long that she finds it easier to do it herself.

Though she would like more help, Sheila is afraid that any further requests will injure their relationship. There seems to be a definite limit to Jan's willingness and desire to help. In addition, Jan does not volunteer for any of the everyday child care and housework. Although Sheila would like a more equitable arrangement, she does not know whether pursuing it is worth a disagreement. She is concerned that although she could obtain some extra help from Jan, it would take a great deal of coaxing and perhaps begin an argument. She wonders whether it is worth the cost.

If Sheila asked you, what advice would you give her?

ACTION / REACTION

How Do Fathers Interact with Infants?

Mothers and fathers interact with their infants differently and for different reasons (Parke, 1995). Mothers are more likely to provide physical care of the children, especially younger ones, and fathers to play with the children (Atkinson, 1987). In addition, fathers play in more physical and emotionally arousing ways, whereas mothers tend to play in a quieter, more verbal manner, using conventional games like peekaboo (Bridges et al., 1988; Hodapp & Mueller, 1982). Fathers also engage in more unconventional, unpredictable play (Lamb, 1977), but mothers are more responsive to infant cues of interest and attention (Power, 1985). These differences remain fairly constant throughout infancy.

These differences in interaction explain why children seek out each parent for different reasons (Biller, 1982). Children who seek out their father to play with and their mother when they need care are manifesting not a function of gender but a function of their differential experience with their two parents. The preference is based on the past experience of the child. This interactional difference is culturally

For Your Consideration ?

Why do fathers interact differently than mothers with their young children in the United States?

determined. Swedish fathers and mothers do not play differently with their infants (Lamb, Frodi, & Hwang, 1983), whereas American fathers and mothers show interactive differences. The qualitative differences between mother-child interactions and father-child interactions decline somewhat in dual-earner families (Stuckey, McGhee, & Bell, 1982).

Do Infants Become Attached to Their Fathers?

Infants form an attachment to their fathers, even though the interaction between fathers and infants is limited (Belsky, 1996). The attachment between father and infant evolves in much the same manner as it does between mother and child. Infants whose fathers are more affectionate and interact more positively with them at 3 months show secure attachments to their fathers at 1 year. Infants who are securely attached to their fathers spend more time looking at their fathers and react emotionally when their fathers enter or leave the room. In addition, "well-fathered" infants are more curious and more likely to explore their environment, are more secure, and are more advanced in motor development (Biller, 1982). The better the entire environment, the more likely fathers will be sensitively involved, and the more likely the child is to form a secure relationship with the father (Belsky, 1996).

The pattern of attachment behavior shown to fathers in the strange situation is about the same as that shown to mothers (Colin, 1996). In fact, infants become attached to many people, not just mother. They show attachment behavior with grandparents with whom they have had frequent contact (Myers, Jervis, & Creasey, 1987). Fathers and mothers mean different things to children, based on the roles the parents choose to fulfill (Parke, 1981). Infants tend to choose mothers over fathers when they are hungry, wet, or under stress, but in a stress-free environment, they show no preference and may even seek out fathers when they want to play. When mother, father, and a stranger are present, the child will stay closer to the mother than to the father and closer to the father than to the stranger (Cohen & Campos, 1974). The attachment to both parents can be quite strong. It is also possible for a child to be securely attached to one parent and insecurely attached to the other.

Fathers as Caregivers

Equating competence and performance in parenting is a mistake. Fathers may not show as many caregiving behaviors as mothers, but they may be capable of them (Parke & Sawin, 1976). Experience is important. One man who had to help care for the baby when his wife returned to her job stated, "There is nothing I can't do for that baby. After his first three months, when Nan returned to work after a three-month unpaid maternity leave, he got so used to my feeding him he complained when I left. Now Nan and I split everything: bathing, feeding, changing—it doesn't matter" (Kammerman, 1980, p. 49). Given the opportunity and enough encouragement, fathers can do a fine job with their children and show many nurturant behaviors.

The infant's attachment to the mother is not the result of any biological rule of nature. Children attach themselves to many people, depending on the nature of the interactions. The quantity of the interactions is not as important as the quality. When one asks just what the father's role is in the family, the answer given by Schaffer (1977, p. 104) is "just what he and his wife choose it to be."

Infants can become attached to their fathers as well as to their mothers.

What factors influence the relationship and attachment of children to their fathers?

Maternal Employment

One of the questions that bothers the Walters is how Lisa's return to full-time employment will affect the children. There are two different findings in this area. First, mothers who are employed generally report being happy and satisfied. They emphasize the benefits of work, including adult contact, stimulation, and higher morale. When employed and nonemployed mothers are compared on measures of personal satisfaction, employed mothers often report being more satisfied. However, we must be careful with generalizations. For mothers with children at home, happiness depends on whether the mother wants to be employed (Gove & Zeiss, 1987; Parke & Buriel, 1998). The positive relationship between dual roles and happiness for women holds only for mothers who want to be employed.

Mothers who want to be employed but cannot for whatever reason tend to show an increase in depressive symptoms. (Field, 1995; Hock & DeMeis, 1990). Women who are employed but prefer to be home do not show increased depression, perhaps because they justify their lifestyle on the basis of family need. They do, however, report greater anxiety about separation from their child (Hock, DeMeis, & McBride, 1987). Employed mothers who want to work have much less anxiety about separation and far more positive attitudes toward leaving children with alternative caregivers.

One important factor in parenting is the mother's satisfaction with her role. Satisfaction is related to better parenting and maternal health and better child-rearing outcomes (Gottfried et al., 1995). The more satisfied the woman is, the more likely she is to interact better with her family (Rutter, 1981). The woman who is satisfied being at home is just as happy as the employed woman.

These attitudes are important. Consider the woman who believes that only she can raise her child. Employment is bound to upset her. Both nonemployed mothers who are more concerned about their careers and employed mothers who are anxious about leaving their infants have infants who exhibit more negative behaviors than infants of mothers who express no role conflict (Hock, 1980).

Datagraphics **Married with Young Children ... and in the Labor Force**

The percentage of married women with children below the age of six who are employed has risen sharply over the years.

Source: U.S. Bureau of Labor Statistics

The majority of mothers with preschoolers are now in the labor force.

Highly anxious employed mothers are more intrusive than less anxious employed mothers. An intrusive, overstimulating style of interactions is linked to anxious avoidant attachment. These mothers who find themselves under time constraints and feeling guilty about separations may be very sensitive to their infants' needs but may overcompensate and become very controlling rather than following baby's interests. Mothers' attitude toward employment is related to their perceptions of their children's behavior. Mothers who are employed and believe that this is good for children generally report that their children are doing well; mothers who are not employed and believe this is good for children also report their children are doing well (NICHD, 1998a).

The second finding concerning maternal employment emphasizes the problem that mothers in dual-earner families have in accomplishing everything they want to. It is difficult for a woman to work a full-time job, return home to do most of the housework, spend time with her children and spouse, and find some time for herself in a 24-hour day. In fact, some refer to employed mothers who perform so much of the housework and child care activities while working full-time as "supermoms" (DeMeis & Perkins, 1996). Employed mothers compensate by performing about half the housework that nonemployed mothers do and becoming more efficient at it (DeMeis & Perkins, 1996). However, employed and nonemployed mothers engage in basically the same behaviors. The experience of being a mother is filled with same set of household chores regardless of employment status.

Do Employed Women Interact Differently with Their Children Than Full-time Homemakers?

Mothers employed for more than 20 hours per week spend less time with their infants and preschool children (South & Spitze, 1994). This difference declines as the mother's education increases. Often, educated mothers compensate for the lack of time spent with their children during the week by increasing the amount of time they spend with their children on weekends and during off-the-job hours (Hoffman, 1989).

The most interesting and controversial finding is that there may be a difference in the way parents in single- and dual-earner families treat their sons and daughters. Employed parents with more time urgency on their job tend to devote fewer weekday hours to their sons in particular (Greenberger, O'Neil, & Nagel, 1994). When mothers are employed, they interact more positively with their daughters and less positively with their sons, while when mothers are full-time homemakers, they interact more positively with their sons (Stuckey et al., 1982). When interviewed, employed mothers of preschoolers described their daughters in more positive terms than their sons. Perhaps boys, who tend to be somewhat more active and less compliant, receive harsher words and generally less nurturant treatment.

One difference that is more accepted is that employed mothers emphasize independence training far more than nonemployed mothers (Hoffman, 1989). In contrast to mothers who are not employed, these mothers stress being able to do things for oneself and being self-sufficient (Volling & Feagans, 1995). Girls appear to benefit from such training, but boys may not (Parke & Buriel, 1998). Stressing independence too early in sons has negative social consequences, being related to less positive peer interactions.

Mothers who are employed full-time tend to stress independence training for their children more than mothers who are not employed.

Some people believe that a mother who works outside the home and who is very committed to her job will have very little time and patience with her children, tending not to communicate well with them. However, this is not the case as long as the mother is also highly committed to parenting. In fact, when there is both a high commitment to work and family, employed mothers use a style of parenting called authoritative, which combines openness to communication with children with the use of firm but flexible rules (Greenberger & Goldberg, 1989).

Effects of Maternal Employment on Children

Everyone has some opinion about how maternal employment affects the children. Whatever differences have been found—and there have not been many—depend on the child's gender and social class. Maternal employment does not have any negative effects on girls and may actually be a positive influence on a girl's development. Daughters of employed mothers tend to be higher achievers, and the mother may serve as an achieving role model (Hoffman, 1979, 1989; Parke & Buriel, 1998). Sons of employed mothers do not have the traditional gender stereotypes that children of full-time homemakers frequently have. Children of employed women are more likely to believe that women can be competent, though this finding is stronger for daughters than for sons. Generally, daughters of employed mothers are very well-adjusted, do well in school, and have higher career aspirations.

Social class is another variable. Generally, maternal employment does not adversely affect the cognitive development of lower-income males, and some studies find higher scores on measures of cognitive development among sons of working-class employed mothers. The research findings on the cognitive development of middle-class boys are inconsistent. Some studies of middle-class boys show differences in cognitive development favoring boys whose mothers are not employed full time (Lerner & Abrams, 1994). This is not the case for daughters of middle-class employed mothers (Desai, Chase-Lansdale, & Michael, 1989; Parke & Buriel, 1998). These studies find the grades of middle-class males are somewhat lower; work habits are poorer; and they display less resilience, resourcefulness, and adaptability in the classroom (Greenberger et al., 1994). Some researchers believe that the development of these qualities may require more extended parental supervision, at least in boys, who may be more affected by the lack of parental availability and involvement. Other studies do not find any differences. A study of the school performance and conduct of middle-class elementary school children between the ages of 9 and 12 found no significant differences (Crouter, MacDermid, McHale, & Perry-Jenkins, 1990). No differences in school competence were found between the children of employed and nonemployed mothers if they shared activities such as reading, playing, and talking (Moorehouse, 1991). It may be that more parental involvement when parents come home after school is required. When a disadvantage in cognitive development is found, it occurs only when mothers are employed full-time and not when mothers work part-time (Gottfried et al., 1988). The evidence, then, as far as the effect of mothers' employment status on the cognitive development of middle-class males is mixed, and there is need for additional research in this area.

Minor differences appear in social behavior between children of employed mothers and children of mothers who stay home full-time. Preschool children of employed mothers are more peer-oriented and self-sufficient (Schachter, 1981). Children of nonemployed mothers seek out more help and protection and show more jealousy. No differences in emotional adjustment are found.

Guideposts

How does maternal employment affect child-rearing behaviors?

Guideposts

According to the research, how does maternal employment affect children's development?

In summary, the effects of maternal employment can be either negative or positive, depending on many factors. Maternal employment neither hurts nor encourages children's development. Children of mothers who are employed are not at risk for poor self-esteem, noncompliant behavior (Harvey, 1999), psychological maladjustment, immature social behavior, or adjustment problems (Gottfried et al., 1995). Perhaps this is because other variables are much more important. For example, regardless of whether parents are employed, when children are less well-monitored, they receive lower grades than better-monitored youngsters (Crouter et al., 1990). Such factors as parental attitudes, level of education, the nature of the home environment, and how the child is treated after parents come home from work are all important variables. Finally, most women who are employed need to find substitute care for their children, and the quality of this care may affect the child's development.

Day Care

Many people think of day care only in terms of large, urban day care centers, but most day care does not take place in such centers. As you can see in Figure 7.3, children are much more likely to be cared for by a relative in their own home or in someone else's home than in a group day care center. There is a recent trend toward using more formal, organized day care facilities because they offer greater educational experiences, provide more reliable care, and are more likely to be regulated by some governmental agency, but the majority of children still are not found in such settings (Hellmich & Peterson, 1996).

Many children are cared for in family day care homes that generally serve six or fewer children. Such homes are conveniently found in many neighborhoods, and every state has some regulations for these facilities, although only a small percentage are licensed or registered with their individual states (Frankel, 1994). Parental satisfaction is high, and when providers are well trained, they do a better job. When family day care is good, it is very good; when it is bad, it can be horrible (Frankel, 1994).

Even when both mother and father are employed, some parents are able to care for their children because their working hours allow split shift parenting. That is, one parent takes care of the children during the day while the other is at the job, and at night the roles are reversed. This requires both parents to be significantly involved in child care.

Figure 7.3   Child Care in the United States

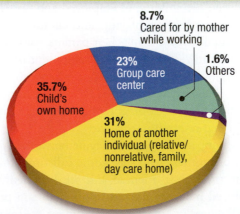

8.7%
Cared for by mother while working

23%
Group care center

1.6%
Others

35.7%
Child's own home

31%
Home of another individual (relative/ nonrelative, family, day care home)

SOURCE: Gomby et al. (1996)

Split Shift

Esteban and Camille were thrilled at the prospect of becoming parents. They both have excellent jobs that they enjoy and are sensitive, loving parents. Camille originally planned to take extensive, nonpaid, maternity leave. Unfortunately, they need both incomes, so she has to return to work.

They are concerned about child care but think they have worked out a good compromise. Esteban comes home at about 5:00 P.M. and Camille can go to work as a nurse for the evening shift beginning at 6:00 P.M. They see each other for about 15 minutes right before she leaves for work.

They reason that since Camille is caring for the child during the day and Esteban at night the child is always cared for by a loving parent. They also realize that they will not be seeing each other very much and wonder whether it will affect their marriage.

Do you think such split-shift parenting works?

ACTION / REACTION

Most people cannot use the split shift solution and must seek out daycare. To do justice to the research on the effects of day care on a child's development, the topic is divided into two sections, depending on the child's age when entering day care.

Day Care and Attachment

Research described earlier leaves no doubt about the importance of attachment for infants, so it is fair to ask whether infant day care affects attachment. Certainly, children in day care form relationships with, and an attachment to, their substitute caregivers (Lewis, 1987). The extent of this attachment depends on the quality of the day care worker's interaction with the child (Anderson, Nagle, Roberts, & Smith, 1981). Children show high levels of attachment to high-interaction, competent caregivers and low levels of attachment to low-interaction caregivers. Again, the quality, not the quantity, of interaction is most important for the development of positive relationships.

Some research shows differences between home-reared and day care children on measures of attachment in the strange situation. Negative effects are sometimes found for children who begin day care before their first birthday. Infants whose mothers are employed and experience day care in their own homes by an unrelated person are more likely to show the anxious/avoidant attachment pattern in the strange situation than infants whose mothers remain at home. However, more than half of those infants whose mothers are employed show secure attachment, and some as yet unidentified factors must moderate the effects of daily separations for these securely attached infants (Barglow, Vaughn, & Molitor, 1987). Some evidence, then, does exist relating infant day care to anxious attachment (Belsky, 1988; Belsky & Rovine, 1988). When these findings occur, sons are more vulnerable to anxious attachment (Chase-Lansdale & Owen, 1987).

Many studies, however, fail to find any heightened risk of anxious avoidant patterns (Phillips, McCartney, & Scarr, 1987; Roggman, Langlois, Hobbs-Tait, & Reiser-Danner, 1994). When children were followed in Sweden, some of whom had begun out-of-home care at various ages and some of whom had no day care experiences, those who had entered day care in the second half of their first year were both better adjusted and later academically superior at ages 8 and 13 years to children who had begun day care at a later age or had no day care experience (Andersson, 1989, 1992). Others claim that the risk is somewhat higher but not

The majority of children in infant day care show secure attachments to their mothers.

dramatically so (Clarke-Stewart, 1988, 1989). In addition, having a secure attachment to an alternative caregiver may even compensate for anxious attachment to a mother (Howes et al., 1988). Good day care may serve a protective function in some areas of social involvement and self-esteem (Egeland & Heister, 1995). Anxiously attached children who received early day care show more positive adaptations in many areas compared with anxiously attached children raised at home.

Current research goes beyond the question of whether day care affects attachment by asking under what circumstances infant day care might influence development. A large, well-designed study of infant child care and its effects on attachment substantially clarified the situation (Chira, 1995; NICHD, 1996, 1997, 1998b).

First, the mothers of secure infants were more sensitive and better adjusted psychologically than mothers of anxiously attached children. They were also better off economically. This is not surprising and matches much of the available research to date.

Second, substitute child care features, in and of themselves, were *not* related to anxious attachment as long as the home care situation was good. Rates of attachment security were not related to variations in the quality of day care, the amount of care, the age of entry into care, or the stability or type of care used. However, infants were less likely to be secure when low maternal sensitivity and responsiveness were combined with poor-quality child care or unstable child care (NICHD, 1997, 1998b). In other words, for vulnerable children, poor child care was related to poor outcomes. Children who experience dual risk—that is, poor home and poor day care quality—have the highest probability of showing anxious attachments to their mothers. It would seem that a good home situation is the most important variable for attachment security and that day care quality is most crucial for those who do not experience good child care at home.

Third, the study found that extensive care for boys and limited care for girls were associated with somewhat elevated rates of insecurity. Perhaps boys are more vulnerable than girls to stress. More research is needed to fully explain these findings.

The report concluded that nonmaternal child care by itself does not constitute a threat to the security of the infant-mother attachment relationship. Nor does it foster secure attachment. However, poor-quality or unstable child care add to the risks already present when the child experiences poor parenting practices, so the combined effects are worse than those of low maternal sensitivity and responsiveness alone (NICHD, 1997). As the results of this major study show, it is probably incorrect to simply blame infant day care; rather, the combination of family characteristics (especially lack of caregiver sensitivity) and poor day care may pose a danger. We can only wait for more on this important subject.

Guideposts

What is the effect of infant day care on attachment patterns?

Early Day Care and Social and Cognitive Development

Attachment is not the only area of interest. The effect of early day care on the social and cognitive aspects of the child's life are also of concern. Preschoolers who enter day care before six months engage in less inactive watching and solitary play and show more cooperative play and positive emotions than those who enter after that age (Field et al., 1988). Attending high-quality day care is associated with greater popularity in elementary school (Field, 1991; Field et al., 1988). However, there is no indication that similar positive results would be found for a sample of children attending poor-quality day care centers.

Many studies of early day care have noted other benefits. Groups of very poor children were randomly assigned to receive extensive university-based intervention group day care or day care in a regular community day care center, and they were compared with a group of children who received little or no day care. The children in the day care groups began their experiences in early infancy—between 6 weeks and 3 months—and continued until kindergarten. The children in both day care situations showed better intellectual development, with the university program being superior (Burchinal, Lee, & Ramey, 1989). Infant day care and day care within the first three years are associated with higher reading and math scores for children from impoverished backgrounds (Caughy, DiPietro, & Strobino, 1994; Desai et al., 1989). It may be that quality day care is positively related to intellectual development, at least for very poor children. Another study found no significant differences in language and intelligence between middle-class 3-year-olds of intact families who had attended high-quality day care since infancy and home-reared children (Ackerman-Ross & Khanna, 1989).

Others argue that children who experience early day care are at risk for heightened aggressiveness, noncompliance, and withdrawal in the preschool and early school years (Belsky, 1988; Belsky & Eggebeen, 1991; Volling & Feagans, 1995). A relatively small but statistically reliable relationship exists between extensive early day care and aggressiveness and social skills problems in kindergarten (Bates et al., 1994).

The quality of the day care situation is the key. Howes (1990) followed a group of middle-class children who entered day care before their first birthday and children who entered between 1 and 4 years of age through their toddler, preschool, and kindergarten years (see Figure 7.4). She found that early entry children in low-quality care had the most difficulty with peers in preschool and were distractible and less considerate of others in kindergarten. Those who entered high-quality child care as infants were not much different from the children who entered high-quality care as older children. When children enrolled in either high- or low-quality day care were examined, children's social competence was related to many factors, including family environment, temperament, and quality of day care experienced. Smaller group size was related to more nurturance and less restrictiveness. Hours of day care and age of entry were not important factors, but quality was. The quality of the day care environment rather than the day care itself had a pronounced effect on social outcomes (Volling & Feagans, 1995). High-quality day care is related to fewer behavioral problems, increased social competence, and greater compliance to mother's suggestions (NICHD, 1998b).

Figure 7.4 Social Adjustment of Children with Varying Child Care Histories

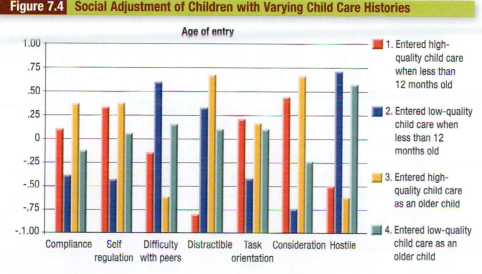

SOURCE: Howes (1990)

For Your Consideration

In your opinion, how does day care affect children?

Day Care after Age 1

It is much easier to discuss day care after age 1 because here the research is fairly consistent. We might assume that if a child from a stimulating environment were to enter a good day care center, little gain or loss should occur. But if a child comes from a nonstimulating environment and goes into a stimulating environment, some gain should result. If a child comes from a stimulating environment and enters a poor day care center, one would expect to see negative effects. Indeed, the research supports these notions (Belsky & Steinberg, 1979). Children who attend day care are more self-confident, outgoing, assertive, verbally expressive, and self-sufficient and less distressed, timid, and fearful in new situations. They are also less polite, agreeable, and compliant with their mother's or caregiver's requests, somewhat louder and more boisterous, more irritable and rebellious, and have more temper tantrums than children who are not in day care. One reason for these findings is that few day care centers teach social skills or effective ways of settling disputes (Clarke-Stewart, Allhusen, & Clements, 1995).

Studies of intellectual performance show that these children do at least as well or better than home-raised children. A longitudinal Swedish study that followed children beginning day care during the toddler years found intellectual benefits for second grade children who had spent considerable time in high-quality center-based day care early in life (Broberg, Wessels, Lamb, & Hwang, 1997). Children from lower-income families are more likely than children from middle-income families to benefit, and the quality of care is more important than the type of care.

Day care has no injurious effects on the cognitive development of low-risk children (Belsky & Steinberg, 1978). For disadvantaged children, an enriched day care program may encourage cognitive development. In some studies, disadvantaged children reared at home showed a decline in intelligence scores over the first three years or so, whereas the scores of those enrolled in day care did not.

Generally, the overall social-emotional adjustment of day care children is good and compares well with that of home-raised children (Deater-Deckard, Pinkerton, & Scarr, 1996; Etaugh, 1980; Watkins & Bradbard, 1984). Most recent studies of behavioral adjustment and out-of-home care find few if any effects (Scarr & Eisenberg, 1993). Although there are differences in social-emotional adjustment, no evidence indicates that day care causes serious emotional or social problems for children.

What are the effects of day care on children's social and cognitive development?

"I Work, but . . . ."

Taneesha is a single parent with a 3-year-old. She worked at a number of part-time jobs while her son Jamal was an infant and toddler, with her mother helping her. But now she has found an excellent opportunity as a paralegal, and the additional income will allow them to move to an apartment in a better neighborhood with better schools. It is an excellent opportunity for her and puts her on a solid career track with a large legal firm. Entailing many responsibilities, it will be a full-time endeavor.

Taneesha will be gone all day. She asked her mother whether she could help, but her mother tactfully refused to take on a daily responsibility. She is in her 70s and not feeling too well. With that in mind, Taneesha is searching for a center for the child.

She feels guilty about leaving her child for the entire day and wonders whether it will interfere with his development. She also admits that she does not know what to look for in a center. She expects to pay for the service, but her ability to pay is limited.

1. *If Taneesha asked you whether she is hurting her child by returning to work full-time, what would you answer?*
2. *If Taneesha asked you what to look for in a day care center, what elements would be most important?*

ACTION / REACTION

Evaluating Day Care

Much depends on the quality of the day care center, especially for vulnerable children in poor child-parent relationships. High-quality, stable child care is associated with positive later outcomes (Howes, 1988; Howes, Phillips, & Whitebook, 1992). All the effects previously described are mediated by the characteristics of the day care center and the home. Vandell and colleagues (1988) observed four-year-olds during play at both good and poor-quality day care centers and again observed these children in play four years later. Those from good day care centers had more friends, showed more friendly interactions with peers, and were rated as more socially competent and happier at age 8 than those who had attended poor-quality day care centers.

Moreover, research shows that programs in more intimate settings with more caregivers lead to better linguistic development and more sophisticated play (Portner, 1995). Better day care is related to better cognitive development. Children's cognitive activity is enhanced when child care facilities offer creative play activities and are staffed by teachers who engage the children in positive social interactions (Burchinal, Ramey, Reid, & Jaccard, 1995; Howes & Smith, 1995).

When evaluating day care centers, both structure and process elements should be noted. *Structural qualities* include child-adult ratio, group sizes, and the physical features of the center. *Process quality* refers to the child's experience in day care, especially the provision of appropriate activities and social interactions with teachers (Hagekull & Bohlin, 1995). Process quality has a stronger relation to child outcomes than does structural quality, but both are important (Howes & Smith, 1995).

Some studies single out certain factors as especially important. One factor is the nature of the program. Although day care should not be thought of in terms of school, such activities as reading to children and playing social games can contribute to social and intellectual growth. Another factor is the caregiver-child ratio. If attention and face-to-face interactions are vital to development in early childhood, the better the caregiver to child ratio, the more likely that day care will be a positive experience (Ruopp, Travers, Glantz & Coelen, 1983). Other structural factors such as safety, ventilation, security, cleanliness, staff turnover, and cost should also be considered.

Guideposts

What structural and process quality variables are important in determining the quality of a day care situation?

The quality of day care in the United States is highly variable (Scarr, Eisenberg, & Deater-Deckard, 1994). Turnover rates of 40% are not unusual, and harsh and detached caregivers are not uncommon (Phillips, Voran, Kisker, Howes, & Whitebrook, 1994). Centers that serve high-income families provide the highest-quality care, probably because the staff is better trained and more sensitive to the children's needs. The most uniformly poor quality of care measured in a variety of ways, including teacher training and appropriateness of activities, is found in centers that serve middle-class children. Centers serving lower-income children often receive government support, and some degree of standards is maintained. Those that serve middle-income children do not receive government support and do not have the financial resources to purchase high-quality care.

The term describing the care that most children receive in day care, according to one major study, is *mediocre*. Some care is so poor that it may be detrimental to children's emotional and intellectual development. Of course, some care is also excellent. Infants and toddlers are in the most danger of receiving poor care, as four in ten are in centers that fail to meet basic health and safety needs (Miller, 1995b). States with more demanding licensing standards have fewer poor-quality programs (Miller, 1995a).

Research to date shows that children given high-quality day care do not suffer, and in some cases they may even benefit from the experience. However, the quality of the day care is a key variable, and parents need to be better informed about what to look for and demand in a day care environment. Unfortunately, some parents may not understand what to look for in a day care situation, while others are thankful to find any reasonable alternative care. The question of what the government's responsibility may be in this area is an important one (see *The School of the 21st Century?* on page 269) and will have a great influence on the future of day care in the United States.

For Your Consideration ❓

What specific factors would you look for in a day care center? Construct a brief checklist of these factors.

Many Roads to Travel

To return to our scenario at the beginning of the chapter, Lisa and Tim Walters now have some of the answers concerning their fear that day care and maternal employment might be harmful to their children. They must be certain that the day care provided is of excellent quality. Tim's attitude toward Lisa's working bears scrutiny, as does his ability and willingness to help with the child care and homemaking chores. Finally, both parents must realize that their responsibilities do not end when they come home from work. They must build active involvement with their children into their schedules. If they choose to leave their children either at a day care center or with the grandmother, the children will develop some attachment to others, but it will not be at the parents' expense.

Much has been said about meeting the needs of the child, and warm, responsive, understanding adults are required if children are to become socially and emotionally healthy. Yet the research shows there is no single way these needs must be met. As Chess and Thomas (1981) note, "Just as the child's nutritional requirements can be met successfully with a wide range of individual variation, so can his psychological requirements" (p. 221).

Many roads can lead to the same destination. Some are more difficult than others. Parents can provide for their children's needs in many ways, taking into account the personality of the child, the child's own needs and requirements, and the family's circumstances.

The School of the 21st Century?

The need for substitute child care in the United States is growing, and many families struggle to find affordable, high-quality child care. The number of young children receiving substitute care has soared over the past decades, driven by the increase in the number of women who are employed and changes in the family structure (Hofferth, 1996).

The major question that arises is how to provide safe, quality day care for everyone who needs it. The research is clear that quality child care programs can help children, while poor day care can stifle their development (Helburn & Howes, 1996). Quality and affordability are key terms, but as quality increases, so do costs. If quality is a major concern, the educational credentials of those who care for children will have to be improved, as will their pay (Gomby et al., 1996).

Parents, the government, and the private sector spend about $40 billion annually on child care (Stoney & Greenberg, 1996). About half comes from parents; 45% from government; and about 5% from business, charity, and other sources. About 85% of the 1,000 largest employers offer some type of child care assistance (Gomby et al., 1996). It is estimated that on an annual basis it costs $7,507 for a baby-sitter, $4,680 for a day care center, and $3,900 for family day care (Deely, 1996). Prices for child care rose in the 1990s after holding steady for quite a while (Hofferth, 1996). For many families, day care is a major expense. Who should pay and how an upgraded day care situation should be financed are great concerns.

At the present time, many government programs and agencies are involved in day care, but to provide affordable day care for every child would require more than double what is being spent today (Gomby et al., 1996). A number of suggestions to improve day care have been made. For example, consolidating existing programs into single block grants to the states might help reduce duplication of effort and increase efficiency. However, this would not necessarily improve quality (Stoney & Greenberg, 1996). Giving child care allowances to families might help, but we must be certain that the money is spent on child care. In addition, this might not improve quality, because many parents may not know what to look for in a day care center (Goldberg, 1996). In fact, when conducting a study of day care quality, parents often rated the day care center much higher in quality than professionals did.

Some European nations are pairing paid parental leave for as much as two years with universally available child care. In Sweden, such leave is provided with 90% pay. In 1993, Congress passed the Family and Medical Leave Act, which requires employers with 50 or more employees to provide up to 12 months of unpaid job-protected leave for parents of a newborn or for serious illness. About 55% of the labor force is eligible for this coverage. Many women cannot afford to take such unpaid leave, however, and one solution may be to provide paid leave, perhaps financed by a payroll tax combined with low-interest government loans that would be repaid much later (Walker 1996). This approach would certainly help in the light of research showing that mothers who either reported

more depressive symptoms or who perceived their infant as having a more difficult temperament and who had short maternal leave showed poorer parenting behaviors compared with a group of mothers who had longer leaves (Clark, Hyde, Essex, & Klein, 1997). Short maternal leave when combined with another risk factor has negative consequences for the mother-child relationship. However, an increase in payroll taxes is politically difficult, and the question of the economic consequences on job creation and competitiveness raise issues that must be solved.

Another suggestion that is becoming more popular is the creation of what is known as the School of the 21st Century, which would provide day care for 3-, 4-, and 5-year-olds directly through the elementary school year-round (Zigler & Finn-Stevenson, 1996). It would also provide after school care for children through age 12. The school also offers outreach services that can include parent education and other support services (see Figure A on the next page). These elements ensure a comprehensive array of services and eliminate the distinction between child care and education. The model is now implemented in more than 400 schools in 13 states. It is funded through parent fees, government grants, local taxes, and help from local business and civic groups. One of its most attractive features is that it uses a community resource that already exists: the school.

The School of the 21st Century, though, will not provide infant and toddler care. Many businesses also cannot do so, and the need for child care for infants and toddlers remains a very difficult question (Gomby et al., 1996). Although more centers are admitting very young

Figure A | **Service Components of the School of the 21st Century**

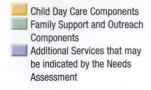

Child Day Care Components
Family Support and Outreach Components
Additional Services that may be indicated by the Needs Assessment

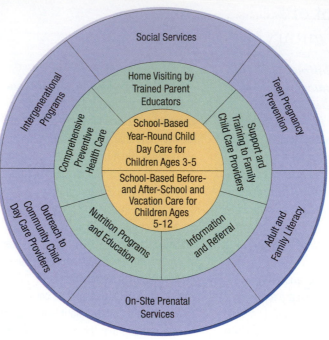

SOURCE: Zigler, Finn-Stevenson, & Marsland (1995)

children, many centers still refuse. Here, there may be a need for some radical rethinking. It may be that work schedules will have to be changed to allow mothers and fathers to care for their infants. Flexible work hours are already permitted in many companies. Part-time jobs, job sharing, and working from home may be the answer for others. Paid parental leave for mothers and fathers may be part of the answer, here, but as noted it is politically controversial in the United States.

The extent to which government has a responsibility for managing day care or requiring the establishment of day care by private industry raises interesting questions. How much day care does the public want to provide? How much is it willing to pay for such services? What is the government's responsibility in this area? We don't expect people to educate their children entirely by themselves, which is why public schools exist. The community as a whole has certain responsibilities, and day care may be one of them. Others argue over the expense of a truly comprehensive day care system or believe day care is a family responsibility.

In the end, though, many of these arguments center around the balance between the individual's responsibility and community involvement. As the need for these services increases and their costs rise, the debate over how to provide such services and what part government should play will become more urgent. It is a debate that bears watching into the next century.

What do you think?

To what extent should child care services be provided by government grants for day care and "schools of the future"? How should the cost of such services be apportioned?

You can explore the questions above using InfoTrac College Edition. Hint: enter search terms *Childcare* and *government*.

Summary

1. According to differential emotions theory, infants' early emotions are innate. These are called primary emotions. Secondary emotions require greater cognitive sophistication, including some understanding of the self as different from others. Other secondary emotions, such as pride, require the child to evaluate his state against some criteria. Children begin to recognize themselves between 15 and 18 months, and begin to evaluate themselves a bit later.

2. Infants can recognize the difference between some facial expressions early in infancy, while recognition of other expressions takes more time to develop. It is only after about 6 months that infants understand the meaning behind the emotional expressions of others. By 1 year, children use social referencing, in which they look at their caregivers in ambiguous circumstances and are affected by the facial expressions of their caregivers. Infants are also affected by the vocal quality and gestures of others.

3. The smile is an important emotional communicator. Infants as young as three weeks smile to both social and nonsocial stimuli, but as infants develop, social stimuli become more salient. Infants show empathic reactions to other infants, which some psychologists believe is the forerunner of more involved empathic responses that require cognitive sophistication.

4. Infants must attach themselves to a caregiver if they are to develop in a healthy manner. Children who have not had the opportunity to do so often experience significant developmental problems. The tragic consequences of maternal deprivation may be reduced if the child receives excellent care later on.

5. Attachment behaviors can be measured using a standardized procedure of brief separations and reunions known as the strange situation. Four classifications of attachment behavior have surfaced: secure attachment, anxious/avoidant attachment, anxious/resistant attachment, and anxious/disorganized-disoriented attachment. Children classified as securely attached are superior to anxiously attached children on a variety of measures. Children's attachment status is related to later behavior. Maternal sensitivity is related to attachment quality.

6. Many factors affect the parent-child relationship, including the parents' emotional state, their own attachment status, their ages, and their attitudes and expectations concerning their new role as parents. The infant's abilities, temperament, and gender also affect the relationship.

7. A child's fear of strangers may begin sometime in the second half of the first year and lasts through most of the second year. The child will show less fear of strangers if the stranger is another child, is female or if the child is allowed to get used to the stranger. Beginning at about 8 months of age and peaking somewhere between 12 and 16 months, children show separation anxiety.

8. Men's contribution to childcare and household chores has increased substantially, especially when their wives are also employed. Even so, mothers still do much more of the housework and child care than fathers do. Increased father involvement is related to better cognitive development and adjustment in their children.

9. Infants form attachments to their fathers as well as to their mothers. Mothers and fathers interact differently with their infants, with mothers often performing more of the daily caregiving chores and fathers playing more physically with their children. Infants often seek out their fathers when they want to play and their mothers when they're in distress.

10. Maternal employment is related to greater satisfaction as long as the mother wants to work. Employed mothers have less time to spend with their families, but they cut down on housework and become more efficient. Employed mothers emphasize independence training more than nonemployed mothers. Maternal employment may positively influence daughters because working mothers may serve as an achieving role model for their daughters. There is still some question about the effects of maternal employment on the cognitive development of middle-class boys. The differences in social behavior between children of employed and non-employed mothers are minor.

11. Most children in day care are cared for by relatives. Family day care homes are also popular. Some studies of children who enter day care before their first birthday show that these children are somewhat more likely to develop anxious attachment patterns, although the majority of such infants show secure attachment patterns. New research shows that poor quality or extensive infant day care combined with poor-quality care at home may lead to anxious attachment patterns.

12. Children who enter day care after their first birthday show few differences compared with children raised at home. Day care children tend to be more peer oriented and more boisterous.

13. The day care experience may be a positive, neutral, or negative one, depending on the quality of the day care, the attitudes of the parents, and the parent-child interactions after work.

Review

According to (1)_____ theory, infants are born with the ability to show particular emotions. (2)_____ emotions are those that are shown early and appear to be innate. (3)_____ and (4)_____ factors are also important factors in the development of emotional expression.

(5)_____ emotions such as pride and shame require some understanding of the self as different from others. Children at about 1 year can be guided by information received from others, a phenomenon called (6)_____. When infants hear other infants cry, they often show (7)_____ by doing the same.

The emotional attachment of an infant that endures over time and space is called a/an (8)_____, while the child's behavior that ensures proximity to the caregiver when frightened is called (9)_____. According to (10)_____, attachment is a product of evolution and helps ensure survival. Konrad Lorenz investigated the rigid relationship of goslings to the first thing they saw, called (11)_____. Infants who have not formed a relationship to a caregiver suffered emotional disturbances and mental retardation as well as other symptoms that Renee Spitz called (12)_____. Wayne Dennis claimed that the difficulties infants showed when they suffered very poor care were due to (13)_____. Harry Harlow found that infant monkeys raised on either a cloth or a wire surrogate mother, when frightened, would always run to the (14)_____ mother no matter which mother fed the infant. Harlow claimed that mammals had a need for (15)_____.

Researchers often use the relatively simple procedure called the (16)_____ to measure the quality of attachment. Infants who greet their caregiver happily and try to establish contact after being separated are categorized as (17)_____ attached. Infants who do not react at all to either the separation or their reunion with their caregivers are described as (18)_____. Infants who are very stressed by the separation from the caregiver and both seek and resist contact after reunion are classified as showing (19)_____ attachment. Infants categorized as (20)_____ show many disturbed behaviors, some of them contradictory, such as approaching the caregiver without looking at the individual. The majority of infants in typical samples are classified as (21)_____ attached. Children who are classified as (22)_____ attached are superior socially and emotionally compared with children who are considered (23)_____ attached. The central concept differentiating the maternal caregiving patterns of securely and anxiously attached children is maternal or caregiver (24)_____. Mothers of children classified as avoidant have mothers who are more (25)_____, while mothers of children classified as resistant are best described by the term (26)_____. Mother's attachment status as measured in the Adult Attachment Interview predicts the child's attachment. Mothers who are classified as (27)_____ tend to have secure relationships with their infants; mothers who are classified as (28)_____ tend to have infants who are avoidant, and mothers who are classified as (29)_____ have children who are classified as resistant. Mothers who are classified as (30)_____ most often have children who show disorganized/disoriented patterns of behavior in the strange situation. The coordinated, second-by-second interaction between caregiver and child is called (31)_____. The most important

child-related characteristic that influences attachment is
(32)_____ . Beginning at six months, infants
often show (33)_____ in which they show
of fear of new people. Fathers are somewhat
(34)_____ (more, less) involved with their
children when mother is employed, and infants do become
attached to their fathers.

Women who want employment but must be home
to care for their children are more prone to
(35)_____ . Women who are employed but
would prefer to be at home with their children show more
(36)_____ about leaving their children.
Mothers who are employed tend to reduce the number of
hours they spend doing (37)_____ . Some
studies show that full-time employed mothers interact more
positively with their (38)_____ than
(39)_____ . Evidence demonstrates that
maternal employment does not affect most children
adversely, but there is some room for concern about the
(40)_____ development of middle-class
boys.

Most children in substitute day care are cared for by
(41)_____ . A major study found that day
care was not related to security of attachment as long as
mothers were competent, but poor-quality day care is related
to (42)_____ if it is combined with poor
parenting. Generally, the studies of children who enter day
care after age 1 shows that the day care experience is not
injurious, but the most important factor is the
(43)_____ of the day care situation. The
quality of day care is variable, and generally the worst day
care serves children from (44)_____ class
families.

InfoTrac

For additional readings, explore InfoTrac
College Edition, our online library.
Go to http://www.infotrac-college.com/wadsworth.
Hint: enter the search terms *Attachment and Separation
Anxiety, Child Care System, Father and Child.*

What's on the web

The School of the 21st Century
http://www.yale.edu/bushcenter/21C/

Issues Involved in Child Care
http://www.bconnex.net/~cspcc/daycare/

How Attachment is Measured
http://www.psy.sunysb.edu/ewaters/mainmenu.htm

The Wadsworth Psychology Study
Center Web Site
Go to the Wadsworth Psychology Study Center at
http://psychology.wadsworth.com/ for quiz questions,
research updates, hot topics, interactive exercises, and
suggested readings in the InfoTrac College Edition
related to this chapter.

Answers 1. differential emotions; **2.** Primary; **3.** Learning; **4.** cognitive; **5.** Secondary; **6.** social referencing; **7.** empathy; **8.** bond;
9. attachment behavior; **10.** John Bowlby; **11.** imprinting; **12.** hospitalism; **13.** lack of stimulation; **14.** cloth; **15.** contact comfort; **16.** strange
situation; **17.** security; **18.** anxious/avoidant; **19.** anxious/ambivalent (anxious resistant); **20.** anxious/disorganized/disoriented; **21.** securely;
22. securely; **23.** anxiously; **24.** sensitivity; **25.** rejecting; **26.** inconsistent; **27.** autonomous; **28.** dismissing; **29.** preoccupied; **30.** unresolved;
31. synchrony; **32.** temperament; **33.** stranger anxiety; **34.** more; **35.** depression; **36.** anxiety; **37.** housework; **38.** daughters; **39.** sons;
40. cognitive; **41.** relatives; **42.** anxious attachment; **43.** quality; **44.** middle

PART THREE

Early Childhood

8   Physical and Cognitive Development
in Early Childhood

9   Social and Personality Development
in Early Childhood

Physical *and* Cognitive

CHAPTER OUTLINE

The Time-Life Remover

Physical Development in the
Preschool Years

Children's Art

Nutrition: Why Preschoolers Eat
What They Eat

Children's Health: A World View

Brain Development

Cognitive Development:
The Preoperational Stage

Recent Challenges to Piaget's Views

Information-Processing Abilities

The Preschooler's Environment:
Home, Television, and Preschool

A Final Thought

ARE THESE STATEMENTS
True *or* False?

1. The rate of growth slows during the preschool years.
2. Most preschoolers will select a nutritionally balanced diet on their own because internal mechanisms operate to make certain children choose foods with the correct nutrients.
3. If a preschooler rejects a healthy food at one time, parents should never again offer the child that particular food until the child asks for it.
4. Most 3-year-olds cannot put 10 sticks in size order.
5. Preschool children believe the taller a person, the older that person is.
6. Most preschoolers believe that cartoon characters are real.
7. Preschoolers forget material more quickly and forget more of the material than elementary school-aged children.
8. Preschoolers are more rigid in their understanding of the order in which events occur at a restaurant or in their preschool classes than older children.
9. There is evidence that watching *Sesame Street* has a positive effect on the cognitive development of preschoolers.
10. Children who attend a Head Start program are less likely to be retained in grade and more likely to graduate high school compared with peers who do not attend a Head Start class.

ANSWERS: 1. *True.* 2. *False.* 3. *False.* 4. *True.* 5. *True.* 6. *False.* 7. *True.* 8. *True.* 9. *True.* 10. *True.*

Development *in* Early Childhood

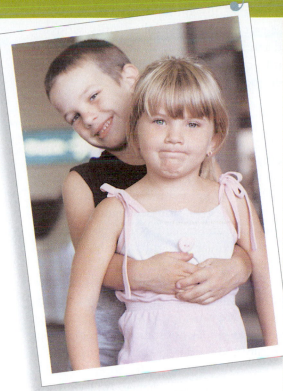

Five-year-old Brent Meldrum saved the life of six-year-old Tanya Branden by using the Heimlich maneuver. Brent had seen it on television.

The Time-Life Remover

"She (turned) almost full blue. My mother was screaming at me to get away from her. I ignored her. I knew what to do. I said to my mother, 'I saw this on Benson' *(the television situation comedy). I lifted her up and banged her on her feet. She bended over and she coughed and it plopped out."*

This is how 5-year-old Brent Meldrum describes how he saved the life of 6-year-old Tanya Branden, who had something stuck in her throat. Brent is the youngest person ever known to have used the Heimlich maneuver, which he calls "the time-life remover" ("Hero," 1986).

In another incident, a 5-year-old child whose mother collapsed in front of him called 911 and calmly waited for the ambulance outside the house as he had been told to do by the police. He learned to call 911 in kindergarten (Burke, 1990).

These incidents demonstrate some impressive physical and cognitive advances. In both incidents, the children showed an ability to translate what they learned into action and performed the proper act in an emotionally charged atmosphere.

Anyone who works with preschoolers will be impressed by these children's new-found abilities. Yet, we are often surprised when preschoolers have difficulty with seemingly simple concepts, such as understanding that squat 8-ounce cups and tall 8-ounce glasses hold the same amount of liquid. Young children seem to confuse reality with fantasy, sometimes believing that if they wish for something it will come true (Woolley, 1997). It is this combination of cognitive and behavioral advancement, along with a distinctive way of viewing the world, that makes preschoolers so engaging.

Physical Development in the Preschool Years

Preschoolers' expanding motor abilities allow them to attend to what is going on around them rather than having to concentrate just on how they walk and hold things. Preschoolers can now easily take part in many physical activities, satisfying some of their curiosity about the world and learning from their experiences. Their physical skills give them more independence. They now interact more frequently with other children and learn from their social interactions.

Growth and Development

The rate of growth slows during the early childhood years. About twice as much growth occurs between the first and the third years as between the third and the fifth years (Cratty, 1986). Growth is still readily apparent, however, during this period, and the child grows about 2.5 to 3 inches per year (see Figure 8.1). Boys are a bit taller and heavier throughout this stage and remain so until about the age of 11 (Hamill, 1977). Weight gain shows a similar pattern, with the preschool child adding about 4 pounds per year during this period (see Figure 8.2).

Figures can be misleading, though, because variation from the statistical average can be expected. Scientists usually speak of a range of heights and weights (between the 25th and 75th percentiles) that are usual for a child of a certain age in a particular culture. Deviations from this range may not indicate a problem, but they may alert doctors to a possible difficulty and encourage them to look into the situation.

During the preschool period, body proportions also change. At 2 years, the head is about one-fourth the total body size, while by 5.5 years, it is one-sixth the body size (Cratty, 1970). The preschooler gradually loses that babylike appearance. The amount of fat decreases during this period, with the added weight resulting from the growth and development of muscle tissue. Generally, boys have more muscle tissue, while girls have a bit more fat, but many individual differences can be found. At the beginning of the preschool period, children generally have their full set of baby teeth, and by the end of the period they begin to shed them. Preschoolers look forward to visits from the "tooth fairy," which bring glee and money (as much as a dollar per tooth in some families).

Motor Abilities

By the beginning of the early childhood period, children have mastered the basics of walking. They are as likely to run as to walk, their movements are smoother, and they turn corners better. Large muscles are still much better developed than fine

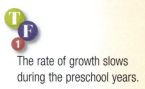

The rate of growth slows during the preschool years.

What changes in height and weight occur during the preschool years?

muscles, but by age 4 years the child can hold a pencil in something that resembles an adult's style and can fold a paper diagonally (Heinicke, 1979). Children at this stage master many fundamental motor skills, including running, jumping, hopping, skipping, and climbing (see Table 8.1).

Figure 8.1 Growth in Early Childhood (50th Percentile)

Throughout the preschool stage, the average boy is a little taller than the average girl.

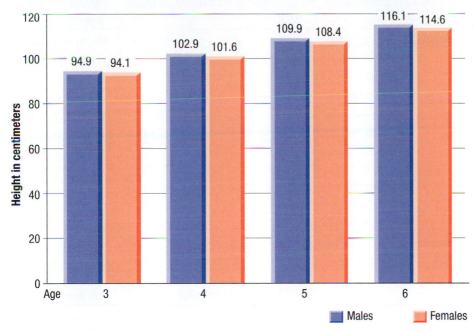

NOTE: Stature is given in centimeters. To convert to inches, multiply by .39.
SOURCE: Hamill et al. (1977)

Figure 8.2 Weight in Early Childhood

Preschool boys are somewhat heavier than preschool girls.

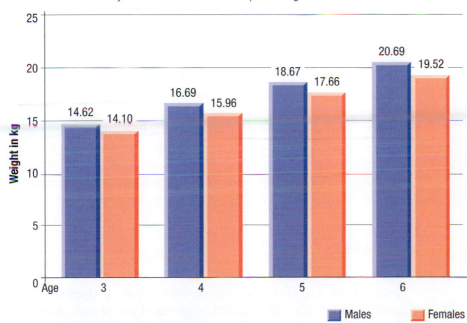

NOTE: All data are given in kilograms. To convert to pounds multiply by 2.2.
SOURCE: Hamill et al. (1977)

Table 8.1	Development of Locomotor Skill		
	3-year-old	**4-year-old**	**5-year-old**
Running	Runs with lack of control in stops and starts	Runs with control over starts, stops, and turns Speed is increasing	Running well established and used in play activities Speed is increasing
Jumping	42% are proficient Jumping pattern lacks differentiation	72% are proficient Jumping pattern characterized by more preliminary crouch	81% are skillful Overall jumping pattern more smooth and rhythmic
Hopping	Can hop 10 times consecutively on both feet Great difficulty experienced with hop pattern	33% are proficient	79% become proficient during this year
Climbing	Ascends stairs using mark time foot pattern During this year ascending stairs is achieved with alternate foot Descending stairs mostly with mark time foot pattern	Ascends and descends stairs with alternate foot pattern	Climbing skill increases 70% can climb a rope ladder with bottom free
Skipping	Skip is characterized by a shuffle step	14% can skip One-footed skip still prevalent Overall movement stiff and undifferentiated	Skips mostly on balls of feet 72% are skillful Can skip with alternate foot pattern

SOURCE: Corbin (1980)

Fine-Motor Control

The 3-year-old riding a tricycle is the picture many people have when they think of a preschooler. Indeed, the development of gross-motor skills, such as running, hopping, and climbing, is readily visible. But the advances in fine-motor control are also impressive, although fine-motor control lags behind gross-muscle development and control. The more subtle development of fine-motor control shows itself in the way a child controls a crayon.

If you give crayons to children of various ages and watch how they hold and use them, the progress is easy to see. Babies use their entire fists. Toddlers progress to holding the crayon fairly well but use their wrist for drawing, while preschoolers by about age 5 have improved to the point where they are now holding the crayon better and using the small muscles in the fingers for control. Still, they must concentrate, and their effort lacks the smoothness it will have later. Both maturation and practice are responsible for this improvement in control and coordination.

Handedness

We live in a right-handed world. Many classrooms do not have any left-handed desks. Demonstrations in class are usually performed by a right-handed teacher for right-handed students. Even the English language glorifies right-handedness. We tell others that their actions are "right on," and the boss's confidant is her "right-hand man," while we give people a "left-handed compliment." Right-handedness is prevalent in all societies

Preschoolers are motivated to master challenges and take pride in what they accomplish.

(Corballis, 1989). Only about 10% of all males and 8% of all females are left-handed, and archaeological evidence suggests that these figures have remained about the same for thousands of years ("Sinister Origins," 1997).

The evidence is strong for some genetic involvement in handedness (Cratty, 1986), but it cannot be a simple pattern of transmission. A child with two right-handed parents has a 91% probability of being right-handed; a child with two left-handed parents has a probability of 63% of being left-handed. If one parent is right-handed and the other left-handed, the child has a 78% chance of being right-handed ("Sinister Evolution," 1995).

Obviously, other factors must be involved. Some believe that prenatal factors may be important. Identical twins frequently do not share handedness, perhaps because they lie differently in the womb (Halpert & Coren, 1990). Environmental factors also play a part. Some parents strongly encourage their children to be right-handed by placing implements in the right hand or handing them toys in a way that forces them to use their right arm. In some parts of the world, left-handedness is socially unacceptable, and children are forced to be right-handed.

Some researchers argue that the precursors of handedness are shown very early. Sonograms of fetal thumb sucking show that more than 90% of fetuses who suck their thumb do so with their right hand (Hepper, Shahidollah, & White, 1990). In addition, observations of infants only 2 days old find that about two-thirds of the infants preferred to lie with their heads turned to the right. At 5 months of age, these infants preferred to reach for things with their right hands, and almost all babies who preferred to lie with their heads to the left reached for things with their left hands (Michel, 1981).

Still, a rigid preference is not found in infancy. Most 6- to 9-month-olds use their left or right hands interchangeably without showing a preference (McCormick & Maurer, 1988). When infants and toddlers were videotaped as they played with toys that required two hands, the 9-month-olds used both their hands equally, but the 13-month-olds showed a preference (Cornwell, Harris, & Fitzgerald, 1991). As the toddler matures, that preference becomes more definite. Still, 4- and 5-year-olds may still use one hand for one activity, such as eating with a spoon, and the other hand for another activity, such as throwing a ball. Usually, by the kindergarten year, the presence is well established (McManus et al., 1988), although in some cases, handedness does not fully show itself until 6, 7, or even 8 years of age (Black & Puckett, 1996).

Handedness is an outgrowth of brain lateralization, the process in which particular abilities are located in either the left or right hemisphere of the brain. Generally, children who develop their handedness early show better motor skills (Gebbard, Hart, & Gentry, 1985). It makes no difference whether that preference is right or left, just so long as there is some preference.

Children's Art

Children have a natural affinity for drawing and painting, and their artistic ability can be viewed within a developmental framework, as shown in Table 8.2 on page 282. Give a 1-year-old a crayon and a piece of paper, and the scribbling will begin, but the sweeping motion of the arm and the manner in which the crayon is held testify to the immaturity of the child. The scribblings may not remain confined to the paper. There is a kinesthetic enjoyment in scribbling. This lack of voluntary control belongs to the early scribbling stage—the first stage of artistic development (Allen & Herley, 1975; Toomela, 1999). Later, eye-hand coordination and small-muscle control will improve, so that the child can better control a writing instrument.

For Your Consideration ?

Some people believe that left-handed people experience difficulties because they live in a right-handed world. What might be the problems a left-handed person faces in society? (If you aren't left-handed, you might want to discuss this with someone who is.)

Guideposts

What factors influence handedness?

Table 8.2 Emergence of Scribbling, Printing, and Drawing

The child's ability to write and draw develops in the sequence shown here. The sequence is relatively fixed, but the age at which each ability is first shown varies. Children should be encouraged to draw, but it is wise to appreciate just where they are developmentally.

Year	Selected Behaviors
1	Scribbling emerges, repetitive in radial or circular patterns
2	Multiple and single line crossings
	Variety of scribbling patterns, various positions on a page
3	Simple cross may be drawn, using two lines
	Enclosed space; a variety of patterns emerge
	Figures placed in simple combinations using two figures
	Aggregates, more than two figures combined
4	"Suns" drawn with extra lines, sometimes forming faces
	Human figures emerge, crudely drawn
	Crude buildings and houses appear
	Human figures contain more detail; trunks usually absent; "stick" arms, legs, and fingers
	Boats and cars crudely drawn
	Circles and squares may be drawn
5	Animals drawn; trees appear in drawings
	Refined buildings and houses
	Better drawings of means of transportation—cars, airplanes, boats, etc.
6	
	Triangles drawn reasonably well
7	
	Diamonds drawn
8	
9	
	Three-dimensional geometrical figures drawn
10	
11	
	Linear perspective seen in drawings
12	

SOURCE: Cratty (1979)

During this advanced scribbling stage, the child can stay within the confines of the paper, and more voluntary control is evident. At about age 3, such basic forms as circles, crosses, and ovals appear in drawings over and over again. The transition between drawing these basic forms and the pictorialism of later childhood art is exhibited in drawings of mandalas, suns, and radials at about age 4 or 5. A mandala is a circle or a square divided by one or more lines inside it (Allen & Herley, 1975). Suns are not necessarily round but may be square or rectangular. After this stage, shapes are combined to form human beings.

Drawing is a valuable childhood activity. It helps children develop fine-motor and eye-hand coordination skills, and it gives them an opportunity to display their creativity. Yet, adults often judge children's art by their own standards. Consider the 5-year-old boy who, after seeing a baby hippo at the zoo, became fascinated with the animal. At home, the child began to draw purple hippos with pink noses and ears. A knowledgeable first-grade neighbor told the boy that hippos weren't purple, and the boy received similar feedback from other children and

Children's drawing indicate their stage of development. These two drawings by Laurie Kaplan, one drawn at age 5 and the other at age 10, show her progress.

well-meaning adults. The boy stopped drawing hippos and later began to draw the standard scene consisting of a house in the middle of the paper near the bottom with a tree on one side, a few flowers on the other side, and a blue sky (Whitener & Kersey, 1980). Children subjected to such comments often give up and produce the standard scene. Children learn to conform to their parents' view of the world and keep their creativity within the bounds of adult acceptance. Certainly children must learn the difference between reality and fantasy, but this need not mean having to draw absolute realism. Rain can be green or pink or purple without injuring a child's sense of reality.

Parents can help their children in this area by providing materials that allow them the freedom to express their creativity. Children require the room, the appropriate clothing (especially for painting), and a variety of materials so they can experiment with color and texture. Adults are wise to avoid interpreting children's art, and often children are so excited that they will tell you what they have drawn. The parent can then write a title for the work on the top of the drawing (with the child's permission) to show that words can be used to describe a scene. The nature of a child's drawings will depend on the child's physical and cognitive development as well as on any experiences with art materials.

Guideposts

How does a childs ability for self-expression through art develop?

Safety

One of the pleasant characteristics of the preschool stage is children's ability to do things on their own. They can dress themselves with some degree of care, eat by themselves, and play by themselves for significant periods of time. Preschoolers' advances in both gross- and fine- motor control open new opportunities for private play. Yet, children's motor skills and desire for independence are greater than their mental ability to understand what is good for them.

Accidents are the leading cause of death during the preschool years, mostly motor vehicle accidents, drowning, fires, and poisoning (U.S. Department of Commerce, 1998). Recently, the use of helmets for preschoolers riding tricycles has been suggested to prevent head injuries (CDC, 1997). Although not all accidents can be avoided, precautions—such as using restraints in cars, fencing and locking pools, and placing poisons in locked storage cabinets—can prevent many of them.

Nutrition: Why Preschoolers Eat What They Eat

Infants eat—or don't eat—what you give them. However, preschoolers know what foods are in the house and can tell you what they want. They may want a particular cereal and cry until they get it, refusing anything else. Three- and four-year-old children can rank-order their food preferences, and these preferences are related to eating habits (Birch & Fisher, 1996).

Conflicts between parents and their young children over nutrition revolve around two areas: what preschoolers' eat and the amount they eat. Research into both of these areas show that parents often have a poor understanding of their children's nutritional needs and make serious mistakes in the way they feed their young children.

Parents are often concerned about the foods their children eat, with good reason. Children's food preferences are the major determinant of their food intake, and children do not eat what they do not like (Birch & Fisher, 1996). A preference for sweet and rejection of sour or bitter foods is present in newborn infants (see Chapter 5). Although neonates are neutral in their response to salt, some preference is shown by 4 months of age. This preference is modifiable and children who are fed lower-salt diets show less of a preference for salt than children who are fed a higher-salt diet (Harris, Thomas, & Booth, 1990). The preference for salt shown by young children is largely based on their experience with salt. In fact, children show a preference for foods to which they are exposed over a long period of time. If they are used to heavily sugared or salted food, they prefer them (Sullivan & Birch, 1990).

Why do children seem to prefer foods high in sugar, fat, carbohydrates, and salt, which are not very nutritious? First, as noted, an innate preference for sugar exists, making these foods more palatable. Second, rich foods are often served at holidays and special occasions, providing an association between these foods and pleasant occasions. Third, substances that impart flavor to food are often fat-soluble (they are absorbed by the fat in the food) so that high-fat foods are often very flavorful (Birch & Fisher, 1996). Fourth, foods that are nutritious, such as vegetables, are also more likely to be the ones associated with parents' coercion and the resulting tension and pressure. Parents are more likely to demand children eat their vegetables than their ice cream sundae. Fifth, many sugary foods are advertised on television, making them even more appealing. Spend a Saturday morning watching children's television, and you'll find that the commercials are often more colorful and impressive than the programs themselves! The cartoon characters selling sugar-coated cereals are appealing to the preschoolers. Most commercials glorify processed and sweet foods, encouraging poor eating habits. It is not surprising that the diet of many preschoolers is filled with high-calorie, low-nutrition foods—especially snacks—since preschoolers receive much of their information about food from watching television. Finally, many parents use sweets as rewards.

Preschoolers' food preferences are shaped by many factors. They will prefer foods that their peers select (Birch, 1986, 1987). Parents and nursery school teachers also act as models.

Parents who do not eat vegetables but are always snacking on potato chips may find their children doing the same. Preschoolers who have the greatest amount of fat in their diet by choice are those with parents who have such diets (Fisher & Birch, 1995). Parents may offer their children the sugary, high-fat foods that they themselves prefer. Cultural factors also enter the picture. For example, in the traditional Mexican village, children are regularly exposed to older siblings and parents eating and enjoying hot peppers, often in hot sauces. This encourages the young child to like the burn of these peppers, which is not innately preferred (Rozin, 1996).

Many people incorrectly believe that children will innately choose the most healthy foods and will seek out the necessary nutrients. Except for a few substances such as salt, the evidence for "natural wisdom" is quite weak, even in animals (Galef, 1991). This belief is often based on a misunderstanding of a classic study conducted by Clara Davis (1928, 1939), in which youngsters were allowed to eat what they wanted from a variety of foods they themselves chose, and, indeed, they thrived. This has been incorrectly interpreted as meaning that people will eat a healthy diet due to some internal mechanism. What is rarely stated is that Davis selected what foods children were offered, and in this case only healthy foods were available.

Parents often complain that their young children reject new foods, especially those that are healthy and low in fat and refined sugars. This is typical behavior for preschoolers who, beginning at about the age of 3, assert their independence (Rolfes, DeBruyne, & Whitney, 1998). With repeated opportunities to eat the food, this aversion is sometimes reduced. It may take a number of exposures and tastings. Many parents believe that a child's initial rejection represents some unchangeable dislike. The child is then viewed as finicky and the food never offered again. Since children's food preferences and selection are linked to familiarity of foods, offering these foods again at a later date increases familiarity and makes them more palatable. It is best to offer one new food at a time, in small amounts and at the beginning of the meal when children are most likely to be hungry. The child makes the decision to accept or reject the food; no power struggles should ensue. Children who are coerced or forced to try new foods are less likely to try them again than if they are given the choice themselves (Birch, 1987). This is true even if the coercion takes the form of positive reinforcement (Rolfes et al., 1998).

Parents, then, have the responsibility to choose what foods to make available to their children. This, incidentally, was also Davis's advice. Given sufficient experience with healthy foods in a noncoercive environment, children learn to accept a wide variety of foods of sufficient nutritional quality.

The second area of parental concern is how much the child should eat. Many parents overestimate the amount of food that young children need to eat. When their children prefer to eat less than parents consider healthy, parents become anxious and reason that their children cannot control their portion size. This conclusion is incorrect.

Children's appetites are variable, usually decreasing at about 12 months, probably in accord with the decrease in the rate of growth (Rolfes et al., 1998). Children need and demand more food during periods of rapid growth than during slower periods (Whitney, Cataldo, & Rolfes, 1994). Preschoolers often have periods in which they eat very little. They will eat at one meal and then pick at their food at the next. Parents need not control their children's portion size to make them eat more. Preschoolers have the ability to modulate the amount of food they eat. A natural internal mechanism does this.

Young children are sensitive to the energy density of their foods—that is, the extent to which a particular food provides carbohydrates, proteins, and fats, which are energy nutrients (Birch & Fisher, 1996). Young children adjust their meal size on the basis of energy density, eating larger quantities of less energy-dense foods and smaller quantities of energy-rich foods. Even infants do this, consuming more of dilute formula than richer formula so that their total energy intake is similar to that of infants fed the standard formula (Fomon, 1993). This same effect is found in preschoolers (Birch, Johnson, Jones, & Peters, 1991; Kern, McPhee, Fisher, Johnson, & Birch, 1993). When 2- to 5-year-old children were offered the same menus on six days with no limitations, their intake of meals was quite variable, but total energy intake was relatively constant for each child over a 24-hour period.

T F 2 Most preschoolers will select a nutritionally balanced diet on their own because internal mechanisms operate to make certain children choose foods with the correct nutrients.

T F 3 If a preschooler rejects a healthy food at one time, parents should never again offer the child that particular food until the child asks for it.

A high energy intake at one meal was often followed by a low energy intake at the next and vice versa (Birch et al., 1993). Children, then, have an internal sense of how much to eat and can regulate their meal sizes quite successfully.

Unfortunately, some parents teach their children to ignore their inner feelings of satiety and pay attention to external cues. Parents may reward their children for finishing everything on their plates or restrict them from doing some activity until they have eaten what parents feel is a reasonable amount. Other parents act in an authoritarian manner during feeding ("Eat what I give you right now!"). This teaches preschoolers to pay attention to external cues and makes them less sensitive to their internal cues (Johnson & Birch, 1994). When children pay attention to their internal cues of being satisfied, they tend to eat less; when they are focused on external cues, they do not respond to the energy density of their foods and eat more (Birch et al., 1987). If parents are truly concerned about the amount their child is consuming, they should consult a physician, but placing external pressure on their young children to eat more is usually counterproductive.

Guideposts

What misconceptions do parents have concerning their preschoolers' eating patterns?

ACTION / REACTION

"He Eats Only Junk Food"

Emil is a 4-year-old who seems to survive on junk food. Potato chips, ice cream, hot dogs, and cookies seem to be his favorite foods. He will drink milk but won't eat vegetables or fruits. His mother tries to limit junk food but has not been successful.

Both of Emil's parents work full-time. He attends a nursery school and then stays with a neighbor until they return home from work. The nursery school teacher informed Emil's mother last week that he throws away most of his lunch, eating only the two cookies she packs with the sandwich.

Emil's mother and father are both very busy earning a living, taking care of one grandmother who is ill and homebound, and taking a couple of classes to improve their skills. They admit they don't eat right, either. Still, they are concerned about Emil's eating habits. One of their friends argues that this is only a "child thing" and he will grow out of it, while another warns that this will become a habit.

What can Emil's parents do to improve his diet?

ACTION / REACTION

Children's Health: A World View

Children's death from disease is very rare in Western countries. However, this is not the case in most of the world. One death in every three in the world is a child under the age of 5 (Grant, 1988). The leading cause of death in young children is diarrhea. Most of these children can be saved if they receive a therapy known as oral rehydration therapy, a system of actions that begins with parents giving children a special solution that parents can make from sugar, salt, and water in the correct proportions. Other steps are taken to prevent dehydration. If the diarrhea persists, the child is given a specially formulated mixture called ORS, or oral rehydration salts.

Other diseases such as measles, tetanus, and whooping cough kill millions each year. Polio is rare in the United States, but outbreaks are not uncommon in underdeveloped nations. These diseases can all be eliminated through vaccinations costing about $5 dollars.

Acute respiratory infections also kill many children and can sometimes be prevented or treated using antibiotics administered by community health workers.

Still, many parents do not know how to distinguish between a bad cough and a more serious lung infection.

Last, undernutrition and malnutrition contribute to perhaps as many as one-third of all childhood deaths. Nutritional problems are related to economic status, with poor children much more likely to be malnourished than rich children (Bellamy, 1996). Although food is still lacking in many places, in some areas the problem is the lack of information about how to feed and when to seek professional help. This information must cover breast-feeding, inoculations, ways of preventing illness, special feeding during and after illness, and when to consult a doctor. Safe water is also necessary, as is information about sanitary waste disposal.

The fact that children are dying of maladies that can be easily prevented or cured is tragic. In addition, the health and mortality rate of the world's children is being affected by the destruction of their communities from violence and war. Yet, tremendous progress has been and is still being made, often under the direction or prodding of the United Nations through such international organizations as UNICEF. In almost all areas of the world, the mortality rate for infants, toddlers, and preschoolers has been reduced (see Figure 8.3). In the Middle East and North Africa, the rate of children's death is now a quarter of what it was in 1960 (Bellamy, 1996). Better preventive medical care and medical treatment, as well as access to clean water, are responsible for this improvement.

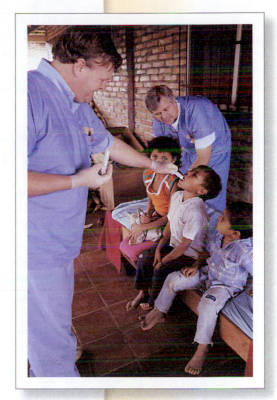

The health of young children from underdeveloped countries has improved due to special international programs, but much remains to be done.

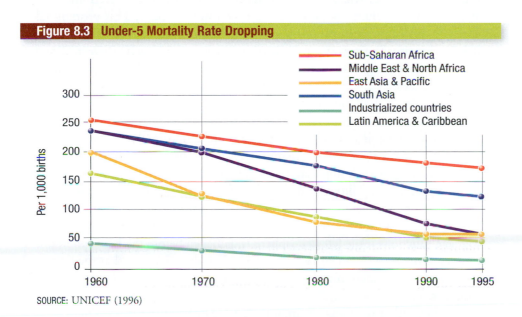

Figure 8.3 **Under-5 Mortality Rate Dropping**

- Sub-Saharan Africa
- Middle East & North Africa
- East Asia & Pacific
- South Asia
- Industrialized countries
- Latin America & Caribbean

Per 1,000 births

SOURCE: UNICEF (1996)

Although a good deal of progress has been made, a great deal more remains to be done. The emergence of low-cost ways of dealing with major health problems opens up new and exciting opportunities for improving the health of the world's children, and progress will continue to be made well into the future.

The health of children within the United States is also a great concern. Most children are covered by medical plans, but about 13.7% are not (U.S. Department of Commerce, 1997). Access to medical care is related to economic status. Poor children are much less likely to see the doctor, both for preventive medicine and when they are ill (USDHHS, 1995). Providing access to adequate medical care for

Guideposts

What are the trends in the health of children around the world?

all is an important concern within the United States. In addition, many children raised in poverty receive nutritional supplements as part of their public assistance. In an age of welfare reform with more stringent eligibility requirements and the growth in the number of working poor, many more children are at risk for having poor nutrition.

Brain Development

The nervous system continues to develop during the preschool period and is related to behavioral change. For example, *myelinization*, the development of the myelin sheath around the axon, allows the neuron to transmit its electrical impulse faster. The myelinization of most of the sensory structures are finished within a year after birth, and those for the motor structures before age 2. However, the myelinization of the higher brain areas involved in complex cognitive functioning is much slower, continuing into adolescence (Korner, 1991). The degree of myelinization in these brain areas is associated with changes in language, planning, and attention. The increasing speed of neural transmission allows the child to process information more quickly and efficiently. Myelinization also insulates the neuron, resulting in less leakage of electrical impulses and making certain that only the correct set of neurons are activated. This reduces interference, increasing the child's ability to attend to a stimulus (Dempster, 1992).

The density of synapses in the brain follows a distinctive developmental course. The fact that synapses are overproduced and experience determines which ones remain and which ones do not was noted in Chapter 5. This pruning takes place at a different rate in various parts of the brain. In some regions of the brain, such as the visual cortex, synaptic density reaches adult levels between 2 and 4 years; for other areas, such as the prefrontal cortex (responsible for planning and executive decisions), it is not until 10 to even 20 years (Johnson, 1998). This allows for greater flexibility in learning, memory, and the development of higher mental functions.

The most fascinating changes, though, are found in the differences in the functioning of the right and left hemispheres of the brain (see page 170). Studies show that the overwhelming majority of people have their language comprehension and production abilities located in the left hemisphere. If a brain injury occurs early in childhood, there is evidence of greater recovery than when it occurs later in childhood (Johnson, 1998). It seems that the right hemisphere can take over language functions if the left hemisphere is damaged before the hemispheres have completed their development (Kalat, 1998). One theory argues that the increased differentiation in function is due to the maturation of the brain (Satz, Strauss, & Whitaker, 1990).

Other authorities disagree, arguing that the hemispheres process material differently (Witelson, 1987). The right hemisphere processes information as a whole. For example, when scanning a face or listening to a melody, the parts are molded into a unified stimulus. The left hemisphere organizes material sequentially as in the perception of a series of words that constitute a sentence. Understanding speech depends on this type of processing. It may be that as children mature, the number and types of cognitive skills to be processed sequentially by the left side increase. This theory leads to the conclusion that it is not that the left hemisphere is specialized for language but that the type of processing that language requires—analytical, serial processing of content that arrives in a structured sequence—is performed by the left hemisphere (Hoff-Ginsberg, 1997).

An interesting study found that the amount of electrical activity in the left and right hemispheres differ significantly (Thatcher, Walker, & Guidice, 1987). The development of the right hemisphere is relatively continuous, but the amount of electrical activity in the left hemisphere shows jumps and spurts. In fact, an extensive jump is found during the preschool years, corresponding to the preoperational stage described by Piaget.

Children improving motor and cognitive development can be related to brain development.

Cognitive Development: The Preoperational Stage

The distinct manner in which preschoolers think was described by Piaget, who argued that children from age 2 to age 7 years progress through the **preoperational stage.** It is a period marked by many advances but also by many limitations (see Table 8.3).

By the time children enter the preoperational stage, preschoolers can use symbols—that is, use one thing to represent another (Siegler, 1998). Children may use a spoon to represent a hammer or a toy person to represent the mail carrier. Children can also use some language. Words represent particular concepts and objects. Another example of representation first seen at the end of the sensori-motor stage is deferred imitation. The child can see something occur, store the information, and perform the action at a later date. To do this, the child must preserve a symbolic representation of the behavior during the intervening time.

Table 8.3 The Preoperational Stage

In this stage, children can use symbols and can judge on the basis of appearance. However, they cannot perform mental operations such as reversibility. This stage is a long one, lasting from about 2 to 7 years of age. Children in the later part of the stage are much more advanced than those in the earlier part. Remember, it is incorrect to use age alone to judge cognitive abilities, because children enter and leave a stage at their own individual rates.

Characteristic	Explanation	Example
Symbolic function	The ability to use one thing to represent another	A child can use a spoon to represent a hammer. The ability to use words also requires the use of symbols.
Deferred imitation	The ability to observe an act and imitate it at a later time	A preschooler can see the teacher exercising and can imitate similar actions at a later time without the teacher's presence.
Inability to seriate	The process of placing objects in size order	Preschoolers cannot place 10 blocks of wood in size order.
Inability to classify	The process of placing objects in different groupings	Younger preschoolers cannot group plastic objects of varying shapes and colors by shape or color. Older preschoolers make progress in this area.
Appearance and reality	The tendency to judge on the basis of appearance	A child shown a red car will correctly identify the color. If a filter that makes the car look black covers the car, the child will say the car is black. When the filter is removed, the child will again identify the car as red.
Inability to conserve	The inability to understand that quantities remain the same despite changes in their appearance	If shown two equal-sized lumps of clay, the preschooler will know they are equal. If one is flattened out, the child will believe that the lumps are no longer the same size.
Centering	The tendency to attend to only one dimension at a time	When comparing the contents of a small, thin beaker and a short, fat beaker, the preschooler will do so by comparing only one dimension of each, probably height, and will ignore the differences in width.
Irreversible thinking	The inability to begin at the end of an operation and work back to the start	Preschoolers do not understand that if you add 4 and 2 to make 6, then you can take 2 away from 6 to make 4 again.
Egocentrism	The inability to understand someone else's point of view	If shown a display and asked how someone standing opposite them is seeing it, preschoolers will not be able to visualize the other person's perspective. Preschoolers believe that the world revolves around them.
Animism	The belief that inanimate objects have a consciousness or are alive. Young preschoolers attribute the characteristics of living things to inanimate objects.	A preschooler believes that the balloon soared to the ceiling because it did not want to be held.
Artificialism	The belief that natural phenomena are caused by human beings	A preschooler will see a lake and say it was made by a group of people digging and then filling it up with water from hoses.

For example, hours after a child sees a sibling doing exercises, the child may do a version of the same exercises.

Language Development in Early Childhood

From ages 3 through 6 years, the child's vocabulary as well as the average number of words used in a sentence increase. The child's style of speech also improves. By the end of the second and into the third year, young children use words to coordinate their actions with others, protesting others' actions, suggesting ideas to others, and responding to questions (Eckerman & Didow, 1996). Their use of language becomes more social and pragmatic (see Table 8.4). At 3 years of age, the child's sentences are well formed but very simple. By age 6, the child is using all parts of speech, making fewer grammatical errors, and using language in a much more efficient and effective manner.

The improvement in grammar is noteworthy. Preschoolers are learning the rules of language. When 4-year-olds were presented with novel words such as a *wug* referring to a ducklike animal, they were able to pluralize *wug* to *wugs*, although children had never encountered the word before (Berko, 1958). In fact, once children begin to acquire some of the basic rules of their language, they often overgeneralize or **overregularize** them (Goodluck, 1986). Children will sometimes overuse the rules of language, saying "seed" and "goed" instead of "saw" and "went." Some children show this tendency more than others. Overregularizations are relatively uncommon; preschoolers show them between 2.5% and 8.3% of the

| Table 8.4 | Linguistic Advancements During the Preschool Stage |

During the preschool stage, the child shows great progress in language acquisition.

Age	Number of Words Used	Numbers of Words per Sentence	New Developments
3	900	3–4	Sentences show subject and verb but are simple; uses present tense; uses words such as *when, time, today*; begins to use plurals and some prepositions; uses commands
3.5	1,200	4–5	Rate of speech increases; asks permission ("*May I?*"); uses *couldn't* and *if* as conjunctions
4	1,500	5–5.5	Demands reasons why and how; rhymes; questions a great deal; uses words such as *even, almost, like,* and *but*; understands most questions; has difficulty with *how* and *why*
4.5	1,800	5.5–6	Does not command or use demands as often; completes most sentences
5	2,200	6	Asks meanings of a particular word; asks function of items and how they work; uses many types of clauses; discusses feelings; understands *before* and *after*
5.5	2,300	6.5	Makes fewer grammatical errors; sentences become more sophisticated
6	2,500	7	Uses all parts of speech to some extent; can define by function

SOURCE: Adapted from Kaplan (1991); Owens (1988); Weiss & Lillywhite (1976)

overregularize
A type of error in which children overuse the basic rules of language. For instance, once they learn to use plural nouns they may say "mans" instead of "men".

Young children engage in a great deal of private speech. Piaget and Vygotsky disagree on the meaning of private speech.

Guideposts

What improvements in language usage occur during the preschool years?

collective monologue

Egocentric exchanges in which young children take turns speaking, but each child's communication has little to do with the content of what the other speaker is saying.

time, so children are most likely to use the correct forms (Marcus, 1995; Marcus et al., 1992). Still, these errors show their increasing knowledge of the use of grammatical rules. With experience, most children gradually learn the exceptions with little or no formal training.

Preschoolers' conversations differ significantly from those of older children and adults. Consider the following example of a conversation between 4-year-olds doing a project (Schoeber-Peterson & Johnson, 1991):

> Child 1: *I'm gonna put on my gloves. Are you finished making your dog, Honey?*
>
> Child 2: *Almost.*
>
> Child 1: *Good.*
>
> Child 2: *I'm gonna get his nose on. Some of the parts are the same. This mechanical dog is more than I thought it was gonna be. He's taking it back. This will work.*
>
> Child 1: *This is nice. Oh, this is nice.*

This conversation contains some real exchanges as when child two answered child one's question. It also contains a number of statements that seem as if the child is talking to herself about the toy dog they are putting together, and child's two's comments are unrelated to anything child one said.

This pattern of some conversation and a great deal of monologue is common in preschoolers (Hoff-Ginsberg, 1997). Piaget believed that young children were not capable of much real conversation and produced a monologue with occasional interactions with others. These interactions, called **collective monologues,** occur because the child cannot understand the other person's perspective. This point raises the issue of what the function of the monologue might be.

The functions of this private speech are controversial. According to Vygotsky (1962), the primary purpose is behavioral self-guidance. Vygotsky argued that people's cognitive skills arise first in social interaction and then are internalized (see pages 64–67). For example, an adult shows a young child how to cut out paper dolls. The child may use private speech as a way of guiding the behavior before the speech is internalized as thought. This private speech helps guide behavior. The frequency of private speech while in contact with peers begins to decline around 5 or 6 years (Berk, 1992). Piaget argues that this reduction in private speech occurs because the child becomes less egocentric; Vygotsky argues that this occurs because children begin to internalize the regulatory function of language. It is possible that both are correct.

Although private speech is certainly common in the preschoolers' conversations, it would be wrong to believe that they do not have meaningful conversations, even though they tend not to be of long duration. When the interactions of preschoolers were observed, children could sustain sequences of conversation from 4 to 12 or even more exchanges, and most of the children's statements were dependent on the verbal or nonverbal behavior of the other children (Garvey & Hogan, 1973). Most conversations between preschoolers are short, but occasionally relatively long conversations occur (Schoeber-Peterson & Johnson, 1989). By the end of the period, children can sustain a conversation longer, have more focused conversations, and attend longer to one topic of conversation.

Despite the preschoolers' limited vocabulary and conversation skills, their linguistic improvements are obvious. This allows us to better understand how preschoolers reason and think.

How Preschoolers Reason

Adults reason either inductively or deductively. **Inductive reasoning** proceeds from the specific to the general. For instance, after examining a number of cases of children who do their homework, we might conclude that children who do their homework receive good grades. Adults also use **deductive reasoning**, beginning with a general rule and proceeding to specifics. They may form a rule concerning homework and grades and then apply the rule to specific cases.

Children as young as 2.5 years can use some inductive reasoning (Gelman & Coley, 1990). Children were shown a picture of a collie and told that it helps take care of sheep. Then they were shown pictures of collies, other dogs, along with a caribou and a condor. The children understood that the collies and other dogs could do the same, but very few extended this idea indiscriminately to other animals (Waxman, Lynch, Casey, & Baer, 1997). Young children do not use deductive reasoning to solve problems, if one measures the ability to use deductive reasoning as understanding that the conclusions deduced are a logical necessity—that is, they must be true. (Siegler, 1991). If you give young children the rule relating homework and good grades, they do not perceive the deduction (Susan does her homework, therefore she gets good grades) as a logical necessity, just as a likely outcome. Children may solve problems that seemingly require deduction using their own experience rather than reasoning. A child who is told "Children who are good receive a treat. Sharon is good; will she receive a treat?" will say yes, a correct answer, but the answer is based on their experience, not logical deduction.

Preschool children, though, often use a different and unique type of reasoning, called **transductive reasoning**—that is, they reason from particular to particular. The simplest example of such reasoning is that if A causes B, then, according to the preschooler, B causes A. The child's understanding of causality is based on how close one event is to another. For example, when he and his father are stuck in a huge traffic jam, the preschooler suggests that his father honk the horn. Since, in the past, the father's use of the horn reminded another driver to go as a red light turned green, the preschooler believes that the horn caused the other car to move and reasons the same will happen in the traffic jam.

Seriation and Classification

Parents are often surprised when their preschoolers have difficulty with a particular problem that seems so simple to adults. For instance, preschoolers between the ages of 2 and 4 years simply cannot seem to put a series of 10 sticks in order from biggest to smallest, an operation called **seriation.** Later in the preoperational stage children can place sticks into size places, but, as shown in Figure 8.4 on page 294, if given a display and asked to insert a new stick into the display, they cannot do so (Piaget, 1952; Siegler 1991).

Nor can they classify items, at least at the beginning of the preoperational stage (see Figure 8.5 on page 295). When young children are given a number of plastic shapes, including squares, triangles, and circles of different colors, and are asked to put things that are alike into a pile, most children younger than 5 years do not organize their choices on any particular logical basis. They may put a red triangle and a blue triangle together, but then throw in a red square. No central organizing principle is evident. Late in the preoperational stage, some progress in **classification** is made. Children can sort items on the basis of one overriding principle—most often form—but they fail to see that multiple classifications are possible.

inductive reasoning

Reasoning that proceeds from specific cases to the formation of a general rule.

deductive reasoning

Reasoning that begins with a general rule and is then applied to specific cases.

transductive reasoning

Preoperational reasoning in which young children reason from particular to particular.

seriation

The process of placing objects in size order.

classification

The process of placing objects into different classes.

Guideposts

What types of reasoning do preschoolers use?

Most 3-year-olds cannot put 10 sticks in size order.

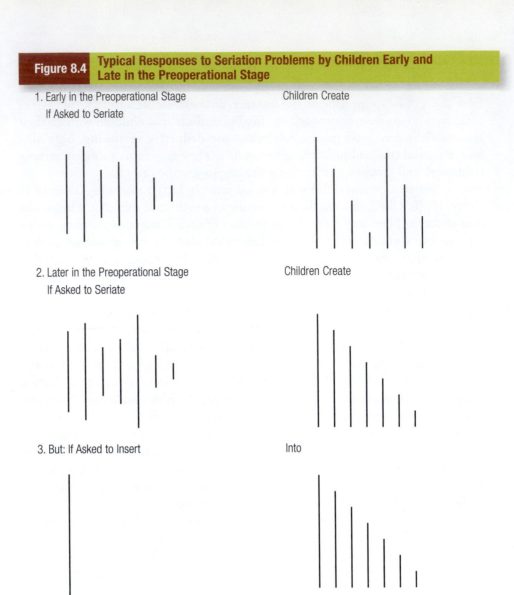

Figure 8.4 Typical Responses to Seriation Problems by Children Early and Late in the Preoperational Stage

1. Early in the Preoperational Stage If Asked to Seriate

Children Create

2. Later in the Preoperational Stage If Asked to Seriate

Children Create

3. But: If Asked to Insert

Into

Children First Try

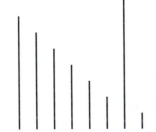

Then Try

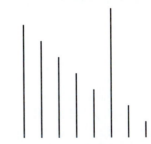

And So On.

SOURCE: Siegler (1998)

Preschool children also have difficulty understanding subordinate and superordinate classes (see Figure 8.6). For example, a child may be shown seven green beads and three white beads, all made of wood, and asked whether there are more green beads or more wooden beads. The child will usually say more green beads (Thomas, 1995). Preschoolers have difficulty with these problems (called **class inclusion** problems) because they cannot seem to make comparisons across levels.

class inclusion

Understanding the relationship between class and subclass.

Figure 8.5 Classification

Young children have difficulty with tasks that require the ability to classify items into various groupings.

Figure 8.6 Class Inclusion (Subordinate/Classification)

Are there more green beads or wooden beads? Young children answer more green beads because they have difficulty making comparisons across levels.

"Are there more green beads or wooden beads?"

"Green beads."

Transitive Inferences

Preschoolers also cannot seem to understand **transitive inferences.** If Susan is taller than Donna, and Shirley is taller than Susan, who is the tallest (Artman & Cahan, 1993)? The preoperational child views comparisons as absolute and does not understand that an object can be larger than one thing and at the same time smaller than another (Piaget & Inhelder, 1974).

transitive inferences
Statements of comparison, such as "If X is taller than Y, and Y is taller than Z, then X is taller than Z."

Present a young child with two identical half-filled beakers of water, the child will tell you they are equal. However, if you transfer one to a tall, thin beaker, the child will then believe that the tall beaker has more liquid.

Guideposts

How do preschoolers handle problems that require seriation, classification, class inclusion, and conservation abilities?

For Your Consideration ?

The most important cognitive skill that preschoolers lack is the ability to conserve. What are the behavioral implications of a child's inability to understand conservation? You may also be able to test Piaget's ideas in this area with children of varying ages.

conservation

The principle that quantities remain the same despite changes in their appearance.

Conservation

Nowhere are the preschooler's differences in perception so obvious than in the child's inability to solve conservation problems (Howes, 1990) (see Figure 8.7). **Conservation** involves the ability to comprehend that quantities remain the same regardless of changes in their appearance. This can be tested in a number of ways. Take two equal lumps of clay and roll each one into a ball. Then, while the child watches, roll one ball into a worm shape and ask the child which form has more clay. The preschooler fails to understand that the forms still contain the same amount and believes that one has more clay. Or show a preschooler two identical half-filled beakers of water. The child will tell you the amounts of water are equal. Transfer the water from one beaker to a squat cup and ask the child which container has more water. The answer usually is that the taller beaker contains more liquid.

Preschoolers' inability to understand the concept of conservation explains some of what seems to adults as strange behavior. Many preschoolers become upset if someone tries to give them a dollar for four quarters or a thin dime for two big nickels. They have difficulty understanding that what they are being given in exchange is equivalent to what they are giving up. But why can't preschoolers solve what seem to adults to be simple tasks? The answer lies in certain characteristics of a preschooler's thinking.

Figure 8.7 | **Conservation**

When presented with the problems seen here, preschoolers give answers (indicated in the right column) that differ from those of older children. Preschoolers have difficulty with conservation problems.

Conservation of number			
Two equal lines of checkers.	Spread out one line of checkers.	Which line has more checkers?	The longer one.

Conservation of liquid			
Two equal glasses of liquid.	Pour one into a squat glass.	Which glass contains more?	The taller one.

Conservation of matter			
Two equal balls of clay.	Roll one into a long, thin shape.	Which piece has more clay?	The long one.

SOURCE: Kaplan, *Child's Odyssey* 2nd (1991)

Characteristics of a Preschooler's Thinking

Most preschool children can concentrate on only one dimension at a time (Piaget & Inhelder, 1969). This is known as **centering**. For instance, try to explain to a preschooler that a cup and a glass hold the same amount of liquid. Because the containers are shaped differently, the preschooler believes that one container is larger than the other. Preschoolers rely on visual comparison and believe that a tall glass contains more liquid than a fat cup.

Centering is not confined to laboratory tasks. Children in the preoperational stage often use height as a means of estimating age. The taller the person, the older the child thinks he is (Piaget, 1969). Young children center on size and height cues. When they are not distracted by these cues, young children can use others, such as facial characteristics, which are more likely to lead to a better guess (Bjorklund, 1995).

Preschool children believe the taller a person is, the older that person is.

Appearance and Reality

Generally, preschoolers confuse how things look with what they really are. Show a 3-year-old a red toy car. A child who knows color will tell you it is red. Now cover the car with a green filter that makes it look black. The child will tell you that it is now black. Now hand the car (without the filter) to the child and the child will say it is now red again (Flavell, 1986).

Preschoolers are perception bound, basing their judgments simply on how things look to them at the present time, and they have difficulty going beyond the information given. The ability to separate reality from appearance increases markedly between 3 and 5 years of age (Gopnik & Astington, 1988).

While young children generally judge by appearances, care should be taken not to overestimate children's difficulties in this area (Deak & Bauer, 1996). Children show the greatest difficulties when deception is involved, such as the problem just described using the filter (Woolley & Wellman, 1990). Preschoolers easily distinguish toys, pictures, and pretend actions from reality. Children know that people who are playing at something are just playing and that a picture is a picture and not real. Young children understand very well that a cactus cannot be made into a porcupine, no matter how much the cactus looks like a porcupine (Keil, 1989). The appearance-reality difficulty depends on the type of situation presented to the child.

Irreversibility

Preschoolers also cannot **reverse** operations. If a clay ball is rolled into a worm shape in front of them, they cannot mentally rearrange the clay back to its original form. Show a child three balls of the same size, each of which is a different color. Place the balls in a cylinder in a certain order (for example, blue, green, yellow). The preschooler has no difficulty understanding that the balls will come out the bottom of the cylinder in the same order. If, however, you rotate the cylinder 180 degrees, the child will continue to predict the original order and is surprised that the balls leave the cylinder in the opposite order (Piaget, 1967). This inability to reverse an operation affects a preschooler's answers to what seem like simple questions. When a preschooler was asked whether he had a sister, he answered yes and gave her name. When asked whether his sister had a brother, he replied no.

centering
> The tendency to attend to only one dimension at a time.

reversibility
> Beginning at the end of an operation and working one's way back to the start.

Transformations

When preschoolers notice that change has occurred, they can point to the beginning and the end but do not realize the sequence involved in the change. For example, when young subjects were asked to draw the successive movements of a bar falling from a vertical position, the children did not draw, nor did they later understand, that it went through a series of intermediate positions between the first and last position (Phillips, 1975).

Egocentrism

For Your Consideration

Are preschoolers as egocentric as Piaget believed? If you can gain the permission of a parent, stand opposite a preschooler and ask the child to raise the right hand while you raise yours. Does the child raise the right or left hand? If the child raises the left hand, how would you interpret the mistake?

Underlying all the child's reasoning processes is a basic **egocentrism**. Piaget (1954) argued that children see everything from their own viewpoint and are incapable of taking someone else's view into account. Young children believe that everything has a purpose that is understandable in their own terms and relevant to their own needs. Preschoolers see the entire world as revolving around them. The sun and moon exist to give them light; mothers and fathers exist to give them warmth and take care of them.

This egocentrism is seen in children's interpretations of their physical world and their social world. Children who know their left hand from their right may not be able to correctly identify the left and right hands of a person standing opposite them. Nursery school teachers are aware of this, and when facing preschoolers they often raise the left hand when requesting that the children raise their right (Davis, 1983).

Egocentrism is found in many social behaviors as well. I can remember coming home on a particularly hard day. It was 98 degrees and the humidity was horrendous. The car had broken down, and a number of other smaller catastrophes had occurred. Seeing me tired and upset, my 4-year-old came over and asked me whether I wanted her to read a story to me. Since stories make her feel better, she supposed they would do the same for me.

Guideposts

How does egocentrism affect children's behavior?

Young children are animistic. This child may play with her two dolls equally so that one does not get jealous of the other.

egocentrism

A thought process in which young children believe everyone is experiencing the environment in the same way they are. Children who are egocentric have difficulty understanding someone else's point of view.

animism

The preschooler's tendency to ascribe the attributes of living things to inanimate objects.

Animism and Artificialism

One of the charming aspects of early childhood is the child's tendency to attribute the characteristics of animate objects to inanimate ones, which is called **animism**. A preschooler may bump into a desk, smack it, and say, "Bad desk." A book that falls from a shelf didn't want to be with the other books. A balloon that has soared to the ceiling didn't want to be held. One youngster made certain she played with all her dolls for the same amount of time so none would become jealous! Animism is most characteristic of the early part of this stage, and it becomes less evident as children reach the age of 4 or 5 years (Bullock, 1985).

The young child's reasoning also reflects **artificialism**, the belief that natural phenomena are caused by human beings. This is a natural outgrowth of what children see around them. Since children view everything as intentional and organized for human use, they explain the world in terms of human causation. Thus, the lake near Geneva was created not by natural forces but by a group of men digging (Pulaski, 1980).

Children interpret their world in terms of what they have experienced in their daily life. One of my daughters was travelling in our car late at night. A beautiful, bright half moon was clearly visible. My daughter turned to me and asked, "Who cut the moon in half?" Since she was familiar with how her parents cut her sandwiches in half, she believed that someone had to have cut the moon in half as well.

Magical Thinking

Children also believe in magical thinking to some extent (Piaget, 1930). Children may believe that it is raining outside because they wished it. Indeed, half of all 4-year-olds in one study believed that a fairy does magic in the real world, and three quarters believed that a magician does real magic, while many fewer 6- or 8-year-olds believed so (Phelps & Woolley, 1994). When 3-year-olds were asked to imagine an object inside an empty box, many of these children claimed that the object would then appear (Woolley & Willman, 1993). When 4- to 6-year-old children were told that a child in a drawing was making a wish to try to influence another person and asked about the effectiveness of the wish, most believed that wishing could make it so (Vikan & Clausen, 1993). As children proceed through this period, they become more skeptical about the effectiveness of wishing, with fewer older than younger preschoolers believing that wishes come true (Woolley, Phelps, Davis, & Mandell, 1999).

Although children younger than 4 years may have difficulty understanding the nature of reality, for other children the problem is not a confusion between fantasy and reality but rather a lack of knowledge about physical phenomena. Children may simply evoke magic to explain events that violate their expectations or for which they simply don't have adequate physical explanations (Woolley, 1997; Woolley et al., 1999).

Guideposts
How do preschoolers show animistic and artificial thought?

For Your Consideration ?
Why do young children sometimes believe that Santa Claus or the tooth fairy is real?

Guideposts
What are the central characteristics of preschoolers' thought processes, according to Piaget?

Recent Challenges to Piaget's Views

After all this, it must seem that preschoolers are described more by what they cannot do than by what they can (Beilen, 1992; Flavell, 1985), and their charm is due to their ignorance. Of course, preschoolers' reasoning appears reasonable to them; it only seems illogical from an adult perspective.

The observations Piaget made of preschoolers using his standard testing procedures are well founded, and no one seriously doubts their reliability (Gelman & Baillargeon, 1983). If you test a preschooler the same way Piaget did, you will get the same results. However, the assumption that because preschoolers fail these tests they cannot seriate, classify, or decenter is questionable. Perhaps if we tested the children differently, they might succeed. Indeed, this is exactly what researchers have found.

At times, simple modifications in Piaget's method change the results of the experiment. For example, Inhelder and Piaget (1964) argued that children can seriate if they can place the items in correct order, put additional items into the series, and correct any errors. So far, this is reasonable. But Piaget used a total of 10 sticks in his observations and concluded that true seriation did not occur at this stage.

artificialism
The belief that natural phenomena are caused by human beings.

When a similar approach is taken with 4 sticks instead of 10, three quarters of the 3- and 4-year-olds could place the sticks in size order, about four-fifths could insert new sticks into the order, and all the children could correct the incorrect insertions (Koslowski, 1980). These children possess the ability to seriate, but 10 sticks is simply too many for the preschooler to deal with at one time.

Piaget noted that children had difficulty with class inclusion problems. Yet, studies show that children sometimes do understand simple superordinate and subordinate classes. Even 2- and 3-year-olds understand that a hammer is a type of tool and a cabinet is a type of furniture (Blewitt, 1994). When shown a number of familiar pictures and asked to pick out the animals, they have no difficulty choosing turtles and monkeys as animals, although they may not get them all.

Even the concept of animism is under fire. Only a third of all the 3-year-olds tested in one study attributed emotional states to dolls (Gelman, Spelke, & Meck, 1983). Although some preschoolers think cartoons and dolls are real, most do not (Prawat, Anderson, & Hapkiewicz, 1989). While there are certainly areas in which children are animistic, we must be careful not to overgeneralize. The point is not that Piaget was wrong but rather that he underestimated young children's abilities because some of the tasks he used were too demanding.

Other Piagetian skills have been taught to children at younger ages than thought possible. Children can be trained to conserve by teaching them to respond to relevant cues and to ignore the apparent visual ones (Gelman, 1969). Preschoolers have also been taught to solve class inclusion problems that they could not originally solve (McCabe & Siegel, 1987). Although there are some doubts about the degree to which children transfer their learning to other situations, these studies do demonstrate that young children are more flexible in the development of their reasoning processes than first thought.

Some of Piaget's ideas have been greatly expanded. At the end of the sensorimotor stage, children develop the ability to represent—that is, to use one object to stand for another. An 18-month-old may pretend that a paper plate is a hat and put it on his head. Representation goes far beyond this simple idea, as shown by a series of intriguing studies performed by Judy DeLoache and her colleagues (1987, 1991; DeLoache, Kolstad, & Anderson, 1991). Consider this situation. A young child watches as a miniature toy dog is hidden somewhere in the scale model of a room. The scale model exactly corresponds to the room. The child is then asked to find a larger miniature toy dog hidden in the same place in the real room. For example, if the miniature toy dog is hidden behind the couch in the model, a somewhat larger but similar toy dog is hidden in the room behind the couch. Will the children be able to use the scale model as a guide to discover where the item in the larger room is hidden? When these and other similar studies are conducted, most of the 3-year-olds but very few 2.5-year-old children use the models and succeed at the task. Younger children seem to understand everything except the relationship of the model to the room. DeLoache argues that the failure of the younger children is due to the dual nature of the model. To succeed in the task, children have to be able to think about the model as both representing the larger room and as a thing in itself. The younger children could not think about the model in two different ways at the same time, but the 3-year-olds could (DeLoache, 1987). The younger children looked at the scale model as an interesting object in itself and not as a symbol.

In fact, when 2.5-year-old children are shown where an object is hidden in a picture of the room rather than a model, they do much better at this task and do use the picture as a guide. DeLoache theorizes that even very young children understand that a two-dimensional picture is a symbol and not the thing itself. They know that a picture of a dog is a representation of a dog. The picture does not require a dual orientation, and so even the 2.5-year-old children can succeed at the

Guideposts

What are the recent challenges to Piaget's ideas?

For Your Consideration ?

Some critics note that the Piagetian preoperational stage seems to emphasize what children can't do rather than what they can. Is this a fair criticism?

task (DeLoache, 1991). These studies show that although a child may be in the pre-operational stage and is therefore capable of using symbols in some fashion, this does not mean that they do so in the same way as older children and adults do.

Piaget's conception of egocentrism has also been the focus of much criticism. Under specific circumstances, preschoolers are not egocentric—that is, they can understand the viewpoint of others. Preschoolers understand that objects with different sides, such as a house, look different from various perspectives but that objects with identical sides, such as a ball, look the same (Flavell, Flavell, Green, & Wilcox, 1981). In another experiment, 1- to 3-year-old children were given a hollow cube with a picture pasted to the bottom of the inside. The children were asked to show the picture to an observer sitting across from them. Almost all the children who were 2 years or older turned the cube away from them and toward the observer, demonstrating some understanding of the other person's perspective (Lempers, Flavell, & Flavell, 1977).

Young children, then, can take someone else's perspective at certain times but not others, perhaps because two levels of perspective taking exist (Flavell et al., 1993). Young children understand that another person does not always see the object in the exact same fashion as the child does. This is basically an all-or-none concept; the child simply understands that others may see it differently. The older child, beginning at about age 4, begins to develop a more mature understanding of the conflicting ways that objects can be represented.

Other important cognitive changes occur at about age 4 as well—for example, the ability to understand the distinction between reality and a deceptive appearance. In the standard test, children are shown an object that looks like one thing but is really something else, such as a sponge that looks like a rock, and are asked an appearance question, such as "What does it look like?" and a reality question, such as "What is it really?" Children under the age of 4 believe that it is not only a sponge but also looks like a sponge (Flavell, Flavell, & Green, 1983). Four-year-olds understand that it looks like a rock but is a sponge. The older child realizes that an object can be represented in more than one way, depending on how one looks at it. Some new evidence indicates that young children fail to understand this due to information-processing limitations; that is, they cannot hold in mind two conflicting object identities at the same time (Rice, Koinis, Sullivan, Tager-Flusberg, & Winner, 1997). When these information-processing requirements are reduced, children who fail the standard test succeed. When 3-year-olds who failed

Ask a child under the age of 4 years, "What does this look like?", and "What is it really?" Children under age 4 believe it is not only sponge but looks like a sponge.

the standard task were presented with an eraser that looked like a peanut, along with a real eraser and a real peanut that were identical in appearance, and asked the reality and appearance questions, the 3-year-olds answered correctly (Brenneman & Gelman, 1993). The presence of both objects helped the young children hold both identities in mind.

These changes in thinking at about age 4 are also shown in children's understanding of the nature of beliefs. In one standard task, a child watches as something, perhaps candy, is hidden in a box. The child is then asked to leave the room and the box is filled with something else, such as pencils, while the candy is moved to another box. When the child returns and is asked where the candy is hidden, the child obviously guesses in the original box. Now if this happened to an older child or adult, they would understand that they had held a false belief and simply change their mind as to where it was hidden. They would understand that another person would make the same mistake, in the absence of any other information. Three-year-olds, though, argued that another child would actually believe there were pencils in the box and stated that they, themselves, always believed that (Gopnik & Astington, 1988). Four-year-olds, though, after realizing they had been tricked, laughed and understood that another child would still think there was candy in the original box. They understood the nature of their false belief and that their representation of the items' location could be wrong and simply changed their beliefs.

In a classic study, young children were shown a skit in which a doll named Maxi left his chocolate in one location for safekeeping (Wimmer & Perner, 1983). When Maxi was out of the room, the chocolate was moved to another location. Maxi returns and the young child is asked, "Where will Maxi look for the candy?" Most young preschoolers believe Maxi will look where the candy presently is hidden. Why? Some argue that children's failure is due to a reality bias; that is, when evaluating a belief, they first consult reality. Reality exerts a stronger influence than the mental state of the character (Saltmarsh, Mitchell, & Robinson, 1995). Another explanation is that young children reason on the basis of desire— that is, what the character wants (Bartsch, 1996)—while others argue that both explanations are correct (Cassidy, 1998).

Under most conditions, children reason on the basis of belief at age 4, but locational beliefs are not the only ones that emerge at this age. Three-year-olds who were told that other children thought it acceptable to bite another child or wear pajamas to school refused to accept the idea that others could believe this (Flavell, Mumme, Green, & Flavell, 1994). Older children have the ability to understand the nature of these false beliefs. This finding holds despite situations in which younger children are given great help to understand the nature of these beliefs (Sullivan & Winner, 1993).

The understanding of false beliefs is part of psychologists' interest in how children understand the nature of mental processes such as dreams, memories, and beliefs. The development of a *theory of mind*, an understanding of the nature of various mental activities and how they influence intention and predict the behavior of others, is of great interest today (Bjorklund, 1995; Sabbagh & Callanan, 1998). As young children mature, they gain a more sophisticated understanding of representation and beliefs. Four year olds seem to have a great advantage over younger children in this area (Schaffer, 1996), and 5-year-olds perform even better (Call & Tomasello, 1999). At 4 years, children's thinking changes as they begin to understand that the same world can be experienced in many different ways by different people, and that each person may have a different belief about reality. They begin to infer mental states in others and see them as an explanation for behavior. They understand that people's beliefs are important and that some of them are false.

Guideposts

How has our understanding of the concept of representation changed recently?

These changes, which begin to appear at age 4, show a new awareness of the nature of the world and demonstrate that even very young children are not as egocentric as Piaget believed. Children's understanding of the world is a great deal more sophisticated than Piaget believed, although it is admittedly incomplete.

Harmonizing the Views

Putting this new information into perspective is difficult. At first glance the research seems contradictory, but it really is not. Under certain circumstances, preschoolers can do things Piaget did not think possible. However, if the situation is complicated or requires more memory and verbal skills than they have, preschoolers fail at these tasks.

The key phrase here is "under certain circumstances." Preschool skills are fragile and delicate, and children's abilities in these areas are just developing. Preschoolers can classify and seriate and are not as egocentric if they have experience in a particular skill, if the task is clear and does not tax their memory, and if the children can understand the verbal instructions. On the other hand, if the situation is complicated or requires more memory and verbal skills than they have, preschoolers fail at these tasks.

These findings have practical implications. People working with preschoolers must design an environment in which tasks are simplified and memory requirements are minimized, and they must be certain that preschoolers understand what is required of them if these newly developing skills are to brought out. Under these circumstances, preschoolers can do some surprising things. Situational and task factors are crucial. We should not underestimate children's abilities, drawing the incorrect conclusion that preschoolers cannot do this or that. This is not to say that a child at any age can learn anything. There are limitations. However, too often people have reached conclusions about what young children can and cannot do, only to find that preschoolers can do more than they thought possible.

Information-Processing Abilities

The importance of the demands of the task are also shown in the preschool child's developing information-processing abilities.

Attention

Two aspects of attention are most commonly studied: **attention span,** which is the time period a child can spend on a given task, and **selective attention,** which is the ability to concentrate on one stimulus and ignore extraneous stimuli. Children's attention span increases significantly during early childhood (Dempster, 1992; Ruff & Lawson, 1990). A fourfold increase in attention span is found between the ages of 1 and 4 years (Anderson & Levin, 1976).

Young children's ability to consciously attend to a particular stimulus when faced with competing stimuli is limited but improves throughout the preschool period. Preschoolers do not spontaneously restrict their attention to important stimuli unless the stimuli stand out or unless the children receive training (Woody-Ramsey & Miller, 1988). They are easily confused when the situation becomes too complex

attention span
> The time period during which an individual can focus psychological resources on a particular stimulus or task.

selective attention
> The ability to concentrate on one stimulus and ignore extraneous stimuli.

The preschooler's ability to concentrate improves greatly during early childhood.

(Miller & Harris, 1988). In fact, preschoolers' attention is affected more by such stimulus characteristics as color, movement, and novelty than older children's and adults' attention. Older children and adults have a greater ability to tune out a physically attractive stimulus and pay attention to another less attractive but more important stimulus. As children mature, their ability to control their attention, to discriminate between what is and is not most important, and to adapt their attention to the demands of a situation improves (Bjorklund, 1995; Flavell et al., 1993). These abilities are just developing in the preschooler and continue to develop throughout the elementary school years.

In addition, preschoolers pay attention to messages that they understand. The preschooler's lack of sustained attention requires that material be presented in small segments. The task must be simple and the directions given in a way that young children understand. Specific instructions as to where to place their attention, then, may be of some help (Hochman, 1996). Because preschoolers are more easily distracted, teachers or parents should reduce or eliminate competing environmental stimuli if they want preschoolers to concentrate.

Memory Skills

Preschoolers have memory skills far superior to those of toddlers. Between 2 and 4 years, their already good recognition skills improve. Even young children can show an impressive memory for events. When children who were 3 or 4 years of age when they went to Disneyworld were interviewed many months later, all the children remembered a great deal about their trip, even 18 months after the trip. Older children remembered more details and did not require as many prompts (Bjorklund, 1995).

Any parent will tell you that children are rather selective in what they remember. Children always seem to remember the toy that you said you might buy them. In fact, interest is an important factor in what they remember for preschoolers as well as toddlers as young as 2 years (Somerville, Wellman, & Cultice, 1983).

Preschoolers show some interesting limitations in the memory strategies they use. Suppose you were shown a group of pictures and asked to remember them. You might first group them into categories (foods, buildings, people), then rehearse them. Preschoolers do not use these strategies on their own (Schneider & Pressley, 1989). Preschoolers do rehearse if they are instructed to do so, and their memory for the list consequently improves (Flavell & Wellman, 1977). In other words, young children apparently can use these strategies but do not unless they are told to do so.

Again, as in the case of Piagetian tasks, we must be careful not to overgeneralize because the characteristics of the task and the test conditions are most important. When 18- to 24-month-old children watched an experimenter hide a toy, were told to remember its location so that they could find the item later, and then were distracted for a few minutes, these children actively tried to remember where it was. They frequently interrupted their play to talk about the hidden toy and its location, which suggests that the idea that preschoolers are completely nonstrategic needs rethinking (DeLoache, Cassidy, & Brown, 1985). Preschoolers do use some strategies for remembering, such as pointing and looking, but their use of particular verbal strategies, such as rehearsal, is limited (Kail & Hagen, 1982).

Young children also may not understand the demands of the task. When 4-, 7-, and 11-year-old children were presented with one of two different instructions:

Guideposts

What are the developmental trends in attention during the preschool years?

"Look at the pictures" or "Remember the pictures," 4-year-olds did not react any differently when presented with either instruction, but older children did (Appel et al., 1972). Preschoolers don't seem to know that the problem requires some voluntary, purposeful cognitive activity. Perhaps preschoolers show such poor use of memory strategies because they do not understand what is involved in the memory tasks (Flavell & Wellman, 1977).

Developmental differences in forgetting also exist. Young children forget more quickly and forget more material than older children (Howe, 1991). They show the same interference effects; that is, something they learn presently can interfere and cause forgetting of something they learned earlier and vice versa (Howe, 1995). Their forgetting can be reduced by reminding the preschoolers of some part of the memory at a later time, a process known as reinstatement (Howe, Courage, & Bryant-Brown, 1993). Such reinstated memories are more durable and less likely to be forgotten than the original memories (Howe et al., 1993).

Taken as a group, the studies in cognition and memory should keep us from generalizing about what abilities children do or do not have. Children who may not show these abilities when tested in a certain way do not necessarily lack them. Instead, it is important to note the situations in which children can and cannot successfully perform particular tasks.

The Importance of Prior Knowledge

One reason for the limitations preschoolers show is their inexperience. Psychologists know that the more people know, the easier it is for them to lay down new memories. This may occur because people who have some prior knowledge have already formed what cognitive psychologists call **schemata.** The term as used by Piaget was introduced in Chapter 2. Its use by information-processing psychologists is a bit different.

A **schema** is an organized body of knowledge that functions as a framework describing objects and relationships that generally occur (Leahy & Harris, 1997). Schemata (the plural of schema) can contain both knowledge about and rules for using knowledge. A schema for a dog may contain ideas about the dog's physical features and activities and different aspects of a dog's behavior as well as ways of treating dogs. If a situation resembles previous situations represented in a schema, the schema is activated, encouraging better organization and interpretation of the information (Schneider & Pressley, 1989).

Consider a preschool teacher talking about hospital procedures and telling students about a nurse taking a patient's blood pressure. Children with some prior knowledge of hospitals would understand or visualize this scenario better than students without this knowledge. Such prior knowledge might involve the roles of various people at the hospital, hospital procedures, and the types of instruments used in hospitals. These schemata underlie our understanding of events and allow us to interpret and clarify what we experience or learn (Chi & Glaser, 1985). The more one knows about hospitals and their procedures, the easier it is to understand what goes on in a hospital.

Schemata allow children to encode additional information more meaningfully, since new information can be linked to already encoded information. It also allows children to fill in gaps and to infer. For example, if you tell someone that the cake is baking, the person knows from past knowledge that the cake is baking in an oven. As children mature, their schemata become more complicated, richer,

Preschoolers forget material more quickly and forget more of the material than elementary school-aged children.

Guideposts

How do the memory abilities of preschoolers compare with those of older children?

schema (information processing)

An organized body of knowledge that functions as a framework describing objects and relationships that generally occur.

and more flexible. A child's background may contain a rich amount of information in one area and a poor amount in another. Since preschoolers generally do not have very rich experiential knowledge, it is not unusual for these children to have difficulty remembering some things while easily remembering others (Eiser, Eiser, & Jones, 1990). Some of the differences between preschoolers and children in middle childhood are due to the richer memory of the latter.

Scripts

A similar concept to schema is **script**, a type of schema that involves knowledge of the events that make up an episode as well as the sequence of the events (Eiser, Eiser, & Jones, 1990). Numerous scripts exist, including those for birthday parties, job interviews, and a schoolday. Adults show a great deal of agreement on these scripts, as do young children on familiar scripts. Four-year-olds and even younger children describe daily events at home, in a day care center, or at a McDonald's restaurant in much the same way as an adult would (Nelson, 1978).

Scripts give order to the child's life (Fivush, Kuebli, & Clubb, 1992). Young children find it easier to remember memories that fit into their regular scripts. Preschoolers have a limited ability for future planning, and scripts seem to help them anticipate future events (Hudson, Shapiro, & Sosa, 1995).

Scripts form the base for remembering familiar stories and events. Prior knowledge represented by the script makes the story easier to follow. When young children are presented with a script that contains an event that is out of order and are asked to recall the event, they either omit the misordered event or put it in the place that is in keeping with their knowledge of how it usually is (Bauer & Thal, 1990; Nelson & Gruendel, 1981).

The knowledge of scripts also affects how children make inferences. Children who are told that Renaldo went to a restaurant and is drinking milk do not need to be told that Renaldo probably looked at a menu or had a glass that held his milk. They infer it because they are familiar with the script. Script knowledge also affects behavior. Preschoolers who are familiar with scripts interact more easily and scripts facilitate turn taking, play, and conversation (Furman & Walden, 1990).

Preschoolers are more rigid in their ideas of what should take place and when (Wimmer, 1980). Older children also produce more alternative paths in their scripts. For instance, when describing an activity such as making a campfire, they offer more possible paths to accomplishing the task than younger children do.

Preschoolers will often rebel if people do things that are not in keeping with their idea of the script. A 2-year-old who usually was given a bath after dinner became very upset when given a bath before dinner because she thought she would not be fed (Hudson, 1990). Preschoolers may become confused or annoyed if a baby-sitter or substitute preschool teacher does things differently than their parents or regular teachers. Scripts become more flexible and more complex as children develop. Both scripts and schemata are culturally dependent. When people move to another country, or even a different part of the same country, the scripts and schemata may change. Research on children's information-processing abilities is especially relevant today, as questions are raised about the accuracy and completeness of children's testimony as they relate what they have seen or experienced (*Children Testifying in Court* on pages 307–309).

Guideposts

How do the concepts of script and schema help explain preschoolers' behavior?

8

Preschoolers are more rigid in their understanding of the order in which events must occur at a restaurant or in their preschool classes than older children.

For Your Consideration ?

How can the concept of script be used to understand a young child's annoyance when his mother shortens a game because she has other things to do

script

A structure that describes an appropriate sequence of events in a particular context.

The Child in the 21st Century

Children Testifying in Court

You are a member of a jury who has just heard a case in which a preschooler describes seeing the defendant with blood on his shirt and a gun in his hand right after a murder. Although the prosecution presents some additional evidence, the case really boils down to whether you believe the testimony of the child. The adult accused of the crime claims innocence. The prosecution argues that the child has the ability to identify the murderer and that the child's memory of the incident can be believed. The defense claims that the child is so young and his memory so faulty that you cannot believe him. The defense also angrily denounces the questioning of the child by the police and social worker, claiming that their questioning led the child to identify the defendant from a lineup. How would you evaluate the evidence?

Claims of sexual abuse are made against a teacher in a preschool. The community is shocked by the possibility that a number of children have been abused. The testimony of the children who have been interviewed repeatedly is the key evidence. Some of the children describe being touched in intimate places. The defendant claims that it never happened. How can you determine whether these events really happened?

Children are sometimes important witnesses in court cases. Testifying in court is a very stressful situation for young children (Flin, Kearney, & Murray, 1996). Many states have changed their laws to encourage children to tell what they know in a more comfortable setting than the courtroom. They allow a child to testify behind a one-way screen so that the child does not see the defendant, or in a video, or they permit professionals such as therapists to describe what the children said to them, an exception to the hearsay rules of evidence (Ceci & de Bruyn, 1993).

People often ask the simple question "Can I believe a 4-year-old's testimony?" Unfortunately, the answer is not simple, because a variety of important factors have to be taken into account (Flin et al., 1996; Priestley; Roberts, & Pipe, 1999). When children of all ages are asked what they remember about an event without any prompting or leading questioning, they usually provide accurate information (Pipe, Gee, Wilson, & Egerton, 1999; Powell & Thomson, 1994). However, children relating an event from memory often give incomplete information. The amount of information offered depends largely on the child's age, with preschoolers providing relatively little information in this free-recall condition (Gordon & Follmer, 1996). Young children simply do not tell the entire story. Errors of omission are more common than errors of commission. In other words, children are more likely to leave things out of their testimony than to give incorrect information.

Young children's vocabularies are limited, adjectives and adverbs are frequently absent, and their schemata lacks the richness that it will have later on (Flin et al., 1996). Children may also be reluctant to relate what happened at all.

In many cases, especially those involving sexual abuse, it may be difficult to get a child to relate what happened, especially if the abuse is perpetrated by a relative and the child is told not to say anything.

Faced with incomplete, or sometimes the lack of any, testimony about an event that the child experienced or witnessed, it may be necessary to ask specific, probing questions. These questions do provide greater information but are open to higher error rates. Nonsuggestive questions—"What did he say to you?" or "What did the lady look like?"—that require children to answer in their own words are likely to lead to accurate information. Questions that are suggestive—"Where did she touch you?" or "She touched you there, right?"—are much more likely to lead to incorrect information (Poole & White, 1991). Not all leading questions are suggestive but some are. The use of leading, suggestive questions reduces the witnesses' credibility with jurors (Karla & Heath, 1997)

It is these suggestive questions that cause the most problems. Younger children are more influenced by suggestions from interviewers than older children (Ceci & De Bruyn, 1993; Ceci & Huffman, 1997; Ceci, Ross, & Toglia, 1987). In fact, preschoolers show a special vulnerability to suggestion, manipulation, and coercion (Lamb, Sternberg, & Esplin, 1995).

This was amply shown in a study in which a man identified as Sam Stone entered a preschool classroom while a teacher was reading to the 3- to 6-year-old children (Leichtman & Ceci, 1995). The man said hello to the teacher, commented briefly on the story ("I know that story; it's one of my favorites"), walked around the classroom, and then left.

Some of the children received information about Stone's personality before his visit to the school. He was depicted as kind, well meaning, but very clumsy, accidentally breaking things. This created a stereotype in the children's mind. Another group did not receive any information before the event but after the visit was interviewed four times by interviewers using suggestive, leading questions, indicating to the children that Stone had ripped a book and soiled a teddy bear. For example, the children were asked when Stone got the bear dirty or whether he did so on purpose or accidentally. A third group received both the initial information and the suggestive interviewing, while a control group received neither. The children were interviewed by a different interviewer a fifth time in a neutral manner during which the interviewer simply asked the children to relate what happened on the day Stone had visited the classroom.

Both the initial stereotyping and the postincident suggestion had significant effects on children's memories. Children in the control condition provided the most accurate reports, children in the stereotype group gave a modest number of false reports, and those in the suggestive group offered a substantial number of false reports. Children who had received both stereotyped information and suggestions offered the highest number of false reports. Older preschoolers were less likely to be influenced than younger preschoolers.

The researchers selected some videotaped interviews of these children and showed them to experts in the field, asking them to determine whether the incidents actually happened. These authorities were unable to do so correctly. Many experts were totally confident that the children were telling the truth, even though the incidents never

transpired. Some of the young children even related details of events that had never happened. Perhaps many young children want to please these adult interviewers, whom they perceive as honest and credible.

The results of this and other studies lead to the conclusion that the usefulness of the testimony depends on the way the child is interviewed and the bias the child may have. When interviews are conducted with an understanding of these problems, the testimony can be elicited so that it is not tainted. For example, some interviewers begin from the hypothesis that sexual abuse has occurred, and they fail to look at other possible explanations. When faced with an obvious bias from the examiner, preschool children often change their stories to meet the interviewer's suggestions and expectations and give inaccurate information (Bruck & Ceci, 1995).

Even the use of repeated questions can cause difficulties. If very young children are asked the same question, especially a yes/no question, repeatedly within an interview, they frequently change their answers (Poole & White, 1991). Children may reason that they are being asked again because the first answer they gave was wrong (Davies et al., 1996). That is one reason that some authorities argue that children should be told that it is alright to say that it didn't happen (Powell & Thomson, 1994). In addition, repeating the story over and over to different interviewers can lead to a story that is strangely devoid of emotion (Steward & Steward, 1996).

Although there is ample concern about the interview techniques used with young children, some authorities question whether the poor interview techniques used in sensational cases are really typical (Lyon, 1995). In addition, we are justly afraid that children will be led to accuse

someone of something that is not true, but what about the opposite problem—that abused children will fail to reveal abuse unless direct and sometimes leading questions are asked?

Sexual abuse is embarrassing, and leading questions may be necessary. In fact, 3-year-olds are reluctant to acknowledge that their parents kissed them in the bathtub if they are told that such behavior is naughty (Ceci, Leichtman, Putnick, & Nightingale, 1993). Many 4- and 5-year-olds will keep secrets when asked to do so by a wrongdoer (Ceci & Bruck, 1993). In one study, 72% of sexually abused children denied having been abused when questioned by a family member or an investigator, even though the abuse was later proven (Sorenson & Snow, 1991). A trade-off exists between false denials and false allegations. Specific questions enable and encourage children to tell what they know, and some authorities argue that they are appropriate when other evidence exists, such as a spontaneous declaration from the child or suspicious medical evidence that indicates that the child knows more than he or she is saying (Lyon, 1995).

How does this research relate to the situation in which a juror must decide a case on the basis of a child's evidence? Obviously, there is no definite answer to the question of whether a 4-year-old's memory is good enough to convict an assailant. Some children are more suggestible than others, and individual differences should be kept in mind (Ceci & Bruck, 1994). Adults and older children make mistakes on identifications as well, and we may be holding children up to a higher standard than others. Elementary school children are neither as suggestible or coachable as some defense advocates believe, nor are they as resistant as some authorities favorable to the prosecution believe (Ceci & deBruyn, 1993). The situation with preschoolers is different. Preschoolers' memory for novel incidents is good, but preschoolers often do not tell the complete story, so some careful questioning is necessary. On the other hand, preschoolers are more suggestible, and so questioners must be very careful not to lead a child to say something that may not be accurate. To be certain that the questioning does not prejudice the child, all conversations with the preschooler in a criminal case should be recorded so that it may be determined that the child has not been led to a conclusion that is counter to the best interests of justice (Davies et al., 1996; McGough, 1995).

What do you think?

What procedures could be used to improve the accuracy and reduce the possibility of errors when questioning a 4-year-old who has witnessed a crime?

You can explore the questions above using InfoTrac College Edition. Hint: enter search terms *Preschool Children, Children's Testimony*.

The Preschooler's Environment: Home, Television, and Preschool

Preschoolers are exposed to a much greater number and variety of environmental influences than are younger children. Three areas of influence on preschoolers' cognitive development are their home, what they watch on television, and what they experience in the preschool.

The Home

The characteristics of the home environment can help or hinder the development of the child's cognitive abilities. Children who are more cognitively advanced come from homes in which language is used expansively. Such children are encouraged to express themselves, to label the environment, and to describe their world. Parents who give information, explain events, read to their children, and encourage curiosity and exploration help develop their children's minds so that when the children enter elementary school, they are ready for new challenges (Katz, 1980).

Even when not directly involved in a parent-child interaction, children observe those around them. An environment filled with books is not stimulating unless the books are read. If preschoolers see their parents and older siblings enjoying reading, they are more likely to develop a positive attitude toward the activity.

Parents can help their children develop their cognitive abilities in a number of ways. Almost every activity can be a learning experience and made enjoyable. Children can learn to recognize similarities, shapes, and colors and explore their environments in a safe and secure manner. Reading to children is especially important. While reading, parents can ask open-ended questions that elicit children's responses (Whitehurst et al., 1994) and talk about pictures and the meaning of the story (Reese & Cox, 1999). Reading, then, encourages the active participation of the child.

There are two models here. The first views parents as environmental engineers who, at the appropriate times, provide materials and opportunities that help their children explore and learn about the world. These parents construct an environment rich in opportunities, allowing their children to discover the world at their own pace and stimulating them

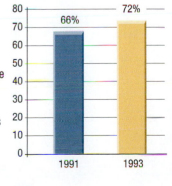

Trends in Development

Ready to Learn: Family-Child Reading and Storytelling
Has the United States increased the percentage of 3- to 5-year-olds whose parents read to them or tell them stories regularly?

Source: National Education Goals Panel (1998).

to think. Although Piaget never listed recommendations on child rearing, this type of strategy is in line with his thinking. The child learns through discovery, and readiness is taken into consideration. Formal instruction is deemphasized. The child's everyday experiences are educational. A simple walk around the neighborhood becomes a learning experience. There are traffic signs, people working, and a hundred different things to discuss. The other approach emphasizes formal instruction. Parents are encouraged to teach their preschooler skills, with less emphasis on self-discovery and more on planned activities that impart knowledge to the child.

Both extreme positions should be questioned. The parent who merely produces an environment suitable for a child but does not actively interact with the youngster is not maximizing the child's experiences. On the other hand, too formal or unnatural a structure may cause a child to resent the parents and reject the instruction. It becomes a "grim business" (Zinsser, 1981), with no joy, only pressure.

Television

Some 98% of all American households have television sets, and many have more than one. Children begin watching television before their first birthday and have favorite programs by their second or third birthday. They spend more time viewing television than doing anything else except sleeping (Dorr & Rabin, 1995). Preschoolers view about 3 hours of television a day (West, Hausken, & Chandler, 1992), and other estimates are somewhat higher (Condry, 1989). Many parents use the television set as a baby-sitter, and the children of such parents may not watch appropriate programming. However, some shows are produced just for young children.

Barney and Friends Many toddlers absolutely love Barney, the purple dinosaur that appears on a television show called *Barney and Friends*. Barney is constantly upbeat, singing songs and reminding children to do such things as brush their teeth and be nice to each other. The show takes place in a suburban school yard. The gestures are exaggerated, and there are no ultramodern graphics. The show features happy children singing happy songs and learning simple lessons. The show seems based on the idea that children need security and a sense of pure love and acceptance (Walsh, 1993).

Parents and other adults don't always feel very positively toward Barney, probably because the show is so unabashedly sweet. However, the show is not produced for them. The more serious criticisms of the show are that it does not recognize the existence of unpleasant realities. Giggles and unconditional love, a place where everyone must be happy and every conflict resolved at once, is appealing, but is it the message that ought to be shown (Levy, 1994)? There is no pain, sorrow, or frustration—natural feelings that are present in the lives of young children as well as everyone else. Barney changes sadness to happiness instantly. For example, when Barney trips on a toy and falls, he is bruised and in pain but giggles. Barney convinces a child who is afraid to get a shot that there is nothing to be afraid of at all. Would it be better in the first instance if he had shown the pain and in the second if the child were told that the shot would hurt only for a second? These are debatable points but require some discussion.

Sesame Street   Big Bird. Grover. Bert and Ernie. Oscar the Grouch. Most preschoolers know these characters quite well. *Sesame Street's* goal is to promote intellectual growth and cultural awareness, especially in disadvantaged preschoolers (Comstock & Paik, 1991). It emphasizes cognitive concerns, although over the years it has covered prosocial behavior and tolerance for others. The show stresses literacy and interpersonal communication, and it counters stereotypes by showing nontraditional role models (Van Evra, 1990; Walsh, 1996).

The producers of *Sesame Street* knew that to be successful the program had to compete with commercial television (O'Bryan, 1980) and be entertaining as well as educational. The show was fitted to the needs and level of its intended audience. The pace is varied and quick, the now-famous Muppets are present, and animation, splashy color, repetition, and music are used. The show is fun to watch, and children from all ethnic and socioeconomic backgrounds do so (Rice et al., 1990). It is broadcast in 130 countries, and 14 countries have coproductions of the program tailored to their own cultures, including a mixed-race South African *Sesame Street* and a peaceful Israeli-Palestinian version. A Russian production features a lovable free spirit from a Russian fairy tale as Bert and Ernie's friend. Its values include racial harmony, peaceful dispute resolution, respect for the environment, and equal rights for women (Cooperman, 1996).

Children who watch *Sesame Street* regularly learn its central concepts and have advantages over those who do not watch it (Anderson, 1998). These advantages hold regardless of the viewer's socioeconomic level, sex, or ethnicity (Ball & Bogatz, 1970, 1972). Watching *Sesame Street* boosts a child's readiness for school, while extensive viewing of cartoons and adult material has a negative effect on readiness for school (Walsh, 1995). Watching *Sesame Street* also has a positive effect on the vocabulary development of children in the age group of 3 to 5 years (Rice, Huston, Truglio, & Wright, 1990).

The show has been criticized for having a very fast, perhaps frenetic pace (Cooperman, 1996). *Sesame Street* also shows negative behaviors such as violence and trickery. Finally, some have criticized its approach to literacy, saying that although learning letters is important, emphasizing the meaning of written passages would be better (Mates & Strommen, 1995). There are no signs or posters to

Barney is a favorite character of very young children.

There is evidence that watching Sesame Street has a positive effect on the cognitive development of preschoolers.

read, and few vignettes involve written material, such as reading menus, letters, or written directions. Little is said or shown about the usefulness of reading or of reading for pleasure.

Mr. Rogers' Neighborhood A show with a completely different format is *Mister Rogers' Neighborhood*. This is a slower-paced show that emphasizes interpersonal skills, imagination, and understanding of one's emotions (Rawson, 1996; Singer & Singer, 1976; Tower, Singer, Singer, & Biggs, 1979). This program emphasizes acceptance and valuing each child as a unique individual (Guy, 1996; Laskas, 1996). It focuses on relatively simple discoveries; the neighborhood visits are filled with adventures, and the child is invited to respond to them (Wehmiller, 1996). The show deals with such emotions as anger, grief, love, loss, and disappointment (Rawson, 1996). The show is hosted by Mr. Rogers (not "Fred"), who is a gentle authority figure (Zuckerman, 1996).

Research on *Mister Rogers' Neighborhood* shows that the program is successful in promoting prosocial behaviors, although the effect is not lasting (Friedrich & Stein, 1973). When preschool children were exposed to daily viewing of *Mister Rogers' Neighborhood*, aggressive cartoons, or neutral programs, the children who saw *Mister Rogers* improved in task persistence and prosocial behavior, such as cooperation. Watching *Mister Rogers* also led to an increase in fantasy play and imagination (Singer & Singer, 1976). This increase is noteworthy, since fantasy and pretend play are considered important aspects of a child's development (Rubin, Fein, & Vandenberg, 1983).

Mister Rogers' Neighborhood has also been criticized. Its slow pace sometimes makes young children restless (Singer & Singer, 1976), and some parents may have difficulty getting their children to watch the program. But there is a trade-off in pacing. In one study, kindergarten and first-grade children attended more to fast-paced programs but showed greater recall for the material in slow-paced shows (Wright et al., 1984).

Television has a great potential for helping preschoolers develop cognitively and socially. Commercial television has learned something from the success of these shows, and its offerings have improved. However, television has a long way to go to reach its potential in this area.

Guideposts

How do *Barney and Friends*, *Sesame Street*, and *Mr. Rogers' Neighborhood* differ in their approaches?

compensatory education

The use of educational strategies in an attempt to reduce or eliminate some perceived difference between groups of children

---

ACTION / REACTION

How Much TV Is Too Much TV?

Both Indra and Mohan have a problem with their two sons, who are ages 4 and 6. They seem addicted to the television set. While it is true that the younger one watches *Sesame Street* and a couple of other programs that they believe are appropriate for him, his brother loves cartoons and situation comedies. The younger one is now beginning to watch more and more of these shows as well.

Both children are bright and doing well. The younger one attends a nursery school, and his skills seem well developed for a 4-year-old, while the older one attends first grade and is also progressing nicely. Still, Indra and Mohan are very concerned because they don't like the violence on the cartoons, and the tricks, sexual innuendoes, and values shown on the comedies.

At the same time, they must admit that after a hard day at work, playing with the children after they come home, and doing the other thousand things they must do, they enjoy watching television as well.

1. *Do Indra and Mohan have any reason to be concerned?*
2. *If so, what should they do?*

ACTION / REACTION

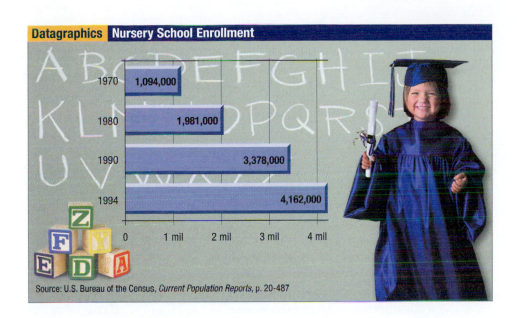

Year	Enrollment
1970	1,094,000
1980	1,981,000
1990	3,378,000
1994	4,162,000

Source: U.S. Bureau of the Census, *Current Population Reports*, p. 20-487

Preschool Education

The third environmental factor influencing cognitive development is preschool education. Nursery school attendance has shown consistent growth in the United States over the past 30 years.

Preschool programs are collectively grouped under the heading of early childhood care and education (ECCE) (Gomby, Larner, Stevenson, Lewit, & Behrman, 1995). One additional term should be introduced here—**compensatory education,** which involves an attempt to compensate for some difference between one group and another. Many preschool programs, such as Project Head Start (discussed later), help children from economically disadvantaged families develop the attitudes and skills necessary for later success in school.

Nursery schools vary greatly. The traditional nursery school emphasizes social and emotional development and may not follow any specific educational theory (McClinton & Meier, 1978). Activities may include story time, listening to music, moving to music, all types of artistic endeavors, trips within the neighborhood (perhaps to the fire department or a donut shop), growing plants, and observing the environment, along with free play. Children are encouraged to cooperate and share and develop the attitude that learning is enjoyable.

Montessori schools, which use the approach developed by Maria Montessori at the beginning of the 20th century, have gained popularity all over the world. They stress the importance of educating through the senses (Northwoods, 1990) because Montessori believed there is a close relationship between the senses and the intellect. Training the senses lays the groundwork for reading and writing. As children physically trace letters with their index finger, listen to the name of the letters, and then write them with a pencil, the child links the sound of the alphabet with touch, sight, and muscular coordination (Deasey, 1978).

Many Montessori activities are self-correcting, so that children can proceed at their own rate and no pressure is placed on them. There is no punishment for not finishing an exercise, nor is there much use of reinforcement. Montessori believed that children negotiated sensitive periods during which they showed strong but transient tendencies to learn or

Trends in Development

Preschool Participation

Has the United States reduced the gap (in percentage points) in preschool participation between 3- to 5-year-olds from high- and low-income families?

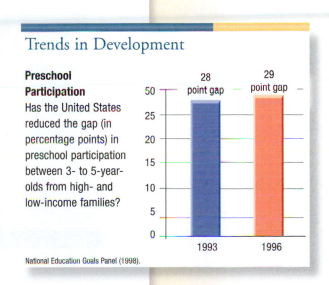

National Education Goals Panel (1998).

develop their abilities. For example, a 2-year-old's sensitivity to touch helps the child learn the shapes of letters using sandpaper letters and to exercise the intellect by classifying things by textures and shapes (Northwoods, 1990).

Montessori's system is not without its critics. Play is not emphasized, and this is troubling to those who consider play to be an important part of a child's development (Rubin et al., 1983). Understanding one's emotions is also not a primary goal. Social interaction is present, but it is not really stressed, either. Children do not act out plays, nor does the teacher tell stories. There is little use of imagination. These activities are not forbidden, but they are not encouraged. Montessori's methods have been in and out of favor with many educators around the world since their inception. Today, with the emphasis on cognitive growth, they are again in fashion.

Some preschools specifically follow Piaget's ideas of learning through doing. Piagetian-based preschools stress play as a learning activity. During play, children are exposed to the viewpoints of others, which challenge their egocentric view of the world. The goals of Piagetian preschools are to develop curiosity, independence, and self-confidence; to learn to cooperate; and to gain physical control of the environment. In the Piagetian preschool, children are not given formal instruction. Instead, teachers act as guides, helping children discover things through active participation (Marcon, 1999). The children are exposed to a wide range of materials that help them gain experience in classification and seriation.

Some preschools are more definitive in the educational goals that they seek to achieve. For example, a behaviorally based program called DISTAR focuses on teaching children the concepts that are considered necessary by the educational staff. The teacher has an objective and presents the material to small groups of children in a standardized fashion for about 20 minutes or so, with periods of rest, music, or other activities alternating with instructional periods. The exchanges are rapid, and the teacher reinforces the children for giving correct answers. This is a teaching approach, and it is based on the idea that children can be taught the desired concepts if the material is presented clearly and appropriately.

Guideposts

How do nursery schools differ from each other?

For Your Consideration ?

If you had your choice of sending your child to any of the four types of preschools discussed in the chapter, where would you enroll your child? Why?

ACTION / REACTION

The Nursery School Gambit

Anna and Al decided to send their 3-year-old daughter, Lindsay, to nursery school, choosing a school that was close to home and that had an excellent reputation. They believe that Lindsay is very bright, and they wanted the teacher to introduce their daughter to letter sounds and concepts that will lead to early reading and writing.

After Lindsay spent three months in the school, Anna and Al saw no visible improvement and went to see the teacher, Ms. Baxter. The teacher explained that the purpose of nursery school is not to teach children to read but to help them develop social skills and a feeling that learning is enjoyable. In the school's program, children learn to cooperate with one another and learn about the world in which they live. They are even "studying" dinosaurs. Ms. Baxter also noted that forcing children to read at an early age is undesirable, because children will learn when they are ready. But Anna and Al are not satisfied. They believe that Lindsay is ready for more than she is getting. They wonder whether they should switch to another nursery school.

1. *If you were Lindsay's parents, what would you do?*
2. *If you were Lindsay's teacher, would you have explained the school's philosophy any differently?*

ACTION / REACTION

Do Nursery Schools Foster Development?

Generally speaking, nursery schools accomplish their purposes. Children who attend nursery schools are generally more advanced than their nonattending peers. This is especially true for children in lower-income groups (Minuchin & Shapiro, 1983). Children who attend preschool programs are more socially competent, outgoing, self-assured, curious, independent, and persistent on a task than those who do not attend (Clarke-Stewart & Fein, 1983).

There is no question that nursery school has a positive effect on children from low-income areas and for children at risk for developing later problems in school. The question of the benefits of nursery school for middle-class children and those not in the at-risk category is somewhat less clear, but some advantages are found in reading and language skills for boys who had attended a preschool. No effect is found for girls (Larsen & Robinson, 1989).

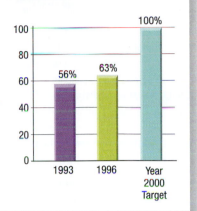

Trends in Development

Children with Disabilities, Ages 3 to 5, Enrolled in Preschool
The figure is moving in the right direction, but it does not approach the goal.

- 1993: 56%
- 1996: 63%
- Year 2000 Target: 100%

Source: USDHHS, 1998

Project Head Start

Children raised in poverty start elementary school behind their middle-class peers in such skills as word knowledge, counting/sorting, and knowledge of letters (Stipek & Ryan, 1997). They enter school with equal motivation, but their cognitive skills are lower, and they tend to fall further behind as they progress through elementary school. Failure to improve the cognitive skills of these children before they enter school may set disadvantaged children on the road to poor academic achievement, and lack of achievement could reduce their motivation in the first few years of school.

Perhaps if these children could attend a preschool that would help compensate for their different experiences, this cycle could be stopped, and such children would have a reasonable chance for academic success. This was partly the thinking behind one of the greatest educational social experiments of the past 50 years, **Project Head Start.** Since its inception in 1964, millions of children have taken part in Head Start, and the program continues to expand. The hope is that a program instituted early enough could give children living in poverty a head start in school and reduce or eliminate the social class differences in education achievement (Zigler & Berman, 1983).

Head Start programs have broader goals than most other preschool programs. All Head Start programs must provide services in four areas: education, health, social (and psychological) services, and parent involvement (Barnett, 1995; Head Start, 1995). Children learn to work and play independently, become able to accept help and direction from adults, gain competence and worth, sharpen and widen their language skills, become curious, and grow in ability to channel inner, destructive impulses.

Project Head Start
A federally funded compensatory education program aimed at reducing or eliminating the differences in educational achievement between poor and middle-class youngsters.

Project Head Start is a successful program to help young children.

Students who participate in Head Start as well as other preschool programs are significantly less likely to be retained in grade or to be found in special education classes. They are also much more likely to graduate from high school (Barnett, 1995). The results of studies on reading and mathematics achievement for children who attended a Head Start program are mixed, with some showing Head Start children achieving more in mathematics and reading than children from other preschool programs (Darlington et al., 1980; Lazar & Darlington, 1982). Head Start is also given some of the credit for the improvement in SAT scores among minority youth (Carmody, 1988).

Children who attend Head Start programs show gains in cognitive ability as measured by intelligence scores, but those gains do not continue as children progress through second and third grade (Currie & Duncan, 1997; Westinghouse Learning Corporation, 1969). This is often called the *fadeout phenomenon*; that is, the gains in intelligence are temporary and fade out by the second grade or so. One reason for this is that many children who graduate from Head Start attend substandard schools (Viadero, 1994).

How can Head Start and other preschool programs lead to better outcomes despite their temporary influence on IQ? First, even the temporary enhancement in intelligence may ease the transition to elementary school, reducing the likelihood of tracking and increasing the probability of immediate success that may carry over into later grades. Second, it may influence parents as well as teachers to have more positive expectations for these children (Entwisle, 1995). Head Start may also lead to better self-esteem, academic motivation, and social competence (the ability of young children to select and carry out their interpersonal goals), which influence school performance (Barnett, 1995; Zigler & Berman, 1983).

The Future of Head Start and Early Childhood Programs

Most Americans support government sponsorship of Head Start programs. Recent additions to the Head Start menu include demonstration projects to help low-income students maintain and enhance the benefits they received in their earlier years in Head Start and programs to aid infants and toddlers (Head Start, 1995). Evidence exists that extending compensatory education programs into the elementary school years can improve reading achievement and lower the rate of grade retention, and that infant and toddler early intervention programs are often successful (Reynolds & Temple, 1998).

Head Start, though, must also look at the quality of its program as it seems to vary considerably among centers (Barnett, 1995). Children in higher-quality Head Start classes perform better on objective measures of preacademic skills, regardless of the quality of their home environment (Bryant, Burchinal, Lau, & Sparling, 1994). In addition, it must serve even more children as presently it serves only about a third of those preschoolers eligible (Currie & Duncan, 1997). Some even argue that it should be expanded to include those children who are slightly above the poverty level (Zigler & Muenchow, 1992). It must also strengthen its parent programs and its health and nutrition segments, which are so important to its success.

The need for such comprehensive early childhood programs is growing and Head Start, as well as other preschool programs, have much to offer. Head Start, though, is not an antidote for poverty, but it does offer hope that children from backgrounds traditionally not characteristic of school success will have a better chance to prosper.

Kindergarten

Do you remember your kindergarten experience? Chances are you attended for a half day, you were never tested for anything, except perhaps your vision, and you spent the day in playlike activities designed to stimulate your curiosity and social competence. Visit most kindergartens today, and you will be very surprised at the changes.

The most obvious change is that today's kindergartners are much more likely to attend a full school day (Olsen & Zigler, 1989). The change to a full day was made for many reasons. Some claim that we now expect kindergartners to accomplish more in that year and that only a full-time program can meet these goals. Others argue for a more practical reason: parents who are employed want their children to attend a school full-time as soon as possible (Honig, 1995). In addition, many children have had some preschool experience and are used to time away from the home, making day-long kindergartens more practical. Some authorities, though, question whether the full-day kindergarten is developmentally appropriate.

Another significant change is the increasing use of screening and readiness tests at these young ages. Screening to identify children at risk has become more common both in preschool and in kindergarten. Some tests are used to screen students to discover whether students have a problem that would prevent them from succeeding in school. Such students may then be referred for a more rigorous examination or be placed in some special program (Kaplan, 1990; Walsh, 1989). Other tests, called **readiness tests**, are more concerned with the skills that children have or have not already acquired. They are used to make instructional decisions. They measure whether students have the necessary skills to master a new skill, such as reading. If a teacher receives information that a student does not have a particular skill, some program might be instituted to help the child develop the skill.

The most profound and controversial change in kindergarten is in curriculum. Over the past two decades, there has been an increasing emphasis placed on academic skills. In the past, play was the basis for the kindergarten movement, but this is changing. Programs now are more likely to stress academic skills and group instruction and to use commercially prepared materials more (Marcon, 1999; Nall, 1982). Kindergarten reading programs are now pencil and paper oriented, with dittos, texts, and workbooks (Willert & Kamii, 1985). Some believe that "kindergarten is what first grade used to be" (Walsh, 1989, p. 385). The pressures for this change come from state-mandated standards that require skill mastery, first-grade teachers who want their students to have certain skills prior to entering the grade, and parents who want their children to read as quickly as possible (Walsh, 1989).

Children who attend full-day kindergarten show significantly greater achievement (Fusaro, 1997). Some studies find that the more extended periods of time spent on academics, including language, reading, and mathematics, do increase standardized test scores, especially on some readiness tests (Olsen & Zigler, 1989). This is especially true for children from at-risk populations, such as children with mild disabilities. The findings on middle-class children are more mixed but again positive. Whether these children do better in the long run is still questionable. There is much less evidence to support changes in motivation or

Kindergarten has changed in many ways, but the most controversial is the increasing emphasis on academic skills.

readiness tests
Tests that measure whether a child has attained the skills necessary to master a new skill.

general intellectual ability that might lead to significant long-term change (Olsen & Zigler, 1989). Other studies find that the development and achievement of inner-city boys is fostered by kindergarten programs that emphasize socioemotional growth over academics (Marcon, 1993). More research is certainly required on this issue.

Questions for the Future

Perhaps the most significant question surrounding preschools and kindergarten is whether we are making inappropriate demands on young children, overemphasizing fine-motor skills and desk work. Are we rushing children into reading and academic enterprises that they are not ready for? This is a difficult question to answer. Others argue that this narrowing emphasis does not place enough importance on problem solving, motivation, interest in learning, and social competence. Should the emphasis be on academic skills or more social-motivational ones? One expert, Bettye Caldwell (1989), argues that it is not an either/or situation. The question is not whether to educate or care for preschool children. She believes that preschools and kindergarten must provide a blend of education and care, which she labels *educare*. Preschools must offer a "developmentally appropriate mixture of education and care, of stimulation and nurture, of work and play" (Caldwell, 1989, p. 266).

For Your Consideration

Are we expecting too much from kindergartners? Should the emphasis be placed on academic work (learning letters, reading) or on improving social skills and self-esteem?

A Final Thought

The preschoolers' physical and cognitive development is impressive. Piaget described the preschooler's abilities and limitations, while new research shows just how sensitive young children are to the type of task and environment surrounding the challenge. Psychologists now have a better understanding of how important it is for children to be ready for the formal school experience and of the part the home, television, and preschool programs can play in fostering a child's cognitive development.

Yet in the midst of the tremendous interest in preschool education and cognitive development, two cautions are necessary. First, there is a real danger of overemphasizing early cognitive education, making parents quasi-teachers who grimly and joylessly drum facts and skills into children's heads (Zinsser, 1981). Second, a child's social and personality development may be submerged in the rush to "school" our children. Social and personality development are just as important, and people sometimes forget that children learn much through interacting with other people and during play. It is to the preschooler's development in these areas that we turn next.

Summary

1. During the preschool years, a child's rate of growth declines. Preschoolers develop a number of motor skills, including jumping, running, and hopping. The development of the large muscles precedes that of the fine muscles.

2. The leading cause of death among preschoolers is accidents, some of which can be prevented.

3. Although death from disease is rare in Western countries, many preventable diseases as well as malnutrition take many lives in underdeveloped countries. There has been great progress in reducing the death rate, improving inoculation rates and water quality, and providing medical care. New, inexpensive treatments are now available. The challenge is not only to offer medical treatment and food but also to provide information and to change attitudes.

4. According to Piagetian theory, children between about 2 and 7 are in the preoperational stage. These children can use symbols and have the capacity to view an action, remember it, and repeat it later. Grammar improves significantly throughout the preschool stage. Young children begin to converse with others. Young children's conversations often involve a monologue. Piaget believed that young children produced monologues because they are egocentric, while Vygotsky believed children used them to guide behavior.

5. Children in the preoperational stage tend to be egocentric (see everything from their own point of view), sometimes believe inanimate objects possess animate qualities, and reason transductively (from specific event to specific event). Preschoolers have difficulty placing things in size order (seriation) and, at least at the beginning of this stage, have problems sorting items into different classes (classification).

6. Preschoolers cannot solve conservation problems (challenges that involve the understanding that quantities remain the same even if their appearance changes). Their tendency to center on one dimension and their inability to reverse operations and to understand transformations are responsible for their problems in this area.

7. New evidence shows that many of these abilities are present if preschoolers are tested on tasks that are meaningful to them, simple, and clearly defined. However, these abilities are fragile, and preschoolers will not show these skills all the time.

8. The attention span of preschoolers is superior to that of toddlers, and it will continue to improve as the child matures. Children are attracted by many aspects of a situation, such as movement, color, and loud noise. As children age, their ability voluntarily to focus their attention in a planned, organized manner increases. This ability is not well developed in preschoolers.

9. Preschoolers generally do not spontaneously use verbal strategies such as rehearsal as memory aids, but they do show such strategies as looking and pointing. Children do better in familiar situations and with tasks that are meaningful.

10. The child's knowledge base affects memory and performance on many tasks. Both children and adults possess a number of scripts or structures describing the sequence of events in a particular situation. These form the basis for understanding events.

11. Parents who label the environment, encourage their children's curiosity, and read to their children tend to maximize their children's cognitive development.

12. *Barney and Friends*, *Sesame Street*, and *Mister Rogers' Neighborhood* are successful television programs combining entertainment with education.

13. More and more preschoolers are attending early childhood education programs. These programs differ from one another in philosophy and teaching methods. The evidence generally shows that children who attend preschools gain from the experience.

14. Project Head Start is an attempt to provide experiences to help close the gap between children from lower socioeconomic backgrounds and their peers from middle-class backgrounds. While the immediate gains in intelligence are not sustained throughout elementary school, children who attend these programs are less likely to be left back or to be found in special education classes. Some studies show that they do better in mathematics and reading as well.

15. The kindergarten experience has recently changed. Full-day kindergartens have become more popular, more screening and readiness tests are being administered, and the curriculum has become more academically oriented. All of these changes are very controversial, with some authorities claiming that the emphasis on academics at this age is inappropriate.

Review

The rate of physical growth (1)_____ during the preschool years. By the end of the preschool period, most children are showing a definite preference for using the (2)_____ hand. Children have a natural ability to determine the (3)_____ of food they eat, but parents must actively determine the (4)_____ of foods offered to children. The most frequent cause of death for preschoolers is (5)_____.The leading cause of death for children around the world is (6)_____, but there are very effective ways of treating it. The mortality rate for young children has significantly (7)_____ over the past 20 years.

According to Piaget, between the ages of 2 and 7 years, the child negotiates the (8)_____ stage. Reasoning from specific instances to a general rule is called (9)_____ reasoning, while reasoning from a general rule to a specific instance is called (10)_____ reasoning. Young children use some (11)_____ logic but often reason from one specific instance to another, a type of reasoning called (12)_____ reasoning. Young preschoolers cannot place sticks in size order, an operation called (13)_____ . Young preschoolers also have difficulty placing things in categories, an operation called (14)_____ . This improves significantly during the stage. Preschoolers often have difficulty with class inclusion problems. If a child is shown a display of five roses and three tulips and asked whether there are more roses or flowers, the young child will say more (15)_____ . Preschoolers do not understand that an item may be larger than one thing yet smaller than another item, a comparison called a/an (16)_____ inference. The most important cognitive difficulty is the preschoolers' lack of understanding that quantities remain the same despite changes in appearance, called (17)_____ .

Preschool children can concentrate on only one dimension at a time, a phenomenon called (18)_____ . They judge everything on the (19)_____ of the item and will make mistakes, especially if deception is involved. Preschoolers are (20)_____ , believing that everyone is perceiving the world the way they are. Young preschoolers show (21)_____ in that they ascribe the attributes of living things to inanimate objects. They also show (22)_____ , explaining natural phenomena by using human causation. Piaget's ideas have been criticized.

During the preschool stage, the child's ability to spend time on a particular task called (23)_____ improves as does the child's ability to concentrate on one stimulus and ignore other extraneous stimuli called (24)_____ . The memory of preschoolers improves as well. An important factor in whether a preschooler will remember something is (25)_____ . Preschoolers' ability to use (26)_____ memory strategies on their own is limited. Preschoolers also forget (more/less) (27)_____ quickly than elementary school age children.

One reason children show limitations in cognitive functions is due to their inexperience. They do not have the experiences necessary to form general frameworks useful for understanding things called (28)_____ . The sequence of events that occur in a particular situation is called a (29)_____ . The preschoolers' understanding of the order of events is more (30)_____ than the older child's.

Preschool children spend more time (31)_____ than in any other activity except sleeping. A television show based on the idea that children need pure love and acceptance is (32)_____ . Children who watch (33)_____ learn its central concepts and are more ready for school than children who do not watch it. A show that emphasizes imagination and emotional awareness is (34)_____ .

Many young children attend nursery school. (35)_____ education programs serve children living in poverty and try to make up for the differences in experiences between poor and middle-class youth. (36)_____ nursery schools emphasize social and emotional development, while the (37)_____ school educates the senses since there is a belief that a close relationship between the senses and the intellect exists. (38)_____ preschools emphasize play, social interaction, and discovery, while preschools based on (39)_____ theory actively teach concepts to young children and use reinforcement. Children living in poverty who regularly attend (40)_____ programs are less likely to be left back and less likely to require special educational services. The program has the temporary effect of raising (41)_____ . The most important change in kindergarten is an increased emphasis on (42)_____ .

InfoTrac

For additional readings, explore InfoTrac College Edition, our online library.
Go to http://www.infotrac-college.com/wadsworth.
Hint: enter the search terms *Preschool Children, Children's Drawings, Children's Testimony,* and *Preoperational Stage.*

What's on the web

Children's Nutrition Research Center
http://www.checnet.org/chec/index.html

The State of the World's Children
http://www.unicef.org/sowc98/

Starting Smart - How Early Experience Affect Brain Development
http://www.bcm.tmc.edu/civitas/links/ounce.html

The Wadsworth Psychology Study Center Web Site
Go to the Wadsworth Psychology Study Center at http://psychology.wadsworth.com/ for quiz questions, research updates, hot topics, interactive exercises, and suggested readings in the InfoTrac College Edition related to this chapter.

Answers 1. decreases; **2.** right; **3.** amount; **4.** type; **5.** accidents; **6.** diarrhea; **7.** declined; **8.** preoperational; **9.** inductive; **10.** deductive; **11.** inductive; **12.** transductive; **13.** seriation; **14.** classification; **15.** roses; **16.** transitive; **17.** conservation; **18.** centering; **19.** appearance; **20.** egocentric; **21.** animism; **22.** artificialism; **23.** attention span; **24.** selective attention; **25.** interest; **26.** verbal; **27.** more; **28.** schemata; **29.** script; **30.** rigid; **31.** watching television; **32.** *Barney and Friends;* **33.** *Sesame Street;* **34.** *Mr. Rogers' Neighborhood;* **35.** Compensatory; **36.** Traditional; **37.** Montessori; **38.** Piagetian; **39.** behavioral; **40.** Head Start; **41.** intelligence scores; **42.** academics

Social *and* Personality

CHAPTER OUTLINE

The Land of Make-Believe

The Self-Concept in the Preschool Years

Play

Parents and Preschoolers

Sibling Relationships: Is It Always "Sibil War"?

Peers: A New Relationship

Gender Role Acquisition

Atypical Development: Child Abuse

ARE THESE STATEMENTS True *or* False?

1. Children raised in happy and secure environments may still develop such fears as fear of the dark or of being alone.
2. The pretend play of boys and girls differs.
3. Boys who engage in rough-and-tumble play are less popular and have poorer social skills than boys who do not engage in such play.
4. Children are most self-reliant and independent if their parents have few rules and make few demands on their children.
5. Play-oriented and positive behaviors are more common in sibling relationships than are arguments and fights.
6. When parents treat their children unequally, it always leads to resentment and poor sibling relationships.
7. The most common type of family violence occurs among siblings.
8. The total amount of aggression shown by preschoolers declines with age.
9. The difference in aggression between boys and girls is disappearing, but gender differences in cognitive abilities, such as math or verbal skills, are increasing.
10. Children who are physically abused are less aggressive than children who are not abused because they understand the consequences of violence.

ANSWERS: 1. *True.* 2. *True.* 3. *False.* 4. *False.* 5. *True.* 6. *False.* 7. *True.* 8. *True.* 9. *False.* 10. *False.*

Development *in* Early Childhood

The Land of Make-Believe

"Let's play Barbie dolls," Annie said to her reluctant baby-sitter as she dumped her dolls onto the carpet. She proceeded to set the scene, telling her sitter exactly what she expected her to do. This time Barbie was Cinderella, and her sitter was to play assorted parts in the fairy tale. The time before, Annie was the mommy and the sitter played the part of the children. During that domestic scene, the children were told that their parents were going out and they couldn't come along because it would be too late. After telling them a story, Annie put the children to bed, but only after she checked to be certain that the night light worked so that the children, who were afraid of the dark, would go to sleep.

Annie has an 8-year-old brother whose sole goal in life, according to Annie's parents, is the emotional torture of his younger sister. The children constantly argue, and Annie is often left in tears after her brother supposedly said or did something to her. Yet, they are not certain whether to intervene or let the children straighten things out themselves.

The life of a preschooler differs greatly from that of a toddler. Preschoolers interact with a wider variety of people and have a good idea of what they want and what they don't want. Their interactions with their parents are more verbal, since they can both express themselves better and understand others with greater ease. Their expanding world offers new challenges in getting along with others as they seek satisfying interpersonal relationships outside the family. At the same time, they become more aware of their environment and begin to develop some idea of how boys and girls act in their society, which forms the basis for their later understanding of gender roles.

A Sense of Initiative

During early childhood, preschoolers are able to plan, and they enjoy being on the move and taking the initiative (Erikson, 1963). They become increasingly involved in independent efforts to accomplish some task—for example, riding a bicycle or planning to make a building with blocks. They are curious about their environment. They strike out on their own, attempting to achieve some goal, and make more of their own choices. Preschoolers have plenty of energy, and they easily forget failures, learning from them to approach the task more accurately and skillfully next time.

Erikson considers **initiative** the positive outcome of this preschool stage, while the negative outcome is **guilt.** The preschool child is eager to master skills and to interact with others. Since simple motor skills like walking have been mastered, the child is free to try new activities such as climbing. Preschoolers enjoy planning and cooperating with others on activities with easy-to-understand future outcomes, such as getting a room ready for a friend, and will participate enthusiastically in such activities (Black & Puckett, 1996). If parents react with encouragement to children's socially acceptable plans and behaviors, children develop a confidence in selecting goals and persevere in reaching them (Erikson, 1963). A major activity in which children show this sense of initiative is in their play, during which they master difficult challenges and tasks through experimentation and repeated effort.

The psychosocial crisis of the preschool stage is initiative versus guilt. If parents encourage their children in their attempts to plan activities, they develop a positive sense of initiative.

initiative

The positive outcome of the psychosocial crisis of the preschool period, involving development of a respect for one's own wishes and desires.

Some initiatives are accomplished independently, such as building a castle with blocks, while others, such as baking a cake or playing baseball, require the active participation of others, both adults and peers. If a child's curiosity and self-initiated activities become a bother to parents and they react with scorn and unnecessary restrictions, the child is likely to become timid and fearful. If the child's many questions are met by impatience and negativity, the child may become less curious about the world. The child develops an unhealthy sense of guilt and requires an excessive amount of assurance from adults. The child does not try new activities, initiate interactions with others, or show any joy in the new abilities that are developing. The child with a positive sense of initiative will show the virtue of purpose—that is, the courage to pursue socially acceptable goals without undue fear of punishment or guilt.

Sometimes, the child's initiatives are misdirected and may result in aggression, such as pushing others to get to the cookies first, or coercion, such as telling another child that if the child doesn't do something, he can't come to the birthday party (Black & Puckett, 1996). At other times, the initiatives may result in dangerous behavior. The parent must guide the child to show the sense of initiative in a socially appropriate manner, giving the child choices, and neither undercontrolling or overcontrolling the child. Preschool children need caregivers who will answer their questions with patience and understanding. They need caregivers who will encourage their interests and abilities while protecting these young children from danger and helping them develop socially appropriate styles of interacting with others.

 Guideposts

What is the meaning of psychosocial crisis of early childhood?

The Self-Concept in the Preschool Years

For many years, psychologists have been interested in the child's emerging self-concept. The **self-concept** is the picture people have of themselves. In early childhood, the self-concept is based on external factors such as physical characteristics (Burns, 1979), possessions (Damon & Hart, 1982), and activities such as "I play baseball" (Keller, Ford, & Meacham, 1978). Self-descriptions focus on what is visible and tangible (Damon & Hart, 1988). The preschooler describes concrete observable behaviors and specific examples but tends not to generalize. A girl may like basketball and baseball but does not say she likes sports, or a boy may like cats and dogs but not say he likes animals. It is not until middle childhood that personality characteristics take center stage and personal comparisons with others, such as "I am taller" become common.

Preschoolers do show the beginnings of a psychological sense of who they are (Eder, 1989). Preschoolers can produce descriptions of inner states and emotions. They sometimes make statements such as "I don't feel good with grownups" or "I usually play with friends." The self-concept is cumulative; what is formed in early childhood can be modified if there is some major change in the child's life. The child's experiences form the basis for later generalizations.

Other people help define the nature of this self-concept both by the way they treat the child (for example, not letting a little girl get dirty but allowing a little boy to do so) or by evaluating some behavior or desire, perhaps by telling children that they are good (or bad) at drawing (Durkin, 1995). Preschoolers who are told that their socially acceptable initiatives are good are likely to evaluate themselves positively. Such early experiences can directly affect behavior. There is a significant correlation between self-concept and cooperative behavior; that is, preschoolers

guilt

The negative outcome of the psychosocial crisis of the preschool period, resulting in a sense that the child's acts and desires are bad.

self-concept

The picture people have of themselves.

Guideposts

What is the basis of the self-concept during the preschool years?

who have a positive sense of themselves are more likely to show cooperation and other helping behaviors (Cauley & Tyler, 1978). Young children usually evaluate themselves very positively, but with increasing age and experiences, they learn about their strengths and weaknesses so that their evaluations become somewhat less positive and more highly related to actual skills, accomplishments, or the evaluations from others (Marsh, Craven, & Debus, 1998).

Emotional Expression in Early Childhood

The preschooler shows a wider range of emotional expressions than younger children, and these emotions change quickly in response to changing circumstances. Children show some ability to restrain their emotions compared with their ability at age 2, but are still less capable of handling their emotions than they will be during the middle childhood years.

Childhood Fears The child's expanding world is sometimes frightening, and fears are quite common in young children. Between ages 2 and 6 years, children average four or five fears (Wicks-Nelson & Israel, 1997). The number and intensity of fears experienced by children decline with age (King et al., 1989). Children differ greatly in their fears; some fear the dark, for example, and others don't. Some react to fears quietly and withdraw, while others cling desperately to their parents. Some of the more common fears are of darkness, being alone, storms, ghosts and monsters, animals and insects, and separation. Many children raised in happy, secure environments still develop fears. In fact, almost every child develops some sort of fear during the course of childhood (Poznansky, 1973).

Certain fears are more common at particular ages: for instance, a fear of strangers in 6- to 9-month-olds, of imaginary creatures during the second year, fear of the dark among 4-year-olds, and social fears and fear of failure in older children. As the child comes to understand that ghosts and monsters are not real, these fears fade away, while they may develop other, less fantastic fears (Bauer, 1976). Most young children's fears are transient, about half disappearing in three months (Wenar, 1994). Preschoolers' limited experience, fragmentary information base, and misconceptions about the world may lead to some of these fears (Black &

T **F**
1

Children raised in happy and secure environments may still develop such fears as fear of the dark or of being alone.

Preschoolers whose initiatives are valued are likely to develop a positive image of themselves.

Puckett, 1996; Harris, 1991). The preschooler's vivid imagination also contributes to fears of darkness, strange creatures, monsters, and goblins. Children at this age magnify and distort events, thinking of the terrible things that could happen (Ross Laboratories, 1979).

At times, a particular experience can make a child quite fearful. A sudden move from a dog or commotion in the street during the night can be the basis for a fear. Some television programs might frighten preschool children, who may insist that the light be kept on in their room to guard against some imaginary creature. At other times, children's real experiences may lead to fears. Parents' actions may threaten children's security. For example, a parent at a shopping mall may threaten that if the child doesn't stop whining the parent will leave her there. A child who is punished for asking for something when his mother comes home from work may show a fear response when he wants to talk to his mother (Bugental & Goodnow, 1998). Of course, not all fears are childish or harmful; some may even be adaptive. A fear of traffic or strange animals may lead to fewer accidents, and children who do not fear these things may take dangerous risks (Black & Puckett, 1996).

Children's fears may be learned through classical conditioning, such as the pairing of the doctor with the pain of a vaccination leading to a fear of the doctor or the surroundings. Children also notice how adults react to particular stimuli, such as insects, dogs, and the dark. If a parent stands on a chair and screams at the sight of a spider, the child learns to fear spiders. Children tend to show many of the same fears their parents have (Bandura & Menlove, 1968).

Children usually outgrow their early fears. Most of the time, calm parental reassurance is sufficient for a child to be able to cope with fears, and the need for clinical treatment is relatively rare (Skuse, 1997). Parents should not ridicule children for their fears or shame them before others. It may also be harmful to force children to face their fears. Children's fears should be respected, and parents are wise to give children time to get used to the environment before helping children adjust to the feared object. If a child is afraid of dogs, parents should allow a child to stay close to the parents and away from a feared dog for a while. Sometimes, if children watch other children cope with the feared stimulus, their fear reactions may be reduced. When preschool children with a fear of dogs were exposed to a model situation in which a 4-year-old child approached a dog in a confident manner, many showed less avoidance of the dogs. Thus, a peer model, patience, and understanding appear to help children overcome their fears (Bandura, Grusek, & Menlove, 1967).

Preschoolers have a number of fears, most of which are transient and disappear.

Guideposts

What fears do young children show? How should parents deal with these fears?

Play

Play is such a natural part of childhood that we tend not to think very much about it. **Play** is an activity that is performed for sheer enjoyment with no ulterior motive. The focus of play is on the child rather than on what the child is holding, bouncing, or coloring. Play activities are performed for their own sake, with no payoff or reward in candy, attention, or money involved (Fogel, Nwokah, & Karns, 1993). Finally, play is enjoyable.

play
An enjoyable activity dominated by the child and performed for its own sake.

The Development of Play

The ability to play follows a developmental pattern (see Table 9.1). Babies are not involved much with other children. Anything that occurs may be of interest to the infant for only a few seconds. Such **unoccupied behavior** is the first stage of play during which babies may stroke their bodies, play with their hands, or hug a stuffed animal. Later in the first year, children play with simple toys, banging them against something or dropping them. They are basically exploring the properties of the toy and are uninvolved with any other children around them. They may play simple peekaboo games with a parent, but the other person is essentially a toy, and no mutuality is evidenced.

Table 9.1	Types of Play	
Unoccupied Play	hugs stuffed animal, basically sensorimotor, explores properties of objects	First year
Solitary play	playing by oneself	Continuing
Onlooker play	watches others, may follow other children around, cannot participate	Later in first year and continuing through second year
Parallel play	plays in proximity to other children but not with other children	2-year-olds and some 3-year-olds
Dramatic Play (Pretend play)	plays various roles, use of imagination	beginning second year, increases through early childhood
Associative play	plays with other children but cannot sustain interactions	third and fourth year
Cooperative play	can sustain interactions, takes roles and play them more easily	fifth or sixth year

Solitary or **independent play** can be seen in young children and remains important in the second and third years of life and, indeed, throughout childhood. However, the transition to a more social type of play can be seen in what Mildred Parten (1932), the pioneer researcher on play, called **onlooker play.** During this stage, children watch others with considerable interest and frequently ask questions about what the other children are doing. They are not yet able to join in and thus remain on the outside. This leads to a type of play in which children may seek out the company of others but do not yet interact with them.

After the second year, children are often brought together with their peers. These 2-year-olds engage in **parallel play.** They play in the presence of other children but not with them. They do not really interact or cooperate with one another. One gets the feeling that if one child were to leave, the other child could go on alone without any problem. The quality of the sand castle built by either child does not depend on the participation of the other child. Parallel play is found throughout the preschool period, but it decreases with age. It is the primary play behavior in 2-year-olds and some 3-year-olds.

Active interaction with others emerges during the preschool period. Annie, for example, can play by herself, with her parents and sitter, and with children her own age. Preschoolers engage in **associative play,** as they actively interact with each other, share, have verbal arguments, and play together, but few of these periods are sustained. There is a flightiness to preschooler's play, and they do not regularly sustain their interactions with others for long periods of time. Much of the

---

unoccupied behavior

A type of play in which children sit and look at others or perform simple movements that are not goal-related.

solitary or independent play

Independent play in which the child plays by himself or herself.

onlooker play

A classification of play in which the child watches others play and shows some interest but is unable to join in.

parallel play

A type of play common in 2-year-olds in which children play in the presence of other children but not with them.

associative play

A type of play seen in preschoolers in which they are actively involved with one another but cannot sustain these interactions.

cooperative play

A type of play seen in the later part of the preschool period and continuing into middle childhood, marked by group play, playing specific roles, and active cooperation for sustained periods of time.

play of preschoolers involves physical practice of skills that have been or are being mastered. Preschoolers' play is active and often physically exhausting.

Beginning in the later part of the preschool period and continuing into middle childhood, children actively engage in **cooperative play** with one another. This involves a more or less unified group of children playing a particular game, often in which one or two children lead. Children are able to take specific parts in a game, and they have a more mature understanding of what their role is in the group. There are often distinct rules to the game. Some children act as leaders and allot roles to the others. Sometimes rebellions break out in the ranks, but children's need for one another is obvious. As children develop, the amount of their social play increases, as does their ability to sustain their attention during play, which allows for longer interactions (Huff & Lawson, 1990).

More recent research confirms this developmental progression in children's play but finds that preschoolers are somewhat less socially-oriented in their play when compared with children's play 40 years earlier (Barnes, 1971). Perhaps certain societal changes are responsible: the amount of time spent in front of television, the advent of modern toys that are more conducive to solitary play, or the possibility that children receive more parental reinforcement for playing by themselves.

Two-year-olds are often involved in parallel play (left) while preschoolers begin interacting with other children in associative play (middle). In middle childhood, children actively cooperate with one another in play (right).

Guideposts

How does the ability to play with others develop throughout childhood?

ACTION / REACTION

Saving the World from Invaders

Terrence, age 5, and his older brother Dean, age 10, love computer games. Some of these games are "shoot-'em-ups," in which the player saves the universe from invaders, while others require the players to solve some riddle or find some treasure. Terrence seems to be imitating his brother in this "obsession" with computer games.

Mrs. K. is especially concerned about Terrence because his behavior seems to be affected more by these games, becoming somewhat wilder after play. He plays with his brother's computer games, which she believes are inappropriate for him. She doesn't like the "shoot-'em-up" games, believing that a young child should be playing more socially. Mr. K. sees nothing wrong with these games since Terrence sometimes plays these games with friends, and perhaps this will make him more interested and familiar with computers.

1. *If you were Terrence's parents, would you limit his play with computer games?*
2. *Are there computer games that you would not let your child play with? If yes, which ones?*
3. *If you would limit Terrence's play, how would you deal with his annoyance and belief that he should be able to do anything he wants with his spare time?*

ACTION / REACTION

For Your Consideration ?

A study published in 1971 found that children are less social than they were in the 1930s when the original study by Parten was conducted. If another study was conducted today, do you think there would be a further erosion of social play? Why or why not?

Pretend Play

Annie enjoys playing pretend games. **Pretend** or **dramatic play** involves taking the roles of others, which requires the ability to imitate and place oneself in another person's position. The latter ability is primitive in preschoolers and develops slowly as children find themselves in different social situations. Most dramatic play centers on common home situations and everyday challenges. Some involves participation in fantasy, including children protecting others from monsters and putting themselves in fairy tales as specific characters. This is seen in Annie's play with her sitter.

Objects can take on new functions and identities in imaginary play, and new roles are spontaneously adopted as a scenario unfolds (de Lorimier, Doyle, & Tessier, 1995). This dramatic play is spontaneous and flexible, and its sophistication increases with age. Children who engage in a great deal of such play are better at perspective taking, role taking, and are more socially competent.

Pretend play can start as early as toddlerhood, because children at age 2 years can use symbols (Piaget, 1962). These toddlers may pretend to talk on a toy telephone. Dramatic play declines as children enter middle childhood but does not disappear (Johnson & Yawkey, 1988). Gender differences are common. Boys more often refer to building and repairing vehicles, and girls more often prepare meals or care for babies (Wall, Pickert, & Bigson, 1989).

As children proceed through the preschool stage, they do not require as many concrete props in their pretend play, and they show better control of their fantasies. Their ability to take the perspective of other people develops slowly but adds to the sophistication of their pretend play. Through pretend play, children cope with their problems, master difficult situations, and explore the roles of those around them (de Lorimier, 1995). Pretend play is, then, a very developmentally important phenomenon.

The themes of pretend play are also related to culture. Korean American children's play includes everyday activities and family role themes much more than Anglo-American children, who enact themes of fantasy and suspected danger in the environment much more often (Farver & Shin, 1997). Anglo-American children spend more time describing their own actions and use more commands, while Korean American children describe their partner's actions more and use more polite requests. Anglo-American children are more individualistic and direct in their communication. These patterns reflect cultural differences in the communication patterns and behaviors they see around them.

Rough-and-Tumble Play

One type of play that adults observe often with some displeasure is **rough-and-tumble play.** Such behaviors as play fighting, chasing, wrestling, sneaking up on someone, carrying another child, holding, and pushing can fall into this category (Humphreys & Smith, 1987). The amount of such play increases from early to middle childhood, peaking at about age 11 years, after which it declines substantially (Pellegrini & Smith, 1998). It is much more common in boys than in girls. Adults often discourage rough-and-tumble play because they are afraid someone will get hurt, that it will escalate into real fighting, or they believe it will teach antisocial or aggressive behavior (Pellegrini & Perlmutter, 1989).

The chances of someone being injured by accident are greater in rough-and-tumble play than if children are busy drawing pictures, but rough-and-tumble play should not be confused with aggression (Pellegrini, 1995). Rough-and-tumble play

T F
2

The pretend play of boys and girls differs.

Guideposts

What are the special benefits of pretend play?

dramatic play (pretend play)

A type of play in which children take on the roles of others.

rough-and-tumble play

Physical play, such as play fighting, chasing, and wrestling.

takes place when no dispute is occurring, whereas aggressive behavior often occurs in the course of disputes, especially those involving property. In rough-and-tumble play, children take turns playing roles, whereas in aggression this is not the case. When rough-and-tumble play ends, children do not separate or have angry feelings toward one another. The opposite pattern is found in aggressive behavior (Humphreys & Smith, 1987).

Recently, psychologists have called for greater tolerance of rough-and-tumble play. Besides providing the obvious practice of physical skills, such play, some claim, can improve social skills and competence (Pelligrini, 1995; 1987). Rough-and-tumble play is related to boys' social problem solving, popularity, and negotiation skills (Humphreys & Smith, 1987).

Both popular and unpopular children engage in a similar amount of rough-and-tumble play (Coie & Kupersmidt, 1983). However, when popular children engage in this sort of play, it does not escalate into aggression, whereas such play by unpopular or rejected children often does (Pellegrini, 1988). Unpopular children may not have the social skills to understand the limits of rough-and-tumble play. Also, unpopular, aggressive children may interpret rough-and-tumble play as a provocation, thereby eliciting aggressive responses from them (Dodge & Frame, 1982).

Gender Differences in Play

Gender differences in play begin early. Boys are more aggressive and engage in more rough-and-tumble play (Pellegrini & Smith, 1998). These differences appear in cultures around the world, whether the culture is essentially tribal or technologically advanced (Whiting & Whiting, 1975). Girls also exchange more information during their interactions (Lansford & Parker, 1999). When same-gender groups of 4.5-year-old children were brought in small groups into a mobile home from which the furnishings had been removed and some toys provided, boys and girls played differently. The girls organized themselves and made rules (DiPietro, 1981). They argued, but they did not resort to physical means of persuasion. The boys played more roughly, often wrestling. They did not seem angry, nor did they attempt to injure one another; they simply played differently from the girls.

T / F

3

Boys who engage in rough-and-tumble play are less popular and have poorer social skills than boys who do not engage in such play.

Guideposts

Why is rough-and-tumble play misunderstood?

Guideposts

What gender differences exist in play?

Children show gender differences in play quite early.

While some may argue that males are biologically predisposed to these patterns, other explanations are possible. Since various societies may expect males to act more aggressively, males may then simply be complying with society's expectations. The possible presence of some biological predisposition does not negate the importance of learning.

The Benefits of Play

People tend to overlook the contributions play makes to a child's development. The physical benefits of play are the most obvious. Children tossing a ball around are exercising their muscles and improving their eye-hand coordination. Play often involves muscular activity, which is vital for optimal physical development (Isenberg & Quisenberry, 1988). As children repeat their newly acquired skills, they increase the strength of the neurological structures that underlie these skills, opening up new opportunities for further learning (McCune, 1998).

In the psychosocial realm, play provides practice in social skills. Play allows children to handle social situations involving dominance and leadership, and it teaches them to share power, space, and ideas (Rubin & Howe, 1986). As children play, they can express their feelings and work through conflicts, thereby regulating their aggressive impulses (Hamburg, 1994; Kramer, 1996). Play also encourages children to take the perspectives of others, helping them become less egocentric and develop their verbal skills (Rogoff, 1998).

In the cognitive realm, play encourages children to improve their planning and problem-solving abilities. It provides a format that allows young children to integrate their experiences into a coherent structure. Preschoolers must learn about what things happen and when, and during pretend play, children figure out the scripts that occur in various situations and practice adult skills (Case, 1998). Play also promotes creativity and flexibility because it allows children to experiment without fear of consequences.

Many theorists have argued for the importance of play. For Freud, play provided children with an avenue for wish fulfillment and a way to master traumatic events. As children play, they allow their emotions to show and work out their problems. Erikson (1977), in some ways similar to Freud, emphasized how play allows children to express some of their anger in a safe situation and to master their problems. Play, then, is an outlet for pent-up frustration and anger. Children act out their problems and thereby reduce their anxieties (Erikson, 1959). One 4-year-old girl played house with small doll-like figures. At home, this girl had to share the attention of her parents with her baby sister, who naturally required much care. In her play, Daddy would come home and, instead of kissing her and going to see the baby, he would say, "I want to play only with you, not that silly baby. I don't care about her." In her play, she was expressing her true feelings. In fact, some psychologists use play situations as therapy to gain deeper insights into the nature of a child's problems (Axline, 1969).

Piaget (1952) looked at play as an activity that encouraged cognitive development and allowed children to exercise their cognitive abilities and practice their newly learned skills. Play allows the child, through the process of assimilation, to incorporate new ideas, objects, or situations into existing ways of thinking. The child plays in a variety of ways, using abilities that he or she already possesses. For others, play is a self-initiated activity that satisfies a child's innate need to explore and master the environment (Berlyne, 1960). Finally, Bruner (1972) sees play as a vehicle for learning skills that will be useful as children mature. Skills can be mastered in a nonthreatening environment and then used to solve problems later in life. Perhaps when children play with building blocks, they learn something about mechanics, spatial relationships, and tool use that may be helpful at a later time.

Many of the preschoolers' interpersonal interactions occur in the context of play, and during the preschool years, the child's relationships with parents, siblings, and peers change dramatically.

Guideposts
Why is play an important developmental phenomenon?

Parents and Preschoolers

There is a fundamental paradox in the preschooler-parent relationship. Preschoolers have a greater sense of independence and can do things on their own. Yet, they have a need to be near parents, to be protected and comforted when they are frightened or must face new challenges. At this stage, parents also expect their preschoolers to have some control of their basic actions, especially aggressive responses (Mills & Rubin, 1990). Parents approve of the use of stricter discipline when they are convinced the child can understand the rules and act appropriately (Dix, Rible, & Zambarano, 1989). For example, what if a 2-year-old breaks a figurine that was sitting on the coffee table? A parent who does not believe that the child understood or is responsible for the behavior will react with disappointment, perhaps even annoyance, yet with understanding. However, the parent who believes the child does understand is more likely to yell or punish. Most parents believe that preschoolers can control their actions, at least to some degree, so a somewhat sterner type of discipline is seen in these years than in the toddler years.

Guideposts
How does the relationship between parents and their preschoolers change?

Parenting Styles

Parents differ in the ways they control their children's behavior. Parenting styles have been perceived in terms of two factors: responsiveness and demandingness (Baumrind, 1988). *Responsiveness* refers to expressing parental warmth, considering the needs of the child, and using a reasoning approach to discipline. *Demandingness* refers to the extent to which parents set firm rules and expect good behavior from their children.

Some parents exercise a great deal of direct control, while others believe that having fewer rules is better. Some parents are much more responsive than others. The effect of differing parenting styles was investigated by Diana Baumrind (1967, 1971, 1978, 1980) and further developed by other psychologists (Maccoby & Martin, 1983) (see Table 9.2).

Authoritarian parents try to control their children's conduct by establishing rules and regulations. Obedience is greatly valued, and these parents use the threat of force to correct behavior. Their decisions cannot be questioned; their word is law. Authoritarian parents are very controlling but are less responsive to their children.

Table 9.2	Parenting Styles	
Style	**Demandingness Level**	**Responsiveness Level**
Authoritarian parents	High	Low
Permissive parents	Low	High
Neglecting/Rejecting	Low	Low
Authoritative	High	High

authoritarian parenting

A style of parenting in which parents rigidly control their children's behavior by establishing rules and value obedience while discouraging questioning.

Permissive parents make few demands on their children. They are nonpunishing, are open to communication, and do not attempt to shape the children's behavior. The children regulate their own activities. When necessary, permissive parents use reason rather than power to control their children. They don't place much emphasis on conformity to rules, and self-regulation is emphasized (Fagot, 1995). Permissive parents are noncontrolling and nondemanding but some are relatively warm.

Rejecting-neglecting parents are essentially not engaged with their children. They are neither responsive nor demanding. They do not monitor their children's activities and provide little or no structure. Some may actively reject their own children, while others simply neglect their responsibilities.

Authoritative parents encourage verbal give-and-take and explain the reasons behind family policies. Both autonomy and discipline are valued. Limits are set, but the child's individuality is taken into consideration. The parents are warm and do not see themselves as infallible (Baumrind, 1971).

As a group, the children of authoritarian parents are discontented, withdrawn, and distrustful. The children of permissive parents are not self-reliant or self-controlled, nor do they explore the environment. Children of neglectful and rejecting parents are perhaps the worst off of any of the other groups (Schaffer, 1996). Adolescents from such homes score the poorest on measures of adjustment, psychosocial competence, and show psychological and behavioral dysfunction (Lamborn, Mounts, Steinberg, & Dornbusch, 1991). They are at risk for drug abuse, delinquency, and aggression (Lamborn et al., 1991; MacKinnon-Lewis, Starnes, Volling, & Johnson, 1997). The children of authoritative parents are the most self-reliant, self-controlled, explorative, and contented. They have higher levels of self-esteem and better impulse control (Paikoff & Brooks-Gunn, 1995).

The children of authoritative parents, then, seem to thrive. Authoritative parents combine firm control, encouragement of individuality, grant appropriate autonomy, and have open communication with their children, leading to children who are independent and competent. They are also warmer and more nurturant than authoritarian parents. Some permissive parents are warm; others show a coolness and detachment toward their children. Authoritative parents are certainly demanding, but they are also warm, rational, and receptive to the child. This combination of high demandingness and positive encouragement of the child's independent striving is best. Parental control does not interfere with independence as long as children are given an opportunity to develop their own abilities and make their own decisions, within limits. Yet the total parental control that authoritarian parents use produces children who are less competent, less contented, and suspicious. Warmth and discipline are the keys to producing independent, competent children.

Discipline Style

A parent's attempts to control a child's behavior can be placed under one of two headings. **Power-assertive discipline** involves physical punishment, yelling, shouting, and forceful commands, while **love-oriented discipline** involves praise, affection, reasoning, a show of disappointment, and the withdrawal of love (Maccoby & Martin, 1983). Each of the three parenting styles uses discipline in a different way, resulting in different outcomes. Authoritarian parents rely on punishment, which gets them obedience in the short term and rebellion in the long term. Permissive parents rarely use any type of discipline, which can result in a child who lacks direction and self-control. When they do discipline their children, they use

T F
4

Children are most self-reliant and independent if their parents have few rules and make few demands on their children.

Guideposts

How do the parenting styles of authoritarian, permissive, authoritative, and rejecting/neglecting parents differ?

permissive parenting
A style of parenting marked by open communication and a lack of parental demand for good behavior.

rejecting-neglecting
A parenting style in which parents are not involved in their children's lives, being neither demanding nor responsive.

reasoning, a love-oriented approach. Authoritative parents use both approaches, depending on the situation, but they encourage independence by allowing children freedom within limits. Perhaps authoritative parents notice the change in a child's verbal and physical abilities and tailor the discipline to the child's emerging abilities.

These discipline styles interact with the emotional tone of the parent-child relationship. When restrictiveness occurs within a context of warmth and acceptance, it can lead to such positive outcomes as obedience and nonaggressiveness. When it occurs in the presence of hostility, it leads to withdrawal and anxiety (Becker, 1964). In investigating techniques of discipline, both the type of approach (power-assertive or love-oriented) and the emotional tone of the relationship (warm or hostile) must be considered.

Preschoolers' ability to use language gives parents more options in dealing with their misbehavior. As children mature, they respond to a more rational approach. Preschoolers respond better to suggestions, while toddlers respond better to simple commands (McLaughlin, 1983). Parents who realize that their preschoolers' verbal abilities give them more options are likely to change their discipline strategy and use more complicated verbal techniques instead of mere commands.

Although the terms are often used interchangeably, discipline and punishment are not the same. The word **discipline** comes from an old English word meaning "instruction," and, indeed, the purpose of discipline is to help children learn how to behave so that they can satisfy their needs in a socially acceptable manner. They learn to control their undesirable urges and develop self-control. Punishment involves the application of sanctions for the purpose of reducing the frequency of an undesirable behavior. While punishment teaches children what not to do, discipline is intended to teach the child what to do and how to properly express such emotions as anger.

The emphasis on discipline rather than punishment translates into child-rearing policies that help teach children to control their own behavior (Bigner, 1994). A number of parenting programs are available that emphasize this positive view of discipline (Cowan, Powell, & Cowan, 1998). Some, such as the STEP (Systematic Training for Effective Parenting) program, argue that all behavior is goal directed and misbehavior is based on the child's faulty beliefs. Misbehavior is related to such goals as the desire to gain attention, seek revenge, express feelings of inadequacy, or obtain power (Dreikurs & Stoltz, 1964). In these programs, parents learn how to positively deal with misbehavior (see Table 9.3 on page 336) and to use encouragement to help children attempt new behaviors. Parents also learn to provide logical consequences to their children's behaviors. For example, if a child is told that throwing a toy will break it and he continues to do so and the toy breaks, the child must do without the toy. If an older child comes home late for a meal, the child must make his own meal or eat something that is cold. If an older child breaks something, the child must clean up the breakage and replace the broken object or reimburse the owner (Gilbert, 1988). These consequences are known by the child before the child engages in the behavior. Children learn that their behavior has consequences and how to take responsibility for their actions. Evaluations of the STEP program are positive (Burnett, 1986; Krebs, 1986).

Another program is the popular Parent Effectiveness Training (PET) program that teaches parents how to communicate effectively with their children to resolve conflicts and create a positive environment for their children (Gordon, 1980). Most parent education programs encourage parents to be more positive and less punitive with their young children, prevent misbehavior, and deal more logically with misbehavior when it arises.

Guideposts

How can the two discipline styles that parents use be described?

authoritative parenting
A style of parenting in which parents establish limits but allow open communication and some freedom for children to make their own decisions in certain areas.

power-assertive discipline
A type of discipline relying on the use of power, such as physical punishment or forceful commands.

love-oriented discipline
A type of discipline relying on the use of reasoning or love.

discipline
An attempt to control others in order to hold undesirable impulses in check and to encourage self-control.

| Table 9.3 | The Goals of Misbehavior |

Child's Faulty Belief	Child's Goal*	Parent's Feeling and Reaction	Child's Response to Parent's Attempts at Correction	Alternatives for Parents
I belong *only* when I am being noticed.	Attention	*Feeling*: Annoyed *Reaction*: Tendency to remind and coax	Temporarily stops misbehavior. Later resumes same behavior or disturbs in another way.	Ignore behavior when possible. Give attention for positive behavior when child is not making a bid for it.
I belong *only* if I am in control or am boss, or when I am proving no one can boss me!	Power	*Feeling*: Angry, provoked, as if one's authority is threatened *Reaction*: Tendency to fight or give in	Active- or passive-aggressive behavior is intensified, or child submits with "defiant compliance."	Withdraw from conflict. Help child see how to use power constructively by appealing for child's help and enlisting cooperation. Realize that fighting or giving in only increases the child's desire for power.
I belong *only* by hurting others as I feel hurt. I cannot be loved.	Revenge	*Feeling*: Deeply hurt *Reaction:Tendency* to retaliate or get even	Seeks further revenge by intensifying misbehavior or choosing another weapon	Avoid feeling hurt. Avoid punishment and retaliation. Build trusting relationship; convince child that he or she is loved.
I belong *only* by convincing others not to expect anything from me. I am unable; I am helpless.	Display inadequacy	*Feeling*: Despair; hopelessness; "I give up" *Reaction*: Tendency to agree with child that nothing can be done	Passively responds or fails to respond to whatever is done; shows no improvement	Stop all criticism. Encourage any positive attempt, no matter how small; focus on assets. Above all, don't be hooked into pity, and don't give up.

*To determine a child's goal, you must check your feelings and the child's response to your attempts to correct him or her. Goal identification is simplified by observing (1) your own feelings and reactions to the child's behavior and (2) the child's response to your attempts at correction. By considering your situation in terms of the chart, you will be able to identify the goals of the misbehavior.

SOURCE: Dinkmeyer, D., & McKay, G. D. (1981). *Parents' handbook: Systematic training for effective parenting*. Reprinted by permission of American Guidance Service, Publishers' Building, Circle Pines, MN. Copyright © 1981. All rights reserved.

Subculture and Discipline

Does this analysis of parenting style hold in other cultures or subcultures? Child-rearing methods are directed toward producing people who can thrive within a particular culture, and various cultures and subcultures have different ideas of what the ideal child and child-rearing strategy might be. In mainstream American and many other Western societies, autonomy and independence are valued, especially today, while in other countries more emphasis is placed on interdependence and feeling a part of a larger group. This can lead to different child-rearing strategies. For example, Mayan mothers strongly disapprove of the Western middle-class custom of allowing infants to sleep alone, and they reacted to an explanation of such Western customs with shock, disapproval, and pity for the child, regarding it as something close to child neglect (Morelli et al., 1992). Their child-rearing methods are targeted toward establishing closeness with their infants that they hope will endure. North American mothers place a great deal emphasis on stimulation compared with both Dutch and Japanese mothers (Corter & Fleming, 1995). Societies differ in the types of relationships they wish to form with their children, the child-rearing strategies they use, as well as their attitudes toward parenting in general (Bornstein et al., 1998; Corter & Fleming, 1995; Holden, 1995).

Even within a particular Western society, parenting styles may differ among groups. For example, the stricter, more authoritarian discipline of African American parents is not associated with behavioral problems such as aggression and is positively related to school achievement (Baumrind, 1993; Deater-Deckard,

Dodge, Bates, & Pettit, 1996). These more restrictive methods of discipline may have a different meaning here. In European American families, more intensive discipline implies a harsh, overly controlling, parent-centered household; but a lack of formal discipline among African American parents may indicate a lack of interest in the child. This analysis only holds for nonabusive discipline. Very harsh discipline, which is outside the norm and physical abuse itself, predicts aggression and psychological problems in children across socioeconomic and ethnic groups (Weiss, Dodge, Bates, & Petit, 1992).

This same analysis holds for Asian American youths (Baumrind, 1972; Darling & Steinberg, 1993). Chinese and other East Asian parents often rate very highly on scales measuring authoritarianism and restrictiveness and low on authoritativeness (Chao, 1994). Among American middle-class children this parenting style is related to a lack of achievement, but Asian children do very well in school under this type of parenting (Dornbusch et al., 1987). Strictness is sometimes equated with parental hostility, mistrust, and aggression in some segments of American society, while many Asian societies interpret a desire for obedience and strictness in terms of caring and involvement. It does not have the meaning of domination that it has in Western societies.

The Chinese term *chiao shun* means training or educating, and Asian parents often see such child-rearing strategies as educating or training children in the self-discipline necessary for academic and vocational success. The training takes place in the context of a supportive, highly involved, and physically close mother-child relationship. In this culture, parental care, concern, and involvement are synonymous with firm control of the child. This control and governance called *guan* has positive connotations. What might be labeled authoritarianism is what traditional Chinese parents might label training, which goes well beyond the authoritarian concept.

The idea of parenting styles is valuable, but to truly understand parenting techniques, an ecological viewpoint is most appropriate. Parental goals, the methods used to reach these goals, and the style of parenting are influenced by cultural practices that reflect specific beliefs about the relationship of the person with society (Darling & Steinberg, 1993).

Child Rearing in African American Homes

No minority group family has been subjected to more analysis than the African American family. African American families are characterized as having one of three structures. A large number of basically middle-class or working-class families that do not differ greatly in structure from majority families make up one group. Another group is poor African Americans with a stable family structure and a potential for economic and social mobility. The third is a group of families with unstable structures, composed of people with poor job skills and insufficient education.

Multigenerational family structures are somewhat more common in African American families than the general public, with grandparents being more involved in the child rearing. Older children often help take care of their younger siblings and have after-school child care responsibilities. A strong work ethic can be found in these families. Adolescents often enter the work force before their white cohorts and help their family with their income.

Guideposts

How do culture and subculture influence child rearing outcome?

Multigenerational family structures are somewhat more common in African American families, with grandparents being more involved in the childrearing.

Child-rearing practices also differ. Often, the emphasis is placed on a people orientation rather than an object orientation. For example, when African American children reach for an object or surface, their attention is often redirected to the person holding them. The interaction between mother and child tends to be a rhythmic volley of speak and respond. Many African American children are accustomed to a higher-energy, fast-paced home with a great deal of concurrent stimulation. Extended kinship networks are a source of strength, with cousins and other relatives often involved. Traditional values stress interdependence, security, a positive self-image, perseverance in the face of adversity, and a positive racial identity (McAdoo, 1991). Socializing children to deal with prejudice and racism is common as well. Organized religion and spirituality are important community resources and sources of inspiration.

Child rearing stresses obedience and respect for elders. African American parental disciplinary practices are somewhat more authoritarian and parent focused (Baumrind, 1972). Such practices may be seen as necessary for safety reasons, because many of these children are being raised in dangerous neighborhoods racked by violence and poverty (Kelley, Power, & Wimbush, 1992; Kelley, Sanchez-Huckles, & Walker, 1993).

The ecological view is especially important here. African Americans growing up in a ghetto area use functional child-rearing strategies, even though they differ from middle-class techniques. These strategies teach self-reliance, resourcefulness, the ability to manipulate situations, mistrust of people in authority, and the ability to ward off attack (Ogbu, 1982).

Child Rearing in Latino Homes

Latinos come from many different countries but are united by a common language. Certain attitudes and family features are shared in Latino families, but differences also occur. For example, mothers originally from the Dominican Republic have child-rearing attitudes reflecting more strictness than mothers from Puerto Rico (Wasserman et al., 1990).

Families emphasize sharing and cooperation rather than competition. Often the individualism and competition of American schools is in conflict with the child's learning at home (Delgado-Gaitan & Trueba, 1985). A sense of family pride and loyalty is also nurtured. The orientation is usually present tense, and a belief in destiny is instilled. A sense of individual dignity not based on economic status is emphasized, which differs somewhat as the general society tends to value people based on their economic or social positions (Garcia Coll, Meyer, & Brillon, 1995).

The traditional role expectations demand that men be virile, somewhat aggressive, and protective of women—the well-known machismo attitude (Bigner, 1994). Machismo has often been criticized, but it actually refers more to the male's responsibility to the family. Family loyalty supersedes individual interests, and older children often have child care responsibilities. In the past, multigenerational family structure was typical, but this arrangement is somewhat less common today. The roles of mothers and fathers are often clearly defined, with fathers being more authoritarian and mothers more involved in child rearing. Traditional male and female role expectations have been somewhat relaxed, with more joint parental decision making today (Garcia Coll et al., 1995).

Frequently, Latino mothers differentiate between the roles of mothers and teachers, emphasizing the maternal role. Latino families are warm and nurturant, showing some indulgence toward young children (Vega, 1990). The emphasis is placed on close mother-child relationships, interpersonal competence, the

For Your Consideration ?

Why would a stricter type of child rearing be supportive of achievement in lower-income African American homes?

Guideposts

How do the parenting practices of African Americans differ from those used by European Americans?

development of proper demeanor, and a sense of pride (Harwood, Schoelmerichs, Schulze, & Gonzalez, 1999). A child should be calm, obedient, courteous, and respectful toward adults (Garcia Coll et al., 1995). Latino parents endorse stricter disciplinary standards than other parents. There is less of an emphasis on reaching early developmental milestones and achievement. Many Latino children do not get as much cognitive stimulation in their early years as Anglo children do. Generally, parents are more concerned with physical well-being and behavior than with the development of cognitive skills.

Guideposts

How do the parenting attitudes of Latinos differ from Anglo parents?

Child Rearing in Asian American Homes

Many Asian American children experience a very different child-rearing regimen compared with most other Americans. For instance, most non-Asian American children sleep by themselves and have their own toys. American parents foster self-reliance, assertiveness, and speaking one's own mind, but Asian American children, especially from the Pacific Rim, are taught to view their role within the society and the family in terms of obligations. Asian American children are taught to think of family first and to subjugate their own desires and concerns. For many Asian Americans, individual behavior reflects either shame or pride on the family (Morrow, 1987).

Child rearing differs in various cultures. Many Chinese parents see child rearing strategies as educatiing or training children in self-discipine, and this translates into firm control.

Asian American families stress the individual as secondary to the family. Expressions of anger and displeasure are to be avoided, and social customs demand strict adherence. Communication is often indirect (Slonim, 1991). Child-rearing practices in infancy and early childhood are indulgent but become more demanding after 5 years. These lenient, nurturant, and permissive ways are due to the belief that young children are not capable of understanding what they do (Kelley & Tseng, 1992). As children above that age are thought to be capable of such understanding, child-rearing practices become stricter, and demands for emotional self-control and self-discipline increase (Garcia Coll et al., 1995). Asian American children are accustomed to a fairly structured formal setting. Parental control, obedience, discipline, an emphasis on education, filial piety, respect for elders, a desire to minimize conflict, and respect for obligations and tradition are common features of Asian American child rearing (Lin & Fu, 1990).

Asian American parents view their primary role as one of teacher (Kelley & Tseng, 1992). Children are taught that through hard work, moral living, and diligence, they will fulfill their potential and make the family proud.

Guideposts

How do the parenting practices of Asian American parents, especially from the Pacific Rim, differ from mainstream American practices?

Child Rearing among Native Americans

The federal government recognizes more than 500 Native American tribal units, and 200 distinct tribal languages are actively spoken (Brown, 1993). With so many tribes, a general Native American child-rearing strategy or culture is difficult to discern. The traditional Native American community is collective and cooperative, with extensive noncompetitive social networks (Harrison, Wilson, Pine, Chan, & Buriel, 1990). In Native American families, responsibilities for child rearing are typically shared among many caring adults, including parents and extended

Guideposts

What qualities do Native Americans want to instill in their children?

For Your Consideration ?

Each society and subculture has an idea of what characteristics it wants to instill in its children. What is the "ideal" child in the Anglo, African American, Latino, Asian American, or Native American culture? How would child-rearing strategies that attempt to instill these characteristics differ from each other?

family members. A great value is placed on age and life experience, and parents often seek advice from older family members or elders. Children are treated somewhat permissively, and there is less interference in the affairs of others and regulation of activities (Williams, 1979). For instance, Navajo children do not need permission to eat or sleep. They eat when they are hungry and sleep when tired (Phillips & Lobar, 1990). Children master self-care skills and participate in household responsibilities fostering self-sufficiency (Garcia Coll et al., 1995). Being part of a group and blending in are important virtues, and asserting one's individuality is not encouraged (Nazarro, 1981; Satler, 1988).

Sharing is an important value that is learned very early, as it is in some other cultures. However, people in authority are supposed to share what they have (Lewis & Ho, 1979). Saving for the future, an ideal among the dominant culture (although not always practiced) is relatively unimportant. One's worth is measured by one's willingness and ability to share; therefore, the accumulation of wealth is not as respected (Slonim, 1991). Strong extended family structures are common, although not as prevalent as years ago.

Patience is a virtue that many Native American tribes teach. Sometimes, Native American children who have been taught to be patient may not seem competitive in the dominant society because they have been taught to wait for their turn without being assertive. Native American children are also frequently given choices and participate in adult activities (Pepper, 1976).

These differences in child-rearing philosophy and attitudes are, of course, very general, and such an analysis runs the risk of stereotyping. Parents differ greatly in their identification with the traditional values of their culture, and the longer they are in this country, the more they take on at least some of the values of the dominant culture. Despite this needed caution concerning overgeneralization, it is clear that any analysis of child rearing must take cultural background, and the cultural goals and prescriptions for child rearing, into account.

Sibling Relationships: Is It Always "Sibil War"?

Annie's older brother enjoys teasing her. He sometimes hides her favorite stuffed animal and will change the channel on the television set while she is watching a program. At the same time, they often play together, and he can sometimes be very kind to her.

The very presence of siblings affects a child's development. Unlike friends, siblings do not leave the home at night. Contact can be limited, but siblings cannot completely be avoided. Siblings compete for parental attention, and their joy and pain affect everyone in the household.

More than 80% of American children have one or more siblings (Eisenberg & Mussen, 1989), and by the time a child enters kindergarten, he or she has spent twice as much time in the company of siblings as with parents (Bank & Kahn, 1975). It stands to reason that sibling relationships are important.

Discussions of siblings usually revolve around sibling rivalry, but siblings also encourage prosocial actions and fill definite psychological needs. Not only do siblings play together and experience one another's joy and pain firsthand, but they often help one another (Brody, Zolinda, MacKinnon, & MacKinnon, 1985). They can sometimes provide the support and affection that may not be forthcoming from the parents (Dunn & Kendrick, 1982).

Sibling interaction is fairly predictable. Older children initiate more prosocial as well as combative behaviors, and younger children imitate more (Abramovitch, Corter, Pepler, & Stanhope, 1986; Vandell & Bailey, 1992). Brother-brother relationships experience the most conflict (Stoneman & Brody, 1993; Vespo, Pedersen, & Hay, 1995). Older siblings clearly dominate the younger ones (Erel, Margolin, & John, 1998). The distinctions lessen over time, but birth order rather than age is the cause of the domination. Although combative behaviors occur, prosocial and play-oriented behaviors constitute a majority of the interactions.

Sibling relationships, then, should not be seen as primarily combative or negative. Positive social interactions increase significantly as children age, and siblings can cooperate in game behaviors. In addition, even children as young as 3 years of age can show distress for their younger siblings (Dunn, 1983). Friendly sibling relationships are associated with the ability to take the perspective of the other person (Howe & Ross, 1990). Sibling relationships are more likely to be pleasant when mothers discuss with an older child how the younger child feels (Dunn & Kendrick, 1982). Temperamental differences also affect sibling relationships (Stocker, Dunn, & Plomin, 1989). Children who are highly active and emotionally intense experience more conflict (Brody, Stoneman & Burke, 1987). Finally, parental behavior may be linked to sibling behavior. Punitive and restrictive maternal child rearing is associated with more quarrelsome and aggressive sibling behavior (Brody, Stoneman, & MacKinnon, 1986).

Children often think that parental attention and treatment is unequal, and this perception *can* negatively affect sibling relationships (Brody, Stoneman, & McCoy, 1992; McHale, Crouter, McGuire, & Updegraff, 1995). Evidence exists that unequal sibling treatment is related to sibling conflict and antagonism (Brody et al., 1985; Furman & Buhrmester, 1985). When parents are more affectionate toward one child than the other, jealousies can grow, and fewer helpful interactions between siblings occur (Volling & Belsky, 1992). Children compare the attention and interest parents show to each sibling and remember preferential treatment. Even in adulthood, people can tell stories of such unfair treatment (Baker & Daniels, 1990).

T F 5

Play-oriented and positive behaviors are more common in sibling relationships than are arguments and fights.

Guideposts

What is the relationship between older and younger siblings?

Unequal treatment, however, does not always lead to these problems. Children's attributions of *why* differential treatment is accorded is the crucial factor mediating between the perception of unequal treatment and its consequences. For example, children may feel it is appropriate to set different bedtimes for their older or younger siblings or to visit a room more often because a little one is afraid of the dark. Yet they may not accept differential parental treatment in complimenting each child when they have done an equally good job (Kowal & Kramer, 1997). This acceptance of treatment differences is commonly the case. Seventy-six percent of all elementary school children in one study who believed differential treatment existed did not see it as unfair because they saw it in terms of sibling needs (Reid, Ramey, & Burchinal, 1990).

Children who are beginning elementary school can understand the reasons behind differential treatment better than younger children. Children with disabilities often require additional care, and such differential parental treatment does not impair the quality of the sibling relationships (McHale & Pawletko, 1992).

There are developmental differences in children's ability to understand these needs. Younger children prefer a completely equal allocation of resources and are less sensitive to contextual elements than older children (Sigelman & Waitzman, 1991). Children younger than 5 years are most interested in what they get, and their egocentrism leads to self-interest. As noted in Chapter 8, they center on only one dimension. In this case, young children center on their own needs and have difficulty considering the needs of others at the same time. Around 5 or 6 years of age, a more mature understanding of the different needs of siblings becomes evident, although even some 4-year-olds can understand the differing needs of their sibling if informed of them. Perhaps older children have more sophisticated verbal skills and the ability to attribute reasons for different treatment (Kowal & Kramer, 1997).

Sibling Arguments

Sibling conflict is inevitable and common, sometimes averaging as often as seven times per hour in families with two preschool-aged children (Dunn & Munn, 1986). In its mild form, it is an annoying problem for parents; in its extreme form, it is the most common form of family violence (Reid & Donovan, 1990).

Sibling quarrels can be classified into three categories (Acus, 1982). *Nuisance quarrels* start when children are bored or in a bad mood. They are noisy and begin over nothing at all. They end quickly, usually cause no damage, and are forgotten as fast as they start. Parents can't follow them, and trying to get to the bottom of one of these quarrels is next to impossible. A second type, called *verbal debate quarrels,* can be constructive. This type of quarrel involves rational disagreements that, although loud and strident at times, can serve as training in debating and assertiveness techniques. Each sibling forcefully gives an opinion, although most siblings will not be budged from their opening position. If the two siblings begin viciously attacking each other, however, this type of quarrel can easily turn into the third kind—the *destructive quarrel.* The destructive quarrel can cause physical or emotional damage to at least one of the participants. If the quarrel is physical, the smaller child is likely to be hurt. If it is verbal, it often entails picking on the weakest point in a child's armor.

Parents frequently intervene in quarrels between young children, especially when one child is very young. Gender is also a consideration, as mothers respond more consistently to aggression by male preschoolers than aggression by female preschoolers. Perhaps mothers have an idea of the level of aggression to accept in their sons but not in their daughters (Kendrick & Dunn, 1983).

When parents treat their children unequally, it always leads to resentment and poor sibling relationships.

How does differential parental treatment of siblings influence their attitudes and behaviors?

The most common type of family violence occurs among siblings.

Should They Intervene?

Sometimes Ira and Gregory seem more like enemies than brothers. Ira is 8 years old and often teases his 5-year-old brother. Gregory will sometimes hit his brother when he can't keep up with the argument, at which point 8-year-old Ira will hit back and the younger one will complain to his mother.

Their father does not believe in intervention and is ready to accept even the screaming that continually disrupts the house. It does not seem to bother him at all, but causes their mother a headache. She sends them to their rooms for five minutes at a time (time-out), which helps for a little while, until, later, another argument occurs. It is difficult for her to ask her husband to help since he doesn't think it is a problem and believes the boys can work it out by themselves. Their mother believes that Ira is taking advantage of his size and abilities and that Gregory will suffer. When she does intervene, Ira accuses her of taking Gregory's side.

If you were their parents what, if anything, would you do to reduce the sibling conflict?

ACTION / REACTION

Should parents intervene in sibling quarrels? Opponents of intervention argue that, by entering the quarrel, parents judge which sibling has the more valid claim and in the end take sides in a dispute which they know little about. In addition, children won't learn to resolve their own conflicts if parents intervene on a regular basis.

Others argue that without intervention the stronger child will win and the weaker will develop learned helplessness, a belief that nothing he or she does will be effective in reducing the distress (Bennett, 1990). The child simply accepts being a victim. After all, the younger child is not only physically smaller but mentally unequal to the task. Proponents of intervention note that parents tend to intervene in sibling disputes in an unbiased manner, although children may not see it that way. Those in favor of intervention argue that intervention may reduce conflict because nonintervention may be interpreted as an endorsement of aggressive conflict.

There is a middle position on this question that advocates that parents only intervene in the most intense disputes, which may involve physical violence, verbal abuse, or when children seem to be losing control. They should avoid taking sides, and the intervention should focus on problem solving, encouraging each child to take the other child's perspective, and improving communication (Dunn, 1995). It becomes a learning situation. Yet, in disputes that are intensely emotional, this may be especially difficult.

Parents must decide whether to intervene in sibling disputes.

Parents do intervene in some sibling conflicts, especially if parents believe their interventions will be successful (Perozynski & Kramer, 1999). Parents intervene when the fights are more intense and especially when preschoolers are crying. Parents tend not to intervene if the conflict is winding down, if one child complies with the sibling's request, if younger children are holding their ground, or if the quarrel is short. Parents use reasoning and explanation about half the time they intervene, but their superior position as adults is also used. Parents often do ask children to explain their conflict and draw attention to their perspectives. After these interventions, children use less aggression and are more likely to invoke positive strategies (Perlman & Ross, 1997). Vygotsky's concept of a zone of proximal development (see pages 64–65) may explain this finding as interaction with parents exposes children to a slightly more sophisticated way of handling disputes and children learn these strategies. Whether parents use reasoning or a more punishment-oriented means of intervention depends on both their belief about the effectiveness of the strategy and their feelings of self-efficacy—that is, whether they can carry out the strategy itself (Perozynski & Kramer, 1999).

Sibling disputes are probably inevitable, and certainly parents need not intervene in every dispute, especially when trying to judge blame involves something akin to listening to testimony in a court case. If the possibility of physical harm is present, a parent must intervene. If one child is verbally abusing the other child, parents must intervene to teach children better ways of handling the disputes.

Guideposts

What are the advantages and disadvantages of trying to solve a sibling quarrel?

The Only Child

Not all children have siblings. About 10% of all marriages result in the birth of one child. The so-called only child has been the victim of many generalizations, few of them flattering. Some people pity the only child because of a lack of siblings; others consider these children spoiled or selfish or even believe that the only child might be more likely have problems interacting with others (Falbo & Piston, 1993).

Modern studies do not find the only child to be disadvantaged and, in fact, find some definite advantages. A review of many studies on the only child found that only children have very positive relationships with their parents, and mothers of only children spend more time with them, engage in more conversation, and give them more information (Falbo & Polit, 1986; Polit & Falbo, 1987). The size of these differences is not large when only children are compared with those with a few siblings, but the differences become somewhat more distinct when only children are compared with children from larger families (Furman, 1996).

A great deal of research on the only child is conducted in China, where an ongoing national policy to encourage families to have only one child seeks to reduce the population growth. Young people are encouraged to marry later, public education is given regarding methods of birth control, and economic incentives are used to encourage parents to have only one child (Yang, Ollendick, Dong, Xia, & Lin, 1995). When this program was begun, there was some question as to how this emphasis on one child per family, quite alien to traditional Chinese ideals, would affect the academic ability and personality of the children. The research evidence has been surprising. In the academic area, the results are clear that only children are more advanced in cognitive development (Yang et al., 1995). They show superior school achievement when compared with those with siblings (Wan, Fan, Lin, & Jing, 1994). This is found in Western studies as well.

In the personality areas, the research is somewhat more complicated, but few differences are found and none are consistent (Falbo & Piston, 1993). Only children are somewhat less anxious, fearful, and less likely to be depressed (Yang et al., 1995). Some studies show no differences in interpersonal skills (Wan et al., 1994). Authorities feared that these children would be little emperors, overindulged and spoiled. Although some studies show they are a bit more likely to be self-centered (Falbo & Piston,

About 10% of all marriages result in the birth of one child. Recent evidence shows the experience of the only child to be a positive one.

1993), they are not spoiled. They are well adjusted, and their social skills are similar to firstborns who have siblings (Falbo & Polit, 1986). The evidence, then, shows that only children show superior cognitive and academic skills, and the differences in personality are neither great nor negative. Children don't seem to suffer from their experience as the only child in the family.

Guideposts
What personality and achievement patterns are found in "only" children?

Peers: A New Relationship

It is during the preschool stage that the concept of friendship emerges. Preschoolers react in a more positive manner and are more responsive to their friends than to other children. The evidence points to both stability and change in preschool friendships. While children maintain some friendships over the years, most children regularly experience making new friends and separating from old ones (Howes, 1988).

Preschool friendships tend to be fragile (Corsaro, 1981), and many, but not all, are fleeting. The qualification for friendship is simply being physically present and willing to play (Rubin, 1980). Friendships often form and disintegrate quickly, and friendships are not based on any real intimacy. Young children describe a friend as someone who is rewarding to be with, whereas older children describe friends in terms of empathy, understanding, and trustworthiness (Bigelow & LaGaipa, 1975). For the preschooler, then, a friend is a playmate.

Some preschoolers form friendships easily, while others have difficulties. Those children who form friendships easily have superior social and communication skills, including the ability to say something relevant to the interaction and direct it properly to other children as well as respond appropriately (Hazen & Black, 1989). Children who do not form friendships use stronger tactics, including aggression, to settle their conflicts than do those who form friendships easily (Gottman, 1983).

One tendency that begins in early childhood and that will become commonplace in middle childhood is having mostly same-sex friends (Lewis & Feiring, 1989). This tendency becomes stronger as children negotiate early childhood. There are many possible reasons for this change. Perhaps children see same sex peers as more compatible in their play. That is, boys may be aware that other boys will allow them to use rough-and-tumble play. Perhaps same-sex children see each other as more similar, or perhaps adults reinforce children for playing with other children of the same sex. The development of gender role stereotypes may also be a factor (Gottman, 1986). Another possibility is that girls find it difficult to influence boys. As children negotiate early childhood, there is an increase in their attempts to influence one another. Girls make polite suggestions, whereas boys use more direct demands. Boys are becoming less responsive to polite suggestions. Girls' style of influence, then, is more effective with other girls than with boys. It may also be a function of the different types of games and play styles. For whatever reason, as children get older, they play more with children of their own gender and less with children of the other gender.

Guideposts
What is the nature of preschool friendships?

Prosocial Behavior

If you observe preschoolers at play, you will notice that sometimes they share and help, while at other times they flatly refuse to do so. Behaviors such as sharing, helping others in need, and comforting others are called **prosocial behaviors** (Eisenberg et al., 1996). A specific type of prosocial behavior, called **altruism,** involves actions that help people, that are internally motivated, and for which no reward is expected. Generally, older children show more prosocial behavior than younger children.

Preschoolers infrequently share with, help, and comfort others (Eisenberg-Berg & Hand, 1979). They are much more likely to agree to help when asked to do so by adults than when their peers make the request (Eisenberg et al., 1985). When they conform to a request from adults, they usually are doing so in obedience to an authority figure. Although peers make more requests for help, compliance with requests from adults is much more common. Altruistic behavior is rare, and relatively few helping behaviors are self-initiated. Yet, most preschoolers perform such self-initiated behavior at some time or another. In other words, preschoolers are indeed capable of self-initiated helping behavior but do not offer it very often (Stockdale, Hegland, & Chiaromonte, 1989). Significant individual differences exist. Some preschoolers respond with comforting to their peers' distress much more than others. Children with easy temperaments, and those who have a friendly relationship with the child in distress, are more likely to help (Farver & Branstetter, 1994). Children who show the most prosocial behavior have excellent social skills and are able to delay gratification (Eisenberg et al., 1996; Fabes, Eisenberg, Karbon, Troyer, & Switzer, 1994). Preschoolers will show more prosocial behavior if they attend a nursery school in which these behaviors are valued and promoted.

Prosocial behavior increases with age, perhaps because older children are more adept at taking the perspective of other children and can empathize more. This explains why even among preschoolers the ability to experience empathy and to take on the roles of others is related to prosocial behavior (Roberts & Strayer, 1996). Older children, being somewhat less egocentric, are much more likely to possess these skills and to share when there is no reward or adult pressure to do so. When they do, they justify their behavior on altruistic grounds.

Conflict

Preschoolers engage in fewer arguments than one might think, and those that occur are relatively brief and end without parental interference. Conflicts are quickly resolved in mostly nonaggressive ways. The most common conflicts involve possessions (Lauresen & Hartup, 1989; Ross, 1996). One child wants a toy that the other is playing with at the time. The second most common are conflicts over another child's actions or lack of action, as when a child acts the wrong part while playing or refuses to take on a role assigned to him or her. The third category involves factual disputes, which are far less common than the other two types of conflict. By about 4.5 or 5 years of age, disputes in the first two categories are occurring at about equal rates (Shantz, 1987).

The most common way of solving conflicts in this period is insistence (Eisenberg & Garvey, 1981). Conflicts are most likely to end when one child surrenders the toy to the other or keeps it by defending it. The second most common strategy is simply to explain why the child should give up the toy to someone else. Preschoolers communicate verbally in the course of the conflict, often explaining their actions and feelings (Vespo, Pedersen, & Hay, 1995). They also have some idea of property rights (Ross, 1996). Other strategies, such as suggesting alternatives and compromise, are not used very often, even though they are more likely to end the conflict. In most conflicts, there is one definite winner and one definite loser.

Guideposts

What is the nature of prosocial behavior during the early childhood years?

prosocial behaviors
Voluntary actions that are intended to help or benefit another individual or group.

altruism
A type of prosocial behavior that involves actions that help people, that are internally motivated, and for which no reward is expected.

In about a quarter of the conflicts, verbal and/or physical aggression is used (Hay & Ross, 1982), but this percentage decreases with age. Aggression itself decreases with age. Aggression can be divided into two categories (Hartup, 1984). **Instrumental aggression** involves struggles over possessions. It is not personal, and its aim is to secure an item. **Hostile aggression,** on the other hand, is person-oriented. This aggression is aimed at injuring the other party. Most young children act aggressively to wrench a toy from someone else or to gain space. The finding that aggression decreases with age probably stems from the striking decrease in instrumental aggression. As children mature, verbal alternatives replace physical means (Parke & Slaby, 1983).

Aggression itself, though, is a fairly stable characteristic (Ladd & Burgess, 1999; Olweus, 1979). Aggressive children in early childhood tend to become aggressive children in middle childhood even though the overall amount of aggression they show declines.

The total amount of aggression shown by preschoolers declines with age.

Guideposts

Why does aggression decline with age?

Gender Role Acquisition

By Annie's age, children understand that people can be placed into two categories, male and female, and they are beginning to understand role and behavioral differences. Gender is one of the first and most obvious distinctions that children make in classifying others. Most infants can visually discriminate males from females by 9 months, although it may occur a bit earlier (Ruble & Martin, 1998; Walsh, Katz, & Downey, 1991). Infants base their discrimination on the basis of hair length rather than facial features or bodily form (Fagot & Lenbach, 1993). By about 2 years, toddlers can understand the labels of boy and girl (Etaugh, Grinnell, & Etaugh, 1989; Fagot & Lenbach, 1989). Children can accurately label their gender and place a picture of themselves with other same-sex children by around 24 to 36 months of age, although variability is common (Ruble & Martin, 1998). By 3 or 4 years, most children can accurately apply gender-stereotyped labels to toys, activities, household tasks, and even adult occupations (Turner & Gervai, 1995). From about 3 years, consistent gender differences are found in preferred toys and play activities: boys play more with toy vehicles, balls, and blocks, whereas girls engage more in artistic activities and play with dolls and dress up (Huston, 1983). Gender differences in personality and social interaction are less pronounced at this age and appear somewhat later (Turner & Gervai, 1995).

Gender Differences

Do boys and girls really differ on any attributes or is it all a matter of the subjective interpretation of behavior? The term **gender differences** describes those differences between the genders that have been established by scientific research. For example, the average female matures more rapidly than the average male. Maccoby and Jacklin (1974) reviewed the scientific research concerning gender differences and concluded that only four differences appeared consistently. Most studies indicate that (1) males are generally more aggressive than females (a finding that is common across many cultures), (2) girls have greater verbal ability, (3) boys excel in visual-spatial ability, and (4) boys excel in mathematical ability. Gender differences are not always stable. Gender differences in cognitive abilities are disappearing, but sex differences in aggression are not (Knight, Fabes, & Higgins, 1996).

The difference in aggression between boys and girls is disappearing, but gender differences in cognitive abilities, such as math or verbal skills, are increasing.

gender differences

The differences between males and females that have been established through scientific investigation.

As valuable as it is, Maccoby and Jacklin's work is not the last word on the subject. Some technical objections to the way the review was conducted surfaced immediately (Block, 1976). Others reviewed much of the same literature and came to different conclusions, indicating that girls are more suggestible and more fearful and that boys were more active (Eagly, 1978; Eaton & Ennis, 1996). Some, but not all, studies find that girls are more empathic and compliant and seek more approval from adults than boys (Turner & Gervai, 1995).

Three Considerations

Three considerations should be kept in mind whenever anyone announces a positive finding on gender differences. First, even though a difference between the genders on some characteristic, such as verbal ability, is found, it tells us nothing about its cause. Are males generally more aggressive than females because of some environmental factor, such as reinforcement, because of some genetic or hormonal factor, or because of some interaction between the two? Even the finding that some genetic or hormonal element may underlie the behavior does not mean the behavior itself cannot be modified. Genetic contribution does not imply immutability. Rather, the individual's genotype may influence the range of possible behaviors, but the environment determines the behavior itself.

Second, most gender differences should not be seen as absolute. The overlap between males and females is tremendous. The average difference between the genders on any particular trait is normally very small, even if it does exist. The differences between individuals within the same gender are far greater than the average differences between males and females. Thus, although males generally seem to perform better at advanced mathematics, you will find excellent female math students and males who receive terrible mathematics grades. Stating that males are better in one trait or that females are superior in another should not blind us to the overlap that exists in these skills or characteristics. The genders are more similar than they are different.

The third consideration is that a gender difference might be found in one circumstance but not another, making global statements about one trait or another questionable. For example, consider a study of the social interactions of preschoolers. Some of the children have same-sex partners, while others have opposite-sex partners. What if you found that when paired with boys, girls showed more passive behavior, allowing the boys to play with the toys as the girls watched? However, when paired with other girls, the girls showed no evidence of passivity, and intense social interaction was the rule. Could you fairly conclude that girls are more passive? Frequently, gender differences are situational, and making a general statement is often incorrect (Maccoby, 1990).

Gender Identity, Gender Stability, and Gender Consistency

The extent to which the development of the understanding of being a male or female is biological or social has been the focus of much dispute. It is a difficult question to answer since boys are not only biologically and genetically male but raised as male. In rare instances, that is not the case. Early research on hermaphrodites (children born with ambiguous genitals) found that as long as the gender assignment is done early, before 18 to 30 months, and it is consistent, there are few problems, although children with the XY genotype raised as females will show more aggressive tendencies (Money & Ehrhardt, 1972). However, recently a case was reported of a child with a damaged penis and an XY genotype who underwent surgery at an early age and was raised as a female. At age 14, the child rejected this sex assignment and changed, now living successfully as a male (Diamond & Sigmundson, 1997).

If the question of the cause of gender assignment is still controversial, the manner in which children develop an understanding of male and female is well understood. Children develop their understanding of gender in a particular developmental progression (Slaby & Frey, 1975). First, children establish a **gender identity**—that is, an awareness of being male or female. Evidence indicates that at about age 2, children become aware of the labels "boy" and "girl" although they don't correctly use them all the time (Ruble & Martin, 1998). After establishing gender identity, children learn that their gender is **stable.** In other words, children know that they were boys or girls when they were younger and will become men and women when they grow up. Finally, children develop **gender consistency** (also called **gender constancy**), the understanding that boys remain boys whether or not they have long hair or play female-oriented games (Szkrybalo & Ruble, 1999). Gender identity is more easily understood by children than gender consistency, with gender stability lying somewhere between. The mean (average) age of attaining these understandings differs widely. A complete understanding is not found until between 5 and 7 years, although there are wide individual variations (Ruble & Martin, 1998).

This developmental progression explains some of the unusual behavior seen in young children. If children have not gained an understanding of gender consistency, they may believe that if Daddy grows his hair long, he will become a female like Mommy. A little girl might believe that if her brother wears a dress, he will become a girl like her.

Sex Typing and Gender Roles

Consider the following statement: "Women cook, take care of the children, ask for help, are rescued from trying circumstances (by men), and play with dolls. Men work full-time jobs, don't ask for help, are action-oriented, and are strong." Such generalizations still exist in our society. **Sex typing** is the process by which an individual acquires values and behaves in a manner more appropriate to one gender or the other. Sex-typed behavior can be seen in many areas of development; for example, boys play with trucks, and girls play with dolls. Such behavior patterns as methods of aggression, behavior while dissecting a frog, and emotional expressiveness are examples of sex-typed behavior. Girls learn that crying is acceptable when they are sad; boys learn to hold their sadness in. Boys avoid showing an interest in babies; females pay more attention to infants (Blakemore, 1981). These stereotyped behaviors have recently been treated differently and more realistically by psychologists. Instead of determining whether particular behaviors and traits are masculine or feminine, psychologists now ask whether particular behaviors are more likely to be found in one gender than another (Stangor & Lange, 1994).

Children develop their ideas about which activities and objects are more likely to be performed or used by males and females rather early. By 26 months they are aware of differences in possessions (men wear ties, women wear dresses), physical appearance, and roles (Weinraub et al., 1984). Knowledge of such stereotypes increases rapidly between 3 and 5 years, reaching a very high level of awareness by kindergarten (Martin & Little, 1990). During the elementary school years, these stereotypes remain, although they become somewhat less rigid. Children become aware of the exceptions and become more flexible, with girls being more flexible than boys (Signorella, Bigler, & Liben, 1993).

Guideposts

How does a child develop an appreciation of the meaning of gender?

gender identity
One's awareness of being a male or a female.

gender stability
Children's knowledge that they were of a particular gender when younger and will remain so throughout life.

gender consistency (constancy)
Children's knowledge that they will remain boys or girls regardless of how they act, dress, or groom.

sex typing
The process by which an individual acquires the attitudes, values, and behaviors viewed as appropriate for one gender or the other in a particular culture.

By engaging in counter stereotypical activities, parents can help deter their children from developing rigid gender stereotypes.

When we add up all the behavior patterns and psychological characteristics that seem appropriate for each gender, we are describing the concept of **gender roles,** which permeate many other roles. Just how children acquire the behaviors that are considered appropriate for their gender is a matter of great interest and controversy. No single approach adequately explains it, but each has something to offer.

Biological Contributions

There is no true biological approach to understanding gender development. Instead, a number of biological factors are suggested that may be taken into account when studying gender roles.

Hormones   Males produce more testosterone; females produce more estrogen. In some unusual situations, a young girl may have a hormonal imbalance, having more testosterone in her system than is typical, and these girls show a tendency to play with more stereotyped male toys, such as helicopters and construction toys rather than with stereotyped feminine toys, such as kitchen sets (Berenbaum & Hines, 1992). Research links the hormone testosterone to aggressive behavior (Buchanan, Eccles, & Becker, 1992; Ruble & Martin, 1998). Perhaps males are more inclined to be aggressive than are females. Despite this inclination, however, every psychologist notes the overwhelming importance of learning in this area.

There is also evidence that hormone levels during sensitive periods in early life may have an organizing effect on the brain, encouraging the development of certain neurons. The brains of animals given doses of hormones show changes, and these may relate to behavioral changes in aggression, parenting behaviors, and rough-and-tumble play (Ruble, 1988).

Differences in Maturation   The average female is born more ready for life than the average male. Females are more advanced in central nervous system development and bone formation (Doyle & Paludi, 1991). They reach their developmental milestones before boys. Some gender differences (for example, why boys have more problems learning to read than girls) may be caused by the interaction of rates of maturation and the environment surrounding the child. Females have a longer attention span, and their eyes are better developed by the time they enter school. Female superiority in reading does not excuse males from learning to read. It only suggests that the average male may find language skills more difficult and may require additional instruction.

Genetic Differences   Genetic differences on the twenty-third chromosome may also affect behavior. The male Y chromosome contains many fewer genes than the female X chromosome, and some characteristics—such as color blindness—are sex linked. There is evidence that this may also be true of spatial ability.

Even if you are impressed by the biological approach, assignment of unequal roles on the basis of biological argument cannot be either condoned or justified by the evidence. In the case of gender roles and behavior, biology is not destiny. Currently, the biological contribution to our understanding of how a child acquires a gender role is a large question mark.

gender roles
Behaviors expected of people in a given society on the basis of whether an individual is male or female.

Whenever any biological factor is raised to explain some aspect of gender differences, people become concerned. People assume that biological contributions are stable, universal, and immutable, while social contributions are easy to alter. As was emphasized in Chapter 3, this belief is not true, and biological predispositions may be relatively easy to modify, while certain social factors (for example, poverty) may be more difficult to change (Ruble & Martin, 1998).

Behavior Theories

The most obvious reason that males and females act differently is that they learn to do so. Children's learning experiences can be roughly divided into two categories: (1) boys and girls are treated differently and reinforced for different behaviors, and (2) the role models that surround boys and girls differ, and children learn at least some of their gender role by observing others.

Different Treatment for Sons and Daughters   Although parents may not consciously reinforce young children for playing with gender-stereotyped toys (boys with trucks, girls with dolls), they actively channel their children into such standard play (Eisenberg et al., 1985). The same parents who may say it would not bother them if their son played with dolls are apt to provide him with only balls, gloves, and trucks and encourage him to play with them.

Girls are viewed as more fragile, and parents play with sons more roughly than they do with daughters. Adults perceive infant boys as stronger and less sensitive than girls, even when the labeled sex of the infant is manipulated (Burnham & Harris, 1992). Boys are also more likely to be discouraged by adults and peers from engaging in "gender-inappropriate" behavior (Langlois & Downs, 1980). Adults purchase gender-typed toys especially for boys, but, of course, children may be requesting these toys. When not requested, adults do purchase more neutral toys (Fisher-Thompson, 1993). Boys receive more encouragement for gross-motor activities and more freedom from supervision, whereas girls receive more affectionate behavior and more immediate help when they request it (Ruble & Martin, 1998).

ACTION / REACTION

"But He's a Boy!"

The day Greg P. came home from the hospital, his father bought a football and put it in his crib. Greg's father dreamed of his son being an "All-American." As Greg grew, Mr. P. continued to give him tennis rackets, baseball gloves, basketballs, and the like. But last week 4-year-old Greg asked for a Cabbage Patch doll, and his father hit the ceiling. "My son is not going to be a sissy and play with dolls. No way." Greg's mother sees nothing wrong with Greg's playing with dolls. In fact, she secretly bought him one a few months ago but allows Greg to play with it only when his father is not home so he won't find out.

Greg's nursery school teacher told Mr. P. that there was nothing wrong with a boy playing with dolls and that he was old-fashioned to think that way. Mr. P. refused to believe that it wouldn't hurt the child and took offense at the teacher's comments.

1. *If you were Greg's mother, how would you handle the situation?*
2. *How would you rate the teacher's handling of the problem?*

ACTION / REACTION

When differences are found, fathers are more likely than mothers to treat sons and daughters differently (Lytton & Romney, 1991). A father is more likely to criticize his son when he sees him playing with dolls than he is to criticize a daughter who is observed beating up a Bobo doll. Today, some parents are making a conscious effort not to sex-type their children's play activities (Idle, Wood, & Desmarais, 1993).

In their analysis, Maccoby and Jacklin (1974) concluded that child-rearing practices were similar for boys and girls with a few consistent differences: infant boys receive more physical stimulation, boys are punished as well as praised more, and parents encourage gender-typed behavior and discourage other gender behavior especially for boys.

In another analysis, the only areas in which parents treated sons and daughters differently were the encouragement of sex-typed activities and perceiving sex-stereotyped characteristics, and even here the findings are modest (Lytton & Romney, 1991). In the United States and Canada there were no significant differences in such variables as parental warmth, encouragement of dependence, restrictiveness, interaction, encouragement of achievement, or verbal interaction. Boys are not necessarily reinforced more than girls for aggressiveness (Maccoby & Jacklin, 1974).

The fact that parents emphasize sex stereotypes in play activities and household chores may have far-reaching effects. For example, boys' toys provide more opportunity for manipulation and visual spatial skills, which may lead to better skills in these areas (Block, 1983). Some authorities, however, are more impressed by the similarities than the differences (Lytton & Romney, 1991; Maccoby & Jacklin, 1974). The evidence in most areas is very weak for differential treatment. In the end, the question is not whether boys and girls are treated differently, but whether these differences are enough to explain later sex-typed behavior patterns. Although some differences in treatment do exist, it is difficult to see how they could be the sole causes of later personality and behavioral differences between the sexes. They are, then, only one part of the puzzle.

Role Models and Imitation   The use of modeling and imitation to explain the acquisition of gender role is appealing. A boy who sees his father cooking dinner and enjoying it gets the idea that it is manly to cook dinner for the family. Because parents are the most important people in the life of preschoolers, the children may model themselves after them (Mischel, 1970). For example, daughters of mothers employed outside the home hold less traditional role concepts and have higher aspirations than girls whose mothers are not employed. They benefit from observing that mother as well as father is valued in the labor market and is performing useful functions outside the home. Mothers who participate more in traditionally male household chores and child care tasks have children who are less typical in their gender activity preferences (Serbin, Powlishta, & Gulko, 1993).

Parents are not the only models in their children's lives. Children are also exposed to models in the outside world—for example, peers, teachers, and characters in children's books and on television. Males are overrepresented on most television programs, with males shown as problem solvers, while females follow males' lead (Ruble & Martin, 1998). In fact, children who are heavy TV viewers have more stereotyped beliefs about gender than lighter viewers (Huston et al., 1992). While it is difficult to analyze the effect these other models have on a child's understanding of gender roles, their role should not be minimized.

Psychoanalytic Theory: Identifying with Parents

No theory is more controversial than Freud's ideas about the development of sex-typed behavior. According to Freud (1924), the development of gender roles arises from events that occur during the **phallic stage.** Until early childhood, both boys and girls have similar psychosexual experiences, but during the phallic stage, the **Oedipus complex** occurs. The little boy experiences sexual feelings toward his mother, views his father as a rival for his mother's affection, and resents his father. The child fears that his father will find out how he feels and retaliate by castrating him. At the same time, the father is respected as a model of masculinity who is superior to the child. As he matures, the little boy represses his feelings toward his mother and identifies with the father. In this way, he becomes like his father and takes on the "appropriate" gender role.

The process with females is more convoluted. It is sometimes called the **Electra complex.** The little girl is also originally sexually attached to the mother but slowly turns her attention to her father when she realizes she does not have a penis (Mullahy, 1948). Blaming her mother for her lack of a penis, she competes with her mother for the father's attention. She does not have to resolve this situation fully, since she doesn't have to worry about castration, but acquires her role by building on her relationship with her mother.

An important idea underlying the psychoanalytic concept of gender roles is **identification.** Children identify with the parents of the same sex and thereby acquire the appropriate gender role. Perhaps the most controversial portion of this theory involves Freud's argument that the girl's discovery that she lacks the male organ is a turning point in her life. Freud sees every imaginable character trait of females beginning with this "penis envy," including feelings of inferiority, physical modesty, envy, and psychosexual difficulties. In the end, however, Freud's ideas in this realm have been largely rejected by developmental psychologists because evidence is lacking (Ruble & Martin, 1998; Sears, Roe, & Alpert, 1965). The clinical problems Freud noted can be interpreted in terms of the social roles traditionally thrust on women by society (Horney, 1939, 1967). In addition, even though the Oedipus complex has been found in a number of societies (Kline, 1972), it is not universal (Mead, 1974).

Gender Schema Theory

An ingredient that is missing from all these theories is the cognitive component. After all, people judge what is appropriate for each gender, with some people having more flexible ideas than others. According to **gender schema theory,** once a child develops gender identity, the idea that he is a boy or she is a girl at about age 2 (Carter & Levy, 1988), children develop a gender schema, or a body of knowledge about what boys and girls do. This is a network of gender-related information that influences perception and behavior. This body of knowledge helps people organize and interpret information and influences preferences and activities (Bem, 1981, 1993; Martin, & Halverson, 1981). Gender schema acts as a lens through which children perceive and think (Bem, 1993).

To understand how schemata may function in sex typing, consider a little girl presented with a doll. The girl knows that dolls are for girls and that she is a girl; therefore, dolls are for her. The girl will then explore the doll and ask questions and obtain information about it. What if that same girl is offered a truck? The girl may think that trucks are for boys, and since she is a girl, she'll decide that trucks are not for her. The result is avoidance, and no further information will be actively

phallic stage
Freud's third psychosexual stage, occurring during early childhood, in which the sexual energy is located in the genital area.

Oedipus complex
The conflict in Freudian theory in which the boy experiences sexual feelings toward his mother and wishes to rid himself of his father.

Electra complex
The female equivalent to the Oedipus complex, in which the female experiences sexual feelings toward her father and wishes to do away with her mother.

identification
The process by which children take on the characteristics of another person, most often a parent.

gender schema theory
A theory of gender role acquisition in which, after developing gender identity, the child acquires a body of knowledge about the behaviors of each gender. This helps the child organize and interpret information and helps guide behavior.

gathered (Martin, 1995). In fact, children will play with a less attractive toy that is considered "gender-appropriate" than a more attractive one that is neutral but labeled for the other gender (Martin, Eisenbud, & Rose, 1995).

As children acquire society's gender schema, they learn which characteristics are related to their own gender—and therefore to themselves—and which are not. Sandra Bem (1981) notes that part of the gender schema for boys is strength; nurturance is part of the schema for girls. The strong-weak dimension appears to be absent from the female gender schema; the nurturant dimension is almost absent from the male gender schema. Children apply the same schema to themselves and choose to attend only to the possible dimensions of personality and behavior that are applicable to their own gender.

One of the advantages of gender schema theory is that it explains why children maintain their gender stereotypes even when confronted with contrary information. Once a child learns his or her schema, such knowledge biases the way information is processed. Most research shows that gender-consistent information is remembered better than gender-inconsistent information (Liben & Signorella, 1993; Signorella & Liben, 1984). Children remember best information that fits their gender schema and may even change information that is inconsistent so that it is now in keeping with their beliefs (Welch-Ross & Schmidt, 1996). For example, if a child thinks that boys are soldiers and is told a story of a female soldier, the child may later change the gender of the soldier.

Gender Role Theories Reconsidered

No single theory can adequately explain how a child acquires a gender role, but each can add greatly to our knowledge (Turner & Gervai, 1995). A number of relatively new findings have changed the way we look at sex typing and gender role formation. For example, at first people thought that gender role acquisition was basically completed before children enter school. Today we know that a great deal of change occurs in middle childhood and, indeed, across the life span. It was also once assumed that parents were the primary socializers, but today the focus expands to others' influences, including siblings, peers, teachers, and the media. Finally, it was once thought that it was important and even necessary for children to form traditional sex-typed behaviors, but today we know that it may not be adaptive, and individual differences in the gender schema are to be expected (Katz & Ksansnak, 1994).

Atypical Development: Child Abuse

Few situations can cause as much psychological, developmental, and physical harm to the child as child abuse (Cicchetti & Toth, 1998). **Child abuse** occurs when parents intentionally injure their children. **Neglect** refers to a situation in which the physical care and supervision of the child is inadequate or inappropriate—for example, a child who comes to school each day dressed inadequately for bitterly cold weather. Acts of neglect include inadequate supervision, abandonment, and refusal of needed medical care (Goodman, Emery, & Haugaard, 1998). All states now require such professionals as doctors, nurses, and teachers to report suspected cases of child abuse or neglect. Over half the reports are of neglect and another 25% for physical child abuse. Despite the widespread publicity surrounding some celebrated cases of abuse in day care centers and foster care settings, only 2% of the

Guideposts

What factors influence a child's gender role acquisition?

For Your Consideration

In your opinion, should parents make a special effort to treat their sons and daughters the same in every area? Are there any areas in which you believe differential treatment because of the gender of a child is warranted?

child abuse

A general term used to denote an injury intentionally perpetrated on a child.

child neglect

A term used to describe a situation in which the care and supervision of a child is insufficient or improper.

Datagraphics | **Reports of Abused and Neglected Children**

3.5 mil
3 mil
2.5 mil
2 mil
1.5 mil
1 mil
500,000
0

2,086,000
2,559,000
2,960,000
3,032,000

1986   1990   1995   1996

Child abuse remains a serious problem.

Source: The National Committee to Prevent Child Abuse
and the National Center on Child Abuse and Neglect

confirmed cases occur in these settings, and that figure has been consistent over the past nine years (National Committee to Prevent Child Abuse [NCPCA], 1997). In 1996, more than 1,000 children died from abuse and neglect.

The results of child abuse are serious and extensive, and the earlier the abuse starts and the more often it occurs, the more serious the consequences (Bolger, Patterson, & Kupersmidt, 1998). They include language delays, poor self-concept, aggression, social and emotional withdrawal, and poor social relationships with peers (Hennessy, Rabideau, Cicchetti, & Cummings, 1994; Mason, 1993). The most common finding is that physically abused children, especially males, are more aggressive than nonabused and even neglected children (Goodman et al., 1998). Children who are abused have lower intelligence scores and are at an increased risk for depression, suicide, and drug problems (Wisdom, 1989). They show greater difficulty regulating their emotions (Cummings, Hennessy, Rabideau, & Cicchetti, 1994; Hennessy et al., 1994), have problems maintaining and developing friendships (Parker & Herrera, 1996), and are more likely to experience failure in school (Cicchetti, Toth, & Hennessy, 1993).

The increased aggressiveness can be explained using an information-processing model (Dodge, Bates, & Pettit, 1990). The experience of early physical abuse is associated in 5-year-olds with perceptions of hostility on the part of others. These children become more aggressive as they interpret the world as more threatening and hostile. In addition, the example of a parent using physical force may become a model.

Sexual Abuse

Sexual abuse may be defined as forced, tricked, or coerced sexual behavior between a younger person and an older person (Gelles & Conte, 1990). Sexual abuse is the least reported type of abuse and is generally considered to be grossly underreported, partly because it is often not recognized as abuse (Clark, 1993). When children between the ages of 10 and 16 years were interviewed, the rate of attempted or completed sexual abuse was 10.5% (Finkelhor & Dziuba-Leatherman, 1994), and other figures are higher.

For Your Consideration ?

Reports of child abuse continue to rise. Is this increase due to greater awareness on the part of the public or to a true increase in abuse?

T F
10

Children who are physically abused are actually less aggressive than children who are not abused because they understand the consequences of abuse.

sexual abuse
Forced, tricked, or coerced sexual behavior between a younger person and an older person.

According to reported incidents, sexual abusers are mostly men, and girls constitute the majority of victims (Gelles & Conte, 1990; Goodman et al., 1998). Sexual abuse is most likely to occur between people who are related, but a child may also be victimized by a stranger.

The consequences of sexual abuse can be both physical—such as venereal disease and pregnancy—and emotional. Long-term effects include depression, self-destructive behavior, anxiety, feelings of isolation and stigma, social withdrawal and isolation, poor self-esteem, difficulty trusting others, substance abuse, and sexual maladjustment (Trickett & McBride-Chang, 1995; Clark, 1993). Although two-thirds of sexually abused child abuse victims show symptoms, they vary considerably and do not fit into one consistent pattern (Kendall-Tackett, Williams, & Finkelhor, 1993). One-fifth of all victims of sexual abuse develop serious long-term psychological problems (American Medical Association's Council, 1992). Sometimes, symptoms may subside within two years following disclosure, but for between 10% and 24%, symptoms may increase over time or a delayed response may ensue.

Parents should remind their children not to accept money or favors from strangers or accept a ride to go anywhere with someone they do not know. Children should be told that if they think they are in danger, it's OK to make a scene by running away and screaming for help. Because the sexual abuser may be someone they know and trust, children should be told that they do not have to agree to demands for physical closeness—even from relatives. Finally, children should be encouraged to report any instances of people touching them in intimate places or asking them to do the same.

Many schools have programs that teach young children about sexual abuse. At this point it is not possible to demonstrate whether these educational efforts are successful in reducing sexual abuse, but studies do show that children learn these lessons and their knowledge improves (MacMillan, MacMillan, Offord, Griffith, & MacMillan, 1994a, 1994b). One concern of sexual abuse prevention programs is that they might have a negative effect on children by making children frightened of strangers or uncomfortable about physical affection. Studies generally show that this does not occur (Wurtele & Mill-Perrin, 1987a, 1987b). These programs should be included in the school's regular health curriculum.

Emotional Abuse

Not all child abuse is physical. Consider the parent who constantly yells at and berates his or her children. Imagine a 4-year-old who has just spilled some juice hearing a parent shout, "You're a stupid, rotten kid. If I had any sense I'd give you away!" Consider a parent who tells a child who refuses to put his face in the water during a swim class that the child is a coward and has made his parents ashamed.

Defining **emotional abuse,** sometimes called **psychological maltreatment,** is difficult (Baumrind, 1994; Goodman et al., 1998; Rosenberg, 1987). It is often defined as persistent and extreme thwarting of a child's basic emotional needs (Cicchetti & Toth, 1998). Certain parental actions can lead to a loss of self-esteem in the child and interfere with the child's emotional development, but defining these actions and describing remedial steps can be difficult. Conceptually, such parental behaviors as rejecting, isolating, terrorizing, ignoring, and corrupting constitute psychological maltreatment (Garbarino, Guttman, & Seeley, 1986). The most frequent form of emotional abuse is verbal aggression or threats (Davis, 1996). These forms of abuse frequently produce emotional and behavioral

emotional abuse (psychological maltreatment)
Psychological damage perpetrated on the child by parental actions that often involve rejecting, isolating, terrorizing, ignoring, or corrupting.

problems in children (Hart & Brassard, 1987). Unfortunately, an objective definition of emotional maltreatment is not yet available that would allow mandatory intervention to reduce such abuse (Kelton & Davison, 1987). In the absence of such specific guidelines, the courts have taken a hands-off attitude toward everything but the most extreme forms. In fact, only 5% of all cases of reported child abuse are reports of emotional maltreatment (Goodman et al., 1998).

Why Are Children Abused?

It is not easy to understand why a parent would harm a defenseless child. A contextual view that looks at the parents, the child, the situation, and the society is needed to understand child abuse (Cicchetti & Lynch, 1993; Cicchetti & Toth, 1998).

Abusing Parents   As a group, parents who physically abuse their children are impulsive; have unmet dependency needs, a poor self-concept, and a poor sense of identity; are defensive; and project their problems onto their children (Green, Gaines, & Sandgrund, 1974). They believe in the value of physical punishment, are afraid of spoiling their children, and have difficulty empathizing with their offspring (Kelley, Grace, & Elliott, 1990). They evaluate their children's behavior more negatively and have more unrealistic child-related expectations (Milner & Chilamkurti, 1991). The picture that emerges of abusive parents is that they derive little enjoyment from parenting or from life in general and show little satisfaction with or expressed affection for the child. They are isolated from the community and do not encourage autonomy or independence, yet they still hold high, sometimes unrealistic, standards of achievement for their children (Trickett, Aber, Carlson, & Cicchetti, 1991). They are lacking in impulse control, especially when stressed, and respond to stress with more intense emotions and greater arousal (Cicchetti & Toth, 1998).

These characteristics are general ones. Many parents who are impulsive and isolated, for example, do not physically abuse their children, and this fact has led many professionals to deny that there is any definite "abusive" personality (Green et al., 1974). A personality profile of a parent is not an accurate predictor of abuse, so instead professionals look at the child-rearing practices of abusive and nonabusive parents.

Abusive parents have lower rates of interaction, more negative interactions with their children, and use more verbal and nonverbal aggression and fewer positive responses when managing behavior (Chilamkurti & Milner, 1993). Physically abusing parents also use more severe forms of punishment, such as striking the child's face, hitting the child with an object, or pulling the child's hair (Trickett & Kuczynski, 1986). They see their children as committing much more misbehavior and use fewer reasoning techniques (Trickett & Kuczynski, 1986).

Do Abused Children Grow Up to Abuse Their Own Children?   About 30% of parents who were abused as children abuse their own children (Kaufman & Zigler, 1987; Wisdom, 1989). This means that the general statement that abused children grow up to abuse their own children is greatly overstated. Although certainly children who are abused are more likely than the general population to do so, and a relationship exists between early maltreatment and later abusive and aggressive behavior (Maxfield & Wisdom, 1996), most children who suffer maltreatment do not become maltreating parents.

Those parents who have broken the cycle of abuse tend to have higher intelligence scores and are more emotionally stable (Egeland, 1988). Those who continue the cycle of abuse experience significantly more life stress and more anxiety and are more dependent, immature, and depressed (Egeland, Jacobovitz, & Sroufe, 1988). Those who do not abuse their children have received emotional support from a nonabusive adult sometime during childhood, participated in therapy at some time in their life, or had a nonabusive, more emotionally stable mate with whom they shared a satisfying relationship. Therefore, the presence and influence of other supportive and nonabusing adults and/or a helpful counseling relationship are two factors that may reduce the possibility of abuse. Since those who continue the cycle experience more stress, teaching stress reduction and problem-solving skills may help them.

The Abused Child   Certain characteristics of a child may predispose that child to being a victim of abuse. Children who are premature, who are physically challenged, or who have mental retardation are abused more often (Friedrich & Boriskin, 1976). The common characteristic in all these groups is the need for special care. The child whose needs are greater is at risk for abuse.

Abusing parents often hold unreasonable expectations for their children and distorted perceptions of what their children can do (Chilamkurti & Milner, 1993). Children with physical, emotional, or mental disabilities cannot meet their parents' expectations and are more likely to be abused. Consider the premature baby, who requires a great deal of care. The demand may be more than an impulsive, unrealistic parent can handle, and the parent may resort to violence to quiet the child. As the child grows, the pattern is reinforced; physical violence keeps the child in line until it becomes well established and continues throughout childhood. These abused children often justify the parent's actions on the basis of their own behavior, believing themselves to be generally bad (Dean, Malik, Richards, & Stringer, 1986). The child whose needs are greater or who is difficult to care for is more likely to set in motion abusive parental responses that may become the standard parent-child interaction.

The Situation   Any situation that raises the level of tension and stress can promote abuse. For instance, neglect and abuse increase when economic problems within the community increase (Steinberg, Catalano, & Dooley, 1981). Unemployment and underemployment cause stress. Parents may displace—that is, transfer their feelings from one person or object to another. Thus, the child may become the object of a parent's anger toward the boss or the life situation in general. Although child abuse and maltreatment can be found in all social groups and neighborhoods, it is more prevalent in areas where people are poor and isolated and unemployment is high (Coulton, Korbin, Su, & Chow, 1995).

Acceptance of Violence   We live in a society that largely condones violence with respect to children. Ninety percent of families report physically punishing their children at some point in their children's development (Clapp, 1988). In fact, laws covering physical abuse are relatively new. In the 19th century, the Society for the Prevention of Cruelty to Animals went to court, arguing that because children were human beings and human beings were animals, children should be protected at least as much as dogs or cats (Goodman et al., 1998). Shortly after this, some tentative steps toward protection were taken. Physical punishment is often accepted in the United States, even though other methods for discipline are available (see *To Spank or Not to Spank* on pages 359–360).

Guideposts

What are the causes of child abuse and neglect?

The Child in the 21st Century

To Spank or Not to Spank

Your child is playing with another child when he gets up and hits that child, who then starts to cry.

Your child used his crayons to write on the newly painted walls of his room, after you told him not to do so.

Your child refuses to eat a sandwich that he asked for and you spent 15 minutes preparing.

Your child refused to say hello to his aunt who came for a visit.

Your child runs into the street to fetch a baseball without looking for traffic.

Under which, if any, of these circumstances do you believe it is appropriate to spank a child?

In the area of discipline, no topic is as controversial as spanking or corporal (physical) punishment. Some parents have a "spare the rod" philosophy, believing strongly in corporal punishment, while others rarely or never resort to it. Feelings often run high, and the emotional debate over spanking has been going on for years.

In Sweden, as well as several other countries, it is against the law for parents or teachers to use corporal punishment. The legislation is not part of the criminal code, but rather acts as a statement of national policy. It is also used to identify parents who need help disciplining their children. The 1979 Swedish law states that "a child may not be subjected to physical punishment or other injurious or humiliating treatment" (Haeuser, 1990, p.

53). Other forms of discipline, including time-out, the judicious use of rewards, denial of privileges, and talking out conflicts, are advocated.

The situation differs in the United States as well as other countries where spanking remains accepted as a disciplinary technique. Spanking is the most common form of physical punishment. Somewhere between 70% and 90% of American parents spank their children at least once in a while (Wauchope & Straus, 1990). Spanking is most commonly used when children are between 3 and 5 years of age and then declines (Lytton, Watts & Dunn, 1988). Even older children, though, are physically punished, and one out of three

15-year-old children is still punished in a physical manner (Straus, 1991). Children are also often threatened with a spanking if they do not behave, so the threat of physical punishment is even more common (Davis, 1996).

Despite the seemingly widespread acceptance of physical punishment, there are some homes in which none or very little corporal punishment goes on. Many factors influence the amount of corporal punishment used. One obvious factor is the attitude parents have toward physical punishment; those who believe it is effective and acceptable are much more likely to use it extensively. In addition, some groups are more likely to use punishment, including those who have less

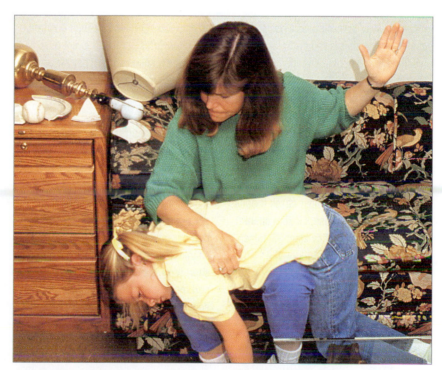

Spanking is one of the most controversial aspects of child rearing. In some countries it is illegal to do so. Is spanking an appropriate punishment for a child? Under what, if any, circumstances might you defend the practice?

education and are younger (Day, Peterson, & McCracken, 1998). Their use of physical punishment is also related to having experienced such punishment when they were growing up and considering it appropriate, as well as not knowing that there are alternative strategies available. Even so, many educated and older parents also use physical punishment (Holden, Coleman, & Schmidt, 1995).

A number of arguments are made both in favor and in opposition to the use of physical punishment. Those in favor of spanking argue that it is a discipline technique, nothing more, although more and more advocates are seeing it as a technique of "last resort" (Davis, 1994). They view it as essentially a natural, normal, and harmless technique that is frequently effective. Verbal and physical threats are regarded as a way to warn children and give them an opportunity to change the behavior. Advocates argue that spanking is a clear, short-lived, and immediate way to discipline. When the spanking ends, that is the end of the punishment and people can then go about their business (Davis, 1994).

Advocates cry foul when critics of physical punishment claim it leads to child abuse or serious physical harm. They are also opposed to child abuse but do not see a swat on the behind as abuse. After all, many parents use corporal punishment, and in most cases it does not lead to serious abuse. Linking spanking with child abuse, they claim, is false logic that only serves to muddy the debate.

Advocates also argue that spanking is an answer to the problems of wholesale permissive child rearing,

which, these advocates believe, leads to antisocial behavior and a lack of self-control (Davis, 1994). Spanking, then, has become a symbol of nonpermissive parenting. Advocates may even claim that parents who do not spank are actually lax and lazy.

Critics of spanking argue that it is an ineffective type of punishment that can lead to very serious consequences. They link it to emotional abuse because they see it as demeaning to the child (Davis, 1994). Spanking may work in the immediate situation but is ineffective in the long term, as it causes resentment and does not lead to internalization and better self-control. Children will stop their behavior out of fear but have not learned how to behave when the authority figure is not present. Meaningful discipline, they argue, involves teaching children self-control, while spanking only teaches that might makes right. Spanking also teaches children that aggression and violence are acceptable, and parents serve as aggressive models for their children. Too often, critics argue, it is not a reasoned response but rather an emotional one as a parent strikes out at the child when angry (Dix, Reinhold, & Zambarano, 1990). Critics also turn the lazy parent argument around, claiming that spanking is the lazy parents' way to discipline, because other, more sound methods require more time and effort.

Lately, another argument against spanking has been added. Critics argue that parents can become addicted to spanking. If it stops the behavior in the short term, parents will use it more and more. It becomes the major and sometimes most important discipline technique.

Finally, some critics argue that physical punishment is related to a whole range of negative developmental outcomes including delayed impulse control, impaired psychological adjustment, delinquency, later child abuse, and aggression (Holden et al., 1995; McCord, 1991; Straus, 1991).

The spanking debate demonstrates how child-rearing strategies can become emotional topics with symbolic meanings. Whenever I discuss spanking and physical punishment in class, these arguments come out, often with considerable fervor. Each side tends to discount what the other side is saying; those in favor of corporal punishment cast their critics as "permissive," while those against corporal punishment consider the others "abusive" or at least "inadequate" parents. Those favoring corporal punishment would like to see things stay as they are and their discipline technique accepted. Those opposed to corporal punishment do not necessarily want legislation as much as they would like to educate people on alternative ways to discipline children. The aim of both sides in this debate is to capture the hearts and minds of American parents as the new century opens.

What do you think?

How would you react to a law, similar to the one currently in effect in Sweden, that would make spanking illegal in the United States?

You can explore the questions above using InfoTrac College Edition. Hint: enter search terms *Corporal Punishment,* and *Spanking.*

Children are influenced and affected by the way their parents handle disputes.

Witnessing Domestic Violence

In homes in which domestic violence occurs, children are 15 times as likely to be physically abused or neglected (McCloskey, Figueredo, & Koss, 1995; Osofsky, 1995). Millions of children, though, live in homes in which they are not physically abused themselves but do witness violence regularly (Jaffe, Wolfe, & Wilson, 1990). These children, are often physically punished, frequently by both parents (McCloskey et al., 1995). Battered women often leave their husbands because they are worried about the possibility of their children becoming the next victims (Hilton, 1992). These children are sometimes called the "silent victims" or "invisible victims" because they show no physical signs of having been abused and are often overlooked by researchers.

Children who witness domestic violence are at risk for emotional and behavioral difficulties including aggression, withdrawal, and regressive behaviors (Kolbo, Blakely, & Engleman, 1996; Sternberg et al., 1993). Some children who continually witness spousal violence may respond with a numbing of their responsiveness to violence. They may even identify with the abuser or the victim, identifying with the father and becoming more abusive or with the mother and becoming a victim (Wisdom, 1989). Children may come to see violence as an appropriate way of settling disputes or as a typical part of a relationship (Jaffe, Wilson, & Wolfe, 1988).

People sometimes assume that preschoolers are too young to be affected by witnessing domestic violence, perhaps because they cannot adequately express themselves, but young children may actually be more vulnerable (Eth, Silverstein, & Pynoos, 1985). Preschoolers are often dealing with normal developmental concerns about safety and both real and fantastic fears (Groves, Zuckerman, Marans, & Cohen, 1993). The youngster's attempts to master these fears are defeated when additional concerns about what is going on in the home must be considered. During the early childhood years, parents are important sources of stability, comfort, and protection. When these adults are either victims or combatants, the child can no longer consider the world safe and secure, and often no reassurance is available (Groves et al., 1993). These preschoolers exhibit emotional distress, immature behavior, somatic complaints, and regression in toileting and language (Bell, 1995; Osofky, 1995). Sleeplessness, disorganized behavior, and agitation are also

Reducing the Child Abuse Rate Some of the increase may be due to greater public awareness and better reporting methods.

22.6 — 1986
41.9 — 1993
Below 22.6 — Goal

Source: National Center for Health Statistics (1997).

Guideposts

Why does witnessing domestic violence promote aggression in children?

Guideposts

How can child abuse be prevented?

posttraumatic stress disorder (PTSD)

A psychological disorder marked by such symptoms as diminished ability to concentrate, persistent sleep disturbances, flashbacks, disordered attachment behaviors, sudden startling, hypervigilance, and a fatalistic orientation.

---

observed in young children, but their caregivers often deny these problems (Eth & Pynoos, 1994).

Children who witness such abuse are also much more likely to develop **posttraumatic stress disorder (PTSD),** a psychological disorder marked by such symptoms as diminished ability to concentrate in school, persistent sleep disturbances, flashbacks, disordered attachment behaviors, sudden startling, hypervigilance, and a fatalistic orientation to the future that leads to increased risk taking in adolescence (Groves et al., 1993; Kilpatrick, Litt, & Williams, 1997). When the cause of stress is a person whom the child loves and respects, the child may be doubly affected with loyalty problems added to the mix (Kilpatrick et al., 1997). Such children may feel more vulnerable to their own destruction and not be able to express it. One little boy who witnessed the violent death of his mother drew pictures of boys with gaping mouths screaming silently. It was the only way to communicate his terror (Groves et al., 1993).

Certainly, not all children exposed to violence react severely. Many factors are involved, including the frequency, duration, and intensity of the violence; the type of violence; whether the child is also physically abused; maternal stress; family disadvantage; the presence of other stresses in life; and the presence of others who may help the child through the hard times (Kolbo et al., 1996). More attention needs to be paid to these "silent victims" of domestic violence.

Preventing Child Abuse

Programs to deal with child abuse have focused on both prevention and treatment. Prevention programs vary widely. Some offer courses in high school on child development, in which students are taught child care techniques, given information concerning children's nutritional and emotional needs, and told where parents can turn for help. Other programs include giving information at health fairs and promoting drop-in centers where parents can talk with other parents, social workers, or counselors (McCauley, 1992). The most effective prevention programs involve home visits from trained professionals who help parents develop better parenting skills and cope with the many challenges of parenting (MacMillan et al., 1994a).

Many approaches are used to treat child abusers. Individual and family therapy, self-help groups such as Parents Anonymous that provide emotional support, and group therapy can all claim some success.

The victims of abuse need help. Many improve somewhat even when only mild to moderate changes occur in the home situation. Early identification is one factor in successful treatment. Child abuse in any form is a tragedy, and all family members need some form of help. More needs to be done if these children are to recover and develop in a healthy manner.

Summary

1. According to Erikson, the psychosocial crisis of the preschool years can be expressed as initiative versus guilt. Preschoolers can express their desires and act on them. Their self-concept is described in terms of their physical characteristics and possessions. The child's self-concept can affect behavior.

2. Preschoolers experience a number of fears, including fear of the dark and monsters. Most fears are transitory, and calm reassurance can reduce the anxiety.

3. Play is an activity performed for sheer enjoyment with no ulterior motive. Play helps develop a child's mental, physical, and social abilities. It allows the child to experiment with new roles. The complexity of play increases with age. Both pretend play and rough-and-tumble play have important developmental benefits. Boys play more roughly than girls.

4. Four types of parenting styles have been identified. Authoritarian parents seek to control a child's every action, causing the child to become suspicious and withdrawn. Permissive parents allow almost total freedom and rarely use discipline. Their children do not show much self-control or self-reliance. Authoritative parents give their children freedom within limits. Their children are competent and self-controlled. Neglectful parents do not show concern for their children, and their children suffer from the greatest number of behavioral and emotional problems.

5. Child-rearing strategies depend on the parents' goals, repertoire of strategies, and parenting style. Culture and subcultural affiliation influence the goals and parenting strategies used.

6. Siblings may offer support and help as well as serve as sources of discord. Although antagonistic behavior among siblings is common, most interactions are positive and play-oriented. Research shows that the only child does not suffer from the experience.

7. Preschoolers have more contact with peers than when they were toddlers. Although some preschool friendships last throughout the year, most are temporary and lack intimacy. Friendship is defined in the play situation.

8. Preschoolers do show some prosocial behavior but little altruistic behavior. Prosocial behavior increases with age. Most children's conflicts are settled without the aid of adults, most often when one child gives in to another. Aggression declines with age because children are less likely to try to take things from others as they mature, but children who are most aggressive remain so in middle childhood.

9. Research generally finds that males are more aggressive than females, that girls have greater verbal abilities, and that boys excel in visual-spatial tasks and ability in mathematics. Gender differences tell us nothing about the cause of the differences, and the differences between individuals within the same gender are greater than the average differences between males and females.

10. Gender roles involve the behavioral patterns and psychological characteristics appropriate for each sex. Biological factors—including hormonal, genetic, and maturational differences—have been advanced as factors contributing to these differences between the genders, but a completely biological explanation is untenable. Children learn their gender roles through operant conditioning and imitation of role models in the environment. Freud saw gender roles in terms of the resolution of the Oedipus complex in the phallic stage, when children identify with the parent of the same sex. Gender schema theory argues that once a child knows his or her gender, the child develops a body of knowledge about what boys and girls do that helps children organize and interpret information and influences their preferences and activities.

11. Abuse and neglect are major societal problems. To understand abuse, the characteristics of the parents, child, and situation must be taken into account. Sexual abuse is the least reported type of abuse, and its incidence is underreported. Psychological or emotional abuse involves such actions as rejecting, isolating, terrorizing, ignoring, and corrupting. Children who witness domestic violence but are not abused themselves are at risk for identifying with the aggressor or the victim and are adversely affected by what they witness. Many parents who physically abuse their children can be helped to stop abusing them.

Review

The positive outcome of the psychosocial crisis of early childhood is a sense of (1)_____. If parents react to a child's wishes and plans with scorn, the child is likely to leave early childhood with a sense of (2)_____. The picture a person has of him- or herself is called the (3)_____. In early childhood, the self-concept is based on (4)_____ factors.

Infants may hold onto a stuffed animal but are not involved with others. Such play is called (5)_____ play. When children play by themselves, they are engaging in (6)_____ play. Later, children engage in (7)_____ play in which they watch others but cannot join in. Two-year-olds engage in (8)_____ play in which they play in the presence of others but not with them. Preschoolers actively play with each other, practicing their motor skills, but this (9)_____ play is not sustained. Finally, at the end of the preschool period and continuing into middle childhood, children show (10)_____ play in which children can use rules and can sustain their interactions.

A type of play in which children take on the roles of others is called (11)_____ play. One type of play that adults discourage is (12)_____ play because they fear it will lead to injury or aggression. This type of play is more likely to lead to aggression in children who lack the (13)_____ necessary to understand its limits.

Parents tend to believe that preschoolers are more responsible for their actions, so a (14)_____ form of discipline is used. Parenting styles can be conceived as differing in two elements, (15)_____ and (16)_____. (17)_____ parents give orders and do not allow for any questioning, leading to children who are suspicious and mistrusting of authority. (18)_____ parents use little discipline, and their children tend to lack direction. (19)_____ parents have rules but encourage communication, and their children are the most self-reliant. (20)_____ parents do not regulate their children's behavior, nor do they communicate with them, leading to the worst outcomes. Some parents use threats and force called (21)_____ discipline, while others use reasoning and shows of disappointment called (22)_____ discipline. In Western societies the ideal child is (23)_____, while this may not be the case in other societies. The meaning of parenting style differs in various (24)_____. In many African American homes, child-rearing practices have a/an (25)_____ orientation rather than an object orientation. Latino families often emphasize (26)_____. Latino mothers differentiate between the roles of (27)_____ and (28)_____. Asian American children are often taught the overriding importance of (29)_____ obligations. (30)_____ child rearing attitudes often stress sharing and fitting into the group.

Most children have siblings. (31)_____ siblings initiate more playful as well as antagonistic exchanges. Most interactions between siblings are (32)_____ (friendly/combative)

Generally, preschool friendships are (strong/fragile) (33)_____, and the prerequisite for being a friend is being present and willing to (34)_____. As children negotiate the period of early childhood, they tend to play more with children of the same (35)_____. The term (36)_____ behavior is used to describe any behavior that helps others, while the term (37)_____ refers to helping others with no thought of reward. The term to describe the frequency of preschoolers' helping behavior is (38)_____. The ability to identify emotionally with the other child is a feeling of (39)_____, as well as the ability to take the role of the other and promote prosocial behavior. Most conflicts between peers in the preschool stage are settled through (40)_____. Aggression (41)_____ with age. Two types of aggression are found. (42)_____ aggression involves using aggression to take something from someone else, while (43)_____ aggression is more personal.

Gender differences in (44)_____ are narrowing, but not those in (45)_____. The first step in the development of an understanding of gender is the appreciation that some people are male and some female, called (46)_____. In the second stage, called (47)_____, children begin to understand that they were of the same gender when they were born and will remain so as they age. Finally, at a later age, they appreciate the fact that even if they change their appearance they still remain the same gender, a stage called (48)_____. (49)_____ is the process by which an individual acquires values and behaves in a manner more appropriate to one gender or the other. There are many factors that contribute to the acquisition of gender role. Biological factors, such as (50)_____ differences (boys have more testosterone and girls more estrogen), and genetic factors may contribute somewhat. The (51)_____ approach emphasizes the fact that boys and girls are treated differently. According to Freud, sex roles arise from the resolution of the Oedipus/Electra complex through the process of (52)_____. (53)_____ argues that first children learn their gender and then create a cognitive framework, a body of knowledge, about what boys and girls do.

Child abuse is the intentional injury to a child, while (54)_____ is the inadequate or inappropriate care for a child. Most reports to authorities are for (55)_____. The most common problem behavior found in physically abused children, especially males, is (56)_____. (57)_____ abuse occurs when the child's basic psychological needs are thwarted. About (58)_____ percent of abused children grow up to abuse and neglect their own children. Children who witness domestic violence in their own homes are (59)_____ (more/less) likely to be abused. In severe cases, these children may develop a disorder called (60)_____, which involves a diminished ability to concentrate in school, persistent sleep disturbances, flashbacks, disordered attachment behaviors, sudden startling, and hypervigilance. For those at risk for abusing their children, the most successful prevention strategy is (61)_____.

InfoTrac

For additional readings, explore InfoTrac College Edition, our online library.
Go to http://www.infotrac-college.com/wadsworth.
Hint: enter the search terms *Children's Play, Sibling Rivalry,* and *Gender Role Attitudes.*

What's on the web

Today's Parent
http://www.todaysparent.com/

National Committee to Prevent Child Abuse
http://childabuse.org

Educational Resources Information Center (ERIC)
http://ericps.ed.uiuc.edu/npin/respar/texts/fampeer.html

The Wadsworth Psychology Study Center Web Site
Go to the Wadsworth Psychology Study Center at http://psychology.wadsworth.com/ for quiz questions, research updates, hot topics, interactive exercises, and suggested readings in the InfoTrac College Edition related to this chapter.

Answers 1. initiative; 2. guilt; 3. self-concept; 4. physical; 5. unoccupied; 6. solitary; 7. onlooker; 8. parallel; 9. associative; 10. cooperative; 11. pretend (dramatic); 12. rough-and-tumble; 13. social skills; 14. stricter; 15. responsiveness; 16. demandingness; 17. Authoritarian; 18. Permissive; 19. Authoritative; 20. Rejecting/neglecting; 21. power-assertive; 22. love-oriented; 23. independent/autonomous; 24. cultures (subcultures); 25. person; 26. cooperation; 27. parent; 28. teacher; 29. familial; 30. Native American; 31. Older; 32. friendly; 33. fragile; 34. play; 35. gender; 36. prosocial; 37. altruism; 38. infrequent/rare; 39. empathy; 40. insistence; 41. decreases; 42. instrumental; 43. hostile; 44. cognitive abilities; 45. aggression; 46. gender identity; 47. gender stability; 48. gender constancy (gender consistency); 49. Sex typing; 50. hormonal; 51. behavioral; 52. identification; 53. Gender schema theory; 54. neglect; 55. neglect; 56. aggression; 57. Emotional/Psychological; 58. 30l 59. more; 60. posttraumatic stress disorder; 61. home visits by professionals

PART FOUR

Middle
Childhood

10 Physical and Cognitive Development
in Middle Childhood

11 Social and Personality Development
in Middle Childhood

CHAPTER TEN

Physical *and* Cognitive

CHAPTER OUTLINE

Books, Baseball, and Potato Chips

Physical Development in Middle Childhood

The Stage of Concrete Operations

Information-Processing Skills

Language Development in Middle Childhood

Children's Humor

The Elementary School Experience

Success in School

Boys, Girls, and the School Experience

Bilingual Children in School

Ebonics

Atypical Development: Children with Exceptional Needs

The Total Child in School

ARE THESE STATEMENTS
True *or* False?

1. Most fourth graders choose their own breakfast, lunch, and snacks.
2. Most overweight elementary school children will be normally weighted adults.
3. Children, on average, weigh less today than they did 20 years ago because they eat better diets and are more physically active.
4. Elementary school children often overestimate how well they will do on a physical task.
5. When elementary school children say they understand something, a person can be reasonably certain that they do.
6. Children in middle childhood do not understand irony at all.
7. American children start elementary school with more knowledge than Japanese and Chinese students but soon fall behind children from these countries.
8. Most bilingual children in the United States live in poverty.
9. Children with attention deficit/hyperactivity disorder (ADHD) are treated with tranquilizers to reduce their symptoms.
10. Most children with high intelligence scores have significant adjustment problems and poor peer relationships.

ANSWERS: 1. *True.* 2. *True.* 3. *False.* 4. *True.* 5. *False.* 6. *False.* 7. *False.* 8. *True.* 9. *False.* 10. *False.*

Development *in* Middle Childhood

Books, Baseball, and Potato Chips

"Books, baseball, and potato chips."

    This is how a mother of two sons, 8 and 10 years of age, described her children's lives. Attending elementary school dominates all their activities, and school is not only a place to learn but to meet their friends. When they come home, they often run out to play, taking a snack with them. During the middle childhood period, children become more independent and make many of their own decisions.

Physical Development in Middle Childhood

Middle childhood is a time of horizontal growth. The physical changes transpire at a slower rate and are less obvious than in earlier years. Gradually, the child's forehead becomes flatter, the arms and legs more slender, the nose larger, the shoulders squarer, the abdomen flatter, and the waistline more pronounced.

Height and Weight

The rate of growth continues to decline during middle childhood. Girls are a bit shorter than boys at the beginning of this period, but because girls experience their adolescent growth spurt about two years earlier than boys, girls are taller for a couple of years later in middle childhood. By age 14 or so, boys regain their height advantage (Tanner, 1989) (see Figure 10.1).

Guideposts

What is the pattern of growth and weight in middle childhood?

Because most children in elementary school choose their own breakfast, lunch, and snacks their nutritional value is often poor.

| Figure 10.1 | Growth in Middle Childhood |

Boys are taller at the beginning of this period of development, but girls become taller at about age 10 because they experience their prepubertal growth spurt about two years earlier than boys.

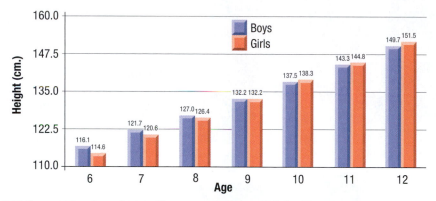

NOTE: Stature is given in centimeters. To convert to inches, multiply by .39.
SOURCE: Hamill et al. (1977)

Boys and girls weigh about the same amount at 8 years of age (Black & Puckett, 1996). Then, girls become heavier at about 9 or 10 and stay heavier until they are about 14.5 years, when boys equal or surpass girls (Tanner, 1989) (see Figure 10.2).

Nutrition in Middle Childhood: "I'll Choose It Myself!"

No one doubts the importance of nutrition. Children who are chronically hungry and malnourished often suffer growth retardation and severe cognitive impairment. When hunger is temporary and nutritional deficiencies mild, they experience more subtle problems such as poor academic performance (Whitney & Rolfes, 1996). Poor eating habits, such as missing breakfast, are related to lower performance on measures of school performance (Kruesi & Rapoport, 1986).

The middle childhood years are the parents' best and perhaps last chance to influence food choices, but nutritional supervision wanes during

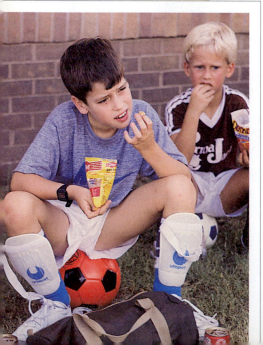

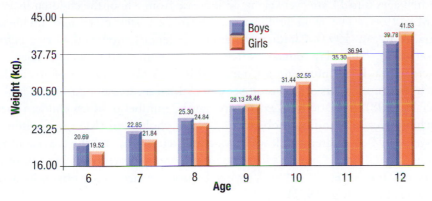

Figure 10.2 **Weight Gain in Middle Childhood**

Boys are heavier than girls until about age 8 or 9 when girls weigh more for a few years.

NOTE: All data are given in kilograms. To convert to pounds multiply by 2.2
SOURCE: Hamill et al. (1977)

this period. Most children in the fourth through eighth grades choose their own breakfast, lunch, and snacks (National Center for Nutrition and Dietetics, 1991). They are deeply affected by what they see on television. The commercials for sugar-coated foods, overindulgence, and an emphasis on tastiness are influential, encouraging them to make poor choices. The most common TV commercials aimed at children are for toys and games, cereals and candy, soda, and other snacks (Condry, Bence, & Scheibe, 1987), and children ask their parents for these foods (Taras, Sallis, Patterson, Nader, & Nelson, 1989).

Relatively few studies have been conducted on the eating habits of elementary school children. One major study, the Bogalusa Heart Study, found a consistent pattern of overconsumption of foods high in saturated fat, sugar, and salt, with snack or junk foods high in these elements, accounting for about one-third of the children's total caloric intake (Berenson et al., 1982). This is unfortunate, because children and adolescents with a high cholesterol level are much more likely to have an elevated cholesterol level in adulthood. Children should be encouraged to eat a low-fat, low-cholesterol diet (Lane, 1991).

The effects of poor diet begin early. At least 40% of elementary school children show at least one risk factor related to later heart disease, such as high blood pressure, high cholesterol or obesity (Black & Puckett, 1996). Latino and African American children are less likely than white children to meet the government's nutritional guidelines (Portner, 1997). Nutritional education is certainly an important concern.

Childhood Obesity

Parents often fall victim to the "baby fat" theory, thinking that a fat child is a healthy child. Other parents argue that school-age children who are obese will grow out of it. Both points of view are wrong. Obese children are not especially healthy, and juvenile obesity is related to adult obesity (Pierce & Wardle, 1997). Between 50% and 80% of all overweight children will be overweight adults (van Dyke, 1995). The longer a child is obese, the more difficult it is to modify the condition.

Most fourth graders choose their own breakfast, lunch, and snacks.

Most overweight elementary school children will be normally weighted adults.

Children are heavier today than they were 20 years ago, having gained about 5 pounds over the past two decades (Whitney & Rolfes, 1996). About 14% of all children ages 6 to 11 are overweight, an increase from 8% of the children in 1980 (JAMA, 1997). The main problem appears to be a lack of exercise (Schlicker, Borra, & Regan, 1994). Children live a more sedentary lifestyle than ever before. Fewer than half play outside after school, while 80% watch television (International Food Information Council [IFIC], 1992). A quarter of all children watch 4 or more hours of television per day (Andersen, Crespo, Bartlett, Cheskin, & Pratt, 1998). A relationship exists between the number of hours children spend watching television and both obesity and blood cholesterol (Klesges, Shelton, & Klesges, 1993). Children snack while watching television, and the television may become a conditioned stimulus for eating if children repeatedly eat in front of the television (Epstein et al., 1995). Viewing TV also replaces more physically active endeavors (Van Dyke, 1995).

Obese children are less active than nonobese children. Obese children prefer sedentary activities even when given the option of being more active (Epstein, Smith, Vara, & Rodefer, 1991). Parents are also models, and if their most athletic activity of the day is switching the channels on the television set's remote, this does not encourage physical activity in their children.

Children, on average, weigh less today than they did 20 years ago because they eat better diets and are more physically active.

Obese children are more likely to be shunned, have fewer friends, and have a poor body image (Mendelson & White, 1985). They may suffer discrimination and be teased (Pierce & Wardle, 1997). They often begin puberty earlier but stop growing at a shorter height (DeBruyne & Rolfes, 1990).

Obesity in children is difficult to correct. Because very heavy dieting can injure children as they develop, it is usually not recommended. One promising approach is to feed children in a nutritious way that will help them maintain a constant weight while they grow. This promotes normal development while restricting the accumulation of body fat (Cataldo & Whitney, 1986). Other approaches involve providing psychological support and increasing the amount of exercise the child gets. Any dietary plan should be executed under a doctor's care.

Guideposts
Why is childhood obesity considered a major problem?

Physical Fitness and Health

Children who are physically fit are healthier and more resistant to fatigue and stress (Krogman, 1980). Physical activity is also needed to support normal growth and development. For example, exercise increases bone width and mineralization (Bailey, 1985). It also has social benefits, since group sports are often important social activities and being excluded may interfere with a child's social development (Williams & Stith, 1980). Physically fit children have better self-concepts than children who are not fit (Sherrill & Holguin, 1989). Exercise is also a form of entertainment. Finally, children who exercise during the school day show improved academic performance (Bailey, 1975).

Unfortunately, many children in school do not get enough exercise or, for that matter, engage in any strenuous physical activity (Parcel et al., 1987). Children seem more interested in watching television and playing computer games (Hellmich, 1997). Many children are turning into "high-tech couch potatoes" (Manzo, 1997).

Very few states require all students to take daily physical education or participate in after-school activities to promote fitness (Manzo, 1997). For those who do receive physical education in the schools, too much of it falls under the heading of competitive sports (Krogman, 1980). The traditional system focuses on the athletically gifted or the early maturing child, leaving the vast majority of other students with little interest in physical activity.

Guideposts
Why are American children generally physically unfit?

Health Education

Nutritional and physical education are parts of a larger program called *health education*, which deals with both physical and emotional health. Health education programs focus on how certain practices, such as drinking and smoking, affect the body. These programs can be beneficial if they are comprehensive. Children in grades 3 through 12 who have taken at least three years of health education are less likely to drink alcohol, smoke, take other drugs, or ride with a driver who has been drinking, than children of the same age who have one year or less of health education (Brody, 1989). These children are also more likely to exercise regularly, wear seat belts, eat breakfast every day, and brush their teeth. When third grade students' school lunches were made more nutritious, and the physical education curriculum was changed to address eating habits, exercise, and cigarette smoking, children engaged in more physical activity, and they consumed foods lower in cholesterol and fat (JAMA, 1996).

Another area of health education is safety and accident prevention (see Table 10.1 on page 374). The most common cause of death in middle childhood is accidents, many of which involve motor vehicles (Pillitteri, 1992). Some accidents may result from failure to follow simple rules, such as looking both ways when crossing the street. Other accidents are caused by errors in judgement when children overestimate their abilities and perhaps run through traffic believing they are faster than they really are. Children in middle childhood often overestimate their ability to perform tasks both just beyond and well beyond their ability (Plumert, 1993). Elementary school children believe themselves to be more capable than they really

Table 10.1	Preventing Accidents in the School-Age Child
Accident	**Preventive Measure**
Motor vehicle accidents	Encourage children to use seat belts in car; role-model their use.
	Teach street-crossing safety; stress that streets are no place for roughhousing, pushing, or shoving.
	Teach bicycle safety, including advice not to take "passengers" on a bicycle and to use a helmet.
	Teach parking lot and school bus safety (do not walk behind parked cars, wait for crossing guard, etc.).
Community	Teach to avoid areas specifically unsafe, such as train yards, grain silos, back alleys. Teach not to go with strangers (parents can establish a code word with child; child does not leave school with anyone who does not know the word).
	Teach to say no to anyone who touches them whom they do not wish to do so, including family members (most sexual abuse is by a family member, not a stranger).
Burns	Teach safety with candles, matches, campfires—fire is not fun. Teach safety with beginning cooking skills (remember to include microwave oven safety such as closing door firmly before turning on oven, not using metal containers).
	Teach not to climb power poles.
Falls	Teach that roughhousing on fences, climbing on roofs, etc., is hazardous.
	Teach skateboard safety.
Sports injuries	Wearing appropriate equipment for sports (face masks for hockey, knee braces for football, batting helmets for baseball) is not babyish but smart.
	Teach not to play to a point of exhaustion or in a sport beyond physical capability (pitching baseball or ballet on toes for a grade school child).
	Teach to use trampolines only with adult supervision to avoid serious neck injury.
Drowning	Children should learn how to swim, and that dares and roughhousing when diving or swimming are not appropriate.
	Teach not to swim beyond limits of capabilities.
Drugs	Teach to avoid all recreational drugs and to take prescription medicine only as directed.
Firearms	Teach safe firearm use. Parents should keep firearms in locked cabinets with bullets separate from gun.
General	Teach school-agers to keep adults informed as to where they are and what they are doing.
	Be aware that the frequency of accidents increases when parents are under stress and therefore less attentive; special precautions must be taken at these times.
	Some children are more active, curious, and impulsive and therefore more vulnerable to accidents than others.

SOURCE: Pillitteri (1992)

Elementary school children often overestimate how well they will do on a physical task.

are and take physical risks, such as riding bicycles too fast or climbing too high (Black & Pucket, 1996). This is especially true for younger elementary school children (McKenzie & Forbes, 1992) and for those who are highly extroverted and impulsive (Schwebel & Plumert, 1999).

Organized Sports: Pro and Con

About 25 million American boys and girls are involved in organized sports. Most organized sports—for example, baseball, football, or soccer—involve competition between teams of children.

Every year, newspaper articles trumpet the abuses of organized competition, including poor coaching, parents who either act out at games or show disappointment in their children's performance, and children being made to feel that they have nothing to offer their teams. Those who defend organized sports readily admit to these problems but claim that, despite these excesses, competitive sports have value. These excesses may be the exceptions, not the norm. If we could end these abuses, would organized sports have value, or are they inherently flawed?

Supporters argue that participating in organized sports leads to good fitness habits and improves self-esteem as children contribute to the team effort. They offer an opportunity for socializing and just having fun (Micheli & Jenkins, 1990). If competition is handled properly, which translates into trying hard and accepting losing and winning graciously, organized sports are a positive experience. Learning what it is to win and lose is part of life and everyone can play, enjoy the games, and contribute something (Leo, 1993). While some children are better than others, that is true in all endeavors, and a realistic view of oneself is not necessarily a negative one. In addition, many team sports combine cooperation and competition, thereby emphasizing both. For example, in basketball five people work as a team and compete with another team.

Others forcefully argue that these benefits are illusions. Competition by its very nature, they ague, undermines self-esteem, injures relationships with others, and may hold children back from doing their best. Any benefits from competitive sports can better be achieved through cooperative activities (Kohn, 1990). Many competitive games can be changed into cooperative games. Most children have played the game "musical chairs" in which there is one more child than the number of chairs (for example, seven children and six chairs). When the music stops, they must all sit down, and the one who does not have a seat is out. The game can be changed so that the object is for everyone to sit on a diminishing number of chairs. Everyone becomes a winner as children cooperate and work toward a group goal. Some argue that competition, especially at a young age, can harm children as they feel embarrassed or inadequate, and they may give up and refuse to participate in other physical activities. It is not an excess in competition that injures children but competition itself.

Evidence that competition can be injurious is easy to find, although much of it is not directly relevant to the type of competition found on the Little League field. In one study, students were given puzzles to solve. Competing children were told that the one who solved the most puzzles would be the winner and could select a prize. Noncompeting children were told there would be a prize for participating. Children who competed and lost viewed themselves as incapable and experienced negative emotions. Competing children who won devalued those who lost and had inflated ideas about their own abilities. Competitive success, though, was more valued than noncompetitive success (Ames & Ames, 1978).

Another criticism is that poor coaching can potentially injure a child. All Canadian and Australian coaches must be certified by examination, but that is not true in the United States (Micheli & Jenkins, 1990). A coach without proper knowledge may unwittingly injure a child—for example, by encouraging a young pitcher to throw a curveball long before his arm is ready for the strain (Wolff, 1993). Other coaches specialize young children, making them play one position on a team when they should be learning all the skills. Some point to the problem of coaches injuring the child psychologically through what they say. Children require the approval of coaches and are very sensitive to criticism. Coaches may produce a negative self-appraisal when they are highly critical of a child, which may cause a lifelong avoidance of physical activity (Wolff, 1993). In one training program, Little League coaches received instructions on praising effort as well as good performance, encouraging children when mistakes are made, giving corrective instruction in an encouraging fashion, and learning specific game strategies. The children on these teams were compared with those on teams whose coaches had

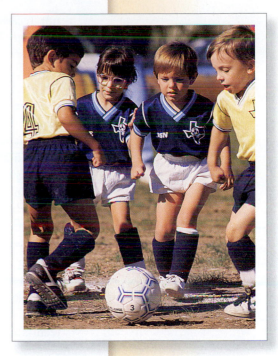

Organized sports are very popular during the elementary school years. Some believe participation is valuable and positive, while others emphasize their potential for harm.

For Your Consideration ❓

Many of you have participated in competitive activities. Do you feel that they have enhanced your development or, in some way, injured you? Would you encourage your children to play Little League or engage in competitive activities?

not received this training. Children with trained coaches were evaluated more positively by players, the players had more fun, and the relationships among players was more positive even though win-loss records were similar. Boys with low self-esteem who played for trained coaches showed significant increases in general self-esteem, while children who played for the untrained coaches did not. If children are to benefit from physical activity, competitive or noncompetitive, the problems in training and coaching must be eliminated, and every child's contribution appreciated.

Since it is doubtful that the popularity of competitive sports will diminish, perhaps it would be better if psychologists looked at the conditions under which children are least likely to be injured by competition. Competition works best when the consequences of winning and losing are not great or do not generate much anxiety (Johnson & Johnson, 1974; Kaplan, 1990). Competition may work if everyone has an opportunity to win (contribute to the team). Competition is likely to lead to negative consequences if the pressure to win is too high or if one team is so much better than the other that there is no chance for one team to compete. Not all competition involves one person or team against another. Competing against oneself and one's prior achievements can be quite a useful motivational technique.

Guideposts

What are the arguments for and against competitive sports?

Dentition

The shedding of baby teeth, called **deciduous teeth,** is perhaps the most obvious physical occurrence during early middle childhood. For children, losing their teeth is a sign that they are growing up, but the gaps left in the mouth can cause temporary cosmetic problems as well as difficulty in pronunciation.

Human beings have a complement of 20 baby teeth and 32 permanent teeth. The first permanent tooth is usually the "6-year molar," which does not replace any baby tooth (Smart & Smart, 1978). This tooth may erupt at any time between 4.5 and 8 years of age (Krogman, 1980). It is not easily recognizable, and it may become decayed and lost if not properly cared for. Many parents do not put much effort into dental care for their young children, thinking they have "only baby teeth" anyway. This is unfortunate, because premature loss can lead to dental problems, including difficulties with the bite. As a rule, girls lose their baby teeth before boys do.

Motor Skill Development

By the time children enter elementary school, they have developed many motor skills. They can run, climb, gallop, and hop. Skipping is just being mastered, as are throwing, catching, and kicking, and balancing is reasonably good. During the next 6 years, motor skills are refined and modified (DeOreo & Keogh, 1980).

During middle childhood, running speed increases and the ability to jump for distance improves. The ability to throw both for accuracy and for distance also improves (Cratty, 1986), as does balance. These developments are due both to maturation and to practice.

Boys are superior in running speed and throwing, while girls excel in tasks that require agility, rhythm, and hopping (Cratty, 1986). Boys are also stronger than girls during this period, but girls show more muscular flexibility. As with almost all gender differences, the overlap between boys and girls is great (Lockhart,

deciduous teeth

The scientific term for baby teeth.

376

1980). In fact, gender differences account for about 10% of the differences among children, and most of the differences are due to practice and training (Krombholz, 1997).

Readiness for School

Think of all the physical, mental, and behavioral skills necessary for academic success. Children must be able to sit in one place, listen to an adult, and attend to lessons. They must be intellectually mature enough to understand what is going on, be emotionally emancipated from their parents so that they can form relationships with others, and have some measure of self-control. In almost every culture, children begin to attend school sometime between the ages of 5 and 7 years.

Traditionally, the child's chronological age is used to indicate school readiness, but only a very weak case can be made for this practice. Many children are simply not ready to master schoolwork (Ames, 1986). For example, a mental age of about 5.5 is considered necessary for acquiring reading skills. This presents a problem because some children may not be mentally, physically, or emotionally mature enough to tackle the challenge. Some children may not have the ability to focus on the reading matter, or they may lack a left-right sequence. They may be too immature to sit in a chair, listen to the teacher, and follow instructions. If children cannot recognize shapes, they cannot begin to learn their letters. Parents may read to their children, provide a home where reading is considered an enjoyable activity, and generally instill in their children a positive attitude toward learning, but even with this excellent background, some children, especially boys, will not be ready for reading instruction by the first grade (Ilg & Ames, 1972). Since children develop at their own rate, some children will be ready to read before others—a point anxious parents should keep in mind.

Do older, more mature children do better than younger, less mature children in kindergarten and first grade? Some evidence indicates that older children in kindergarten and first grade perform a bit better academically, but these differences are very small, and age is not the most important factor (Breznitz & Teltsch, 1989; Shepard & Smith, 1986). Other factors, such as the home and even socioeconomic status, are more important (Jones & Mandeville, 1990). Both younger and older students make comparable progress in school. Age at entrance is not a good predictor of either learning or academic risk (Morrison, Griffith, & Alberts, 1997).

Guideposts

Why is the concept of readiness important?

The Stage of Concrete Operations

The school experience is so important that the middle childhood years are often called the school years. As children enter first grade, at about the age of 6, the long preoperational stage is drawing to a close, and children are just entering the **stage of concrete operations.** The shift from the preoperational stage to the concrete operational stage is gradual. The child does not go to sleep egocentric, unable to fully understand classification and conservation, and wake up with fully developed abilities in these areas. These skills develop gradually over the years (see Table 10.2).

During the concrete operational stage, children can deal with real objects when considering change, but not with abstractions (Siegler, 1998). Children in this stage who are presented with a purely verbal problem that involves hypotheses cannot solve the problem, but they have no difficulty with it if it is explained in

concrete operational stage

Piaget's third stage of cognitive development, lasting roughly from 7 years of age through 11 years, in which children develop the ability to perform logical operations, such as conservation.

Table 10.2 The Concrete Operational Stage

In the stage of concrete operations, children can deal with information that is based on something they can see or imagine. They can mentally operate on objects but cannot deal with abstractions.

Characteristic	Explanation	Example
Conservation	Children in this stage understand that things remain the same despite changes in appearance.	A child develops the ability to understand that a ball of clay can change shape and still contain the same amount of clay.
Ability to classify	Students can place objects into various categories.	Elementary school students can now group different animals as mammals.
Ability to seriate	Students can place things in size order.	Children can arrange a series of sticks in terms of length or weight.
Ability to reverse operations	Students can follow a process from beginning to end and then back again.	If a teacher rolls a ball of clay into a long, wormlike structure, a child in this stage can mentally re-create the ball of clay.
Inability to use abstractions	Students cannot deal with abstract material, such as ideas and statements not tied to something observable or imaginable.	Children may find political cartoons and proverbs puzzling because they cannot understand their abstract meaning.

real, concrete terms. This is one reason that children have difficulty understanding the long-range, probable effects of such behaviors as poor nutrition and find it easier to understand direct, concrete, and immediate cause-and-effect relations involved in safety related concerns (Olvera-Ezzell, Power, Cousins, Guerra, & Trujillo, 1994).

The Decline of Egocentrism

Elementary school children become less egocentric. They understand that other people see the world differently and seek to validate their own view of the world. This is accomplished through social interaction, during which they can share their thoughts and verify their view of the world (Piaget, 1928). In addition, they can now take the other person's perspective and can imagine what others are thinking of them in a relatively simple way (Harter, 1983). They are capable of being more sensitive to the feelings of others and imagining how others would feel in various situations. Language becomes less egocentric. Preschoolers often use such pronouns as *he* and *she* without offering adequate information to the listener. They reason that since they know who they are talking about, so does the listener (Pulaski, 1980). As the child matures, this tendency is greatly reduced.

Reversibility, the Ability to Decenter and Transformations

During middle childhood, the limitations of preoperational thought begin to fade slowly. Children develop the ability to reverse operations—to realize that if they roll a clay ball into a long worm, they can reverse the operation and re-create the ball of clay. One 6-year-old proudly told his mother that he learned that 3 plus 2 equals 5. After praising him, his mother asked how much is 2 plus 3? The child answered that he didn't know; he hadn't learned that one yet (Bjorklund, 1995). The older child, in the concrete stage of operations, understands reversibility and has no difficulty with this. Children develop the ability to decenter—to take into consideration more than one dimension. Children now realize that the increase in the length of the clay worm compensates for the decrease in its width. They also begin to understand transformations—to understand that as objects change position or shape, they progress through a series of intermediate points. Piaget did not find these abilities in the preschooler.

Conservation

The crowning achievement of the concrete operational stage is the ability to conserve (see page 296) (Bisanz, Morrison, & Dunn, 1995). Children, though, do not show conservation of number, substance, weight, and volume all at the same time. A child may be able to solve conservation of number problems but not problems involving conservation of volume. Piaget (1952) noted that a child may understand the underlying principle but may not be able to apply it across all contexts, calling this uneven performance **horizontal decalage.**

Conservation of Number Show children displays of seven pennies in which the coins either are grouped closely together or are spread out. The 4-year-old is certain that the spread-out group has more coins than the other group. The 6- or 7-year-old develops a sense of conservation of number and knows that the spacing does not matter.

Conservation of Weight When one of two equal balls of clay is made into a worm-shaped object and then reformed into a ball, the 7-year-old will probably understand that no clay has been lost in transforming the ball to a worm and back again. However, the child probably will not understand that the two shapes still-weigh the same. Conservation of weight comes later, at about age 9 or 10 years (Piaget & Inhelder, 1969).

Conservation of Volume The last conservation problem to be solved correctly is conservation of volume. Make two balls of clay and show them to the child. The child should understand that the clay balls are equally large and equally weighted. Then put the clay balls in two identical beakers containing equal amounts of water and show that the balls displace the same volume of liquid because they cause the level of the water to rise the same amount. Finally, change the shape of one of the balls and ask the child whether the ball would still make the water rise to the previous height (Diamond, 1982). Typically, conservation of volume problems are the last to be solved, and the ability may first emerge at about age 11 or 12 (Piaget & Inhelder, 1969).

Seriation and Classification

School-age children further develop the ability to seriate and to classify. They can easily arrange a series of sticks in terms of length and later by weight and finally by volume (Bjorklund, 1995). Their ability to classify also greatly improves. In fact, school-age children are known for their propensity to collect things (Kegan, 1982). They will collect anything and thereby practice their skills of classification.

horizontal decalage
A term used to describe the unevenness of development in which a child may be able to solve one type of problem but not another, even though a common principle underlies them both.

The elementary school child collects things and realizes that an item can be classified in many ways and can belong to a great many classes at the same time.

They begin to realize that an item can be classified in many ways and can belong to a great many classes at one time. In Figure 10.3, children are presented with problems in which stimuli vary along two dimensions, such as shape and color or color and number or shape and size, and asked to choose the correct figure for the blank space from a group of choices (Inhelder & Piaget, 1964). (Piaget also asked children to justify their choices). This task requires children to identify the two relevant classes and choose an object that satisfies the requirement (Siegler, 1998). Four- to six-year-old children select objects that include one of the desired dimensions, but very few correctly choose the object that has both. By 9 or 10 years, most can do so.

Figure 10.3 Multiple Classification

Which of the choices on the right side fits in best? Each item involves three questions: (1) finding the correct picture, (2) justifying this choice, and (3) stating whether one or two of the other pictures might fit in as well or better. Notice that these choices vary along two or more dimensions.

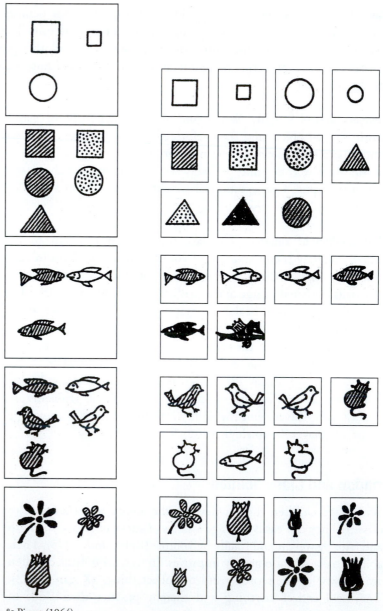

SOURCE: Inhelder & Piaget (1964)

How the School-Age Child Thinks

The school-age child's thought processes are certainly a great improvement over those of the preschooler. The more logical, less egocentric ways of the elementary school child are more recognizable. School-age children develop a quantitative attitude toward tasks and problems. They now understand that problems have precise, quantifiable solutions that can be obtained by logical reasoning and measurement operations. For example, take nine Legos® and lay them in a perfectly straight line (see Figure 10.4). Then take nine Legos and place them end to end but in a jagged fashion. The display of nine Legos placed in a straight line looks longer than the display placed in a jagged line. Now tell preschoolers and school-age children that these Lego lines are two roads and ask them who makes the longest trip—the person who drives the car the entire length of the first (straight) road or the driver who drives the entire length of the second (jagged) road. The preschooler is fooled by the appearance of the roads and says the first. The school-age child answers that they are the same (Flavell, 1977). The older child is not fooled by how the roads look and recognizes that the total length of each road can be divided into subparts and measured.

Guideposts

What gains in cognitive functioning occur during the stage of concrete operations?

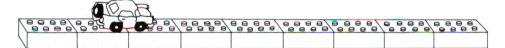

| Figure 10.4 | Through the Child's Eyes |

The first road looks longer than the second road, causing the preschooler to think that it will take the driver of the first car longer than the driver of the second car to get to the end of the road.

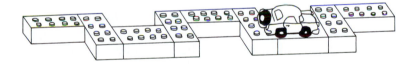

Limitations of Concrete Operational Thought

The cognitive abilities of school-age children still show a number of limitations. For instance, ask 7-year-olds to interpret a proverb such as "You can lead a horse to water, but you can't make it drink." You will be very surprised at the answer. These children may say something about not being able to force an animal to drink, or they may show a puzzled expression, or they may attempt a literal interpretation of the saying. They do not understand the more general, abstract meaning of the saying. Political cartoons require the ability to think in the abstract, and children do not understand them very well. Teachers who are aware of this may attempt to explain difficult concepts, such as democracy, in more concrete terms that children can understand, perhaps through elections in class, rather than trying to define concepts in abstract, dictionary terms.

Children also have difficulty with hypothetical situations or hypotheses that are contrary to fact. Ask a child, "If all dogs were pink and I had a dog, would it be pink, too?" Children often rebel at such statements (Ault, 1977). They insist that dogs are not pink, and that's that. Children in the concrete stage of operations

For Your Consideration ?

Using the material on cognitive advances and limitations during middle childhood, how would you teach a concept such as buoyancy (what floats and what sinks)?

have great difficulty accepting hypothetical situations. In the area of health, children in the concrete operational stage believe germs cause all illness and that to be healthy all you need do is follow some rigid rules.

Information-Processing Skills

Success in elementary school requires the ability to place one's attention on the important aspects of the lesson and remember what is being taught. The elementary school child's information-processing skills are superior to the preschool child's skills.

Attention

Preschoolers' ability to voluntarily place their attention on a relevant stimulus is limited, and they are easily distracted. The ability to pay attention despite interference improves with age, as does their attention span (Dempster, 1992). During middle childhood, children can also switch attention from one task to another more quickly (Bjorklund, 1995; Pearson & Lane, 1991).

Recall, Recognition, and Memory Strategies

Short-term memory improves with age. The typical 5-year-old can recall four or five numbers after a single presentation; a 10-year-old can recall six or seven (Williams & Stith, 1980). Recognition memory is generally good at all ages, but it too shows improvement with age, as does recall. Retention is also superior in both recall and recognition.

Children in middle childhood also begin to use verbal memory strategies on their own. During first and second grade, young children can often use an organizational strategy such as rehearsal when prompted, but they fail to apply the strategies spontaneously when given a memory task (Alexander & Schwanenflugel, 1994). Later in elementary school, they use these strategies on their own and spontaneous rehearsal becomes more common (Flavell et al., 1966, 1993).

As children progress through middle childhood, they also become aware that some strategies are superior to others. Second graders show no preference for categorization over rehearsal, while sixth graders demonstrate a clear preference for more sophisticated strategies, such as categorization (Justice, 1985). Progress in understanding the relative effectiveness of different strategies continues through the elementary school years.

During middle childhood, rates of forgetting decline significantly (Brainerd & Reyna, 1995). Children also process material much faster (Eaton & Ritchot, 1995; Kail, 1991). This increase in speed is partly due to the increasing myelinization of brain systems during childhood and adolescence (Bjorklund & Harnishfeger, 1990).

Metamemory

"After you study the names of the presidents and know them well, come downstairs and I'll test you," said Sean's mother. With that, 8-year-old Sean ran upstairs and studied. A little while later, he was ready. Asked whether he knew the presidents,

Guideposts

How do elementary school children's ability to concentrate and remember material differ from the abilities that preschoolers' show?

Children often do not know what they know and don't know. This problem in metamemory may cause parents to lose patience unnecessarily.

he confidently answered yes. However, it soon became apparent that he knew very few. Sean's mother got angry, and Sean ran upstairs.

This scene is relatively common in many homes. Although it is possible that Sean was pulling a fast one on his mother, it is just as probable that he really thought he knew them. Sean may have a problem with **metamemory,** an individual's knowledge of the memory process (Flavell, 1985).

Just because a child says he or she understands the material does not mean that the child does understand. In fact, academic progress may be related to a child's ability to comprehend his or her own level of understanding. Good students may be those who often say they do not understand, because they are aware of their level of knowledge. Poor students may not really know whether they understand the material. As one author noted, "The problem is not to get students to ask us what they don't know; the problem is to make them aware of the difference between what they know and what they don't" (Holt, 1964, p. 29). Metamemory improves with age, and older children have a more realistic and accurate picture of their own memory abilities and limitations than younger children (Short, Schatschneider, & Friebert, 1993).

A number of factors influence metamemory. Children must understand the directions, have some idea of their own memory abilities, and grasp the nature of the task and the strategies needed to succeed. For example, young children overestimate the number of items they can remember and have difficulty separating the important material from the not-so-important material. They also do not understand the nature of the task. When 6-, 8-, and 10-year-olds were told that they would be tested on their recognition of pictures after a few minutes, a day, or a week, only the older children studied longer when told they would have to remember the material for a longer period of time (Rogoff, Newcombe, & Kagan, 1974). In addition, as children mature, they gain the ability to use different strategies and to understand the situations in which one strategy is more useful than another.

Language Development in Middle Childhood

During middle childhood, children's linguistic abilities improve. Their vocabulary increases significantly throughout the elementary school years. Children's vocabularies increase by 9,000 words between first and third grade and by 20,000 words between third and fifth grade (see Figure 10.5 on page 384). A great deal of this

For Your Consideration

How can metamemory problems lead to difficulties in elementary school?

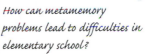

When elementary school children say they understand something, a person can be reasonably certain that they do.

Guideposts

How does metamemory influence learning?

metamemory
A person's knowledge of his or her own memory process.

increase is due to elementary school children's ability to decipher new words they had not heard before because they understand affixes (additions to words as in *sad* + *-ness*, *preach* + *-er*, or *pre* + *-test*). Elementary school children can easily pick up words from the context of the narrative without explicit labeling, which is necessary for it is the only way children encounter new words after the preschool years (Hoff-Ginsburg, 1997). Having a good vocabulary is an advantage in life, and there is a relationship between vocabulary knowledge and reading skills, but the direction of effect is difficult to unravel. The more words children know, the better they can understand what they are reading (Stanovich, 1986). On the other hand, the more children read, the better their vocabulary because they have more exposure to new words. This translates into a policy of encouraging exposure to print as a means of developing better vocabularies.

The elementary school child uses more elaborate phrasing and masters the passive voice, as in *was sad, got lost,* or *was chased.* After 7 years of age, the child understands the adverb suffix *-ly* and verb agreement with irregular nouns, such as "The sheep is eating," improves greatly. The child begins to use past participles, such as *eaten,* and perfect tenses, such as *has been.* These tenses develop slowly, and even though some forms are produced early in this stage, their use may be uneven until later in the period.

The gradual nature of language development typifies this period. For example, the conjunctions *if, so,* and *because* are used much earlier, but their full development does not occur until later in the period. Some forms, such as *although* and *therefore,* may not be used until late elementary school or early adolescence.

Children's ability to add something relevant to a conversation also increases, most significantly between second and fifth grade (Dorval & Eckerman, 1984). This translates into longer conversations (see Figure 10.6). Elementary school children also show an improved ability to tell a story in a coherent way. For example, preschoolers often tell incomplete stories, leaving out important sections. By 6 years, children can tell a single-episode story that includes the setting, place, characters, events, and a resolution. During the elementary school years, beginning

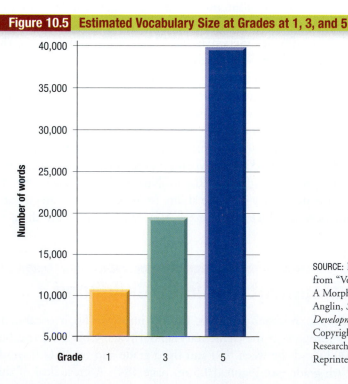

Figure 10.5 Estimated Vocabulary Size at Grades at 1, 3, and 5

SOURCE: Hoff-Ginsberg (1997), from "Vocabulary Development: A Morphological Analysis," by J. M. Anglin, *Society for Research in Child Development,* 58, Serial No. 238. Copyright © 1993 The Society for Research in Child Development, Inc. Reprinted by permission.

at age 8, children can produce more complicated stories with multiple events and talk about the internal motivations and mental states of the characters (Hoff-Ginsberg, 1997).

One communication problem that preschoolers have is their inability to recognize when a message is inadequate or unclear. When children are asked to look at the quality of incomplete messages, young children don't see the message as unclear. This skill improves greatly, especially in the later elementary school years (Hoff-Ginsberg, 1997).

Pragmatically, one of the significant developments, as most parents well know, is the school-age child's ability to use language more subtly. Children's ability to get what they want now improves because children in the middle years of childhood can understand things from other people's point of view. This gives the child the ability to ask for things indirectly, as in "Gee, that cowboy hat looks great." Most parents understand that this is an indirect request. The school-age child can gain attention in a more socially acceptable manner, ask for things giving a reason, and more easily direct the actions of others. The child can now introduce a topic into the conversation, keep the conversation going for a while, and close the conversation less abruptly than can preschoolers.

Guideposts

What linguistic improvements take place in middle childhood?

| **Figure 10.6** | **Developmental Changes and the Percentage of Speaker Turns Occuring in Brief, Medium, and Long Dialogues** |

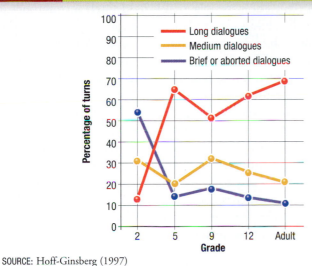

SOURCE: Hoff-Ginsberg (1997)

Children's Humor

Progress in cognitive development and language usage shows itself in many areas of children's lives, including their understanding of humor. Humor serves many purposes. It enhances human relationships, and children with a sense of humor are more popular with their peers (Masten, 1986). Children who have a good sense of humor are viewed by teachers as more attentive, cooperative, responsive and productive. Laughter can also reduce tension. In fact, young children who experience some frightening situation that turns out to be harmless will laugh at it (Smart & Smart, 1978). Humor helps children deal with problems and feelings, such as powerlessness. Children in the middle years of childhood often use adults and teachers as the butt of jokes. Humor may also be used to hide embarrassment or uncertainty. A child may trip and then laugh.

But what makes children laugh? A key to understanding humor is *incongruity*, or the difference between what is expected and what is perceived. Things that do not go together can sometimes be funny. Elementary school children were presented with a series of riddles, each with three answers, and their appreciation of the humor was analyzed (Schultz, 1974). For example:

Why did the cookie cry?
1. Because its mother had been a wafer so long.
2. Because its mother was a wafer.
3. Because it was left in the oven too long.

Answer 1 is incongruous, but it is resolved by interpreting wafer as "away for." Answer 2 is incongruous, but it lacks a resolution, a way of rendering the incongruity understandable within the context of the joke. Answer 3 eliminates incongruity. Younger children appreciated only the incongruity, while the older children found the resolvable answer the most humorous and the other alternatives less humorous. Young children, then, appreciate humor only in incongruity, while older children appreciate humor based on incongruity and resolution (Shultz & Horibe, 1974).

In addition, the incongruity can be too simple or too complex (Chapman & Sheehy, 1987). A moderate amount of incongruity produces the most humor. Too much incongruity, and the joke is difficult to understand; too little, and the joke is too simple (McGhee, 1976). The same joke that is moderately incongruous to a younger child and makes the child roll with laughter is too simple and produces little incongruity in the older child. Understanding jokes and riddles requires some mental effort. If the jokes and riddles do not require any mental effort, they are too obvious and do not cause laughter. If they require too much mental effort, they are too difficult and again fail to cause laughter.

Children's understanding of humor develops along with their cognitive abilities and knowledge base. Children can interpret the joke or riddle only in terms of what they know. A joke about a sailor on a ship only makes sense if the child understands what a sailor and a ship are. The relationship between cognitive abilities and appreciation of humor is easy to demonstrate. Preschoolers do not understand "knock, knock" jokes because these jokes require a knowledge of the double meanings of words that preschoolers simply do not have (Bjorklund, 1995). Children in grades 1, 2, and 5, and also graduate students were tested on jokes that required a knowledge of conservation. For example: "Joey lives near an ice cream store where they give really big scoops of ice cream. One day Joey asked for two scoops, and the man asked if he wanted them in one dish or two. 'Oh, just one dish,' said Joey, 'I could never eat two dishes of ice cream' " (McGhee, 1976, p. 422).

About half the first and second graders could conserve on weight tasks while the other half could not. First and second grade children who could conserve found the jokes funny, while the nonconserving children did not understand the humor. However, although all the fifth graders and adults understood the jokes, they did not find them very funny, because as noted previously, the jokes were too

Children's understanding of a joke depends upon their cognitive abilities.

simple, and they required too little mental effort. For these young first and second graders who had just developed the ability to conserve, the degree of incongruity and the mental effort required was perfect.

In another study, McGhee (1976) initially discovered which first, second and fifth graders could successfully solve class inclusion problems (see page 294). Jokes that required a knowledge of class inclusion were then read to the children. For example:

> *Johnny, Tom, and Alice all go to kindergarten. One day the teacher asked: "Who has the most different kinds of animals at home?" Johnny said "I've got a dog and a cat." Tom said "I've got three, a dog, a cat and a bird." Finally, Alice stood up and said, "I've got you all beat! I've got 81 guppies" (McGhee, 1976, p. 424).*

Again, the children who had just recently acquired the capacity to understand class inclusion found the jokes more humorous than those children who did not understand class inclusion or who had understood class inclusion for years.

There is some dispute as to when humor is first experienced by a child. Some believe that even infants as young as 4 months can understand some forms of humor. They laugh when incongruous events are presented in safe situations (Chapman & Sheehy, 1987). However, the humorous situation is not verbally presented, nor is any symbolism required to comprehend the humor. The capacity to understand humor that requires symbols first appears at between 18 and 24 months, but it is not until after 2 years of age that the child begins to understand some verbal jokes (McGhee, 1979). Some 2-year-olds find it funny when a dog says "meow," and preschoolers find it very funny when someone incorrectly labels something, such as calling a cat "doggie."

Preschoolers may find absurdity very appealing and laugh at a picture of an elephant trying to take a bath in the bathtub. Preschoolers also find rhyming words very funny. Children are active in producing humor through silliness, teasing, and absurdity (Gratch, 1974).

Children in middle childhood have more sophisticated language skills and a greater knowledge base. They are more likely to appreciate humor based on the double meanings of words and phrases. Most 7-year-olds can represent two meanings of a single word simultaneously. Children in middle childhood enjoy plays on words and puns. For example:

> *A man was locked up in a house with a calendar and a bed. How did he stay alive?*
>
> *Answer: He ate dates from the calendar and drank water from the springs on the bed (Williams & Stith, 1980, p. 402)*

School-age children like short jokes with a surprise ending. There is a marked change from early to middle childhood, as surprise and resolution of the joke become as important as incongruity (Shultz, 1974). Children's humor develops beyond very simple jokes as their knowledge base and cognitive abilities, such as conservation and class inclusion, expand. The theme of children's humor changes during middle childhood. Before fourth grade (ages 9 to 10), most jokes are "clean" and involve playing with language (for example, What did the jack say to the car? "Need a lift?"). After that age, especially for boys, more antisocial, impolite comments, or jokes that contain profanity become more common (Socha & Kelly, 1994). This is not to say that girls do not produce antisocial humor, but a greater proportion of boys tell these jokes and produce a greater number of them. In fact, much humor in the middle years of childhood is off-color and deals with taboo

For Your Consideration ?

If you have access to children of different ages, get a book of jokes from the library and see whether the concepts of incongruity, surprise, and resolution are age related.

subjects such as body functions. Children often use humor to express hostility and make older people, especially authority figures, look foolish.

In daily life, humor often occurs in the form of verbal irony—for example, the person who drops his cup of coffee, looks up, and says, "What a great way to start the morning!" Ironic criticism, as when a diving instructor witnessing his student do a belly flop, says, "Yes, that was a great dive," mutes the criticism, making it less harsh. Irony also functions as a type of humor (Dews, Kaplan, & Winner, 1995).

Do children understand irony and appreciate its humor? Children between the ages of 5 and 6 years, 8 and 9 years, and adults were shown film clips from children's television programming that showed irony (Dews et al., 1996). For example:

> *Garfield thought he was safe from an obnoxious companion because the companion is in a different city for the day, only to get a phone call from that person. His companion yells through the phone so loudly that the phone booth in which Garfield is standing explodes. Garfield says, "Great connection." (Dews et al., 1996, p. 3084)*

Subjects were also shown examples of literal criticism, in which the person directly and accurately expresses criticism, and literal compliments, in which the speaker's intention and statement both are complimentary. Few 5-year-old children understood the irony, but many 6-year-olds did. As long as children understood the concept of irony, they considered ironic criticism as less mean. Younger children, though, judge both the literal and ironic criticism as equally funny, while the older children and adults considered the ironic criticism much funnier. By age 8 or 9, the humor function of irony is well understood. Irony is perceived as funny because of the discrepancy between the intended meaning and the literal meaning, and this appreciation increases with age.

Sometimes irony is complicated and involves more than the speaker meaning the opposite of what he says. Sometimes, it is more indirect. For example:

> *Jim and Sally were in the same diving class at summer camp. On the first day, the instructor asked everyone to dive into the lake from the dock. Then he asked everyone to dive off the diving board. Finally, it was Sally's turn. She got onto the board, did a huge belly flop, and splashed into the water. After class, Jim said to Sally:*
>
> *1. You sure are a graceful diver. (direct irony)*
> *2. I guess diving is going to be your favorite class. (indirect irony)*
> *3. You really can't dive very well. (literal criticism)*

The youngest group found direct and indirect irony equally humorous, while the older group of children and adults found indirect irony much funnier. Indirect irony is more subtle, and children who do not grasp the full impact of the statement do not appreciate it. At about 11 or 12 years, some of the more subtle ambiguities of humor are understood.

Children's understanding of humor, then, is associated with developmental changes in their cognitive abilities. The study of children's humor is important in itself, since humor plays a part in interpersonal relations. It also reminds us of the many diverse ways in which cognitive development affects different areas of life.

Children in middle childhood do not understand irony at all.

How does a sense of humor develop in children?

The Elementary School Experience

The ages between 6 and 12 years are dominated by the school experience. Children in elementary school are expected to master the basics of reading, writing, and arithmetic. This mastery is crucial because it forms the basis for later success in school and influences how children see themselves. Erik Erikson viewed the psychosocial crisis of this stage in terms of **industry versus inferiority.** Children who do not measure up to other children in these skills may feel inferior, while children who do well develop a positive sense of achievement.

Reading

Reading is fundamental to school achievement, and learning to read at the appropriate time is crucial to academic success. Failure to learn to read by the end of first grade is associated with later academic failure. When first graders were followed into 11th grade, first grade reading ability strongly predicted 11th grade reading ability, comprehension, vocabulary, and general knowledge, even when intelligence was compensated for statistically (Cunningham & Stanovich, 1997). This does not mean that a poor reader in the second grade cannot be helped, but without special help, children who are behind tend to stay behind. If they receive this help, they can recover. In fact, children who lag in reading in first grade but catch up by third or fifth grade have a good prognosis for future reading achievement.

Unfortunately, students spend relatively little time reading in or out of school (Rothman, 1990). About half the students in grades 4, 8, and 12 report reading ten or fewer pages each day for schoolwork. This is troublesome because the more children read, the better their tested skills. Exposure to print and reading time is related to better reading (Echols, West, Stonovich, & Zehr, 1996). Poor readers read less and often find themselves reading material that is too difficult for them (Cunningham & Stanovich, 1997). This leads to a vicious cycle in which poor reading skills make the activity unrewarding, which leads children to avoid reading, in turn resulting in less practice and poorer skills, and so on.

Although time spent reading is related to reading achievement, about half of all students read ten or fewer pages each day.

Guideposts

Why do good readers improve and poor readers fall further behind?

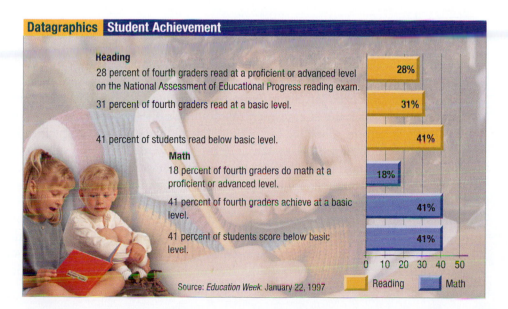

Datagraphics Student Achievement

Reading

28 percent of fourth graders read at a proficient or advanced level on the National Assessment of Educational Progress reading exam. — 28%

31 percent of fourth graders read at a basic level. — 31%

41 percent of students read below basic level. — 41%

Math

18 percent of fourth graders do math at a proficient or advanced level. — 18%

41 percent of fourth graders achieve at a basic level. — 41%

41 percent of students score below basic level. — 41%

0 10 20 30 40 50

Reading   Math

Source: *Education Week,* January 22, 1997

industry versus inferiority

The fourth psychosocial stage, in which the positive outcome is a sense of confidence concerning one's accomplishments and the negative outcome is a sense of inadequacy concerning one's achievements.

Parental involvement is a key to boosting children's reading. Parents who read and show they value the activity influence their children (Madden, 1996). If parents read for enjoyment, children may do the same. In addition, parents can listen to the child read and can encourage reading by providing a wide choice of materials (Carbo & Cole, 1995).

Reading and Television

Both parents and teachers often blame television for children's lack of reading skills. Television, the argument goes, has replaced reading as a leisure activity, thereby reducing reading ability. A negative relationship exists between television viewing and reading, and between television viewing and academic achievement (Johnson, Cooper, & Chance, 1982).

Television has an especially severe adverse effect on reading when the skill is being acquired, during the early years of elementary school (Van Evra, 1990). It may take away valuable practice time. Those who view more television do read less, and the relationship between television and poor reading skills is greatest for those who are heavy viewers (Comstock & Paik, 1991).

Yet, television viewing may not be the cause but a symptom of the problem. Children who find it difficult to read are frustrated and turn to television as an outlet. In addition, television viewing displaces more than just reading; it displaces physical activity and, in fact, any activity that is valued less than television viewing (Huston, Wright, Marquis, & Green, 1999).

It would be a mistake to blame poor reading skills on television viewing. The child's cognitive abilities, the values of the home and school, and the child's attitude toward reading are also important factors that enter the equation. Some excellent readers watch quite a bit of television (Neuman, 1982). Television may be one factor that inhibits reading, but it cannot shoulder the entire blame, which must be shared with the home and the school (Comstock & Paik, 1991). However, restricting television viewing can improve reading, at least in the short term (Gadberry, 1980).

Writing is also an important skill that requires practice. Too often, writing in school is an activity that is not related to anything useful, and the importance of editing is not taught. Modern writing programs emphasize the use of writing as a skill to communicate and teach writing as a process.

Math Skills

Mathematics is another core subject. American students spend less time on and do more poorly in mathematics than do children in many other societies. First and fifth grade students from Japan and Taiwan are superior to elementary school students in the United States in basic mathematical skills (Geary, Salthouse, Chen, & Fan, 1997; Stevenson, Chen, & Lee, 1993). The differences can be explained by the time devoted to these skills as well as by the practice demanded of students.

The picture most people have of learning mathematics is a child sitting at a desk memorizing a multiplication table. Indeed, mathematics does involve some learning by rote, but many experts have criticized this aspect of mathematics instruction, advocating that thinking and the child's approach to problems are more important than merely obtaining the correct answer (Kamii, 1982). The new methods of teaching math recognize the importance of basic math facts and practice but also take into consideration the cognitive level of the child; introduce mathematics on a concrete level; and emphasize thinking, discovery, and problem solving.

For Your Consideration ?

Design a program that might encourage a poor reader to read more. Base each suggestion on some theory discussed in the text.

Guideposts

What is the relationship between viewing television and reading ability?

Guideposts

What changes in teaching math are taking place?

Computer Literacy: The New Basic

Recently, the schools have been asked to teach a new basic skill: **computer literacy**, the skills and knowledge that will allow a person to function successfully in an information-based society (Upchurch & Lochhead, 1987). This involves knowing how to use computers as well as understanding what they can do. Computer literacy can be taught in many ways. Some schools offer minicourses. At other times, elements of computer literacy are integrated into the regular academic classroom.

Computers are used about 1.75 hours per student per week in the average elementary school, mostly as electronic workbooks for practice and drill (Mergendoller, 1997). The promise of using the computer as an educational tool, though, goes beyond these uses. Many elementary schools are connecting to the Web and teaching students to use computer-related materials for project and research purposes. Writing can be furthered by using a "key pals" program so students can write and send E-mail to other students in foreign lands or around the country. Others can use material on the Web to study areas of interest, such as archeology or weather (Foa, Schwab, & Johnson, 1996).

Evaluations have faulted schools for not using technology effectively. Many schools boast that they have computers, but on-site technical support is lacking and professional development is poor (Viadero, 1996b). More time and effort must be spent investigating the best use of such technology (Woronov, 1994). All too often, computers are found only in isolated labs. Teachers have difficulty scheduling classes or find the software available does not meet their educational needs (Whitehead et al., 1994). Teachers must become comfortable with the independent, project-focused, and problem-solving work that may result from the use of computers (Foa et al., 1996).

Not everyone is enamored with the use of computers in schools. Some argue that access to information is being confused with real knowledge and that endless surfing of the Web is not necessarily educational (Conte, 1998). Knowing how to use the computer and understanding how it is used in society are admirable goals in our information-rich environment. However, the technical problems, staff developmental issues, and the best way to integrate the use of computers into the classroom are important concerns that require further study.

▷**Guideposts**

How are computers used in elementary school?

Computer literacy is now considered one of the basic skills a child must learn.

computer literacy

A term used to describe general knowledge about computers that includes some technical knowledge of hardware and software, the ability to use computers to solve problems, and an awareness of how computers affect society.

Rating the Schools

We live in an age of dissatisfaction with schools. A recent Gallup poll found Americans rate the quality of schools as the nation's most pressing problem, ahead of crime, the economy, and health care (Gregory et al., 1996). Yet, parents are not dissatisfied with their local schools. Parents rate the schools in their community superior to the nation's schools. More than half the parents who send their children to a local public school give it an A or a B, while only 16% give those grades to the nation's schools (Rose & Gallup, 1998; Rose, Gallup, & Elam, 1997). Other interesting results of this poll are found in Table 10.3.

Elementary schools have largely escaped the criticisms of the educational system; almost all of the discontent seems directed at the secondary school. Polls consistently find more parental and community support and approval for elementary schools than secondary schools. Half of all elementary school students give their school an A or A- overall rating, but only a third of the secondary school students do so. The parental totals show a similar trend, with more parents rating their neighborhood elementary school higher than their local high school. Many more children rate their elementary school teacher A or A- than secondary school students, and, again, this trend is found for parents as well.

A number of factors may be at work here. Elementary school children stay in one class with one teacher for most of the day; secondary school students have many teachers. It is likely that students and their parents have closer relationships with elementary school teachers. Parents also understand what their children are learning in elementary school but may have more difficulty understanding high school lessons. In addition, the mandate of the elementary school to teach the basics is understandable and clear to the general public; the mandate of the secondary school is somewhat more ambiguous (Bracey, 1996). When elementary schools are criticized, it is most often for failing to address the difficulties of children from minority groups. This is important, for by the year 2025, 50% of all students in public schools will be from minority groups (Jones, 1997).

How are American children doing in elementary school? Generally, American children show reasonably good gains in math and science since 1980 but relatively small gains in reading and writing, especially over the past decade (Frankey, 1995; Gregory et al., 1996; Henry, 1997). The emphasis on higher standards and accountability may be the cause of these improvements (Ashford, 1997). Yet, many students are not doing well; for example, more than a third of all students in math and about a third in science have less than a basic knowledge of these subjects (Lawton, 1997).

One problem in evaluating how students are doing is that the same test results can be interpreted differently. For example, the Third International Math and Science study found that American fourth graders outperformed all but Korean and Japanese students in science and were outperformed by 7 of the 26 countries in math (Henry, 1997b). *USA Today*'s headline announced "U.S. Fourth-Graders Score Well in International Math, Science Study," with a banner headline stating "U.S. Students Reaching for World-Class Stature" (Henry, 1997b). The American Psychological Association's newspaper stated, "America Still Lags Behind in Mathematics Test Scores" (Murray, 1997, p. 44).

Many African American and Latino children do not achieve as well as would be desirable. The gaps between various racial and ethnic groups have narrowed, though (Sommerfeld, 1996). Between a third and a half of the gap in achievement between African Americans and white Americans was closed between the 1970s

Table 10.3 Rating Public Schools

Students are often given the grades A, B, C, D, and FAIL to denote the quality of their work. Suppose the public schools themselves, in this community, were graded in the same way. What grade would you give the public schools here—A, B, C, D, or FAIL?

	National Totals		No Children in School		Public School Parents		Nonpublic School Parents	
	'98 %	'97 %	'98 %	'97 %	'98 %	'97 %	'98 %	'97 %
A & B	46	46	43	42	52	56	39	26
A	10	10	8	8	15	15	8	9
B	36	35	35	34	37	41	31	17
C	31	32	31	33	33	30	24	35
D	9	11	9	11	9	10	16	21
FAIL	5	6	5	7	4	3	7	13
Don't know	9	5	12	7	2	1	14	5

How about the public schools in the nation as a whole? What grade would you give the public schools nationally—A, B, C, D, or FAIL?

	National Totals		No Children in School		Public School Parents		Nonpublic School Parents	
	'98 %	'97 %	'98 %	'97 %	'98 %	'97 %	'98 %	'97 %
A & B	18	22	19	23	16	23	12	24
A	1	2	*	3	2	2	4	2
B	17	20	19	20	14	21	8	22
C	49	48	48	49	52	46	52	38
D	15	15	15	15	13	16	19	15
FAIL	5	6	6	6	4	4	7	6
Don't know	13	9	12	7	15	11	10	17

What do you think are the biggest problems with which the public schools in this community must deal?

	National Totals		No Children in School		Public School Parents		Nonpublic School Parents	
	'98 %	'97 %	'98 %	'97 %	'98 %	'97 %	'98 %	'97 %
Fighting/violence/gangs	15	12	14	12	20	12	10	16
Lack of discipline/more control	14	15	15	15	9	12	29	22
Lack of financial support/funding/money	12	15	13	15	11	14	2	4
Use of drugs/dope	10	14	10	14	12	14	8	9
Overcrowded schools	8	8	5	6	11	10	22	17
Concern about standards/quality of education	6	8	6	7	5	8	9	10
Difficulty getting good teachers/quality teachers	5	3	6	3	4	4	*	*
Pupils' lack of interest/poor attitudes/truancy	5	6	4	6	5	6	15	3
None	3	2	2	2	5	3	7	*
Don't know	16	10	19	13	10	6	8	4

NOTE: *Less than one-half of 1%.
SOURCE: Rose & Gallup (1998)

and 1980s, but the progress has recently slowed (U.S. Department of Education, 1993b). Unfortunately, so much emphasis has been placed on the underachievement of African American children that it has led to a stereotype of these children as underachievers (Slaughter-Defoe, Nakagawa, Takanishi, & Johnson, 1990). This is unfair, as many children from minority group backgrounds do succeed.

Much of the problem concerning the academic achievement of minority students is directly related to poverty and all the factors that go with poverty, including poor housing, greater exposure to violence, lower parental education, poor access to health care, and lack of family stability (Ford & Harris, 1996). Academically successful African American elementary school students come from supportive home environments, smaller families, families that are above the poverty line, and those with mothers who are more intelligent and relatively better educated (Luster & McAdoo, 1996). The opposite is true for those who are not achieving.

A similar situation exists among some Latino children. Proficiency in reading, math, and science have improved but a significant gap remains (U.S. Department of Education 1995b). Much of the problem that Latinos experience in achievement relates to poverty as well, but other problems also exist, the most important one being language (Duran, 1989).

The elementary school has changed over the years and will continue to do so, but more quietly and more gradually than the high school. Formal recitations are gone and discipline is not as strict. It is a more pleasant place. Newer methods of learning including cooperative learning (in which students work as a team), experiential learning, projects, and exhibitions are more common (Darling-Hammond, 1994). Parental involvement is also being emphasized and such cooperation can be effective (Whitehurst et al., 1994). There is an increasing emphasis on assuring that children are ready for school and on easing the transition from preschool to elementary school (see Table 10.4 for some suggestions) (Fleck, 1995).

Guideposts

How are children achieving in elementary school?

Success in School

The general achievement of any student in elementary school depends on a number of factors, including the nature of the school experience, the child's home, and the student's personal characteristics.

The School Experience

Each school has its own atmosphere, its own feeling. Some schools are orderly; others have a carnival atmosphere. Some schools are doing a better job than others. Such factors as a safe and orderly environment, an understanding of the goals of the school, administrative leadership, a climate of high expectations, allocation of time to instruction in the basic skills, and frequent monitoring of student progress have been suggested as ones that differentiate schools that are more successful from those that are less successful (Lezotte, 1982). A good relationship between the home and the school is also important. Especially in the early grades, and in schools where students require remedial work, smaller classes are an advantage (Rutter, 1983). One suggestion for improving achievement is to lengthen the number of days children spend in school from the usual 180 to 220. This would naturally increase the amount of time spent in school learning basic skills. It would

Table 10.4 | **Suggestions for Easing the Transition between Home and School**

The first day of school is an important milestone in the life of both parents and child. Parents play an important role in helping to prepare their young children and giving them the self-confidence necessary to negotiate the new environment. Here are some suggestions for doing so:

1. Recognize that the first day of school is an important event.	For some children, this is the first real separation from parents, while for others with extensive nursery school experience it may not be. Nevertheless, it is a new environment. Young children need support and encouragement.
2. Remember that learning to like school and liking to learn are related.	The child begins to form an attitude toward school from the first day, and parents must show positive attitudes toward learning and schooling.
3. Explain to the child what to expect and answer questions honestly.	Children often want to know how long school will be and how they will get there and back. Answering these practical questions helps a child prepare for the day.
4. Allow the child to visit the kindergarten if possible.	Some school districts have a day set aside to allow next year's class to visit a kindergarten and perhaps even meet their teachers during the spring before they enter the class.
5. Create a normal routine atmosphere in the home.	It is important to create a routine during the first few days of school—for example, getting up at a certain time, eating breakfast, following a routine when the child arrives home after school, and the like. This gives the child a sense of security.
6. Show an interest in the child's day.	Children often are excited about what is going on in school and want to share it with parents. The attention paid to the child's day shows just how important parents consider the school experience.
7. Give the child a chance to play at home.	After spending a great deal of time in a structured atmosphere, the child needs free time to play.
8. Accent the positive.	It is best to praise children when they have done something positive. Too often, parents and teachers focus on the negative.
9. Treat going to school as a normal part of the day.	School attendance is something to be expected. If the child shows anxiety, try to find out why and offer gentle encouragement.
10. Help the child with the frustrations and disappointments that occur every so often.	Every now and then, something will not turn out the way the child would like. The child needs to learn to cope with these little disappointments. It is important to acknowledge the child's feelings and neither belittle nor exaggerate what has transpired.
11. Avoid comparisons between children.	Any comparisons can be harmful and set up a competitive situation that is not in the best interest of either of the children.
12. Get to know the teacher and participate in school activities.	A good relationship and good communication between parent and teacher helps keep parents aware of what is going on in class and how the child is doing. Becoming involved in school-related activities, such as the Parent-Teacher Association and volunteering when possible, reflects the parents' interest level and seriousness about the child's education.

SOURCE: Adapted partially from USDHHS (1985)

also prevent some of the forgetting that occurs during the long summer vacations, which would be somewhat shorter under this system. Kindergartners who attended a traditional school were matched on background characteristics and compared with students attending an extended-year program (Frazier & Morrison, 1998). The results showed those attending for the longer school year outperformed traditional students in reading and general knowledge, and this improvement was not due to differences in the quality or intensity of the educational program (see Figure 10.7 on page 396).

Everyone knows that some teachers do a better job than others, but it is difficult to discover just what qualities are common to superior teachers. In fact, no single pattern predominates (Centra & Potter, 1980). To be effective today,

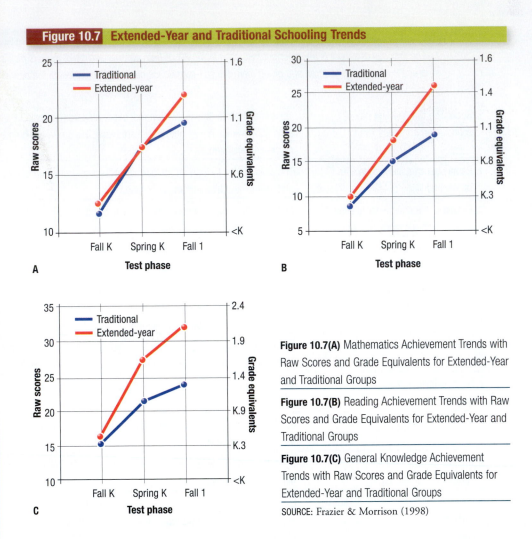

Figure 10.7 **Extended-Year and Traditional Schooling Trends**

Figure 10.7(A) Mathematics Achievement Trends with Raw Scores and Grade Equivalents for Extended-Year and Traditional Groups

Figure 10.7(B) Reading Achievement Trends with Raw Scores and Grade Equivalents for Extended-Year and Traditional Groups

Figure 10.7(C) General Knowledge Achievement Trends with Raw Scores and Grade Equivalents for Extended-Year and Traditional Groups

SOURCE: Frazier & Morrison (1998)

teachers must be aware of the culture and background of the children they teach. For example, a teacher in a rural community is teaching students how to tell time. After telling them when the big hand is on the 12 and the little hand is on the 10, it is 10 o'clock, she asks the students what time is showing on the clock. Many white children raise their hands but no African American children. She incorrectly concludes that her African American children do not understand. However, whereas the white children most probably grew up in families in which children were routinely quizzed about colors and shapes, in some African American families, questions are posed only when someone really needs the information. Parents don't hold up a picture and say, "What color is this?" and children are not asked for information that the person already knows. The African American children may be asking themselves, "What is she asking us for, since she just told us the time?" (Viadero, 1996).

The Home

Children who live in poverty do not do as well as their age mates who are more advantaged. Poverty is negatively related to academic achievement across all racial and ethnic groups (Duncan, Brooks-Gunn, & Klebanov, 1994; Greenberg et al., 1999). Children from poor families live in crowded conditions, have poorer health care, are not exposed to such middle-class experiences as trips and books, have lower career aspirations, and may not know how to succeed in public school (Kaplan, 1990). Children from lower socioeconomic backgrounds generally come to school less advanced cognitively. These conditions may lead to failure, and a vicious cycle can ensue: failure leads to lack of interest and motivation, which leads to more failure.

Although socioeconomic status is correlated with achievement, it can explain only about 5% of the final results in academic achievement. Many parents living in poverty do help their children achieve, and concentrating on these home variables, which might be easier to change, might be valuable. Children from low-income homes that are unstable and stressful are more likely to have difficulty in school than those whose homes are stable (Ackerman, Kogos, Youngstrom, Schoff, & Izard, 1999). No matter what the socioeconomic level of the family, homes in which children are intellectually stimulated produce children with higher intrinsic motivation (that is, they enjoy learning) and these children learn more (Gottfried, Fleming, & Gottfried, 1998). Some measures of intellectual stimulation for elementary school students are found in Table 10.5.

At the same time, certain social behaviors lead to better achievement. Parents who are involved yet not overcontrolling and who exercise moderate levels of supervision rather than very high or low levels are likely to have children who are

Guideposts

What school- and home-related factors lead to superior achievement?

Table 10.5 Cognitively Stimulating Home Environment Variables

Instruments and Items

Home Observation for the Measurement of the Environment

Family has a television, and it is used judiciously, not left on continuously.

Family encourages child to develop or sustain hobbies.

Child is regularly included in family's recreational hobby.

Family provides lessons or organizational membership to support child's talents.

Child has ready access to at least two pieces of playground equipment in immediate vicinity.

Child has ready access to a library card, and family arranges for child to go to library once a month.

Family member has taken child or arranged for child to go to a scientific, historical, or art museum within the past year.

Family member has taken child or arranged for child to take a trip on a plane, train, or bus within the past year.

Home Environment Survey

Does your child have access to a real musical instrument?

Does your child have his/her own subscription to a magazine or book club?

Is your child receiving private lessons?

How many different magazines or journals does your family receive at home each month?

Is there a personal computer at home that the child has had experience working with?

How much education do you expect your child to achieve?

Family Environment Scale

We often talk about political and social problems.

We rarely go to lectures, plays, or concerts.

Learning about new and different things is very important in our family.

We are not that interested in cultural activities.

We rarely have intellectual discussions.

Someone in our family plays a musical instrument.

Family members often go to the library.

Watching TV is more important than reading on our family.

Family members really like music, art, and literature.

SOURCE: Gottfried et al. (1998)

To Change Teachers or Not to Change: That Is the Question.

Mr. And Mrs. D. have a problem, but they don't know with whom. Their third grade son, Mark, does not like his teacher. He claims that the teacher yells at the class, does not call on him when he knows the answer, and is always criticizing him. Mark's parents had a conference with the teacher who frankly told them that Mark's attitude and work was poor. She showed them some of his written work, which showed little effort and was rife with careless mistakes. The teacher seemed pleasant enough and suggested that Mr. and Mrs. D. work with Mark to produce a better product. She also told them that Mark sometimes talks back and whenever she asked Mark to stop talking, he counters with "I'm not talking."

The next day they spoke to Mark, asking him about his work and conduct. He told them that he didn't talk back and claimed that she always picks on him whenever anyone does anything wrong. He wants to change classes. Mark accused them of taking the teacher's side and believing her over him.

The principal does not like to change students' classes. She claims that this opens up all types of problems with children wanting to change to be with friends or because one teacher gives more work. She believes Mark's teacher is demanding but fair.

Mr. and Mrs. D. don't know what to do. On the one hand, Mark must learn to get along with his teachers, but on the other hand he doesn't seem to be actively engaged in learning. He liked his first grade teacher and tolerated his second grade teacher. They are not certain what the best course would be.

If you were Mark's parents, what would you do?

ACTION / REACTION

Many American families provide a stimulating atmosphere for their preschoolers but become uninvolved in their children's elementary school education. Parental involvement is one of the keys to academic achievement.

higher achievers (Ginsburg & Bronstein, 1993; Kurdek, Fine, & Sinclair, 1995). Such activities as praising children for their successes, stating expectations in a non-challenging manner, acknowledging children's feelings and needs, and providing choices and alternatives, are positively related to achievement (Ginsburg & Bronstein, 1993; Levitt, Guacci-Franco, & Levitt, 1994). Parents who read to their children, help them with homework, take them to the library, and expand on their language are giving their children a boost. Since we know these home variables predict academic achievement, parents can be educated to change the way they interact with their children. By concentrating on home environment instead of socioeconomic status, we turn the attention away from a particular group and toward particular parent-child relationships, home variables, and child-rearing strategies. Socioeconomic status may mask truly important home variables that are good predictors of academic achievement.

Unfortunately, many parents become less involved with their children's cognitive development when they enter elementary school. American children often enter school with more knowledge and motivation than Asian children in Japan and China, but soon Japanese and Chinese students are achieving more. Many American families provide a stimulating atmosphere for their preschoolers, including reading to them and taking them to museums and on outings. When

American children enter elementary school, however, parents often seem to believe that it is solely the school's job to educate the child (Rothman, 1991). This attitude hinders the achievement of American children.

Parents are aware of the importance of being involved, and 87% of all parents with elementary school children believe it is "extremely" or "very important" to be involved in school work, according to a recent survey. Parents, however, rate themselves only a C+ when it comes to actually being involved. Children are keenly aware of how involved parents are in their education and value their parents' time and effort (Hellmich, 1995).

Attitudes, Motivation, and Work Habits

Highly motivated students with positive attitudes toward school do better than children who dislike learning and school and don't care how they do. Also, children who know how to study and how to take tests are likely to do better than those who don't. Work habits and study skills can be taught. Students who know how to use their time effectively, pay attention to the lessons, and involve themselves in classroom activities also do better (Alexander, Entwisle, & Dauber, 1993). Both cognitive and motivational variables together predict success (Kreitler, Zigler, Kagan, Weissler, & Kretler, 1995).

Intelligence

Of all the factors that contribute to academic achievement, none is more controversial than intelligence. **Intelligence** has been defined as the ability to profit from one's experiences, a cluster of cognitive abilities, the ability to do well in school, and whatever an intelligence test measures (Kaplan, 1990). A more applied definition views intelligence as "an ability to solve problems or to fashion a product which is valued in one or more cultural settings" (Gardner, 1987, p. 25). Piaget viewed intelligence not as a "thing" but rather as an ongoing process by which children use qualitatively different ways to adapt to their environment.

Most people see intelligence in terms of those skills which relate to academic achievement. One of the more popular and newer conceptions of intelligence is called the **Theory of Multiple Intelligences** (Gardner, 1983, 1987a, 1987b). Gardner argues that seven different types of intelligence exist, including linguistic, logical-mathematical, musical, spatial, bodily kinesthetic, interpersonal (social skills), and intrapersonal (the understanding of one's own feelings) (see Figure 10.8 on page 400). Schools that have adopted this definition focus on developing children's abilities in all these areas, and one type of intelligence is not necessarily considered superior to any other type (Murray, 1996).

Clearly, the definition one uses affects the way intelligence tests will be constructed. Most intelligence tests are targeted at school-age populations. A high correlation exists between school achievement and performance on intelligence tests (about .6), and an even higher one between scores on standardized achievement tests and those on intelligence tests (between .7 and .9) (Kubiszyn & Borich, 1987). That is, children who score very high are likely to do better in school. Intelligence tests, then, have predictive power in the area of school success, and children who score very low may have

T **F** **7**
American children start elementary school with more knowledge than Japanese and Chinese students but soon fall behind children from these countries.

intelligence
The ability to profit from experience; a cluster of abilities, such as reasoning and memory. The ability to solve problems or fashion a product valued in one's society.

theory of multiple intelligences
A conception of intelligence advanced by Howard Gardner, who argues that there are seven different types of intelligence.

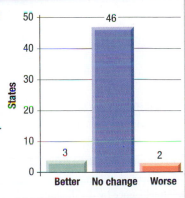

Trends in Development

Parental Involvement in Schools: Principals' Perspective
Since 1991, have states and the District of Columbia reduced the percentage of public school principals reporting that lack of parental involvement in their school is a serious problem?

Source: National Education Goals Panel (1998).

Figure 10.8 **Gardner's Conception of Intelligence**

Linguistic

Language skills include a sensitivity to the subtle shades of the meaning of words.

Logical-Mathematical

Both critics and supporters acknowledge that IQ tests measure this ability well.

Musical

Like Language, music is an expressive medium—and this talent flourishes in prodigies.

Spatial

Sculptors and painters are able to accurately perceive, manipulate, and recreate forms.

Bodily-kinesthetic

At the core of this kind of intelligence are body control and skilled handling of objects

Interpersonal

Skill in reading the moods and intentions of others is displayed by politicians, among others.

Intrapersonal

The key is understanding one's own feelings—and using that insight to guide behavior.

SOURCE: From "7 Ways to Be Bright," *U.S. News and World Report.* Copyright © November 23, 1987, U.S. News and World Report.

difficulty in school (Brody, 1995). However, notice that the correlation is not perfect, meaning that other factors, including motivation, background, and work habits, affect how a child performs in school.

The Stanford-Binet and Wechsler Tests   In the early 1900s, Alfred Binet created a test to identify students who could not benefit from traditional education. He used a series of tests that measured a sample of children's abilities at different age levels. At each level, some children performed better than others. Binet simply compared children's performances on these tests with those of others in the age group. If a child had less knowledge than the average child of the same age, that child was said to be less intelligent; if the child knew more, the child's intelligence was said to be higher. Binet used the term **mental age** to describe the age at which the child was functioning. A child's **intelligence quotient,** or IQ, is arrived at by taking the mental age of the child, dividing it by the child's chronological age (age since birth), and then multiplying by 100 to remove the decimal. The problem with the IQ is that it assumes a straight-line (linear) relationship between age and intelligence. This is not the case, especially after age 16. The original Binet test has gone through a number of revisions and today is called the Stanford-Binet Intelligence Test.

mental age

The age at which an individual is functioning.

intelligence quotient (IQ)

A method of computing intelligence by dividing the mental age by the chronological age and multiplying by 100.

In the late 1930s, David Wechsler began developing another set of individualized intelligence tests. The Wechsler Intelligence Scale for Children (WISC; third edition) contains a number of subtests that can be divided into two categories: verbal and performance. The verbal subtests measure verbal skills such as information and similarities, while the performance subtests measure nonverbal skills such as completing pictures and putting together puzzle pieces (Wechsler, 1991). A composite, or total, intelligence score may also be obtained.

Today, a statistically sophisticated way of calculating the intelligence score, called a *deviation IQ*, is used. This involves a comparison of a child's performance with the average performance of a large group of children of the same age. The average is still 100. If every 8-year-old child in the United States were to receive an intelligence test, most scores would cluster around the middle, with fewer scores being found on each extreme. Scores closer to the average are much more common that those further way. Over two-thirds of all children have intelligence scores between 85 and 115, and very few—less than 3%—have scores above 130 or below 70. There are far fewer people with very low or very high intelligence scores than people of average intelligence.

The Wechsler Intelligence Scale for Children includes subtests that measure verbal and performance abilities. This block design task is one of the performance subtests.

How Intelligence Tests Can Be Misused   In recent years, much controversy has arisen over the use of intelligence tests (Laosa, 1996). Some criticism has been directed at the possible cultural bias against minorities (Hickson, Blackson, & Reis, 1995). In 1971, a group of parents of African American children who were placed in classes for children with mental retardation sued in federal court, claiming that the placements were discriminatory because they were based on intelligence tests that were culturally biased. Eight years later, the court ruled that IQ tests were culturally biased. This famous decision, *Larry P. v. Riles*, meant that intelligence tests could no longer be used as the sole basis for placing children in special classes (Rothstein, 1995).

Opponents of the use of intelligence tests often emphasize the negative social outcomes of testing, such as the overrepresentation of students from minority groups in special education. They argue that analyzing the consequences of test usage is as serious a concern as whether the tests are technically fair (Laosa, 1996). Children from minority groups may be unfairly stigmatized as less intelligent. Others point to the different experiences of minority group children. On an older version of a standardized intelligence test, a child is asked, "What would you do if you were sent to buy a loaf of bread and the grocer said he did not have any more?" Professionals constructing the test thought the answer "Go to another store" was reasonable, and it certainly is. Yet, more than a quarter of all children from minority groups said they would go home—a seemingly incorrect answer. When asked why they answered this way, the children simply told investigators there were no other stores in the neighborhood (Hardy, Welcher, Mellits, & Kagan, 1976).

Many such examples show that minority group students may have different experiences that can affect the way they answer questions on intelligence tests. This leads some psychologists to argue that IQ tests discriminate against test takers who don't fit into the white middle-class profile. (On some intelligence tests, a child may be asked to explain the answer and be given credit if the answer is logical).

Vocabulary, too, can cause difficulties because some words and phrases may be inappropriate for children for whom English is not the primary language (Kaplan, 1996). In addition, children from the majority culture may be very comfortable with the testing setting, the format of the test and the types of questions asked. Children from various minority group cultures may not be as comfortable (Duran, 1989).

Another problem is the interpretation of intelligence as if it were a fixed quality etched in stone. As we have noted many times, it is not. Intelligence can change with one's experience. Finally, although scores on an intelligence test correlate with academic achievement, there is a tendency to overrate the test's predictive abilities and to rigidly categorize children (Kaplan, 1977). For example, one of my acquaintances was shocked when her child's fifth grade teacher told her that her son was doing fine, considering he had an IQ of "only" 105. If intelligence test scores are used in such a manner, the child can truly suffer.

Proponents of testing argue that the problem with intelligence tests is the way they are used, not their construction or what they indicate. They do predict, albeit not perfectly, academic success across ethnic groups (U.S. Department of Education, 1993a). If some children from both minority and dominant groups do not score well, intelligence tests would then predict poor achievement (which is too often the case) (Hunt, 1995). Criticizing the messenger (the test) is not helpful. Intelligence tests scores do not indicate the cause of the difference in intelligence between groups of children, just that one exists. Recently, studies report that poverty and home environment explain the overwhelming majority of this difference. In fact, when poverty and home environmental variables are controlled, differences between African American and white children on intelligence tests are narrowed considerably and all but eliminated (Brooks-Gunn, Klebanov, & Duncan, 1996).

A major problem, a proponent of testing would argue, lies in the definition of intelligence used by the general public and some educators. The type of intelligence measured by intelligence tests relates to academic skills, but not what many people often regard as intelligence, such as "common sense" or being able to solve problems in the community or life. It does not really measure adaptation to life or interpersonal skills. This point is readily admitted even by those who prepare intelligence tests (Wechsler, 1991). In fact, some argue that intelligence tests may be related to success in school, but emotional intelligence—which includes delaying gratification, persistence, and other personal and emotional qualities—is a better predictor of success in life after school. They argue that the school should pay more attention to these areas (Goleman, 1995).

If people would realize that these tests measure particular skills related to school achievement and understand that they are not global measures of functioning, these tests would be appreciated for what they are. These tests do not measure overall learning potential in every area but do predict how well the child will do in the schools as they are now constructed (U.S. Department of Education 1993a). A child's low score on a test would translate into a lack of particular skills necessary to negotiate schools the way they are now structured. Low scores indicate a need for action rather than an indictment of the child.

Properly used, the tests would then become sources of diagnostic help for the teacher. Test scores would only be considered part of an assessment and other sources of information would be used to obtain a more complete picture of the child's functioning. No standardized test can provide such a picture.

In an attempt to free standardized tests of any bias, culture-fair tests have been formulated that depend less on language abilities and speed of responding and eliminate items that reflect differential cultural or social experiences. Such tests use matching, picture completion, copying, block designs, analogies, spatial relations, and ability to see relations between patterns (Brown, 1983). But a perfect culture-free test has yet to be invented, and some argue that culture-fair tests are impossible (Cahan & Cohen, 1989). Even if such a test is formulated, it is questionable whether it will predict school performance as well as our present standardized tests.

Boys, Girls, and the School Experience

Even though no gender differences exist in intelligence, girls perform better than boys on measures of reading, verbal fluency, spelling, and mathematical computation, while boys are superior in mathematics reasoning and problems involving spatial analysis (Halpern, 1986; Marshall & Smith, 1987). A great deal of overlap occurs, with some girls performing better than boys in mathematics and some boys reading better than girls. Boys believe they are more competent in math and science, while girls believe that they are more competent in reading even in first grade before they have had much experience in school (Eccles, 1993). Girls also spend more time in academic activities (Posner & Vandell, 1999). Females are also less likely to repeat grades, and they show higher writing proficiency in elementary school (U.S. Department of Education, 1995a). Yet, as children negotiate elementary school, boys remain confident in their abilities and often overestimate them, while girls show an increasing tendency to underestimate their academic competence (Cole, Martin, Peeke, Seroczynski, & Fier, 1999). This may have an impact on achievement as these children enter secondary school.

Girls may have an advantage over boys in elementary school. The atmosphere of elementary school is feminine, with its great percentage of female teachers and its emphasis on obedience and activities that require fine-motor coordination. Boys and girls experience school in different ways, and both male and female teachers value the stereotyped feminine traits of obedience and passivity rather than aggressiveness and independence (Etaugh & Hughes, 1975).

Teachers interact with boys and girls differently. A study by the American Association of University Women (1992) found widespread discrimination by teachers and in texts and tests. Teachers pay less attention to girls, and some tests remain biased against girls or stereotype or ignore women. Even though girls get better grades, they are still shortchanged. When teachers were observed over a 3-year period, teachers called on boys more often than girls, offered boys more detailed and constructive criticisms, and allowed boys to shout out answers but reprimanded girls for this practice (Sadker & Sadker, 1985). When children demand attention, teachers respond to boys with instructions and girls with nurturance (Beal, 1994). Girls are frequently told they are right or wrong and given the correct answers. These differences are not deliberate, and even female teachers show these patterns (Kerr 1991).

Not everyone agrees with the conclusion that girls are shortchanged. Some authorities question the quality of some of the research reviewed, noting that some research findings run contrary to these assertions and that the strides in educational achievement made by women are often disregarded (Schmidt, 1994).

One area of increasing importance is opening up technology to girls. The media often depicts males as experts in technology, and teachers often direct questions about technical material to boys. Computers are more likely to be found in the boy's bedroom than the girl's bedroom or in a common area, so fewer girls are familiar with the computer (Koch, 1994). Female students do not attend the computer room during lunch as often as males do. No one actively stops them from attending, but they do not come because some girls believe that computers and

For Your Consideration ?

In your opinion, are girls shortchanged in elementary school?

math are not their domain. They must be encouraged to come to the computer room if they are to be familiar with computers (Sadker & Sadker, 1994). Girls are somewhat more ambivalent about technology, although about an equal number of males and females use the Web. Women often see computers in terms of aiding communication, while boys see it in terms of technical problem solving (Brunner & Bennett, 1998).

Bilingual Children in School

Many children today live in homes in which more than one language is used. In some of these homes, English is used very sparingly. English is the second language for these children, and their success in the United States depends partly on learning English.

Knowing more than one language can be a great advantage. Bilingual children score higher in verbal and nonverbal intelligence scores and show more cognitive flexibility compared with their monolingual peers (Segalowitz, 1981). These children also enjoy advantages in concept formation and creativity (Padilla et al., 1991). These advantages are found when children show competence in both languages (Winsler, Diaz, Espinoza, & Rodriguez, 1999).

Many bilingual children, though, do not do well in school. Most bilingual students are raised in poverty, and many come from immigrant families. The difficulties encountered by bilingual students are not due to their bilingualism but to poverty and the clash of cultures (Diaz, 1985). In addition, many bilingual children actually have a poor knowledge of their primary language (Crawford, 1987). That is, their grammar and vocabulary are poor. Bilingual students often are not given an opportunity to continue to study their native language, so they do not improve usage and vocabulary in it.

Everyone agrees that all children in the United States need to learn Standard English. If children leave school knowing mathematics, science, and social studies but functioning poorly in such language-related areas as reading, writing, and speaking, their prospects for educational advancement and jobs will be poor. Many programs have been instituted to teach English to children whose primary language is something other than English (see *Bilingual Programs: Are They Needed? Do They Work?* on pages 405–406).

8

Most bilingual children in the United States live in poverty.

How does being bilingual affect cognitive performance?

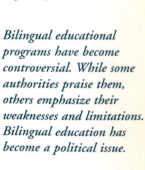

How do the experiences of boys and girls differ in elementary school?

Bilingual educational programs have become controversial. While some authorities praise them, others emphasize their weaknesses and limitations. Bilingual education has become a political issue.

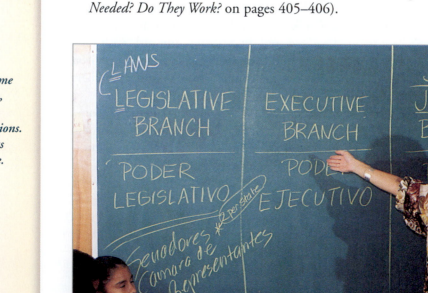

The Child in the 21st Century

Bilingual Programs: Are They Needed? Do They Work?

The number of children in the United States whose first language is not English is expected to continue growing into the 21st century. About 3.2 million limited English-proficient children (LEP) attend American public schools (Schnaiberg, 1997). Nine of ten LEP elementary school students come from impoverished backgrounds (U.S. Department of Education, 1993b). Their success in climbing out of poverty depends on their academic achievement and partly on learning Standard English, but what is the best way to teach English to children whose native language is something other than English?

Many people do not understand the differences between the experience immigrant groups face now and what immigrants faced at the beginning of the 20th century. Although discrimination has always existed, the need for advanced education and training has not. Fifty years ago, an advanced education was not required, and the importance of academic advancement could be minimized. We could afford to wait generations for a family's education and language abilities to develop to the extent that they could succeed in advanced training or higher education.

Today, we do not have this luxury. Most jobs that provide a reasonable standard of living require education. We now look at children entering schools with poor English skills, and our goal is not just to teach them basic English but to help them gain the necessary academic skills to succeed in high school and

perhaps beyond. Every child who spends a great deal of time in the United States will eventually learn enough English to function in the community. However, the type of English used in advanced schooling differs. It is more abstract, technically more exacting, and uses a higher level vocabulary. A child learns the type of social English necessary for conversation within three years, but the more academic school-related language takes much longer, between five and seven years (U.S. Department of Education, 1993b). It is only recently that educators have been asked to accomplish this feat and teach advanced language skills, not in a matter of generations, but in a relatively few years.

How can this be accomplished? A number of new approaches are being tried in communities across the country. Generally, these programs can be viewed as a continuum between the active encouragement and use of the primary language on one side, sometimes called *native language emphasis*, and the increased focus on English called *sheltered English* or *structured immersion* on the other (Gerstein & Woodward, 1994).

Some educators propose that a bilingual program be introduced in the school and that subjects such as math and social studies be taught to Spanish-speaking students in Spanish until the children gain sufficient ability in English to function effectively in English. At the same time, these children would receive instruction in Standard English. Advocates of such an approach, such as Jim Cummins (1989), argue that the use of the native language empowers these students and reinforces their cultural

identity. He argues that when children learn to read in Spanish they do not have to learn to read all over again. They transfer what they have learned. Under this system, students are encouraged to use their native language around the school, signs are provided in different languages, people who can tutor in the native language are recruited, books in the native language are read, and writing in the student's native language assigned.

The structured immersion or sheltered English approach assumes that proficiency in English can be best attained through well-designed content instruction that uses English, but at a level that is constantly modified and expanded as the child's abilities increase. Teachers control their classroom vocabulary, use concrete objects and gestures to enhance understanding, and use many instructional strategies so students understand the academic material. In some cases, students receive native language instruction for 30 to 90 minutes a day at school, but English is used the majority of the teaching day.

Students in such programs learn English while they are developing basic academic abilities and skills. This is the approach used successfully in Quebec, Canada with English-speaking students, with Southeast Asian immigrants in elementary school, and, to a somewhat more limited but increasing extent, with Latino youth at the secondary level (Gerstein & Woodward, 1994). Other approaches, such as two-way programs, also exist. In these programs, part of the day both English- and Spanish speaking children are taught in English, while at other times of the day, both groups of

The Child in the 21st Century

Bilingual Programs: Are They Needed? Do They Work? *continued*

children are taught in Spanish. During the Spanish-speaking part of the day, Spanish-speaking students explain lessons to their English-speaking peers; during the English part, of the day the roles are reversed. This peer tutoring encourages students to depend on each other, respect each other, and communicate. Unlike traditional bilingual programs, two way programs don't segregate students (Donegan, 1996).

Research to date has not generally shown much difference in the achievement between children taught with either emphasis (Ramirez, 1992). A New York City study found that students in English as a Second Language programs (ESL) who spent most of their time learning English fared better than those in bilingual programs (New York City Board of Education, 1994), but its methodology has been criticized. Some evidence shows that bilingual programs have helped students achieve scholastically (Crawford, 1987; Willig, 1985), while other studies show the opposite (Porter, 1990; Schnaiberg, 1997).

Bilingual education has become a political issue, with some state initiatives to curb bilingual programs being sent to voters (Schnaiberg, 1998). Questions about the nature and effectiveness of bilingual programs are raised by all groups in society, including Latinos and Asian Americans who most frequently receive these services. What started out as an educational program to give new immigrants a better chance at success about 25 years ago has turned into a $10 billion political football. For some, bilingual education has become a rallying point for safeguarding one's own culture and the programs look more like a cultural studies program (Schnaiberg, 1997). Those opposed see such programs as dangerous attempts to

divide society by emphasizing cultural divisions and deemphasizing the learning of English. Those who advocate a more English-intensive approach are accused of being anti-immigrant; those who favor bilingual methods are branded as self-serving protectors of the bilingual educational bureaucracy who care more for cultural advancement than for educational advancement (Schnaiberg, 1997).

No matter where one stands on the issue of bilingual education, serious practical shortcomings are all too clear. Too often, programs have been inflexible and unresponsive to parents' and children's needs. For example, one young student of Puerto Rican descent was born in Brooklyn. Although his mother was born in Puerto Rico, only English was spoken at home. The child was placed in a regular classroom until the third grade when he was moved to a program that taught him in Spanish for all but 45 minutes a day. Seeing his lack of progress, his mother begged to have her son returned to an English-only class. Her request was met with the question "Why, don't you feel proud to be Hispanic?" (Headden, 1996).

Students are also staying much too long in programs that were supposed to be transitional, some for as long as nine years. Bilingual education programs were meant to allow children to remain current in all other subjects while they learn English. After three or four years, children should switch over to classes taught exclusively in English. Children would then, theoretically, be fluent in two languages. Unfortunately, some students hear English for as little as 30 minutes a day.

A serious charge is that some Latino children are placed in bilingual programs not because they show deficiencies in

English but because they simply don't read well. They require remedial not bilingual help.

Other practical problems involve questions about what should be done when parents do not want their children in such classes (Donegan, 1996), and how to coordinate programs when in some districts many languages are spoken. For example, in one Virginia county, children come from 182 different countries and speak more than 100 languages (Jones, 1997).

These practical problems and political questions do not mean that bilingual education is a failure and should be stopped. Many worthy programs have practical flaws that can be addressed. It is obvious, though, that we need to better define our goals for bilingual education and solve the practical problems that plague inflexible programs. Solid, impartial research evaluating programs is also required (Schnaiberg, 1997). What is needed is a relatively quick way of teaching children Standard English, while keeping students current in their other subjects. Any successful strategy requires a complex balance between use of native language and the language to be acquired (Gerstein & Woodward, 1994). Hopefully, new experimentation in the next decade will provide educators with an answer to this challenge.

What do you think?

Bilingual programs are controversial. Why is it so difficult to demonstrate whether they have been a success? How would you vote on a referendum to eliminate such programs from the schools? Why?

You can explore the questions above using InfoTrac College Edition. Hint: enter search term *Bilingual Education.*

Ebonics

"By the time I get there, he will have gone."

"Time I git dere, he be done gone."

If you were asked which of these sentences would be best received by an English professor, you would certainly choose the first. While the first sentence illustrates Standard English, or marketplace English (Lovett & Neely, 1997), the second is what used to be called Black English and now **Ebonics** (Fox, 1997). Ebonics contains a consistent, logical, and coherent grammar and is spoken by 60% of inner-city African Americans (Labov, 1970; Longres & Harding, 1997). In some ways, it is even more precise than Standard English. When a teacher asks an African American child why his father couldn't make a meeting the night before, the child might answer, "He sick." However, when asked why the father has not attended any of the meetings during the year, the child says, "He be sick" (Raspberry, 1970). The use of *be* means that the quality is not limited but reflects past, present, and future; it is ongoing (Smitherman, 1997). The pronunciation of some words may also differ—for example, "sista"—because many West African languages do not have the "r" sound (Smitherman, 1997).

In December 1996, the Oakland California School Board created controversy by labeling Ebonics a language and advocating its use as a bridge to learning marketplace English. The resolution noted that Ebonics is a primary language of many students in the district and called on teachers to learn this system of communication (Lee, 1997).

The uproar was immediate and came from both African American and white political leaders and educators (Fox, 1997). More than 2,500 editorials, articles, columns, and letters resulted from this decision (Barnes, 1998). Many African Americans saw it as an unnecessary step complicating the development of marketable language skills (Verdelle, 1997) and as an insult, with the connotation that African American children could not be expected to learn the same language skills as other children (Fox, 1997). Some argued that this was an attempt to legitimize what they considered stigmatizing behavior, since its usage is linked with poverty and the problems of urban life (Fox, 1997). Many thought it would encourage poor grammar and further isolate inner-city youths (School Board News, 1997). Older African Americans and more educated people have a much more negative concept of Ebonics than younger people, who are somewhat less likely to reject it (Lovett & Neely, 1997; Smitherman & Cunningham, 1997).

Supporters were equally vocal, arguing that Ebonics should be recognized as a language and that the resolution was misunderstood. Everyone agrees that all children need to learn marketplace language skills; the question is how this is to be accomplished. The board's purpose was only to use the children's linguistic style as a way of helping them learn language.

Whether Ebonics is a language on its own or a dialect of English (which is what it is considered by the federal government) depends on one's definition of language (Woodford, 1997). Some people fear that teachers who consider Ebonics to be inferior to Standard English may reject urban African American children's ideas, essentially turning them off and reducing communication between themselves and their students. Students may also develop feelings of inferiority. Ebonics, they argue, should be respected and not scorned (Smitherman & Cunningham, 1997; Woodford, 1997). When a teacher misunderstands Ebonics, it may also lead to frustrating situations for both teacher and pupil. Some African American children read the words *I saw it* as *I see it*, since both *see* and *saw* are pronounced "see" in this dialect (Dale, 1972). Correcting this error is difficult, because children do not understand that this is an error.

Ebonics

A type of linguistic communication with a consistent, logical, and coherent grammar used by some African Americans.

The possible use of Ebonics as a bridge to learning English is not a new idea and has been suggested since the 1960s (Baratz, 1969). For example, one program allowed students to proceed from the familiar Ebonics to the less familiar Standard English by first being presented with a story totally written in Ebonics, then one written half in Ebonics and half in Standard English, and finally one written all in Standard English (Simpkins, Holt, & Simpkins, 1974).

Years ago, people thought of Ebonics as a **linguistic deficit,** something children had to give up along the way, but a more modern approach sees it in terms of a **linguistic difference.** Children must be able to deal with their environment, and therefore Ebonics has its uses; but while it is reasonable in some environments it is not acceptable in others (Lovett & Neely, 1997). Learning to speak Standard English is a necessity if children are to succeed in school and in the world of work. When African American college women were sent for interviews, those who used Ebonics were given shorter interviews and fewer offers, and more often for lower-paying positions (Raloff, 1982).

Perhaps there has been too much focus on the deficit and difference hypotheses and not enough on how one teaches children a different dialect that they will not hear very much around their homes or neighborhoods. More research is needed on ways of teaching Standard English to children who speak other dialects.

Atypical Development: Children With Exceptional Needs

About 10.6% of all children between the ages of 6 and 17 years receive special education services (U.S. Department of Education, 1997b). These include children who have learning disabilities, communication disorders, mental retardation; show behavior disorders; have visual or auditory impairments; or are physically challenged (see Table 10.6). The overwhelming majority have mild disabilities (Kaplan, 1996). Most disabilities are diagnosed during the elementary school years. When increasing academic demands are made on the child, these previously undetected problems surface.

The most important law mandating educational services for children with disabilities is the Individuals with Disabilities Education Act (IDEA), Public Law 94–142 (Kaplan 1996). This law does not cover gifted children, who comprise about 3% of the school population, although many districts have special programs for gifted children. The law requires all children with disabilities to receive a free, appropriate education and provides procedures to safeguard the rights of children with disabilities. The law also requires accountability, because educators must develop an individualized education program (IEP), which states the goals of the child's schooling and the methods for attaining them. Parents have the right to participate in all phases of their children's placement and education. The law also mandates that the child be placed in the least restrictive environment. This means that each student with a disability must be educated in an environment that is no more restrictive than absolutely necessary. New rules require the regular education teacher to participate in developing the IEP (Clay, 1998) and encourage more parental participation (Sack, 1997).

Today, a relatively new movement called **full inclusion** maintains that all children with disabilities should be served in the regular classroom with the aid of various professionals and aides. The classroom teacher would have the primary responsibility for educating all children and would have the help of a support team.

For Your Consideration ?

What are the pros and cons of using Ebonics as a teaching device in inner-city schools

Guideposts

Why has Ebonics become a controversial subject?

linguistic deficit

The belief that a dialect, such as Black English, is a hindrance to learning.

linguistic difference

The belief that a dialect, such as Black English, is different from Standard English but not a deficit.

full inclusion

A movement that would provide children with disabilities all special services within the regular classroom.

Table 10.6 Students Age 6 to 21 Served under IDEA, Part B, 1995–1996, by Disability

Disability Category	1995–1996	Percentage of Total
Specific learning disabilities	2,597,231	51.2
Speech or language impairments	1,025,941	20.2
Mental retardation	585,308	11.5
Serious emotional disturbance	438,217	8.6
Multiple disabilities	94,156	1.9
Hearing impairments	68,070	1.3
Orthopedic impairments	63,200	1.2
Other health impairments	133,419	2.6
Visual impairments	25,484	0.5
Autism	28,827	0.6
Deaf-blindness	1,362	0.0*
Traumatic brain injury	9,443	0.2

*This percentage is rounded to the nearest tenth. The actual percentage is 0.026.
SOURCE: U.S. Department of Education, Office of Special Education Programs, Data Analysis System (DANS).

The entire educational system, the school, and the classroom would be adapted so that students with disabilities receive virtually all their education with their peers who do not have disabilities (Stainback & Stainback, 1984, 1991).

Some authorities doubt the wisdom of full inclusion. They argue that there are times when the child with a disability is best served outside of the classroom and that full inclusion is neither always realistic or desirable (Vann, 1997).

Learning Disabilities

There are children who, despite attending class and having the same teachers as their peers, do not learn well. More children with disabilities are diagnosed as having a learning disability than any other disability. Children with learning disabilities show significant difficulties acquiring and using listening, speaking, reading, writing, or reasoning skills or mathematics. They do not achieve up to their age and ability in some basic skill. The problem cannot be the result of sensory

Guideposts

What are the key provisions of the Individuals with Disabilities Education Act?

Proponents of the full inclusion movement believe that all services to children with disabilities ought to be delivered within the regular classroom.

learning disability

A group of disorders marked by significant difficulties in acquiring and using listening, speaking, reading, writing, reasoning skills, or mathematics.

handicaps such as blindness, mental retardation, emotional disturbance, or any environmental, cultural, or economic disadvantage ("Education of Handicapped Children," 1977; Gaskill & Brantley, 1996).

Children with learning disabilities may show problems in perception, motor skills, communication, and memory strategies. For example, they may have difficulty discriminating a *p* from a *b*, or they may not perceive the position of the stimuli correctly, reversing letters or words and reading *saw* for *was*. These problems are common in young children, but they persist in children with learning disabilities. They often do not use memory or learning strategies such as rehearsal appropriately and show poor organization skills and short-term memory problems (Swanson, 1994).

Today, psychologists believe a primary feature of learning disability is a deficit in phonological awareness (McBride-Chang, 1995; Wagner, Torgesen, & Rashotte, 1994). Phonological awareness involves a number of skills, for example, understanding that words can be divided into sounds such as "c" + "a" + "t" for *cat*. Other such skills involve being able to blend sounds such as "fl" in *flower* or recognizing the beginning sound of a word. The inability to blend, segment, rhyme, and manipulate sounds can cause children to have problems recognizing words (Hansen & Bowey, 1994; O'Connor, Jenkins, & Slocum, 1995). Because of these phonological problems, children with learning disabilities have trouble abstracting and transferring. For example, when taught to read *pine* and *shark*, children with learning disabilities are not better able to identify *fine* and *dark* (Lovett et al., 1994). Studies show children can be directly taught these phonological skills, and when they are integrated with reading instruction, children with learning disabilities make significant progress (Hatcher, Hulme, & Ellis, 1994).

Children with learning disabilities are most often diagnosed in elementary school as problems appear. Two approaches are used to help these children. Direct instructional methods pinpoint academic problems and teach children these skills. Another approach is to teach children learning strategies, such as how to approach a task, how to monitor their progress, as well as organizational skills (Butler, 1995; Lovett et al., 1994).

Attention Deficit/Hyperactivity Disorder

If you spend a few minutes with a child who is easily distracted, hyperactive, and impulsive, you begin to appreciate the patience and skill required for dealing with such children. Children who show these symptoms are classified as having an **attention deficit/hyperactivity disorder (ADHD).** These children have difficulty in school, and their relationships with their teachers are often strained. It is estimated that between 3% and 5% of all children have ADHD (Burcham & Carlson, 1995; Fowler, 1991), but others find a lower incidence (Viadero, 1993). Boys are much more likely to be diagnosed as having ADHD than girls (Barabasz & Barabasz, 1996). Many children with ADHD show conduct difficulties, including fighting, disobedience, and rule breaking (Weiss, 1990).

Children with ADHD are inattentive, impulsive, and, in many cases, show hyperactivity (Fowler, 1991). Three specific types of ADHD are recognized today: one in which inattention predominates, another in which hyperactivity and impulsivity are the primary symptoms, and a third in which all three major symptoms exist (American Psychiatric Association, 1994). Children with ADHD have social problems; they often are seen as bothersome, socially awkward, disruptive, talkative, loud, and aggressive (Wicks-Nelson & Israel, 1997). The disorder appears to be caused by difficulties in the functioning of specific parts of the brain,

Guideposts

What does the diagnosis of learning disability mean?

attention deficit/ hyperactivity disorder

A diagnostic classification involving a number of symptoms including inattention, impulsivity and hyperactivity.

especially the frontal lobes that play a major part in performing executive functions, such as planning and implementing goal-oriented strategies and controlling impulses (Aman, Roberts, & Pennington, 1998).

As these children mature, between 30 and 50% carry some of the symptoms of hyperactivity into adulthood. They do not fidget as much, but they are likely to be impulsive and have difficulty forming relationships.

Two basic approaches are being used to treat ADHD. Children with ADHD are most often treated with stimulant medications, most commonly Ritalin, to reduce the symptoms of the disorder (Elia, Ambrosini, & Rapoport, 1999; Goldman, Genel, Bezman, & Stanetz, 1998). This seems unusual, but scientists understand how this works. Neurons "communicate" with other neurons through the use of special chemicals called *neurotransmitters*. One neurotransmitter that inhibits the firing of other neurons is dopamine, and Ritalin increases the activity of dopamine in the child's brain (Joelker, 1998; Kalat, 1998). This produces an increase in attention because it decreases activity in many brain areas, thereby reducing background noise and narrowing attention to one stimulus and away from competing stimuli (Mattay et al., 1996). Under such medication, children with ADHD become calmer, more attentive, more compliant, and less aggressive (Forness & Kavale, 1988). About 70% to 75% show increased attention, reduced impulsivity and activity levels, and some academic and behavioral improvement.

The use of these medications has been widely criticized because the drugs treat only the symptoms, not the underlying cause, and may produce unpleasant side effects such as insomnia and decreased appetite (Elia et al., 1999). In addition, evidence indicates that although effective in reducing the symptoms in the short run, medication is not effective in the long run unless given with other treatments, probably because the aggressive and antisocial behavior is not being treated (Weiss, 1990). The overall benefits may not be long lasting and may disappear when the medication is halted (Hinshaw & Erhardt, 1993). No one claims that drug therapy will improve intelligence or even schoolwork, only that it reduces the symptoms.

T F

9

Children with attention deficit/hyperactivity disorder (ADHD) are treated with tranquilizers to reduce their symptoms.

Another approach to treating ADHD (which may be used in combination with medication) involves manipulating the environment and its reinforcers. For example, providing structure and solid routines and using positive reinforcers can be helpful (Abramowitz & O'Leary, 1991). In some home-school programs, teachers complete a brief checklist that indicates whether the child has met specific behavioral goals for the day. The checklist is sent home, signed by the parent, and returned to the school. The parents provide appropriate reinforcers at home that have been carefully designed for the child. If the child has not met the criteria for success, some privilege is forfeited. A serious problem, though, is that behavior modification programs may not generalize to other behaviors or carry over to other environments, and when treatment stops the symptoms may return (Barabasz & Barabasz, 1996). Sometimes, programs to improve academic performance are offered as well, and academic success may also help children in the areas of attention and behavior (Wicks-Nelson & Israel, 1997).

Mental Retardation

The public holds many stereotypes of people with mental retardation. They are often surprised to learn that most people with mental retardation cannot be identified by their physical appearance and that many can work in competitive employment. Today, the future of children with mental retardation is somewhat brighter than in the past, with many being able to live productive and meaningful lives.

Mental retardation is characterized by significant subaverage intellectual functioning which exists along with limitations in at least two areas of personal functioning such as communication, self-care, home living, social skills, community use, health, and safety. It must be shown before the age of 18 years (American Association on Mental retardation [AAMR], 1992). General intellectual functioning is usually measured by some score on an individualized intelligence test (for example, below 70 on the Wechsler Intelligence Scale for Children), while adaptation is often measured by behavioral scales.

Children with mental retardation are often classified according to their intelligence level, with the overwhelming majority being classified as having mild mental retardation (an intelligence score between 50 or 55 and 70). They often have difficulty with schoolwork and show slow information processing, short-term memory problems, and the inability to generalize from one situation to another similar one (Kaplan, 1996). Children with mild mental retardation are diagnosed in elementary school when it becomes apparent that they are performing on a lower academic level. If they receive proper vocational education, many lead independent lives (Hickson, Blackman, & Reis, 1995; Kaplan, 1990). They require not only job skills but training in social and behavioral skills as well. They can work successfully in unskilled or semiskilled jobs, and studies show them to be effective workers (Gaylord-Ross, Forte, Storey, Gaylord-Ross, & Jameson, 1987; Levy, Jessop, Rimmerman, & Levy, 1992), who frequently have a lower turnover rate than nonretarded workers (Brickey & Campbell, 1990).

People with moderate mental retardation (30 to 50 or 55) will probably not be able to lead an independent existence, since they are very slow, especially in language development. Their educational program stresses self-help skills, proper behavior, and limited simple verbal communication. Moderately retarded individuals are often employed in sheltered workshops or through supported employment where the environment is noncompetitive and friendly. The jobs may include sorting and packaging. These individuals may live in group homes with other retarded or disabled individuals.

Guideposts

How are children with attention deficit/hyperactivity disorder helped?

For Your Consideration ?

If a neighbor came around with a petition against the establishment of a group home for people with mental retardation on your block, would you sign it? Why or why not?

mental retardation

A condition marked by subnormal intellectual functioning and adjustment difficulties that occur before a person is 18 years of age.

Most severely (20–35 IQ) or profoundly retarded (below 20 IQ) children have multiple disabilities, including sensory and motor problems. Special programs that help these children develop basic survival and self-help skills are now available.

While the categories of "mild", "moderate", "severe" and "profound" are still used, a new classification system based upon intensity of support services needed has been advanced by the American Association on Mental Retardation. This new classification system emphasizes the child's functional strengths and weaknesses in the psychological, health, and environmental areas rather than on intelligence level.

Attempts to help people with mental retardation center on educational experiences. Today, the emphasis is on developing the social and personal skills necessary for success in the outside world. There is also a movement toward community-based group homes, where people with mental retardation can live in dignity and with a degree of independence. In this area, the watchword is *normalization*; that is, the trend is to try to integrate the individual into mainstream society as much as possible. The degree to which this can be accomplished depends on the level of support available, the education and social training the person receives, and the public acceptance of people with mental retardation as individuals with full rights in the community.

What is the criteria for being diagnosed as having mental retardation?

Gifted and Talented Children

When the word *gifted* is mentioned, people usually think in terms of people with high intelligence. Children who score considerably above average on intelligence tests are indeed gifted, but people who are artistically or musically gifted or have leadership ability are also gifted (Gifted and Talented Children's Act, 1978). The basic educational assumption is that the unique skills and abilities of these children require special curricular alterations (Hershey, 1988).

Stereotypes of the gifted sometimes prevent society from meeting the special needs of such children. For example, many people believe that the gifted are socially backward, have little or no common sense, and look down on other people (Rickert, 1981). These stereotypes should be laid to rest. Gifted elementary school children tend to be well accepted by other nongifted children and rather popular (Cohen, Duncan, & Cohen, 1994). Gifted children are not generally isolated, and their interpersonal relationships are good (Austin & Draper, 1981). Besides being fast learners and interested in school, gifted children tend to be well adjusted, energetic and physically healthy, intuitive, perceptive, a bit rebellious and original, and show superior concentration skills (MacKinnon, 1978; Scott, 1988). They see relationships among diverse ideas and are curious (Tuttle, Becker, & Sousa, 1988).

Two general approaches to educating gifted children exist. **Acceleration** involves completing courses of study in less time or at a younger age than usual (Reynolds & Birch, 1988). Early admission to school, skipping a grade or course, or special accelerated courses that allow a child, for instance, to do two years of math in one are typical of accelerated programs. Sometimes, students take college courses in high school (Pendarvis, Howley, & Howley, 1990). Some people object to acceleration because they are afraid of creating social problems or gaps in knowledge base, but no evidence exists for any deficits in knowledge or social problems in accelerated students (Sayler & Brookshire, 1993; Swiatek & Benbow, 1991).

Most children with high intelligence scores have significant adjustment problems and poor peer relationships.

acceleration
A major division of services for gifted children in which a student skips a grade or a particular unit, or in which material is presented much more quickly than it would be for an average student.

Guideposts

What educational approaches are used to help gifted children fulfill their potential?

Enrichment programs offer gifted children work that goes much beyond the usual work of students their age, but they stay in grade. Their educational experiences are deeper, more varied, and require curriculum modifications (Schiever & Maker, 1991). It may include Saturday classes, after-school seminars, or doing different work, perhaps in the form of projects (Feldhusen, 1991). The problem with enrichment is that sometimes it translates into simply more work, rather than work that is qualitatively different. Assigning 20 math problems instead of 10 is not enrichment; in some ways it can be seen as a punishment! In any case, gifted children require a program that is qualitatively different from their age mates if they are to fulfill their potential.

It is wrong, however, merely to concentrate on children who are academically gifted. Today, with the expansion of our definitions of intelligence as in Gardner's ideas discussed earlier, many schools are looking at giftedness in a more global sense and trying to serve children who may be gifted in the arts, music, or leadership (Davis & Rimm, 1994).

The Total Child in School

The child's school experience is of paramount importance in middle childhood. As we have seen, the nature of that experience depends on many factors. Although there will always be individual differences in achievement, all children must learn the basic skills and develop a feeling of confidence in their abilities. When children succeed in school, they develop the positive sense of achievement about their work that Erik Erikson calls *industry*, which leads to a higher sense of self-esteem and a more hopeful attitude toward the future.

enrichment

A major division of services for gifted children in which students are given special challenging work that goes beyond what would be usual for the child's age group.

Summary

1. During middle childhood, the rate of growth slows. Children's motor skills improve and are refined with maturation and experience. Physical changes during this stage are gradual.

2. Elementary school children today weigh more than their peers did a generation ago, probably because they are less active. Treatment for obesity may involve following a nutritious diet, providing psychological support, and beginning an exercise routine. Any such plan should be executed under a doctor's care.

3. Teaching good health habits in the areas of nutrition, safety, and exercise is an important part of the parents' and schools' responsibility. Many children overestimate their physical abilities.

4. Proponents of organized sport for children argue that it contributes to physical fitness, improves children's self-esteem, and provides an opportunity for socialization. Critics claim that the competition is injurious to children and there is too much emphasis on winning. Many coaches do not have sufficient training.

5. In almost every society, children begin their education at about 6 years. Still, some children may not be ready to learn to read or to successfully perform school tasks because of physical, cognitive, or behavioral immaturity.

6. According to Piaget, the school-age child is negotiating the stage of concrete operations. Egocentrism declines, and improvements occur in the ability to solve problems that entail reversibility, the ability to decenter, seriation, and classification. The crowning achievement is the development of the ability to conserve. The child develops the ability to conserve number, substance, weight, and then volume.

7. Children in the stage of concrete operations are limited by their inability to understand abstractions and hypothetical problems. Children's language continues to improve. Their understanding of humor depends on their cognitive abilities.

8. During middle childhood, children's ability to voluntarily use attentional strategies improves greatly. In addition, children begin to spontaneously use verbal memory strategies, such as rehearsal and classification.

9. The term *metamemory* describes an individual's knowledge of the memory process. Metamemory abilities increase during the school years.

10. As children proceed through elementary school, they are expected to learn how to read, write, and successfully solve mathematical problems. They are also required to develop some knowledge of computers. Mastering these basic skills influences a child's self-concept and self-esteem. American children's basic skills have improved somewhat over the past 20 years. Elementary schools are rated more positively by parents and students than secondary schools.

11. A child's academic achievement is affected by the nature of the school and teachers, the pupil's socioeconomic status, the home environment, gender, attitudes, motivation, work habits, and intelligence.

12. There are many different approaches to defining intelligence. Performance on intelligence tests is related to school achievement, but other factors—such as motivation and adjustment—are important. Intelligence tests have been criticized for a variety of reasons, most important of which is the possibility that they may be biased against children from some minority groups, and their value is still being debated.

13. Recent studies stress the advantages of bilingualism. Bilingual programs are controversial, and much research concerning the best way to teach English to bilingual students remains to be performed.

14. Ebonics, or Black English, is a type of verbal communication used by many African Americans. It has a consistent grammar of its own. Its use as an educational bridge to learn Standard English is controversial as is its status as a dialect of English or a language on its own.

15. Public Law 94–142 requires schools to provide a free appropriate education for every child. It also mandates educational accountability through an individualized education program. Finally, it requires that children be placed in the least restrictive educational environment. The full inclusion movement advocates providing special educational services in the regular classroom.

16. Children who achieve much below what their intelligence and educational experiences indicate they should be achieving are considered to have a learning disability. This disability may not be the result of cultural differences, socioeconomic level, or sensory disability. Children with attention deficit/hyperactivity disorder are impulsive and distractible. These children often have difficulty in school and with interpersonal relationships.

Review

17. Most children with mental retardation are classified as having mild retardation and can often lead independent lives. Children with moderate mental retardation are taught self-care and some skills, but only rarely can they live independently. Children with severe or profound mental retardation often have multiple disabilities.

18. Gifted children have superior intellectual, creative, or academic capabilities; or manifest talent in leadership or in the performing or visual arts. The gifted are generally well adjusted.

Physical changes take place at a (1)_____ (slower/faster) rate during middle childhood. Concerning weight in middle childhood, children are generally (2)_____ than they were 20 years ago, mostly owing to (3)_____. The most common cause of death in middle childhood is (4)_____. Children in middle childhood often (5)_____ their abilities. Perhaps the most noticeable physical change that occurs in middle childhood is the shedding of one's baby teeth, called (6)_____ teeth.

According to Piaget, children from 7 through about 11 years enter the (7)_____ stage. Children can deal with concrete real objects but have difficulty understanding (8)_____. As children proceed through this stage, they become less (9)_____ as they understand that others are seeing the world differently. The greatest cognitive achievement in this stage, according to Piaget, is an understanding of (10)_____. Sometimes, the child can understand the underlying principle but cannot use it in every context where it would be useful. Piaget called this phenomenon (11)_____.

During middle childhood, children's ability to concentrate and remember things (12)_____. They begin to use verbal strategies, such as (13)_____, on their own. Rates of forgetting (14)_____ over the middle childhood years, and children process information at a (15)_____ rate. People's knowledge of their own memory processes is called (16)_____. Children who understand what they know and what they do not know are better students.

The key to understanding children's humor is (17)_____—that is, a difference between what is expected and what is perceived. In middle childhood, (18)_____ and (19)_____ become as important.

The school experience dominates the middle childhood years. Erikson argued that the psychosocial crisis of this period could be understood in terms of (20)_____ versus (21)_____. Reading, writing, and mathematics are key subjects. Most computer use in elementary school is used for the purpose of (22)_____.

Generally, the public rates the elementary school as (23)_____ to the secondary school. The gap between how minority and majority group students achieve has (24)_____. Besides students' personal characteristics and ability, (25)_____ and (26)_____ variables predict academic achievement. Parental involvement (27)_____ in the elementary school years.

Intelligence may be defined in many ways. Gardner proposed the theory of (28)_____, which argues that seven types of intelligence exist. A high correlation exists between scores on standardized intelligence tests and (29)_____. The two most commonly used intelligence tests are the (30)_____ and the (31)_____. Some psychologists argue that they should not be used because they may be biased against children from (32)_____. Recent studies find that (33)_____ and (34)_____ environments are the most important factors explaining the differences in intelligence scores. In an attempt to free these achievement tests from bias, some psychologists have constructed (35)_____ tests, but it is doubtful that they will be as useful as traditional tests.

Children who are bilingual have some cognitive advantages over their monolingual peers. Many have not done well in school due to (36)_____. The federal government considers Ebonics a (37)_____, while others consider it a language.

The Individuals with Disabilities Education Act, Public Law 94–142, guarantees a free, appropriate education to children with (38)_____. All children with disabilities must have a plan that states the individual goals for the child called a/an (39)_____. The child also has the right to be placed in the (40)_____ environment—that is, the educational environment no more separate than absolutely necessary. Today, some believe that all children with disabilities should receive the services in a regular classroom, an idea called (41)_____. The most common diagnosis for children who receive special education services is (42)_____. Today, psychologists argue that the primary feature of such a disorder is a deficit in (43)_____ awareness. Children with attention deficit/hyperactivity disorder are often treated with (44)_____ medications. Children with mental retardation have significant subaverage intelligence scores, but must also show problems in (45)_____ before their 18th birthday. Gifted children generally have (46)_____ interpersonal relationships. The two approaches to helping the gifted child maximize potential are (47)_____ and (48)_____.

InfoTrac

For additional readings, explore InfoTrac College Edition, our online library. Go to http://www.infotrac-college.com/wadsworth. Hint: enter the search terms *Giftedness* and *Bilingual Education*.

What's on the web

Suggestions for Helping Girls Develop Interest in Science and Computing
http://math.rice.edu/~lanius/club/girls.html

Success For All—Restructuring Program for Elementary Schools
http://www.successforall.net/aboutsfa1.html

The Wadsworth Psychology Study Center Web Site
Go to the Wadsworth Psychology Study Center at http://psychology.wadsworth.com/ for quiz questions, research updates, hot topics, interactive exercises, and suggested readings in the InfoTrac College Edition related to this chapter.

Answers 1. slower; 2. heavier; 3. lack of exercise; 4. accidents; 5. overestimate; 6. deciduous; 7. concrete operational; 8. abstractions; 9. egocentric; 10. conservation; 11. horizontal decalage; 12. improves; 13. rehearsal; 14. decline; 15. faster; 16. metamemory; 17. incongruity; 18. surprise; 19. resolution; 20. industry; 21. inferiority; 22. drill/practice; 23. superior; 24. declined (narrowed); 25. school; 26. home; 27. declines; 28. multiple intelligences; 29. academic achievement; 30. Stanford-Binet; 31. Wechsler Intelligence Scale for Children; 32. minority groups; 33. poverty; 34. home; 35. culture fair; 36. poverty; 37. dialect; 38. disabilities; 39. individualized education program; 40. least restrictive; 41. Full inclusion; 42. learning disabilities; 43. phonological; 44. stimulant; 45. personal functioning (adjustment); 46. good; 47. acceleration; 48. enrichment.

CHAPTER ELEVEN

Social *and* Personality

CHAPTER OUTLINE

Through a Child's Eyes

Looking at Middle Childhood

"How I See Myself": The Self-Concept and Self-Esteem

Child Rearing during Middle Childhood

The Changing Family

Best Friends

Moral Development

Prosocial and Antisocial Behavior

Atypical Development: Children and Stress

Middle Childhood in Perspective

ARE THESE STATEMENTS
True *or* False?

1. Children's self-esteem in middle childhood declines with age.
2. Temper tantrums and the number of disciplinary encounters decline markedly between ages 3 and 9 years.
3. After a divorce, the custodial parent usually becomes stricter and the noncustodial parent more lenient but less available.
4. Children living in single-parent families are much more likely to live in poverty than children from intact families.
5. Sons have a more difficult time adjusting to the entrance of a new stepfather into the family than daughters.
6. Despite the many challenges, most homeless children are doing well in school.
7. The overwhelming majority of children raised by gay or lesbian parents consider themselves heterosexual.
8. As children mature, they tend to share with other children more often.
9. Aggressive children are more likely to view the world as a hostile, threatening place than nonaggressive children.
10. Children exposed to a great deal of stress yet are doing well prefer to be by themselves and are deeply involved with their family problems.

ANSWERS: 1. *True.* 2. *True.* 3. *True.* 4. *True.* 5. *False.* 6. *False.* 7. *True.* 8. *True.* 9. *True.* 10. *False.*

Development *in* Middle Childhood

Through a Child's Eyes

Karen quickly picked the wallet up and put it in her pocket. She carefully looked around. No one had noticed. The wallet contained three $50 bills and a couple of $5 bills, and Karen had so many things she wanted to buy. She could return the wallet, since she knew the man who had lost it, a wealthy businessman. Karen's parents would want her to return the wallet, but they were busy with their own problems. They were always arguing, and Karen's mother threatened to divorce her father just last week. Karen was considered the "bad one" anyway. Her parents were always saying how dumb she was, and her father usually lost his patience when trying to explain something to her. The only adult Karen had any respect for was her aunt, who frequently listened to her, tried to help her, and would give her a kind word.

Then Karen saw her best friend, Linda, and got an idea. Linda was very poor, and Karen would enjoy sharing the money with Linda and perhaps with her small group of friends. She could buy Linda some nice slacks, and they could go to the movies. To Karen's surprise, Linda didn't think they should keep the wallet, because it "wasn't right." Karen valued Linda's opinion and realized that if she returned the wallet, she might receive a nice reward. Yet, she still couldn't decide what to do. Now that Linda knew about the wallet, Karen had to make up her mind quickly.

In middle childhood, the number and importance of friendships increase.

Looking at Middle Childhood

Children's social networks expand significantly during middle childhood, and the number and importance of their friendships increase (Ladd & Le Sieur, 1995). Children of this age receive feedback from many more sources and develop a sense of their own abilities, strengths, and weaknesses. At the same time, elementary school children's relationship with their parents undergoes a subtle but definite shift toward greater independence (Collins, Harris, & Susman, 1995). Children are considered more responsible for their own actions and develop a sense of right and wrong. They are likely to be faced with moral and ethical dilemmas concerning cheating, lying, and stealing, as well as to face situations calling for helping and cooperating with others. These changes take place slowly over a number of years, and the theme of more gradual change is found throughout this period of development.

Measuring Up

School-age children become more project oriented and are faced with many academic challenges. During this stage, children take comparisons seriously. If parents compare a child's work unfavorably with that of a sibling's, the child may stop trying. One of the more difficult parenting tasks is valuing the competencies of each child in the family, especially when one child may be better than the others in a number of areas. Even if parents avoid direct comparisons, implicit comparisons are still present.

For Your Consideration ?

How could a parent or teacher show children who do not seem to compare well to their peers in a number of areas that they are worthy and valuable people?

ACTION / REACTION

The All-American Boy's Brother

Everyone is proud of Oliver. He is a top student, an excellent musician who can play both classical and rock guitar, one of the top scorers on the high school basketball team as a freshman, and popular with everyone. In fact, the local newspaper just did a story on Oliver's interview with the governor of the state, who offered him a summer internship.

Jesse is also proud of his brother but simply can't compete. He is not a top student, can't play any musical instrument well, is not great at any sport, and is not very popular, although he has some good friends. Jesse does not act out in class; he simply stops trying. He does just enough work to get by. It is clear to his parents and his teacher that he could do a lot better.

At a recent conference with the guidance counselor and Jesse's teacher, Jesse's parents said that they understood that it was difficult for Jesse but that they tried hard not to compare the two boys. Jesse's father noted that since Jesse often was cited for not doing his homework or his best, some of the communication between them takes the form of criticism, but he never brought Oliver's achievements up as an example of what Jesse can do. Jesse's mother noted that at a recent newspaper photo session they made certain Jesse was included in a picture of them with Oliver, but Jesse really didn't want to be in the picture. Jesse, according to the mother, has become somewhat sullen.

1. *What can Jesse's parents do to help Jesse?*
2. *If you were Jesse's teacher, what would you do?*

ACTION / REACTION

If children succeed, they resolve the psychosocial crisis of middle childhood in a positive manner and gain what Erikson called a sense of **industry,** the sense that their work and efforts are valued. Children with a sense of industry enjoy learning about new things and experimenting with new ideas. If they do not succeed, they develop a sense of **inferiority,** a belief that they are incompetent and do not measure up to their peers.

Guideposts

How do Erikson's ideas about middle childhood relate to children's experiences in school?

The Latency Stage

In Freudian theory, the child has now negotiated the Oedipus conflict and enters the **latency stage.** A boy resolves his Oedipus complex by identifying with his father ("Me and you, Dad") and repressing his feelings toward his mother, and indeed all females. Girls experience less pressure to completely resolve their conflicts in this stage, and many do not fully do so. Sexuality in this stage lies dormant, and the segregation of children by gender becomes stronger. Boys play with boys, and girls play with girls.

Freudians argue that this segregation occurs because children have repressed their feelings toward the other gender to resolve their Oedipus conflict, and contact might reawaken these disturbing emotions. In addition, because girls are developmentally ahead of boys, such grouping allows each gender to explore issues in sexual curiosity and fantasies at its own rate in a more comfortable and less stimulating manner (Solnit, Call, & Feinstein, 1979).

"How I See Myself": The Self-Concept and Self-Esteem

In early childhood, the self-concept is based on external factors, such as physical characteristics, possessions, and such abilities as playing a sport well. In middle childhood, especially after age 8, a shift from physical to psychological conceptions of the self takes place, and personality characteristics take center stage (Damon & Hart, 1982). Children often make statements referring to personal attributes, interests, beliefs, attitudes, and values, and fewer statements concerning possessions and appearance.

The self-concept evolves from a combination of feedback children receive from peers, parents, and teachers and their evaluation of their own subjective experiences. Children whose parents continually tell them that they have "no brains" and are "stupid" may believe it. Children, though, are not just passive recipients of feedback. Children evaluate their own experiences. They experience themselves as being good, bad, aggressive, calm, or honest, and compare their experience against a standard set by society, parents, peers, and finally themselves. Even in the absence of direct feedback, they evaluate these experiences. If a child's experience is not in keeping with the youngster's sense of self, the child may reject the subjective experience. For instance, children may believe they are honest and have difficulty coming to grips with the fact that they copied from a friend during an exam or, as in Karen's case, kept something that didn't belong to them. The experience of dishonesty may not match their conception of themselves as honest.

industry

The positive outcome of the psychosocial crisis in the middle years of childhood, involving a feeling of self-confidence and pride concerning one's achievements.

inferiority

The negative outcome of the psychosocial crisis in the middle years of childhood, involving the child's belief that his or her work and achievements are below par.

latency stage

The psychosexual phase, occurring during middle childhood, in which sexuality is dormant.

self-concept

The picture people have of themselves.

Children's self-concept is determined by the feedback they receive from others and their evaluation of their own experience.

In middle childhood, the situation becomes complicated because children receive feedback from many more sources. They encounter more children and adults, not all of whom will like them. Some feedback is likely to be negative, or at least conflicting. In addition, children's newly developing cognitive skills affect the self-concept. Children in the concrete operational stage can reason more logically, making it possible for them to verify the attributes of their self. Children become especially good at developing a self-theory from inductive (specific) experience. They may conclude that they are smart because they are good at reading and mathematics (Harter, 1983), or honest because they returned something they found. Children now develop the ability to take another person's point of view. They test their self-concepts by comparing themselves with others, and because they are no longer as egocentric, they develop the ability to imagine what others are thinking of them. The self-concept affects how information is processed. If children think they are bad, they will believe such feedback from other people. In this way, the self-concept can set a self-fulfilling prophecy in motion. Believing that someone will say something negative causes children to anticipate poor evaluations, reject positive feedback, and even to interpret neutral feedback as negative.

Self-Esteem: Valuing Oneself

Karen was reading in class when she came upon a difficult phrase. After trying to sound it out, she slammed her book shut and just stared at it. Her teacher came over to her and asked about the problem. "I guess I'm just stupid," Karen said. "I can't do it."

Karen's teachers have commented on what they call her poor self-esteem and discussed how they could help her. There is no single accepted definition of the term (Cross, 1997). Generally, **self-esteem** refers to judgments that one places on the self-concept or various aspects of the self (Frey & Carlock, 1989). While the self-concept is usually viewed in descriptive and nonjudgmental terms, self-esteem is self-evaluative (Scott, Murray, Martens, & Dustin, 1996).

One problem with this definition of self-esteem is that it could appear rather self-centered and selfish. People with high-self-esteem who like themselves and value their contributions might be seen as uncaring about others. Some definitions of self-esteem emphasize not only appreciating one's own worth and importance, but having the character to be accountable for oneself and to act responsibly toward others (California State Department of Education, 1990). This extends the definition to include personal responsibility and caring for others (Scott et al., 1996). Some authorities emphasize the importance of an overall global self-esteem; others argue that different aspects of the self will be evaluated differently. An academic self-concept will have a particular valuation, while an interpersonal aspect may be valued differently. The two most common divisions of self-esteem are worthiness (feelings of self-worth, liking and value as a person) and competence or self-efficacy (feeling that one can get something done successfully) (Hakim-Larson & Mruk, 1997).

Children in early childhood evaluate themselves very positively in ways that have no relationship to objective factors (Cole, 1991). This changes in middle childhood when children become aware that they are succeeding or failing compared with others (Harter, 1993). Self-esteem declines with age (Davies & Brember, 1995). Perhaps the judgments and comparisons, some of them critical, that come with school and with the child's expanding social network are to blame.

For Your Consideration ?

Why does self-esteem decline with age?

T
F
1

Children's self-esteem in middle childhood declines with age.

Does high self-esteem influence achievement? Does achieving produce high self-esteem? Although there is a relationship between self-esteem and achievement, the direction of that relationship is still in question.

Positive self-esteem is related to better adjustment, more independence, less defensive behavior, greater acceptance of others, sociability, motivation to learn, and better school achievement (Francis, 1997; Gurney, 1987). Children with high self-esteem expect to do well and believe their successes are due to their own efforts and abilities (Kohn, 1994). They have a sense of control over their lives. They take mistakes and even failures in stride and learn from them (Brooks, 1994). Children with high self-esteem also cope with stressful encounters better (Ruble & Thompson, 1992). A positive relationship between self-esteem and prosocial behavior is found beginning at the fourth grade level (Eisenberg & Fabes, 1998). Low-self esteem, on the other hand, is related to anxiety and depression (Francis, 1997; Kohn, 1994).

Signs of low self-esteem vary from child to child and from situation to situation. Karen feels "dumb" in the classroom but has a positive view of her physical self because she is one of the faster runners in the school. While some children show their poor self-esteem directly through statements such as "I'm stupid" and "I always do the wrong things," others may show it by the way they cope with challenges (Brooks, 1992). When children with low self-esteem are faced with difficult tasks, they may quit, avoid them, cheat, bully others, clown, or make excuses to escape the challenge (Davies & Brember, 1995).

Teachers believe that lack of self-esteem stunts children's academic performance (Cross, 1997). They are convinced that raising self-esteem can be accomplished and have definite ideas about how to do it. Most strategies involve showing children that they are liked and valued, demonstrating that they can succeed, and avoiding statements that compromise the child's self-esteem through ridicule or impatience.

Unfortunately, the situation is not so simple. First, the relationship between high self-esteem and academic success is positive but relatively low, meaning that other factors are involved (Hansford & Hattie, 1982; Kohn, 1994). Second, research results relating high self-esteem to positive outcomes are based on correlations and do not demonstrate cause and effect (see pages 24–25). Even if there is some causative relationship, there is considerable doubt about the direction of that relationship. It may be that high self-esteem has a positive effect on achievement, but it is also possible that doing well in school leads to high self-esteem (Cross, 1997; Kahne, 1996). If the latter is the case, all the positive comments may not succeed with children who don't read or do math well, and extra help in the academic areas is required (Kagan, 1996). On the other hand, both may be true (Davies & Brember, 1995).

Guideposts

Why is self-esteem considered an important attribute of children?

Guideposts

What are signs of low self-esteem in children?

self-esteem

A term that refers to judgments that one places on the self-concept or various aspects of the self. Newer definitions suggest self-esteem involves not only appreciating one's own worth and importance, but being accountable for oneself and acting responsibly toward others.

Building Self-Esteem

Fostering self-esteem is not a simple process and helping a child who already has poor self-esteem is even more difficult. Some school programs and even some commercially available programs may sound reasonable, but few objective evaluations are available (Cross, 1997; Kohn, 1994). Often, attempts to raise self-esteem are artificial and divorced from reality. School programs that involve catchy sayings such as "I can do anything" and "I like me" are of questionable value (Kohn, 1994; Scott et al., 1996). This is especially true for children who have low self-esteem who may mouth words but not believe them (Paul, 1997).

The most powerful forces shaping a child's self-esteem are family, peers, and teachers. The best way to help foster self-esteem is to create an environment at home and at school that reinforces the probability of success and to attribute this success to the child's efforts and motivation. This requires a certain degree of choice, personal control and responsibility, and developing a feeling that they are contributing to the home, school, and community (Brooks, 1994). Few children are competent at everything, but every child has some areas of competence that can be reinforced. Doing so in one area may create a ripple effect and lead to enhanced self-esteem in other areas (Rutter, 1985). For example, one child who showed very little interest in school but saw himself competent in pet care took care of various animals that were sometimes brought into the elementary school. He wrote a brief manual about pet care that was bound and placed in the school library. He had never been motivated to write, but with his teacher's encouragement and assistance, he produced a fine and valuable work because he had something to offer (Brooks, 1994).

Helping children achieve may also improve self-esteem. Although children should realize that they are worthy individuals even if they do not achieve well in school, school achievement may help an individual develop a sense of self-efficacy.

For Your Consideration ?

Why do you think simple programs to raise students' self-esteem have not been very successful?

Child Rearing During Middle Childhood

The family remains the most powerful influence on the child's development during the elementary school years. As middle childhood proceeds, the relationship between parents and children changes. Parents show less physical affection for their children, are not as protective, and generally spend less time with them (Maccoby, 1980). Parents try to use reason more. As in previous years, mothers have more frequent interactions with their children involving caregiving and household tasks, while fathers engage in more physical and outdoor play. Parents expect children to regulate their own behavior and show greater autonomy and independence at home. They encourage their children to take on more responsibility (Collins, Harris, & Susman, 1995). Children show fewer temper tantrums, and the frequency of disciplinary encounters declines significantly between the ages of 3 and 9 years. When disciplinary exchanges do take place, parents less frequently engage in physical punishment and are more likely to use other techniques, such as forfeiting children's privileges, reminding children of responsibility, and appealing to them. Despite these changes, which are due to the child's increasing age and abilities, general parenting values remain stable. That is, a parent who is very punishing remains so, and a parent who is responsive remains responsive (McNally, Eisenberg, & Harris, 1991).

Children also perceive their parents differently. During the early years of middle childhood, children strive to please their parents and teachers and live up

T F 2

Temper tantrums and the number of disciplinary encounters decline markedly between ages 3 and 9 years.

to their parents' expectations. Later in this stage, the importance of peers increases, and it becomes important to fit in and be accepted in the group. Children begin to identify less with adults and more with their peers. They become more argumentative, discourteous, and rebellious and complain of what they perceive as unfairness. They now see parents as human beings who can be—and often are—arbitrary and wrong. They see their parents' authority as having limits (Smetana, 1989). Ten-year-olds believe that decisions about who their friends are, and other decisions that affect only them, are outside their parents' authority (Tisak, 1986). Children question more, and parents may get a bit tired of explaining the reasons for certain rules.

Guideposts
How does the relationship between parents and their children change in middle childhood?

Child-Rearing Strategies Reconsidered

The original studies on child-rearing strategies performed by Diana Baumrind (see Chapter 9) were based on observations of children in nursery school. She continued her studies, looking at the behavior of these children when they were 8 or 9 years old. The problems of authoritarian-raised children continued at those ages, especially for boys. Boys showed less interest in achievement and withdrew from social contact. Children who were raised permissively lacked self-confidence and were not achievement oriented. The authoritative-raised children were, again, superior. The combination of firm rule enforcement, demands for more mature, yet age-appropriate, behavior, better communication, and warmth led to a desirable outcome.

Neither the unbridled use of power nor the permissive style benefits most children. Demanding either total, unquestioning obedience or nothing at all does not lead to independence or social maturity. Children of authoritarian parents (such as Karen's parents) lack social competence with peers, do not take the initiative, lack spontaneity, and have external rather than internal moral orientations to right and wrong. Children from permissive families are impulsive and aggressive, lacking independence and a sense of responsibility. Children of authoritative parents are independent, take the initiative in the cognitive and social areas of life, are responsible, control their aggressive urges, have self-confidence, and have high self-esteem (Maccoby & Martin, 1983). As noted in Chapter 9, these conclusions are most valid for children of European ancestry, and more research is needed to extend these conclusions to children living in a variety of circumstances or who belong to different ethnic groups.

Taken as a whole, the research on parenting in middle childhood yields no surprises. Children benefit when their parents show warmth and acceptance, set appropriate rules and enforce them, listen to their children and are responsive to them. Children also benefit from having some room for personal choice, responsibility, and freedom. In middle childhood, parental behavior has to strike a delicate balance between assistance and respect for the autonomy of the child (Krappman, 1989).

Do Parents Agree on How to Raise Their Children?

Parents do not always agree on their child-rearing strategies, and these disagreements become more intense as children mature. We all know families in which one parent is more authoritarian than another and have wondered whether this would make much of a difference. Minor disagreements in child rearing probably occur in every family. Generally, high agreement between parents indicates more adaptive functioning than low agreement, which often is related to conflict and familial disorganization (Simons, McCluskey, & Mullett, 1985).

When parents have major disagreements over parenting, less effective parenting is often the result (Minuchin, 1985). This is only half the story, however, for parents who use more effective child-rearing strategies tend to agree with each other, while parents using less effective strategies tend to disagree with each other. Parents who agree with each other are most often characterized by positive interactions both between spouses and between parents and children, confront problems in a positive way, have good communication, and use rational discipline techniques (Deal, Halverson, & Wampler, 1989). In addition, parents who agree with each other also have much in common with other effective parents.

The story is different, however, with parents who disagree with each other on child-rearing strategies. These parents often use poor strategies, and they disagree both with their spouses and with the other effective and ineffective parents. There is no consensus at all. The great Russian novelist Tolstoy summed this up well when he claimed that all happy families resemble one another; every unhappy family is unhappy in its own way (Deal et al., 1989).

The Changing Family

The American family today is a far cry from what it was even 30 years ago. The number of single-parent families has increased substantially, and about one million children each year are affected by divorce (Ensign, Scherman, & Clark, 1998). If trends continue, more than half of all American children will spend some part of their childhood in a single-parent household before their 18th birthday. Since most divorced mothers and fathers remarry, many children will experience a series of marital transitions, from intact-family to single-parent family to stepfamily relationships.

The Experience of Divorce

A divorce is not an event for a child but rather a process that unfolds over many years (Goodman, Emery, & Haugaard, 1998). Divorce itself brings many changes. The child's world is torn asunder, and the child's entire lifestyle may be disrupted. Conflicts between parents may continue, and children may find themselves in the middle of these disputes. Children's sense of security is threatened as parents are deeply involved in their own problems, and less adequate parenting often results (Goodman et al., 1998). Contact with one parent is generally reduced. Financial problems may force the family to move to a new neighborhood, altering the child's daily routine (Hines, 1997). Most children do not see such changes in a positive light, even years after the divorce (Wallerstein, Corbin, & Lewis, 1988).

Immediate Reactions to Divorce   Almost all children find divorce a painful experience, and most children show some disruptions in their functioning in the first two years (Bray & Hetherington, 1993). The early symptoms may include anger, depression, and guilt (Weinraub & Gringlas, 1995). Some children show regression, sleep disturbances, aggression, noncompliance, or fear (Hetherington, Hagan, & Anderson, 1989). Parent-child relationships often change. The custodial parent, usually the mother, becomes stricter and more controlling, while the other parent becomes permissive and understanding, though less accessible. Both parents make fewer demands on children to mature, become less consistent in their discipline and less responsive, and have more difficulty communicating with the

T F
3

After a divorce, the custodial parent usually becomes stricter and the noncustodial parent more lenient but less available.

children (Hetherington, Cox, & Cox, 1978; Katz & Goffman, 1998). Parents' discipline practices become poorer, and parents do not monitor their children as well (Hetherington & Clingempeel, 1992).

After the initial period, some children show a remarkable ability to recover, while others do not. Some adapt well in the early stages and show delayed effects (Hetherington & Bray, 1993). How quickly children recover from the initial shock depends on whether a stable environment is created after the divorce and on the social supports available to the child (Kurdek, 1981).

Often, such supports are not available. Parents are confused and must rearrange their own lives. Relatives are often judgmental, and their relationships with both the parents and the children may change. Peer relationships may suffer, as some children feel guilty about what is happening. Family friends may be forced to take sides and maintain contact with only one parent. Economic problems, especially for women, are common, and a reduction in living standard adds to the difficulties (Morrison & Cherlin, 1995).

Guideposts

How do parent-child relationships change right after divorce? How can parents buffer their children against the problems caused by divorce?

Long-term Effects of Divorce   Many of the initial reactions either become less severe or disappear by the end of the first year to 18 months (Hetherington, 1993; Portes, Howell, Brown, Echenberger, & Mas, 1992). The long-term effects of divorce on children, though, can be severe. In one study of children whose parents divorced during their middle childhood years, the functioning of half had improved, while about one-fourth of the subjects had become significantly worse (Kelly & Wallerstein, 1976).

It isn't difficult to find studies showing that children from divorced families are at risk when compared with children of intact families. Children from one-parent families do not differ in academic ability or intelligence, but they are absent from school more often, are more disruptive, have lower grades, are viewed by teachers as less motivated, and are more likely to drop out of school (McLanahan, 1996; Zill, Morrison. & Coiro, 1993). Children of divorced parents show more behavioral problems, such as aggression, depression, low self-esteem, and anxiety, than children in intact families (Coughlin & Vuchinish, 1996; Davies & Cummings, 1998). When children whose parents were divorced when they were

Children whose parents are divorcing are somewhat at risk, but there is much the parents can do to prevent difficulties.

in middle childhood were followed, Wallerstein (1987) found feelings of sadness, neediness, and an increased sense of vulnerability expressed by a majority of these older children. Even though it had been ten years since the divorce, the children spoke sadly of their loss of the intact family, and especially of the lack of contact with their noncustodial parent. They expressed a great concern of being betrayed in relationships, and anxiety about personal commitments was high. Half the boys and one-fourth of the girls were considered poorly adjusted and at high risk at this 10-year follow-up. Some of these effects continue into adulthood (Amato & Keith, 1991; Coontz, 1997).

Although this may sound impressive and rather frightening, the differences between children in intact families and those who have experienced the divorce of their parents is modest in magnitude in most studies (Goodman et al., 1998), so a listing of differences tells only half the story. There is no evidence for extensive mental health problems for children from divorced families, and most children successfully cope with divorce (Goodman et al., 1998; Peterson, 1997). The problems described are not inevitable and are often based on the worst-case scenario.

In addition, much of what is blamed on divorce may be due to the problems that existed before the divorce (Hines, 1997; Shaw, Winslow, & Flanagan, 1999). Family turmoil—whether it ends in divorce or not—creates problems for children (Cherlin et al., 1991; Katz & Goffman, 1998). Marital problems may affect child-rearing practices (Erel, Margolin, & John, 1998). Mothers in troubled marriages depend more on the use of power than reasoning, which may lead to undesirable behavior in their children, such as increased aggressiveness. When an improvement in the home climate takes place, children benefit greatly. In fact, in high-conflict families, children have higher levels of well being as young adults if their parents divorced than if they stayed together. This is not the case in low-conflict marriages (Amato, Loomis, & Booth, 1995). After the high-conflict marriage ends in divorce, the improvement in atmosphere is significant and obvious. When parents get divorced in a low-conflict relationship, the children may be surprised by the divorce and may not perceive any beneficial change in the home environment. Low-conflict marriages ending in divorce are not uncommon, with many divorcing couples reporting that they simply drifted apart and became estranged from each other (Wolf, 1996).

This does not mean that all the problems are caused by turmoil before the divorce. Divorce is also a stressor, but care should be taken about blaming all the problems on the divorce (Bray & Hetherington, 1993).

Most important, the extent of the child's difficulties will depend greatly on what happens after the divorce (Sandler, Tein, & West, 1994). Postdivorce adjustment is much better if parents can cooperate after divorcing (Bronstein, Stoll, Caluson, Abrams, & Briones, 1994). If parents continue to quarrel whenever they talk to each other after the divorce, children will suffer (Portes, Haas, & Brown, 1991). Unfortunately, many parents, about 50%, continue to argue after the divorce is final (Ahrons, 1994).

Children do better when their parents maintain a warm relationship with them. Good relationships between parents and children may buffer the child against the problems of divorce (Wierson, 1989). Adjustment problems will be less severe if financial problems and parental conflict are minimized and if social supports exist (Gohm, Oishi, Darlington, & Diener, 1998; Kurdek, 1981). Unfortunately, parents' difficulties involving finances, loneliness, fear, anxiety about the future, and the loss of social supports reduce their ability to give the children what they need to soften the blow (Weinraub & Gringlas, 1995).

That Seven-Letter Word: Divorce

The fighting was unbearable. The only practical solution was divorce, as far as Stanley and Christina were concerned. However, their feelings were not matched by their children's. Emil, age 11, and Rose, age 9, both blamed their mother for "throwing their father out." In truth, Christina did ask Stanley to leave after a particularly bad argument, and they both agreed to seek a divorce.

During the legal proceedings, the relationship between the parents worsened. Stanley would complain that Christina's lawyer was trying to get all his money. Christina became angry, believing that Stanley was turning the children against her.

Now that the divorce is final, things haven't changed much. Whenever Christina and Stanley talk to each other, they argue. The children still blame Christina and want to live with their father. Christina has had to be stricter with the children but finds it difficult. She must work to supplement her income and comes home tired and depressed.

Recently, Christina was called to school because Emil had been caught lying about his homework and forging his mother's signature on notes. Stanley blames it on Christina and her "active" social life. Christina quips back that if Stanley would give her more financial support and stop undercutting her authority, things would be better.

If you were Christina or Stanley, what would you do?

Divorce and the Age of the Child   Children of various ages experience divorce somewhat differently. Some people believe that young preschoolers aren't aware of what is going on and aren't affected as much. This is incorrect. Children who experience parental divorce before age 6 exhibit more behavioral disturbances than their peers who experienced the divorce of their parents later in childhood (Pagani, Bouerlice, Tremblay, & Vitaro, 1997). Preschoolers react quite negatively, often showing regressive behavior and separation anxiety, although most do recover from the initial shock after a year or so (Allison & Furstenberg, 1989). The preschooler does not understand what is going on, and parents don't explain much to preschoolers. Preschoolers may blame themselves and fear abandonment by their parents (Wallerstein et al., 1988).

Elementary school children experience loyalty problems, including feelings that they have to choose between their parents. Children in elementary school feel powerless and frightened and frequently are angry at one or both parents. They may support one parent against the other. About half show severe declines in achievement during the first year (Wallerstein et al., 1988).

Adolescents may be better able to deal with trauma and may insulate themselves through peer relationships. Teens are likely to know that they didn't cause the divorce and do not blame themselves as often. Yet, since adolescence is a time of being concerned about relationships, they may find it difficult to believe that relationships can be stable and faithful, and trust may become a critical question (Wallerstein & Blakeslee, 1989). Adolescents may have a difficult time coping with anger, often showing acute depression, acting-out behaviors, emotional and social withdrawal, and anxiety about their future. They are often disturbed by the fact that the family's financial problems no longer allow them to buy what they could in the past. They are also more susceptible to peer pressure (Coughlin & Vuchinich, 1996).

For Your Consideration ❓

Why does it appear that boys are more sensitive to marital turmoil and the effects of divorce than girls?

Guideposts

How does the age and gender of children affect their reaction to divorce?

For Your Consideration ❓

Your friends are divorcing and have two young children. Based on the research, what specific advice would you give them to help their children adjust to their new circumstances?

Does Divorce Affect Boys and Girls Differently?   One generally accepted, but not unanimous, research finding is that the long-term effects of divorce are greater for boys than for girls (Morrison & Cherlin, 1995; Mott, Kowaleski-Jones, & Menaghhan, 1997). Boys are much more likely to suffer psychologically, socially, and academically and to show acting-out behaviors than are girls (Hetherington et al., 1989). They seem more sensitive to marital turmoil and divorce, often showing an increase in disruptive behaviors and noncompliance (Mott et al., 1997). Girls adjust more quickly and may internalize dissatisfaction.

The reasons for this gender difference are not known. In the majority of cases, mothers gain custody, and perhaps the absence of the male authority figure may have an especially injurious effect on boys (Huston, 1983). Others simply argue that girls are more resilient to stress, at least until adolescence.

On the other hand, perhaps girls are affected as much. Girls become more argumentative and have more conflict with their mothers (Wallerstein & Blakeslee, 1989). In addition, psychologists now appreciate the influence fathers have on their daughters' development. Girls raised by their mother have more difficulty relating to men later on. Girls from divorced families are more flirtatious, sexually precocious, and seductive, while girls raised in widowed families are more withdrawn (Hetherington, 1972). Therefore, paternal absence affects daughters as well as sons.

Prescriptions for Divorcing Parents   The research on divorce is substantial and leads to the following conclusions:

1. Children encounter a wide range of emotional, relationship, and economic stressors during and after divorce.
2. Divorce is a risk factor, and children who have experienced the family turmoil and divorce are more vulnerable to behavioral difficulties, but only a minority of children experience significant psychological problems as a result of divorce.
3. There are individual differences in children's outcomes, depending on how families manage the process of divorce.
4. Even parents who cope well will find that their children may have painful memories and regrets (Goodman et al., 1998).

The effects, then, of divorce on children depend on many factors, including the quality of the family life after the divorce. Children must accept the divorce, work through their feelings, reestablish routines, and reformulate relationships with both parents (Wallerstein, 1983). They must disengage from the conflict and resume their normal activities. If parents make an effort to maintain good relationships with the children, reestablish stable and healthy living patterns, agree on child-rearing issues, and understand what the children are going through, the negative effects of divorce can be minimized.

The Child in a Single-Parent Family   Children living in single-parent families have most of their contact with the custodial parent. The extent of their contact with the other parent is quite variable. Some noncustodial parents rarely or never see their child; others see them quite often. The relationship with the noncustodial parent is important, as children who report more positive and warm social interactions with fathers who are not living with them obtain higher scores on achievement tests in school (Coley, 1998). Sometimes, other adults can help. African American children, who are statistically more likely to reside with a single parent than white children, often have grandparents or other extended family living with them who may provide emotional support (USDHHS, 1996).

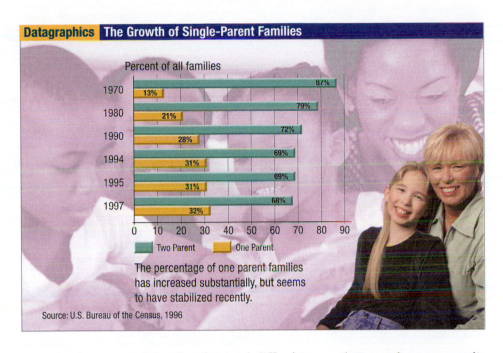

Datagraphics **The Growth of Single-Parent Families**

Percent of all families

Year	One Parent	Two Parent
1970	13%	87%
1980	21%	79%
1990	28%	72%
1994	31%	69%
1995	31%	69%
1997	32%	68%

0 10 20 30 40 50 60 70 80 90

Two Parent   One Parent

The percentage of one parent families has increased substantially, but seems to have stabilized recently.

Source: U.S. Bureau of the Census, 1996

Single parents claim that financial difficulties are their number one postdivorce problem (Amato & Partridge, 1987). About half the single-parent families live in poverty, while 1 in 10 two-parent families do (McLanahan & Booth, 1991). Even if the mother and children have not fallen into poverty, their standard of living declines significantly. One reason for low income is lack of child support payment from those who can pay (Sorensen, 1997).

Many divorced people overcome these economic and social problems, although it takes a significant amount of time and effort to do so. Single mothers often must increase the number of hours they work to improve their lot financially, which makes supervision of their children difficult. Children in single-parent families often must grow up faster, and these children, most often daughters, take on household tasks at an earlier age. Monitoring is more difficult, and sons, especially, are less likely to receive adequate supervision (Hetherington & Stanley-Hagan, 1995). Children in single-parent families also have more power in family decision making.

The everyday problems of single-parent families should not be forgotten. It is often difficult for the single parent to transport children to after-school activities and to find adequate day care or after-school care. Single parents are less organized, and mothers report feeling overloaded by all that they have to accomplish (Hetherington & Stanley-Hagan, 1995). They perceive themselves as more able parents but do report more child-rearing stresses, especially in the area of monitoring and control of children (Hetherington, 1993). Single mothers also report pride in their ability to handle their newfound role and sometimes, if they have just joined the labor force, some boost in self-esteem.

Most single custodial parents are mothers, but some fathers find themselves in this role. Fathers who have custody have their own problems. Many must learn a child-rearing routine that is foreign to them, and they suffer the same problems of loneliness and lack of child care that single mothers do.

Despite these problems, the change to a single-parent family can sometimes bring an improvement in the atmosphere of the home. If the home was filled with violence, it is less violent now. If it was fraught with emotional conflict, the conflict is reduced. Children do better in a happy one-parent family than a conflicted two-parent family (Goodman et al., 1998). On the other hand, many single parents find that they have turned in one set of problems for another.

T F
4
Children living in single-parent families are much more likely to live in poverty than children from intact families.

For Your Consideration

Parental monitoring is very important. How would you handle a preteen who claims you don't trust him or her because you always have to know everything about where he or she is and with whom he or she is associating?

Table 11.1	Successful Single Parent Families
1. Acceptance of responsibilities and challenges	These parents showed a positive attitude toward parenting and life in general. Problems were neither minimized or maximized.
2. Parenting as a priority	Parents wanted to be the best possible single parent and were willing to sacrifice time, money, and energy. Many thought there would be time for themselves later on.
3. Use of consistent, nonpunitive discipline	The household had a structure and logical consequences followed any misbehavior.
4. Open communication encouraged	Trusting relationships were formed through an honest expression of feelings.
5. Individuality fostered within a supportive family	Children's individuality and independence was supported. Each person was seen as having particular skills and interests.
6. Recognition of needs for self-nurturance	Despite the fact that the parent lacked time for herself, an attempt to continue to grow was made through physical, spiritual, emotional, or social means.
7. Respect of rituals and traditions	The family had specific routines, such as at bedtimes, and holiday celebrations were common.

SOURCE: Adapted from Olson & Haynes (1993)

A tendency exists to emphasize the problems and negative stereotypes of single-parent families. Many children in single-parent families do well, and an examination of these children found seven themes related to successful single parenting (see Table 11.1) (Olson & Haynes, 1993). The best conclusion is that single parenting is a challenge, but one with which many parents adequately cope.

Stepfamilies

Life in a single-parent household is often a temporary condition, as about two-thirds of divorced women and three-quarters of divorced men eventually remarry (Glick, 1989). Often people see stepfamilies as identical to nuclear families, but they are very different. Not only are children living with a new parent, but each individual comes to the new family after having experienced a loss. The children must adjust to a new set of rules, and the stepparent and biological parent must learn to share the children with the other biological parent who lives elsewhere. In addition, the stepparent may have his or her own children, so children may need to learn to live with stepbrothers and stepsisters. On the positive side, the remarried mother often experiences a financial improvement and gains some additional emotional support (Hetherington & Stanley-Hagan, 1995).

In the period following a remarriage, children must accept the remarriage and resign themselves to the fact that their biological parents will not get back together again. Children may resent their new stepparent's attempts to discipline and feel that the entrance of the new parent threatens the relationship they have with their biological parents (Hetherington et al., 1989). Stepparent-child relationships are somewhat more detached, conflicted, and less warm than relationships with biological parents (Bray & Berger, 1993).

Directly following the remarriage, the children may show more problem behaviors. Most younger children eventually form a reasonably good relationship with a competent stepparent, but adolescents may have more difficulty. Younger children become attached to, and benefit from, stepparents more easily than adolescents, who may actively challenge the new family (Hetherington et al., 1989). Still, only about 1 in 5 children have a bad relationship with a stepparent (Elias, 1997).

There is some evidence that girls have more difficulty adjusting to remarriage than boys (Brand, Clingempeel, & Bowen-Woodward, 1988; Hetherington & Clingempeel, 1992). In fact, over time preadolescent boys in families with stepfathers are more likely than girls to show improvements in their adjustment. Perhaps girls have developed a very strong relationship to their mothers during the time when their mothers were unmarried and see the entrance of the new male stepparent as a threat to this relationship. Perhaps the presence of a male increases the tension in the family more for a daughter than for a son.

Sons have a more difficult time adjusting to the entrance of a new stepfather into the family than daughters.

Adjustment to the new family structure takes time. Successful stepfathers initially spend more time observing how the family functions and establishing good relationships with their stepchildren and are warm and involved, but they do not assert too much parental authority (Hetherington & Stanley Hagan, 1995). If stepparents build a close relationship with their stepchildren, support the biological parent's discipline, but do not immediately seek control, chances of success improve (Hetherington, 1993). Stepmothers are more active and involved in discipline than stepfathers. When positive relationships exist between stepparents and stepchildren, the children are less aggressive and show higher levels of self-esteem (Clingempeel & Segal, 1986).

There is some controversy over just how well children in stepfamilies do. Some evidence does not indicate a "marital benefit" for children, despite the improved financial position. Some studies find that children in stepfamilies have about the same number of adjustment problems as children in single-parent families and more than children in intact families, although the differences are modest (Demo & Acock, 1996; Hanson, McClanaham, & Thomson, 1996). This is somewhat surprising because many of the problems associated with single-parent homes involve economic difficulties (McLanahan & Sandefur, 1994). Any remarriage benefit is greatest for those children who experience very little or no conflict in their families, so conflict may be one key. What goes on within a family is probably more important than the structure of that family (Demo, 1997; Silverstein & Auerbach, 1999).

On the other hand, positive research findings also exist. Some studies that compare children in stepfamilies with those in nuclear families in areas of adjustment or cognitive functioning find little or no difference (Clingempeel & Segal, 1986). In some cases, the presence of a stepfather reduces some of the negative effects of divorce for boys, and males score higher both on measures of cognitive development and adjustment (Hetherington, 1993; Oshman & Manosevitz, 1976).

One reason for these diverse findings is the many variables associated with stepparenting, including the children's attitudes and the parents' abilities. Although stepfamilies are faced with many adjustments, research shows that living in a stepfamily can be a positive, negative, or neutral experience, depending on the quality of the relationship between parents and children.

Many children in stepfamilies may have to make two gifts, one for their biological mother or father and one for their stepmother or stepfather.

Guideposts

What can stepparents do to increase the probability that the children will cope well with the new situation?

What's a Mother to Do?

When Manny and Sandra were married, they knew that Sandra's children from her first marriage Angela, aged 9, and Alexandra, aged 7, were not happy. Although Manny was nice to the girls throughout their courtship, the girls were distinctly cool to him, although they never talked back.

Sandra was divorced 3 years ago, and Angela and Alexandra's biological father sees them every weekend. He is a very competent and loving father who had no problems with the remarriage. He is not going with anyone, but when he met Manny at a birthday party, he thought Manny was a "nice guy" and wished them luck. The girls do not agree. They blame Manny for the breakup of their parent's marriage. This is nonsense since Sandra first met Manny a year after the divorce.

After the remarriage, Sandra and the girls moved from their small two-bedroom apartment into Manny's bigger home where the girls have their own rooms. The schools are also somewhat better in their new neighborhood. The girls resented the move, however.

Manny believes that eventually the girls will come around and accept him, but Sandra isn't so sure. It has been 8 months and Sandra sees no improvement, especially in Angela. The girls basically ignore Manny. The situation is somewhat complicated by a promise Sandra made to Manny who was never married before and has no children. Sandra agreed to have another child. They agreed to begin trying a year after the marriage. She loves Manny very much, and they get along very well. Now, with the girls not taking well to the situation, Sandra is not certain that having another child is the best course. She knows that her refusal will injure the marital relationship, perhaps showing a lack of commitment. She can wait a little longer but not too much longer, and, although Manny has not yet mentioned it, she is beginning to feel pressure.

1. *Why are the girls acting that way toward Manny?*
2. *If you were Sandra or Manny, what would you do?*
3. *If you were Sandra, would you now keep your promise to have another child? Why or why not?*

ACTION / REACTION

Latchkey or Self-Care Children

When Karen comes home from school, neither of her parents is home, and she spends about 2.5 hours after school alone. No one knows for certain how many children are in this situation, but estimates are that 1.6 million children, some 7.6% of all children between the ages of 5 and 14, are alone after school (Field, 1994). The public is greatly concerned about the safety and development of latchkey children (Campbell & Flake, 1985).

Some studies find a pattern of few, if any, differences in social development (popularity, adjustment, or competence) between latchkey children and children who have a parent waiting for them at home (Galambos & Garbarino, 1983; Vandell & Corasaniti, 1988). When self-care children were compared with children with adult care on such variables as self-esteem, locus of control, social adjustment, and interpersonal relationships, no significant differences were found (Rodman, Pratto, & Nelson, 1985).

The public, though, is most concerned about the possibility of unsupervised children getting into trouble, especially since lack of parental monitoring is related to substance abuse, delinquency, and poor achievement (Bradley, 1995). Indeed, eighth graders in California urban areas who spent considerable time in self-care were more likely to abuse drugs (Richardson et al., 1993). Some studies show that latchkey children are more likely to show behavior problems and lower achievement in school (Diamond, Kataria, & Masser, 1989).

Many children do not go directly home after school, "hanging out" at malls or street corners, while others go home, call their parents, and do their homework. When susceptibility to peer pressure in children grades 5 through 9 was measured, children and adolescents who report home after school were not significantly different from other children, but children who did not go directly home were more susceptible to peer pressure to engage in antisocial activity (Steinberg, 1986). Children who do not go home after school are more likely to be involved with deviant peers, have poor self-images, and show problem behavior. Adolescents whose parents know their children's whereabouts are less susceptible to peer influence even if the supervision is somewhat lax. Unfortunately, nearly half of the self-care youngsters do not go directly home (Steinberg, 1988). Parental monitoring is a crucial factor (Pettit, Bates, Doyle, & Meece, 1999) and even long-distance monitoring, such as when children call their parents at work to tell them that they're home, can be useful. Negative effects are most likely when children are not monitored regularly (Golambos & Maggs, 1991).

With the number of self-care children increasing, some organizations offer courses for children and their parents that encourage parents to evaluate their children's maturity level and ability to be alone. They also teach children safety and survival skills, such as how to talk to strangers on the phone, discriminate between emergencies and nonemergencies, and care for younger siblings. Children who take these courses feel more confident about handling both emergencies and everyday situations. However, the children strongly wish that a parent was home with them or would call them. They experience a sense of independence and accomplishment, but they also feel frightened, lonely, and bored (Freiberg, 1996; Gray & Coolsen, 1987). Some communities offer telephone helplines, which children can call for help with minor domestic emergencies, conversation, information, or advice concerning problems with friends (Peterson, 1990).

There is an important difference between those children who come directly home and whose parents use some sort of supervision and those who do not. Parents should be encouraged to provide long-range supervision for their children. Another possibility is the establishment of meaningful after-school programs which may provide academic help, a supervised place for students to socialize, and a place to play (Lamb, 1998).

Many elementary schoolchildren return home from school to an empty house. New research has discovered the importance of parents knowing where their children are and communicating with them on a regular basis.

Guideposts
How does being in self-care affect children?

Homeless Families

The fastest-growing segment of the homeless population today is families with children (Anderson & Koblinsky, 1995; Wright, 1993). Nine of ten homeless families are headed by a single mother, most likely in her late 20s, with an average of two children (Koblinsky, Morgan, & Anderson, 1997). Many are members of minority groups (Anderson & Koblinsky, 1995). About half of the mothers have completed high school, but most have not worked for longer than one month (Bassuk & Rosenberg, 1988).

Many families become homeless because of a crisis event, most commonly job loss, eviction, and overcrowded conditions (Koblinsky et al., 1997). Overcrowded conditions may at first seem to be a surprising reason, but often after losing the apartment, the next step is doubling or tripling up with other families (Foscarinis, 1991). This sharing continues until the family is asked to leave, possibly because of the constant tension of overcrowding. Having little or no income and nowhere to go, these families then become homeless.

latchkey or self-care children
Elementary school children who must care for themselves after school hours. (Some include junior high school students in the definition.)

Homeless children show many deficits, especially in language. Their families need permanent housing and extensive social services.

Homeless families are more similar to than different from other poor families, but homeless parents have experienced more disruptions in their early life than other poor people (Milburn & D'Ercole, 1991). One-third of the mothers heading homeless families report having been abused during childhood, and two-thirds have experienced major family disruptions, such as divorce in their early life. The physical abuse continues into their adult relationships, and homeless mothers have higher rates of spousal violence than poor but housed women (Browne & Bassuk, 1997). Homeless mothers are more likely than poor single mothers who have housing to report an early experience that includes being in a foster home, running away for a week or more, or living on the street for a time (Bassuk & Rosenberg, 1988; Bassuck et al., 1997).

The frequency of alcohol and other drug problems as well as serious psychiatric problems is also greater among homeless mothers than among poor, housed mothers (Bassuk et al., 1997; Hausman & Hammen, 1993), although only about 10% report they have been hospitalized for mental illness or treated for substance abuse (Robertson, 1991). Homeless mothers often have less social support, and their relationships are often filled with conflict (Bassuk et al., 1997; Vostanis, Grattan, Cumella, & Winchester, 1997). They may have some contact with family members, but presently they have no one to turn to and are isolated, often because they are likely to have stayed with these family members or friends in the past. Homeless families generally do not live on the streets but in emergency shelters, which are crowded and noisy, with little privacy (Anderson & Koblinsky, 1995; Buckner, Bassuk, Weinreb, & Brooks, 1999).

Being homeless impairs a mother's ability to parent (Hausman & Hammen, 1993). Homeless mothers are preoccupied with housing, food, and providing for the basic needs of the family. This limits the amount of time available for nurturing and teaching. The physical environment of many shelters is not conducive to children's development, and in many shelters mothers relinquish their parenting duties to others so do not feel in control (Koblinsky et al., 1997). Homeless mothers offer a great deal less cognitive and social stimulation to their children and are less likely to praise them or to respond when children ask questions.

Despite these problems, some homeless mothers are organized and optimistic. One homeless mother notes:

We may be homeless but we're not going to live like it. I get up at 6:00 every morning and clean and do my laundry. I fix up my room with nice things— my family pictures, my grandma's tablecloth, Keisha's art projects from Head Start. . . . Every night I work with Keisha on her letters and numbers. . . . I know there's better things ahead for us. (Koblinsky et al., 1997, p. 45)

Studies comparing homeless children to housed children who are very poor find that homeless children are at a greater risk for medical, developmental, and educational problems (Hausman & Hammer, 1993). For example, homeless children experience a greater number of both acute and chronic health problems than other poor children (Rafferty & Shinn, 1991). They are more likely to have delayed immunization schedules and to show higher rates of abuse and neglect (Alperstein, Rappoport, & Flanigan, 1988). Fewer homeless mothers receive adequate prenatal care and the rate of prematurity is higher (Chavkin, Kristal, Seabron, & Guiogli, 1987). Homeless children are also more likely to show developmental problems than poor but housed children (Hausman & Hammen, 1993; Molnar, Rath, & Klein, 1990). The most common problem is a lag in language development (Vostanis et al., 1997), but other problems, for example, in visual motor development are also found (Rescorla, Parker, & Stolley, 1991). Homeless children are also more likely to show such psychological problems as depression and anxiety (Buckner, Bassuk, Weinreb, & Brooks, 1999; Bassuk, Rubin, & Laurist, 1986). Sleep disturbances, withdrawal, and aggression are also relatively common (Hausman & Hammen, 1993; Bassuk & Rubin, 1987). Some of these increased difficulties may be due to the greater amount of stress in homeless children's lives as well as their lack of housing (Buckner et al., 1999).

Most homeless children are enrolled in public school, but their attendance is spotty, and they are more likely to drop out of school (Hausman & Hammen, 1993; Molnar et al., 1990). Homeless children are also more likely to read and do mathematics below grade level and to be retained in grade (Rafferty & Shinn, 1991; Rubin et al., 1996).

Although the long-term effects of homelessness on children are not yet known, it is clear that this is a population not only at risk but currently suffering physical, emotional, and psychological damage. What can be done? If temporary shelters are required, such shelters must provide children with day care, Head Start Programs, medical care, and space for physical activity. Obviously, affordable, permanent housing is required, but there is a shortage of low-cost housing, and the larger the family size, the less likely the family to find permanent housing (Rocha, Johnson, McChesney, & Butterfield, 1996). Such affordable housing must be safe housing, for many of these homeless women and children are separated from abusive mates (Browne & Bassuk, 1997). The more quickly families can be moved from shelters to permanent housing the better (Huttman & Redmond, 1992). Some areas offer transitional housing programs or reduced-rent apartments for a year or two while parents complete their education or job training (Bassuk, 1991). Homeless families also require extensive special services—including child care, social support, self-help programs, job services, health care, mental health care, substance abuse counseling and treatment, transportation assistance, and programs such as Head Start—but service enriched permanent housing is often unavailable (Rog, Holupka, & McCombs-Thornton, 1995a). It is clear that both affordable housing and extensive social services are necessary if these at-risk children are to develop in a healthy manner.

Despite the many challenges, most homeless children are doing well in school.

What is the effect of being homeless on children?

Gay and Lesbian Households

About 20% of all gay men have been married, and about half have at least one child (Allen & Demo, 1995). About a third of all lesbians have been married, and half have children (Falk, 1989). Some lesbians have borne children through artificial insemination (Seligmann, 1990).

In the past, gays and lesbians have been prevented from adopting children and have lost child custody cases just because of their sexual orientation. This is unjust because these decisions are based on incorrect assumptions. For example, some people believe that children raised by gays or lesbians will have more difficulties with their gender roles or will be more likely to be abused. Others fear that having gay parents would lead to homosexual preferences. These views are all false. Studies of children living with gay or lesbian parents show that the overwhelming majority become heterosexual (Green, 1978, 1982). In fact, over 90% of the adult children of gay fathers are heterosexual (Bailey, Barbrow, Wolfe & Mikach, 1995).

This does not mean that being raised in a gay or lesbian environment has no effect on the child. One would expect any child raised in a loving and warm environment with gay or lesbian parents to be more accepting of such relationships, and the evidence shows this. When children raised with lesbian or heterosexual mothers were followed from childhood into early adulthood, they were somewhat more likely to admit to same-gender sexual attraction, but otherwise no significant differences were found. When asked about sexual identity, the overwhelming majority of young adults with lesbian mothers identified themselves as heterosexual (Golombok & Tasker, 1996). Significantly more of the young adults from lesbian families, even though they were heterosexual, stated that they had previously considered or thought it was a future possibility that they might experience some same-sex gender attraction or have a same-sex gender relationship. This was true, especially for daughters and, indeed, the young adults raised by lesbian mothers were more likely to have had such a relationship. People raised by lesbian mothers are more open to these relationships than those raised in heterosexual homes, but the overwhelming majority become heterosexual.

The overwhelming majority of children raised by gay or lesbian parents consider themselves heterosexual.

Research evidence shows that the children of gay and lesbian parents do quite well and should put to rest the prejudice against their adopting and raising children.

Children reared in gay or lesbian homes do not differ significantly in intellectual functioning when compared with children raised in heterosexual households. When children raised by lesbian couples who had the child through artificial insemination were compared with matched heterosexual families, no significant differences in the children's cognitive functioning or behavioral adjustment were found. The quality of the couple's relationships and child-rearing practices were similar (Flaks, Ficher, Masterpasqua, & Joseph, 1995). No current research shows significant differences in parenting or outcomes between lesbian and heterosexual mothers (Chan et al., 1998; Falk, 1989).

Although the division of housework and decision making are shared in lesbian households, biological mothers are more involved in the child care and nonbiological mothers spend more time in paid employment (Patterson, 1995). Just as in heterosexual married households, when lesbian couples share the child care more evenly, mothers are more satisfied and children better adjusted.

Gay fathers can also be effective parents, and those living in stable relationships provide good-quality parenting. Most gay fathers have positive relationships with their children, and gay fathers want their children to have stable environments. In summary, no evidence exists showing that being raised by gay or lesbian parents injures children in any way (Patterson, 1992)

For Your Consideration ❓

How would you explain the fact that the overwhelming majority of children raised by gay or lesbian parents are heterosexual?

Guideposts

What is the influence on the child of being raised by gay or lesbian parents?

Best Friends

During middle childhood, the influence of peers and friends grows substantially. Peer interactions are very different from adult-child interactions. Interactions between children involve companionship and amusement; adult-child interactions involve protection, care, and instruction (Damon, 1983). Children turn to parents for affection and reliable aid, but they turn to their friends when they want companionship (Furman & Buhrmester, 1985). Having friends is related to better adjustment, more positive attitudes toward school, and better academic involvement (Wentszel & Caldwell, 1997).

During the elementary school years, children's ideas about friendship change, and they now see support, helping, sharing, and affection as more important and view physical characteristics as less important (Rubin, Bukowski, & Parker, 1998). As children mature, they begin to look at psychological compatibility. In fact, friends tend to be similar to each other in both prosocial and antisocial behavior (Hartup, 1996). Children's definition of friendship also changes from the self-centered orientation of perceiving friendships as self-satisfying to perceiving friendships as mutually satisfying, and from an emphasis on the momentary or transient positive interactions between individuals to a relationship that endures over time and through conflict. For these changes to occur, advances in cognitive functioning are necessary. Children cannot develop mutuality unless they can take a friend's point of view into consideration, an ability that develops in middle childhood.

Children in middle childhood typically have more than one "best friend." In fact, children are often found in small groups (Berndt, 1989). Children are aware of the standards of the group, and much of the communication in these friendship groups is in the form of gossip (Parker & Gottman, 1989). This gossip concentrates on an exploration of the similarities among group members, reveals attitudes and beliefs that members share, and often involves criticizing other children. As children gossip, they are affirming their norms and the values of the group. For example, they may criticize another child because he is bossy and aggressive, tells lies, or is a tattletale.

Acceptance and Rejection

Not all children make friends easily. Some children are more popular and make friends more easily than others. Children who are popular and have many friends are physically attractive; share interests with other children; are friendly, outgoing, and enthusiastic; know how to give positive reinforcement; and have interpersonal skills, including the ability to regulate their emotions (Dunn & McGuire, 1992; Fabes et al., 1999). Late in middle childhood, such traits as loyalty and empathy become important.

Two patterns are found in unpopular and rejected children. First, there are children who can be described as anxious, lonely, depressed, and having low self-esteem (Patterson, Kupersmidt, & Griesler, 1990). Rejected boys who are not aggressive are often rated by their teachers as being shy, passive, and socially insensitive (Dunn & McGuire, 1992). Second, there are unpopular children who are aggressive (Dodge et al., 1990). These patterns are relatively stable (Stormshak et al., 1999). Children who show aggressive patterns in second grade show acting-out behavior in fifth grade, and children who are socially incompetent and isolated in second grade show anxiety and depression later in elementary school (Hymel, Bowker, & Woody, 1990). The effect of rejection can be long standing. Rejection is related to poorer school achievement, lower aspirations, and less participation in social activities years later, while having friends and low levels of rejection are related to positive outcomes (Bagwell, Newcomb, & Bukowski, 1998).

Aggressive and unpopular children do have friends. They usually play with other aggressive or unpopular children (Cairns, Cairns, Neckerman, Gest, & Gariepy, 1988), with whom aggression is more accepted (Stormshak et al., 1999). Aggressive children are often members of very solid peer clusters throughout elementary school. They may be generally rejected by the majority of children, but they do find other children with whom they can share a relationship, and their relationships are no less meaningful to them. Some aggressive children are more likely to be rejected than others. Those who use aggression indiscriminately and who are prone to tantrums or outbursts are more likely to be rejected than those who use aggression as a tactic to gain social dominance in groups, although their aggression is not sanctioned by peers (Pope & Bierman, 1999).

Friendship Patterns and Gender

Same-gender friendships are the rule during middle childhood. Boys and girls do talk with each other, but their relationships lack intimacy and involvement. Active rejection of the other gender is rare; avoidance is the usual course of action, although teasing is not uncommon (Boulton, 1992, 1993). This segregation reaches its peak during the late elementary school. Of course, individual differences do exist, and some fast-developing children may be ready to develop cross-gender friendships.

Many reasons may underlie this segregation. Boys and girls see a lack of compatibility in play; boys don't expect girls to want to join in their games. They perceive girls as having different interests and participating in different activities. Parents may encourage same-gender friendships and the formation of gender role stereotypes (Hartup, 1983). Children may also be aware of the relationships between the genders that await them during adolescence, including dating, romance, and sex. Peer pressure may also be a factor. A sixth-grade boy interested in forming a relationship with a girl may find himself under peer pressure not to do so. The young girl may also be the butt of rumors and jokes and find it easier to avoid a boy than to risk her friends' criticism. Whatever the reason, the growth

Guideposts

Why are some children rejected by other children?

For Your Consideration ?

Why are popularity and unpopularity stable characteristics throughout childhood?

empathy

An emotional response resulting from understanding another person's state or condition

Segregation by gender is one of the hallmarks of middle childhood.

of same-gender friendships during this period helps the child develop the ideals of friendship and intimacy that prove so important when the child begins to form cross-gender relationships in adolescence.

Gender Stereotypes in Middle Childhood

As children proceed through middle childhood, they become more flexible in their understanding of gender relations and show more tolerance for others (Katz & Kasansnak, 1994). They become somewhat less rigid in their stereotypes. After about age 7, children no longer accept such stereotypes as absolute and are willing to make exceptions (Carter & Patterson, 1982). This tendency should not be overemphasized, for children have limits to what they will accept, and the resistance of boys to change is likely to be greater than that of girls (Katz & Walsh, 1991). Whereas boys show an increased preference for male stereotyped activities in middle childhood, girls do not show the same growing preference for stereotyped female activities (Carter & Patterson, 1982). Boys still have much stricter ideas about gender role preferences than girls do, and boys greatly value their own stereotyped competencies.

Moral Development

The moment Karen picked up the wallet, she was faced with a moral question. Moral issues are very much in the news and concern about instilling values in youth is growing (see *Rasing a Moral Child* on pages 448–449).

Piaget's Theory of Morality

Piaget viewed morality in terms of how a child develops a sense of justice and a respect for the social order. He argued that children's understanding of rules follows a general sequence. Preschoolers and children in the early school years consider rules sacred and untouchable and created by an all-powerful authority figure.

Ask a young child who did worse, a child who broke one dish trying to sneak a cookie from the chookie jar or another child who broke three dishes trying to help mother clean the table? Most children below age seven will say the child who broke more dishes did worse.

Guideposts

How will a child in the stage of moral relativism differ from a child in the stage of moral realism?

moral realism

The Piagetian stage of moral reasoning, during which rules are viewed as sacred and justice is whatever the authority figure says.

moral relativism

The Piagetian stage of moral reasoning, in which children weigh the intentions of others before judging their actions right or wrong.

In this stage, called **moral realism,** rules are viewed as inflexible, and justice is whatever the authority or law commands. The letter, not the spirit, of the law is important, and children become upset if people try to change the rules. Children believe in the absoluteness of values, and during these years, they evaluate acts on the basis of their consequences and not on an individual's intent or motivation.

At about age 7 or 8, children reach the intermediate stage. Children now interact with peers and develop some type of reciprocal give-and-take understanding. What is fair is more important than the position of authority. Punishments may or may not be fair, depending on the "crime" committed.

The stage called **moral relativism** emerges at about age 11 or 12. Children become more flexible and allow rules to be changed. They take extenuating circumstances into account and weigh them in their moral judgments. For example, ask a young child, "Who was naughtier—the child who broke one dish trying to sneak into the refrigerator to get some jam or the child who broke three dishes trying to help her mother?" Children in the stage of moral realism claim that the second child was naughtier, but children in the stage of moral relativism argue that the first child committed the worse act. Children younger than 7 years old rely primarily on consequences when evaluating another person's actions. Children older than age 10 or so rely on intentions. Between about age 7 and age 10, children rely on either one of these (Ferguson & Rule, 1982).

Children gain a better understanding of morality through social interaction and cognitive growth (Piaget, 1932). For instance, as children progress through the concrete stage of operations, they become less egocentric and are able to understand another person's intentions and motivations. They can also take more than one element into consideration at a time when evaluating a complex dilemma.

Piaget's ideas in this area have been criticized. First, making judgments about who is naughtier is a very special type of moral judgment. Piaget does not deal with questions about what a child should do (Rest, 1983). Second, studies have varied such factors as the amount of damage and the degree of intentionality and found that under certain circumstances, even small children understand that deliberate damage is naughtier. Piaget's findings are valuable, despite the narrow area of moral development covered. The most complete theory of moral reasoning, though, was developed by Lawrence Kohlberg.

Kohlberg's Theory of Moral Reasoning

Heinz's wife has cancer. There is a drug that might cure her, but the only dose is owned by a pharmacist who wants a great deal of money for it. Heinz doesn't have the money. Should he steal the drug? Kohlberg (1969, 1976) presented dilemmas like this to many subjects, and after careful study, he proposed a three-level, six-stage model that describes the development of moral reasoning. These stages are sequential and universal; that is, they are applicable to every culture, and no stage is ever skipped. Each stage requires more sophisticated skills than the one that precedes it. As we review Kohlberg's levels and stages, keep in mind that it is the moral reasoning, not the answer itself, that determines one's stage of moral development.

Level I: Preconventional Morality   At the preconventional level, people make decisions on the basis of reward or punishment and the satisfaction of their own needs.

If Karen reasoned at this level, she might keep the wallet because it satisfies her immediate desires. On the other hand, she might not, because she is afraid of getting caught and being punished. Morality is defined strictly by the physical consequences of the act.

Stage 1: Punishment and Obedience Orientation   An individual in stage 1 avoids breaking rules because it might lead to punishment. This person shows complete deference to rules. The interests of others are not considered.

Stage 2: Instrumental-Relativist Orientation   In stage 2, the right actions are those that satisfy one's own needs and only sometimes the needs of others. However, the only reason for helping others is that they will then owe you something, to be collected at a later time. There is a sense of fairness in this stage, and a deal is acceptable.

Level II: Conventional Morality   At the conventional level, conformity is the most important factor. The individual conforms to the expectations of others, including the general social order. Karen might keep the wallet if she reasons that anyone would keep it—and it's just too bad for the owner. On the other hand, she might not keep it if she reasons that it is against the rules and she would not be doing the "right" thing or being a good girl.

Stage 3: Interpersonal Concordance, or "Good-Boy/Nice-Girl" Orientation   Living up to the expectations of others and being good are the important considerations for a person in stage 3. The emphasis is on gaining approval from others by being nice.

Stage 4: "Law-and-Order" Orientation   A person in stage 4 is oriented toward authority and maintaining the social order. The emphasis is on doing one's duty and showing respect for authority. Sometimes people in this stage reason, "If everyone did it, then . . . ."

Level III: Postconventional Morality   People in the postconventional level have evolved moral values that have been internalized. These values are individualized and do not depend on membership in any particular group. This involves being able to weigh the ethics of various viewpoints and reasoning, and creating abstract guidelines to direct one's behavior (Kohlberg & Kramer, 1969; Turiel, 1998). For example, in Heinz's dilemma, an individual may reason that the abstract concept of protecting life or respect of property prevails rather than think of the specific consequences of the action (Thompson, 1995). Usually, such moral reasoning does not occur until adolescence at the earliest, so we would not expect Karen to show such reasoning. However, if this dilemma occurred at a later age, she might return the wallet because she herself values honesty and integrity, even if it means she has to do without something. In Karen's case, the reasoning for keeping the wallet is admittedly strained. However, she might reason that her friend had a greater need for the money than the man who lost it, and she would be helping another human being in need—her friend. Karen's values of friendship, loyalty, and giving to others would become most important here.

Stage 5: Social Contract, Legalistic Orientation   In stage 5, correct behavior is defined in terms of individual rights and the consensus of society. Right is a matter of personal values and opinions, but the emphasis is on the legal point of view.

Kohlberg's theory stresses the importance of the reasoning behind an act— Why this child would do_____, not whether he (she) did or did not do it.

preconventional level
Kohlberg's first level of moral reasoning, in which satisfaction of one's own needs and rewards and punishment serve as the basis for moral decision

conventional level
Kohlberg's second level of moral reasoning, in which conformity to the expectations of others and society in general serves as the basis for moral decision making.

postconventional level
Kohlberg's third level of moral reasoning, in which moral decisions are made on the basis of individual values that have been internalized.

Stage 6: Universal Ethical Principle Orientation In this the highest stage, the correct behavior is defined as a decision of conscience in accordance with self-chosen ethical principles that are logical, universal, and consistent (Turiel, 1998).

When people are asked to consider various moral dilemmas, their reasoning often cannot be placed neatly into only one stage. Kohlberg argued that some variability exists. While most of the reasoning reflects a particular stage of moral reasoning (for example, stage 3), some reasoning might be indicative of the two surrounding stages (stages 2 and 4). Improvements in moral reasoning are signified by a gradual shift in the percentage of reasoning from one stage to the next higher stage (Walker, 1988; Walker & Taylor, 1991).

Is Moral Reasoning Related to Moral Behavior? Would a person reasoning at Kohlberg's stage 5 act differently from a person reasoning at stage 1? As the individual progresses toward stage 6, we would think that moral behavior such as honesty and resisting temptation would increase. Most studies do find a relationship between moral reasoning and moral action (Blasi, 1980; Kohlberg, 1987), but the strength of the relationship varies from area to area. Some support is found for the idea that people at higher moral stages are more honest, but only relatively weak associations are found between progressing to higher levels of moral reasoning and whether a child will cheat, yield to temptation, or behave altruistically if there is a personal cost attached to it (Maccoby, 1980). For example, college students were found to cheat less as the level of their moral reasoning increased. However, although subjects low in moral judgment cheated more, those high in moral judgment also cheated when the temptation became strong (Malinowski & Smith, 1985). Therefore, although a relationship between moral reasoning and moral behavior exists, other factors help determine whether a person will perform a particular act.

Moral Reasoning and Gender Think about the descriptions of Kohlberg's stages for a moment. The emphasis on justice and individual rights is unmistakable (Thompson, 1995). Higher moral reasoning has little to do with interpersonal relationships or the context of the dilemma. According to Gilligan (1982), women have a different orientation to moral questions than men. Women see moral issues more in terms of how these issues affect interpersonal relationships, while men are more likely to stress individual rights and abstract principles.

The differences in moral reasoning are rooted in the varying experiences boys and girls have in childhood. For example, boys learn to be independent, assertive, achievement oriented, individualistic, and to attach great importance to the rule of law. This is similar to Kohlberg's stage 4 perspective. On the other hand, women are raised to be more concerned with the needs of others and to be interested in interpersonal relationships (Hotelling & Forrest, 1985). They are more oriented toward interpersonal connectedness, care, sensitivity, and responsibility to other people than toward abstract principles of justice (Muuss, 1988). Women tend to see moral difficulties as conflicts between what they, themselves, want and the needs and wants of others, and they may base their decisions on how relationships with others will be affected. Harmony rather than justice may be the guiding principle. This emphasis on care reads more like the stage 3 perspective. Gilligan notes, however, that neither reasoning is superior, just different, and the differences should be understood and respected. Gilligan argues that Kohlberg's theory devalues women's unique way of looking at issues (Thompson, 1995). A morality of care for others as a principle consideration is overlooked because of the emphasis on justice (Turiel, 1998). Karen may, then, look at how her actions might

Guideposts

What is the nature of Kohlberg's three levels and six stages of moral reasoning?

affect her relationships with others rather than simply looking at some abstract rules of justice.

Gilligan's ideas are controversial, with studies generally failing to find consistent gender differences (Galotti, 1989; Walker, 1984, 1989, 1991). In addition, research generally shows that only a minority of people exclusively use either a care or justice orientation; most use both (Gilligan & Antonucci, 1988). People invoke different forms of moral judgment in response to different types of dilemmas.

In fact, both men and women use more justice-based than care-based moral arguments (Wark & Krebs, 1996), although a tendency is sometimes found for females to use a care orientation a bit more than males on some issues. It seems that both genders have access to both orientations (Haste & Baddeley, 1991). Although there may be a tendency or a trend here, the patterns are not clear-cut. Even the idea that these two orientations must be separate is questionable. A commitment to others' health and well-being may be considered just (Colby & Damon, 1992).

Even though consistent gender differences do not occur, Gilligan has made a substantial contribution to the field. Her outlook broadens the view of moral reasoning to include the idea that the moral person may integrate concepts of abstract justice and the concern for others (Muuss, 1988). This was demonstrated in a study in which people were asked to list the characteristics of a highly moral person, and these descriptions were then classified into major categories. As shown in Table 11.2, people view the moral person as having strongly held values and principles in keeping with Kohlberg's ideas, but also as having compassion and caring as Gilligan notes (Walker & Pitts, 1998). The situation is even more complicated as people also see the moral individual as having certain personality characteristics, such as dependability, loyalty, integrity, trustworthiness and confidence.

Evaluating Kohlberg's Theory   Kohlberg offers a valuable framework for understanding moral development, but some serious criticisms have arisen. One problem is Kohlberg's emphasis on moral reasoning rather than behavior, as the

For Your Consideration ?

In your experience, do men and women reason differently about moral issues?

Guideposts

How does Carol Gilligan differentiate the moral thinking of males and females?

Table 11.2   Who Is the Moral Person?

People were asked to "write down the characteristics and attributes of a highly moral person." The results show a complicated picture of a principled, caring individual who has a number of personal characteristics. Six distinct clusters were isolated as shown here, with a few examples of the attributes included in each cluster.

Principled—Idealistic	Caring—Trustworthy	Dependable—Loyal
concerned about doing right	caring	responsible
has strong beliefs	honest	reliable
maintains high standards	trustworthy	dependable
self-disciplined	helpful	respected
has clear values	considerate	loyal

Fair	Integrity	Confident
virtuous	consistent	strong
fair	conscientious	self-assured
just	rational	self-confident
	hard-working	
	has integrity	

SOURCE: Walker & Pitts (1998)

discrepancy between reasoning and action is troublesome. For whatever reason, people sometimes proceed in ways they think are theoretically best, and sometimes they do not (Chandler & Boyes, 1982). In addition, it is possible to reason at any level and still find a reason to cheat, lie, or steal. More predictability is needed.

Kohlberg's theory also assumes that a person should reason fairly consistently in different situations. That is, a person predominantly reasoning at stage 4 would reason mostly at this stage and a little at the two surrounding stages. The available research does not support this consistency (Hoffman, 1988; Wark & Krebs, 1996). It seems that when people begin to reason at higher stages, they retain the ability and the willingness to reason at the lower stages as well (Carpendale & Krebs, 1995). Others object to the view of morality exclusively in terms of reasoning, as Kohlberg's theory ignores emotion and the characteristics of the person (Walker & Pitts, 1998).

Kohlberg's use of hypothetical dilemmas is also problematic. We know a great deal about hypothetical dilemmas, such as the case of Heinz, but very little about real-life moral judgments (Wark & Krebs, 1996). Kohlberg's theory would be somewhat more useful if it were based on actual life experiences rather than on verbal responses to hypothetical situations (Vitz, 1990).

A final question concerns the influence of culture on moral development, with some arguing that more collectivist cultures such as Japan, India, and China may look at some moral questions differently than more individualistic cultures, such as those found in the United States, Canada, or England (Markus & Kitayama, 1991). For example, children in the United States are taught a rights-driven morality, while those in India are raised more on a duty-based morality (Shweder, Mahapatra, & Miller, 1987).

The Psychoanalytic Conception of Morality

Psychologists who are followers of Freud view morality as based on the development of the **superego,** which consists of two parts: the ego ideal and the conscience. The **ego ideal** involves the individual's standards of perfect conduct, formed when the child identifies and internalizes the ideals and values of the adults around him or her. The **conscience** causes the child to experience guilt when misbehaving (Eidelberg, 1968; Freud, 1933).

The concept of **identification** is most important. Before the superego is formed, all resistance to temptation exists outside the individual (Solnit et al., 1979). The child is afraid that he or she will lose the parents' love or that the parents will punish the child. As the child identifies with the parent(s) and the superego is formed, the regulation is internalized. Even if the parents are not present, the child acts in ways that would make the parents proud and experiences guilt when acting badly.

Research on the psychoanalytic conception of morality is mixed. Children do identify with older people, including their parents (Kline, 1972), but their moral values are hardly carbon copies of their parents' values. Although some similarity exists, the idea that children totally copy their parents is unacceptable (Damon, 1983).

The Learning Theory Approach to Morality: Studying the Behavior Itself

Some psychologists approach moral development by studying the behavior itself—including sharing, helping, and giving, as well as lying, stealing, and being aggressive—instead of looking at the moral reasoning of the individual. They

superego
In Freudian theory, the part of the mind that includes a set of principles, violation of which leads to feelings of guilt.

ego ideal
The individual's positive and desirable standards of behavior.

identification
The process by which children take on the characteristics of another person, often a parent.

conscience
Part of the superego that causes the individual to experience guilt when transgressing.

explain moral behavior in terms of the situation, the child's background, the models available to the child, and the reinforcers present in the environment.

Behaviorists argue that moral behavior, like any other behavior, is learned. Operant conditioning explains some of it. Children who are reinforced for giving and sharing are more likely to give and share. Observation learning is also important. Much behavior is influenced by watching how others—both adults and peers—deal with life's challenges (Bandura, 1986). If we observe people we respect helping others or giving to charity, we are more likely to do so ourselves. This may not always be the case, since we do not imitate everything we see, and such factors as the character of the model, the consequences of the behavior, and our own characteristics affect whether we imitate (Bandura, 1977).

Critics of the learning theory approach note that cognitive factors, such as perception and information processing, are important to understanding moral behavior. Without taking these factors into consideration, a complete view of moral development cannot be obtained.

Parents act as models for their children in many ways.

Prosocial and Antisocial Behavior

It is tempting to divide the world into those who are honest and helpful and those who are not, those who give and share and those who are selfish. This trait-like approach has not worked well. In their landmark studies, Hartshorne and May (1928) tested thousands of children on a number of different tasks. They concluded that children's behavior varied with the situation. A child could be honest in one situation and not in another. One who cheated on an athletics test might or might not cheat on an arithmetic test (Cairns, 1979). This situational view of honesty prevailed for some time, but later research discovered a carryover of honesty from one situation to the next, although it was not very strong (Burton, 1963). It seems that some people are more honest than others, but we cannot say that a person will be honest in every situation.

Sometimes, nothing helps us feel better than the encouragement and reassurance of a friend.

Helping Others

Why do some children help others while other children sit back and do nothing? Social scientists have identified a number of factors that affect prosocial behavior. One of them is culture. Americans pride themselves on being prosocial, and indeed they donate a good deal of money to charity. Yet, American children are not as willing to share or to give as children in other societies such as India, Kenya, Okinawa, Mexico, and the Philippine Islands. Differences were found between the three societies that showed the most prosocial behavior—Kenya, Mexico, and the Philippines—and the other three. Prosocial behaviors were encouraged in cultures where children lived in extended families, had greater responsibilities, and the social structure was simpler (Eisenberg & Mussen, 1989). Cultures that emphasize obligation to the community, trust, and cooperation rather than individualism and self-reliance are more likely to produce people who are prosocial but also are more conforming (Stevenson, 1991).

Raising a Moral Child

Parents, schools and communities are wrestling with the problem of raising children who are decent and moral. At a time when supervision of children is more tenuous and life is infinitely more complicated, the question of how to raise virtuous children becomes more urgent. Serious evidence of social disintegration involving arrests and criminality are splashed all over the news; we seem very much to be a society in crisis. We also see the problems of intolerance and bigotry and wonder whether anything can be done to improve children's moral development. One survey found that 71% of all Americans believe it is more important to teach values than academic subjects, and respect for others topped the list (Wagner, 1996).

Years ago, special programs called values clarification courses were advocated. These emphasized the importance of children experiencing the process of valuing, rather than attempting to transmit a group of values to children (Raths, Harmin, & Simon, 1966). Students were challenged to discover their own values. The teacher offered a number of anecdotes, simulations, and other activities aimed at getting students to freely adopt and clarify their own values.

These courses were severely criticized because so much stress is placed on process and so little on the end product (Ryan, 1981). There is no right or wrong (Bauer, 1987). Some authorities claim that fostering values cannot be left to self-discovery, and students cannot be allowed to find their own values without input from adults (Ryan & Greer, 1990). Such a hands-off approach runs the risk of children developing antisocial or prejudiced values without the correction of adults. Such an open-ended format is rarely practiced today (Herbert & Daniel, 1996).

A similar approach uses Kohlberg's dilemmas, such as the case of Heinz, in an attempt to improve moral reasoning. Students are encouraged to play the role of different characters within the dilemmas. A dilemma is offered to the class in the form of a story, and the students determine how the situation should be resolved, giving reasons for their solutions, which are shared in group discussion. Kohlberg also argued for trans-

forming schools into *just communities*, which involves establishing democratic structures and student participation in making and enforcing rules and policies (Oser, 1990).

On the surface, agreement on the type of values to be transmitted would seem easy to obtain. However, problems abound, especially in the area of priorities (Wagner, 1996). If you were a school administrator responsible for a new program to instill values in your students, how would you rank-order the following values in order of their importance to your program?

____ A. self-discipline
____ B. altruism
____ C. respect for the environment
____ D. respect for authority
____ E. tolerance for others who may be different
____ F. patriotism
____ G. compassion
____ H. obedience
____ I. self-sacrifice
____ J. courage

Two sets of values, espoused by two different philosophical approaches, vie for public support (Narvaez, Getz, Rest, & Thoma, 1999). One might be called

Another variable is child rearing. Parents who use reasoning techniques combined with affection outside the discipline situation raise children who practice prosocial behavior. This is especially true if parents make an effort to point out to children the effect of such behavior on others. Explaining rules clearly, and linking these rules to their consequences is also important (Robinson, Zahn-Waxler, & Emde, 1994). These explanations should be delivered with emotion and not blandly. In addition, children who observe their parents helping and sharing are more likely to do so.

Another factor is age. Older children have more experiences and more knowledge about what to do in a situation. Cooperation and sharing increases somewhat with age, probably owing to a decline in egocentrism and improvements in evaluating the emotional states and signals of others (Durkin, 1995; Eisenberg,

8

As children mature, they tend to share with other children more often.

character education and emphasizes such values as self-discipline, patriotism, respect for authority, obedience, perseverance, and courage. These are often perceived as conservative virtues, sometimes religious in nature (although they are not associated with any particular religion). On the other side are the citizenship values, which include altruism, concern for democratic values, civility, tolerance, respect for the environment, compassion, and self-esteem. The argument today rages over which values our children should be taught. Those who emphasize more traditional values often claim the breakdown of society is due in some measure to the loss of these values, to indulgent parenting, and advocate a return to respect and deference to authority, firmness, and character training. Those who favor citizenship values are concerned by the fact that traditional values are often "preachy," and they consider them more divisive than citizenship values (Wagner, 1996).

Parents can use both verbal and action-oriented methods to foster moral development in their children. Parents who encourage their children to participate in discussions of moral issues, especially those that present other points of view, promote moral reasoning in their children (Walker & Taylor, 1991a). An action component is also important, and children must be encouraged to put their values into action. There are many ways

to do this, including helping elderly people, collecting and distributing food at shelters, and providing special holiday gifts for homeless and needy children (Spade, 1995). Unless a concerted effort is made to build opportunities to put their values into practice, children may verbalize these values without really internalizing them.

The same emphasis on action is needed to reduce prejudice. Just placing children together does not encourage tolerance and respect for others. When many schools were integrated, it was assumed that physical proximity would encourage interaction, dispel prejudice, and reduce intergroup problems. However, the results have not been particularly promising (Weyant, 1986). We have not seen the expected precipitous drop in racial prejudice, for example, or the increases in interaction between African Americans and whites. The findings are similar for the research on integrating children with disabilities into the regular classroom (Kaplan, 1996).

The lack of progress should have been predicted. Allport (1954) argued that to succeed in reducing prejudice, contact needs to be planned to fulfill three characteristics: (1) the groups must have equal status, (2) they should share a common goal, and (3) they must engage in activities supported by authority figures. Unfortunately, status differences are often maintained, and many

classrooms do not encourage cooperation. Active cooperation can be increased, however, by using cooperative learning strategies in which two or more students work together to reach some common goal. By sharing the same goal, students can overcome their prejudices.

In the 21st century, children will face significant social and economic challenges. The need for tolerance and understanding between groups, self-discipline, and the ability to delay gratification will be as great as ever. Activity-based programs will supplement programs aimed at attitude change so that students will be encouraged to live their ideals and practice what they preach. The school and community will have to actively confront the social and moral problems that so plague our society if we are to prosper in the 21st century.

What do you think?

Some people believe that the United States and other Western countries are in the middle of a crisis of morality. Others disagree. What is your opinion?

You can explore the questions above using InfoTrac College Edition. Hint: enter search terms *Moral Development and Ethics, Social Aspects.*

Murphy, & Shepard, 1997). These improvements lead to an increase in empathy, the emotional response that results from understanding another person's state or condition (Eisenberg et al., 1996). A positive relationship exists between the ability to experience empathy and prosocial behavior (Eisenberg, 1989; Roberts & Strayer, 1996). Children show more empathy if their parents show nurturance, are responsive, accept their feelings, and if fathers are positively involved in child rearing (Koestner, Franz, & Weinberger, 1997).

A final important variable is the situation. A child will be more likely to help another if the personal cost is low rather than if it is high. Asking a 5-year-old to share green beans is likely to be greeted with joy, but ask the same child to share a piece of cake and you may get a different reaction.

Guideposts

What are the "ingredients" that produce a child who is willing to help and share with others?

Aggression and Antisocial Behavior

Almost all parents have to handle aggression in their young children at one time or another, and aggression is a growing problem at home, in the schools, and in the community (Henry, 1994). Concern about being the victim of aggression is widespread in young children. When children between the ages of 7 and 12 years were asked about their worries, concerns about physical harm or attack by others was the single most frequent response reported by children, and this survey was not conducted in a high-crime area (Silverman, La Greca, & Waserstein, 1995).

Physical aggression declines throughout the early childhood years, although verbal aggression increases, especially between ages 2 and 4. This decline may be due to improvements in language; children can now talk about what they want and what is bothering them. Children with linguistic problems and delays are more likely to be aggressive (Coie & Dodge, 1998). The increase in the ability to delay gratification may also help as children have a bit more patience. Aggression continues to decline during the elementary school years (Nagin & Tremblay, 1999). Aggressive behaviors become more person oriented rather than property centered and are often responses to teasing, perceived threats, or disagreements over some aspects of a game (Bouton, 1993).

Some children, though, are clearly more aggressive than their peers and these children show deficits in social skills; they don't interact well with other children and often criticize others (Patterson et al., 1990). Aggressive children often aggress against each other, and these children are more aggressive while interacting with other aggressive children than when they are interacting with nonaggressive children (Coie, Dodge, & Christopoulus, 1991). When aggressive children are placed in small groups with children who are not aggressive, their rates of problem behavior decrease (Dishion, Patterson, Stoolmiller, & Skinner, 1991). Since aggressive children often do poorly in school, they are often tracked together in a class, giving them less opportunity to interact with better-adjusted children.

Aggressive children are likely to be male, and boys are also more likely to be targets of aggression. The gender differences are rather constant across age and culture. Some argue that hormones predispose males toward aggression (Maccoby & Jacklin, 1980), and the evidence for this hormonal theory in animals is strong.

As children mature, more of their aggressive acts are aimed directly at others, called hostile aggression, rather than aimed at taking things away from others, or instrumental aggression.

The question is whether it holds for human beings, and here the evidence is far from conclusive, with some arguing that it is an important factor and others denying it (Schaffer, 1996). The argument will continue for many years, but both sides readily acknowledge that social factors are involved in aggressive behavior.

It is wishful thinking to believe that aggressive children will grow out of it (Coie & Dodge, 1998). Aggression is rather stable over long periods of time for both boys and girls (Coie & Dodge, 1998; Olweus, 1977, 1979, 1982). When children were followed from middle childhood through early adulthood, the more aggressive 8-year-olds developed into the more aggressive 30-year-olds (Huesman, Lagerspetz, & Eron, 1984).

Creating the Aggressive Child

Culture, personality factors, family relationships, and cognitive factors operate to influence aggressive children. Certain cultures encourage, or at least tolerate, aggressiveness. If aggressiveness is modeled in society, it is thought to be the proper way to deal with problems. Our own society seems to have a love/hate relationship with violence. On the one hand, violence is condemned and punished (albeit violently). On the other hand, our heroes use violence freely, sometimes without regard for the law, and children see violence—some of which is rewarded—all around them.

Family variables are also important. Many aggressive children experience family backgrounds of great stress, poor parental monitoring, and the overuse of power by parents (Dishion, 1990). Fathers who reject their children, show a lack of warmth, and especially those who harshly punish their children are most likely to have children who are aggressive (DeKlyen, Bierbaum, Speltz, & Greenberg, 1998).

Children who witness violence in the home may believe that it is acceptable to use violence as a means of settling disputes (Comer, 1995). In a series of studies, young children were exposed to live or filmed models acting aggressively against a Bobo doll. They were then given the opportunity to play with the doll. Usually, the young children imitated whatever they saw. If exposed to aggressive actions, they acted aggressively; if shown constructive actions, they imitated those actions (Bandura, 1986; Bandura, Ross, & Ross, 1961).

A child may also be rewarded for aggression, leading to more violent behavior (Becker, Barham, Eron, & Chen, 1994). If a child takes things away from other children and is allowed to keep them, the child learns that the consequences are positive and will continue to do so. Aggression becomes a characteristic method of dealing with desires and frustration.

Certain child-rearing strategies are related to aggression in children (Sears et al., 1957). Such strategies include permissiveness and punitiveness. Parents who are very permissive tend to raise aggressive children. In addition, the more punishing the parents, the more aggressive their children. The combination of permissiveness and punitiveness leads to the most aggressive children. If parents allow their children to vent their aggressive impulses, children think it is acceptable. Then they are harshly punished for it, which causes frustration and anger, which in turn leads to further aggression. Often, aggressive children are not monitored properly, and their homes are plagued by inconsistent discipline (Kazdin, 1994). Their parents often use physical punishment in response to just about any transgression and expect more problems from their children (Strassberg, 1995).

The process by which some highly aggressive patterns of behavior may develop has been described by Patterson (1986; Patterson, DeBaryshe, & Ramsey,

For Your Consideration ?

Why is physical aggression more common in males than in females?

Guideposts

What "ingredients" produce children who are aggressive?

1989). Any criticism from the parent brings an immediate aggressive response from the child, which causes the parent to withdraw from the interaction. The child, then, is reinforced for the aggressive response. The child uses coercion to get what is desired. A child whose early aggressive behavior has been rewarded by parents through a process of coercion will continue to use this pattern with other people (Patterson, Reid, & Dishion, 1992). Aggression results in a short-term payoff as other children give in to the child's intimidation or demands, reinforcing the aggression. The longer-term consequences are rejection and fewer opportunities to learn social skills. As other children react negatively, the aggressive child believes that he must defend himself from the hostile world. He becomes sensitive to what others are saying and more aggressive. This, in turn, just increases the child's rejection. Aggressive children then begin to associate with other aggressive, rejected children who share their beliefs. They become less involved in school and more isolated from other children (Loeber, 1990).

Peer groups also influence aggressive behavior (Parke & Slaby, 1983). This may occur in three ways. First, children may model themselves after a violent individual, especially if the model gains something of value through violence. Second, the peer group may reinforce the violent deeds. Although aggressive individuals are often rejected by the majority of children, they may find a group in which this behavior is acceptable. This leads us to the third point—the social norms of the peer group. Some groups reject violence more than others.

In addition, cognitive factors must be taken into consideration. Aggressive behavior can be viewed in terms of a stage-like decision-making process, and at every stage differences between aggressive and nonaggressive individuals exist. First, elements of the social situation are encoded and interpreted. Children who are aggressive attribute more aggressiveness to others, seeing peer behavior as more provocative and hostile than it really is and then retaliating (Crick & Dodge, 1994, 1996). This stems from aggressive children's view of the world as a more hostile place, sometimes as a result of a history of being harshly punished (Egan, Monson, & Perry, 1998). If children are asked to imagine that someone spills water on them during lunchtime and are given no additional information, aggressive children are much more likely to believe that it was done on purpose than nonaggressive children (Hudley & Graham, 1993). The next step involves clarification of goals. A child's goals in a social situation may include avoiding embarrassment, being first in line, or showing strength. Aggressive children may want to get even with a peer or avoid feelings of failure.

This is followed by the construction of a response, which depends on the number of behavioral alternatives generated and the content of these responses. Aggressive children often do not understand that other alternatives are available in a social situation. The decision is then evaluated. Aggressive children evaluate their actions positively, as they expect positive outcomes from their own aggressiveness. Finally, the behavior is enacted (Crick & Dodge, 1994).

Exposure to Crime and Violence

While emphasizing the factors that contribute to aggression, the influence of the child's neighborhood may be underestimated (Osofsky, Wewers, Hann, & Fick, 1993). Taking a more ecological view leads us to examine this important influence (Greenberg, Lengua, Coie, & Pinderhughes, 1999). Children who live in neighborhoods where poverty flourishes are exposed to more antisocial behaviors by other children and do not have as many nonaggressive models. Young children living in high-crime areas deal with death more frequently and at a much younger

T F 9

Aggressive children are more likely to view the world as a hostile, threatening place than nonaggressive children.

age (Allison et al., 1999). When elementary school children living in a very high-crime area were surveyed, almost all had witnessed a violent act, and over half had been victims of some form of violence. Weapons were a common sight, and some of the violence occurred within their family. Fears of violence were intense, and many children showed stress reactions, including a pervasive sense of fear and vulnerability and an inability to concentrate. Some admitted becoming violent themselves and adopting an uncaring attitude. Such patterns as hypervigilance, withdrawal, suspicion, reduced impulse control, and increased risk taking were common (Martinez & Richters, 1993). Many of these children were taught "avoidance" skills, including to dive or run when they heard shots or not to sit near windows.

These reactions are commonly found among children in battle zones around the world (Lorion & Saltzman, 1993), and there are similarities between people living in such communities and those living in combat areas (Cairnes & Dawes, 1996). Aggression may be the response to living in unsafe stressful environments, and children may learn to anticipate aggression and meet it with violence (Kupersmidt et al., 1995).

Not all children living in these areas are so affected, just as not all children living in war zones suffer from major behavioral problems—about 20% do (Garbarino & Kostelny, 1996). Some children cope with these oppressive circumstances (Punamaki, 1996), perhaps because their families provide a buffer from the violence (Zahr, 1996). Youth exposed to crime and violence represent a population at significant risk for developing a number of psychological problems including anxiety, depression, phobias and aggressive disorders (Berman et al., 1996), and parents often underestimate the amount of violence to which their children are exposed.

Television and Antisocial Behavior

By the time children leave elementary school, they have witnessed 8,000 murders and 100,000 other acts of violence (Huston, Watkins, & Kunkel, 1989). Does viewing violent television increase the probability of aggression?

Few authorities claim that violent television is the only or even the main culprit causing children's aggression, but evidence certainly indicates that viewing violent television increases the probability of violent action (Hughes & Hasbrouck, 1996). Short-term effects are easy to document (Wood, Wong, & Chackere, 1991). If two groups of children who are similar in aggressiveness are compared after one group sees a violent program and the other doesn't, the first group will react more aggressively. The same short-term effects are found for studies of children who play violent video games; that is, such play is related to increased aggressiveness (Griffiths, 1991).

Children of both genders and of all ages, social classes, ethnic groups, and personality characteristics may be affected (Huesmann, Eron & Lefkowitz, 1984). Although children at every age are susceptible, a particularly sensitive period during late middle childhood, around 8 or 9 years of age—has been found (Eron, Huesmann, Brice, Fischer, & Mermelstein, 1983). Exposure to violence peaks at about the third grade, but the correlation between aggressiveness and viewing violence increases until ages 10 to 11, suggesting a cumulative effect beyond this sensitive period.

Seeing violence that appears justified and realistic has a greater effect on children than seeing violence that appears unjustified or brings negative consequences to the aggressor. These realistic and violent shows are very popular with children (Gable,

For Your Consideration ?

What television programs would you forbid your elementary school–age children to watch? Why?

Guideposts

How does television influence antisocial behavior?

For Your Consideration ?

Will the v-chip help reduce children's exposure to violence? Would you use it if you were a parent?

1994). Although television violence can have an effect even if the viewer is not emotionally aroused, its effect is greater if the viewer is initially angry or frustrated.

Television may influence children's aggressiveness in a number of ways (Liebert & Sprafkin, 1988). First, some children may directly imitate; they simply copy what they see on television. Obviously other factors are involved, as most children do not imitate such behavior. Aggressive children, though, may learn different ways to aggress by watching television. Second, televised violence disinhibits aggression. People have certain inhibitions against violence, and witnessing aggression may reduce these inhibitions. Third, television violence may lead to antisocial attitudes and encourage children to accept violence as a way of dealing with problems. Children become desensitized to violence on television and come to accept it as a normal part of life, not taking it seriously (Coie & Dodge, 1998).

There is a positive statistical relationship between aggression and television violence (Hughes & Hasbrouck, 1996). Children who are heavy viewers of television violence are more likely to respond with aggression to conflict situations. However, such a relationship does not demonstrate cause and effect. For example, television may lead to aggressiveness in children, but aggressive children may also simply watch more aggressive television (Eron, 1987). There is some truth to this, as aggressive children do prefer more violent television (Eron, 1982). Children who are aggressive are often heavy viewers of crime dramas, adventure shows, and cartoons, especially those with high levels of violence (Sprafkin, Watkins, & Gadow, 1990). These children are more likely to identify with the violent characters than nonaggressive children (Sprafkin, Gadow, & Abelman, 1992).

Whatever the reasons, the link between aggression and viewing violence on television is well established (Comstock & Paik, 1994). Exposure to violent programming not only increases the probability of aggressive behavior but reduces prosocial behavior as well (Donnerstein, Slaby, & Eron, 1994). It is estimated that between 5% and 15% of all antisocial or illegal acts can be linked to exposure to violent television programming (Comstock & Paik, 1994; Graham, 1994; Silver, 1996).

Television can reduce the violent content of its programs, and some surveys show reductions ("Study," 1996). The v-chip, which allows parents to program out objectionable television shows, may make limiting children's exposure to violence somewhat easier for parents. The v-chip, which is now required on new television sets, is activated by a rating sent out electronically with the program. Parents can establish the level of violence they want to screen out (Carney, 1996). Nothing, though, will take the place of parental monitoring and parents explaining to children the consequences of violent actions. Some argue that teaching children to evaluate the violence on television, and to understand the consequence of real violence, is of greater benefit to children than the v-chip (Marano, 1997).

Atypical Development: Children and Stress

All children are exposed to stressful situations, but some children must cope with severe and multiple stressors (Kliewer, Fearnow, & Miller, 1996). Positive correlations are found between children's stress and their experience of anxiety, depression, behavior problems, delinquency, physical illness, and accidents (Clapp, 1988; Greenberg et al., 1999). Stress also adversely affects intellectual functioning. As many as 35% of all American children are estimated to experience stress-related health problems ("Children under Stress," 1986).

Despite many problems and challenges, most children do grow up to be independent, well-functioning adults (Herrenkohl, Herrenkohl, & Egolf, 1994). Even some homeless children are resilient and rise above their difficulties (Hausman & Hammen, 1993). Why do some children exposed to tremendous amounts of stress develop some difficulty while others seem to do well?

Children who do well despite experiencing great stressors are called **stress-resistant** or, more recently, **stress-resilient** children (Rutter, 1985; Wyman et al., 1999). These children bounce back and can cope with pressures that seem at times to be too much for any child. A number of factors differentiate stress-resilient children from their peers who are greatly affected.

Resilient children have easy temperaments, as the more flexible, adaptable, and easygoing child is more likely to cope better with stress than the child with a difficult temperament (Wertlieb, Weigel, Springer, & Feldstein, 1987). The more adaptable child also receives more positive responses from others, which reduce the stress (Rutter, 1985). Resilient children show a strong social orientation as well as autonomy, even during the preschool period (Werner, 1993; Werner & Smith, 1989). Their social skills may help them gain social support and positive reinforcement from others (Neher & Short, 1998). They seem to lack fear and are self-reliant. Stress-resilient children often use hobbies and outside interests as a refuge from the problems of the family. They are active in after-school activities, which allows them to be away from the poor home environment. These children also use better problem-solving strategies and are less likely to catastrophize—that is, make a mountain out of a molehill. They do not focus on the negative aspects of a situation (Brown, O'Keeffe, Sanders, & Baker, 1986).

Many of these children have something about them that is special and allows them to garner whatever emotional resources the family has to offer (Radke-Yarrow & Sherman, 1991). For example, one such child was the only healthy child in the family, while another had some musical talent. Children who have experienced nurturant and responsive caregiving are more likely to be resilient, probably because they have a good basis from which to deal with the world (Wyman et al., 1999).

Generally, resilient children use active coping strategies. They think about a solution to a problem and seek help from others when they need it (Sandler, Tein & West, 1994). Their coping strategies may be affected by how their parents cope with stress. Homeless children who are resilient often have mothers who are deemed to be resilient as well (Hausman & Hammen, 1993). Children who see their parents use active strategies (for example, looking at the stressor in a different manner and actively doing something about it) tend to do the same (Kliewer & Lewis, 1995). Resilient children have high self-esteem, including both self-liking and self-efficacy, which derive from their school work and hobbies; elements of their experience that are outside the home (Werner, 1993).

Of all the protective factors, though, a good relationship with an adult is the greatest buffer or protective device for children (Clapp, 1988). The positive relationship with an adult does not have to be with a parent. Sometimes an older sibling, a grandparent, or another adult—perhaps a teacher—can serve as a role model and confidant. Stress-resilient children are very active in finding these adults whose social support effectively moderates the effect of stress (Werner, 1984; Wertlieb, Weigel, & Feldstein, 1989). In Karen's case, her relationship with her parents is very poor, but she has a good relationship with her aunt, and this may help her adjust to the stresses in her family.

T F 10 Children exposed to a great deal of stress yet are doing well prefer to be by themselves and are deeply involved with their family problems.

stress resistant (stress-resilient) children
Children who do not appear to be negatively affected by stress or are able to cope with it and turn out healthy in the long run.

For Your Consideration
Using the research on stress-resilient children, construct a community program that might help children who are presently dealing with highly stressful situations.

Children who are resilient are frequently involved in taking care of others, most commonly younger siblings. This concept is called *required helpfulness* (Werner & Smith, 1982). Helping and caring for others may increase their coping skills and morale and generally give them a sense of purpose.

Finally, children seem to be able to deal with a single stressor but have difficulty dealing with multiple stressors. If a child must deal with some stress, such as the death of a loved one or failure, it is then best to try to maintain stability in other areas of life. This is why divorce, which brings about multiple changes in a child's life, can have such negative consequences. If possible, the number of changes that are introduced into a child's life following divorce should be as few as possible so that the child has the opportunity to adjust to the divorce.

This emphasis on stress-resilient children is refreshing. Instead of looking at the factors that cause behavioral problems, we are looking at why some children are able to transcend or cope with these stressors while others are not.

Guideposts

What characteristics describe a child who is considered stress-resilient?

Middle Childhood in Perspective

The elementary school period is often considered one of horizontal growth. Middle childhood is viewed as the calm before the storm of change that occurs in adolescence. Unfortunately, this has led to the mistaken notion that middle childhood is a stagnant period, which is untrue. Unlike the early years, when cognitive, physical, and social growth are obvious, changes during middle childhood are more gradual. We must look harder to find them, but significant changes are taking place. The child's social world is expanding, as friends and teachers become more important. Children are given more freedom and responsibility at home. Because parents will not be with them all the time, children must develop their own sense of right and wrong and decide how they will handle their interpersonal relationships.

These trends are seen in Karen's dilemma. There are no parents or even adult figures present to tell Karen what to do. Karen must reason and act on her own and decide whether to give the wallet back or keep it. Her background, her relationships with her parents, her self-concept, and numerous other factors will influence her reasoning and final behavior.

It comes as no surprise, then, that psychologists find that children who emerge from middle childhood with positive self-esteem, good working relationships with their parents, a healthy relationship with friends, and a good feeling about their own academic and social capabilities, are ready to tackle the challenges that await them during adolescence.

Summary

1. Children's social network expands significantly in middle childhood. According to Erikson, the positive outcome of middle childhood is the development of a sense of industry, while the negative outcome is a feeling of inferiority.

2. Freud noted that upon resolving the Oedipus complex, children next enter a latency phase, when sexuality is hidden. Boys' and girls' groups are segregated.

3. During middle childhood, the self-concept shifts from physical to psychological characteristics. Children receive feedback from many different people. Their self-concept develops from a combination of this feedback and their own evaluation of their subjective experiences. Self-esteem is the valuation that people place on aspects of their self. It is divided into self-liking and self-efficacy. High levels of self-esteem are related to many positive behaviors. It is not easy to raise a child's self-esteem, especially a child who already has low self-esteem.

4. Children's relationships to their parents change during middle childhood. Children become more independent and later in the stage are greatly influenced by peers. They also become more argumentative and question parental judgment more often.

5. Children's immediate reaction to divorce involves anger, depression, and guilt. Normally, children recover from the initial shock after a year or so, but the long-term effects of divorce can be serious if parents continue to argue, if serious financial problems exist, and if social supports are unavailable.

6. The stepfamily situation requires adjustment on everyone's part. Stepfathers who attempt to build a good relationship with the children before trying to discipline them do better than if they do not first attend to the personal relationships.

7. Children who must take care of themselves after school are called latchkey or self-care children. Evidence indicates that if the child comes right home after school and parents monitor the child even from a distance, the experience does not yield negative results. However, many children do not go straight home after school and are not monitored. Some schools and social agencies offer training for self-care children.

8. Most homeless families are headed by mothers, many of whom have suffered serious disruptions in their early lives. Homeless children experience many more health problems, developmental problems such as lags in language development, and psychological problems such as depression compared with children who are poor but housed. Homeless families need permanent, affordable housing and intensive psychological and social services.

9. Friendships in middle childhood are based upon psychological compatibility. Children's conceptions of friendship change over time as children become more cognitively sophisticated. Children who are popular tend to be friendly, have good social skills, share interests with their peers, and are physically appealing. Rejected children are anxious, depressed, or aggressive.

10. In middle childhood, children become somewhat more flexible in their understanding of gender roles. Boys show an increased preference for male-stereotyped activities, while girls do not show such a preference for stereotyped female activities.

11. Piaget and Kohlberg both advanced theories of moral reasoning. Piaget noted that young children do not take intention into consideration when judging actions and that they see rules as unchangeable. Older children are more flexible and consider intent when judging actions. Kohlberg explained the development of moral reasoning in terms of three levels, each of which contains two stages. It is the reasoning behind the moral decision, not the decision itself, that determines the level of moral reasoning.

12. Carol Gilligan argues that, while males are oriented toward individual rights and legal issues, women are more concerned with how their decision will affect their social and interpersonal relationships. Although there is evidence that two different styles of moral reasoning exist, the idea that there are distinct gender-related styles of moral reasoning does not fit the evidence.

13. Freud viewed morality in terms of the development of the superego. The child identifies with the parent of the same sex and internalizes ideals and values.

14. Behaviorists are more interested in studying moral behaviors—such as cheating and altruism—than in the reasoning behind the behavior. The environment as well as the situation itself affects moral behavior.

15. Some cultures encourage more prosocial behavior than others. Children are more likely to show prosocial behavior when parents use rational methods of discipline and point out how the child's behavior helps others. The models children observe around them, as well as the reinforcements they experience or witness, are also important. Children's prosocial behavior increases with age because they become less egocentric.

Review

16. Children who observe a great deal of aggressive behavior at home, who are harshly disciplined, or who are taught that aggressiveness is an acceptable method of getting what they want tend to be aggressive. Aggressive children interpret the actions of others as provocative and are more likely to use violence as a response. Living in a violent neighborhood may affect children's development and behavior.

17. Most studies indicate that observing violent behavior on television makes it more likely that a child will act aggressively. It also desensitizes children to violence.

18. Children often cope well with a single stressor, but when exposed to multiple stressors, they are more likely to develop stress-related problems. Some children are stress-resistant or stress-resilient. These resilient children show a strong social orientation and are flexible and more adaptable. They tend to be active in after-school activities and use better problem-solving strategies than other children. A good adult-child relationship can be a buffer against the negative consequences of stress. Children who take care of others are more resilient as well.

Erik Erikson argued that the positive outcome of the middle years of childhood is a sense of (1)_____, while the negative outcome is a sense of (2) _____. During middle childhood, according to Freud, children enter the (3)_____ stage, when their sexuality is dormant. The child's (4)_____ during the elementary school years is based on psychological conceptions, such as personality attributes and interests. The term *self-esteem* refers to the valuation people put on aspects of their self as well as the character to be responsible for one's actions and caring for others. It is often divided into two distinct areas: (5)_____ and self-(6)_____. (7)_____ self-esteem is related to many positive behaviors, while having a low opinion of oneself is related to avoidance of challenges and other problems. As children proceed through middle childhood, their self-esteem (8)_____.

The relationship of parents to their children changes in middle childhood, but children raised by adults using the parenting style called (9)_____ are superior. The structure of the family has changed as children are more likely to be raised in a single-parent family than in the past. Children often see divorce as a stressor but may recover if (10)_____ is minimized and (11)_____ are available. Many people blame the problems of children on the divorce, but studies show that some of the problems are due to (12)_____ that occurred before the divorce. Single-parents claim that their most difficult problem is (13)_____. Most divorced people remarry. When a stepfather is involved, (14)_____ have a greater difficulty adjusting. Stepparents do best if they (15)_____ how the family functions and (16)_____ with their stepchildren.

Another term for *latchkey children* is (17)_____ children. The most important factor moderating the effect of the latchkey situation is parental (18)_____. Homeless children are at risk for many developmental problems, most commonly (19)_____ difficulties. Gays and lesbians have been denied adoption due to prejudice. Studies show that children raised by gays and lesbians have a (20)_____ sexual orientation.

Friendships develop in middle childhood as children look at friends in terms of mutuality and relationships are somewhat more stable. This requires cognitive advancements, especially a decline in (21)_____. Much of the communication between friends is in the form of (22)_____. Children who are very (23)_____ or (24)_____ tend to have fewer friends. Cross-gender friendships are (25)_____ (usual/unusual) during this period. Gender stereotypes generally tend to (26)_____ (increase/decline), with (27)_____ (boys/girls) being more flexible.

Jean Piaget argued that children below the age of 7 in the stage of moral reasoning called (28)_____ view right and wrong in terms of what authority figures command. After age 10 or so, children enter the stage of (29)_____ in which they become more flexible and take (30)_____ into account when judging right and wrong. Lawrence Kohlberg viewed moral reasoning as a stage-like progression consisting of (31)_____ levels and (32)_____ stages. In Level I or the (33)_____ level, people reason on the basis of gaining reward or avoiding punishment. People reason on the basis of rules and conformity if they reason at the (34)_____ level of moral reasoning. At the highest level, the (35)_____ level, people reason on the basis of self-accepted principles. There is a (36)_____ relationship between level or stage of moral reasoning and moral behavior, but it is far from perfect. Carol Gilligan argues that men and women reason differently about moral issues, with men arguing from a/an (37)_____ viewpoint and women from a/an (38)_____ standpoint. Studies show that men and women can use both ways of reasoning about moral issues.

Freud argued that children learn morality through the process of (39)_____. (40)_____ argue that instead of studying moral reasoning psychologists should study moral behavior and that people learn to act morally through operant conditioning and observation learning.

Many factors influence children's helping behavior, called (41)_____ behavior, including culture, child rearing, and age as well as situational variables. Aggressive children are influenced by these same factors. Children who are physically punished often are (42)_____ (more/less) likely to be aggressive. Children who witness aggression in the home are (43)_____ (more/less) likely to be aggressive. Patterson noted that some children's aggressive behavior is met by parental withdrawal which encourages these children to intimidate and use more aggression. These children obtain what they want through a process of (44)_____. Aggressive children also view the world as (45)_____. Studies show that viewing violent television (46)_____ (increases/decreases) the probability of becoming violent, and that aggressive children tend to watch more (47)_____ programs.

Despite tremendous amounts of stress, some children develop well. These children are called (48)_____. Often they have a good relationship with at least one adult, are sociable, independent, and have many outside interests.

InfoTrac

For additional readings, explore InfoTrac College Edition, our online library. Go to http://www.infotrac-college.com/wadsworth. Hint: enter the search terms *Childhood Stress, Moral Development, Children* and *Self-Esteem.*

What's on the web

Suggestions for Building a Sense of Positive Self-Esteem in Children:
http://childparenting.miningco.com/msub6a.htm

Kohlberg's Theory of Moral Development:
http://snycorva.cortland.edu/
~andersmd/kohl/content.html

Topics Related to Family Interactions:
http://family.go.com/Categories/Parenting/
?clk=NAV8_parenting

The Wadsworth Psychology Study Center Web Site
Go to the Wadsworth Psychology Study Center at http://psychology.wadsworth.com/ for quiz questions, research updates, hot topics, interactive exercises, and suggested readings in the InfoTrac College Edition related to this chapter.

Answers 1. industry; 2. inferiority; 3. latency; 4. self-concept; 5. worthiness; 6. efficacy; 7. High; 8. declines; 9. authoritative; 10. conflict; 11. social supports; 12. turmoil; 13. financial; 14. girls (daughters); 15. observe; 16. build a relationship; 17. self-care; 18. monitoring; 19. language; 20. heterosexual; 21. egocentrism; 22. gossip; 23. aggressive; 24. fearful; 25. unusual; 26. decline; 27. girls; 28. moral realism; 29. moral relativism; 30. intention; 31. three; 32. six; 33. preconventional; 34. conventional; 35. postconventional; 36. positive; 37. abstract principles (justice/individual rights); 38. caring (interpersonal, harmony); 39. identification; 40. Behaviorists; 41. prosocial; 42. more; 43. more; 44. coercion; 45. hostile; 46. increases; 47. violent; 48. stress-resilient (stress-resistant)

PART FIVE

Adolescence

12 Physical and Cognitive Development
in Adolescence

13 Social and Personality Development
in Adolescence

Physical *and* Cognitive

CHAPTER OUTLINE

Will the Real Teenager Please Stand Up!

Puberty and Adolescence

The Timing of Puberty

The Health of Teenagers Today

Nutrition, Physical Activity, and Sleep

Atypical Development: Eating Disorders

Cognitive Advances in Adolescence

Adolescent Thought Processes
  and Risk Taking

Morals and Values in Adolescence

Sexual Expression

Adapting to Change

ARE THESE STATEMENTS

True *or* False?

1. The growth rate during early adolescence is greater than for any other time since age 1 year.
2. Parents believe they experience more stress from early-maturing daughters than on-time or late-maturing daughters.
3. Adolescents who talk about committing suicide are more likely to do so.
4. Most teenage girls whose weight is within the normal range still want to weigh less.
5. Most girls who suffer from anorexia nervosa, an eating disorder marked by self-starvation, come from poverty-stricken families and are considered rebellious by their families.
6. When teenagers walk into the room, they believe that everyone is observing and evaluating them.
7. Adolescents who are religious are less likely to use drugs and more likely to show altruistic behavior.
8. Adolescents tend to overestimate the percentage of teens who are engaging in sexual intercourse.
9. More than three-quarters of all teens say they used a condom the last time they had sexual intercourse.
10. Most people who are gay can be recognized by their physical appearance.

ANSWERS: **1.** *True.* **2.** *True.* **3.** *True.* **4.** *True.* **5.** *False.* **6.** *True.* **7.** *True.* **8.** *True.* **9.** *False.* **10.** *False.*

Development
in Adolescence

Will the Real Teenager Please Stand Up!

When asked what first comes to mind when they think about today's teenagers, two-thirds of all American adults reach for negative adjectives such as "rude," irresponsible," or "wild" (Public Agenda, 1997). Parents of teens claim that their children have too much time on their hands and show poor work habits, and these negative views are shared by white, African American, and Latino parents (see Table 12.1). Many people consider adolescence a period of life marked by emotional swings, unrealistic ideas, and selfishness. The media constantly trumpets stories of adolescents involved in violent crimes and drug abuse, leaving the impression that adolescence is a hopeless period and the serious problems of adolescents today predict a dismal future for our society (Wagner, 1996).

Although the problems and challenges are real, this crisis-based perception of adolescence is inadequate. Most adolescents are not involved in drug abuse or violence and are optimistic about their future. And too little research has been conducted into adolescent prosocial behavior and the volunteer community work they often perform (Eisenberg, 1990). Adolescence can better be viewed more positively, as a series of "firsts" (Siegel & Shaughnessy, 1995).

Table 12.1 | Views on Teenagers

"Now I'm going to describe different types of teenagers and ask if you think they are common or not. How about teenagers who [INSERT ITEM]? Are they common, somewhat common, not too common, or not common at all?"

% saying "very common"	General public	Parents	Parents of teens	African American parents	Hispanic parents	White parents
Face social problems like drugs, gangs, or crime	62%	66%	62%	71%	72%	64%
Get into trouble because they have too much free time	50%	51%	45%	63%	61%	49%
Have poor work habits and lack self discipline	41%	40%	43%	49%	46%	38%
Lack good role models	36%	36%	35%	43%	34%	36%
Are wild and disorderly in public	30%	33%	30%	49%	43%	31%
Are lively and fun to be around	29%	25%	24%	35%	25%	25%
Are friendly and helpful toward their neighbors	12%	10%	12%	16%	14%	10%
Treat people with respect	12%	9%	9%	17%	11%	8%

NOTE: *Teenagers were defined for respondents as 13 to 17 years old.
Sample sizes: General public = 2,000; parents = 763; parents of teens = 162; parents of children = 293; African American parents = 367; Latino parents = 348; white parents = 596; youth = 600.
SOURCE: Public Agenda (1997)

For Your Consideration ?

Why do people have such a negative impression of the stage of adolescence?

It is the time of one's first kiss, first dance, first job, first date, first crush, and first love. It is a time of looking at the world in a new and different way, of forming new ideas and ideals. It is the first time for experiencing the intense feelings that come with deeper relationships.

Puberty and Adolescence

The terms **puberty** and **adolescence** are often used synonymously. Actually, **puberty** refers to the physiological changes involved in the sexual maturation of the individual as well as to other body changes that occur during this period (Sommer, 1978). Body changes directly related to sexual reproduction, including maturation of the testes in males and of the ovaries in females, are called **primary sex characteristics.** Changes that are not directly related to reproduction but that distinguish boys from girls are called **secondary sex characteristics.** These changes include beard growth in males and breast development in females. Adolescence refers to the stage from puberty to adulthood, covering all the psychological experiences of the person during that period.

Adolescence is a lengthy period of life, and changes occur quite rapidly throughout. The interests of a 12-year-old are certainly not the same as those of an 18-year-old. For convenience, adolescence is divided into three age groups. The period between the beginning of puberty and 15 years is called *early adolescence*, the years from 15 through 17 are considered *middle adolescence*, while *late adolescence*

Guideposts

What is the difference between puberty and adolescence?

begins at 18 years. At present, there is no agreement on the age at which adolescence ends (Steinberg, 1996).

The sequence of changes that takes place in adolescence is predictable, but the timing of the changes varies considerably from person to person. For example, the average age of the first menstrual flow among American teens is approximately 12.8 years (Tanner, 1990), but a girl may begin menstruating any time between ages 10 and 16.5 years and still be within the typical range.

Development of the Female Adolescent

The growth spurt is one of the earliest and most recognizable body changes. It begins at about age 10 or 11 for females and 12 or 13 years for males (Rolfes et al., 1998). Because this spurt begins much earlier in girls than in boys, early adolescent girls are generally a bit taller and heavier than early adolescent boys (Tanner, 1970). The growth rates during this period are exceeded only by those during the prenatal stage and the first year of life (Wagner, 1996). People often observe that young adolescents seem to spurt upward, which is accurate. The peak velocity of growth for girls is age 12 and for boys age 14. Girls reach their adult height well before boys (see Figure 12.1) (Brooks-Gunn & Petersen, 1984). Changes in weight are also readily apparent (see Figure 12.2)

The growth rate during early adolescence is greater than for any other time since age 1 year.

Figure 12.1 Growth During Adolescence

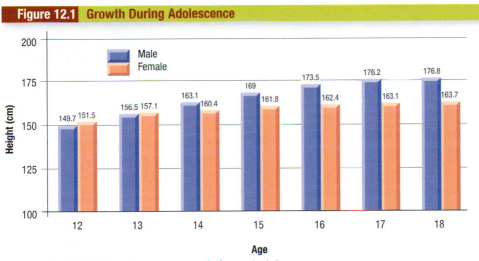

Stature is given in centimeters. To convert to inches, multiply by .39.

Figure 12.2 Changes in Weight during Adolescence

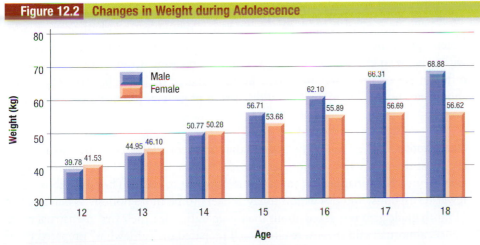

All data are given in kilograms. To convert to pounds multiply by 2.2.
SOURCE: P.V.V. Hammill, (1977)

puberty
Physiological changes involved in sexual maturation, as well as other body changes that occur during the teen years.

adolescence
The psychological experience of the child from puberty to adulthood.

primary sex characteristics
Body changes directly associated with sexual reproduction.

secondary sex characteristics
Physical changes that distinguish males from females but are not associated with sexual reproduction

Because girls begin their growth spurt a year or two sooner than boys, there is a time when they are taller than boys of their own age.

Women champions in the Olympics are often younger than their male counterparts, partly because of their earlier maturation.

Shortly after the growth spurt begins, girls develop breast buds, and the breadth of their hips increases. Then, when the growth spurt is at its maximum, changes in the genital organs take place. They include maturation of the uterus, vagina, labia, and clitoris as well as the breasts. When physical growth slows considerably, menarche (the onset of menstruation) takes place. At this point, a number of other changes in fat and muscle composition also occur. Following menarche, most of the changes are nonsexual, including further changes in body shape and voice (Krogman, 1980).

Even though all females progress through these physical changes, each adolescent girl experiences them as novel and challenging. Each person develops within her own environment, specific culture, and subculture and is exposed to a different set of peers and parents. The importance of her subjective experience should not be lost in any biological discussion of general physical development or norms.

Menstruation Of all the body changes that occur in adolescence, menstruation is the most dramatic. Today, most female adolescents receive at least some information about what is happening (or about to happen) to them. They are subjected to fewer restrictions, and discussion today is likely to be more honest. When a group of ninth grade girls was asked about their preparation for their first menstrual experience, almost all said they were either well prepared or "somewhat" prepared (Koff & Rierdan, 1995).

Most girls consider menstruation mildly stressful and greet it with mixed feelings (Koff & Rierdan, 1995). Some physical distress is reported as well as an immediate desire for privacy. Girls who are less prepared, or who begin menstruating very early, are most likely to evaluate the experience negatively. Although the experience produces some confusion and ambivalence, it is not as traumatic as once thought (Brooks-Gunn & Ruble, 1982; Ruble & Brooks-Gunn, 1982).

Development of the Male Adolescent

The first signs of puberty in males are the growth of the testes and scrotum along with the appearance of pubic hair. This is followed about a year later by a spurt in height. The trunk and legs elongate. Leg length reaches its adult proportions before body breadth. The last growth change to occur is a widening of the shoulders. The voice deepens, and facial hair appears. Muscles develop, in part because of the secretion of testosterone, and the heart and lungs increase dramatically, as does the number of red blood cells.

The Secular Trend: Taller, Earlier, and Heavier

In the past 100 years or so, each new generation has been taller and heavier than the preceding one. In addition, each new generation has entered puberty at a slightly earlier age. These, as well as other developmental tendencies, are known collectively as the **secular trend.** Since 1900, children each decade have been growing taller at the rate of approximately 1 centimeter and heavier by half a kilogram (1.1 pounds) (Katchadourian, 1977). Menstruation is also starting earlier. Between 1880 and 1970, the age of menarche averaged some three to four months earlier per decade, although the decline was greater in some decades than in others (Tanner, 1990). Secondary sex characteristics, such as breast enlargement and the appearance of pubic hair, are also occurring at younger ages, as is the peak adolescent growth spurt (Herman-Giddens et al., 1997).

The secular trend is due to an improvement in nutrition, a decline in growth-retarding illnesses during the first five years of life, and better medical care. The secular trend is leveling off, and some authorities believe it may even have stopped in the United States and Western Europe (Tanner, 1990), possibly indicating that there are limits to how much these factors can influence the course of the physical changes that occur during adolescence. However, not all evidence points to this. A recent study found that adolescent girls today are taller than those studied 20 years ago. Women's average height has risen from 5 foot 3 inches in 1980 to 5 foot 4 3/8 inches (Temple, 1997).

Guideposts

What do most scientists think causes the secular trend?

What Causes Puberty?

Three structures are thought to be primarily responsible for puberty: the hypothalamus (a part of the brain); the pituitary gland; and the gonads, or sex organs—the testes in males and the ovaries in females (Chiras, 1993). The hypothalamus produces chemicals known as releasing factors that are carried in the bloodstream to the pituitary gland, stimulating it to produce substances called *gonadotropins*, which stimulate the gonads. The gonads then produce the sex hormones that cause pubertal changes in the body (see Figure 12.3 on page 468) (Sommer, 1978).

secular trend

The trend toward earlier maturation today, compared with past generations.

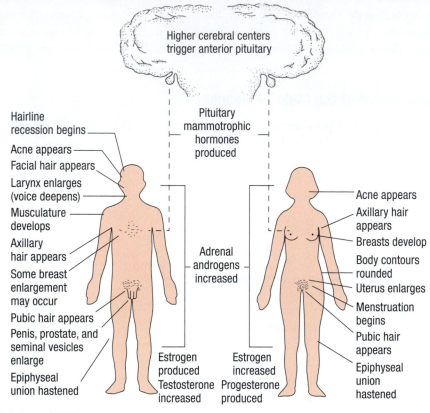

Figure 12.3   Observable Effects of Sex Hormones

Sex hormones produce many observable physical changes.

Higher cerebral centers trigger anterior pituitary

Pituitary mammotrophic hormones produced

Hairline recession begins

Acne appears

Facial hair appears

Larynx enlarges (voice deepens)

Musculature develops

Axillary hair appears

Some breast enlargement may occur

Pubic hair appears

Penis, prostate, and seminal vesicles enlarge

Epiphyseal union hastened

Adrenal androgens increased

Estrogen produced
Testosterone increased

Estrogen increased
Progesterone produced

Acne appears

Axillary hair appears

Breasts develop

Body contours rounded

Uterus enlarges

Menstruation begins

Pubic hair appears

Epiphyseal union hastened

SOURCE: Jensen (1985)

The level of hormones in the body is kept in balance. During childhood, the level of gonadotropins is quite low, but secretion of these hormones increases in later childhood. The gonads grow and produce more sex hormones. The hypothalamus is sensitive to sex hormones circulating in the body. As the amount of sex hormones increases, the output of the releasing factors from the hypothalamus decreases, thereby reducing the pituitary's output of gonadotropins and regulating the amount of sex hormones in the body. As the individual matures, the hypothalamus becomes less sensitive to these hormones, increasing the amount of gonadotropin-releasing hormones in the system, and the pituitary output of gonadotropins climbs. This rise increases the production of sex hormones, inducing puberty (Chiras, 1993).

The changes that take place during adolescence, then, are largely determined by hormones, one group of which is the sex hormones. Scientists use the term **androgens** to refer to the group of male hormones, including testosterone, and the term **estrogens** to denote a group of female hormones, including estradiol. Although both males and females produce both sets of hormones, males produce more androgens and females produce more estrogens. During adolescence, the sex hormones are secreted into the bloodstream in great quantities. The androgens cause secondary sex characteristics—such as lower voice, beard growth, the growth of hair on the chest and in the underarm and pubic areas. Estrogens encourage breast development and broadening of the hips (Kalat, 1981).

Guideposts

What biological factors cause puberty?

androgens

A group of male hormones, including testosterone.

estrogens

A group of female hormones, including estradiol.

The Timing of Puberty

As any observer of adolescence can attest, the timing of growth and development varies widely. Adolescents of similar ages can be more or less developed. Physical development brings about psychological and emotional changes. Some teens feel awkward and sensitive about their newly emerging bodies, especially when they compare their own development with that of their peers.

For many years, the question of puberty's timing was simply explained in terms of genetics and dietary factors (Moffitt, Caspi, Belsky, & Silva, 1992). In societies where medical care and nutrition are reasonable, developmental differences between people were ascribed to genetic factors. Although everyone agrees genetic factors are important, they do not account for all the variation (Steinberg, 1989). Some authorities point to environmental factors as possible codeterminants of pubertal timing (Belsky, Steinberg, & Draper, 1991).

In some specific cases, environmental factors can even override genetic factors in this area. Very intensive physical training can delay puberty and menstruation (Warren, Brooks-Gunn, Hamilton, Hamilton, & Warren, 1986; Warren et al., 1991). Teen dancers, for example, have later ages of menarche than other girls. Usually, mothers and daughters are quite similar in age of menarcheal timing (Garn, 1980). When girls enrolled in dance company schools were compared with girls who did not attend such schools, a relationship between mother's and daughter's age of menarche was found only for the nondancers, not for the dancers (Brooks-Gunn & Warren, 1988).

Other psychosocial factors have also been implicated. Family conflict and father absence in childhood predict a moderately earlier age of menarche (Moffitt et al., 1992). Better family relations, including lack of conflict, the presence of the father, and lower amounts of stress, are associated with later onset of menarche (Graber, Brooks-Gunn, & Warren, 1995). The mechanisms linking family relationships and status to pubertal development are not yet identified, although hormonal pathways are probably involved (Graber et al., 1995).

Early and Late Maturation

Most adolescents are neither very early maturing nor very late, but fall somewhere in between. Teens who mature either very early or very late may be affected by this experience. Early-maturing males have a substantial social advantage over late maturers. Adults rate early maturers more positively than late maturers. Early-maturing boys are considered more masculine, more attractive, and better groomed. They also have advantages in athletic competition, which may lead to popularity and increased self-esteem (Dusek, 1996; Spencer, Dupress, Swanson, & Cunningham, 1998). They have more self-confidence and are more satisfied with their physical appearance.

The picture is not entirely positive, as they are also more likely to show behavioral problems at school, to be truants and delinquent, and to use drugs more than their later-maturing peers (Andersson & Magnusson, 1990; Duncan, Ritter, Dornbusch, Gross, & Carlsmith, 1985). Early-maturing boys may form friendships with older boys and may be drawn into such behaviors. In addition, early-maturing boys become less active, more submissive, and less curious as they mature (Peskin, 1967, 1973).

Late maturers are considered tense and childish and are seen as always seeking attention. Peers see them as bossy, restless, less attractive, and having less leadership ability (Jones & Bayley, 1950). Late maturers are also viewed as more rebellious and dependent, demonstrating a basic conflict in their personalities (Mussen & Jones, 1957). Not all the findings are negative, however, as late maturers also are more assertive and insightful. Whereas the early-maturing boy may have a social advantage, the later maturer is superior in some intellectual areas, and later in life early maturers become more conforming and rigid, whereas the late maturers remain more flexible and more insightful (Jones, 1965).

The results of studies of early maturation in females are inconsistent, and the effects are more transient (Aro & Taipale, 1987). Early-maturing girls are more optimistic about their future, are more popular with boys, and date both more often and earlier than later-maturing girls (Gargiulo, Attie, Brooks-Gunn, & Warren, 1987; Simons & Blyth, 1987). They are more independent but more likely to be delinquent, use drugs, have eating disorders, misbehave in school, and obtain poor grades (Aro & Taiple, 1987; Koff & Rierdan, 1993). They are more likely than their on-time or late-maturing peers to associate with older peers and to experience pressure to have early sexual intercourse and break rules, and, indeed, they are more likely to engage in sexual intercourse at an earlier age (Magnusson, 1988). They are also more vulnerable to peer pressure to perform antisocial acts or take risks, compared to on-time and late-maturing peers (Ge, Conger & Elder, 1996). Early-maturing girls have the advantage of being more socially accepted by boys but don't have the time to adjust to the pubertal changes and gain the coping skills necessary for the types of social interactions they will have (Petersen & Crockett, 1985). They also may look older, and people may attribute greater social maturity to them than they really have (Caspi et al., 1993). This causes additional stresses. In fact, early maturers admit to experiencing more frequent and intense emotional distress than average-maturing girls (Ge et al., 1996; Peskin, 1973).

Late-maturing girls are more likely to be anxious and show higher levels of self-doubt, but they are under far less social pressure. Since girls mature about two years earlier than boys, later-maturing girls may develop along with their male peers.

These problems don't occur in every early-maturing girl, and perhaps early maturation simply increases problems that are already present. When early-, on-time, and late-maturing girls were compared, an increase in problem behaviors for the early-maturing girls (ages 13 and 15 years) was found. When early-maturing girls with a history of problem behavior were compared with those who did not have such a history, only those girls with a history of problems showed the increase in behavioral problems (Caspi & Moffitt, 1991). Those early maturers without a history of behavioral problems were no different than those girls who were on-time maturers. Early maturation is a stress that magnifies the individual differences that exist even before adolescence.

Early-maturing girls are somewhat less satisfied with their physical characteristics than later maturers (Duncan et al., 1985; Brooks-Gunn & Warren, 1985). Later-maturing girls tend to be somewhat taller and thinner, more nearly approximating the cultural ideal of beauty in Western society, while early-maturing girls are shorter and have more body fat. Most of these differences are significantly reduced or even, in some cases, nonexistent by 10th grade.

Parents perceive less conflict with early-maturing sons than with moderate- or late-maturing sons. On the other hand, early-maturing daughters are perceived to be a source of more stress and anxiety for their parents than late- and on-time maturing daughters (Savin-Williams & Small, 1986). Perhaps early-maturing girls date older boys, and monitoring them becomes more difficult. The early-maturing boy is less likely to date and be involved with older teenage girls.

Guideposts

What are the effects of early and late maturation on male and female adolescents?

For Your Consideration ?

Why are parents so much more worried about their early-maturing daughters than their early-maturing sons?

T
F
2

Parents believe they experience more stress from early-maturing daughters than on-time or late-maturing daughters.

The Health of Teenagers Today

Traditionally, adolescence has been viewed as a time at which health is excellent. The mortality rate of adolescents is lower than any other group, with the exception of young children (Millstein, 1989). Adolescents are rarely hospitalized and have low rates of both disability and chronic disease.

This does not mean that this generation of adolescents is especially healthy. In fact, according to some experts, this generation is less healthy, less cared for, and less prepared for life than their parents were at the same age (Carnegie Council, 1995). The health problems of adolescents are mainly, but not exclusively, found in the behavioral areas, including violent behavior, early sex, drug use, and poor eating habits. This generation is also less physically fit.

The relationship between these behaviors and health is obvious in some cases, such as drinking and traffic accidents. In other cases, it may not show up for many years. Smoking, lack of exercise, and poor eating patterns may take their toll later on. Even when teenagers are in a high-risk group, they do not change their behavior. Teenagers who were determined to be at risk for later heart disease due to high blood pressure, obesity, and family history consumed saturated fats and large amounts of salt, did not exercise, drank alcohol, and smoked cigarettes with no thought to their future health status (Adyanju, 1990). Young people's health is jeopardized by their own risky behaviors rather than disease (Moore, Gullone, & Kostanski, 1997; Wilson & Jaffe, 1995).

Accidents remain the leading cause of death for adolescents, and the accident rate for adolescents 19 years and younger is higher than for any other age group (Sells & Blum, 1996). More than three-quarters of these incidents are motor vehicle accidents, and three-quarters of these involve males (National Safety Council, 1998). There is some optimism, though, for the mortality rate has been reduced owing to safer cars; an increase in the legal age of drinking; greater use of seat belts; and until recently, lower speed limits.

The second most common case of death is homicide. Deaths from violence have increased greatly, especially among young people, and homicide is the number one cause of death among African American males (USDHHS, 1996). Recently, a reduction in the homicide rate among youth has occurred, but it remains a serious problem (Cole, 1999). The general level of violence throughout society is a national issue, and violence and delinquency will be further discussed in Chapter 13.

Suicide

Suicide is the third leading cause of death among people between 15 and 24 years of age (Worsnop, 1991). Each year, more than half a million young people attempt suicide, and, unfortunately, about 5,000 succeed (U.S. Department of Commerce, 1998). Males complete suicide four times as often as females, but females try three times more often than males. The difference is probably due to the more lethal methods of suicide (often firearms) used by males. Whites have higher suicide rates than African Americans, but the highest suicide rate is among Native Americans.

The most common cause of suicide is depression (Comer, 1995; Weissman et al., 1999). A sense of hopelessness pervades the victim. When psychological autopsies (analyses of why suicides occur after they have already taken place) are performed, certain factors appear, including drug and alcohol use, prior suicide attempts, depression, antisocial or aggressive behavior, psychopathology, and family histories of suicide behavior (Garland & Zigler, 1993; Mazza, 1997).

For Your Consideration ❓

Why don't teenagers who are at risk for later developing health problems change their behavior to eat healthier diets and exercise?

The presence of mental illness coexisting with suicidal behavior is common (Brent, 1995; Brent et al., 1995). Most adolescents who attempt suicide have experienced many stressful events in childhood, with a marked increase in stress in the year preceding the attempt.

Whenever a suicide occurs in a community, people start looking for answers and clues. Indeed, in a majority of cases, clues are found. About 80% of the adolescents communicate their feelings and intentions to other people before attempting suicide (Shafii, Carrigan, Whittinghill, & Derrick, 1985). Research provides some clues to predict the possibility of suicide, but unfortunately people do not always pay attention to them. For instance, many believe that people who talk about suicide never actually do it. But this is not so. People who talk about suicide are actually *more* likely to attempt it (Marttunen et al., 1998). Other warning signs include giving treasured items away and talking about "ending it." A previous attempt at suicide is also a warning that a future attempt might be made if the predisposing factors are not controlled or adequately dealt with (see Table 12.2 for potential warning signs) (Colt, 1983).

Some schools offer classes that teach students to recognize the warning signs and introduce students to the community resources available for help. Some evaluations are positive, showing gains in understanding suicide prevention techniques and an increased likelihood that teens will use a hotline to help themselves (Nelson, 1987; Viadero, 1987).

Other evaluations are not positive (Mazza, 1997; Williams, 1997). Some authorities are concerned by the possible negative effect such programs might have on already troubled students and doubt their effectiveness (Mazza, 1997; Shaffer, Garland, Vieland, Underwood, & Busner, 1991). A review of prevention programs found that the most effective programs were based on sound empirical knowledge, including a clear understanding of risk, and collected evaluative data (Price, 1989). Most suicide prevention programs fail on both accounts. Programs are not based on research on what is known about suicide. In an attempt to destigmatize suicide, the programs often deny that suicide victims experience mental disturbance. Suicide is sometimes incorrectly portrayed as a reaction to common stress (Mazza, 1997). The incidence of suicide is also exaggerated in many cases. Deemphasizing the link between emotional disturbances and suicide does not do a service to anyone, and many students only remember the link between stress and suicide. Many

Adolescents who talk about committing suicide are more likely to do so.

Table 12.2	Warnings of a Potential Suicide Attempt
1.	Preoccupation with themes of death or expressing suicidal thoughts
2.	Giving away prized possessions or making a will or other "final arrangements"
3.	Changes in sleeping patterns—too much or too little
4.	Sudden and extreme changes in eating habits or losing or gaining weight
5.	Withdrawal from friends and family or major behavioral changes
6.	Changes in school performance, lowered grades, cutting classes, dropping out of activities
7.	Personality changes such as nervousness, outbursts of anger, or apathy about appearance and health
8.	Use of drugs or alcohol
9.	Recent suicide of a friend or relative
10.	Previous suicide attempts
11.	Feelings of hopelessness and depression
12.	Recent loss of people who are close to them

prevention programs also do not reach the populations at greatest risk, which include dropouts, runaways, youths who are arrested and incarcerated, and especially youths who have been exposed to suicides (Eggert, Thoimpson, Herring, & Nicholas, 1995). Targeting suicide education toward at-risk populations may be the most effective way of preventing suicide (Garland & Zigler, 1993). Finally, reducing the availability of firearms would certainly help.

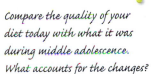

Guideposts

What are the warning signs that a suicide attempt might be forthcoming?

Physical Activity and Nutrition

The recommended daily allowances increase for most vitamins and minerals, especially calcium, during the teenage years (Barr, 1994; Rolfes & DeBruyne, 1990). In fact, nutritional needs are greater during adolescence than during any other time of life, with the exception of pregnancy or lactation (Whitney et al., 1994). Eating patterns among teens are variable, and no one pattern is found. Some teenagers have good diets, while the diets of others are deficient. The most common problems are skipping breakfast and snacking excessively (Hertzler & Frary, 1989). Adolescents consume about 20% more fat than recommended by nutritional experts (Kimm, Gergen, Malloy, Dresser, & Carroll, 1990). Eating patterns are affected by peers. If an adolescent's friends perceive drinking milk as babyish and choose soft drinks instead, skip meals, or snack on the run, these patterns influence others in their group (DeBruyne et al., 1998).

For Your Consideration ?

Compare the quality of your diet today with what it was during middle adolescence. What accounts for the changes?

Physical Activity

Although adolescence is often considered a physically active time of life, the facts speak otherwise. Many teenagers lead a sedentary life (Savage & Scott, 1998). Physical activity declines as the years of adolescence roll by (USDHHS, 1996). High school students today take less physical education (see Figure 12.4) and enrollment in physical education classes falls drastically from ninth to twelfth grades (Elias, 1994). In most American high schools physical activity is tied to team sports, and those who don't make varsity tend to abandon sports as well as other kinds of physical activity ("Why Physical Activity Drops," 1997). Once teens

| **Figure 12.4** | **Daily Participation in Physical Education by High School Students** |

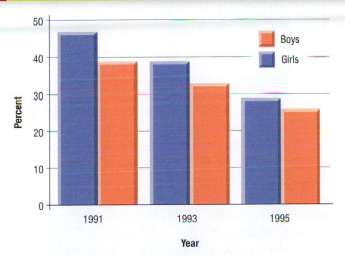

SOURCE: Centers for Disease Control (CDC), National Youth Risk Behavior Survey

Adolescents are less active today than they were years ago, leading to questions about their physical fitness.

Guideposts

Why do physical activity and fitness decline during adolescence?

learn to drive, they walk and bicycle less. Girls become physically inactive earlier than boys. Barriers to exercise include time problems and social factors (having no one to exercise with) (Myers & Roth, 1997).

"I'm Really Fat": Teenagers and Body Image

The primary focus of concern for adolescents, especially in early adolescence, is their body (Emmons, 1996). Although some teens cope very well with physical changes, they are not always comfortable with their new bodies. Many want to change aspects of their physical selves—mostly their height, weight, and complexion (Burns, 1979). The combination of peer pressure and media advertising encourages teens to try to meet a stereotyped socially approved body image. As teens proceed through adolescence, their wish for physical changes that they cannot have, such as being taller, declines (Bybee, Glock, & Zigler, 1990).

A good part of one's self-esteem in adolescence is determined by body image (Guinn, Semper, & Jorgensen, 1997; Rosenblum & Lewis, 1999). There is a link between physical attractiveness and high self-esteem and between dissatisfaction with one's body and low self-esteem (Grant & Fodor, 1986). Girls are much more likely to experience problems with their body image than boys and are generally less satisfied with their bodies (Galambos, Almeida, & Petersen, 1990; Paxton et al., 1990). For example, although 81% of the girls in one study were assessed to be within the ideal weight range or even underweight, 78% wanted to weigh less, and only 14% were satisfied with their current weight (Eisele, Hertsgaard, & Light, 1986). Many more girls consider themselves overweight than are really overweight (Pritchard, King, & Czajka-Narins, 1997), and most teenage girls whose weight is within the normal range state that they still want to weigh less. This dissatisfaction with body weight is so common in girls that it is sometimes called a "normative discontent" (Foster, Wadden, & Vogt, 1997; Rodin, 1993). Teenage girls often misperceive themselves, thinking they weigh more or are larger than their actual

Trends in Development

Proportion of Students in Grades 9 to 12 Who Participate in Daily School Physical Education
Fewer students receive daily physical education today.

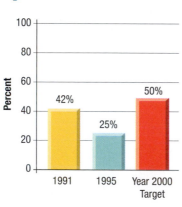

Source: USDHHS, 1998

Most teenage girls whose weight is within the normal range still want to weigh less.

measurements. This dissatisfaction with body measurements increases between ages 12 and 18 (Pritchard et al., 1997; Rosenblum & Lewis, 1999). There is a cultural aspect to these perceptions. White and Latino females tend to show greater discontent and want a lower body weight than African American females (Emmons, 1996; Halpern, Udry, Campbell, & Suchinderan, 1999).

These concerns begin early. About a third of all 9-year-olds and more than half the 10-year-olds report fear of becoming fat and perceive themselves as overweight even though they aren't (Mellin, Irwin, & Scully, 1992). Extreme weight concern in these young girls is predictive of symptoms of eating disorders later on (Killen et al., 1994a, 1994b). In middle school (fifth through eighth grade), these concerns are even more prevalent, and extreme weight control behaviors are sometimes unfortunately found (see Table 12.3) (Childress, Brewerton, Hodeges, & Jarrell, 1993). These behaviors and attitudes are associated with depressive symptoms, lower self-esteem, and feelings of inadequacy and worthlessness (Killen et al., 1994a, 1994b; Lewinsohn, Hops, Roberts, Seeley, & Andrews, 1993).

A natural part of pubertal development for girls is an increase in body fat, and with this often comes a decline in body satisfaction and an increase in weight concerns (Koff & Rierdan, 1991; Richards, Casper, & Larson, 1990). As teens develop, they move away from the thinness of prepubertal status and become less satisfied with their bodies (Swarr & Richards, 1996). Higher rates of body fat are associated with a chronic risk for eating problems (Graber, Brooks-Gunn, Paikof, & Warren, 1994). The fact that early-maturing girls tend to be heavier than on-time or late-maturing girls (who experience themselves as thinner) explains why the former are somewhat more prone to eating problems and the latter have a more positive body image (Blyth, Simmons, & Zakin, 1985; Graber et al., 1994; Richards & Larson, 1993).

Most girls, even if they are within the normal weight range, believe they are too heavy. Teenage girls often misperceive their weight.

Table 12.3	KIDS Items Endorsed by Middle School Students: Comparisons by Gender		
	Percentage	Gender	
	Endorsed	Female	Male
Items	(N = 3,129)	(N = 1,559)	(N = 1,530)
Wanted to lose weight*	42.0	55.0	28.5
Felt looked fat*	41.4	54.4	27.8
Afraid of weight gain*	23.0	32.5	13.0
Dieted*	31.4	42.6	19.7
Fasted*	8.7	11.2	6.0
Vomited	4.8	5.6	3.9
Exercised*	32.6	37.8	27.3
Used diet pills*	2.4	3.6	1.1
Used diuretics	1.5	2.2	0.8
Used laxatives	1.5	2.3	0.7
Binged*	16.2	6.5	26.3

NOTE: *indicates significant differences between males and females
SOURCE: Childress et al. (1993)

It is not objective weight status, though, that predicts adolescent eating problems but the perception of weight. Poor body image, irrespective of the real weight status, is related to disordered eating in female adolescents and the onset of depressive symptoms (Paxton et al., 1991; Rierdan & Koff, 1997). Between one-half and two-thirds of all high school girls in the United States are on a diet at any particular time, most of them unnecessarily since the majority of female dieters are not overweight (Cauffman & Steinberg, 1996). Most of this dieting involves adopting a low-fat or low-calorie diet, eating less and perhaps increasing physical activity, behaviors that can usually be considered healthy (French, Perry, Leon, & Fulkerson, 1995). However, a substantial number of adolescents use dangerous and unhealthy activities to reduce weight such as fasting or fad diets. These unhealthy weight loss practices have been reported by girls as young as 9 years of age (Berg, 1992).

Some of this obsession with weight is based on girls' perception of social attitudes. When students in high school were questioned about their attitudes toward weight and dating, male students were less tolerant of overweight partners than female students (Sobal, Nicolopoulos, & Lee, 1995). Females are more stigmatized by being overweight than men. In addition, many models in magazines and television are ridiculously thin, and teenage girls often believe they have to measure up to an impossible cultural stereotype.

ACTION / REACTION

Mirror, Mirror on the Wall

Lisa's parents understand what adolescence is like. They know that their daughter wants to be accepted into the crowd and is very concerned about her physical image. They were prepared for her spending quite a bit of time fixing her hair and makeup and talking for hours on the telephone with her friends. They were not prepared, however, for some of her other behaviors.

Lisa is of about average weight but still considers herself overweight. She sometimes diets stringently, refusing to eat, and then breaks the diet and overeats. She refuses to shop with her mother, insisting that she go with her friend and buy her own clothing. Lisa's mother allows her to do it, but she is genuinely unhappy with the clothing that her daughter buys. She does not think that her daughter is wearing clothing that makes her look her best or, for that matter, is wearing her hair and makeup in a way that is flattering.

Lisa seems to take what Lisa's mother considers to be minor events, such as being invited to a party, as overwhelmingly important, and Lisa's mother is especially concerned because Lisa's grades are not as good as they could be. All Lisa says is that her parents do not understand and have never felt rejected. Lisa also is talking back more, which is causing a strain on the whole family.

Lisa's parents understand the importance of the peer group and the problems involved in adolescence, but they do not know how they should react. You are a good friend of the family, and they ask you the following questions.

1. *How should they react to Lisa's eating behavior and her appearance?*
2. *How should they deal with her talking back?*
3. *How should they deal with their daughter's dependence on her peers?*

ACTION / REACTION

Males have largely been ignored in this analysis of problems with body image. With the exception of obesity, few researchers have looked at male difficulties with body image. However, there is cause for concern here as well, as recent findings indicate males are also falling victim to body image difficulties. Some male wrestlers have engaged in very unhealthy dieting, and runners also show an intense concern for weight control and a tendency toward disordered eating patterns (Parks & Read, 1997).

Another major problem is the increased use of steroids and performance-enhancing drugs. The prescribed cultural stereotype for males, especially male athletes, is a very angular, muscular body. In addition, with the emphasis on the importance of athletic performance, steroid use has become a great concern (Porcerelli & Sandler, 1995). To reach the goals of greater muscularity and improved athletic performance, some males use anabolic steroids, male hormones that build tissue, as well as other performance-enhancing drugs (Wang & Yesalis, 1994). They often do this despite being told of the long-term risks and side effects, which include breathing difficulties, skin problems, elevated heart rate, risk of heart disease, and aggressiveness and hostility, to name just a few. These consequences show why steroids are dangerous and, indeed, illegal substances (NASM Policy Statement, 1992; Ropp, 1992). Male athletes also are taking a myriad of other performance-enhancing substances. Most have not been the focus of much controlled research, and the future consequences of their consumption are unknown. The use of steroids by adolescents is significantly related to their use by friends, who most probably are also heavily involved in these athletic activities (Yarnold, 1998).

Guideposts
How do teenage boys and girls evaluate their body images?

Atypical Development: Eating Disorders

Until recently major eating disorders, such as anorexia and bulimia, were considered rare, but the number of reported cases has increased substantially. This trend may reflect an actual increase in eating disorders or simply greater awareness of them and better reporting. Revelations of anorexic and bulimic behavior by Karen Carpenter and Princess Diana have led to increased public interest and news coverage of eating disorders (Wicks-Nelson & Israel, 1997).

Anorexia Nervosa

Anorexia nervosa is a disorder marked by self-imposed starvation and involves an abnormal fear of becoming obese, a disturbance of body image, significant weight loss, and a refusal to maintain even a minimal normal body weight. It is fatal in about 10% of all cases (American Psychiatric Association, 1994). About 96% of all anorexics are female, and the onset is most often during the teen years.

Anorexics usually show little overt rebellion toward their parents, but they suffer deep conflict on the dependent-independent dimension. They are often raised in educated, success-oriented, middle-class families that are quite weight-conscious. They are also perfectionistic and are described by their parents as model children (Smart, Beaumont, & George, 1976).

Anorexics are obsessed with food, weight loss, and compulsive dieting and are physically active. Their physical activity may be part of a socially accepted activity, such as participation in sports, or unusual, such as running up and down the driveway until exhausted (Wenar, 1994). Once they achieve significant weight loss, anorexics do not stop, but continue until they are too thin to be physically healthy. Losing weight becomes an obsession, and they fear they will lose control if they eat a normal diet. Controlling their weight becomes the passion of life. Changes in their physiology, thinking, and personality occur. They misperceive their weight,

Most girls who suffer from anorexia nervosa, an eating disorder marked by self-starvation, come from poverty-stricken families and are considered rebellious by their families.

anorexia nervosa
A condition of self-imposed starvation found most often among adolescent females.

believing they are fat or about to become so. In fact, they often complain about feeling bloated after eating very small amounts of food (Wenar, 1994). Their condition becomes serious as their body begins to waste away. Menstruation ceases, they become ill and anemic, they cannot sleep, they suffer from low blood pressure, and their metabolism rate decreases (Bruch, 1978). In most cases, depression is also found (Herzog, Keller, Sacks, Yeh, & Levori, 1992).

The cause of anorexia is still a mystery. There is evidence for a genetic predisposition, as studies find a much higher concordance rate in identical than fraternal twins (Kendler et al., 1991). One theory emphasizes the effects our society's view of the glamorous female as very thin has on girls (Nagel & Jones, 1992). An analysis of articles in a women's magazine aimed at teens found that the models became thinner and the hips narrower over the years, and the primary reason for eating a good diet was to look attractive, not to be healthy (Guillen & Barr, 1994). Yet, females often find themselves surrounded by calorie-rich foods during social functions. Unable to integrate these messages, the anorexic develops a fear of losing control and of eating too much and gaining weight. There must be more to this, for only a minority of those exposed to such media messages develop these eating disorders (Cauffman & Steinberg, 1996).

Those emphasizing a family approach note that anorexics come from rigid, overprotective families in which conflicts are avoided and people are overinvolved with each other. This interferes with the formation of a personal identity. Still others believe that there is some basis in biology or that a neurological dysfunction exists (Muuss, 1985).

Bulimia

Bulimia involves recurrent episodes of overeating followed by a number of different behaviors intended to control weight and body shape, including vomiting and the misuse of laxatives. Bulimics maintain relatively normal weights, and the fluctuations in body weight are rarely extreme enough to be life-threatening, but the behaviors are abnormal, and purging can cause serious physical problems. A characteristic set of disturbed attitudes to shape and weight, sometimes referred to as the "morbid fear of fatness," exists (Fairburn et al., 1991). The overwhelming majority of bulimics are women.

Bulimics are aware that their behavior is abnormal but are afraid of losing control over their eating. Depression and extreme self-criticism are common after the binge. Often the food is sweet, easy to chew, high in calories, and is eaten very quickly. The binge eating may be brought on by some emotional difficulty, such as stress, loneliness, depression, rejection, or rage (Muuss, 1986). Bulimia is often preceded by a diet (American Psychiatric Association, 1994).

Bulimics have an all-or-none way of thinking, believing that if they eat a small portion of a forbidden food they will completely lose control. They often jump from one eating fad to another. They make lists of forbidden foods and begin by denying themselves these foods. Later, they break down and binge. They have unreasonably high goals and may believe that if they gain any weight at all they will be fat or that if they can't stick to a diet they are failures (Muuss, 1986).

Bulimics are perfectionistic, high achievers, and fearful of losing control. They often believe that others are watching them, and they are constantly worried about how others perceive them. Bulimics are likely to have histories of mood swings, are more extroverted than anorexics, become easily frustrated and bored, and may abuse drugs (Fahy & Eisler, 1993). Bulimics are very concerned about

For Your Consideration ?

Social pressures are often blamed for serious eating disorders, especially among girls. While all teen girls receive messages about being overly thin from the media, not all will develop serious eating disorders. What other factors do you believe are important?

Guideposts

What are the symptoms and possible causes of anorexia and bulimia?

bulimia

An eating disorder marked by episodic binge eating and purging.

pleasing men and being attractive, a difference between them and anorexics, who do not care about attracting others or sexual activities (Comer, 1995).

The treatment for anorexia and bulimia is varied. The first priority is to restore a reasonable weight, which sometimes requires hospitalization. In severe cases, intravenous feeding is necessary for anorexics. Family therapy that focuses on the relationships among family members and behavior modification to reinforce the anorexic to eat properly may be required (Muuss, 1985). Therapy for both anorexics and bulimics challenges misconceptions and attitudes about eating and weight control (Wilson & Fairburn, 1993). It is important to change the way these adolescents think—for example, their belief that weight determines one's value as a person, and the bulimic's low self-esteem and perfectionalism (Garner, Fairburn, & Davis, 1987). Longer-term therapy focuses on body image and interpersonal problems, making anorexics more aware of underlying difficulties with autonomy and to find other ways to assert their independence (Bruch, 1986). Separate treatment for depression may be needed. Therapy can be very effective, but relapses are not uncommon (Sarafino, 1994).

Obesity

Between 10% and 15% of all teenagers are obese (Dusek, 1996), and other figures are as high as 20% to 24% (USDHHS, 1998), depending on one's definition of obesity. Obesity has increased over the past 20 years, probably because teens are less active than they were. It heightens risks for hypertension and coronary disease. Obese teenagers also have more difficulty developing a coherent identity (Shestowsky, 1983). Obesity creates a social problem for the teen. Because our society's view of beauty and attractiveness is equated with being thin, the obese person is out of step with current fashion. The obese person also faces discrimination by peers (Fowler, 1989).

Obese children become obese teens, and obese teens become obese adults (Epstein, 1987). Parental supervision of eating habits wanes during the teen years as the adolescent gains personal freedom. Social and academic pressure may lead to increased caloric intake. Many students use food to quiet their anxiety, and the less physically active life many older teens lead runs counter to the more active life of childhood (American Athletic Union, 1989). Even though less active, many teenagers are eating diets that are high in fat and sugar and do not cut back on their consumption of these foods (Carruth & Goldberg, 1990).

There is no easy cure for obesity. Certainly, nutritional information is needed because teens eat an enormous amount of junk food, and their diet is often rich in starch but deficient in basic nutrients (Miller, 1980). In addition, many teens use crash diets, semistarvation, or fad diets in a desperate attempt to lose or maintain weight. These approaches can cause physical damage, especially to the kidneys, and are not effective in the long run. Perhaps a combination of increased physical activity under a doctor's supervision, nutritional information, a reduction in the consumption of junk food, and psychological support provided by peer group and family members can help the obese teen lose weight and keep it off. However, long-term weight loss is difficult, and the battle against fat is a lifelong process.

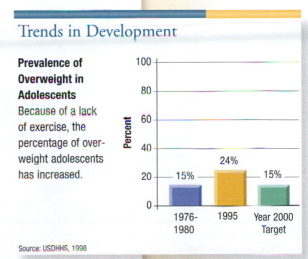

Trends in Development

Prevalence of Overweight in Adolescents
Because of a lack of exercise, the percentage of overweight adolescents has increased.

Source: USDHHS, 1998

Sleep: Why Many Teenagers Are Always Tired

The average teenager does not get enough sleep. Between the ages of 10 through 18 years, the amount of sleep adolescent boys and girls get each night declines substantially from about 10 hours during middle childhood to about 7 hours at age 18 (see Table 12.4) (Carskadon, 1990; Wolfson & Carskadon, 1998). Optimal sleep time for adolescents is about 9.2 hours, which is about the same amount of time that teenagers say they need when asked (Carskadon, Harvey, & Duke, 1980). Teens go to bed earlier and rise earlier on school days through age 18 (Manber et al., 1995). Almost half the high school students go to bed after midnight on school nights, and 90% do so on weekends (Carskadon & Mancuso, 1988). Teenagers sleep later on weekends but also stay up somewhat later as well.

Teens today get less sleep, about 90 minutes less, than their great-grandparents did (Harris, 1995). Teenagers sleep less for many reasons. Parents become much less likely to demand or even suggest specific bedtimes as the years of adolescence pass by. Adolescents also like staying up later, using the later time to watch television, study, and socialize. Social and academic pressures and earlier starting times in high school are cited as the main reasons for staying up later and getting less sleep. Some evidence also suggests that a shift to a later bedtime may partially be due to pubertal changes (Carskadon et al., 1997).

A common but incorrect belief is that adolescents do not really need as much sleep as preadolescents. This view is patently false. Teenagers require as much sleep

Table 12.4   Self-Reported Sleep Patterns in Adolescents

	Age	Bedtime	Girls Risetime	Sleep Time	Bedtime	Boys Risetime	Sleep Time
School nights	10*	9:30	7:15	9h 45m	9:09	7:00	9h 51m
	11*	9:30	7:05	9h 35m	9:40	7:00	9h 20m
	12*	9:45	6:55	9h 10m	9:50	7:05	9h 15m
	13*	10:06	6:50	8h 44m	10:28	7:00	8h 32m
	14*	10:10	5:56	7h 46m	10:16	6:15	7h 59m
	15*	10:24	6:05	7h 41m	10:43	6:27	7h 44m
	16*	10:52	6:13	7h 21m	11:08	6:38	7h 30m
	17*	10:58	6:26	7h 28m	11:14	6:45	7h 31m
	18†	1:15 A.M.	8:18	7h 3m	1:30 A.M.	8:36	7h 6m
Weekend nights	10*	10:25	8:10	9h 45m	10:22	7:45	9h 23m
	11*	10:22	8:25	9h 3m	10:50	7:45	8h 55m
	12*	10:55	8:35	9h 40m	11:05	8:35	9h 40m
	13*	11:20	8:45	9h 25m	11:42	8:45	9h 3m
	14*	11:57	9:14	9h 17m	12:06 A.M.	9:12	9h 6m
	15*	12:11 A.M.	9:24	9h 13m	12:27 A.M.	9:25	8h 58m
	16*	12:28 A.M.	9:21	8h 53 m	12:44 A.M.	9:37	8h 52m
	17*	12:39 A.M.	9:21	8h 42m	12:51 A.M.	9:29	8h 38m
	18†	2:48 A.M.	10:39	7h 51m	2:43 A.M.	10:40	7h 57m

*From previous surveys.
†From college freshmen.
SOURCE: Carskadon (1990)

Adolescents get less sleep than they, themselves, think they need, and this constant tiredness can affect academic performance and mood.

or even more than they did when they were younger (Carskadon, 1990). Even when sleeping as much as younger adolescents, older teenagers report being sleepy and tired during the day (Carskadon et al., 1980). When the amount of sleep was held steady in an experimental situation, teenagers' reports of sleepiness increased with age, showing that the need for sleep certainly does not decline in adolescence. Sleep is especially important at a time of rapid physiological change, and some modifications in the brain's electrical activity during sleep in adolescence may signal organizational changes in the brain (Harris, 1995). A majority of teens report being sleepy and needing more sleep than they get (Andrade, Bendito-Silva, Domenice, Arnhold, & Menna-Barreto, 1993). When asked, 87% said they needed more sleep than they get, with a self-reported sleep need of 9 hours (Wolfson & Carskadon, 1998).

This constant tiredness may lead to lack of attention in school and poor academic performance (Wolfson & Carskadon, 1998). Greater amounts of sleep, earlier bedtimes, and later weekday risings are associated with better grades. Students who report poor academic performance are more likely to sleep less, go to bed later, and have more irregular sleep habits (Kowalksi & Allen, 1995; Link & Ancoli-Israel, 1995). Teenagers getting less sleep report greater levels of depressive moods, and insufficient sleep may be one source of the irritability and moodiness that some adolescents show (Wolfson & Carskadon, 1998).

These studies are correlational, and the direction of effects can be questioned. It may be that greater amounts of sleep help students perform better, but it is also possible that students who do better in school sleep more. Perhaps a third factor, such as personality characteristics, may be involved. Lack of sleep may even be dangerous, as many teenagers drive, and being sleepy at the wheel may lead to accidents (Carskadon, 1990).

Part of the increased freedom of being a teen is staying up later. However, the evidence indicates that teens are not getting enough sleep and often say they are tired and that this lack of sleep may be associated with academic and behavioral problems. These research results can be used to help teenagers and their parents understand the importance of sleep during this time.

Why don't adolescents get enough sleep?

Cognitive Advances in Adolescence

Adolescents are capable of perceiving the world as other people do and evaluating themselves as they think others will. Their self-consciousness stems from their ability to consider how other people might be evaluating them and then to act to influence this assessment. The attitude that "People will think I am . . ." is especially powerful in early and middle adolescence. At the same time, other cognitive changes that relate directly to behavior are taking place, although they are less obvious. These changes allow teens to think differently from elementary schoolchildren and begin to develop their own values.

The Stage of Formal Operations

During Piaget's fourth and last stage of cognitive development, the stage of formal operations, adolescents develop the ability to generate and explore hypotheses, to make logical deductions and to use abstractions (Inhelder & Piaget, 1958; Piaget, 1972, 1987). Their thinking can be described as formal, scientific, and logical (Miller, 1993) (see Table 12.5). These abilities and patterns of thinking are rarely if ever seen prior to adolescence (Moshman, 1998).

| Table 12.5 | The Formal Operations Stage |

In the stage of formal operations, adolescents develop the ability to deal with abstract information and theoretical propositions. They can formulate and test hypotheses in a scientific manner.

Characteristic	Explanation	Example
Combinational logic	The ability to find all the possible alternatives	When asked what the president could have done in a certain situation, a teenager will produce a great many alternatives, some real, some impractical. If given five jars of colorless liquid and told that some combination will yield a yellow liquid, an adolescent will use an efficient and effective strategy that will produce all possible alternatives.
Separating the real from the possible	The ability to separate oneself from the real world and consider different possibilities. The ability to accept propositions that are contrary to reality.	A teenager can imagine other realities, other life styles and think about what could be rather than what is. A teenager can readily discuss propositions such as, "What if all human beings were green?"
Using abstractions	The ability to deal with material that is not observable	An adolescent understands higher-level concepts such as democracy and liberty as well as the abstract meaning in proverbs.
Hypothetical-deductive reasoning	The ability to form hypotheses and use scientific logic	A teenager uses deductive logic to test a hypothesis.

formal operations stage
The last Piagetian stage of cognitive development, in which a person develops the ability to deal with abstractions and to reason in a scientific manner.

Combinational Logic   When elementary school children are given a problem in which they must find all the possible alternatives, they do not approach the task in a scientific manner. For example, subjects of varying ages were presented with five jars containing a colorless liquid and told that some combination of these chemicals would yield a yellow liquid (Inhelder & Piaget, 1958). Preschoolers, who are in the preoperational stage, simply poured one into another, making a mess. Children in the concrete stage of operations combined the liquids but did not approach the task with a systematic strategy. Adolescents formed a strategy for making all possible combinations of liquids and finally solved the problem.

Adolescents can give all the possible solutions to a particular problem. If asked why something might happen, they understand that there are many different motives behind behavior. If you ask adolescents to answer the question "Why didn't Justin do his homework?" you'll get a number of answers—some possible and many improbable. This demonstrates another similar skill—being able to divorce oneself from what is real.

Adolescents in the formal stage of cognitive development can understand political cartoons because they can appreciate abstractions.

Separating the Real and the Possible   Adolescents can separate themselves from their present situation and consider other alternatives. They can think about other lifestyles and consider many other possible alternatives. At times, what is possible may be more important to adolescents than reality (Piaget & Inhelder, 1951/ 1975).

Some parents may have difficulty with adolescents who suggest alternatives that may not be feasible or that parents simply do not like. The separation of what is from what could be allows adolescents to think about a better world. Their "why" questions are sometimes based on possibilities divorced from reality, and they are capable of suggesting other alternatives. Adolescents begin to understand that the particular reality in which they live is only one of many imaginable realities. This leads them to think about alternative possibilities and investigate questions concerning truth, justice, and morality (Siegler, 1998). But their lack of experience in the real world limits their ability to consider these possibilities in practical terms.

Using Abstractions   The ability adolescents have to separate themselves from the trappings of what is real stems partly from their newfound ability to create and use abstractions and the theoretical (Siegler, 1998). Children in the stage of concrete operations have difficulty understanding political cartoons and such sayings as "You can lead a horse to water, but you can't make him drink." They are still reality bound and have difficulty with abstract thought. These children may actually picture a horse being led to water. But adolescents develop an ability to interpret abstractions, which allows them to develop internal systems of overriding principles. They can now speak in terms of ideals and values. Freedom, liberty, and justice take on added significance when they are separated from their specific situational meanings. Adolescents are now able to form their own values based on these overriding principles.

Hypothetical-Deductive Reasoning   These emerging abilities allow the adolescent to engage in hypothetical-deductive reasoning—the ability to form a hypothesis, which then leads to certain logical deductions. Some hypotheses can be tested while others cannot be. Ask a young child, "What if all humans were green?" and the youngster may insist that human beings are not green. But adolescents can accept a proposition contrary to fact and separate themselves from the real world (Markovitz & Vachon, 1989). Adolescents can reflect on a verbal hypothesis even though its elements do not exist in real life. They can think in a scientific and logical manner.

Thinking about Thinking   Adolescents also develop the ability to think about thinking, to reflect on their thought processes and critically analyze their own thinking (Moshman, 1998). This ability allows them to consider the development of their own concepts and ideas as well as considering how others are thinking.

Piaget considered the attainment of formal operations the crowning achievement in human cognitive abilities. He viewed formal operational reasoners as scientists who devise experiments on the basis of theoretical considerations and interpret their results within a logical framework.

Evaluating Piaget's Ideas

These abilities sound quite impressive, and they are. But not all adolescents—or, for that matter, even all adults—reason on this level (Keating, 1991; Neimark, 1975, 1982). Although older adolescents tend to be further along in using formal operational thinking, they do not use it on every problem where it would be appropriate (Morris & Sloutsky, 1998; Rutter & Rutter, 1993). Only about half the adult population attains the final stage of formal operations (Muuss, 1982).

In addition, studies of formal operations in non-Western cultures show that people in these cultures generally perform more poorly when presented with Piagetian tasks that require formal operational reasoning (Dasen & Heron, 1981). It may be that Piaget's stage of formal operations is basically applicable only to adolescents in Western technological societies who are exposed to a great deal of formal education. Indeed, schooling is an important variable in determining whether people reach the formal operational stage. Schooled non-Western adolescents do better on these tests than unschooled non-Western adolescents (Rogoff, 1981). Piaget viewed it as the ultimate achievement, but that may be so only in Western cultures. We have little idea what may constitute the ideal last stage of cognitive growth in other societies.

Such evidence led Piaget (1972) to reevaluate this area of his theory. He recognized that education, vocational interests, and the society and culture determine performance on tests of formal operations.

Cognitive Functioning Beyond Formal Operations

Piaget believed that no important changes in cognitive abilities occurred after the stage of formal operations, but some psychologists disagree, arguing that qualitative changes in cognitive abilities can be found beginning in late adolescence and continuing through early adulthood. These styles of reasoning are collectively called **postformal operational reasoning.**

As adolescents negotiate the later part of the stage and enter the adult world, they are faced with challenges that are more practical, and their solutions have to be more realistic (Labouvie-Vief, 1980, 1984, 1990). The type of abstract, principle-based logic of formal operations may not be as useful in dealing with these practical problems. For example, adolescents using formal operational reasoning may look at all the alternative solutions to a problem as if the problem existed in a vacuum, but older adolescents and young adults often cannot and do not do this. These older adolescents or early adults may take into consideration such practical constraints as money, time, and political concerns, which limit which solutions they will investigate.

While flexibility is the theme for formal operations, commitment, responsibility and practicality is found in post-formal operational thought (Labouvie-Vief, 1990). Commitment to job and family may require a pragmatic viewpoint, and

Guideposts

What cognitive changes occur during the stage of formal operations?

postformal operational reasoning

An expression used to describe any qualitatively different reasoning style that goes beyond formal operational reasoning and develops in the later part of adolescence and during adulthood.

the endless generating of "ifs" and "whens" may no longer be adaptive. People faced with an issue or a problem may need to strike a balance between what is most logical and what is the most practical solution. This more pragmatic viewpoint differs greatly from the theoretical, abstract concept of cognitive functioning that characterizes formal operations (Labouvie-Vief, 1984).

Postformal operations are contextual, meaning that people now see problems within a particular context, not in the abstract, theoretical manner that younger adolescents see it (Rybash, Roodin, & Hoyer, 1995).

Postformal reasoning is also often **relativistic,** meaning that knowledge depends on the subjective experiences and perspectives of the individual (Sinnott, 1981, 1984). Such reasoning is shown by some during the high school years, but further development occurs as adolescents mature (Leadbeater, 1991; Leadbeater & Kuhn, 1988).

An important study showing postformal relativistic thinking was conducted by William Perry (1968), who interviewed a group of Harvard students over their 4 years at the school. Freshmen approached intellectual and ethical problems from a perspective that there was one and only one correct response and the professors would teach them the right answer. Later, this belief in one answer was replaced by the complete belief in subjective experience. Students came to believe that everything was relative, and they experienced difficulties, since if all knowledge and values are relative, they seem equally right and equally wrong. Finally, Perry found that these students reached a level where they became committed to a viewpoint in addition to accepting the relative nature of truth. They came to believe that some viewpoints were better researched and had more evidence supporting them than others. Perry (1981) argued for a progression in which people begin with a belief in absolute truth then develop into a belief in full relativism, and finally to a new equilibrium of commitment in the face of relativism.

Postformal thought differs greatly from formal operational abilities. Postformal thought is more practical and realistic; it admits that knowledge is relative and not absolute, and it emphasizes the importance of context rather than believing that absolute, hypothetical principles operate in every context (Kramer, 1983; Rybash, 1995). Although postformal operational thought is hardly one theory, the idea that qualitatively different patterns of thought emerge in late adolescence and early adulthood is an intriguing one which requires further study.

Adolescent Thought Processes and Risk Taking

The self-consciousness of adolescents (especially early adolescents) is legendary. In fact, early adolescent eighth graders in one study were found to be significantly more self-conscious than both younger children and older adolescents (Elkind & Bowen, 1979). Adolescents often look at themselves in the mirror and imagine what others will think about them. Adolescents can now think about thoughts—both their own and those of others. However, although teenagers can understand the thoughts of others, they fail to differentiate between the objects toward which the thoughts of others are directed and those that are the focus of their own thoughts (Buis & Thompson, 1989). Because teens are concerned primarily with themselves, they believe everyone else is focusing on them, too, and that others are as obsessed with their behavior and appearance as they are. The inability to differentiate between what one is thinking and what others are thinking constitutes what David Elkind (1967) called **adolescent egocentrism.** This leads to two interesting phenomena: the imaginary audience and the personal fable.

Guideposts

How do the qualitative changes in reasoning that occur after the stage of formal operations influence the way decisions are made?

For Your Consideration ?

Why might parents thinking on a postformal level have difficulties with adolescents thinking on a formal operational level?

relativistic reasoning
Thinking that involves the appreciation that knowledge depends on the subjective experiences and on the perspective of the individual.

adolescent egocentrism
The adolescent failure to differentiate between what one is thinking and what others are considering.

The Imaginary Audience

Adolescents often believe that when they walk into a room everyone focuses their attention on them. Then they anticipate the reactions. Adolescents are always onstage when in front of others (Elkind, 1985). Teenagers create an imaginary audience, believing that everyone is looking at and evaluating them. The people in this "audience" are real, but the audience is imaginary because most of the time the adolescent is not the focus of attention.

The **imaginary audience** phenomenon leads to self-consciousness and the adolescent's mania for privacy (Peterson & Roscoe, 1991). The self-consciousness stems from the conviction that others are seeing and evaluating them in the same way that they see themselves. The mania for privacy may come either from what Elkind calls a reluctance to reveal one-self or from a reaction to being constantly scrutinized by others. Privacy becomes a vacation from evaluation.

As adolescents dress, act, and groom, they imagine how others will see them. Elkind notes that when the boy who combed his hair for hours and the girl who carefully applied makeup meet, both are more concerned with being observed than with being the observer. Teens who score high on a scale that measures the imaginary audience do more poorly in school, probably because they believe everyone is carefully evaluating their performance, and often protect their self-concepts by creating excuses for failure (Montgomery et al., 1996).

The imaginary audience is a normal part of development that diminishes greatly by later adolescence. Predictably, self-consciousness also declines from midadolescence to late adolescence (Hudson & Gray, 1986; Ryan & Kuczkowski, 1994). Older teens understand that people may not react to them the way they think they will. They also realize that people are not as interested in them as they thought.

The Personal Fable

"You can't know how it feels to be in love with someone who doesn't know you exist," one adolescent told his parents. He was convinced that only he could suffer such feelings of unrequited love, of loneliness, of despair. As adolescents reflect on their own thoughts and experiences, they come to believe that what they are thinking and experiencing is absolutely unique in the annals of human history. The belief that what they are experiencing and thinking is original, new, and special is known as the **personal fable.** Teenagers who believe that they are unique may also believe they are invulnerable to harm, resulting in one of the most controversial behaviors found in adolescence: risk taking.

Risk Taking

Almost 33% of all adolescents questioned admit to having five or more drinks in the past month. Almost 10% have tried cocaine. Nearly 20% say they never wear seat belts. One-third have ridden in the past month with someone who had been drinking. About 18% admit to carrying a gun, knife, or club in the prior month (CDC, 1998). The leading cause of death in adolescence is automobile accidents. Young drivers, particularly young males, engage in risky driving practices, such as speeding, more often than other aged drivers (Vavrik, 1997). Risk taking seems to

Adolescents are quite self-conscious. They believe others see and evaluate them in the same way as they see themselves.

When teenagers walk into the room, they believe that everyone is observing and evaluating them.

What is the imaginary audience and personal fable? How do they influence adolescent behavior?

imaginary audience
A term used to describe adolescents' belief that they are the focus of attention and being evaluated by everyone.

personal fable
Adolescents' belief that their experiences are unique and original.

be a pattern; adolescents who engage in one risk are much more likely to engage in others, so a common cause may underlie them (Arnett & Balle-Jensen, 1993).

Although certain types of risk taking are related to injury (Jelalian, Spirito, & Rasile, 1997), not all risk taking is dangerous. Participating in a new sport; taking on a project and thereby risking failure; or walking up to a classmate whom you would like to get to know and asking her or him out, risking embarrassment and rejection, may lead to new opportunities for growth (Moore, 1997). Some risk taking, then, may be adaptive and lead to greater self-confidence and a broadened view of one's abilities. Even so, the fact that teenagers often show risky behavior involving unprotected sex, drug use, or irresponsible driving makes concern about risk taking reasonable.

Some risk taking is explained by the personal fable. Teenagers are told that they are at the height of their physical and mental powers, that their future is bright and unlimited, and that they are unique individuals. They may believe that they are invincible and that nothing can happen to them. "It won't happen to me" is the philosophy that makes risk taking easy. Some sexually active adolescents explain their lack of using contraception with some variation of "I thought I (or my partner) couldn't get pregnant" (Quadrel, Fischoff, & Davis, 1993).

Adolescents think they are less vulnerable than others to negative events (Smith, Gerrard, & Gibbons, 1997). When asked to consider their personal risk to a sexually transmitted disease, they conjure up an image of someone who is particularly vulnerable to that disorder and compare themselves with that image. This leads to an underestimation of the likelihood of, for example, getting into an accident while driving under the influence of alcohol or contracting a sexually transmitted disease from unprotected sex. The personal fable declines at a much slower rate than the imaginary audience (Lapsley, Milstead, & Quintana, 1986).

The personal fable cannot be the total explanation for adolescent risk taking. Adolescents are able to discriminate risky behaviors from safer ones and understand the possible negative consequences of their behaviors (Alexander et al., 1990; Dolcini et al., 1989). Some studies find little or no difference between adolescents' and adults' understanding of the consequences of a particular risky action, such as driving while drunk (Beyth-Marom, Austin, Fischoff, Palmgren, & Jacobs-Quadrel, 1993). And a variation of the personal fable is found in adults as well. Adolescents and adults both see themselves as at less risk than others (Quadrel et al., 1993). When adolescents involved in risky sexual practices are questioned, some do, indeed, feel invulnerable, while just as many recognize the risks but continue these risky practices anyway (Moore & Rosenthal, 1990). The immediate benefits are far more attractive than the fear of possible consequences in the future (Moore et al., 1997). If they engage in a risky activity and there are no immediate negative consequences, they may never consider the long-term outcomes. They accept the risks by underestimating them or by believing that everything will turn out well in the end. Perhaps risk taking in the face of understanding the possible negative consequences is simply a show of bravado or courage.

Another explanation for risk taking relates it to teenagers' desire for sensation seeking (Arnett, 1992). Sensation seeking provides adolescents with novelty and an intense experience. The need for variety and sensation are highest in adolescence and declines thereafter. Both individual and cultural differences are involved in sensation seeking. In cultures characterized by individualism and independence, such as American culture, there is less parental monitoring and fewer restrictions on self-expression. These individualistic cultures are more likely to spawn sensation seeking than cultures that emphasize obedience and conformity (Arnett & Belle-Jensen, 1993).

Still others point to a number of social factors, including the need to show independence by not conforming to standards of older people (Lavery et al., 1993). Adolescents may also take risks as a way of dealing with feelings of inadequacy or to gain inclusion into a group (Gonzalez et al., 1994).

Guideposts

Why do teens seem to take so many more unnecessary risks than older people?

Morals and Values in Adolescence

Adolescents' newfound cognitive abilities allow them to formulate their own personal principles and ideas about right and wrong. They realize that there are other roads to travel and other possibilities. They begin to think about how the world can be changed and to question the nature and meaning of justice and morality (Siegler, 1998). As thinking becomes more abstract, idealism grows, but so does a sense of uncertainty as older, established beliefs are modified (Rutter & Rutter, 1993).

Cognitive Development and Moral Reasoning

Lawrence Kohlberg, whose theory of moral reasoning was discussed in Chapter 11, argued that moral reasoning is related to cognitive growth. As adolescents develop their formal operational skills, they begin to show higher levels of moral reasoning (Kohlberg, 1987). Teens become concerned about the world of ideas and willingly debate various moral and political perspectives (Miller, 1993).

Using Kohlberg's system, stage 4 involves reasoning that is oriented toward doing one's duty and maintaining the social order for its own sake. Stages 5 and 6 comprise the postconventional level. Stage 5 involves a contractual legalistic orientation that emphasizes not violating the rights of others and respecting the welfare and majority will of others. Stage 6 is a more individualistic orientation, in which decisions are made involving one's own conscience and principles. Adolescents who are developing formal operational skills are better able to reason at these higher levels of moral reasoning. But even if they have this ability, many adolescents do not function at this level. In fact, most people do not develop beyond stage 4 (Shaver & Strong, 1976).

The individual's stage of moral reasoning affects behavior. The higher the stage of moral reasoning, the less likely an individual is to engage in risky sexual behavior (Hubbs-Tait & Garmon, 1995). For example, the relationship between knowledge about AIDS and changes in sexual behavior is dependent on the level of moral reasoning. AIDS knowledge and risky sexual behavior are inversely correlated; that is, as knowledge increases, risky sexual behavior decreases for higher-level reasoners but not for lower-level reasoners. Generally, people who reason at higher stages of moral reasoning tend to use their knowledge in a different manner, allowing that knowledge to influence their behavior.

A number of reasons explain why some people use stage 6 reasoning while others do not. Cognitive advancement makes more sophisticated moral reasoning possible but does not assure it. Other factors may enter the picture, such as the content of the problem (Fischer, 1980), and the consequences of the moral decision. When people are faced with a dilemma in which the personal consequences are great, they are likely to demonstrate lower-level moral thinking (Sobesky, 1983). When people are confronted with a problem, their cognitive skills form the upper limits of their abilities to reason, but the situation itself will affect the actual behavior.

The adolescent's moral reasoning cannot be neatly placed in a single stage (Kohlberg, 1969). At times, adolescents operate on a higher level, but at other times they operate on a lower one (Holstein, 1976). Moral reasoning, then, may be inconsistently applied to various problems, and parents may have difficulty understanding their adolescent's highly moral stand on one issue and lower-level reasoning on another.

Guideposts

Why are adolescents capable of using formal operational abilities better able to reason at Kohlberg's postconventional level?

For Your Consideration ?

Why does adolescents' moral behavior seem so inconsistent?

Values and Attitudes

Since 1966, the attitudes and values of college freshmen have been surveyed, uncovering some interesting trends (see Table 12.6). In the late 1960s, students were more interested in social interpersonal morality. By 1975, however, the climate had changed: students were more interested in personal achievement, and this trend, although moderating, has continued. For example, many more

Table 12.6	Changes in Freshmen's Attitudes

Alexander Astin and his colleagues surveyed nearly six million first-year college students. Some of their results are described here.

Percentage Who	1970	1995
Identify themselves as politically liberal	34	21.1
Identify themselves as middle-of-the-road politically	45	54.3
Identify themselves as politically conservative	17	20.3
	1966	**1991**
Plan to major in business	14	15.3
	1968	**1995**
Plan to pursue elementary or secondary teaching careers	21.7	9.3
	1986	**1995**
Are involved in programs to clean up the environment	15.9	22.5
	1967	**1995**
Believe it is essential or very important to be very well-off financially	44	74.1
Believe the activities of married women are best confined to the home and family	57	24.3
Believe it is essential or very important to develop a meaningful philosophy of life	83	41.9

SOURCE: Data from Sax et al. (1995)

adolescents in the 1960s believed that it was essential to develop a meaningful philosophy of life than in 1995, and many more adolescents in 1995 believed it was important to be well off financially (Sax, Astin, Korn, & Mahoney, 1995). The changes in freshmen's views of social roles are startling. In the late 1960s, more than half believed that married women should stay home and look after their families, whereas less than one-quarter believed the same in 1995.

Adolescents see law and politics differently from the way younger children see them. Preadolescents look at law and government in terms that are concrete, absolute, and authoritarian and evaluate them on the basis of how they affect particular individuals—for example, seat belts are necessary to protect the driver and passengers. Older subjects are less authoritarian and more sensitive to individual rights and personal freedom. Between 14 and 16 years, teenagers begin to use the term *rights* to describe a person's just claims to control one's own destiny (Ruck, Abramovitch, & Keating, 1998). Adolescents may see the conflict between requiring seat belts for the good of everyone and the loss of personal freedom that comes with regulation—a conflict that younger children do not see.

The political attitudes of today's freshmen are different from what they were just two decades ago. More college students identify themselves as middle-of-the-road or conservative than in years past (Sax et al., 1995). Unfortunately, interest in keeping up-to-date with political affairs declined drastically between 1966 and 1995, and one-third believe there is little an individual can do to change society (Sax et al., 1995). Freshmen appear to be less interested in national issues and politics but are becoming more liberal on personal freedom. The belief that homosexual relationships should be prohibited continues to decline, even since the 1980s.

Religious Beliefs

Adolescence is a time of questioning and examining belief systems, and religious beliefs and affiliations are areas that are reevaluated. Indeed, cross-sectional studies show a decline in religiousness during adolescence (Donahue & Benson, 1995). By the end of adolescence, teenagers are less involved in religious activities than they were as young teenagers (Benson, Donahue, & Erickson, 1989). This is often seen as a natural stage in religious development when all forms of authority are questioned and thinking becomes more critical.

Guideposts

How have adolescent attitudes and values changed over the past 20 years?

For Your Consideration ?

Fewer adolescents than years ago seem to be taking an interest in politics and social issues. Why don't adolescents feel they can change things? Why do you think there has been such a change in adolescents' thinking?

For Your Consideration ?

Why is there a general decline in religious belief and practice during the teenage years?

Despite the fact that adolescence is a stage of development in which all forms of authority are questioned, most adolescents believe in God, and about three quarters pray at least occasionally.

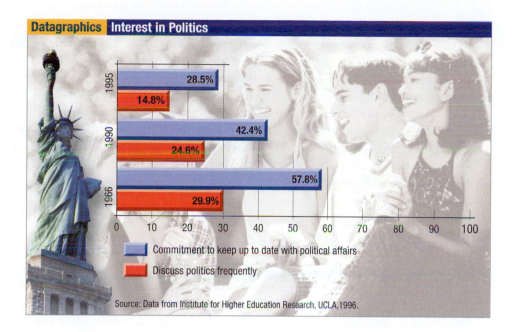

Datagraphics | **Interest in Politics**

Commitment to keep up to date with political affairs
- 1995: 28.5%
- 1990: 42.4%
- 1966: 57.8%

Discuss politics frequently
- 1995: 14.8%
- 1990: 24.6%
- 1966: 29.9%

Source: Data from Institute for Higher Education Research, UCLA, 1996.

Most adolescents believe in God. In one poll, 76% of adolescents 13 to 17 years believe in God, while 74% pray at least occasionally (Donohue & Benson, 1995). Adolescents have a more abstract notion of God than young children and do not see a Supreme Being as a physical entity. Many adolescents claim that their religious beliefs are important to them (Bachman, Johnston, & O'Malley, 1993; Benson, 1993). Generally, women are more religious than men and African Americans more so than white Americans (Donahue & Benson, 1995; USDHHS, 1996).

Religion can affect behavior and attitudes. People who are religious are less likely to engage in premarital sex or use drugs (Donohue & Benson, 1995). It is also related to altruism, as religious youth are more likely to be involved in service projects. Lower rates of violence are also related to religiousness, and adolescents who see religion as a meaningful part of their lives are less likely to be depressed (Wright et al., 1993; Wright, Frost, & Wisecarver, 1997). Religious belief and practices, then, do affect behavior, but it is one influence among many. It is more salient for some than others, but it would be a mistake to ignore religion as an influence.

T F 7 Adolescents who are religious are less likely to use drugs and more likely to show altruistic behavior.

Guideposts

What role does religion play in the lives of adolescents?

Sexual Expression

The physical changes that occur in adolescence bring sexuality into stronger focus. The cognitive changes allow adolescents to develop their own values and guide the choices that adolescents make in this area. Sexuality is a basic concern of adolescence. According to Freud, adolescents enter the **genital stage,** during which the libido—hidden during the latency phase—reappears. Physical drives are strong and cannot easily be repressed, and as a result, adolescents turn their attention to heterosexual relationships (Freud, 1925/1953).

The Revolution in Sexual Attitudes

The traditional attitude concerning sexuality reflects the double standard. Males were permitted sexual freedom; females were denied it. Males were encouraged to

genital stage

The final psychosexual stage, occurring during adolescence, in which adult heterosexual behavior develops.

experiment, yet sanctions against female sexuality were great. The sexual needs of males were recognized, but females' desires were denied, even within marriage. At least to some degree the double standard has declined, although it still influences socialization practices (Bingham & Crockett, 1996). Attitudinal differences between males and females have narrowed.

Generally, attitudes have changed in the direction of greater acceptance and a live-and-let-live orientation to sex. Sexual behavior is considered more a matter of personal choice than the business of society (Chilman, 1983). The attitudes of adolescents are likely to be much more permissive than those of their parents. Parents often underestimate the sexual activity of their adolescent teens, and teens underestimate their mother's level of disapproval for such behavior (Jaccard, Dittus, & Gordon, 1998). This is especially true if there is poor communication between parents and children.

The revolution in attitudes has been greater for females than for males, probably because women had more conservative attitudes to start with. Yet the idea that sex itself is looked on casually or that the attitudes of males and females are identical is false. Males have more liberal attitudes toward sexuality than females, and females are more likely to view sex as part of a loving relationship (De Gaston, Weed, & Jensen, 1996; Wilson & Medora, 1990). Females are also more likely to believe that people having sex should always use some method of birth control and a person should not be pressured into having sex (Carver, Kittleson, & Lacey, 1990). More women are committed to abstinence, somewhat less permissive in their views, and more likely to see sexual activity as a barrier to future goal attainment (Harvey & Spigner, 1995).

Both males and females become more permissive as the relationship gets more serious. And both believe that more sexual intimacy is proper when one is in love or engaged than when one is dating without affection or even with affection but without love (Roche, 1986). However, males and females show differences in what they believe is appropriate at the beginning stages of dating, with males being more permissive than females. In the later stages—which include dating only one person, being in love, and engagement—the differences narrow substantially. Males, then, expect sexual intimacy earlier in the relationship, while females tie sexual intimacy to love and commitment.

Dating

One of the most noticeable developmental changes in adolescence is the increase in social interactions between males and females. Adolescents spend much more time with teens of the other gender than they did when they were younger (Csikszentmihalyi & Larson, 1984).

The age at which teens begin to date has declined. In 1924, girls started to date at age 16 years, while today it is about 13 years (Thornton, 1990). Girls complain more about their parents' rules concerning dating than boys, probably because parents are stricter with girls. Because girls date somewhat older boys, they experience increased pressure for sexual activity, which often leads parents to be more protective (De Gaston et al., 1996).

Dating affords an opportunity to interact and learn about others and to try out different relationships (Cox, 1990). Later in adolescence and continuing into early adulthood, dating may become somewhat more serious as the possibility of finding a mate enters the picture.

For Your Consideration ?

It is common to argue that the double standard of sexuality has changed. In your opinion, does it still exist and if so, in what contexts?

Forming meaningful relationships and considering the meaning and expression of sexuality are important issues facing teenagers as they negotiate adolescence.

In fact, two different dating goals appear in adolescence. One involves using dating as a way to explore different roles and identities and as a way of achieving independence from family. The other involves sharing intimate thoughts and feelings (Sanderson & Cantor, 1995). When dating is viewed in terms of intimacy, then mutual dependence and open communication is common. When dating is used as a way of exploring roles and identities, dating many people is common, and the relationships have less commitment and closeness.

Dating Violence and Acquaintance Rape

One serious problem that has recently received attention is acquaintance rape (also called date rape) and dating violence. It is not rare, but reliable figures are very difficult to obtain (Truman, Tokar, & Fischer, 1996). One study of college students found that 40% of the women and 30% of the men either received or inflicted violence on their date, and between 15% and 25% of all women experience date rape (Finkelson & Oswalt, 1995; Lane & Gwartney-Gibbs, 1985; Ward, Chapman, Cohn, White, & Williams, 1991).

Most women do not report date rapes to the authorities because they believe that their own behavior would be judged critically, they feel embarrassed, or they feel some responsibility because they were under the influence of alcohol at the time (Finkelson & Oswalt, 1995). Others do not acknowledge that it was rape (Koss et al., 1987) because it does not meet the stereotyped image of rape—that of being attacked by a stranger (Strong & DeVault, 1995). This is false. The great majority of rapes are committed by someone the victim knows, even well. In fact, about half the rapes are by first dates, casual dates, or romantic acquaintances.

Some date rape is the result of men who see their date solely as a source of sexual pleasure, or who do not want to believe that their date's refusal to allow certain sexual activities is real. Men expect sex earlier in relationships than women do, and women often face the problem of how to encourage a relationship without engaging in more sexual activity than they want (Komarovsky, 1985). Men who rape their dates are likely to have coercive fantasies, are aggressive, and accept the myth that women want to be coerced or believe that women really don't mean no when they say no (Greendlinger & Byrne, 1987; Spade, 1997). Their belief in these false ideas allows them to blame the victim (Blumberg & Lester, 1991).

Attitudes toward rape need to be changed, as studies repeatedly reveal misconceptions and ignorance. In a study of high school students, more than half believed that some women provoke men into raping them, and about half believed that some girls encourage rape just by the way they dress (Kershner, 1996). Forced intercourse in some situations is not always seen as wrong by some adolescent males and females, an incredible belief (Feltey, Ainslie, & Geib, 1991). High school seniors were asked to read a vignette describing an obvious date rape. Some students were shown a picture of the victim dressed in provocative dress, others the victim conservatively dressed, and the rest were not shown any photograph. The findings are shown in Table 12.7 on page 494. Notice about one-third of the students shown the provocative picture believed that the girl was partially responsible and that the boy was justified, or denied the girl in the vignette was even raped (Cassidy & Hurrell, 1995). Since no gender differences were found, both males and females need rape education.

Women can take steps to reduce the possibility of date rape—for example, by communicating limits, being assertive, not placing themselves in vulnerable situations, not accepting pressure, and avoiding the excessive use of alcohol and other drugs (American College Health Association, 1986). For men, accepting a

Table 12.7	Percentage of Responses by Photographic Condition			
Item		Percentage Provocative	Percentage Conservative	Percentage No Photo
Jennifer was responsible for John's behavior.	Agree	37	4.3	5.5
	Disagree	63	95.7	94.5
John was justified in having sex with Jennifer.	Agree	31.5	6.9	7.3
	Disagree	68.5	93.1	92.7
John raped Jennifer.	Agree	63	89.7	84.4
	Disagree	37	10.3	15.6

SOURCE: Cassidy & Hurrell, (1995)

woman's decision (no means no), improving communication, and avoiding alcohol and other drugs are advised. There is also a movement to place antirape education in the high schools (Rich, 1991), and many colleges have initiated programs aimed at reducing acquaintance rape.

Sexual Behavior

Most people believe that a sexual revolution, a tremendous increase in the rate of sexual intercourse, has taken place. Has there been a revolution in sexual behavior?

There is no doubt that more teenagers are experiencing sexual intercourse at an earlier age than did so in generations past, although some progress has been made in convincing younger teens to delay the age at which they begin to have sex. Still, American men and women are more likely than ever to have intercourse by age 18 years. Among those born between 1963 to 1973, 61% of the men and 58% of the women had intercourse by age 18. For those born 30 years earlier, the percentages were 43% for males and 32% for females (Hollander, 1996). By the end of the teen years, more than half are sexually active (Sellers, McGraw, & McKinlay, 1994; Stryker, 1997).

Nevertheless, adolescents generally overestimate the percentage of their peers engaging in sex, which may exert some subtle, or perhaps some not so subtle, pressure on teens to sexually experiment at a younger age (Leland & Barth, 1992). Indeed, one great concern is that teens are beginning their sexual experiences earlier. A third of the boys and more than a quarter of the girls have their first sexual experience by their fifteenth birthday (Carnegie Council, 1995).

Certain personality and social variables differentiate those teens who become sexually active at very early ages (in their early teens) from those who become active at age 17 or after. Early sexual intercourse is considered a problem because it is related to an increased risk of teen pregnancy, transmission of sexually transmitted diseases, drug use, poor school achievement, delinquency, behavioral problems, depression, and poor family relationships (Crockett, 1996; Tubman, Windle, & Windle, 1996). Perhaps the troubled behavior is indicative of poor impulse control and is related to sensation seeking and risk taking. Teens engaging in sexual intercourse at an early age have comparatively poorer communication with parents (Casper, 1990) and are less well-monitored (Capaldi, Crosby, & Stoolmiller, 1996; Meschke & Silbereisen, 1997). The poor family relationships and rebellion cause the young adolescent to seek acceptance from peers through sexual activity.

A different way of conceptualizing the relationship between early sex and problem behaviors is to look at the conditions that were present before adolescence. Researchers find that poor family relationships and other difficulties set the stage for early and often unprotected sexual behavior and later developmental problems,

Guideposts

What is date rape? How can its incidence be reduced?

8

Adolescents tend to overestimate the percentage of teens who are engaging in sexual intercourse.

What trends in teenage sexual behavior have been identified by recent studies?

including excessive risk taking. Perceived in this manner, the problems are not the result of the timing of intercourse as much as part of a general pattern of poor development and familial relationships that appear before adolescence and continue into this period (Bingham & Crockett, 1996). However it is viewed, there is a group of adolescents whose very early sexual behavior is related to personal and familial difficulties, and their profiles may differ from those who begin having sex later in adolescence.

Most researchers now accept the increase in premarital sex. However, whether one wants to call this a revolution or an evolution depends on one's personal point of view. The change in attitudes has been more radical than the change in behavior. The explanations for the increase are many and varied. Some explain it in terms of its more open coverage by the media, the reduction of sanctions against premarital sex, the movement toward women's equality, the increased availability of contraceptives and abortion, earlier maturation, and the faster pace of our society.

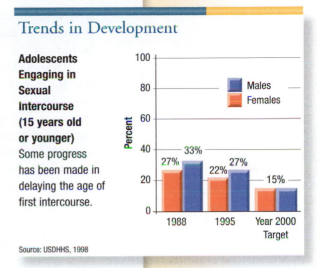

Trends in Development

Adolescents Engaging in Sexual Intercourse (15 years old or younger) Some progress has been made in delaying the age of first intercourse.

Source: USDHHS, 1998

Contraceptive Use

If rates of premarital sex have increased substantially and attitudes are more liberal, what about contraceptive use? The statistics are depressing. Between 45% and 59% of all women used contraception at their first intercourse (Mauldon & Luker, 1996). Only about half of all sexually active teens reported using a condom the last time they had intercourse (CDC, 1995). Many teens who do use condoms use them inconsistently (CDC, 1992a, 1992b), and most sexually active teens have had intercourse at least once without using any form of birth control (Morton, Nelson, Walsh, Zimmerman, & Coe, 1996). Over half the sexually active students report having had sex when they were drunk or high, and one half of these students had not used any method of birth control on these occasions (Leland & Barth, 1992). In fact, the use of alcohol is highly related to engaging in sexual relations without using any contraception (Gordon, Carey, & Carey, 1997; Harvey & Spigner, 1995). Girls are more likely to depend on contraceptive methods used by the male when they first become sexually active. Early use of contraception begins a pattern of safer sexual practices.

We often think that the sexually active teen is a well-informed person and knowledgeable about the facts of conception, but the research shows otherwise (Morrison, 1985). Many teens do not believe that a pregnancy could result the first time they had intercourse and cannot identify the time during the menstrual cycle when the greatest risk of pregnancy exists. On various tests of sexual knowledge, teens answer only about half of the questions correctly, and teens who are sexually active do not show greater knowledge than those who are abstainers (Carver, Kittleson & Lacey, 1990; Leland & Barth, 1992).

Contraceptive use has increased somewhat lately but is still at a low level. Adolescents know something about the different methods of contraception, with older teens knowing more than younger teens. However, mistakes and misunderstandings are quite common (Padilla & Baird, 1991).

Attitudes toward contraception are negative or neutral at best. Many teens simply do not consider the possibility that they will get pregnant, and if they do think about it, they do so fleetingly. Some show mistaken beliefs about fertility, are indifferent to becoming pregnant, don't know where to obtain contraceptives, or

More than three-quarters of all teens say they used a condom the last time they had sexual intercourse.

What are the trends in teenage contraceptive use?

have negative attitudes toward contraceptive devices themselves (Morrison, 1985; White & DeBlassie, 1992). Some teenagers do not visit a family planning clinic because they are under the erroneous impression that they need their parents' consent (Brooks-Gunn & Furstenberg, 1989). Others are afraid of using an oral contraceptive or say that they are not in a continuous sexual relationship. The fact that contraception must be planned and that planned sex seems to lose its romantic quality and spontaneity may be another reason for the sporadic use of contraceptives. Many teens also deny that they are sexually active and may not be mature enough to admit that they are engaging in intercourse (Dreyer, 1982). The first sexual encounter is rationalized as an accident—a moment of passion or a chance event. Most methods of birth control demand that the person acknowledge that he or she is sexually active and view sexual encounters realistically (Pestrak & Martin, 1985). The need for sex education would seem obvious, but what to teach and the effects of sex education are areas of controversy (see *Sex Education: Just the Facts?* on page 497).

Guideposts

What prevents teenagers from always using contraception when they have sexual intercourse?

For Your Consideration ?

Considering the problems involving the transmission of STDs and teenage pregnancy, what strategies could increase the use of condoms?

ACTION / REACTION

What Did You Find?

As Lois was putting the laundry away, she found an opened pack of condoms in her 15-year-old son's drawer. She was shocked and concerned because she does not think he is very mature. She believes that he is too young and is worried that through some mistake his girlfriend will become pregnant. That night she privately told her husband about the condoms. Her husband just shrugged his shoulders, snickered, and went back to reading the newspaper. She did not like his attitude at all. Later, sensing his wife's unhappiness, Larry told her that their son Dennis was taking precautions and didn't think there was anything he should do.

Lois is annoyed with her husband but also confused about what to say to her son, or even whether she should say anything.

1. *If you were Lois, what would you do?*
2. *If you were Larry, how would you have reacted to your wife's findings?*
3. *If, instead of the adolescent being a male, the child was a daughter and you found condoms in her drawer, would you react any differently?*

ACTION / REACTION

Sexually Transmitted Diseases

One in six sexually experienced teens have had a sexually transmitted disease (Sellers et al., 1994), and more than three million teens a year contract a sexually transmitted disease (STD) (Grimley & Lee, 1997). Concern about STDs has increased with the spread of AIDS. The increasing prevalence of other sexually transmitted diseases including syphilis, gonorrhea, herpes, and chlamydia is of great concern since these diseases can lead to serious health consequences if left untreated. While the prevalence of STDs in other industrialized nations remains low, the rate in the United Sates shows a rapid rise (Ericksen & Trocki, 1994). About 20% of all the HIV-positive adults contracted the virus in adolescence (Brown et al., 1996). Teens may be HIV-positive and not know it. The long incubation period for the disease, averaging 11 years for the HIV infection, means that many people infected as teens will develop AIDS in their 20s or 30s (Rosenberg & Biggar, 1998; Sellers et al., 1994). AIDS prevention is vital in adolescence since the behaviors of some adolescents put them at risk for acquiring the virus.

The Child in the 21st Century

Sex Education: Just the Facts?

Everyone agrees that reducing the prevalence of adolescent pregnancy and combating the spread of AIDS and other sexually transmitted diseases (STDs) are worthy goals (Leland & Barth, 1992). The question that divides the public is how to attain these goals (Frost & Forrest, 1995).

People generally agree that the family should be the basic transmitter of education about sexuality. Parents do talk to their teens about sex, but these discussions are often very general and incomplete. Although teens cite their parents as the most important source of information on sex, pregnancy, and contraception, only a third discuss contraception with their parents. Those who discuss it are about twice as likely as those who don't to use contraceptives, if they are sexually active (Pick & Palos, 1995; Wattleton, 1987). When a great deal of communication occurs, teens are also more likely to share the sexual values of their parents. It is difficult for parents to talk with their children on these sensitive topics, though, and such communication is often incomplete or even nonexistent.

The schools also have a responsibility in the area of sex education, and state education departments either strongly recommend or mandate the teaching of sex education and AIDS education (Haffner, 1992; Kirby et al., 1994). As many as 80% of all parents favor sex education in the schools, although those opposed are often a very vocal minority (Miller, 1995; Barron, 1987). When sex education is offered in school, less than

3% of all parents refuse to let their children participate (Scales, 1984).

Once we get past offering students the basic biological information on sex, the divisions begin to show. Some want abstinence to rule the program, and at least 23 states now require abstinence instruction. In contrast, only 11 require teaching about contraception or disease control (Stryker, 1997). Most parents want contraception taught, and about 65% of all American adults support condom availability in the schools (Roper Organization, 1991). Some are concerned that condom availability or explicit sex education will encourage sexual activity, but this is not so (Stryker, 1997). Studies of HIV prevention programs that included promotion and distribution of condoms do not find an increase in sexual activity among adolescents (Sellers, McGraw, &

McKinlay, 1994). In an important study, packets consisting of condoms, an instruction sheet, and a card warning that condoms are not completely effective in preventing AIDS but abstinence is were available at a Los Angeles County high school. A year later, *no* significant increases in the percentage of males or females having intercourse occurred, but a significant increase in condom use by those who were sexually active was reported (Schuster, Bell, Berry, & Kanouse, 1998). Even the most comprehensive sex education programs do not lead to sexual experimentation (Kirby et al., 1994).

Most sex education programs do not include condom distribution. Do these sex education programs help students postpone becoming sexually active or encourage contraceptive use? The findings are

The majority of parents favor sex education in the schools, and programs are becoming more common. However, it is estimated that less than 15% of American children receive comprehensive sex education.

mixed. Many sex education programs have failed to achieve their goals or have only had a small positive effect, while others have been successful (Firestone, 1994; U.S. Office of Technology Assessment, 1992). For example, a large national representative survey found that the likelihood that a teenager will use some contraceptive method at first intercourse increases by about one-third following instruction about birth control (Mauldon & Luker, 1996). Generally, programs emphasizing delay are more effective with younger adolescents. Among older adolescents, comprehensive sex education programs significantly increase the percentage of sexually active adolescents who consistently use contraceptives (Frost & Forrest, 1996; Mitka, 1999).

The real question, then, is why some programs succeed while others fail. One major reason for failure is that many unsuccessful programs spend too much time on safe, noncontroversial topics, such as providing simple biological information, and so little time on contraception and disease prevention issues. Discussions of risk taking are far too

general (Alan Guttmacher Institute, 1989). Sex education also frequently comes too late, after students have already begun having intercourse (Rodriguez & Moore, 1995). Some programs also fail to present a clear focus against unprotected sex. They may try to use a nonbiased, nonjudgmental model, encouraging students to simply make their own decisions (Kirby et al., 1994). Studies show that this is not an effective approach, probably because spontaneous, unprotected sex is often considered romantic and produces short-term immediate pleasure, while waiting or using contraception involves long-range considerations. Ineffective programs are also often lecture centered: an adult offers biological information or warnings without dealing with the pressures to have sex that are so common in teenage life.

One interesting program was conducted in Baltimore in which junior and senior high school students received not only sex education but also information presented by social workers in their homerooms dealing with the services offered at a clinic. For several hours each day, staff members assigned to each

school made themselves available for individual counseling. After school, a special clinic across the street or a few blocks away offered open group discussion and individual and group counseling that emphasized personal responsibility, goal setting, parental communication, and health care, including contraception. The results showed more knowledge of sex and contraception, as well as a delay in the age of first intercourse. Students attended the clinic sooner after initiating sexual activity, and sexually active students increased their use of contraception. This behavior was especially noticeable among the younger teens, who usually show less responsible sexual behavior. The program altered behavior partially because access to high-quality free services, including professional counseling, was assured (Zabin, Kantner, & Zelnik, 1986). Competent sex education and confidential sex-related health services are among the most effective ways of stemming teen pregnancy rates and the spread of STDs ("Sex Education," 1996).

Yet, there are those who want a federal law passed allowing parents to

For Your Consideration ?

Although many studies have shown that comprehensive sex education and condom distribution in the schools do not lead to increased sexual activity, people continue to believe it. Why is it so difficult to counter this belief?

Adolescents are the highest risk group for nearly all STDs (Rosenthal, Biro, Succop, Bernstein, & Stanberry, 1997). Teens are especially at risk because they often have multiple partners and are less likely to take action to prevent STDs (Biro & Rosenthal, 1992; Grimley & Lee, 1997). A history of drinking and drug taking, and having a number of sexual partners, increase the risk of contracting STDs (Ericksen & Trocki, 1994; Rosenthal et al., 1997). Generally, boys engage in more high-risk sexual activities than girls (Leland & Barth, 1992). Girls report having fewer sexual partners and question their partners about high-risk sexual behaviors more often, although evidence shows lying about one's sexual history is very common (Leland & Barth, 1992). Failure to disclose having previous sexual partners, not using condoms, and failure to disclose testing positive for HIV or other STDs occurs quite often both among men and women (Desiderato & Crawford, 1995; Kalichman, Kelly, & Rompa, 1997).

The most important variable influencing the use of safer sexual practices is perception of vulnerability (Campbell, Peplau, & DeBro, 1992). People are more likely to use condoms if they feel vulnerable to disease or becoming pregnant (Bryan, Aiken, & West, 1997). Logic would dictate that unprotected sex could lead to these consequences, but situational variables are crucial. An adolescent may object to their children receiving contraception as well as explicit information on AIDS. This is part of the "parental rights movement," which seeks to give parents a larger say in the education and health areas (Donovan, 1997; Gavora, 1997). Advocates argue that parents should have the right to know when their children are receiving contraceptive devices or receiving explicit information about sex that may be contrary to the values of the home. While one can sympathize with parents who feel excluded, such a requirement for parental notification or approval would have devastating consequences for teens who would not visit clinics to receive contraceptive or prenatal help because they are afraid that their parents will find out. Many states now allow teens to receive such help in a confidential manner because of the society's overriding need to reduce the transmission of STDs and reduce teen pregnancy. Federal policy has emphasized confidentiality for many years.

Successful school-based programs share a number of elements. Effective programs focus on reducing sexual risk-taking behaviors that lead to HIV and other STDs or pregnancy. They may recommend abstinence but also talk about contraception and tell students how to obtain contraceptive devices. They all emphasize goal setting and teach resistance skills—that is, learning how to say no to sex, and, most importantly, negotiate and communicate within relationships (Ku, Sonenstein, & Pleck, 1993). Comprehensive sex education programs also explore the context for and meaning of sex. They emphasize values and choices (Stryker, 1997). It is also important to dispel the myth that almost everyone has sex by the ages of 15 or so, something that is a prominent belief that leads to pressure to have early sex.

Every successful program devotes time to communication, negotiation, and refusal skills. These programs are not value-free. They reinforce values and group norms against unprotected sex and are tailored to the students' experience and needs (Kirby et al., 1994).

As we enter the 21st century, communities will continue to debate the type of sex education programs they want. Hopefully, the old and now discredited arguments about sex education or condom availability encouraging teen sexuality will be put to rest, as will programs that do not have a solid value orientation. Unfortunately, many communities still use programs that are ineffective. Now that we have learned a great deal about what works and what doesn't, communities should insist that their sex education programs be based upon the research on effectiveness rather than on habit or wishful thinking.

What do you think?

A 17-year-old high school junior wants to attend classes on sex education, while the parents object strenuously to such classes which are comprehensive in scope. Should parents have the right to exclude their children from taking such courses if their teenagers want to attend? What rights should parents have in determining what courses their children take in school?

You can explore the following questions using InfoTrac College Edition. Hint: enter search terms *Sex Education for Youth* and *Parents Rights*.

say that he will use a condom, but the emotional nature of the moment may influence his actual behavior. Perceptions of risk and vulnerability vary with the emotional content of the situation. For example, if a male knows that a very appealing female has had a number of partners and did not consistently use condoms, he certainly cannot conclude that there is little risk of disease transmission. Yet, many reach that illogical conclusion because they are motivated to use irrelevant information—for example, that she is an honor student—to reduce their perception of risk (Blanton & Gerrard, 1997). When people are motivated to find a way around their perception of risk, they rationalize and find one. Educational programs need to take motivation and justification into account if teens are to be helped to reduce their chances of getting an STD or becoming pregnant.

Teenage Pregnancy

As many teens are engaging in unprotected sex, it is not surprising to find that more than one million teenagers become pregnant each year and about 60% carry to term (Henshaw, 1994). One in five 14-year-old girls today will become pregnant before reaching the age of 18. This is a serious problem among all groups, but it is most serious among minority group youth, who are even more likely to become pregnant in adolescence. Some progress has been made here, as the teenage birth rate has dropped nearly 12% since 1991. Even so, the United States still has the highest teenage birth rate of all developed countries (Wickham, 1998; Zabin, Sedivy, & Emerson, 1994).

Consequences of Teenage Pregnancies   The vast majority of teen childbearing is unintended. The consequences of adolescent pregnancies are serious for the entire family.

The Infant   Infants born to teenage mothers have more health problems than the average infant. Babies born to teenagers have lower birth weights, are more often premature, and have a greater chance of having a birth defect (Carver et al., 1990). These children are also more likely to live in poverty, and the rate of child abuse is higher as well.

The Mother   Pregnancy is a major reason that female students drop out of school (Ladner, 1987). Having a child before age 20 significantly reduces schooling by almost three years among females in all major ethnic and racial groups (Klepinger, Lundberg, & Plotnick, 1995). Perhaps as a direct consequence to this lack of educational attainment, mothers who have babies in their teens have lower incomes, hold lower-prestige jobs, and are more likely to live in poverty than their classmates (Weissberg & Greenberg, 1998).

Some teens are at high risk for becoming mothers. Those who live with single parents, initially had sex before age 16, use no form of contraception, and those who use alcohol are most at risk (Rodriguez & Moore, 1995). In many cases, their parents have talked with them about sex too late. They are not close to their families and do not think that they have bright futures; teenagers who see a future for themselves are less likely to become pregnant.

Teenage pregnancy is a national problem. More than one million teenagers become pregnant each year.

The Young Mother as Parent   The young mother does not seem to be ready for her role. Most of the children of teenage mothers will live in homes where the father is not present and are very likely to live in poverty. Adolescent mothers tend to be impatient, insensitive, and prone to punish their children. They show less empathy toward their children (Baranowski, Schilmoeller, & Higgins, 1990). Their behavior is characterized as highly physical and less verbal than that of more adult mothers (Garcia Coll, Hoffman, & Oh, 1987). They are also less responsive and involved, show less positive emotion toward their children, and create a less stimulating home environment. Adolescent mothers know less about their infant's development and do not understand what their infants can do (Karraker & Evans, 1996).

Children born to adolescent mothers lag behind their peers in cognitive, social, and academic performance and are at greater risk than peers for maladjustment (Dubow & Luster, 1990). Teenage parents require help if they are to successfully raise their children. If support is received from the mother's family, the general outlook on life as well as psychological adjustment improves (Schilmoeller, Baranowski, & Higgins, 1991).

Programs to improve the interactions between teenage parents and their children are quite successful (Murray, 1995). They also significantly lower the child abuse rate. One program sends child development specialists to homes on a weekly basis for about two years. It offers child care services, allowing mothers to attend school and prepare for a better life, as well as providing instruction on child rearing. Young parents are taught the difference between harsh and firm parenting. After participation, these young parents have more realistic expectations for child rearing and development. Other programs involve fathers as well. These programs are cost effective because they reduce costs due to delinquency, abuse, and unemployment.

The Father Only a minority of children born to teenage mothers are fathered by teenagers (Weinstein & Rosen, 1994); most fathers are 20 years old or older. When the father is an adolescent, he may not admit parenthood, perhaps out of ignorance, disbelief, or refusal to accept the obligations of fatherhood (Furstenberg, Brooks-Gunn, & Chase-Lansdale, 1989). Teenage fathers are often poorly educated and face an uphill climb to succeed in the world of work (Hardy & Duggan, 1988; Ladner, 1987).

Many teenage fathers are concerned about supporting a new family, finishing school, tending to the welfare of the child and mother, and developing their relationship with their in-laws. Feelings of alienation are great (Elster & Panzarine, 1983). Many have some contact with the baby, but often it is not extensive and does not continue. The degree of contact depends on the continuing nature of their relationship with the mother. These fathers often do not provide much, if any, financial support (Toledo-Dreves, Zabin, & Emerson, 1995).

The Extended Family The quality of the relationship between the pregnant teen and her parents during the pregnancy determines what will happen after the birth. If the bond is close, the young mother is much less likely to marry and is apt to stay with her parents (Furstenberg, 1981).

Most young mothers will stay at home if their mother signals a desire to help them. In fact, young mothers who are helped by their parents, especially until the child is attending school, are in a better economic position than others who leave to be on their own. Grandmothers provide much of the child care in these situations. Many young mothers who return to school are better off years later, although problems do exist, and the benefits should not be overstated. As the child matures, family relationships may deteriorate. The child's mother remains in a subordinate position to her parents because she is dependent on them.

Siblings may also be affected. They may need to help out, and sometimes their share of the family's resources may be reduced if the mother returns to the home with the child. Older sisters also seem to serve as role models: the younger sisters of childbearing adolescents are at risk of bearing children themselves as adolescents (East, 1996).

It is clear that young parents need help. Whether or not they marry, and whether they live at home or try to make it on their own, teenage parents need counseling and support from the time the pregnancy begins through the prenatal period and delivery and into the early years of parenthood. Because subsequent pregnancies are common, sex education is also necessary.

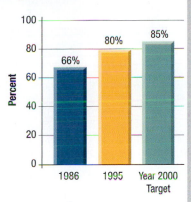

Trends in Development

Adolescents 13 to 18 Who Have Discussed Sexuality with Their Parents
Good progress has been made toward meeting this goal.

1986: 66%
1995: 80%
Year 2000 Target: 85%

Source: USDHHS, 1998

Guideposts
What are the consequences of teenage pregnancy for the mother, child, father, and extended family?

Sexual Orientation: Homosexual Behavior

For some adolescents, their sexuality is expressed in relationships with people of the same sex. Between 3% and 10% of all men define themselves as gay, and between 1% and 3% of all women define themselves as lesbian (Fay, Turner, Klasssen, & Gagnon, 1989; Strong & De Vault, 1995). The number of people who have engaged in homosexual behavior, often as teenagers, is much greater, but when such behavior occurs only once or twice, it does not necessarily mean that the person is gay (Rice, 1989). Despite this contact, most become exclusively heterosexual.

The term *gay* is now used to describe both males and females whose primary sexual orientation is toward members of the same sex. The term *lesbian* is used only to describe women whose sexual orientation is to other women. The term *bisexual* describes sexual behavior directed toward members of both the same and the opposite sex. Homosexuality does not define one's sex role, personality, attitudes toward life, or physical appearance, only one's sexual orientation.

The origins of homosexuality are controversial. Recent work shows that homosexuality may have a genetic component (Hershberger, 1997; Savin-Williams, 1988). Indeed, twin studies offer evidence of genetic involvement. When one identical twin is homosexual, more than 50% of the time the other twin is also homosexual. The percentage is reduced to less than 20% for fraternal twins or other siblings (Bailey & Pillard, 1991; Whitman, Diamond, & Martin, 1993). Since the concordance rate for twins is not near perfect, there is much evidence for other causative factors as well.

Physiological differences have also been found, especially in the hypothalamus (LeVay, 1991). It is possible that some early experience, a chemical or hormonal event, causes changes in the structure and organization of the brain (Berenbaum & Schneider, 1995). Although there is no single child rearing pattern found among people who have homosexual identities, a pattern in which mothers are domineering or overprotective and fathers ignore the child is found with some frequency (Bell, Weinberg, & Hammersmith, 1981). A similar argument is made for lesbians, who as a group perceive their mothers as cold and distant (Bell et al., 1981). These patterns do not hold, though, for all and may be important only if certain genetic or biological predispositions exist. Obviously, many pieces are missing in our attempt to explain the origins of homosexuality. The findings of genetic and biological differences, though, do match the feelings of many homosexuals who claim that sexual orientation is not a choice as such. It is fair to say that sexual orientation is probably shaped by a complex interaction of social and biological influences (Money, 1987; Paul, 1993).

For adolescents whose primary orientation is toward members of the same sex, the teenage years may be difficult. Most are confused about it, and half try to deny it (Newman & Muzzonigro, 1993). These teenagers may reject their sexual orientation, hide it from their family, and find that it is very difficult to cope with their feelings. They may fear family rejection (Townsend, Wallick, Pleak, & Cambre, 1997) or the rejection and ridicule of their peers (Waldner-Haugrud & Magruder, 1996). Parental reactions to being told that their child is gay are varied. About half of all parents respond with disbelief, denial, or negative comments suggesting that it is only a phase (Robinson, Walters, & Skeen, 1992). Some parents don't discuss the issue, hoping it will disappear (Cohen & Savin-Williams, 1996). Most parents do eventually arrive at a tolerance or acceptance of their child's sexual orientation (Savin-Williams & Dube, 1998). Generally, the better the relationship before the disclosure, the better the relationship after disclosure.

For Your Consideration ?

Why is there such prejudice against homosexuals?

For Your Consideration ?

Some people reacted very positively to the findings that there may be biological/genetic factors involved in the cause of homosexuality, reasoning that it might counter the idea that it is a "choice." On the other hand, others argue that looking at the "cause" merely makes it seem like a disease or a type of psychopathology. Should scientists continue to look for the "cause" of homosexuality?

Our society certainly does not endorse such sexual orientations, and discrimination, taunting, and violence are common. Society often shows *homophobia*, or a fear of homosexuality. Even people who do not show homophobia may believe myths about homosexuality. For instance, some people believe that gays are readily recognized and that they show a particular behavior pattern. The truth is that most gays cannot be identified simply by looking at them or observing their behavior (Greenberg, Buess, Mullen, & Sands, 1989). Some also believe that all gay men are effeminate. Actually, only about 15% of all male gays are effeminate (Voeller, 1980). Those who do show "effeminate" behavior tend to stand out, but the great majority who do not show this behavior go unnoticed. In addition, people sometimes confuse sexual orientation with gender identity. Contrary to many people's opinions, gays are comfortable with their gender and do not want to change (Comer, 1995). There is also no identifiable homosexual personality, nor are people who engage in homosexuality more prone to psychopathology. Last, some people consider homosexuality, itself, to be some sort of mental illness rather than a sexual orientation, yet the American Psychiatric Association (1994) does not consider homosexuality a mental disorder.

Usually, the adolescent experiences homosexual feelings years before identifying himself as gay. The average gay male does not identify himself as gay until age 19 or 21 years (Strong & DeVault, 1995). Often the first phase in acquiring such an identity involves awareness of one's own feelings and recognition of emotional and physical desires. This phase is marked by fears of discovery and confusion. In the second phase, the individual actually acknowledges these feelings. The third phase involves a self-definition of being gay; this is difficult, for it is considered deviant in our society. Families must deal with this acknowledgment. Some gays may go through two additional phases. One involves entrance into a gay subculture, including acquiring gay friends and frequenting gay bars and clubs. The final phase involves entrance into a gay or lesbian love affair, and most gay individuals have experienced at least one long-term relationship (Strong & DeVault, 1995).

Not all gays, though, "come out"—that is, publicly acknowledge their gayness. Some may acknowledge their own feelings but may not wish to publicly identify with the gay subculture. Coming out is often difficult and may create a crisis situation in the family, but gradually most families accept the situation and adjust to it (Holtzen & Agresti, 1990).

Prejudice, discrimination, and even violence against homosexuals are common. The extent of the prejudice is shown by a national survey of white, African American, and Latino adolescents concerning their attitudes toward homosexuality and homosexuals. Ethnicity and race were not factors. The majority (59%) disagreed either "a lot" or "a little" with the idea that "I could be friends with a gay person" (Marsiglio, 1993). As in so many areas we have looked at, there is need for education.

Homosexuality is a sexual orientation. It says nothing about one's personality, abilities, or vocational interests.

Guideposts

What are some of the myths about homosexuality?

Most people who are gay can be recognized by their physical appearance.

Adapting to Change

It is easy to recite the list of physical changes that occur in adolescence, but more important than any list is an understanding of the subjective experience of each adolescent in coping with these changes. Although it is more difficult to cite the cognitive changes that take place during adolescence, they are just as important, and their contribution to adolescent behavior should be appreciated.

Adolescents face many challenges, and it would be folly not to take the problems associated with body image and sexual activity seriously. Yet, most cope with the challenges well. Much of the difficulty and the uneasiness teens experience is due to the novelty of these challenges and teenagers' lack of experience dealing with social situations. It takes time, patience, knowledge, understanding from others, and experience to accept oneself and to feel confident in what one believes and how one acts. Viewing adolescence as a time of "firsts" may provide the focus for a better understanding of the adolescent years and a more optimistic portrayal of adolescence.

Summary

1. Puberty refers to the physiological changes leading to sexual maturity, while adolescence refers to the individual's psychological experiences during this period of life. The sequence of physical changes during adolescence are predictable, although the age at which each change occurs varies from person to person.

2. Females normally experience their growth spurt before males do. After the growth spurt, the genital organs and breasts develop. Menstruation then occurs. In males, growth of the testes, scrotum and the appearance of pubic hair occur before the growth spurt. Deepening of the voice and widening of the shoulders occur later.

3. The fact that each new generation for the past 100 years or so has been taller and heavier and menstruated earlier than the previous one is known as the secular trend.

4. Early maturation in males is a social advantage during adolescence and early adulthood. Later in life, however, early maturers tend to be less flexible and less insightful. Early-maturing girls are more likely to date early, have sex early, and show behavioral difficulties, perhaps because they are drawn into associations with older adolescents. These problems may not be due to early maturation but a combination of preexisting family problems with early maturation adding to the stress. Early-maturing girls are not as pleased with their bodies as later-maturing girls, but these differences disappear by late adolescence.

5. Teenagers' health is usually considered excellent. Today, however, there are grave doubts about the health of teenagers, based on their tendency to engage in behaviors that have negative health consequences both for the near and the long term.

6. Accidents, homicide, and suicide are the leading causes of adolescent death. Most suicide victims are depressed and have a pervading sense of hopelessness. Many give clues, such as talking about suicide or giving treasured items away, or have a history of a previous suicide attempt or a suicide in their family.

7. Generally, teens consume too much fat in their diet. Adolescents focus on their bodies, and girls are less satisfied with their bodies than boys. Many girls whose weight is within the normal range believe they are overweight, and girls are more likely to experience problems with body image than are males. Physical activity declines during adolescence, and much unnecessary dieting could be reduced if physical activity and good eating patterns were practiced.

8. Eating disorders are not uncommon in adolescence. Anorexia nervosa, a disorder involving self-imposed starvation, can be fatal. Bulimia involves engaging in binge eating and then purging the system. Obesity is a major medical and social problem.

9. Adolescents do not get enough sleep and often complain of being tired. Lack of sleep is related to academic and behavioral difficulties.

10. During the stage of formal operations, adolescents develop the ability to find possible alternatives to problems, to separate the real from the possible, to form hypotheses and test them out, to interpret abstractions, and to think about their own thoughts. Formal operational reasoning is abstract, scientifically logical, and often not contextual.

11. Some authorities believe that qualitative differences in thinking can be found in later adolescence and continue to develop into early adulthood. Older adolescents and early adults often deal with problems that are more practical and realistic. Problems are now seen within a context, and solutions constrained by practical factors including money and time. Knowledge is considered relative; that is, knowledge depends on one's perspective.

12. Adolescents often have difficulty differentiating between their own thoughts and those of others, leading to egocentric thinking. Out of this egocentrism comes the imaginary audience, in which adolescents often believe everyone else is looking at them, and the personal fable, in which they believe their experiences and thoughts are absolutely unique in the annals of human history.

13. Adolescent risk taking may be related to the personal fable but is also influenced by the adolescent's desire for new experiences, sensation seeking, and variety. Some adolescent risk takers do so to flaunt their courage or to show their nonconformity or opposition to authority.

14. According to Kohlberg, adolescents' more sophisticated cognitive abilities allow them to function at higher levels of moral reasoning. However, most people do not develop past Kohlberg's stage 4. In adolescence, there is a positive relationship between the level of moral reasoning and prosocial behavior.

15. During the past 20 years, values relating to personal achievement have become more prominent than those involving societal issues. Most adolescents believe in God, and religious beliefs can have an effect on behavior.

Review

16. Adolescent attitudes toward sexuality are more liberal than in the past. Females are still more conservative than males, although the gap is narrowing. Males expect intimacy sooner in a relationship than females do. Teenagers are beginning to have sex at earlier ages than years ago. Sexually transmitted diseases are a major problem.

17. Many sexually active teens do not use contraception regularly. Use increases with age, and there has been some rise in usage recently, although it remains inconsistent. Many teens do not use any contraceptive device because they deny their sexuality, do not believe they can become pregnant, believe that contraception diminishes the romantic nature of the experience, are ignorant of the biological facts of life, or use cognitive strategies to reduce their feelings of vulnerability.

18. Teen pregnancy is a widespread problem for everyone concerned. Infants born to teenage mothers have more health problems, and teen mothers are more likely to drop out of school. Teenage mothers engage in fewer behaviors that would optimize the child's development. Teenage fathers are often found in dead-end jobs.

19. Most parents favor sex education in schools. Sex education is most effective when it offers not only the biological information but also information on contraception and enhances communication and decision making skills. There is no evidence that sex education or condom distribution encourages sexual intercourse, and sexually active young women who are exposed to sex education are less likely to become pregnant.

20. The teenage years are frequently difficult for teenagers whose primary orientation is homosexual, and these teens may have difficulty coping with feelings. Homosexuality seems to have genetic and biological roots, but there is still much not known about the origins of homosexuality. People hold a number of myths about homosexuality. Most gay males are not effeminate and are comfortable with their own gender identity. Homosexuality is not a mental disturbance. Acquiring an identity as gay occurs in a number of distinct phases.

The physiological changes that take place during the teenage years are called (1)_____. Bodily changes that relate directly to sexual reproduction are called (2)_____ characteristics, while those that are not directly related to reproduction but differentiate boys from girls are called (3)_____ characteristics. (4)_____ refers to the psychological aspects of the individual during this period. The earliest and most noticeable pubertal change is the (5)_____. (6)_____ (Girls/Boys) mature before (7)_____. The trend for adolescents to be taller than their parents and to enter puberty earlier is known as the (8)_____ trend. The three structures responsible for puberty are the (9)_____, (10)_____, and (11)_____. Most adolescents are neither early nor late but rather average. However, (12)_____ maturing boys have a social advantage in adolescence and early adulthood. (13)_____ maturing girls date earlier but are more likely to have poorer grades in school and show behavioral problems. The leading cause of death among adolescents is (14)_____, with (15)_____ ranking second. (16)_____ is the third leading cause of death among adolescents.

Body image is an important factor in self-esteem, and (17)_____ are more likely to suffer from poor body image and are very likely to see themselves as overweight even though they are not. (18)_____ (Early-, On-time, Late-) maturing girls are more likely to develop eating disorders. The eating disorder known as (19)_____ involves self-induced starvation and can be fatal. Another eating disorder called (20)_____ entails eating large quantities of food and purging the system.

Important cognitive changes also take place in adolescence as teenagers enter Piaget's final stage in which they begin to show (21)_____ operations. Adolescents develop the ability to find all possible alternatives called (22)_____ logic. Adolescents can understand proverbs and political cartoons because they can now appreciate (23)_____. They also can reason in a logical and scientific manner as they show (24)_____ reasoning. Piaget believed that there were no further qualitative changes in reasoning, but others argue that reasoning in later adolescence changes. These later changes in reasoning are collectively known as (25)_____ reasoning. These psychologists argue that in very late adolescence and early adulthood thinking becomes more (26)_____, and often people understand that knowledge depends upon the subjective experience of the individual, a type of thinking known as (27)_____ thinking.

Adolescents can anticipate how others will react to them, but they fail to differentiate between what they are thinking and what others are thinking, a difficulty called adolescent (28)_____. Teens often show the

(29) _____, a belief that when they enter a room everyone is watching and observing them. They also believe that their experiences are unique and they are relatively invulnerable, a belief known as the (30) _____. This is one of the explanations for adolescent (31) _____.

Adolescent cognitive advancements allow them to think about a better world and formulate their own morals and values. Most people do not progress past Kohlberg's (32) _____ stage, which involves doing one's duty and maintaining the social order for its own sake. Fewer reason at Kohlberg's higher levels.

Adolescents in the 1960s were more interested in a/an (33) _____ morality involving social issues, while beginning in the middle 1970s and continuing until today, adolescents are more interested in (34) _____. Adolescents are most likely to have values that are similar to those held by their parents if they have experienced a/an (35) _____ style of parenting. Religious beliefs may affect behavior as there is a/an (36) _____ relationship between holding strong religious beliefs and refraining from premarital sex and not using drugs. Religiousness shows a/an (37) _____ (decline/increase) during the adolescent years, but most adolescents say they believe in God.

The traditional attitude that males were entitled to sexual expression but not women is known as the (38) _____. This view is declining. Adolescent sexual attitudes are more (39) _____ (liberal/conservative) than those of their parents. The age at which teens start to date has (40) _____. Rates of premarital sex have (41) _____ (increased/decreased). Adolescents are engaging in sexual intercourse at an earlier age than in years past, but adolescents (42) _____ (overestimate/underestimate) the percentage of adolescents having sex.

About (43) _____ of all teens have used contraception the last time they had sexual intercourse. The most important variable influencing the use of safer sexual practices is a sense of (44) _____. The developed country with the highest teenage pregnancy rate is (45) _____. The health of infants born to teenage mothers is often compromised, and they are likely to be raised in poverty.

Homosexuality defines one's (46) _____, but not one's sex role or attitudes toward life. The term (47) _____ is used to describe a person whose primary sexual orientation is to people of the same gender.

InfoTrac

For additional readings, explore InfoTrac College Edition, our online library.

Go to http://www.infotrac-college.com/wadsworth. Hint: enter the search terms *Puberty and Adolescence, Sex Education for Youth,* and *Eating Disorders in Children.*

What's on the web

Anorexia Nervosa and Related Eating Disorders
http://www.anred.com

Youth Crime Watch
http://www.ycwa.org

New York Online Access to Health - Sexually Transmitted Diseases
http://www.noah.cuny.edu/pregnancy/march_of_dimes/stds/stdsbro.html

The Wadsworth Psychology Study Center Web Site
Go to the Wadsworth Psychology Study Center at http://psychology.wadsworth.com/ for quiz questions, research updates, hot topics, interactive exercises, and suggested readings in the InfoTrac College Edition related to this chapter.

Social *and* Personality

CHAPTER OUTLINE

Rites of Passage

The Self-Concept and Self-Esteem in Adolescence

In Search of an Identity

Achieving Emotional and Behavioral Autonomy

The Secondary School Today

Career Choice

Atypical Development: Drug Abuse and Violence

Exploding the Myths

ARE THESE STATEMENTS True *or* False?

1. Generally, males show higher self-esteem in middle and late adolescence than females.
2. Adolescent boys show more symptoms of depression than adolescent girls.
3. Periods of confusion in adolescence usually signal the probability of mental illness.
4. Teenagers generally report feeling close to their parents and having a good relationship with them.
5. Parents tend to underestimate the differences in opinions on various issues between themselves and their adolescent children, and adolescents tend to overestimate the differences in opinions between themselves and their parents.
6. When parents communicate with their adolescent children, they tend to explain their own views rather than try to understand their teens' opinions and attitudes.
7. Junior high school and high school students read at lower levels today than they did 20 years ago.
8. High school students who are employed for more than 20 hours a week are most often motivated students who show outstanding grade point averages and excellent citizenship.
9. Drug use among teenagers has declined substantially throughout the 1990s.
10. Children who witness domestic violence are less likely to engage in violent behavior because they are aware of its consequences.

ANSWERS: **1.** *True.* **2.** *False.* **3.** *False.* **4.** *True.* **5.** *True.* **6.** *True.* **7.** *False.* **8.** *False.* **9.** *False.* **10.** *False.*

Development *in* Adolescence

Rites of Passage

In some Native American tribes, each 14- or 15-year-old male is taken to a sweat lodge where the body and spirit are purified by the heat. A medicine man advises and assists him with prayers. The adolescent is then brought to an isolated spot where he fasts for four days. He prays, reflects on the medicine man's words, and awaits a vision that reveals to him his path of life as a man in society (Heinrich, Corbine, & Thomas, 1990).

*A **rite of passage** is a ritual that marks the movement of a person from one social position to another (Schultz & Levenda, 1987). These almost universal ceremonies most often involve a separation from society, some preparation or instruction from an elder, a transition (usually a special ceremony), and a welcoming back into the society with some acknowledgment of the changed status (Delaney, 1995). Some faiths have rites of passage—for example, the Bar and Bat Mitzvah in Judaism, a ceremony that Jewish boys and girls, respectively, participate in during early adolescence that marks their spiritual arrival at adulthood.*

Although some see high school graduation as a rite of passage, it is a weak one at best since it lacks the moral and spiritual function prominent in traditional rites of passage.

High school graduation is a rite of passage in a technological society. Adolescents are isolated in schools from the rest of society for a good part of the day. They are taught by teachers who are older and specially chosen by society. The graduation ceremony, with its special dress and formal setting, may be thought of as a transition (Delaney, 1995). But not all adolescents graduate or attend their graduation. More importantly, the teacher-student relationship lacks the moral and spiritual function so prominent in rites of passage. The bond with society is not necessarily strengthened. This rite of passage is very weak compared to those in more traditional societies. Sometimes, young people create their own rites of passage, such as attempts to imitate adult behavior through cigarette smoking, drinking and early sex. The change in status is acknowledged by peers and some social solidarity exists, but the lack of adult leadership and continuity with society makes such transitions incomplete.

Our society presents adolescents with no real ceremony that functions as a rite of passage, especially if we consider the spiritual and communal point of view. After puberty, children are faced with a long period of transitional status not really marked by a specific end point that would universally signify their arrival at adult status. Some communities are moving toward providing such transitions. In an attempt to combat the social problems in their neighborhoods, some African American communities have initiated programs to restore traditional African values such as interdependence, spirituality, and respect for elders (Warfield-Copock, 1992). These rites of passage are modeled after traditional rites in some African tribes (Harvey & Brauch, 1997). Adolescents are instructed in many areas, some philosophical and some practical, and an overnight retreat is planned by elders.

For Your Consideration ?

When does adulthood begin? What criteria would you use to determine whether an individual is an "adult"?

Middle adolescents list conflicting descriptions of their selves and are bothered by them. In later adolescence, they will be able to integrate them and accept the full range of their emotions and behaviors.

The Self-Concept and Self-Esteem in Adolescence

The self becomes more differentiated with age. When asked to describe themselves, adolescents give different descriptions of the self as they play different roles. The teen may experience a "sarcastic" self with parents but a "comforting" self with friends (Harter & Monsour, 1992). This differentiation is due to an increased awareness of the social roles they play and their emerging cognitive ability to use abstractions.

Early adolescents construct simple abstractions about the self. They realize that they are extroverted because they like to talk and are loud or depressed because they are embarrassed and feel alone (Harter, 1988). They may construct opposites, seeing themselves as "outgoing," "self-conscious," "angry," and "calming," but do not compare these abstractions to each other. They are not aware of the contradictions, perhaps because these behaviors are separated by time (Fischer, 1980), nor are they bothered by them.

Adolescents develop the cognitive skills necessary for such comparisons in middle adolescence and find these conflicting descriptions (being outgoing and yet introspective) a source of distress. In late adolescence, these opposites are integrated into a coherent whole, and adolescents understand that they can be both "introverted" and "extroverted" with different people (Harter, 1988). It is not only acceptable but desirable to show different sides of the self to different people. The number of such opposites peaks

at middle adolescence (9th grade) and then declines somewhat in 11th grade (see Figure 13.1). This decline becomes even more substantial in 12th grade (Harter & Carlson, 1988).

Many adolescents, especially during the middle adolescent years, become concerned about which of these contradictions is their "real self" or "real me" (Harter & Monsour, 1992). They are concerned about being phony and acting falsely—that is, acting in ways that do not reflect their true self (Harter, 1998; Harter, Marold, Whitesell, & Cobbs, 1996).

Adolescents may act falsely to make a good impression on others (acting happy and self-assured at an interview when they don't feel that way), to experiment with new roles and behaviors, and, because they must conform to the expectations of others, to be valued and accepted. Adolescents often know why they are acting falsely (Harter et al., 1996). Those who cite behaving falsely because others do not value their real feelings and behaviors show the highest levels of false behavior and report low self-esteem and more depressive symptoms. Those reporting more role experimentation show the most positive outcomes, with those using false behavior to garner approval and make a good impression somewhere in the middle.

Adolescents are especially upset when they feel they cannot act or express their feelings because important people in their lives do not accept them for whom they are. They believe parents will only value and support them if they express opinions that are similar to their parents'. This causes adolescents to suppress their real selves. Parents' acceptance and support is dependent on being what others want them to be, and teenagers do not perceive this conditional support as true support (Harter, Marold, & Whitesell, 1992). Higher levels of behaving falsely are reported by adolescents who receive a low level of support as well as support they perceive as conditional.

Guideposts

What changes in the self take place in adolescence?

Figure 13.1 Developmental Differences in Adolescents' Perception of Opposing and Conflicting Self-Attributes

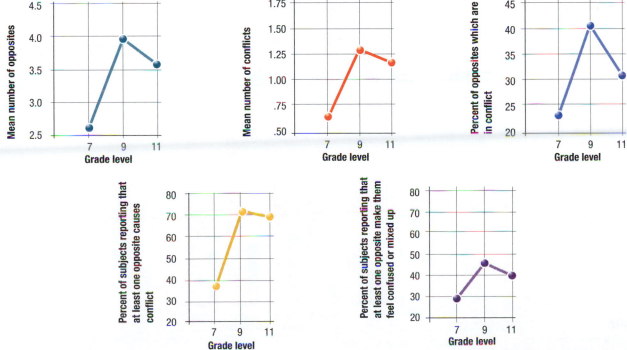

SOURCE: Harter & Monsour (1988)

Some argue that girls are more likely to believe they cannot voice their true feelings and show their real self because they are taught to identify with the cultural role of the polite, quiet person (Gilligan, 1982; Gilligan, Lyons, & Hammer, 1989). Women are taught not to express their opinions assertively, thereby leading to a suppression of self. Carol Gilligan (Gilligan, 1988; Gilligan, Brown, & Rogers, 1990) argues that in adolescence, women are faced with a dilemma. They have been raised to value human relationships and to define themselves in terms of their relationships with others. Part of this is the ethic of caring, which encourages women to be more sensitive to the needs and desires of others than their own (Gilligan, 1993). If they begin to think and act in a manner in which they allow their own desires and goals to show and to become self-sufficient, they label themselves, and risk being labeled by others, as selfish. Yet the selfless giving to others may not allow their own strivings to be realized. The conflict is based on concerns of inclusion and exclusion. *Inclusion* involves being connected with and giving to others and is a central value for women. *Exclusion* involves being centered on oneself and one's own desires and needs. Gilligan (1988) notes that selfishness connotes the exclusion of others and selflessness the exclusion of self. Women may believe that their need to become more autonomous means that their need for connectedness must be ignored (Lytle et al., 1997). Often, women's solution to this dilemma is to silence their special and distinctive voice, not to offer opinions, and thus they lose confidence in themselves. This pattern may continue through adulthood. Young women, then, must find an answer to the dilemma of inclusion and exclusion.

Others argue that there are no real gender differences here (Harter, Waters, Whitesell, & Kastelic, 1998). Rather, there are dramatic individual differences that can be predicted by perceived support and gender orientation. The higher the level of support for speaking out and being oneself, the more adolescents of both genders will be able to voice their true convictions without fear of being ridiculed or losing love (Figure 13.2). In addition, those women who combine both masculine and feminine traits, a situation called **androgyny,** rather than scoring very high only on femininity are more likely to voice their opinions. Finally, expressing oneself is often situational, and even those who may not voice their opinions in a group or in school may do so with parents or with close fiends.

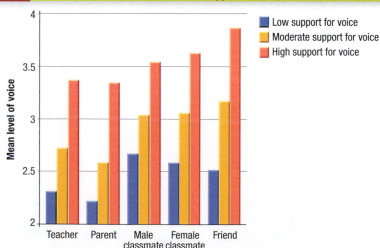

Figure 13.2 **Level of Voice as a Function of Support for Voice within Relational Contexts**

SOURCE: Harter et al. (1998)

Self-esteem in adolescence is related to many significant outcomes. High self-esteem is related to academic success and to an internal locus of control, feeling that one is basically in control of one's life (Chubb, Fertman, & Ross, 1997). Teens with high self-esteem are less preoccupied with peer approval and are less susceptible to peer pressure than those with low self-esteem (Thorne & Michaelieu, 1996). High self-esteem is also related to closer, more positive interpersonal relationships (Fullerton & Ursano, 1994). Low self-esteem is associated with depression, delinquency, substance use, and poor academic outcomes (Zimmerman, Copeland, Shope, & Dielman, 1996).

Two trends are found when researchers investigate self-esteem throughout the teenage years. First, self-esteem shows moderate consistency throughout adolescence (Alsaker & Olweus, 1992; Chubb et al., 1997). Adolescents with high self-esteem or low self-esteem tend to stay that way. Since only moderate stability is found, there is some room for change. Some individuals show substantial but not radical changes in self-esteem (Block & Robins, 1993; Hirsh & Dubois, 1991).

Second, males generally show higher self-esteem than females after early adolescence (Bolognini, Plancherel, Bettschart, & Halfon, 1996). More girls report low self-esteem during middle and late adolescence (Cairns, McWhirter, Duffy, & Barry, 1990; Chubb et al., 1997). While the self-esteem of males increases from early adolescence to early adulthood, many—but certainly not all—females fail to show such increases (Block & Robins, 1993; Zimmerman et al., 1997). One reason centers on body image, which tends to be more positive for males than for females (Thorne & Michaelieu, 1996). It may also result from different messages sent to males and females about their adequacy (Chubb et al., 1997). Perhaps society values the more stereotyped competencies of males and devalues the female emphasis on caring and helping.

Depressive symptoms are also more common among adolescent girls than boys (Wichstrøm, 1999). This is a switch from childhood, when depressive symptoms were more prevalent among boys (Nolen-Hoeksema, Girgus, & Seligman, 1991). The reversal occurs at around age 13 or 14 years (Ge et al., 1994). Girls' symptoms increase, while boys' remain relatively stable after this age. Boys react more negatively to stressors in childhood, but the pattern seems to be reversed in adolescence. Although stressful events affect both boys and girls, they seem to affect girls somewhat more in adolescence.

Puberty marks a change in vulnerability to stress for girls, and girls are more disrupted by changes in peer relations. Girls are more concerned with body image and may be more troubled by these physical changes than boys (Gavin & Furman, 1989). Perhaps fundamental conflicts in society's view of females make it more difficult for girls to form an identity and to mesh their personal desires with the interpersonal orientation that is a basic part of their socialization (Leaper, 1994). Boys and girls may differ in their search for an identity, but this search is difficult for both.

In Search of an Identity

Who am I?
Where do I belong?
Where am I going?

These three questions typify the adolescent's search for a personal identity (Ruittenbeck, 1964). Erik Erikson (1959) saw the positive outcome of adolescence as the formation of a solid, personal **identity,** while the negative outcome of adolescence is an aimlessness known as **role confusion** (the state of not knowing who

Generally, males show higher self-esteem in middle and late adolescence than females.

Guideposts

What gender differences in self-esteem develop during adolescence?

Adolescent boys show more symptoms of depression than adolescent girls.

identity

The sense of knowing who you are. (The positive outcome of adolescence in psychosocial theory).

role confusion

In psychosocial theory, the negative outcome of adolescence, which involves feelings of aimlessness and a failure to develop a personal identity.

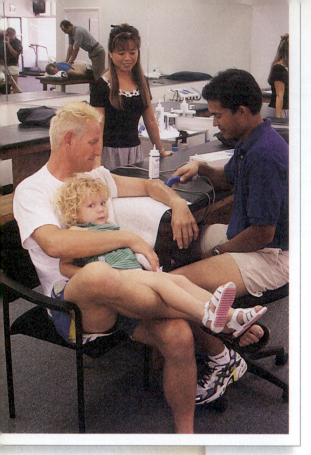

People explore many vocational opportunities. They then make commitments and follow a course of study.

one really is). Two central components of identity include finding a vocational identity and developing a personal ideology—that is, key central values, spiritual beliefs, and a connection with family and community.

Forming an identity is probably more difficult today than it was in the past. Years ago, women were expected to be wives and mothers and men to follow their father's trade. Today, adolescents have more avenues of choice open to them and more freedom to choose.

Although it is possible to speak about a global identity, identity has many aspects, including the personal, religious, occupational, interpersonal, and racial/ethnic identity (see *Identity, Minority Status, and the Bicultural Experience* on pages 518–519). An individual may be well along in forming one of these and not another (Meeus & Dekovic, 1995). Achieving an identity requires exploration, which one researcher called the "work" of adolescence (Grotevant, 1987). Adolescents have a difficult course to chart. If they are to function as adults, they must be able to make their own decisions. They cannot simply be carbon copies of their parents. On the other hand, the attitudes and values gained from parents during childhood serve as anchors, providing security in a sea of change. Adolescents who totally abandon these values may become bewildered and utterly confused. In addition, surrendering older ideals assumes all such ideals to be worthless, a conclusion that is difficult to support.

The Four Identity Statuses

Achieving an identity depends on two variables: exploration (sometimes referred to as crisis) and commitment (Marcia, 1967; Meeus & Dekovic, 1995). During a period of **exploration,** one actively faces and questions aspects of one's personal identity. For instance, a college student may have to choose a major and be faced with this decision when approaching the junior year. In the personal sphere, the student may be dating someone for a while and may have to decide whether to get more deeply involved. **Commitment** relates to the presence or absence of a decision (Flum, 1994). An individual making a commitment follows a plan of action that reflects the decision. A person who investigates many vocational choices and decides on a particular career will follow the appropriate course of study. The decision to end a relationship or to become engaged leads to different behavioral paths.

Adolescents differ in the extent to which they have experienced crises or made commitments. A prominent researcher in this field, James Marcia (1967, 1980), grouped adolescents into four categories, according to their experiences with crises (exploration) and commitments (see Table 13.1). Because identity status is related to specific attitudes and behaviors, it is worth taking a more detailed look at each status.

Identity Diffusion An individual who shows **identity diffusion** may or may not have explored various alternatives but has not made any commitments and is not presently in the process of forming any. Identity-diffused people may actively seek noncommitment, avoiding demanding situations. They are unwilling or unable to make commitments (Valde, 1996). They may appear aimless, aloof, drifting, confused and empty (Orlofsky, Marcia, & Lesser, 1973). They find it difficult to plan ahead or make firm decisions (Flum, 1994). They often show excessive dependence on peers and do not believe they are in control. The excessive conformity to group

exploration (crisis)
In psychosocial theory, a time in which a person actively faces and questions aspects of his or her own identity.

commitment
In psychosocial theory, making a decision concerning some question involved in identity formation and following a plan of action reflecting the decision.

identity diffusion
An identity status resulting in confusion, aimlessness, and a sense of emptiness.

Table 13.1	James Marcia's Four Identity Statuses
Identity Status	**Definition**
Identity diffusion	An identity diffuser may or may not have experienced doubt over goals and values; he or she does not evidence a serious or realistic inclination to examine concerns about goals and values; he or she expresses no commitment similar to an ideology or to career plans.
Identity foreclosure	A foreclosure displays a commitment similar to that of the identity achiever but has not appraised alternatives to personal goals and values; choices often express parental preferences.
Identity moratorium	A moratorium has questioned goals and values and considered alternatives but is still doubtful and uncommitted; an active effort to become informed and to make suitable choices is predominant.
Identity achievement	An identity achiever has experienced doubt (crisis) in personal goals and values, has considered alternatives, and is committed, at least tentatively, to some expressed value positions and career plans.

SOURCE: Hummel & Roselli (1983)

expectations means that very little individual growth takes place. Identity diffusion is not a sign of mental disturbance. It only becomes a problem when a person leaves adolescence without making tentative steps toward commitments. A period of confusion often precedes establishment of a firm identity (Erikson, 1959). In fact, there may be two different types of diffusion; one that is a permanent status and one that is a temporary state (Flum, 1994).

Identity Foreclosure   The **identity-foreclosed** group consists of teens who have not experienced a crisis; they have not explored alternatives but have made commitments anyway. These teens have made premature commitments. They identify very well—perhaps too well—with their parents. For example, some people may go into their parents' business because they were always expected to. They were not permitted—or did not permit themselves—to search for other alternatives. In another situation, a young woman may have married very early in life and not explored other possible choices or alternatives to early marriage. Identity-foreclosed people are very certain about their future plans and spend little time on self-examination (Flum, 1994).

Identity foreclosure can be a secure status, and teens in this status are frequently envied by their peers. After all, they have a definite direction in life that they are following. This security is purchased at a price, however. The path is not one they might have chosen, and foreclosed individuals may find themselves mired in an unhappy lifestyle later in life.

Identity Moratorium   Adolescents who are presently experiencing a crisis but whose commitments are vague are considered to be in the **moratorium** status—a period of delay in which a person is not yet ready to make definite commitments (Erikson, 1968). They are exploring many possibilities, some of them radical, but their final commitments tend to be more conservative.

The moratorium status is not a happy one. Adolescents engaged in identity exploration show more self-doubt, apprehension, confusion, and conflict with parents and other authority figures (Flum, 1994; Kidwell, Dunham, Bachno, Pastorino, & Portes, 1995). They are often found alone, thinking about and considering their options.

T **F**
3

Periods of confusion in adolescence usually signal the probability of mental illness.

identity foreclosure
An identity status marked by a premature identity decision.

identity moratorium
An identity status in which a person is actively searching for an identity.

Identity moratorium is the least stable of all the statuses (Marcia et al., 1993; Waterman, 1982), but it may be necessary for a person to experience it. When a person does make a commitment, it is his or her own, made after a period of searching for answers.

Identity Achievement   **Identity achievers** have made it. They have explored their alternatives and made their commitments. These independent personal identities are not carbon copies of their parents' identities, nor are they totally the opposite. Their identity includes some of their parents' values and attitudes and omits others. They are well adjusted (Bernard, 1981) and have good relationships with both peers and authority figures (Donovan, 1975). Identity achievers have the highest grade-point averages of any of the other statuses (Cross & Allen, 1970) and better study habits (Waterman & Waterman, 1971).

Becoming an identity achiever is not something that is commonly accomplished in early or middle adolescence. The number of identity achievers increases with age and the number of adolescents in the foreclosure and, especially, diffusion statuses declines (Waterman, 1993). The years between 18 and 21 years seem especially crucial to development of an identity. Before this time, the overwhelming number of adolescents are either foreclosed or diffused (Archer, 1982; Meilman, 1979), and only very limited changes occur before or during the high school years (Meuus, 1996; Waterman, 1982). Generally, older adolescents are more oriented toward, and concerned with, their future (Adamson & Lyxell, 1997), and the older an adolescent, the more exploration and the greater the commitment (Markstrom-Adams & Adams, 1995).

Identity status is not carved in stone. People can move from one group to another as they experience a crisis or make a new commitment. An unusual experience might lead one back to a moratorium. For example, after spending a number of years preparing to become a newspaper reporter, one young woman found she could not find a job and had to search for an occupational identity all over again. A divorced person may have to search anew for a personal or social identity because the original one is no longer viable.

One's identity status is linked to depth of intimacy developed in early adulthood. The psychosocial crisis of young adulthood can be expressed as **intimacy versus isolation** (Erikson, 1968). *Intimacy* involves the development of very close personal relationships, while *isolation* involves a lack of commitment. Intimacy requires that two people share their identities without a complete merging of selves. Problems may occur for people who choose marriage or parenthood as a way out of an identity dilemma. These people really have not resolved the identity issue—it is still on the back burner, waiting for an opportunity to show itself. People in the moratorium and achievement statuses experience deeper levels of intimacy than people in the other two statuses (Fitch & Adams, 1983; Orlofsky et al., 1973).

Although the basic relationship between identity and intimacy is correct, it may be somewhat different for males and females. Some women can deal successfully with intimacy issues prior to identity, but very few men can (Bartle-Haring & Strimple, 1996; Schiedel & Marcia, 1985). Men may not be able to achieve intimacy unless they have already made substantial progress on the identity front, but the relationship does not necessarily apply for all women.

For Your Consideration ?

Why would the years between 18 and 21 be critical for identity development?

Guideposts

What are the four identity statuses? What types of behavior would you expect to find in a teen in each of these statuses?

For Your Consideration ?

How can parents encourage their adolescent children to develop a coherent personal identity?

identity achievement

An identity status in which a person has developed a solid personal identity.

intimacy versus isolation

The sixth psychosocial stage, occurring during young adulthood, in which the positive outcome is a development of deep interpersonal relationships and the negative outcome is a flight from close relationships.

Do Males and Females Take Different Paths to Identity Formation?

Males and females may approach identity formation from different perspectives. Traditionally, males tended to focus on intrapersonal factors, such as vocational identity and personal identity, while women were more likely to tie their identities to interpersonal relationships (Erikson, 1968; Schiedel & Marcia, 1985). Relational identities are stronger, more important and are developed at a higher level than occupational identity for most women, which is not the case for men (Meeus & Dekovic, 1995; Waterman, 1993). Today, though, with women so actively involved in the labor force, many women's search includes an exploration of both family and career possibilities (Kroger, 1997). Women are trying to blend interpersonal and intrapersonal identities, while men still appear to emphasize the intrapersonal sphere (Lytle, Bakken, & Romig, 1997).

Women are accurately perceiving their new role as both worker and family caregiver. Men may not yet see their dual responsibility in these balanced terms and this may have far reaching consequences later in adulthood. As discussed in Chapter 7, women often find themselves with two full-time jobs, one at their place of employment and another at home, while men do not. There may be conflicts between what Hochschild (1989) describes as "faster-changing women and slower-changing men" (p. 11). Women may expect a more equal sharing of the homemaking and child-rearing chores, while men, who do not see their role or identity as changing that much, may not. The differing expectations may form a basis for dissatisfaction and interpersonal problems.

Concerns about Identity Status

Marcia's view of identity status is a useful way of looking at identity but has its critics. First, it lacks a process orientation (Valde, 1996). Identity status concepts have been more useful in noting individual differences than in tracing developmental patterns (Grotevant, 1998). The process by which one travels from status to status remains unexplained.

Second, it seems that once a person has reached identity achiever status, the search for identity ends. Yet, this is often not the case. The identity achiever status may be split between those who are inflexible and closed and those who continue their search even though they have made commitments (Valde, 1996). For example, someone who has considered political philosophies and made a commitment may be considered an achiever, but what if no further development takes place? This individual would be considered an achiever but closed to new exploration. Other achievers may be open to new experience. Those who remain open score higher in sensitivity, realism, spontaneity, and self-acceptance (Valde, 1996).

Finally, the concept of identity status appears more relevant to Western than Eastern societies. The individual is viewed as searching for his or her own individual identity, as distinct from others, achieving autonomy and emancipation from parents. Exploration is seen as relatively unrestricted. This may not be the case in some Eastern societies where a set of values is communicated, conformity to these values expected, and responsibility to one's family and community of origin is most important.

Guideposts

How does the identity search of males and females differ?

For Your Consideration

Arlie Hochschild argues that women are changing their ideas about their role faster than men and this could lead to difficulties. Do you agree with Hochschild's ideas about "faster-changing women and slower-changing men"?

The Child in the 21st Century

Identity, Minority Status, and the Bicultural Experience

Identity development is a complex task for all youth, but it is particularly complicated for adolescents belonging to ethnic and racial minority groups (Spencer & Markstrom-Adams, 1990). Often, these adolescents have to come to terms with rejection and hostility at the same time that they try to accept themselves (Burnette, 1995). They must also reject the stereotypes that are common in the outside world.

Ethnic identity takes on increased importance and meaning as teens negotiate adolescence. Adolescents become more aware of the relationship of their ethnic group to the majority group (Phinney, Catu, & Kurty, 1997). Achieving a satisfying ethnic identity is related to self-confidence, a sense of purpose in life, and self-esteem (Martinez & Dukes, 1997), although it is certainly not the only or even most important predictor of self-esteem (Bagley & Copeland, 1994; Phinney & Alipuria, 1990). Exploration of ethnic issues is significantly greater among minority group college students than among those in the majority group (Phinney et al., 1997).

One basic approach to understanding the development of ethnic identity uses Erikson's and Marcia's work (Phinney, 1989, 1993). Many minority youth begin by internalizing the views held by the majority group of their own group. This is similar to identity foreclosure in that people may without question take on the values to which they have been exposed. Erikson (1968) assumed that minority youth would accept the negative self-images projected onto them

by society and be prone to developing a negative identity. However, studies do not show this to be so, as positive self-attitudes are commonly found (Spencer & Markstrom-Adams, 1990). Other processes must be at work, perhaps in the community or at home, to counter any negative messages from outside sources.

Some minority youth have not been faced with issues of ethnicity yet and therefore give little thought to them. This might be considered diffusion, but little research has been conducted in this area. Phinney sees these two statuses as constituting a general first stage in identity formation.

A period of exploration or moratorium then ensues, which involves experimentation, inquiry, and an attempt to clarify personal implications of ethnicity (Phinney & Tarverim 1988). The search

process takes various paths, including reading relevant books, taking courses, having discussions, and becoming politically involved. This is hypothesized as the second stage of the process.

Last, there is identity achievement during which questions are resolved and commitments made. People feel better about who they are and feel confident. This entails an acceptance of themselves as members of a minority group.

Minority group youth often find themselves in two cultures; a dominant culture that sometimes does not give full credit to their group's contributions, and a culture shaped by their ethnicity or race. Living in two cultures can be difficult. Cultural values may be in conflict. One culture may value individual achievement, and another more group-oriented achievement. One culture may

Minority group youth develop an ethnic identity. It is important to be able to live in two cultures and accept a bicultural identity.

value school achievement and another see it as "selling out" and requiring a surrendering of group identity (Fordham, 1988).

When dealing with the majority culture and society, people from ethnic and racial minorities have four different choices. They can *separate* from the dominant group and emphasize their unique values and culture, having little or no interaction with the dominant culture. Another choice is *assimilation*, where the minority group members choose identification with the dominant society and cut all ties to their own group. *Integration* is a third option that involves identification and involvement in both the dominant culture and the minority culture, while *marginality* is a lack of involvement in either the minority or the majority culture. Minority group members who can be classified as integrated show better psychological adjustment and have higher self-esteem than those choosing the other options (Phinney, Chavira, & Williamson, 1992).

Minority group members who opt for full assimilation may find they are rejecting their own minority group culture. This may pose the problem of nonacceptance in both the majority and minority culture. Separation and embeddedness in one's

own culture poses problems as well. It assumes that all the ideals and beliefs of the majority group are of less value, and that there is nothing to be learned from its culture and experiences. The rejection of the dominant culture makes participation in society difficult. The bicultural alternative, in which people see themselves as existing both in the dominant culture as well as their own culture, is one answer. There is respect for both and an ability to behave appropriately in different culturally defined situations.

People can successfully exist in two cultures. It is possible to achieve a sense of belonging to two cultures without sacrificing a sense of cultural/ethnic identity (LaFramboise, Coleman, & Gerton, 1993). A choice need not be made between them or an assumption made that one is superior to the other. A person may use one language when interacting with people from the majority group, and another when speaking to someone in their own ethnic group.

When questionnaires measuring values and attitudes were administered to children from the Lakota tribe (Plas & Bellet, 1983), the younger children provided the expected cultural answers. However, the older children maintained their preference for Native American

values of community and style of relating to others, but adopted the majority value toward school achievement. Differences in world views and value conflicts are real, but people can develop solid ethnic identities and bicultural competence. In fact, bicultural Native American students are better adjusted in college, particularly in the academic and cultural domains, than their nonbicultural counterparts (LaFramboise et al., 1993).

If minority group adolescents are to succeed in the mainstream as well as develop a meaningful ethnic/racial identity, they must be able to exist in two worlds—that is, be biculturally competent. Although the task may not be an easy one, it is both possible and desirable to do so.

What do you think?

What are the consequences to choosing assimilation, separation, integration, or marginality as a guiding principle in determining the relationship between a person and society? What might influence a person to adopt any of these strategies?

You can explore the questions above using InfoTrac College Edition. Hint: enter search terms *Minority Youth*.

Achieving Emotional and Behavioral Autonomy

In Western cultures, adolescence is a time of achieving autonomy. **Emotional autonomy** involves shifting away from the emotional dependency on parents and forming new relationships. **Behavioral autonomy** involves being able to behave competently when on one's own.

Achieving Emotional Autonomy: Renegotiating Relationships with Parents

G. Stanley Hall was responsible for the first modern look at adolescence. His two detailed volumes, published in 1904, brought together much of what was known about adolescence (White, 1994). Hall believed adolescence was a period of great

Guideposts

What is meant by the concept of bicultural competence?

emotional autonomy
Shifting away from the emotional dependency on parents and forming new relationships.

behavioral autonomy
Being able to behave competently when on one's own.

G. Stanley Hall perceived adolescence as a time of "storm and stress" and is responsible for making adolescence a specialty. However, modern research does not show that adolescence is a long period of intense conflict.

Guideposts

What was G. Stanley Hall's conception of adolescence?

For Your Consideration ?

Is the media portrayal of adolescence accurate? What film or television program do you feel reflects adolescence in a realistic manner?

Teenagers generally report feeling close to their parents and having a good relationship with them.

change where new beliefs and behaviors were established and therefore a period of great vulnerability to stress and difficulties (Cairns, 1998). He saw adolescence as a time of great upheaval; as a period of "storm and stress". It is a time marked by intense conflict between the adolescent and the parents as the teen makes the break from dependence on family to a more independent existence. The individual exiting adolescence is a fundamentally different person from the person who entered it.

This view was accepted for quite some time. The changing relationship between parents and adolescents was seen as a process of progressive detachment and distancing of oneself from the family (Jani, 1997). At the same time, parental values and behaviors are challenged and often devalued. Peer relationships become increasingly important and replace parental attachments. These processes were considered necessary and led to the storm and stress of the adolescent years which was considered natural, inevitable and necessary. This remains a popular conception of adolescence, especially in Hollywood films, which often portray adolescents as confused, alienated, and buffeted between the old and useless standards and beliefs of the older generation and the more modern but dangerous examples of their peers. Relationships with parents are viewed as argumentative, and slavish devotion to peers is shown as the norm.

About 20 years ago, psychologists began taking a different perspective. The data simply did not fit Hall's conception. Most adolescents report having a positive relationship with their parents (Phares & Renk, 1998; Steinberg, 1989), and the most autonomous and well-adjusted adolescents were still firmly connected with their families. Nineteen-year-old adolescents report feeling just as close to their parents as fourth graders (Hunter & Youniss, 1982).

In addition, many adolescents do not experience tremendous conflict with their families. Although no one denies that some conflict occurs, the more modern view does not see intense and continuous conflict as inevitable (Larson & Ham, 1993). There is no general upheaval in personality or self-concept.

Today, the process of achieving emotional autonomy is viewed in terms of a transformation of family relationships (Grotevant, 1998). Relationships in adolescence shift, and power is renegotiated, but achieving emotional autonomy occurs within a context of remaining emotionally involved with parents. The adolescent continually seeks to redefine the relationship to be consistent with a new sense of self and with individual dreams and expectations for the future (Jory, Rainbolt, Karns, Freeborn, & Greer, 1996).

Developing emotional autonomy is a process that continues throughout adolescence and probably into early adulthood. When adolescents from the fifth through the ninth grade were questioned, four aspects of emotional autonomy were followed: (1) nondependence (a reduction in childish dependence but not absolute freedom from parental influence), (2) deidealization (not seeing parents as all powerful), (3) individuation (a sense of being an autonomous, responsible individual human being), and (4) seeing parents as people. The first three show impressive increases as adolescents move through the teenage years (see Figure 13.3) (Steinberg

Figure 13.3 **Age Differences in Four Aspects of Emotional Autonomy**

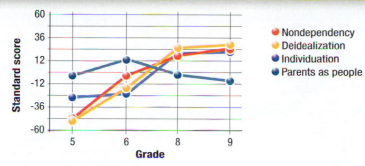

SOURCE: Steinberg & Silverberg (1986)

Guideposts
How does modern psychological thought differ from Hall's ideas?

& Silverberg, 1986). The only measure that does not show this impressive increase is "seeing parents as people," which may develop very late in adolescence or in early adulthood (Smoller & Younis, 1985).

Behavioral Autonomy: The Issue of Conformity and Independent Action

During early adolescence, teens become more behaviorally autonomous from parents but less from friends (Steinberg & Silverberg, 1986). Some argue that dependence on parents simply switches to a dependence on peers, but this is not really the case.

One way to investigate just how adolescents spend their time is to use the *experience sampling method (ESM)*. Teens are asked to carry beepers and at different times are prompted to report their behaviors and feelings in self-report booklet forms provided for them. As adolescents negotiate the period, time spent with family declines dramatically while time spent alone or with peers increases (Larson & Richards, 1991). By the time youngsters are seniors in high school, they are spending only 14% of their waking hours with family, compared with about 35% in the fifth grade (Larson, Richards, Moneta, Holmbeck, & Duckett, 1996) (see Figure 13.4 on page 522). This disengagement is not necessarily caused by difficult family relationships, but simply by the pull of forces outside the family as well as having access to cars and permission to stay out later.

Peers help adolescents with their striving for independence and provide them with an understanding partner. Since peers are presently negotiating the same pressures and stresses, teens feel that other teens understand what they are presently experiencing. Adolescents often turn to their friends for advice and comfort (Fuligni & Eccles, 1993), and peers help adolescents develop social skills and an identity (Coleman, 1981). The peer group also serves as a reference group through which teens can evaluate their own actions.

Adolescents' self-esteem and emotional well-being are linked to having positive friendships. Adolescents who describe their friendships more positively have higher self-esteem and fewer emotional disorders (Barrera, Chassin, & Rogosch, 1993). When adolescents are not popular, having just one good friend may be sufficient to buffer the teen from the isolation and low self-esteem that may result from the unpopularity (Bishop & Inbertditzen, 1995).

As adolescents become more emotionally autonomous and idealize their parents less, they depend somewhat less on their parents and more on their peers. This is accompanied by increased susceptibility to peer influences (Steinberg &

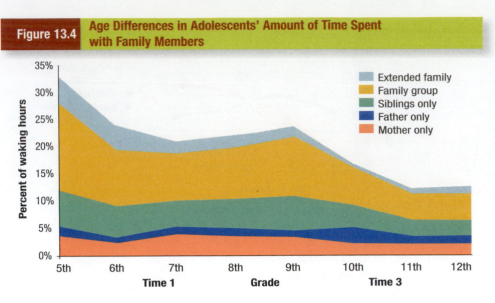

Figure 13.4 Age Differences in Adolescents' Amount of Time Spent with Family Members

SOURCE: Larson et al. (1996)

Silverberg, 1986). One problem in studying peer influence is determining exactly how it operates. Do friends influence a teen to change attitudes and behavior, or do teens simply choose friends who feel and act the same way they do? Peers with particular needs, personalities, and interests select others who are similar for friendships. People who drink, smoke, or show high levels of aggression seek each other out, as do people who show high or low levels of school achievement (Cairns et al., 1988; Hogue & Steinberg, 1995). Teenagers who internalize—that is. experience a great deal of depression and anxiety—choose friends who show similar levels of internalized distress (Hogue & Steinberg, 1995).

Friends also shape or reinforce others who show these attributes, and this is a type of socialization (Hogue & Steinberg, 1995). It is very difficult to tease apart the influence of selection and socialization. Research shows that both are important; for example, adolescents who are aggressive form relationships with other aggressive children, and then these adolescents influence each other through modeling and reinforcement. This is a pattern suggested for drug use, in which drug users both select other users as friends and then influence each other to continue their usage (Fletcher, Darling, Steinberg, & Dornbusch, 1995).

Peer influence is usually considered negative but it shouldn't be. Peers may influence each other for or against a particular behavior (Brown, Clasen, & Eicher, 1986). For example, peers may influence adolescents to use or not to use drugs and alcohol, to achieve or not to achieve in school (Mounts & Steinberg, 1995). In addition, peers and parents may exert influence in the same way, connecting parent and peer support (Meuus, 1993; Meuus & Dekovic, 1995).

Parents are often uneasy about the extent of peer group conformity. What will a teenager do if parents would like their teenage child to behave in one way and the peer group a different way? It depends on the situation. Adolescents perceive peers and parents as competent guides in different areas (Brittain, 1963). The peer group is viewed as more knowledgeable in surface and social areas, such as styles and feelings about school. Adolescents are more likely to conform to peers' opinions in these short term day-to-day social matters of style and dress, music, and leisure-time activities, especially in the junior high and early years of high school (Steinberg, 1996). When behavior reflects deeper values involving family, education, or financial affairs, adolescents report being closer to their parents, as long as the relationship is

good. With age, adolescents report turning to those they see as experts for advice (Sebald, 1989). It is a mistake, though, to view adolescents as completely buffeted between parents and peers without minds of their own. The decisions adolescents make often show a reasonable sense of independent judgement.

Susceptibility to peer pressure increases substantially as youngsters move through early adolescence, peaking at age 14 or so, and declining thereafter. But conformity for antisocial acts peaks a bit later during the early part of middle adolescence, in ninth grade or so, and declines thereafter (Berndt, 1979).

Arguments between parents and children are most frequent during early adolescence and the first year or so of middle adolescence, as the push for independence is particularly strong at this point. During middle adolescence, behavioral autonomy increases and this increase continues through late adolescence. These are general trends and some children are more oriented toward parents and others toward their peers.

Peer relationships are influenced by family relationships. Autonomous youngsters come from homes in which authoritative methods of child rearing are used. Peer-oriented children come from homes that are less nurturant and either very controlling or very permissive (Steinberg, 1996).

Peers can have an enormous influence on adolescent behavior, particularly in such areas as dress, general appearance, and adoption of special slang or jargon.

Guideposts

In what areas are peers and parents most influential?

Conflict between Parents and Adolescents

Although psychologists no longer view adolescence as a time of constant and intense conflict, any parent or teen will tell you it is not free of conflict either. Sometimes the battle is fought over the timing of being allowed to do something. Adolescents generally believe that they should be able to do things at a younger age than their parents do. They hold a different timetable for independence, which causes some conflict (Collins et al., 1997). It is not that parents refuse to accept their children's growing independence and competencies; they just see specific privileges and behaviors as appropriate at a later time. When sixth graders were asked to decide the age at which they expected to engage in certain behaviors, their estimations were often somewhat earlier than those of their parents (see Table 13.2). The researchers surveyed only the parents of boys but suggest that since the parents of girls are usually even more conservative, they would expect the differences to be somewhat greater. When these behaviors are ranked in terms of the ages at which both parents and peers think something should be allowed, the order is very similar (Feldman & Quatman, 1988).

Parents are sometimes reluctant to grant too much autonomy too early as they fear that too much freedom may require more self-direction than the youth can handle (Dornbusch, Ritter, Mont-Reynaud, & Chen, 1990). At the same time, if the desire for independence is continually thwarted, frustration and resentment may grow. Parents' and adolescents' views on the appropriateness of activities converge over time, and then this matter becomes less of an issue.

Table 13.2 When Should Children Be Allowed to Participate in Specific Activities?

Average age at which teenagers and parents believe activities should begin or when children should be allowed to:

	Generation	
	Child	Parent
Overall timetable	15.6	16.6
Composite scores		
Oppositional autonomy	15.0	15.6
Autonomy	15.7	16.6
Social	15.3	16.2
Leisure	14.7	16.4
Items		
1. Choose hairstyle, even if your parents don't like it.	14.8	14.1
2. Choose what books, magazines to read.	13.2	14.3
3. Go to boy-girl parties at night with friends.	14.8	13.9
4. Not have to tell parents where you are going.	17.2	18.9
5. Decide how much time to spend on homework.	13.0	15.0
6. Drink coffee.	16.0	17.5
7. Choose alone what clothes to buy.	13.7	14.7
8. Watch as much TV as you want.	14.3	14.7
9. Go out on dates.	15.4	16.1
10. Smoke cigarettes.	20.3	20.5
11. Take a regular part-time job.	16.2	16.6
12. Make own doctor and dentist appointments.	17.4	17.9
13. Go away with friends without any adults.	15.8	18.5
14. Be able to come home at night as late as you want.	17.7	19.4
15. Decide what clothes to wear, even if your parents disapprove.	15.8	16.0
16. Go to rock concerts with friends.	16.1	17.3
17. Stay home alone rather than go out with your family.	14.5	15.0
18. Drink beer.	18.9	19.3
19. Be able to watch any TV, movie, or video show you want.	15.3	17.4
20. Spend money (wages or allowance) however you want.	13.4	14.1
21. Stay home alone if you are sick.	13.4	14.2

SOURCE: Feldman & Quatman (1988)

Not all areas are equal candidates for conflict (Smetana & Asquith, 1994). Parents yield power more often and more easily in some areas than others. For example, both parents and children see personal issues, such as what programs to watch on television and what clothes to wear, as determined by the child to a great extent. There are also some moral issues that both see as legitimate concerns for parents, but as adolescents proceed through this period, more issues are deemed personal and their own business. Large discrepancies are found between adolescent and parental judgment of the limits of parental rights in areas of personal safety and friendship issues, and most battles involving autonomy are fought over these issues.

Guideposts

What types of conflict occur between parents and adolescents?

ACTION / REACTION

How Much? How Soon?

Lorraine is a 15-year-old high school sophomore who feels that her parents do not understand her needs and don't trust her. The other day she asked her parents if she could go with her friend into the city by train and "see the sights." She guaranteed she would be home at 11 o'clock at the latest. They refused, saying that without an adult supervising, they did not think two 15-year-old girls should be walking around, especially after dark.

Lorraine's mother still checks her homework, and Lorraine always has to tell her mother where she is and whom she is with. She resents the fact that her best friend in class, Sheryl, does not have to do this. "They trust her," Lorraine tells her parents. "You don't trust me."

Lorraine goes out with her boyfriend on weekends but has a strict 11 o'clock curfew. Her parents do allow her to stay out later if she calls or if there is a special occasion, but Lorraine resents having to call her parents and check in.

For their part, Lorraine's parents do not consider their rules arbitrary or unreasonable. They understand her desire to be independent, but they believe she is not yet ready for more freedom. There is quite a bit of tension in the home, which makes things rather unpleasant.

1. *If you were Lorraine's parents, would you change any of your rules?*
2. *What can be done to reduce the tension in the home?*

ACTION / REACTION

Conflict is more frequent in divorced and stepfamilies than in intact families (Demo, 1997). However, the differences within groups of divorced, intact, or stepfamilies are greater than the differences among them, meaning that family processes are more important than family structure (Demo, 1997). Some families, no matter what their composition, experience less conflict and better conflict resolution than others.

Conflict, itself, does not weaken the parent-child relationship, but the inability to settle conflict in a satisfactory manner may. Parents and adolescents might get along better if they tried to understand issues from each other's viewpoint and stopped making each issue a battle of wills. If more time was spent defining the issue rather than testing each other's will, parents and adolescents might arrive at a solution that both can live with more often. An argument over a messy room, for example, can be resolved by a cleaning schedule that both can live with (Steinberg & Levine, 1990).

The ability to solve conflict depends on the family climate. A family atmosphere of warmth and supportiveness promotes successful negotiation of disagreements and keeps conflict to low or moderate levels. When the conditions are hostile or coercive, no one truly listens and conflict escalates sometimes to unhealthy levels. Unfortunately, the frequency of conflict between teens and parents increases during early adolescence and remains relatively high in middle adolescence in family environments that are hostile and coercive, while parent-adolescent relationships tend to improve gradually in warm supportive environments (Rueter & Conger, 1995). Families that do not resolve disputes successfully find that these become long-running, festering problems that weaken the parent adolescent relationship. In fact, adolescent reports of severe and unresolved disagreements are associated with many adjustment and conduct problems, as well as alcohol and drug abuse (Rueter & Conger, 1995).

Communication with Parents and Peers

Adolescents and parents often misperceive the opinions of each other. Adolescents were asked to note their opinions on major questions and then to write down how they thought their parents would answer these questions. Then, parents were asked to note their opinions and to answer the questions the way their adolescent children would. The actual differences were mostly in intensity, a matter of degree, with one agreeing or disagreeing more strongly with some statement. Their perceptions of the other generation, however, were often mistaken.

Parents see their adolescent's views as closer to their own, and adolescents were likely to think that their views were much different from their parents (Lerner, Karson, Meisels & Knapp, 1975). Parents underestimate the differences, and teens overestimate them. Perhaps parents want to see themselves as closer to their children, while adolescents are motivated to separate themselves more from their parents. This could also reflect poor communication between the generations.

Communication with peers differs greatly from communication with parents during adolescence. Parents are more directive, sharing their wisdom, whereas communication with peers often shows greater mutuality and sharing of similar experiences (Hunter, 1984). This communication difference may spring from the nature of the parent-child relationship, which, by its very nature, is dominated by parents, while peer relationships tend to show more give-and-take (Fuligni & Eccles, 1993). Parents may not like to listen to their adolescents who are in the process of formulating their own values and opinions, especially if their children are taking positions that are different from theirs. Parents may counter these unwanted views with a long lecture, which is usually an ineffective method of

Parents tend to underestimate the differences in opinions on various issues between themselves and their adolescent children, and adolescents tend to overestimate the differences in opinions between themselves and their parents.

Guideposts

In what ways do parents and teens misunderstand each other?

It is important for parents and teenagers to talk with each other. Unfortunately, adults are frequently more interested in explaining their point of view to teens than in listening to them.

communication. Parents tend to concentrate more on explaining their own viewpoints than on trying to understand their child's views (Hunter, 1985).

Much parental communication is delivered in the form of criticism. This is unfortunate, because positive and supportive communication enables children to explore their identity in greater depth. Good communication requires family members to listen to each other, express views with clarity and in a self-assertive manner, yet be flexible and open, showing respect and sensitivity (Rathunde, 1997). Mothers tend to be more open with adolescents and talk to adolescents more on a daily basis than fathers, and teens report more satisfaction with their relationship with their mother (Rathunde, 1997). Generally, fathers are more controlling. Parents who support their adolescents by creating an atmosphere that fosters respect for the opinions of others, mutuality, and tolerance make it possible for their children to explore identity alternatives (Grotevant & Cooper, 1986).

Adolescents perceive the communicational differences between parents and peers more clearly than parents do. They see significantly less openness and more problems in intergenerational communication (Barnes & Olson, 1985). However, communication problems exist on both sides.

Different Views: Same Family

Parents and adolescents often do not see the family as operating in the same manner. Parents tend to rate themselves more positively in their parenting skills than do adolescents (Paulson, 1994). Parents perceive the family as more loving, closer, as showing more understanding, and parents rate family communication more open and less problematic than their adolescents do (Noller & Callan, 1986; Noller, Seth-Smith, Bouma, & Schweitzer, 1992). Perhaps adolescents are distancing themselves from their families and seeing them in this way makes it easier to become autonomous and later leave the home. Perhaps parents are motivated to see the family they created as better than it really is. Perhaps adolescents have unrealistic ideas about how families should function (Noller & Callan, 1986). Some researchers find that adolescents want the family to be high in cohesion and very adaptable to their wishes and desires—a tall order and not necessarily always a desirable one (Noller et al., 1992).

Successful Parenting in Adolescence

Successful parenting in adolescence requires some change in parenting practices, and most parents understand that a renegotiation of power is necessary. This change toward greater mutuality and sharing power is not an easy one for parents. Parents need to relax some of the earlier restrictions and give their adolescents more opportunities for independence and decision making. Not all parents can do this. Some parents simply believe that high levels of restrictiveness are best, while others believe their children are not yet ready for any increase in autonomy perhaps because of behavioral problems. Yet, if this is not done, adolescents may become more alienated from the family and turn away from parents. Adolescents who see no change in parental restrictiveness and no increase in self-determination report higher levels of peer advice seeking and a greater orientation toward peers compared with those who perceive a decline in parental restrictiveness and more decision-making opportunities. When excessive parental control occurs along with coldness and punitiveness, adolescents rebel against parents standards in an attempt to become independent (Hill & Holmbeck, 1986). Adolescents whose parents refuse to grant reasonable curfews stay out the latest.

When parents communicate with their adolescent children, they tend to explain their own views rather than try to understand their teens' opinions and attitudes.

Guideposts

How does communication with parents differ from communication with peers?

For Your Consideration

Why are adolescents and their parents motivated to see the family as operating differently?

On the other hand, some parents take a hands-off attitude. Parental permissiveness, though, is related to susceptibility to antisocial peer influence (Steinberg, 1987). The idea that parents of young adolescents should back off and let children "grow up" is simply wrong; supervision and monitoring are required (Carnegie Council, 1995; Pettit, Bates, Dodge, & Meece, 1999). Adolescents who are not monitored or supervised get into more trouble, and a rapid reduction in parental monitoring may be seen as a loss of parental interest.

These two views are not really in conflict. If control is viewed in terms of monitoring and supervision; making certain homework is done, and knowing where the adolescent is and what he or she is doing, such control is related to competence and is positive. However, trying to control every facet of adolescent life, being confrontational, and not allowing adolescents any freedom to make decisions are not related to positive outcomes (Kurdek & Fine, 1994).

Cultural Differences

These analyses and prescriptions seem reasonable, but cultural differences and expectations must be taken into account. Adolescents raised in diverse cultural backgrounds may have different expectations about autonomy and their parents may have distinct ideas about how to raise adolescents. For example, compared with Anglo mothers, Latino mothers from the southwestern United States score higher on scales measuring control, inconsistent discipline, and cohesion, but these family patterns do not translate into differences in the mental health of early adolescents (Knight, Virdin, & Roosa, 1994). Perhaps family cohesion is more important, and some of these behaviors are traditionally expected. Highly acculturated Latino mothers are similar to Anglo mothers.

In more traditional, less individualistic societies, parent-adolescent relationships may revolve around questions of obligation, responsibility, and respect for elders (Fuligni, Tseng, & Lamm, 1999). This may cause a clash in a society in which the cultural group holds one ideal and the society in which they live holds another, such as individual autonomy. It is argued that this is one problem among some Southeast Asian refugees living in poverty. High rates of delinquency, gang behavior, and juvenile arrests may occur because parents do not understand their part in this new society. In certain Southeast Asian cultures, boys are regarded as adults by age 12 and can actually marry and become fathers. Girls marry around that time and, until marriage, parents are very restrictive. This traditional culture does not prepare adults to set limits for adolescents or allow many options for daughters. The parent-child relationship must be considered within a family's cultural context.

In American society, relationships between parents and their children are relatively informal and teens are expected to create their own individual lives outside the family. In some cultural groups, however, this is not as much the case. Adolescents are expected to give support, respect, and show a formality in their relationships within the family, especially toward their fathers. Their academic performance and behavior is seen as bringing pride or shame to the entire family and does not reflect just on the individual.

When the values and relationships among Mexican, Vietnamese, Filipino, and Chinese teens, and adolescents of European descent were measured among California college students, interesting differences were found. Adolescents from all cultural groups believed families should make sacrifices to guarantee a good education for their children. Mexican, Chinese, and Vietnamese adolescents endorsed the value of mutual support among siblings and turning to parents and other relatives for help in making important decisions more often. Vietnamese and Chinese adolescents most strongly endorsed the idea of older siblings helping to support the other family members economically. Most teens from these cultures described a pattern of greater responsibility and obligation to their families and deference to their parents. Describing parents and adolescents as renegotiating patterns of authority toward peerlike mutuality is more appropriate for European American families than for more recent immigrants from Asia or Mexico.

Conflict over when one is allowed to do something is common in American families. However, when Asian American teens were compared with American teens from European backgrounds, the adolescents from Asian backgrounds believed they should be allowed to engage in particular behavior at a later age than their Anglo-American peers (Feldman & Quatman, 1988).

The different experiences of adolescents from minority groups, often involving poverty, must also be considered. The perception of many inner-city African American teens is of a shorter life expectancy, less permanence, and an accelerated life course, in which they are exposed to more adultlike situations at an earlier age. The need to help out and care for others may accelerate the entrance into adulthood (Burton, 1995). It is obvious that we must look at the cultural background of the teen when discussing transformation of relationships, which is in keeping with an ecological perspective.

The Secondary School Today

The daily life of most adolescents revolves around the school. It is in the school where most adolescents meet their friends and must deal with the more complex interpersonal relationships found in adolescence. It is in the school where the more advanced academic skills are developed and where information about jobs, college, and future careers is most available to students. The secondary school is a different place today from what it was even 20 years ago.

The Junior High/Middle School Experience

Junior high schools and middle schools were originally designed to bridge the gap between the relatively easy curriculum of the elementary school and the more demanding work of high school (Smith, 1987). They were also advocated on a developmental basis. Early adolescence is a period of rapid physical, cognitive, and social changes. It is a transitional period in which children have different needs that may be best met in a school environment fundamentally different from the elementary school (Walker, Kozma, & Green, 1989). These are critical years, and the potential for increased risk taking in many areas—delinquency, sex, and drugs—calls for a special environment dedicated to the needs of students of this age (Manning & Allen, 1987).

Junior high schools and middle schools differ from elementary schools in a number of ways. Students travel from class to class. Each subject is taught by a different teacher, and each teacher may have different requirements.

Most children adapt well to the change from elementary to a middle/junior high environment. A minority of

Trends in Development

Mathematics Achievement, Eighth Grade
The National Education Goals Panel set its performance standard at the two highest levels of achievement, proficient and advanced, on the National Assessment of Educational Progress (the Nation's Educational Report Card). Have states and the District of Columbia increased the percentages of public school eighth graders who meet the panel's goals for math? Some states have not yet reported.

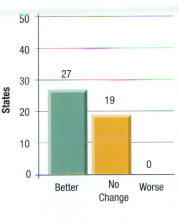

Source: National Education Goals Panel (1998)

Junior high school was developed as a way of easing the transition between elementary school and high school. The most common student complaint is that their teachers do not know who they are.

students will experience problems, and girls are somewhat more likely to do so than boys, perhaps because of the multiple stresses the girls experience at this time. For many girls, the transition to junior high school coincides with many other developmental changes, especially physical ones, whereas this is not the case for the boys (Simmons, Blyth, Van Cleave, & Bush, 1979). Still, most students adjust well and enjoy going to the new school (Nottelman, 1987).

The transition to junior high/middle school does bring some complaints, even from those students who adjust well. Many adolescents feel a sense of anonymity in junior high school that impacts negatively on their self-concept (Thornburg & Glider, 1984). They feel less attached to the school. Students do not believe their teachers are as warm and caring as elementary school teachers. They see their teachers as less supportive and as offering students less encouragement.

Perhaps the most troublesome finding, though, is a reduction in students' academic motivation and an increase in behavioral problems. A decline in school grades is not uncommon (Anderson & Midgley, 1997). Some point to the new peer group and social changes to explain the decline in academic competence and grades (Seidman, Allen, Aber, Mitchell, & Feinman, 1994). Others argue that junior high school teachers grade lower and are stricter in their grading systems (Eccles, Wigfield, Harold, & Blumenfield, 1993). Many educators, though, believe that the structure of the school leads to these problems. Middle schools are characterized by more emphasis on teacher control and discipline and fewer opportunities for student decision making. Teacher-student relationships are less positive and less personal, with very little individual attention and more public evaluation. The lack of personal attention is built into the system if a junior high school teacher teaches five classes of 30 students each, instead of one class of 30 students all day. However, the reduction in decision making is developmentally inappropriate at a time when there is a desire for greater autonomy.

Two detailed reports by the Carnegie Corporation (1995, 1989) argued that middle schools are not meeting young people's needs. A number of changes are suggested, including dividing large middle-grade schools into smaller communities for learning, teaching a core academic program, the elimination of tracking by achievement level, fostering health and fitness, connecting the school with the community through service opportunities, and establishing partnerships with community organizations. They also advocate the use of cooperative learning strategies, social and life skills training and a curriculum that strengthens problem-solving abilities and higher-order thinking. In addition, because students may be overwhelmed by having to satisfy many teachers, they must be taught organizational skills.

Guideposts

How do adolescents adapt to the junior high school experience?

For Your Consideration ?

What can be done to improve the junior high school experience?

The High School

The overwhelming majority of adolescents today attend high school, a change from earlier in the century when the high school graduate was a rarity. However, achievement is a great concern. The congressionally mandated National Assessment of Educational Progress (NAEP) tests fourth, eighth, and twelfth graders (high school seniors) in reading, math, science, and writing. Overall, the results show some modest improvements, especially since the early 1980s, or in some cases no improvement, which is disappointing (see Figures 13.5–13.8).

There is some good news, however. Enrollments in advanced science and math courses have increased (West, 1994). The achievement gap between white and African American students in science math and reading has declined. The gender gap is also narrower than it was 20 years ago (Jacobson, 1997). Graduation rates are up, and the percentage of high school students taking core academic subjects

Junior high school and high school students read at lower levels today than they did 20 years ago.

Figure 13.5 Long-Term Trends in Student Reading Performance

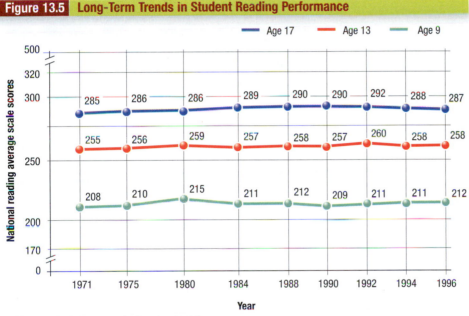

SOURCE: U.S. Department of Education (1998)

Figure 13.6 NAEP Mathematics Average Scale Scores for the Nation

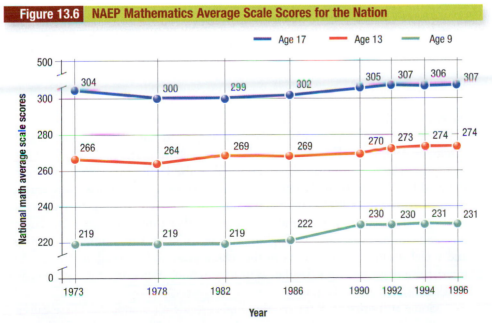

SOURCE: U.S. Department of Education (1998)

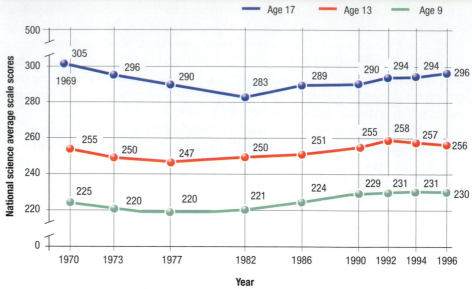

Figure 13.7 NAEP Science Average Scale Scores for the Nation

SOURCE: U.S. Department of Education (1998)

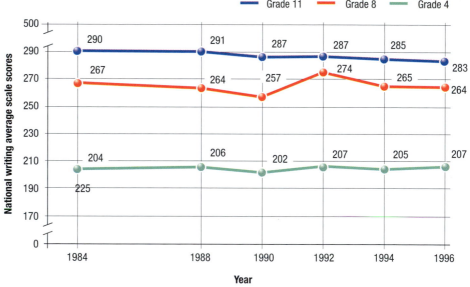

Figure 13.8 NAEP Writing Average Scale Scores for the Nation

SOURCE: U.S. Department of Education (1998)

Guideposts

What are the trends in high school achievement?

increased significantly in the past decade (Toch, Bennefield, & Bernstein, 1996). Achievement on the SAT and ACT tests have improved somewhat (Marklein, 1997; Sandham, 1997), and high school work has become more rigorous.

The school reform movement flowered in the 1970s and 1980s, much of it initiated by The National Commission on Excellence in Education's study entitled *A Nation At Risk* (1981). The commission documented many problems in the educational system and recommended, among other things, stricter requirements for graduation, especially in English, mathematics, science, foreign language, and social studies; a lengthening of the school year; and curriculum reform. The trend toward greater rigor in the secondary school, especially high school, will continue into the near future.

Some authorities call for creating higher academic standards. These calls are partially based on studies showing that American students in high school do not do as well as high school students in other countries, such as China and Japan. These students spend more time in school, more time studying at home, and are exposed to a more rigorous curriculum (Fuligni & Stevenson, 1995; Stevenson et al., 1993). After agreeing that such standards are necessary, it is difficult to go on from there (Applebome, 1996). There is no clear idea of what students should know (Kelly, 1996). Although many states have moved toward developing standards, they are often general and imprecise. Very few states have developed standards that are clear enough to be used as part of a formal curriculum. National standards are difficult because the United States has a long history of local control.

There has also been a call for high schools to focus on health, moral, and family issues. For example, there is a clamor for more drug- and sex-education programs and for courses covering family living that include basic information on child development and relationships.

Other changes are also demanded. A report on the restructuring of high schools called *Breaking Ranks* advocated some far-reaching structural changes. Many high school students feel that few people really know them, and anonymity is a major problem, as it is in junior high (Maeroff, 1996). Limiting high schools to 600 students would help solve this problem. In addition, each student should have a personal adult advocate who meets regularly with the teenager and can serve as a liaison between the student and others in the school environment. More practical learning is also emphasized, and a warrantee guaranteeing that students can meet performance standards in entry-level jobs issued. It would permit employers to return students lacking basic skills to high schools for additional training (Henry, 1996). Each student would be given an individualized plan to guide his or her education. A full-time teacher should be asked to teach no more than 90 students per day to foster individualized attention. Schools should be required to develop a long-term plan for using computers and other technologies. The report also advocates teaching a core set of values stressing that possession of weapons, drugs, and violence will not be tolerated, as well as providing students with some role in decision making within the school. The practicality of these structural changes is questionable in the present environment (Henry, 1996).

School reform is not easy, and schools differ in their ability to implement reforms. Change is often a messy and inexact process (Olson, 1998).

High Schools: A Different View

Almost all suggestions for change center on how to alter the structure of the school to make it more responsive to students. However, a startling analysis of high school education points to a teen culture that does not value academic achievement as the key problem. After group discussions with many students and parents, Steinberg, Brown, and Dornbusch (1996) argue that all the improvement in curriculum and standards will not work unless a change takes place in students' attitudes. Students must come to school interested in and committed to learning. They found that roughly 40% of the students admitted they were just going through the motions in school.

Disengagement was pervasive. Some students surveyed reported deliberately hiding their capabilities due to concerns about what friends might think. Few students believe their friends think it is important to get good grades. Most said that they could bring home grades of C or worse without their parents getting upset, and many students said they do not do the homework they are assigned. American students are much busier watching television, socializing, and working part-time than students in other countries, with academics not being given the same attention.

Some authorities call for reforms in school, while others emphasize the need to change students' attitudes and commitment to learning.

For Your Consideration ?

If you agree with Steinberg's ideas about students and parents being disengaged from high school, what can be done about it?

Guideposts

Why is Steinberg's approach to achievement concerns so controversial?

Parents are also disengaged from the educational process and do not attend school functions, such as open school week and teacher conferences; nor do a quarter of all parents have an idea of how their children are doing. This is an important point because parenting style and involvement are related to academic achievement in secondary school, and parents become less involved in secondary school (Paulson, 1994). Parental involvement does not mean tutoring students with advanced chemistry but rather giving encouragement, holding high expectations, showing interest in school work, monitoring progress, and being involved in school functions. Adolescents who report parental demandingness, responsiveness and involvement show high achievement (see Table 13.3) (Dornbusch, Ritter, Leiderman, Roberts, & Fraleigh, 1987). Adolescents who perceive parents as having higher achievement values, being more interested in work, and involved in school functions have higher grades. Of course, other factors including peer relationships, ability, and motivation are important as well (Paulson, 1994).

Steinberg argues for more parenting education to draw parents into the children's schools, adopting a system of national academic standards and examinations, cutting back student work hours, and making it harder for students to go through the motions. This analysis is sure to be cause controversy (Viadero, 1996). Some do not believe that adolescents are any more disengaged than years ago and that their conclusions are overgeneralized. Others argue that curriculum and school reforms are meaningful and more practical than trying to change home or peer group reactions.

Gender and Achievement in High School

In elementary school, girls do at least as well as boys, and perhaps better. Elementary school teachers value female competencies, and females may find that their teachers greatly value and praise their noncompetitive, highly social, more obedient behavior. Boys have a more difficult time and receive more punishment. In middle school, girls continue to outperform boys, but in the high school boys improve considerably, and the gap between males and females closes rapidly (Henry, 1997; U.S. Department of Education, 1997).

Table 13.3 — Sample Items from the Demandingness, Responsiveness, and Parental Involvement Scales

Demandingness Items

I would describe my mother as a strict parent.

My mother usually wants to know where I am going.

My mother gives me chores to do around the house routinely.

My mother has few rules for me to follow.

It is okay with my mother if I do not follow certain rules.

Responsiveness Items

My mother expects me to tell her when I think a rule is unfair.

My mother encourages me to talk with her about things.

My mother expects me to do what she says without having to tell me why.

My mother seldom praises me for doing well.

My mother usually tells me the reasons for rules.

Values toward Achievement Items

My mother tries to get me to do my best on everything I do.

My mother has high aspirations for my future.

My mother thinks that getting ahead in life is very important.

Interest in Schoolwork Items

My mother makes sure that I have done my homework.

My mother usually knows the grades I get.

My mother seldom looks at my tests and papers from school.

Involvement in School Functions Items

My mother usually goes to parent-teacher conferences.

My mother usually goes to activities in which I am involved in school.

My mother sometimes does volunteer work at my school.

NOTE: For paternal parenting, *mother* was changed to *father* in each item. For parental reports, items were reworded: "My mother usually knows the grades I get" was written "I usually know the grades my adolescent gets." In calculating scores, some items were reverse scored.

SOURCE: Paulson (1994)

The fact that males catch up and females lag in high school does not tell us anything about the reasons it happens. Theories abound, but few real facts have been offered. Women have an achievement orientation equal to that of men. They are also as persistent as men.

The areas of greatest concern are science and math. Two recent studies found that many teachers of math and science ignore girls in favor of boys. Those girls who do well do not continue. Teachers consistently underestimate their female students' abilities in math (Kimball, 1989). Female students have less confidence in their math abilities, and with loss of confidence comes loss of performance (Junge & Dretzke, 1995). Differential teacher attitudes and behaviors may discourage female students from taking advanced science and math courses. Simple training can improve teacher behaviors in this area.

In some cases, school personnel including teachers, administrators, and guidance counselors discourage girls from taking particular courses. A bright adolescent female may be advised not to take an advanced math course because what is she

Guideposts

What happens to the achievement of males and females in high school?

going to do with it anyway. This type of blatant sexism has been held up to public scrutiny and criticized as it should be. But such statements are probably less common than the subtle communication of expectations. In many schools and homes today, females are not actively restricted from these areas. They are simply not encouraged to take such courses (Sadker & Sadker, 1994). Females do not have to be actively dissuaded from achieving. Lack of encouragement produces similar results.

Female students do not take as many science and math courses in high school (Terwilliger & Titus, 1995). This reduced interest in science and math may begin when students are in the middle school (Sadker & Sadker, 1994). By the time advanced courses in high school are chosen, a considerable gender difference is found. Girls take advanced biology, and boys choose physics and advanced chemistry. As girls proceed through high school, they see science and math as less and less relevant to their futures. Once girls avoid high school math, they close out some career options or at least make them more difficult (Murray, 1995b). Things are changing somewhat. The gender gap in math and science is much narrower than what it was in 1960. This is gratifying, but there is obviously still work to be done.

Minorities in High School

Over the past 20 years, measures of academic achievement in reading, writing, and mathematics for both African American and Latino youth have improved but still remain below their white peers (Toch et al., 1996). The overall achievement of African Americans and Latinos is still a great concern, and especially those who come from low-income groups are at increased risks for school failure (Reyes, Gillock, & Kobus, 1994). College attendance is also lower for minority group youth (DeBlassie & DeBlassie, 1996).

Grouping these youths from different cultural groups together under the heading of minority youth is poor practice, though. These young people come from different cultural, environmental, and social backgrounds and may have different difficulties. For example, some Latinos, as well as some youth belonging to other minorities, have poor English skills and require specific help in this area. In addition, many Latinos come from a background that emphasizes cooperation more than individual achievement, which does not mesh with the more individualized achievement orientation of American schools. For Native American children, there is also less of an emphasis on individual achievement and much more on group-oriented achievement. This may also lead to difficulties in school (LaFromboise & Low, 1989). The family values of interdependence with others and sharing may not be reflected in school. In addition, there may be a reluctance to talk in school, and communication patterns may be different.

African American youth face a combination of social and environmental problems. A disproportionate number of African American children live in poverty, often in substandard housing and in crime-ridden areas. Many are born into single-parent families (Edelman, 1985). Children born into single-parent families are especially vulnerable to

Some Latinos experience difficulties in language and have a culture that emphasizes cooperation more than individualized achievement.

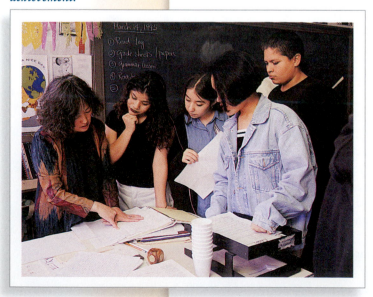

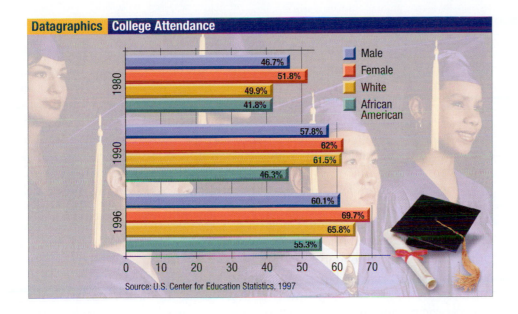

Datagraphics | **College Attendance**

1980
- Male: 46.7%
- Female: 51.8%
- White: 49.9%
- African American: 41.8%

1990
- Male: 57.8%
- Female: 62%
- White: 61.5%
- African American: 46.3%

1996
- Male: 60.1%
- Female: 69.7%
- White: 65.8%
- African American: 55.3%

Source: U.S. Center for Education Statistics, 1997

school failure, since they are more likely to live in poverty, their health is poorer, and their mothers are less likely to promote optimal development and are under more stress (Comer, 1985). Programs that aim at overcoming these problems can help, especially if they emphasize parental involvement (Comer, 1985). Many schools in primarily African American neighborhoods are starved for funds and are lacking in a safe and orderly environment.

Asian Americans have always been thought to do well, and indeed they have achieved. However, the stereotype of the bright, conscientious, quiet Chinese or Japanese student is very limiting, and teachers may have unreasonable expectations based only on ethnic identity. These students frequently have limited skills in English and may also have difficulties negotiating a culture whose values differ greatly from those at home (Nogata, 1989).

One common thread that unites many minority youth is poverty. Often, students from poverty backgrounds have a poor history with the schools and have been labeled unintelligent and channeled into less challenging programs. Their attitudes toward school and motivation may be poor, and they often see little relationship between what they learn in school and their real world. They may have no safe and quiet place to study, and the level of family support may be low. They experience higher suspension and dropout rates (Reed, 1988). Another factor is the largely impersonal high school environment and an estrangement from adults in the school (Reyes et al., 1994). Poor academic achievement is more often a consequence of cultural, social, and environmental factors than of lack of ability (Gibbs & Huang, 1989).

That is not to say that individual factors are unimportant. Ability and motivation are certainly factors that predict achievement for at-risk, low-income minority group students (Anderson & Keith, 1997). Motivation, as measured by effort in school and the belief in one's ability to succeed, is affected by many variables within the home, community, and school.

There is no single answer to the problem of underachievement among adolescents. We must rid ourselves of the idea that all students learn or can be taught in the same way. Students coming from different cultural and experiential backgrounds may respond to different teaching styles and methods. Teachers who will teach minority youth can become more knowledgeable about their students' cultural and family backgrounds and can observe other teachers who are very effective with these teens (Kaplan, 1990).

Guideposts

What trends are found in the achievement of students from minority groups in high school?

Dropping Out of School

Although the majority of students finish high school, a large minority do not. High school dropouts are more likely to live at or near the poverty level, experience unemployment, and depend on government for support (Steinberg, 1989). Most have average intelligence. Students from minority groups, who often live in poverty, have a higher dropout rate than middle-class youths (McNeal, 1997). In the past, African Americans dropped out of school at a much higher rate than whites, but today the percentage is narrowing substantially (Henry, 1994). Latinos, though, still lag behind in high school completion (DeBlassie & DeBlassie, 1996). Many Latinos drop out before or in the early years of high school ("Hispanic Dropouts," 1993).

The most common signs of possible early school withdrawal are consistent failure, grade-level placement below average, poor attendance, active antagonism to teachers, disinterest in school, low reading ability, unhappy family situations, and conduct problems in school (Brooks-Gunn, Guo, & Furstenberg, 1993; Horowitz, 1992). School holds little promise for dropouts, who as a group are poor readers. Many of these students have been left back a grade. They often come from large families or have backgrounds of poverty, discord, and divorce (Zmiles & Lee, 1991). Dropouts often have friends who have also dropped out. Dropouts often cite disliking school, poor grades, and disciplinary problems as most important reasons for leaving school (Janosz, LeBlanc, Boulerice, & Tremblay, 1997).

Most factors that differentiate graduates from dropouts are present before these teens drop out. Low self-esteem, higher rates of delinquency, and higher rates of drug abuse are found before the students stop attending school, so these factors are not consequences of dropping out. Dropouts are less engaged in school generally and are involved in fewer extracurricular activities (Mahoney & Cairns, 1997). In fact, the school dropout rate is much lower for at-risk students who participate in such activities as clubs, school newspaper, theater or athletics. Early school failure sets the stage for negative attitudes toward school and feelings of rejection and alienation (Kaplan, Beck, & Kaplan, 1997). These students associate with others who also share these feelings and attitudes. Dropping out is not an event as much as it is the result of a long process of failure, disengagement, poor adjustment, low aspirations, low intellectual stimulation, and poverty.

Many school districts recognize the seriousness of the problem and that bold new approaches are required. Some school districts have instituted promising programs in which potential dropouts attend alternative schools or work-study programs and receive more attention and tutoring in basic academic skills.

Career Choice

"If only I knew what I wanted to be, I'd be able to do better in school." This is one of the more common complaints of adolescents. Vocational identity was acknowledged by Erikson (1968) as being a key to identity formation. In fact, college students who chose occupations that mirror their measured abilities and interests show more successful resolutions of Erikson's first six stages, including identity formation in adolescence (Munley, 1975, 1977).

The process of vocational development starts in childhood as children observe the occupations around them and imagine themselves working in them (Super, 1953, 1980). But it is in high school that students begin to realize that they are facing a career decision. The two most important factors in career choice are knowledge of the job market and knowledge of oneself. Knowing the job market involves understanding the vocational alternatives and the requirements for entry-level positions. Knowing oneself includes understanding what one wants in a job or career, having a realistic appraisal of one's abilities and personal resources, and understanding one's personal characteristics. For example, personality dimensions and problem-solving orientation can affect career choice (Holland, 1973; Prediger, Swaney, & Mau, 1993). People who are task oriented or who prefer to work independently tend to enter scientific vocations. There is some evidence that when people enter fields congruent with these characteristics they are more satisfied (Osipow, 1990).

But vocational choice is a conscious choice only when people can consider what they want to do and then follow some program of study or training to achieve it (Drummond & Ryan, 1995). For some women and members of many ethnic and racial minority groups, this is not always the case.

Women and Careers

Most adolescent girls realize their future involves employment (Dennehy & Mortimer, 1993; McCracken & Weitzman, 1997). By 2005, women will comprise from between 46% and 48% of the labor force in the United States (U.S. Department of Labor, 1996). Studies investigating the vocational choices of women contradict each other. Some studies show little difference in vocational choice between male and female students in high school (Kramer, 1986); others show lower aspirations for females (Delisle, 1992).

Women experience both internal and external barriers in making vocational decisions to enter fields in math and the physical sciences. The external barriers include sexism, discrimination, and lack of role models. The internal barriers include fear of being considered too bright and falling back onto very traditional societal roles (Delisle, 1992).

The picture, though is not a simple one. Although women are still overrepresented in certain fields, such as clerical and service positions and some professional fields, such as elementary school teachers and librarians, more women are entering nontraditional fields. A nontraditional field is one in which the overwhelming majority, more than two-thirds, are workers of the opposite gender (Hayes, 1986). Women are making substantial, though uneven, progress, as shown in Figure 13.9. The percentage of women who are doctors, lawyers, computer scientists, and architects has increased significantly.

Figure 13.9 Percentage of Women in Non-traditional Professions

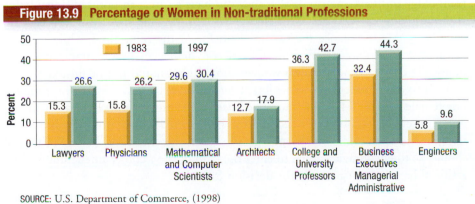

SOURCE: U.S. Department of Commerce, (1998)

The percentage of female doctors, lawyers, computer scientists, and architects has increased significantly in the past few decades.

For Your Consideration ❓

How is the process of vocational exploration different for men and women?

Guideposts

What prevents many bright women from viewing the sciences and technology as career options?

Many women face problems in career planning that males do not. Men are socialized to accept the role of breadwinner, but women have developed a dual role as mother and worker, which often limits their career choices. Women are sometimes reluctant to enter careers in the sciences because they see problems combining family life and a career in this area. Although women are now entering nontraditional careers such as law and medicine, the woman entering chemistry, physics, and engineering is still a rarity.

Why? Women are sometimes discouraged from pursuing a particular career because of their belief in the inappropriateness of achieving in that area held by some parents, teachers, and even peers. Television programs and movies rarely show women in scientific fields, and when they do, the women seem to be incapable of having a satisfying family life along with a career. Parents sometimes propagate sexist attitudes by discouraging daughters from achieving in certain fields.

In the past, women were divided into those who were career oriented and those who were oriented toward home and family—in other words, those who were traditionally minded and those who weren't. These divisions are no longer as useful (O'Brien & Fassinger, 1993). Since most women want families and careers, they realize they must plan to balance both, and many struggle to do so (McCracken & Weitzman, 1997). Many do not believe it is possible to do so in the sciences.

There is *no* evidence that the trend for women to enter occupations that were previously male dominated is associated with plans for nontraditional lives. Rather, females who want both career and family must understand that it is possible to have both and find ways to do so. It is this mistaken belief that they cannot be combined, rather than traditional gender beliefs, that often affect career plans (O'Connell, Betz, & Kurth, 1989). For example, one gifted female student told me that she would love to go into the computer software field but felt that if she took off three or more years from the job to raise her children when they were young, she would return without adequate knowledge and skills since the field changes so quickly.

It is not so much that science and math careers are seen as the total province of males (Lightbody & Durndell, 1996) but the question of balance that seems to be a troublesome ingredient in the career choice of many highly intelligent women. The key, then, may be not to convince women that women can be successful with technology but to demonstrate that they can have a career in nontraditional fields without giving up their desire for family. Perhaps showing successful women who have been able to balance the two might help. At the same time, while concern about vocational choice and artificial barriers to achievement are important, some politically correct view of how a woman should live should not be foisted on students. Too often, older stereotypes have been replaced by newer ones. For instance, one female student felt rather guilty because she wanted to pursue a career in elementary school teaching. Her decision was not greeted with approval by her counselor, her teacher, and some friends who believed she could "do better." The goal should be to encourage women to enter the field of their choice unencumbered by artificial barriers, not to make the decision for them.

High-achieving minority professionals may serve as role models for minority group youth without a history of success with the system.

Socioeconomic Status

Career choice is a misnomer for the poor, many of whom belong to minority groups. Many poor adolescents do not have any choices, or at least do not see any. Many poor African American males have no real career exploration period. They may take a job in their teens, but after that job, they may have a succession of unrelated jobs for 50 years, with no discernible career ladder. Occupational choice may also be limited by lack of academic skills and economic resources or by racial discrimination, and complicated by the lack of high-achieving role models.

Adolescents from middle-class families believe they can influence their own futures; that is, they have an internal locus of control. But this is not the case with poorer youngsters, who often have an external locus of control and see themselves as at the mercy of the system, the outside world, or luck. They are more fatalistic in their outlook (Farmer, 1978). If they don't have the power to change things, why plan?

There is both good and bad news concerning career choices for minorities. The proportion of African Americans and Latinos in white-collar, professional jobs, and technical specialties has increased (see Figure 13.10). The progress, though, has been slow (Jaccoby, 1999). In addition, the unemployment rate is higher for minority youth than for white youths (Lewis, 1999). This higher unemployment rate probably reflects both the lack of skills and the high percentage of school dropouts found among minority youths.

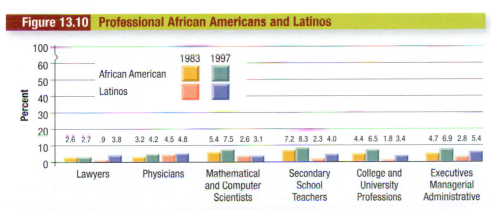

Figure 13.10   Professional African Americans and Latinos

NOTE: In 1997, African Americans comprised about 12.1% of the U.S. population and Latinos about 10.7%.
SOURCE: Data from U.S. Department of Commerce (1998)

A number of areas need to be addressed. First, minority group youth know less about different types of occupations than majority youth, and since occupational knowledge does influence choice, this is one place to start (Drummond & Ryan, 1995). A successful work-experience program for minority students may involve providing better occupational information, relating academic skills learned to future career requirements, giving students some job-related experience, and teaching job-finding and interview skills. This can be accomplished through informational seminars, career luncheons with role models, job fairs, career tours, and counseling (Miller & Cunningham, 1992).

Second, beliefs must be changed. African Americans and some members of other minority groups have a long history of discrimination and lack of opportunity. The majority and some minority groups who have achieved view school as the gateway to these higher-paying jobs. But the African American community has a history of negative experiences. Difficulties in achievement may be caused by prior negative experiences and a history of discrimination that now pervades the culture. African American and Latino youth often believe that they will face a labor market that will not offer them rewards equal to the effort they put in and the educational credentials they may attain. A lack of motivation may then be a response to the belief that educational effort may not pay off (Ogbu, 1978, 1981, 1992). To change perceptions, job opportunities within the general society must be opened up for minority group members so they can see for themselves the value of schooling. Role models must be available as well. Unfortunately, in many poverty-stricken communities, those who succeed move out to other communities, and the role models of successful business and professional people may not be at hand.

Third, schools in poverty neighborhoods must be given the resources to do their mission and students must be given an opportunity to learn in schools that are safe and secure, with an environment conducive for learning.

Guideposts

Why has the progress of minority group members entering the professions been so slow?

Teenagers and Work

Many high school students hold part-time jobs during the school year. Twenty years ago, this entrance into the world of work was greeted with approval. It was universally believed that work gives teenagers a greater understanding of the job market, builds a sense of responsibility, and develops both self-esteem and a work ethic (Meyer, 1987). Teenagers who work can learn the value of a dollar, as they spend the money on personal items (Shanahan, Elder, Burchinal, & Conger, 1996). Work encourages teens to think about their future occupational goals, and perhaps they may even learn some job skills which may help them in their future. Both teenage boys and girls show better psychological adjustment when their jobs are perceived as providing such skills (Mortimer, Finsh, Shanahan, & Ryu, 1992 a, 1992b). At the least, they may learn how to acquire a job, fill out an application, meet supervisor's expectations, and get along with the public (Mortimer, Finch, Ryu, Shanahan, & Call, 1996). Employment is related to self-reported punctuality, dependability, and a sense of personal responsibility (Greenberger & Steinberg, 1986). Public attitudes toward teenagers working are very favorable (Phillips & Sandstrom, 1990).

This positive view was recently challenged. Most jobs open to teens provide no training in useful skills and little opportunity for growth or challenge (Greenberger & Steinberg, 1986). Even governmental programs designed to give minority teenagers work experience often do not teach skills that are later needed in the world of work (Foster, 1995). Most high school seniors say they work in jobs they describe as not being acceptable for their future and work only for the money (Bachman et al., 1993). One exception, though, are some work-study jobs that do teach important job-related skills.

These studies also found that teenagers who work more than 20 hours have lower grades and show poorer school achievement than nonworkers (Steinberg, Greenberger, Garduque, & McAuliffe, 1982). Teenagers who work long hours are more likely to show adjustment problems, to smoke, use alcohol immoderately, use other drugs, and to be delinquent (Steinberg, Fegley & Dornbusch, 1993; Steinberg et al., 1982). Working is related to lower engagement and involvement with school, as measured by time spent doing homework, participation in extracurricular activities, and achievement (Steinberg et al., 1993). When thousands of students were studied, the results showed a positive relationship between number of working hours and drug use as well as interpersonal difficulties. This was true even when background and educational success were controlled (Bachman & Schulenberg, 1993).

Working long hours may also interfere with the process of forming an identity. Work may take up the time necessary to explore different roles, and students may have difficulties juggling home, schoolwork, and extracurricular activities.

Perhaps the relationship between working long hours and these undesirable consequences is best explained by the concept of **pseudomaturity,** or the premature entrance into the adult role. Pseudomaturity involves withdrawal from the preadult adolescent student role and a premature commitment to an adult lifestyle (Bachman & Schulenberg, 1993). One of the consequences of this pseudomaturity is alcohol use and smoking. Youths who work long hours don't get much sleep, don't eat breakfast, don't exercise, and do not report much satisfaction in leisure-time activities. This premature entrance into adulthood does not allow time for after-school activities, forming social relationships, and participating in community activities. Teenagers who work many hours take on adult responsibilities and adult lifestyles without developing the coping abilities necessary to succeed (Greenberger & Steinberg, 1986). Although teens may learn something about punctuality and responsibility from working, the other results do not look very promising.

These negative outcomes are found mostly for teens who work 20 or more hours a week. Students who work fewer hours do not seem to suffer. In addition, some teens work in jobs that are related to possible future skills such as construction, coaching sports, helping children after school, or caring for the elderly (Roscoe, Morgan, & Peebles, 1996). And those who work to save money for college may be different from those who do not. Finally, the poor grades and drinking problems may actually precede working long hours rather than extensive work experience leading to poorer grades and drinking problems (Steinberg, Fegley, & Dornbusch, 1993). Perhaps, some common factor underlies both. As is often the case, the direction of the relationship is difficult to establish. Perhaps both are correct. Although many students who are doing poorly work extra hours, taking a job for more than 20 hours a week further disengages the students from school. Leaving employment after working long hours leads to improvements in school performance but not a reversal of other negative effects (Steinberg et al., 1993). Perhaps these students have already been indoctrinated into this life pattern and have friends who smoke or use drugs.

In the end, limited work experience may have some benefits. However, teens must be monitored so that their schedules allow sufficient time for school-related activities, social interaction, and community involvement, which are so necessary for growth during these important years.

High school students who are employed for more than 20 hours a week are most often highly motivated students who show outstanding grade point averages and excellent citizenship.

Guideposts

What is the effect of part-time work on adolescent adjustment and academic achievement?

pseudomaturity

The premature entrance into adulthood, which involves taking on adult roles before one is ready.

Atypical Development: Drug Abuse and Violence

When adolescents between the ages of 12 and 17 years are asked about the most important problems facing people their age, they report (1) drugs and (2) crime (Center on Addiction and Substance Abuse, 1994). The general public is also very concerned about these problems.

Drug Use

With only 5% of the world's population, Americans consume almost 50% of the illegal drugs in the world (Segal & Stewart, 1996). Since 1975, the Monitoring the Future Study has measured the extent of drug use among students by sampling thousands of secondary school students from all around the United States (NIDA Capsules, 1995; USDHHS, 1997). Some of the results of two surveys are shown in Table 13.4. An analysis of the full data for these surveys leads to three conclusions. First, after a marked decline throughout the 1980s, drug usage has increased substantially since the early 1990s before showing a small decline very recently (Johnston, Bachman, & O'Malley, 1995; Stephenson, Henry & Robinson, 1996; USDHHS, 1997). The levels of illicit drug use are still well below the peak during the late 1970s, but the trend is worrisome (Johnston et al., 1995; USDHHS, 1997). Second, a trend exists for youngsters to become involved in drugs at an earlier age (Leshner, 1995). Substance use has increased substantially for the youngest teens, those in the sixth through ninth grades (Stephenson et al., 1996). Third, the percentage of adolescents who appreciate the dangers of drugs has declined greatly (Johnston et al., 1995; Leshner, 1995). This leads to an increase in peer tolerance for drug taking and eventually to increased usage.

Alcohol   Alcohol is the most frequently used drug (Johnston et al., 1995). Monthly alcohol use has remained fairly stable over the past few years, but it remains at a very high level. Although people tend not to take alcohol use seriously, the facts prove otherwise. More than half of the jailed inmates convicted of violent crimes were drinking before they committed the offense (Greenfeld, 1998; New York State Council on Alcoholism, 1986). Adolescents driving under the influence of alcohol are involved in a little less than half of all fatal motor vehicle accidents (Wodarski, 1990). The carnage on our highways has caused an outcry, with the legal age for drinking being raised to 21 years in many states. Higher minimum drinking ages, stricter laws, and increased educational efforts have had some effect, leading to some decline in the number of alcohol-related automobile accidents involving young people. Drinking, especially binge drinking on college campuses, has become alarming and many parents are shocked at the level of such drinking (O'Neal, 1998; Temple, 1998). Often, teens see drinking all around them and perceive warnings from adults as hypocritical.

Nicotine   Despite all the studies linking smoking to cancer, heart disease, and so many other health-related problems, smoking remains a national problem (Johnston et al., 1995; Nelson et al., 1995; NIDA Capsules, 1995). A greater percentage of high school seniors smoke than adults. Most adolescent smokers say they will quit in a few years, but this does not happen. White teenage girls are most likely to smoke, but smoking among African American male youth has doubled since 1991

Guideposts

What are the trends in drug usage over the past 20 years?

T F 9

Drug use among teenagers has declined substantially throughout the 1990s.

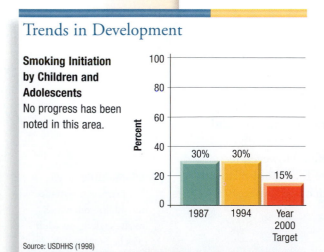

Trends in Development

Smoking Initiation by Children and Adolescents
No progress has been noted in this area.

Percent

1987	1994	Year 2000 Target
30%	30%	15%

Source: USDHHS (1998)

Table 13.4	Monitoring the Future Study: Trends in Prevalence of Various Drugs for 8th Graders, 10th Graders, and High School Seniors					
	8th Graders		**10th Graders**		**12th Graders**	
	1991	**1995**	**1991**	**1995**	**1991**	**1995**
Marijuana/hashish						
Lifetime	10.2%	19.9%	23.4%	34.1%	36.7%	41.7%
Annual	6.2	15.8	16.5	28.7	23.9	34.7
30-day	3.2	9.1	8.7	17.2	13.8	21.2
Daily	0.2	0.8	0.8	2.8	2.0	4.6
Cocaine						
Lifetime	2.3	4.2	4.1	5.0	7.8	6.0
Annual	1.1	2.6	2.2	3.5	3.5	4.0
30-day	0.5	1.2	0.7	1.7	1.4	1.8
Daily	0.1	0.1	0.1	0.1	0.1	0.2
Crack cocaine						
Lifetime	1.3	2.7	1.7	2.8	3.1	3.0
Annual	0.7	1.6	0.9	1.8	1.5	2.1
30-day	0.3	0.7	0.3	0.9	0.7	1.0
Daily	*	*	*	*	0.1	0.1
Heroin						
Lifetime	1.2	2.3	1.2	1.7	0.9	1.6
Annual	0.7	1.4	0.5	1.1	0.4	1.1
30-day	0.3	0.6	0.2	0.6	0.2	0.6
Daily	*	*	*	*	*	0.1
Stimulants						
Lifetime	10.5	13.1	13.2	17.4	15.4	15.3
Annual	6.2	8.7	8.2	11.9	8.2	9.3
30-day	2.6	4.2	3.3	5.3	3.2	4.0
Daily	0.1	0.2	0.1	0.2	0.2	0.3
Alcohol†						
Lifetime	70.1	54.5	83.8	70.5	88.0	80.7
Annual	54.0	45.3	72.3	63.5	77.7	73.7
30-day	25.1	24.6	42.8	38.3	54.0	51.3
Daily	0.5	0.7	1.3	1.7	3.6	3.5
Cigarettes (any use)						
Lifetime	44.0	46.4	55.1	57.6	63.1	64.2
Annual	NA	NA	NA	NA	NA	NA
30-day	14.3	19.1	20.8	27.9	28.3	33.5
1/2 pack + per day	3.1	3.4	6.5	8.3	10.7	12.4

*Less than 0.5%.

†The wording of the questionnaire was changed in 1993; the new questionnaire requires heavier use to elicit a positive response.

SOURCE: Data from National Institute on Drug Abuse, Monitoring the Future Study, 1995

(Friend, 1996). Smoking is not just an American problem but one that is growing worldwide (Abernathy, Massad, & Romano-Dweyer, 1995).

Marijuana   Teenage use of marijuana has increased significantly since the early 1990s at every grade level (Pina, 1995; USDHHS, 1995). Some marijuana users believe that no lasting effects occur after the high wears off. This is not true, as shown by a study of college students who were marijuana users but had not smoked for most of a month before testing. Heavy users still performed worse on measures of attention and general learning (Painter, 1996).

Cocaine and Crack   Cocaine is a stimulant, affecting the central nervous system and producing feelings of euphoria. Physiological changes include extreme changes in blood pressure, increases in heart and respiration rates, insomnia, nausea, tremors, and convulsions. Cocaine use can lead to paranoid behavior, and potent forms such as crack are especially addictive.

The use of cocaine and crack has increased for eighth and tenth graders and use by twelfth graders stays relatively stable (Johnston et al., 1995). The percentage of students in each grade who felt that people are at great risk of harming themselves by trying crack cocaine has decreased markedly since 1991.

Can Drug Abuse Be Predicted?   If we could predict who is most likely to become a drug abuser, we could commit our resources more effectively. The factors predictive of drug abuse can be broadly placed in three categories: individual characteristics, family (parent-child) factors, and peer group influence.

Individual Characteristics   Although there is no single personality pattern that is predictive of drug abuse, some characteristics do stand out. A pattern of undercontrol and antisocial behavior at young ages predicts drug abuse (Shedler & Block, 1990). Children who are described as undercontrolled, are aggressive or disruptive in nursery school, kindergarten, and elementary school, are more likely to abuse drugs (Block, Block, & Keyes, 1988; Dobkin, Tremblay, Masse, & Vitaro, 1995).

Abusers tend to have poor impulse control; have high anxiety in interpersonal relationships; be chronically angry, depressed, and bored; have a low frustration tolerance; and show denial (Segal & Stewart, 1996). They are more likely to have low self-esteem, equate drug use with entertainment, and have weaker family ties, while nonusers of alcohol and drugs equate them with negative consequences, show higher self-esteem and stronger family ties. Light to moderate users are found somewhere in the middle (DeAngelis, 1994). This pattern in which heavy users differ from light and nonusers is commonly found with many drugs, such as marijuana. For example, regular heavy users are much more rebellious and angry, show a lack of responsibility, and score high on measures of sensation seeking (Brook, Whiteman, Brook, & Gordon, 1981). They see themselves as inadequate, have friends who smoke marijuana heavily, often come from turbulent homes filled with discord, and show an inability to conform to rules. The differences between light and nonusers are more subtle; nonusers have more affectionate relationships with their fathers (Brook et al., 1981), while users are more defensive and rebellious (Mayer & Ligman, 1989).

Family Relations   Adolescents who describe their family lives as troubled and who are alienated from family at the age of 7 years are more frequent users and abusers of drugs in adolescence (Shedler & Block, 1990). Marital discord is related to substance abuse, as is physical and sexual abuse (Mayes, 1995). In addition, if parents use drugs, teenagers are more likely to do so as well (Mayes, 1995). Children whose parents smoke are three times more likely to smoke by age 15 (Males, 1997b).

Certain types of parenting seem to predispose adolescents to abuse drugs. Problem drinkers and illicit drug users often describe having experienced inconsistent parenting, a lack of family cohesiveness, and more conflict. Less conflict and a warm parent-child bond is associated with less adolescent drug abuse (Brook, Nomura, & Cohen, 1989). Parents who abused drugs may show poorer parenting strategies that may predispose their children to the use of drugs. When these children grow up and have their own children, they may continue this type of parenting (Stein, Newcomb, & Bentler, 1993). Warm family relations provide a buffer against the use of drugs, perhaps by reducing the need for escape and providing models and lessons in how to deal with stress (Bogenschneider, Wu, Raffaelli, & Tsay, 1998; Stephenson et al., 1996). Lack of supervision is also related to drug use.

Peers   Most parents believe that peer pressure is the primary reason teens use drugs; indeed two-thirds of the adolescents cite peer pressure as one reason. However, the overwhelming majority of teenagers say they use alcohol and other drugs for the high or use them to forget their problems (Boeck & Lynn, 1995). Peer pressure is certainly a factor, but despite the availability of alcohol, cigarettes, and marijuana, many teenagers do not smoke or drink excessively. Having friends who smoke or drink excessively influences the adolescent, but peer pressure does not operate in a vacuum (Graham, 1991). Peer influence is mediated by the quality of the relationship with parents (Chassin et al., 1993). The better the relationship, the less likely peer influence for use of drugs will be effective. This is only half the story, though. Adolescents who take drugs or are at risk for taking drugs may select as friends other adolescents with similar interests and outlook on life who then expose them to drugs and both model and reinforce their usage (Swain, Oetting, Edwards, & Beauvais, 1989).

Not all adolescents, even those at risk, will become drug abusers. A number of protective factors exist mediating between risk and outcome. For example, a positive attitude toward school and health, placing personal value on academic achievement, and an understanding of the health consequences of drug use predict less drug-taking behavior. Warm relationships with parents who show interest and discuss problems as well as parental supervision deter drug abuse by improving family relationships, regulating time, and clearly showing what behaviors are and are not valued (Jeffor et al., 1995). One way to combat drug abuse is to reduce factors that lead to at-risk status and increase those factors that seem to buffer the child against drug abuse.

In this analysis, these areas have been separated, but they really can be combined. For example, particular parent-child difficulties may be related to such personality traits as tolerance for deviance, risk taking, or rebellion that may lead to the selection of drug-using friends who encourage the teen's drug taking (Brook et al., 1997). The child's personality characteristics may also influence the parenting practices used. For example, the child's aggressiveness may cause parents to resort to inconsistent and inappropriate discipline, which may then lead to poor family relationships that encourage drug use (Stice & Brown, 1995).

Guideposts

What personality, family, and peer factors seem to lead to drug abuse?

When Daniel Comes Home from College . . . Drunk

Daniel is home after completing his first year in college. One Saturday evening he came home drunk. His parents weren't happy but did not say much. This occurred again two weeks later. In a casual conversation with a daughter of a friend who goes to the same school, Daniel's parents discovered that Daniel binge drinks frequently at college and once got in trouble with the campus authorities for it.

They told Daniel how shocked they were by his behavior and that they think he might need substance abuse counseling. Daniel reacted sharply to this, stating that he "wasn't an alcoholic" and "almost everyone drinks at school." Daniel told his parents that he never drives when he drinks and not to worry: "I know what I'm doing." Daniel also admitted using marijuana "occasionally."

Daniel's parents are concerned. They don't like the pattern they are seeing and think it will get worse. They feel he is flirting with danger and his behavior is a sign of deeper problems, while their son does not seem to agree.

1. *If you were Daniel's parent, would you consider his behavior a problem?*
2. *If you were Daniel's parent, what, if anything, would you do?*
3. *If you were Daniel's parent and found marijuana in his room, how would you deal with the situation?*

Drug Education   Americans favor a broad-based strategy to prevent and combat drug use consisting of education, treatment, and law enforcement (Brown, 1995; Office of National Drug Control Policy, 1995). Drug prevention should start early, since studies show that children are starting to use drugs at an earlier age (Jones, McDonald, Fiore, Arrington, & Randall, 1990). Students whose parents communicate with them about drugs and are involved in community and school activities are half as likely to use drugs (Manning, 1994).

Unfortunately, many drug prevention programs have not been very successful (Goodstadt, 1987; Tobler, 1986), and many that seem promising suffer from inadequate evaluations (Gorman, 1997). One reason for their ineffectiveness is that these programs cannot remove the social problems that may lead to drug abuse or the adult models that surround teens (Males, 1997b). An adolescent may abuse drugs for immediate pleasure, as a means of experimentation, to show rebelliousness, and because of peer pressure to use drugs. These reasons are easy to understand. However, drugs may also be used as an escape from the harsh realities of life, such as failure, rejection, and family problems (Tower, 1987). These are much more difficult to remedy (Forbes, 1987). To be effective, drug education programs must deal with the issue of how to help teenagers find alternative ways of dealing with their problems.

Teenagers certainly need factual information about the dangers of drug taking, and correcting misconceptions about the percentage of users can even reduce drug use. For example, as is true for adolescents of all ages, college students often overestimate the number of students who drink heavily on campus. When students are meaningfully informed of the real figures, student perceptions change in line with the facts, and this somewhat reduces alcohol consumption on campus (DeAngelis, 1994). The same is true for cigarette smoking (Robinson & Klesges, 1997).

Trends in Development

High Schools Providing Antismoking Education

There is significant movement in the right direction.

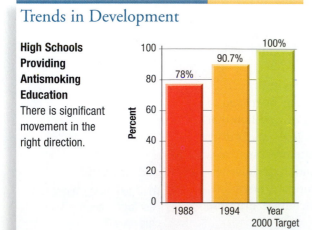

Most modern drug education programs go beyond just saying no or telling adolescents why they should say no and teach them *how* to say no (Murray, 1995a). These programs build drug resistance skills and improve the adolescent's involvement in community and school since so many drug-taking youth are alienated from family, community and society in general (Murray, 1995a).

No single drug prevention program will work for everyone. Some adolescents, such as those who are homeless or runaway teens who have used drugs, need more help (Edmonds, 1995). Drug treatment is also required, and this service reduces crime in the community. For every dollar spent on treatment, the public saves seven dollars in criminal justice and health costs (Office of National Drug Control Policy, 1996).

For Your Consideration ?

If you were in charge of the nation's drug abuse prevention program and had adequate funds at your disposal, what type of program would you design?

Violence and Delinquency

"Teenage Time Bombs: Violent juvenile crime is soaring—and it's going to get worse." These words appeared with a picture of a youth in handcuffs on the cover of the March 25, 1996, issue of *U.S. News and World Report*. The article describes in detail the violence that is of such a concern to the American public. Recently, a string of seemingly senseless shootings at schools have heightened the public's awareness of teen violence (Peterson, 1998).

The fear of crime and violence affects the routine of both adults and children. According to a Harris Poll of junior and senior high school students, one-third have been involved in fights involving weapons and many avoid particular parks and playgrounds (Henry, 1996a). Even young 7- to 10-year-old children are anxious about violence and have a fear of violence and death. There is a link between violence and drug use; adolescents who carry guns are almost fifteen times as likely to use cocaine and much more likely to drink and smoke marijuana (Manning, 1994).

At the same time, it is important not to paint with a broad stroke. Teenagers are not uniquely violent or crime-prone, and adolescents object with good reason to this stereotype of them (Males, 1997b).

The most modern view of violence and delinquency sees it as a developmental problem that may begin very early in life (Henry, Caspi, Mofitt, & Silva, 1996). A number of risk factors exist that can be categorized as family, individual/peer, school and community. These factors often interact, making it difficult to separate one from the other.

Violence is a continuing problem, and fear of crime and violence affects the routine of both adults and children.

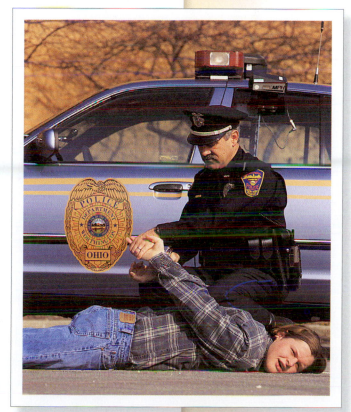

Family Processes and Relationships Children who are rejected by their parents, who grow up in conflict-filled homes, or who are not properly supervised are at a great risk of becoming delinquents (Wright & Wright, 1995). Cold, unloving families who are over-critical often produce aggressive children. Very often, the parents of delinquents use discipline that is either very severe and punitive or very lax (Fox, 1985). A link between child abuse and witnessing violence in the home and later aggression is often found (Holden & Ritchie, 1991; Mason, 1993). Witnessing violence

Children who witness domestic violence are less likely to engage in violent behavior because they are aware of its consequences.

or experiencing abuse teaches children to solve their problems with violence, and prevents them from feeling empathy for others as well as reduces their ability to deal with stress (Siegel & Senna, 1991).

Individual/Peer Factors   The personality profiles of delinquent teens differ from their non-aggressive peers. Children with background factors related to delinquency were identified when they were in fourth grade. When these children reached 12 or 13 years, those who were delinquent were compared with those who were not. As a group, the delinquents were more unempathetic, egocentric, manipulative, and had poor impulse control (Figure 13.11) (John, Caspi, Robins, Moffitt, & Stouthamer-Loeber, 1994). Remember that this is a comparison to others with similar backgrounds and risk factors who did not become delinquent. Delinquents are resentful, socially assertive, defiant, suspicious, and lacking in self-control (Henry et al., 1996). They are often described as explosive and impulsive and show histories of aggression. Perhaps the most disturbing trait that differentiates highly violent teens from others is their lack of empathy; many of these adolescents do not feel the distress or agony of their victims (Peterson, 1998). This undercontrolled behavior may also have an aversive impact on parents, peers, and teachers, causing others to react negatively. Family factors pose risks for offending in general (both violent and nonviolent), and personality features may distinguish those who become violent from those who do not.

Peers also both model and reinforce aggressive behavior. Aggressive children and adolescents seek out peers with the same characteristics and then reinforce each other for their aggressive behavior.

Trends in Development

Student Victimization
Has the United States reduced the percentage of tenth grade students reporting that they were threatened or injured at school during the previous year? There has been some progress here.

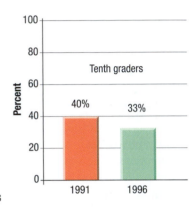

Source: National Education Goal Panel (1998)

Guideposts

What factors lead to adolescent violence?

School and Community Factors   Many adolescents witness violence in their homes, schools, and communities, which contributes to their own violence. Adolescents raised in communities with high rates of violence may believe that this is the way disagreements ought to be settled, and the atmosphere of violence may permeate their everyday lives.

Figure 13.11	Mean-Level Differences Between Delinquent and Nondelinquent Groups on Personality Traits

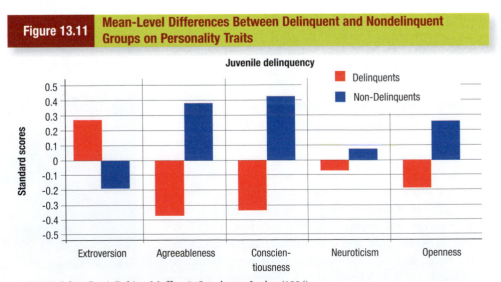

SOURCE: John, Caspi, Robins, Moffitt, & Stouthamer-Loeber (1994)

Protective Factors These factors are cumulative, and the greater the number that exist the more likely the child will show aggressive behavior and delinquency (Catalano & Hawkins, 1995). Yet, care must be taken not to overstate each of these factors. Not all children who grow up in violent homes become violent adults (Wright & Wright, 1995). Along with risk factors, protective factors also function. Such personal characteristics as being warm, flexible, and socially-oriented are related to less delinquency. Families that are marked by greater amounts of support, affection, and supervision serve as buffers against violence. Peers who do not accept violence also serve as checks, as do community programs that emphasize inclusion and school programs that enhance social and academic competence.

Can Violence Be Curbed? Psychologists know enough about what makes a child violent to fashion effective prevention programs. Since there are many paths to violence, many different programs can be successful. Some successful prevention programs attempt to improve family relationships and begin in the first five years (Bilchik, 1995). Programs that prevent abuse, improve parenting abilities, and reduce violence in the family are very successful.

Programs that prevent academic failure and promote social competence also prevent delinquency. Some preschool programs are very successful in reducing later delinquency, although this wasn't their original intention. When the social and intellectual development of children as young as 3 or 4 years old is fostered, children grow up with a greater sense of social competence, and later they commit fewer criminal acts (High/Scope Educational Research Foundation, 1993).

Programs that emphasize conflict resolution and social skills training look promising as well (Lawton, 1994). Students today need such skills desperately. In 1993, a Louis Harris poll found that more than half the teenagers surveyed said it was almost impossible to back off from a confrontation (Rubin, 1995). Many violent incidents in middle and high school escalate from trivial events (Lockwood, 1997). With the increasingly violent reaction of some students, yesterday's couple of punches is a shootout today. Conflict resolution programs can help. For example, in New York City, the "Resolving Conflict Creatively" program aims at reducing violence and promoting cooperation by offering students peer mediation and a special curriculum dealing with how to resolve conflicts. Evaluations are positive, with teachers and administrators reporting less physical violence in the classroom (Bilchik, 1995).

Other programs seek to improve the alienated teen's attachment to the community through social and work programs. Some community efforts focus on creating a positive adult-teen relationship by offering a mentoring program, while other programs attempt to provide a safe haven in the community for teens to socialize (Carnegie Council, 1994; Grossman & Garry, 1997). These community-based programs can reduce the violence in a community, but few localities make extensive efforts in these areas.

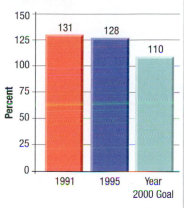

Trends in Development

Physical Fighting among Adolescents 14 to 17 Years (incidents per 100 students per month) A small amount of progress has occurred here.

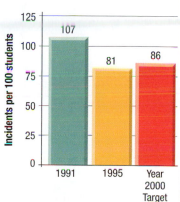

Trends in Development

Weapon Carrying by Adolescents (14–17 years) Progress has been made in this area.

Source: USDHHS, 1998

Exploding the Myths

The popular belief that adolescents surrender their dependence on parents and form a total dependence on peers is incorrect. The commonly held belief that parents' relationships with their adolescents are uniformly poor must also be reevaluated in view of recent research. The popular view that most adolescents are involved in antisocial behavior or abusing drugs must also be laid to rest.

During adolescence, young people are faced with important decisions in every area of life and must be prepared for them. As we have seen, parents need not abdicate their special relationship with their children during this stage. Supervision and guidance are part of a parent's responsibilities, but so is preparation for independent adulthood. Constant criticism, harsh punishment, and strict warnings are often ineffective, especially if they occur in a cold, hostile environment. Adolescents are affected most by what they see and experience—and communication is extremely important. As Haim Ginott (1969) said:

> Character traits cannot be taught directly: no one can teach loyalty by lectures, courage by correspondence, or manhood by mail. Character education requires presence that demonstrates and contact that communicates. A teenager learns what he lives, and becomes what he experiences. To him, our mood is the message, the style is the substance, the process is the product. (p. 243)

Summary

1. There is no real rite of passage marking the entrance to adulthood in our society. Some groups are trying to create ceremonies and experiences that provide such rites of passage.

2. The self becomes more differentiated in adolescence. During middle adolescence, teens become concerned about the conflicts in their self and being phony. These conflicts are integrated into a coherent self in later adolescence. Carol Gilligan argues that adolescent women experience a conflict between being feminine and voicing their opinions and true feelings. Others argue that there are no gender differences, and displaying the real self is dependent on parental support and other factors. Self-esteem is generally higher for males than for females beginning in middle adolescence. Teenage girls are more prone to depression than teenage boys.

3. Erik Erikson viewed the formation of a personal identity as the positive outcome of adolescence. Role confusion, the failure to answer fundamental questions of identity, is the negative outcome of the stage. Identity formation involves exploration (crisis) and commitment. Erikson emphasized the importance of the vocational and ideological domains. There are many other areas, including ethnic/racial, gender, and religious identities.

4. James Marcia extended Erikson's conception of identity to include four identity statuses. Identity diffusion is a status in which a person has not begun to make any commitments. This status is considered negative only when an individual leaves adolescence without making reasonable progress toward finding an identity. Identity foreclosure is a status in which a person has made commitments prematurely. Identity moratorium is a temporary status in which an individual is not ready to make commitments but may be exploring possibilities. Identity achievers have gone through their crises and made their commitments. People who are identity achievers are generally more ready to form intimate relationships. Two types of identity achievement have been suggested, one in which there is continued exploration and one in which exploration stops after commitment.

5. Males and females may take different paths to identity formation. Males focus on intrapersonal factors, while women tend to tie their identities to interpersonal relationships. Some changes are taking place in this area, however, as many women now seek to balance a career with family responsibilities.

6. Emotional autonomy involves shifting away from the emotional dependency on parents and forming new

relationships. Most adolescents achieve emotional autonomy while remaining connected with their families and have good relationships with their parents. A renegotiation of the relationship between parents and their adolescent children occurs. Although adolescence is not a period of continual storm and stress, conflict does occur.

7. Behavioral autonomy involves being able to behave competently when on one's own. Peer influence increases in adolescence but does not replace that of parents. Peer influence peaks in early adolescence, but conformity to antisocial behavior peaks in the early part of middle adolescence. Peer influence is greater in the areas of social interaction, styles, and attitudes toward school than in the realm of deeper values.

8. Parents are more likely to be directive, to want to share their wisdom, and to explain their views than to listen to the opinions of their teens. Peer communication shows more give-and-take.

9. The junior high school and middle school were established to ease the transition to high school and to provide for the rapidly changing needs of young adolescents. Although most children adapt well to the transition, a minority do have problems. Junior high schools have been criticized for not providing students with an adequate educational experience.

10. High school academic work is becoming more rigorous, and more students are taking advanced science and math courses, but achievement remains a concern, especially for some minority group youth.

11. Most high school dropouts have average intelligence scores but lack academic skills, have little interest in school, and show a history of school-related problems. They are more likely to come from poor, large families or families with discord and divorce. Dropouts are more likely than graduates to find themselves in dead-end jobs.

12. The choice of a vocation affects one's entire lifestyle. For many female and minority youths, vocational choice is limited. However, women have made progress entering male-dominated occupations, and more members of minority groups are now entering the professions. Many minority adolescents do not have high vocational aspirations, lack adequate role models, and find their choices limited by lack of academic skills and economic resources or by discrimination. These youths are less likely to believe that they have the power to influence their own futures.

Review

13. Drug use among teenagers has increased significantly since the early 1990s, and adolescents are using drugs at an earlier age. Teens also have less knowledge of the consequences of drug use than years ago. Some individual characteristics, such as undercontrolled and antisocial behavior, troubled family relationships, and peers who reinforce and model drug taking increase the risk of drug abuse. Drug education must give the facts but also build drug resistance skills.

14. Violence is a national concern. Factors that influence violence include personality characteristics, such as poor impulse control, parental behaviors such as parental rejection, and peer reinforcement and models. Some violence prevention programs appear to be successful.

Modern technological societies do not have strong, spiritually meaningful ceremonies called (1)_____ that acknowledge a change in status, such as the assumption of adult privileges and responsibilities. The self-concept becomes more (2)_____ in early adolescence. Adolescents become most concerned about behaving falsely in (3)_____ adolescence, but in (4)_____ adolescence they integrate these opposites. Carol Gilligan argues that women see these opposites and experience a conflict between (5)_____ and (6)_____ . If teens are to express their own opinions they require parental (7)_____ . Beginning in middle adolescence, self-esteem is (8)_____ in males than in females. Depressive symptoms are more common in adolescent (9)_____ .

Erik Erikson argued that the psychosocial crisis of the adolescent years can be expressed as (10)_____ versus (11)_____ . Two processes central to acquiring an identity are (12)_____ and (13)_____ . James Marcia identified four identity statuses. Adolescents who make premature commitments before they have done any exploration are said to be identity (14)_____ . Those who may or may not have explored but are unwilling or unable to make commitments are categorized as identity (15)_____ . Teens who are presently questioning and exploring but have not yet made any commitments are in the identity (16)_____ group, and those who have explored and made commitments can be placed in the identity (17)_____ group. Those in the (18)_____ group show superior adjustment and higher grade point averages than those in the other statuses. There is also a relationship between having a solid identity and the positive outcome of the psychosocial stage of early adulthood called (19)_____ . The negative outcome of that stage is a sense of (20)_____ . Traditionally, psychologists argued that men based their identities on (21)_____ factors such as competitive success, while women's identities were more involved with (22)_____ factors. Today, though, women are exploring both (23)_____ and (24)_____ opportunities and trying to blend them into a coherent identity and life style.

During the period of adolescence, teenagers are trying to achieve a shift of emotional dependency from their parents and form new relationships called (25)_____ autonomy. A pioneer in adolescent study, G. Stanley Hall, considered adolescence a time of (26)_____ . Today, the process of achieving autonomy is viewed in terms of a (27)_____ of family relationships. Most adolescents consider their relationships with their parents as (28)_____ . The ability to behave competently in various situations when teens are on their own is called (29)_____ autonomy. During adolescence the influence of (30)_____ increases. The general influence of other adolescents peaks during (31)_____ adolescence, while conformity to antisocial behavior peaks during (32)_____ adolescence.

Parents are more (33)_____ in their communication than peers. Parents also tend to (34)_____ the differences in opinions and beliefs between themselves and their adolescent children, while teenagers tend to (35)_____ the differences between what they and their parents believe.

Most adolescents adjust well to junior high school, but they complain about (36)_____ . High school work has become more (37)_____ in the past few years. Lately, there has been call for stricter and higher (38)_____ . Many want structural changes made in secondary schools, but some argue that students and parents are more (39)_____ from school. Educators are concerned about the achievement of students from some minority groups. One common thread running throughout these communities is (40)_____ . The gap between African American and white teens graduating from high school has (41)_____ , but the graduation rates of (42)_____ continue to be a source of concern.

The percentage of women entering male-dominated occupations and the percentage of members of minority groups entering the professions is (43)_____ . Many teenagers work part-time during the school year. Research evidence shows that teens who work (44)_____ or more hours show poorer grades and are more likely to use alcohol and smoke cigarettes.

Drug use has (45)_____ since the early 1990s. Drug use is also starting at a/an (46)_____ age. The most commonly used drug is (47)_____ .

Aggressive adolescents have frequently experienced very (48)_____ or extremely (49)_____ discipline. Many have witnessed violence in their homes and neighborhoods. (50)_____ programs, which teach adolescents to resolve their conflicts in a peaceful manner, may be helpful.

InfoTrac

For additional readings, explore InfoTrac College Edition, our online library.
Go to http://www.infotrac-college.com/wadsworth.
Hint: enter the search terms *Adolescence Identity, Teenage Violence,* and *Autonomy in Adolescence*

What's on the web

Impact of Television on Children and Adolescents
http://interact.uoregon.edu/MediaLit/FA/MLmediaviolence.html

New Hampshire Teen Institute/Prevention Programs for Middle and Senior High School Youth
http://www.mv.com/ipusers/nhteen/

Self-Esteem/Key to Student Learning
http://www.academicinnovations.com/sesteem.html

The Wadsworth Psychology Study Center Web Site
Go to the Wadsworth Psychology Study Center at http://psychology.wadsworth.com/ for quiz questions, research updates, hot topics, interactive exercises, and suggested readings in the InfoTrac College Edition related to this chapter.

Glossary

acceleration   A major division of services for gifted children in which a student skips a grade or a particular unit, or in which material is presented much more quickly than it would be for an average student.

accommodation   The process by which one's existing structures are altered to fit new information.

adolescence   The psychological experience of the child from puberty to adulthood.

adolescent egocentrism   The adolescent failure to differentiate between what one is thinking and what others are considering.

altruism   A type of prosocial behavior that involves actions that help people, that are internally motivated, and for which no reward is expected.

amniocentesis   A procedure in which fluid is taken from a pregnant woman's uterus to check fetal cells for genetic and chromosomal abnormalities.

anal stage   The second psychosexual stage, in which sexuality is centered on the anal cavity.

androgens   A group of male hormones, including testosterone.

androgyny   Possessing some characteristics considered typical of males and others considered typical of females.

animism   The preschooler's tendency to ascribe the attributes of living things to inanimate objects.

anorexia nervosa   A condition of self-imposed starvation found most often among adolescent females.

anxious/avoidant attachment   A type of attachment behavior shown in the "strange situation" in which the child avoids reestablishing contact with the mother as she reenters the room after a brief separation.

anxious/disorganized-disoriented attachment   A type of attachment behavior shown during the "strange situation," in which the child shows a variety of behaviors, such as fear of the caregiver, or contradictory behaviors, such as approaching while not looking at the caregiver, during the mother's reentrance after a brief separation.

anxious/resistant attachment   A type of attachment behavior shown during the "strange situation" in which the child both seeks close contact and yet resists it during the mother's reentrance after a brief separation.

Apgar Scoring System   A relatively simple system that gives a gross measure of infant survivability.

artificialism   The belief that natural phenomena are caused by human beings.

assimilation   The process by which information is altered to fit into one's already existing cognitive structures.

associative play   A type of play seen in preschoolers in which they are actively involved with one another but cannot sustain these interactions.

attachment   An emotional tie binding people together over space and time.

attachment behavior   Actions by a child that result in the child gaining proximity to caregivers.

attention deficit/hyperactivity disorder   A diagnostic classification involving a number of symptoms including inattention, impulsivity, and hyperactivity.

attention span   The time period during which an individual can focus psychological resources on a particular stimulus or task.

authoritarian parenting   A style of parenting in which parents rigidly control their children's behavior by establishing rules and valuing obedience while discouraging questioning.

authoritative parenting   A style of parenting in which parents establish limits but allow open communication and some freedom for children to make their own decisions in certain areas.

autonomy   The positive outcome of the second stage of Erikson's psychosocial stage: an understanding that the child is someone on his or her own.

babbling   Verbal production of vowel and consonant sounds strung together and often repeated.

Babinski reflex   The reflex in which stroking the soles of a baby's feet results in the baby's toes fanning out.

behavioral autonomy   Being able to behave competently when on one's own.

behaviorist   A psychologist who explains behavior in terms of the processes of learning, such as classical and operant conditioning, and emphasizes the importance of the environment in determining behavior.

blastocyst   The stage of prenatal development in which the organism consists of layers of cells around a central cavity forming a hollow sphere.

Brazelton Neonatal Behavior Scale   An involved system for evaluating an infant's reflexes and sensory and behavioral abilities.

Broca's area   An area in the brain responsible for producing speech.

bulimia   An eating disorder marked by episodic binge eating and purging.

canalization   The self-righting process in which the child catches up in growth despite a moderate amount of stress or illness.

caregiver sensitivity (maternal sensitivity)   A construct related to security of attachment that describes the degree to which a caregiver is aware of infant cues, interprets them correctly, and responds appropriately and promptly to the infant.

carrier   A person who possesses a particular gene or group of genes for a trait who does not show the trait but can pass it on to his or her offspring.

case study   A method of research in which a person's progress is followed for an extended period of time.

centering   The tendency to attend to only one dimension at a time.

cephalocaudal principle   The growth principle stating that growth proceeds from the head downward to the trunk and feet.

cesarean section   The birth procedure by which the fetus is surgically delivered through the abdominal wall and uterus.

child abuse   A general term used to denote an injury intentionally perpetrated on a child.

child neglect   A term used to describe a situation in which the care and supervision of a child is insufficient or improper.

chorionic villus sampling   A diagnostic procedure in which cells are obtained from the chorion during the 8th to 12th weeks of pregnancy and checked for genetic abnormalities.

chromosomes   Rod-shaped structures that carry the genes.

class inclusion   Understanding the relationship between class and subclass.

classical conditioning   A learning process in which a neutral stimulus is paired with a stimulus that elicits a response until the originally neutral stimulus elicits that response.

classification The process of placing objects into different classes.

cohort effect The effect of belonging to a particular generation and of being raised in a certain historical time.

collective monologue Egocentric exchanges in which young children take turns speaking, but each child's communication has little to do with the content of what the other speaker is saying.

commitment In psychosocial theory, making a decision concerning some question involved in identity formation and following a plan of action reflecting the decision.

communication The process of sharing information.

compensatory education The use of educational strategies in an attempt to reduce or eliminate some perceived difference between groups of children

computer literacy A term used to describe general knowledge about computers that includes some technical knowledge of hardware and software, the ability to use computers to solve problems, and an awareness of how computers affect society.

concordance rate The degree of similarity between twins on any particular trait.

concrete operational stage Piaget's third stage of cognitive development, lasting roughly from 7 years of age through 11 years, in which children develop the ability to perform logical operations, such as conservation.

conditioned response The learned response to the conditioned stimulus.

conditioned stimulus The stimulus that the organism has learned to associate with the unconditioned stimulus.

conscience Part of the superego that causes the individual to experience guilt when transgressing.

conservation The principle that quantities remain the same despite changes in their appearance.

contact comfort The need for physical touching and fondling.

conventional level Kohlberg's second level of moral reasoning, in which conformity to the expectations of others and society in general serves as the basis for moral decision making.

cooing Verbal production of single-syllable sounds, such as "oo."

cooperative play A type of play seen in the later part of the preschool period and continuing into middle childhood, marked by group play, playing specific roles, and active cooperation for sustained periods of time.

correlation A term denoting a relationship between two variables.

critical period The period during which a particular event has its greatest impact.

cross sectional study A research design in which people at different ages are studied to obtain information about changes in some variable.

crossing over The process occurring during meiosis in which genetic material on one chromosome is exchanged with material from the other.

crowning The point in labor at which the baby's head appears.

cystic fibrosis A severe genetic disease marked by respiratory problems.

deciduous teeth The scientific term for baby teeth.

deductive reasoning Reasoning that begins with a general rule and is then applied to specific cases.

defense mechanism An automatic and unconscious strategy that reduces or eliminates feelings of anxiety or emotional conflict.

deferred imitation The ability to observe an act and imitate it at a later time.

delivery of the placenta The third and last stage of birth, in which the placenta is delivered.

dependent variable The factor in a study that will be measured by the researcher.

development The sequence of physical, cognitive, social and personality changes that occur to human beings as they age.

differential emotions theory The theory that neonates show a limited number of emotions that are biologically determined.

dilation The first stage of labor, in which the uterus contracts and the cervix flattens and dilates to allow the fetus to pass.

discipline An attempt to control others in order to hold undesirable impulses in check and to encourage self-control.

discrimination The process by which a person learns to differentiate among stimuli.

dizygotic (fraternal) twins Twins resulting from fertilization of two eggs by two different sperm and whose genetic composition is no more similar than any other pair of siblings.

dominant traits Traits that require the presence of only one gene.

Down syndrome A disorder caused by the presence of an extra chromosome, leading to a distinct physical appearance and mental retardation of varying degree.

dramatic play (pretend play) A type of play in which children take on the roles of others.

dynamic systems theory A theory of motor development emphasizing the interaction between the organism and the environment.

early intervention programs Systematic efforts to assist young children between the ages of birth and 3 years and their families. Programs attempt to enhance development, minimize potential developmental delays, remediate existing problems, and improve overall family functioning.

Ebonics A type of linguistic communication with a consistent, logical, and coherent grammar used by some African Americans.

ego The part of the mind in Freudian theory that mediates between the real world and the desires of the id.

ego ideal The individual's positive and desirable standards of behavior.

egocentrism A thought process in which young children believe everyone is experiencing the environment in the same way they are. Children who are egocentric have difficulty understanding someone else's point of view.

Electra complex The female equivalent to the Oedipus complex, in which the female experiences sexual feelings toward her father and wishes to do away with her mother.

embryonic stage The stage of prenatal development, from about 2 to about 8 weeks, when bone cells begin to replace cartilage.

emotional abuse (psychological maltreatment) Psychological damage perpetrated on the child by parental actions that often involve rejecting, isolating, terrorizing, ignoring, or corrupting.

emotional autonomy Shifting away from emotional dependency on parents and forming new relationships.

empathy An emotional response resulting from understanding another person's state or condition

enrichment A major division of services for gifted children in which students are given special challenging work that goes beyond what would be usual for the child's age group.

environmentality The proportion of the variation between people in a given population on a particular characteristic that is caused by environmental factors.

epigenetic principle The preset developmental plan in Erikson's theory consisting of two elements: that personality develops according to maturationally determined steps, and that each society is structured to encourage challenges that arise during these stages.

equilibration In Piagetian theory, the process by which children seek a balance between what they know and what they are experiencing.

estrogens A group of female hormones, including estradiol.

event-related potentials Transient changes in the brain's electrical activity that reflect the activity of neurons in response to a particular stimulus.

exosystem Settings in which the individual is not actively involved, at least at the present time, but yet affect the individual.

experience-dependent information Information acquired through experiences that are unique to the individual.

experience-expectant information Environmental information acquired through experiences that are common to all members of the species, such as receiving visual information.

experimental study A research strategy using controls that allows the researcher to discover cause-and-effect relationships.

exploration (crisis) In psychosocial theory, a time in which a person actively faces and questions aspects of his or her own identity.

expressive children Children who use words involved in social interactions, such as stop and bye-bye.

expulsion The second stage of birth, involving actual delivery of the fetus.

extinction The weakening and disappearance of a learned response.

fear of strangers A common phenomenon beginning in the second half of the first year, consisting of a fear response to new people.

fetal alcohol effect An umbrella term used to describe damage to a child caused by the mother's imbibing alcohol during pregnancy. It is somewhat less pronounced than fetal alcohol syndrome.

fetal alcohol syndrome A number of characteristics—including retardation, facial abnormalities, growth defects, and poor coordination—caused by maternal alcohol consumption during pregnancy.

fetal stage The stage of prenatal development beginning at about 8 weeks and continuing until birth.

fine-tuning theory A theory noting that parents tune their language to a child's linguistic ability.

fontanels The soft spots on the top of a baby's head.

formal operations stage The last Piagetian stage of cognitive development, in which a person develops the ability to deal with abstractions and to reason in a scientific manner.

full inclusion A movement that would provide children with disabilities all special services within the regular classroom.

gametes The scientific term for the sex cells.

gender consistency (constancy) Children's knowledge that they will remain boys or girls regardless of how they act, dress, or groom.

gender differences The differences between males and females that have been established through scientific investigation.

gender identity One's awareness of being a male or a female.

gender roles Behaviors expected of people in a given society on the basis of whether an individual is male or female.

gender schema theory A theory of gender role acquisition in which, after developing gender identity, the child acquires a body of knowledge about the behaviors of each gender. This helps the child organize and interpret information and helps guide behavior.

gender stability Children's knowledge that they were of a particular gender when younger and will remain so throughout life.

gene The basic unit of heredity.

genetic counselors Specially educated professionals who help couples understand the genetic risks involved in producing offspring.

genital stage The final psychosexual stage, occurring during adolescence, in which adult heterosexual behavior develops.

genotype The genetic configuration of the individual.

germinal stage The earliest stage of prenatal development, lasting from conception to about 2 weeks.

grammar A general term that refers to the total linguistic knowledge of phonology, morphology, syntax, and semantics.

guilt The negative outcome of the psychosocial crisis of the preschool period, resulting in a sense that the child's acts and desires are bad.

habituation The process by which organisms spend less and less time attending to familiar stimuli.

heritability The proportion of the measured differences between people in a given population on a particular characteristic that is due to genetic factors.

holophrase One word used to stand for an entire thought.

horizontal decalage A term used to describe the unevenness of development in which a child may be able to solve one type of problem but not another, even though a common principle underlies them both.

hospitalism A condition found in children from substandard institutions. It is marked by emotional disturbances, failure to gain weight, and retardation.

id The portion of the mind in Freudian theory that serves as the depository for wishes and desires.

identification The process by which children take on the characteristics of another person, most often a parent.

identity The sense of knowing who you are. (The positive outcome of adolescence in psychosocial theory).

identity achievement An identity status in which a person has developed a solid personal identity.

identity diffusion An identity status resulting in confusion, aimlessness, and a sense of emptiness.

identity foreclosure An identity status marked by a premature identity decision.

identity moratorium An identity status in which a person is actively searching for an identity.

imaginary audience A term used to describe adolescents' belief that they are the focus of attention and are being evaluated by everyone.

implantation The process by which the fertilized egg burrows into the lining of the mother's uterus and obtains nourishment from the mother's system.

imprinting An irreversible, rigid behavior pattern of attachment.

independent variable The factor in a study that will be manipulated by the researcher.

inductive reasoning Reasoning that proceeds from specific cases to the formation of a general rule.

industry The positive outcome of the psychosocial crisis in the middle years of childhood, involving a feeling of self-confidence and pride concerning one's achievements.

industry versus inferiority The fourth psychosocial stage, in which the positive outcome is a sense of confidence concerning one's accomplishments and the negative outcome is a sense of inadequacy concerning one's achievements.

infancy The first year of life.

infant amnesia The inability of adults to recall events that occur during infancy and toddlerhood.

inferiority The negative outcome of the psychosocial crisis in the middle years of childhood, involving the child's belief that his or her work and achievements are below par.

information-processing theory An approach to understanding cognition that delves deeply into the way information is taken in, processed, and then acted on.

initiative The positive outcome of the psychosocial crisis of the preschool period, involving development of a respect for one's own wishes and desires.

intelligence The ability to profit from experience; a cluster of abilities, such as reasoning and memory. The ability to solve problems or fashion a product valued in one's society.

intelligence quotient (IQ) A method of computing intelligence by dividing the mental age by the chronological age and multiplying by 100.

intimacy versus isolation The sixth psychosocial stage, occurring during young adulthood, in which the positive outcome is a development of deep interpersonal relationships and the negative outcome is a flight from close relationships.

labor A term used to describe the general process of expelling the fetus from the mother's womb.

language The use of symbols to represent meaning in some medium.

language acquisition device An assumed biological device used in the acquisition of language.

lanugo The fine hair that covers a newborn infant.

latchkey or self-care children Elementary school children who must care for themselves after school hours. (Some include junior high school students in the definition.)

latency stage The psychosexual phase, occurring during middle childhood, in which sexuality is dormant.

learning disability A group of disorders marked by significant difficulties in acquiring and using listening, speaking, reading, writing, reasoning skills, or mathematics.

learning Relatively permanent changes in behavior due to interaction with the environment.

libido In Freudian theory, the energy emanating from the sex instinct.

linguistic deficit The belief that a dialect, such as Black English, is a hindrance to learning.

linguistic difference The belief that a dialect, such as Black English, is different from Standard English but not a deficit.

longitudinal study A research design in which subjects are followed over an extended period of time to note developmental changes in some variable.

love-oriented discipline A type of discipline relying on the use of reasoning or love.

macrosystem The ideology or belief system inherent in social institutions including ethnic, cultural, and religious influences, as well as the economic and political systems that exist.

mass to specific principle A principle of muscular development stating that control of the mass, or large muscles, precedes control of the fine muscles.

maturation A term used to describe changes that are due to the unfolding of an individual's genetic plan. These changes are relatively immune to environmental influence.

meiosis The process by which sex cells divide to form two cells, each containing 23 chromosomes.

mental age The age at which an individual is functioning.

mental retardation A condition marked by subnormal intellectual functioning and adjustment difficulties that occur before a person is 18 years of age.

mesosystem The interrelationships among two or more settings in which the person actively participates.

metamemory A person's knowledge of his or her own memory process.

microsystem The immediate interactions between the individual and the environment.

mistrust The negative outcome of Erikson's first psychosocial stage; an attitude of suspiciousness.

monozygotic (identical) twins Twins who develop from one fertilized egg and have an identical genetic structure.

moral realism The Piagetian stage of moral reasoning during which rules are viewed as sacred and justice is whatever the authority figure says.

moral relativism The Piagetian stage of moral reasoning in which children weigh the intentions of others before judging their actions right or wrong.

Moro reflex A reflex elicited by a sudden loud noise or momentary change in position, causing arching of the back, an extension of the arms and legs, and finally their contraction into a hugging position.

morpheme The smallest unit of meaning in a language.

morphology The study of the patterns of word formation in a particular language.

motherese The use of simple repetitive sentences with young children.

multifactorial traits Traits that are influenced both by genes and by the environment.

nativist explanation An explanation of language development based on biological or innate factors.

naturalistic observation A method of research in which the researcher observes people in their natural habitat.

neonate The scientific term for the baby in the first month of life.

nonshared environmental factors Environmental factors that are unique to the individual.

object permanence The understanding that an object exists even when it is out of one's visual field.

social learning theory The theoretical view emphasizing the process by which people learn through observing others and imitating their behaviors.

Oedipus complex The conflict during the phallic stage in which a boy experiences sexual feelings toward his mother and wishes to do away with his father.

onlooker play A classification of play in which the child watches others play and shows some interest but is unable to join in.

operant conditioning The learning process in which behavior is governed by its consequences.

operation An internalized action that is part of the child's cognitive structure.

oral stage The first psychosexual stage, in which sexuality is centered on the oral cavity.

overregularize A type of error in which children overuse the basic rules of language. For instance, once they learn to use plural nouns they may say "mans" instead of "men".

palmar grasp The reflex in which placing something in the palm of an infant's hand causes a tight grasp.

parallel play A type of play common in 2-year-olds in which children play in the presence of other children but not with them.

permissive parenting A style of parenting marked by open communication and a lack of parental demand for good behavior.

personal fable Adolescents' belief that their experiences are unique and original.

phallic stage Freud's third psychosexual stage, occurring during early childhood, in which the sexual energy is located in the genital area.

phenotype The observable characteristics of the individual.

phenylketonuria (PKU) A recessive genetic disorder marked by the inability to digest a particular amino acid and leading to mental retardation if not treated.

phonology The study of the sounds of language, the rules for combining the sounds to make words, and the stress and intonation patterns of the language.

play An enjoyable activity dominated by the child and performed for its own sake.

pleasure principle   The principle by which the id operates, involving the achievement of satisfaction as quickly as possible through the reduction of discomfort and tension.

polygenic or multigenic traits   Characteristics that are influenced by more than one pair of genes.

postconventional level   Kohlberg's third level of moral reasoning, in which moral decisions are made on the basis of individual values that have been internalized.

postformal operational reasoning   An expression used to describe any qualitatively different reasoning style that goes beyond formal operational reasoning and develops in the later part of adolescence and during adulthood.

posttraumatic stress disorder (PTSD)   A psychological disorder marked by such symptoms as diminished ability to concentrate, persistent sleep disturbances, flashbacks, disordered attachment behaviors, sudden startling, hypervigilance, and a fatalistic orientation.

power-assertive discipline   A type of discipline relying on the use of power, such as physical punishment or forceful commands.

pragmatics   The study of how people use language in various contexts.

preconventional level   Kohlberg's first level of moral reasoning, in which satisfaction of one's own needs and rewards and punishment serve as the basis for moral decision making.

prematurity   Infants weighing less than 5.5 pounds or born at or before 37 weeks after conception.

preoperational stage   Piaget's second stage of cognitive development, marked by the appearance of language and symbolic function and the child's inability to understand logical concepts such as conservation.

preterm infants   Infants born at or before the 37th week of gestation.

primary circular reactions   Actions that are repeated again and again by infants.

primary emotions   Emotions that appear early in infancy, are innately determined, can be recognized through facial expressions, and reflect a subjective experience.

primary sex characteristics   Body changes directly associated with sexual reproduction.

Project Head Start   A federally funded compensatory education program aimed at reducing or eliminating the differences in educational achievement between poor and middle-class youngsters.

prosocial behaviors   Voluntary actions that are intended to help or benefit another individual or group.

proximodistal principle   The growth principle stating that development occurs from the inside out—that the internal organs develop faster than the extremities.

pseudomaturity   The premature entrance into adulthood, which involves taking on adult roles before one is ready.

puberty   Physiological changes involved in sexual maturation, as well as other body changes that occur during the teen years.

qualitative changes   Changes in process, function, structure, or organization

quantitative changes   Changes that can be considered solely in terms of increases or decreases, such as changes in height or weight.

quasi-experimental design   A research design used when sufficient control over the variables under study is lacking. Because of the lack of control, definitive statements about cause and effect cannot be made.

readiness   The point in development at which a child has the necessary skills to master a new challenge.

readiness tests   Tests that measure whether a child has attained the skills necessary to master a new skill.

reality principle   The process by which the ego satisfies the organism's needs in a socially appropriate manner.

recall   A way of testing retention in which the subject must produce the correct responses given very limited cues.

recessive traits   Traits that require the presence of two genes.

reciprocal determinism   A concept in social learning theory referring to the idea that a complex reciprocal interaction exists among individual factors, behavior, and environmental stimuli, and that each of these components influences the others.

reciprocal interaction   The process by which an individual constantly affects and is affected by the environment.

recognition   A way of testing retention in which the subject is required to choose the correct answer from a group of choices.

referential children   Children whose early language is used to name objects, such as dog or bed.

reflex   A relatively simple automatic reaction to a particular stimulus.

reinforcer   Any event that increases the likelihood that the behavior that preceded it will reoccur.

rejecting-neglecting parenting   A parenting style in which parents are not involved in their children's lives, being neither demanding nor responsive.

relativistic reasoning   Thinking that involves the appreciation that knowledge depends on the subjective experiences and on the perspective of the individual.

replication   The duplication or repetition of an experiment or a piece of research. The description of a study must be so detailed that other researchers may reproduce the study.

representation   The ability to go beyond physical actions and to use symbols to portray events and feelings mentally.

reversibility   Beginning at the end of an operation and working one's way back to the start.

Rh factor   An antibody often, but not always, found in human beings.

role confusion   In psychosocial theory, the negative outcome of adolescence, which involves feelings of aimlessness and a failure to develop a personal identity.

rooting reflex   The reflex in which a stroke on a cheek causes an infant to turn in the direction of the stimulus.

rough-and-tumble play   Physical play, such as play fighting, chasing, and wrestling.

rubella   A disease responsible for many cases of birth defects.

saltatory growth   Growth marked by brief spurts and stops.

schema Piagetian theory   A method of dealing with the environment that can be generalized to many situations.

schema (information processing)   An organized body of knowledge that functions as a framework describing objects and relationships that generally occur.

schizophrenia   A severe mental disorder marked by hallucinations, delusions, and emotional disturbances.

script   A structure that describes an appropriate sequence of events in a particular context.

secondary circular reactions   Repetitive actions that are intended to create some environmental reaction.

secondary emotions   Emotions that begin to appear in the second year of life and require sophisticated cognitive abilities, for example envy and pride.

secondary sex characteristics   Physical changes that distinguish males from females but are not associated with sexual reproduction

secular trend   The trend toward earlier maturation today, compared with past generations.

secure attachment A type of attachment behavior in which the infant in the "strange situation" uses the mother as a secure base of operations.

selective attention The ability to concentrate on one stimulus and ignore extraneous stimuli.

self-concept The picture people have of themselves.

self-efficacy A person's belief about whether he or she can successfully perform a behavior related to a personal goal.

self-esteem A term that refers to judgments that one places on the self-concept or various aspects of the self. Newer definitions suggest self-esteem involves not only appreciating one's own worth and importance, but being accountable for oneself and acting responsibly toward others.

semantics The study of the meaning of words.

semiotic function (symbolic function) the ability to use one thing to stand for another.

sensorimotor stage The first stage in Piaget's theory of cognitive development, in which the child discovers the world using the senses and motor activity.

separation anxiety Fear of being separated from caregivers, beginning at 8 or 9 months and peaking at between 12 and 16 months.

sequential design The use of at least two cross-sections or two longitudinal analyses in the same study.

seriation The process of placing objects in size order.

sex chromosomes The 23rd pair of chromosomes that determines the gender of the organism.

sex selection Techniques that allow couples to choose the gender of their child.

sex typing The process by which an individual acquires the attitudes, values, and behaviors viewed as appropriate for one gender or the other in a particular culture.

sex-linked traits Traits that are inherited through genes found on the sex chromosomes.

sexual abuse Forced, tricked, or coerced sexual behavior between a younger person and an older person.

shame or doubt The negative outcome of Erikson's second psychosocial stage, in which the child has a sense of shame or doubt about being a separate individual.

shared environmental factors Environmental factors, such as socioeconomic status or parental child-rearing styles, that are shared by siblings.

sickle cell anemia An inherited defect in the structure of red blood cells found mostly in African Americans and Latinos.

small-for-date infants Infants born below the weight expected for their gestational age.

social referencing The phenomenon in which a person uses information received from others to appraise events and regulate behavior.

solitary or independent play Play in which the child plays by himself or herself.

sonogram An image of the developing organism taken through the use of sound waves.

stimulus generalization The tendency of an organism that has learned to associate a certain behavior with a particular stimulus to show this behavior when confronted with similar stimuli.

strange situation An experimental procedure used to measure attachment behaviors.

stress resistant (stress-resilient) children Children who do not appear to be negatively affected by stress or are able to cope with it and turn out healthy in the long run.

subcultures Groups with a system of values, attitudes, modes of behavior, and life styles which are distinct from, but related to, the dominant culture of a society.

sucking reflex A reflex found in young infants in which an infant automatically sucks when something is placed in the mouth.

sudden infant death syndrome (SIDS) The diagnosis given to young infants whose cause of death cannot be determined.

superego In Freudian theory, the part of the mind that includes a set of principles, violation of which leads to feelings of guilt.

survey A method of study in which data are collected through written questionnaires or oral interviews from a number of people.

synchrony The coordination between infant and caregiver in which each can respond to the subtle verbal and nonverbal cues of the other.

syntax The rules for combining words to make sentences.

Tay-Sachs disease A fatal genetic disease most commonly found in Jews who can trace their lineage to Eastern Europe.

telegraphic speech Sentences in which only the basic words necessary to communicate meaning are used, with helping words such as *a* or *to* left out.

temperament A group of characteristics reflecting an individual's way of responding to the environment. These are thought to be genetic.

teratogen Any agent that causes birth defects.

tertiary circular reactions Repetitive actions with some variations each time.

theory of multiple intelligences A conception of intelligence advanced by Howard Gardner, who argues that there are seven different types of intelligence.

time lag study A study that compares data presently gathered to data gathered at an earlier time, before the study was contemplated.

toddler A term designating the child between the ages of 1 and 3 years.

transductive reasoning Preoperational reasoning in which young children reason from particular to particular.

transition A period late in labor in which the contractions become more difficult.

transitive inferences Statements of comparison, such as "If X is taller than Y, and Y is taller than Z, then X is taller than Z."

trust The positive outcome of Erik Erikson's first psychosocial stage, a feeling that one lives among friends.

unconditioned response The response to the unconditioned stimulus.

unconditioned stimulus The stimulus that elicits the response prior to conditioning.

unoccupied behavior A type of play in which children sit and look at others or perform simple movements that are not goal-related.

vernix caseosa A thick liquid that protects the skin of the fetus.

visual cliff A device used to measure depth perception in infants.

Wernicke's area An area in the brain responsible for comprehension of language.

zone of proximal development Vygotsky's term for the difference between the child's actual developmental level as determined by independent problem solving and the higher level of potential development determined by problem solving under adult guidance or in cooperation with more capable peers.

zygote A fertilized egg.

References

A

AAP statement on infant sleeping position. (1997). *American Family Physician, 55,* 706.

Abernathy, T. J., Massad, L., & Romano-Dweyer, L. (1995). The relationship between smoking and self-esteem. *Adolescence, 30,* 899–907.

Abramovitch, R., Corter, C., Pepler, D. J., & Stanhope, L. (1986). Sibling and peer interaction: A final follow-up and a comparison. *Child Development, 57,* 217–229.

Abromowitz, A. J., & O'Leary, G. (1991). Behavioral interventions for the classroom: Implications for students with ADHD. *School Psychology Review, 20,* 220–234.

Ackerman, B. P., Kogos, J., Youngstrom, E., Schoff, K., & Izard, C. (1999). Family instability and the problem behaviors of children from economically disadvantaged families. *Developmental Psychology, 35,* 258–268.

Acredolo, L, & Goodwyn, S. (1988) Symbolic gesturing in normal infants. *Child Development, 59,* 450–466.

Acredolo, L., & Goodwyn, S. (1985) Symbolic gesturing in language development. *Human Development, 28,* 40–49.

Acus, L. K. (1982, January 24). Quarreling kids? How to handle them. *Newsday,* 16ff.

Adams, P. F., & Benson, V. (1990). Current estimates from the National Health Interview Survey, 1989. DHHS Pub. No. PHS 90–1504. *Vital and Health Statistics Series* 10, No. 176. Hyattsville, MD: National Center for Health Statistics.

Adams, R. J. (1987). An evaluation of color preference in early infancy. *Infant Behavior and Development, 10,* 143–150.

Adams, R. J. (1989). Newborns' discrimination among mid- and long-wavelength stimuli. *Journal of Experimental Child Psychology, 47,* 130–141.

Adams, R. J. (1995). Further exploration of human neonatal chromatic-achromatic discrimination. *Journal of Experimental Child Psychology, 60,* 344–360.

Adamson, L., & Lyxell, B. (1996). Self-concept and questions of life: Identity development during late adolescence. *Journal of Adolescence, 19,* 569–582.

Adeyanju, M. (1989). Adolescent health status, behaviors and cardiovascular disease. *Adolescence, 25,* 155–169.

Adler, L. L. (1982). Cross-cultural research and theory. In B. B. Wolman (Ed.), *Handbook of developmental psychology* (pp. 76–88). Upper Saddle River, NJ: Prentice Hall.

Adler, T. (1991). Seeing double? Controversial twins study is widely reported, debated. *APA Monitor, 22,* 1+.

Adler, T. (1995, March 11). Infants' deaths become less mysterious. *Science News,* p. 151.

Ahmed, A., & Ruffman, T. (1998) Why do infants make A not B errors in a search task, yet show memory for the location of hidden objects in a nonsearch task. *Developmental Psychology, 34,* 441-454.

Ahrons, C. R. (1994). *The good divorce: Keeping your family together when your marriage comes apart.* New York: HarperCollins.

Ainsworth, M. D. S. (1979). Infant-mother attachment. *American Psychologist, 34,* 932–938.

Ainsworth, M. D. S. (1967). *Infancy in Uganda: Infant care and growth of attachment.* Baltimore: Johns Hopkins University Press.

Ainsworth, M. D. S. (1974). The development of infant-mother attachment. In B. Caldwell & H. Riciutti (Eds.), *Review of child development* (Vol. 3). Chicago: University of Chicago Press.

Ainsworth, M. D. S., Blehar, M. C., Waters, E., & Wall, S. (1978). *Patterns of attachment.* Hillsdale, NJ: Erlbaum.

Ainsworth, M. D. S., & Wittig, B. A. (1969). Attachment and the exploratory behavior of one-year-olds in a strange situation. In B. M. Foss (Ed.), *Determinants of infant behavior* (Vol. 4, pp. 113–136). London: Methuen.

Akhtar, N., Carpenter, M., & Tomasello, M. (1996). The role of discourse novelty in early word learning. *Child Development, 67,* 635–645.

Akiyama, M. M. (1984). Are language-acquisition strategies universal? *Developmental Psychology, 20,* 219–229.

Akiyama, M. M. (1985). Denials in young children from a cross-linguistic perspective. *Child Development, 56,* 95–102.

Alan Guttmacher Institute. (1989). *Risk and responsibility: Teaching sex education in America's schools today.* New York: Author.

Aleser, K. H., Brix, K. A., Fine, L. J., Kallenbach, L. R., & Wolfe, R. A. (1989). Occupational mercury exposure and male reproductive health. *American Journal of Independent Medicine, 15,* 517–529.

Alessandri, S.M., Bendersky, M., & Lewis, M. (1998) Cognitive functioning in 8-to 18-month old drug exposed infants. *Developmental Psychology, 34,* 565–573.

Alexander, C. S., Youth, Y. J., Ensminger, M., Johnson, K .E., Smith, B., & Dolan, L. J. (1990). A measure of risk taking for young adolescents: Reliability and validity assessments. *Journal of Youth and Adolescence, 19,* 559–569.

Alexander, J. M., & Schwanenflugel, P. J. (1994). Strategy regulation: The role of intelligence, metacognitive attributions, and knowledge base. *Developmental Psychology, 30,* 709–723.

Alexander, K. L., Entwisle, D. R., & Dauber, S. L. (1993). First-grade classroom behavior: Its short-and-long term consequences for school performance. *Child Development, 64,* 801–814.

Allen, A. W., & Harley, D. (1975). *Art through your child's eyes.* New York: Allen & Harley.

Allen, K. R., & Demo, D. H. (1995). The families of lesbians and gay men: A new frontier in family research. *Journal of Marriage and the Family, 57,* 111–127.

Allgood-Merten, B., & Lewinsohn, P. (1990, June 6). (Research cited in *Education Week,* p. 9.)

Allison, K.W., Burton, L., Marshall, S., Perez-Febles, A., Yarington, J., Kirsh, L.B., & Merriwether-DeVries, C. (1999) Life experiences among urban adolescents: Examining the role of context. *Child Development, 70,* 1017–1029.

Allison, P. D., & Furstenberg, F. F. (1989). How marital dissolution affects children: Variation by age and sex. *Developmental Psychology, 25,* 540–549.

Allport, G. W. (1954). *The nature of prejudice.* Reading, MA: Addison-Wesley.

Alperstein, G., Rappaport, C., & Flanigan, J. M. (1988). Health problems of homeless children in New York City. *American Journal of Public Health, 78,* 1232–1233.

Alsaker, F. D., & Olweus, D. (1992). Stability of global self-evaluations in early adolescence: A cohort longitudinal study. *Journal of Research on Adolescence, 2,* 123–145.

Alton, E. (1996, February 1). Gene therapy. *New England Journal of Medicine, 334,* 332.

Aman, C.J., Roberts, R.J. Jr., & Pennington, B.F. (1998) A neuropsychological examination of the underlying deficit in attention deficit hyperactivity disorder: Frontal lobe versus right parietal lobe theories. *Developmental Psychology, 34,* 956–970.

Amato, P.R., & Keith, B. (1991) Parental divorce and the well-being of children: A meta-analysis. *Psychological Bulletin, 110,* 26–46

Amato, P.R., Loomis, L.S., & Booth, A. (1995) Parental divorce, marital conflict, and offspring well-being during early adulthood. *Social Forces, 73,* 895–915.

Amato, P. R., & Partridge, S. (1987). Women and divorce with dependent children: Maternal, personal, family, and social well being. *Family Relations, 36,* 316–320.

American Academy of Pediatrics Task Force on Infant Positioning and SIDS. (1996). Positioning and SIDS, update. *Pediatrics, 98,* 1216–1218.

American Academy of Pediatrics (1999) Reduce the risk of sudden infant death syndrome (SIDS). U.S. Public Health Service, American Academy of Pediatrics, SIDS Alliance, and Association of SIDS and Infant Mortality Programs.

American Association of University Women. (1992). *How schools short-change girls*. Washington, DC: AAUW Educational Foundation.

American Association on Mental Retardation. (1992). *Mental retardation: Definition, classification, and systems of supports* (9th ed.). Washington, DC: Author.

American Athletic Union. (1989). *Physical fitness trends in American youth*. Washington, DC: Author.

American College Health Association. (1986). *Acquaintance rape: Is dating dangerous?* Rockville, MD: Author.

American Home Economics Association. (1986). Preventing adolescent pregnancy: Promising new approaches. *Journal of Home Economics, 78*, 42–47.

American Medical Association's Council on Scientific Affairs. (1992, June 17). Violence against women: Relevance for medical practitioners. *Journal of the American Medical Association*, p. 3185.

American Psychiatric Association. (1994). *Diagnostic and statistical manual of mental disorders* (4th ed.). Washington, DC: Author.

Ames, C., & Ames, R. (1978) The thrill of victory and the agony of defeat: Children's self and interpersonal evaluations in competitive and noncompetitive learning environments. *Journal of Research and Development in Education, 12*, 79–87.

Ames, L. B. (1986, Summer). Ready or not. *American Educator*, pp. 30–34.

Anand, K. J. S., & Hickey, P. R. (1987). Pain and its effects in the human neonate and fetus. *New England Journal of Medicine, 317*, 1321–1329.

Anderman, E. M., & Midgley, C. (1997). Changes in achievement goal orientations, perceived academic competence, and grades across the transition to middle-level schools. *Contemporary Educational Psychology, 22*, 269–298.

Anderson, C. W., Nagle, R. J., Roberts, W. A., & Smith, J. W. (1981). Attachment to substitute caregivers as a function of center quality and caregiver involvement. *Child Development, 52*, 53–61.

Anderson, D. R. (1998). Educational television is not an oxymoron. *Annals of the American Academy of Political and Social Science, 557*, 24–39.

Anderson, D. R., & Levin, S. R. (1976). Young children's attention to Sesame Street. *Child Development, 47*, 806–811.

Anderson, E. A., & Koblinsky, S. A. (1995). Homeless policy: The need to speak to families. *Family Relations, 44*, 13–18.

Anderson, E. S., & Keith, T. Z. (1997). A longitudinal test of a model of academic success for at-risk high school students. *Journal of Educational Research, 90*, 259–269.

Anderson, G. L., Sedmak, D. D., & Lairmore, M. D. (1994). Placenta as barrier. In P. A. Pizzo & C. M. Wilfert (Eds.), *Pediatric AIDS: The challenge of HIV infection in infants, children, and adolescents* (2nd ed., pp.159–169). Baltimore: Williams & Wilkins.

Anderson, K. E., Lytton, H., & Romney, D. M. (1986). Mothers' interactions with normal and conduct-disordered boys: Who affects whom? *Developmental Psychology, 22*, 604–609.

Andersen, R. E., Crespo, C. J., Bartlett, S. J., Cheskin, L. J., & Pratt, M. (1998, March 25). Relationship of physical activity and television watching with body weight and level of fatness among children. *Journal of the American Medical Association, 279*, 938–942.

Andersson, B. E. (1989). Effects of public day-care: A longitudinal study. *Child Development, 60*, 857–866.

Andersson, B. E. (1992). Effects of day-care on cognitive and socioemotional competence of thirteen-year-old Swedish schoolchildren. *Developmental Psychology, 63*, 20–36.

Andersson, T., & Magnusson, D. (1990). Biological maturation in adolescence and the development of drinking habits and alcohol abuse among young males: A prospective longitudinal study. *Journal of Youth and Adolescence, 19*, 33–42.

Andolsek, K. M. (1997, January). Advice from family physicians on infant sleeping patterns. *American Family Physician, 55*, 295–299.

Andrade, M.M., Bendito-Silva, A.A., Domenice, S., Arnhold, I.J.P. & Mena-Barreto, L. (1993) Sleep characteristics of adolescents: A longitudinal study. *Journal of Adolescent Health, 14*, 401–406.

Angell, M. (1990). New ways to get pregnant. *New England Journal of Medicine, 323*, 1200–1202.

Angier, N. (1990a, September 21). Team cures cells in cystic fibrosis by gene insertion. *New York Times*, p. 1+.

Angier, N. (1990b, December 14). Gene-treated girl is raising hopes. *New York Times*, p. A24.

Anisfield, M. (1991). Neonatal imitation. *Developmental Review, 11*, 60–97.

Annas, G. J. (1995). Editorial: Genetic prophecy and genetic privacy: Can we prevent the dream from becoming a nightmare? *American Journal of Public Health, 85*, 1196–1197.

Annas, G. J. (1998, July 2). Why we should ban human cloning. *New England Journal of Medicine, 339*, 122–125.

Annis, L. F. (1978). *The child before birth*. Ithaca, NY: Cornell University Press.

Antell, S. E., Caron, A. J., & Myers, R. S. (1985). Perception of relational invariants by newborns. *Developmental Psychology, 21*, 942–948.

Antonarakis, S. E. (1991, March 28). Parental origin of the extra chromosome in trisomy 21 as indicated by analysis of DNA polymorphisms: Down syndrome collaborative group. *New England Journal of Medicine, 324*, 872–876.

Apgar, V. (1953). A proposal for a new method of evaluation of the newborn infant. *Current Researches in Anesthesia and Analgesia, 32*, 260–267.

Apgar, V., & Beck, J. (1974). *Is my baby all right?* New York: Pocket Books.

Apgar, V., Holaday, D. A., James, L. S., Weisbrot, I. M., & Berien, C. (1958). Evaluation of the newborn infant: Second report. *Journal of the American Psychological Association, 168*, 1985–1988.

Appel, L. F., Cooper, R. G., McCarrell, N., et al. (1972). The development of the distinction between perceiving and memorizing. *Child Development, 43*, 1365–1381.

Applebaum, M. I., & McCall, R. B. (1983). Design and analysis in developmental psychology. In P. H. Mussen (Ed.), *Handbook of child psychology* (4th ed., Vol. 1, pp. 415–477). New York: Wiley.

Applebome, P. (1996, March 27). Education summit calls for tough standards to be set by states and local school districts. *New York Times*, p. B9.

Archer, S. L. (1982). The lower boundaries of identity development. *Child Development, 53*, 1555–1556.

Armon-Lotem, S. (1995). Locating parameters: Evidence from early word-order. In E. V. Clark (Ed.), *The child language research forum* (pp. 71–81). N.p.: Center for the Study of Language and Information, Leland Stanford Junior University.

Arnett, J. (1992). Reckless behavior in adolescence: A developmental perspective. *Developmental Review, 12*, 339–373.

Arnett, J., & Balle-Jensen, L. (1993). Cultural bases of risk behavior: Danish adolescents. *Child Development, 64*, 1842–1855.

Aro, H., & Taipale, V. (1987). The impact of timing of puberty on psychosomatic symptoms among fourteen-to sixteen-year old Finnish girls. *Child Development, 58*, 261–268.

Artman, L., & Cahan, S. (1993). Schooling and the development of transitive inference. *Developmental Psychology, 19*, 753–759.

Arvey, R. D., Bouchard, T. J., Segal, N. L., & Abraham, L. M. (1989). Job satisfaction: Environmental and genetic components. *Journal of Applied Psychology, 74*, 187–192.

Asendorpf, J. B., Warkentin, V., & Baudonniere, P. (1996). Self-awareness and other-awareness II: Mirror self-recognition, social contingency awareness, and synchronic imitation. *Developmental Psychology, 32*, 313–321.

Ashford, E. (1997). How schools boost minority achievement. *School Board News, 17*, 1, 4.

Aslin, R. N. (1987). Visual and auditory development in infancy. In J. Osofsky (Ed.), *Handbook of infant development* (2nd ed., pp. 5–98). New York: Wiley.

Aslin, R. N., & Dumais, S. T. (1980). Binocular vision in infants: A review and a theoretical framework. In L. Lipsitt & H. Reese (Eds.), *Advances in child development and behavior.* New York: Academic Press.

Aslin, R. N., Jusczyk, P. W., & Pisoni, D. B. (1998). Speech and auditory processing. In W. Damon (Editor in Chief) & D. Kuhn & R. S. Siegler (Vol. Eds.), *Handbook of child psychology* (5th ed., Vol. 2, pp. 147–198). New York: Wiley.

Atkinson, A. M. (1987). Fathers' participation and evaluation of family day care. *Family Relations, 36,* 146–151.

Ault, R. (1977). *Children's cognitive development.* New York: Oxford University Press.

Austin, A. B., & Draper, D. C. (1981). Peer relationships of the academically gifted: A review. *Gifted Child Quarterly, 25,* 129–133.

Axline, V. M. (1969). *Play therapy* (rev. ed.). New York: Ballantine.

Axworthy, D., Brock, D.J.H., Bobrow, M., & Marteau, T.H. (1996) Psychological impact of population-based carrier testing for cystic fibrosis: 3-year-follow-up. *The Lancet, 347,* 1443–1444.

Azar, B. (1994, December). Psychology weighs in on Bell Curve debate. *APA Monitor, 25,* 1, 22.

Azar, B. (1995, May). Several genetic traits linked to alcoholism. *APA Monitor, 26,* 21–22.

Azar, B. (1996, December). Research seeks to soothe infant pain. *APA Monitor,* p. 21.

B

Bachman, J. G., & Schulenberg, J. (1993). How part-time work intensity relates to drug use, problem behavior, time use, and satisfaction among high school seniors: Are these consequences or merely correlates. *Developmental Psychology, 29,* 223–235.

Bachman, J. G., Johnston, L. D., & O'Malley, P. M. (1993). *Monitoring the future: Questionnaire responses from the nation's high school seniors, 1992.* Ann Arbor: Institute for Social Research, University of Michigan.

Badger, E., Burns, F., & Vietze, P. (1981). Maternal risk factors as predictors of developmental outcome in early childhood. *Infant Mental Health Journal, 2,* 151–162.

Bagley, C. A., Copeland, E. J. (1994). African and African American graduate students' racial identity and personal problem-solving strategies. *Journal of Counseling & Development, 73,* 157–173.

Bagwell, C. L., Newcomb, A. F., & Bukowski, W. M. (1998). Preadolescent friendship and peer rejection as predictors of adult adjustment. *Child Development, 69,* 140–153.

Bailey, D. A. (1975). The growing child and the need for physical activity. In M. S. Smart & R. C. Smart (Eds.), *School-age children: Development and relationships* (pp. 50–61). New York: Macmillan.

Bailey, J. M. (1995, December). Sexual orientation revolution. *Nature Genetics, 2,* 353–354.

Bailey, J. M., & Pillard, R. C. (1991). A genetic study of male sexual orientation. *Archives of General Psychiatry, 48,* 1089–1096.

Bailey, J. M., Bobrow, D., Wolfe, M., & Mikach, S. (1995). Sexual orientation of adult sons of gay fathers. *Developmental Psychology, 31,* 124–129.

Bailey, W. T. (1994). A longitudinal study of fathers' involvement with young children: Infancy to age 5 years. *Journal of Genetic Psychology, 155,* 331–339.

Baillargeon, R. (1987). Object performance in 3 ½- and 4 ½-month infants. *Developmental Psychology, 23,* 655–665.

Baillargeon, R., & Graber, M. (1988). Evidence of location memory in 8-month-old infants in a nonsearch AB task. *Developmental Psychology, 24,* 502–512.

Baillargeon, R., Spelke, E. S., & Wasserman, S. (1985). Object permanence in five-month-old infants. *Cognition, 20,* 191–208.

Baird, P. A., & Sadovnick, A. D. (1987). Life expectancy in Down syndrome. *Journal of Pediatrics, 849,* 110.

Baker, L.A., & Daniels, D. (1990) Nonshared environmental influences and personality differences in adult twins. *Journal of Personality and Social Psychology, 58,* 103–110.

Balaban, M.T., Anderson, L.M., & Wisniewski, A.B. (1998) Lateral asymmetries in infant melody perception. *Developmental Psychology, 34,* 39–49.

Balinsky, B. I. (1970). *An introduction to embryology* (3rd ed.). Philadelphia: Saunders.

Ball, S., & Bogatz, G. (1970). *The first year of "Sesame Street:" An evaluation.* Princeton, NJ: Educational Testing Service.

Baltes, P. B., Lindenberger, U., & Staudinger, U. M. (1998). Life-span theory in developmental psychology. In W. Damon (Editor in Chief) & R. M. Lerner (Vol. Ed.), *Handbook of child psychology* (5th ed., Vol. 1, pp. 1029–1143). New York: Wiley.

Bandura, A. (1982). Self-efficacy mechanism in human agency. *American Psychologist, 37,* 122–147.

Bandura, A. (1977). *Social learning theory.* Upper Saddle River, NJ: Prentice Hall.

Bandura, A. (1986). *Social foundations of thought and action: A social cognitive theory.* Upper Saddle River, NJ: Prentice Hall.

Bandura, A., Barbaranelli, C., Caprara, V., & Pastorelli, C. (1996). Multifaceted impact of self-efficacy beliefs on academic functioning. *Child Development, 67,* 1206–1222.

Bandura, A., Grusek, J. E., & Menlove, F. L. (1967). Vicarious extinction of avoidance behavior. *Journal of Personality and Social Psychology, 5,* 516–523.

Bandura, A., & Menlove, F. L. (1968). Factor determining vicarious extension of avoidance behavior. *Journal of Personality and Social Psychology, 8,* 99–108.

Bandura, A., Ross, D., & Ross, S. A. (1961). Transmission of aggression through imitation of aggressive models. *Journal of Abnormal and Social Psychology, 63,* 575–582.

Bank, S., & Kahn, M. D. (1975). Sisterhood-brotherhood is powerful: Sibling subsystems and family therapy. *Family Process, 14,* 311–337.

Banks, M. S., & Salapatek, P. (1983). Infant visual perception. In P. H. Mussen (Ed.), *Handbook of child development* (4th ed., Vol. 2, pp. 435–573). New York: Wiley.

Barabasz, M., & Barabasz, A. (1996). Attention deficit disorder: Diagnosis, etiology and treatment. *Child Study Journal, 26,* 1–14.

Baranowski, M. D., Schilmoeller, G. L., & Higgins, B. S. (1990). Parenting attitudes of adolescent and older mothers. *Adolescence, 25,* 781–789.

Barglow, P., Vaughn, B. E., & Molitor, N. (1987). Effects of maternal absence due to employment on the quality of infant-mother attachment in a low-risk sample. *Child Development, 58,* 945–955.

Barkley, R. A. (1990). *Attention deficit hyperactivity disorder.* New York: Guilford.

Barlte-Haring, S., & Strimple, R. E. (1996). Association of identity and intimacy: An exploration of gender and sex-role identity. *Psychological Reports, 79,* 1255–1264.

Barnat, S. B., Klein, P. J., & Meltzoff, A. N. (1996). Deferred imitation across changes in context and object: Memory and generalization in 14-month-old infants. *Infant Behavior and Development, 19,* 241–251.

Barnes, H. L., & Olson, D. H. (1985). Parent-adolescent communication and the circumplex model. *Child Development, 56,* 438–447.

Barnes, K. E. (1971). Preschool play norms: A replication. *Developmental Psychology, 5,* 99–103.

Barnes, S. L. (1998). Ebonics and public awareness. *Journal of Black Studies, 29,* 17–34.

Barnett, W. S. (1995). Long-term effects of early childhood programs on cognitive and school outcomes. *The Future of Children, 5,* 25–51.

Barney, J., & Koford, J. (1987, October). Schools and single parents. *Education Digest,* pp. 40–43.

Barr, S. I. (1994). Associations of social and demographic variables with calcium intakes of high school students. *Journal of the American Dietetic Association, 94,* 260–266, 269.

Barrera, M. E., & Maurer, D. (1981). Recognition of mother's photographed face by the three-month-old infant. *Child Development, 52,* 715–716.

Barrera, M., Jr., Chassin, L., & Rogosch, F. (1993). Effects of social support and conflict on adolescent children of alcoholic and nonalcoholic fathers. *Journal of Personality and Social Psychology, 64,* 602–612.

Barret, R. L., & Robinson, B. E. (1981). Teenage fathers: A profile. *Personnel and Guidance Journal, 60,* 226–228.

Barrett, M., Harris, M., & Chasin, J. (1991). Early lexical development and maternal speech: A comparison of children's initial and subsequent uses of words. *Journal of Child Language, 18,* 21–40.

Barron, J. (1987, November 8). Sex education programs that work in public schools. *New York Times,* Section 12, pp. 16–19.

Bartholomew, K. & Horowitz, L. (1991) Attachment styles among young adults: A test of a four-category model. *Journal of Personality and Social Psychology, 61,* 226–244.

Barton, S. (1994). Chaos, self-organization, and psychology. *American Psychologist, 49,* 5–14.

Bartsch, K. (1996). Between desires and beliefs: Young children's action predictions. *Child Development, 67,* 1671–1685.

Basseches, M. A. (1980). A framework for the empirical study of the development of dialectical thinking. *Human Development, 23,* 400–421.

Basseches, M. A. (1984). *Dialectical thinking and adult development.* Norwood, NJ: Ablex.

Bassuk, E. L. (1991). Homeless families. *Scientific American, 265,* 66–74.

Bassuk, E. L., Buckner, J. C., Weinreb, L. F., Browne, A., Bassuk, S., Dawson, R., & Perloff, J. N. (1997). Homelessness in female-headed families: Childhood and adult risk and protective factors. *American Journal of Public Health, 87,* 241–248.

Bassuk, E., & Rosenberg, L. (1988). Why does family homelessness occur? A case-control study. *American Journal of Public Health, 78,* 783–787.

Bassuk, E., & Rubin, L. (1987). Homeless children: A neglected population. *American Journal of Orthopsychiatry, 57,* 279–286.

Bassuk, E., Rubin, L., & Lauriat, A. (1986). Characteristics of sheltered homeless families. *American Journal of Public Health, 76,* 1097–1100.

Bates, B. A. (1988). Maternal depression and motherese: temporal and intonational features. *Child Development, 59,* 1089–1096.

Bates, J. E. (1987). Temperament in infancy. In J. Osofsky (Ed.), *Handbook of infant development* (2nd ed., pp. 1101–1150). New York: Wiley.

Bates, J. E. (1989). Concepts and measures of temperament. In G. A. Kohnstamm, J. E. Bates, & M. K. Rothbart (Eds.), *Temperament in childhood* (pp. 3–26). Chichester: Wiley.

Bates, J. E., Marvinney, D., Kelly, T., Dodge, K. A., Bennett, D. S., & Pettit, G. S. (1994). Child-care history and kindergarten adjustment. *Developmental Psychology, 30,* 690–700.

Bateson, C. (1975). Mother-infant exchanges: The epigenesis of conversational interaction. In D. Aronson & R. Rieber (Eds.), Development psycholinguistics and communication disorders. *Annals of the New York Academy of Sciences, 263,* 101–113.

Bauer, G. (1987, March). Teaching morality in the classroom. *Education Digest,* pp. 2–5.

Bauer, P. J., & Thal, D. J. (1990). Scripts or scraps: Reconsidering the development of sequential understanding. *Journal of Experimental Psychology, 50,* 287–304.

Baumrind, D. (1967). Child care practices anteceding three patterns of preschool behavior. *Genetic Psychology Monographs, 75,* 43–88.

Baumrind, D. (1971). Current patterns of parental authority. *Developmental Psychology Monograph, 4(1),* Part 2.

Baumrind, D. (1978, March). Parental disciplinary patterns and social competence in children. *Youth and Society, 9,* 239–276.

Baumrind, D. (1985). Research using intentional deception: Ethical issues revisited. *American Psychologist, 40,* 165–175.

Baumrind, D. (1986). Sex differences in moral reasoning: Response to Walker's conclusion that there are none. *Child Development, 57,* 511–521.

Baumrind, D. (1989). Rearing competent children. In W. Damon (Ed.), *Child development today and tomorrow* (pp. 349–379). San Francisco: Jossey-Bass.

Baumrind, D. (1993). The average expectable environment is not good enough: A response to Scarr. *Child Development, 64,* 1299–1318.

Baumrind, D. (1994). The social context of child maltreatment. *Family Relations, 43,* 360–368.

Baydar, N., & Brooks-Gunn, J. (1991). Effects of maternal employment and child-care arrangements on preschoolers' cognitive and behavioral outcomes: Evidence from the Children of the National Longitudinal Survey of Youth. *Developmental Psychology, 27,* 932–945.

Bayley, N. (1969). *The Bayley Scales of Infant Development.* New York: Psychological Corporation.

Beal, C. R. (1994). *Boys and girls: The development of gender roles.* New York: McGraw-Hill.

Becker, J. (1988). The success of parents' indirect techniques for teaching their preschoolers pragmatic skills. *First Language, 8,* 173–182.

Becker, J. V., Barham, J., Eron, L. D. & Chen, S. A. (1994). The present status and future directions for psychological research on youth violence. In L. D. Eron, J. H. Gentry, & P. Schlegel (Eds.), *Reason to hope: A psychosocial perspective on violence and youth* (pp. 435–447). Washington, DC: American Psychological Association.

Becker, W. C. (1964). Consequences of different kinds of parental discipline. In M. L. Hoffman & H. W. Hoffman (Eds.), *Review of child development research* (Vol. 1). New York: Russell Sage Foundation.

Beilin, H. (1992). Piaget's enduring contribution to developmental psychology. *Developmental Psychology, 28,* 191–205.

Beilin, Y., Leibowitz, A.B., Bernstein, H.H., & Abramovitz, S.E. (1999) Controversies of labor epidural analgesia. *Anesthesia and Analgesia, 89,* 969–978.

Belkin, L. (1997, October 26). Pregnant with complications. *New York Times Magazine,* pp. 34–40+.

Bell, A., Weinberg, M., & Hammersmith, S. (1981). *Sexual preference: Its development in men and women.* Bloomington: Indiana University Press.

Bell, C. (1995, January 6). Exposure to violence distresses children and may lead to their becoming violent. *Psychiatric News,* pp. 6–8, 15.

Bell, R. Q. (1968). A reinterpretation of the direction of effects in socialization. *Psychological Review, 75,* 81–95.

Bell, R. Q. (1979). Parent, child, and reciprocal influences. *American Psychologist, 34,* 821–827.

Bell, S. M., & Ainsworth, M. D. (1972). Infant crying and maternal responsiveness. *Child Development, 43,* 1171–1190.

Bellamy, C. (1996). *The state of the world's children, 1996.* Oxford: Oxford University Press.

Belsky, J. (1984). The determinants of parenting: A process model. *Child Development, 55,* 83–96.

Belsky, J. (1988). The "effects" of infant day care reconsidered. *Early Childhood Research Quarterly, 3,* 235–273.

Belsky, J. (1996). Parent, infant, and social-contextual antecedents of father-son attachment security. *Developmental Psychology, 32,* 905–913.

Belsky, J. (1997). Theory testing, effect-size evaluation, and differential susceptibility to rearing influence: The case of mothering and attachment. *Child Development, 68,* 598–600.

Belsky, J., & Cassidy, J. (1994) Attachment: Theory and evidence. in M. Rutter, D. Hay, & S.K. Baron-Cohen (Eds.). *Developmental principles and clinical issues in psychology and psychiatry.* Oxford: Blackwell, Science Publishers.

Belsky, J., & Most, R. K. (1982). Infant exploration and play. In J. Belsky (Ed.), *In the beginning* (pp. 109–121). New York: Columbia University Press.

Belsky, J., & Rovine, M. (1987). Temperament and attachment security in the strange situation: An empirical rapprochement. *Child Development*, 58, 787–795.

Belsky, J., & Steinberg, L. D. (1979, July–August). What does research teach us about day care? *Children Today*, pp. 21–26.

Belsky, J., Campbell, S. B., Cohn, J. F., & Moore, G. (1996). Instability of infant-parent attachment security. *Developmental Psychology*, 32, 921–924.

Belsky, J., Steinberg, L., & Draper, P. (1991). Childhood experience, interpersonal development, and reproductive strategy: An evolutionary theory of socialization. *Child Development*, 62, 647–670.

Belsky, J., Woodworth, S., & Crnic, K. (1996). Trouble in the second year: Three questions about family interaction. *Child Development*, 67, 556–578.

Bem, S. L. (1993). *The lenses of gender: Transforming the debate on sexual inequality.* New Haven, CT: Yale University Press.

Bem, S. L. (1981). Gender schema theory: A cognitive account of sex typing. *Psychological Review*, 88, 354–364.

Benbow, C. P. (1991). Mathematically talented children: Can acceleration meet their educational needs? In N. Colangelo & G. Davis (Eds.), *Handbook of gifted education* (pp. 154–166). Needham Heights, MA: Allyn & Bacon.

Bendersky, M., & Lewis, M. (1998) Arousal modulation in cocaine-exposed infants. *Developmental Psychology*, 34, 555–565

Bennett, J. C. (1990). Nonintervention into siblings' fighting as a catalyst for learned helplessness. *Psychological Reports*, 66, 139–145.

Benoit, D., & Parker, K. (1994). Stability and transmission of attachment across three generations. *Child Development*, 65, 1444–1456.

Benson, J. B., Cherny, S. S., Haith, M. M., & Fulker, D. W. (1993). Rapid assessment of infant predictors of adult IQ: Midtwin-midparent analyses. *Developmental Psychology*, 29, 434–447.

Benson, P. L. (1993). *The troubled journey: A portrait of 6th–12th grade youth.* Minneapolis, MN: Search Institute.

Benson, P., Donahue, M., & Erickson, J. (1989). Adolescence and religion: Review of the literature from 1970–1986. *Research in the Social Scientific Study of Religion*, 1, 153–181.

Berenbaum, S. A., & Hines, M. (1992). Early androgens are related to childhood sex-typed toy preferences. *Psychological Science, 3*, 203–206.

Berenbaum, S. A., & Snyder, E. (1995). Early hormonal influences on childhood sex-typed activity and playmate preferences: implications for the development of sexual orientation. *Developmental Psychology*, 31, 31–42.

Berenson, G., Frank, G., Hunter, S., Srinivasan, S., Voors, A., & Webber, L. (1982). Cardiovascular risk factors in children: Should they concern the pediatrician. *American Journal of Diseases of Children*, 136, 855–862.

Berg, F. (1992 July/August). Harmful weight loss practices are widespread among adolescents. *HWJ Obesity & Health*, 6, 69–72.

Berg, F. M. (1995). Health risks of weight loss. *Healthy Weight Journal.* Hettinger, ND: Healthy Living Institute.

Berg, W. K., & Berg, K. M. (1979). Psychophysiological development in infancy: State, sensory functioning, and attention. In J. Osofsky (Ed.), *Handbook of infant development* (pp. 283–344). New York: Wiley.

Berg, W. K., Adkinson, C. D., & Strock, B. D. (1973). Duration and frequency of periods of alertness in the newborn. *Developmental Psychology*, 9, 434.

Berger, C. S., Sorensen, L., Gendler, B., & Fitzsimmons, J. (1990). Cocaine and pregnancy: A challenge for health care providers. *Health and Social Work*, 15, 310–316.

Berger, E. P. (1995). *Parents as partners in education* (4th ed.). Upper Saddle River, NJ: Prentice Hall.

Berk, L.E. (1992) Children's private speech: An overview of theory and the status of research. in R.M. Diaz & L.E. Berk (Eds). *Private speech: from social interaction to self-regulation* (pp.17–54) Hillsdale, NJ: Erlbaum.

Berko, J. (1958) The child's learning of English morphology. *Word*, 14, 159–177.

Berkowitz, G. S., Skovron, M. L., Lapinski, R. H., & Berkowitz, R. L. (1990). Delayed childbearing and the outcome of pregnancy. *New England Journal of Medicine*, 322, 659–663.

Berlyne, D. E. (1960). *Conflict, arousal, and curiosity.* New York: McGraw-Hill.

Berman, A. L., & Jobes, D. A. (1995). Suicide prevention in adolescents (age 12–18). *Suicide and Life Threatening Behaviors*, 25, 143–154.

Bernard, H. S. (1981). Identity formation during late adolescence: A review of some empirical finding. *Adolescence*, 16, 349–356.

Berndt, T. J. (1979). Developmental changes in conformity to peers and parents. *Developmental Psychology*, 15, 608–617.

Berndt, T. J. (1981). Relations between social cognition, nonsocial cognition, and social behavior: The case of friendship. In J. H. Flavell & L. Ross (Eds.), *Social cognitive development.* Cambridge: Cambridge University Press.

Berndt, T. J. (1989). Friendships in childhood and adolescence. In W. Damon (Ed.), *Child development: Today and tomorrow* (pp. 332–349). San Francisco: Jossey-Bass.

Berndt, T. J., & Hoyle, S. G. (1985). Stability and change in childhood and adolescent friendship. *Developmental Psychology*, 21, 1007–1015.

Berndt, T. J., & Keefe, K. (1995). Friends' influence on adolescents' adjustment to school. *Child Development*, 66, 1312–1329.

Bernhardt, B., & Rauch, J.B. (1993) Genetic family histories: an aid to social work assessment. *Families in Society*, 74, 195–205.

Bertenthal, B. L. & Bai, D. L. (1989). Infants' sensitivity to optical flow for controlling posture. *Developmental Psychology*, 25, 936–945.

Bertenthal, B. L. & Campos, J. J. (1987). New directions in the study of early experience. *Child Development*, 58, 560–567.

Besharov, D. J. (1989, Fall). Children of crack. *Public Welfare*, pp. 6–11.

Bettelheim, A. (1998, Dec.4). AIDS update. *CQ Researcher*, 8, 1051-1066.

Beyth-Marom, R., Austin, L., Fischoff, B., Palmgren, C., & Jacobs-Quadrel, M. (1993). Perceived consequences of risky behaviors: Adults and adolescents. *Developmental Psychology*, 29, 549–563.

Bhatt, R. S., & Rovee-Collier, C. (1996). Infants' forgetting of correlated attributes and object recognition. *Child Development*, pp. 172–187.

Bigelow, B. J., & La Gaipa, J. J. (1975). Children's written descriptions of friendship: A multidimensional analysis. *Developmental Psychology*, 11, 857–858.

Bigner, J. J. (1994). *Parent-child relations: An introduction to parenting* (4th ed.). New York: Macmillan.

Bilchik, S. (1995). *Delinquency prevention works.* Washington, DC: Office of Juvenile Justice and Delinquency Prevention, U.S. Justice Department.

Biller, H. B. (1982). Fatherhood: Implications for child and adult development. In B. B. Wolman (Ed.), *Handbook of development psychology* (pp. 702–720). Upper Saddle River, NJ: Prentice Hall.

Bingham, C. R., & Crockett, L. J. (1996). Longitudinal adjustment patterns of boys and girls experiencing early, middle and late sexual intercourse. *Developmental Psychology*, 32, 647–658.

Birch, H. G. (1971, March). Functional effects of fetal malnutrition. *Hospital Practice*, pp. 1134–1148.

Birch, L. L. (1979). Preschool children's food preferences and consumption patterns. *Journal of Nutrition Education*, 11, 189–192.

Birch, L. L. (1986). Children's food preferences: Developmental patterns and environmental influences. In G. Whitehurst & R. Vasta (Eds.), *Annals of child development* (Vol. 4). Greenwich, CT: JAI.

Birch, L. L. (1987). The acquisition of food acceptance patterns in children. In R. A. Boakes, D. A. Popplewell, & M. J. Burton (Eds.), *Eating habits: Food, physiology and learned behavior.* New York: Wiley.

Birch, L. L., & Fisher, J. A. (1996). The role of experience in the development of children's eating behavior. In E. D. Capaldi (Ed.), (pp. 113–145). Washington, DC: American Psychological Association.

Birch, L. L., Johnson, S. L., Andresen, G., Petersen, J. C. & Schulte, M. C. (1991). The variability of young children's energy intake. *New England Journal of Medicine, 324,* 232–235.

Birch, L. L., Johnson, S. L., Jones, M. B., & Peters, J. C. (1993). Effects of a non-energy fat substitute on children's energy and macronutrient intake. *American Journal of Clinical Nutrition, 58,* 326–333.

Birch, L. L., McPhee, L., Shoba, B. C., Pirok, E., & Steinberg, L. (1987). What kind of exposure reduces children's food neophobia? *Appetite, 9,* 171–178.

Biro, F. M., & Rosenthal, S. L. (1992). Psychological sequelae of sexually transmitted diseases in adolescents. *Obstetric and Gynecologic Clinics of North America, 19,* 209–218.

Bisanz, J. Morrison, F.J., & Dunn, M. (1995) Effects of age and schooling on the acquisition of elementary quantitative skills. *Developmental Psychology, 31,* 221–236.

Bishop, J. A., & Inderbitzen, H. M. (1995). Peer acceptance and friendship: An investigation of their relation to self-esteem. *Journal of Early Adolescence, 15,* 476–489.

Bjorklund, D. E. (1995). *Children's thinking: Developmental function and individual differences.* Pacific Grove, CA: Brooks/Cole.

Bjorklund, D. F., & Green, B. L. (1992). The adaptive nature of cognitive immaturity. *American Psychologist, 47,* 46–54.

Black, J. K., & Puckett, M. B. (1996). *The young child: Development from prebirth through age eight.* Upper Saddle River, NJ: Merrill/Prentice Hall.

Blackburn, B. (1997, September 24). Moms starting families in 40s test odds. *USA Today,* p. A14.

Blakemore, J. E. O. (1981). Age and sex differences in interaction with a human infant. *Child Development, 52,* 386–388.

Blakeslee, S. (1986, October 7). Fetus returned to womb following surgery. *New York Times,* p. C1.

Blakeslee, S. (1989, February 14). Crib death: Suspicion turns to the brain. *New York Times,* pp. C1, C3.

Blakeslee, S. (1991, January 1). Research on birth defects turns to flaws in sperm. *New York Times,* p. B1+.

Blanton, H., & Gerrard, M. (1997). Effect of sexual motivation on men's risk perception for sexually transmitted disease: there must be 50 ways to justify a lover. *Health Psychology, 16,* 374–379.

Blasi, A. (1980). Bridging moral cognition and moral action: A critical review of the literature. *Psychological Bulletin, 88,* 1–45.

Blass, E. M., Ganchrow, J. R., & Steiner, J. E. (1984). Classical conditioning in newborn humans 2–48 hours of age. *Infant Behavior and Development, 7,* 223–235.

Blewitt, P. (1994). Understanding categorical hierarchies: The earliest levels of skill. *Child Development, 65,* 1279–1298.

Block, J. H. (1976). Assessing sex differences: Issues, problems, and pitfalls. *Merrill-Palmer Quarterly, 22,* 283–308.

Block, J.H. (1983) Differential premises arising from differential socialization of the sexes: Some conjectures. *Child development, 54,* 1335–1354.

Block, J. H. (1979). Socialization influences on personality development in males and females. *American Psychological Association's Master Lecture Series.* Washington, DC: American Psychological Association.

Block, J. H., Block, J., & Gjerde, P. F. (1986). The personality of children prior to divorce: A prospective study. *Child Development, 57,* 827–840.

Block, J. H., & Robins, R.W. (1993). A longitudinal study of consistency and change in self-esteem from early adolescence to early adulthood. *Child Development, 54,* 1335–1354.

Block, J., Block, J. H., & Keyes, S. (1988). Longitudinally foretelling drug usage in adolescence: Early childhood personality and environmental precursors. *Child Development, 59,* 336–355.

Bloom, L. (1998). Language acquisition in its developmental context. In W. Damon (Ed.), *Handbook of child psychology* (4th ed., Vol. 2, pp. 309–370). New York: Wiley.

Bloom, L. M. (1975). Language development. In F. D. Horowitz (Ed.), *Review of child development research* (Vol. 4). Chicago: University of Chicago Press.

Bloom, L., Margulis, C., Tinker, E, & Fujita, N. (1996). Early conversation and word learning: Contributions from children and adults. *Child Development, 67,* 3154–3166.

Blumberg, M. L., & Lester, D. (1991). High school and college students' attitudes towards rape. *Adolescence, 26,* 727–720.

Blyth, D. A., Simmons, R. G., & Zakin, D. F. (1985). Satisfaction with body image for early adolescent females: the impact of pubertal timing within different school environments. *Journal of Youth and Adolescence, 14,* 207–225.

Boeck, S., & Lynn, G. (1995, December. 27). Why teens choice to use. *USA Today,* p. 1A.

Bogatz, G., & Ball, S. (1971). *The second year of "Sesame Street": A continuing evaluation.* Princeton, NJ: Educational Testing Service.

Bogenschneider, K., Wu, M.Y., Raffaelli, M., & Tsay, J. C. (1998). Parent influences on adolescent peer orientation and substance use: The interface of parenting practices and values. *Child Development, 69,* 1672–1688.

Bohannon, J. N., & Marquis, A. L. (1977). Children's control of Adult Speech. *Child Development, 48,* 1002–1008.

Bohannon, J. N., & Stanowicz, L. (1988). The issue of negative evidence: Adult responses to children's language errors. *Developmental Psychology, 24,* 684–689.

Bohannon, J. N., MacWhinney, B., & Snow, C. (1990). No negative evidence revisited: Beyond learnability—or who has to prove what to whom. *Developmental Psychology, 26,* 221–227.

Bohannon, J. N., Padgett, R. J., Nelson, K. E., & Mark, M. (1996). Useful evidence on negative evidence. *Developmental Psychology, 32,* 551–555.

Bolero, J. M., Moore, S. M., & Rosenthal, D. A. (1992). Intention, context, and safe sex: Australian adolescents' response to AIDS. *Journal of Applied Social Psychology, 22,* 1357–1397.

Bolger, K.E., Patterson, C.J., & Kupersmidt, J.B. (1998) Peer relationships and self-esteem among children who have been maltreated. *Child Development, 69,* 1171-1197.

Bolognini, M., Plancherel, B., Bettschart, W., & Halfon, O. (1996). Self-esteem and mental health in early adolescence: Development and gender differences. *Journal of Adolescence, 19,* 233–245.

Bornstein, M. H. (1991). Approaches to parenting in culture. In M.H. Bornstein (Ed.), *Cultural approaches to parenting* (pp. 3–19). Hillsdale, NJ: Erlbaum.

Bornstein, M. H. (1995). Parenting infants. In M. H. Bornstein (Ed.), *Handbook of parenting* (pp. 3–41). Mahwah, NJ: Erlbaum.

Bornstein, M.H., Haynes, O.M., Azuma, H., Galperin, C., Maital, S., Ogino, M., Painter, K., Pascual, L., Pecheux, M.G., Rahn, C., Toda, S., Venuti, P., Vyt, A., & Wright, B. (1998) A cross-national study of self-evaluations and attributions in parenting: Argentina, Belgium, France, Israel, Italy, Japan, and the United States. *Developmental Psychology, 34,* 687–697.

Borstelmann, L. J. (1983). Children before psychology: Ideas about children from antiquity to the late 1800s. In P. H. Mussen (Ed.), *Handbook of child psychology* (4th ed., Vol. 1, pp. 1–41). New York: Wiley.

Bouchard, T. J. (1984). Twins reared together and apart: What they tell us about human diversity. In S. W. Fox (Ed.), *Individuality and determinism.* New York: Plenum.

Bouchard, T. J., Lykken, D. T., McGue, M., Segal, & Tellegen, A. (1990). Sources of human psychological differences: The Minnesota study of twins reared apart. *Science, 250,* 223–228.

Boulton, M. J. (1992). Participation in playground activities at middle school. *Educational Research, 34,* 167–182.

Boulton, M. J. (1993). Proximate causes of aggressive fighting in middle school children. *British Journal of Educational Psychology, 63,* 231–244.

Bowerman, M. (1981). Language development. In H. C. Triandis & A. Heron (Eds.), *Handbook of cross-cultural psychology* (Vol. 4, pp. 93–187). Boston: Allyn & Bacon.

Bowerman, M., De Leon, L., & Choi, S. (1995). Verbs, particles, and spatial semantics: learning to talk about spatial actions in typologically different languages. In E. V. Clark (Ed.), *The child language research forum* (pp. 101–111). N.p.: Center for the Study of Language and Information, Leland Stanford Junior University.

Bowlby, J. (1969). *Attachment and loss*. New York: Basic Books.

Bowlby, J. (1980). *Attachment and loss: Vol. 3. Sadness and depression*. New York: Basic Books.

Bowlby, J. (1982). Attachment and loss: Retrospect and prospect. *American Journal of Orthopsychiatry, 52*, 664–678.

Boyatzis, C. J., Matillo, G. M., & Nesbitt, K. M. (1995). Effects of "The Mighty Morphin Power Rangers" on children's aggression with peers. *Child Study Journal, 22*, 45–55.

Bracey, G. W. (1996). 75 years of elementary education. *Principal, 75*, 17–21.

Brack, C. J., Orr, D. P., & Ingersoll, G. (1988). Pubertal maturation and self-esteem. *Journal of Adolescent Health Care, 9*, 280–285.

Brackbill, Y. (1979). Obstetrical medication and infant behavior. In J. D. Osofsky (Ed.), *Handbook of Infant development* (pp. 76–125). New York: Wiley.

Brackbill, Y. (1982). Lasting effects of obstetrical medication on children. In J. Belsky (Ed.), *In the beginning* (pp. 50–55). New York: Columbia University Press.

Bradley, R. H. & Caldwell, B. M. (1980). The relation of home environment, cognitive competence and IQ among males and females. *Child Development, 51*, 1140–1148.

Bradley, R. H. (1989). Home measurement of maternal responsiveness. In M. H. Bornstein (Ed.), *Maternal responsiveness: Characteristics and consequences* (pp. 63–75). San Francisco: Jossey-Bass.

Bradley, R. H. (1995). Environment and parenting. In M. H. Bornstein (Ed.), *Handbook of parenting* (Vol. 2, pp. 235–261). Mahwah, NJ: Erlbaum.

Bradsher, K. (1995, October 27). Widest gap in incomes? Research points to U.S. *New York Times*, p. D2.

Brainerd, C. J. (1978). *Piaget's theory of intelligence*. Upper Saddle River, NJ: Prentice Hall.

Brainerd, C. J., & Reyna, V. F. (1995). Learning rate, learning opportunities, and the development of forgetting. *Developmental Psychology, 31*, 251–262.

Brand, E., Clingempeel, W. E., & Bowen-Woodward, K. (1988). Family relationships and children's psychological adjustment in stepmother and stepfather families: Findings and conclusions from the Philadelphia Stepfamily Research Project. In E. M. Heatherington & J. D. Arasteh (Eds.), *Impact of divorce, single parenting and stepparenting on children* (pp. 299–324). Hillsdale, NJ: Erlbaum.

Bray, J. H, & Hetherington, E. M. (1993). Families in transition: Introduction and overview. *Journal of Family Psychology, 7*, 3–8.

Bray, J. H. (1988). Children's development during early remarriage. In E. M. Hetherington & J. D. Arasteh (Eds.), *Impact of divorce, single parenting and stepparenting on children* (pp. 279–298). Hillsdale, NJ: Erlbaum.

Bray, J.H. & Berger, S.H. (1993) Developmental issues in stepfamilies research project: Family relationships and parent-child interactions. *Journal of Family Psychology, 7*, 1–17.

Brazelton, T. B. (1981). *On becoming a family: The growth of attachment*. New York: Delacorte.

Brazelton, T. B. (1990). Saving the Bathwater. *Child Development, 61*, 1661–1671

Bremner, J. G. (1988). *Infancy*. New York: Blackwell.

Brems, C., Baldwin, M., & Baxter, S. (1993). Empirical evaluation of a self psychologically oriented parent education program. *Family Relations, 42*, 26–30.

Brenneman, K., & Gelman, R. (1993, March). Reasoning about object identifies in the appearance-reality situation. Cited in Rice, C., et al. When 3-year-olds pass the appearance-reality test. *Developmental Psychology, 33*, 54–61.

Brenner, R. A., Simons-Morton, B. G., Bhaskar, B., Mehta, N., Melnick, V. L., Revenis, M., Berendes, H. W., & Clemens, J. D. (1998, July 22/29). Prevalence and predictors of the prone sleep position among inner-city infants. *Journal of the American Medical Association, 280*, 341–346.

Brent, D. A. (1995). Risk factors for adolescent suicide and suicidal behavior; Mental and substance abuse disorders, family environmental factors and life stress. *Suicide and Life Threatening Behaviors, 25*, 52–63.

Brent, D. A., Perper, J. A., Moritz, G., Allman, C. J., Friend, A., Roth, C., Schweers, J., Balach, L., & Baugher, M. (1993). Psychiatric risk factors for adolescent suicide: A case control study. *Journal of the American Academy of Child and Adolescent Psychiatry, 32*, 521–529.

Breznitz, Z., & Teltsch, T. (1989). The effect of school entrance age on academic achievement and social-emotional adjustment of children: Follow-up study of fourth graders. *Psychology in the Schools, 26*, 62–68.

Brickey, M., & Campbell, K. (1981). Fast food employment for moderately and mildly mentally retarded adults. *Mental Retardation, 19*, 113–116.

Bridges, F. A., & Cicchetti, D. (1982). Mothers' ratings of the temperament characteristics of Down's syndrome infants. *Developmental Psychology, 18*, 238–244.

Bridges, L. J., Connell, J. P., & Belsky, J. (1988). Similarities and differences in infant-mother and infant-father interaction in the strange situation: A component process analysis. *Developmental Psychology, 24*, 92–101.

Brierly, J. (1976). *The growing brain*. Windsor, England: NFER.

Brittain, C. V. (1963). Adolescent choices and parent-peer cross-pressures. *American Sociological Review, 28*, 385–391.

Broberg, A. G., Wessels, H., Lamb, M. E., & Hwang, C. P. (1997). Effects of day care on the development of cognitive abilities in 8-year olds: A longitudinal study. *Developmental Psychology, 33*, 62–69.

Brody, G. H., & Forehand, R. (1988). Multiple determinants of parenting: Research findings and implications of the divorce process. In E. M. Hetherington & J. D. Arasteh (Eds.), *Impact of Divorce, single parenting, and stepparenting on children* (pp. 117–135). Hillsdale, NJ: Erlbaum.

Brody, G. H., Stoneman, Z., & Burke, M. (1987). Family system and individual child correlates of sibling behavior. *American Journal of Orthopsychiatry, 57*, 561–569.

Brody, G. H., Stoneman, Z., & MacKinnon, C. (1986). Contributions of maternal childrearing practices and play concepts to sibling interactions. *Journal of Applied Developmental Psychology, 7*, 225–236.

Brody, G. H., Stoneman, Z., & McCoy, J. K. (1992). Associations of maternal and paternal direct and differential behavior with sibling relationships: Contemporaneous and longitudinal analyses. *Child Development, 63*, 391–400.

Brody, G. H., Zolinda, S., MacKinnon, C. E., & MacKinnon, R. (1985). Role relationships and behavior between preschool-aged and school-aged siblings. *Developmental Psychology, 21*, 124–129.

Brody, J. E. (1980). Tending to obesity, inbred tribe aids diabetes study. *New York Times*, pp. C1, C5.

Brody, J. E. (1989, August 10). Breast feeding. *New York Times*, p. B10.

Brody, J. E. (1990, May 24). Preventing children from joining yet another unfit generation. *New York Times*, p. B14.

Brody, R. (1981). Visual short-term memory in infancy. *Child Development, 52*, 242–250.

Bronfenbrenner, U. (1979). *The ecology of human development*. Cambridge, MA: Harvard University Press.

Bronfenbrenner, U. (1986). Ecology of the family as a context for human development: Research perspectives. *Developmental Psychology, 22*, 723–743.

Bronfenbrenner, U., & Ceci, S. J. (1994). Nature-nurture reconceptualized in developmental perspective: A bioecological mode. *Psychological Review*, 101, 568–586.

Bronfenbrenner, U., & Crouter, A. C. (1983). The evolution of environmental models in developmental research. In P. H. Mussen (Ed.), *Handbook of child development* (4th ed., pp.357–415). New York: Wiley.

Bronfenbrenner, U., & Morris, P. A. (1998). The ecology of developmental processes. In W. Damon (Editor in Chief) & R. M. Lerner (Vol. Ed.), *Handbook of child psychology* (5th ed., Vol. 1, pp. 993–1028). New York: Wiley.

Bronson, G. (1968). The development of fear. *Child Development*, 39, 409–432.

Bronson, G. W. (1994). Infants' transitions toward adult-like scanning. *Child Development*, 65, 1243–1261.

Bronstein, P., Stoll, M., Caluson, J. A., Abrams, C. L., & Briones, M. (1994). Fathering after separation or divorce: Factors predicting children's adjustment. *Family Relations*, 43, 460–473.

Brook, J. S., Nomura, C., & Cohen, P. (1989). Prenatal, perinatal, and early childhood risk factors and drug involvement in adolescence. *Genetic, Social, and General Psychology Monographs*, 115, 221–241.

Brook, J. S., Whiteman, M., Balka, E. B., Win, P., & Gursen, M.D. (1997). African-American and Puerto Rican drug use: A longitudinal study. *Journal of the American Academy of Child and Adolescent Psychiatry*, 36, 1260–1268.

Brook, J. S., Whiteman, M., Brook, D. W., & Gordon, A. S. (1981). Paternal determinants of male adolescent marijuana use. *Developmental Psychology*, 17, 841–847.

Brooke, H. (1996, March/April). Sudden infant death syndrome. *World Health*, 49, 16–17.

Brookins, C. C. (1997). Promoting ethnic identity development in African American youth: The role of rites of passage. *Journal of Black Psychology*, 22, 388–417.

Brooks, R. B. (1994). Children at risk: Fostering resilience and hope. *American Journal of Orthopsychiatry*, 64, 545–553.

Brooks, R. B. (1992). Self-esteem during the school years: Its normal development and hazardous decline. *Pediatric Clinics of North America*, 39, 537–550.

Brooks-Gunn, J., & Furstenberg, F. F. (1989). Adolescent sexual behavior. *American Psychologist*, 44, 249–157.

Brooks-Gunn, J., Guo, G., & Furstenberg, F. F. (1989). Who drops out of and who continues beyond high school? A twenty-year follow-up of black urban youth. *Journal of Research on Adolescence*, 3, 271–294.

Brooks-Gunn, J., Klebanov, P. K., & Duncan, G. J. (1996). Ethnic differences in children's intelligence test scores: Role of economic deprivation, home environment, and maternal characteristics. *Child Development*, 67, 396–409.

Brooks-Gunn, J., Klebanov, P., & Liaw, F. (1995). The learning, physical, and emotional environment of the home in the context of poverty: The Infant Health and Development Program. *Journal of Research on Adolescence*, 3, 271–294.

Brooks-Gunn, J., & Petersen, A. C. (1984). Problems in studying and defining pubertal events. *Journal of Youth and Adolescence*, 13, 181–196.

Brooks-Gunn, J., & Ruble, D. N. (1982). The development of menstrual-related beliefs and behavior during adolescence. *Child Development*, 53, 1567–1577.

Brooks-Gunn, J., & Warren, M. P. (1988). Mother-daughter differences in menarcheal age in adolescent dancers and nondancers. *Annals of Human Biology*, 15, 35–43.

Brooten, D., & Jordan, C. (1983) Caffeine and pregnancy: A research review and recommendations for clinical practice. *JOGN Nursing*, 12, 190–195

Brown, A. L., Bransford, J. D., Ferrara, R. A., & Campione, J. C. (1983). Learning, remembering, and understanding. In J. H. Flavell & E. M. Markman (Eds.), *Handbook of child psychology* (4th ed., pp. 77–167). New York: Wiley.

Brown, B. B., Clasen, D. R., & Eicher, S. A. (1986). Perceptions of peer pressure, peer conformity, dispositions, and self-reported behavior among adolescents. *Developmental Psychology*, 22, 521–530.

Brown, B. R., Baranowski, M. D., Kulig, J. W., & Stephenson, J. N. (1996). Searching for the Magic Johnson effect: AIDS, Adolescence, and celebrity disclosure. *Adolescence*, 31, 253–265.

Brown, C. (1993, October 11). The vanished Native Americans. *The Nation*, 257, 384–389.

Brown, F. G. (1983). *Principles of educational and psychological testing*. New York: Holt, Rinehart & Winston.

Brown, J. E. (1995). *Nutrition Now*. St. Paul, MN: West.

Brown, J. M., O'Keeffe, J., Sanders, S. H., & Baker, B. (1986). Developmental changes in children's cognition to stressful and painful situations. *Journal of Pediatric Psychology*, 11, 343–357.

Brown, L. (1995). *Statement by White House drug czar Lee P. Brown on the 1995 Monitoring the Future survey*, Washington, DC: Office of National Drug Control Policy.

Brown, R. (1973). Development of the first language in the human species. *American Psychologist*, 28, 97–106.

Browne, A., & Bassuk, B. A. (1997). Intimate violence in the lives of homeless and poor housed women: Prevalence and patterns in an ethnically diverse sample. *American Journal of Orthopsychiatry*, 67, 261–278.

Bruch, H. (1978). *The golden cage: The enigma of anorexia nervosa*. Cambridge, MA: Harvard University Press.

Bruch, H. (1986). Anorexia nervosa: The therapeutic task. In K. D. Brownell & J. P. Forey (Eds.), *Handbook of eating disorders: Physiology, psychology, and treatment of obesity, anorexia, and bulimia*. New York: Basic Books.

Bruck, M., & Ceci, S. J. (1995). Amicus brief for the case of Sate of New Jersey v Michaels presented by Committee of Concerned Social Scientists. *Psychology, Public Policy, and Law*, 1, 272–322.

Bruner, J. (1972). The nature and uses of immaturity. *American Psychologist*, 27, 687–708.

Bruner, J. (1978a). Learning how to do things with words. In J. S. Bruner & A. Garton (Eds.), *Human growth and development: Wolfson College lectures* (pp. 62–85). Oxford: Clarendon.

Bruner, J. (1978b, September). Learning the mother tongue. *Human Nature*, pp. 11–19.

Bruner, J. S. (1983). The acquisition of pragmatics commitments. In R. M. Golinkoff (Ed.), *The transition from prelinguistic to linguistic communication* (pp. 27–42). Hillsdale, NJ: Erlbaum.

Brunner, C., & Bennett, D. (1997). Technology perceptions by gender. *NASSSP Bulletin*, 81, 46–51.

Bruskin/Goldring Research, Parental Discipline. (1993, may 19). *Education Week*, p. 3.

Bryan, A. D., Aiken, L. S., & West, S. G. (1997). Young women's condom use: The influence of acceptance of sexuality, control over sexual encounter, and perceived susceptibility to common STDs. *Health Psychology*, 16, 468–479.

Bryant, D. M., Burchinal, M., Lau, L. B., & Sparling, J. J. (1994). Family and classroom correlates of Head Start children's developmental outcomes. *Early Childhood Research Quarterly*, 9, 289–309.

Brynie, F. H. (1995). *Genetics and human health*. Brookfield, CT: Millbrook.

Buchanan, C. M., Eccles, J. S., & Becker, J. B. (1992). Are adolescents the victims of raging hormones. Evidence for activation effects of hormones on moods and behaviors at adolescence. *Psychological Bulletin*, 111, 62–107.

Buckner, J. C., Bassuk, E. L., Weinreb, L. F., & Brooks, M. G. (1999). Homelessness and its relation to the mental health and behavior of low-income school-age children. *Developmental Psychology*, 35, 246–257.

Bugental, D. B., & Goodnow, J. J. (1998). Socialization processes. In W. Damon (Editor in Chief) & N. Eisenberg (Vol. Ed.), *Handbook of child psychology* (5th ed., Vol. 3, pp. 389–462). New York: Wiley.

Bugental, D. B., & Goodnow, J. J. (1998). Socialization processes. In W. Damon (Editor in Chief) & N. Eisenberg (Vol. Ed.), *Handbook of child psychology* (5th ed., Vol. 3, pp. 369–463). New York: Wiley

Buis, J. M., & Thompson, D. N. (1989). Imaginary audience and personal fable: A brief review. *Adolescence*, 24, 773–781.

Bullock, M. (1985). Animism in childhood thinking: A new look at an old question. *Developmental Psychology, 21,* 217–226.

Bullock, M., & Lutkenhaus, P. (1988). The development of volitional behavior in the toddler years. *Child Development, 59,* 664–675.

Bulmer, M. G. (1970). *The biology of twinning in man.* London: Oxford University Press.

Burcham, B., & Carlson, L. (1995, March). Attention deficit hyperactivity disorder. *Education Digest,* pp. 42–44.

Burchinal, M. R., Campbell, F. A., Bryant, D. M., Wasik, B. H., & Ramey, C. T. (1997). Early intervention and mediating processes in cognitive performance of children of low-income African American families. *Child Development, 68,* 955–970.

Burchinal, M. R., Ramey, S. L., Reid, M. K., & Jaccard, J. (1995). Early child care experiences and their association with family and child characteristics during middle childhood. *Early Childhood Research Quarterly, 10,* 33–61.

Burchinal, M. R., Roberts, J. E., Nabors, L. A., & Bryant, D. M. (1996). Quality of center child care and infant cognitive and language development. *Child Development, 67,* 606–620.

Burchinal, M., Lee, M., & Ramey, C. (1989). Type of day-care and preschool intellectual development in disadvantaged children. *Child Development, 60,* 128–138.

Burke, J. R. (1990, July 13). "Super" son, 5, aids mother by dialing 911. *Newsday,* pp. 20, 26.

Burnett, P. C. (1986). Evaluation of Adlerian parenting programs. *Individual Psychology, 44,* 63–76.

Burnette, E. (1995, June). Black males retrieve a noble heritage. *APA Monitor,* pp. 1 & 32.

Burnham, D. K., & Harris, M. B. (1992). Effects of real gender and labeled gender on adults' perceptions of infants. *Journal of Genetic Psychology, 153,* 165–183.

Burns, A., & Scott, C. (1994). *Mother-headed families and why they have increased.* Hillsdale, NJ: Erlbaum.

Burns, K., Chethik, L., Burns, W., & Clark, R. (1991). Dyadic disturbances in cocaine-abusing mothers and their infants. *Journal of Clinical Psychology, 47,* 316–319.

Burns, R. B. (1979). *The self-concept: Theory, measurement, development, and behavior.* New York: Longman.

Burton, R. V. (1963). Generality of honesty reconsidered. *Psychological Review, 70,* 481–499.

Bushnell, I. W. R., Sai, F., & Mullin, J. T. (1989). Neonatal recognition of the mother's face. *British Journal of Developmental Psychology, 7,* 3–15.

Buskens, E., Steyerberg, E. W., Hess, J., Wladimiroff, J. W., & Grobbee, D. E. (1997). Routine prenatal screening for congenital heart disease: What can be expected? A decision-analytic approach. *American Journal of Public Health, 76,* 962–966.

Buss, A. H., & Plomin, R. (1984). *Temperament: Early developing personality traits.* Hillsdale, NJ: Erlbaum.

Bussey, K., & Bandura, A. (1984). Influence of gender constancy and social power on sex-linked modeling. *Journal of Personality and Social Psychology, 47,* 1292–1302.

Butler, D. L. (1995). Promoting strategic learning by postsecondary students with learning disabilities. *Journal of Learning Disabilities, 28,* 170–190.

Butler, N., Goldstein, H., & Ross, K. (1972). Smoking in pregnancy and subsequent child development. *British Journal of Medicine, 4,* 573–575.

Butterfield, E. C., & Siperstein, G. N. (1972). Influence of contingent auditory stimulation upon non-nutritional suckle. In J. F. Bosma (Ed.), *Third symposium on oral sensation and perception: The mouth of the infant.* Springfield, IL: Thomas.

Bybee, J., Glock, M., & Zigler, E. (1990). Differences across gender, grade level, and academic track in the content of the ideal self-image. *Sex Roles, 22,* 349–359.

Byrnes, J. P. (1988). Formal operations; A systematic reformulation. *Developmental Review, 8,* 66–87.

C

Cadoff, J. (1995). Can we prevent SIDS? *Parents,* 30–32.

Cahan, S., & Cohen, N. (1989). Age versus schooling effects on intelligence development. *Child Development, 60,* 1239–1249.

Cairns, E., & Dawes, A. (1996). Children: Ethnic and political violence- A commentary. *Child Development, 67,* 129–140.

Cairns, E., McWhirter, L., Duffy, U., & Barry, R. (1990). The stability of self-concept in late adolescence: Gender and situational effects. *Personality and Individual Differences, 11,* 937–944.

Cairns, R. B. (1979). *Social development: The origins and plasticity of interchanges.* San Francisco: Freeman.

Cairns, R. B. (1998). The making of developmental psychology. In W. Damon (Editor in Chief) and R. M. Lerner (Vol. Ed.), *Handbook of child psychology* (5th ed., Vol. 1, pp. 25–105). New York: Wiley.

Cairns, R. B., Cairns, B. D., Neckerman, H. J., Gest, S. D., & Gariepy, J. L. (1988). Social networks and aggressive behavior: Peer support or peer rejection? *Developmental Psychology, 24,* 815–823.

Cairns, R. B., Leung, M. C., Buchanan, L., & Cairns, B. D. (1995). Friendships and social networks in childhood and adolescence: Fluidity, reliability, and interrelations. *Child Development, 66,* 1330–1345.

Caldwell, B. M. (1989). All-day kindergarten-assumptions, precautions, and overgeneralizations. *Early Childhood Research Quarterly, 4,* 261–267.

California State Department of Education. (1990). *Toward a state of esteem: The final report of the task force to promote self-esteem and personal social responsibility.* Sacramento, CA: Author.

Calkins, S., & Fox, N. (1992). The relations among infant temperament, security of attachment, and behavioral inhibition at twenty-four months. *Child Development, 63,* 1456–1472.

Call, J., & Tomasello, M. (1999) A nonverbal false belief task. The performance of children and great apes. *Child Development, 70,* 381–395.

Campbell, F. A., & Ramey, C. T. (1994). Effects of early intervention on intellectual and academic achievement: A follow-up study of children from low-income families. *Child Development, 65,* 684–699.

Campbell, L. P., & Flake, A. E. (1985). Latchkey children—What is the answer? *The Clearing House, 58,* 381–383.

Campbell, R L., & Christopher, J. C. (1996). Moral development theory: a critique of its Kantian presuppositions. *Developmental Review, 16,* 1–47.

Campbell, S. M., Peplau, L. A., & DeBro, S. C. (1992). Women, men and condoms: Attitudes and experiences of heterosexual college students. *Psychology of Women Quarterly, 16,* 273–288.

Campos, J., Langer, A., & Krowitz, A. (1970). Cardiac responses on the visual cliff in prelocomotor human infants. *Science, 170,* 196–197.

Camras, L. A., & Sachs, V. B. (1991). Social referencing and caregiver expressive behavior in a day care setting. *Infant Behavior and Development, 14,* 27–36.

Canetto, S. S. (1997). Meanings of gender and suicidal behavior during adolescence. *Suicide and Life-Threatening Behavior, 27,* 339–351.

Canfield, R.L. & Haith, M.M. (1991) Active expectations in 2-and 3-month old infants: Complex event sequences. *Developmental Psychology, 27,* 198–208.

Capaldi, D. M., Crosby, L., & Stoolmiller, M. (1996). Predicting the timing of first sexual intercourse for at-risk adolescent males. *Child Development, 67,* 344–359.

Capell, E. J., Vugia, D. J., Mordaunt, V. L., Marelich, W. D., Ascher, M. S., Trachtenberg, A. I., Cunningham, G. C., Arnon, S. S., & Kizer, K. W. (1992). Distribution of HIV type 1 infection in childbearing women in California. *Journal of Public Health, 82,* 254–256.

Carbo, M., & Cole, R.W. (1995, January). Nurture love of reading and test scores. *Instructional Leader, 8,* 1–3, 12

Carmody, D. (1988, September 21). Head Start gets credit for rise in scores. *New York Times*, p. B9.

Carnegie Council on Adolescent Development. (1990). *Turning points.* New York: Carnegie Corporation.

Carnegie Council on Adolescent Development. (1994). *A matter of time: Risk and opportunity in the out-of-school hours.* New York: Carnegie Corporation.

Carnegie Council on Adolescent Development. (1995). *Great transitions: Preparing adolescents for the new century.* Washington, DC: Author.

Carney, D. (1996, March 2). Members eye new efforts to police and airways. *Congressional Quarterly Weekly Report, 54,* 553–555.

Carpendale, J. I. M., & Krebs, D. L. (1995). Variations in level of moral judgment as a function of type of dilemma and moral choice. *Journal of Personality, 63,* 289–313.

Carr, J. (1994). Annotation: Long term outcome for people with Down Syndrome. *Journal of Child Psychology, Psychiatry and Allied Disciplines, 35,* 425–439.

Carroll, D. W. (1994). *Psychology of language.* Pacific Grove, CA: Brooks/Cole.

Carruth, B., & Goldberg, D. (1990). Nutritional issues of adolescents. *Journal of Early Adolescence, 10,* 122–140.

Carskadon, M.A. & Mancuso, J. (1988) Daytime sleepiness in high school adolescents: Influence of curfew. *Sleep Research, 17,* 75.

Carskadon, M.A., Acebo, C., Richardson, G.S., Tate, B.A., & Seifer, R. (1997) An approach to studying circadian rhythms of adolescent humans. *Journal of Biological Rhythms, 12,* 278–279.

Carskadon, M.A., Harvey, K. & Duke, P. (1980) Pubertal changes in daytime sleepiness. *Sleep, 2,* 453–460.

Carskadon, M.A. (1990) Patterns of sleep and sleepiness in adolescents. *Pediatrician, 17,* 5–12.

Carter, D. B., & Levy, G. D. (1988). Cognitive aspects of children's early sex-role development: The influence of gender schemas on preschoolers' memories and preferences for sex-typed toys and activities. *Child Development, 59,* 782–793.

Carter, D. B., & Patterson, C. J. (1982). Sex roles as social conventions: The development of children's conceptions of sex-role stereotypes. *Developmental Psychology, 18,* 812–825.

Carver, V. C., Kittleson, M. J., & Lacey, E. P. (1990). Adolescent pregnancy: A reason to examine gender knowledge in sexual knowledge, attitudes and behavior. *Health Values, 14,* 24–29.

Case, R. (1985). *Intellectual development: Birth to adulthood.* Orlando, FL: Academic Press.

Case, R., Hayward, S., Lewis, M., & Hurst, P. (1988). Toward a neo-Piagetian theory of cognitive and emotional development. *Developmental Review, 8,* 1–51.

Casiro, O. (1994, March). When pregnant women drink. *NEA Today,* p. 17.

Caskey, C. T. (1997, June 18). Medical genetics. *Journal of the American Medical Association, 277,* 1869–1870.

Casper, L. M. (1990). Does family interaction prevent adolescent pregnancy? *Family Planning Perspectives, 22,* 109–114.

Caspi, A., & Moffitt, T. E. (1991). Individual differences are accentuated during periods of social change: The sample case of girls at puberty. *Journal of Personality and Social Psychology, 61,* 157–168.

Caspi, A., & Silva, P. A. (1995). Temperamental qualities at age three predict personality traits in young adulthood: longitudinal evidence from a birth cohort. *Child Development, 66,* 486–498.

Caspi, A., Elder, G. H., & Bem, D. J. (1987). Moving against the world: Life-course patterns of explosive children. *Developmental Psychology, 23,* 308–313.

Cassidy, K.W. (1998). Preschoolers' use of desires to solve theory of mind problems in a pretense context. *Developmental Psychology, 34,* 503–511.

Cassidy, L., & Hurrell, R. M. (1995). The influence of victim's attire on adolescents' judgments of date rape. *Adolescence, 30,* 319–324.

Catalano, R. F., & Hawkins, J. D. (1995). *Risk focused prevention: Using the social development strategy.* Seattle, WA: Developmental Research and Programs.

Cataldo, C. B., & Whitney, E. N. (1986). *Nutrition and diet therapy: Principles and practices.* St. Paul, MN: West.

Catania, A. C. (1998). *Learning* (4th ed.). Upper Saddle River, NJ: Prentice Hall.

Catron, T. F., & Masters, J. C. (1993). Mothers' and children's conceptualizations of corporal punishment. *Child Development, 64,* 1815–1828.

Cauffman, E., & Steinberg, L. (1996). Interactive effects of menarcheal status and dating on dieting and disordered eating among adolescent girls. *Developmental Psychology, 32,* 631–635.

Caughy, M. O., DePietro, J. A., & Strobino, D. M. (1994). Day-care participation as a protective factor in the cognitive development of low-income children. *Child Development, 65,* 457–471.

Cauley, K., & Tyler, B. (1989). The relationship of self-concept to prosocial behavior in children. *Early Childhood Research Quarterly, 4,* 51–61.

Cavalli-Sforza, L. L. (1991). Genes, people and languages. *Scientific American, 265,* 104–111.

Cazden, C. B. (1981). Language development and the preschool environment. In C. B. Cazden (Ed.), *Language in early childhood education.* Washington, DC: National Association for the Education of Young Children.

Ceci, S. J., & Bruck, M. (1993). Suggestibility of the child witness: A historical review and synthesis. *Psychological Bulletin, 113,* 403–439.

Ceci, S. J., & DeBruyne, E. (1993). Child witnesses in court: A growing dilemma. *Children Today, 22,* 5–9.

Ceci, S. J., & Huffman, M. L. (1997). How suggestible are preschool children? Cognitive and social factors. *Journal of the American Academy of Child and Adolescent Psychiatry, 36,* 948–958.

Ceci, S. J., Leichtman, M. D., Putnick, M., & Nightingale, M. N. (1993). The suggestibility of children's recollections. In D. Cicchetti & S. Toth (Eds.), *Child abuse, child development, and social policy* (pp. 117–137). Norwood, NJ: Ablex.

Ceci, S. J., Ross, D., & Toglia, M. (1987). Age differences in suggestibility: Psycholegal implications. *Journal of Experimental Psychology: General, 117,* 38–49.

Ceci, S. J., Toglia, M., & Ross, D. (1988). On remembering . . . more or less. *Journal of Experimental Psychology: General, 118,* 250–262.

Census paints a new picture of family life. (1994, August 30). *New York Times,* p. A17.

Center on Addiction and Substance Abuse. (1995, August 2). A matter of opinion. *Education Week,* p. 4.

Centers for Disease Control and Prevention, Ad Hoc Working Group for the Development of Standards for Pediatric Immunization Practices. (1993, April 14). Standards for pediatric immunization practices. *Journal of the American Medical Association,* pp. 1818–1821.

Centers for Disease Control and Prevention. (1995). Suicide among children, adolescents, and young adults: United States, 1980–1992. *Morbidity and Mortality Weekly Report, 44,* 289–291.

Centers for Disease Control and Prevention. (1995, March 24). *CDC Surveillance Summaries, MMWR, 44* (No. SS-1).

Centers for Disease Control and Prevention. (1998a). Assessment of infant sleeping position—selected states, 1996. *MMWR, 280,* 1899.

Centers for Disease Control and Prevention. (1998b). *The Youth Risk Behavior Surveillance Survey.* Atlanta: Author.

Centers for Disease Control. (1992a). Selected behaviors that increase risk for HIV infection among high school students-United States, 1990. *Morbidity and Mortality Weekly Report, 41,* 237–240.

Centers for Disease Control. (1992b). Sexual behavior among high school students—United States, 1990. *Morbidity and Mortality Weekly Report, 40,* 885–888.

Centers for Disease Control. (1997). Bicycle helmets: getting people to use them. *Injury Control Newsletter.* Atlanta: Author, U.S. Department of Health and Human Services.

Centra, J. A., & Potter, D. A. (1980). School and teacher effects: An interrelational model. *Review of Educational Research, 50,* 273–290.

Cernoch, J. M., & Porter, R. H. (1985). Recognition of axillary odors by infants. *Child Development, 56,* 1593–1598.

Chan, R.W., Raboy, B., & Patterson, C.J. (1998) Psychosocial adjustment among children conceived via donor insemination by lesbian and heterosexual mothers. *Child Development, 69,* 443–457.

Chandler, M., & Boyes, M. (1982). Social-cognitive development. In B. B. Wolman (Ed.), *Handbook of developmental psychology* (pp. 387–400). Upper Saddle River, NJ: Prentice Hall.

Chao, R. K. (1994). Beyond parental control and authoritarian parenting style: Understanding Chinese parenting through the cultural notion of training. *Child Development, 65,* 1111–1119.

Chaos comes to psychology (1993 May/June) *Psychology today, 26,* 21.

Chase-Lansdale, P. L., Cherlin, A. J., & Kiernan, K. E. (1995). The long-term effects of parental divorce on the mental health of young adults: A developmental perspective. *Child Development, 66,* 1614–1634.

Chasnoff, I. J. (1987). Perinatal effects of cocaine. *Contemporary Ob/Gyn, 26.* (March of Dimes reprint, entire issue.)

Chasnoff, I. J., Burns, W. J., Schnoll, S. H., & Burns, K. (1985). Cocaine use in pregnancy. *New England Journal of Medicine, 313,* 666–669.

Chasnoff, I. J., Griffith, D. R., Freier, C. & Murray, J. (1992). Cocaine/polydrug use in pregnancy: Two-year follow-up. *Pediatrics, 89,* 284–289.

Chassin, L., Pillow, D. R., Curran, P. L., Molina, B. S., & Barrera, M. (1993). Relation of parental alcoholism to early adolescent substance use: A test of three mediating mechanisms. *Journal of Abnormal Psychology, 102,* 3–19.

Chavkin, W., Kristal, A., Seabron, C. & Guiogli, P. E. (1987). Reproductive experience of women living in hotels for the homeless in New York City. *New York State Journal of Medicine, 87,* 10–13.

Cherlin, A. J., Furstenberg, F. F., Chase-Lansdale, P. L., Kiernan, K. E., Robins, P. K., Morrison, D. R., & Teitler, J. O. (1991). Longitudinal studies of effects of divorce on children in Great Britain and the United States. *Science, 252,* 1386–1389.

Chess, S., & Thomas, A. (1981). Infant bonding: mystique and reality. *American Journal of Orthopsychiatry, 52,* 213–222.

Chi, M. T. H., & Glaser, R. (1985). Problem solving ability. In R. J. Sternberg (Ed.), *Human abilities: An information processing approach.* New York: Freeman.

Chilamkurti, C., & Milner, J. S. (1993). Perceptions and evaluations of child transgressions and disciplinary techniques in high-and low-risk mothers and their children. *Child Development, 64,* 1801–1814.

Children under stress. (1986, October 27). *U.S. News and World Report.*

Children's Defense Fund. (1992, January). *Children's Defense Fund, Medicaid and childhood immunizations: A national study* (pp. 7–8). Washington, DC: Author.

Childress, A. C., Brewerton, T. D., Hodeges, E. L., & Jarrell, M. P. (1993). The kids' eating disorders survey (KEDS): A study of middle school students. *Journal of the American Academy of Child and Adolescent Psychiatry, 32,* 843–850.

Chilman, C. S. (1983). *Adolescent sexuality in a changing American society* (2nd ed.). New York: Wiley.

Chira, S. (1996, April 21). Study says babies in child care keep secure bonds to mothers. *New York Times,* pp. A1, A31.

Chiras, D. D. (1993). *Biology: The web of life.* St. Paul, MN: West.

Chiu, L. H. (1987). Child-rearing attitudes of Chinese, Chinese-American, and Anglo-American mothers. *International Journal of Psychology, 22,* 409–419.

Chomitz, V. R., Cheung, I. W. Y., & Lieberman, E. (1995 Spring). The role of lifestyle in preventing low birth weight. *The Future of Children, 5,* 121–138.

Chomsky, N. (1959). A review of B. F. Skinner's verbal behavior. *Language, 35,* 26–58.

Chomsky, N. (1965). *Aspects of the theory of syntax.* Cambridge, MA: MIT Press.

Chomsky, N. (1972). *Language and mind* (enlarged ed.). New York: Harcourt, Brace, Jovanovich.

Chubb, N. H., Fertman, C., & Ross, J. L. (1997). Adolescent self-esteem and locus of control: A longitudinal study of gender and age differences. *Adolescence, 32,* 113–130.

Churchill, E. (1997, January). Genes and society: Puzzles, promises and policy. *Annals of the American Academy of Political and Social Science, 549,* 173–185.

Cicchetti, D., & Lynch, M. (1993). Toward an ecological/transactional model of community violence and child maltreatment: Consequences for children's development. *Psychiatry, 56,* 257–281.

Cicchetti, D., & Toth, S. L. (1998). Perspectives on research and practice in developmental psychopathology. In W. Damon (Editor in Chief) & I. E. Sigel & K. A. Renninger (Vol. Eds.), *Handbook of child psychology* (5th ed., Vol. 4, pp. 479–584). New York: Wiley.

Cicchetti, D., Toth, S. L., & Hennessy, K. (1993). Child maltreatment and school adaptation: Problems and promises. In D. Cicchetti, & S. L. Toth (Eds.), *Child abuse: Child development, and social policy* (pp. 301–330). Norwood, NJ: Ablex.

Cicero, T. J. (1994). Effects of paternal exposure to alcohol on offspring development. *Family Planning Perspectives, 18,* 37–41.

Ciffone, J. (1993). Suicide prevention: A classroom presentation to adolescents. *Social Work, 38,* 196–203.

Cipriani, D. C. (1996). Stability and change in personality across the life span: Behavioral-genetic versus evolutional approaches. *Genetic, Social, and General Psychology Monographs, 122,* 57–74.

Clapp, G. (1988). Television: Today's most important socializer? In G. Clapp (Ed.), *Child study research* (pp. 57–85). Lexington, MA: Lexington.

Clark, C. A., Worthington, E. L., Jr., & Danser, D. B. (1988). The transmission of religious beliefs and practices from parents to first born early adolescent sons. *Journal of Marriage and the Family, 50,* 463–472.

Clark, C. S. (1993, January 15). Child sexual abuse. *CQ Researcher, 3,* 38–44.

Clark, R., Hyde, J. S., Essex, M. J., & Klein, M. H. (1997). Length of maternity leave and quality of mother-infant interactions. *Child Development, 68,* 364–383.

Clark, S. L., & DeVore, G. R. (1989). Prenatal diagnosis for couples who would not consider abortion. *Obstetrics and Gynecology, 73,* 1035–1037.

Clarke, A. M., & Clarke, A. D. B. (1976). *Early experience: Myth and evidence.* New York: Free Press.

Clarke-Stewart, K. A. (1988). The "effects" of infant day care reconsidered. *Developmental Psychology, 3,* 293–319.

Clarke-Stewart, K. A. (1989). Infant day care: Maligned or malignant? *American Psychologist, 44,* 266–274.

Clarke-Stewart, K. A., & Fein, G. G. (1983). Early childhood programs. In M. M. Haith & J. J. Campos (Eds.), *Handbook of child psychology* (Vol. 2, pp. 917–1001). New York: Wiley.

Clarke-Stewart, K. A., Allhusen, V. D., & Clements, D. C. (1995). Nonparental caregiving. In M. H. Bornstein (Ed.), *Handbook of parenting* (Vol. 3, pp. 161–176). Mahwah, NJ: Erlbaum.

Clay, R. A. (1998). New laws aid children with disabilities. *APA Monitor,* p. 18.

Clingempeel, W. G., & Segal, S. (1986). Stepparent-stepchild relationships and the psychological adjustment of children in stepmother and stepfather families. *Child Development, 57,* 474–484.

Cloninger, C. R. (1987). Neurogenetic adaptive mechanisms in alcoholism. *Science, 236,* 410–416.

Cogan, R. (1980). Effects of childbirth preparation. *Clinical Obstetrics and Gynecology, 23,* 1–14.

Cohen, A. R. (1998, July 2). Sickle cell disease-new treatments, new questions. *New England Journal of Medicine, 330,* 42–45.

Cohen, K. M., & Savin-Williams, R. C. (1996). Developmental perspectives on coming out to self and others. In R. C. Savin-Williams & K. M. Cohen (Eds.), *The lives of lesbians, gays, and bisexuals: Children to adults* (pp. 113–151). Fort Worth, TX: Harcourt Brace.

Cohen, L. B., DeLoache, J. S., & Strauss, M. S. (1979). Infant visual perception. In J. Osofsky (Ed.), *Handbook of infant development* (pp. 393–439). New York: Wiley.

Cohen, L., & Campos, J. (1974). Father, mother and stranger as elicitors of attachment behavior in infancy. *Developmental Psychology, 10,* 146–154.

Cohen, R., Duncan, M., & Cohen, S. L. (1994). Classroom peer relations of children participating in a pull-out enrichment program. *Gifted Child Quarterly, 38,* 33–37.

Cohn, J. F., & Tronick, E. Z. (1988). Mother-infant face-to-face interaction: Influence in bidirectional and unrelated to periodic cycles in either partner's behavior. *Developmental Psychology, 24,* 386–393.

Cohn, J. F., & Tronick, E. Z. (1989). Specificity of infants' response to mothers' affective behavior. *Journal of the American Academy of Child and Adolescent psychiatry, 28,* 242–248.

Cohn, J. F., Campbell, S. B., Matias, R., & Hopkins, J. (1990). Face-to-face interactions of postpartum depressed and nondepressed mother-infant pairs at 2 months. *Developmental Psychology, 26,* 15–23.

Cohn, J. F., Matias, R., Tronick, E. Z., Connell, D., & Lyons-Ruth, D. (1986). Face-to-face interactions of depressed mothers and their infants. In E. Z. Tronick & T. Field (Eds.), *Maternal depression and infant disturbance* (pp. 31–45). San Francisco: Jossey-Bass.

Coie, J. D., & Dodge, K. A. (1998). Aggression and antisocial behavior. In W. Damon (Editor-in Chief) & N. Eisenberg (Vol. Ed.), *Handbook of child psychology* (Vol. 3, pp. 779–862). New York: Wiley.

Coie, J. D., & Kupersmidt, J. B. (1983). A behavioral analysis of emerging social status in boy's groups. *Child Development, 54,* 1400–1416.

Coie, J. D., Dodge, K. A., & Christopoulos, K. (1991). Cited in T. J. Dishion, G. R. Patterson, M. Stoolmiller, & M. L. Skinner. Family, school, and behavioral antecedents to early adolescent involvement with antisocial peers. *Developmental Psychology, 27,* 172–280.

Colby, A., & Damon, W. (1992). *Some do care: Contemporary lives of moral commitment.* New York: Free Press.

Cole, D. A. (1991). Change in self-perceived competence as a function of peer and teacher evaluation. *Developmental Psychology, 27,* 682–688.

Cole, D. A., Martin, J. M., Peeke, L. A., Seroczynski, A. D., & Fier, J. (1999). Children's over-and underestimation of academic competence: A longitudinal study of gender differences, depression and anxiety. *Child Development, 70,* 459–473.

Cole, T. B. (1999, January 6). Ebbing epidemic: Youth homicide rate at a 14-year low. *Journal of the American Medical Association, 281,* 25–26.

Coleman, E. (1981). Counseling adolescent males. *American Personnel and Guidance Journal, 60,* 215–219.

Coleman, M., Ganong, L. H., & Ellis, P. (1985). Family structure and dating behavior of adolescents. *Adolescence,* 537–543.

Coles, A. D. (1999, May 12). Falling teenage birthrate fuels drop in overall U.S. rate. *Education Week,* p. 13.

Coley, R. L. (1998). Children's socialization experiences and functioning in single-mother households: The importance of fathers and other men. *Child Development, 69,* 219–230.

Colin, V.L. (1996) *Human attachment* New York: McGraw Hill.

Colletta, N. (1981). Social support and the risk of maternal rejection by adolescent mothers. *Journal of Psychology, 109,* 191–197.

Collins, F. S., & Fink, L. (1995a). Genetic maps provide blueprint for human genome. *Alcohol Health and Research World, 19,* 192–194.

Collins, F. S., & Fink, L. (1995b). Tools of genetic research. *Alcohol Health and Research World, 19,* 190–196.

Collins, J.S. (1982) cited in A Bandura's (1986) *Social foundations of thought and action* Englewood Cliffs, NJ: Prentice Hall.

Collins, N.L., & Read, S.J. (1990) Adult attachment, working models, and relationship quality in dating couples. *Jounal of Personality and Social Psychology, 58,* 644–663.

Collins, W. A., Harris, M. L., & Susman, A. (1995). Parenting during middle childhood. In M. H. Bornstein (Ed.), *Handbook of parenting* (Vol. 1, pp. 57–67). Mahwah, NJ: Erlbaum.

Colombo, J., & Horowitz, F. D. (1987). Behavioral state as a lead variable in neonatal research. *Merrill-Palmer Quarterly, 33,* 234–437.

Colt, G. H. (1983, September–October). Suicide. *Harvard Magazine,* pp. 46–53, 63–66.

Coltrane, S. (1996). *Family man.* New York: Oxford University Press.

Comer, R. J. (1995). *Abnormal psychology* (2nd ed.). New York: Freeman.

Comstock, G., & Paik, H. (1991). *Television and the American child.* San Diego, CA: Academic Press.

Condon, J. T., & Hilton, C. A. (1980). A comparison of smoking and drinking behaviors in pregnant women: Who abstains and why? *Obstetrics and Gynecology Survey, 44,* 51–53.

Condon, W. S., & Sander, L. W. (1974). Synchrony demonstrated between movements of the neonate and adult speech. *Child Development, 65,* 456–462.

Condry, J. (1989). *The psychology of television.* Hillsdale, NJ: Erlbaum.

Condry, J., Bence, P., & Scheibe, C. (1988). Nonprogram content of children's television. *Journal of Broadcasting and Electronic Media, 32,* 255–269.

Conger, J. J., & Petersen, A. C. (1984). *Adolescence and youth* (3rd ed.). New York: Harper & Row.

Conger, R. D., McCarty, J., Yang, R., Lahey, B., & Kropp, J. (1984). Perception of child, child-rearing values, and emotional distress as mediating links between environmental stressors and observed maternal behavior. *Child Development, 54,* 2234–2247.

Conte, C. (1998, January). Technology in schools: Hip or hype? *Education Digest,* 28–33.

Cook, P. S., Petersen, R. C., & Moore, D. T. (1990). *Alcohol, tobacco, and other drugs may harm the unborn.* Rockville, MD: U.S. Department of Health and Human Services.

Cooke, R. A. (1982). The ethics and regulation of research involving children. In B. B. Wolman (Ed.), *Handbook of developmental psychology* (pp. 149–175). Upper Saddle River, NJ: Prentice Hall.

Coontz, S. (1997, November 17). Divorcing reality. *The Nation,* pp. 21–24.

Cooper, M. H. (1992a, June 9). Infant mortality. *CQ Researcher, 5,* 489–509.

Cooper, M. H. (1992b, July 31). Technology and Choice. *CQ Researcher, 5,* 643–663.

Cooper, M. H. (1995, June 9). Combating infectious disease, *CQ Researcher, 5,* 489–469.

Cooper, M.L., Shaver, P.R., & Collins, R. (1998) Attachment styles, emotion regulation, and adjustment in adolescence. *Journal of Personality and Social Psychology, 74,* 1380–1397.

Cooperman, A. (1996, February 12). Bert and Ernie go to Moscow. *U.S. News and World Report,* pp. 4–5.

Copans, S. A. (1974). Human prenatal effects: Methodological problems and some suggested solutions. *Merrill-Palmer Quarterly, 20,* 43–52.

Corballis, D. (1989). Laterality and human evolution. *Psychological Review, 96,* 492–505.

Corbin, C. B. (1980a). Childhood obesity. In C. B. Corbin (Ed.), *A textbook of motor development* (pp. 121–128). Dubuque, IA: Brown.

Corbin, C. B. (1980b). The physical fitness of children: A discussion and point of view. In C. B. Corbin (Ed.), *A textbook of motor development* (pp. 100–107). Dubuque, IA: Brown.

Corbin, C. B. (1980c). *A textbook of motor development* (2nd ed.). Dubuque, IA: Brown.

Cordier, S., Deplan, F., Mandereau, L., & Hermon, D. (1991). Paternal exposure to mercury and spontaneous abortions. *British Journal of Industrial Medicine, 48,* 375–381.

Corey, L., & Spear, P. G. (1986). Infections with herpes simplex viruses. *New England Journal of Medicine, 314,* 749–754.

Cornwell, K. S., Harris, L. T., & Fitzgerald, H. E. (1991). Task effects in the development of hand preferences in 9, 13, and 20 month old infant girls. *Developmental Neuropsychology, 7,* 19–34.

Corsaro, W. A. (1981). Friendship in the nursery school: social organization in a peer environment. In S. R. Asher & J. M. Gottman (Eds.), *The development of children's friendships* (pp. 207–242). Cambridge, MA: Harvard University Press.

Corter, C. M., & Fleming, A. S. (1995). Psychobiology of maternal behavior in human beings. In M. H. Bornstein (Ed.), *Handbook of parenting* (Vol. 2. pp. 87–116). Mahwah, NJ: Erlbaum.

Cotton, D., Currier, J. S., & Wofsy, C. (1994). Information for caretakers of children women infected with HIV. In P. A. Pizzo & C. M. Wilfert (Eds.), *Pediatric AIDS: The challenge of HIV Infection in infants, children, and adolescents* (2nd ed., pp. 83–97). Baltimore: Williams & Wilkins.

Coughlin, C., & Vuchinich, S. (1996). Family experience in preadolescence and the development of male delinquency. *Journal of Marriage and the Family, 58,* 491–502.

Coulton, C. J., Korbin, J. E., Su, M., & Chow, J. (1995). Community level factors and child maltreatment rates. *Child Development, 66,* 1262–1276.

Cowan, P. A. (1997). Beyond meta-analysis: A plea for a family systems view of attachment. *Child Development, 68,* 601–603.

Cowan, P. A., Powell, D., & Cowan, C. P. (1998). Parenting interventions: A family systems perspective. In W. Damon (Editor in Chief) and I. E. Sigel, & K. A. Renninger (Vol. Eds.), *Handbook of child psychology* (5th ed., Vol. 4, pp. 3–72). New York: Wiley.

Cox, F. D. (1984). *Human intimacy: Marriage, the family and its meaning* (3rd ed.). St. Paul: West.

Cox, M., Owen, M., Henderson, V. & Margand, N. (1992). Prediction of infant-father and infant-mother attachment. *Developmental Psychology, 28,* 474–483.

Crain, W. (1992). *Theories of development: Concepts and applications* (2nd ed.). Upper Saddle River, NJ: Prentice Hall.

Cratty, B. J. (1986). *Perceptual and motor development in infants and children* (3rd ed.). Upper Saddle River, NJ: Prentice Hall.

Cratty, B. J. (1970). *Perceptual and motor development in infants and children.* New York: Macmillan.

Crawford, J. (1987, March 25). Bilingual education works, study finds. *Education Week,* p. 16.

Creedy, K. B. (1994, November/December). What makes your child tick? *Adoptive Families,* pp. 8–13.

Crichton, M. (1989). *Jurassic park.* New York: Ballantine.

Crick, N. R., & Dodge, K. A. (1996). Social information-processing mechanisms in reactive and proactive aggression. *Child Development, 67,* 993–1002.

Crick, N. R., & Dodge, K. A. (1994). A review and reformulation of social information-processing mechanisms in children's social adjustment. *Psychological Bulletin, 115,* 74–101.

Crockenberg, S. (1987). Support for adolescent mothers during the postnatal period: Theory and research. In C. Boukydis (Ed.), *Research on support for parents and infants in the postnatal period* (pp. 3–24). Norwood, NJ: Ablex.

Crockenberg, S., & McCluskey, K. (1986). Change in maternal behavior during the baby's first year of life. *Child Development, 57,* 746–754.

Croen, L. A., & Shaw, G. M. (1995). Young maternal age and congenital malformations: A population-based study. *American Journal of Public Health, 85,* 710–713.

Cross, B. (1997). Self-esteem and curriculum: Perspectives from urban teachers. *Journal of Curriculum and Supervision, 13,* 70–92.

Cross, H. J., & Allen, J. G. (1970). Ego identity status, adjustment, and academic achievement. *Journal of Consulting and Clinical Psychology, 34,* 288.

Crouter, A. C., MacDermid, S. M., McHale, S. M., & Perry-Jenkins, M. (1990). Parental monitoring and perceptions of children's school performance and conduct in dual- and single-earner families. *Developmental Psychology, 26,* 649–657.

Csikszentmihalyi, M., & Larson, R. (1984). *Being adolescent: Conflict and growth in the teenage years.* New York: Basic Books.

Cummings, E. M., & Davies, P. (1994). *Children and marital conflict: The impact of family dispute and resolution.* New York: Guilford.

Cummings, E. M., Hennessy, K., Rabideau, G., & Cicchetti, D. (1994). Responses of physically abused boys to interadult anger involving their mothers. *Development and Psychopathology, 6,* 31–42.

Cummings, E. M., Iannotti, R. J., & Zahn-Waxler, C. (1989). Aggression between peers in early childhood: Individual continuity and developmental change. *Child Development, 60,* 887–896.

Cummings, M. R. (1995). *Human heredity: Principles and issues* (3rd ed.). St. Paul, MN: West.

Cunningham, A. E., & Stanovich, K. E. (1997). Early reading acquisition and its relation to reading experience and ability 10 years later. *Developmental Psychology, 33,* 934–945.

Currie, J., & Thomas, D. (1997). Can Head Start lead to long term gains in cognition after all? *SRCD Newsletter, 40* (2).

Curry, K., & Rosensteel, L. (1995). National vaccination week: Marketing vaccinations to Hispanics in Newark, DE. *Public Health Reports, 110,* 202.

Curtis, S. (1977). *Genie: A psychological study of a modern-day wild child.* New York: Academic Press.

D

Dale, P.S. (1972) *Language Development: Structure and function* Hinsdale, IL: Dryden Press.

Damon, W. (1983). *Social and personality development.* New York: Norton.

Damon, W., & Hart, D. (1982). The development of self-understanding from infancy through adolescence. *Child Development, 53,* 841–864.

Damon, W., & Hart, D. (1988). *Self-understanding in childhood and adolescence.* Cambridge: Cambridge University Press.

Daniels, D., & Plomin, R. (1985). Origins of individual differences in infant shyness. *Developmental Psychology, 21,* 118–122.

Daniels, D., Plomin, R., & Greenhalgh, J. (1984). Correlates of difficult temperament in infancy. *Child Development, 55,* 1184–1194.

Dannemiller, J. L. & Stephens, B. R. (1988). A critical test of infant pattern preference models. *Child Development, 59,* 210–217.

Darling, N., & Steinberg, L. (1993) Parenting style as context: An integrative model. *Psychological Bulletin, 113,* 487–496.

Dasen, P., & Heron, A. (1981). Cross-cultural test of Piaget's theory. In H. C. Triandis & A. Heron (Eds.), *Handbook of cross-cultural psychology* (Vol. 4, pp. 295–343). Boston: Allyn & Bacon.

Davidson, R. J., & Fox, N. A. (1989). Frontal brain asymmetry predicts infants' response to maternal separation. *Journal of Abnormal Psychology, 98,* 127–131.

Davies, D., Cole, J., Albertella, G., McCulloch, L., Allen, K., & Kekevian, H. (1996). A model for conducing forensic interviews with child victims of abuse. *Child Maltreatment, 1,* 189–199.

Davies, J., & Brember, I. (1995). Change in self-esteem between year 2 and year 6: A longitudinal study. *Educational Psychology, 15,* 171–181.

Davies, P. T., & Cummings, E. M. (1998). Exploring children's emotional security as a mediator of the link between marital relations and child adjustment. *Child Development, 69,* 124–139.

Davis, C. M. (1928). Self-selection of diet by newly weaned infants. *American Journal of Diseases of Children, 36,* 651–679.

Davis, C. M. (1939). Results of the self-selection of diets by young children. *Canadian Medical Association Journal, 95,* 759–764.

Davis, G. A., & Rimm, S. B. (1994). *Education of the gifted and talented* (3rd ed.). Needham Heights, MA: Allyn & Bacon.

Davis, G.A. (1983) *Educational psychology: Theory and practice* Reading MA: Addison-Wesley.

Davis, P. W. (1994). The changing meanings of spanking. In J. Best (Ed.), *Troubling children: Studies of children and social problems* (pp. 133–153). New York: Aldine de Gruyter.

Davis, P. W. (1996). Threats of corporal punishment as verbal aggression: A naturalistic study. *Child Abuse & Neglect, 20,* 289–304.

Davis, R. A. (1989). Teenage pregnancy: A theoretical analysis of a social problem. *Adolescence, 24,* 19–27.

Day, R. D., Peterson, G. W., & McCracken, C. (1998). Predicting spanking of younger and older children by mothers and fathers. *Journal of Marriage and the Family, 60,* 79–93.

De Gaston, J. F., Weed, S., & Jensen, L. (1996). Understanding gender differences in adolescent sexuality. *Adolescence, 31,* 217–231.

de Haan, M., & Nelson, C. A. (1997). Recognition of the mother's face by six-month-old infants: A neurobehavioral study. *Child Development, 68,* 187–210.

de Lormier, S., Doyle, A. B., & Tessier, O. (1995). Social coordination during pretend play: Comparisons with nonpretend play and effects on expressive content. *Merrill-Palmer Quarterly, 41,* 497–516.

de Roiste, A., & Bushness, I. W. R. (1996). Tactile stimulation: Short-and long-term benefits for pre-term infants. *British Journal of Developmental Psychology, 14,* 41–53.

de Wolff, M. S., & van IJzendoorn, M. H. (1997). Sensitivity and attachment: A meta-analysis on parental antecedents of infant attachment. *Child Development, 68,* 571–592.

Deak, G. O., & Bauer, P. J. (1996). The dynamics of preschoolers' categorization choices. *Child Development, 67,* 740–767.

Deal, J. E., Halverson, C. F., & Wampler, K. S. (1989). Parental agreement on childrearing orientations: Relations to parental, marital, family, and child characteristics. *Child Development, 22,* 617–626.

Dean, A. L., Malik, M. M., Richards, W., & Stringer, S. A. (1986). Effects of parental maltreatment on children's conceptions of interpersonal relationships. *Developmental Psychology, 22,* 617–626.

DeAngelis, T. (1993, July). Science meets practice on PKU findings. *APA Monitor,* pp. 16–17.

DeAngelis, T. (1994, December). Perceptions influence student drinking. *APA Monitor,* p. 35.

Deasey, D. (1978). *Education under six.* New York: St. Martin's.

Deater-Deckard, K., & Plomin, R. (1999). An adoption study of the etiology of teacher and parent reports of externalizing behavior problems in middle childhood. *Child Development, 70,* 144–154.

Deater-Deckard, K., Dodge, K.A., Bates, J.E., & Petit, G.S. (1996). Physical discipline among African American and European American mothers: Links to children's externalizing behaviors. *Developmental Psychology, 32,* 1063–1072.

Deater-Deckard, K., Pinkerton, R., & Scarr, S. (1996). Child care quality and children's behavioral adjustment: A four-year longitudinal study. *Journal of Child Psychology and Psychiatry, 37,* 937–948.

DeBlassie, A. M., & DeBlassie, R. R. (1996). Education of Hispanic youth: A cultural lag. *Adolescence, 31,* 205–215.

DeBruyne, L. K., & Rolfes, S. R. (1989). *Life cycle nutrition: Conception through adolescence.* St. Paul, MN: West.

DeCasper, A. J., & Fifer, W. P. (1980). Of human bonding: Newborns prefer their mothers' voices. *Science, 208,* 1174–1176.

DeCasper, A. J., & Spence, M. J. (1986). Prenatal maternal speech influences newborns' perception of speech sounds. *Infant Behavior and Development, 9,* 133–150.

Deely, K. (1996, May). Who's doing what? *Parenting,* p. 44.

DeKlyen, M., Biernbaum, M.A., Speltz, M.L., & Greenberg, M.T. (1998) Fathers and preschool behavior problems. *Developmental Psychology, 34,* 264–275.

Dekovic, M., & Meeus, W. (1997). Peer relations in adolescence: Effects of parenting and adolescents' self-concept. *Journal of Adolescence, 20,* 165–176.

Delaney, C. H. (1995). Rites of passage in adolescence. *Adolescence, 30,* 891–898.

Delgado-Gaitan, C., & Trueba, H. T. (1985). Ethnographic study of participant structures in task completion: Reinterpretation of "Handicaps" in Mexican children. *Learning Disability Quarterly, 8,* 67–75.

Delisle, J. R. (1992). *Guiding the social and emotional development of gifted children.* New York: Longman.

DeLoache, J. S. & Todd, C. M. (1988). Young children's use of spatial categorization as a mnemonic strategy. *Journal of Experimental Child Psychology, 46,* 1–20.

DeLoache, J. S. (1987). Rapid change in the symbolic functioning of very young children. *Science, 238,* 1556–1557.

DeLoache, J. S. (1991). Symbolic functioning in very young children: Understanding of pictures and models. *Child Development, 62,* 736–753.

DeLoache, J. S., & Marzolf, D. P. (1995). The use of dolls to interview young children: Issues of symbolic representation. *Journal of Experimental Child Psychology, 60,* 155–173.

DeLoache, J. S., Cassidy, D. J., & Brown, A. L. (1985). Precursors of mnemonic strategies in very young children's memory. *Child Development, 56,* 125–137.

DeLoache, J. S., Kolstad, V., & Anderson, K. N. (1991). Physical similarity and young children's understanding of scale models. *Child Development, 62,* 111–126.

DeLuccie, M. F. (1996). Mothers: Influential agents in father-child relations. *Genetic, Social, and General Psychology Monographs, 122,* 285–307.

DeMeis, D. K., & Perkins, H. W. (1996). "Supermoms" of the nineties. *Journal of Family Issues, 17,* 777–792.

Demo, D. H. (1997, Spring). Family type and adolescent adjustment. *Stepfamilies, 17,* 13–14.

Demo, D. H., & Acock, A. C. (1996). Family structure, family process, and adolescent well-being. *Journal of Research on Adolescence, 6,* 457–488.

Dempster, F. N. (1992). The rise and fall of the inhibitory mechanism: Toward a unified theory of cognitive development and aging. *Developmental Review, 12,* 45–75.

Dennehy, K., & Mortimer, J. T. (1993). Work and family orientations of contemporary adolescent boys and girls. In J. C. Hood (Ed.), *Men, work, and family* (pp. 87–107). Newbury Park, CA: Sage.

Dennis, W. (1960). Causes of retardation among institutional children: Iran. *Journal of Genetic Psychology, 96,* 47–59.

Dennis, W. (1973). *Children of the creche.* New York: Appleton-Century-Crofts.

Dennis, W., & Dennis, M. G. (1940). Cradles and cradling customs of the Pueblo Indians. *American Anthropologist, 42,* 107–115.

Dennis, W., & Najarian, P. (1957). Infant development under environmental handicap. *Psychological Monographs, 71,* 1–13.

DeOreo, K., & Keough, J. (1980). Performance of fundamental motor tasks. In C. B. Corbin (Ed.), *A textbook of motor development* (2nd ed., pp. 76–91). Dubuque, IA: Brown.

Deruelle, C., & de Schonen, C. (1995) Pattern processing in infancy: Hemispheric differences in the processing of shape and location of visual components. *Infant Behavior and Development, 18,* 123–132.

Deruelle, C., & de Schonen, S. (1991) Hemispheric asymmetries in visual pattern processing in infancy. *Brain and Cognition, 16,* 151-179.

Desai, S., Chase-Lansdale, P. L., & Michael, R. T. (1989). Mother or market? Effects of maternal employment on the intellectual ability of 4-year-old children. *Developmental Psychology, 26,* 545–561.

Desiderato, L. L., & Crawford, H. J. (1995). Risky sexual behavior in college students: Relationships between number of sexual partner, disclosure of previous risky behavior, and alcohol use. *Journal of Youth and Adolescence, 24,* 55–68.

Deutsch, F. M., Lussier, J. B., & Servic, L. J. (1993). Husbands at home: predictors of paternal participation in childcare and housework. *Journal of Personality and Social Psychology, 65,* 1154–1166.

deVilliers, J. G., & deVilliers, P. A. (1978). *Language acquisition.* Cambridge, MA: Harvard University Press.

DeVries, M. W., & Sameroff, A. J. (1984). Culture and temperament: Influences on infant temperament in three East African societies. *American Journal of Orthopsychiatry, 54,* 83–96.

Dews, S., Winner, E., & Kaplan, J. (1995). Why not say it directly? The social functions of irony. *Discourse Processes, 19,* 347–368.

Dews, S., Winner, E., Kaplan, J., Rosenblatt, E., Hunt, M., Lim, K., McGovern, A., Qualter, A., & Smarsh, B. (1996). Children's understanding of the meaning and functions of verbal irony. *Child Development, 67,* 3071–3985.

Diamond, A., Cruttenden, L., & Neiderman, D. (1994). AB with multiple wells: 1. Why are multiple wells sometimes easier than two wells? 2 memory or memory + inhibition? *Developmental Psychology, 30,* 192–205.

Diamond, J. M., Kataria, S., & Messer, S. C. (1989). Latchkey children: A pilot study investigating behavior and academic achievement. *Child and Youth Care Quarterly, 18,* 131–140.

Diamond, M., & Sigmundson, K. (1997). Sex reassignment at birth: Long-term review and clinical implications. *Archives of pediatric Adolescent Medicine, 151,* 298–304.

Diamond, N. (1982). Cognitive theory. In B. B. Wolman (Ed.), *Handbook of developmental psychology* (pp. 3–23). Upper Saddle River, NJ: Prentice Hall.

Diaz, R. M. (1985). Bilingual cognitive development: Addressing three gaps in current research. *Child Development, 56,* 1376–1388.

Dickover, R. E., Garratty, E. M., Herman, S. A., Sim, M. S., Plaeger, S., Boyer, P. J., Keller, M., Deveikis, A., Stiehm, E. R., & Bryson, Y. J. (1996, February 28). Identification of levels of maternal HIV-1 RNA associated with risk of perinatal transmission. *Journal of the American Medical Association, 275,* 599–605.

DiLalla, L. F., & Watson, M. W. (1988). Differentiation of fantasy and reality: Preschoolers' reactions to interruptions in their play. *Developmental Psychology, 24,* 286–292.

Dion, K. K. (1973). Young children's stereotyping of facial attractiveness. *Developmental Psychology, 9,* 183–188.

DiPietro, J. (1981). Rough and tumble play: A function of gender. *Developmental Psychology, 17,* 50–58.

Dishion, T. J. (1990). The family ecology of boys' peer relations in middle childhood. *Child Development, 61,* 874–892.

Dishion, T. J., Patterson, G. R., Stoolmiller, M., & Skinner, M. L. (1991). Family, school, and behavioral antecedents to early adolescent involvement with antisocial peers. *Developmental Psychology, 27,* 172–280.

Dix, T., Reinhold, D., & Zambarano, R. (1990). Mothers' judgments in moments of anger. *Merrill-Palmer Quarterly, 36,* 465–486.

Dobkin, P. L., Tremblay, R. E., Masse, L. C., & Vitaro, F. (1995). Individual and peer characteristics in predicting boys' early onset of substance abuse: A seven-year longitudinal study. *Child Development, 66,* 1198–1214.

Dodd, B. J. (1972). Effects of social and vocal stimulation on infant babbling. *Developmental Psychology, 7,* 80–83.

Dodge, K. A., & Frame, C. L. (1982). Social cognitive biases and deficits in aggressive boys. *Child Development, 53,* 620–635.

Dodge, K., Bates, J., & Pettit, G. S. (1990). Mechanisms in the cycle of violence. *Science, 250,* 1678–1683.

Dolan, C. V., & Molenaar, C. M. (1995). A note on the scope of developmental behavior genetics. *International Journal of Behavioral Development, 18,* 749–760.

Dolan-Mullen, P., Ramirez, G., & Groff, J. Y. (1994). A meta-analysis of randomized trials of prenatal smoking cessation interventions. *American Journal of Obstetrics & Gynecology, 171,* 1328–1334.

Dolcini, M. M., Cohn, L. D., Adler, N. E., Millstein, S. G., Irwin, C. E., Kegeles, S. M., & Stone, G. C. (1989). Adolescent egocentrism and feelings of invulnerability: Are they related? *Journal of Early Adolescence, 9,* 409–418.

Donahue, M., & Benson, P. L. (1995). Religion and the well-being of adolescents. *Journal of Social Issues, 51,* 145–161.

Dondi, M., Simion, F., & Caltran, G. (1999). Can newborns discriminate between their own cry and the cry of another newborn infant? *Developmental Psychology, 35,* 418–426.

Donegan, C. (1996, January 19) Debate over bilingualism. *CQ Researcher,* 49–70.

Donnerstein, E., Slaby, R. G., & Eron, L. D. (1994). The mass media and youth aggression. In L. D. Eron, J. H. Gentry, & P. Schlegel (Eds.), *Reason to hope: A psychosocial perspective on violence & youth* (pp. 219–251). Washington, DC: American Psychological Association.

Donovan, J. M. (1975). Identity status and interpersonal style. *Journal of Youth and Adolescence, 4,* 37–55.

Donovan, P. (1998). The Colorado parental rights amendment: How and why it failed. *Family Planning Perspectives, 29,* 187–191.

Dornbusch, S. M., Ritter, P. L., Mont-Reynaud, R., & Chen, Z. Y. (1990). Family decision making and academic performance in a diverse high school population. *Journal of Adolescent Research, 5,* 143–160.

Dorr, A., & Rabin, B. E. (1995). Parents, children, and television. In M. H. Bornstein (Ed.), *Handbook of parenting* (Vol. 4, pp. 323–353). Mahwah, NJ: Erlbaum.

Dorval, B., & Eckerman, C.O. (1984) Developmental trends in the quality of conversation achieved by small groups of acquainted peers. *Monographs of the Society for Research in Child Development, 49,* (serial number 206).

Dougherty, T. M., & Haith, M. M. (1997). Infant expectations and reaction time as predictors of childhood speed of processing and IQ. *Developmental Psychology, 23,* 146–156.

Douglas, M. J. (1991). Potential complications of spinal and epidural anesthesia for obstetrics. *Seminars in Perinatology, 15,* 368–374.

Doussard-Roosevelt, J. A., Porges, S. W., Scanlon, J. W., Alemi, B., & Scanlon, K. B. (1997). Vagal regulation of heart rate in the prediction of developmental outcome for very low birth weight preterm infants. *Child Development, 68,* 173–186.

Doyle, J. A., & Paludi, M. A. (1991). *Sex and gender: The human experience* (2nd ed.). Dubuque, IA: Brown.

Dreher, M. C., & Hayes, J. S. (1993). Triangulation in cross-cultural research of child development in Jamaica. *Western Journal of Nursing Research, 15,* 216–229.

Dreikurs, R., & Stoltz, V. (1964) *Children: The challenge,* New York: Meredith Press.

Dreyer, P. H. (1982). Sexuality during adolescence. In B. B. Wolman (Ed.), *Handbook of developmental psychology* (pp. 559–602). Upper Saddle River, NJ: Prentice Hall.

Drummond, R. J., & Ryan, C. W. (1995). *Career counseling: A developmental approach.* Upper Saddle River, NJ: Prentice Hall.

Dubow, E. F., & Luster, T. (1990). Adjustment of children born to teenage mothers: The contribution of risk and protective factors. *Journal of Marriage and the Family, 52,* 393–404.

Dubow, E. F., & Tisak, J. (1989). The relation between stressful life events and adjustment in elementary school children: The role of social support and social problem-solving skills. *Child Development, 60,* 1412–1424.

Dubowitz, V. (1997, February 27). The muscular dystrophies: Clarity or chaos. *New England Journal of Medicine, 336,* 650–651.

Duke, M.P. (1994). Chaos theory and psychology: Seven propositions. *Genetic, Social, and General Psychology Monographs, 120,* 267–286.

Dullea, A. (1989, October 12). Opening the world to a generation. *New York Times,* pp. C1, C6.

Duncan, G. J., Brooks-Gunn, J., & Klebanov, P. K. (1994). Economic deprivation and early childhood development. *Child Development, 65,* 296–318.

Dunham, P. J., Dunham, F., & Curwin, A. (1993). Joint-attentional states and lexical acquisition at 18 months. *Developmental Psychology, 29,* 827–831.

Dunn, H., & Plomin, R. (1990). *Separate lives: Why siblings are so different.* New York: Basic Books.

Dunn, J. (1983). Sibling relationships in early childhood. *Child Development, 54,* 787–812.

Dunn, J. (1995). *From one to two.* New York: Ballantine.

Dunn, J., & Kendrick, C. (1982). *Siblings: Love, envy and understanding.* Cambridge, MA: Harvard University Press.

Dunn, J., & McGuire, S. (1992). Sibling and peer relationships in childhood. *Journal of Child Psychology and Psychiatry, 33,* 67–105.

Dunn, J., & Munn, P. (1986). Sibling quarrels and maternal intervention: Individual differences in understanding and aggression. *Journal of Child Psychology and Psychiatry, 27,* 583–595.

DuPaul, G. J., & Barkley, R. A. (1993). Behavioral contributions to pharmacotherapy: The utility of behavioral methodology in medical treatment of children with attention deficit hyperactivity disorder. *Behavior Therapy, 24,* 47–64.

Duran, R. P. (1989). Assessment and instruction of at-risk Hispanic students. *Exceptional Children, 56,* 154–159.

Durkin, K. (1995). *Developmental social psychology.* Cambridge, MA: Blackwell.

Dusek, J. B. (1996). *Adolescent development and behavior* (3rd ed.). Upper Saddle River, NJ: Prentice Hall.

Duwa, S. M., Wells, C., & Lalinde, P. (1993). Creating family-centered programs and policies. In D. M. Bryant & M. A. Graham (Eds.), *Implementing early intervention* (pp. 92–124). New York: Guilford.

Dworezysky, J.P. (1984) *Introduction to child development.* St. Paul, MN: West.

E

Eagly, A. H. (1978). Sex differences in influence-ability. *Psychological Bulletin, 85,* 86–116.

East, P. L. (1996). The younger sisters of child-bearing adolescents: Their attitudes, expectations, and behaviors. *Child Development, 67,* 267–282.

Eaton, W. O., & Ennis, L. R. (1986). Sex differences in human motor activity level. *Psychological Bulletin, 100,* 19–28.

Eaton, W. O., & Ritchot, K. F. M. (1995). Physical maturation and information-processing speed in middle childhood. *Developmental Psychology, 31,* 967–972.

Eccles, J. S., Midgley, C., Wigfield, A., Buchanan, C. M., Reuman, D., Flanagan, C., & MacIver, D. (1993). Development during adolescence: The impact of stage-environment fit on young adolescents' experience in schools and families. *American Psychologist, 48,* 90–101.

Eccles, J., Wigfield, A., Harold, R. D., & Blumenfield, P. (1993). Age and gender differences in children's self-and task perceptions during elementary school. *Child Development, 64,* 830–847.

Echols, L. D., West, R. F., Stonovich, K. E., & Zehr, K. S. (1996). Using children's literacy activities to predict growth in verbal cognitive skills: A longitudinal investigation. *Journal of Educational Psychology, 88,* 296–304.

Eckenrode, J., Laird, M., & Doris, J. (1993). School performance and disciplinary problems among abused and neglected children. *Developmental Psychology, 29,* 53–62.

Eckerman, C. O., & Didow, S. M. (1996). Nonverbal imitation and toddlers' mastery of verbal means of achieving coordinated action. *Developmental Psychology, 32,* 141–152.

The Economist (1995, March 4) Extra dry. *The Economist, 334,* p.80.

Edelman, M. W. (1985). The sea is so wide and my boat is so small: Problems facing black children today. In H. P. McAdoo & J. L. McAdoo (Eds.), *Black children* (pp. 72–85). Beverly Hills, CA: Sage.

Eder, A. (1995). *Changes of having twins.* Parent Resource Center on the Web.

Eder, R.A. (1989). The emergent personalogist: The structure and content of 3 1/2, 5 1/2, and 7 1/2-year-olds' concepts of themselves and other persons. *Child Development, 60,* 1218–1229.

Editorial note. (1998, April 1). *Journal of the American Medical Association, 279,* 985–986.

Edmonds, P. (1995, November 29). They're lost in the system and out on their own. *USA Today,* p. A6.

Education of handicapped children. (1977). U.S. Office of Education. *Federal Register, 42,* 65082–65085.

Edwards, C. P. (1995). Parenting toddlers. In M. H. Bornstein (Ed.), *Handbook of parenting* (Vol. 1, pp. 41–63). Mahwah, NJ: Erlbaum.

Egan, S.K., Monson, T.C., & Perry, D.G. (1998) Social-cognitive influences on change in aggression over time. *Developmental Psychology, 34,* 996–1006.

Egeland, B. (1988). Breaking the cycle of abuse: Implications for prediction and intervention. In K. Browne, C. Davies, & P. Stratton (Eds.). *Early prediction and prevention of child abuse.* New York: Wiley.

Egeland, B., & Hiester, M. (1995). The long-term consequences of infant day-care and mother-infant attachment. *Child Development, 66,* 474–485.

Egeland, B., Jacobovitz, D., & Sroufe, L. A. (1988). Breaking the cycle of abuse. *Child Development, 59,* 1080–1089.

Eggert, L. L., Thompson, E. A., Herring, J. R., & Nicholas, L. J. (1995). Reducing suicide potential among high-risk youth: Tests of school-based prevention programs. *Suicide and Life-Threatening Behavior, 25,* 276–296.

Ehrenhaft, P. M., Wagner, J. L., & Herdman, R. C. (1989). Changing prognosis for very low birth weight infants. *Obstetrics and Gynecology, 74,* 528–535.

Eidelberg, L. (Ed.). (1968). *Encyclopedia of psychoanalysis.* New York: Free Press.

Eisele, J., Hertsgaard, D., & Light, H. K. (1986). Factors related to eating disorders in young adolescent girls. *Adolescence, 21,* 283–290.

Eisen, L. M., Field, T. M., Bandsrtra, E. S., Roberts, J. P., Morrow, C., Larson, S. K., & Steele, B.M. (1991). Perinatal cocaine effects on neonatal stress behavior and performance on Brazelton scale. *Pediatrics, 88,* 477–479.

Eisenberg, N. (1989). The development of prosocial and aggressive behavior. In M. H. Bornstein & M. E. Lamb (Eds.), *Social, emotional and personality development* (pp. 461–486). Hillsdale, NJ: Erlbaum.

Eisenberg, N. (1990). Prosocial development in early and mid-adolescence. In R. Montemayor, G. R. Adams, & P. T. Gulotta (Eds.), *From childhood to adolescence: A transitional period?* (pp. 240–268). Newbury Park, CA: Sage.

Eisenberg, N., & Fabes, R. A. (1994). Mothers' reactions to children's negative emotions: Relations to children's temperament and anger behavior. *Merrill-Palmer Quarterly, 40,* 138–156.

Eisenberg, N., & Fabes, R. A. (1998). Prosocial development. In W. Damon (Editor in Chief) & N. Eisenberg (Vol. Ed.), *Handbook of child psychology* (Vol. 3, pp. 701–778). New York: Wiley.

Eisenberg, N., & Garvey, C. (1981). Children's use of verbal strategies in resolving conflicts. *Discourse Processes, 4,* 149–170.

Eisenberg, N., & Mussen, P. H. (1989). The roots of prosocial behavior in children. New York: Cambridge University Press.

Eisenberg, N., & Mussen, P. H. (1989). *The roots of prosocial behavior in children.* Cambridge: Cambridge University Press.

Eisenberg, N., Fabes, R.A., Murphy, B., Karbon, M., Smith, M., & Maszk, P. (1996). The relations of children's dispositional empathy-related responding to their emotionality, regulation, and social functioning. *Developmental Psychology, 32,* 195–209.

Eisenberg, N., Miller, P.A., Shell, R., McNalley, S., & Shea, C. (1991). Prosocial development in adolescence: A longitudinal study. *Developmental Psychology, 27,* 849–857.

Eisenberg, N., Murphy, B., & Shepard, S. (1997). The development of empathic accuracy. In W. Ickes (Ed.), *Empathic accuracy* (pp. 73–116). New York: Guilford.

Eisenberg, N., Wolchik, S. A., Hernandez, R., & Pasternack, J. F. (1985). Parental socialization of young children's play: A short-term longitudinal study. *Child Development, 56,* 1506–1513.

Eisenberg, R. B. (1970). The organization of auditory behavior. *Journal of Speech and Hearing Research, 13,* 461–464.

Eisenberg-Berg, N., & Hand, M. (1979). The relationship of preschoolers' reasoning about prosocial moral conflicts to prosocial behavior. *Child Development, 50*, 356–363.

Elder, G. H., Modell, J., & Parke, R. D. (Eds.). (1993). *Children in time and place*. Cambridge: Cambridge University Press.

Elder, G., Liker, J., & Cross, C. (1984). Parent-child behavior in the great depression: Life course and intergenerational influences. In P. Baltes & O. Brim (Eds.), *Life-span development and behavior* (Vol. 6, pp. 109–158). Orlando, FL: Academic Press.

Elia, J., Ambrosini, P. J., & Rapoport, J. L. (1999, March 11). Treatment of attention-deficit-hyperactivity disorder. *New England Journal of Medicine, 340*, 780–788.

Elias, M. (1994, November 8). Fewer teens exercise their workout option. *USA Today*, p. D1.

Elias, M. (1997, August 11). Kids tend to take after oft-divorced parents. *USA Today*, p. D1.

Elicker, J., Englund, M., & Sroufe, L. A. (1992). Predicting peer competence and peer relationships in childhood from early parent-child relationships. In R. D. Parke & G.W. Ladd (Eds.), *Family-peer relationships: Modes of linkage*. Hillsdale, NJ: Erlbaum.

Elkind, D. (1967). Egocentrism in adolescence. *Child Development, 38*, 1025–1034.

Elkind, D. (1985). Egocentrism redux. *Developmental Review, 5*, 218–226.

Elkind, D., & Bowen, R. (1979). Imaginary audience behavior in children and adolescence. *Developmental Psychology, 15*, 38–44.

Elkins, I. J., McGue, M. M., & Iacono, W. G. (1997). Genetic and environmental influences on parent-son relationships: Evidence for increasing genetic influence during adolescence. *Developmental Psychology, 33*, 351–363.

Elsen, H. (1995). Linguistic team-work: The interaction of linguistic modules in first language acquisition. In E. V. Clark (Ed.), *The child language research forum* (pp. 123–137). N.p.: Center for the Study of Language and Information, Leland Stanford Junior University.

Elster, A. B., & Panzarine, S. (1983). teenage fathers: Stresses during gestation and early parenthood. *Clinical Pediatrics, 22*, 700–703.

Emde, R. N. (1992). Individual meeting and increasing complexity: Contributions of Sigmund Freud and Rene Spitz to developmental psychology. *Developmental Psychology, 28*, 347–360.

Emde, R. N., Izard, C., Huebner, R., Sorce, J. F., & Klinnert, M. (1985). Adult judgments of infant emotions: Replication studies within and across laboratories. *Infant Behavior and Development, 8*, 79–88.

Emery, R. E. (1982). Interparental conflict and the children of discord and divorce. *Psychological Bulletin, 92*, 310–330.

Emmons, L. (1996). The relationship of dieting to weight in adolescents. *Adolescence, 31*, 167–179.

Emory, E. K., Schlackman, L. J., & Fiano, K. (1996). Drug-hormone interactions on neurobehavioral responses in human neonates. *Infant Behavior and Development, 19*, 213–220.

Engen, T., Lipsitt, L. P., & Peck, M. B. (1973). Ability of newborn infants to discriminate sapid substances. *Developmental Psychology, 10*, 741–744.

Ensign, J., Scherman, A., & Clark, J. J. (1998). The relationship of family structure and conflict to levels of intimacy and parental attachment in college students. *Adolescence, 33*, 575–582.

Entwisle, D. R. (1995). The role of schools in sustaining early childhood program benefits. *The Future of Children, 5*, 133–145.

Entwisle, D. R., & Alexander, K. L. (1987). Long-term effects of cesarean delivery on parents' beliefs and children's schooling. *Developmental Psychology, 23*, 676–682.

Epstein, J. L. (1990). What matters in the middle grades-grade span or practices? *Phi Delta Kappan*, 438–444.

Epstein, L. H. (1987). Behavioral treatment of childhood obesity. *Psychological Bulletin, 101*, 331–342.

Epstein, L.H., Smith, J.A., Vara, L.S., & Rodefer, J.S. (1991) Behavioral economic analysis of activity choice in obese children. *Health Psychology, 10*, 311–316.

Erel, O., Margolin, G., & John, R.S. (1998) Observed sibling interaction: Links with the marital and the mother-child relationship. *Developmental Psychology, 34*, 288–299.

Ericksen, K. P., & Trocki, K. F. (1994). Sex, alcohol and sexually transmitted diseases: A national survey. *Family Planning Perspectives, 26*, 257–263.

Erikson, E. (1963). *Childhood and society*. New York: Norton.

Erikson, E. (1968). *Identity: Youth and crisis*. New York: Norton.

Erikson, E. H. (1959). The problem of ego identity. Reprinted in Erikson, E. (1980). *Identity and the life cycle*. New York: Norton.

Erikson, E. (1975). *Life history and the historical moment*. New York: Norton.

Eron, L. D. (1982). Parent-child interaction, television violence, and aggression of children. *American Psychologist, 37*, 197–212.

Eron, L. D., Huesmann, L. R., Brice, P., Fischer, P., & Mermelstein, R. (1983). Age trends in the development of aggression, sex typing, and related television habits. *Developmental Psychology, 19*, 71–78.

Etaugh, C. (1980). Effects of nonmaternal care on children: Research evidence and popular views. *American Psychologist, 35*, 309–319.

Etaugh, C., & Hughes, V. (1975). Teachers' evaluations of sex-typed behaviors in children: The role of teacher sex and school setting. *Developmental Psychology, 11*, 394–395.

Etaugh, C., Grinnell, K., & Etaugh, A. (1989). Development of gender labeling: Effect of age of pictured children. *Sex Roles, 26*, 129–147.

Eth, S., & Pynoos, R. (1994). Children who witness the homicide of a parent. *Psychiatry, 57*, 287–306.

Eth, S., Silverstein, S., Pynoos, R. S. (1985). Mental health consultation to a preschool following the murder of a mother and child. *Hospital Community Psychiatry, 36*, 73–76.

Etzel, B. C., & Gewirtz, J. L. (1967). Experimentation model of caretaker-maintained heart-rate operant crying in a six and a twenty week old infant: Extinction of crying with reinforcement of eye contact and smiling. *Journal of Experimental Child Psychology, 5*, 303–317.

Evaloff, H. H. (1971). Some cognitive and affective aspects of early language development. *Child Development, 42*, 1895–1907.

Evaluation of telephoned computer-generated reminders to improve immunization coverage at inner-city clinics. (1993, July/August). *Public Health Reports, 108*, 426–430.

Extra dry. (1995, March 4). *The Economist, 334*, 80.

F

Fabes, R. A., Eisenberg, N., Jones, S., Smith, M., Guthrie, I., Poulin, R., Shepard, S., & Friedman, J. (1999). Regulation, emotionality, and preschoolers' socially competent peer interactions. *Child Development, 70*, 432–442.

Fabes, R. A., Eisenberg, N., Karbon, M., Troyer, D., & Switzer, G. (1994). The relations of children's emotion regulation to their vicarious emotional responses and comforting behavior. *Child Development, 65*, 1678–1693.

Face up to sex education. (1993, June 8). *USA Today*, p. A12.

Fagen, J. F. (1973). Infants' delayed recognition memory and forgetting. *Journal of Experimental Child Psychology, 16*, 424–450.

Fagot, B. I. (1978). The influence of sex of child on parental reactions to toddler children. *Child Development, 49*, 459–465.

Fagot, B. I. (1995). Parenting boys and girls. In M. H. Bornstein (Ed.), *Handbook of parenting* (Vol. 1, 163–183). Mahwah, NJ: Erlbaum.

Fagot, B. I. (1997). Attachment, parenting, and peer interactions of toddler children. *Developmental Psychology, 33*, 489–499.

Fagot, B. I., & Hagan, R. (1991). Observations of parent reactions to sex-stereotyped behaviors: Age and sex effects. *Child Development, 62*, 617–628.

Fagot, B. I., & Kavanagh, K. (1993). Parenting during the second year: Influences of age, sex of child and attachment classification. *Child Development, 63,* 258–271.

Fagot, B. I., & Lenbach, M. D. (1989). The young child's gender schema: Environmental input, internal organization. *Child Development, 60,* 663–672.

Fagot, B. I., Hagan, R., Leinbach, M. D., & Kronsberg, S. (1985). Differential reactions to assertive and communicative acts of toddler boys and girls. *Child Development, 56,* 1499–1505.

Fahy, T. A., & Eisler, I. (1993). Impulsivity and eating disorders. *British Journal of Psychiatry, 162,* 193–197.

Fairburn, C. G., Jones, R., Pevel, R. C., Carr, S. J., Solomon, R. A., O'Connor, M. E., Burton, J., & Hope, R. A. (1991). Three psychological treatments for bulimia nervosa. *Archives of General Psychiatry, 48,* 463–469.

Falbo, T., & Polit, D. (1986). Quantitative review of the only child literature: Research evidence and theory development. *Psychological Bulletin, 100,* 176–189.

Falbo, T., & Poston, D. L., Jr. (1993). The academic, personality, and physical outcomes of only children in China. *Child Development, 64,* 18–35.

Falk, P. J. (1989) Lesbian mothers: Psychosocial assumptions in family law. *American Psychologist, 44,* 941–947.

Fantz, R. L. (1961, May). The origin of form perception. *Scientific American,* pp. 16–21.

Fantz, R. L. (1963). Pattern vision in newborn infants. *Science, 140,* 296–297.

Fantz, R. L., & Miranda, S. B. (1975). Newborn infant's attention to form of contour. *Child Development, 46,* 224–228.

Farmer, A. (1996, December). The genetics of depressive disorders. *International Review of Depressive Disorders, 8,* 369–373.

Farmer, H. S. (1978). Career counseling implications for the lower social class and women. *Personnel and Guidance Journal, 56,* 467–472.

Farver, J. A. M., & Branstetter, W. H. (1994). Preschoolers' responses to their peers' distress. *Developmental Psychology, 30,* 334–341.

Farver, J. A. M., & Shin, Y. L. (1997). Social pretend play in Korean- and Anglo-American preschoolers. *Child Development, 68,* 544–556.

Fay, R., Turner, C., Klassen, A., & Gagnon, J. (1989, January 20). Prevalence and patterns of same-gender sexual contact among men. *Science, 243,* pp. 338–348.

Feeney, J. A., & Noller, P. (1991) Attachment style and verbal descriptions of romantic partners. *Journal of Social and Personal Relationships, 8,* 187–215.

Feinman, S., & Lewis, M. (1983). Social referencing at ten months: A second-order effect in infants' responses to strangers. *Child Development, 54,* 878–888.

Feldhusen, J. F. (1991). Saturday and summer programs. In N. Colangelo & G. A. Davis (Eds.), *Handbook of gifted education* (pp. 197–209). Needham Heights, MA: Allyn & Bacon.

Feldman, J. F., Brody, N., & Miller, S. A. (1980). Sex differences in non-elicited neonatal behaviors. *Merrill-Palmer Quarterly, 26,* 63–73.

Feldman, M. W., & Lewontin, R. C. (1975). The heritability hang-up. *Science, 190,* 1163–1168.

Feldman, S. S., & Quatman, T. (1988). Factors influencing age expectations for adolescent autonomy: A study of early adolescents and parents. *Journal of Early Adolescence, 8,* 325–343.

Felice, M. (1986). Reflections on caring for Indochinese children and youths. *Journal of Developmental and Behavioral Pediatrics, 7,* 124–128.

Feltey, K., Ainslie, J. J., & Geib, I. (1991). Sexual coercion attitudes among high school students. *Youth and Society, 23,* 229–250.

Ferguson, A. (1993, November 29). Barney backlash. *National Review,* pp. 80–81.

Ferguson, T. J., & Rule, B. G. (1982). Influence of inferential set, outcome intent, and outcome severity on children's moral judgments. *Developmental Psychology, 18,* 843–851.

Fernald, A. & Simon, T. (1984). Expanded intonation contours in mothers' speech to newborns. *Developmental Psychology, 20,* 104–113.

Fernald, A. (1985). Four-month-old infants prefer to listen to mothers. *Infant Behavior and Development, 8,* 181–195.

Fernald, A. (1993). Approval and disapproval: Infant responsiveness to vocal affect in familiar and unfamiliar languages. *Child Development, 64,* 657–674.

Fernald, A., & Kuhl, P. (1987). Acoustic determinants of infant preference for mothers speech. *Infant Behavior and Development, 10,* 279–293.

Fernald, A., & Morikawa, H. (1993). Common themes and cultural variations in Japanese and American mothers' speech to infants. *Child Development, 64,* 637–657.

Field, T. (1986). Interventions for premature infants. *Journal of Pediatrics, 109,* 183–190.

Field, T. (1991). Quality infant day care and grade school behavior and performance. *Child Development, 62,* 863–870.

Field, T. (1992). Infants of depressed mothers. *Developmental Psychology, 4,* 49–66.

Field, T. (1995). Psychologically depressed parents. In M. H. Bornstein (Ed.), *Handbook of parenting* (Vol. 4, pp. 85–101). Mahwah, NJ: Erlbaum.

Field, T. (1996). Attachment and separation in young children. *Annual Review of Psychology, 47,* 541–561.

Field, T. M., Woodson, R. W., Cohen, D., Greenberg, R., Garcia, R., & Collins, R. (1983). Discrimination and imitation of facial expressions by term and preterm neonates. *Infant Behavior and Development, 6,* 485–489.

Field, T., Fox, N., Pickens, J., & Nawrocki, R. (1995). Relative right frontal EEG activation in 3-to 6-month old infants of "depressed" mothers. *Developmental Psychology, 31,* 358–363.

Field, T., Masi, W., Goldstein, S., Perry, S., & Pearl, S. (1988). Infant day care facilitates preschool social behavior. *Early Childhood Research Quarterly, 3,* 341–359.

Fields, G. (1994, May 20–22). 1.6 million kids home alone. *USA Today,* p. A1.

Finkelhor, D., & Dziuba-Letherman, J. (1994). Children as victims of violence: A national survey. *Pediatrics, 94,* 413–420.

Finkelson, L., & Oswalt, R. (1995). College data rape: incidence and reporting. *Psychological Reports, 77,* 526.

Finn, C. E. (1995, January). For whom it tolls. *Commentary, 99,* 76–81.

Finster, M., Pedersen, H., & Morishima, H. O. (1984). Principles of fetal exposure to drugs used in obstetric anesthesia. In B. Krauer, F. Krauer, F. E. Hytten, & E. del Pozo (Eds.), *Drugs and pregnancy* (pp. 95–101). New York: Academic Press.

Firestone, W. A. (1994). The content and context of sexuality education: An exploratory study in one study. *Family Planning Perspectives, 26,* 125–131.

First, J. A., & Wey, W. L. (1995). Parent education outcomes: Insights into transformative learning. *Family Relations, 44,* 104–109.

Fischer, K. W. (1980). A theory of cognitive development: The control and construction of hierarchies of skills. *Psychological Review, 87,* 477–531.

Fischer, K. W. (1987). Commentary-relations between brain and cognitive development. *Child Development, 58,* 623–633.

Fisher, C. B., & Lerner, R. M. (1994). Foundations of applied developmental psychology. In C. B. Fisher & R. M. Lerner (Eds.), *Applied developmental psychology* (pp. 3–23). New York: McGraw-Hill.

Fisher, C. B., & Tryon, W. W. (1988). Ethical issues in the research and practice of applied developmental psychology. *Journal of Applied Developmental Psychology, 9,* 27–39.

Fisher, C., & Tokura, H. (1996). Acoustic cues to grammatical structure in infant-directed speech: Cross-linguistic evidence. *Child Development, 67,* 3192–3218.

Fisher, J. A. & Birch, L. L. (1995). Fat preferences and fat consumption of 3- to 5-year-old children are related to parental adiposity. *Journal of the American Dietetic Association, 95,* 759–764.

Fisher-Thompson, D. (1993). Adult toy purchase for children: Factors affecting sex-typed toy selection. *Journal of Applied Developmental Psychology, 14,* 385–406.

Fitch, S. A., & Adams, G. R. (1983). Ego identity and intimacy: Replication and extension. *Developmental Psychology, 19,* 839–845.

Fivush, R., Kuebli, J., & Clubb, P.A. (1992). The structure of events and event representations: A developmental analysis. *Child Development, 63,* 188–201.

Flaks, D. K., Ficher, I., Masterpasqua, F., & Joseph, G. (1995). Lesbians choosing motherhood: A comparative study of lesbian and heterosexual parents and their children. *Developmental Psychology, 31,* 105–115.

Flavell, J. H. (1977). *Cognitive development.* Upper Saddle River, NJ: Prentice Hall.

Flavell, J. H. (1985). *Cognitive development* (2nd ed.). Upper Saddle River, NJ: Prentice Hall.

Flavell, J. H. (1986). The development of children's knowledge about the appearance-reality distinction. *American Psychologist, 41,* 418–426.

Flavell, J. H. (1992). Cognitive development: Past, present and future. *Developmental Psychology, 28,* 998–1006.

Flavell, J. H., & Miller, P. H. (1998). Social cognition. In W. Damon (Editor in Chief) & D. Kuhn & R. S. Sielger (Vol. Eds.), *Handbook of child psychology* (5th ed., Vol. 2, pp. 851–899). New York: Wiley.

Flavell, J. H., & Wellman, H. M. (1977). Metamemory. In R. V. Kail & J. W. Hagen (Eds.), *Perspectives on the development of memory and cognition.* Hillsdale, NJ: Erlbaum.

Flavell, J. H., Beach, D. H., & Clinsky, J. M. (1966). Spontaneous verbal rehearsal in memory tasks as a function of age. *Child Development, 37,* 283–299.

Flavell, J. H., Flavell, E. R., Green, F. L., & Wilcox, S. A. (1981). The development of three spatial perspective-taking rules. *Child Development, 52,* 356–358.

Flavell, J. H., Miller, P. H., & Miller, S. A. (1993). *Cognitive development* (3rd ed.). Upper Saddle River, NJ: Prentice Hall.

Flavell, J. H., Mumme, D. L., Green, F. L., & Flavell, E. R. (1992). Young children's understanding of different types of beliefs. *Child Development, 63,* 960–978.

Fleck, K.M. (1995, November) Easing into elementary school. *The Education Digest, 4,* 25–27.

Fletcher, A. C., Darling, N. E., Steinberg, L., & Dornbusch, S. M. (1995). The company they keep: Relation of adolescents' adjustment and behavior to their friends' perceptions of authoritative parenting in the social network. *Developmental Psychology, 31,* 300–310.

Flin, R., Kearney, B., & Murray, K. (1996). Children's evidence: Scottish research and law. *Criminal Justice and Behavior, 23,* 358–376.

Floyd, R. L., Rimer, B. K. Giovino, G. A., Mullen, P. D., & Sullivan, S. E. (1993). A review of smoking in pregnancy: Effects on pregnancy outcomes and cessation efforts. *Annual Review of Public Health, 14,* 379–411.

Flum, H. (1994). Styles of identity formation in early and middle adolescence. *Genetic, Social, and General Psychology Monographs, 120,* 435–467.

Foa, L., Schwab, R. L., & Johnson, M. (1996, May 1). Upgrading school technology. *Education Week,* pp. 40, 52.

Fogel, A. (1984). *Infancy: Infant, family and society.* St. Paul, MN: West.

Fogel, A., Nwokah, E., & Karns, J. (1993). Parent-infant games as dynamic social systems. In K. MacDonald (Ed.), *Parent-child play.* Albany: State University of New York Press.

Fogelman, K. (Ed.). (1983). *Growing up in Great Britain.* London: Macmillan.

Fomon, S. J. (1993). *Nutrition of normal infants.* St. Louis, MO: Mosby.

Fonteyn, V. J., & Isada, N. B. (1988). Nongenetic implications of childbearing after age 35. *Obstetrical and Gynecological Survey, 43,* 709–719.

Forbes, D. (1987). Saying no to Ron and Nancy: School-based drug abuse prevention program in the 1980s. *Journal of Education, 169,* 80–90.

Ford, D. & Harris, J.J. III (1996) Perceptions and attitudes of black students toward school achievement, and other educational variables. *Child Development, 67,* 1141-1152

Ford, M. E. (1979). The construct validity of egocentrism. *Psychological Bulletin, 86,* 1169–1188.

Fordham, S. (1988). Racelessness as a factor in Black students' school success: Pragmatic strategy or pyrrhic victory. *Harvard Educational Review, 58,* 54–84.

Forness, S. R., & Kavale, K. A. (1988). Psychopharmacological treatment: A note on classroom effects. *Journal of Learning Disabilities, 21,* 144–147.

Foscarinis, M. (1991). The politics of homelessness: A call to action. *American Psychologist, 46,* 1232–1238.

Foster, E. M. (1995). Why teens do not benefit from work experience programs: Evidence from brother comparisons. *Journal of Policy Analysis and Management, 14,* 393–414.

Foster, G. D., Wadden, T. A., & Vogt, R. A. (1997). Body image in obese women before, during, and after weight loss treatment. *Health Psychology, 16,* 226–229.

Fowler, B. A. (1989). The relationship of body image perception and weight status to recent change in weight status of the adolescent female. *Adolescence, 24,* 557–567.

Fowler, M. (1991, September). *Attention deficit disorder.* Washington, DC: National Information Center for Children and Youth with Disabilities.

Fox, R., Anderson, R., Fox, T., & Rodriguez, M. (1991, September). STAR parenting: A model for helping parents effectively deal with behavioral difficulties. *Young Children,* pp. 54–60.

Fox, S. (1997, November). The controversy over Ebonics. *Phi Delta Kappan,* pp. 237–240.

Fox, V. (1985). *Introduction to criminology* (2nd ed.). Upper Saddle River, NJ: Prentice Hall.

Fraley, R.C., & Shaver, P.R. (1997) Adult attachment and the suppression of unwanted thoughts. *Journal of Personality and Social Psychology, 73,* 1080–1092.

Francis, H. (1975). *Language in childhood: Form and function in language development.* New York: St. Martin's.

Francis, L. J. (1997). Coopersmith's model of self-esteem: Bias toward the stable extravert? *Journal of Social Psychology, 137,* 139–143.

Frankel, A. J. (1994). Family day care in the United States. *Families in Society: The Journal of Contemporary Human Services, 75,* 550–560.

Frankel, B. (1995 August 16). Reining in out-of-control schools. *USA Today,* p. D4.

Frankel, K.A., & Bates, J.E. (1990) Mother-toddler problem solving: Antecedents in attachment, home behavior, and temperament. *Child Development, 61,* 810–820.

Franklin, M. E. (1992). Culturally sensitive instructional practices for African-American learners. *Exceptional Children, 59,* 115–123.

Frazier, J.A., & Morrison, F.J. (1998) The influence of extended-year schooling on growth of achievement and perceived competence in early elementary school. *Child Development, 69,* 495–517.

Freiberg, P. (1996, September). Latchkey kids not always trouble-prone. *APA Monitor,* p. 48.

Freidrich, L. K., & Stein, A. H. (1975). Prosocial television and young children: The effects of verbal labeling and role playing on learning and behavior. *Child Development, 46,* 27–38.

French, S. A., Perry, C. L., Leon, G. R., & Fulkerson, J. A. (1995). Dieting behaviors and weight change history in female adolescents. *Health Psychology, 14,* 548–555.

Freud, S. (1953). *General introduction to psychoanalysis.* New York: Doubleday. (Originally published 1935.)

Freud, S. (1957). The interpretation of dreams. In J. Strachey (Ed.), *The standard edition of the complete psychological works of Sigmund Freud* (Vol. 4). London: Hogarth. (Originally published 1900.)

Freud, S. (1961). *New introductory lectures on psychoanalysis.* New York: Norton. (Originally published 1933.)

Freud, S. (1962). *The ego and the id.* New York: Norton. (Originally published 1923.)

Freund, L. S. (1990). Maternal regulation of children's problem-solving behavior and its impact on children's performance. *Child Development, 61,* 113–127.

Frey, D., & Carlock, C. J. (1989). *Enhancing self esteem.* Muncie, IN: Accelerated Development.

Friedman, M. A., & Brownell, K.D. (1995). Psychological correlates of obesity: Moving to the next research generation. *Psychological Bulletin*, 117, 3–20.

Friedman, S., & Carpenter, G. C. (1971). Visual response decrement as a function of age of human newborn. *Child Development, 42*, 1967–1973.

Friedrich, L., & Stein, A. (1973). Aggressive and prosocial television programs and the natural behavior of preschool children. *Monographs of the Society for Research in Child Development, 4*, Serial No. 151.

Friedrich, W. N., & Boriskin, J. A. (1976). The role of the child in abuse: A review of the literature. *American Journal of Orthopsychiatry, 46*, 580–591.

Friend, T. (1994, November 1). Genes may cause manic depression. *USA Today*, p. D1.

Friend, T. (1996, May 24–27). Teen smoking rate highest since 1970s. *USA Today*, p. A1.

Frost, J. J., & Forrest, J. D. (1995). Understanding the impact of effective teenage pregnancy prevention programs. *Family Planning Perspectives, 27*, 188–195.

Fuligni, A. J. & Stevenson, H. W. (1995). Time use and mathematics achievement among American, Chinese, and Japanese high school students. *Child Development, 66*, 830–842.

Fuligni, A. J., & Eccles, J. S. (1993). Perceived parent-child relationships and early adolescents' orientation toward peers. *Developmental Psychology, 29*, 622–632.

Fuligni, A.J., Tseng, V., & Lam, M. (1999) Attitudes towards family obligations among American adolescents with Asian, Latin American, and European Backgrounds. *Child Development, 70*, 1030–1044.

Fullerton, C. S., & Urbano, R. J. (1994). Preadolescent peer friendships: A critical contribution to adult social relatedness. *Journal of Youth and Adolescence, 23*, 43–63.

Furman, L. N., & Walden, T. A. (1990). Effect of script knowledge on preschool children's communicative interactions. *Developmental Psychology, 26*, 227–233.

Furman, W. (1996). Parenting siblings. In M. H. Bornstein (Ed.), *Handbook of parenting* (Vol. 1., pp. 143–162). Mahwah, NJ: Erlbaum.

Furman, W., & Buhrmester D. (1985a). Children's perceptions of the personal relationships in their social networks. *Developmental Psychology, 21*, 1016–1024.

Furman, W., & Buhrmester, D. (1985b). Children's perceptions of the qualities of sibling relationships. *Child Development, 56*, 448–461.

Furstenberg, F. F. (1981). Implicating the family: Teenage parenthood and kinship involvements. In T. Ooms (Ed.), *Teenage pregnancy in a family context: Implications for policy* (pp. 131–165). Philadelphia: Temple University Press.

Furstenberg, F. F., Brooks-Gunn, J., & Chase-Lansdale, L. (1989). Teenaged pregnancy and childbearing. *American Psychologist, 44*, 313–320.

Furstenberg, F., Jr. (1976). The social consequences of teenage parenthood. *Family Planning Perspectives, 8*, 148–164.

Fusaro, J. A. (1997). The effects of full-day kindergarten on student achievement: A meta-analysis. *Child Study Journal, 27*, 269–280.

Futterman, D., & Hein, K. (1994). Medical management of adolescents with HIV infection. In P. A. Pizzo & C. M. Wilfert (Eds.), *Pediatric AIDS: The challenge of HIV Infection in infants, children, and adolescents* (2nd ed., pp. 757–7752). Baltimore: Williams & Wilkins.

G

Gabbard, C., Hart, S., & Gentry, V. (1995). General motor proficiency and handedness in children. *Journal of Genetic Psychology, 156*, 411–417.

Gable, D. (1994, May 10). Reality-based violence hits harder. *USA Today*, p. DD.

Gadberry, S. (1980). Effects of restricting first graders' TV-viewing on leisure time use, IQ change, and cognitive style. *Journal of Applied Developmental Psychology, 1*, 45–57.

Galambos, N. L., Almeida, D. M., & Petersen, A. C. (1990). Masculinity, femininity, and sex role attitudes in early adolescence: Exploring gender intensification. *Child Development, 61*, 1905–1914.

Galef, B. G., Jr. (1991). A contrarian view of the wisdom of the body as it relates to dietary self-selection. *Psychology Review, 98*, 759–764.

Gallup, G. H., Jr., & Bezilla, R. (1992). *The religious life of young Americans*. Princeton, NJ: George H. Gallup International Institute.

Galotti, K. M. (1989). Gender differences in self-reported moral reasoning: A review and new evidence. *Journal of Youth and Adolescence, 18*, 475–487.

Garbarino, J., & Kostelny, K. (1996). The effects of political violence on Palestinian children's behavior problems: A risk accumulation model. *Child Development, 67*, 33–46.

Garcia Coll, C. T., Meyer, E. C., & Brillon, L. (1995). Ethnic and minority parenting. In M. H. Bornstein (Ed.), *Handbook of parenting* (Vol. 2, pp. 189–209). Mahwah, NJ: Erlbaum.

Garcia-Coll, C., Hoffman, J., & Oh, W. (1987). The social ecology of early parenting of Caucasian adolescent mothers. *Child Development, 58*, 955–964.

Gardner, H. (1983). *Frames of mind*. New York: Basic Books.

Gardner, H. (1987). *The theory of multiple intelligences*. Annals of Dyslexia, 37, 19–35.

Gardner, H. (1993). *Multiple intelligences: The theory in practice*. New York: Basic Books.

Gargiulo, J., Attie, I., Brooks-Gunn, J., & Warren, M. P. (1987). Girls' dating behavior as a function of social context and maturation. *Developmental Psychology, 23*, 730–737.

Garland, A. F., & Zigler, E. (1993). Adolescent suicide prevention: Current research and social policy implications. *American Psychologist, 48*, 169–182.

Garn, S. M. (1980). Continuities and change in maturational timing. In O. G. Brim, Jr., & J. Kagan (Eds.), *Constancy and change in human development* (pp. 113–162). Cambridge, MA: Harvard University Press.

Garner, D. M., Fairburn, C. G., & Davis, R. (1987). Cognitive behavioral treatment for bulimia nervosa: A critical appraisal. *Behavioral Medicine, 11*, 398–431.

Garnica, O. K. (1977). Some prosodic and paralinguistic features of speech directed to young children. In C. E. Snow & C. A. Ferguson (Eds.), *Talking to children: Language input and acquisition*. Cambridge: Cambridge University Press.

Garvey, C., & Hogan, R. (1973) Social speech and social interaction: Egocentrism revisited. *Child Development, 44*, 562–568.

Gaskill, F. W., & Brantley, J. C. (1996). Changes in ability and achievement scores over time: Implications for children classified as learning disabled. *Journal of Psychoeducational Assessment, 14*, 220–228.

Gates, H. L. (1994, November 7). Don't blame Darwin. *New Republic, 211*, 10–13.

Gavin, L. A., & Furman, W. (1989). Age differences in adolescents' perceptions of their peer groups. *Developmental Psychology, 25*, 827–834.

Gavora, J. (1997, March/April). Courts cast pall over parental-rights bill. *Policy Review, 82*, 12–14.

Gaylord-Ross, R. J., Forte, J., Storey, K., Gaylord-Ross, C., & Jameson, D. (1987). Community-referenced instruction in technological work settings. *Exceptional Children, 54*, 112–120.

Ge, X., Conger, R. D., & Elder, G. H. (1996). Coming of age too early: Pubertal influences on girls' vulnerability to psychological distress. *Child Development, 67*, 3386–3400.

Ge, X., Lorenz, F. O., Conger, R. D., Elder, G. H., Jr., & Simons, R. L. (1994). Trajectories of stressful life events and depressive symptoms during adolescence. *Developmental Psychology, 30*, 467–483.

Geary, D. C., Salthouse, T. A., Chen, G. P., & Fan, L. (1996). Are East Asian versus American differences in arithmetic ability a recent phenomenon? *Developmental Psychology, 32*, 254–262.

Geber, M., & Dean, R. F. A. (1957). The state of development of newborn African children. *The Lancet, 272*, 1216–1219.

Gelles, R. J. (1978). Violence toward children in the United States. *American Journal of Orthopsychiatry, 48*, 580–592.

Gelles, R. J., & Conte, J. R. (1990). Domestic violence and sexual abuse of children: A review of research in the eighties. *Journal of Marriage and the Family, 52*, 1045–1058.

Gelman, D., with Foote, D. (1992, February 24). Born or Bred? *Newsweek*, pp. 46–53.

Gelman, R. (1969). Conservation acquisition: A problem of learning to attend to relevant attributes. *Journal of Experimental Child Psychology, 7*, 167–187.

Gelman, R., & Baillargeon, R. A. (1983). A review of some Piagetian concepts. In P. H. Mussen (Ed.), *Handbook of child psychology* (4th ed. Vol. 3, pp. 167–231). New York: Wiley.

Gelman, R., Spelke, E., & Meck, E. (1983). What preschoolers know about animate and inanimate objects. In D. Rogers & J. Sloboda (Eds.), *The acquisition of symbolic skills* (pp. 232–252). New York: Plenum.

Gelman, S.A., & Coley, J.D. (1990) The importance of knowing a dodo is a bird: Categories and inferences in 2 ½-year-old children. *Developmental Psychology, 26*, 796–804.

Genetic testing for cystic fibrosis. (1997, May 21). *Journal of the American Medical Association, 277*, 1507.

Gerber, P. J., Ginsberg, R., & Reiff, H. B. (1992). Identifying alterable patterns in employment success for highly successful adults with learning disabilities. *Journal of Learning Disabilities, 25*, 475–487.

Gerbner, G. (1996). Fred Rogers and the significance of story. In M. Collins & M. M. Kimmel (Eds.), Mister Rogers' Neighborhood: *Children, television and Fred Rogers* (pp. 3–14). Pittsburgh, PA: University of Pittsburgh Press.

Gershkoff-Stowe, L., Thal, D. J., Smith, L. B., & Namy, L. L. (1997). Categorization and its developmental relations to early language. *Child Development, 68*, 843–860.

Gerstein, T., & Woodward, J. (1994) The language-minority student and special education issues, trends and paradoxes. *Exceptional Children, 61*, 310–322.

Gewirtzman, R., & Fodor, I. (1987). The homeless child at school: From welfare hotel to classroom. *Child Welfare, 66*, 237–245.

Giardiello, F. M., Brensinger, J. D., Petersen, G. M., et al. (1997). The use and interpretation of commercial APC gene testing for familial adenomatous polyposis. *New England Journal of Medicine, 336*, 823–827.

Gibbs, J. T., & Huang, L. N. (1989). A conceptual framework for assessing and treating minority youth. In *Children of color: Psychological interventions with minority youth* (pp. 1–30). San Francisco: Jossey-Bass.

Gibson, E. J., & Walk, R. D. (1960, April). The "visual cliff." *Scientific American*, pp. 64–71.

Gifted and Talented Children's Act of 1978. PL 96–561, Section 902.

Gilbert, J. I. (1986). Logical consequences: A new classification. *Individual Psychology, 42*, 243–254.

Gilligan, C. (1982). *In a different voice.* Cambridge, MA: Harvard University Press.

Gilligan, C. (1988). Exit-voice dilemmas in adolescent development. In C. Gilligan, J. V. Ward, J. M. Taylor, & B. Bardige (Eds.), *Mapping the moral domain.* Cambridge, MA: Harvard University Press.

Gilligan, C., & Attanucci, J. (1988). Two moral orientations: Gender differences and similarities. *Merrill-Palmer Quarterly, 34*, 223–237.

Gilligan, C., Brown, L. M., & Rogers, A. G. (1990). Psyche embedded: A place for body, relationships, and culture in personality theory. In A. I. Rabin, R. A. Zuker, R. A. Emmons, & S. Frank (Eds.), *Studying persons and lives.* New York: Springer.

Gilligan, C., Lyons, N., & Hammer, T.J. (1989). *Making connections.* Cambridge, MA: Harvard University Press.

Gilroy, F. & Steinbacher, R. (1991) Sex selection technology utilization: Further implications for sex ratio imbalance. *Social Biology, 38*, 285–288.

Gilroy, F., & Steinbacher, R. (1983) Preselection of child's sex: Technological utilization and feminism. *Psychological Reports, 53*, 671–676.

Ginott, H. G. (1969). *Between parent and teenager.* New York: Macmillan.

Ginsburg, G. S., & Bronstein, P. (1993). Family factors related to children's intrinsic/extrinsic motivational orientation and academic performance. *Child Development, 64*, 1461–1474.

Gjerdingen, D. K., Ireland, M., & Chaloner, K. M. (1996). Growth among Hmong children. *Archives of Adolescent Medicine, 150*, 1295–1298.

Gleason, J. B. (1985). *The development of language.* Columbus, OH: Merrill/Prentice Hall.

Glick, P. C. (1989). Remarried families, stepfamilies, and stepchildren: A brief demographic profile. *Family Relations, 38*, 24–27.

Goertzel, V., & Goertzel, M. G. (1962). *Cradles of eminence.* Boston: Little, Brown.

Gohm, C.L., Oishi, S., Darlington, J., & Diener, E. (1998) Culture, parental conflict, parental marital status, and the subjective well-being of young adults. *Journal of Marriage and the Family, 60*, 319–335.

Golambos, N. L., & Maggs, J. L. (1991). Out-of-school care of young adolescents and self-reported behavior. *Developmental Psychology, 27*, 644–655.

Goldenberg, R. L., & Rouse, D. J. (1998, July 30). Prevention of premature birth. *New England Journal of Medicine, 339*, 313–319.

Goldenberg, R. L., Tamura, T., Neggers, Y., Cooper, R. L., Johnston, K. E., DuBard, M. B., & Hauth, J. C. (1995). The effect of zinc supplementation on pregnancy outcome. *Journal of the American Medical Association, 274*, 463–468.

Goldfield, B. A. (1990). Pointing, naming, and talk about objects: Referential behavior in children and mothers. *First Language, 10*, 231–242.

Goldfield, B. A., & Reznick, J. S. (1989). Early lexical acquisition: Rate, content, and the vocabulary spurt. Journal of *Child Language, 17*, 171–183.

Goldfield, E. C., Kay, B. A., & Warren, W. H., Jr. (1993). Infant bouncing: The assembly and tuning of action systems. *Child Development, 64*, 1128–1143.

Goldman, G., Pineault, R., Potvin, L., Blais, R., & Bilodueau, H. (1993). Factors influencing the practice of vaginal birth after cesarean section. *American Journal of Public Health, 83*, 1104–1131.

Goldman, L. S., Genel, M., Bezman, R. J., & Stanetz, P. J. (1998, April 8). Diagnosis and treatment of attention-deficit/hyperactivity disorder in children and adolescents. *Journal of the American Medical Association, 279*, 1100–1107.

Goldsmith, E. (1987). The analysis of illustration in theory and practice. In D. M. Willows & H. A. Houghton (Eds.), *The psychology of illustration* (Vol. 2, pp. 53–82). New York: Springer.

Goldsmith, H. H. (1996). Studying temperament via construction of the toddler behavior assessment questionnaire. *Child Development, 67*, 218–235.

Goldsmith, H. H., Buss, K. A., & Lemery, K. S. (1997). Toddler and childhood temperament: Expanded content, stronger genetic evidence, new evidence for the importance of the environment. *Developmental Psychology, 33*, 891–905.

Goldsmith, H., Buss, A. H., Plomin, R., Rothbart, M. K., Thomas, A., Chess, S., Hinde, R. A., & McCall, R. B. (1987). What is temperament? Four approaches. *Child Development, 58*, 505–529.

Goldsmith, H.H., & Alansky, J.A. (1987) Maternal and infant temperamental predictors of attachment: A met-analytic review. *Journal of Consulting and Clinical Psychology, 55*, 805–816.

Goleman, D. (1989, June 6). New research overturns a milestone of infancy. *New York Times*, pp. C1+.

Goleman, D. (1995). *Emotional intelligence: Why it can matter more than IQ.* New York: Bantam.

Goleman, D. G. (1986, September 2). The roots of terrorism are found in brutality of shattered childhood. *New York Times*, pp. C1, C8.

Golombok, S., & Tasker, F. (1996). Do parents influence the sexual orientation of their children? Findings from a longitudinal study of lesbian families. *Developmental Psychology, 32*, 3–12.

Golombok, S., Cook, R., Bish, A., & Murray, C. (1995). Families created by the new reproductive technologies: Quality of parenting and social and emotional development of the children. *Child Development, 66*, 285–298.

Gomby, D. S., Krantzler, N., Larner, M. B., Stevenson, C. S., Terman, D. L., & Behrman, R. E. (1996). Financing child care: Analysis and recommendations. In *The future of children* (Vol. 6, pp. 5–25). Los Altos, CA: David and Lucile Packard Foundation.

Gomby, D. S., Larner, M. B., Stevenson, C. S., Lewit, E. M., & Behrman, R. E. (1995). Long-term outcomes of early childhood programs: Analysis and recommendations. In *The future of children* (Vol. 5, pp. 6–25). Los Altos, CA: David and Lucile Packard Foundation.

Gonzalez, J., Field, T., Yando, R., Gonzalez, K., Lasko, D., & Bendell, D. (1994). Adolescents' perception of their risk-taking behavior. *Adolescence, 79,* 701–710.

Gonzalez, J., Field, T., Yando, R., Gonzalez, K., Lasko, D., & Bendell, D. (1994). Adolescents' perceptions of their risk-taking behavior. *Adolescence, 29,* 701–711.

Gonzalez-Mena, J. (1986). Toddlers: What to expect. *Young Children, 42,* 85–90.

Goodluck, H. (1986). Language acquisition and linguistic theory. In P. Fletcher & M. Garman (Eds.), *Language acquisition* (2nd ed., pp. 49–69). London: Cambridge University Press.

Goodman, G. S., Emery, R. E., & Haugaard, J. J. (1998). Developmental psychology and law: Divorce, child maltreatment, foster care, and adoption. In W. Damon (Editor in Chief) & I. E. Sigel & K. A. Renninger (Vol. Eds.), *Handbook of child psychology* (5th ed., Vol. 4, pp. 775–874). New York: Wiley.

Goodman, R., & Stevenson, J. (1989). A twin study of hyperactivity. 2. The aetiological role of genes, family relationships and perinatal adversity. *Journal of Child Psychology and Psychiatry, 30,* 691–709.

Goodstadt, M. S. (1987, February). School-based drug education: What is wrong: *Education Digest,* pp. 44–47.

Goodwyn, S., & Acredolo, L. (1993) Symbolic gesture versus word: Is there a modality advantage for the onset of symbol use? *Child Development, 64,* 688–701.

Gopnick, A., & Meltzoff, A. (1987). The development of categorization in the second year and its relation to other cognitive and linguistic developments. *Child Development, 58,* 1523–1531.

Gopnik, A., & Astington, J. W. (1988). Children's understanding of representational change and its relation to the understanding of false belief and the appearance-reality distinction. *Child Development, 59,* 26–37.

Gordon, B. N., & Follmer, A. (1994). Developmental issues in judging the credibility of children's testimony. *Journal of Clinical Child Psychology, 23,* 283–294.

Gordon, C. M., Carey, M. P., & Carey, K. B. (1997). Effects of a drinking event on behavioral skills and condom attitudes in men: Implications for HIV risk from a controlled experiment. *Health Psychology, 16,* 490–495.

Gordon, P. (1990). Learnability and feedback. *Developmental Psychology, 26,* 217–221.

Gorman, D. M. (1997, February). The failure of drug education. *The Public Interest, 129,* 50–61.

Gorsuch, R. L., & Key, M. A. (1974). Abnormalities of pregnancy as a function of anxiety and life stress. *Psychosomatic Medicine, 36,* 352–362.

Gottesman, I. I. (1966). Genetics and personality. Cited in Hutt, J. J., & Hutt, C. (Eds.). (1973). *Early human development* (pp. 17–25). London: Oxford University Press.

Gottesman, I. I. (1978). Schizophrenia and genetics: Where are we? Are you sure? In L. C. Wynne (Ed.), *The nature of schizophrenia.* New York: Wiley.

Gottesman, I. I., & Shields, J. (1972). *Schizophrenia and genetics: A twin study vantage point.* New York: Academic Press.

Gottfried, A. E., Bathurst, K., & Gottfried, A. W. (1994). Role of maternal and dual-earner employment status in children's development: A longitudinal study from infancy through early adolescence. In A. E. Gottfried & A. W. Gottfried (Eds.). *Redefining families: Implications for children's development* (pp. 55–97). New York: Plenum.

Gottfried, A. E., Gottfried, A. W., & Bathurst, K. (1988). Maternal employment, family environment, and children's development: Infancy through the school year. In A. E. Gottfried & A. W. Gottfried (Eds.), *Maternal employment and children's development: Longitudinal research* (pp. 11–58). New York: Plenum.

Gottfried, A. E., Gottfried, A. W., & Bathurst, K. (1995). Maternal and dual-earner employment status and parenting. In M. H. Bornstein (Ed.), *Handbook of parenting* (Vol. 2, pp. 139–160). New York: Wiley.

Gottlieb, G. (1991). Experiential canalization of behavioral development: Theory. *Developmental Psychology, 27,* 4–14.

Gottman, J. (1983). *How children become friends. Monographs of the Society for Research in Child Development, 48,* Serial No. 201.

Gottman, J., & Mettetal, G. (1986). Speculations about social and affective development: Friendship and acquaintanceship through adolescence. In J. M. Gottman & J. G. Parker (Eds.), *Conversations of friends: Speculations on affective development* (pp. 192–241). New York: Cambridge University Press.

Goubet, N., & Clifton, R. K. (1998) Object and event representation in 6 ½- month-old infants. *Developmental Psychology, 34,* 63–77.

Gove, W. R., & Zeiss, C. (1987). Multiple roles and happiness. In F. J. Crosby (Ed.), *Spouse, parent, worker* (pp. 125–137). New Haven, CT: Yale University Press.

Graber, J. A., Brooks-Gunn, J., & Warren, M. P. (1995). The antecedents of menarcheal age: Heredity, family environments, and stressful life events. *Child Development, 66,* 346–359.

Graber, J. A., Brooks-Gunn, J., Paikoff, R. L., & Warren, M. P. (1994). Prediction of eating problems: An 8-year study of adolescent girls. *Developmental Psychology, 30,* 823–834.

Graber, J., Brooks-Gunn, J., Paikoff, R., & Warren, M. (1994). Prediction of eating problems: An 8-year- study of adolescent girls. *Developmental Psychology, 30,* 823–834.

Graham, J. (1994, January 28). TV executives lash out at violence study. *USA Today,* p. D1.

Grant, C. L., & Fodor, I. G. (1986). Adolescent attitudes toward body image and anorexic behavior. *Adolescence, 21,* 269–281.

Grant, J. P. (1988). *The state of the world's children 1988.* New York: Oxford University Press for UNICEF.

Gratch, G. (1979). The development of thought and language in infancy. In J. Osofsky (Ed.), *Handbook of infant development* (pp. 439–461). New York: Wiley.

Gratch, G., Appel, K. J., Evans, W. F., LeCompte, G. K., & Wright, N. K. (1974) Piaget's stage 4 object concept error: evidence of forgetting or object conception? *Child Development, 45,* 71–77.

Gray, E., & Coolsen, P. (1987, July/August). How do kids really feel about being home alone? *Children Today,* pp. 30–32.

Greaney, V. (1980). Factors related to amount and type of leisure time reading. *Reading Research Quarterly, 15,* 337–357.

Green, A. H., Gaines, R. W., & Sandgrund, A. (1974.). Child abuse: Pathological syndrome of family reaction. *American Journal of Psychiatry, 131,* 882–886.

Green, J. A., Gustafson, G. E., & McGhie, A. C. (1998) Changes in infants' cries as a function of time in a cry bout. *Child Development, 69,* 271–280.

Green, R. (1978). Sexual identity of 37 children raised by homosexual or transsexual parents. *American Journal of Psychiatry, 135,* 692–697.

Green, R. (1982). The best interests of the child with lesbian mother. *Bulletin of the American Academy of Psychiatry and the Law, 10,* 7–15.

Green, R. (1987). *The "sissy boy" syndrome and the development of homosexuality.* New Haven, CT: Yale University Press.

Greenberg, J. S., Buess, C. E., Mullen, K. D., & Sands, D. W. (1989). *Sexuality: Insights and issues.* Dubuque, IA: Brown.

Greenberg, M. T., Lengua, L. J., Coie, J. D., & Pinderhughes, E. E. (1999). Predicting developmental outcomes at school entry using a multiple-risk model: Four American communities. *Developmental Psychology, 35,* 403–417.

Greenberger, E., O'Neil, R., & Nagel, S. K. (1994). Linking workplace and homeplace: Relations between the nature of adults' work and their parenting behaviors. *Developmental Psychology, 30,* 990–1002.

Greendlinger, V., & Byrne, D (1987). Coercive sexual fantasies of college men as predictors of self-reported likelihood of rape and overt sexual aggression. *Journal of Sex Research, 23,* 1–11.

Greene, S. (1994). Reactivity in infants: A cross-national comparison. *Developmental Psychology, 30,* 342–345.

Greenfeld, L. A. (1998). *Alcohol and crime,* NCJ 168632. Washington, DC: NCJRS.

Greenfield, P. M., & Suzuki, L. K. (1998). Culture and human development: Implications for parenting, education, pediatrics, and mental health. In W. Damon (Editor in Chief) & I. E. Sigel & K. A. Renninger (Vol. Eds.), *Handbook of child psychology* (5th ed., pp. 1059–1112). New York: Wiley.

Greenough, W. T., Black, J. E., & Wallace, C. S. (1987). Experience and brain development. *Child Development, 58,* 539–560.

Griffith, D. R. (1992, September). prenatal exposure to cocaine and other drugs: Developmental and educational prognoses. *Phi Delta Kappan,* pp. 30–34.

Griffiths, M. D. (1991). Amusement machine playing in childhood and adolescents: A comparative analysis of video games and machines. *Adolescence, 14,* 53–73.

Grimley, D. M., & Lee, P. A. (1997). A condom and other contraceptive use among a random sample of female adolescents: A snapshot in time. *Adolescence, 32,* 771–779.

Groome, L. J., Swiber, M. J., Atterbury, J. L., Bentz, L. S., & Holland, S. B. (1997). Similarities and differences in behavioral state organization during sleep periods in the perinatal infant before and after birth. *Child Development, 68,* 1–11.

Grossman, J. B., & Garry, E. M. (1997). *Mentoring: A proven delinquency prevention strategy.* NCJ 164834. Washington, DC: NCJRS.

Grossman, K.E., & Grossman, K. (1990) The wider concept of attachment in cross-cultural research. *Human Development, 33,* 31–47.

Grotevant, H. D. (1987). Toward a process model of identity formation. *Journal of Adolescent Research, 2,* 203–222.

Grotevant, H. D. (1998). Adolescent development in family contexts. In W. Damon (Editor in Chief) & N. Eisenberg (Vol. Ed.), *Handbook of child psychology* (5th ed., pp. 1097–1140). New York: Wiley.

Grotevant, H. D., & Cooper, C. R. (1986). Individuation in family relationships. *Human Development, 29,* 82–100.

Groves, B. M., Zuckerman, B., Marans, S., & Cohen, D. J. (1993, January 13). Silent victims: Children who witness violence. *Journal of the American Medical Association, 269,* 262–264.

Guerra, N. G., & Slaby, R. (1990). Cognitive mediators of aggression in adolescent offenders: 2. Intervention. *Developmental Psychology, 26,* 269–277.

Guillen, E. O., & Barr, S. I. (1994). Nutrition, dieting, and fitness messages in a magazine for adolescent women, 1970–1990). *Journal of Adolescent Health, 15,* 464–472.

Guinn, B., Semper, T., & Jorgensen, L. (1997). Mexican American female adolescent self-esteem: The effect of body image, exercise behavior, and body fatness. *Hispanic Journal of Behavioral Sciences, 13,* 439–456.

Guntheroth, W. G. (1982). *Crib death: Sudden infant death syndrome.* Mount Kisco, NY: Futura.

Gurney, P. (1987). Self-esteem enhancement in children: A review of research findings. *Educational Research, 29,* 130–135.

Gustafson, G. E., & Harris, K. L. (1990). Women's responses to young infants' cries. *Developmental Psychology, 26,* 144–152.

Guy, W. (1996). The theology of *Mister Rogers' Neighborhood.* In M. Collins & M. M. Kimmel (Eds.), Mister Rogers' Neighborhood: *Children, television and Fred Rogers* (pp. 101–122). Pittsburgh, PA: University of Pittsburgh Press.

Guyer, M. S., & Collins, F. S. (1993). The human genome project and the future of medicine. *American Journal of Diseases in Childhood, 147,* 1145–1152.

H

Haager, D., & Vaughn, S. (1995). Parent, teacher, peer, and self-reports of the social competence of students with learning disabilities. *Journal of Learning disabilities, 28,* 205–215, 231.

Hack, M., Klein, N. K., & Taylor, H. G. (1995). Long-term developmental outcomes of low birth weight infants. In *The future of children: Low birthweight* (pp. 176–197). Los Altos, CA: David and Lucile Packard Foundation.

Hadeed, A., & Siegel, S. R. (1989). Maternal cocaine use during pregnancy: Effect on the newborn infant. *Pediatrics, 84,* 205–210.

Hadjistavropoulos, H.D., Craig, K.D., Grunau, R.V.E., & Johnston, C.C. (1994) Judging pain in newborns: Facial and cry determinants. *Journal of Pediatric Psychology, 19,* 485–491.

Haeuser, A. A. (1990). Can we stop physical punishment of children? *Holistic Education Review, 3,* 53–56.

Haffner, D. W. (1992). *1992 report card on the states: Sexual rights in America.* SIECUS Report 20, 1–7.

Haft, W. L., & Slade, A. (1989). Affect attunement and maternal attachment: A pilot study., *Infant Mental Health Journal, 10,* 157–172.

Hagekull, B., & Bohlin, G. (1995). Day care quality, family and child characteristics and socioemotional development. *Early Childhood Research Quarterly, 10,* 505–526.

Hagerman, R. J. (1996). Biomedical advances in developmental psychology: The case of fragile X syndrome. *Developmental Psychology, 32,* 416–424.

Haith, M. M. (1966). The response of the human newborn to visual movement. *Journal of Experimental Child Psychology, 3,* 237–243.

Haith, M. M. (1980). *Rules babies look by: The organization of newborn visual activity.* Hillsdale, NJ: Erlbaum.

Haith, M. M. (1990). Progress in the understanding of sensory and perceptual processes in early infancy. *Merrill-Palmer Quarterly, 36,* 1–26.

Haith, M. M., & Benson, J. B. (1998). Infant cognition. In W. Damon (Ed.), *Handbook of child psychology* (4th ed., Vol. 2, pp. 199–254). New York: Wiley

Hakim-Larson, J., & Mruk, C. (1997). Enhancing self-esteem in a community mental health setting. *American Journal of Orthopsychiatry, 67,* 655–659.

Hall, C. W., & Rouse, B. D. (1996). Teenagers knowledge about prenatal exposure to cocaine. *Perceptual and Motor Skills, 83,* 122.

Hall, M. (1994, November 2). Violence up in 38% of schools. *USA Today,* p. A1.

Halpern, C. T., Udry, J. R., Campbell, B., & Suchindran, C. (1999). Effects of body fat on weight concerns, dating, and sexual activity: A longitudinal analysis of black and white adolescent girls. *Developmental Psychology, 35,* 721–736.

Halpern, D. F. (1986). *Sex differences in cognitive abilities.* Hillsdale, NJ: Erlbaum.

Halpern, S. (1989). Infertility: Playing the odds. *Ms.,* pp. 147–151, 154–156.

Halsey, C. L., Collin, M. F., & Anderson, C. L. (1996). Extremely low-birth-weight children and their peers. *Archives of Pediatric and Adolescent Medicine, 150,* 790–794.

Hamachek, D. E. (1988). Evaluating self-concept and ego development within Erikson's psychosocial framework: A formulation. *Journal of Counseling and Developing, 66,* 354–360.

Hamburg, D. A. (1994). *Today's children: Creating a future for a generation in crisis.* New York: Times Books.

Hamill, P. V. V. (1977). *NCHS growth curves for children.* Vital and Health Statistics, Series 11, Data from the National Health Survey, No. 165. Washington, DC: U.S. Government Printing Office (DWEH no. 78–1650).

Hamilton, E. M. N., Whitney, E. N., & Sizer, F. S. (1985). *Nutrition: Concepts and controversies* (3rd ed.). St. Paul, MN: West.

Hansen, J., & Bowey, J. A. (1994). Phonological analysis skills, verbal working memory, and reading ability in second-grade children. *Child Development, 65,* 938–950.

Hansford, B. C., & Hattie, J. A. (1982). The relationship between self and achievement/performance measures. *Review of Educational Research, 52,* 135–153.

Hanson, T. L., McLanahan, S. S., & Thomson, E. (1996). Double jeopardy: Parental conflict and stepfamily outcomes for children. *Journal of Marriage and the Family, 58,* 141–155.

Hardy, J. B., Welcher, D. W., Mellits, E. D., & Kagan, J. (1976). Pitfalls in the measurement of intelligence: Are standardized tests valid for measuring the intellectual potential of urban children? *Journal of Psychology, 94,* 43–51.

Hardy, J., & Duggan, A. (1988). Teenage fathers and the fathers of infants of urban, teenage mothers. *American Journal of Public Health, 78,* 919–922.

Harlap, S., & Shiono, P. (1980, July 26). Alcohol and incidence of spontaneous abortions in the first and second trimester. *The Lancet,* pp. 173–176.

Harlow, H. F. (1959, July). Love in infant monkeys. *Scientific American,* 68–74.

Harlow, H. F. (1971). *Learning to love.* San Francisco: Albion.

Harlow, H. F., & Harlow, M. K. (1962). Social deprivation in monkeys. *Scientific American, 207,* 136–146.

Harlow, H. F., & Suomi, S. J. (1971). Social recovery by isolation-reared monkeys. *Proceedings of the National Academy of Science, 68,* 1534–1538.

Harris, G., Thomas, A., & Booth, D. (1990). Development of salt taste in infancy. *Developmental Psychology, 26,* 534–539.

Harris, J. C. (1995). *Developmental neuropsychiatry* (Vol.1). New York: Oxford University Press.

Harris, M. B. & Turner, P. H. (1985/1986). Gay and lesbian parents. *Journal of Homosexuality, 12,* 101–113.

Harris, M., Barlow-Brown, F., & Chasin, J. (1995). The emergence of referential understanding: Pointing and the comprehension of object names. *First Language, 15,* 19–34.

Harris, P. L. (1989). Object permanence in infancy. In A. Slater & G. Bremner (Eds.), *Infant development.* Hillsdale, NJ: Erlbaum.

Harrison, A. O. Wilson, M .N., Pine, C. J., Chan, S. Q., & Buriel, R. (1990). Family ecologies of ethnic minority children. *Child Development, 61,* 347–362.

Hart, B. (1991). Input frequency and children's first words. *First Language, 11,* 289–300.

Hart, B., & Riley, T. R. (1992). American parenting of language-learning children: Persisting differences in family-child interactions observed in natural home environments. *Developmental Psychology, 28,* 1096–1105.

Hart, C. H., Ladd, G. W., & Burleson, B. R. (1990). Children's expectations of the outcomes of social strategies: Relations with sociometric status and maternal disciplinary styles. *Child Development, 61,* 127–138.

Hart, S. N., & Brassard, M. R. (1987). A major threat to children's mental health: Psychological maltreatment. *American Psychologist, 42,* 160–166.

Harter, S. (1983). Developmental perspective on the self-system. In P. H. Mussen (Ed.), *Handbook of child psychology* (4th ed., Vol. 4, pp. 275–387). New York: Wiley.

Harter, S. (1993). Visions of self: Beyond the me in the mirror. In J. Jacobs (Ed.), *Developmental perspectives on the self* (pp. 99–144). Nebraska Symposium on Motivation 1992. Lincoln: University of Nebraska Press.

Harter, S. (1998). The development of self-representations. In W. Damon (Editor in Chief) & N. Eisenberg (Vol. Ed.), *Handbook of child psychology* (5th ed., pp. 553–617), New York: Wiley.

Harter, S., & Carlson, J. (1988). Developmental and gender differences in the conflict caused by opposing attributes within the adolescent self. Unpublished manuscript cited in Harter, S., & Monsour, A. (1992). Developmental analysis of conflict caused by opposing attributes in the adolescent self-portrait. *Developmental Psychology, 28,* 251–260.

Harter, S., & Monsour, A. (1992). Developmental analysis of conflict caused by opposing attributes in the adolescent self-portrait. *Developmental Psychology, 28,* 251–260.

Harter, S., Marold, D. B., Whitesell, N. R., & Cobbs, G. (1996). A model of the effects of parent and peer support on adolescent false self behavior. *Child Development, 67,* 360–374.

Harter, S., Marold, D.B., Whitesell, N.R., & Cobbs, G. (1996) A model of the effects of parent and peer support on adolescent false self behavior. *Child Development, 67,* 160–174.

Harter, S., Waters, P. L., & Whitesell, N. R. (1998). False self behavior and lack of voice among adolescent males and females. *Developmental Psychology.*

Harter, S., Waters, P. L., Whitesell, N. R., & Kastelic, D. (1998). Level of voice among female and male high school students: Relational context, support, and gender orientation. *Developmental Psychology, 34,* 892–901.

Hartshorne, H., & May, M. A. (1928). *Studies in the nature of character* (Vol. 1). New York: Macmillan.

Hartup, W. W. (1983). Peer relations. In P. H. Mussen (Ed.), *Handbook of child psychology: Socialization, personality, and social development* (4th ed., Vol. 4, pp. 103–197). New York: Wiley.

Hartup, W. W. (1989). Social relationships and their developmental significance. *American Psychologist, 44,* 120–127.

Hartup, W. W. (1996). The company they keep: friendships and their developmental significance. *Child Development, 67,* 1–13.

Harvey, A. R., & Brauch, J. B. (1997). A comprehensive Afrocentric rites of passage program for black male adolescents. *Health & Social Work, 22,* 30–38.

Harvey, E. (1999). Short-term and long-term effects of early parental employment on Children of the National Longitudinal Survey of Youth. *Developmental Psychology, 35,* 445.

Harvey, S. M., & Spigner, C. (1995). Factors associated with sexual behavior among adolescents: A multivariate analysis. *Adolescence, 30,* 253–264.

Harwood, R. L. (1992). The influence of culturally derived values on Anglo and Puerto Rican mothers' perceptions of attachment behavior. *Child Development, 63,* 822–839.

Harwood, R.L., Schoelmerich, A., Schulze, P.A., & Gonzalez, Z. (1999) Cultural differences in maternal beliefs and behaviors: A study of middle-class Anglo and Puerto Rican mother-infant pairs in four everyday situations. *Child Development, 70,* 1005–1016.

Haste, H., & Baddeley, J. (1991). Moral theory and culture: the case of gender. In W. M. Kurtines & J. L. Gewirtz (Eds.), *Handbook of moral behavior and development: Vol. 1 Theory* (pp.222–249). Hillsdale, NJ: Erlbaum.

Hatcher, P. J., Hulme, C., & Ellis, A. W. (1994). Ameliorating early reading failure by integrating the teaching of reading and phonological skills: The phonological linkage hypothesis. *Child Development, 65,* 41–57.

Hauser-Cram, P. (1996). Mastery motivation in toddlers with developmental disabilities. *Child Development, 67,* 236–248.

Hausman, B., & Hammen, C. (1993). Parenting in homeless families: The double crisis. *Journal of Orthopsychiatry, 63,* 358–369.

Hay, D. F., & Ross, H. S. (1982). The social nature of early conflict. *Child Development, 53,* 105–113.

Hayes, R. (1986). Men's decisions to enter or avoid nontraditional occupations. *Career Development Quarterly, 34,* 89–101.

Hayne, H. (1990). The effect of multiple reminders on long-term retention in human infants. *Developmental Psychology, 23,* 453–477.

Hayne, H., & Rovee-Collier, C. (1995). The organization of reactivated memory in infancy. *Child Development, 66,* 893–906.

Haynes, H., White, B. L., & Held, R. (1965). Visual accommodation in human infants. *Science, 148,* 528–530.

Hayslip, B., & Panek, P. E. (1993). *Adult development and aging* (2nd ed.). New York: HarperCollins.

Hazan, C., & Hutt, M.J. (1990, July) Continuity and change in inner working models of attachment (unpublished paper) cited in Kirkpatrick, L.A. & Davis, K.E. (1994) Attachment style, gender, and relationship stability: A longitudinal Analysis. *Journal of Personality and Social Psychology, 66,* 502–512.

Hazan, C., & Shaver, P.R. (1990) Love and work: An attachment-theoretical perspective. *Journal of Personality and Social Psychology, 59,* 270–280.

Hazen, N. L., & Black, B. (1989). Preschool peer communication skills: The role of social status and interaction context. *Child Development, 60,* 867–877.

Head Start. (1995). Program characteristics. In *The future of children: Long-term outcomes of early childhood programs* (Vol. 5, pp. 212–213). Los Altos, CA: David and Lucile Packard Foundation.

Headden, S. (1996, September 25) Tongue-tied in the schools. *U.S. News and World Report,* pp. 44–46.

Healey, J. (1995). Proposed electronic "V-chip" complicates the view. *Congressional Quarterly Weekly Report,* 53, 1994–1997.

Healthy People 2000: Midcourse review and 1995 Revisions. (1995). Washington, DC: U.S. Department of Health and Human Services, U.S. Public Health Service.

Heath, D. T. (1994). The impact of delayed fatherhood on the father-child relationship. *Journal of Genetic Psychology,* 155, 511–531.

Hebberler, K. M., Smith, B. J., & Black, T. L. (1991). A history of legislation for the early intervention of children with handicaps. *Exceptional Children,* 58, 104–112.

Heckman, J. J. (1995, March). Cracked bell. *Reason,* 26, 49–56.

Hegde, M. N. (1995). *Introduction to communication disorders* (2nd ed.). Austin, TX: Pro-Ed.

Heinicke, C. M. (1979). Development from two and one-half to four years. In J. D. Noshpitz (Ed.), *Basic handbook of child psychiatry* (Vol. 1, pp. 167–178). New York: Basic Books.

Heinig, M.J., & Dewey, K.G. (1996) Health advantages of breast feeding for infants: A critical review. *Nutrition Research Reviews,* 9, 89–110.

Heinrich, R., Corbine, J., & Thomas, K. (1990). Counseling Native Americans. *Journal of Counseling and Development,* 69, 128–132.

Heinrichs, C., Munson, P. J., Counts, D. R., Cutler, G. B., & Baron, J. (1995, April 21). *Science,* 268, 443–444.

Helburn, S. W., & Howes, C. (1996). Child care cost and quality. In *The future of children* (Vol. 6, pp. 62–82). Los Altos, CA: David and Lucile Packard Foundation.

Hellerstedt, W. L., Himes, J. H., Story, M., Alton, I. R., & Edwards, L. E. (1997). The effects of cigarette smoking and gestational weight change on birth outcomes in obese and normal-weighted women. *American Journal of Public Health,* 87, 591–595.

Hellmich, N. (1995, August 30). PTA learns new ways to get help. *USA Today,* p. D4.

Hellmich, N. (1997, April 24). Oldest new mom is 63. *USA Today,* p. D1.

Hellmich, N. (1997, July 1). Few kids get daily exercise. *USA Today,* p. D1.

Hellmich, N., & Peterson, K. S. (1996, April 24). More parents putting kids in formal day care. *USA Today,* pp. 1, 2.

Hellmich, N., & Peterson, K. S. (1997, April 25). Giving birth to controversy: Is it ever too late to have kinds? *USA Today,* pp. D1, D2.

Hennessy, K., Rabideau, G., Cicchetti, D., & Cummings, E. M. (1994). Responses of physically abused children to different forms of interadult anger. *Child Development,* 65, 815–828.

Henry, B., Caspi, A., Mofitt, T., & Silva, P. (1996). Temperamental and familial predictors of violent and nonviolent criminal convictions: Age 3 to age 18. *Developmental Psychology,* 32, 614–623.

Henry, B., Silva, P. A., Caspi, A., & Moffitt, T. E. (1996). Temperamental and familial predictors of violent and nonviolent criminal convictions. *Developmental Psychology,* 32, 614–623.

Henry, T. (1994, January 6). Violence in schools grows more severe. *USA Today,* p. D1.

Henry, T. (1996a, February 22). Principals urge broad changes in high schools. *USA Today,* p. D1.

Henry, T. (1996b, March 13). Fear of crime change kids daily routine. *USA Today,* p. D1.

Henry, T. (1997a, May 7). Gender gap in math skills grows slim. *USA Today,* p. D1.

Henry, T. (1997b, February 28–March 2). Math scores up, but still just average. *USA Today,* pp. A1, D4.

Henry, T. (1997c). U.S. students reaching for world-class stature. *USA Today,* pp. A1, D6.

Henshaw, S. K. (1994). *U.S. teenage pregnancy statistics.* New York: Alan Guttmacher Institute.

Henslin, J. M. (1999). *Sociology* (4th ed.). Boston: Allyn & Bacon.

Hepper, P. G., Shahidollah, S., & White, R. (1990). Origins of fetal handedness. *Nature,* 347, 431.

Herbert, W., with Daniel, M. (1996, June 3). The moral child. *U.S. News and World Reports,* pp. 52–59.

Herman-Giddens, M. E., Slora, E., Wasserman, R., Bourdony, C., Bhapkar, M., Koch, G., & Hasemeier, C. (1997). Secondary sexual characteristics and menses in young girls seen in office practice: A study from the Pediatric Research in Office Settings Network. *Pediatrics,* 99, 505–512.

Herman-Giddens, M., Slora, E., Wasserman, R., Bourdony, C., Bhapkar, M., Koch, G., & Hasemeier, C. (1997) Secondary sexual characteristics and menses in young girls seen in office practice: A study from the pediatric Research in office Settings network. *Pediatrics,* 88, 505–512.

Hernandez, D. J. (1995). Changing demographics: Pat and future demands for early childhood programs. *The Future of Children,* 5, 156–161.

Hernandez, D. J. (1997). Child development and the social demography of childhood. *Child Development,* 68, 149–170.

Hernandez, H. (1989). *Multicultural education: A teacher's guide to content and process.* New York: Merrill/Prentice Hall.

Hero, 5, can do it but can't say it. (1986, August 7). *Los Angeles Times,* p. 2.

Heron, A., & Kroeger, E. (1981). Introduction to developmental psychology. In H. C. Triandis & A. Heron (Eds.), *Handbook of cross-cultural psychology* (Vol. 4, pp. 1–17). Boston: Allyn & Bacon.

Herrenkohl, E. C., Herrenkohl, R. C., & Egolf, B. (1994). Resilient early school age children from maltreating homes: Outcome in late adolescence. *American Journal of Orthopsychiatry,* 64, 301–309.

Herrnstein, R. J., & Murray, C. (1994). *The bell curve: Intelligence and class structure in American life.* New York: Free Press.

Hershberger, S. L. (1997). A twin registry study of male and female sexual orientation. *Journal of Sex Research,* 34, 212–223.

Hershey, M. (1988, February). Gifted child education. *The Clearing House,* pp. 280–282.

Hertzler, A. A., & Frary, R. B. (1989). Food behavior of college students. *Adolescence,* 24, 349–355.

Herzog, D. B., Keller, M. B., Sacks, N. R., Yeh, C. J., & Levori, P. W. (1992). Psychiatric comorbidity in treatment-seeking anorexics and bulimics. *Journal of the American Academy of Child and Adolescent Psychiatry,* 31, 810–818.

Hess, R. D., Hiroshi, A., & Kashiwagi, K., et al. (1986). Family influences on school readiness and achievement in Japan and the United States: An overview of longitudinal study. In H. Stevenson, H. Azuma, & K. Makuta (Eds.), *Child development and education in Japan* (pp. 147–166). New York: Freeman.

Hess, R., & Shipman, V. (1967). Parents as teachers: How lower and middle class mothers teach. Cited in Lavatelli, C. S., & Stendler, F. (Eds.). (1972). *Readings in child behavior and development* (3rd ed., pp. 436–446). New York: Harcourt Brace Jovanovich.

Hetherington, E. M. (1972). Effects of father absence on personality: Development in adolescent daughters. *Developmental Psychology,* 7, 313–321.

Hetherington, E. M. (1993). An overview of the Virginia Longitudinal Study of divorce and remarriage with a focus on early adolescence. *Journal of Family Psychology,* 7, 39–56.

Hetherington, E. M., & Clingenpeel, W.G. (1992). Coping with marital transitions: Family systems perspective. *Monographs of the Society for Research in child Development,* 57, 2–3 Serial No. 227.

Hetherington, E. M., & Stanley-Hagan, M. M. (1995). Parenting in divorced and remarried families. In M.H. Bornstein (Ed.), *Handbook of parenting* (Vol. 3, pp. 233–254). Mahwah, NJ: Erlbaum.

Hetherington, E. M., Cox, M., & Cox, R. (1978). The development of children in mother headed families. In H. Hoffman & D. Reiss (Eds.), *The American family: Dying and developing.* New York: Plenum.

Hetherington, E. M., Hagan, M. S., & Anderson, E. R. (1989). Marital transitions: A child's perspective. *American Psychologist, 44,* 303–313.

Hickson, L., Blackman, L. S., & Reis, E. M. (1995). *Mental retardation: Foundations of educational programming.* Boston: Allyn & Bacon.

Higgins, B. S. (1990). Couple infertility: From the perspective of the close-relationship model. *Family Relations, 39,* 81–86.

High/Scope Educational Research Foundation. (1993). *Significant benefits: The High/Scope Perry Preschool study through age 27.* Ypsilanti, MI: High/Scope Educational Research Foundation.

Hill, J., & Holmbeck, G., (1986) Attachment and autonomy during adolescence. in G. Whitehurst (Ed.). *Annals of child development,* Greenwich, CT: JAI Press.

Hilton, N. Z. (1992). Battered women's concerns about their children witnessing wife abuse. *Journal of Interpersonal Violence, 7,* 77–86.

Hines, A. M. (1997). Divorce-related transitions, adolescent development, and the role of the parent-child relationship: A review of the literature. *Journal of Marriage and the Family, 59,* 375–388.

Hinshaw, S. P., & Erhardt, D. (1993). Behavioral treatment in V. B. Van Hasselt & M. Hersen (Ed.), *Handbook of behavior therapy and pharmacotherapy for children: A comparative analysis.* Boston: Allyn & Bacon.

Hirsh, B. J., & Debois, D. L. (1991). Self-esteem in early adolescence: the identification and prediction of contrasting longitudinal trajectories. *Journal of Youth and Adolescence, 20,* 53–71.

Hirshberg, L. M., & Svejda, M. (1990). When infants look to their parents: I. Infants' social referencing to mothers compared to fathers. *Child Development, 59,* 62–634.

Hispanic dropouts. (1993, November 3). *Education Week,* p. 3.

Hochschild, A. (1989). *The second shift.* New York: Viking.

Hock, E. (1980). Working and nonworking mothers and their infants: A comparative study of maternal caregiving characteristics and infant social behavior. *Merrill-Palmer Quarterly, 26,* 79–101.

Hock, E., & DeMeis, D. (1990). Depression in mothers of infants; the role of maternal employment. *Developmental Psychology, 26,* 285–291.

Hock, E., DeMeis, D., & McBride, S. (1987). Maternal separation anxiety: Its role in the balance of employment and motherhood in mothers of infants. In A. Gottfried & A. W. Gottfried (Eds.), *Maternal employment and children's development: Longitudinal research* (pp. 191–229). New York: Plenum.

Hodapp, R. M., & Mueller, E. (1982). Early social development. In B. B. Wolman (Ed.), *Handbook of developmental psychology* (pp. 284–298). Upper Saddle River, NJ: Prentice Hall.

Hofer, M. A. (1988). On the nature and function of prenatal behavior. In W. P. Smotherman & C. R. Robinson (Eds.), *Behavior of the fetus* (pp.3–19). Caldwell, NJ: Telford.

Hofferth, S. (1996). Child care in the United States today. In *The future of children* (Vol. 6, pp. 41–61). Los Altos, CA: David and Lucile Packard Foundation.

Hoff-Ginsberg, E. (1986). Function and structure in maternal speech: Their relation to the child's development of syntax. *Developmental Psychology, 22,* 155–163.

Hoffman, L. (1974). Effects of maternal employment on the child: A review of the research. *Developmental Psychology, 10,* 204–228.

Hoffman, L. W. (1979). Maternal employment. *American Psychologist, 34,* 859–865.

Hoffman, L. W. (1984). Work, family, and the socialization of the child. In R. D. Parke (Ed.), *Review of child development research* (The Family). (Vol. 7, pp. 223–282). New York: Russell Sage Foundation.

Hoffman, L. W. (1989). Effects of maternal employment in the two-parent family. *American Psychologist, 44,* 283–292.

Hoffman, M. L. (1988). Moral development. In M. H. Bornstein & M. E. Lamb (Eds.), *Personality, emotional and personality development* (2nd ed., pp. 497–541.). Hillsdale, NJ: Erlbaum.

Hogue, A., & Steinberg, L. (1995). Homophily of internalized distress in adolescent peer groups. *Developmental Psychology, 31,* 897–906.

Holden, G. W. (1995). Parental attitudes toward childrearing. In M. H. Bornstein (Ed.), *Handbook of parenting* (Vol. 3, pp. 359–392). Mahwah, NJ: Erlbaum.

Holden, G. W., & Ritchie, K. L. (1991). Linking extreme marital discord, child rearing, and child behavior problems: Evidence from battered women. *Child Development, 62,* 311–327.

Holden, G. W., Coleman, S. M., & Schmidt, K. L. (1995). Why 3-year-old children get spanked: Parent and child determinants as reported by college educated mothers. *Merrill-Palmer Quarterly, 41,* 431–452.

Holland, J. (1973). *Making vocational choices.* Upper Saddle River, NJ: Prentice Hall.

Hollander, D. (1996). Nonmarital childbearing in the United States: A governmental report. *Family Planning Perspectives, 28–32, 41.*

Holmes, D. S. (1976a). Debriefing after psychological experiments: I. Effectiveness of post-deception dehoaxing. *American Psychologist, 31,* 858–868.

Holmes, D. S. (1976b). Debriefing after psychological experiments: II. Effectiveness of post-experimental desensitization. *American Psychologist, 31,* 868–876.

Holstein, C. B. (1976). Irreversible, stepwise sequence in the development of moral judgement: A longitudinal study of males and females. *Child Development, 47,* 51–61.

Holt, J. (1964). *How children fail.* New York: Pitman.

Holtzen, D. W., & Agresti, A. A. (1990). Parental responses to gay and lesbian children. *Journal of Social and Clinical Psychology, 9,* 390–399.

Holtzman, N. A., Kronmal, R. A., Van Doornick, W., Azen, C., & Koch, R. (1986). Effect of age at loss of dietary control on intellectual performance and behavior of children with phenylketonuria. *New England Journal of Medicine, 314,* 593–597.

Honig, A. S. (1988). The art of talking to a baby. *Baby, 3,* 12–14, 16–17.

Honig, A. S. (1995). Choosing child care for young children. In M. H. Bornstein (Ed.), *Handbook of parenting* (Vol. 4, pp. 411–435). Mahwah, NJ: Erlbaum.

Honig, B. (1997). Research-based reading instruction: The right way. *The School Administrator, 54,* 6–15.

Horbar, J. D., & Lucey, J. F. (1995, Spring). Evaluation of neonatal intensive care technologies. In *The future of children: Low birth weight* (pp. 139–161). Los Altos, CA: David and Lucile Packard Foundation.

Horgan, J. (1995). The mystery of SIDS. *Science, 33–35*

Horn, J. M. (1983). The Texas adoption project: Adopted children and their intellectual resemblance to biological and adoptive parents. *Child Development, 54,* 268–275.

Horn, J. M. (1985). Bias? Indeed! *Child Development, 56,* 779–781.

Horn, J. M., Loehlin, J. C., & Willerman, L. (1979). Intellectual resemblance among adoptive and biological relatives: The Texas adoption project. *Behavior Genetics, 9,* 177–207.

Horney, K. (1939). *New ways in psychoanalysis.* New York: Norton.

Horney, K. (1967). *Feminine psychology.* New York: Norton.

Hornik, R., & Gunnar, M. R. (1988). A descriptive analysis of infant social referencing. *Child Development, 59,* 626–635.

Horowitz, T. R. (1992). Dropout: Mertonian or reproduction scheme? *Adolescence, 27,* 451–459.

Hotelling, K., & Forrest, L. (1985, November). Gilligan's theory of sex-role development: A perspective for counseling. *Journal of Counseling and Development, 64,* 183–186.

Householder, J., Hatcher, R., Burns, W. & Chasnoff, I. (1982). Infants born to narcotic-addicted mothers. *Psychological Bulletin, 2,* 453–468.

How poor are the poor? (1994, October 1). *The Economist, 323,* 106.

Howard, M. (1985). Postponing sexual involvement among adolescents: An alternative approach to prevention of sexually transmitted diseases. *Journal of Adolescent Health Care, 6,* 271–277.

Howe, M. L. (1991). Misleading children's story recall: Forgetting and reminiscence of the facts. *Developmental Psychology, 27,* 746–762.

Howe, M. L. (1995). Interference effects in young children's long-term retention. *Developmental Psychology, 31,* 579–596.

Howe, M. L., Courage, M. L., & Bryant-Brown, L. (1993). Reinstating preschoolers' memories. *Developmental Psychology, 29,* 854–869.

Howe, N., & Ross, H. S. (1990). Socialization, perspective-talking, and the sibling relationship. *Developmental Psychology, 26,* 160–165.

Howell, J.C. (1994). *Gangs.* Fact Sheet #12. Washington, DC: U.S. Department of Justice, Office of Juvenile Justice and Delinquency Prevention.

Howes, C. (1988a). Peer interaction of young children. *Monographs of the Society for Research in Child Development, 53* (1), Serial No. 217.

Howes, C. (1988b). Same- and cross-sex friends: Implications for interaction and social skills. *Early Childhood Research Quarterly, 3,* 21–37.

Howes, C. (1990). Can the age of entry into child care and the quality of child care predict adjustment in kindergarten. *Developmental Psychology, 26,* 292–304.

Howes, C., & Hamilton, C. E. (1992a). Children's relationships with caregivers: Mothers and child care teachers. *Child Development, 63,* 859–866.

Howes, C., & Hamilton, C. E. (1992b). Children's relationships with child care teachers and concordance with parental attachments. *Child Development, 63,* 867–878.

Howes, C., & Smith, E. . (1995). Relations among child care quality, teacher behavior, children's play activities, emotional security, and cognitive activity in child care. *Early Childhood Research Quarterly, 10,* 381–404.

Howes, C., Hamilton, C.E., & Philipsen, L.C. (1998) Stability and continuity of child-caregiver and child-peer relationships. *Child Development, 69,* 418–427.

Howes, C., Phillips, D. A., & Whitebook, M. (1992). Thresholds of quality: Implications for the social development of children in center-based child care. *Developmental Psychology, 63,* 449–460.

Howes, M. B. (1990). *The psychology of human cognition.* New York: Pergamon.

Hronsky, S., & Emory, E. (1987) Neurobehavioral effects of caffeine on the neonate. *Infant Behavior and Development, 10,* 61–80.

Hubbs-Tait, L., & Garmon, L. C. (1995). The relationship of moral reasoning and AIDS knowledge to risky sexual behavior. *Adolescence, 30,* 549–564.

Hudley, C., & Graham, S. (1993). An attributional intervention to reduce peer-directed aggression among African-American boys. *Child Development, 66,* 984–998.

Hudson, J. A. (1990). Constructive processing in children's event memory. *Developmental Psychology, 26,* 180–187,

Hudson, J. A., Shapiro, L. R., & Sosa, B. B. (1995). Planning in the real world: Preschool children's scripts and plans for familiar events. *Child Development, 66,* 984–998.

Hudson, L., & Gray, W. (1986). Formal operations, the imaginary audience, and the personal fable. *Adolescence, 21,* 751–765.

Huesman, L. R. (1986). Psychological processes promoting the relation between exposure to media violence and aggressive behavior by the viewer. *Journal of Social Issues, 42,* 125–139.

Huesmann, L. R., & Miller, L. S (1994). Long-term effects of repeated exposure to media violence in childhood. In L. R. Huesmann (Ed.), *Aggressive behavior: Current perspectives* (pp. 153–186). New York: Plenum.

Huesmann, L. R., Eron, L. D., Lefkowitz, M. M., & Walder, L. O. (1984). Stability of aggression over time and generations. *Developmental Psychology, 20,* 1120–1134.

Huesmann, L. R., Lagerspetz, K. M. J., & Eron, L. D. (1984). Intervening variables in the TV violence aggression relation: Evidence from two countries. *Developmental Psychology, 20,* 746–775.

Huff, H. A., & Lawson, K. R. (1990). Development of sustained, focused attention in young children during free play. *Developmental Psychology, 26,* 85–93.

Huffman, L., Bryan, Y.E., del Carmen, R., Pedersen, F.A., Doussard-Roosevelt, J.A., & Porges, S.W. (1998) Infant temperament and cardiac vagal tone: Assessments at twelve weeks of age. *Child Development, 69,* 624–635.

Hughes, D., & Simpson, L. (1995, Spring). The role of social change in preventing low birth weight. In *The future of children: Low birth weight* (pp. 87–102). Los Altos, CA: David and Lucile Packard Foundation.

Hughes, J. N., & Cavell, T. A. (1995). Cognitive-affective approaches to enhancing competence in aggressive children. In G. Cartledge & J. F. Milburn (Eds.), *Teaching social skills to children and youth* (3rd ed. pp. 199–236). Needham Heights, MA: Allyn & Bacon.

Hughes, J. N., & Hasbrouck, J. E. (1996). Television violence: Implications for violence prevention. *School Psychology Review, 25,* 134–151.

Hultsman, W. (1993). The influence of others as a barrier to recreation participation among early adolescents. *Journal of Leisure Research, 25,* 150–164.

Humphreys, A. P., & Smith, P. K. (1987). Rough and tumble friendship and dominance in school children: Evidence for continuity and change with age in middle childhood. *Child Development, 58,* 201–212.

Hunt, J. M. (1961). *Intelligence and experience.* New York: Ronald.

Hunt, J.R., Kristal, A.R., White, E., Lynch, J.C., & Fries, E. (1995) Physician recommendations for dietary change. Their prevalence and impact in a population-based sample. *American Journal of Public Health, 85,* 722–726.

Hunter, F. T. (1984). Socializing procedures in parent-child and friendship relations during adolescence. *Developmental Psychology, 20,* 1092–1100.

Hunter, F. T. (1985). Adolescents' perception of discussions with parents and friends. *Developmental Psychology, 21,* 443–450.

Hunter, F. T., & Youniss, J. (1982). Changes in functions of three relations during adolescence. *Developmental Psychology, 18,* 806–812.

Hura, S. L., & Echols, C. H. (1996). The role of stress and articulatory difficult in children's early production. *Developmental Psychology, 21,* 165–176.

Huston, A. C. (1983). Sex-typing. In E. H. Hetherington (Ed.), *Handbook of child psychology* (4th ed., Vol. 4, pp. 387–469). New York: Wiley.

Huston, A. C., Dunnerstein, E., Fairchild, H., Feshbach, N. D., Katz, P. A., Murray, J. P., Rubinstein, E. A., Wilcox, B. L., & Zuckerman, D. (1992). *Big world, small screen: The role of television in American society.* Lincoln: University of Nebraska press.

Huston, A. C., McLoyd, V. C., & Coll, C. G. (1994). Children and poverty: Issues in contemporary research. *Child Development, 65,* 275–283.

Huston, A. C., Watkins, B. A., & Kunkel, D. (1989). Public policy and children's television. *American Psychologist, 44,* 424–433.

Huston, A.C., Wright, J.C., Marquis, J. & Green, S.B. (1999) How young children spend their time: Television and other activities. *Developmental Psychology, 35,* 912–925.

Huttenlocher, J. (1974). The origins of language comprehension. In R. L. Solso (Ed.), *Theories in cognitive psychology.* Potomac, MD: Erlbaum.

Huttman, E., & Redmond, S. (1992). Women and homelessness: evidence of need to look beyond shelters to low term social service assistance and permanent housing. *Journal of Sociology and Social Welfare, 19,* 89–111.

Huttunen, M. O. (1989). Maternal stress during pregnancy and the behavior of the offspring. In S. Dopxiadis (Ed.), *Early influences shaping the individual* (pp. 175–182). New York: Plenum.

Hymel, S., Bowker, A., & Woody, E. (1993). Aggressive versus withdrawn, unpopular children: Variations in peer and self-perceptions in multiple domains. *Child Development, 64,* 879–896.

I

Idle, T., Wood, E., & Desmarais, S. (1993). Gender role socialization in toy play situations: Mothers and fathers with their sons and daughters. *Sex Roles, 28,* 679–690.

Ilg, F. L., & Ames, L. B. (1972). *School readiness.* New York: Harper & Row.

Illingworth, R. S. (1974). *The development of the infant and young child: Normal and abnormal.* Edinburgh: Livingstone.

Impact of vaccines universally recommended for children: United States 1900–1998. (1999). *MMWR, 48,* 243–248.

Infant Health and Development Program. (1990). Enhancing the outcomes of low birth weight, premature infants: A multisite randomized trial. *Journal of the American Medical Association, 263,* 3035–3042.

Infant mortality. (1992, July 31). *CQ Researcher, 2,* 641–664.

Ingersoll, E. W., & Thomas, E. B. (1998). Sleep/wake states of preterm infants: Stability, developmental change, diurnal variation, and relation with caregiving activity. *Child Development, 70,* 1–10.

Inhelder, B., & Piaget, J. (1958). *The growth of logical thinking.* New York: Basic Books.

Inhelder, B., & Piaget, J. (1964). *The early growth of logic in the child.* New York: Harper & Row.

International Food Information Council. (1992). *Kids make the nutritional grade.* Washington DC: Author.

Intons-Peterson, M. J., & Reddel, M. (1984). What do people ask about a neonate? *Developmental Psychology, 20,* 358–360.

Isabella, R. (1993). Origins of attachment: Maternal interactive behavior across the first year. *Child Development, 64,* 605–621.

Isabella, R. A., & Belsky, J. (1991). Interactional synchrony and the origins of infant-mother attachment: A replication study. *Child Development, 62,* 373–384.

Isabella, R. A., Belsky, J., & Von Eye, A. (1989). The origins of infant-mother attachment: An examination of interactional synchrony during the infant's first year. *Developmental Psychology, 25,* 12–21.

Isenberg, J., & Quisenberry, N. L. (1988, February). Play: A necessity for all children. *Childhood Education,* pp. 138–145.

Istomina, Z. M. (1982). The development of voluntary memory in preschool-age children. Cited in Paris, S. G., & Lindauer, B. K. The development of cognitive skills during childhood. In B. B. Wolman (Ed.), *Handbook of developmental psychology* (pp. 333–349). Upper Saddle River, NJ: Prentice Hall.

Iverson, J.M., Capirci, O., & Caselli, M.C. (1994) From communication to language in two modalities. *Cognitive Development, 9,* 23–43.

Izard, C. E. (1994). Innate and universal facial expressions: Evidence from developmental and cross-cultural research. *Psychological Bulletin, 115,* 288–299.

Izard, C. E., & Malatesta, C. Z. (1987). Perspectives on emotional development 1: Differential emotions theory of early emotional development. In J. D. Osofsky (Ed.), *Handbook of infant development* (pp. 494–555). New York: Wiley.

Izard, C. E., Haynes, O. M., Chisholm, G., & Baak, K. (1991). Emotional determinants of infant-mother attachment. *Child Development, 62,* 906–917.

Izard, C. E., Huebner, R., Risser, D., McGinnes, G., & Dougherty, L. (1980). The young infant's ability to produce discrete emotion expressions. *Developmental Psychology, 16,* 132–140.

J

Jaccard, J., Dittus, P. J., & Gordon, V.V. (1998). Parent-adolescent congruency in reports of adolescent sexual behavior and communications about sexual behavior. *Child Development, 69,* 247–261.

Jack, B. W., & Culpepper, L. (1990). Preconception care. *Journal of the American medical Society, 264,* 1147–1149.

Jackson, J. F. (1993). Human behavioral genetics, Scarr's theory, and her views on interventions: A critical review and commentary on their implications for African-American children. *Child Development, 64,* 1318–1333.

Jacobson, A. L. (1978, July). Infant day care: Toward a more human environment. *Young Children.*

Jacobson, J. L., & Wille, D. E. (1986). The influence of attachment pattern on developmental changes in peer interaction from the toddler to the preschool period. *Child Development, 57,* 338–347.

Jacobson, J. L., Jacobson, S. W., Fein, G., Schwartz, P. M., & Dowler, J. K. (1984). Prenatal exposure to an environmental toxin: A test of the multiple effects model. *Developmental Psychology, 20,* 523–533.

Jacobson, J. L., Jacobson, S. W., Padgett, R. J., Brumitt, G. A., & Billings, R. L. (1992). Effects of prenatal PCB exposure on cognitive processing efficiency and sustained attention. *Developmental Psychology, 28,* 297–306.

Jacobson, L. (1997, September 3). Long-term achievement study shows gains, losses. *Education Week,* p. 12.

Jaffe, P. G., Wilson, S. K., & Wolfe, D. (1988). Specific assessment and intervention strategies for children exposed to wife battering: preliminary empirical investigation. *Canadian Journal of Community Mental Health, 7,* 157–163.

Jaffe, P. G., Wolfe, D. A., & Wilson, S. K. (1990). *Children of battered women.* Newbury Park, CA: Sage.

Jahoda, G. (1983). European "lag" in the development of an economic concept: A study in Zimbabwe. *British Journal of Developmental Psychology, 1,* 113–120.

JAMA (1997a, May 21) Genetic testing for cystic fibrosis. *JAMA, 277,* 1507

JAMA (1997B, April 9) Opposition to human cloning. *JAMA, 277,* 1105

JAMA (1998, April 1) Editorial note, *JAMA, 279,* 985–986.

Jani, S. (1997). Changing relationships with parents. In J. D. Noshpitz (Editor in Chief) and L.T. Flaherty & R. M. Sarles (Vol. Eds.), *Handbook of child and adolescent psychiatry* (Vol. 3, pp. 87–97). New York: Wiley.

Janosz, M., LeBlanc, M., Boulerice, B., & Tremblay, R. E. (1997). Disentangling the weight of school dropout predictors: A test on two longitudinal samples. *Journal of Youth and Adolescence, 26,* 733–762.

Jaroff, L. (1989, March 20). The gene hunt. *Time,* pp. 62+.

Jelalian, E., Spirito, A., & Rasile, D. (1997). Risk taking, reported injury, and perception of future injury among adolescents. *Journal of Pediatric Psychology, 22,* 513–531.

Jencks, C. (1972). *Inequality: A reassessment of the effects of family and schooling in America.* New York: Basic Books.

Jensen, L.C. (1985) *Adolescence: Theories, Research, Applications.* St. Paul, Mn: West.

Jessor, R., Van Den Bos, J., Vanderryn, J., Costa, F. M., & Turbin, M. S. (1995). Protective factors in adolescent problem behavior: Moderator effects and developmental change. *Developmental Psychology, 31,* 923–933.

Joekler, N. (1998, August 26) Dopamine defect and ADHD. *JAMA, 280,* 687.

Joffe, L. S., & Vaughn, B. E. (1982). Infant-mother attachment: Theory, assessment, and implications for development. In B. B. Wolman (Ed.), *Handbook of developmental psychology* (pp. 190–204). Upper Saddle River, NJ: Prentice Hall.

Johnson, D.W., & Johnson, R.T. (1974) Instructional goal structure: Cooperative, competitive or individualistic. *Review of Educational Research, 44,* 218–240.

Johnson, J. E., & Yawkey, T. D. (1988). Play and integration. In T. D. Yawkey & J. E. Johnson (Eds.), *Integrative processes and socialization* (pp. 97–119). Hillsdale, NJ: Erlbaum.

Johnson, J. S., & Newport, E. L. (1991). Critical period effects on universal properties of language: The status of subagency to the acquisition of a second language. *Cognition, 39,* 715–758.

Johnson, M. H. (1998). The neural basis of cognitive development. In W. Damon (Editor in Chief) & D. Kuhn & R. S. Siegler (Vol. Eds.), *Handbook of child psychology* (5th ed., Vol. 2, pp. 1–50). New York: Wiley.

Johnson, M. H., Dziurawiec, S., Ellis, H. D., & Morton, J. (1991). Newborns' preferential tracking of face-like stimuli and its subsequent decline. *Cognition, 40,* 1–19.

Johnson, R. R., Cooper, H. I. & Chance, J. (1982). The relation of children's television viewing to school achievement and I.Q. *Journal of Educational Research, 76,* 294–297.

Johnson, S. L., & Birch, L. L. (1994). Parents' and children's adiposity and eating style. *Pediatrics*, 94, 653–661.

Johnson, S. P., & Aslin, R. N. (1995). Perception of object unity in 2-month-old infants. *Developmental Psychology*, 31, 739–745.

Johnson, S. P., & Nanez, J. E. Sr. (1995). Young infants' perception of object unity in two-dimensional displays. *Infant behavior and Development*, 18, 133–143.

Johnston, L., Bachman, J., & O'Malley, P. (1995). *Monitoring the future: National High School Seniors Survey*. Ann Arbor, Michigan: University of Michigan Survey Research Center.

Johnston, R. B., & Staples, D. A. (1998). Use of folic acid-continuing supplements among women of childbearing age: United States, 1997. *MMWR*, 131–134.

Jones, C. (1997, September 24). Increase in diversity is challenge for educators. *USA Today*, pp. A1, A2.

Jones, K. L., Smith, D. W., Streissguth, A. P., and Myrianthopoulus, N. (1974). Outcomes in offspring of chronic alcoholic women. *The Lancet*, 1, 1076–1078.

Jones, M. C. (1965). Psychological correlates of somatic development. *Child Development*, 36, 899–911.

Jones, M. C., & Bayley, N. (1950). Physical maturing among boys as related to behavior. *Journal of Educational Psychology*, 41, 129–148.

Jones, M. M., & Mandeville, G. K. (1990). The effect of age at school entry on reading achievement scores among South Carolina students. *Remedial and Special Education*, 11, 56–62.

Jones, R. T., McDonald, D. W., Fiore, M. F., Arrington, T., & Randall, J. (1990). A primary preventive approach to children's drug refusal behavior: The impact of rehearsal plus. *Journal of Pediatric Psychology*, 15, 211–223.

Jones, S.S. & Raag, T. (1989) Smile production in older infants: the importance of a social recipient for the facial signal. *Child Development*, 60, 811–818.

Jordan, W. J., Lara, J., & McPartland, J. M. (1996). Exploring the causes of early dropout among race-ethnic and gender groups. *Youth and Society*, 28, 62–94.

Jory, B., Rainbolt, E., Karns, J. T., Freeborn, A., & Greer, C. V. (1996). Communication patterns and alliances between parents and adolescents during a structured problem solving task. *Journal of Adolescence*, 19, 139–146.

Jost, K. (1993). Childhood immunizations. *CQ Researcher*, 23, 531–551.

Junge, M. E., & Dretzke, B. J. (1995). Mathematical self-efficacy gender differences in gifted/talented adolescents. *Gifted Child Quarterly*, 39, 22–28.

Jusczyk, P. W. (1995). Infants' detection of the sound patterns of words in fluent speech. *Cognitive Psychology*, 29, 1–23.

Jusczyk, P. W., Cutler, A., & Redanz, N. J. (1993). Infants' preference for the predominant stress patterns of English words. *Child Development*, 64, 675–687.

Justice, E. (1985). Categorization as a preferred memory strategy: Developmental changes during elementary school. *Developmental Psychology*, 21, 1105–1110.

K

Kagan, J. (1979a). The form of early development. Cited in Mussen, P. H., Conger, J. J., & Kagan, J. (Eds.). (1980). *Readings in child and adolescent psychology: Contemporary perspectives* (pp. 18–22). New York: Harper & Row.

Kagan, J. (1979b). Overview: Perspectives on human infancy. In J. Osofsky (Ed.), *Handbook of Infant Development* (pp. 1–29). New York: Wiley.

Kagan, J. (1984). *The nature of the child*. New York: Basic Books.

Kagan, J. (1992). Yesterday's premises, tomorrow's promises. *Developmental Psychology*, 28, 990–998.

Kagan, J. (1996, January 12). The misleading abstractions of social scientists. *Chronicle of Higher Education*, p. A52.

Kagan, J. (1997). Temperament and the reactions to unfamiliarity. *Child Development*, 68, 139–143.

Kagan, J., Reznick, J. S., & Snidman, N. (1987). Physiology and psychology of behavioral inhibition. *Child Development*, 59, 1459–1473.

Kahn, P. H., Jr. (1992). Children's obligatory and discretionary moral judgments. *Child Development*, 63, 416–430.

Kahne, J. (1996, Spring). The politics of self-esteem. *American Educational Research Journal*, 35, 3–22.

Kail, R. (1993). Processing time decreases globally at an exponential rate during childhood and adolescence. *Journal of Experimental Child Psychology*, 56, 254–265.

Kail, R., & Hagen, J. W. (1982). Memory in childhood. In B. B. Wolman (Ed.), *Handbook of developmental psychology* (pp. 350–367). Upper Saddle River, NJ: Prentice Hall.

Kalat, J. W. (1981). *Biological psychology*. Belmont, CA. Wadsworth.

Kaler, S. R., & Kopp, C. (1990). Compliance and comprehension in very young toddlers. *Child Development*, 61, 1997–2003.

Kalichman, S. C., Kelly, J. A., & Rompa, D. (1997). Continued high-risk sex among HIV seropositive gay and bisexual men seeking HIV prevention services. *Health Psychology*, 16, 369–373.

Kalra, B., & Heath, W. P. (1997). Perceptions of a child as witness: effects of leading question and the type of relationship between child and defendant. *Psychological Reports*, 80, 979–986.

Kamii, C. (1985). Leading primary education toward excellence. *Young Children*, 40, 3–9.

Kamii, C., & Radin, N. (1967). Class differences fin the socialization practices of Negro mothers. In R. Staples (Ed.), *The Black family: Essays and studies*. Belmont CA: Wadsworth.

Kammerman, S. B. (1980). *Parenting in an unresponsive society: Managing work and family life*. New York: Free Press.

Kandel, D. B., Wu, P., & Davies, M. (1994). Maternal smoking during pregnancy and smoking by adolescent daughters. *American Journal of Public Health*, 84, 1407–1413.

Kandel, E.R., Schwartz, J.H., & Jessell, T.M. (1995). *Principles of neural science*. Norwalk, CT: Appleton & Lange.

Kaplan, D. S., Beck, B. ., & Kaplan, H. B. (1997). Decomposing the academic failure-dropout relationship: A longitudinal analysis. *Journal of Educational Research*, 90, 331–344.

Kaplan, P. S. (1977, March 13). It's the I.Q. tests that flunk. *New York Times*, p. 26.

Kaplan, P. S. (1990). *Educational psychology for tomorrow's teacher*. St. Paul, MN.: West.

Kaplan, P. S. (1996). *Pathways for Exceptional Children*, St. Paul, MN: West.

Karen, R. (1990, February). Becoming attached. *Atlantic Monthly*, pp. 35–50, 63–70.

Karraker, K. H., & Evans, S. L. (1996). Adolescent mothers' knowledge of child development and expectations for their own infants. *Journal of Youth and Adolescence*, 25, 651–666.

Kashani, J. H., Goddard, P., & Reid, J. C. (1989). Correlates of suicidal ideation in a community sample of children and adolescents. *Journal of the American Academy for Child and Adolescent Psychiatry*, 28, 912–917.

Katchadourian, H. (1977). *The biology of adolescence*. San Francisco: Freeman.

Kato, P., & Mann, T. (1996). *Handbook of diversity issues in health psychology*. New York: Plenum.

Katz, L. F., & Gottman, J. M. (1997). Buffering children from marital conflict and dissolution. *Journal of Clinical Child Psychology*, 26, 157–171.

Katz, L. G. (1980, August). Should you be your child's parents? *Parents*, pp. 88–90.

Katz, P. A., & Ksansnak, K. R. (1994). Developmental aspects of gender role flexibility and traditionality in middle childhood and adolescence. *Developmental Psychology*, 30, 272–282.

Katz, P. A., & Walsh, P. V. (1991). Modification of children's gender-stereotyped behavior. *Child Development*, 62, 338–351.

Kaufman, J., & Zigler, E. (1987). Do abused children become abusive parents? *American Journal of Orthopsychiatry*, 57, 186–192.

Kazdin, A. E . (1994). Interventions for aggressive and antisocial children. In L. D. Eron, U. H. Gentry, P. Schlegel (Eds.), *Reason to hope: A psychosocial perspective on violence and youth*. (pp. 341–383). Washington, DC: American Psychological Association.

Kearsley, R. B. (1973). The newborn's response to auditory stimuli: A demonstration of orientation and defensive behavior. *Child Development, 44,* 582–590.

Keating, D.P. (1990) Structuralism, deconstruction, reconstruction: The limits of reasoning (pp.299–319) in W.F. Overton (Ed.). Reasoning, necessity, and logic: *Developmental perspectives.* Hillsdale, NJ: Erlbaum.

Keefer, C. S., Dixon, E., Tronick, L. B., & Brazelton, T. B. (1978). Gusii infants' neuromotor behavior: Use of the Neonatal Behavioral Assessment Scale in cross-cultural studies. Cited in D. A. Wagner & H. W. Stevenson (Eds.), *Cultural perspectives on child development* (pp. 20–54). San Francisco: Freeman, 1982.

Kegan, R. (1982) *The evolving self: Problem and process in human development.*, Cambridge, MA: Harvard University Press.

Keil, F. C. (1989). *Concepts, word meanings, and cognitive development.* Cambridge, MA: MIT Press.

Keller, A., Ford, L. M. & Meacham, J. A. (1978). Dimensions of self-concept in preschool children. *Developmental Psychology, 14,* 483–489.

Kelley, M. L., & Tseng, H. (1992). Cultural differences in child rearing: A comparison of immigrant Chinese and Caucasian American mothers. *Journal of Cross-Cultural Psychology, 23,* 444–455.

Kelley, M. L., Grace, N., & Elliott, S. N. (1990). Acceptability of positive ad punitive discipline methods: Comparisons among abusive, potentially abusive, and nonabusive parents. *Child Abuse & Neglect, 14,* 219–226.

Kelley, M. L., Power, T. G., & Wimbush, D. D. (1992). Determinants of disciplinary practices in low-income Black mothers. *Child Development, 63,* 573–582.

Kelley, M. L., Sanchez-Huckles, J., & Walker, R. R. (1993). Correlates of disciplinary practices in working-to-middle-class African-American mothers. *Merrill-Palmer Quarterly, 39,* 252–264.

Kellman, P. J., & Banks, M. S. (1998). Infant visual perception. In W. Damon (Editor in Chief) & D. Kuhn & R. S. Siegler (Vol. Eds.), *Handbook of child psychology* (5th ed., Vol. 2, pp. 103–146). New York: Wiley.

Kellogg, R. (1970). *Analyzing children's art.* Palo Alto, CA: Mayfield.

Kelly, B. T., Loeber, R., Keenan, K., & DeLamatre, M. (1997). Developmental pathways in boys' disruptive and delinquent behavior. *Juvenile Justice Bulletin.* Washington, DC: U.S. Department of Justice.

Kelly, D. (1996, April 3). Understanding standards. *USA Today,* p. D4.

Kelly, J. B., & Wallerstein, J. S. (1976). The effects of parental divorce: Experiences of the child in early latency. *American Journal of Orthopsychiatry, 46,* 20–33.

Kendler, K. S., MacLean, C., Neale, M., Kessler, R., Heath, A., & Eaves, L. (1991)The genetic epidemiology of bulimia nervosa. *American Journal of Psychiatry, 148,* 1627–1637.

Kendrick, C., & Dunn, J. (1983). Sibling quarrels and maternal responses. *Developmental Psychology, 19,* 62–71.

Kermis, M. D. (1984). *The psychology of human aging.* Boston: Allyn & Bacon.

Kern, D. L., McPhee, L., Fisher, J., Johnson, S., & Birch, L.L. (1993). The postingestive consequences of fat condition preferences for flavors associated with high dietary fat. *Physiology & Behavior, 54,* 71–76.

Kerr, B. (1991). Educating gifted girls. In N. Colangelo & G. A. Davis (Eds.), *Handbook of gifted education* (pp.402–416). Needham Heights, MA: Allyn & Bacon.

Kershner, R. (1996). Adolescent attitudes about rape. *Adolescence, 31,* 29–33.

Khoury, M. J., and the Genetics Working Group. (1996). From genes to public health: The applications of genetic technology in disease prevention. *American Journal of Public Health, 86,* 1717–1722.

Kidwell, J. S., Dunham, R. M., Bachno, R. A., Pastorino, E., & Portes, P. R. (1995). Adolescent identity exploration: A test of Erikson's theory of transitional crisis. *Adolescence, 30,* 785–793.

Killen, J. D., Hayward, C., Wilson, D. M., Taylor, C. B., Hammer, L .D., Litt, I., Simmonds, B., & Haydel, F. (1994a). factors associated with eating disorder symptoms in a community sample of 6th and 7th grade girls. *International Journal of Eating Disorders, 15,* 357–367.

Killen, J. D., Taylor, C. B., Hayward, C., Wilson, D. M., Haydel, K. F., Hammer, L. D., Simmonds, B., Robinson, T. N., Litt, I., Varady, A., & Kraemer, H. (1994b). Pursuit of thinness and onset of eating disorder symptoms in a community sample of adolescent girls: A three-year prospective analysis. *International Journal of Eating Disorders, 16,* 227–238.

Kilpatrick, K. L., Litt, M., & Williams, L. M. (1997). Post-traumatic stress disorder in child witnesses to domestic violence. *American Journal of Orthopsychiatry, 67,* 639–644.

Kim, J.E., Hetherington, E.M., & Reiss, D. (1999) Associations among family relationships, antisocial peers, and adolescents' externalizing behaviors: Gender and family type differences. *Child Development, 70,* 1209–1230.

Kimball, M. (1989). A new perspective on women's math achievement. *Psychological Bulletin, 105,* 198–214.

Kimble, G. A. (1993). Evolution of the nature-nurture issue in the history of psychology. In R. Plomin & G. E. McClearn (Eds.), *Nature, nurture, and psychology* (pp. 3–27). Washington, DC: American Psychological Association.

Kinney, H. C., Filiano, J. J., Sleeper, L. A., Mandell, F., Valdes-Dapena, & White, W. F. (1995). Decreased muscarinic receptor binding in the arcuate nucleus in sudden infant death syndrome. *Science, 269,* 1446–1450.

Kirby, D., et. al. (1994). School-based programs to reduce sexual risk behaviors: A review of effectiveness. *Public Health Reports, 109,* 339–360.

Kirk, S. A., & Gallagher, J. J. (1989). *Educating exceptional children* (6th ed.). Boston: Houghton Mifflin.

Kirkpatrick, L.A., & Davis, K.E. (1994) Attachment style, gender, and relationship stability: a longitudinal analysis. *Journal of Personality and Social Psychology, 66,* 502–512.

Klepinger, D. H., Lundberg, S., & Plotnick, R. D. (1995). Adolescent fertility and the educational attainment of young women. *Family Planning Perspectives, 27,* 23–28.

Klesges, R. C., Shelton, M. L., & Klesges, L. M. (1993). Effects of television on metabolic rate: Potential implications for childhood obesity. *Pediatrics, 91,* 281–286.

Klesges, R. E., et al. (1991). Parental influence on food selection in young children and its relationships to childhood obesity. *American Journal of Clinical Nutrition, 53,* 859–864.

Kliewer, W., & Lewis, H. (1995). Family influences on coping processes in children and adolescents with Sickle Cell Disease. *Journal of Pediatric Psychology, 20,* 511–525.

Kliewer, W., Fearnow, M. D., & Miller, P. A. (1996). Coping socialization in middle childhood: Tests of maternal and paternal influences. *Child Development, 67,* 2339–2357.

Klimes-Dougan, B., & Kistner, J. (1990). Physically abused preschoolers' responses to peer distress. *Developmental Psychology, 26,* 599–602.

Klimes-Dougan, B., Lopez, J. A., Nelson, P. & Adelman, H. S. (1992). Two studies of low income parents' involvement in schooling. *Urban Review, 24,* 185–202.

Kline, P. (1972). *Fact and fancy in Freudian theory.* London: Methuen.

Klinnert, M. D., Emde, R .N., Butterfield, P., & Campos, J. J. (1986). Social referencing: The infant's use of emotional signals from a friendly adult with mother present. *Developmental Psychology, 22,* 427–432.

Klonoff-Cohen, H., & Edelstein, S. (1995). A case-control study of routine and death scene sleeping position and sudden infant death syndrome in Southern California. *Journal of the American Medical Association, 273,* 790–794.

Knight, G., Virdin, L., & Roosa, M. (1994).Socialization and family correlates of mental health outcomes among Hispanic and Anglo American children: Consideration of cross-ethnic scalar equivalence. *Child Development, 65,* 212–224.

Knothe, H., & Dette, G. A. (1985). Antibiotics and pregnancy: Toxicity and teratogenicity. *Infection*, 49, 13.

Knowles, M., & Boucher, R. (1996, February 1). Gene therapy. *New England Journal of Medicine*, pp. 333, 334.

Koblinsky, S. A., Morgan, K. M., & Anderson, E. A. (1997). African-American homeless and low-income housed mothers: Comparison of parenting practices. *American Journal of Orthopsychiatry*, 67, 37–47.

Koch, M. (1994, Fall). Opening up technology to both genders. *Technos*, 3, 14–19.

Koestner, R., Weinberger, J., & Franz, C. (1997). The family origins of empathic concern: A 26-year longitudinal study. *Journal of Personality and Social Psychology*, 58, 709–717.

Koff, E., & Rierdan, J. (1991). Perceptions of weight and attitudes toward eating in early adolescent girls. *Journal of Adolescent Health*, 12, 307–312.

Koff, E., & Rierdan, J. (1995). Preparing girls for menstruation: Recommendations from adolescent girls. *Adolescence*, 30, 795–811.

Kohlberg, L. (1969). Stage and sequence: The cognitive-developmental approach to socialization. In D. A. Goslin (Ed.), *Handbook of socialization theory and research*. Chicago: Rand-McNally.

Kohlberg, L. (1976). Moral stages and moralization: The cognitive-developmental approach. In T. Lickona (Ed.), *Moral development and behavior*. New York: Holt, Rinehart & Winston.

Kohlberg, L. (1987a). The development of moral judgment and moral action. In L. Kohlberg (Ed.), *Child psychology and childhood education: A cognitive-developmental view* (pp. 259–329). New York: Longman.

Kohlberg, L. (1987b). The young child as a philosopher. In L. Kohlberg (Ed.), *Child psychology and childhood education* (pp. 13–43). New York: Longman.

Kohlberg, L., & Kramer, R. (1969). Continuities and discontinuities in childhood and adult moral development. *Human Development*, 12, 83–120.

Kohn, A. (1994, December). The truth about self-esteem. *Phi Delta Kappan*, pp. 272–285.

Kolata, G. (1989, December 5). *Understanding Down syndrome: A chromosome holds the key*. New York Times, pC3.

Kolbo, J. R., Blakely, E. H., & Engleman, D. (1996). Children who witness domestic violence: A review of empirical literature. *Journal of Interpersonal Violence*, 11, 281–293.

Komarovsky, M. (1985). *Women in college*. New York: Basic Books.

Kopp, C. (1992). Emotional distress and control in young children. *New Directions for Child Development*, 55, 41–56.

Kopp, C. B., & Kaler, S. R. (1989). Risk in infancy. *American Psychologist*, 44, 244–231.

Kopp, C. B., & Krakow, J. B. (Eds.). *The child: Development in a social context*. Reading, MA: Addison-Wesley.

Kopp, C. B., & Parmelee, A. H. (1979). Prenatal and perinatal influences on infant behavior. In J. D. Osofsky (Ed.), *Handbook of infant development* (pp. 29–75). New York: Wiley.

Korner, A. F. (1973). Sex differences in newborns with special reference to differences in the organization of oral behavior. *Journal of Child Psychology and Psychiatry*, 14, 17–29.

Koslowski, B. (1980). Quantitative and qualitative changes in the development of seriation. *Merrill-Palmer Quarterly*, 26, 391–405.

Koss, M., et al. (1987, April). The scope of rape: Incidence and prevalence of sexual aggression and victimization in a national sample of higher education students. *Journal of Consulting and Clinical Psychology*, 55, 162–170.

Koup, R. A., & Wilson, C.B . (1994). Clinical immunology of HIV-infected children in *Pediatric AIDS: The challenge of HIV Infection in infants, children, and adolescents* (2nd ed., pp.129–159). Baltimore: Williams & Wilkins.

Kowal, A., & Kramer, L. (1997). Children's understanding of parental differential treatment. *Child Development*, 68, 113–126.

Kowalski, N. & Allen, R. (1995) School sleep lag is less but persists with a very late starting high school. *Sleep Research*, 24, 124.

Kraemer, H. C., Korner, A., Anders, T., Jacklin, C. N., & Dimiceli, S. (1985). Obstetric drugs and infant behavior: A reevaluation. *Journal of Pediatric Psychology*, 10, 345–353.

Kramer, D. (1983). Post-formal operations? A need for further conceptualization. *Human Development*, 16, 91–105.

Kramer, L. (1996). What's real in children's fantasy play? Fantasy play across the transition to becoming a sibling. *Journal of Child Psychology and Psychiatry*, 37, 329–337.

Kramer, L. R. (1986). Career awareness and personal development: A naturalistic study of gifted adolescent girls' concerns. *Adolescence*, 21, 123–131.

Krappman, L. (1989). Family relationships and peer relationships in middle childhood: an exploratory study of the associations between children's integration into the social network of peers and family development. In K. Kreppner & R. M. Lerner (Eds.), *Family systems and life-span development* (pp. 93–104). Hillsdale, NJ: Erlbaum.

Krebs, D. L., & Van Hesteren, F. (1994). The development of altruism: Toward an integrative model. *Developmental Review*, 14, 103–158.

Krebs, L. L. (1986). Current research on theoretically based parenting programs. *Individual Psychology*, 42, 375–387.

Kreitler, S., Zigler, E., Kagan, S., Weissler, K., & Kretler, H. (1995). Cognitive and motivational determinants of academic achievement and behaviour in third and fourth grade disadvantaged students. *British Journal of Educational Psychology*, 65, 297–316.

Kremenitzer, J. P., Vaughn, H. G., Kurtzberg, D., & Dowling, K. (1979). Smooth-pursuit eye movements in the newborn infant. *Child Development*, 50, 442–448.

Kreppner, K., & Lerner, R. M. (1989). Family systems and life-span development: Issues and perspectives. In K. Kreppner & R. M. Lerner (Eds.), *Family systems and life-span development* (pp. 1–15). Hillsdale, NJ: Erlbaum.

Kreutzer, M. A., & Charlesworth, W. R. (1973). Infants' reactions to different expressions of emotion. In C. A. Nelson, The recognition of facial expressions in the first two years of life: Mechanisms of development. *Child Development*, 58, 889–909.

Kroger, J. (1997). Gender and identity: The intersection of structure, content and context. *Sex Roles*, 36, 747–770.

Krogman, W. M. (1980). *Child growth*. Ann Arbor: University of Michigan Press.

Krombholz, H. (1997). Physical performance in relation to age, sex, social class and sports activities in kindergarten and elementary school. *Perceptual and Motor Skills*, 84, 1168–1170.

Kroninger, S. (1995, September 25). That's entertaining. *Forbes*, p. 31.

Kruesi, M. J., & Rapoport, J. L. (1986). Diet and human behavior: How much do they affect each other? *Annual Reviews of Nutrition*, 6, 113–130.

Ku, L. C., Sonenstein, F. L., & Pleck, J. H. (1993). Factors affecting first intercourse among young men. *Public Health Reports*, 108, 680–694.

Kubiszyn, T., & Borich, G. (1987). *Educational testing and measurement* (2nd ed.). Glenview, IL: Scott, Foresman.

Kuhn, L., & Stein, Z. (1997). Infant survival, HIV infection, and feeding alternatives in less-developed countries. *American journal of Public Health*, 87, 926–928.

Kurdek, L. (1991a). Predictors of increases in marital distress in newlywed couples: A 3-year prospective longitudinal study. *Developmental Psychology*, 27, 627–636.

Kurdek, L. (1991b). The relations between reported well-being and divorce history, availability of a proximate adult, and gender. *Journal of Marriage and the Family*, 53, 71–78.

Kurdek, L. A., & Fine, M. A. (1994). Family acceptance and family control as predictors of adjustment in young adolescents: Linear, curvilinear, or interactive. *Child Development*, 64, 1137–1146.

Kurdek, L. A., Fine, M. A., & Sinclair, R. J. (1995). School adjustment in sixth graders: Parenting transitions, family climate, and per norm effects. *Child Development*, 66, 430–445.

Kurtzweil, P. (1996, August). How folate can help prevent birth defects. *FDA Consumer Magazine Reprint*, pp. 96–2306.

Kurzweill, S. R. (1988). Recognition of mother from multisensory interactions in early infancy. *Infant Behavior and Development*, 11, 235–243.

L

Labouvie-Vief, G. (1980). Beyond formal operations: Uses and limits of pure logic in life-span development. *Human Development*, 23, 141–161.

Labouvie-Vief, G. (1984). Logic and self-regulation from youth to maturity: A model. In M. L. Commons, F. A. Richards, & C. Armon (Eds.), *Beyond formal operations* (pp. 158–181). New York: Praeger.

Labouvie-Vief, G. (1990). Wisdom as integrated thought: Historical and developmental perspectives. In R. J. Sternberg (Ed.), *Wisdom: Its nature, origins, and development* (pp. 52–87). Cambridge: Cambridge University Press.

Labov, W. (1977). The study of nonstandard English. In V. P. Clark, P. A. Eshholz, & A. F. Rosa (Eds.), *Language* (2nd ed., pp. 439–450). New York: St. Martin's.

Ladd, G. W. (1990). Having friends, keeping friends, making friends, and being liked by peers in the classroom: Predictors of children's early school adjustment. *Child Development*, 61, 1081–1100.

Ladd, G.W., & Burgess, K.B. (1999) Changing the relationship trajectories of aggressive, withdrawn, and aggressive/withdrawn children during early grade school. *Child Development*, 70, 910–929.

Ladd, G. W., & Le Sieur, K. D. (1995). Parents and children's peer relationships. In M. H. Bornstein (Ed.), *Handbook of parenting* (Vol. 4, pp. 377–411). Mahwah, NJ: Erlbaum.

Ladd, G. W., & Price, J. M. (1993). Play styles of peer-accepted and peer-rejected children on the playground. In C. H. Hart (Ed.), *Children on playgrounds: Research perspectives and applications* (pp. 130–161). Albany: State University of New York Press.

Ladner, J. (1987). Black teenager pregnancy: A challenge for educators. *Journal of Negro Education*, 56, 53–63.

LaFromboise, T. D. & Low, K. G. (1989). American Indian children and adolescents. In *Children of color: Psychological interventions with minority youth* (pp. 114–148). San Francisco: Jossey-Bass.

LaFromboise, T., Coleman, H. L. K., & Gerton, J. (1993). Psychological impact of biculturalism: Evidence and theory. *Psychological Bulletin*, 114, 395–412.

Lamaze, F. (1970). *Painless childbirth*. Chicago: Regnery.

Lamb, M. E. (1988). Social and emotional development in infancy. In M. H. Bornstein & M. E. Lamb (Eds.), *Social, emotional and personality development* (pp. 359–411). Hillsdale, NJ: Erlbaum.

Lamb, M. E. (1998). Nonparental child care: Context, quality, correlates, and consequences in W. Damon (Editor in Chief) & I. E. Sigel & K. A. Renninger (Vol. Eds.), *Handbook of child psychology* (5th ed., Vol. 4, pp. 73–134). New York: Wiley.

Lamb, M. E., Frodi, M., Hwang, C. P., & Frodi, A. M. (1983). Effects of paternal involvement on infant preferences for mothers and fathers. *Child Development*, 54, 450–458.

Lamb, M. E., Sternberg, K. J., & Esplin, P. W. (1995). Making children into competent witnesses: Reactions to the amicus brief *In re Michaels*. *Psychology, Public Policy, and Law*, 1, 438–449.

Lamborn, S., Mounts, N., Steinberg, L., & Dornbusch, S. (1991). Patterns of competence and adjustment among adolescents from authoritative, authoritarian, indulgent and neglectful homes. *Child Development*, 62, 1049–1065.

Lampl, M., Cameron, N., Veldhuis, J. D., & Johnson, M. L. (1992). Salutation and status: A model of human growth. *Science*, 258, 801–803.

Lampl, M., Cameron, N., Veldhuis, J. D., & Johnson, M. L. (1995, April 21). Response *Science*, 268, 445–447.

Lancashare, J. (1995). National center for health statistics data line. *Public Health Reports*, 110, 105–106.

Landau-Stanton, J., & Clements, C. D., & Associates. (1993). *AIDS Health and Mental Health: A Primary Sourcebook*. New York: Brunner/Mazel.

Lane, E. (1991, April, 9). Low-fat diets at 2 urged. *Newsday*, pp. 4, 34.

Lane, E. (1995, April 11). Teen surveys vs. parental consent. *Newsday*, p. B29.

Lane, K.E., & Gwartney-Gibbs, P.A. (1985) Violence in the context of dating and sex. *Journal of Family Issues*, 6, 45–49.

Langlois, J. H., & Downs, A. C. (1980). Mothers, fathers, and peers as socialization agents of sex-typed play behavior in young children. *Child Development*, 51, 1237–1247.

Lansford, J. E., & Parker, J. G. (1999). Children's interactions in triads: Behavioral profiles and effects of gender and patterns of friendships among members. *Developmental Psychology*, 35, 80–93.

Laosa, L. M. (1996). Intelligence testing and social policy. *Journal of Applied Developmental Psychology*, 17, 153–173.

Lapsley, D. K., Milstead, M., & Quintana, S. M. (1986). Adolescent egocentrism and formal operations: Tests of a theoretical assumption. *Developmental Psychology*, 22, 800–807.

Larroque, B., Karminski, M., Dehaene, P., Subtil, D., Delfosse, M. J., & Querleu, D. (1995). Moderate prenatal alcohol exposure and psychomotor development at preschool age. *American Journal of Public Health*, 85, 1654–1661.

Larsen, J. M., & Robinson, C. C. (1989). Later effects of preschool on low-risk children. *Early Childhood Research Quarterly*, 4, 133–144.

Larson, J. (1992, June). Understanding stepfamilies. *American Demographics*, pp. 36–42.

Larson, R. W., Richards, M. H., Moneta, G., Holmbeck, G., & Duckett, E. (1996). Changes in adolescents' daily interactions with their families from ages 10 to 18: Disengagement and transformation. *Developmental Psychology*, 32, 744–754.

Larson, R., & Ham, M. (1993). Stress and "storm and stress" in early adolescence: The relationship of negative events with dysphoric affect. *Developmental Psychology*, 29, 130–140.

Laskas, J. M. (1996). What is essential is invisible to the eye. In M. Collins & M. M. Kimmel (Eds.), Mister Rogers' Neighborhood: *Children, television and Fred Rogers* (pp. 15–36). Pittsburgh, PA: University of Pittsburgh Press.

Laughlin, H. P. (1970). *The ego and its defenses*. New York: Appleton-Century-Crofts.

Lauresen, B., & Hartup, W. W. (1989). The dynamics of preschool children's conflicts. *Merrill-Palmer Quarterly*, 35, 281–297.

Lavery, B., Siegel, A. W., Cousins, J., & Rubovits, D. S. (1993). Adolescent risk-taking: An analysis of problem behaviors in problem children. *Journal of Experimental Child Psychology*, 55, 277–294.

Lawrence, R. (1991). Breast-feeding trends: A cause for action. *Pediatrics*, 88, 867–868.

Lawrence, V. W., & Shipley, E. F. (1996). Parental speech to middle-and working-class children from two racial groups in three settings. *Applied Psycholinguistics*, 17, 233–255.

Lawton, M. (1991, April 10). More than a third of teens surveyed say they have contemplated suicide. *Education Week*, p. 5.

Lawton, M. (1994, November 9). Violence-prevention curricula: What works best? *Education Week*, pp. 1, 10.

Lawton, M. (1996, May 22). Board endorses draft play for NAEP overhaul. *Education Week*, pp. 1, 11.

Lawton, M. (1997, October 29). Science proves a big mystery to U.S. pupils. *Education Week*, pp. 1, 14.

Lazar, I., & Darlington, R. (1982). Lasting effects of early education: A report from the consortium for longitudinal studies. *Monographs of the Society for Research in Child Development*, 47 (2–3), Serial No. 195.

Leadbeater, B. J., & Bishop, S. J. (1994). Predictors of behavior problems in preschool children of inner-city Afro-American and Puerto Rican adolescent mothers. *Child Development*, 65, 638–649.

Leadbeater, B. J., Bishop, S. J., & Raver, C. C. (1996). Quality of mother-toddler interactions, maternal depressive symptoms, and behavior problems in preschoolers of adolescent mothers. *Developmental Psychology*, 32, 280–288.

Leadbeater, B., & Kuhn, D. (1988) Interpreting discrepant narratives: Hermeneutics in adult cognition in J. Sinnott (Ed.). *Everyday problem solving*, (pp. 175–200). New York: Praeger.

Leahy, T. H., & Harris, R. J. (1997). *Learning and cognition* (4th ed.). Upper Saddle River, NJ: Prentice Hall.

Leaper, C. (1994). Exploring the consequences of gender segregation on social relationships. In C. Leaper (Ed.), *The development of gender and relationships: New directions for child development*. (pp. 67–86). San Francisco: Jossey-Bass.

Learner, R. M. (1991). Changing organism-context relations as the basis process of development. *Developmental Psychology, 27,* 27–33.

Leary, M.R. (1995) *Behavioral Research Methods* (2nd ed). Pacific Grove, Cal: Brooks-Cole.

LeClere, F. B., & Wilson, J. B. (1997, July 25). *Smoking behavior of recent mothers, 18–44 years of age, Before and after pregnancy: United States, 1990.* DHHS Pub. No. PHS 97–1250. Hyattsville, MD: U.S. Department of Health and Human Services.

Lee, T. J. (1997). How can there be free speech if it's only in English? *Human Rights, 24,* 10–13.

Leger, D. W., Thompson, R. A., Merritt, J. A., & Benz, J. J. (1996). Adult perception of emotion intensity in human infant cries: Effects of infant age and cry acoustics. *Child Development, 67,* 3238–3249.

Legerstee, M., Anderson, D., & Schaffer, A. (1998) Five- and eight-month-old infants recognize their faces and voices as familiar and social stimuli. *Child Development, 69,* 1–270.

Leichtman, M. D., & Ceci, S. J. (1995). The effects of stereotypes and suggestions on preschoolers' reports. *Developmental Psychology, 31,* 568–578.

Leinbach, M. D. & Fagot, B. I. (1993). Categorical habituation to male and female faces: Gender schematic processing in infancy. *Infant Behavior and Development, 16,* 317–332.

Leland, N. L., & Barth, R. P. (1992). Gender differences in knowledge, intentions, and behaviors concerning pregnancy and sexually transmitted disease prevention among adolescents. *Journal of Adolescent Health, 13,* 589–599.

Leland, N. L., Petersen, D. J., Braddock, M., & Alexander, G. R. (1995). Variations in pregnancy outcomes by race among 10–14 year-old mothers in the United States. *Public Health Reports, 110,* 53–58.

Lemery, K. S., Goldsmith, H. H., Klinnert, M. D., & Mrazek, D. A. (1999). Developmental models of infant and childhood temperament. *Developmental Psychology, 35,* 189–204.

Lempers, J. D., Flavell, E. R., & Flavell, J. H. (1977). The development in very young children of tacit knowledge concerning visual perceptions. *Genetic Psychology Monographs, 95,* 3–53.

Lenneberg, E. H. (1967). *Biological foundations of language.* New York: Wiley.

Lerman, C., Hughes, C., Trock, B. J., Myers, R. E., Main, D., Bonney, B., Abbaszadegan, M. R., Harty, A. E., Franklin, B. A., Lynch, J. F., & Lynch, H. T. (1999, May 5). Genetic testing in families with hereditary nonpolyposis colon cancer. *Journal of the American Medical Association, 281,* 1618–1622.

Lerner, J.V., & Abrams, L.A. (1994) Developmental correlates of maternal employment influences on children. in C.B. Fisher & R.M. Lerner (Eds). *Applied developmental psychology.* (pp. 174–192). New York: McGraw-Hill.

Lerner, R. M, Karson, M., Meisels, M., & Knapp, J. R. (1975). Actual and perceived attitudes of late adolescents and their parents: The phenomenon of the generation gap. *Journal of Genetic Psychology, 126,* 195–207.

Lerner, R. M. (1984). *On the nature of human plasticity.* New York: Cambridge University Press.

Leshner, A. I. (1995). *Statement of Alan I Leshner, director, National Institute on Drug Abuse, National Institute of Health*, Washington, DC: U.S. Department of Health & Human Services.

Lesko, S. M., Corwin, M. J., Vezina, R. M., Hunt, C. E., Mandell, F., McClain, M., Heeren, T., & Mitchell, A. A. (1998, July 22/29). Changes in sleep position during infancy. *Journal of the American Medical Association, 280,* 336–340.

Lester, B. M., & Dreher, M. (1989). Effects of marijuana use during pregnancy on newborn cry. *Child Development, 60,* 765–771.

Lester, B. M., Heidelise, A., & Brazelton, T. B. (1982). Regional obstetric anesthesia and newborn behavior: A reanalysis towards synergistic effects. *Child Development, 53,* 687–692.

LeVay, S. (1991). A difference in hypothalamic structure between heterosexual and homosexual men. *Science, 253,* 1034–1037.

Levine, K., & Mueller, E. (1988). In T. D. Yawkey & J. E. Johnson (Eds.), *Integrative processes and socialization: Early to middle childhood* (pp. 207–225). Hillsdale, NJ: Erlbaum.

Leviton, A. (1995). Editorial: Reform without change? Look beyond the curriculum. *American Journal of Public Health, 85,* 907–908.

Levitt, M., Guacci-Franco, N., & Levitt, J. L. (1994). Social support and achievement in childhood and early adolescence: A multicultural study. *Journal of Applied Developmental Psychology, 15,* 207–222.

Levy, C.W. (1994, February). The bad news about Barney. *Parents,* pp. 191–192

Levy, D. (1997, March 20). Moms' nicotine levels found in newborns. *USA Today,* p. D1.

Levy, G. D., & Carter, D. B. (1989). Gender schema, gender constancy, and gender-role knowledge: The roles of cognitive factors in preschoolers' gender-role stereotype attributions. *Developmental Psychology, 25,* 444–450.

Levy, J. M., Jessop, D. J., Rimmerman, A., & Levy, P. H. (1992). Attitudes of Fortune 500 corporate executives toward the employability of persons with severe disabilities: A national study. *Mental Retardation, 30,* 67–75.

Lewis, M. & Rosenblum, L. A. (1975). *Friendship and peer relations.* New York: Wiley.

Lewis, M. (1987). Social development in infancy and early childhood. In J. D. Osofsky (Ed.), *Handbook of infant development* (pp. 419–494). New York: Wiley.

Lewis, M., & Brooks-Gunn, J. (1972). The relations of infants to people. In J. Belsky (Ed.), *In the beginning* (pp. 166–172). New York: Columbia University Press.

Lewis, M., & Brooks-Gunn, J. (1979). *Social cognition and the acquisition of self.* New York: Plenum.

Lewis, M., & Feiring, C. (1989a). Early predictors of childhood friendship. In T. J. Berndt & G. W. Ladd (Eds.), *Peer relationships in child development* (pp. 246–274). New York: Wiley.

Lewis, M., & Feiring, C. (1989b). Infant, mother, and mother-infant interaction behavior and subsequent attachment. Child Development, 60, 831–838.

Lewis, M., Alessandri, S. M., & Sullivan, M. W. (1992). Differences in shame and pride as a function of children's gender and task difficulty. *Child Development, 63,* 630–638.

Lewis, M., Stanger, C., & Sullivan, M. W. (1989). Deception in 3-year-olds. *Developmental Psychology, 25,* 439–443.

Lewis, M., Stanger, C., & Sullivan, M.W. (1989) Self development and self-conscious emotion. *Child Development, 60,* 146–156.

Lewis, R. G., & Ho, M. K. (1979). Social work with Native Americans. *Social Work, 20,* 379–392.

Lewit, E. M., & Baker, L. S. (1995). Health insurance coverage. *The Future of Children: Long-Term Outcomes of Early Childhood Programs, 5,* 192–204.

Lewkowicz, D. J. (1996). Infants' response to the audible and visible properties of the human face 1. Role of lexical-syntactic content, temporal synchrony, gender, and manner of speech. *Developmental Psychology, 32,* 347–366.

Leyendecker, B., Lamb, M. E., Fracasso, M. P., Scholmerich, A., & Larson, C. (1997). Playful interaction and the antecedents of attachment: A longitudinal study of Central American and Euro-American mothers and infants. *Merrill-Palmer Quarterly, 43,* 24–47.

Lezotte, L. W. (1982, November). Characteristics of effective schools and programs for realizing them. *Education Digest,* pp. 27–29.

Liben, L. S., & Signorella, M. L. (1993). Gender-schematic processing in children: The role of initial interpretations of stimuli. *Developmental Psychology, 29,* 141–149.

Lieberman, A. F. (1993). *The emotional life of the toddler*. New York: Macmillan.

Lieberman, E., & Ryan, K. J. (1989, December 28). Birth-day choices. *New England Journal of Medicine*, 321, 1824–1825.

Lieberman, E., Gremy, I., Lang, J. M., & Cohen, A. P. (1995). Low birthweight at term and the timing of fetal exposure to maternal smoking. *American Journal of Public Health*, 84, 1127–1131.

Liebert, R. M., & Sprafkin, J. (1988). *The early window: Effects of television on children and youth* (3rd ed.). New York: Pergamon.

Light, D., Keller, S., & Calhoun, C. (1989). *Sociology* (7th ed.). New York: Knopf.

Lightbody, P., & Durndell, A. (1996). The masculine image of careers in science and technology: Fact or fantasy? *British Journal of Educational Psychology*, 66, 231–246.

Lin, C. C., & Fu, V. R. (1990). A comparison of child-rearing practices among Chinese, immigrant Chinese, and Caucasian-American parents. *Child Development*, 61, 429–433.

Lindberg, M. (1980). The role of knowledge structures in the ontogeny of learning. *Journal of Experimental Child Psychology*, 30, 401–410.

Link, S.C. & Ancoli-Israel, S. (1995) Sleep and the teenager. *Sleep Research*, 24, 184.

Lipsitt, L. (1982). Perinatal indicators and psychophysiological precursors of crib death. In J. Belsky (Ed.), *In the beginning: Readings on infancy* (p. 74). New York: Columbia University Press.

Lipsitt, L. P., & Kaye, H. (1964). Conditioned sucking in the newborn. *Psychonomic Science*, 1, 29–30.

Lipsitt, L. P., & Levy, N. (1959). Electrotactual threshold in the neonate. *Child Development*, 30, 547–554.

Little, B. B., Snell, L. M., Gilstrap, L. C., Gant, N. F., & Rosenfeld, C. R. (1989). Alcohol abuse during pregnancy: Changes in frequency in a large urban hospital. *Obstetrics and Gynecology*, 74, 547–550.

Little, R. E., & Sing, C. F. (1987). Father's drinking and infant birth weight: Report of an association. *Teratology*, 36, 59–65.

Lobel, T. E., & Menashri, J. (1993). Relations of conceptions of gender-role transgressions and gender constancy to gender-typed toy preferences. *Developmental Psychology*, 29, 150–155.

Lockhart, A. S. (1980). Motor learning and motor development during infancy and childhood. In C. B. Corbin (Ed.), *A textbook of motor development* (2nd ed., pp. 246–253). Dubuque, IA: Brown.

Lockwood, D. (1997). *Violence among middle school and high school students: analysis and implications for prevention*. NCJ 166363. Washington, DC: NCJRS.

Loeber, R. (1990). Development and risk factors of juvenile antisocial behavior and delinquency. *Clinical Psychology Review*, 10, 1–42.

Loehlin, J. C. (1992). *Genes and environment in personality development*. Newbury Park, CA: Sage.

Loehlin, J. C., Horn, J. M., & Willerman, L. (1989). Modeling IQ change: Evidence from the Texas Adoption Project. *Child Development*, 60, 993–1005.

Lombroso, P., Pauls, D. L., & Leckman, J. F. (1994). Genetic mechanisms in childhood psychiatric disorders. *Journal of the Academy of Child Adolescent Psychiatry*, 33, 921–938.

Londerville, S., & Main, M. (1981). Security, compliance and maternal training methods in the second year of life. *Developmental Psychology*, 17, 289–299.

Longres, J. F., & Harding, S. (1997). Ebonics and social work education. *Journal of Social Work Education*, 33, 222–225.

Longstreth, L. E. (1981). Revisiting Skeel's final study: A critique. *Developmental Psychology*, 17, 620–625.

Lonsway, K. A., & Fitzgerald, L. F. (1994). Rape myths: In review. *Psychology of Women Quarterly*, 18, 133–164.

Lorenz, K. (1937). The companion in the bird's world. *Auk*, 54, 245–273.

Lorion, R. P., & Saltzman, W. (1993). Children's exposure to community violence: following a path from concern to research to action. *Psychiatry*, 56, 55–65.

Lourenco, O. & Machado, A. (1996). In defense of Piaget's theory: A reply to 10 common criticisms. *Psychological Review*, 103, 143–164.

Lovett, M. W., Borden, S. L., DeLuca, T., Lacerenza, L., Benson, N. J., & Brackstone, D. (1994). Treating the core deficits of developmental dyslexia: Evidence of transfer of learning after phonologically-and strategy-based reading training programs. *Developmental Psychology*, 30, 805–822.

Lovett, M., & Neely, J. (1997). On becoming bilingual. *Journal of Black Psychology*, 23, 242–245.

Lowrey, G. (1978). *Growth and development of children* (7th ed.). Chicago: Year Book Medical.

Lucas, A., Morley, R., Cole, T. J., Lister, G., & Leeson-Payne. (1992). Breast milk and subsequent intelligence quotient in children born preterm. *Lancet*, 339, 261–264.

Luster, T., & McAdoo, H. P. (1994). Factors related to the achievement and adjustment of young African American children. *Child Development*, 65, 1080–1094.

Lynch, L. (1996, July/August). The new genetics. *Adoptive Families*, pp. 8–11.

Lyon, T. D. (1995). False allegations and false denials in child sexual abuse. *Psychology, Public Policy, and Law*, 1, 429–437.

Lyon, T. D., & Flavell, J. H. (1993). Young children's understanding of forgetting over time. *Child Development*, 64, 789–800.

Lyons-Ruth, K. (1992). Maternal depressive symptoms, disorganized infant-mother attachment relationships and hostile-aggressive behavior in the preschool classroom: A prospective longitudinal view from infancy to age five. In D. Cicchetti & S. L. Toth (Eds.), *Developmental perspectives on depression* (pp. 131–171). Rochester, NY: University of Rochester Press.

Lyons-Ruth, K., Connell, D., Grunebaum, H., & Botein, S. (1990). Infants at social risk: Maternal depression and family support services as mediators of infant development and security of attachment. *Child Development*, 61, 85–98.

Lyons-Ruth, K., Easterbrooks, M. A., & Cibelli, C. D. (1997). Infant attachment strategies: Infant mental lag, and maternal depressive symptoms: Predictors of internalizing and externalizing problems at age 7. *Developmental Psychology*, 33, 681–692.

Lytle, L. J., Bakken, L., & Romig, C. (1997). Adolescent female identity development. *Sex Roles*, 37, 175–185.

Lytton, H., & Romney, D. M. (1991). Parents differential socialization of boys and girls: A meta-analysis. *Psychological Bulletin*, 109, 267–296.

Lytton, H., Singh, J. K., & Gallagher, L. (1995). Parenting twins. In M. H. Bornstein (Ed.), *Handbook of parenting* (Vol. 1, pp. 185–208). Mahwah, NJ: Erlbaum.

Lytton, H., Watts, D., & Dunn, B. E. (1988). Continuity and change in child characteristics and maternal practices between ages 2 and 9: An analysis of interview responses. *Child Study Journal*, 18, 1–15.

M

Maccoby, E. E. (1980). *Social development: Psychological growth and the parent-child relationship*. New York: Harcourt Brace Jovanovich.

Maccoby, E. E. (1990). Gender and relationships: A developmental account. *American Psychologist*, 45, 513–521.

Maccoby, E. E., & Jacklin, C. N. (1974). *The psychology of sex differences*. Stanford, CA: Stanford University Press.

Maccoby, E. E., & Jacklin, C. N. (1980). Sex differences in aggression: A rejoinder and reprise. *Child Development*, 51, 964–980.

Maccoby, E. E., & Martin, J. A. (1983). Socialization in the context of the family: Parent-child interaction. In P. H. Mussen (Ed.), *Handbook of child development* (4th ed., Vol. 4, pp. 1–103). New York: Wiley.

MacDormand, M. F., & Rosenberg, H. M. (1993). Trends in infant mortality by cause of death and other characteristics. *Vital Health Statistics, 1993*; DHHS Publication PHS 93–1857.

MacFarlane, A. (1975). Olfaction in the development of social preferences in the human neonate. Cited in Brazelton, T. B. (1981). *On becoming a family: The growth of attachment*. New York: Delacorte.

MacKinnon, D. (1978). *In search of human effectiveness*. Buffalo, NY: Creative Education Foundation.

MacMillan, H. L., MacMillan J. H., Offord, D. R., Griffith, L., & MacMillan, A. (1994b). Primary prevention of child sexual abuse: A critical review. Part II. *Journal of Child Psychology and Psychiatry and Applied Disciplines, 35*, 857–876.

MacMillan, H. L., MacMillan, J. H., Offord, D. R., Griffith, L., & MacMillan, A. (1994a). Primary prevention of child abuse and neglect: A critical review. *Journal of Child Psychology and Psychiatry and Allied Disciplines, 35*, 835–856.

Madden, M. (1996, June 18). Kids take parents' lead to read and succeed. *USA Today*, p. D1.

Maeroff, G. I. (1996, March 6). Apathy and anonymity: Combating the twin scourges of modern post-adolescence. *Education Week*, pp. 46, 60.

Magnusson, D. (1988). *Individual development from an interactional perspective: A longitudinal study*. Hillsdale, NJ: Erlbaum.

Mahoney, J. L., & Cairns, R. B. (1997). Do extracurricular activities protect against early school dropout? *Developmental Psychology, 33*, 241–253.

Main, M., & Cassidy, J. (1988). Categories of response to reunion with the parent at age 6: Predictable from infant attachment classifications and stable over a 1-month period. *Developmental Psychology, 24*, 415–427.

Main, M., & Goldwyn, R. (1985) Adult attachment classification and rating system, cited in V.L. Colin (1996) *Human Attachment*. New York McGraw Hill.

Main, M., & Soloman, J. (1990) Procedures for identifying infants as disorganized/disoriented during the Ainsworth strange situation. In M. Greenberg, D., Cicchetti, & M. Cummings (Eds). *Attachment in the preschool years: Theory, research, and intervention*. (pp.121–160) Chicago: University of Chicago Press.

Main, M., Kaplan, N., & Cassidy, J. (1985). Security in infancy, childhood and adulthood: A move to the level of representation. In I. Bretherton & E. Waters (Eds.), *Growing points in attachment theory and research. Monographs of the Society for Research in child Development, 50*, 66–104.

Makin, J. W., & Porter, R. H. (1989). Attractiveness of lactating females' breast odors to neonates. *Child Development, 60*, 803–811.

Making money by making babies (1992), June 10). *New York Times*, p. A22.

Malatesta, C. Z., Culver, C., Tesman, J. R., & Shepard, B. (1989). The development of emotion expression during the first two years of life. *Monographs of the Society for Research in Child Development, 54*(1–2), Serial No. 219.

Males, M. A. (1997a, December). Debunking 10 myths about teens. *Education Digest*, pp. 48–50.

Males, M. A. (1997b). Stop blaming kids and TV. *The Progressive*, 61, 25–28.

Malinoski-Rummell, R., & Hansen, D. (1993). Long-term consequences of physical abuse. *Psychological Bulletin*, 114, 68–79.

Malinowski, C. I., & Smith, C. P. (1985). Moral reasoning and moral conduct: An investigation prompted by Kohlberg's theory. *Journal of Personality and Social Psychology, 49*, 1016–1027.

Manber, R., Pardee, R.E., Bootzin, R.R., Kuo, T., Rider, A.M., Rider, S.P., & Bergstrom, L. (1995) Changing sleep patterns in adolescence. *Sleep Research*, 24, 106

Mandel, D. R. (1995). Chaos theory, sensitive dependence, and the logistic equation. *American Psychologist*, 50, 106–107.

Mandel, D. R., Jusczyk, P. W., & Pisoni, D. B. (1995). Infants' recognition of the sound patterns of their own names. *Psychological Science*, 6, 314–317.

Mandler, J. M. (1990). A new perspective on cognitive development in infancy. *American Scientist*, 78, 236–243.

Mandler, J. M. (1998). Representation. In W. Damon (Editor in Chief) & D. Kuhn & R. S . Siegler (Vol. Eds.), *Handbook of child psychology* (5th ed., Vol. 2, pp. 255–308).

Mandler, J., & Johnson, N. (1977). Remembrance of things passed: Story structure and recall. *Cognitive Development*, 9, 111–151.

Manning, A. (1994, October 21). Trouble follows armed students. *USA Today*, p. D1.

Manning, M. L., & Allen, M. G. (1987). Social development in early adolescence. *Childhood Education*, 18, 172–176.

Manzo, K. K. (1997, November 5). U.S. schools need to pump up physical education, report warns. *Education Week*, p. 14.

Marano, H. E. (1997, May/June). A chip of fools? *Psychology Today*, p. 10.

March of Dimes. (1983). *Be good to your baby before it is born*. White Plains, NY: Author.

March of Dimes. (1986a). *PKU*. Public Health Education Information Series. White Plains, NY: Author.

March of Dimes. (1986b). *Sickle cell anemia*. Public Health Education Information Sheet: Genetic Series. White Plains, NY: Author.

March of Dimes. (1986c). *Tay-Sachs*. Public Health Education Information Series. White Plains, NY: Author.

March of Dimes. (1987). *Down syndrome*. Public Health Education Information Sheet: Genetic Series. White Plains, NY: Author.

March of Dimes. (1989). *VDT facts*. Public Health Education Information Sheet. White Plains, NY: Author.

Marcia, J. (1967). Ego identity status: Relationship to change in self-esteem, "general maladjustment," and authoritarianism. *Journal of Personality*, 35, 118–133.

Marcia, J. (1980). Identity in adolescence. In J. Adelson (Ed.), *Handbook of adolescent psychology*. New York: Wiley.

Marcon, R. A. (1993). Socioemotional versus academic emphasis: Impact of kindergartners' development and achievement. *Early Child Development and Care*, 96, 81–91.

Marcon, R. A. (1999). Differential impact of preschool models on development and early learning of inner-city children: A three cohort study. *Developmental Psychology*, 5, 358–375.

Marcus, G. F., Pinker, S., Ullman, M., Hollander, M., Rosen, T. J., & Xu, F. (1992). Overregularization in language acquisition. *Monographs of the Society for Research in Child Development*, 57, Serial No. 228.

Marcus, G.F. (1995) Children's overregularization of English plurals: A quantitative analysis. *Journal of Child Language*, 22, 447–460.

Mare, R. D. (1995). Changes in educational attainment and school enrollment. In R. Farley (Ed.), *State of the union: America in the 1990s* (pp. 155–213). New York: Russell Sage Foundation.

Marean, G. C., Werner, L. A., & Kuhl, P. K. (1992). Vowel categorization by very young infants. *Developmental Psychology*, 28, 396–405.

Marklein, M. B. (1997, August 27). SAT scores up, but so is grade inflation. *USA Today*, p. A1.

Markovits, H., & Vachon, R. (1989) Reasoning with contrary-to-fact propositions. *Journal of Experimental Child Psychology*, 47, 398–412.

Markstrom-Adams, C., & Adams, G.R. (1995). Gender, ethnic group, and grade differences in psychosocial functioning during middle adolescence. *Journal of Youth and Adolescence*, 24, 397–417.

Markus, H. R., & Kitayama, S. (1991). Culture and the self: Implications for cognition, emotion, and motivation. *Psychological Review*, 98, 224–253.

Marsh, H.W., Craven, R., & Debus, R., (1998) Structure, stability, and development of young children's self-concepts: A multicohort-multioccassion study. *Child Development*, 69, 1030–1053.

Marshall, S. P., & Smith, J. D. (1987). Sex differences in learning mathematics. A longitudinal study with item and error analysis. *Journal of Education Psychology*, 79, 372–381.

Marsiglio, W. (1993). Attitudes toward homosexual activity and gays as friends: A national survey of heterosexual 15- to 19- year-old males. *Journal of Sex Research*, 30, 12–17.

Martin, B. (1975). Parent-child relationships. In F. D. Horowitz (Ed.), *Review of child development research* (Col. 4, pp. 463–540). Chicago: University of Chicago Press.

Martin, C. L. & Little, J. K. (1990). The relation of gender understanding to children's sex-typed preferences and gender stereotypes. *Child Development*, 61, 1427–1439.

Martin, C. L., & Halverson, C. F. (1981). A schematic processing model of sex-typing and stereotyping in children. *Child Development, 52,* 1119–1132.

Martin, C. L., Eisenbud, L., & Rose, H. (1995). Children's gender-based reasoning about toys. *Child Development, 66,* 1453–1471.

Martin, G. B., & Clark, R. D. (1982). Distress crying in neonates: Species and peer specificity. *Developmental Psychology, 18,* 3–9.

Martin, S. (1995, October). Practitioners may misunderstand black families *Monitor,* p. 36.

Martin, S. L., Ramey, C.T., & Ramey, S. (1990). The prevention of intellectual impairment in children of impoverished families: Findings of a randomized trial of educational day care. *American Journal of Public Health, 80,* 844–847.

Martinez, F. D., Wright, A. L., Taussig, L. M., & the Group Health Medical Associates. (1994). The effect of paternal smoking on the birthweight of newborns whose mothers did not smoke. *American Journal of Public Health, 84,* 1489–1491.

Martinez, P., & Richters, J. E. (1993). The NIMH community violence project II. Children's distress symptoms associated with violence exposure. *Psychiatry, 56,* 22–35.

Martinez, R. O., & Dukes, R. L. (1997). The effects of ethnic identity, ethnicity, and gender on adolescent well-being. *Journal of Youth and Adolescence, 26,* 503–516.

Marttunen, M. J., Henriksson, M. M., Isometsa, E. T., Heikkinene, M. E., Aro, H. M., & Lonnqvist, J. K. (1998). Completed suicide among adolescents with no diagnosable psychiatric disorder. *Adolescence, 33,* 669–681.

Marwick, C. (1998, September 23/30). Challenging report on pregnancy and drug abuse. *Journal of the American Medical Association, 280,* 1039–1040.

Masataka, N. (1996). Perception of motherese in a signed language by 6-month-old deaf infants. *Developmental Psychology, 21,* 874–879.

Masataka, N., (1999) Preference for infant-directed singing in 2-day-old hearing infants of deaf parents. *Developmental Psychology, 35,* 1001–1005.

Mascola, M.A., Van Vunakis, H., Tager, I.B., Speizer, F.E., & Hanrahan, J.P. (1998) Exposure of young infants to environmental tobacco smoke: Breast-feeding among smoking mothers. *American Journal of Public Health, 88,* 893–896.

Mason, J. O. (1993). The dimensions of an epidemic of violence. *Public Health Reports, 108,* 1–4.

Matas, L., Arend, R., & Sroufe, L. A. (1978). Continuity of adaptation in the second year: The relationship between quality of attachment and later competence. *Child Development, 49,* 547–556.

Mates, B. F., & Strommen, L. (1995, December). Why Ernie can't read: Who reads on Sesame Street? *Reading Teacher, 49,* 300–306.

Mattay, V.S., Berman, K.F., Ostrem, J.L., Esposito, G., Van Horn, J.D., Bigelow, L.B., & Weinberger, D.R. (1996) Dextroampetamine enhances "neural network-specific" physiological signals: A positron-emission tomography rCBF study. *Journal of Neuroscience, 15,* 4816–4822.

Mauldon, J., & Luker, K. (1996). The effects of contraceptive education on method use at first intercourse. *Family Planning Perspectives, 28,* 19–24, 41.

Maurer, D., & Salapatek, P. (1976). Developmental changes in the scanning of faces by young infants. *Child Development, 47,* 523–527.

Maxfield, M., & Wisdom, C. (1996). The cycle of violence: Revisited 6 years later. *Archives of Pediatric Adolescent Medicine, 150,* 390–395.

Mayaux, M. J., Burgard, M., Telas, J. P., Cottalorda, J., Keivine, A., Simon, F., et al. (1996, February 28). Neonatal characteristics in rapidly progressive perinatally acquired HIV-1 disease. *Journal of the American Medical Association, 275,* 506–610.

Mayer, J. E., & Ligman, J. D. (1989). Personality characteristics of adolescent marijuana users. *Adolescence, 24,* 965–975.

Mayes, L. C. (1995). Substance abuse and parenting. In M. H. Bornstein (Ed.), *Handbook of parenting* (Vol. 4, pp. 101–125). Mahwah, NJ: Erlbaum.

Mayes, L. C., Granger, R. H., Bornstein, M. H., & Zuckerman, B. (1992). The problem of prenatal cocaine exposure: A rush to judgment. *Journal of the American Medical Association, 267,* 406–408.

Maynard, R., & Rangarajan, A. (1994). Contraceptive use and repeat pregnancies among welfare-dependent teenage mothers. *Family Planning Perspectives, 26,* 198–205.

Maziade, M., Boudreault, M., Cote, R., & Thivierge, J. (1986). Influence of gentle birth delivery procedures and other perinatal circumstances on infant temperament: Developmental and social implications. *Journal of Pediatrics, 108,* 134–136.

Mazza, J. J. (1997). School-based suicide prevention programs: Are they effective? *School Psychology Review, 26,* 382–397.

McAdoo, H. P. (1991). Family values and outcomes for children. *Journal of Negro Education, 60,* 361–365.

McBride, B. A., & Darragh, J. (1995). Interpreting data on father involvement: implications for parenting programs for men. *Families in Society, 78,* 490–497.

McBride, B., & Mills, G. (1993). A comparison of mothers' and fathers' involvement with their preschool age children. *Early Childhood Research Quarterly, 8,* 457–477.

McBride-Chang, C. (1995). What is phonological awareness? *Journal of Educational Psychology, 87,* 179–192.

McCabe, A. E., & Siegel, L. S. (1987). The stability of training effects in young children's class inclusion reasoning. *Merrill-Palmer Quarterly, 33,* 187–194.

McCabe, L. (1996). Efficacy of a targeted genetic screening program for adolescents. *American Journal of Human Genetics, 59,* 762–763.

McCall, R. B. (1981). Nature-nurture and the two realms of development: A proposed integration with respect to mental development. *Child Development, 52,* 1–12.

McCall, R. B. (1987). Developmental function, individual differences, and the plasticity of intelligence. In J. J. Gallagher & C. T. Ramey (Eds.), *The malleability of children* (pp. 15–25). Baltimore, MD: Brookes.

McCall, R. B., Hogarty, P. S., & Hurlburt, N. (1972). Transitions in infant sensorimotor development and the prediction of childhood I.Q. *American Psychologist, 27,* 728–748.

McCauley, E., Kay, T., Ito, J., & Treder, R. (1987). The Turner syndrome: Cognitive deficits, affective discrimination, and behavior problems. *Child Development, 58,* 464–474.

McCauley, K. (1992). Preventing child abuse through the schools. *Children Today, 21,* 8–11. Washington, DC: Administration for Children and Families, Department of Health & Human Services.

McClanahan, S., & Booth, K. (1991). Mother-only families: Problems, prospects, and politics. In A. Booth (Ed.), *Contemporary families: Looking forward, looking back.* Minneapolis, MN: National Council on Family Relations.

McClearn, G. E. (1993). Behavioral genetics: The last century and the next. In R. Plomin & G. E. McClearn (Eds.), *Nature, nurture, and psychology* (pp. 27–55). Washington, DC: American Psychological Association.

McClinton, B. S., & Meier, B. G. (1978). *Beginnings: The Psychology of early childhood.* St. Louis, MO: Mosby.

McCloskey, L. A., Figeredo, A. J., & Koss, M. P. (1995). The effects of systematic family violence on children's mental health. *Child Development, 66,* 1239–1261.

McCord, J. (1991) Questioning the value of punishment. *Social Problems, 38,* 167–179.

McCormick, C. M., & Maurer, D. M. (1988). Unimanual hand preferences in 6-month-olds: Consistency and relation to familial handedness. *Infant Behavior and Development, 11,* 21–29.

McCracken, R. S., & Weitzman, L. M. (1997). Relationship of personal agency, problem-solving appraisal, and traditionality of career choice to women's attitudes towards multiple role planning. *Journal of Counseling Psychology, 40,* 149–159.

McCune, L. (1995). A normative study of representational play at the transition to language. *Developmental Psychology*, 31, 198–206.

McDonald, J. L. (1997). Language acquisition: The acquisition of linguistic structure in normal and special populations. *Annual Review of Psychology*, 48, 215–241.

McGhee, P.E. (1979) *Humor: Its origin and development* San Francisco, Cal.:W.H. Freeman.

McGough, L. S. (1995). For the record: Videotaping investigative interviews. *Psychology, Public Policy, and Law*, 1, 370–386.

McGraw, M. B. (1940). Neural maturation as exemplified in achievement of bladder control. *Journal of Pediatrics*, 16, 580–589.

McGue, M. (1993). From proteins to cognitions: The behavioral genetics of alcoholism in R. Plomin & G. E. McClearn (Eds.), *Nature, nurture, and psychology* (pp. 245–269). Washington, DC: American Psychological Association.

McGue, M., Bacon, S., & Lykken, D. T. (1993). Personality stability and change in early adulthood: A behavioral genetic analysis. *Developmental Psychology*, 29, 96–110.

McGuinness, D. (1976). Sex differences in the organization of perception and cognition. In B. Lloyd & J. Archer (Eds.), *Exploring sex differences* (pp. 123–157). London: Academic Press.

McGuinness, D. (1979). How schools discriminate against boys. In S. Hochman & P. S. Kaplan (Eds.), *Readings in psychology: A soft approach* (rev. ed., pp. 74–79). Lexington, MA: Ginn.

McHale, S. M., & Pawletko, T. M. (1992). Differential treatment of siblings in two family contexts. *Child Development*, 63, 68–81.

McHale, S. M., Crouter, A. C., McGuire, S.A., & Updegraff, K. A. (1995). Congruence between mothers' and fathers' differential treatment of siblings: Links with family relations and children's well being. *Child Development*, 66, 116–128.

McHale, S.M., Crouter, A.C., & Tucker, C.J. (1999) Family context and gender role socialization in middle childhood: Comparing girls to boys and sisters to brothers. *Child Development*, 70, 990–1004.

McIntosh, D. N., Silver, R. C., & Wortman, C. B. (1993). Religion's role in adjustment to a negative life event: Coping with a loss of a child. *Journal of Personality and Social Psychology*, 65, 812–821.

McKusick, V. A. (1989, April 6). Mapping and sequencing the human genome. *New England Journal of Medicine*, pp. 921–915.

McLanahan, S. S., & Sandefur, G. (1994). *Growing up with a single parent: What hurts, what helps*. Cambridge, MA: Harvard University Press.

McLaughlin, B. (1983). Child compliance to parental control techniques. *Developmental Psychology*, 19, 667–674.

McLoyd, V. C. (1990). The impact of economic hardship on black families and children: Psychological distress, parenting, and socioemotional development. *Child Development*, 61, 311–317.

McLoyd, V. C. (1998a). Children in poverty: Development, public policy, and practice. In W. Damon (Editor in Chief) & I. E. Sigel & K. A. Renninger (Vol. Eds.), *Handbook of child psychology* (5th ed., pp. 135–208). New York: Wiley.

McLoyd, V. C. (1998b). Socioeconomic disadvantage and child development. *American Psychologist*, 53, 185–205.

McLoyd, V. C., & Wilson, L. (1991). The strain of living poor: Parenting, social support, and child mental health. In A. C. Huston (Ed.), *Children in poverty* (pp. 105–136). New York: Cambridge University Press.

McNally, S., Eisenberg, N., & Harris, J. D. (1991). Consistency and change in maternal child-rearing practices and values: A longitudinal study. *Child Development*, 62, 190–198.

McNeal, R. B., Jr. (1997). High school dropouts: A closer examination of school effects. *Social Science Quarterly*, 78, 209–213.

McNeill, D. (1970). The development of language. In P. H. Mussen (Ed.), *Carmichael's manual of child psychology* (3rd ed.). New York: Wiley.

Mead, M. (1974). On Freud's view of female psychology. In J. Strouse (Ed.), *Women and analysis*. New York: Grossman.

Meeus, W. (1996). Studies on identity development in adolescence: An overview of research and some new data. *Journal of Youth and Adolescence*, 25, 569–598.

Meeus, W., & Dekovic, M. (1995). Identity development, parental, and peer support in adolescence: Results of a national Dutch study. *Adolescence*, 30, 931–944.

Meier, R. P., & Newport, E. L. (1990). Out of the hands of babes: On a possible sign advantage in language acquisition. *Language*, 66, 1–23.

Meilman, P. W. (1979). Cross-sectional age changes in ego identity status during adolescence. *Developmental Psychology*, 15, 230–231.

Meldrum, D. R., & Gardner, D. K. (1998, August 27). Two-embryo transfer: The future looks bright. *New England Journal of Medicine*, 339, 624.

Mellin, L. M., Irwin, C. E., & Scully, S. (1992). Prevalence of disordered eating in girls: A survey of middle-class children. *Journal of the American Dietetic Association*, 92, 851–853.

Mellins, C. A., Gatz, M., & Baker, L. (1996). Children's methods of coping with stress: A twin study of genetic and environmental influences. *Journal of Child Psychology and Psychiatry*, 37, 721–730.

Meltzer, J., & Sherman, T. M. (1997). 10 commandments to implement technology. *NAASP Bulletin*, 81, 23–32.

Meltzoff, A. N. (1977). Imitation of facial and manual gestures by human neonates. *Science*, 198, 75–78.

Meltzoff, A. N. (1988). Imitation of televised models by infants. *Child Development*, 59, 1221–1229.

Meltzoff, A. N., & Moore, M. K. (1983). Newborn infants imitate adult facial gestures. *Child Development*, 54, 702–709.

Meltzoff, A. N., & Moore, M. K. (1989). Imitation in newborn infants: Exploring the range of gestures imitated and the underlying mechanisms. *Developmental Psychology*, 25, 954–963.

Melzack, R. (1984). The myth of painless childbirth. *Pain*, 19, 321.

Mendelson, B. K., & White, D. R. (1985). Development of self-body in overweight youngsters. *Developmental Psychology*, 21, 90–97.

Mendelson, J. H., & Mello, N. K. (1985). *Alcohol, use and abuse in America*. Boston: Little, Brown.

Mendrum, D.R., & Gardner, D.K. (1998, August 27) Two-embryo transfer-The future looks bright. *The New England Journal of Medicine*, 339, p.624.

Menyuk, P. (1977). *Language and maturation*. Cambridge, MA: MIT Press.

Mercer, J. (1998). *Infant development: A multidisciplinary approach*. Pacific Grove, CA: Brooks/Cole.

Mergendoller, J. R. (1997). Technology and learning: The research. *Principal*, 76, 12–14.

Mervis, C. B., & Bertrand, J. (1994). Acquisition of the novel name-nameless category (N3C). principle. *Child Development*, 65, 1646–1662.

Meschke, L. L., & Silbereisen, R. K. (1997). The influence of puberty, family processes, and leisure activities on the timing of first sexual experience. *Journal of Adolescence*, 20, 403–418.

Metcalf, R. D. (1979). Organizers of the psyche and EEG development: Birth through adolescence. In R. L. Noshpitz (Ed.), *Basic handbook of child psychiatry* (Vol. 1, pp. 63–72). New York: Basic Books.

Metcoff, J., Coistiloe, P., Crosby, W. M., Sandstread, H. H., & Milne, D. (1989). Smoking in pregnancy: Relation of birth weight to maternal plasma carotene and cholesterol levels. *Obstetrics and Gynecology*, 64, 302–308.

Meyer, J., & Sobieszek (1972). Effect of a child's sex on adult interpretations of its behavior. *Developmental Psychology*, 6, 42–48.

Meyer, K. A. (1987). The work commitment of adolescents: Progressive attachment to the work force. *Career Development Quarterly*, 36, 140–147.

Meyer-Bahlburg, H. F. L., Ehrhardt, A. A., Rosen, L. R., Gruen, R. S., Verdiano, N. P., Vann, F. H., & Neuwalder, H. F. (1995). Prenatal estrogens and the development of homosexual orientation. *Developmental Psychology*, 31, 12–21.

Michel, G.F. (1981). Right handedness: A consequence of infant supine head-orientation. *Science*, 212, 685–687.

Michelsson, K., Rinne, A., & Paajanen, S. (1990). Crying, feeding and sleeping patterns in 1- to 12-month-old infants. *Child, Health and Development*, 16, 99–111.

Midgley, C., Feldlaufer, H., & Eccles, J. S. (1989). Student/teacher relations and attitudes toward mathematics before and after the transition to junior high school *Child Development*, 60, 981–992.)

Milburn, N. G., & Booth, J. (1990). Sociodemographic, homeless state and mental health characteristics of women in shelters: Preliminary findings. *Urban Research Review*, 12, 1–4.

Milburn, N., & D'Ercole, A. (1991). Homeless women, children, and families. *American Psychologist*, 46, 1159–1160.

Milewski, A. E. (1976). Infants' discrimination of internal and external pattern elements. *Journal of Experimental Child Psychology*, 22, 229–246.

Miller, L. (1995a, February 8). Child-care study finds mediocre level of services. *Education Week*, pp. 1, 11.

Miller, L. (1995b, July 12). Children and families. *Education Week*, p. 9.

Miller, L. (1995c, November 8). Inadequate laws put children in day care at risk, CDF says. *Education Week*, p.16.

Miller, M. J. (1980). Cantaloupes, carrots, and counseling: Implications of dietary interventions for counselors. *Personnel and Guidance Journal*, 58, 421–425.

Miller, P. H. (1989). *Theories of developmental psychology.* New York: Freeman.

Miller, P. H. (1993). *Theories of developmental psychology* (3rd ed.). New York: Freeman.

Miller, P. H., & Harris, Y.R. (1988). Preschoolers' strategies of attention on a same-different task. *Developmental Psychology*, 24, 628–634.

Miller, R. W. (1974). Susceptibility of the fetus and child to chemical pollutants. *Science*, 184, 812–813.

Miller, S. A. (1988). Parents' beliefs about children's cognitive development. *Child Development*, 59, 259–286.

Miller, S. A. (1998). *Development research methods* (2nd ed.). Upper Saddle River, NJ: Prentice Hall.

Miller, S., & Cunningham, B. (1992). A guided look experience program for minority students. *Journal of College Student Development*, 33, 373–374.

Mills, J. L., Braubard, B. I., Harley, E. E., Rhoads, G. G., & Berendes, H. W. (1984, October 12). Maternal alcohol consumption and birth weight: How much drinking during pregnancy is safe? *Journal of the American Medical Association*, 252, 1875–1879.

Mills, R. S. L., & Rubin, K. H. (1990). Parental beliefs about problematic social behaviors in early childhood. *Child Development*, 61, 138–152.

Millstein, S. G. (1989). Adolescent health: Challenges for behavioral scientists. *American Psychologist*, 44, 837–843.

Millstein, S. G., & Moscicki, A. (1995). Sexually transmitted disease in female adolescents: effects of psychosocial factors and high risk behaviors. *Journal of Adolescent Health*, 17, 83–90.

Milunsky, A. (1989). *Choices not chances.* Boston: Little, Brown.

Minard, J., Coleman, D., Williams, G., & Ingledyne, E. (1968). Cumulative REM of three to five day olds: Effect of normal external noise and maturation. *Psychophysiology*, 5, 232.

Minkoff, H. L., & Duerr, A. (1994). Obstetric issues-relevance to women and children in *Pediatric AIDS: The challenge of HIV Infection in infants, children, and adolescents* (2nd ed., pp.809–828). Baltimore: Williams & Wilkins.

Minuchin, P. (1985). Families and individual development: Provocations from the field of family therapy. *Child Development*, 56, 289–302.

Minuchin, P. P., & Shapiro, E. K. (1983). The school as a context for social development. In E. M. Hetherington (Ed.), *Handbook of child psychology: Socialization, personality, and social development* (4th ed., Vol. 4, pp. 197–275). New York: Wiley.

Mirsky, A. F., & Duncan, C. C. (1986). Etiology and expression of schizophrenia: Neurobiological and psychosocial factors. *Annual Review of Psychology*, 37, 291–321.

Mischel, W. (1970). Sex-typing and socialization. In P. H. Mussen (Ed.), *Carmichael's manual of child psychology* (3rd ed.). New York: Wiley.

Mitchell, J. J ., Capua, A., Clow, C., & Scriver, C. R. (1996). Twenty-year outcome analysis of genetic screening programs for Tay-Sachs and B-thalassemia disease carriers in high schools. *American Journal of Human Genetics*, 59, 793–798.

Mitka, M. (1999, January 6). Public health targets teens' private acts. *Journal of the American Medical Association*, 281, 21–22.

Miyake, K., Chen, S., & Campos, J. (1985). Infants' temperament, mothers' mode of interaction and attachment in Japan: An interim report. In I. Bretherton & E. Waters (Eds.), Growing points of attachment theory and research. *Monographs of the Society for Research in Child Development*, 50 (1–2), 276–297, Serial No 109.

MMWR (1998) National, state, and urban area vaccination coverage levels among children aged 19–35 months—United States, July 1996- June 1997. *MMWR*, 47, 108–116.

MMWR (1999a) Impact of vaccines universally recommended for children—United States 1900–1998. *MMWR*, 48, 243–248.

MMWR (1999b) Recommended childhood immunization schedule, United States, 1999. *MMWR*, 48, 12–16.

Moerk, E. L. (1989). The LAD was a lady and the tasks were ill-defined. *Developmental Review*, 9, 21–57.

Mofenson, L. M., & Wolinsky, S. M. (1994). Current insights regarding vertical transmission in *Pediatric AIDS: The challenge of HIV Infection in infants, children, and adolescents* (2nd ed., pp.179–203). Baltimore: Williams & Wilkins.

Moffitt, T. E., Caspi, A., Belsky, J. & Silva, P. A. (1992). Childhood experience and the onset of menarche: A test of a sociobiological model. *Child Development*, 63, 47–58.

Mohar, C. J. (1988). Applying the concept of temperament to child care. *Child and Youth Care Quarterly*, 17, 221–238.

Molnar, J. M., Rath, W. R., & Klein, T. P. (1990). Constantly compromised: The impact of homelessness on children. *Journal of Social Issues*, 46, 109–124.

Monaco, N. M., & Gayer, E. L. (1987). Developmental level and children's responses to the explosion of the space shuttle Challenger. *Early Childhood Research Quarterly*, 2, 83–95.

Money, J. (1987). Sin, sickness, or status? Homosexual gender identity and psychoneuroendocrinology. *American Psychologist*, 42, 384–399.

Money, J., & Ehrhardt, A. A. (1972). *Man and woman. Boy and girl.* Baltimore: Johns Hopkins University Press.

Montgomery, R. L., Haemmerlie, F. M., et al. (1996). The "imaginary audience," self-handicapping and dr9inking patterns among college students. *Psychological Reports*, 79, 783–787.

Moon, S. M., & Dillon, D. R. (1995). Multiple exceptionalities: A case study. *Journal for the Education of the Gifted*, 18, 111–130.

Moore, K. L., & Persaud, T. V. N. (1993). *Before we are born* (4th ed.). Philadelphia: Saunders.

Moore, S. M., & Rosenthal, D. A. (1991). Adolescent invulnerability and perception of AIDS risk. *Journal of Adolescent Research*, 6, 160–180.

Moore, S. M., Gullone, E., & Kostanski, M. (1997). An examination of adolescent risk-taking using a story completion task. *Journal of Adolescence*, 20, 369–379.

Moorehouse, M.J. (1991) Linking maternal employment patterns to mother-child activities and children's school competence. *Developmental Psychology*, 27, 295–303.

More women drink during pregnancy. (1997, April 25). *Newsday*, p. A19.

Morelli, G. A., Rogoff, B. I, Oppenheim, D., & Goldsmith, D. (1992). Cultural variation in infants' sleeping arrangements: Questions of independence. *Developmental Psychology*, 28, 604–613.

Moreno, A., & Thelen, M. (1993). A preliminary prevention program for eating disorders in a junior high school population. *Journal of Youth and Adolescence, 22,* 109–124.

Morgan, J. L. (1996). Finding relations between input and outcome in language acquisition. *Developmental Psychology, 32,* 556–559.

Morrell, P., & Norton, W. T. (1980). Myelin. *Scientific American, 242,* 88–119.

Morris, A.K., & Sloutsky, V.M. (1998) Understanding of logical necessity: Developmental antecedents and cognitive consequences. *Child Development, 69,* 721–741.

Morrison, D. M. (1985). Adolescent contraceptive behavior: A review. *Psychological Bulletin, 98,* 538–568.

Morrison, D. R., & Cherlin, A. J. (1995). The divorce process and young children's well-being: A prospective analysis. *Journal of Marriage and the Family, 57,* 800–812.

Morrison, F. J., Griffith, E. M., & Alberts, D. M. (1997). Nature-nurture in the classroom: Entrance age, school readiness, and learning in children. *Developmental Psychology, 33,* 254–262.

Morrison, G. S. (1988). *Early childhood education today* (4th ed.). Columbus, OH: Merrill/Prentice Hall.

Morrison, G. S. (1991). *Early childhood education today* (5th ed.). Columbus, OH: Merrill/Prentice Hall.

Morrow, R. D. (1987, November). Cultural differences—Be Aware! *Academic Therapy, 23,* 143–149.

Mortimer, J. T., Finch, M. D., Ryu, S., Shanahan, M. J., & Call, K. T. (1996). The effects of work intensity on adolescent mental health, achievement, and behavioral adjustment: New evidence from a prospective study. *Child Development, 67,* 1243–1261.

Mortimer, J. T., Finch, M., Shanahan, M., & Ryu, S. (1992a). Adolescent work history and behavioral adjustment. *Journal of Research on Adolescence, 2,* 59–80.

Mortimer, J. T., Finch, M., Shanahan, M., & Ryu, S. (1992b). Work experience, mental health, and behavioral adjustment in adolescence. *Journal of Research on Adolescence, 2,* 25–57.

Morton, M., Nelson, L., Walsh, C., Zimmerman, S., & Coe, R. M. (1996). Evaluation of a HIV/AIDS education program for adolescents. *Journal of Community Health, 21,* 23–36.

Moshman, D. (1998). Cognitive development beyond childhood in W. Damon (Editor in Chief), D. Kuhn, & R. S. Siegler (Vol. Eds.), *Handbook of child psychology* (5th ed., Vol. 2, pp. 947–978). New York: Wiley

Mott, F. L., Kowaleski-Jones, L., & Menaghan, E. G. (1997). Paternal absence and child behavior: Does a child's gender make a difference? *Journal of Marriage and the Family, 59,* 103–118.

Motulsky, A. G. (1997, May 1). Screening for genetic diseases. *New England Journal of Medicine, 336,* 1314–1316.

Muir, D., & Field, J. (1979). Newborn infants orient to sounds. *Child Development, 50,* 431–436.

Mullahy, P. (1948). *Oedipus: Myth and complex.* New York: Hermitage.

Mumme, D. L., Fernald, A., & Herrera, C. (1996). Infants' responses to facial and vocal emotional signals in a social referencing paradigm. *Child Development, 67,* 3219–3237.

Munley, P. H. (1975). Erik Erikson's theory of psychosocial development and career development. *Journal of Counseling Psychology, 22,* 314–319.

Munley, P. H. (1977). Erikson's theory of psychosocial development and career development. *Journal of Vocational Behavior, 10,* 261–269.

Murray B. (1995c, November). Programs go beyond "just saying no." *APA Monitor,* p. 41.

Murray, B. (1995a, November). Gender gap in math scores is closing. *APA Monitor,* p. 43.

Murray, B. (1995b, November). Key skill for teen parents: Having realistic expectations. *APA Monitor,* p. 51.

Murray, B. (1996, April). Students stretch beyond the "three R's." *APA Monitor,* p. 46.

Murray, B. (1997, January). America still lags behind in mathematics test scores. *APA Monitor,* p. 44.

Murray, L., Fiori-Cowley, A., Hooper, R., & Cooper, P. (1996). The impact of postnatal depression and associated adversity on early mother-infant interactions and later infant outcome. *Child Development, 67,* 2512–2526.

Murray, S. F., Dolby, R. M., Nation, R. L., & Thomas, D. B. (1981). Effects of epidural anesthesia on newborns and their mothers. *Child Development, 52,* 71–82.

Mussen, P. H., & Jones, M.C . (1957). Some conceptions, motivations, and interpersonal attitudes of late- and early-maturing boys. *Child Development, 28,* 242–256.

Muuss, R. E. (1982). *Theories of adolescence* (4th ed.). New York: Random House.

Muuss, R. E. (1985). Adolescent eating disorder: Anorexia nervosa. *Adolescence, 20,* 525–536.

Muuss, R. E. (1986). Adolescent eating disorder: Bulimia. *Adolescence, 21,* 257–267.

Muuss, R. E. (1988). Carol Gilligan's theory of sex differences in the development of moral reasoning during adolescence. *Adolescence, 23,* 235–243.

Myers, J.E. B. (1995). New era of skepticism regarding children's credibility. *Psychology, Public Policy, and Law, 1,* 387–398.

Myers, R. S., & Roth, D. L. (1997). Perceived benefits of and barriers to exercise and stage of exercise adoption in young adults. *Health Psychology, 16,* 277–283.

N

Nachmias, M., Gunnar, M., Mangelsdorf, S., Parritz, R., & Buss, K. (1996). Behavioral inhibition and stress reactivity: The moderating role of attachment security. *Child Development, 67,* 508–522.

Naeye, R. L., & Peters, E. C. (1984). Mental development of children whose mothers smoked during pregnancy. *Obstetrics & Gynecology, 64,* 601–607.

Nagel, K. L., & Jones, K. H. (1992). Sociological factors in the development of eating disorders. *Adolescence, 27,* 107–113.

Nagin, D. & Temblay, R.E. (1999) Trajectories of boys' physical aggression, opposition, and hyperactivity on the path to physically violent and nonviolent juvenile delinquency. *Child Development, 70,* 1181–1196.

Nall, S. W. (1982). Bridging the gap: Preschool to kindergarten. *Childhood Education, 59,* 107–110.

Namy, L.L., & Waxman, S.R. (1998) Words and gestures: Infants' interpretations of different forms of symbolic reference. *Child Development, 69,* 295–309.

Narvaez, D., Getz, I., Rest, J. R., & Thoma, S. J. (1999). Individual moral judgment and cultural ideologies. *Developmental Psychology, 35,* 476–488.

Nathanielsz, P. W. (1995). The role of basic science in preventing low birth weight. In *The future of children: Low birth weight* (pp. 57–70). Los Altos, CA: David and Lucile Packard Foundation.

National Association of State Boards of Education. (1990). *Code Blue: Uniting for healthier youth.* Alexandria, VA: Author.

National campaign launched to reduce risk of sudden infant death syndrome. (1994). *Children Today, 23,* 3–5.

National Center for Health Statistics. (1993). Advance report of final mortality statistics. *Monthly and Vital Statistics Report, 41*(7). Hyattsville, MD: U.S. Department of Health and Human Services, Public Health Service, CDC.

National Center for Health Statistics. (1997). *Healthy People 2000 review, 1997.* Hyattsville, MD: Public Health Service.

National Commission on Excellence in Education (1981). *A nation at risk.* Washington, DC: U.S. Department of Education.

National Committee to Prevent Child Abuse. (1994). *Current trends in child abuse reporting and fatalities: The results of the 1993 annual fifty state survey.* Chicago: Author.

National Committee to Prevent Child Abuse. (1996). *Current trends in child abuse reporting and fatalities: The results of the 1995 annual fifty state survey.* Chicago: Author.

National Committee to Prevent Child Abuse. (1998). *Current trends in child abuse reporting and fatalities: The results of the 1997 annual fifty state survey.* Chicago: Author.

National Safety Council. (1998). *Accident facts.* Itasca, IL: Author.

National Vaccine Advisory Committee. (1991, September 18). The measles epidemic: The problems, barriers and recommendations. *Journal of the American Medical Association,* 266, 1547–1552.

National, state, and urban area vaccination coverage levels among children aged 19–35 months: United States, July 1996–June 1997. (1998). *MMWR,* 47, 108–116.

Navarick, D. J. (1979). *Principles of learning: From laboratory to field.* Reading, MA: Addison-Wesley.

Nazarro, J. N. (Ed.). *Culturally diverse exceptional children.* Reston, VA: Council for Exceptional Children.

Needelman, R., Zuckerman, B., Anderson, G. M., Mirochnik, M., & Cohen, D. J. (1993). Cerebrospital fluid monoamine precursors and metabolites in human neonates following in utero cocaine exposure: A preliminary study. *Pediatrics,* 92, 55–60.

Neher, L. S., & Short, J. L. (1998). Risk and protective factors for children's substance use and antisocial behavior following parental divorce. *American Journal of Orthopsychiatry,* 68, 154–161.

Neiderhiser, J. M., Reiss, D., Hetherington, E. M., & Plomin, R. (1999). Relationships between parenting and adolescent adjustment over time: Genetic and environmental contributions. *Developmental Psychology,* 35, 680–692.

Neimark, E. D. (1975). Intellectual development during adolescence. In F. D. Horowitz (Ed.), *Review of child development research* (Vol. 4). Chicago: University of Chicago Press.

Neimark, E. D. (1982). Adolescent thought: transition to formal operations. In B.B. Wolman (Ed.), *Handbook of human development* (pp. 486–503). Upper Saddle River, NJ: Prentice Hall.

Nelkin, D., & Lindee, M. S. (1995). *The DNA mystique.* New York: Freeman.

Nelson, C. A. (1987). The recognition of facial expressions in the first two years of life: Mechanisms of development, *Child Development,* 58, 889–910.

Nelson, C. A., & Horowitz, F. D. (1983). The perception of facial expressions and stimulus motion by two- and five-month-old infants using holographic stimuli. *Child Development,* 54, 868–878.

Nelson, D. E., Giovino, G. A., Shopland, D. R., Mowery, P. D., Mills, S. L., & Eriksen, M. P. (1995). Trends in cigarette smoking among US adolescents, 1974 through 1991. *American Journal of Public Health,* 85, 34–40.

Nelson, F. L. (1987). Evaluation of a youth suicide school program. *Adolescence,* 22, 813–825.

Nelson, K. (1973). Structure and strategy in learning to talk. *Monograph of the Society for Research in Child Development,* 38 (1–2), Serial No. 149.

Nelson, K. (1974). Concept, word, and sentence. *Psychological Review,* 81, 267–285.

Nelson, K. (1978). How children represent knowledge of their world in and out of language: A preliminary report. In R. S. Siegler (Ed.), *Children's thinking: What develops.* Hillsdale, NJ: Erlbaum.

Nelson, K. (1981). Individual differences in language development: Implications for development and language. *Developmental Psychology,* 17, 170–188.

Nelson, K., & Gruendel, J. (1981). Generalized event representations: basic building blocks of cognitive development. In M. E. Lamb & A. L. Brown (Eds.), *Advances in developmental psychology* (Vol. 1). Hillsdale, NJ: Erlbaum.

Ness, R. B., Grisson, J. A., Hirschinger, N., Markovic, N., Shaw, L. M., Day, N. L., & Kline, J. (1999). Cocaine and tobacco use and the risk of spontaneous abortion. *New England Journal of Medicine,* 340, 333–339.

Neuman, S. B. (1982). Television viewing and leisure reading: A qualitative analysis. *Journal of Educational Research,* 75, 299–304.

Neuspiel, D. R., & Hamel, S. C. (1991). Cocaine and infant behavior. *Developmental and Behavioral Pediatrics,* 12, 55–64.

New York City Board of Education. (1994). *Educational progress of students in bilingual and ESL programs: A longitudinal study, 1990–1994.* New York City Board of Education.

New York State Council on Alcoholism. (1986). *Alcohol Abuse.* New York State Division of Alcohol and Alcohol Abuse.

New York State Department of Health. (1979). *DES: The wonder drug women should wonder about.* New York: Author.

Newman, B. M. (1989). The changing nature of the parent-adolescent relationship from early to late adolescence. *Adolescence,* 96, 915–923.

Newman, B. S., & Muzzonigro, P. G. (1993). The effects of traditional family values on the coming out process of gay male adolescents. *Adolescence,* 28, 213–226.

Newman, D.L., Caspi, A., Moffitt, T.E., & Silva, P.A. (1997) Antecedents of adult interpersonal functioning: Effects of individual differences in age 3 temperament. *Developmental Psychology,* 33, 206–217.

Newman, P. R., & Newman, B. M. (1988). Differences between childhood and adulthood: the identity watershed. *Adolescence,* 92, 551–557.

NICHD Early Child Care Research Network. (1999) Chronicity of maternal depressive symptoms, maternal sensitivity, and child functioning at 36 months. *Developmental Psychology,* 35, 1297–1310.

NICHD. (1996). *Infant child care and attachment security: Results of the NICHD study of early child care.* Symposium, International Conference on Infant Studies, Providence, RI.

NICHD. (1996). *Infant child care and attachment security: Results of the NICHD study of early child care.* Washington, DC: Author.

NICHD. (1997). The effects of infant child care on infant-mother attachment security: Results of the NICHD study of early child care. *Child Development,* 68, 860–879.

NIDA Capsules. (1995). *Facts about teenagers and drug abuse.* Washington, DC: National Institute on Drug Abuse.

Nielsen, L. (1996). *Adolescence: A contemporary view.* Fort Worth, TX: Harcourt Brace.

Nigg, J. T., & Goldsmith, H. H. (1994). Genetics of personality disorders: Perspectives from personality and psychopathology research. *Psychological Bulletin,* 115, 346–380.

Nisbett, R. (1994, October 31). Blue genes. *New Republic,* 211, 15–16.

Nix, R.L., Pinderhughes, E.E., Dodge, K.A., Bates, J.E., Pettit, G.S., & McFadyen-Ketchum, S.A. (1999) The relation between mothers' hostile attribution tendencies and children's externalizing behavior problems: The mediating role of mothers' harsh discipline practices. *Child Development,* 70, 896–909.

Nogata, D. K. (1989). Japanese American children and adolescence. In J. T. Gibbs & L. N. Huang (Eds.), *Children of color* (pp. 67–114). San Francisco: Jossey-Bass.

Nolen-Hoeksema, S., Girgus, J. S., & Seligman, M. E. P. (1992). Predictors and consequences of childhood depressive symptoms: A 5-year-longitudinal study. *Journal of Abnormal Psychology,* 101, 405–422.

Noller, P., & Callan, V. J. (1986). Adolescent and parent perceptions of family cohesion and adaptability. *Journal of Adolescence,* 9, 97–106.

Northwoods Montessori School (1990) Northwoods Montessori Center School Publication.

Nottelman, E. D. (1987). Competence and self-esteem during transition from childhood to adolescence. *Developmental Psychology,* 23, 441–451.

Nunnally, J. C. (1982). The study of change: measurement, research strategies and methods of analysis. In B. B. Wolman (Ed.), *Handbook of Developmental Psychology* (pp. 133–149). Upper Saddle River, NJ: Prentice Hall.

Nye, R. D. (1975). *Three views of man.* Monterrey, CA: Brooks/Cole.

Nyhan, W. L. (1986). Neonatal screening for inherited disease. *New England Journal of Medicine,* 313, 43–44.

Nyiti, R. M. (1982). The validity of "cultural differences explanations" for cross-cultural variation in the rate of Piagetian cognitive development. In D. A. Wagner & H. W. Stevenson (Eds.), *Cultural perspectives on child development* (pp. 144–166). San Francisco: Freeman.

O

O'Brien, K. M., & Fassinger, R. E. (1993). A causal model of the career orientation and career choice on adolescent women. *Journal of Counseling Psychology*, 40, 456–469.

O'Brien, M. (1996). Child-rearing difficulties reported by parents of infants and toddlers. *Journal of Pediatric Psychology*, 21, 433–446.

O'Brien, S. F., & Bierman, K. L. (1988). Conceptions and perceived influence of peer groups: Interviews with preadolescent and adolescents. *Child Development*, 59, 1360–1365.

O'Bryan, K. G. (1980). The teaching face: A historical perspective. In E. L. Palmer & A. Dorr (Eds.), *Children and the faces of television: Teaching, violence, selling* (pp. 5–16). New York: Academic Press.

O'Connell, L., Betz, M., & Kurth, S. (1989). Plans for balancing work and family life: do women pursuing nontraditional and traditional occupations differ? *Sex Roles*, 20, 35–45.

O'Connor, M. J., Sigman, M., & Kasari, C. (1993). Interaction model for the association among maternal alcohol use, mother-infant interaction, and infant cognitive development. *Infant Behavior and Development*, 16, 177–192.

O'Connor, M. L. (1997). By six months postpartum, many teenagers are not using method effectively. *Family Planning Perspectives*, 29, 289–291.

O'Connor, R. E., Jenkins, J. R., & Slocum, T. A. (1995). Transfer among phonological tasks in kindergarten: Essential instructional content. *Journal of Educational Psychology*, 87, 202–217.

O'Hare, W. P., & Frey, W. H. (1992, September). Booming, suburban and black. *American Demographics*, pp. 30–38.

O'Neal, G. (1998, March, 30). Colleges run bars to battle binges. *USA Today*, p. D4.

Obarzanek, E., et al. (1994). Energy intake and physical activity in relation to indexes of body fat: The National Heart, Lung, and Blood Institute Growth and Height Study. *American Journal of Clinical Nutrition*, 60, 15–22.

Office of National Drug Control Policy. (1996). *President Clinton's accomplishments in the fight against drugs in defense of our children and our families*. Washington, DC: Author.

Ogbu, J. U. (1978). *Minority education and caste*. New York: Academic Press.

Ogbu, J. U. (1981). Origins of human competence: A cultural-ecological perspective. *Child Development*, 52, 413–429.

Ogbu, J.U. (1992). Understanding cultural diversity and learning. *Educational Researcher*, 21, 5–14.

Olim, E. G., Hess, R. D., & Shipman, V. C. (1967). Role of mothers' language styles in mediating their preschool children's development. *School Review*, 78, 414–424.

Olness, K. N. (1986). Reflections on caring for Indochinese children and youth. *Journal of Developmental and Behavior Pediatrics*, 7, 129–130.

Olsen, D., & Zigler, E. (1989). An assessment of the all-day kindergarten movement. *Early Childhood Research Quarterly*, 4, 167–187.

Olshan, A. F., & Faustman, E. M. (1993). Male-mediated developmental toxicity. *Annual Review of Public Health*, 14, 159–181.

Olson, L. (1998, April 1). Study: Schoolwide reform not easy. *Education Week*, pp. 1, 17.

Olson, M. R., & Haynes, J. A. (1993). Successful single parents. *Families in Society*, 259–267.

Olson, S. L., Bates, J. E., & Bayles, K. (1984). Mother-infant interaction and the development of individual differences in children's cognitive competence. *Developmental Psychology*, 20, 166–179.

Olvera-Ezzell, N., Power, T. G., Cousins, J. H., Guerra, A. M., & Trujillo, M. (1994). The development of health knowledge in low-income Mexican-American children. *Child Development*, 65, 416–427.

Olweus, D. (1977). Aggression and peer acceptance in adolescent boys: Two short-term longitudinal studies of ratings. *Child Development*, 48, 1301–1313.

Olweus, D. (1979). Stability and aggressive reaction patterns in males: A review. *Psychological Bulletin*, 86, 852–875.

Olweus, D. (1982). Development of stable aggressive reaction patterns in males. In R. Blanchard & C. Blanchard (Eds.), *Advances in the study of aggression* (Vol. 1). New York: Academic Press.

Onorato, I. M., Gwinn, M., & Dondero, T. J. (1994). Applications of data from the CDC family of surveys. *Public Health Reports*, 109, 204–212.

Oppel, W. C., Harper, P. A., & Rider, R. V. (1968). The age of attaining bladder control. *Pediatrics*, 42, 614–626.

Oppenheim, J., Boegehold, B., & Brenner, B. (1984). *Raising a confident child*. New York: Viking.

Opposition to human cloning. (1997, April 9). *Journal of the American Medical Association*, 277, 1105.

Orenberg, C. L. (1981). *DES: The complete story*. New York: St. Martin's.

Orlofsky, J. L, Marcia, J. E., & Lesser, T. M. (1973). Ego identity status and the intimacy versus isolation crisis of young adulthood. *Journal of Personality and Social Psychology*, 27, 211–219.

Ortho Diagnostic Systems. (1981). *What every Rh negative woman should know about Rho GAM*. Raritan, NJ: Author.

Oser, F. K. (1990). Kohlberg's educational legacy. In D. Schrader (Ed.), *The legacy of Lawrence Kohlberg* (pp. 81–89). San Francisco: Jossey-Bass.

Oshman, H. P., & Manosevitz, M. (1976). Father absence: Effects of stepfathers upon psychosocial development in males. *Developmental Psychology*, 12, 477–480.

Osipow, S. H. (1990). Convergence in theories of career choice and development: Review and prospect. *Journal of Vocational Behavior*, 36, 122–131.

Osofsky, J. D. (1995). Children who witness domestic violence: The invisible victims. *Social Policy Report: Society for Research in Child Development*, 9, 1–17.

Osofsky, J. D., Wewers, S., Hann, D. M., & Fick, A. C. (1993). Chronic community violence: What is happening to our children? *Psychiatry*, 56, 36–45.

Owen, M. T., & Mulvihill, B. A. (1994). Benefits of a parent education and support program in the first thee years. *Family Relations*, 43, 206–212.

Owens, R. E. (1988). *Language development*. Columbus, OH: Merrill/Prentice Hall.

Owens, R. E. (1992). *Language development* (3rd ed.). Columbus, OH: Merrill/Prentice Hall.

Owens, R.E . (1994). Development of communication, language, and speech. In G. H. Shames, E. H. Wiig, & W. A. Second (Eds.), *Human communication disorders* (4th ed., pp. 36–82). New York: Macmillan.

Oxtoby, M. J. (1994). Vertically acquired HIV infection in the United States, In P. A. Pizzo & C. M. Wilfert (Eds.), *Pediatric AIDS: The challenge of HIV infection in infants, children, and adolescents* (2nd ed., pp. 3–21). Baltimore: Williams & Wilkins.

P

Pachter, L. M., & Harwood, R. L. (1996). Culture and child behavior and psychosocial development. *Developmental and Behavioral Pediatrics*, 17, 191–198.

Padilla, A. M., & Baird, T. L. (1991). Mexican-American adolescent sexuality and sexual knowledge: An exploratory study. *Hispanic Journal of Behavioral Sciences*, 13, 95–104.

Padilla, A. M., Lindholm, K. J., Chen, A., Duran, R., Hakuta, K., Lambert, W., & Tucker, G. R. (1991). The English-only movement: Myths, reality, and implications for psychology. *American Psychologist*, 46, 120–131.

Pagani, L., Boulerice, B., Tremblay, R. E., & Vitaro, F. (1997). Behavioural development in children of divorce and remarriage. *Journal of Child Psychology, Psychiatry, and Allied Disciplines*, 38, 769–781.

Painful jabs. (1995, July 1). *The Economist*, 336, 20–22.

Painter, K. (1996, February 21). Heavy marijuana use may impair learning. *USA Today*, p. D1.

Palkovitz, R. (1985). Father's birth attendance, early contact, and extended contact with their newborns: A critical review. *Child Development*, 56, 392–407.

Paneth, N. S. (1995). The problem of low birth weight. In *The future of children: Low birth weight* (pp. 19–43). Los Altos, CA: David and Lucile Packard Foundation.

Parcel, G. S., Simons-Morton, B. G., O'Hara, N. M., Baranowski, T., Kolbe, L. J., & Bee, D. E. (1987). School promotion of healthful diet and exercise behavior: an integration of organizational change and social learning theory interventions. *Journal of School Health*, 57, 150–156.

Parens, E. (1996, July/August). Taking behavioral genetics seriously. *Hastings Center Report*, 26, 13–18.

Parish, T. S. (1990). Evaluations of family by youth: Do they vary as a function of family structure, gender, and birth order. *Adolescence*, 25, 353–356.

Parke, K. A., & Waters, E. (1989). Security of attachment and preschool friendships. *Child Development*, 60, 1076–1082.

Parke, R. D. (1981). *Fathers*. Cambridge, MA: Harvard University Press.

Parke, R. D. (1995). Fathers and families. In M.H. Bornstein (Ed.), *Handbook of parenting* (Vol.3, pp. 27–63). Mahwah, NJ: Erlbaum.

Parke, R. D., & Buriel, R. (1998). Socialization in the family: Ethnic and ecological perspectives in W. Damon (Editor in Chief) & N. Eisenberg (Vol. Ed.), *Handbook of child psychology* (5th ed., Vol. 3, pp. 463–552). New York: Wiley.

Parke, R. D., & Collmer, C. W. (1975). Child abuse: An interdisciplinary analysis. In E. M. Hetherington (Ed.), *Review of child development research* (Vol. 5). Chicago: University of Chicago Press.

Parke, R. D., & Sawin, D. B. (1976). The father's role in infancy: A reevaluation. *Family Coordinator*, 25, 365–371.

Parke, R. D., & Slaby, R. G. (1983). The development of aggression. In E. M. Hetherington (Ed.), *Handbook of child psychology: Socialization, personality, and social development* (4th ed., Vol. 4, pp. 547–643). New York: Wiley.

Parke, R. D., Ornstein, P. A., Reiser, J. J., & Zahn-Waxler, C. (1994). *Reflections on a century of developmental psychology*. Washington, DC: American Psychological Association.

Parker, J. G., & Asher, S. R. (1987). Peer relations and later adjustment: Are low-accepted children "at risk"? *Psychological Bulletin*, 102, 357–389.

Parker, J. G., & Gottman, J. M. (1989). Social and emotional development in a relational context. In T. J. Berndt & G. W. Ladd (Eds.), *Peer relationships in child development* (pp. 95–133). New York: Wiley.

Parker, J. G., & Herrera, C. (1996). Interpersonal processes in friendship: A comparison of abused and nonabused children's experiences. *Developmental Psychology*, 32, 1025–1038.

Parks, P.S.M., & Read, M.H. (1997) Adolescent male athletes: Body image, diet, and exercise. *Adolescence*, 32, 593–603.

Parmelee, A. H., & Sigman, M. D. (1983). Perinatal brain development and behavior. In P. H. Mussen (Ed.), *Handbook of child development* (3rd ed.. Vol. 2, pp. 95–157). New York: Wiley.

Parmelee, A. H., Wenne, W. H., & Schulz, H. R. (1964). Infant sleep patterns from birth to sixteen weeks of age. *Journal of Pediatrics*, 65, 576–582.

Parten, M. (1932). Social participation among preschool children. *Journal of Abnormal and Social Psychology*, 27, 243–269.

Pascalis, O., De Schonen, S., Morton, J., Deruelle, C., & Fabre-Grenet, M. (1995). Mothers' face recognition by neonates: A replication and extension. *Infant Behavior and Development*, 18, 79–85.

Patterson, C .J. (1992). Children of lesbian and gay parents. *Child Development*, 63, 1025–1042.

Patterson, C. J. (1995). Families of the lesbian baby boom: Parents' division of labor and children's adjustment. *Developmental Psychology*, 31, 1215–1254.

Patterson, C. J., Kupersmidt, J. B., & Griesler, P. C. (1990). Children's perceptions of self and of relationships with others as a function of sociometric status. *Child Development*, 61, 1335–1350.

Patterson, G. R. (1986). Performance models for antisocial boys. *American Psychologist*, 41, 432–444.

Patterson, G. R., DeBaryshe, B. D., & Ramsey, E. (1989). A developmental perspective on antisocial behavior. *American Psychologist*, 44, 329–335.

Patterson, G. R., Reid, J. B., & Dishion, T. J. (1992). *Antisocial boys*. Eugene OR: Castalia.

Paul, A. M. (1997, September). If you say so. *Psychology Today*, p. 12.

Paul, J. (1993). Childhood cross-gender behavior and adult homosexuality: The resurgence of biological models of sexuality. *Journal of Homosexuality*, 24, 41–54.

Paulson, S. E. (1994). Relations of parenting style and parental involvement with ninth-grade students' achievement. *Journal of Early Adolescence*, 14, 250–267.

Paxton, S. (1993). A prevention program for disturbed eating and body dissatisfaction in adolescent girls: A 1 year follow-up. *Health Education Research*, 8, 43–51.

Paxton, S. J., Wertheim, E. H., Gibbons, K., Szmukler, G. I., Hillier, L., & Petrovich, J. L. (1991). Body image satisfaction, dieting beliefs, and weight loss behaviors in adolescent girls and boys. *Journal of Youth and Adolescence*, 20, 361–379.

Pearson, D. A., & Lane, D. M. (1991). Auditory attention switching; A developmental study. *Journal of Experimental Child Psychology*, 51, 320–334.

Peckham, C., & Gibb, D. (1995). Mother-to-child transmission of the human immunodeficiency virus. *New England Journal of Medicine*, 333, 298–302.

Pederson, D. R., & Moran, G. (1996). Expressions of the attachment relationship outside of the strange situation. *Child Development*, 67, 915–927.

Pederson, D.R., Gleason, K.E., Moran, G., & Bento, S. (1998) Maternal attachment representations, maternal sensitivity, and the infant-mother attachment relationship. *Developmental Psychology*, 925–933.

Pedlow, R., Sanson, A., Prior, M., & Oberklaid, F. (1993). Stability of maternally reported temperament from infancy to 8 years. *Developmental Psychology*, 29, 998–1007.

Peeck, J. (1987). The role of illustrations in processing and remembering. In D. M. Willows & H. A. Houghton (Eds.), *The psychology of illustration* (Vol.1, pp. 115–151). New York: Springer.

Pellegrini, A. D. (1988). Elementary-school children's rough-and-tumble play and social competence. *Developmental Psychology*, 24, 802–807.

Pellegrini, A. D. (1995). A longitudinal study of boys' rough-and-tumble play and dominance during early adolescence. *Journal of Applied Developmental Psychology*, 16, 77–93.

Pellegrini, A. D., & Perlmutter, J. C. (1989). Classroom contextual effects on children's play. *Developmental Psychology*, 25, 289–297.

Pellegrini, A.D., & Smith, P.K. (1998) Physical activity play: The nature and function of a neglected aspect of play. *Child Development*, 69, 577–599.

Pendarvis, E. D., Howley, A. A., & Howley, C.B . (1990). *The abilities of gifted children*. Upper Saddle River, NJ: Prentice Hall.

Pepper, E. C. (1976). Teaching the American Indian child in mainstream settings. In R. L. Jones (Ed.), *Mainstreaming and the minority child*. Reston VA: Council for Exceptional Children.

Perlman, M., & Ross, H. S. (1997). The benefit of parent intervention in children's disputes: An examination of concurrent changes in children's fighting styles. *Child Development*, 64, 690–700.

Perlmutter, M., & Myers, N. A. (1979). Recognition memory development in two- to four-year-olds. *Developmental Psychology*, 15, 73–83.

Perozynski, L., & Kramer, L. (1999). Parental beliefs about managing sibling conflict. *Developmental Psychology, 35,* 489–499.

Perry, W. B. (1968). *Forms of intellectual and ethical development in the college years: A scheme.* New York: Holt, Rinehart & Winston.

Perry, W. B. (1981). Cognitive and ethical growth: The making of meaning. In A. Chickering (Ed.), *The modern American college* (pp. 76–117). San Francisco: Jossey-Bass.

Peskin, H. (1973). Influence of the developmental schedule of puberty on learning and ego functioning. *Journal of Youth and Adolescence,* 14, 191–206.

Pestrak, V. A., & Martin, D. (1985). Cognitive development and aspects of adolescent sexuality. *Adolescence, 20,* 981–987.

Peters, A. M. (1986). Early syntax. In P. Fletcher & M. Garman (Eds.), *Language acquisition* (2nd ed., pp. 307–326). London: Cambridge University Press.

Peters, D. L. (1977). Early childhood education: An overview and evaluation. In H. L. Hom & P. A. Robinson (Eds.), *Psychological processes in early education* (pp. 1–23). New York: Academic Press.

Petersen, A. C., & Crockett, L. (1985). Pubertal timing and grade effects on adjustment. *Journal of Youth and Adolescence,* 14, 191–206.

Peterson, C., & Rideout, R. (1998) Memory for medical emergencies experienced by 1-and 2-year olds. *Developmental Psychology,* 34, 1059–1073.

Peterson, K. L. & Roscoe, B. (1991). Imaginary audience behavior in older adolescent females. *Adolescence,* 26, 195–200.

Peterson, K. S. (1997, July 14). Split decision on how divorce affects kids. *USA Today,* p. D6.

Peterson, K. S. (1998, June 1). Lack of empathy seen as key to spotting troubled youth. *USA Today,* p. D6.

Peterson, L. (1990). PhoneFriend: A developmental description of needs expressed by child callers to a community telephone support system for children. *Journal of Applied Developmental Psychology,* 11, 105–122.

Petitpas, A. (1978). Identity foreclosure: A unique challenge. *American Personnel and Guidance Journal,* 56, 558–562.

Petitto, L. (1988) "Language" in the prelinguistic child in F.S. Kessel (Ed.). *The development of language and language researchers: Essays in honor of Roger Brown* (pp. 187–221). Hillsdale, NJ: Erlbaum.

Petrill, S. A., Saudino, K., Cherny, S. E., Emde, R. N., Hewitt, J. K., Fulker, D. W., & Plomin, R. (1997). Exploring the genetic etiology of low general cognitive ability from 14 to 36 months. *Developmental Psychology,* 33, 544–548.

Pettit, G. S., & Bates, J. E. (1989). Family interaction patterns and children's behavior problems from infancy to 4 years. *Developmental Psychology,* 25, 413–421.

Pettit, G. S., Bates, J. E., Dodge, K. A., & Meece, D. W. (1999). The impact of after-school peer contact on early adolescent externalizing problems is moderated by parental monitoring, perceived neighborhood safety, and prior adjustment. *Child Development,* 70, 768–778.

Pfannenstiel, J.C., & Seltzer, D.A. (1989) New parents as teachers: Evaluation of early parent education programs. *Early Childhood Research Quarterly,* 4, 1–18.

Pfeffer, K., & Barnecutt, P. (1996). Children's auditory perception of movement of traffic sounds. *Child: Care, Health and Development,* 22, 129–137.

Phares, V., & Renk, K. (1998). Perceptions of parents: A measure of adolescents' feelings about their parents. *Journal of Marriage and the Family,* 60, 646–660.

Phelps, K. E., & Woolley, J. D. (1994). The form and function of young children's magical beliefs. *Developmental Psychology,* 30, 385–394.

Phillips, D. A., Voran, M., Kisker, E., Howes, C., & Whitebook, M. (1994). Child care for children in poverty: Opportunity or inequity? *Child Development,* 65, 472–492.

Phillips, D., McCartney, K., & Scarr, S. (1987). Child-care quality and children's social development. *Developmental Psychology,* 23, 537–543.

Phillips, J. L. (1975). *The origins of intellect: Piaget's theory* (2nd ed.). San Francisco: Freeman.

Phillips, R. B., Sharma, R., Premachandra, B. R., Vaughn, A. J., & Reyes-Lee, M. (1996). Intrauterine exposure to cocaine: Effect on neurobehavior of neonates. *Infant Behavior and Development,* 19, 71–81.

Phillips, S. C. (1994, April 8). Reproductive ethics. *CQ Magazine,* pp. 289–310.

Phillips, S., & Lobar, S. L. (1990). Literature summary of some Navajo child health beliefs and rearing practices within a transcultural nursing framework. *Journal of Transcultural Nursing,* 1, 13–20.

Phillips, S., & Sandstrom, K.L. (1990) Parental attitudes towards youth work. *Youth and Society,* 22, 160–183.

Phinney, J. S. (1989). Stages of ethnic identity development in minority group adolescents. *Journal of Early Adolescence,* 9, 34–49.

Phinney, J. S. (1993). A three-stage model of ethnic identity development in adolescence. In M. E. Bernal & G. P. Knight (Eds.), *Ethnic identity: Formation and transmission among Hispanics and other minorities.* New York Press: Albany.

Phinney, J. S., & Alipuria, L. L. (1990). Ethnic identity in college groups from four ethnic groups. *Journal of Adolescence,* 13, 171–183.

Phinney, J. S., & Tarver, S. (1988). Ethnic identity search and commitment in black and white eighth graders. *Journal of Early Adolescence,* 8, 265–277.

Phinney, J. S., Cantu, C. L., & Kurtz, D. A. (1997). Ethnic and American identity as predictors of self-esteem among African American, Latino, and white adolescents. *Journal of Youth and Adolescence,* 26, 165–186.

Phinney, J. S., Chavira, V., & Williamson, L. (1992). Acculturation attitudes and self-esteem among high-school and college students. *Youth and Society,* 23, 299–312.

Piaget, J. & Inhelder, B. (1974). *The child's construction of quantities: Conservation and atomism.* London: Routledge & Kegan Paul.

Piaget, J. (1928). *Judgment and reasoning in the young child.* New York: Harcourt, Brace, & World.

Piaget, J. (1929). *The child's conception of the world.* London: Kegan Paul, Trench, & Trubner.

Piaget, J. (1930). *The child's conception of physical causality.* London: Kegan Paul, Trench, & Trubner.

Piaget, J. (1932). *The moral judgment of the child.* London: Routledge & Kegan Paul.

Piaget, J. (1952a). *The child's conception of number.* New York: Humanities Press.

Piaget, J. (1952b). *The origins of intelligence in children.* New York: Norton.

Piaget, J. (1954). *The construction of reality in the child.* New York: Basic Books. (Originally published 1937.)

Piaget, J. (1962a). *Play, dreams, and imitation in childhood.* New York: Norton.

Piaget, J. (1962b). The stages of intellectual development of the child. *Bulletin of the Menninger Clinic,* 26, 120–128.

Piaget, J. (1965). *The moral judgment of the child* (M. Gabain, Trans.). New York: Free Press. (Originally published 1932.)

Piaget, J. (1967). *Six psychological studies.* New York: Vintage.

Piaget, J. (1968). *On the development of memory and identity.* Worcester, MA: Clark University Press.

Piaget, J. (1969). *The child's conception of the world.* Totowa, NJ: Littlefield & Adams.

Piaget, J. (1970). *Genetic epistemology.* New York: Columbia University Press.

Piaget, J. (1972). Intellectual evolution from adolescence to adulthood. *Human Development,* 15, 1–12.

Piaget, J. (1974). *Understanding causality.* New York: Norton.

Piaget, J. (1983). Piaget's theory. In P. H. Mussen (Ed.), *Handbook of child psychology* (Vol. 1, pp. 103–129). New York: Wiley. (Originally published 1970.)

Piaget, J. (1987). *Possibility and necessity* (2 vols.). Minneapolis: University of Minnesota press. (Original work published 1981 & 1983).

Piaget, J., & Inhelder, B. (1969). *The psychology of the child.* New York: Basic Books.

Pick, S., & Palos, P.A. (1995). Impact of the family on the sex lives of adolescents. *Adolescence*, 119, 667–674.

Pickens, J. (1994). Perception of auditory-visual distance relations by 5-month-old infants. *Developmental Psychology*, 30, 537–544.

Pickens, J., & Field, T. (1993). Facial expressivity in infants of depressed mothers. *Developmental Psychology*, 29, 986–988.

Pierce, J. W., & Wardle, J. (1997). Cause and effect beliefs and self-esteem of overweight children. *Journal of Child Psychology and Psychiatry and Allied Discipline*, 38, 645–650.

Pike, A., & Plomin, R. (1996). Importance of nonshared environmental factors for childhood and adolescent psychology. *Journal of the American Academy of Child and Adolescent Psychiatry*, 35, 560–570.

Pillitteri, A. (1992). *Maternal and child health nursing: Care of the childbearing and childrearing family*. Philadelphia: Lippincott.

Pina, P. (1995, September 13). More teenagers using marijuana. *USA Today*, p. D7.

Pipe, M. E., Gee, S., Wilson, C., & Egerton, J. M. (1999). Children's recall 1 or 2 years after an event. *Developmental Psychology*, 35, 781–789.

Plas, J. M., & Bellet, W. (1983). Assessment of the value-attitude orientations of American Indian children. *Journal of School Psychology*, 21, 57–64.

Pleck, J. (1983). Husbands' paid work and family roles: Current research issues. In Z. Lopata & J. Pleck (Eds.), *Research in the interweave of social roles: Families and jobs* (vol. 3, pp. 251–333). Greenwich, CT: JAI.

Plomin, R., & Daniels, D. (1987). Why are children in the same family so different from each other. *Behavioral and Brain Sciences*, 10, 1–16.

Plomin, R., & DeFries, J. C. (1980). Genetics and intelligence: Recent data. *Intelligence*, 4, 15–24.

Plomin, R., & Rutter, M. (1998) Child development, molecular genetics, and what to do with genes once they are found. *Child Development*, 69, 1223–1243.

Plomin, R., DeFries, J. C., & McClearn, G. E. (1990). *Behavioral genetics: A primer* (2nd ed.). New York: Freeman.

Plomin, R., Emde, R. N., Braungart, J. M., Campos, J., Corley, R., Fuler, D. W., Kagan, J., Reznick, J. S., Robinson, J., Zahn-Waxler, C., & DeFries, J. C. (1993). Genetic change and continuity from 14 to 20 months: The MacArthur Longitudinal Twin Study. *Child Development*, 64, 1354–1377.

Plumert, J. M. (1995). Relations between children's overestimation of their physical abilities and accident proneness. *Developmental Psychology*, 31, 866–876.

Polak, A., & Harris, P.L. (1999) Deception by young children following noncompliance. *Developmental Psychology*, 35, 561–568.

Polit, D. F., & Falbo, T. (1987). Only children and personality development: A quantitative review. *Journal of Marriage and the Family*, 49, 309–325.

Pollock, R. (1994). Shots in the dark. *Reason*, 26, 51–54.

Pomerleau, A., Bolduck, D., Malcuit, G., & Cossette, L. (1990). Pink or blue: Environmental gender stereotypes in the first two years of life. *Sex Roles*, 22, 359–367.

Poole, D. A. & White, L. T. (1991). Effects of question repetition on the eyewitness testimony of children and adults. *Developmental Psychology*, 27, 975–986.

Pope, A. W., & Bierman, K. L. (1999). Predicting adolescent peer problems and antisocial activities: The relative roles of aggression and dysregulation. *Developmental Psychology*, 35, 235–246.

Porcerelli, J.H., & Sandler, B.A. (1995) Narcissism and empathy in steroid users. *American Journal of Psychiatry*, 152, 1672–1675.

Porter, R. P. (1990, May 17). Tongue-tied by bilingual education. *Newsday*, p. 36.

Portes, P. R., Haas, R., & Brown, J. H. (1991). Predicting children's adjustment to divorce. *Journal of Divorce*, 15, 87–103.

Portes, P. R., Howell, S. C., Brown, J. H., Eichenberger, S., & Mas, C. A. (1992). Family functions and children's postdivorce adjustment. *American Journal of Orthopsychiatry*, 62, 613–617.

Portner, J. (1995, April 19). Two studies link high-quality day care and child development. *Education Week*, p. 6.

Portner, J. (1997, September 10). New report on children's dietary habits disappoints educators. *Education Week*, p. 8.

Posner, J.K., & Vandell, D.L. (1999) After-school activities and the development of low-income urban children: A longitudinal study. *Developmental Psychology*, 35, 868–879.

Powell, C., & Grantham-McGregor, S. (1989). Home visiting of varying frequency and child development. *Pediatrics*, 84, 157–164.

Powell, M. B. & Thomson, D. M. (1994). Children's eyewitness-memory Research: implications for practice. *Families in Society*, 75, 204–216.

Power, T. (1985). Mother- and father-infant play: A developmental analysis. *Child Development*, 56, 1514–1525.

Poznansky, E. O. (1954). Children with excessive fears. *American Journal of Orthopsychiatry*, 43, 428–438.

Prawat, R. S., Anderson, A. H., & Hapkiewicz, W. (1985). Is the scariest monster also the least real? An examination of children's reality justifications. *Journal of Genetic Psychology*, 146, 7–12.

Prediger, D., Swaney, K., Mau, W. C. (1993). Extending Holland's hexagon: Procedures, counseling applications, and research. *Journal of Counseling and Development*, 71, 422–428.

Price, R.C., Cowen, E.L., Lorion, R.P. & Ramos-McKay, J. (1989) The search for effective prevention programs: What we learned along the way. *American Journal of Orthopsychiatry*, 59, 49–58.

Priestley, G., Roberts, S., & Pipe, M.E. (1999) Returning to the scene: Reminders and context reinstatement enhance children's recall. *Developmental Psychology*, 35, 1006–1019.

Pritchard, M. E., King, S. L., & Czajka-Narins, M. (1997). Adolescent body mass indices and self-perception. *Adolescence*, 128, 863–879.

Psychological Corporation. (1993). *The Bayley Scales of infant development* (2nd ed.). San Antonio, Texas: Author.

Public Agenda (1997). *Kids these days: What Americans really think about the next generation*. New York: Author.

Public Health Reports (1993, July/August) Evaluation of telephoned computer-generated reminders to improve immunization coverage at inner-city clinics. *Public Health Reports*, 108, 426–430.

Pulaski, M. A. S. (1980). *Understanding Piaget: An introduction to children's cognitive development* (rev. ed.). New York: Harper & Row.

Punamaki, R. L. (1996). Can ideological commitment protect children's psychosocial well-being in situations of political violence? *Child Development*, 67, 55–70.

Q

Quadrel, M. J., Fischoff, B., & Davis, W. (1993). Adolescent (in)vulnerability. *American Psychologist*, 48, 102–116.

Quilligan, E. J. (1995). Obstetrics and gynecology. *Journal of the American Medical Association*, 273, 1700–1701.

R

Radke-Yarrow, M., & Sherman, T. (1991). Hard growing: children who survive. In J. Rolf et al. (Eds.), *Risk and protective factors in developmental psychopathology* (pp. 97–120). New York: Cambridge University Press.

Rafferty, Y., & Shinn, M. (1991). The impact of homelessness on children. *American Psychologist*, 46, 1170–1179.

Ragone, H. (1994). *Surrogate motherhood: Conception in the heart*. Boulder, CO: Westview.

Raloff, J. (1982). Reports from the 1982 meeting of the American Speech Language Hearing Association's meeting in Toronto, Canada. *Science News*, 122, 360.

Ramey, C. T., & Ramey, S .L. (1992). Effective early intervention. *Mental Retardation, 50,* 180–187.

Ramey, C. T., & Ramey, S. L. (1998). Early intervention and early experience. *American Psychologist, 53,* 109–120.

Ramirez, J.D. (1992) Executive summary. bilingual *Research Journal,* 16, 1–62.

Rapkin, I. (1997). Autism. *New England Journal of Medicine,* 337, 97–103.

Rasmussen, K. M., & Adams, B. (1997). Annotation: Cigarette smoking, nutrition and birthweight. *American Journal of Public Health,* 87, 543–545.

Raspberry, W. (1970, April). Should ghettoese be accepted? *Today's Education,* pp. 30–31, 34–41.

Raths, L. E., Harmin, M., & Simon, S. B. (1966). *Values and teaching.* Columbus, OH: Merrill/Prentice Hall.

Rathunde, K. (1997). Parent-adolescent interaction and optimal experience. *Journal of Youth and Adolescence,* 26, 669–689.

Ray, W.J. (1997) *methods: Toward a science of behavior and experience* (5th ed). Pacific Grove, Cal: Brooks-Cole

Razel, M. (1988). Call for a follow-up study of experiments on long-term deprivation of human infants. *Perceptual and Motor Skills,* 67, 147–158.

Recommended childhood immunization schedule, United States, 1999. (1999). *MMWR,* 48, 12–16.

Reed, R. (1988). Education and achievement of young black males. In J. T. Gibbs (Ed.), *Young, black, and male in America: An endangered species.* Dover, MA: Auburn House.

Reese, E., & Cox, A. (1999). Quality of adult book reading affects children's emergent literacy. *Developmental Psychology,* 35, 20–28.

Reese, H. W., & Lipsitt, L. P. (1973). *Experimental Child Psychology.* New York: Academic Press.

Reichelt, P. (1982). Cited in P. H. Dreyer, Sexuality during adolescence. In B. B. Wolman (Ed.), *Handbook of developmental psychology* (pp. 559–601). Upper Saddle River, NJ: Prentice Hall.

Reid, M., Ramey, S. L., & Burchinal, M. (1990). Dialogues with children about their families. *New Directions for Child Development,* 48, 5–27.

Reid, W. J. & Donovan, T. (1990). Treating sibling violence. *Journal of Family Therapy,* 17, 49–59.

Reiss, D. (1993). Genes and the environment: Siblings and synthesis. In R. Plomin & G.E. McClearn (Eds.), *Nature, nurture, and psychology* (pp. 417–433). Washington, DC: American Psychological Association.

Reissland, N. (1988). Neonatal imitation in the first hour of life: Observations in rural Nepal. *Developmental Psychology,* 24, 464–470.

Repacholi, B.M. (1998) Infants' use of attentional cues to identify the referent of another person's emotional expression. *Developmental Psychology,* 34, 1017–1026.

Repp, A. C., Nieminen, G. S., Olinger, E., & Brusca, R. (1988). Direct observation: Factors affecting the accuracy of observers. *Exceptional Children,* 55, 29–36.

Rest, J. R. (1983). Morality. In P. H. Mussen (Ed.), *Handbook of child psychology: Cognitive development* (4th ed., Vol. 3, pp. 556–630). New York: Wiley.

Restak, R. M. (1988). *The mind.* New York: Bantam.

Revelle, W. (1995). Personality processes. *Annual Review of Psychology,* 46, 295–328.

Reyes, O., Gillock, K., & Kobus, K. (1994). A longitudinal study of school adjustment in urban, minority adolescents: Effects of a high school transition program. *American Journal of Community Psychology,* 22, 341–369.

Reynolds, A. J. (1995). Effects of a preschool plus follow-on intervention for children at risk. *Developmental Psychology,* 30, 787–804.

Reynolds, A. J., & Temple, J. A. (1998). Extended early childhood intervention and school achievement: Age 13 findings from the Chicago Longitudinal Study. *Child Development,* 231–245.

Reynolds, M.C., & Birch, J.W. (1988) *Adaptive mainstreaming* (3rd ed.). New York: Longman.

Reznick, J. S., & Goldfield, B. A. (1992). Rapid change in lexical development in comprehension and production. *Developmental Psychology,* 28, 406–413.

Rheingold, H., & Cook, K. (1975). The contents of boys' and girls' rooms as an index of parents' behavior. *Child Development,* 46, 459–463.

Rheingold, H. L., & Eckerman, C.O. (1973). Fear of the stranger: a critical examination. In H. W. Reese (Ed.), *Advances in child development and behavior* (Vol. 8). New York: Academic Press.

Rhoads, G. G., et al. (1989, March 9). The safety and efficacy of chorionic villus sampling for early prenatal diagnosis of cytogenetic abnormalities. *New England Journal of Medicine,* 320(10), 609–617.

Ricciuti, H. (1974). Fear and development of social attachments in the first year of life. In M. Lewis & L. A. Rosenblum (Eds.), *The origins of human behavior: Fear.* New York: Wiley.

Ricciuti, H. N. (1980). Developmental consequences of malnutrition in early childhood In E. M. Hetherington & R. D. Parke (Eds.), *Contemporary readings in child psychology* (2nd ed.). New York: McGraw-Hill.

Rice, C., Koinis, D., Sullivan, K., Tager-Flusberg, H., & Winner, E. (1997). When 3-year-olds pass the appearance-reality test. *Developmental Psychology,* 33, 54–62.

Rice, F. P. (1996). *The adolescent: Development, relationships, and culture.* Boston: Allyn & Bacon.

Rice, K. (1995). Phonological variability in language acquisition: A representational account. In E. V. Clark (Ed.), *The child language research forum* (pp. 7–19). N.p.: Center for the Study of Language and Information, Leland Stanford Junior University.

Rice, M. L. (1989). Children's language acquisition. *American Psychologist,* 44, 149–157.

Rice, M. L., & Woodsmall, L. (1988). Lessons from television: Children's word learning when viewing. *Child Development,* 59, 420–429.

Rice, M. L., Burh, J. C., & Nemeth, M. (1990). Fast mapping word-learning abilities of language-delayed preschoolers. *Journal of Speech and Hearing Disorders,* 55, 33–42.

Rice, M. L., Huston, A. C., Truglio, R., & Wright, J. (1990). Words from "Sesame Street": Learning vocabulary while viewing. *Developmental Psychology,* 26, 421–429.

Rich, M. (1991, May 1). Y.W.C.A. official discusses the need for anti-rape education. *Education Week,* pp. 6, 7.

Richards, M. H., Casper, R. C., & Larson, R. (1990). Weight and eating concerns among pre- and young adolescent boys and girls. *Journal of Adolescent Health Care,* 11, 203–209

Richards, M. S., & Larson, R. (1993). Weight and eating concerns among pre-and young adolescent boys and girls. *Journal of Research in Adolescence,* 3, 145–169.

Richards, M. (1998) Annotation: Genetic research, family life, and clinical practice. *Journal of Child Psychology and Psychiatry and Allied Disciplines,* 39, 291–305.

Richmond, J. (1990). Low-birth-weight infants: Can we enhance their development? *Journal of the American Medical Association,* 263, 3069–3070.

Richmond-Abbott, M. (1983). *Masculine and feminine.* Reading, MA: Addison-Wesley.

Rickelman, K. E. (1986). Childhood cross-sex friendship: An investigation of trends and possible explanatory theories. Cited in J. M. Gottman, The world of coordinated play: Same and cross sex friendship in young children. In J. M. Gottman & J. G. Parker (Eds.), *Conversations of friends: Speculations on affective development* (pp. 139–192). New York: Cambridge University Press.

Rickert, E. S. (1981). Media mirrors of the gifted: E. Susanne Rickert's review of the film "Simon." *Gifted Child Quarterly,* 25, 3–4.

Rickman, M. D., & Davidson, R. J. (1994). Personality and behavior in parents of temperamentally inhibited and uninhibited children. *Developmental Psychology,* 30, 346–354.

Rierdan, J., & Koff, E. (1997). Weight, weight-related aspects of body image, and depression in early adolescent girls. *Adolescence,* 32, 615–625.

Rist, M. C. (1990, January). "Crack babies" in school. *American School Board Journal,* pp. 19–24.

Ristow, M., Moller-Wieland, D., Pfeiffer, A., Krone, W., & Kahn, C. R. (1998, October 1). Obesity associated with a mutation in a genetic regulator of adipocyte differentiation. *New England Journal of Medicine, 339,* 953–959.

Ritchie, K. (1995, April). Marketing to Generation X. *American Demographics,* pp. 34–39.

Rivera, S.M., Wakeley, A., & Langer, J. (1999) The drawbridge phenomenon: Representational reasoning or perceptual preference? *Developmental Psychology, 35,* 427–435.

Roach, M.A., Barratt, M.S., Miller, J.F., & Leavitt, L.A. (1998) The structure of mother-child play: Young children with Down Syndrome and typically developing children. *Developmental Psychology, 34,* 77–88.

Roberge, J. R., & Flexer, B. K. (1979). Further examination of formal operational reasoning abilities. *Child Development, 50,* 478–484.

Roberts, E. M. (1997). Neighborhood social environments and the distribution of low birthweight in Chicago. *American Journal of Public Health, 87,* 597–605.

Roberts, W., & Strayer, J. (1996). Empathy, emotional expressiveness, and prosocial behavior. *Child Development, 67,* 449–470.

Robertson, M. J. (1991). Homeless women with children. *American Psychologist, 46,* 1198–1204.

Robinson, B. E., Walters, L. H., & Skeen, P. (1989). Response of parents to learning that their child is homosexual and concern over AIDS: A national study. *Journal of Homosexuality, 18,* 59–80.

Robinson, J. L., Kagan, J., Reznick, J. S., & Corley, R. (1992). The heritability of inhibited and uninhibited behavior: A twin study. *Developmental Psychology, 28,* 1030–1038.

Robinson, L. A., & Klesges, R. C. (1997). Ethnic and gender differences in risk factors for smoking onset. *Health Psychology, 16,* 499–505.

Rocha, C., Johnson, A. K., McChesney, K. Y., & Butterfield, W. H. (1996). Predictors of permanent housing for sheltered homeless families. *Families in Society,* 50–57.

Rochat, P., Querido, J.G., & Striano, T. (1999) Emerging sensitivity to the timing and structure of protoconversation in early infancy. *Developmental Psychology, 35,* 950–957.

Roche, A. F. (1979). Secular trends in stature, weight, and maturation. In A. F. Roche (Ed.), *Secular trends in growth, maturation, and development of children. Monographs of the Society for Research in Child Development, 44,* 3–27.

Roche, J. P. (1986). Premarital sex: Attitudes and behavior by dating stage. *Adolescence, 81,* 107–121.

Rock, A.M.L., Trainor, L.J., & Addison, T.L. (1999) Distinctive messages in infant-directed lullabies and play songs. *Developmental Psychology, 35,* 527–534.

Rodin, J. (1993). Cultural psychosocial determinants of weight concerns. *Annals of Internal Medicine, 119,* 643–645.

Rodman, H., Pratto, D. J., & Nelson, R. S. (1985). Child care arrangements and children's functioning: A comparison of self-care and adult-care children. *Developmental Psychology, 21,* 413–418.

Rodriquez, C., & Moore, N.B. (1995). Perceptions of pregnant/parenting teens: Reframing issues for an integrated approach to pregnancy problems. *Adolescence, 30,* 685–706.

Roffwarg, H .P., Muzio, J. N., & Dement, W. C. (1966). Ontogenic development of the human sleep-dream cycle. *Science, 152,* 604–619.

Rog, D. J., Holupka, C. S., McCombs-Thornton, K. L. (1995). Implementation of the homeless families program: 1. Service models and preliminary outcomes. *American Journal of Orthopsychiatry, 65,* 502–513.

Rogers, C. R. (1980). *A way of being.* Boston: Houghton Mifflin.

Roggman, L. A., Langlois, J. H., Hobbs-Tait, L., & Rieser-Danner, L. A. (1994). Infant day-care attachment, and the "file drawer problem" *Child Development, 65,* 1429–1443.

Rogoff, B. (1981). Schooling and the development of cognitive skills. In H. C. Triandis & A. Heron (Eds.), *Handbook of cross-cultural psychology: Vol. 4. Developmental psychology* (pp. 233–295). Boston: Allyn & Bacon.

Rogoff, B., & Morelli, G. (1989). Culture and American children: Section introduction. *American Psychologist, 44,* 341–343.

Rogoff, B., Newcombe, N., & Kagan, J. (1974). Planfulness and recognition memory. *Child Development, 45,* 972–977.

Rolfes, S. R., & DeBruyne, L. K. (1990). *Life span nutrition.* St. Paul, MN: West.

Rolfes, S. R., DeBruyne, L. K., & Whitney, E. N. (1998). *Life span nutrition: Conception through life* (2nd ed.). Belmont, CA: Wadsworth.

Rollins, B. C. (1989). Marital quality at midlife. In S. Hunter & M. Sundel (Eds.), *Midlife myths: Issues, findings, and practical implications* (pp. 184–195). Newbury Park, CA: Sage.

Rondal, J. A. (1988). Language development in Down's syndrome: a life-span perspective. *International Journal of Behavioral Development, 11,* 21–36.

Rooks, J. P., Weatherby, N. L., Eunice, K. M., Stapleton, S., Rosen, D., & Rosenfield, A. (1989). Outcomes of care in birth centers. *New England Journal of Medicine, 321,* 1804–1810.

Roper Organization. (1991). *AIDS: Public attitudes and education needs.* New York.

Ropp, K.L. (1992, Dec). No-win situations for athletes. *FDA Consumer,* pp.8–12.

Rose, L. C., & Gallup, A. M. (1998, September). The 30th Annual Phi Delta Kappa/Gallup Poll of the Public's Attitudes Towards Public Schools. *Phi Delta Kappan,* pp. 41–56.

Rose, L. C., Gallup, A. M., & Elam, S. M. (1997). The 29th Annual Phi Delta Kappan/ Gallup Poll of the public's attitudes toward the public schools. *Phi Delta Kappan,* pp. 41–57.

Rose, R. J. (1995). Genes and human behavior. *Annual Review of Psychology, 46,* 615–654.

Rose, S. A. (1981). Developmental changes in infants' retention of visual stimuli. *Child Development, 52,* 227–233.

Rose, S. A., & Feldman, J. F. (1996). Memory and processing speed in preterm children at eleven years: A comparison with full-terms. *Child Development, 67,* 2005–2021.

Rose, S. A., & Feldman, J. F. (1997). Memory and speed: Their role in the relation of infant information processing to later IQ. *Child Development, 68,* 630–641.

Rose, S. A., & Wallace, I. F. (1985). Visual recognition memory: A predictor of later cognitive functioning. *Child Development, 56,* 853–861.

Rose, S. A., Feldman, J. F., Futterweit, L. R., & Jankowski, J. J. (1998). Continuity in tactual-visual cross-modal transfer: Infancy to 11 years. *Developmental Psychology, 34,* 435–440.

Rose, S.A., & Feldman, J.F. (1997) Memory and speed: Their role in the relation of infant information processing to later IQ. *Child Development, 68,* 630–642.

Rose, S.A., Gottfried, A.W., & Bridger, W.H. (1981) Cross-modal transfer in 6-month-old infants. *Developmental Psychology, 27,* 723–737.

Rosen, K. S., & Burke, P. B. (1999). Multiple attachment relationships within families: Mothers and fathers with two young children. *Child Development, 35,* 436–444.

Rosen, K. S., & Rothbaum, F. (1993). Quality of parental caregiving and security of attachment. *Developmental Psychology, 29,* 358–367.

Rosen, W. D., Adamson, L. B., & Bakeman, R. (1992). An experimental investigation of infant social referencing: Mothers' messages and gender differences. *Developmental Psychology, 28,* 1172–1178.

Rosenberg, M. S. (1987). New directions for research on the psychological maltreatment of children. *American Psychologist, 42,* 166–172.

Rosenberg, P. S., & Biggar, R. J. (1998), June 17). Trends in HIV incidence among young adults in the United States. *Journal of the American Medical Association, 279,* 1894–1899.

Rosenberg, Z. F., & Fauci, A. S. (1994). Immunopathology and pathogenesis of HIV infection. In *Pediatric AIDS: The challenge of HIV infection in infants, children, and adolescents* (2nd ed., pp.115–128). Baltimore: Williams & Wilkins.

Rosenblum, G. D., & Lewis, M. (1999). The relations among body image, physical attractiveness, and body mass in adolescence. *Child Development, 70,* 50–64.

Rosenham, D. L., & Seligman, M .E. P. (1995). *Abnormal psychology* (3rd ed.). New York: Norton.

Rosenstein, D., & Oster, H. (1988). Differential facial responses to four basic tastes. *Child Development, 59*, 1555–1569.

Rosenthal, E. (1990, February 4). When a pregnant woman drinks. *New York Times Magazine*, pp. 30–32+.

Rosenthal, E. (1992, May 26). Cost of high-tech fertility: too many tiny babies. *New York Times*, pp. C1, C10.

Rosenthal, S. L., Biro, F. M., Succop, P. A., Bernstein, D. I., & Stanberry, L. R. (1997). Impact of demographics, sexual history, and psychological functioning on the acquisition of STDs in adolescents. *Adolescents, 32*, 758–769.

Rosenzweig, M. R., Bennett, E. L., & Diamond, M. C. (1972, February). Brain changes in response to experience. *Scientific American*, pp. 22–29.

Ross Laboratories. (1977). *Your child's fears*. Columbus, OH: Ross Laboratories.

Ross, H. S. (1996). Negotiating principles of entitlement in sibling property disputes. *Developmental Psychology, 32*, 90–101.

Rothman, R. (1990, June 13). Students spend little time reading or writing in school, NAEP finds. *Education Week*, pp. 1, 9.

Rothman, R. (1991, March 13). Psychologist's cross-national studies in math show U.S.'s long road to "first in the world". *Education Week*, pp. 6–7.

Rothstein, L. E. (1995). *Special Education Law* (2nd ed.). White Plains, NY: Longman.

Rovee-Collier, C. (1987). Learning and memory in infancy. In J. Osofsky (Ed.), *Handbook of infant development* (2nd ed., pp. 98–149). New York: Wiley.

Rovee-Collier, C., & Boller, K. (1995). Current theory and research on infant learning and memory: Application to early intervention. *Infants and Young Children, 7*, 1–12.

Rowe, D. C., & Waldman, I. D. (1993). The question "how?" reconsidered. in R. Plomin & G.E. McClearn (Eds.), *Nature, nurture, and psychology* (pp. 355–375). Washington, DC: American Psychological Association.

Rozin, P. (1996). Sociocultural influences on human food selection. In E. D. Capaldi (Ed.), *Why we eat what we eat* (pp. 233–267). Washington, DC: American Psychological Association.

Rubenstein, A.J., Kalakanis, L., & Langlois, J.H. (1999) Infant preferences for attractive faces: A cognitive explanation. *Developmental Psychology, 35*, 848–855.

Rubin, A. M. (1995, July 21). Using pop culture to fight teen violence. *Chronicle of Higher Education*, p. A5.

Rubin, D. H., Erickson, C. J., Agustin, M. S. Cleary, S. D., Allen, J. ., & Cohen, P. (1996). Cognitive and academic functioning of homeless children compared with housed Children. *Pediatrics, 93*, 289–294.

Rubin, J., Provenzano, F., & Luria, Z. (1974). The eye of the beholder: Parents' views of sex of newborns. *American Journal of Orthopsychiatry, 43*, 720–731.

Rubin, K. H., & Howe, N. (1986). Social play and perspective taking. In G. Fein & M. Rivkin (Eds.), *The young child at play: Reviews of research* (Vol. 4, pp. 113–125). Washington, DC: National Association for the Education of Young Children.

Rubin, K. H., Bukowski, W., & Parker, J. G. (1998). Peer interactions, relationships, and groups In W. Damon (Editor in Chief) & I. E. Sigel & N. Eisenberg (Vol. Ed.), *Handbook of child psychology* (5th ed., Vol. 3, pp. 619–700). New York: Wiley.

Rubin, K. H., Fein, G. G., & Vandenberg, B. (1983). Play. In P. H. Mussen (Ed.), *Handbook of child psychology* (4th ed., Vol. 4, pp. 693–775). New York: Wiley.

Rubin, K. H., Hastings, P. D., Stewart, S. L., Henderson, H. A., & Chen, X. (1997). The consistency and concomitants of inhibition: Some of the children, all of the time. *Child Development, 68*, 47–484.

Rubin, K., Bukowski, W., & Parker, J. G. (1998). Peer interactions, relationships, and groups. In W. Damon (Editor in Chief) & N. Eisenberg (Vol. Ed.), *Handbook of child psychology* (5th ed., Vol. 3, pp. 619–700). New York: Wiley.

Rubin, K.H., (1998) Social and emotional development from a cultural perspective. *Developmental Psychology, 34*, 611–616.

Rubin, R. A., & Balow, B. (1979). Measures of infant development and socioeconomic status as predictors of later intelligence and school achievement. *Developmental Psychology, 15*, 225–227.

Rubin, Z. (1980). *Children's friendships*. Cambridge, MA: Harvard University Press.

Ruble, D. N. (1988). Sex role development. In M. H. Bornstein & M. E. Lamb (Eds.), *Social, emotional and personality development* (2nd ed., pp. 411–451). Hillsdale, NJ: Erlbaum.

Ruble, D. N., & Brooks-Gunn, J. (1982). The experience of menarche. *Child Development, 53*, 1557–1566.

Ruble, D. N., & Martin, C. L. (1998). Gender development. In W. Damon (Editor in Chief) & W. Damon & N. Eisenberg (Vol. Eds.), *Handbook of child psychology* (5th ed., Vol. 3, pp. 933–1016). New York: Wiley.

Ruble, D. N., & Thompson, E. P. (1992). The implications of research on social development for mental health: an internal socialization perspective. In D. N. Ruble, P. R. Costanzo, & M. E. Oliveri (Eds.), *The social psychology of mental health: Basic mechanisms and applications*. New York: Guilford.

Ruck, M. D., Abramovitch, R., & Keating, D. P. (1998). Children's and adolescents' understanding of rights: Balancing nurturance and self-determination. *Child Development, 64*, 404–417.

Ruddy, M. G. & Bornstein, M. H. (1982). Cognitive correlates of infant attention and maternal stimulation over the first year of life. *Child Development, 53*, 183–188.

Rueter, M. A., & Conger, R. D. (1995). Antecedents of parent-adolescent disagreements. *Journal of Marriage and the family, 57*, 435–448.

Ruff, H. A., & Lawson, K. R. (1990). Development of sustained, focused attention in young children during free play. *Developmental Psychology, 26*, 85–93.

Rugh, R., & Shettles, L. B. (1971). *From contraception to birth: The drama of life's beginnings*. New York: Harper & Row.

Ruittenbeck, H. M. (1964). *The individual and the crowd: A study of identity in America*. New York: New American Library.

Ruopp, R., Travers, J., Glantz, F., & Coelen, C. (1983). Children at the center (final report of the National Day Care Study). Cited in E. Zigler & S. Muenchow, Infant day care and infant-care leaves: A policy vacuum. *American Psychologist, 38*, 91–95.

Rushworth, G. (1971). On postural and righting reflexes. In C. B. Kopp (Ed.), *Readings in early development: For occupational and physical therapy students* (pp. 6–21). Springfield, IL: Thomas.

Russell, C. (1995, December). The baby boom turns 50. *American Demographics*, pp. 23–33.

Russell, C. (1997, December). What's wrong with kids? *American Demographics*, pp. 12–16.

Rutter, M. (1979). Maternal deprivation, 1972–1978: New findings, new concepts, new approaches. *Child Development, 50*, 283–305.

Rutter, M. (1981). Social-emotional consequences of day care for pre-school children. *American Journal of Orthopsychiatry, 51*, 4–29.

Rutter, M. (1983). School effects on pupil progress: Research findings and policy implications. *Child Development, 54*, 1–29.

Rutter, M. (1985). Resilience in the face of adversity: Protective factors and resistance to psychiatric disorder. *British Journal of Psychiatry, 147*, 598–611.

Rutter, M., & Rutter, M. (1993). *Developing minds*. New York: Basic Books.

Ryan, E. J. (1994, February). Will multiculturalism undercut student individuality? *Education Digest*, pp. 26–28.

Ryan, K. (1981). *Questions and answers on moral education*. Bloomington, IN: Phi Delta Kappa Educational Foundation.

Ryan, K., & Greer, P. (1990, January). Putting moral education back in schools. *Education Digest*, pp. 31–34.

Ryan, R. M., & Lynch, J. H. (1989). Emotional autonomy versus detachment: Revising the vicissitudes of adolescence and young adulthood. *Child Development, 60*, 340–356.

Rybash, J. M., Roodin, P. A., & Hoyer, W. J. (1995). *Adult development and aging* (3rd ed.). Dubuque, IA: Brown & Benchmark.

Rychlak, J. F. (1985). Eclecticism in psychological theorizing: Good and bad. *Journal of Counseling and Development,* 63, 351–354.

S

Sabbagh, M. A., & Callanan, M. A. (1998). Metarepresentation in action: 3-, 4-, and 5- year-olds' developing theories of mind in parent-child conversations. *Developmental Psychology,* 34, 491–502.

Sachs, B., Kobelin, C., Castro, M. A., & Frigoletto, F. (1999, January 7). The risks of lowering the cesarean-delivery rate. *New England Journal of Medicine,* 340, 54–57.

Sack, J. L. (1997, December 3). Education officials cite concerns about implementing IDEA rules. *Education Week,* p. 24.

Sack, J. L. (1997, May 28). Advocacy group issues guides for diagnosing ADHD. *Education Week,* p. 9.

Sadker, M., & Sadker, D. (1985). Sexism in the schoolroom in the '80s. *Psychology Today,* 19, 54–57.

Sadker, M., & Sadker, D. (1994). *Failing at fairness: How America's schools cheat girls.* New York: Macmillan.

Saffran, J. R., Aslin, R. N., & Newport, E. C. (1996). Statistical learning by 8-month-olds *Science,* 274, 1926–1928.

Salend, S. J., & Taylor, L. (1993). Working with families: A cross-cultural perspective. *Remedial and Special Education,* 14, 25–32, 39.

Salk, L. (1960). The effects of the normal heartbeat sound on the behavior of newborn infants: Implications for mental health. *World Mental Health,* 12, 168–175.

Salkind, N. J. (1981). *Theories of human development.* New York: Van Nostrand.

Saltmarsh, R., Mitchell, P., & Robinson, E. (1995). Realism and children's early grasp of mental representation: Belief-based judgments in the state change task. *Cognition,* 57, 247–325.

Sameroff, A. J., & Cavanagh, P. J. (1979). Learning in infancy: A developmental perspective. In J. Osofsky (Ed.), *Handbook of infant development* (pp. 344–393). New York: Wiley.

Sameroff, A. J., & Chandler, M. J. (1975). Reproductive risk and the continuum of care-taker causality. In F. D. Horowitz (Ed.), *Review of child development research* (Vol. 4). Chicago: University of Chicago Press.

Sampson, P. D., Bookstein, F. L., Barr, H. M., & Streissguth, A. P. (1994). Prenatal alcohol exposure, birthweight, and measures of child size from birth to age 14 years. *American Journal of Public Health,* 84, 1421–1428.

Sande, M. A. (1986). Transmission of AIDS: The case against casual contagion. *New England Journal of Medicine,* 314, 380–382.

Sanders, J. (1987). Closing the computer gender gap in school cited. In P. Lightbody, & A. Durndell (1996). The masculine image of careers in science and technology: Fact or fantasy? *British Journal of Educational Psychology,* 66, 231–246.

Sanderson, C. A., & Cantor, N. (1995). Social dating goals in late adolescence: Implications for safer sexual activity. *Journal of Personality and Social Psychology,* 68, 1121–1134.

Sanders-Phillips, K., Strauss, M. E., & Gutberlet, R. L. (1988). The effect of obstetric medication on newborn infant feeding behavior. *Infant Behavior and Development,* 11, 251–263.

Sandham, J. L. (1997, September 3). Math scores rise, verbal scores stay flat on SAT, ACT. *Education Week,* p. 12.

Sandler, I. N., Tein, J. Y., & West, S. G. (1994). Coping, stress, and the psychological symptoms of children of divorce: A cross-sectional and longitudinal study. *Child Development,* 65, 1744–1763.

Sansavini, A., Bertoncini, J., & Giovanelli, G. (1997). Newborns discriminate the rhythm of multisyllable stressed words. *Developmental Psychology,* 23, 3–12.

Santrock, J. W. (1972). Relation of type and onset of father absence to cognitive development. *Child Development,* 43, 455–469.

Sarafino, E. P. (1994). *Health psychology.* New York: Wiley.

Sarafino, E. . (1996). *Principles of behavior change.* New York: Wiley.

Sarnoff, I. (1971). *Testing Freudian concepts: An experimental social approach.* New York: Springer.

Satcher, D. (1995, June 9). Is the new vaccines for children program improving immunization rates in the United States. Yes. *CQ Researcher,* 5, 505.

Satz, P., Strauss, E., & Whitaker, H. (1990) The ontogeny of hemispheric specialization: Some old hypotheses revisited. *Brain and Language,* 38, 596–614.

Saudino, K. J., & Plomin, R. (1996). Tester-rated temperament at 14, 20 and 24 months: Environmental change and genetic continuity. *British Journal of Developmental Psychology,* 14, 129–144.

Saunders, S. E., & Carroll, J. (1988). The use of Whole cow's milk in infancy. *Journal of the American Dietetic Association,* 88, 213–215.

Sautter, R. C. (1992, November). Crack: Healing the children. *Phi Delta Kappan* (Kappan Special Report), pp. K1–K12.

Savage, M. P., & Scott, L. B. (1998). Physical inactivity and rural middle school adolescents. *Journal of Youth and Adolescence,* 27, 245–252.

Savin-Williams, R. C. (1988). Theoretical perspectives accounting for adolescent homosexuality. *Journal of Adolescent Health Care,* 9, 95–105.

Savin-Williams, R. C. (1996). Ethnic-and sexual-minority youth. In R.C. Savin-Williams & K. M. Cohen (Eds.), *The lives of lesbians, gays, and bisexuals: Children to adults* (pp. 152–165). Fort Worth, TX: Harcourt Brace.

Savin-Williams, R. C., & Dube, E. M. (1998). Parental reactions to their child's disclosure of a gay/lesbian identity. *Family Relations,* 47, 7–13.

Savin-Williams, R. C., & Small, S. A. (1986). The timing of puberty and its relationship to adolescent and parent perceptions of family interactions. *Developmental Psychology,* 22, 342–348.

Savitz, D. A. Schwingle, P. J., & Keels, M. A. (1991). Influence of paternal age, smoking, and alcohol consumption on congenital anomalies. *Teratology,* 44, 429–440.

Sax, L. J., Astin, A. W., Korn, W. S., & Mahoney, K. M. (1995). *The American freshman: National norms for 1995.* Los Angeles: Higher Education Research Institute, UCLA.

Sayler, M. E., & Brookshire, W. K. (1993). Social, emotional, and behavioral adjustment of accelerated students, students in gifted classes, and regular students in eighth grade. *Gifted Child Quarterly,* 37, 150–154.

Scales, P. (1984). Sex education policies and the primary prevention of teenage pregnancy. Cited in Allgeier, E. R., & Allgeier, A. R., *Sexual interactions.* Lexington, MA: Heath.

Scarr, S. (1986). How plastic are we? *Contemporary Psychology,* 31, 565–567.

Scarr, S. (1992). Developmental theories for the 1990s: Development and individual differences. *Child Development,* 63, 1–20.

Scarr, S. (1993). Biological and cultural diversity: The legacy of Darwin for development. *Child Development,* 64, 1333–1354.

Scarr, S. (1998). American child care today. *American Psychologist,* 53, 95–108.

Scarr, S., & Eisenberg, M. (1993). Child care research: Issues, perspectives, and results. *Annual Review of Psychology,* 44, 613–644.

Scarr, S., & Kidd, K. K. (1983). Developmental behavior genetics. In P. H. Mussen (Ed.), *Handbook of child psychology* (4th ed., Vol. 2, pp. 345–433). New York: Wiley.

Scarr, S., & McCartney, K. (1983). How people make their own environments: A theory of genotype-environment effects. *Child Development,* 54, 424–435.

Scarr, S., Eisenberg, M., & Deater-Deckard, K. (1994). Measurement of quality in child care centers. *Early Childhood Research Quarterly,* 9, 131–151.

Scarr, S. (1998) American child care today. *American Psychologist,* 53, 95–108.

Scarr-Salapatek, S. (1975). Genetics and the development of intelligence. In E. M. Hetherington, S. Scarr-Salapatek, & G. M. Siegel (Eds.), *Review of child development research* (Vol. 4, pp. 1–58). Chicago: University of Chicago Press.

Schachter, F. F. (1981). Toddlers with employed mothers. *Child Development, 52,* 958–964.

Schachter, J. (1989). Why we need a program for the control of chlamydia trachomatis. *New England Journal of Medicine, 320,* 802–803.

Schaffer, H. R. (1996). *Social development,* Oxford: Blackwell.

Schaffer, K. F. (1981). *Sex roles and human behavior.* Cambridge, MA: Winthrop.

Schaffer, R. (1977). *Mothering.* Cambridge, MA: Harvard University Press.

Schaie, K. W. (1994). The course of adult intellectual development. *American Psychologist, 49,* 304–313.

Scher, A., Tirosh, E., Jaffe, M., Rubin, L., Sadeh, A., & Lavie, P. (1995). Sleep patterns of infants and young children in Israel. *International Journal of Behavioral Development, 18,* 701–711.

Scherling, D. (1994). Prenatal cocaine exposure and childhood psychopathology. *American Journal of Orthopsychiatry, 64,* 9–19.

Schiedel, D. G., & Marcia, J. E. (1985). Ego identity, intimacy, sex role orientation and gender. *Developmental Psychology, 21,* 149–160.

Schiever, S. W., & Maker, C. J. (1991). Enrichment and acceleration: An overview and new directions. In N. Colangelo & G. David (Eds.), *Handbook of gifted education* (pp. 99–111). Needham Heights: MA: Allyn & Bacon.

Schilmoeller, G. L., Baranowski, M. D., & Higgins, B. S. (1991). Long-term support and personal adjustment of adolescent and older mothers. *Adolescence, 26,* 787–797.

Schlicker, S. A., Borra, S. T., & Regan, C. (1994). The weight and fitness status of United States children. *Nutrition Reviews, 52,* 11–17.

Schmidt, P. (1994, September). Idea of "gender" gap" under attack. *Education Week,* pp. 1, 16.

Schmitt, M. H. (1979, July). Superiority of breast-feeding: Fact or fancy. *American Journal of Nursing,* pp. 1488–1493.

Schmitz, S., Saudino, K. J., Plomin, R., Fulker, D. W., & DeFries, J. C. (1996). Genetic and environmental influences on temperament in middle childhood: Analyses of teacher and tester ratings. *Child Development, 67,* 409–422.

Schnaiberg, L. (1996a, January 17). Educating Rafael. *Education Week,* pp. 18–26.

Schnaiberg, L. (1996b, August 7). Hispanic immigrants trail other groups, study says. *Education Week,* pp. 12.

Schnaiberg, L. (1997a, April 30). Language and program limits at issue across states. *Education Week,* p. 6.

Schnaiberg, L. (1997b, May 5). The politics of language. *Education Week,* pp. 25–27.

Schnaiberg, L. (1998, January 14). Bilingual ed. initiative all set to go before voters in June. *Education Week,* p. 28.

Schneider, M.L., Roughton, E.C., & Lubach, G.R. (1997) Moderate alcohol consumption and psychological stress during pregnancy induces attention and neuromotor impairments in primate infants. *Child Development, 68,* 747–759.

Schneider, W., & Bjorklund, D. F. (1998). Memory, In W. Damon (Ed.), *Handbook of child psychology* (4th ed., Vol. 2, pp. 467–523). New York: Wiley.

Schneider, W., & Pressley, M. (1989). *Memory development between 2 and 20.* New York: Springer.

Schneider-Rosen, K., & Wenz-Gross, M. (1990). Patterns of compliance from eighteen to thirty months of age. *Child Development, 61,* 104–112.

Schoeber-Peterson, D., & Johnson, C.J. (1991) Non-dialogue speech during preschool interactions. *Journal of Child Language, 18,* 153–170

School Board News. (1997, January 14). Ebonics: Rush to judgment? Author: National School Boards Association.

Schuckit, M. A. (1986). Genetic and clinical implications of alcoholism and affective disorder. *American Journal of Psychiatry, 143,* 140–153.

Schuckit, M. A. (1987). Biological vulnerability to alcoholism. *Journal of Consulting and Clinical Psychology, 55,* 301–309.

Schuckit, M. A. (1994). A clinical model of genetic influences in alcohol dependence. *Journal of the Studies of Alcohol, 55,* 5–17.

Schuckit, M. A., Tsuang, J. W., Anthenelli, R. M., Tipp, J. E., & Nurnberger, J. I. (1996). Alcohol challenges in young men from alcohol pedigrees and control families: A report from the COGA project. *Journal of the Studies of Alcohol, 57,* 368–377.

Schuklenk, U., & Ristow, M. (1996). The ethics of research into the cause(s). of homosexuality. *Journal of Homosexuality, 31,* 5–30.

Schultz, E. A., & Levenda, R. H. (1987). *Cultural anthropology.* St. Paul, MN: West.

Schuster, M. A., Bell, R. M., Berry, T., & Kanouse, W. F. (1998). Impact of a high school condom availability program on sexual attitudes and behaviors. *Family Planning Perspectives, 30,* 67–73.

Schwebel, D. C., & Plumert, J. M. (1999). Longitudinal and concurrent relations among temperament, ability estimation, and injury proneness. *Child Development, 70,* 700–712.

Scott, C. G., Murray, G. C., Mertens, C., & Dustin, E. R. (1996). Student self-esteem and the school system: Perceptions and implications. *Journal of Educational Research, 89,* 286–294.

Scott, C. S ., Shifman, L., Or, L., Owen, R. G., & Fawcett, N. (1988). Hispanic and black American adolescents' beliefs relating to sexuality and contraception. *Adolescence, 23,* 667–688.

Scott, M. E. (1988, Spring). Learning strategies can help. *Teaching Exceptional Children,* pp. 30–34.

Seachrist, L. (1995, July 15). Nicotine plays deadly role in infant death. *Science News,* p. 39.

Searey, S. (1988). Developing self-esteem. *Academic Therapy, 23,* 453–460.

Sears, R. R., Maccoby, E. E., & Levin, H. (1957). *Patterns of child rearing.* New York: Harper & Row.

Sears, R. R., Roe, L., & Alpert, R. (1965). *Identification and child rearing.* Stanford, CA: Stanford University Press.

Sebald, H. (1989). Adolescents' peer orientation: Changes in the support system during the past three decades. *Adolescence, 96,* 937–945.

Segal, B. M., & Stewart, J. C. (1996). Substance use and abuse in adolescence: An overview *Human Development, 26,* 193–210.

Segalowitz, N. S. (1981). Issues in the cross-cultural study of bilingual development. In H. C. Triandis & A. Heron (Eds.), *Handbook of cross-cultural psychology* (Vol. 4, pp. 55–93). Boston: Allyn & Bacon.

Seifer, R., Schiller, M., Sameroff, A., Resnick, S., & Riordan, K. (1996). Attachment, maternal sensitivity, and infant temperament during the first year of life. *Developmental Psychology, 32,* 12–25.

Seitz, V., & Apfel, N. H. (1994). Effects of a school for pregnant students on the incidence of low-birthweight deliveries. *Child Development, 65,* 409–414.

Seligman, M. (1991) Family systems and beyond: Conceptual issues. in M. Seligman (ed). *The family with a handicapped child.* 2nd ed. Boston: Allyn & Bacon

Seligmann, J. (1990, Winter/Spring). Variation on a theme. *Newsweek* (special ed., The 21st Century Family), pp. 38–46.

Selkoe, D. J. (1991, November). Amyloid protein and Alzheimer's disease. *Scientific American,* pp. 68–78.

Sellers, D. E., McGraw, S. A., & McKinlay, J. B. (1994). Does the promotion and distribution of condoms increase teen sexual activity? Evidence from an HIV prevention program for Latino youth. *American Journal of Public Health, 84,* 1952–1959.

Sells, C. W., & Blum, R. M. (1996). Morbidity and mortality among US adolescents: An overview of data and trends. *American Journal of Public Health, 86,* 513–519.

Selman, R. L. (1981). The child as a friendship philosopher. In S. R. Asher & J. M. Gottman (Eds.), *The development of children's friendships* (pp. 242–273). Cambridge, MA: Cambridge University Press.

Serbin, L. A., Powlishta, K. K., & Gulko, J. (1993). The development of sex typing in middle childhood. *Monographs of the Society for Research in Child Development, 58*(2), Serial No. 232.

Serrano, J. M., Iglesias, J., & Loeches, A. (1995). Infants' responses to adult static facial expressions. *Infant Behavior and Development, 18,* 477–482.

Sex education fires controversy over teaching "hostile" values. (1996, October 25). *CQ Researcher, 6,* 946–948.

Sexias, J. S., & Youcha, G. (1985). *Children of alcoholism.* New York: Crown.

Shaffer, D., Garland, A., Vieland, V., Underwood, M., & Busner, C. (1991). The impact of curriculum-based suicide prevention programs for teenagers. *Journal of the American Academy of Child and Adolescent Psychiatry, 30,* 588–596.

Shafii, M., Carrigan, S., Whittinghill, J. R., & Derrick, A. (1985). Psychological autopsy of completed suicide in children and adolescents. *American Journal of Psychiatry, 142,* 1061–1064.

Shalala, D. E. (1993, April). Giving pediatric immunizations the priority they deserve. *Journal of the American Medical Association,* p. 1845.

Shanks, D. (1993, January 30). Breaking Chomsky's rules. *New Scientist,* pp. 26–29.

Shantz, C. U. (1983). Social cognition. In J. H. Flavell & E. M. Markman (Eds.), *Handbook of child psychology* (4th ed., Vol. 3, pp. 495–556). New York: Wiley.

Shantz, C. U. (1987). Conflicts between children. *Child Development, 58,* 283–306.

Shatz, M. (1983) Social cognition. In P.H. Mussen (Ed.) *Handbook of child psychology: Cognitive development* (4th ed, pp. 841–891). New York: Wiley.

Shaver, J. P., & Strong, W. (1976). *Facing value decisions: Rationale-building for teachers.* Belmont, CA: Wadsworth.

Shaw, D. S., & Vondra, J. I. (1993). Chronic family adversity and infant attachment security. *Journal of Child Psychology and Psychiatry, 34,* 1205–1215.

Shaw, D. S., Keenan, K., & Vondra, J. I. (1994). Developmental precursors of externalizing behavior: Ages 1 to 3. *Developmental Psychology, 30,* 355–364.

Shaw, D. S., Winslow, E. M., & Flanagan, C. (1999). A prospective study of the effects of marital status and family relations on young children's adjustment among African American and European American families. *Child Development, 70,* 742–755.

Shedler, J., & Block, J. (1990). Adolescent drug use and psychological health: A longitudinal inquiry. *American Psychologist, 45,* 612–630.

Shell, R., & Eisenberg, N. (1990). The role of peers' gender in children's naturally occurring interest in toys. *International Journal of Behavioral Development, 13,* 373–388.

Shepard, L. A., & Smith, M. L. (1986). Synthesis of research on school readiness and kindergarten retention. *Educational Leadership, 44,* 78–86.

Shestowsky, B. (1983). Ego identity development and obesity in adolescent girls. *Adolescence, 71,* 550–559.

Shinn, M., Knickman, J. R., & Weitzman, B. C. (1991). Social relationships and vulnerability to becoming homeless among poor families. *American Psychologist, 46,* 1180–1187.

Shiono, P. H., & Behrman, R. E. (1995, Spring). Low birth weight: Analysis and recommendations. In *The future of children: Low birth weight* (pp. 4–18). Los Altos, CA: David and Lucile Packard Foundation.

Shiono, P. H., Rauh, V. A., Park, M., Lederman, S. A., & Zuskar, D. (1997). Ethic differences in birthweight: The role of lifestyle and other factors. *American Journal of Public Health, 87,* 787–793.

Shirley, M. M. (1931). *The first two years: A study of twenty-five babies: Vol. 1. Postural and locomotor development.* Minneapolis: University of Minnesota Press.

Shirley, M. M. (1933). *The first two years: A study of twenty-five babies: Vol. 2. Intellectual development.* Minneapolis: University of Minnesota Press.

Shonkoff, J. P., & Hauser-Cram, P. (1987). Early intervention for disabled infants for disabled infants and their families: A quantitative analysis. *Pediatrics, 80,* 650–658.

Shore, R. E. (1995). Editorial: Epidemiologic data in risk assessment-imperfect but valuable. *American Journal of Public Health, 85,* 474–475.

Short, E. J., Schatschneider, C. W., & Friebert, S. E. (1993). Relationship between memory and metamemory performance: A comparison of specific and general strategy knowledge. *Journal of Educational Psychology, 85,* 412–423.

Shultz, T.R. (1974) Development of the appreciation of riddles. *Child Development, 45,* 100–105.

Shweder, R. A., Mahapatra, M., & Miller, J.G. (1987). Culture and moral development. In J. Kagan & S. Lamb (Eds.), *The emergence of morality in young children* (pp. 1–83). Chicago: University of Chicago Press.

Sibinga, M. S., & Friedman, C. J. (1971). Complexities of parental understanding of phenylketonuria. *Pediatrics, 48,* 216–224.

Siegel, J., & Shaughnesy, M. F. (1995). There's a first time for everything: Understanding adolescence. *Adolescence, 30,* 217–222.

Siegel, L. J., & Senna, J. J. (1991). *Juvenile delinquency* (4th ed.). St. Paul, MN: West.

Siegel, O. (1982). Personality development in adolescence. In B. B. Wolman (Ed.), *Handbook of developmental psychology* (pp. 537–549). Upper Saddle River, NJ: Prentice Hall.

Siegler, R. S. (1991). *Children's thinking* (2nd ed.). Upper Saddle River, NJ: Prentice Hall.

Siegler, R. S. (1998). *Children's thinking* (3rd. ed.). Upper Saddle River, NJ: Prentice Hall.

Sigelman, C. K., & Waitzman, K. A. (1991). The development of distributive justice orientations: Contextual influences on children's resource allocations. *Child Development, 62,* 1367–1378.

Signorella, M. L., Bigler, R. S., & Liben, L. S. (1993). Developmental differences in children's gender schemata about others: A meta-analytic review. *Developmental Review, 13,* 147–183.

Signorella, M. L., & Liben, L. S. (1984). Recall and reconstruction of gender-related pictures: Effects of attitude, task difficulty, and age. *Child Development, 55,* 393–405.

Silver, L.B. (1990) Attention deficit hyperactivity disorder: Is it a learning disability or a related disorder? *Journal of Learning Disabilities, 23,* 394–397.

Silverman, E. H. (1995). *Speech, language, and hearing disorders.* Needham, MA: Allyn & Bacon.

Silverman, W. K., La Greca, A. M. & Waserstein, S. (1995). What do children worry about? Worries and their relation to anxiety. *Child Development, 66,* 671–686.

Silverstein, L. B., & Auerbach, C. F. (1999). Deconstructing the essential father. *American Psychologist, 54,* 397–407.

Simkin, P., Whalley, J., & Keppler, A. (1984). *Pregnancy, childbirth, and the newborn.* Deephaven, MN: Meadowbrook.

Simmons, R. G., & Blyth, D. A. (1987). *Moving into adolescence: the impact of pubertal change and school context.* Hawthorne, NJ: Aldine.

Simmons, R. G., Blyth, D. A., Van Cleave, E. F., & Bush, D. M. (1979). Entry into early adolescence: The impact of school structure, puberty, and early dating on self-esteem. *American Sociological Review, 38,* 553–568.

Simner, M. L. (1971). Newborn's response to the cry of another infant. *Developmental Psychology, 5,* 136–150.

Simons, C., McCluskey, K., & Mullett, M. (1985). Interparental ratings of temperament for high and low risk infants. *Child Psychiatry and Human Development, 15,* 1678–1679.

Simons, R. G., & Blyth, D. A. (1987). *Moving into adolescence: the impact of pubertal change and school context.* Hawthorne, NY: Aldine & deGruyter.

Singer, D. G., & Singer, J. L. (1976). Family television viewing habits and the spontaneous play of preschool children. *American Journal of Orthopsychiatry, 46,* 496–502.

Singer, J. L., & Singer, D. G. (1983). Psychologists look at television: Cognitive, developmental, personality, and social policy implications. *American Psychologist, 38,* 826–835.

Singer, J.D., Fuller, B., Keiley, M.K. & Wolf, A. (1999) Early child-care selection: Variation by geographic location, maternal characteristics, and family structure. *Developmental Psychology, 34,* 1129–1144.

Singer, L.T., Salvator, A., Guo, S., Collin, M., Lilien, L., & Baley, J. (1999, March 3). Maternal psychological distress and parenting stress after the birth of a very low-birth-weight infant. *Journal of the American Medical Association, 281,* 799–805.

Singer, S., & Hilgard, H. R. (1978). *The biology of people.* San Francisco: Freeman.

Sinister evolution. (1995, August 26). *The Economist, 336,* 69–71.

Sinister origins. (1997, February 15). *The Economist,* pp. 80–83.

Sinnott, J. D. (1981). The theory of relativity. *Human Development, 24,* 293–311.

Sinnott, J. D. (1984). Postformal reasoning: The relativistic stage. In M. L. Commons, F. A. Richards, & C. Armon (Eds.), *Beyond formal operations* (pp. 298–326). New York: Praeger.

Sirignano, S. W., & Lachman, M. E. (1985). Personality change during the transition to parenthood: The role of perceived infant temperament. *Developmental Psychology, 21,* 558–567.

Sizer, F. S., & Whitney, E. N. (1988). *Life choices: Health concepts and strategies.* St. Paul, MN: West.

Skarin, K. (1977). Cognitive and contextual determinants of stranger fear in six- and eleven-month-old infants. *Child Development, 48,* 537–544.

Skeels, H. M. (1966). Adult status of children with contrasting early life experiences: A follow-up study. *Monographs of the Society for Research in Child Development, 31*(3).

Skinner, B. F. (1957). *Verbal behavior.* New York: Appleton-Century-Croft.

Skuse, D. (1997). Editorial. *Journal of Child Psychology and Psychiatry, 38,* 387–388.

Slaby, R. G., & Frey, K. S. (1975). Development of gender constancy and selective attention to same-sex models. *Child Development, 46,* 849–856.

Slater, A., Johnson, S. P., Kellman, P. J., & Spelke, E. S. (1994). The role of three dimensional depth cues in infants' perception of partly occluded objects. *Early Development and Parenting, 3,* 187–191.

Slaughter-Defoe, D., Nakagawa, K., Takanishi, R., & Johnson, D. J. (1990). Toward cultural/ecological perspectives on schooling and achievement in African-and Asian-American children. *Child Development, 61,* 363–383.

Slobin, D. I. (1972, July). Children and language: They learn the same way all around the world. *Psychology Today,* pp. 18+.

Slonim, M. B. (1991). *Children, culture and ethnicity.* New York: Garland.

Small, M. Y. (1990). *Cognitive Development,* San Diego, CA: Harcourt, Brace, Jovanovich.

Smart, D. E., Beaumont, P. J., & George, G. C. (1976). Some personality characteristics of patients with anorexia nervosa. *British Journal of Psychiatry, 128,* 57–60.

Smart, M. S., & Smart, R. C. (1978). *School-age children: Development and relationships* (2nd ed.). New York: Macmillan.

Smetana, J. G. (1986). Preschool children's conceptions of sex-role transgressions. *Child Development, 57,* 862–871.

Smetana, J. G. (1989). Adolescents' and parents' reasoning about actual family conflict. *Child Development, 60,* 1052–1067.

Smetana, J.G., & Asquith, P. (1994) Adolescents' and parents' conceptions of parental authority. *Child Development, 65,* 1147–1162.

Smith, C., & Lloyd, B. (1978). Maternal behavior and perceived sex of infant: Revisited. *Child Development, 49,* 1263–1265.

Smith, G. E., Gerrard, M., & Gibbons, F. X. (1997). Self-esteem and the relation between risk behavior and perceptions of vulnerability to unplanned pregnancy in college women. *Health Psychology, 16,* 137–146.

Smith, R. E., & Smoll, F. L. (1990). Self-esteem and children's reactions to youth sport coaching behaviors: A field study of self-enhancement. *Developmental Psychology, 26,* 987–993.

Smith, S. (Ed.). *Two-generation programs for families in poverty: A new intervention strategy.* Norwood, NJ: Ablex.

Smith, T. E. C. (1987). *Introduction to education.* St. Paul, MN: West.

Smitherman, G. (1997). Black language and the education of Black children: One mo' once. *Black Scholar, 27,* 28–36.

Smitherman, G., & Cunningham, S. (1997). Moving beyond resistance: Ebonics and African American youth. *Journal of Black Psychology, 23,* 227–233.

Snow, C.W. (1998) *Child development* (2nd ed.). Upper Saddle River, NJ: Prentice Hall.

Snyderman, M., & Rothman, S. (1987). Survey of expert opinion on intelligence and aptitude testing. *American Psychologist, 42,* 137–144.

Sobal, J., Nicolopoulos, V., & Lee, J. (1995). Attitudes about overweight and dating among secondary school students. *International Journal of Obesity, 19,* 376–381.

Sobesky, W. E. (1983). The effects of situational factors on moral judgments. *Child Development, 54,* 575–584.

Socalar, R. S., & Stein, R. E. K. (1996). Maternal discipline of young children: Context, belief, and practice. *Developmental and Behavioral Pediatrics, 17,* 1–8.

Socha, T. J., & Kelly, B. (1994). Children making "fun": Humorous communication, impression management, and moral development. *Child Study Journal, 24,* 237–252.

Sodowsky, G. R., & Carey, J. C. (1988). Relationship between acculturation-related demographics and cultural attitudes of an Asian-Indian immigrant group. *Journal of Multicultural Counseling and Development, 16,* 117–136.

Sokolov, J. L. (1993). A local contingency analysis of the fine-tuning hypothesis. *Developmental Psychology, 29,* 1008–1023.

Solnit, A. J., Call, J. D., & Feinstein, C. B. (1979). Psychosexual development: Five to ten years. In J. D. Noshpitz (Ed.), *Basic handbook of child psychiatry* (pp. 184–190). New York: Basic Books.

Somerville, S. C., Wellman, H. M., & Cultice, J. C. (1983). Young children's deliberate reminding. *Journal of Genetic Psychology, 143,* 87–96.

Sommer, B. B. (1978). *Puberty and adolescence.* New York: Oxford University Press.

Sommerfeld, M. (1996, May 8). Math, science test scores up, NSF reports. *Education Week,* p. 6.

Sontag, L. W. (1941). The significance of fetal environmental differences. *American Journal of Obstetrics and Gynecology, 42,* 996–1003.

Sontag, L.W. (1944). War and the fetal-maternal relationship. *Marriage and Family Living, 6,* 3–4.

Sorce, J. F., Emde, R. N., Campos, J., & Klinnert, M. D. (1985). Maternal emotional signaling: Its effect on the visual cliff behavior of 1-year-olds. *Developmental Psychology, 21,* 195–200.

Sorensen, E. (1997). A national profile of non-resident fathers and their ability to pay child support. *Journal of Marriage and the Family, 59,* 785–797.

Sorenson, R. C. (1973). *The Sorenson report: Adolescent sexuality in contemporary America.* New York: World.

Sorenson, T., & Snow, B. (1991). How children tell: The process of disclosure in child sexual abuse. *Child Welfare, 70,* 3–15.

South, S. J., & Spitze, G. (1994). Housework in marital and nonmarital households. *American Sociological Review, 59,* 327–347.

Spade, J.Z. (1996). Fraternities and collegiate rape culture. *Gender and Society, 10,* 133–148.

Spaide, D. (1995). *Teaching your kids to care: How do discover and develop the spirit of charity in your children.* New York: Citadel.

Spelke, E. S., & Newport, E. L. (1998). Nativism, empiricism, and the development of knowledge. in W. Damon (Editor in Chief) & R. M. Lerner (Vol. Ed.), *Handbook of child psychology* (5th ed., Vol. 1, pp. 275–340). New York: Wiley.

Spencer, M. B., & Markstrom-Adams, C. (1990). Identity processes among racial and ethnic minority children in America. *Child Development, 61,* 290–311.

Spencer, M. B., Dupress, D., Swanson, D. P., & Cunningham, M. (1998). The influence of physical maturation and hassles on African American adolescents' learning behaviors. *Journal of Comparative Family Studies, 27,* 189–200.

Sperber, A. N., & L. F. Jarvik (Eds.). (1976). *Psychiatry and genetics.* New York: Basic Books.

Spitz, R. (1945). Hospitalism: An inquiry into the genesis of psychiatric conditions in early childhood. *Psychoanalytic Study of the Child, 1*, 53.

Spitz, R. (1965). *The first year of life: A psychoanalytic study of normal and deviant development of object relations.* New York: International Universities Press.

Sprafkin, J. N., Liebert, R. M., & Poulos, R. W. (1975). Effects of a prosocial televised example on children's helping. *Journal of Experimental Child Psychology, 20,* 119–126.

Sprafkin, J., Gadow, K. D., & Abelman, R. (1992). *Television and the exceptional child: A forgotten audience.* Hillsdale, NJ: Erlbaum.

Sprafkin, J., Watkins, L. T., & Gadow, K. D. (1990). Efficacy of television literacy curriculum for emotionally disturbed and learning disabled children. *Journal of Applied Developmental Psychology, 11,* 225–244.

Sprintall, N. A., & Collins, W. A. (1984). *Adolescent psychology: A developmental view.* New York: Random House.

Sroufe, L. A. (1985). Attachment classification from the perspective of infant-caregiver relationships and infant temperament. *Child Development, 56,* 1–14.

Sroufe, L. A., & Wunsch, J. (1972). The development of laughter in the first year of life. *Child Development, 43,* 1326–1344.

Sroufe, L. A., Carlson, E., & Shulman, S. (1993). Individuals in relationships: Development from infancy through adolescence. In D. C. Funder, R. D. Parke, C. Tomlinson-Keasey, & K. Widaman (Eds.), *Studying lives through time* (pp. 315–343). Washington, DC: American Psychological Association.

St. Pierre, R., Layzer, J., & Barnes, H. (1995). Two-generation programs: Design, cost, and short-term effectiveness. *Future of Children, 5,* 76–93.

Stack, D.M., & Muir, D.W. (1992) Adult tactile stimulation during face-to-face interactions modulates five-month-olds' affect and attention. *Child Development, 63,* 1509–1525.

Stagno, S., & Whitley, R. J. (1985). Herpes simplex virus and varicella-zoster virus infections. *New England Journal of Medicine, 313,* 1327–1329.

Stainback, S., & Stainback, W. (1991). Schools as inclusive communities. In S. Stainback, & W. Stainback (Eds.), *Controversial Issues confronting special education* (pp. 27–44). Needham Heights, MA: Allyn & Bacon.

Stainback, W., & Stainback, S. (1984). A rationale for the merger of special and regular education. *Exceptional Children, 51,* 102–111.

Stangor, C., & Lange, J. E. (1994). Mental representation of social groups: Advances in understanding stereotypes and stereotyping. *Advances in Experimental Social Psychology, 26,* 357–416.

Stanovich, K.E. (1986) Matthew effects in reading: Some consequences of individual differences in the acquisition of literacy. *Reading Research Quarterly, 21,* 360–406.

Stark, E. (1986, May). Friends through it all. *Psychology Today,* pp. 54–60.

Statistical Abstract, U.S. Department of Commerce. (1996). *Statistical abstract of the United States.* Washington, DC: Author.

Stechler, G., & Halton, A. (1982). Prenatal influences on human development. In B. B. Wolman (Ed.), *Handbook of developmental psychology* (pp. 175–189). Upper Saddle River, NJ: Prentice Hall.

Steele, H., Steele, M., & Fonagy, P. (1996). Associations among attachment classifications of mothers, fathers, and their infants. *Child Development, 67,* 541–555.

Stefanatou, A., & Bowler, D. (1997). Depiction of pain in the self-drawings of children with sickle cell disease. *Child: Care, Health and Development, 23,* 135–155.

Stehlin, D. (1995). Feeding baby: Nature and nurture. *FDA Consumer,* Publication Number (FDA) 95–2236.

Stein, J. A., Newcomb, M. D., & Bentler, P. M. (1993). Differential effects of parent and grandparent drug use on behavior problems of male and female children. *Developmental Psychology, 29,* 31–43.

Steinbacher, R., & Gilroy, F.D. (1996) Technology for sex selection: Current status and utilization. *Psychological Reports, 79,* 28–731.

Steinberg, L. (1987). Single parents, stepparents, and the susceptibility of adolescents to antisocial peer pressure. *Child Development, 58,* 269–275.

Steinberg, L. (1988). Reciprocal relation between parent-child distance and pubertal maturation. *Developmental Psychology, 24,* 122–128.

Steinberg, L. (1989a). *Adolescence* (2nd ed.). New York: McGraw-Hill.

Steinberg, L. (1989b). Pubertal maturation and parent-adolescent distance: An evolutionary perspective. In G. Adams, R. Montemayor, & T. Gulotta (Eds.), *Advances in adolescent development* (Vol.1, pp. 82–114). Beverly Hills, Cal.: Sage.

Steinberg, L. (1996). *Adolescence* (4th ed.). New York: McGraw-Hill.

Steinberg, L. D., Catalano, R., & Dooley, D. (1981). Economic antecedents of child abuse. *Child Development, 52,* 975–985.

Steinberg, L. D., Fegley, S., & Dornbusch, S. M. (1993). negative impact of part-time work on adolescent adjustment: Evidence from a longitudinal study. *Developmental Psychology, 29,* 171–180.

Steinberg, L., & Levine, A. (1991). *You and your adolescent: A parents' guide for ages 10 to 20.* New York: Harper Perennial.

Steinberg, L., & Silverberg, S. B. (1986). The vicissitudes of autonomy in early adolescence. *Child Development, 57,* 841–851.

Steinberg, L., Brown, B., & Dornbusch, S. (1996). *Beyond the classroom: Why school reform has failed and what parents need to do.* New York: Simon & Schuster.

Steinberg, L., Elmen, J. D., & Mounts, N. S. (1989). Authoritative parenting, psychosocial maturity, and academic success among adolescents. *Child Development, 60,* 1424–1436.

Steinberg, L., Greenberger, E., Garduque, L., & McAuliffe, S. (1982). Students in the labor force: Some costs and benefits to schooling and learning. *Evaluation and Policy Analysis, 4,* 363–372.

Steinberg, M. H. (1999, April 1). Management of sickle cell disease. *New England Journal of Medicine, 340,* 1021–1029.

Stephenson, A. L., Henry, C. , & Robinson, L. C. (1996). Family characteristics and adolescence substance abuse. *Adolescence, 31,* 59–77.

Stephenson, J. (1997, April 2). Threatened bans on human cloning research could hamper advances. *Journal of the American Medical Association, 277,* 1023–1025.

Stephenson, J. (1998, October 21). Human genome project on fast track. *Journal of the American Medical Association, 280,* 1298.

Stephenson, J. (1999, January 13). New method to repair faulty genes stirs interest in chimeraplasty technique. *Journal of the American Medical Association, 281,* 119–121.

Stern, D. N., Spieker, S., & MacKain, K. (1982). Intonation contours as signals in maternal speech to prelinguistic infants. *Developmental Psychology, 18,* 727–736.

Stern, R. C. (1997, February 13). The diagnosis of cystic fibrosis. *New England Journal of Medicine,* pp. 487–491.

Sternberg, K. J., Lamb, M. E., Greenbaum, C., Cicchetti, D., Dawud, S., Cortes, R. M., Krispin, O., & Lorey, F. (1993). Effects of domestic violence on children's behavior problems and depression. *Developmental Psychology, 29,* 44–52.

Sternberg, R. J. (1985). General intellectual ability. In R. J. Sternberg (Ed.), *Mechanisms of cognitive development* (pp.163–187). New York: Freeman.

Stevens-Long, J., & Commons, M. L. (1992). *Adult Life* (Fourth Edition). Mountain View, Cal.: Mayfield.

Stevenson, H. W. (1991). The development of prosocial behavior in large-scale collective societies: China and Japan. In R. A. Hinde & J. Groebel (Eds.), *Cooperation and prosocial behaviour.* Cambridge: Cambridge University Press.

Stevenson, H. W., Chen, C., & Lee, S. Y. (1993). Mathematics achievement of Chinese, Japanese & American children: Ten years later. *Science,* pp. 259, 53–58.

Stevenson, R. E. (1973). *The fetus and newly born infant: Influences of the prenatal environment.* St. Louis, MO: Mosby.

Steward, M. S., & Steward, D. S. (1996). Interviewing young children about body touch and handling. *Monographs of the Society for Research in Child Development, 61,* Serial No. 248, Nos. 4–5.

Stice, E., & Barrera, M. Jr. (1995) A longitudinal examination of the reciprocal relations between perceived parenting and adolescents' substance use and externalizing behaviors. *Developmental Psychology*, 31, 322–334.

Stipek, D. J., Gralinski, H., & Kopp, C. B. (1990). Self-concept development in the toddler years. *Developmental Psychology*, 26, 972–977.

Stipek, D., Feiler, R., Daniels, D., & Milburn, S. (1995). Effects of different instructional approaches on young children's achievement and motivation. *Child Development*, 66, 209–223.

Stipek, D.J., & Ryan, R.H. (1997) Economically disadvantaged preschoolers: Ready to learn but further to go. *Developmental Psychology*, 33, 711–726.

Stockdale, D. F., Hegland, S. M., & Chiaromonte, T. (1989). Helping behaviors: An observational study of preschool children. *Early Childhood Research Quarterly*, 4, 533–544.

Stocker, C., Dunn, J., & Plomin, R. (1989). Sibling relationships: Links with child temperament, Maternal behavior, and family structure. *Child Development*, 60, 715–728.

Stoneman, Z., & Brody, G. H. (1993). Sibling temperaments, conflict, warmth, and role asymmetry. *Child Development*, 64, 1786–1800.

Stoney, L., & Greenberg, M. H. (1996). The financing of child care: Current and emerging trends. In *The future of children* (Vol. 6, pp. 83–102). Los Altos, CA: David and Lucile Packard Foundation.

Stormshak, E. A., Bierman, K. L., Bruschi, C., Dodge, K. A., Coie, J. D., and the Conduct Problems Prevention Research Group. (1999). The relation between behavior problems and peer preference in different classroom contexts. *Child Development*, 70, 169–182.

Strassberg, Z. (1995). Social information processing in compliance situations by mothers of behavior-problem boys. *Child Development*, 66, 176–189.

Straus, M. A. (1991a). Discipline and deviance: Physical punishment of children and violence and other crime in adulthood. *Social Problems*, 38, 133–152.

Straus, M. A. (1991b). New theory and old canards about family violence research. *Social Problems*, 38, 180–197.

Streri, A., & Poohoux, M. G. (1986). Tactual habituation and discrimination of form in infancy: A comparison with vision. *Child Development*, 57, 100–104.

Strong, B., & DeVault, C. (1995). *The marriage and family experience* (6th ed.). St. Paul, MN: West.

Stryker, J. (1997, June, 16). Abstinence or Else! *Nation*, 264, 19–22.

Stuckey, M. R., McGhee, P. E., & Bell, N. J. (1982). Parent-child interaction: The influence of maternal employment. *Developmental Psychology*, 18, 635–644.

Study: Less violence on TV. (1996, October 16). *Newsday*, p. A10.

Stunkard, A. J., Soresen, T. I. A., Hanis, C., Teasdale, T. W., Chakraborty, R., Schull, W. J., & Schulsinger, F. (1986). An adoption study of human obesity. *New England Journal of Medicine*, 314, 193–198.

Subbotsky, E. V. (1994). Early rationality and magical thinking in preschoolers: Space and time. *British Journal of Developmental Psychology*, 12, 97–108.

Sullivan, K., & Winner, K. (1993). Three-year-olds' understanding of mental states: The influence of trickery. *Journal of Experimental Child Psychology*, 56, 135–148.

Sullivan, S. Birch, L. L. (1990). Pass the sugar, pass the salt: Experience dictates preference. *Developmental Psychology*, 26, 536–552.

Super, C. M. (1981). Cross-cultural research on infancy. In H. C. Triandis & A. Heron (Eds.), *Handbook of cross-cultural psychology* (Vol. 4, pp. 17–55). Boston: Allyn & Bacon.

Super, D. (1953). A theory of vocational development. *American Psychologist*, 8, 185–190.

Sutton, H. E. (1980). *An introduction to human genetics* (3rd ed.). Philadelphia: Saunders.

Swain, I. U., Zelazo, P. R., & Clifton, R. K. (1993). Newborn infants' memory for speech sounds retained over 24 hours. *Developmental Psychology*, 29, 312–323.

Swain, R. C., Oetting, E. R., Edwards, R. W., & Beauvais, F. (1989). Links from emotional distress to adolescent drug use: A path model. *Journal of Consulting and Clinical Psychology*, 57, 227–231.

Swanson, H. L. (1994). Short-term memory and working memory: Do both contribute to our understanding of academic achievement in children and adults with learning disabilities? *Journal of Learning Disabilities*, 27, 34–50.

Swarr, A. E., & Richards, M. H. (1996). Longitudinal effects of adolescent girls' pubertal development, perceptions of pubertal timing and parental relations on eating problems. *Developmental Psychology*, 32, 636–646.

Swiatek, M. A., & Benbow, C. P. (1991). Ten-year longitudinal follow-up of ability-matched accelerated and unaccelerated gifted students. *Journal of Educational Psychology*, 83, 528–538.

Symons, D. K., & Moran, G. (1987). The behavioral dynamics of mutual responsiveness in early face-to-face mother-infant interactions. *Child Development*, 58, 1488–1496.

Szkrybalo, J., & Ruble, D. N. (1999). "God made me a girl": Sex-category constancy judgments and explanations revisited. *Developmental Psychology*, 35, 392–402.

T

Tafarodi, R.W., & Swann, W. B., Jr. (1995). Self-liking and self-competence as dimensions of global self-esteem: initial validation of a measure. *Journal of Personality Assessment*, 65, 322–342.

Tanner, J. M. (1970). Physical growth. In P. H. Mussen (Ed.), *Carmichael's manual of child development* (3rd ed., pp. 77–155). New York: Wiley.

Tanner, J. M. (1990). *Fetus into man*. Cambridge, MA: Harvard University Press.

Taras, H. L., Sallis, J. F., Patterson, T. L., Nader, P. R., & Nelson, J. A. (1989). Television's influence on children's diet and physical activity. *Developmental and Behavioral Pediatrics*, 10, 176–180.

Taskinen, H., Antitila, A., Lindbohm, M. L., Sallmen, M., & Hemminki, K. (1989). Spontaneous abortions and congenital malformations among the wives of men occupationally exposed to organic solvents. *Scandinavian Journal of Work Environment: Health*, 15, 345–352.

Temple, L. (1997, June 2). Today's girls taller and standing taller too. *USA Today*, pp. C1, C6.

Temple, L. (1998, March 30). Drinking in tradition: College students keep alcohol in core curriculum. *USA Today*, pp. D1, D2.

Templeton, A., & Morris, J. K. (1998 August 27). Reducing the risk of multiple births by transfer of the two embryos after in vitro fertilization. *New England Journal of Medicine*, 339, 573–577.

Termine, N. T., & Izard, C. E. (1988). Infants' responses to their mothers' expressions of joy and sadness. *Developmental Psychology*, 24, 223–230.

Terwilliger, J. S., & Titus, J. C. (1995). Gender differences in attitudes and attitude changes among mathematically talented youth. *Gifted Child Quarterly*, 39, 29–35.

Tessor, A. (1993). The importance of heritability in psychological research: The case of attitudes. *Psychological Review*, 100, 129–142.

Teti, D. M., Gelfand, D. M., Messinger, D. S., & Isabella, R. (1995). Maternal depression and the quality of early attachment: An examination of infants, preschoolers, and their mothers. *Developmental Psychology*, 31, 364–376.

Thapar, A., & McGuffin, P. (1994). A twin study of depressive symptoms in childhood. *British Journal of Psychiatry*, 165, 259–265.

Thatcher, R.W., Walker, R.A., & Giudice, S. (1987) Human cerebral hemispheres develop at different rates and ages. *Science*, 236, 1110–1113.

Thelen, E. & Ulrich, B. D. (1991). Hidden skills. *Monographs of the Society for Research in Child Development*, 56(1), Serial No. 223.

Thelen, E. (1986). Treadmill-elicited stepping in seven-month-old infants. *Child Development*, 57, 1498–1506.

Thelen, E. (1987). The role of motor development in developmental psychology: A view of the past and an agenda for the future. In N. Eisenberg (Ed.), *Contemporary topics in developmental psychology* (pp. 3–34). New York: Wiley.

Thelen, E. (1989). Self-organization in developmental processes: Can systems approaches work? In M. Gunnar & E. Thelen (Eds.), *Minnesota symposia in child psychology* (Vol. 22, pp. 77–117). Hillsdale, NJ: Erlbaum.

Thelen, E., & Adolph, K. E. (1992). Arnold L., Gesell: The paradox of nature and nurture. In R. D. Parke et al. (Eds.), *A century of developmental psychology* (pp.357–389). Washington, DC: American Psychological Association.

Thelen, E., & Fisher, D. M. (1982). Newborn stepping: An explanation for a "disappearing" reflex. *Developmental Psychology, 18,* 760–775.

Thelen, E., & Smith, L. B. (1998). Dynamic systems theory. In W. Damon (Editor in Chief) & R. M. Lerner (Vol. Ed.), *Handbook of child psychology* (5th ed., Vol. 1, pp. 563–634). New York: Wiley.

Thomas, A., Chess, S., & Birch, H. G. (1970, August). The origins of personality. *Scientific American,* pp. 102–109.

Thomas, H. (1995). Modeling class inclusion strategies. *Developmental Psychology, 31,* 170–179.

Thomas, R. (1996). Reflective dialogue parent education design: Focus on parent development. *Family Relations, 45,* 189–200.

Thomas, R. M. (1979). *Comparing theories of child development.* Belmont, CA: Wadsworth.

Thompson, C. J. (1995, Fall). A contextualist proposal for the conceptualization and study of marketing ethics. *Journal of Public Policy and Marketing, 14,* 177–192.

Thompson, R .A. (1998). Early sociopersonality development. In W. Damon (Editor in Chief) & W. Damon & N. Eisenberg (Vol. Ed.), *Handbook of child psychology* (5th ed., Vol. 3, pp. 25–104). New York: Wiley.

Thompson, R. A. (1990). Vulnerability in research: A developmental perspective on research risk. *Child Development, 61,* 1–17.

Thompson, R. A. (1997). Sensitivity and security: New questions to ponder. *Child Development, 68,* 595–597.

Thornburg, H. D. (1986, January). Is the beginning of identity the end of innocence? *The Clearing House,* pp. 217–219.

Thornburg, H. D., & Glider, P. (1984). Dimensions of early adolescent social perceptions and preferences. *Journal of Early Adolescence, 4,* 387–406.

Thorne, A., & Michaelieu, Q. (1996). Situating adolescent gender and self-esteem with personal memories. *Child Development, 67,* 1374–1390.

Thornton, A (1990). The courtship process and adolescent sexuality. *Journal of Family Research, 11,* 239–273.

Tisak, M. S. (1986). Children's conceptions of parental authority. *Child Development, 57,* 166–176.

Tobler, N. S. (1986). Meta-analysis of 143 adolescent drug prevention programs: Quantitative outcome results of program participants compared to a control or comparison group. *Journal of Drug Issues, 16,* 537–568.

Toch, T., Bennefield, R. M., & Bernstein, A. (1996, April 1). The case for tough standards. *U.S. News and World Reports,* pp. 52–56.

Toledo-Dreves, V., Zabin, L. S., & Emerson, M. R. (1995). Durations of adolescent sexual relationships before and after conception. *Journal of Adolescent Health, 17,* 163–172.

Tomasello, M., & Barton, M. (1994). Learning words in nonostensive contexts. *Developmental Psychology, 30,* 639–650.

Tomasello, M., & Ferrar, J. (1984). Cognitive bases of lexical development: Object permanence and relational words. *Journal of Child Language, 13,* 495–505.

Tomasello, M., & Kruger, A. (1992). Acquiring verbs in ostensive and non-ostensive contexts. *Journal of Child Language, 19,* 311–333.

Tomasello, M., & Mannle, S. (1985). Pragmatics of sibling speech to one-year-olds. *Child Development, 56,* 911–917.

Toomela, A. (1999) Drawing development: Stages in the representation of a cube and a cylinder. *Child Development, 70,* 1141–1150.

Torgersen, A. M. (1989). Genetic and environmental influences on temperamental development: Longitudinal study of twins from infancy to adolescence. In S. Doxiadis (Ed.), *Early influences shaping the individual* (pp. 269–283). New York: Plenum.

Tower, R. B., Singer, D. G., Singer, J. J., & Biggs, A. (1979). Differential effects of television programming on preschoolers' cognition, imagination, and social play. *American Journal of Orthopsychiatry, 49,* 265–281.

Tower, R. L. (1987). *How schools can help combat student drug and alcohol abuse.* Washington, DC: NEA Professional Library.

Townsend, M. H., Wallick, M. M., Pleak, R. R., & Cambre, K. M. (1997). Gay and lesbian issues in child and adolescent psychiatry training as reported by training directors. *Journal of the American Academy of Child and Adolescent Psychiatry, 36,* 764–768.

Travis, J. (1995, December 2). Breathing a bit askew in SIDS babies. *Science News,* pp. 148, 380.

Trehub, S. (1973). Infants' sensitivity to vowel and tonal contrasts. *Developmental Psychology, 9,* 81–96.

Trevarthen, C. (1982). Basic patterns of psychogenetic change in infancy. In T. Bever (Ed.), *Regressions in mental development* (pp. 7–46). Hillsdale, NJ: Erlbaum.

Triandis, H. C., & Brislin, R. W. (1984). Cross-cultural psychology. *American Psychologist, 39,* 1006–1017.

Trickett, P. K., & Kuczynski, L. (1986). Children's misbehaviors and parental discipline strategies in abusive and nonabusive families. *Developmental Psychology, 22,* 115–123.

Trickett, P. K., & Susman, E. J. (1988). Parental perceptions of childrearing practices in physically abusive and nonabusive families. *Developmental Psychology, 24,* 270–276.

Trickett, P.K., & McBride-Chang, C. (1995) The development impact of different forms of child abuse and neglect. *Developmental Review, 15,* 311–337.

Trotter, R.J. (1975, September 15) The new face of birth. *Science News,* pp. 106–108.

Truman, D. M., Tokar, D. M., & Fischer, A. R. (1996). Dimensions of masculinity: Relations to date rape supportive attitudes and sexual aggression in dating situations. *Journal of Counseling and Development, 74,* 555–562.

Tubman, J. G., Windle, M., & Windle, R. C. (1996). The onset and cross-temporal patterning of sexual intercourse in middle Adolescence: Prospective relations with behavioral and emotional problems. *Child Development, 67,* 327–343.

Tucker, T., & Bing, E. (1975). *Prepared childbirth,* New Canaan, CT: Tobey.

Tulkin, S. R., & Kagan, J. (1972). Mother-child interaction in the first year of life. *Child Development, 43,* 31–41.

Turiel, E. (1990). Moral judgment, action, and development. In D. Schrader (Ed.), *The legacy of Lawrence Kohlberg* (pp. 31–51). San Francisco: Jossey-Bass.

Turiel, E. (1998). The development of morality. In W. Damon (Editor in Chief) & N. Eisenberg (Vol. Ed.), *Handbook of child psychology* (5th ed., pp. 863–932). New York Wiley.

Tur-Kaspa, H., & Bryan, T. (1995). Teachers' ratings of the social competence and school adjustment of students with LD in elementary and junior high school. *Journal of Learning Disabilities, 28,* 44–52.

Turner, P. J., & Gervai, J. (1995). A multidimensional study of gender typing in preschool children and their parents: Personality, attitudes, preferences, behavior, and cultural differences. *Developmental Psychology, 31,* 759–772.

Tuttle, E. B., Becker, L. A., & Sousa, J. A. (1988). *Characteristics and identification of gifted and talented students.* Washington, DC: NEA Publications.

Twomey, J. G., Jr., & Fletcher, J. C. (1994). Ethical issues surrounding care of HIV-infected children. *Pediatric AIDS: The challenge of HIV infection in infants, children, and adolescents* (2nd ed., pp.713–724). Baltimore: Williams & Wilkins.

U

The U.N.'s global immunization triumph. (1993, June 18). *CQ Researcher, 3,* 546.

U.S. Bureau of the Census. (1994). *Current population reports* (pp. 20–477). Washington, DC: Author.

U.S. Bureau of the Census. (1996). *Current population reports* (pp. 25–1130). Washington, DC: Author.

U.S. Congress, Office of Technology Assessment. (1992). *Adolescent health: Vol. 2. Effectiveness of selected prevention and treatment services.* Washington, DC: U.S. Government Printing Office.

U.S. Department of Commerce. (1998). *Statistical abstract of the United States.* Washington, DC: Author.

U.S. Department of Education Statistics. (1996). *Digest of educational statistics.* Washington, DC: Author.

U.S. Department of Education. (1993a). *Fifteenth annual report to congress on the implementation of the Education of the Handicapped Act.* Washington, DC: Author.

U.S. Department of Education. (1993b). *National excellence: A case for developing America's talent.* Washington, DC: Author.

U.S. Department of Education. (1995a). *The educational progress of black students.* Washington, DC: Author.

U.S. Department of Education. (1995b). *The educational progress of Hispanic students.* Washington, DC: Author.

U.S. Department of Education. (1997a). *NAEP 1996 trends in academic progress.* NCES 97-085. Washington, DC: U.S. Department of Education.

U.S. Department of Education. (1997b). *To assure the free appropriate public education of all children with disabilities: Nineteenth Annual Report to Congress on the Implementation of The Individuals with Disabilities Education Act.* Washington, DC: Author.

U.S. Department of Education. (1998, September). *NAEP facts.* NCES 98–468. Washington, DC: Author.

U.S. Department of Health and Human Services. (1993). *Eighth special report to the U.S. Congress on Alcohol and Health.* NIH Pub. No. 94–3699. Washington, DC: Author.

U.S. Department of Health and Human Services. (1995a). *Health: United States, 1994.* DHHS Pub. No. (PHS) 95–1232. Hyattsville, MD: Author.

U.S. Department of Health and Human Services. (1995b). *Healthy People 2000: Healthy People 2000 review 1995–1996.* Hyattsville, MD: Author.

U.S. Department of Health and Human Services. (1995c). *HHS news: Annual survey shows increases in tobacco and drug use by youth.* Washington, DC: Author.

U.S. Department of Health and Human Services. (1996a). *Physical activity and health.* Hyattsville, MD: Author.

U.S. Department of Health and Human Services. (1996b). *Trends in the well-being of America's children and youth: 1996.* Washington, DC: Author.

U.S. Department of Health and Human Services. (1997a, December 20). *Drug use survey shows mixed results for nation's youth.* Washington, DC: Author.

U.S. Department of Health and Human Services. (1997b). *Healthy People 2000: Review 1997.* DHHS Pub. No. PHS 98–1256. Hyattsville, MD: Author.

U.S. Department of Health and Human Services. (1998). Washington, DC: Author.

U.S. Department of Labor (1996). *Tomorrow's jobs.* Bulletin 2470–1. Washington, DC: Bureau of Labor Statistics.

United Nations Children's Fund. (1993). *The state of the world's children.* New York: Author.

United Nations Children's Fund. (1996). *UNICEF annual report.* New York: Author.

Upchurch, R. L., & Lochhead, J. (1987). Computers and higher-order thinking skills. In V. Richardson Koehler (Ed.), *Educators' handbook* (pp. 139–165). New York: Longman.

Update: Prevalence of overweight among children, adolescents, and adults: United States, 1988–1994. (1997, April 9). *Journal of the American Medical Association.*

USDHHS (1995) Healthy people 2000. Healthy people 2000 review 1995–1996. Hyattsville, MD: Author

Use of alcohol linked to rise in fetal illness. (1995, April 7). *New York Times,* p. A27.

Uzgiris, I. C. (1968). Situational generality of conservation. In I. E. Sigel & F. H. Hooper (Eds.), *Logical thinking in children: Research based on Piaget's theory.* New York: Holt.

Uzgiris, I. C. (1973). Patterns of cognitive development in infancy. *Merrill-Palmer Quarterly, 19,* 181–204.

Uzgiris, I.C., & Hunt, J. Mc. *assessment in infancy: ordinal scales of psychological development.* urbana: University of Illinois Press, 1975

V

Valde, G. A. (1996). Identity closure: A fifth identity status. *Journal of Genetic Psychology, 157,* 245–254.

van Balen, F. (1996). Child-rearing following in vitro fertilization. *Journal of Child Psychology and Psychiatry and Allied Disciplines, 37,* 687–693.

van den Boom, D. C. (1994). The influence of temperament and mothering on attachment and exploration: An experimental manipulation of sensitive responsiveness among lower-class mother and irritable infants. *Child Development, 65,* 1457–1478.

van den Boom, D. C. (1997). Sensitivity and attachment: Next steps for developmentalists. *Child Development, 68,* 592–594.

van den Boom, D. C., & Hoeksma, J. B. (1994). The effect of infant irritability on mother-infant interaction: A growth-curve analysis. *Developmental Psychology, 30,* 581–590.

Van Dyke, A. (1995, November 27). Nurses share concerns, strategies for combatting childhood obesity. *New York Teacher,* p. 9.

Van Evra, J. (1990). *Television and child development.* Hillsdale, NJ: Erlbaum.

van IJzendoorn, M. H. (1995). Adult attachment representations, parental responsiveness, and infant attachment: A meta-analysis on the predictive validity of the adult attachment interview. *Psychological Bulletin, 117,* 387–403.

van IJzendoorn, M. H., & De Wolff, M. S. (1997). In search of the absent father: Meta-analyses of infant-father attachment: A rejoinder to our discussants. *Child Development, 68,* 604–609.

van IJzendoorn, M. H., Jeffer, F., & Duyvesteyn, M. G. C. (1995). Breaking the intergenerational cycle of insecure attachment: A review of the effects of attachment-based interventions on maternal sensitivity and infant security. *Journal of Child Psychology and Psychiatry, 36,* 225–248.

van IJzendoorn, M.H., & de Wolff, M.S. (1997) In search of the absent father-meta-analyses of infant-father attachment: A rejoinder to our discussants, 68, 571–746

Vandell, D. L., & Bailey, M. D. (1992). Conflicts between siblings. In C. U. Shatz & W. W. Hartup (Eds.), *Conflict in child and adolescent development* (pp. 242–269). Cambridge: Cambridge University Press.

Vandell, D. L., & Corasaniti, M. A. (1988). The relation between third graders' after-school care and social, academic, and emotional functioning. *Child Development, 59,* 868–875.

Vandell, D. L., Henderson, V. K., & Wilson, K. S. (1988). A longitudinal study of children with day-care experiences of varying quality. *Child Development, 59,* 1286–1293.

Vandenberg, B. (1978). Play and development from an ethological perspective. *American Psychologist, 33,* 724–739.

Vandenberg, S. G., & Kuse, A. R. (1979). Spatial ability: A critical review of the sex-linked major-gene hypothesis. In M. Whittig & A. Petersen (Eds.), *Determinants of sex related differences in cognitive functioning.* New York: Academic Press.

Vann, A. S. (1997). Inclusion: How full? *Principal, 76,* 54–56.

Vaughn, B. E., Stevenson-Hinde, J., Water, E., Kotsaftis, A., Shoudice, A., Trudel, M., & Belsky, J. (1992). Attachment security and temperament in infancy and early childhood: Some conceptual clarifications. *Developmental Psychology, 28,* 463–471.

Vaughn, S. (1985). Why teach social skills to learning disabled students? *Journal of Learning Disabilities, 18,* 588–591.

Vavrik, J. (1997). Personality and risk-taking: A brief report on adolescent male drivers. *Journal of Adolescence, 20,* 461–465.

Veatch, R. M. (1997, March 20). Consent, confidentiality, and research. *New England Journal of Medicine, 336,* 869–870.

Vega, W. A. (1990). Hispanic families in the 1980s: A decade of research. *Journal of Marriage and the Family, 52,* 1015–1024.

Veneziano, E., & Sinclair, H. (1995) Functional changes in early child language: The appearance of references to the past and of explanations. *Journal of Child Language, 22,* 557–581.

Verdelle, A. J. (1997, January 27). Classroom rap. *The Nation, 264,* 5–7.

Vereijken, C.M. & Riksen-Walraven, J.M. (1997) Mother-infant relationships in Japan. *Journal of Cross-Cultural Psychology, 28,* 442–463.

Vergason, G. A. (1990). *Dictionary of special education and rehabilitation* (3rd ed.). Denver: Love.

Vernon, P. E. (1976). Environment and intelligence. In V. P. Varma & P. Williams (Eds.), *Piaget, psychology and education* (pp. 31–42). Itasca, IL: Peacock.

Vespo, J. E., Pedersen, J., & Hay, D. F. (1995). Young children's conflicts with peers and siblings: Gender effects. *Child Study Journal, 25,* 189–212.

Viadero, C. (1987, January 28). Panel to develop model suicide-prevention program for schools. *Education Week,* p. 5.

Viadero, C. (1996b, October 15). Few U.S. schools use technology well, 2 studies report. *Education Week,* p. 6.

Viadero, C. (1996c, April 10). Culture clash. *Education Week,* pp. 39–42.

Viadero, D. (1989, May 3). 7 of 10 Handicapped graduates found "productive." *Education Week,* 6.

Viadero, D. (1994, April 20). Fade-out in Head Start gains linked to later schooling. *Education Week,* p. 9.

Viadero, D. (1996a, February 24). Teen culture seen impeding school reform. *Education Week,* pp. 1, 10.

Viadero, D. (1993, May 5). Special education update. *Education Week,* p10.

Vikan, A., & Clausen, S. E. (1993). Freud, Piaget, or neither? Beliefs in controlling others by wishful thinking and magical behavior in young children. *Journal of Genetic Psychology, 154,* 297–314.

Vitz, P. C. (1990). The use of stories in moral development: New psychological reasons for an old education method. *American Psychologist, 45,* 709–720.

Voelker, R. (1996, December 25). The flip side of SIDS decline. *Journal of the American Medical Association, 276,* 1941.

Voeller, B. (1980). Society and the gay movement. In J. Marmor (Ed.), *Homosexual behavior.* New York: Basic Books.

Volling, B. L., & Belsky, J. (1992). The contribution of mother-child and father-child relationships to the quality of sibling interaction: A longitudinal study. *Child Development, 63,* 1209–1222.

Volling, B. L., & Feagans, L. V. (1995). Infant day care and children's social competence. *Infant Behavior and Development, 18,* 177–188.

Volpe, E. P. (1984). *Patient in the womb.* Macon, GA: Mercer University Press.

Volpe, J. J. (1992). Effect of cocaine use on the fetus. *New England Journal of Medicine, 82,* 399–407.

Vorhees, C. V., & Mollnow, E. (1987). Behavioral teratogenesis: Long-term influences on behavior from early exposure to environmental agents. In J. D. Osofsky (Ed.), *Handbook of infant development* (pp. 913–972). New York: Wiley.

Vostanis, P., Grattan, E., Cumella, S., & Winchester, C. (1997). Psychosocial functioning of homeless children. *Journal of the American Academy of Adolescent Psychiatry, 36,* 881–889.

Vulthipongse, P., Bhadrakom, C., Chaisliwattana, P., Boogpisuthipong, A., Chalerchokcharenket, A., & the Thailand Division of HIV/AIDS Collaboration. (1998). Administration of zidovudine during late pregnancy and delivery to prevent perinatal HIV transmission: Thailand, 1996–1998. *MMWR, 47,* 151–154.

Vurpillot, E. (1968). The development of scanning strategies and their relation to visual differentiation. *Journal of Experimental Child Psychology, 6,* 632–650.

Vurpillot, E., & Ball, W. A. (1979). The concept of identity and children's selective attention. In G. Hale & M. Lewis (Eds.), *Attention and cognitive development.* New York: Plenum.

Vygotsky, L. S. (1962). *Thought and language.* Cambridge, MA: MIT Press.

Vygotsky, L. S. (1978). *Mind in society: The development of higher psychological processes.* In M. Cole, V. John-Steiner, S. Scribner, & E. Souberman (Eds.), Cambridge, MA: Harvard University Press.

W

Waddington, C. H. (1957). *The strategy of the genes.* London: Allen & Unwin.

Wade, N. A., Birkhead, G. S., Warren, B. L., Charbonneau, T. T., French, P. T., Wang, L., Baum, J. B., Tesoriero, J. M., & Savicki, R. (1998). Abbreviated regimens of zidovudine prophylaxis and perinatal transmission of the human immunodeficiency virus. *New England Journal of Medicine, 339,* 1409–1414.

Wagner, D. A., & Stevenson, H. W. (Eds.). (1982). *Cultural perspectives on child development.* San Francisco: Freeman.

Wagner, R. K., Torgesen, J. K., & Rashotte, C. A. (1994). Development of reading-related phonological processing abilities: New evidence of bidirectional causality from a latent variable longitudinal study. *Developmental Psychology, 30,* 73–87.

Wagner, T. (1996, October 9). Creating community consensus on core values. *Education Week,* pp. 36, 38.

Wagner, W. G. (1996). Optimal development in adolescence: What is it and how can it be encouraged? *Counseling Psychologist, 24,* 360–399.

Wainryb, C. (1993). The application of moral judgments to other cultures: Relativism and universality. *Child Development, 64,* 924–933.

Walden, T. A., & Ogan, T. A. (1988). The development of social referencing. *Child Development, 59,* 1230–1241.

Waldner-Haugrud, L. K., & Magruder, B. (1996). Homosexual identity expression among lesbian and gay adolescents. *Youth and Society, 27,* 313–333.

Walk, R. D. (1981). *Perceptual development.* Monterey, CA: Brooks/Cole.

Walker, D., Greenwood, C., Hart, B., & Carta, J. (1994). Prediction of school outcomes based on early language production and socioeconomic factors. *Child Development, 65,* 606–621.

Walker, E., & Emory, E. (1985). Commentary: Interpretive bias and behavioral genetic research. *Child Development, 56,* 775–779.

Walker, J. H., Kozma, E. J., & Green, R. P. (1989). *American education: Foundations and policy.* St. Paul, MN: West.

Walker, J. R. (1996). Funding child rearing: Child allowance and parental leave. In *The Future of Children* (Vol. 6, pp. 122–136). Los Altos, CA: David and Lucile Packard Foundation.

Walker, L. J. (1984). Sex differences in the development of moral reasoning: A critical review. *Child Development, 53,* 1330–1336.

Walker, L. J. (1988). The development of moral reasoning. *Annals of Child Development, 5,* 33–78.

Walker, L. J. (1989). A longitudinal study of moral reasoning. *Child Development, 60,* 157–166.

Walker, L. J. (1991). Sex differences in moral reasoning. In W. M. Kurtines & J. L. Gewirtz (Eds.), *Handbook of moral behavior and development: Vol. 2. Research* (pp.333–364). Hillsdale, NJ: Erlbaum.

Walker, L. J., & Taylor, J. H. (1991a). Family interactions and the development of moral reasoning. *Child Development, 62,* 264–283.

Walker, L. J., & Taylor, J. H. (1991b). Stage transitions in moral reasoning: A longitudinal study of developmental processes. *Developmental Psychology, 27,* 330–337.

Walker, L.J., & Pitts, R.C. (1998) Naturalistic conceptions of moral maturity. *Developmental Psychology, 34,* 403–420.

Walker-Andrews, A. S., & Gronlick, W. (1983). Discrimination of vocal expressions by young infants. *Infant Behavior and Development, 6,* 491–498.

Wall, S. M., Pickert, S. M., & Bigson, W B. (1989). Fantasy play in 5- and 6-year-old children. *Journal of Psychology, 123,* 245–256.

Wallace, I., Wallechinsky, D., Wallace, A., & Wallace. S. (1981). *The book of lists: 2.* New York: Bantam.

Wallerstein, J. S. (1983). Children of divorce: The psychological tasks of the child. *American Journal of Orthopsychiatry, 53,* 230–243.

Wallerstein, J. S. (1987). Children of divorce: Report of a ten-year follow-up of early latency-age children. *American Journal of Orthopsychiatry, 57,* 199–211.

Wallerstein, J. S., & Blakeslee, S. (1989). *Second changes: Men, women, and children a decade after divorce.* New York: Ticknor & Fields.

Wallerstein, J. S., Corbin, S. B., & Lewis, J. M. (1988). Children of divorce: A 10-year study. In E. M. Hetherington & J. D. Arasteh (Eds.), *Impact of divorce, single parenting, and stepparenting on children* (pp. 197–215). Hillsdale, NJ: Erlbaum.

Walsh, D. J. (1989). Changes in kindergarten: Why here? Why now? *Early Childhood Research Quarterly, 4,* 377–393.

Walsh, M. (1993, September 22). Experts ponder academic value of Barney. *Education Week,* pp. 14–16.

Walsh, M. (1995, June 7). Study links television viewing, school readiness. *Education Week,* p. 5.

Walsh, M. (1996, December 6). "Sesame Street" incorporates theories on cognition. *Education Week,* p3.

Walsh, P.V., Katz, P.A., & Downey, E.P. (1991) A longitudinal perspective on race and gender socialization in infants and toddlers cited in D.N. Ruble & C.L. Martin (1998) Gender Development. *Handbook of Child Psychology* (5th ed, pp 933–1017). New York: Wiley

Wan, C., Fan, C., Lin, G., & Jing, Q. (1994). Comparison of personality traits of only and sibling children in Beijing. *Journal of Genetic Psychology, 155,* 377–189.

Wang, M.Q. & Yesalis, C.E. (1994) Desire for weight gain and potential risks of adolescent males using anabolic steroids. *Perceptual and Motor Skills, 78,* 267–275.

Ward, M.J., & Carlson, E.A. (1995) Associations among adult attachment representations, maternal sensitivity, and infant-mother relationships. *Child Development, 66,* 69–80.

Ward, S. K., Chapman, K., Cohn, E., White, S., & Williams, K. (1991). Acquaintance rape and the college social scene. *Family Relations, 40,* 65–71.

Warfield-Coppock, N. (1992). The rites of passage movement: A resurgence of African-centered practices for socializing American Youth. *Journal of Negro Education, 61,* 471–481.

Wark, G. R., & Krebs, D. L. (1996). Gender and dilemma differences in real-life moral judgment. *Developmental Psychology, 32,* 220–230.

Warren, M. P., Brooks-Gunn, J., Fox, R., Lancelot, C., Newman, D., & Hamilton, W. G. (1991). Lack of bone accretion and amenorrhea in young dancers: Evidence for a relative osteopenia in weight bearing bones. *Journal of Clinical Endocrinology and Metabolism, 72,* 847–853.

Warren, M. P., Brooks-Gunn, J., Hamilton, L. H., Hamilton, W. G., & Warren, L. F. (1986). Scoliosis and fractures in young ballet dancers: Relationships to delayed menarcheal age and secondary amenorrhea. *New England Journal of Medicine, 314,* 1348–1353.

Waschull, S .B., & Kernis, M. H. (1996). Level and stability of self-esteem as predictors of children's intrinsic motivation and reasons for anger. *Personality and Social Psychology Bulletin, 22,* 4–14.

Waterman, A. S. (1982). Identity development from adolescence to adulthood: An extension of theory and a review of the literature. *Developmental Psychology, 18,* 341–359.

Waterman, A. S., & Waterman, C. K. (1971). A longitudinal study of changes in ego identity status during the freshman year at college. *Developmental Psychology, 5,* 167–173.

Waters, E. (1978). The reliability and stability of individual differences in infant-mother attachment. *Child Development, 49,* 483–494.

Waters, E., & Deane, K. E. (1982). Theories, models, recent data and some tasks for comparative developmental analysis. In L. Hoffman, R. Gandelman, & R. Schiffman (Eds.), *Parenting: Its causes and consequences* (pp. 19–54). Hillsdale, NJ: Erlbaum.

Watkins, H. D., & Bradbard, M. R. (1984, Fall). The social development of young children in day care: What practitioners should know. *Child Care Quarterly,* pp. 169–187.

Wattleton, F. (1987). American teens: Sexually active, sexually illiterate. *Journal of School Health, 57,* 379–380.

Wauchope, B., & Straus, M. A. (1990). Physical punishment and physical abuse of American children: Incidence rates by age, gender, and occupational class. In M. S. Straus & R. J. Gelles (Eds.), *Physical violence in the American family* (pp. 133–148). New York: Doubleday/Anchor.

Waxman, S. R., Lynch, E. B., Casey, K. L., & Baer, L. (1997). Seters and samoyeds: The emergence of subordinate level categories as a basis for inductive inference in preschool-age children. *Developmental Psychology, 33,* 1074–1090.

Weatherley, D. (1964). Self-perceived rate of physical maturation and personality in late adolescence. *Child Development, 35,* 1197–1210.

Wechsler, D. (1991). *Manual for the Wechsler Intelligence Scale for children, III.* San Antonio, TX: Psychological Corporation.

Weiner, E. (1996, March–April). Our bio-future: Exploring the frontiers of human biology. *The Futurist,* 25–28.

Weinraub, M., & Gringlas, M. B. (1995). Single parenting. In M. H. Bornstein (Ed.), *Handbook of parenting* (Vol. 3, pp. 65–87). Mahwah, NJ: Erlbaum.

Weisenfeld, A. R., & Klorman, R. C. (1978). The mother's psychological reactions to contrasting affective expressions by her own and unfamiliar infants. *Developmental Psychology, 14,* 294–304.

Weiss, B., Dodge, K., Bates, J., & Petit, G. (1992). Some consequences of early harsh discipline: Child aggression and a maladaptive social information processing style. *Child Development, 63,* 1321–1335.

Weiss, C. D., & Lillywhite, H. S. (1976). *Communication disorders: A handbook for prevention and early intervention.* St. Louis, MO: Mosby.

Weiss, G. (1990). Hyperactivity in childhood. *New England Journal of Medicine, 323,* 1413–1414.

Weissberg, R. P., & Greenberg, M. T. (1998). School and community competence-enhancement and prevention programs. In W. Damon (Editor in Chief) & I. E. Sigel & K. A. Renninger (Vol. Eds.), *Handbook of child psychology* (5th ed., Vol. 4, pp. 877–954). New York: Wiley.

Weissman, M. M., Wolk, S., Goldstein, R. B., Moreau, D., Adams, P., Greenwald, S., Klier, C. M., Ryan, N. D., Dahl, R. E., & Wickramaratne, P. (1999, May 12). Depressed adolescents grown up. *Journal of the American Medical Association, 281,* 1707–1713.

Welch-Ross, M. K., & Schmidt, C. R. (1996). Gender-schema development and children's constructive story memory: Evidence for a developmental model. *Child Development, 67,* 820–835.

Wellman, H. M., Cross, D., & Bartsch, K. (1987). Infant search and object permanence: A meta-analysis of the A-not-B error. *Monographs of the Society for Research in Child Development, 51*(3), Serial No. 214.

Wells, K. (1987). Scientific issues in the conduct of case studies. *Journal of Child Psychology and Psychiatry and Allied Disciplines, 28,* 783–790.

Wells, L. E., & Rankin, J. H. (1991). Families and delinquency: A meta-analysis of the impact of broken homes. *Social Problems, 38,* 71–93.

Wenar, C. (1994). *Developmental psychopathology* (3rd ed.). New York: McGraw-Hill.

Wendland-Carro, J., Piccinini, C.A., & Millar, W.S. (1999) The role of an early intervention on enhancing the quality of mother-infant interaction. *Child Development, 70,* 713–721.

Wentworth, N., & Haith, M.M. (1992) Event-specific expectations of 2-and 3- month-old infants. *Developmental Psychology, 28,* 842–850.

Wentworth, N., & Haith, M.M. (1998) Infants' acquisition of spatiotemporal expectations. *Developmental Psychology, 34,* 247–258.

Wentzel, K. R., & Caldwell, K. (1997). Friendships, peer acceptance, and group membership: Relations to academic achievement in middle school. *Child Development, 68,* 1198–1209.

Werner, E. E. (1984, November). Resilient children. *Young Children,* pp. 686–692.

Werner, E. E. (1993). Risk, resilience, and recovery: Perspectives from the Kauai Longitudinal Study. *Development and Psychopathology, 5,* 503–515.

Werner, E. E., & Smith, R. S. (1982). *Vulnerable but invincible: A study of resilient children.* New York: McGraw-Hill.

Werner, E. E., & Smith, R. S. (1989). *Vulnerable but invincible: A longitudinal study of resilient children and youth.* New York: Adams-Banister-Cox.

Wertheimer, M. (1961). Psycho-motor coordination of auditory-visual space at birth. *Science, 134,* 1962.

Wertlieb, D., Weigel, C., Springer, T., & Feldstein, M. (1987). Temperament as a moderator of children's stressful experiences. *American Journal of Orthopsychiatry, 57,* 234–245.

Wertsch, J. V., & Tulviste, P. (1992). L. S. Vygotsky and contemporary developmental psychology. *Developmental Psychology, 28,* 548–558.

Wertz, D.C., & Fletcher, J.C. (1998) Ethical and social issues in prenatal sex selection: A survey of geneticists in 37 nations. *Social Science and Medicine, 46,* 255–273.

West, J., Hausken, E. G., & Chandler, K. (1992). *Home activities of 3-to-8-year-olds: Statistics in brief.* Washington, DC: National Center for Education Statistics. (ERIC Document Reproduction Service No ED341 513)

West, P. (1994, October 12). Report links increased enrollments in math, science to reforms of 80s. *Education Week,* p. 11.

Westinghouse Learning Corporation. (1969, June). *The impact of Head Start: An evaluation of effects of Head Start on children's cognitive and affective development.* Executive Summary, Ohio University, Report to the Office of Economic Opportunity (EDO93497). Washington, DC: Clearinghouse for Federal Scientific and Technical Information.

Weyant, J. M. (1986). *Applied social psychology.* New York: Oxford University Press.

Wheeler, D. L. (1995, July 14). Few successes in gene therapy. *Chronicle of Higher Education,* pp. A8, A12.

Whitall, J., & Getchell, N. (1995). From walking to running: Applying a dynamical systems approach to the development of locomotor skills. *Child Development, 66,* 1541–1553.

Whitcomb, D., et al. (1994). *The child victim as a witness.* Washington, DC: Office of Juvenile Justice and Delinquency Prevention.

White, B. (1993). *The first three years of life.* New York: Simon & Schuster.

White, B. L. (1971). *Human infants: Experience and psychological development.* Upper Saddle River, NJ: Prentice Hall.

White, S. D., & DeBlassie, R. (1992). Adolescent sexual behavior. *Adolescence, 27,* 183–191.

White, S. H. (1994). G. Stanley Hall: From philosophy to developmental psychology. In R. D. Parke, P. A., J. Ornstein, J. Rieser, & C. Zahn-Waxler (Eds.), *A century of developmental psychology* (pp.204–225). Washington, DC: American Psychological Association

Whitehead, B. M., Cain, K. C., & Graves, G. (1994, March). Put computers into elementary classrooms-not labs. *American School Board Journal, 181,* 48–49.

Whitehurst, G. J., & Valdez-Menchaca, M. C. (1988). What is the role of reinforcement in early language acquisition? *Child Development, 49,* 430–441.

Whitehurst, G. J., Arnold, D., Epstein, J., Angell, A., Smith, M., & Fischel, J. (1994). A picture book reading intervention in daycare and home for children from low-income families. *Developmental Psychology, 30,* 679–689.

Whitehurst, G. J., Falco, F. L., Lonigan, C. J., Fischel, J. E., DeBaryshe, B. D., Valdez-Menchaca, M. C., & Caulfield, M. (1988). Accelerating language development through picture book reading. *Developmental Psychology, 24,* 552–560.

Whitener, C. B., & Kersey, K. (1980, November/December). A purple hippopotamus? Why not? *Childhood Education,* pp. 18–20.

Whiting, B. B., & Edwards, C. P. (1988). *Children of different worlds: The formation of social behavior.* Cambridge, MA: Harvard University.

Whiting, B. B., & Whiting, J. W. M. (1975). *Children of six cultures.* Cambridge, MA: Harvard University Press.

Whitman, F. L., Diamond, M., & Martin, J. (1993). homosexual orientation in twins: A report on 61 pairs and three triplet sets. *Archives of Sexual Behavior, 22,* 187–206.

Whitney, E. N., & Rolfes, S. R. (1996). *Understanding nutrition* (7th ed.). St. Paul, MN: West.

Whitney, E. N., Cataldo, C. B., & Rolfes, S. R. (1994). *Understanding normal and clinical nutrition.* St. Paul, MN: West.

Why physical activity drops in adolescence (1997, September 26). *CQ Researcher, 7,* 852.

Wichstrom, L. (1999). The emergence of gender difference in depressed mood during adolescence: The role of intensified gender socialization. *Developmental Psychology, 35,* 232–245.

Wickham, D. (1998, May 5). Girls' views change, so pregnancy drops. *USA Today,* p. A13.

Wicks-Nelson, R., & Israel, A. C. (1997). *Behavior disorders of children* (3rd ed.). Upper Saddle River, NJ: Prentice Hall.

Wiesel, T. N., & Hubel, D. H. (1965). Extent of recovery from the effects of visual deprivation in kittens. *Journal of Neurophysiology, 28,* 1060–1072.

Wilfert, C. M. (1996, November 28). Beginning to make progress against HIV. *New England Journal of Medicine, 335,* 1678–1680.

Willemsen, E. (1979). *Understanding infancy.* San Francisco: Freeman.

Willert, M., & Kamii, C. (1985). Reading in kindergarten: Direct vs. indirect teaching. *Young Children, 40,* 3–9.

Williams, H. B. (1979). Some aspects of childrearing practices in three minority subcultures in the United States. *Journal of Negro Education, 48,* 408–418.

Williams, J. W., & Stith, M. (1980). *Middle childhood: Behavior and development* (2nd ed.). New York: Macmillan.

Williams, K. (1997). Preventing suicide in young people: What is known and what is needed. *Child Care, Health and Development, 23,* 173–185.

Williams, R. D. (1994, May). Kid's vaccinations get a little easier. *FDA Consumer,* Publication No. (FDA). 94–9011.

Willig, A. E. (1985). A meta-analysis of selected studies on the effectiveness of bilingual education. *Review of Educational Research, 55,* 269–317.

Wilmut, I. & Campbell, K. et al. (1997). Cloning. *Nature, 385,* 810–813.

Wilson, G. T., & Fairburn, C. G. (1993). Cognitive treatments for eating disorders. *Journal of Consulting and Clinical Psychology, 61,* 261–269.

Wilson, M. D., & Joffe, A. (1995). Adolescent health. *Journal of the American Medical Association, 273,* 1657–1659.

Wilson, R. S. (1983). The Louisville twin study: Developmental synchronies in behavior. *Child Development, 54,* 298–316.

Wilson, R.S. (1977). Mental development in twins. In A. Oliverio (Ed.), *Genetics, environment, and intelligence.* Amsterdam: Elsevier.

Wilson, S. M., & Medora, N. P. (1990). Gender comparisons of college students' attitudes toward sexual behavior. *Adolescence, 25,* 615–627.

Wimmer, H. (1979). Processing of script deviations by young children. *Discourse Processes, 2,* 301–310.

Wimmer, H. (1980). Children's understanding of stories: Assimilation by a general schema for actions or coordination of temporal relations? In F. Wilkening, J. Becker, & T. Trabasso (Eds.), *Information integration by children*. Hillsdale, NJ: Erlbaum.

Wimmer, H., & Perner, J. (1983) Beliefs about beliefs: representation and constraining function of wrong beliefs in young children's understanding of deception. *Cognition*, 13, 103–128.

Wingfield, A., & Byrnes, D. L. (1981). *The psychology of human memory*. New York: Academic Press.

Winick, M. (1976). *Malnutrition and brain damage*. New York: Oxford University Press.

Winsler, A., Diaz, R. M., Espinosa, L., & Rodriguez, J. L. (1999). When learning a second language does not mean losing the first: Bilingual language development in low-income, Spanish-speaking children attending bilingual preschool. *Child Development*, 70, 349–362.

Wisdom, C. S. (1989). Does violence beget violence? A critical examination of the literature. *Psychological Bulletin*, 106, 3–28.

Wodarski, J. S. (1990). Adolescent substance abuse: Practical implications. *Adolescence*, 25, 667–687.

Wolf, R. (1995, October 6). A positive turn for the poor. *USA Today*, p. A6.

Wolf, R. (1996) *Marriages and families in a diverse society*. New York: Harper Collins.

Wolff, P. H. (1969). The natural history of crying and other vocalizations in early infancy. In B. M. Foss (Ed.), *Determinants of Infant Behaviour*, 4, 81–111.

Wolfson, A.R., & Carskadon (1998) Sleep schedules and daytime function in adolescents. *Child Development*, 69, 875–887.

Wolfson, J. C. (1996, January 15). Women with cystic fibrosis defy the odds by having babies. *Newsday*, pp. B17–B18.

Wood, D. (1995, June). Vaccination levels in Los Angeles public health centers: The contribution of missed opportunities. *American Journal of Public Health*, 85, 850–854.

Wood, W., Wong, F., & Chachere, G. J. (1991). Effects of media violence on viewers' aggression in unconstrained social interaction. *Psychological Bulletin*, 78, 371–383.

Woodford, M. (1997). The Black scholar reader's forum: Ebonics. *Black Scholar*, 27, 2–4.

Woodruff, C. W. (1978). The science of infant nutrition and the art of infant feeding. *Journal of the American Medical Association*, 240, 657–661.

Woodward, A. L., Markman, E. M., & Fitzsimmons, C. M. (1994). Rapid word learning in 13-and 18-month-olds. *Developmental Psychology*, 30, 553–566.

Woodyard, C. (1998, Oct. 6). Generation Y. *USA Today*, 1A, 2A.

Woody-Ramsey, J., & Miller, P. H. (1988). The facilitation of selective attention in preschoolers. *Child Development*, 59, 1504–1514.

Woolley, J. D. & Wellman, H. M. (1993). Origin and truth: Young children's understanding of imaginary mental representations. *Child Development*, 64, 1–17.

Woolley, J. D. (1997). Thinking about fantasy: Are children fundamentally different thinkers and believers from adults? *Child Development*, 68, 991–1012.

Woolley, J. D., & Wellman, H. M. (1990). Young children's understanding of realities, nonrealities, and appearances. *Child Development*, 61, 946–961.

Woolley, J. D., Phelps, K. E., Davis, D. L., & Mandell, D. J. (1999). Where theories of mind meet magic: The development of children's belief about wishing. *Child Development*, 70, 571–587.

Worobey, J., & Blajda, V. M. (1989). Temperament ratings at 2 weeks, 2 months, and 1 year: Differential stability of activity and emotionality. *Developmental Psychology*, 25, 257–264.

Woronov, T. (1994, December). Myths about the magic of technology in schools. *Education Digest*, 12–15.

Worsnop, R. L. (1991). Teenage suicide. *CQ Researcher*, 1, 371–391.

Wright, J. (1993). Homeless children: two years later. *American Journal of Disabled Children*, 147, 518–519.

Wright, J. C., Huston, A. C., Ross, R. P., Calvert, S. L., Rolandelli, D., Weeks, L. A., Raeisse, P., & Potts, R. (1984). Pace and continuity of television programs: Effects on children's attention and comprehension. *Developmental Psychology*, 20, 653–667.

Wright, K. N. & Wright, K. E. (1995). *Family life, delinquency, and crime: A policymaker's guide*. Washington, DC: Office of Juvenile Justice and Delinquency Prevention, Department of Justice.

Wright, L. S., Frost, C. J., et al. (1993). Church attendance, meaningfulness of religion, and depressive symptomatology among adolescents. *Journal of Youth and Adolescence*, 22, 559–569.

Wright, R. (1994, October 24). Technology and choice. *New Republic*, 211, 6–7.

Wright, R. (1995, January 2). Dumb bell. *New Republic*, 212, 6–7.

Wrightman, M. J. (1991). Criteria for placement decisions with cocaine-exposed infants. *Child Welfare*, pp. 653–663.

Wurtele, S. K., & Miller-Perrin, C. L. (1987a). Harmful effects of school-based sexual abuse prevention programs? Reassure the parents. In C. C. Tower (Ed.), *How schools can help combat child abuse and neglect* (2nd ed., pp. 146–153). Washington, DC: NEA Library.

Wurtele, S. K., & Miller-Perrin, C. L. (1987b). Sexual abuse prevention: Are school programs harmful? *Journal of School Health*, 57, 228–231.

Wyman, P. A., Cowen, E. L., Work, W. C., Hoyt-Meyers, L., Mgnus, K. B., & Fagen, D. B. (1999). Caregiving and developmental factors differentiating young at-risk urban children showing resilient versus stress-affected outcomes: A replication and extension. *Child Development*, 70, 645–659.

Wyrobek, A. J. (1993). Methods and concepts in detecting abnormal reproductive outcomes of paternal origin. *Reproductive Toxicology*, 7, 3–16.

Wyrobek, A. J., Watchmaker, G., & Gordon, L. (1994). An evaluation of sperm tests as indicators of germ-cell damage in men exposed to chemical or physical agents. *Reproduction: The New Frontier in Occupational and Environmental Health Research*, 160, 385–405.

X

Xu, K., Shi, Z. M., Veeck, L. L., Hughes, M. R., & Rosenwaks, Z. (1999, May 12). First unaffected pregnancy using preimplantation genetic diagnosis for sickle cell anemia. *Journal of the American Medical Association*, 281, 1701–1704.

Y

Yale, M.E., Messinger, D.S., Cobo-Lewis, D., Oiler, D.K. & Eilers, R.E. (1999) An event-based analysis of the coordination of early infant vocalizations and facial actions. *Developmental Psychology*, 35, 505–513.

Yang, B., Ollendick, T. H., Dong, Q., Xia, Y., & Lin, L. (1995). Only children and children with siblings in the People's Republic of China: Levels of fear, anxiety, and depression. *Child Development*, 66, 1301–1311.

Yarnold, B.M. (1998) Steroid use among Miami's public school students, 1992. *Psychological Reports*, 82, 19–25.

Young, D. (1982) Changing childbirth: Family birth in the hospital. Rochester, NY: Childbirth Graphics.

Young, G.Y., & Gagnon, M. (1990) Neonatal laterality, birth stress, familial sinistrality, and left-brain inhibition. *Developmental Neuropsychology*, 6, 127–150.

Youniss, J., & Smollar, J. (1985). *Adolescent relations with mothers, fathers, and friends*. Chicago: University of Chicago Press.

Youniss, J, & Volpe, J. (1978). A relational analysis of children's friendship. In W. Damon (Ed.), *Social cognition: New directions for child development* (pp. 1–22). San Francisco: Jossey-Bass.

Z

Zabin, L. S., Sedivy, V., & Emerson, M. R. (1994). Subsequent risk of childbearing among adolescents with a negative pregnancy test. *Family Planning Perspectives*, 26, 212–217.

Zahr, L. (1996). Effects of war on the behavior of Lebanese preschool children: Influence of home environment and family functioning. *American Journal of Orthopsychiatry*, 66, 401–408.

Zambrana, R. E., Scrimshaw, S. C. M., Collins, N., & Dunkel-Schetter, C. (1997). Prenatal health behaviors and psychosocial risk factors in pregnant women of Mexican origin: The role of acculturation. *American Journal of Public Health, 87,* 1022–1025.

Zelazo, N. A., Zelazo, P. R., Cohen, K. M., & Zelazo, P. D. (1993). Specificity of practice effects on elementary neuromotor patterns. *Developmental Psychology, 29,* 686–691.

Zelazo, P. R., Zelazo, N. A., & Kolb, S. (1972). "Walking" in the newborn. *Science, 176,* 314–315.

Zernicke, R. F., & Schneider, K. (1993). Biomechanics and developmental neuromotor control. *Child Development, 64,* 982–1005.

Zeskind, P. S., Sale, J., Maio, L. W., & Weiseman, J. R. (1985). Adult perceptions of pain and hunger cries: A synchrony of arousal. *Child Development, 56,* 549–554.

Zigler, E. F., & Finn-Stevenson, M. (1996). Funding child care and public education. *The Future of Children* (Vol. 6, pp. 104–121). Los, CA: David and Lucile Packard Foundation.

Zigler, E. F., Finn-Stevenson, M., and Marsland, K. W. (1995). Child day care in the schools: The School of the 21st Century. *Child Welfare, 24*(6), 1301–1326.

Zigler, E., & Berman, W. (1983). Discerning the future of early childhood intervention. *American Psychologist, 38,* 894–907.

Zigler, E., & Muenchow, S. (1992). *Head Start: The inside story of America's most successful educational experiment.* New York: Basic Books.

Zill, N., & Robinson, J. (1995, April). The Generation X difference. *American Demographics,* pp. 24–33.

Zill, N., Morrison, D. R., & Coiro, M. J. (1993). Long-term effects of parental divorce on parent-child relationships, adjustment, and achievement in young adulthood. *Journal of Family Psychology, 7,* 91–103.

Zimmerman, B.J., Bandura, A., & Martinez-Pons, M. (1992) Self-motivation for academic attainment: The role of self-efficacy beliefs and personal goal setting. *American Educational Research Journal, 29,* 663–676.

Zimmerman, M. A., Copeland, L. A., Shope, J. T., & Dielman, T. E. (1997). A longitudinal study of self-esteem: Implications for adolescent development. *Journal of Youth and Adolescence, 26,* 117–141.

Zinsser, C. (1981, October). The preschool pressure cooker. *Working Mother,* pp. 61–64.

Zmiles, H., & Lee, V. E. (1991). Adolescent family structure and educational progress. *Developmental Psychology, 27,* 314–320.

Zuckerman, B., & Frank, D. A. (1992). "Crack kids": Not broken. *Pediatrics, 89,* 337–339.

Zuckerman, E. (1996). Musical notes: An interview with Yo-Yo Ma. In M. Collins & M. M. Kimmel (Eds.), Mister Rogers' Neighborhood: *Children, television and Fred Rogers* (pp. 79–88). Pittsburgh, PA: University of Pittsburgh Press.

Name Index

A

AARP Statement, 176
AARP, 176
Abelman, R., 454
Aber, J. L., 357, 530
Abernathy, T. J., 546
Abrams, C. L., 428
Abrams, L. D., 261
Abromovitch, R., 341, 490
Abromowitz, A. J., 412
Ackerman, B. P., 397
Ackerman-Ross, S., 265
Acock, A. C., 433
Acredolo, L. P., 218
Acus, L. K., 342
Adams, B., 122, 123
Adams, G. R., 516
Adams, P. F., 9
Adams, R. J., 161
Adamson, L., 238, 516
Addison, T. L., 162
Adeyanju, M., 471
Adkinson, C. D., 165
Adler, T., 95, 176
Adolph, K. E., 180
Agresti, A. A., 503
Ahmed, A., 202
Ahrons, C. R., 428
Aikin, L. S., 498
Ainslie, J. J., 493
Ainsworth, M. D., 166, 241, 242, 244, 245, 246
Akhtar, N., 219
Akiyama, M. M., 224
Alan Guttmacher Institute, 498
Alanski, J. A., 251
Alberts, D. M., 377
Alderdice, F., 144
Alemi, B., 144
Aleser, K. H., 133
Alessandri, S. M., 125, 235
Alexander, C. S., 487
Alexander, J. M., 382
Alexander, K. L., 141, 399
Allen, A. W., 281, 282
Allen, J. G., 516
Allen, K. R., 438
Allen, L., 530
Allen, M. G., 529
Allen, R., 481
Allhusen, V. D., 266
Allison, K. W., 453
Allison, P. D., 429
Allport, G. W., 449
Almeida, D. M., 474
Alperstein, G., 437
Alpert, R., 353
Alpipuria, L. L., 518
Alsaker, F. D., 513
Alton, E., 99
Alton, I. R., 122
Aman, C. J., 411

Amato, P. R., 428, 431
Ambrosini, P. J., 411
American Academy of Pediatrics Task Force on Infant Positioning, 175
American Academy of Pediatrics, 186
American Association of University Women, 403
American Association on Mental Retardation, 412
American Athletic Union, 479
American College Health Association, 493
American Medical Association's Council, 356
American Psychiatric Association, 410, 477, 478, 503
Ames, L. B., 377
Anand, K. J. S., 164
Ancoli-Israel, S., 481
Anderman, E. M., 530
Andersen, R. E., 372
Anderson, A. H., 300
Anderson, C. L., 145
Anderson, C. W., 263
Anderson, D., 242, 303, 311
Anderson, E. A., 435, 436
Anderson, E. R., 426
Anderson, E. S., 537
Anderson, G. L., 128
Anderson, G. M., 124
Anderson, K. N., 300
Anderson, L. M., 170
Andersson, B. E., 263
Andersson, T., 469
Andolsek, K. M., 171, 176
Andrade, M. M., 481
Andrews, J. A., 475
Angell, M., 136
Angier, N., 99
Anisfield, M., 167
Annas, G. J., 106, 107
Annis, L. F., 116, 118, 119, 120, 132, 148
Anthenelli, R. M., 104
Antitila, A., 133
Antonaraks, S. E., 101
Antonucci, J., 445
Apfel, N. H., 130
Apgar, V., 129, 148, 149
Appel, L. F., 305
Applebom, M. I., 5, 533
Archer, S. L., 516
Arend, R., 245
Armon-Lotem, S., 220
Arnett, J., 487, 488
Arnold, I. J. P., 481
Aro, H., 470
Arrington, T., 548
Artman, L., 295
Asendorpf, J. B., 236

Ashford, E., 392
Aslin, R. N., 159, 162, 205, 217
Asquith, P., 525
Astin, A. W., 490
Astington, J. W., 297, 302
Atkinson, A. M., 257
Atterbury, J. L., 164
Attie, I., 470
Auerbach, C. F., 433
Ault, R., 198, 200, 201, 381
Austin, A. B., 413
Austin, L., 487
Axline, V. M., 332
Axworthy, D., 106
Azar, B., 97, 164, 241
Azen, C., 101

B

Baak, K., 248
Bachman, J. G., 491, 543, 544
Bachno, R. A., 515
Bacon, S., 86
Baddeley, J., 445
Badger, E., 213
Baer, L., 293
Bagley, C. A., 518
Bagnato, S. J., 191
Bagwell, C. L., 440
Bahrick, O., 11
Bai, D. L., 182
Bailey, D. A., 373
Bailey, J. M., 106, 438, 502
Bailey, M. D., 341
Bailey, W. T., 29
Baillargeon, R., 202, 204, 299
Baird, P. A., 102
Baird, T. L., 495
Bakeman, R., 238
Baker, B., 455
Baker, L. A., 341
Baker, L. S., 92
Bakken, L., 517
Balaban, M. T., 170
Baldwin, M., 213
Balinsky, B. I., 116
Ball, S., 311
Balle-Jensen, L., 487, 488
Baltes, P. B., 55, 64
Bandura, A., 60, 62, 71, 327, 447, 451
Bank, S., 341
Banks, M. S., 159, 161
Barabasz, A., 410, 412
Barabasz, M., 410, 412
Baranowski, M. D., 500
Barbaranelli, C., 62
Barglow, P., 263
Barham, J., 451
Barnat, S. B., 200
Barnecutt, P., 28, 29
Barnes, H. L., 214, 527
Barnes, K. E., 329

Barnes, S. L., 407
Barnett, W. S., 315, 316
Baron, J., 177
Barr, H. M., 123
Barr, S. I., 473, 478
Barratt, M. S., 102
Barrera, M. Jr., 206, 237, 521, 548
Barrett, M., 218, 226
Barron, J., 497
Barry, R., 513
Barth, R. P., 494, 495, 497, 498
Bartholomew, K., 252
Bartle-Haring, S., 516
Bartlett, S. J., 372
Barton, M., 220
Barton, S., 72
Bartsch, K., 201, 302
Bassuk, B. A., 436, 437
Bassuk, E., 435, 436, 437
Bates, B. A., 250
Bates, J. E., 92, 185, 245, 265, 337, 355, 435, 528
Bateson, C., 217
Bathurst, K., 255, 256
Baudonniere, V., 236
Bauer, G., 326, 448
Bauer, P. J., 297, 306
Baumrind, D., 31, 110, 333, 334, 336, 337, 338, 356
Baxter, S., 213
Bayles, K., 185
Bayley, N., 208, 469
Beal, C. R., 403
Beaumont, P. J., 477
Beauvais, F., 547
Beck, B. M., 538
Beck, J., 129
Becker, J. V., 451
Becker, J., 216, 350
Becker, L. A., 413
Becker, W. C., 335
Bee, H., 45
Behrman, R. E., 146, 148, 313
Beilin, H., 299
Belkin, L., 134, 139
Bell, A., 502
Bell, C., 361
Bell, N. J., 258
Bell, R. M., 497
Bell, R. Q., 21
Bell, S. M., 166
Bellamy, C., 287
Bellet, W., 519
Belsky, J., 185, 200, 246, 247, 249, 251, 258, 263, 265, 266, 341, 469
Bem, S. L., 20, 353, 354
Benbow, C. P., 413
Bence, P., 371
Bendersky, M., 125
Bendito-Silva, A. A., 481
Bennefield, R. M., 531

Bennett, D., 404
Bennett, J. C., 343
Benoit, D., 248
Benson, J. B., 203
Benson, P. L., 490, 491
Benson, V., 9
Bentler, P. M., 547
Bentz, L. S., 164
Benz, J. J., 166
Berenbaum, S. A., 350, 502
Berendes, H. W., 124
Berenson, G., 371
Berg, F., 476
Berg, K. M., 164
Berg, W. K., 164, 165
Berger, C. S., 125
Berger, S. H., 432
Berien, C., 149
Berk, E. L., 292
Berko, J., 291
Berkowitz, G. S., 130
Berkowitz, R. L., 130
Berlyne, D. E., 332
Berman, S. L., 453
Berman, W., 315, 316
Bernard, H. S., 516
Berndt, T. J., 439, 523
Bernhardt, B., 110
Bernstein, A., 531
Bernstein, D. I., 498
Berry, R. M., 497
Bertenthal, B. L., 182
Bertoncini, J., 162
Bertrand, J., 219
Besharov, D. J., 125
Bettelheim, A., 127
Bettschart, W., 513
Betz, M., 540
Beyth-Marom, R., 487
Bezman, R. J., 411
Bhatt, R. S., 206
Bierman, K. L., 440
Bigelow, B. J., 345
Biggar, R. J., 496
Biggs, A., 312
Bigler, R. S., 349
Bigner, J. J., 185, 335, 338
Bigson, W. B., 330
Bilchik, S., 551
Biller, H. B., 257, 258
Billings, R. L., 126
Bilodueau, H., 141
Bing, E., 139
Bingham, C. R., 492, 495
Birch, H. G., 20, 89, 132
Birch, J. W., 413
Birch, L. L., 284, 285, 286
Biro, F. M., 498
Bisanz, J., 379
Bish, A., 135
Bishop, J. A., 521
Bishop, S. J., 249, 250
Bjorklund, D. E., 47, 199, 200,
    201, 297, 302, 304, 378, 379,
    382, 386
Bjorklund, D. F., 6, 206, 208, 212
Black, B., 345

Black, J. E., 170
Black, J. K., 281, 324, 325, 326,
    327, 370, 371, 374
Black, T. L., 191
Blackman, L. S., 401, 412
Blais, R., 141
Blajda, V. M., 90
Blakely, E. H., 361
Blakemore, J. E. 0., 349
Blakeslee, S., 137, 172, 174, 429,
    430
Blanck, P. D., 29
Blanton, H., 499
Blasi, A., 444
Blehar, M. C., 244
Blewitt, P., 300
Block, J. H., 348, 352, 513, 546,
    547
Block, J., 546
Bloom, L., 216, 221, 222, 225
Blum, R. M., 471
Blumberg, M. L., 493
Blumenfield, P., 530
Blyth, D. A., 470, 475, 530
Bobrow, D., 438
Bobrow, M., 106
Boeck, S., 547
Boegehold, B., 184
Bogatz, G., 311
Bogenschneider, K., 547
Bohannon, J. N., 224, 226
Bohlin, G., 267
Bohman, M., 104
Bolduck, D., 189
Bolger, K. E., 355
Boller, K., 207
Bolognini, M., 513
Bonamo, K. M., 224
Booth, A., 428
Booth, D., 284, 431
Borich, G., 25, 399
Boris, N. W., 249
Boriskin, J. A., 358
Bornstein, M. H., 16, 125, 165,
    172, 182, 208, 237, 336
Borra, S. T., 372
Botein, S., 249
Bouchard, T. J., 95
Boucher, R., 99
Boudreault, M., 144
Boulerice, B., 429, 538
Boulton, M. J., 440, 450
Bouma, R., 527
Bowen, R., 485
Bowen-Woodward, K., 433
Bowerman, M., 225, 226
Bowey, J. A., 410
Bowker, A., 440
Bowlby, J., 241, 242, 252, 255
Bowler, D., 100
Boyatzis, C. J., 26
Boyes, M., 446
Bracey, G. W., 392
Brackbill, Y., 141
Bradbard, M, R., 266
Bradley, R. H., 209, 243, 434

Bradsher, K., 10
Brainerd, C. J., 382
Brand, E., 433
Branstetter, W. H., 346
Brantley, J. C., 410
Brassard, M. R., 357
Braubard, B. I., 124
Brauch, J. B., 510
Bray, J. H., 426, 427, 428, 432
Brazelton, T. B., 142, 149, 150,
    165, 169, 179, 251
Brember, I., 422, 423
Bremner, J. G., 159, 162, 202
Brems, C., 213
Brenneman, K., 302
Brenner, B., 184
Brenner, R. A., 176
Brent, D. A., 472
Brewerton, T. D., 475
Breznitz, Z., 377
Brice, P., 453
Brickey, M., 412
Bridger, W. H., 163
Bridges, L. J., 249, 257
Brierly, J., 169
Brillon, L., 338
Briones, M., 428
Brittain, C. V., 522
Brix, K. A., 133
Broberg, A. G., 266
Brocks, D. J. H., 106
Brody, G. H., 341
Brody, J. E., 373
Brody, N., 188
Brody, R., 206
Bronfenbrenner, U., 67, 68
Bronson, G. W., 159, 254
Bronstein, P., 398, 428
Brook, D. W., 546
Brook, J. S., 546, 547, 548
Brooke, H., 176
Brooks, M. G., 436, 437
Brooks, R. B., 423, 424
Brooks-Gunn, J., 254, 334, 396,
    402, 465, 467, 469, 470, 475,
    496, 501, 538
Brookshire, W. K., 413
Brooten, D., 126
Brown, A. L., 304
Brown, B. B., 522
Brown, B. R., 496
Brown, B., 533
Brown, C., 339, 402
Brown, J. E., 187, 548
Brown, J. H., 427, 428
Brown, J. M., 455
Brown, L., 177, 512
Brown, R., 220
Browne, A., 436, 437
Bruch, H., 478, 479
Bruck, M., 308
Brummitt, G. A., 126
Bruner, J., 225, 226, 227, 332
Brunner, C., 404
Brusca, R., 23
Bruskin/Goldring Research, 17, 18
Bryan, A. D., 498

Bryant, D. M., 211, 212, 226, 316
Bryant-Brown, L., 305
Buchanan, C. M., 350
Buckner, J. C., 436, 437
Buess, C. E., 503
Bugental, D. B., 21, 327
Buhr, J. C., 219
Buhrmester, D., 341, 439
Buis, J. M., 485
Bukowski, W., 5, 439, 440
Bullock, M., 185, 298
Burcham, B., 410
Burchinal, M. R., 212, 226, 265,
    267, 316, 342, 542
Burgess, K. B., 347
Buriel, R., 257, 259, 260, 261,
    339
Burke, J. R., 277
Burke, M., 341
Burke, P. B., 251, 253
Burnett, P. C., 335
Burnette, E., 518
Burnham, D. K., 351
Burns, A., 10
Burns, F., 213
Burns, K., 125, 126
Burns, R. B., 325, 474
Burns, W., 125, 126
Burton, R. V., 447, 529
Bush, D., 530
Bushnell, I. W. R., 160
Bushness, I. W. R., 146
Buskens, E., 137
Busner, C., 472
Buss, A. H., 89, 91
Buss, K. A., 90, 251
Butler, D. L., 410
Butler, N., 123
Butterfield, E. C., 167
Butterfield, P., 239
Butterfield, W. H., 437
Bybee, J., 474
Byrne, D., 493

C

Cacioppo, J. T.,
Cadoff, J., 176
Cahan, S., 295, 403
Cain, K. C.,
Cairns, B. D., 440
Cairns, E., 453, 513
Cairns, R. B., 39, 49, 53, 54, 63,
    440, 447, 520, 522, 538
Caldera, Y. M., 189
Caldwell, B., 209, 318
Caldwell, K., 439
Caldwell, M. B. A., 209
Calhoun, C., 11
California State Department of
    Education, 422
Calkins, S., 251
Call, J., 302, 421
Call, K. T., 542
Callan, V. J., 527
Callanan, M. A., 302
Caltran, G., 240
Caluson, J. A., 428

Cambre, K. M., 502
Cameron, N., 177
Campbell, B., 475
Campbell, F. A., 211, 212
Campbell, K., 412
Campbell, L. P., 434
Campbell, S. B., 246, 249
Campbell, S. M., 498
Campos, J., 161, 239, 253, 258
Camras, L. A., 239
Cantor, N., 493
Cantu, C. C., 518
Capaldi, D. M., 494
Capell, E. J., 128
Capirci, O., 218
Caprara, V., 62
Capua, A., 105
Carbo, M., 390
Carey, K. B., 495
Carey, M. P., 495
Carlock, C. J., 422
Carlsmith, M. J., 469
Carlson, E., 246, 248
Carlson, J., 511
Carlson, L., 410
Carlson, V., 357
Carmody, D., 316
Carnegie Corporation, 530
Carnegie Council, 471, 494, 528, 552
Carney, D., 454
Carpendale, J. I. M., 446
Carpenter, M., 219
Carrigan, S., 472
Carroll, D. W., 216, 219
Carroll, J., 187
Carroll, M., 473
Carruth, B., 479
Carskadan, M. A., 480, 481
Carta, J., 228
Carter, D. B., 353, 441
Carver, V. C., 252, 492, 495, 500
Case, R., 46, 332
Caselli, M. C., 218
Casey, K. L., 293
Casiro, O., 124
Caskey, C. T., 106
Casper, R. C., 475
Caspi, A., 20, 90, 469, 470, 549, 550
Cassidy, D. J., 304
Cassidy, J., 245, 246, 248
Cassidy, K. W., 302
Cassidy, L., 493
Castro, M. A., 141
Catalano, R., 358, 551
Cataldo, C. B., 131, 177, 285, 373
Catania, A. C., 158
Cauffman, E., 476, 478
Caughy, M., 265
Cauley, K., 326
Cavalli-Sforza, L. L., 91
Cavanaugh, P. J., 167
CDC, 486, 495
Ceci, S. J., 307, 308, 309
Center on Addiction and Substance Abuse, 544

Centers for Disease Control and Prevention, 149, 174, 473
Centra, J. A., 395
Cernock, J. M., 163
Chackere, G. J., 453
Chan, R. W., 439
Chan, S. Q., 339
Chance, J., 390
Chandler, K., 310
Chandler, M., 446
Chao, R. K., 337
Chapman, K., 493
Charles, A. G., 143
Charlesworth, W. R., 237
Chase-Landsdale, P. L., 261, 263, 501
Chasin, J., 218
Chasnoff, I. J., 125, 126
Chassin, L., 521, 547
Chavira, V., 519
Chavkin, W., 437
Chen, C., 390
Chen, G. P., 390
Chen, S., 253, 451
Chen, X., 91
Chen, Z. Y., 524
Cherlin, A. J., 427, 428, 430
Cheskin, L. J., 372
Chess, S., 20, 89, 268
Chethik, L., 125
Chi, M. T. H., 305
Chiaromonte, T., 346
Chilamkurti, C., 357, 358
Children Under Stress, 545
Children's Defense Fund, 172
Childress, A. C., 475
Chilman, C. S., 492
Chira, S., 264
Chiras, S., 140, 467, 468
Chisholm, G., 248
Choi, S., 225
Chomitz, V. R., 132, 147
Chomsky, N., 222
Chow, J., 358
Christianson, R. E., 123
Christopoulus, K., 450
Chubb, N. H., 513
Chung, C., 356
Churchill, E., 99, 105
Cibelli, C. D., 245
Cicchetti, D., 249, 250, 354, 355, 356, 357
Cicero, T. J., 133
Cipriani, D. C., 85, 92
Clapp, G., 358, 454, 455
Clark, C. S., 355, 356
Clark, J. J., 426
Clark, R., 125, 240, 269
Clark, S. L., 137
Clarke, A. D. B., 6, 19, 20
Clarke, A. M., 6, 19, 20
Clarke-Stewart, K. A., 264, 266, 315
Clasen, D., 522
Clausen, S. E., 299
Clay, R. A., 408
Clements, C. D., 128

Clements, D. C., 266
Clifton, R. K., 203, 206
Clingempeel, W. G., 427, 433
Cloninger, C. R., 104
Clow, C., 105
Clubb, P. A., 306
Cobbs, G., 511
Coe, R. M., 495
Coelen, C., 268
Cogan, R., 143
Cohen, A. P., 123
Cohen, A. R., 101
Cohen, D. J., 124, 361
Cohen, D., 167
Cohen, E., 493
Cohen, K. M., 6, 502
Cohen, L. B., 159, 258
Cohen, N., 403
Cohen, P., 547
Cohen, R., 413
Cohen, S. L., 413
Cohn, J. F., 246, 249, 250
Coie, J. D., 331, 450, 451, 452, 454
Coiro, M. J., 427
Coistiloe, P., 123
Colby, A., 445
Cole, D. A., 403, 422
Cole, R. W., 390
Cole, T. B., 471
Cole, T. J., 187
Coleman, D., 164
Coleman, E., 521
Coleman, H. L. K., 519
Coleman, S. M., 360
Coles, A. D., 10
Coley, J. D., 293
Coley, R. L., 430
Colin, V. L., 242, 244, 245, 248, 258
Coll, C. G., 10
Collins, F. S., 78, 105, 523
Collins, J., 62
Collins, M. F., 145
Collins, N., 147, 252
Collins, R., 167, 252
Collins, W. A., 420, 424
Colombo, J., 165
Colt, G. H., 472
Coltrane, S., 256
Comer, R. J., 451, 471, 479, 503, 537
Commons, M. L., 29
Comstock, G., 311, 390, 454
Condon, W. S., 162, 217
Condry, J., 310, 371
Confield, R. L., 162
Conger, R. D., 214, 470, 526, 542
Connell, D., 249, 250
Connell, J. P., 249
Conte, C., 391
Conte, J. R., 355, 356
Cook, P. S., 120
Cook, R., 135
Cooke, R. A., 30
Coolsen, P., 435
Coontz, S., 428

Cooper, C. R., 527
Cooper, H. I., 390
Cooper, M. H., 175
Cooper, M. L., 252
Cooper, P., 249
Cooperman, A., 311
Copans, S. A., 132
Copeland, E. J., 518
Copeland, L. A., 513
Corasaniti, M. A., 434
Corballis, D., 281
Corbin, S. B., 426
Corbine, J., 509
Cordier, S., 133
Corey, L., 127
Corley, R., 91
Cornwell, K. S., 281
Corsaro, W. A., 345
Corter, C. M., 336, 341
Cossette, L., 189
Cote, R., 144
Cotton, D., 128
Coughlin, C., 427, 429
Coulton, C. J., 358
Counts, D. R., 177
Courage, M. L., 305
Cousins, J. H., 378
Cowan, C. P., 95, 335
Cowan, P. A., 95, 96, 98, 110, 248, 335
Cox, A., 309
Cox, F. D., 117, 492
Cox, M., 427
Cox, R., 427
Craig, K. D., 164
Crain, W., 64, 67
Cratty, B. J., 6, 278, 281, 282, 376
Craven, R., 326
Crawford, H. J., 498
Crawford, J., 404, 405
Creasey, G. L., 258
Creedy, K. B., 110
Crespo, C. J., 372
Crichton, M., 71
Crick, N. R., 452
Crnic, K., 185
Crockenberg, S., 214, 250
Crockett, L., 470, 492, 494, 495
Croen, L. A., 130
Crosby, L., 494
Crosby, W. M., 123
Cross, B., 422, 423, 424
Cross, C., 214
Cross, D., 201
Cross, H. J., 516
Crouter, A. C., 67, 68, 261, 262, 341
Cruttenden, L., 201
Csikszentmihalyi, M., 492
Culpepper, L., 129
Cultice, J. C., 304
Culver, C., 234
Cumella, S., 436
Cummings, E. M., 79, 86, 247, 355, 427
Cummings, M. R., 78, 79, 80, 81, 83, 85, 86, 88

Cummins, J., 405
Cunningham, A. E., 389
Cunningham, B., 542
Cunningham, M., 469
Cunnungham, S., 407
Current population reports, 313
Currie, J., 316
Currier, J.S., 128
Curry, K., 174
Curtis, S., 222
Curwin, A., 225
Cutler, A., 217
Cutler, G. B., 177
Czajka-Narins, M., 474

D

Dale, P. S., 407
Damon, W., 325, 421, 439, 445, 446
Daniel, M., 448
Daniels, D., 92, 94, 341
Dannemiller, J. L., 159
Daragh, J., 256
Darling, N., 337, 522
Darling-Hammond, L., 394
Darlington, J., 428
Darlington, R. B., 316
Dasen, P., 484
Data Analysis System, 409
Dauber, S. L., 399
Davidson, R. J., 255
Davies, D., 308, 309
Davies, J., 422, 423
Davies, M., 123
Davies, P. T., 247, 427
Davis, C., 285
Davis, D. L., 299
Davis, G. A., 298, 414
Davis, K., 253
Davis, P. W., 356, 359, 360
Davis, P., 247
Davis, R., 479
Davis, W., 487
Dawes, A., 453
Day, R. D., 360
De Bruyne, E., 307, 309
De Gaston, J. F., 492
De Haan, M., 158
De Lorimier, S., 330
de Roiste, A., 146
De Schonen, S., 160, 170
De Wolff, M. S., 246, 247
Deak, G. O., 297
Deal, J. E., 426
Dean, A. L., 358
Dean, R. F. A., 179
Deane, K. E. 241, 244
DeAngelis, T., 101, 546, 549
Deasey, D., 313
Deater-Deckard, K., 93, 266, 268, 336
DeBaryshe, B. D., 451
DeBlassie, A. M., 536, 538
DeBlassie, R., 496, 536, 538
Debois, D. L., 513
DeBro, S. C., 498

DeBruyne, L. K., 18, 132, 187, 285, 372, 473
Debus, R., 326
DeCasper, A. J., 162
Deely, K., 269
DeFries, J. C., 87, 90, 95
Dekovic, M., 514, 517, 522
Delaney, C. H., 509, 510
DeLeon, L., 225
Delgado-Gaitan, C., 338
Delisle, J. R., 539
DeLoache, J. S., 159, 300, 301, 304
DeLuccie, M. F., 257
DeMeis, D., 259, 260
Dement, W. C., 164
Demo, D. H., 433, 438, 525
Dempster, F. N., 288, 303, 382
Dennehy, K., 539
Dennis, M. G., 179
Dennis, W., 179, 243
DeOreo, K., 376
DePietro, J. A., 265
Deplan, F., 133
D'Ercole, A., 436
Derrick, A., 472
Deruelle, C., 160, 170
Desai, S., 261, 265
Desiderato, L. L., 498
Desmarais, S., 352
Deutch, F. M., 256
DeVault, C., 493, 502, 503
deVilliers, J. G., 217
deVilliers, P. A., 217
DeVore, G. R., 137
deVries, M. W., 91
Dewey, K. G., 187
Dews, S., 388
Diamond, A., 201, 202
Diamond, J. M., 434
Diamond, M., 349, 502
Diamond, N., 201, 202, 203, 379
Diaz, R. M., 404
Dickover, R. E., 128
Didow, S. M., 291
Dielman, T. E., 513
Diener, E., 428
Digest of Education Statistics, 537
DiLalla, L. F., 208, 209
Dillon, D. R., 23
Dinkmeyer, D., 336
DiPietro, J. A., 331
Dishion, T. J., 450, 451, 452
Dittus, P. J., 492
Dix, T., 333, 360
Dixon, E., 179
Dobkin, P. L., 546
Dodge, K. A., 250, 331, 337, 355, 435, 440, 450, 451, 452, 454, 528
Dolan, C. V., 96
Dolan-Mullen, P., 122
Dolby, R. M., 142
Dolcini, M. M., 487
Domenice, S., 481
Donahue, M., 490, 491
Dondi, M., 240

Donegan, C., 406
Dong, Q., 344
Donnerstein, E., 454
Donovan, J. M., 516
Donovan, T., 342
Dooley, D., 358
Dornbusch, S., 334, 337, 469, 522, 524, 533, 534, 543
Dorr, A., 10, 310
Dorval, B., 384
Dougherty, L., 234
Dougherty, T. M., 208
Douglas, M. J., 142
Doussard-Roosevelt, J. A., 144
Dowler, J. K., 126
Dowling, K., 162
Downey, E. P., 347
Downs, A. C., 351
Doyle, A, B., 330
Doyle, J. A., 188, 350
Draper, D. C., 413
Draper, P., 469
Dreher, M., 126
Dreikurs, R., 335
Dresser, C., 473
Dretzke, B. J., 535
Dreyer, P. H., 496
Drummond, R. J., 539, 542
Dube, E. M., 502
Dubow, E. F., 500
Duckett, E., 521
Duerr, A., 128
Duffy, U., 513
Duggan, A., 501
Duke, M. P., 71, 72
Duke, P., 480
Dukes, R. L., 518
Dullea, A., 101
Dumais, S. T., 159
Duncan, C. C., 103
Duncan, G. J., 396, 402
Duncan, M., 413
Duncan, P., 469, 470
Dunham, F., 225
Dunham, P. J., 225
Dunham, R. M., 515
Dunkel-Schetter, C., 147
Dunn, B. E., 359
Dunn, H., 94
Dunn, J., 341, 342, 343, 440
Dunn, M., 379
Dupress, D., 469
Duran, R. P., 394, 402
Durkin, K., 218, 220, 222, 225, 254, 325, 448
Durndell, A., 540
Dusek, J. B., 469, 479
Dustin, E. R., 422
Duwa, S. M., 192
Duyvesteyn, M. G. C., 246
Dwoterzky, J. P., 168
Dziuba-Letherman, J., 355
Dziurawiec, S., 159, 160

E

Eagly, A. H., 348
East, P. L., 501

Easterbrooks, M. A., 245
Eaton, W. 0., 348, 382
Eccles, J. S., 350, 403, 521, 526, 530
Echols, L. D., 389
Eckerman, C. O., 254, 291, 384
Edelman, M. W., 536
Edelstein, S., 172
Eder, A., 79
Eder, R. A., 325
Editorial Note, 172
Edmonds, P., 549
Eduction of Handicapped Children, 410
Edwards, C. P., 184, 186
Edwards, L. E., 122
Edwards, R. W., 547
Egan, S. K., 452
Egeland, B., 264, 358
Egerton, J. M., 307
Eggebeen, D. J., 265
Eggert, L. L., 473
Egolf, B., 455
Ehrenhaft, P. M., 145
Ehrhardt, A., 348
Eichenberger, S., 427
Eicher, S. A., 522
Eidelberg, L., 52, 446
Eisele, J., 474
Eisen, L. M., 125
Eisenberg, M., 266, 268
Eisenberg, N., 189, 341, 346, 351, 423, 424, 447, 448, 449, 463
Eisenberg-Berg, N., 346
Eisenbud, L., 354
Eiser, C., 306
Eiser, J. R., 306
Eisler, I., 478
Elam, S. M., 392
Elardo, R., 209
Elder, G. H., 20, 70, 470, 542
Elder, R., 214
Elia, J., 411
Elias, M., 433, 473
Elicker, J., 246
Elkind, D., 485, 486
Elkins, I. J., 87
Elliott, S. N., 357
Ellis, A. W., 410
Ellis, H. D., 159, 160
Elsen, H., 226
Elster, A. B., 501
Emde, R. N., 53, 234, 239
Emerson, M. R., 500, 501
Emery, R. E., 354, 426
Emmons, L., 474, 475
Emory, E., 97, 126, 142
Engleman, D., 361
Englund, M., 246
Ennis, L. R., 348
Ensign, J., 426
Entwisle, D. R., 141, 316, 399
Epstein, L. H., 372, 479
Erel, O., 341, 428
Erhardt, D., 411
Ericksen, K. P., 496, 498

Erickson, J., 490
Erikson, E. H., 54, 56, 241, 324, 332 , 513, 515, 516, 517, 518, 538
Eron, L. D., 451, 453, 454
Eskenazi, B., 123
Espinosa, L., 404
Esplin, P. W., 307
Essex, M. J., 269
Etaugh, A., 347
Etaugh, C., 266, 347, 403
Eth, S., 361, 362
Etzel, B. C., 240
Evaluation, 175
Evans, S. L., 500
Eveloff, H. H., 240
Extra Dry, 175

F

Fabes, R. A., 346, 347, 423, 440
Fabre-Grenet, M., 160
Fagen, J. F., 206
Fagot, B. I., 184, 189, 246, 334, 347
Fahy, T. A., 478
Fairburn, C, G., 478, 479
Falbo, T., 344, 345
Falk, P., 438
Fan, C., 344
Fan, L., 390
Fantz, R. L., 159, 160
Farmer, A., 93
Farmer, H. S., 541
Farver, J. A. M., 330, 346
Fassinger, R. E., 540
Fauci, A. S., 127
Faustman, E. M., 133
Fay, R., 502
Feagans, L. V., 260, 265
Fearnow, M. D., 454
Feeney, J. A., 252
Fegley, S., 543
Fein, G., 126, 312, 315
Feinman, J., 530
Feinman, S., 239
Feinstein, C. B., 421
Feiring, C., 251, 345
Feldhusen, J. F., 414
Feldman, J. F., 163, 188, 209
Feldman, M. W., 95
Feldman, S. S., 524, 529
Feldstein, M., 455
Feltey, K., 493
Ferguson, T. J., 442
Fernald, A., 217, 226, 227, 238, 239
Ferrar, J., 225
Fertman, C. I., 513
Fiano, K., 142
Ficher, I., 439
Fick, A. C., 452
Field, T. M., 167, 237
Field, T., 146, 249, 253, 259, 264, 434
Fier, J., 403
Fifer, W. P., 162
Figeredo, A. J., 361

Fine, L. J., 133
Fine, M. A., 398, 528
Fink, L., 78
Finkelhor, D., 355, 356
Finkelson, L., 493
Finn, C. E., 96
Finn-Stevenson, M., 269, 270
Finsh, M., 542
Fiore, M. F., 548
Fiori-Cowley, A., 249
Firestone, P. B., 203
Firestone, W. A., 498
Fischer, A. R., 493
Fischer, K. W., 171, 489, 510
Fischer, P., 453
Fischoff, B., 487
Fisher, C. B., 8, 31
Fisher, C., 217
Fisher, D. M., 168, 181
Fisher, J. A., 284, 285
Fisher-Thompson, D., 351
Fitch, S. A., 516
Fitzgerald, H. E., 281
Fitzsimmons, C. M., 219
Fitzsimmons, J., 125
Fivush, R., 306
Flake, A. E., 434
Flaks, D. K., 439
Flanagan, C., 428
Flanigan, J. M., 437
Flavell, E. R., 301, 302
Flavell, J. H., 45, 199, 200, 205, 238, 297, 299, 301, 302, 304, 305, 381, 382, 383
Fleck, K. M., 394
Fleming, A. S., 336, 397
Fletcher, A. C., 522
Fletcher, J. C., 81, 128
Flin, R., 307
Floyd, R. L., 123
Flum, H., 514, 515
Foa, L., 391
Fodor, I. G., 474
Fogel, A., 327
Fogelman, K., 20
Follmer, A., 307
Fomon, S. J., 285
Fonagy, P., 248
Fonteyn, V. J., 130
Forbes, D., 548
Ford, D., 394
Ford, L. M., 325
Fordham, S., 519
Forness, S. R., 411
Forrest, J. D., 497, 498
Forrest, L., 444
Forte, J., 412
Foscarinis, M., 435
Foster, E. M., 542
Foster, G. D., 474
Fowler, B. A., 479
Fowler, M., 410
Fox, N., 251, 255
Fox, S., 407
Fox, V., 550
Fracasso, M. P., 246
Fraleigh, M., 534

Fraley, R. C., 252
Frame, C. L., 331
Francis, L. J., 423
Francis, P. L., 208
Frank, D. A., 126
Frankel, A. J., 262
Frankel, K. A., 245
Franz, C., 449
Frary, R. B., 473
Frazier, J. A., 395, 396
Freeborn, A., 520
Freiberg, P., 435
French, S. A., 476
Freud, S., 50, 242, 353, 446, 491
Freund, L. S., 65
Frey, D., 422
Frey, K. S., 349
Frey, W. H., 15
Friebert, S. E., 383
Friedrich, L., 312
Friedrich, W. N., 358
Friend, T., 546
Frigoletto, F., 141
Frodi, M., 258
Frost, C. J., 491
Frost, J. J., 497, 498
Fu, V. R., 339
Fujita, N., 221
Fuligni, A. J., 521, 526, 528, 533
Fulker, D. W., 90
Fulkerson, J. A., 476
Fullerton, C. S., 513
Furman, L. N., 306
Furman, W., 341, 344, 439, 513
Furstenberg, F. F., 429, 496, 501, 538
Fusaro, J. A., 317
Futterman, D., 128
Futterweit, L. R., 163

G

Gable, D., 453
Gadberry, S., 390
Gadow, K. D., 454
Gagnon, J., 502
Gagnon, M., 170
Gaier, E., 37
Gaines, R. W., 357
Galambos, N. L., 434, 435, 474
Galef, B. G. Jr., 285
Gallagher, L., 79
Gallup, A. M., 392, 393
Galotti, K. M., 445
Garbarino, J., 356, 434, 453
Garcia, R., 167
Garcia-Coll, C., 251, 338, 339, 340, 500
Gardner, D. K., 134
Gardner, H., 46, 96, 399
Garduque, L., 543
Gargiulo, J., 470
Gariepy, J. L., 440
Garland, A. F., 471, 472, 473
Garmon, L. C., 488
Garn, S. M., 469
Garner, D. M., 479
Garnica, 0. K., 226

Garvey, C., 292, 346
Gary, E. M., 552
Gaskill, F. W., 410
Gatch, G., 387
Gatz, M., 92
Gavin, L. A., 513
Gavora, J., 499
Gaylord-Ross, C., 412
Gaylord-Ross, R. J., 412
Ge, X., 470, 513
Geary, D. C., 390
Geber, M., 179
Gee, S., 307
Geib, I., 493
Gelfand, D. M., 249
Gelles, R. J., 355, 356
Gelman, R., 299, 300, 302
Gelman, S. A., 293
Gendler, B., 125
Genel, M., 411
Genetic testing for Cystic Fibrosis, 99
George, G. C., 477
Gergen, P. J., 473
Gerrard, M., 487, 499
Gershkoff-Stowe, L., 219
Gerstein, T., 405
Gerton, J., 519
Gervai, J., 347, 348, 354
Gest, S. D., 440
Getz, I., 448
Gewirtz, J. L., 240
Giardiello, F. M., 107
Gibb, D., 128
Gibbons, F. X., 487
Gibbs, J. T., 537
Gibson, E. J., 161
Gifted and Talented Children's Act, 413
Gilbert, J., 335
Gilligan, C., 444, 445, 512
Gillock, K., 536
Gilroy, F. D., 80
Ginott, H., 552
Ginsburg, G. S., 398
Giovanelli, G., 162
Giovino, G. A., 123
Girgus, J. S., 513
Glantz, F., 268
Glaser, R., 305
Gleason, J. B., 223
Glick, P. C., 432
Glider, P., 530
Glock, M., 474
Goertzel, M. G., 19
Goertzel, V., 19
Gohm, C. L., 428
Goldberg, D., 479
Goldberg, W. A., 261, 269
Goldenberg, R. L., 132, 144
Goldfield, B. A., 219, 220
Goldfield, E. C., 182
Goldman, G., 141
Goldman, L. S., 411
Goldsmith, E., 92
Goldsmith, H. H., 88, 90, 103, 251

Goldstein, H., 123
Goldwyn, R., 248
Goleman, D. G., 16, 254, 402
Golombok, S., 135, 438
Gomby, D. S., 262, 269, 313
Gonzalez, J., 488
Gonzalez, Z., 339
Gonzalez-Mena, J., 184, 186
Goodluck, H., 222, 291
Goodman, G. S., 354, 355, 356,
    357, 358, 426, 428, 430, 431
Goodman, R., 93
Goodnow, J. J., 21, 327
Goodstadt, M. S., 548
Goodwyn, S. W., 218
Gopnick, A., 219
Gopnik, A., 225, 297, 302
Gordon, A. S., 546
Gordon, B. N., 307
Gordon, C. M., 495
Gordon, L., 133
Gordon, P., 224, 335
Gordon, V. V., 492
Gorman, D. M., 548
Gottesman, I. I., 108
Gottfried, A. E., 255, 256, 259,
    261, 262, 397
Gottfried, A. W., 163, 255, 256,
    397
Gottlieb, G., 64, 108
Gottman, J., 345, 439
Goubet, N. N., 203
Gove, W. R., 259
Graber, J., 469, 475
Graber, M., 202, 204
Grace, N., 357
Graham, J., 454, 547
Graham, M. A., 192
Graham, S., 452
Gralinski, H., 122, 236
Granau, R., 164
Granger, R. H., 125
Grant, C. L., 474
Grant, J. P., 286
Gratch, G., 387
Grattan, E., 436
Gray, E., 435
Gray, W., 486
Green, A. H., 357
Green, B. L., 212
Green, F. L., 301, 302
Green, J. A., 166
Green, R., 438, 529
Green, S. B., 390
Greenberg, J. S., 503
Greenberg, M. H., 269
Greenberg, M. T., 147, 396, 452,
    454, 500
Greenberg, R., 167
Greenberger, E., 260, 261, 542,
    543
Greendlinger, V., 493
Greenfeld, L. A., 544
Greenhalgh, J., 92
Greenough, W. T., 170
Greenwood, C., 228
Greer, C. V., 520

Greer, P., 448
Gremy, I., 123
Griesler, P. C., 440
Griffith, D. R., 125, 126
Griffith, E. M., 377
Griffith, L., 356
Griffiths, M. D., 453
Grimley, D. M., 496, 498
Gringlas, M. B., 426, 428
Grinnell, K., 347
Grobbee, D. F., 137
Groff, J. Y., 122
Gronlick, W., 238
Groome, L. J., 164
Gross, R., 469
Grossman, J. B., 552
Grossman, K. E., 248
Grossman, K., 248
Grotevant, H. D., 514, 517, 520,
    527
Group Health Medical Associates,
    123
Groves, B. M., 361, 362
Gruendel, J., 306
Grunebaum, H., 249
Grusec, J. E., 327
Guacci-Franco, N., 398
Guerra, A. M., 378
Guidice, S., 289
Guillen, E. O., 478
Guinn, B., 474
Guiogli, P. E., 437
Gulko, J., 352
Gullone, E., 471
Gunnar, M. R., 238, 251
Guntheroth, W. G., 172, 175
Guo, G., 538
Gurney, P., 423
Gustafson, G. E., 166
Gutberlet, R. L., 142
Guttman, E., 356
Guy, W., 312
Guyer, M. S., 105
Gwartney-Gibbs, P. A., 493

H

Haas, R., 428
Hack, M., 22, 146
Hadjistauropoulis, H. D., 164
Haeuser, A. A., 359
Haffner, D. W., 497
Hagan, M. S., 426
Hagan, R., 189
Hagekull, B., 267
Hagen, J. W., 6, 304
Hagerman, R. J., 103
Haith, H., 159
Haith, M. M., 159, 162, 203, 208
Hakim-Larson, J., 422
Halfon, O., 513
Hall, C. W., 150
Halpern, C. T., 475
Halpern, D. F., 403
Halpern, S., 134
Halsey, C. L., 145
Halton, A., 132
Halverson, C. F., 353, 426

Ham, M., 520
Hamachek, D. E., 55, 56
Hamburg, D. A., 332
Hamel, S. C., 125
Hamill, P. V. V., 177, 278, 279,
    370, 371, 465
Hamilton, C. E., 246, 247
Hamilton, L. H., 469
Hamilton, W. G., 469
Hammen, C., 436, 437, 455
Hammer, T. J., 512
Hammersmith, S., 502
Hand, M., 346
Hann, D. M., 452
Hansen, J., 410
Hansford, B. C., 423
Hanson, T. L., 433
Hapkeiwicz, W., 300
Harding, S., 407
Hardy, J. B., 401, 501
Harlap, S., 124
Harley, D., 281, 282
Harley, E. E., 124
Harlow, H. F., 243
Harlow, M. K., 243
Harmin, M., 448
Harper, P. A., 191
Harris, G., 284
Harris, J. C., 164, 169, 222, 223,
    224, 480, 481
Harris, J. D., 424
Harris, J. J., 394
Harris, K. L., 166
Harris, L. T., 281
Harris, M., 218, 351, 420, 424
Harris, P. L., 203, 237
Harris, R. J., 305
Harris, Y. R., 304
Harrison, A. O., 339
Harrold, R. D., 530
Hart, B., 218, 226, 228
Hart, D., 325, 421
Hart, S. N., 357
Harter, S., 378, 422, 510, 511,
    512
Hartshorne, H., 447
Hartup, W. W., 346, 347, 439,
    440
Harvey, A. R., 510
Harvey, E., 262
Harvey, K., 480
Harvey, S. M., 492, 495
Harwood, R. L., 12, 339
Hasbrouck, J. E., 453, 454
Haste, H., 445
Hastings, P. D., 91
Hatcher, P. J., 410
Hattie, J. A., 423
Haugaard, J. J., 354, 426
Hauser-Cram, P., 184, 192
Hausken, E. G., 310
Hausman, B., 436, 437, 455
Hawkins, J. D., 551
Hay, D. F., 341, 346, 347
Hayes, R., 539
Hayne, H., 206, 207
Haynes, H., 159

Haynes, J. A., 432
Haynes, O. M., 248
Hayslip, B., 30
Hazan, L., 252, 253, 345
Head Start, 315, 316
Headden, S., 406
Healey, J., 10
Heath, D.T., 130
Heath, W. P., 307
Hebberler, K. M., 191
Heckman, J. J., 96, 98
Hedge, M. N., 217
Hegland, S. M., 346
Heidelise, A., 142, 149, 150
Hein, K., 128
Heinicke, C. M., 279
Heinig, M. J., 187
Heinrich, R., 509
Heinrichs, C., 177
Heister, M., 264
Helburn, S. W., 269
Held, R., 159
Hellerstedt, W. L., 122
Hellmich, N., 136, 262, 373, 399
Hemminki, K., 133
Henderson, H. A., 91
Hennessy, K., 355
Henry, B., 549
Henry, C. S., 544
Henry, T., 392, 450, 533, 534,
    538, 549, 550
Henshaw, S. K., 499
Henslin, J. M., 11
Hepper, P. G., 281
Herbert, W., 448
Herdman, R. C., 145
Herman-Giddens, M. E., 467
Hermon, D., 133
Hernandez, D. J., 8, 10, 13
Hernandez, H., 13
Hernandez, R., 189
Heron, A., 484
Herrenkohl, E. C., 455
Herrenkohl, R. C., 455
Herrera, C., 239, 355
Herring, J. R., 473
Herrnstein, R. J., 96
Hershberger, S. L., 502
Hershey, M., 413
Hertsgaard, D., 474
Hertsgaard, L., 245
Hertzler, A. A., 473
Herzog, D. B., 478
Hess, J., 137
Hess, R. D., 228
Hetherington, E. M., 91, 426,
    427, 428, 430, 431, 432, 433
Hickey, P. R., 164
Hickson, L., 401, 412
Higgins, B. S., 134, 500
Higgins, D. A., 347
High/scope Educational Research
    Foundation, 551
Hilgard, H. R., 116
Hill, J. P., 527
Hilton, N. Z., 361
Himes, J. H., 122

Hines, A. M., 426, 428
Hines, M., 350
Hinshaw, S. P., 411
Hirsh, B. J., 513
Hirshberg, L. M., 239
Hispanic Dropouts, 538
Ho, M. K., 340
Hobbs-Tait, L., 263
Hochman, D., 304
Hochschild, A., 256, 517
Hock, E., 259
Hodapp, R. M., 257
Hodeges, E. L., 475
Hoeksma, J. B., 251
Hofer, M. A., 116
Hoff, R., 128
Hofferth, S., 269
Hoff-Ginsberg, E., 288, 292, 384, 385
Hoffman, J., 500
Hoffman, L. W., 240, 241, 256, 260, 261
Hoffman, M. L., 446
Hogan, R., 292
Hogarty, P. S., 209
Hogue, A., 522
Holaday, D. A., 149
Holden, G. W., 336, 360, 550
Holland, J., 539
Holland, S. B., 164
Hollander, D., 494
Holmbeck, G., 521, 527
Holmes, D. S., 19, 31
Holstein, C. B., 489
Holt, G., 408
Holt, J., 383
Holtzen, D. W., 503
Holtzman, N. A., 101
Holupka, C. S., 437
Honig, A. S., 228, 317
Hooper, R., 249
Hopkins, J., 249
Hops, H., 475
Horbar, J. D., 144, 145
Horgan, J., 173, 175
Horn, J. M., 96, 97
Horney, K., 353
Hornik, R., 238
Horowitz, F. D., 165, 208, 237
Horowitz, L., 252
Horowitz, T. R., 538
Hotelling, K., 444
Hovell, M. F., 228
How Poor Are The Poor, 175
Howe, M. L., 305
Howe, N., 332, 341
Howell, S. C., 427
Howes, C., 246, 247, 264, 265, 267, 268, 269, 296, 345
Howley, A. A., 413
Howley, C. B., 413
Hoyer, W. J., 485
Hronsky, S., 126
Huang, L. N., 537
Hubb-Tait, L., 488
Hubel, D. H., 170
Hudley, C., 452

Hudson, J. A., 306
Hudson, L., 486
Huebner, R., 234
Huesmann, L. R., 451, 453
Huff, H. A., 329
Huffman, L., 91
Huffman, M. L., 307
Hughes, D. C., 146
Hughes, J. N., 453, 454
Hughes, M. R., 136
Hughes, V., 403
Hulme, C., 410
Humphreys, A. P., 330, 331
Hunt, C., 173
Hunt, J., 208
Hunt, J. R., 402
Hunter, F. T., 520, 526, 527
Hurlburt, N., 209
Hurrell, R. M., 493
Huston, A. C., 10, 33, 189, 311, 347, 352, 390, 430, 453
Hutt, M. J., 253
Huttman, E., 437
Huttunen, M. O., 132
Hwang, C. P., 258, 266
Hyde, J. S., 269
Hymel, S., 440

I
Iacono, W. G., 87
Idle, T., 352
Iglesias, J., 237
Ilg, F. L., 377
Illingworth, R. S., 169
Impact of Vaccines, 172
Indelgyne, E., 164
Inderbitzen, H. M., 521
Infant Mortality, 172, 173
Ingersoll, E. W., 165
Inhelder, B., 43, 225, 295, 297, 379, 380, 482, 483
International Food Information Council, 372
Intons-Peterson, M. J., 188
Irwin, C. E., 475
Isabella, R. A., 246, 249, 250, 251
Isada, N. B., 130
Isenberg, J., 332
Israel, A. C., 326, 410, 412, 477
Ito, J., 103
Iverson, J. M., 218
Izard, C. E., 234, 235, 248, 251, 397

J
Jaccard, J., 492
Jaccard, M. R., 267
Jack, B. W., 7, 129
Jacklin, C. N., 347, 352, 450
Jackson, J. F., 110
Jacobovitz, D., 358
Jacobson, A. L., 249
Jacobson, J. L., 126
Jacobson, L., 531
Jacobson, S. W., 126
Jacobs-Quadrel, M., 487
Jaffe, P. G., 361

Jahoda, G., 10
JAMA, 372, 373
James, L. S., 149
Jameson, D., 412
Jani, S., 520
Jankowski, J. J., 163
Jarrell, M. P., 475
Jarvis, P. A., 258
Jelalian, E., 487
Jencks, C., 96
Jenkins, J. R., 410
Jensen, L., 492
Jensen, L. C., 468
Jessell, T., 208
Jessop, D. J., 412
Jessor, R., 547
Jing, Q., 344
Joekler, N., 411
Joffe, A., 471
Joffe, L. S., 245
John, O. P., 550
John, R. J., 341
John, R. S., 428
Johnson, A. K., 437
Johnson, C. J., 292
Johnson, D. J., 394
Johnson, D. W., 376
Johnson, J. E., 330
Johnson, J. S., 223
Johnson, M. H., 159, 160, 169, 170, 171, 288
Johnson, M. L., 177
Johnson, M., 391
Johnson, R. R., 390
Johnson, R. T., 376
Johnson, S. L., 285, 286
Johnson, S. P., 158, 205, 222
Johnson, S., 334
Johnston, C., 164
Johnston, L. D., 491, 544, 546
Johnston, R. B., 132
Jones, B. A., 306
Jones, C., 392, 406
Jones, K. H., 478
Jones, K. L., 123
Jones, M. B., 285
Jones, M. C., 469, 470
Jones, M. M., 377
Jones, R. T., 548
Jones, S., 240
Jordan, C., 126
Jorgensen, L., 474
Jory, B., 520
Joseph, G., 439
Jost, K., 172, 174
Juffer, F., 246
Junge, M. E., 535
Jusczyk, P. W., 162, 217
Justice, E., 382

K
Kagan, J., 45, 70, 90, 91, 207, 251, 253, 383, 401, 423
Kagan, S., 399
Kahn, C. R., 88
Kahn, M. D., 341

Kahne, J., 423
Kail, R., 5, 6, 304, 382
Kalakanis, L., 160
Kalat, J. W., 103, 170, 188, 288, 411, 468
Kaler, S. R., 145, 184, 186
Kalichman, S. C., 498
Kallenbach, L. R., 133
Kamii, C., 317, 390
Kammerman, S. B., 258
Kandel, D. B., 123
Kandel, E. R., 208
Kanouse, W. F., 497
Kantner, J., 498
Kaplan, D. S., 538
Kaplan, H. B., 538
Kaplan, J., 388
Kaplan, N., 248
Kaplan, P. S., 9, 48, 97, 98, 102, 191, 192, 240, 291, 296, 317, 376, 397, 399, 401, 402, 408, 412, 449, 537
Karbon, M., 346
Karen, R., 241, 254
Karla, B., 307
Karns, J., 327, 520
Karraker, K. H., 500
Karson, M., 526
Kasansnak, K. R., 441
Kasari, C., 124
Kastelic, D., 512
Kataria, S., 434
Katchadourian, H., 467
Katz, L. G., 309
Katz, P. A., 347, 354, 441
Kaufman, J., 357
Kavale, K. A., 411
Kavanaugh, K., 184
Kay, T., 103
Kaye, H., 167
Kazdin, A. E., 451
Kearney, B., 307
Kearsley, R. B., 162
Keating, D. P., 484, 490
Keefer, C. S., 179
Keels, M. A., 133
Keenan, K., 249
Kegan, R., 379
Keil, F. C., 297
Keith, B., 428
Keith, T. Z., 537
Keller, A., 325
Keller, M. B., 478
Keller, S., 11
Kelley, M. L., 338, 339, 357
Kellman, P. J., 158, 159, 161
Kelly, B., 387
Kelly, D., 533
Kelly, J. A., 498
Kelly, J. B., 427
Kendall-Tackett, K. A., 356
Kendler, K. S., 478
Kendrick, C., 341, 342
Keogh, J., 376
Keppler, A., 127
Kermis, M. D., 84
Kern, D. L., 285

Kerr, B., 403
Kersey, K., 283
Kershner, R., 493
Keyes, S., 546
Khanna, P., 265
Kidd, K. K., 82, 97
Kidwell, J. S., 515
Killen, J. D., 475
Kilpatrick, K. L., 362
Kimball, M., 535
Kimble, G. A., 85
Kimm, S. Y., 473
King, N. J., 326
King, S. L., 474
Kinney, H. C., 171
Kirby, D., 497, 498, 499
Kirkpatrick, L. A., 253
Kisker, E., 268
Kistner, J., 23
Kitayama, S., 446
Kittleson, M. J., 492, 495
Klassen, A., 502
Klebanov, P. K., 396, 402
Klein, M. H., 269
Klein, N. K., 22, 146
Klein, P. J., 200
Klein, T. P., 437
Klepinger, D. H., 500
Klesges, L. M., 372
Klesges, R. C., 372, 549
Kliewer, W., 454, 455
Klimes-Dougan, B., 23
Kline, P., 353, 446
Klinnert, M. D., 90, 234, 239
Klonoff-Cohen, H., 172
Klorman, R. C., 166
Knapp, J. R., 526
Knight, G. P., 347, 528
Knowles, M., 99
Kobelin, C., 141
Koblinsky, S. A., 435, 436, 437
Kobus, K., 536
Koch, M., 403
Koch, R., 101
Koestner, R., 449
Koff, E., 466, 467, 470, 475, 476
Kogos, J., 397
Kohlberg, L., 442, 443, 444, 488, 489
Kohn, A., 423, 424
Koinis, D., 301
Kolata, G., 102
Kolb, S., 180
Kolbo, J. R., 361, 362
Kolstad, V., 300
Komarovsky, M., 493
Kondo-Ikemura, K., 247
Kopp, C. B., 67, 144, 145, 184, 186, 236
Korbin, J. E., 358
Korn, W. S., 490
Korner, A. F., 188, 288
Koslowski, B., 251, 300
Koss, M., 361, 493
Kostanski, M., 471
Kostelny, K., 453
Koup, R. A., 128

Kovalski, N., 481
Kowal, A., 342
Kowaleski-Jones, L., 430
Kozma, E. J., 529
Kraemer, H. C., 142
Krakow, J. B., 67
Kramer, D., 485
Kramer, L., 332, 342, 343, 344, 539
Kramer, R., 443
Krappman, L., 425
Krebs, D. L., 445, 446
Krebs, L. L., 335
Kreitler, S., 399
Kremenitzer, J. P., 162
Kreppner, K., 8
Kretler, H., 399
Kreutzer, M. A., 237
Kristal, A., 437
Kroger, J., 517
Krogman, W. M., 373, 376, 466
Krombholz, H., 377
Krone, W., 88
Kronmal, R. A., 101
Kronsberg, S., 189
Kropp, J., 214
Krowitz, A., 161
Kruesi, M. J., 370
Kruger, A., 220
Krunkel, D., 453
Ksansnak, K. R., 354
Ku, L. C., 499
Kubiszyn, T., 25, 399
Kuczynski, L., 357
Kuebli, J., 306
Kuhl, P. K., 224
Kuhn, D., 485
Kuhn, L., 128, 485
Kunkel, D., 33
Kupersmidt, J. B., 331, 355, 440, 453
Kurdek, L. A., 398, 427, 428, 528
Kurth, S., 540
Kurtz, D. A., 518
Kurtzberg, D., 162
Kurtzweil, P., 132
Kurzweil, S. R., 160

L

Labouvie-Vief, G., 484, 485
Labov, W., 407
Lacey, E. P., 492, 495
Lachman, M. E., 92
Ladd, G. W., 347, 420
Ladner, J., 500, 501
LaFromboise, T., 519, 536
LaGaipa, J. J., 345
Lagerspetz, K. M. J., 451
LaGreca, A. M., 450
Lahey, B., 214
Lairmore, M. D., 128
Lalinde, P., 192
Lam, M., 528
Lamaze, F., 143
Lamb, M. E., 33, 239, 246, 257, 258, 266, 307, 435
Lamborn, S., 334

Lampl, M., 177
Lancashare, J., 122, 130, 142, 147, 148
Landau-Stanton, J., 128
Lane, D. M., 382
Lane, E., 31, 371
Lane, K., 493
Lang, J. M., 123
Lange, J. E., 349
Langer, A., 161
Langer, J., 205
Langlois, J. H., 160, 263, 351
Lansford, J. E., 331
Laosa, L. M., 401
Lapinsky, R. H., 130
Lapsley, D. K., 487
Larner, M. B., 313
Larroque, B., 124
Larsen, J. M., 315
Larson, C., 246
Larson, J., 10
Larson, R., 475, 492, 520, 521, 522
Laskas, J. M., 312
Lau, L. B., 316
Lau, Y. U. L., 105
Laughlin, H. P., 51
Lauresen, B., 346
Lauriat, A., 437
Lavery, B., 488
Lawrence, R., 186
Lawrence, V. W., 209, 228
Lawson, K. R., 303, 329
Lawton, M., 392, 551
Lazar, I., 316
Lazer, J., 214
Le Sieur, K. D., 420
Leadbeater, B. J., 249, 250, 485
Leahy, T. H., 305
Leaper, C., 513
Leary, M. R., 26, 27, 28
Leavitt, L. A., 102
LeBlanc, M., 538
Leboyer, F., 144
Leckman, J. F., 88
Lederman, S. A., 147
Lee, J., 476
Lee, M., 265
Lee, P. A., 496, 498
Lee, S. Y., 390
Lee, T. J., 407
Lee, V. E., 538
Leeson-Payne, D., 187
Lefkowitz, M. M., 453
Leger, D. W., 166
Legerstee, M., 242
Leichtman, M. D., 307, 308
Leiderman, P., 534
Leinbach, M. D., 189, 347
Leland, N. L., 494, 495, 497, 498
Lemery, K. S., 90
Lempers, J. D., 301
Lenbach, M. D., 347
Lengua, L. J., 452
Lenneberg, E. H., 222
Leon, G. R., 476
Lerman, C., 105

Lerner, J. V., 261
Lerner, R. M., 8, 526
Leshner, A. I., 544
Lesko, S. M., 176
Lesser, I, M., 91
Lesser, T. M., 514
Lester, B. M., 126, 142, 149, 150
Lester, D., 493
LeVay, S., 502
Levenda, R. H., 509
Levin, H., 191
Levin, S. R., 303
Levine, A., 525
Levine, K., 227
Levitt, J. L., 398
Levitt, M. J., 398
Levori, P. W., 478
Levy, C. W., 311
Levy, D., 122
Levy, G. D., 353
Levy, J. M., 412
Levy, P. H., 412
Lewinsohn, P., 475
Lewis, H., 455
Lewis, J. M., 426
Lewis, M., 125, 235, 236, 237, 239, 251, 254, 263, 345, 474, 475, 541
Lewis, R. G., 340
Lewit, E. M., 313
Lewkowicz, D. J., 162
Lewontin, R. C., 95
Leyendecker, B., 246
Lezotte, L.W., 394
Liben, L. S., 349, 354
Lidenberger, U., 427
Lieberman, A. F., 182, 184, 191
Lieberman, E., 123, 142
Liebert, R. M., 454
Light, D., 11
Light, H. K., 474
Lightbody, P., 540
Ligman, J. D., 546
Liker, J., 214
Lillywhite, H. S., 220, 291
Lin, C. C., 339
Lin, G., 344
Lin, K. M., 91
Lin, L., 344
Lindbohm, M. L., 133
Lindee, M. S., 106
Lindenberger, U., 55
Link, S. C., 481
Lipsitt, L. P., 163, 167, 174
Lister, G., 187
Litt, M., 362
Little, J. K., 349
Little, R. E., 133
Lloyd, B., 189
Lobar, S. L., 340
Lochhead, J., 391
Lockhart, A. S., 376
Lockwood, D., 551
Loeber, R., 452
Loeches, A., 237
Loehlin, J. C., 92, 94, 96
Lombroso, P. J., 88

Londerville, S., 185, 245
Longres, J. F., 407
Longstreth, L. E., 99
Loomis, L. S., 428
Lorenz, K., 242
Lorion, R. P., 453
Lourenco, O., 205
Lovelace, L., 209
Lovett, M., 407, 408, 410
Low, K. G., 536
Lowrey, G., 177
Lubach, G. R., 124
Lucas, A., 187
Lucey, J. F., 144, 145
Luker, K., 495, 498
Lundberg, S., 500
Luria, Z., 188
Lussier, J. B., 256
Luster, T., 394, 500
Lutkenhaus, R., 185
Lykken, D. T., 86, 95
Lynch, E. B., 293
Lynch, L., 99, 106
Lynch, M., 357
Lynn, G., 547
Lyon, T. D., 308
Lyons, N., 512
Lyons-Ruth, K., 245, 246, 249, 250
Lytle, L. J., 512, 517
Lytton, H., 79, 352, 359
Lyxell, B., 516

M

Maccoby, E. E., 191, 249, 255, 333, 334, 347, 348, 352, 424, 425, 444, 450
MacDermid, S., 261
MacDormand, M. F., 148
MacFarlane, A., 163
Machado, A., 205
MacKain, K., 217
MacKinnon, C. E., 341
MacKinnon, D., 413
MacKinnon, R., 341
MacKinnon-Lewis, C., 334
MacMillan, A., 356
MacMillan, H. L., 356, 362
MacMillan, J. H., 356
MacWhinney, B., 224
Madden, M., 390
Maeroff, G., 533
Maggs, J. L., 435
Magnusson, D., 469, 470
Magruder, B., 502
Mahapatra, M., 446
Mahoney, J. L., 538
Mahoney, K. M., 490
Main, H., 251
Main, M., 185, 244, 245, 248
Maio, I. W., 166
Maker, C. J., 414
Makin, J. W., 163
Making Money, 139
Malatesta, C. Z., 234, 235
Malcuit, G., 189
Males, M. A., 547, 548, 549

Malik, M. M., 358
Malinowski, C. I., 444
Malloy, M., 473
Manber, R., 480
Mancuso, J., 480
Mandel, D. R., 72, 217
Mandell, D. J., 299
Mandereau, L., 133
Mandeville, G. K., 377
Mandler, J., 204, 205, 206
Mangelsdurf, S., 251
Manning, A., 548, 549
Manning, M. L., 529
Mannle, S., 226
Manosevitz, M., 433
Manzo, K. K., 373
Marano, H. E., 454
Marans, S., 361
March of Dimes, 100, 101, 122, 126, 127, 137
Marcia, J., 514, 516, 517
Marcon, R. A., 314, 317, 318
Marcus, G. F., 221, 292
Marean, G. C., 224
Margolin, G., 341, 428
Margulis, C., 221
Mark, M., 224
Marklein, M. B., 532
Markman, E. M., 219
Markovitz, H., 483
Marksrom-Adams, C., 516, 518
Markus, H. R., 446
Marold, D. B., 511
Marquis, A. L., 226
Marquis, J., 390
Marsh, H. W., 326
Marshall, S. P., 403
Marsiglio, W., 503
Marsland, C., 270
Marteau, T. H., 106
Martens, C., 422
Martin, C. L., 119, 347, 349, 350, 351, 353, 354
Martin, D., 496
Martin, G. B., 240
Martin, J. A., 249, 333, 334, 425
Martin, J. M., 403
Martin, J., 502
Martin, S., 211, 354
Martinez, F. D., 123
Martinez, P., 453
Martinez, R. O., 518
Martinez-Pons, M., 62
Marttunen, M. J., 472
Marwick, C., 147
Mas, C. A., 427
Masataka, N., 162, 226
Mascola, M. A., 123
Mason, J. O., 355, 550
Massad, L., 546
Masse, L. C., 546
Masterpasqua, F., 439
Matas, L., 245
Mates, B. F., 311
Matias, R., 249, 250
Mattay, V., 411
Mau, W. C., 539

Mauldon, J., 495, 498
Maurer, D., 159, 206, 237, 281
Maxfield, M., 357
May, M. A., 447
Mayaux, M. J., 128
Mayer, J. E., 546
Mayes, L. C., 125, 547
Maziade, M., 144
Mazza, J. J., 471, 472
McAdoo, H. P., 338, 394
McAuliffe, S., 543
McBride, B., 256, 257, 356
McBride, S., 259
McBride-Chang, C., 410
McCabe, A. E., 300
McCabe, L., 105
McCall, R. B., 5, 97, 209
McCartney, K., 108, 263
McCarty, J., 214
McCauley, E., 103
McCauley, K., 362
McChesney, K. Y., 437
McClearn, G. E., 87
McClinton, B. S., 313
McCloskey, L. A., 361
McCluskey, K., 250, 425
McCombs-Thornton, K. L., 437
McCord, J., 360
McCormick, C. M., 281
McCoy, 341
McCracken, C., 360
McCracken, R. S., 539, 540
McCune, L., 200, 332
McDonald, D. W., 548
McGhee, P. E., 258, 386, 387
McGhie, A. C., 166
McGinnes, G., 234
McGough, L. S., 309
McGraw, M. B., 191
McGraw, S. A., 494, 497
McGue, M., 86, 87, 95, 104, 109
McGuffin, P., 93
McGuire, S., 341, 440
McHale, S. M., 261, 341, 342
McIntosh, D. N., 176
McKay, G. D., 336
McKinlay, J. B., 494, 497
McLanahan, S., 427, 431, 433
McLaughlin, B., 335
McLoyd, V.C., 9, 10, 145, 213, 214, 250
McManus, I. C., 281
McNally, S., 424
McNeal, R. B. Jr., 538
McNeill, D., 224
McPhee, L., 285
McWhirler, L., 513
Meacham, J. A., 325
Mead, M., 353
Meck, E., 300
Medora, N. P., 492
Meece, D. W., 435, 528
Meeus, W., 514, 517
Mehler, J., 217
Meier, B. G., 313
Meier, R. P., 205
Meilman, P. W., 516

Meisels, M., 526
Mellin, L. M., 475
Mellins, C. A., 92
Mellits, E. D., 401
Mello, N. K., 124, 126
Meltzoff, A. N., 167, 200, 205, 219, 225
Melzack, R., 143
Menaghan, E. G., 430
Mendelson, B. K., 372
Mendelson, J. H., 124, 126
Mendrum, D. R., 134
Menlove, F. L., 327
Menna-Barreto, L., 481
Menyuk, P., 228
Mercer, J., 162
Mergendoller, J. R., 391
Mermelstein, R., 453
Merritt, J. A., 166
Mervis, C. B., 219
Meschke, L. L., 494
Messer, S. C., 434
Messinger, D. S., 249
Metcalf, R. D., 254
Metcoff, J., 123
Meuus, W., 516, 522
Meyer, E. C., 338
Meyer, J., 189
Meyer, K. A., 542
Meyer-Bahlberg, H. F. L., 350
Michael, R. T., 261
Michaelieu, Q., 513
Michel, G. F., 281
Michelsson, K., 164
Middle, C., 144
Midgley, C., 530
Mikach, S., 438
Milburn, N., 436
Millar, W. S., 247
Miller, J. F., 102
Miller, J. G., 446
Miller, L., 268, 497
Miller, M. J., 479
Miller, P. A., 454
Miller, P. H., 43, 45, 49, 53, 54, 56, 64, 66, 200, 238, 303, 304, 482, 488
Miller, S. A., 30, 45, 188, 213
Miller, S., 542
Miller-Perrin, C. L., 356
Mills, G., 256, 257
Mills, J. L., 124
Mills, R. S. L., 333
Millstein, S. G., 471
Milne, D., 123
Milner, J. S., 357, 358
Milstead, M., 487
Minard, J., 164
Minkoff, H. L., 128
Minuchin, P., 315, 426
Miranda, S. B., 159
Mirochnik, M., 124
Mirsky, A. F., 103
Mischel, W., 352
Mitchell, C., 530
Mitchell, J. J., 105
Mitchell, P., 302

Mitka, M., 498
Miyake, K., 253
Modell, J., 70
Moerk, E, L., 224
Mofenson, L. M., 128
Moffitt, T, E., 90, 469, 470, 549, 550
Molenaar, C. M., 96
Molfese, V. J., 209
Molitor, N., 263
Moller-Wieland, D., 88
Mollnow, E., 121, 122, 126
Molnar, J. M., 437
Monaco, N., 37
Moneta, G., 521
Money, J., 348, 502
Monsour, A., 510, 511
Montgomery, R., 486
Mont-Reynaud, R., 524
Moore, D. T., 120
Moore, G., 246
Moore, K. L., 116, 117, 119, 121
Moore, M. K., 167
Moore, N. B., 498, 500
Moore, S. M., 23, 471, 487, 488
Moorehouse, M. J., 261
Morelli, G. A., 336
Morgan, J. L., 224
Morgan, K. M., 435
Morikawa, H., 226, 227, 238
Morley, R., 187
Morrell, P., 170
Morris, J. K., 134
Morris, P. A., 67
Morrison, D. M., 495, 496
Morrison, D. R., 427, 430
Morrison, F. J., 377, 379, 395, 396
Morrow, R, D., 339
Mortimer, J. T., 539, 542
Morton, J., 159, 160
Morton, M., 495
Moshman, D., 482, 484
Most, R. K., 200
Mott, F. L., 430
Motulsky, A. G., 101, 106
Mounts, N., 334, 522
Mrazek, D. A., 90
Mruk, C., 422
Mueller, E., 227, 257
Muenchow, S., 316
Muir, D. W., 164
Mullahy, P., 353
Mullen, K. D., 503
Mullen, P. D., 123
Mullett, M., 425
Mullin, J. T., 160
Mulvihill, B. A., 213
Mumme, D. L., 239, 302
Munley, P. H., 538
Munn, P., 342
Munson, P. J., 177
Munson, S. M., 191
Munson, T. C., 452
Murphy, B., 449
Murray, B., 392, 399, 500, 536, 549
Murray, C., 96, 135

Murray, G. C., 422
Murray, K., 307
Murray, L., 249, 250
Murray, S. F., 142
Mussen, P. H., 341, 447, 470
Muuss, R. E., 444, 445, 478, 479, 484
Muzio, J. N., 164
Muzzonigro, P. G., 502
Myers, B. J., 258
Myers, R. S., 474
Myrianthopoulus, N., 123

N
Nabors, L. A., 226
Nachmias, M., 251
Nader, P. R., 371
Naeye, R. L., 123
Nagel, K. L., 478
Nagel, S. K., 260
Nagin, D., 450
Nagle, R. J., 263
Najarian, P., 179
Nakagawa, K., 394
Nall, S. W., 317
Namy, L. L., 218, 219
Nanez, J. E. Sr., 205
Narvaez, D., 448
Nasm Policy Statement, 477
Nathanielsz, P. W., 145
Nation, R. L., 142
National Center for Health Statistics, 148, 149
National Center for Nutrition and Dietetics, 371
National Commission on Excellence in Education, 532
National Committee to Prevent Child Abuse, 355
National Education Goals Panel, 148, 171, 309, 313, 399, 529, 538, 550
National Institute on Drug Abuse, 545
National Safety Council, 471
Navarick, D. J., 61
Nazarro, J. N., 340
Neckerman, H. J., 440
Needlman, R., 124
Neely, J., 407, 408
Neher, L. S., 455
Neiderhiser, J. M., 91
Neiderman, D., 201
Neimark, E. D., 484
Neisworth, J, T., 191
Nelkin, D., 106
Nelson, C. A., 158, 237
Nelson, D. E., 544
Nelson, F. L., 237, 472
Nelson, J. A., 371
Nelson, K., 219, 224, 306
Nelson, L., 495
Nelson, R. S., 434
Nemeth, M., 219
Ness, R. B., 124
Neuman, S. B., 390
Neuspiel, D. R., 125

New York City Board of Education, 406
New York State Council on Alcoholism, 544
New York State Department of Health, 122
Newcomb, A. F., 440
Newcomb, M. D., 547
Newcombe, N., 383
Newman, B. S., 502
Newman, D. L., 90
Newport, E. C., 217
Newport, E. L., 161, 205, 223
Newsday, 123
NICHD, 249, 260, 264, 265
Nicholas, L. J., 473
Nicholopoulos, V., 476
NIDA Capsules, 544
Nieminen, G. S., 23
Nigg, J. T., 88, 103
Nightingale, M. N., 308
Nisbett, R., 98
Nogata, D. K., 537
Nolen-Hoeksema, S., 513
Noll, R. B., 100
Noller, P., 252, 527
Nomura, C., 547
Northwoods, 313, 314
Norton, W. T., 170
Nottelman, E. D., 530
Nunnally, J. C., 29
Nurnberger, J. I., 104
Nwokah, E., 327
Nye, R. D., 52

O
O'Bryan, K. G., 311
O'Connell, L., 540
O'Connor, R. E., 410
O'Keeffe, J., 455
O'Neal, G., 544
Oberklaid, F., 90
O'Brien, K. M., 540
O'Brien, M., 189, 210
O'Connor, M. J., 124
Oetting, E. R., 547
Office of National Drug Control Policy, 548, 549
Office of Special Education, 191, 409
Offord, D. R., 356
Ogan, T. A., 239
Ogbu, J. U., 14, 338, 542
Oh, W., 500
O'Hare, W. P., 15
O'Leary, G., 412
Olim, E. G., 228
Olinger, E., 23
Ollendick, T. H., 344
Olsen, D., 317, 318
Olshan, A. F., 133
Olson, D. H., 527
Olson, L., 533
Olson, M. R., 432
Olson, S. L., 185
Olvera-Ezzell, N., 378
Olweus, D., 347, 451, 513

O'Malley, P. M., 491, 544
O'Neil, R., 260
Oppel, W. C., 191
Oppenheim, J., 184
Opposition to Human Cloning, 105, 107
Orenberg, C. L., 122
Orlofsky, J. L., 514, 516
Ornstein, P. A., 69
Ortho Diagnostic Systems, 129
Oser, F. K., 448
Oshman, H. P., 433
Osipow, S, H., 539
Osofsky, J. D., 361, 452
Oster, H., 163, 235
Oswalt, R., 493
Owen, M. T., 213, 263
Owens, R. E., 215, 220, 221, 291
Oxtoby, M. J., 128

P
Paajanen, S., 164
Pachter, L. M., 12
Padgett, R. J., 126, 224
Padilla, A. M., 404, 495
Pagani, L., 429
Paik, H., 311, 390, 454
Paikoff, R., 334, 475
Painful Jabs, 175
Painter, K., 128, 546
Palkoviz, R., 143
Palmgren, C., 487
Palos, P. A., 497
Paludi, M. A., 188, 350
Panek, P. E., 30
Paneth, N. S., 147
Panzarine, S., 501
Parcel, G. S., 373
Parens, E., 106, 107
Park, M., 147
Parke, K. A., 246
Parke, R. D., 69, 70, 255, 257, 258, 259, 260, 261, 347, 452
Parker, J. G., 5, 331, 355, 439
Parker, K., 248
Parker, R., 437
Parks, P. S. M., 477
Parmelee, A. H., 144, 145, 164, 165
Parritz, R. H., 251
Parten, M., 328
Partridge, S, 431
Pascalis, O., 160
Pasternack, J. F., 189
Pastorelli, C., 62
Pastorino, E., 515
Patterson, C. J., 355, 439, 440, 441, 450
Patterson, G. R., 450, 451, 452
Patterson, T. L., 371
Paul, A. M., 424
Paul, J., 502
Pauls, D. L., 88
Paulson, S. E., 527, 534, 535
Pawletko, T. M., 342
Paxton, S. J., 476
Pearson, D. A., 382

Peckham, C., 128
Pedersen, J., 341, 346
Pederson, D. R., 247
Pediatrics, 173
Pedlow, R., 90
Peeke, L. A., 403
Pellegrini, A.D., 330, 331
Pendarvis, E. D., 413
Pennington, R., 411
Peplau, L. A., 498
Pepler, D. J., 341
Pepper, E. C., 340
Perkins, H. W., 260
Perlman, M., 344
Perlmutter, J. C., 330
Perner, J., 302
Perozynski, L., 343, 344
Perry, C. L., 476
Perry, D. G., 452
Perry, W., 485
Perry-Jenkins, M., 261
Persaud, T. V. N., 116, 117, 119, 121
Peskin, H., 469, 470
Pestrak, V. A., 496
Peters, A. M., 225
Peters, E. C., 123
Peters, J. C., 285
Petersen, A. C., 465, 470, 474
Peterson, C., 207
Peterson, G. W., 360
Peterson, K. L., 486
Peterson, K. S., 136, 262, 428, 549, 550
Peterson, L., 435
Peterson, R. C., 120
Petitto, L., 218
Petrill, S. A., 95, 97
Pettit, G. S., 337, 355, 435, 528
Petty, J., 144
Pfannenstiel, J. C., 213
Pfeffer, K., 28, 29
Pfeiffer, A., 88
Phares, V., 520
Phelps, K. E., 299
Philipson, L. C., 247
Phillips, D., 263, 267, 268
Phillips, J. L., 298
Phillips, K., 142
Phillips, R. B., 124, 125
Phillips, S., 136, 137, 139, 340, 542
Phinney, J. S., 518, 519
Piaget, J., 38, 41, 42, 43, 198, 199, 200, 201, 202, 206, 225, 293, 295, 297, 298, 299, 330, 332, 378, 379, 380, 442, 482, 483, 484
Piccinini, C. A., 247
Pick, S., 497
Pickens, J., 163, 249
Pickert, S. M., 330
Pierce, J. W., 371, 372
Pike, A., 86, 92, 93
Pillard, R. C., 502
Pillitteri, A., 183, 373, 374
Pina, P., 546

Pinderhughes, E. E., 452
Pine, C. J., 339
Pineault, R., 141
Pinkerton, R., 266
Pipe, M. E., 307
Pisoni, D. B., 162, 217
Pitts, R. C., 445
Plancherel, B., 513
Plas, J. M., 519
Pleak, R. R., 502
Pleck, J., 256, 499
Plomin, R., 79, 86, 87, 89, 90, 91, 92, 93, 94, 95, 99, 101, 103, 107, 341
Plotnick, R. D., 500
Plumert, J. M., 373, 374
Polak, A., 237
Poland, R. E., 91
Polit, D., 344, 345
Pollack, R., 172, 173
Pomerleau, A., 189
Poole, D. A., 307, 308
Pope, A. W., 440
Porcerelli, J. H., 477
Porges, S. W., 144
Porter, R. H., 163
Porter, R. P., 406
Portes, P. R., 427, 428, 515
Portner, J., 267, 371
Posner, J. K., 403
Poston, D. L., Jr., 344, 345
Potter, D. A., 395
Potvin, L., 141
Powell, D., 95, 335
Powell, M. B., 307, 308
Power, T., 257, 338, 378
Powlishta, K. K., 352
Poznansky, E. O., 326
Pratt, M., 372
Pratto, D. J., 434
Prawat, R. S., 300
Prediger, D., 539
Prehn, A. W., 123
Premachandra, B. R., 124
Pressley, M., 304, 305
Price, R. H., 472
Priestley, G., 307
Prior, M., 90
Pritchard, M. E., 474, 475
Provenzano, F., 188
Psychological Corporation, 208
Public Agenda, 24, 463, 464
Puckett, M. B., 281, 324, 325, 327, 370, 371, 374
Pulaski, M. A. S., 299, 378
Punamaki, R. L., 453
Putnick, M., 308
Pynoos, R. S., 361, 362

Q
Quadrel, M. J., 487
Quatman, T., 524, 529
Querido, J. G., 240
Quilligan, E. J., 141
Quintana, S. M., 487
Quisenberry, N. L., 332

R
Raay, T., 240
Rabideau, G. 355
Rabin, B. E., 10, 310
Rader, N., 203
Radke-Yarrow, M., 455
Raffaelli, M., 547
Rafferty, Y., 437
Ragone, H., 138, 139
Rainbolt, E., 520
Raloff, J., 408
Ramey, C. T., 22, 211, 212, 265
Ramey, S. L., 22, 211, 212, 267, 342
Ramirez, G., 122
Ramirez, J. D., 406
Ramsey, E., 451
Randall, J., 548
Rapkin, I., 93
Rapoport, J. L., 370, 411
Rappaport, C., 437
Rashotte, C. A., 410
Rasile, D., 487
Rasmussen, K. M., 122, 123
Raspberry, W., 407
Rath, W. R., 437
Raths, L. E., 448
Rathunde, K., 527
Rauch, J. B., 110
Rauh, V. A., 147
Raver, C. C., 249
Ray, B. A., 182
Ray, W. J., 27
Razel, M., 180
Read, M. H., 477
Read, S. T., 252
Recommended Childhood Immunization Schedule, 172
Redanz, N. J., 217
Reddel, M., 188
Redmond, S., 437
Reed, R., 537
Reese, E., 309
Reese, H. W., 163
Regan, C., 372
Reid, J. B., 452
Reid, M., 267, 342
Reid, W. J., 342
Reinhold, D., 360
Reis, E. M., 401, 412
Reiser, J. J., 69
Reiss, D., 87, 88, 91
Reissland, N., 167
Renk, K., 520
Repacholi, B. M., 237
Repp, A. C., 23
Rescorla, L., 437
Resnick, S., 251
Rest, J. R., 442, 448
Restak, R. M., 84
Revelle, W., 109
Reyes, O., 536, 537
Reyes-Lee, M., 124
Reyna, V. F., 382
Reynolds, A. J., 192, 316
Reynolds, M. C., 413
Reznick, J. S., 91, 219, 220, 251

Rheingold, H. L., 254
Rhoads, G. G., 124, 138
Riccardo, E., 11
Ricciuti, H. N., 132
Rice, C., 301
Rice, M. L., 219, 225, 311, 502
Rich, M., 494
Richards, M. H., 100, 475, 521
Richards, W., 358
Richmond, J., 146
Richters, J. E., 453
Rickert, E. S., 413
Rideout, R., 207
Rider, R. V., 191
Rierdan, J., 466, 467, 470, 475, 476
Rieser-Danner, L. A., 263
Riksen-Walraven, J. M., 247
Rimer, B. K., 123
Rimm, S. B., 414
Rimmerman, A., 412
Rinne, A., 164
Riordan, K., 251
Riseley, T. R. 228
Risser, D., 234
Ristow, M., 88
Ritchie, K., 18, 550
Ritchot, K. F. M., 382
Ritter, P., 469, 524, 534
Rivera, S. M., 205
Roach, M. A., 102
Roberts, D., 534
Roberts, E. M., 146, 148
Roberts, J. E., 226
Roberts, R. E., 475
Roberts, R. S., 411
Roberts, S., 307
Roberts, W., 263, 346, 449
Robertson, M. J., 436
Robins, R. W., 513, 550
Robinson, B. E., 502
Robinson, C. C., 315
Robinson, E., 302
Robinson, J. L., 18, 91
Robinson, L. A., 549
Robinson, L.C., 544
Rocha, C., 437
Rochat, P., 240
Roche, J. P., 492
Rock, A. M. L., 162
Rock, S. L., 209
Roder, J. S., 372
Rodin, J., 474
Rodman, H., 434
Rodriguez, C., 498, 500
Rodriguez, J. L., 404
Roe, L., 353
Roffwarg, H. P., 164
Rog, D. J., 437
Rogers, A. G., 512
Rogers, C. R., 60
Rogers, M. F., 128
Roggman, L. A., 263
Rogoff, B., 332, 383, 484
Rogosch, F., 521
Rolfes, S. R., 18, 131, 132, 177, 187, 285, 370, 372, 465, 473

Romano-Dwyer, L., 546
Romig, C., 517
Romney, D. M., 352
Rompa, D., 498
Roodin, P. A., 485
Rooks, J. P., 142
Roosa, M., 528
Roper Organazation, 497
Ropp, K. L., 477
Roscoe, B., 486
Rose, H., 354
Rose, L. C., 392, 393
Rose, R. J., 92, 104
Rose, S. A., 163, 206, 208, 209
Rosen, K. S., 251, 253
Rosen, L. R., 239
Rosen, W. D., 238
Rosenberg, H. M., 148
Rosenberg, L., 435, 436
Rosenberg, M. S., 356
Rosenberg, P. S., 496
Rosenberg, Z. F., 127
Rosenblum, G. D., 474, 475
Rosenblum, L. A., 254
Rosenhan, D. L., 92
Rosensteel, L., 174
Rosenstein, D., 163, 235
Rosenthal, D. A., 487
Rosenthal, E., 123, 124, 134
Rosenthal, R., 29
Rosenthal, S. L., 498
Rosenwaks, Z., 136
Rosenzweig, M. R., 170
Ross Laboratories, 327
Ross, D., 307, 451
Ross, H. S., 341, 344, 346, 347
Ross, J. K., 513
Ross, K., 123
Ross, S. A., 451
Roth, D. L., 474
Rothbaum, F., 253
Rothman, R., 389, 399
Rothman, S., 96, 97
Rothstein, L. E., 401
Roughton, E. C., 124
Rouse, B. D., 150
Rouse, D. J., 144
Rovee-Collier, C., 167, 206, 207
Rovine, M., 263
Rowe, D. C., 88
Rozin, P., 284
Rubenstein, A. J., 160
Rubin, A. M., 551
Rubin, J., 188, 189
Rubin, K. H., 5, 91, 312, 314,
   332, 333, 439
Rubin, L., 437
Rubin, Z., 345
Ruble, D. N., 119, 333, 347, 349,
   350, 351, 353, 423, 467
Ruck, M. D., 490
Ruddy, M. G., 208
Rueter, M. A., 526
Ruff, H. A., 303
Ruffman, T., 202
Rugh, R., 127
Ruittenbeck, H. M., 513

Rule, B. G., 442
Ruopp, R., 268
Rushworth, G., 169
Russell, C., 17
Rutter, M., 16, 20, 242, 259, 394,
   424, 455, 484, 488
Rutter, S., 103, 107
Ryan, C. W., 539, 542
Ryan, E. J., 15
Ryan, K. J., 142, 448
Ryan, R. H., 315
Rybash, J. M., 485
Rychlak, J. F., 70
Ryu, S., 542

S

Sabbagh, M. A., 302
Sachs, B., 141
Sachs, V. B., 239
Sack, J. L., 408
Sacks, N. R., 478
Sadker, D., 403, 404, 536
Sadker, M., 403, 404, 536
Sadovnick, A. D., 102
Saffran, J. R., 217
Sagi, A., 248
Sai, F., 160
Saint Pierre, R., 214
Salapate, P., 159, 161
Sale, J., 166
Salend, S. J., 15
Salk, L., 162
Sallis, J. F., 371
Sallmen, M., 133
Salthouse, T. A., 390
Saltmarsh, R., 302
Saltzman, W., 453
Sameroff, A. J., 91, 167, 251
Sampson, P. D., 123
Sanchez-Huckles, J., 338
Sandberg, E., 138
Sande, M. A., 128
Sandefur, G., 433
Sander, L. W., 162, 217
Sanders, N., 142
Sanders, S. H., 455
Sanderson, C. A., 493
Sandgrund, A., 357
Sandham, J. L., 532
Sandler, B. A., 477
Sandler, I. N., 428, 455
Sands, D. W., 503
Sandstread, H., 123
Sandstrom, K. L., 542
Sansavini, A., 162
Sanson, A., 90
Sarafino, E. P., 479
Satcher, D., 174
Sattler, J. M., 340
Satz, P., 288
Saudino, K. J., 90, 94
Saunders, S. E., 187
Sautter, R. C., 122
Savage, M. P., 473
Savin-Williams, R. C., 470, 502
Savitz, D. A., 133
Sawin, D. B., 258

Sax, L. J., 489, 490
Sayler, M. E., 413
Scales, P., 497
Scanlon, J. W., 144
Scanlon, K. B., 144
Scarr, S., 8, 82, 97, 108, 109, 263,
   266, 268
Scarr-Salapatek, S., 99
Schachter, F. F., 261
Schachter, J., 127
Schaffer, A., 242
Schaffer, H. R., 302, 334, 451
Schaffer, R., 258
Schaie, K. W., 30
Schatschneider, C. W., 383
Scheeringa, M. S., 249
Scheibe, C., 371
Scher, A., 164
Scherling, D. 125
Scherman, A., 426
Schiedel, D. G., 516, 517
Schiever, S. W., 414
Schiller, M., 251
Schilmoeller, G. L., 500
Schlackman, L. J., 142
Schlicker, S. A., 372
Schmidt, C. R., 354
Schmidt, K. L., 360
Schmidt, P., 403
Schmitt, M. H., 187
Schmitz, S., 90
Schnaiberg, L., 102, 405, 406
Schneider, K., 181
Schneider, M. A., 124
Schneider, W., 6, 206, 208, 304,
   305
Schnoll, S. H., 126
Schochetman, G., 128
Schoeber-Peterson, D., 292
Schoff, K., 397
Scholmerich, A., 246, 339
School Board News, 407
Schuckit, M. A., 104
Schulenberg, J., 543
Schultz, E. A., 509
Schulz, H. R., 164
Schulze, P. A., 339
Schumaker, J. B., 228
Schuster, M. A., 497
Schwab, R., 391
Schwanenflugel, P. J., 382
Schwartz, J. H., 208
Schwartz, P. M., 126
Schwebel, D. C., 374
Schweitzer, R., 527
Schwingle, P. J., 133
Scott, C., 10, 422, 424
Scott, L. B., 473
Scott, M. E., 413
Scrimshaw, S. C. M., 147
Scriver, C. R., 105
Scully, S., 475
Seabron, C., 437
Seachrist, L., 172
Sears, R. R., 191, 353, 451
Sebald, H., 523
Sedivy, V., 500

Sedmak, D. D., 128
Seeley, J., 356, 475
Segal, B. M., 544, 546
Segal, N. L., 95
Segal, S., 433
Segalowitz, N. S., 404
Seidman, E., 530
Seifer, R., 251
Seitz, V., 130
Self, P. A., 208
Seligman, M. E. P., 68, 92, 513
Seligmann, J., 438
Sellers, D. E., 494, 496, 497
Sells, C. W., 471
Selman, R. L., 5,
Seltzer, D. A., 213
Semper, T., 474
Senna, J. J., 550
Serbin, L. A., 352
Seroczynski, A. D., 403
Serrano, J. M., 237
Servis, L. J., 256
Seth-Smith, M., 527
Sexias, J. S., 104
Shaffer, D., 472
Shafii, M., 472
Shahidollah, S., 281
Shalala, D. E., 175
Shanahan, M. J., 542
Shanks, D., 225
Shapiro, E. K., 315
Shapiro, L. R., 306
Sharma, R., 124
Shatz, C. U., 346
Shatz, M., 215
Shaughnessy, M. F., 463
Shaver, J. P., 488
Shaver, P. R., 252, 253
Shaw, D. S., 249, 428
Shaw, G. M., 130
Shedler, J., 546, 547
Shelton, M. L., 372
Shepard, B., 234
Shepard, L. A., 377
Shepard, S., 449
Sherman, J. A., 228
Sherman, T., 455
Shestowski, B., 479
Shi, Z. M., 136
Shields, J., 108
Shin, Y. L., 330
Shinn, M., 437
Shiono, P., 124, 146, 147, 148
Shipley, E. F., 209, 228
Shipman, V. C., 228
Shirley, M., 178
Shonkoff, J. P., 192
Shope, J. T., 513
Shore, R. E., 133
Short, E. J., 383
Short, J. L., 455
Shulman, S., 246
Shweder, R. A., 446
Siegel, J., 463
Siegel, L. J., 550
Siegel, L. S., 300

Siegler, R. S., 45, 192, 290, 293, 377, 380, 483, 488
Sigelman, C. K., 342
Sigman, M. D., 165
Sigman, M., 124
Sigmundson, K., 349
Signorella, M. L., 349, 354
Silbereisen, R. K., 494
Silva, P. A., 90, 469, 549
Silver, R. C., 176
Silverberg, S. B., 521, 522
Silverman, E. H., 217
Silverman, W. K., 450
Silverstein, L. B., 433
Silverstein, S., 361
Simkin, P., 127
Simmons, R. G., 470, 475, 530
Simner, M. L., 240
Simon, F., 240
Simon, S. B., 448
Simon, T., 217
Simons, C., 425
Simpkins, C., 408
Simpkins, G., 408
Simpson, L., 146
Sinclair, H., 207
Sinclair, R. J., 398
Sing, C. F., 133
Singer, D. G., 312
Singer, J. J., 312
Singer, L. T., 144
Singer, S., 116
Singh, J. K., 79
Sinister Evolution, 281
Sinister Origins, 281
Sinnott, J. D., 485
Siperstein, G. N., 167
Sirignano, S. W., 92
Sizer, F. S., 131
Skarin, K., 254
Skeels, H. M., 98
Skeen, P., 502
Skinner, B. F., 221
Skinner, M. L., 450
Skovron, M. L., 130
Skuse, D., 327
Slaby, R. G., 347, 349, 452, 454
Slater, A., 158, 205
Slaughter-Defoe, D., 394
Slobin, D. I., 222, 224
Slocum, T. A., 410
Slonim, M. B., 339, 340
Small, S. A., 470
Smart, D. E., 477
Smart, M. S., 376, 385
Smart, R. C., 376, 385
Smetana, J. G., 425, 525
Smith, B. J., 191
Smith, C. P., 444
Smith, C., 189
Smith, D. W., 123
Smith, E. W., 267
Smith, G. E., 487
Smith, J. A., 372
Smith, J. D., 403
Smith, J. W., 263
Smith, L. B., 180, 219

Smith, M. L., 377
Smith, P. K., 330, 331
Smith, R. S., 455, 456
Smith, S., 214
Smith, T. E. C., 529
Smitherman, G., 407
Smollar, J., 521
Snidman, N., 251
Snodgrass, S. E., 29
Snow, B., 308
Snow, C. W., 126, 144, 183, 184, 185, 208
Snow, C., 224
Snyder, E., 502
Snyderman, M., 96, 97
Sobal, J., 476
Sobesky, W. E., 489
Sobieszek, B., 189
Socha, T. J., 387
Sokolov, J. L., 227
Solnit, A. J., 421, 446
Solomon, J., 244
Somerville, S. C., 304
Sommer, B. B., 464, 467
Sommerfeld, M., 392
Sonenstein, F. L., 499
Sontag, L. W., 132
Sorce, J. F., 234, 239
Sorensen, E., 431
Sorensen, L., 125
Sorenson, T., 308
Sosa, B. B., 306
Sousa, J. A., 413
South, S. J., 260
Spade, J. Z., 493
Sparling, J. J., 211, 316
Spear, P. G., 127
Spelke, E., 158, 161, 300
Spence, M. J., 162
Spencer, M. B., 469, 518
Spieker, S., 217
Spigner, C., 492, 495
Spirito, A., 487
Spiro, D. J., 203
Spitz, R., 242
Spitze, G., 260
Sprafkin, J., 454
Springer, T., 455
Sroufe, L. A., 235, 245, 246, 358
Stack, D. M., 164
Stagno, S., 127
Stainback, S., 409
Stainback, W., 409
Stanberry, L. R., 498
Stanetz, P. J., 411
Stanger, C., 235, 237
Stangor, C., 349
Stanhope, L., 341
Stanley-Hagan, M. M., 431, 432, 433
Stanovich, K., 384, 389
Stanowicz, L., 224
Staples, D. A., 132
Starnes, R., 334
Staudinger, U. M., 55
Stechler, G., 132
Steele, H., 248

Steele, M., 248
Stefanatou, A., 100
Stehlin, D., 186, 187
Stein, A., 312
Stein, J. A., 547
Stein, Z., 128
Steinbacher, R., 80
Steinberg, L., 266, 334, 337, 358, 435, 465, 469, 476, 478, 520, 521, 522, 523, 525, 528, 533, 538, 542, 543
Steinhardt, M. H., 100
Stephens, B. R., 159
Stephenson, A., 99, 544, 547
Stephenson, J., 101, 105, 107
Stern, D. N., 217
Stern, R. C., 82
Sternberg, K. J., 307, 361
Sternberg, R. J., 47
Stevens-Long, J., 29
Stevenson, C. S., 313
Stevenson, H. W., 390, 447, 533
Stevenson, J., 93
Stevenson, R. E., 129
Steward, D. S., 308
Steward, M. S., 308
Stewart, J. C., 544, 546
Stewart, S. L., 91
Steyerberg, E. W., 137
Stice, E., 548
Stipek, D. J., 236, 315
Stith, M., 373, 382, 387
Stockadle, D. F., 346
Stocker, C., 341
Stoll, M. F., 428
Stolley, P., 437
Stoltz, V., 335
Stone, L., 192
Stoneman, Z., 341
Stoney, L., 269
Stoolmiller, M., 450, 494
Storey, K., 412
Stormshak, E. A., 440
Story, M. 122
Stouthamer-Loeber, M., 550
Strassberg, Z., 451
Straus, M. A., 359, 360
Straus, M. S., 159
Strauss, M., 142
Strayer, J., 346, 449
Streissguth, A. P., 123
Striano, T., 240
Strimple, R. E., 516
Stringer, S. A., 358
Strobino, D. M., 265
Strock, B. D., 165
Strommen, L., 311
Strong, B., 493, 502, 503
Strong, W., 488
Strouse, E., 288
Strouse, J. S., 288
Stryker, J., 494, 497, 499
Stuckey, M. R., 258, 260
Study, 454
Stunkard, A. J., 86, 88
Su, M., 358
Succop, P. A., 498

Suchindran, C., 475
Sullivan, K., 301, 302
Sullivan, M. W., 235, 237
Sullivan, S. A., 284
Sullivan, S. E., 123
Suomi, S. J., 243
Super, C. M., 179
Super, D., 539
Susman, A., 420, 424
Sutton, H. E., 103
Svejda, M., 239
Swain, I. U., 206
Swain, R. C., 547
Swaney, K., 539
Swanson, D. P., 469
Swanson, H. L., 410
Swarr, A. E., 475
Swiatek, M. A., 413
Swiber, M. J., 164
Switzer, G., 346
Szkrybalo, J., 349

T

Tagar-Flusberg, H., 301
Taipale, V., 470
Takanishi, R., 394
Tanner, J. M., 177, 188, 370, 465, 467
Taras, H. L., 371
Tarver, S., 518
Tasker, F., 438
Taskinen, H., 133
Taussig, L. M., 123
Taylor, H. G., 22, 146
Taylor, J. H., 444, 449
Taylor, L., 15
Tein, J. Y., 428, 455
Tellegen, A., 95
Teltsch, T., 377
Temblay, R. E., 450
Temple, J. A., 316
Temple, L., 467, 544
Templeton, A., 134
Terwilliger, J. S., 536
Tesman, J. R., 234
Tessier, O., 330
Teti, D. M., 249
Thal, D. J., 219, 306
Thapar, A., 93
Thatcher, R. W., 289
The Economist, 172
The U. N.'s Global Immunization Triumph, 175
Thelen, E., 72, 168, 180, 181
Thivierge, J., 144
Thoma, S. J., 448
Thomas, A., 20, 89, 268, 284
Thomas, D. B., 142
Thomas, E. B., 165
Thomas, H., 294
Thomas, K., 509
Thomas, R. M., 41, 57, 63, 213
Thompson, C. J., 174, 443, 444
Thompson, D. N., 485
Thompson, E. A., 473
Thompson, E. P., 423
Thompson, R. A., 31, 166, 247

Thomson, D. M., 307, 308
Thomson, E., 433
Thornburg, H. D., 530
Thorne, A., 513
Thornton, A., 492
Tinker, E., 221
Tipp, J. E., 104
Tisak, M. S., 425
Titus, J. C., 536
Tobler, N. S., 548
Toch, T., 531, 536
Toglia, M., 307
Tokar, D. M., 493
Tokura, H., 217
Toledo-Dreves, V., 501
Tomasello, M., 219, 220, 225, 226, 302
Toomela, A., 281
Torgersen, A. M., 90
Torgesen, J. K, 410
Toth, S. L., 249, 250, 354, 355, 356, 357
Tower, R. B., 312
Tower, R. L., 548
Townsend, M. H., 502
Trainor, L. J., 162
Travers, J., 268
Travis, J., 174
Travis, L. L., 224
Treder, R., 103
Trehub, S., 217
Tremblay, R. E., 429, 538, 546
Treuba, H. T., 338
Trickett, P. K., 356, 357
Trocki, K. F., 496, 498
Tronick, E. Z., 249, 250
Tronick, L. B., 179
Troyer, D., 346
Truglio, R., 311
Trujillo, M., 378
Truman, D. M., 493
Trutter, R. J., 144
Tryon, W. W., 31
Tsay, J. C., 547
Tseng, H., 339
Tseng, V., 528
Tsuang, J. W., 104
Tubman, J. G., 494
Tucker, T., 139
Tulviste, P., 64, 65
Turiel, E., 443, 444
Turner, C., 502
Turner, P. J., 347, 348, 354
Tuttle, E. B., 413
Twomey, J. G. Jr., 128
Tyler, B., 326

U

U. S. Bureau of the Census, 313
U. S. Department of Commerce, 11, 13, 234, 283, 287, 471, 541
U. S. Department of Education Statistics, 537
U. S. Department of Education, 394, 402, 403, 405, 408, 409, 531, 532, 534

U. S. Department of Health and Human Services, 104, 123, 124, 126, 131, 132, 141, 146, 147, 172, 176, 186, 187, 287, 315, 395, 430, 471, 473, 479, 491, 495, 501, 544, 546, 551
U. S. Department of Labor, 539
U. S. News and World Report, 400
U. S. Office of Technology Assessment, 498
U. S. Public Health Service, 172
Udry, J. R., 475
Ulrich, B. D., 181
Underwood, M., 472
UNICEF, 175, 287
Upchurch, R. L., 391
Updegraff, K. A., 341
Urbano, R. J., 513
Uzgiris, I. C., 45, 208

V

Vachon, R., 483
Valde, G. A., 514, 517
Van Balen, F., 134
Van Cleave, E. F., 530
Van den Boom, D. C., 91, 246, 247, 251
Van Doorninck, W., 101
Van Dyke, A., 371, 372
Van Evra, J., 311, 390
Van Ijzendoorn, M. H., 246, 247, 248
Vandell, D., 267, 341, 403, 434
Vandenberg, B., 312
Vann, A. S., 409
Vara, L. S., 372
Vaughn, A. J., 124
Vaughn, B. E., 245, 251, 263
Vaughn, H. G., 162
Vavrik, J., 486
Veatch, R. M., 107
Veeck, L. L., 136
Vega, W. A., 338
Veldhuis, J. D., 177
Veneziano, E., 207
Verdelle, A. J., 407
Vereijken, M. J. L., 247
Vernon, P. E., 212
Vespo, J. E., 341, 346
Viadero, C., 391, 396, 410, 472, 534
Viadero, D., 316, 410
Vieland, V., 472
Vietze, P., 213
Vikan, A., 299
Virdin, L., 528
Vishi, S., 428
Vitaro, F., 429, 546
Vitz, P. C., 446
Voeller, B., 503
Vogt, R. A., 474
Volling, B., 260, 265, 334, 341
Volpe, E. P., 137
Volpe, J. J., 124
Von Eye, A., 246
Vondra, J. I., 249
Voran, M., 268

Vorhees, C. V., 121, 122, 126
Vostanis, P., 436, 437
Vuchinich, S., 427, 429
Vulthipongse, P., 127
Vygotsky, L., 64, 65, 292

W

Wadden, T. A., 474
Waddington, C. H., 177
Wade, N.A., 128
Wagner, J. L., 145
Wagner, R. K., 410
Wagner, T., 448, 449, 463, 465
Waitzman, K. A., 342
Wakeley, A., 205
Walden, T. A., 239, 306
Waldman, I. D., 88
Waldner-Haugrud, L. K., 502
Walk, R. D., 161, 162
Walker, D., 228
Walker, E., 97
Walker, J. H., 529
Walker, J. R., 269
Walker, L. J., 444, 445, 449
Walker, R. A., 289
Walker, R. R., 338
Walker, T., 214
Walker-Andrews, A. S., 238
Wall, S., 244, 330
Wallace, I., 71, 208
Wallace, A., 71
Wallace, C. S., 170
Wallace, S., 71
Wallechinsky, D., 71
Wallerstein, J. S., 426, 427, 428, 429, 430
Wallick, M. M., 502
Walsh, C., 495
Walsh, D. J., 317
Walsh, M., 311
Walsh, P. V., 347, 441
Walters, L. H., 502
Wampler, K. S., 426
Wan, C., 344
Wang, M. Q., 477
Ward, M. J., 248
Ward, S. K., 493
Wardle, J., 371, 372
Warfield-Copock, N., 510
Wark, G. R., 445, 446
Warkentin, V., 236
Warren, L. F., 469
Warren, M. P., 469, 470, 475
Warren, W. H. Jr., 182
Waserstein, S., 450
Wasik, B. H., 211, 212
Wasserman, G. A., 338
Watchmaker, G., 133
Waterman, A. S., 516, 517
Waterman, C. K., 516
Waters, E., 241, 244, 245, 246
Waters, P. L., 512
Watkins, B. A., 33, 453
Watkins, H. D., 266
Watkins, L. T., 454
Wattleton, F., 497
Watts, D., 359

Wauchope, B., 359
Waxman, S. R., 218, 293
Wechsler, D., 401, 402
Weed, S., 492
Weigel, C., 455
Weinberg, M., 502
Weinberger, J., 449
Weiner, E., 105, 106, 107
Weinraub, M., 349, 426, 428
Weinreb, L. F., 436, 437
Weisbrot, I. M., 149
Weiseman, J. R., 166
Weisenfeld, A. R., 166
Weiss, B., 337
Weiss, C. D., 220, 291
Weiss, G., 410, 411
Weissberg, R. P., 147, 500
Weissler, K., 399
Weissman, M. M., 471
Weitzman, L. M., 539, 540
Welcher, D. W., 401
Welch-Ross, M. K., 354
Wellman, H. M., 201, 297, 299, 304, 305
Wells, C., 192
Wells, K., 23
Wenar, C., 326, 477, 478
Wendland-Carro, J., 247
Wenne, W. H., 164
Wentworth, N., 159, 162
Wentzel, K. R., 439
Werner, E. E., 455, 456
Werner, L. A., 224
Wertheimer, M., 162
Wertlieb, D., 455
Wertsch, J. V., 64, 65
Wertz, D. C., 81
Wessels, H., 266
West, J., 310
West, P., 531
West, R. F., 389
West, S. G., 428, 455, 498
Westinghouse Learning Corporation, 316
Wewers, S., 452
Weyant, J. M., 449
Whalley, J., 127
Wheeler, D. L., 99
Whitaker, H., 288
White, B. L., 159
White, B., 180, 210, 214
White, D. R., 372
White, L. T., 307, 308
White, R., 281
White, S. H., 519
White, S., 493, 496
Whitebrook, M., 267, 268
Whitehead, B. M., 391
Whitehurst, G. J., 229, 309, 394
Whiteman, M., 546
Whitener, C. B., 283
Whitesell, N. R., 511, 512
Whiting, B. B., 186, 331
Whiting, J. W. M., 331
Whitley, R. J., 127
Whitman, F. L., 502

Whitney, E. N., 131, 177, 186, 187, 285, 370, 372, 373, 473
Whittinghill, J. R., 472
Why Physical Activity Drops, 473
Wichstrom, L., 513
Wickham, D., 500
Wicks-Nelson, R., 326, 410, 412, 477
Widom, C., 357
Wierson, M., 428
Wiesel, T. N., 170
Wigfield, A., 530
Wilcox, S. A., 301
Willemsen, E., 200
Willerman, L., 96
Willert, M., 317
Williams, G., 164
Williams, H. B., 340
Williams, J. W., 373, 382, 387
Williams, K., 472, 493
Williams, L., 356, 362, 519
Williams, R. D., 172
Willig, A. E., 406
Wilmut, I., 107
Wilson, C., 128, 307
Wilson, G. T., 479
Wilson, L., 9,
Wilson, M. D., 471
Wilson, M. N., 339
Wilson, R. S., 95
Wilson, S. K., 361
Wilson, S. M., 492
Wimbush, D. D., 338
Wimmer, H., 302, 306
Winchester, C., 436
Windle, M., 494

Windle, R. C., 494
Winick, M., 132
Winner, E., 301, 388
Winner, K., 302
Winsler, A., 404
Winslow, E. M., 428
Wisdom, C. S., 355, 357, 361
Wisecarver, S. J., 491
Wisniewski, A. B., 170
Witelson, S. T., 288
Wittig, B. A., 244
Wladimiroff, J. W., 137
Wodarski, J. S., 544
Wofsy, C., 128
Wolchik, S. A., 189
Wolf, R., 10, 428
Wolfe, D. A., 361
Wolfe, M., 438
Wolfe, R. A., 133
Wolff, P. H., 164, 166
Wolfson, A. R., 480, 481
Wolfson, J. C., 99
Wolinsky, S. M., 128
Wong, F., 453
Wood, D., 9
Wood, E., 352
Wood, W., 453
Woodford, M., 407
Woodsmall, L., 219
Woodson, R. W., 167
Woodward, A. L., 219
Woodward, J., 405
Woodworth, S., 185
Woody, E., 440
Woodyard, C., 17, 18
Woody-Ramsey, J., 303

Woolley, J. D., 278, 297, 299
Worobey, J., 90
Woronov, T., 391
Worsnop, R. L., 471
Wortman, C. B., 176
Wright, A. L., 123
Wright, J., 311, 312, 390, 435
Wright, K. E., 550, 551
Wright, K. N., 550, 551
Wright, L. S., 491
Wright, R., 97, 98, 136,
Wrightman, M. J., 125
Wu, M. Y., 547
Wu, P., 123
Wunsch, J., 235
Wyman, P. A., 455
Wyrobek, A. J., 115, 133

X
Xia, Y., 344
Xu, F., 136

Y
Yale, M. E., 216
Yang, B., 344
Yang, R., 214
Yarnold, B. M., 477
Yawkey, T. D., 330
Yeh, C. J., 478
Yesalis, C. E., 477
Youcha, G., 104
Young, D., 144
Young, G. Y., 170
Youngstrom, E., 397
Youniss, J., 520, 521

Z
Zabin, L. S., 498, 500, 501
Zahn-Waxler, C., 69
Zahr, L., 453
Zakin, D., 475
Zambarano, R. J., 333, 360
Zambrana, R. E., 147
Zeanah, C. H., 249
Zehr, K. S., 389
Zeiss, C., 259
Zelazo, N. A., 6, 180
Zelazo, P. D., 6,
Zelazo, P. R., 6, 180, 206
Zelnik, M., 498
Zernicke, R. F., 181
Zeskind, P. S., 166
Zigler, E., 269, 270, 315, 316, 317, 318, 357, 399, 471, 473, 474
Zill, N., 18, 427
Zimmerman, B., 62
ZImmerman, M. A., 513
Zimmerman, S., 495
Zinsser, C., 210, 310, 318
Zmiles, H., 538
Zolinda, S., 341
Zuckerman, B., 124, 125, 126, 361
Zuckerman, E., 312
Zuskar, D., 147

Subject Index

A

AB search error, 201
Abecedarian Project, 211
Abstractions, 483
Abuse, *see* child abuse
Abusive parents, 357
Academic achievement
  in elementary school, 392, 394
  gender and, 403–404
  home and, 396–399
  intelligence and, 399–403
  math and, 390
  motivation and, 399
  reading and, 389–390
  school experience and, 394–396
  socioeconomic status and,
    541–542
Acceleration, 413
Accidents, 283, 471
Accident prevention, 183, 373
Accommodation, 43
Acculturation, 13
Acquaintance rape, 493–494
Acquired Immune Deficiency
  Syndrome,
  adolescents and, 496–497
  education and, 497–498
  prenatal exposure, 127,
Active effects, 109
Adaptation (Piagetian theory), 43
Adolescence,
  behavioral autonomy and,
    521–523
  body image in, 474–477
  career choice in, 538–542
  cognitive development in,
    482–485
  conflict in, 523–526
  contraception in, 495–496
  cultural differences in, 528–529
  dropping out of school in,
    538–539
  drug use in, 544–549
  early and late maturation in,
    469–470
  eating disorders in, 477–479
  egocentrism in, 485
  emotional autonomy in,
    519–521
  growth in, 465
  health in, 471
  high school experience in,
    531–534, 536–538
  homosexuality in, 502–503
  identity formation in, 513–519
  imaginary audience in, 486
  junior high school experience,
    529–530
  morals and values in, 488–489
  nutrition in, 473
  obesity in, 479
  parenting in, 527–529

  peer influence in, 521–523
  personal fable in, 486
  physical activity during,
    473–474
  physical development in,
    465–470
  pregnancy in, 499–502
  puberty and, 464–465
  public attitudes towards
    teens, 464
  relationship with parents
    and peers, 519–527
  religion in, 490–491
  rites of passage in, 509–510
  risk taking in, 486–488
  secular trend, 467
  self-esteem in, 510–513
  sex education during, 497–499
  sexual expression in, 491–498
  sleep in, 480–482
  suicide in, 471–473
  thought patterns in, 482–484
  values in, 489–491
  violence and delinquency in,
    549–552
  weight gain in, 465
  working during, 542–543
Adolescent egocentrism, 485
Adoption studies, 85
Adult Attachment Interview, 248
African Americans,
  achievement in elementary
    school, 394
  achievement in high school,
    531, 536–537
  and career choice, 541–542
  child rearing methods, 337–338
  demography, 11
  and discipline, 337
  and drop out rate, 538
  and identity formation,
    518–519
  intelligence tests and, 401–403
  and language usage, 407–408
  and poverty, 10
  and prematurity, 146, 147–148
  and rites of passage, 510
Age of parents, 130
Age segregation, 421,
Aggression, 5, 196–197, 257–260
  during adolescence, 549–552
  during early childhood, 347
  during middle childhood,
    450–453
  and television, 453–454
AIDS (*see* acquired immune
  deficiency syndrome)
Alcohol,
  use in adolescence, 544
  genetics and, 104
  and pregnancy, 123–124
Alcoholism, 104

Alpha–fetoprotein test, 137–138
Altruism,
  in early childhood, 346
  in middle childhood, 447
Alzheimer's disease, 102
American question, 212
American Sign Language, 215
Amniocentesis, 137
Anal stage, 52
Androgens, 468
Androgyny, 512
Animism, 298
Anorexia nervosa, 477–478
Anxious attachment, 244, 245,
  246, 247, 248
Anxious/ambivalent attachment,
  245, 246, 247, 248
Anxious/avoidant attachment, 245,
  246, 247, 248
Anxious/disorganized-disoriented
  attachment, 244,
Apgar Scoring System, 148, 149
Appearance-reality dimension, 297
Artificialism, 298–299
Artistic development, 281–283
Asian-Americans,
  achievement in high school, 537
  and child rearing methods, 339
  and discipline, 337
  and identity formation,
    518–519
  population, 11
Aspirin, in pregnancy, 126
Assimilation, 43
Associative play, 328–320
Attachment
  and Adult Attachment Interview,
    248
  behavior, 242
  critique of, 253–254
  categories of, 244–245
  consequences of poor, 242–247
  and day care, 263–264
  defined, 241
  and depressed mothers, 249–250
  factors affecting, 246–250
  and fathers, 258
  and later behavior, 245–246,
    252–253
  and maternal sensitivity,
    247–248
  quality of 244–245
  temperament and, 251
Attention,
  in early childhood, 303–304
  in middle childhood, 382
Attention-deficit/hyperactivity
  disorder, 410–412
Attention span, 303
Attitudes, 489–490
Auditory (*see* hearing)

Authoritarian parenting, 333–334,
  425
Authoritative parenting, 333–334,
  425
Autonomy vs. Shame or Doubt,
  55, 183–184

B

Babbling, 217
Babinski reflex, 169
Baby boom generation, 17
Barney and Friends, 310–311
Basic skills, 389–391
Bayley Scales of Infant
  Development, 209–210
Behavioral approach,
  criticisms of, 56
  description of, 57–60
  evaluation, 60
  to gender role acquisition,
    351–352
  to language learning, 221–223
  to moral behavior, 446–447
Behavior traits and genetics, 92–93
Behavioral autonomy, 521–523
Behaviorism, 57–60
Bell Curve, 96–97
Bidirectionality, 21
Bilingual programs, 405–406
Bilingualism, 404,
Bipolar disorder, 93
Birth,
  Cesarean, 140–141
  Lamaze method, 143
  Leboyer method, 144
  premature, 144–147
  stages of, 139–140
Birth centers, 142
Birth control, (*see* contraception)
Black English (*see* Ebonics)
Blastocyst, 116
Body image, 474–477
Bottle feeding, 187
Brain development,
  in infancy and toddlerhood,
    169–171
  in early childhood, 188–189
Brazelton Neonatal Behavior Scale,
  149, 150
Breast feeding, 186–187
Broca's area, 223
Bronfenbrenner's ecological theory,
  67–69
  see ecological theory
Bulimia, 478–479
Butterfly effect, 72

C

Caffeine use in pregnancy, 126
Canalization, 177
Career choice, 538–542 (*see also*
  work)

Caregiver sensitivity, 246, 247–248
Carrier, 82
Case studies, 23–24
Centering, 297
Cephalocaudal development, 178
Cesarean birth, 127, 140–141
Chaos theory, 71–71
Change
  qualitative, 5–6
  quantitative, 5–6
Child Abuse,
  consequences, 355–356
  defined, 354
  emotional, 356–357
  factors in, 357–358
  and neglect, 354
  prevention of, 362
  sexual, 355–356
Child Development
  benefits from studying, 32–34
  and change 5
  definition, 4
  nature, 5
  themes of, 6–22
Child neglect, 354 (see child abuse)
Child rearing, (see also Mother, Father, Parents)
  in African American homes, 337–338
  and aggression, 451–452
  in Asian American families, 339,
  and culture, 326–340
  and first generation, 13–15
  in Latino families, 338–338
  in Native American families, 339–340
  and prosocial development, 448
  strategies in middle childhood, 424–426
Children,
  with exceptional needs, 408–415
  and health, 172–175
  and homelessness, 437–438
Chlamydia, 127
Chomsky's theory of language acquisition, 222–225
Chorionic villus sampling, 137
Chromosomal abnormalities, 101–103
Chromosomes, 78
Classical conditioning, 58, 167
Classification, 293, 379–380
Cloning, 107
Cocaine,
  and pregnancy, 125–126
  use in adolescence, 546
Cognitive development, (see also intelligence, memory, information processing)
  in adolescence, 482–485
  attempts to accelerate, 212
  in early childhood, 290–306
  and contraception, 495–496
  and early daycare, 264–265
  and home, 309–310
  and humor, 385–388

in infancy and toddlerhood, 198–212
  and language development, 225
  in middle childhood, 377–382
  and moral reasoning, 488–489
  and parenting, 210
  theoretical perspectives, 41–49
Cognitive structure, 42–43
Cognitive theory of language acquisition, 225
Cohort effect, 16, 17, 18
Collective monologue, 292
Color vision, 161
Combinational logic, 482
Commitment (identity), 512
Communication, (see language)
  and language, 215
  with parents and peers in adolescence, 527–528
Community,
  as context for development, 9
  and prematurity, 147–148
  and violence and delinquency, 551
Compensatory education, 313–314
Computer literacy, 391–392
Concordance rate, 85
Concrete operational stage, 377–382
Conditioned response, 58
Conditioned stimulus, 59
Conflict, 347–348, 523–526
Conformity, 521–522
Conscience, 50
Conscious mind, 50
Conservation,
  in early childhood, 296,
  in middle childhood, 379
Contact comfort, 243–244
Contexts of development, 8–11
Contextual theory, 40
Continuous development, 21–22
Contraception, 495–496
Control groups, 26
Conventional morality, 443
Cooing, 217
Cooperative play, 329–330
Corporal punishment, 359–260
Correlations, 24–25
Cortex, 169
Crack (see cocaine),
Crisis (identity), 512
Critical period, 121
Cross-cultural research, (see also culture)
Cross-sectional studies, 28–29
Crossing over, 79
Crowning, 140
Crying, 165, 166,
Culture,
  and achievement, 398–400
  in adolescence, 528–529
  and aggression, 451
  and child rearing, 336–340
  as context of development, 1–15
  and diet, 284
  and discipline, 336

and emotional development, 236–237
  and father involvement, 258
  and formal operations, 484
  and health of children, 286–288
  and identity, 517
  and intelligence testing, 401–403
  and language development, 227
  misunderstandings, 13–14
  and motor development, 179
  and prosocial development, 446
  and rites of passage, 509–510
  and secular trend, 467
  and SIDS, 176
  psychosocial development and, 56
  and temperament, 91
Culture fair tests of intelligence, 402–403
Cystic fibrosis, 99–100, 105

D
Date rape (see acquaintance rape)
Dating, 492–493
  dating violence, 493–492
Day care
  and attachment, 263–264
  and cognitive and social influence of, 264–265, 266
  future of, 269–270
  infant, 263–265
  quality of, 267–268
  during toddlerhood, 266, 267
  types of, 262–263
Decenter, 378–379
Deception in research, 31–32
Deductive reasoning, 293
Defense mechanisms, 50, 51
Deferred imitation, 200
Delinquency
  community factors and, 551
  curbing, 551
  family processes and relationships, 550
  individual factors, 550
  peer factors, 550
  protective factors and, 551
Delivery of the placenta, 140
Demographic changes,
  population changes to 2050, 11
Dentition, 376
Dependent variable, 27
Depth perception, 161
Depression,
  in adolescents, 513
  in mothers, 249–250
Development
  benefits to studying, 32–33
  definition, 4
  nature, 5
  and change 5
  themes of, 6–22
Diet (see nutrition)
Diethylstilbestrol, 122
Differential emotions theory, 234–235

Difficult temperament, 89, 92
Dilation, 139
Disabilities,
  children with, 409–413
  law and, 408–409
Discipline,
  generational changes in, 17, 18 (see cohort effect)
  styles of, 334–335
  and subculture, 336
Discontinuous development, 21–22
Discrimination (learning theory), 58
Displacement, 50
Divorce,
  and age of child, 429
  experience of, 426
  gender differences in reaction to, 430
  immediate reactions to, 426–427
  long term effects, 427–428
  children's experience, 426–430
  prescriptions for, 430
Dizygotic twins, 79, 86–88
Domestic abuse, (witnessing), 361
Dominant traits, 82
Down syndrome, 101–102
Dramatic play, 330
Dropping out of school, 538–539
Drug education, 548–549
Drug use
  in adolescence, 544–549
  during pregnancy, 122–127
Dynamic systems theory, 180–182

E
Early childhood,
  aggression in, 347
  altruism in, 346
  and art, 281–283
  attention and, 303–304
  brain development in, 288–289
  child abuse in, 354–358, 361–362
  child rearing and culture during, 326–340
  cognitive development in, 290–306
  conflict in, 347–348
  fears during, 326–327
  gender role development in, 347–354
  growth, 278, 279
  health in, 286–288
  home influences on cognitive development in, 309–310
  information processing in, 303–306
  initiative vs. guilt, 324–325
  language development, 291–292
  memory skills in, 304–306
  motor skills in, 278–280
  nutritional needs in, 284–286
  parenting styles in, 333–325
  peer group in, 345

physical development during, 278–290
play in, 327–333
preoperational stage, 293–303
preschool education during, 312–314
prosocial behavior in, 345–346
safety concerns, 283
self-concept in, 325–326
sibling relationships, 341–344
television viewing in, 310–312
Early childhood care and education,
future of, 316
kindergarten, 317
preschool education, 313–318
Early experience, 16, 18
Early intervention, 126, 191–192, 211–212
Early maturation, 469–470
Easy temperament, 89
Eating disorders, 477–479
Ebonics, 407–408
Eclectic, 70
Ecological theory,
criticisms of, 69
description, 67–68
evaluation, 69
Education,
attitudes, 399
bilingual, 405–406
computer literacy, 391
elementary school, 389–394
experience, 394–395
high school, 531–534
home influences, 396–398
intelligence and, 399–403
junior high school, 529–530
kindergarten, 317–318
math skills, 390
preschool, 313–316
reading and, 389–390
writing skills, 390
Ego, 50
Ego ideal, 50, 446
Egocentrism, 298
decline during middle childhood, 378
Ego integrity vs. Despair, 56
Egocentrism, 44
Egocentrism (adolescent), 485
Electra complex, 52
Elementary school
experience, 393–394
factors for success in, 304–404
Embryonic stage, 119–120
Emotional abuse, 356–357
Emotional autonomy, 519–521
Emotional development,
and fears in childhood, 326–327
and fear of strangers, 254
in infancy, 234–241
and separation anxiety, 254–255
Empathy, 240–241
Enrichment, 413
Environmentality, 85

Epigenetic principle, 54
Equilibration, 42
Erikson's psychosocial theory
(see psychosocial theory)
Eros, 51
Estrogen, 468
Ethics and research, 30–32
Event-related potentials, 158
Evocative effects, 109
Exercise,
in adolescence, 473–474
in middle childhood, 373
Exceptional needs, children with, 408–413
Exosystem, 68
Experience dependent information, 171
Experience expectant information, 170–171
Experience sampling method, 521
Experimental method, 25–27
Expressive children, 219
Expulsion, 140
Extinction, 58

F
Fadeout phenomenon, 316
Family, (see also divorce, parenting, single parenting, stepparenting)
in adolescence, 519–529
and aggressive behavior, 451–452
changes in demographics, 8
and cognitive stimulation, 309–310, 333–340, 396–398
as context of development, 8
discord, 428
in divorce, 430
in early childhood,
in infancy, 240–258
in middle childhood, 424–426
relationships and drug use, 547
Fast mapping, 219
Fathers, (see also child rearing)
adolescent, 501
and attachment, 258
as caregivers, 258–259
child rearing and, 255–257
and infants, 257–258
role during pregnancy, 133
Fear of strangers, 254
Fears, 326–327
Fetal alcohol effect, 124
Fetal alcohol syndrome, 123–124
Fetal monitor, 137
Fetal stage, 119–120
Fine motor development, 280
Fine tuning theory, 227
First word, 218–219
Fontanels, 158
Forgetting, 305
Formal operational stage, 482–484
Fragile X, 103

Freud's psychoanalytic theory,
criticisms of, 53
description, 50–54
evaluation, 53
psychosexual stages, 51–54
Friendships,
in adolescence, 521–523
in early childhood, 249–250
in middle childhood, 439–441
Full inclusion, 408–409

G
Gametes, 78
Gay and Lesbian households, 438–440
Genes, 78, 79, 80, 81, 82, 83
Gene therapy, 105–107
Gender consistency, 349
Gender determination, 80
Gender differences,
attitudes towards sex, 492
at birth, 188
and body image, 474–477
and career choice, 539–540
defined, 347–348
in depression, 537
and effects of divorce, 430
in elementary school experience, 403–404
and friendship patterns, 345, 440–441
in growth, 176–178, 278, 279, 370, 465
in high school, 536–537
and humor, 387
in identity formation, 517
in infancy and toddlerhood, 188–190
in moral reasoning, 444–445
in play, 331–332
in weight, 177, 278, 279, 370, 465
in adolescence, 465
in early childhood, 278, 279
in middle childhood, 370
and adjustment to stepfamilies, 433
and self-esteem, 513
and sexual behavior, 494–495
in taking math and science courses, 536
Gender identity, 348–349
Gender roles,
behavioral approaches, 351–352
biological approaches, 350–351
cognitive approach, 353–354
psychoanalytic approach, 353
social learning approach, 352
Gender schema theory, 353–354
Gender stability, 349
Generalization, 58
Generation X, 17–18
Generation Y, 18
Generativity vs. Stagnation, 56

Genetics
and alcoholism, 104
behavioral traits and, 92
at birth, 148
and disease, 99–103
and environmental interaction, 6–8, 40
and ethical dilemmas, 105–108
and physical characteristics, 88
determining level of contribution, 85–88
and intelligence, 95–99
and interaction, 108–110
misconceptions concerning, 78–79
models of genetic/environmental effects, 109–111
and personality, 92
and physical characteristics, 88–89
and predispositions, 103–104
and psychopathology, 92–93
and rate of development, 94–95
and screening, 105–106
and sibling differences, 93–94
and temperament, 89–92
and transmission, 78–84
Genetic counseling, 81, 105–106
Genital stage, 53, 491
Genome Project, 105–106
Genotype, 83
Genotype/environment effects model, 108–110
Germinal stage, 116
Gifted and talented children, 413–414
Gonorrhea, 127 see also sexually transmitted diseases
Grammar, 216
Grasping reflex, 168, 169
Growth,
in adolescence, 465
in infancy and toddlerhood, 176–178
in early childhood, 278, 279
in middle childhood, 370
Guilt, 446

H
Habituation, 158
Hall, G. Stanley, 519–520
Handedness, 280–281
Head Start, 315–318
Health,
in adolescence, 471
in early childhood, 266–268
in infancy and toddlerhood, 172–175
world view of children's, 286–288
Health education, 373–374
Hearing,
in infancy and toddlerhood, 162–163

Height,
  in adolescence, 465
  in infancy and toddlerhood,
    176–178
  in early childhood, 278, 279
  in middle childhood, 370
Heritability, 85, 95–96
Heredity, see genetics
Heroin, 126, 545
Herpes, 127
High school, 531–534, 536–538
Hispanic, see Latino
Holophrase, 219
Home, (see Family, Parenting,
  Mother, Father)
HOME Scale, 209–210
Homeless families, 435–437
Homosexuality, 106, 502–503
Horizontal decalage, 379
Hormones, 350, 467–468
Hospitalism, 242
Hostile aggression, 347
Humor, (children's understanding
  of), 385–388
Huntington's disease, 105
Hypothetical-deductive reasoning,
  483

I

Id, 50
Identification, 353, 446
Identity,
  achievement, 516–517
  diffusion, 514–515
  foreclosure, 515
  gender differences in, 517
  and intimacy, 516
  minority status and, 518–519
  moratorium, 515–516
  statuses, 514–516
Identity vs. Role confusion, 56,
  513–515
Imaginary audience, 486
Immigration, 13
Imitation, 61–62
  in infancy, 167
Immaturity, functions of, 212
Implantation, 117
Imprinting, 242
In vitro fertilization, 134–136
Inclusion, 408
Independent play, 328
Independent variable, 26
Inductive reasoning, 293
Industry vs. Inferiority, 55, 389,
  420–421
Infancy
  attachment in, 240–255
  brain development, 169–171
  cognitive development in,
    198–206
  crying, 195, 196–197
  day care, 262–264
  defined, 158
  emotional development in,
    234–241
  fear of strangers in, 254

gender differences, 188–190
growth, 176–182
health, 171–176
information processing in,
  206–208
intelligence in, 209–211
learning in, 167
motor development, 178–182
nutrition, 186–187
parenting relationship in,
  247–251, 257–258
principles of growth, 178–179
reflexes, 168–169
sensory development, 158–164
separation anxiety, 254–255
social referencing in, 238–239
sleeping-waking cycle, 164–165
vaccinations in, 172–173
weight, 177
Infant amnesia, 207–208
Infant daycare, 263–265
Infant mortality rate, 148, 149
Infants of teen mothers, 500
Information-processing,
  assumptions of, 47–48
  criticisms of, 49
  description of, 46–49
  evaluation of, 49
  in early childhood, 303–306
  in infancy and toddlerhood,
    206–208
  and later intelligence, 208–209
  in middle childhood, 382–383
Informed consent, 30–31
Initiative vs. Guilt, 55, 324–325
Instrumental aggression, 347
Integrity vs. Despair, 56
Intelligence,
  correlation with academic
    achievement, 399–400
  cultural fairness of tests
    measuring, 401–403
  definition, 399
  genetics and, 95–97
  and home variables, 210
  in infancy and toddlerhood,
    208–210
  misuse of testing for, 401–403
  modifying, 96–99
  predicting, 208–210
  quotient, 400
  tests, 400–401
Intelligence quotient, 400
Intervention,
  and course of development, 22
  early, 191–192, 211–212
  for infants exposed to cocaine,
    125–126
Intimacy vs. Isolation, 56
Irony, 388
Irreversibility, 297–298

J

Japanese children
  and language development,
    227–228
  parenting strategies with, 336

Jobs, (see careers)
Junior high school, 529–530

K

Kindergarten, 317–318
Klinefelter's syndrome, 103
Knowledge, (Piaget's concept), 41
Kohlberg's theory,
  in adolescence, 488–489
  in childhood, 442–446

L

Labor, 139–140
Lamaze method, 143
Language
  and culture, 227
  and communication, 215
  defined, 198
  development of, 216–220
  encouraging competence in, 228
  in early childhood, 291–292
  in middle childhood, 383–385
  nature of, 215–216
  reading and, 229
  and social class, 228
  theories of acquiring, 221–223
  use of, 216, 225–227
Language acquisition device, 223
Lanugo, 158
Latchkey, (see self-care)
Latency stage, 53
Latinos,
  achievement in elementary
    school, 394
  achievement in high school,
    536, 538
  child rearing strategies, 338
  and dropping out, 538
  and identity formation,
    518–519
  and language, 404–407
  population, 11
  and prematurity rate, 147–148
Learning, (see also achievement)
  definition, 7
  in infancy, 167
  and interaction with
    environment, 6–8
Learning disabilities, 409–410
Leboyer method, 144
Lesbian households, 438–440
Libido, 51
Linguistic deficit hypothesis, 408
Linguistic difference hypothesis,
  408
Long-term memory, 48, 206–208,
  304–306, 382–383
Longitudinal research, 29–30
Love-oriented discipline, 334
Low birthweight, 144–147

M

Macrosystem, 68
Magical thinking, 299
Malnutrition,
  during childhood, 174–175, 287
  during prenatal stage, 131–132

Mapping genes, 105
Marijuana, 126, 546
Mass to specific, 178
Maternal age and parenting, 130
Maternal depression, 249–250
Maternal PKU, 101
Maternal serum alphafetoprotein,
  137
Maternal employment,
  effects on children, 261–262
  extent, 233–234
  interaction with children,
    260–261
Maternal nutrition, 130–131
Maternal phenylketonuria, 101
Maternal sensitivity, 246, 247–248
Math skills, 390
Maturation,
  defined, 6
  early and late, 419–420
  gender differences in, 350
  nature of, 6–8
Mechanistic theory, 40
Meiosis, 78
Memory,
  in early childhood, 304–306
  in infancy and toddlerhood,
    206–208
  in middle childhood, 382–383
  models of, 48
  strategies, 382
Menstruation, 466–467
Mental age, 400
Mental retardation,
  children with, 413–414
  and Down syndrome, 101–102
Mesosystem, 67–68
Metamemory, 382–383
Microsystem, 67
Middle childhood
  aggression and antisocial
    behavior in, 450–453
  basic skills learning in, 389–391
  child rearing strategies during,
    424–426
  cognitive development in,
    377–382
  and disabilities, 408–413
  reactions to divorce in, 426–430
  elementary school experience in,
    393–394
  factors in school success,
    394–404
  family relationships in, 424–425
  friendship in, 439–441
  gradual changes in, 456
  growth in, 370
  humor in, 385–388
  industry vs inferiority, 420–421
  information processing in,
    382–383
  language development in,
    383–385
  measuring intelligence in,
    399–400
  memory in, 382–383

moral development in, 441–447,
448–449
motor development in, 376
nutrition, 370
physical development in,
370–377
physical fitness, 373
prosocial behavior in, 447
self-care in, 434–435
self-concept in, 421–422
self-esteem in, 421–424
sports in, 374–376
stress in, 454–456
television viewing and violence
in, 453–454
theoretical approaches to,
420–421
weight gain, 370
Middle school, 529–530
Minority groups, (see also African
American, Asian American,
Latino, Native American)
and career choice, 541–542
and child rearing strategies,
339–340
and identity formation,
518–519
and measurement of intelligence,
401–403
and prematurity, 147–148
Mister Rogers' Neighborhood, 312
Monozygotic twins, 79, 85–86
Montessori schools, 313–314
Moral development,
in adolescence, 488–489
in childhood, 441–447,
448–449
and behavioral approach,
446–447
Kohlberg's theory, 442–446
Piaget's theory, 441–442
and psychoanalytic theory, 446
Moral realism, 442
Moral reasoning, 442
Moral relativism, 442
Morals and values in adolescence,
488–489
Moro reflex, 169
Morpheme, 216
Morphology, 216
Mothers, (see also Parenting)
adolescent, 130, 500, 501
age at pregnancy, 130–131
and infants, 247, 248,
depressed, 249–250
nutrition during pregnancy,
131–132
Motherese, 226
Motor development,
in infancy and toddlerhood,
179–182
in early childhood, 278–280
in middle childhood, 376
Mr. Rogers' Neighborhood, 312
Multifactorial transmission, 83

Multiple births, 79
see monozygotic twins and
dizygotic twins
Myelin sheath, 169, 288

N
Narcotics and pregnancy, 124–126
Native Americans,
child rearing strategies, 339–340
and identity, 518–519
population, 11
Nativist approach, 222–225
Naturalistic observation, 22
Neglect, 354, 357–358
Neonate,
defined, 159
gender differences, 188–189
hearing, 162–163
pain, 164
sense of smell, 163
sense of taste, 163–164
vision, 159–162
Niche taking, 109
Nicotine,
use in adolescence, 544, 546
prenatal effects, 122–123
(see smoking)
Nonshared environmental factors,
93–94
Norms, 177
Nursery school, 313–314
Nutrition,
in adolescence, 473
in early childhood, 284–286
in middle childhood, 370
during pregnancy, 131–132

O
Obesity, 371–372
in adolescence, 479
genetic contribution, 88
in middle childhood, 371–373
Object permanence, 44, 200–205
Observation, 23
Observation learning, 61–62
Obstetrical medication, 141–142
Oedipus complex, 52, 353
Older mothers, 130
Onlooker play, 328
Only child, 344–345
Operant conditioning, 58–59, 167
Operations (Piagetian theory, 42
Oral stage, 52
Organismic theory, 39
Organization (Piagetian theory),
42–43
Over–the–counter drugs, 126
Overregularization, 291–292

P
Pain, in infancy and childhood,
164
Palmar grasp, 168–169
Parallel play, 328
Parentese, 226
Parent Effectiveness Training
(PET), 325

Parental agreement on child
rearing, 425–426
Parents, (see mothers, fathers)
agreement on parenting
strategies, 425–426
and child abuse, 357
and cognitive development, 210,
309
communication with, 526–527
gays and lesbians as, 438–439
promoting cognitive
development, 210
Parenting,
in adolescence, 527–529
and cognitive development,
309–310
and moral behavior, 448–449
differences for sons and
daughters, 189–190
and homeless families, 436–437
and prosocial development, 448
styles, 333–335
in toddlerhood, 184–185
Parenting education, 213–214
Passive effects, 109
Passive smoking, 123
Peers,
in adolescence, 521–523
and aggression, 452
communication with, 439
and drug use, 547–548
in early childhood, 345
influence in adolescence,
521–523
and violent and delinquent
behavior, 550–551
Permissive parenting, 198, 334
Personal fable, 486
Personality
genetic involvement in, 92
and temperament, 89–92
Phallic stage, 353
Phonology, 216
Phenotype, 83
Phenylketonuria, 101
Phonological awareness, 410
Physical activity, 473–474
Physical development,
in adolescence, 465–470
in early childhood, 278–290
in infancy, 158–167, 169–170,
176–182
in middle childhood, 370–377
Physical fitness, 373
Piaget's theory of cognitive
development,
application of, 45
challenges to, 45–46, 203–205,
484
and collective monologues,
292–293
concrete operational stage, 44
criticisms of, 45
description, 41–49
factors in development, 42
formal operational reasoning,
44–45

and knowledge, 41
and language development, 225
preoperational stage and, 44
sensorimotor stage, 43–44,
198–206
summary of, 48
Piaget's theory of moral
development, 441–442
PL94–142, 408
PL99–457, 191
Play,
benefits of, 332–333
defined, 327
development of, 328–331
gender differences, 331–332
pretend, 330
rough-and-tumble, 330–331
Pleasure principle, 50
Pollution, 126
Polygenic inheritance, 83
Postconventional level, 443–444
Postformal operational reasoning,
485–486
Posttraumatic stress disorder, 362
Poverty, (see socioeconomic status)
and career choice, 541–542,
and demographics, 9–10
and homelessness, 437
and school achievement,
396–397
Power-oriented discipline, 334
Pragmatics, 216
Preconception care, 129
Preconscious mind, 50
Preconventional level, 442–443
Predispositions, 103–104
Pregnancy, 129–132
in adolescence, 499–502
age of the mother and, 130–131
alcohol use during, 123–124
cocaine use, 124–126
disease and, 127–128
fathers role during, 129
marijuana use during, 126
medication and, 122
nutrition and, 131–132
and nicotine, 122–123
over-the-counter drug use
during, 126
stress during, 132
and technology, 134–139
Prematurity, 144–147
Prenatal development, 116–122
Preoperational stage, 293–303
Preschool education, 312–314
Pretend play, 330
Preterm infants, 144
Primary circular reactions,
198–199
Primary emotions, 234–235
Primary process, 50
Primary sex characteristics, 464
Project CARE, 211–212
Project Head Start, 315–318
Prosocial behavior,
in early childhood, 345–346
in middle childhood, 447

Proximodistal, 178
Psychoanalytic concept of morality, 446
Psychoanalytic theory
  criticisms of, 53
  description, 50–54
  evaluation, 53
  psychosexual stages, 51–54
Psychological abuse, 356–357
Psychosexual stages,
  anal stage, 52
  description, 51–54
  genital stage, 53, 491
  latency stage, 421
  oral stage, 52
  phallic stage, 52, 353
Psychosocial theory
  and adolescence, 513–519
  criticisms of, 57
  description, 55–57
  evaluation, 57
  in infancy, 166–167
  in early childhood, 324–325
  in middle childhood, 420–421
  during toddlerhood, 183
Pseudomaturity, 543
Puberty,
  cause of, 467–468
  early and late maturation, 469–470
  female development in, 465–466
  male development in, 467
  timing of, 459–460

Q

Qualitative change, 5–6
Quantitative change, 5–6
Quasi-experimental designs, 27–28
Quickening, 120

R

Radiation, 126
Range of reaction model, 108
Readiness for school, 377
Readiness testing, 317
Reading, 389–390
  and television, 390
Reinforcer, 58
Relativistic thinking, 485
Rh factor, 129
Race, (see African American, Asian)
Rapid eye movements, 164
Readiness, 94
Reading,
  and achievement, 389–390
  to children, 228–229
Reality principle, 50
Recall, 206, 382
Recessive traits, 82
Reciprocal determinism, 63
Reciprocal interaction, 21
Recognition, 106, 382
Referential children, 219
Reflexes, 167–169
Rejecting–neglecting parenting, 334

Replication, 22
Reversibility, 97
Risk taking, 485–488
Relativistic thinking, 485
Religion,
  in adolescence, 490–491
Representation, 301–302
Reproductive surrogacy, 138–139
Reproductive technology, 134–136
Research methods, 22–32
  ethical considerations in, 30–32
Reversibility, 297–298, 378
Risk taking in adolescence, 486–488
Rites of passage, 509–510
Ritalin, 411
Role models, 61
Rooting reflex, 168
Rough-and-tumble play, 330–331
Rubella, 127

S

Safety, 283
Salt, intake of, 284
Saltatory growth, 177
Schema (Piagetian), 42
Schema (information processing), 305
Schizophrenia, 103
School,
  as context for development, 9
  in early childhood, 213–215
  elementary, 393–395
  high, 531–538
  junior high, 529–530
  ratings, 392–393
  success, 394–400
School of the 21st Century, 269–270
Script, 306
Secondary circular reactions, 199
Secondary emotions, 235–236
Secondary sex characteristics, 464
Secular trend, 467
Secure attachment, 245, 246, 247, 248
Selective attention, 304
Self-care, 435–435
Self-concept,
  in adolescence, 510–513
  in early childhood, 325–326
  in middle childhood, 421–422
Self-efficacy, 63
Self-esteem, 421–424, 510–513
Semantics, 216
Semiotic function, 200
Sensorimotor stage, 198–205
Sensory development, 158–164
Sensory memory, 48
Separation anxiety, 254–255
Sequential studies, 29–30
Seriation, 293–294, 379–380
Sesame Street, 311–312
Sequencing genes, 107
Sequential designs, 29–30

Sex,
  attitudes in adolescence concerning, 491–493
  behavior, 491–498
  expression in adolescence, 491–493, 494–499
Sex chromosomes, 81
Sex education, 497–499
Sex-linked chromosomal disorders, 103
Sex-linked traits, 84
Sex selection, 81–82
Sex typing, 349–350
Sexual abuse, 355–356
Sexual orientation, 502–504
Sexually transmitted diseases, 496–499
Shared environmental factors, 93–94
Short-term memory, 48
Siblings,
  arguments, 342–344
  differences between, 94–95
  relationships in early childhood, 341–344
  rivalry, 341
  and teen pregnancy, 501
Sickle cell anemia, 100–101
Single-parent families, 8, 430–432
  and poverty, 431
Sleep in adolescence, 480–482
Sleeping-waking cycle, 164–166
Slow to warm up temperament, 89
Small-for-date-infants, 144
Smell,
  in infancy and toddlerhood, 163
Smile, 239–240
Smoking,
  in adolescence, 544, 545, 546
  during pregnancy, 122–123
  and prematurity, 122–123
  passive smoking during pregnancy, 123
Social class,
  and language development, 228
Social interaction and language, 225–227
Social learning theory,
  description, 60–63
  evaluation, 63
Social referencing, 238–239
Social transmission, 42
Sociocultural theory,
  criticisms of, 67
  description, 64–67
  evaluation, 67
Socioeconomic status, 209
  (see poverty)
  and daycare quality, 267
  and language development, 228–229
  and maternal employment, 261–262
  and preschool experience, 315–316
Solitary play, 328
Sonogram, 137

Spanking, 359–360
Sports, 374–376
Stability, 20
Stage theory, 40, 41
Stanford-Binet Intelligence Test, 400
Stepfamilies, 433
Stepping reflex, 168, 169, 181
Stimulus deprivation, 243
Stimulus discrimination, 58
Stimulus generalization, 58
Strange situation, 244 (see also attachment)
Stress,
  in childhood, 455–456
  during pregnancy, 132,
Stress-resilient children (stress-resistant) 454–456
Subcultures,
  in the United States, 11–15
Sucking reflex, 167
Sudden Infant Death Syndrome, 171–176.
Suicide,
  in adolescence, 471–473
Superego, 50, 446
Surrogacy, 138–139
Survey, 24
Symbolic function, 200
Synchrony, 250–251
Syntax, 216
Syphilis, 127 (see sexually transmitted diseases)
Systematic Training for Effective Parenting (STEP), 335, 336

T

Taste,
  in infancy, 163
Tay–Sachs disease, 101
Teachers, 395–396
Technology and pregnancy, 137–138
Technology and reproductive alternatives, 134–137
Teen pregnancy, 499–501
Telegraphic speech, 220
Television,
  in early childhood, 310–312
  and reading, 390
  viewing during early childhood, 310–312
  and violence, 434–435
Temperament, 89–92
  and attachment classification, 251–252
  infant, 90–92
Teratogen, 120, 122–128
Tertiary circular reactions, 200
Testimony in court, (children), 307–309
Theories of development, 37–72
  (see behaviorism, Erikson, Freud, Information processing, Piaget, and Vygotsky)
  evaluation of, 30
  importance of, 38–39

new developments in, 70
types of theories, 39–40
Theory of multiple intelligences, 399–400
Time–lag studies, 30
Time out, 17
Toddlerhood
    accidents in, 183
    and autonomy vs doubt, 55, 183
    brain development, 169–171
    cognitive development in, 200, 202–203
    communication, 219–220
    day care, 266, 267
    defined, 158
    description, 182
    emotional development in, 235–237
    fear of strangers in, 254
    gender differences, 189–190
    growth, 177–178
    information processing, 206, 207
    language development in, 219–220

motor development in, 179–180
sensory development, 158–162
separation anxiety, 254–255
social referencing, 238–239
and terrible twos, 184–185,
toilet training in, 190–191
vaccinations in, 172–175
weight gain during, 177
Toddler language, 219–220
Toilet training, 190–191
Transductive reasoning, 293
Transformations, 298, 379
Transition, 139, 395, 530
Transitive inferences, 295
Trust vs. Mistrust, 55, 166–167
Turner's syndrome, 103
Twin studies, 84–88

U
Unconditioned response, 58
Unconditioned stimulus, 58
Unconscious, 50
Unoccupied play, 328
Uzgiris–Hunt Scales, 208

V
Vaccinations, 172–175
Values, 489–491
Venereal disease (*see* sexually transmitted diseases)
Vernix caseosa, 159
Violence,
    community factors and, 551
    curbing, 551–552
    exposure to, 452–453
    family processes and relationships, 550
    individual factors, 550
    peer factors, 550
    protective factors and, 551
    television and, 453–454
Vision,
    in infancy and toddlerhood, 158–162
Visual cliff, 161–162
Vocabulary, 216, 218, 219, 283, 291
Vygotsky's Sociocultural Theory 64–67
    (*see* Sociocultural theory)

W
Wechsler tests, 401
Weight,
    in adolescence, 465
    in early childhood, 278, 279
    in infancy and toddlerhood, 177
    in middle childhood, 370
Wernicke's area, 223
Women,
    and career choice, 539–540
    and moral reasoning, 444–445
Work (teens and), 542–543
Working memory, 48
Writing, 390, 532

Z
Zone of proximal development, 64–65
Zygote, 116

Photo Credits

Page abbreviations are as follows (t) top, (b) bottom (c) center, (l) left, (r) right, (tl) top left, (tr) top right, (bl) bottom left, (br) bottom right, (frgrd) foreground, (bkgrd) background, (all) all photos on page.

1 © PhotoDisc;

3 © Michael Newman/PhotoEdit;

4 (l) © Mary Kate Denny/PhotoEdit;

(tl) © David Young-Wolff/PhotoEdit;

(tr) © Digital Stock; (bl) © PhotoDisc;

(br) © Digital Vision;

5 © Ellen Senisi/Photo Researchers Inc.;

8 (b) © Jerry Wachter/Photo Researchers Inc.;

(t) © Photodisc;

9 (bl) © Andrew Lichtenstein/The Image Works;

(br) © Bill Bachmann/The Image Works;

(t, frgrd) © Digital Vision; (t, bkgrd) © PhotoDisc;

11 © Sean Sprague/Stock Boston;

15 © Joseph Schuyler/Stock Boston;

16 (l) © Archive Photos;

(c) © Ken Heyman/Woodfin Camp & Assoc.;

(r) © David Young-Wolff/ PhotoEdit;

19 (l) © Y. Karsh/Woodfin Camp & Assoc.;

(r) © CORBIS/Hulton-Deutsch Collection;

23 © Richard T. Nowitz/Photo Researchers Inc.;

25 © David Young-Wolff/PhotoEdit;

28 © Richard Hutchings/PhotoEdit;

33 © Charles Gupton/Stock Boston;

37 © CORBIS;

40 © Charles Gupton/Stock Boston;

41 © Bill Anderson/Monkmeyer;

44 © Tom Prettyman/PhotoEdit;

47 © David Young-Wolff/PhotoEdit;

52 © Ray Ellis/Photo Researchers, Inc.;

55 © Peter Menzel/Stock Boston;

59 © Robin L. Sachs/PhotoEdit;

61 © Courtesy of Albert Banduar, Stanford University;

62 © Elizabeth Crews;

65 © Steve Rubin/The Image Works;

68 © PhotoDisc;

77 © Digital Stock;

79 (l) © Bob Daemmrich/Stock Boston;

(r) © Lawrence Migdale/Stock Boston;

(t, frgrd) © PhotoDisc; (t, bkgrd) © PhotoDisc;

80 © Bob Daemmrich/Stock Boston;

85 © Bob Daemmrich/The Image Works;

86 © Myrleen Ferguson Cate/ PhotoEdit;

92 © Nancy Richmond/The Image Works;

94 © Tony Freeman/PhotoEdit;

95 © Tony Freeman/PhotoEdit;

100 © Archive Photos;

103 © Susan Woog Wagner/Photo Researchers Inc.;

104 © Richard Hutchings/Photo Researchers Inc.;

106 © Will & Deni McIntyre/Photo Researchers Inc.;

109 © Index Stock Imagery;

114 © PhotoDisc;

115 © PhotoDisc;

116 © Andy Walker/Midland Fertility Services/Photo Researchers Inc.;

118–119 (all) © Lennart Nilsson;

122 © Michael Newman/PhotoEdit;

124 © George Steinmetz;

130 © Frank Siteman/Stock Boston;

134 © CC Studio/Science Photo Library/Photo Researchers Inc.;

135 © Michael Tweed/The New York Times Pictures;

137 © Mehau Kulyk/Science Photo Library/Photo Researchers Inc.;

138 © CORBIS/Owen Franken;

143 © Lawrence Migdale/Stock Boston;

145 © Joseph Nettis/Stock Boston;

146 © PhotoDisc;

155 © Digital Vision;

157 (t) © Frank Siteman/Stock Boston;

(b) © PhotoDisc;

159 © Sotographs/Gamma-Liaison;

161 © The Image Works;

163 © D. Rosenstein and H. Oster, Child Development, 1988;

166 © Elizabeth Crews;

167 © from A.N. Meltzoff and M.K. Moore in Science, 1979;

169 © CORBIS/Jennie Woodcock;

181 © Mark Richards/PhotoEdit;

182 © Suzanne Szasz/Photo Researchers Inc.;

186 © Ruth Jenkinson/ MIDIRS/ Science Photo Library/Photo Researchers Inc.;

187 © PhotoDisc;

189 © Nancy Sheehan/PhotoEdit;

190 © Margaret Miller/Photo Researchers Inc.;

191 © Tony Freeman/PhotoEdit;

196 © Digital Vision;

197 © (top) Michael Newman/PhotoEdit;

198 © Michael Newman/PhotoEdit;

199 © M. Siluk/The Image Works;

201 © Hazel Hankin/Stock Boston;

203 © Elizabeth Crews;

207 © Bill Bachmann/The Image Works;

208 © Laura Dwight/PhotoEdit;

209 © Roswell Angier/Stock Boston;

212 © Michelle Bridwell/PhotoEdit;

216 © Alex Farnsworth/The Image Works;

221 © Tony Freeman/PhotoEdit;

227 © Elizabeth Crews;

228 © Laura Dwight/PhotoEdit;

232 © Digital Vision;

233 © Digital Vision;

235 © Courtesy of Carroll E. Izard, University of Delaware;

236 © Laura Dwight/PhotoEdit;

237 © Laura Dwight/PhotoEdit;

238 (all) © Michael Newman/PhotoEdit;

241 © Ulrike Welsch/Photo Researchers Inc.;

242 © David Young-Wolff/ PhotoEdit;

243 © Martin Rogers/Stock Boston;

247 © Stephen Agricola/Stock Boston;

254 © Michael Newman/PhotoEdit;

255 © Mary Kate Denny/PhotoEdit;

256 © Bob Daemmrich/Stock Boston;

259 © Eyewire; (bkgrd) © PhotoDisc;

260 © Robert Brenner/PhotoEdit;

266 © Steven Rubin/The Image Works;

275 © Digital Stock;

277 © AP/Wide World Photos;

280 © Gale Zucker/Stock Boston;

287 © Bob Daemmrich/Stock Boston;

292 © Robert Brenner/PhotoEdit;

296 © Elizabeth Crews;

298 © David J. Sams/Stock Boston;

301 © Bonnie Kamin/PhotoEdit;

303 © David Woo/Stock Boston;

310 © Dorothy Littell Greco/The Image Works;

311 © Index Stock Imagery;

313 © Digital Stock; (bkgrd) © PhotoDisc; (blocks) © PhotoDisc;

315 © Spencer Grant/PhotoEdit;

317 © Bob Daemmrich/The Image Works;

322 © Rubberball;

323 © (b) Digital Stock; © (t) Digital Vision;

324 © M. Siluk/The Image Works;

326 © Digital Vision;

327 © David Young-Wolff/PhotoEdit;

329 (l)© Elizabeth Crews; (r)© Stephen McBrady/PhotoEdit;

331 (l) © M. Siluk/The Image Works;

(r) © Felicia Martinez/PhotoEdit ;

337 © Michael Newman/PhotoEdit;

339 © Robert Brenner/PhotoEdit;

340 © Lawrence Migdale/Photo Researchers Inc.;

343 © Dennis MacDonald/PhotoEdit;

344 © Cindy Charles/PhotoEdit;

350 © Lawrence Migdale/Stock Boston;

355 © PhotoDisc;

359 © David Young-Wolff/PhotoEdit/PNI;

361 © Tom McCarthy/PhotoEdit;

367 © Digital Stock;

369 (c) © Digital Stock;

369 (b) © Digital Vision;

369 (t) © PhotoDisc;

370 © Bob Daemmrich/The Image Works;

375 © Bob Daemmrich/The Image Works;

379 © David Young-Wolff/PhotoEdit;

383 © Myrleen Ferguson Cate/PhotoEdit;

386 © Myrleen Ferguson Cate/PhotoEdit;

389 (t) © Laura Dwight/PhotoEdit;

389 (b) © RubberBall; (b, bkgrd) © Digital Stock;

391 © CORBIS/Julie Houck;

398 © Bob Daemmrich/The Image Works;

401 © Lew Merrim/Monkmeyer;

404 © Bob Daemmrich/The Image Works;

409 © Robin L. Sachs/PhotoEdit;

411 © Bob Daemmrich/Stock Boston;

419 © PhotoDisc;

420 © David M. Grossman;

Figure Credits

192 Table 5.3: From "Service Delivery and Design Study..." by M. A. Graham and L. Stone, *Florida's Cost/Implementation Study for Public Law 99–457.* Copyright © 1991 by CPEIP. Used by permission.

202 Fig. 6.1: From J. G. Bremner, "The Stage IV Search Task" from Infancy, 1988, p. 111.

204 Fig. 6.2: From R. Baillargeon and M. Graber, *Developmental Psychology,* July 1988, p. 505. Copyright © American Psychological Association.

209 Table 6.3: Adapted from R. H. Bradley, "Home Measurement Responsiveness" in M. H. Bornstein (ed.), *Maternal Responsiveness: Characteristics and Consequences. New Directions for Child Development,* no. 43., p. 65. Copyright © 1989. Used by permission.

215 Fig. 6.3: From *Language Development: An Introduction,* 2nd ed., by R. E. Owens, Jr. Copyright © 1988 by Merrill Publishing Co.

223 Fig. 6.4: From "Critical Period Effects on Universal Properties of Language..." (figure 1), by J. S. Johnson and E. L. Newport, *Cognition,* 39: 715–758. Copyright © 1991 by Elsevier Science.

236 Fig. 7.1: From "Differences in Shame and Pride as a Function of Children's Gender and Task Difficulty" (figure 1, p. 633), by M. Lewis, S. M. Alessandri, and M. W. Sullivan, *Child Development,* 63: 630–638. Copyright © 1992 by the Society for Research in Child Development. Used by permission.

238 Fig 7.2: From "Infants' Responses to Adult Static Facial Expressions" (figure 1, page 478), by J. M. Serrano, J. Iglesias, and A. Loeches, *Infant Behavior and Development,* 477–482. Copyright © 1995 by Elsevier Science.

244 Fig. 7.1: From page 36 in *Human Attachment,* by V. Colin. Copyright © 1996 by McGraw-Hill Companies. Used by permission.

252 Table A: From page 515 in "Romantic Love Conceptualized as an Attachment Process," by C. Hazan and P. R. Shaver, *Journal of Personality and Social Psychology,* 59: 522–524. Copyright © 1987 by the American Psychological Association. Used by permission.

265 Fig. 7.4: From "Can the Age of Entry into Child Care and the Quality of Child Care Predict Adjustment in Kindergarten?," by C. Howes, *Developmental Psychology,* 26: 292–303. Copyright © 1990 by the American Psychological Association. Used by permission of the author.

270 Fig. A: From "Child Day Care in the Schools...," by E. F. Zigler, M. Finn-Stevenson, and K. W. Mar, *Child Welfare,* LXXIV(6), 1995, p. 1303. Reprinted by special permission of the Child Welfare League of America.

280 Table 8.1: Adapted from Charles B. Corbin, *A Textbook of Motor Development,* 2nd ed. (table 21.3). Copyright © 1980 W. C. Brown Publishers. Reprinted by permission of The McGraw-Hill Companies.

282 Table 8.2: From *Perceptual and Motor Development in Infants and Children,* by J. B. Cratty. Copyright © 1979. Reprinted by permission of Prentice-Hall, Inc.

287 Fig. 8.3: From page 59 in *The State of the World's Children.* Copyright © 1996 UNICEF. Used by permission.

294 Fig. 8.4: From *Children's Thinking,* 3rd ed., (figure 2.5, p. 48), by R. Siegler. Copyright © 1997 by Prentice-Hall, Inc. Used by permission.

326 Fig. 9.1: From "Fears of Children and Adolescents" (figure 1, p. 779) by N. J. King, et al, *Journal of Child Psychology and Psychiatry,* 30(1989). Copyright © 1989 by Cambridge University Press. Used by permission.

336 Table 9.3: From *The Parent's Handbook from Systematic Training for Effective Parenting (STEP),* by D. Dinkmeyer and C. D. McKay. Reprinted with permission of American Guidance Service, Inc., 4201 Woodland Road, Circle Pines, MN 55014–1796 © 1981. All rights reserved.

372 Table 10.1: From p. 947 in *Maternal and Child Health Nursing,* by A. Pillitteri. Copyright © 1992 by J. B. Lippincott. Used by permission of Lippincott Williams & Wilkins.

378 Fig. 10.3: From pp. 160–161 in *The Growth of Logical Thinking: From Childhood to Adolescence,* by B. Inhelder and J. Piaget. Copyright © 1964 by Harper & Row.

382 Fig. 10.5: From "Vocabulary Development: A Morphological Analysis" by J. M. Anglin, *Society for Research in Child Development,* 58, Serial No. 238. Copyright © 1993 by the Society for Research in Child Development. Reprinted by permission.

383 Fig. 10.6: From *Language Development* (figure 6.5, p. 267) by E. Hoff-Ginsberg. Copyright © 1997 by Brooks/Cole Publishing Co. Used by permission of Wadsworth/Thomson Learning.

391 Table 10.3: From pp. 46, 47, and 51 in "The 30th Annual Phi Delta Kappa/Gallup Poll of the Public's Attitudes Towards Public Schools," by L. C. Rose and A. M. Gallup, *Phi Delta Kappan,* 1998(September), pp. 41–56.

394 Fig. 10.7: From pp. 506 and 507 in "The Influence of Extended-Year Schooling on Growth of Achievement and Perceived Competence in Early Elementary School," by J. A. Frazier and F. J. Morrison, *Child Development,* 69: 495–517. Copyright © 1998 by The Society for Research in Child Development.

397 Table 10.5: From "Children's Academic Intrinsic Motivation: A Longitudinal Study" (table 1, p. 1452) by Gottfried, et al, *Child Development,* 69: 1448–1460. Copyright © 1998 by The Society for Research in Child Development.

398 Fig. 10.8: From "7 Ways to be Bright," *U.S. News and World Report.* Copyright © November 23, 1987, *U.S. News and World Report.* Visit us at our Web site at www.usnews.com for additional information.

430 Table 11.1: Adapted from p. 262 in "From Successful Single Parents," by M. R. Olson and J. A. Haynes, *Families in Society,* pp. 259–267. Copyright © 1993 by Manticore Publishers. Used by permission.

443 Table 11.2: Adapted from p. 410 in "Naturalistic Conceptions of Moral Maturity," by L. J. Walker and R. C. Pitts, *Developmental Psychology,* 34 (1998): 403–419.

462 Table 12.1: "Views on Teenagers" (table 1, p. 37), from *Kids These Days: What Americans Really Think About the Next Generation.* Copyright © 1997 by Public Agenda. Used by permission.

466 Fig. 12.3: From *Adolescence: Theories, Research and Applications* by L. C. Jensen. Copyright © 1985 by West Publishing Company. Used by permission of Wadsworth/Thomson Learning.

473 Table 12.3: From The Kids' Eating Disorders Survey (KEDS)..." (table 2, p. 846), by A. C. Childress, et al, *Journal of the American Academy of Child and Adolescent Psychiatry,* 32: 843–850. Copyright © 1993. Used by permission of Lippincott Williams & Wilkins.

478 Table 12.4: From "Trends in Patterns of Sleep and Sleepiness in Adolescents" (table 1, p. 6), by M. A. Carskadon, *Pediatrician,* 17: 5–12. Copyright © 1990 Karger Publishing Co. Used by permission of S. Karger AG, Basel.

492 Table 12.7: From "The Influence of Victim's Attire on Adolescents' Judgments of Date Rape" (table 1, p. 322), by L. Cassidy and R. M. Hurrell, *Adolescence,* 30(Summer 1995): 319–324. Copyright © 1995 by Libra Publishing. Used by permission.

509 Fig. 13.1: From "Developmental Analysis of Conflict Caused by Oppositional Attributes in the Adolescent Self-Portrait" (figure 2, p. 255), by S. Harter and M. A. Monsour, *Developmental Psychology.* Copyright © 1992 by the American Psychological Association. Used by permission of the author.

510 Fig. 13.2: From "Level of Voice Among Female and Male High School Students..." (figure 1, p. 898), by S. Harter, et al, *Developmental Psychology,* 34: 892–901. Copyright © 1998 by the American Psychological Association. Used by permission of the author.

513 Table 13.1: From "Identity Status and Academic Achievement in Female Adolescents," by R. Hummel and L. L. Roselli. In *Adolescence,* 18. Copyright © 1983 by Libra Publishing. Reprinted by permission.

519 Fig. 13.3: From "The Vicissitudes of Autonomy in Early Adolescence" (figure 1, p. 845), by L. Steinberg and S. B. Silverberg, *Child Development,* 57. Copyright © 1986 by the Society for Research in Child Development. Used by permission.

520 Fig. 13.4: From "Changes in Adolescents' Daily Interactions with Their Families from Ages 10 to 18" (figure 1, p. 748), by R. W. Larson, et al, *Developmental Psychology,* 32: 744–754. Copyright © 1998 by the American Psychological Association. Used by permission of the author.

522 Table 13.2: Adapted from table 1, p. 333 in "Factors Influencing Age Expectations for Adolescent Autonomy," by S. S. Feldman and T. Quatman, *Journal of Early Adolescence.* Copyright © 1988 by Sage Publications, Inc.

533 Table 13.3: From "Relations of Parenting Style and Parental Involvement with Ninth-Grade Students' Achievement" (table 1, p. 256), *Journal of Early Adolescence,* 14: 250–267. Copyright © 1994 by Sage Publications, Inc. Reprinted by permission of Sage Publications, Inc.

548 Fig. 13.11: From "The 'Little Five': Exploring the Nomological Network ..." (figure 1, p. 167), by O. P. John, et al, *Child Development,* 65: 160–178. Copyright © 1994 by Society for Research in Child Development. Used by permission.

Illustrations

Figure, Datagraphics, and Trends in Development art created by Jeff Grunewald Pages: 9, 12, 48, 67, 79, 80, 82, 83, 84, 102, 123, 124, 131, 132, 135,141, 146, 148, 149, 160, 165, 171, 176, 177, 202, 204, 210, 215, 223, 236, 259, 262, 265, 270, 279, 287, 309, 313, 315, 355, 362, 370, 371, 384, 385, 389, 396, 399, 431, 465, 473, 474, 479, 491, 495, 501, 511, 512, 521, 522, 529, 531, 532, 537, 538, 539, 541, 544, 548, 550, 551.